AUTO MECHANICS:
THEORY AND SERVICE

William J. deKryger

Robert T. Kovacik

Saverio G. Bono

IE09   *Published by*
SOUTH-WESTERN PUBLISHING CO.

CINCINNATI   WEST CHICAGO, ILL.   DALLAS   PELHAM MANOR, N.Y.   PALO ALTO, CALIF.

PHOTOS ON COVER, PAGE I AND II.
COURTESY OF CHEVROLET MOTOR DIVISION — GMC

ISBN: 0-538-33090-2

Library of Congress Catalog Card Number: 84-52073

2 3 4 5 6 7 8 9 K 9 8 7 6

Printed in the United States of America

TABLE OF CONTENTS

Contents

Contents

PREFACE

Auto Mechanics: Theory and Service is the cornerstone of a comprehensive learning program. This textbook is designed for the secondary school student who is considering a career in the automotive service industry.

The automobile industry—manufacturing, sales, and service—accounts for almost 20 percent of all employment in the United States. Within this huge industry, career opportunities are expanding most rapidly in the area of automobile service and repair. Automotive mechanics is one of the fastest-growing employment fields in the nation.

For these reasons, *Auto Mechanics: Theory and Service* provides the student with a comprehensive overview of this career field. In addition, the textbook provides valuable insights into the skills and attitudes that lead to job and career success.

The vocational content of the textbook is complemented by in-depth comprehensive technical treatment of the service and repair tasks performed by auto mechanics. The majority of the content is aimed specifically at building job-qualifying skills among students. The total effect is a blend of the theory learned in the classroom with the practical skills acquired in the automotive shop. This blend of knowledge and skill acquisition provides a complete learning experience.

ORGANIZATION

This textbook is organized into nine parts. Each part concentrates upon a major area of knowledge and/or skill involved in automotive service and repair. Within each part are units that represent natural learning experiences for students. These units are divided further into numbered topics. The numbering system provides a convenient and useful system of cross-referencing throughout the textbook. The student is guided swiftly to referenced material through the use of unit numbers in the titles of major discussion topics. Further enhancing this ease of reference is the inclusion of numbered topics in the Table of Contents.

Major systems and components of the automobile are presented in a two-unit format. This arrangement permits a natural and meaningful transition from classroom instruction to hands-on shop experience.

One major exception is made to this format in the interest of a logical learning progression. Part II consists entirely of knowledge units introducing the student to the basic principles of automotive engine design and operation. This information is necessary for a clear understanding of the automotive systems that follow. However, at this stage, the student is not prepared to undertake major engine service procedures. Thus, the service units pertaining to major engine repairs are positioned later in the text, in Part VI.

Each unit is presented in a readable and understandable format. At the beginning of each unit is a *Unit Preview,* which provides a brief overview of the subject matter. Immediately following the preview is a listing of major achievement goals, entitled *Learning Objectives.* These elements provide a focus for the study and practice activities in the unit. These introductory elements also provide both student and instructor with references by which learning performance can be rated.

Throughout this textbook, a strong emphasis is placed on safe working habits. In keeping with this emphasis, skill units include a thorough discussion of *Safety Precautions* pertaining to the tasks in those units.

Unit Highlights at the conclusion of each unit provide a brief summary of the major topics. Important words and phrases defined in the unit are listed under the heading *Terms. Review Questions* are presented in a variety of multiple-choice styles. This format resembles that of the mechanic certification tests administered by the National Institute for Automotive Service Excellence (ASE, formerly NIASE). Finally, *Supplemental Activities* are suggested to enrich and reinforce the knowledge or skills emphasized in the unit.

FEATURES

Illustrations are positioned in direct relationship to the text content to which they apply. All illustrations are cited in the text to provide solid learning reinforcement.

Safety is emphasized throughout the text. An entire unit (Unit 4, "Safety Around the Automobile") is devoted to a thorough discussion of safe working habits. Particular attention is paid to proper use of tools and power equipment. Development of a safety-minded attitude is stressed.

Safety is emphasized further by the inclusion of special cautions for all shop procedures in which potential hazards exist. Each of these cautions, printed in boldface type for emphasis, begins with the words SAFETY CAUTION.

Boldface notations also reinforce other important concepts. Notes introduced by the word CAUTION call for special care to avoid damage to a part during a specific procedure. Notes introduced by the word NOTE call attention to an important concept or to a helpful suggestion in performing a task.

A *Service Manual* complements this textbook. The shop manual contains individual Job Sheet assignments and written Tests. The Job Sheets are step-by-step procedures designed to verify and reinforce the student's shop practice experiences. The Tests are presented in a format similar to that used by ASE in its mechanic certification tests.

ACKNOWLEDGMENTS

The authors wish to thank Russell J. Mukai, auto mechanic instructor at North Hollywood High School, Los Angeles Unified School District, for his valuable contributions as a reviewer and technical consultant.

Photography for this textbook, both color and black-and-white, was done by James L. Camp, except where otherwise credited.

The authors also wish to thank the following companies for supplying illustrations and photographs used throughout this book: Chevrolet Motor Division, Pontiac Motor Division, Oldsmobile Division, Buick Motor Division, and Cadillac Motor Division, General Motors Corporation; Delco-Morraine and Hydra-Matic, Divisions of General Motors Corporation; Chrysler Corporation; Ford Motor Company; American Motors Corporation; American Honda Motor Company, Inc.; American Isuzu, Inc.; Mazda (North America), Inc.; Mercedes-Benz of North America, Inc.; Nissan Motor Corporation in U.S.A.; Toyota Motor Sales, U.S.A., Inc.; Volkswagen of America, Inc.; and Volvo of America, Inc.

Other companies that supplied illustrations and/or photographs are: Champion Spark Plug Company; Snap-On Tools Corporation; Gould, Inc.; Moog Automotive, Inc.; Robert Bosch Corporation; BFGoodrich; Sun Electric Corporation; Inland Manufacturing Company; Kleer-Flo Company; L.S. Starrett Co.; Storm Vulcan; Ammco Tools, Inc.; Sioux Tools, Inc.; Bear Auto Service Equipment Co.; The Black & Decker Mfg. Co.; Fel-Pro, Inc.; Hastings Manufacturing Co.; Dana Corporation; Stanadyne Diesel Systems Group; and TRW, Inc.

CAREER OPPORTUNITIES AND THE AUTOMOBILE

1 CAREERS AND OPPORTUNITIES

UNIT PREVIEW

The automotive industry is the nation's No. 1 provider of jobs and career opportunities. Nearly one-fifth of all workers in the United States are associated, directly or indirectly, with the automotive industry. This book deals with automotive mechanics, one of the fastest-growing of all employment fields. This unit discusses the types of jobs available in the field of automotive service and repair.

LEARNING OBJECTIVES

When you have completed your assignments and exercises in this unit, you should be able to:

☐ Explain why the need for automotive service is increasing.

☐ Identify major types of automotive service businesses.

☐ Identify jobs available in automotive service.

☐ Describe the basic duties of general and specialty mechanics.

☐ Describe characteristics of a good employee.

1.1 THE AUTOMOTIVE INDUSTRY

Automotive mechanics is one of many different occupations included in the automotive industry. Automobiles are manufactured, sold, and used by purchasers. Thus, the automotive industry can be divided into three basic areas of job and career opportunities:

• Manufacturing
• Sales
• Service.

Manufacturing. Included in the manufacturing process are design, engineering, production of parts, and final assembly of automobiles. Automobile manufacturing companies employ people in many different skill areas.

Sales. Automobiles in the United States are sold through independent dealerships, which contract to sell the products of manufacturers. Some automobile dealers carry more than one product line.

Service. This textbook deals with the *servicing* of automobiles. Servicing includes *maintenance* and *repair*. It is the only one of these three areas that applies to the full life of every automobile. To perform properly, an automobile must be maintained on a regular basis. Maintenance is the care and upkeep of mechanical and other parts of an automobile, usually performed according to a schedule. Regular maintenance includes procedures such as oil and filter changes, lubrication, replacement of belts and hoses, and tune-ups. See Figure 1-1. Repair is the replacement or fixing of parts that wear out, break, or malfunction. Some repairs—servicing of brakes or replacement of bolt-on parts, such as shock absorbers or alternators—are considered minor. Other repairs, such as engine or transmission overhauls, are considered major.

1.2 INCREASING NEEDS FOR SERVICE

No part of an automobile is permanent. Thus, the need for service is ongoing. Routine service intervals have been extended on modern automobiles. However, regularly scheduled maintenance is as important as ever. In addition, several factors contribute to the increasing need for trained and certified automotive mechanics. These factors are:

• More complicated automobiles
• Increased average age of automobiles
• Emissions and fuel economy requirements.

Figure 1-1. Regular maintenance procedures are routine parts of a mechanic's job.

More Complicated Automobiles

Modern automobiles have computers and electronic devices that control many aspects of a vehicle's operation. For example, computers may control fuel flow, engine operation, gear shifting (on automatic transmissions), and shock absorber settings. Computerized and electronic systems are lightweight and compact, and they contribute to the operation and comfort of modern automobiles. However, they are expensive.

Servicing these highly technical systems and parts requires special knowledge and new diagnostic equipment. See Figure 1-2. In many cases, parts cannot be repaired. Instead, they are simply removed and replaced if they fail.

Increased Average Age of Automobiles

The average age of the automobiles in service ranges from four to seven years in different parts of the country. At one time, it was common practice for motorists to replace their automobiles every three years. However, increased prices of new automobiles and higher interest rates have persuaded many people to keep their vehicles longer. The longer an automobile is operated, the more maintenance and repairs it requires. Nonetheless, these costs usually are considerably lower than the investment required for a new vehicle.

Emissions and Fuel Economy Requirements

Most states have laws that require periodic inspections of passenger vehicles. In many cases, vehicles must pass exhaust emissions and safety inspections before registration can be renewed. Vehicles that fail such inspections must be brought up to standards at their owners' expense.

Federal regulations governing emissions control and minimum fuel mileage standards require the installation of special devices. These devices require service if they are to function properly. Laws setting emissions and fuel economy standards are increasing the amount of service performed each year on new automobiles.

1.3 AUTOMOTIVE SERVICE BUSINESSES

Automotive mechanics are employed in a variety of automotive businesses. Some of these businesses offer a full range of automotive maintenance and repair services. Some offer only certain types of services. From a career standpoint, two important facts stand out. First, automotive service businesses are great in

Figure 1-2. Diagnostic equipment is used by mechanics to help locate automotive problems.

number. Second, these businesses are needed in every community in the country.

The majority of automotive service businesses fall into one of the following categories:

- New-car dealerships
- Independent garages
- Specialty shops
- Service stations
- Fleet garages
- Auto supply and accessory stores, and department stores.

New-Car Dealerships

Many automotive service functions are performed at dealerships. See Figure 1-3. Dealer service departments usually coordinate all service activities. These

Figure 1-3. New-car dealer service centers usually offer all services required for the automobiles they sell.

activities may include preparing new and used automobiles for delivery to customers, servicing customers' automobiles, and body repairs. Dealerships also serve as manufacturers' representatives in the performance of *warranty* repairs. A warranty is a manufacturer's guarantee that certain parts of an automobile will perform as designed. A warranty repair is the repair or replacement of a defective part at the manufacturer's cost.

Another important function in most dealerships is the parts department. A parts department keeps commonly used parts available for installation by the service department and for sale to the public. A well-run parts department can be the most profitable part of a dealership.

Independent Garages

The *independent garage* is the primary source for automotive servicing in many communities. See Figure 1-4. An independent garage typically offers customers a complete line of services. Maintenance services include oil and filter changes, chassis lubrication, tune-ups, and brake repairs. Most independent garages also perform major and minor mechanical repairs. Some even overhaul engines and transmissions.

Specialty Shops

The automotive *specialty shop* usually concentrates on one type of automotive service, or a limited number of services. This specialization allows the shop owner or manager to maintain close control of operations and expenditures. Examples of specialty shops are tire, muffler, tune-up, and brake repair facilities. See Figure 1-5.

Service Stations

A *service station* is a gasoline station that offers automotive servicing. One or more *service bays,* or work areas, may be used for maintenance and repair

Figure 1-5. A specialty shop offers limited services, usually specializing in one phase of automobile repair and service.

services. Some service stations perform only simple maintenance services and sell and install tires and batteries. Others perform tune-ups, brake repairs, and other maintenance services. Still other service stations may offer major repairs, such as engine overhauls. See Figure 1-6.

In many communities, the availability of a certified mechanic can greatly increase the volume of business done by a service station.

Fleet Garages

Many businesses, government agencies, and other organizations have fleets of automobiles. A *fleet* may consist of as few as two or three automobiles, or it may number in the thousands. Small fleets usually are serviced by independent shops. Large fleets often are serviced in a garage owned by the organization that operates the fleet. Garages for major fleets usually have complete maintenance and repair capabilities. See Figure 1-7.

Figure 1-4. An independent garage can perform many services for different brands of automobiles.

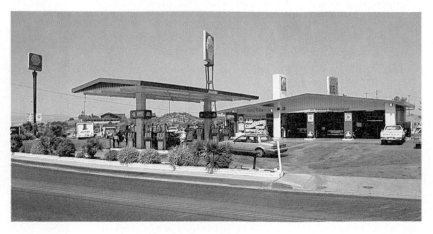

Figure 1-6. Many service stations provide service as well as fuel for automobiles. Some service stations specialize in simple maintenance. Others perform major repairs.

Figure 1-7. Government and private industry have fleets of automobiles that are serviced regularly in fleet garages.

Figure 1-9. Many automotive shops use only ASE (NIASE) certified mechanics.

Auto Supply and Accessory Stores, and Department Stores

Auto supply and accessory stores frequently sell parts at reduced prices when installation is performed in their own service facilities. Many of these stores find it profitable to sell and install certain products.

Most department store chains offer automotive services at some, if not all, of their locations. See Figure 1-8. In many cases, customers find it convenient to use department store credit cards to charge automotive services.

1.4 JOBS IN AUTOMOTIVE SERVICE

Jobs in automotive service have a variety of names. The following discussions apply to basic work functions.

General Automobile Mechanic

The National Institute for Automotive Service Excellence (formerly NIASE, now referred to as ASE) offers tests and certifications for mechanics. See Figure 1-9. Many states recognize ASE certifications and/or base their own certifications on ASE standards.

ASE offers tests and certifications in eight areas of automobile repair, identified below. A mechanic who passes all required tests and meets experience requirements is certified as a *General Automobile Mechanic*.

A general automobile mechanic must be skilled in all areas of automobile maintenance and repair. In many automotive service businesses, mechanics are divided into two general categories:

- Line mechanic—light work
- Line mechanic—heavy work.

Line mechanic—light work. The *line mechanic— light work* performs nonspecialized minor services. See Figure 1-10. These services include oil and filter

Figure 1-8. Major department store chains have service centers. These centers usually install parts and make repairs with parts that are sold through the stores.

Figure 1-10. A line mechanic may perform only light-work duties, such as chassis lubrication.

changes, lubrication, accessory installation, tune-ups, and replacement of belts, hoses, and lights. Also included in this category is inspection of new automobiles prior to delivery to customers.

Line mechanic—heavy work. The *line mechanic—heavy work* performs nonspecialized services, including disassembly, repair, and replacement of parts, and reassembly of major assemblies. These services include engine, transmission, and differential overhauls. See Figure 1-11. The line mechanic in this area must have good overall automotive service experience.

Figure 1-12. A specialty mechanic repairs only one part of an automobile, such as the brake system.

Figure 1-11. A line mechanic who does heavy work repairs larger, more complicated automotive assemblies.

Automotive Specialty Mechanic

The *automotive specialty mechanic* concentrates on servicing a single part of an automobile, such as electrical, brakes, or transmission. See Figure 1-12. These specialties require advanced and continuing training in a particular field. Specialty mechanics often are certified by ASE in one or more service areas. ASE certification tests are given in the following areas:

- Engine Repair
- Automatic Transmission
- Manual Transmission and Rear Axle
- Front End
- Brakes
- Electrical Systems
- Heating and Air Conditioning
- Engine Performance.

Service Writer

The person who greets customers at a service center is the *service writer* or *service advisor*. See Figure 1-13. The service writer must have good knowledge of automobiles, a friendly attitude, and the ability to deal

with people effectively. Customers discuss their automotive problems and needs with the service writer. The service writer then makes a preliminary diagnosis and prepares a cost estimate for the customer.

Shop Foreman

A service department with a number of mechanics usually has one or more shop foremen. The *shop foreman* supervises the work of several mechanics. The foreman must be able to work well with people and must have thorough knowledge of automotive mechanics. The shop foreman schedules work for mechanics and helps to solve mechanical problems. The foreman also will check the completed work to be sure that the customer's automobile has been serviced properly.

Service Manager

All maintenance and repair jobs are controlled by the *service manager*. The service manager must be a good mechanic and have some business knowledge. The service manager is responsible for the profit earned

Figure 1-13. A service writer greets the customer and makes a preliminary diagnosis of a problem for the mechanic.

or lost by the department, as well as for customer satisfaction.

Parts Department

The sale of automotive parts requires a working knowledge of the automobile and servicing. Service departments require parts to perform most repair jobs. A *parts department* maintains a stock of often-used replacement parts. See Figure 1-14. If a needed part is not in stock, the parts department worker must know where to obtain it quickly.

A *parts manager* runs the parts department. The parts manager is responsible for ordering, stocking, and selling parts and accessories.

1.5 TRAINING FOR A CAREER IN AUTOMOTIVE SERVICE

The course in which you are using this text probably is the first—and most important—step in your training. In this course, you will learn the basics of how automobiles operate and how they are serviced.

To move ahead in the automotive field, you should continue your education in one or more specialized areas. See Figure 1-15. You also may be able to obtain valuable training through work in an apprenticeship program. For information on such programs in your community or area, consult with your school counselor or placement office.

Specialized courses in all phases of automotive servicing are available in high schools, community colleges, vocational schools, and the armed forces. You also may be able to work in a service department while attending school. Many dealers and garages offer apprentice programs.

1.6 GOING TO WORK

Becoming a valuable worker requires more than learning job skills. When you get a job, you will enter into a business transaction with your employer. A

Figure 1-15. Automotive classes help students learn more about servicing all systems in an automobile.

business transaction is an exchange of things of value. When you become an employee, you sell your time, skills, and effort. Your employer pays you money for these resources.

Both parties in a business transaction have responsibilities. The obligations of an employer to a worker include:

- Instruction and supervision. You should be told what is expected of you on the job. There should be a supervisor who can observe your work and tell you if it is satisfactory. See Figure 1-16.

- A clean, safe place to work. Automotive mechanics frequently involves dirty work. An employer should provide adequate facilities for you to clean up after work.

- Wages. You should know how much you are to be paid before accepting a job. Your employer should pay you on designated paydays.

Figure 1-14. Parts departments keep a stock of often-used parts. These parts are available to a mechanic when a replacement is necessary to complete a repair.

Figure 1-16. Supervisors rely on their experience to help young mechanics learn needed skills.

- Fringe benefits. When you are hired, you should be advised about any benefits, in addition to wages, that you can expect. Fringe benefits usually include paid vacations and employer contributions to health insurance and retirement plans.

- Opportunity and fair treatment. Opportunity means that you are given a chance to succeed and possibly to advance in a company. Fair treatment means that all employees are treated equally, without prejudice or favoritism.

On the other side of this business transaction, employees have responsibilities to their employers. Your obligations as a worker will include:

- Regular attendance. A good employee is reliable. Businesses cannot operate successfully unless their workers are on the job regularly.

- Following directions. As an employee, you are part of a team. Doing things "your way" may not serve the best interests of the business.

- Responsibility. Be willing to answer for your work-related obligations and your conduct.

- Productivity. Remember, you are paid for your time as well as your skills and effort. You have a duty to use time on the job as effectively as possible.

- Attitude. With a positive attitude, you increase your value beyond your skills and time. One reason for this is that your attitude may have a positive effect on other employees.

- Loyalty. Last but not least, loyalty is expected by any employer. Being loyal means that you act in the best interests of your employer, both on and off the job. Another word for loyalty is trustworthiness.

Getting Along at Work

In addition to your obligations to an employer, you also will have certain responsibilities toward your fellow workers. You will be a member of a team. Teamwork means cooperation with, and caring about, other workers. An important strength of a valuable employee is the ability to work in harmony with fellow employees. You also should strive for harmonious relations with your supervisors and with those you supervise.

Pride in Your Work

Doing your best on the job comes naturally if you take pride in your work. Doing a job right the first time is the pathway to profits. The more proud you are of your work, the more likely a customer is to be satisfied. This satisfaction is bound to be shared by your employer.

Pride in your work means more than just doing the work correctly and well. Also important is your attitude toward customer satisfaction. For example,

stained or soiled upholstery will not please a customer, no matter how well you perform a mechanical repair. See Figure 1-17. Treat other people's property as if it were your own.

Figure 1-17. Many service shops use paper floormats and other protective devices to prevent soiling customers' automobiles.

UNIT HIGHLIGHTS

- Automotive mechanics can be the beginning of a career in servicing—the maintenance and repair of automobiles.

- The automotive industry consists of three main areas of job and career opportunities: manufacturing, sales, and service.

- Manufacturing starts with ideas and raw materials. It concludes with a finished product.

- Automotive service is performed by many different types of businesses.

- Automotive service will always be in demand to keep automobiles operating.

- A variety of jobs are available in automotive servicing.

TERMS

servicing	service manager
maintenance	independent garage
repair	specialty shop
dealer	service station
warranty	service bay
fleet	fleet garage
general automobile mechanic	line mechanic— light work
automotive specialty mechanic	line mechanic— heavy work
service writer	parts department
shop foreman	parts manager

R E V I E W   Q U E S T I O N S

DIRECTIONS: The following questions are similar to those used on mechanic certification tests. On a separate sheet of paper, write the letter of the correct choice.

1. Major automotive job and career areas include all of the following EXCEPT
A. manufacturing.
B. restyling.
C. sales.
D. service.

2. Which of the following statements about large automotive service facilities is true?
   I. A shop foreman is in charge of all the mechanics in the shop.
   II. The service manager is in charge of all the mechanics in the shop.
A. I only   B. II only   C. Both I and II   D. Neither I nor II

3. Mechanic A says that computers and electronics in many modern cars control the operation of automatic transmissions and fuel systems.
   Mechanic B says that the average age of an automobile is 12 years.
   Who is correct?
A. A only   B. B only   C. Both A and B   D. Neither A nor B

4. Which of the following businesses does *not* engage in most types of automotive servicing?
A. Dealership
B. Independent garage
C. Specialty shop
D. Fleet garage

5. Which of the following offer specialized courses in all phases of automotive servicing?
   I. Community colleges and vocational schools
   II. The armed forces
A. I only   B. II only   C. Both I and II   D. Neither I nor II

S U P P L E M E N T A L   A C T I V I T I E S

1. Describe the major stages of automobile manufacturing.
2. Name the duties of a service writer.
3. Describe the role of the fleet garage.
4. Explain the differences in job duties between light-work and heavy-work line mechanics.
5. Describe the operation of a parts department.

2 THE AUTOMOBILE

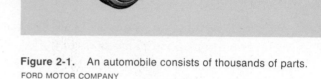

Figure 2-1. An automobile consists of thousands of parts.
FORD MOTOR COMPANY

UNIT PREVIEW

An automobile is made up of many different parts. Many of the mechanical parts work together to provide movement. An engine furnishes power, which is transferred to driving wheels through a series of parts called a drivetrain. An automobile performs a number of functions. It provides space for occupants and cargo; it moves forward or backward; it goes around corners; and it stops. This unit discusses the major mechanical parts that make the automobile work.

LEARNING OBJECTIVES

When you have completed your assignments and exercises in this unit, you should be able to:

☐ Describe the basic parts of a reciprocating piston engine.

☐ Explain how fuel is burned in an automotive engine.

☐ Explain the difference between a transmission and a transaxle.

☐ Describe the major types of automotive body construction.

☐ Explain how drum brakes and disc brakes operate.

2.1 BASIC PARTS OF THE AUTOMOBILE

The automobile uses thousands of different parts, as illustrated in Figure 2-1. However, only four basic assemblies are needed to make the automobile work:

- Engine
- Drivetrain
- Chassis
- Body.

2.2 ENGINE

An *engine* is a machine that converts a form of energy into mechanical motion and force. The most common form of engine in passenger vehicles is the internal-combustion piston engine. An *internal-combustion engine* is one in which combustion, or burning, of air and fuel takes place inside the engine.

Automobile engines produce mechanical motion in the form of rotation. The power of the engine is delivered as a twisting force.

Piston Engine

The most widely used passenger-car engine is the *reciprocating piston engine.* In this type of engine, a piston moves up and down in a cylinder. Refer to Figure 2-2. The major parts of a reciprocating piston engine are:

- Cylinder block
- Cylinder head
- Valve train
- Piston
- Connecting rod
- Crankshaft
- Manifolds.

The following descriptions apply to gasoline engines. Diesel engines share the same major parts, but they do not use a spark to ignite an air-fuel mixture. See Topic 10.7.

Cylinder block. The biggest part of the engine is the *cylinder block,* also called the *engine block.* The block is a large casting of metal that is drilled with holes. The block contains *cylinders,* which are round passageways fitted with pistons. The block houses, or holds, the major mechanical parts of the engine. Figure 2-3 shows an engine block and the parts it encloses.

Cylinder head. The *cylinder head* fits on top of the cylinder block to close off and seal the top of the cylinder. The *combustion chamber* is an area into which the air-fuel mixture is compressed and burned. The cylinder head contains all or most of the combustion chamber. The cylinder head also contains *ports,* passageways through which the air-fuel mixture enters, and burned gases exit, the cylinder.

Valve train. A *valve train* is a series of parts used to open and close the intake and exhaust ports. A *valve* is a movable part that opens and closes a passageway. A *camshaft* controls the movement of the valves (see Figure 2-4).

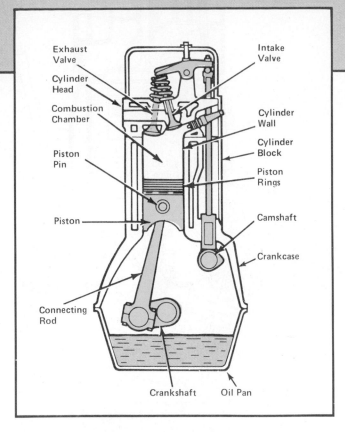

Figure 2-2. The basic parts of a reciprocating piston engine.
CHRYSLER CORPORATION

Piston. The burning of air and fuel occurs between the cylinder head and the top of the *piston*. The piston is a can-shaped part closely fitted inside the cylinder. In an engine with a *four-stroke cycle,* the piston has four strokes, or movements: intake, compression, power, and exhaust. On the intake stroke, the piston moves downward, and a charge of air-fuel mixture is introduced to the cylinder. As the piston travels upward, or reciprocates, the air-fuel mixture is compressed in preparation for burning. When combustion occurs, the piston is forced downward on its power stroke. When it reciprocates, or moves upward again, the piston pushes the burned gases out of the cylinder.

Connecting rod. The movement of the piston is controlled by a *connecting rod*. A connecting rod is a solid bar of metal. The top of the connecting rod is connected to the piston. The bottom of the connecting rod is connected to the crankshaft.

Crankshaft. The *crankshaft* is a shaft located at the bottom of the engine block. A shaft is a cylindrical part used to turn, or to be turned by, other parts. The

Figure 2-3. An engine block houses or holds many different parts that help the engine operate. FORD MOTOR COMPANY

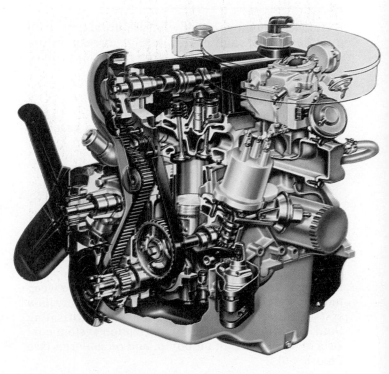

Figure 2-4. A valve train acts to draw in an air/fuel mixture and push out exhaust gases. FORD MOTOR COMPANY

crankshaft is not round along its length. Instead, it has offset, or extended, portions where the connecting rods are attached. The distance that the piston moves, up and down, in the cylinder depends upon the crank pin offset.

As each connecting rod pushes down, it rotates the crankshaft. Thus, engine power is changed from a reciprocating, or up-and-down, motion to a rotating motion.

Manifolds. There are two manifolds, which are metal fixtures attached to the cylinder head (see Figure 2-5). The *intake manifold* delivers air and fuel to the intake ports. The *exhaust manifold* covers the exhaust ports and carries exhaust gases away from the cylinders.

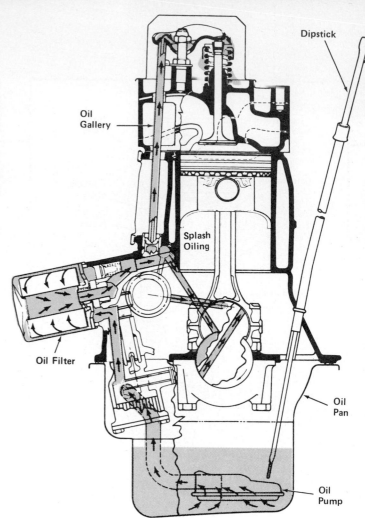

Figure 2-6. A lubrication system distributes oil throughout the engine. BUICK MOTOR DIVISION—GMC

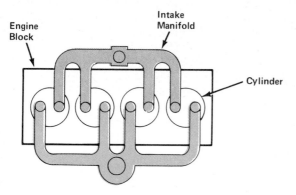

Figure 2-5. A manifold directs gases in and out of combustion chambers.

Automotive engines usually have four, six, or eight cylinders. An engine also has a corresponding number of pistons and connecting rods, all turning a single crankshaft.

Piston Engine Systems

Basic systems required for operation of a gasoline-fueled piston engine are:

- Lubrication
- Cooling
- Fuel
- Exhaust
- Ignition.

Lubrication system. All moving parts in the engine require *lubrication*. Lubrication is the application of an oil or grease to moving parts to reduce friction. *Friction* is the resistance to motion that occurs when two objects rub against one another. Friction between mechanical parts causes heat and wear. A *lubrication system* is used in engines to distribute the lubricating fluid, or motor oil. A typical lubrication system consists of an oil pan, an oil pump, and oil galleries (see Figure 2-6).

The motor oil is stored in an *oil pan* that is bolted to the bottom of the engine block. Oil is drawn from

the oil pan by an *oil pump. Oil galleries,* or small passageways, direct oil to the moving parts of the engine. Extra lubrication is provided by the rotating crankshaft, which delivers oil to the connecting rods and cylinder walls.

Cooling system. The engine operates by burning a fuel mixture, so it becomes very hot. To maintain proper temperatures, a special *cooling system* is built into all automobiles (see Figure 2-7). Most engines are *water-cooled,* or cooled by a liquid. Some engines are *air-cooled,* or cooled by air.

A water-cooled system uses *coolant.* Coolant is a fluid that contains special chemicals mixed with water. Coolant flows through passages in the engine block and through a *radiator.* The radiator accepts hot coolant from the engine block and lowers the coolant temperature. Air flowing around and through a radiator takes heat from the coolant.

Fuel system. For fuel to burn in an automotive engine, it must be mixed with air. This air-fuel mixture is introduced into the cylinder at the cylinder head. Special assemblies, such as *carburetors* or *fuel injection,* mix the fuel and air, then feed the mixture into the cylinder. See Figure 2-8.

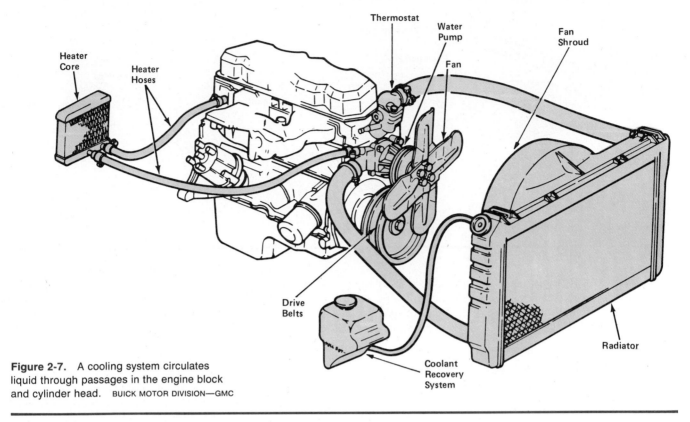

Figure 2-7. A cooling system circulates liquid through passages in the engine block and cylinder head. BUICK MOTOR DIVISION—GMC

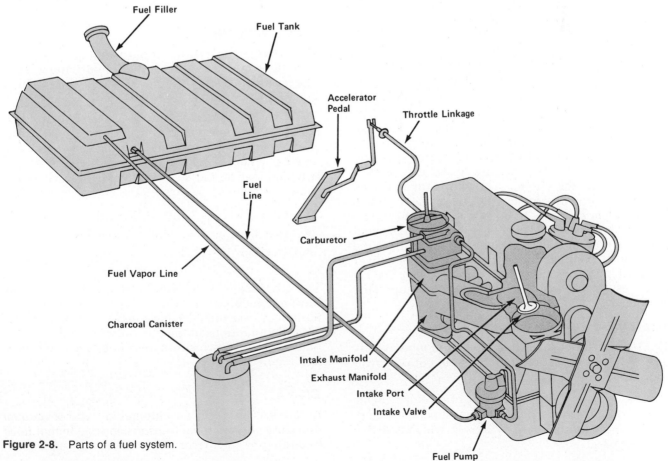

Figure 2-8. Parts of a fuel system.

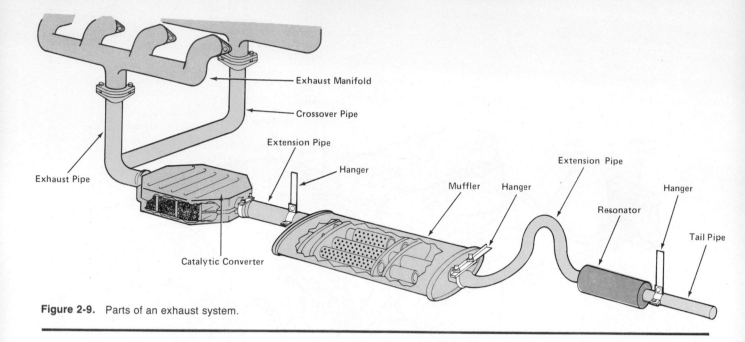

Figure 2-9. Parts of an exhaust system.

Exhaust system. As the piston returns to its upper-most position, it forces the burned air-fuel mixture, or exhaust, out of the engine. The exhaust then passes through the *exhaust system,* a series of parts shown in Figure 2-9.

Ignition system. A *spark plug* is installed in the cylinder head and extends into the combustion chamber. The spark plug has a gap formed by two electrodes. A *distributor* sends electrical current through a wire to the spark plug when ignition is scheduled in that cylinder (see Figure 2-10). When electrical current jumps the spark plug gap, a spark is created, igniting the air-fuel mixture. The spark plug fires only when the piston is nearing the top of its compression stroke.

The ignition system actually is a subsystem within the overall *electrical system* of an automobile. Other subsystems within the electrical system are the starting system, charging system, and accessory circuits. The main parts of the electrical system are the *battery* and the *alternator.* The *starting system* uses battery power to start the engine. The alternator is driven by the engine and provides electrical power while the engine is running. In addition to the alternator, the *charging system* has a *voltage regulator.* The voltage regulator controls the electrical output from the alternator to the battery. Accessory circuits deliver electricity to power the lights, safety systems, and accessories, such as radios and electrically operated equipment.

Alternative Power Sources

The reciprocating piston engine is the most widely used power source for automobiles, but other power sources exist.

Rotary engine. The main parts of a *rotary engine* rotate instead of reciprocate. The most popular rotary engine is the Wankel, used by Mazda, which is shown in Figure 2-11.

Gas turbine engine. The gas turbine engine used in automobiles is similar to the engine that is used in aircraft. Air and fuel are forced into spinning turbines, or rotors.

Battery-operated electric motor. A simple but, so far, impractical power source is an electric motor powered by storage batteries. This power source will remain impractical until, or unless, a more efficient type of battery is invented.

2.3 DRIVETRAIN

The *drivetrain* is a series of parts that carries power from the engine and directs it to the driving wheels. The term *power train* is used to describe the combination of engine and drivetrain.

There are two basic drivetrain designs used on modern passenger vehicles. One type of drivetrain, referred to as conventional drive, has the engine and driving wheels located at opposite ends of the automobile. The parts of a conventional drivetrain, shown in Figure 2-12, are:

- Clutch
- Transmission
- Driveline
- Differential
- Driving axles.

The other major type of drivetrain is the *transaxle.* Most automobiles with transaxles have their engines positioned over their driving wheels. A transaxle combines the functions of the transmission and differential. A transaxle drivetrain does not have a driveline (see Figure 2-13).

Clutch

A *clutch* is used on an automobile with a *manual transmission.* A manual transmission is one that must be shifted by the driver when changing gears.

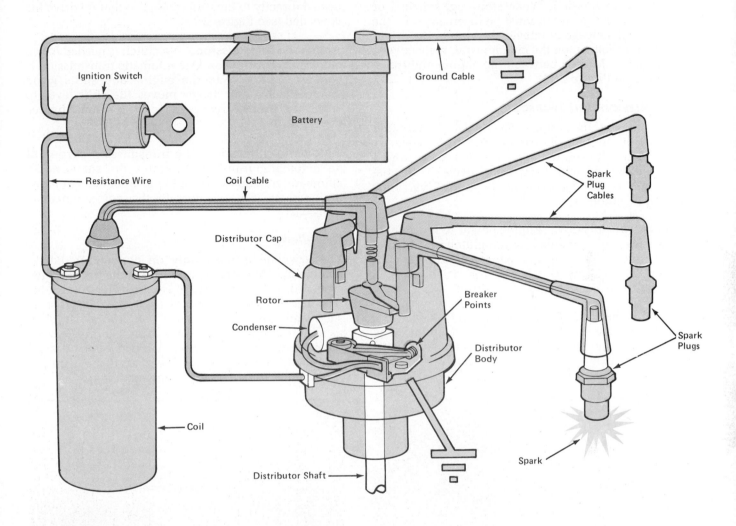

Figure 2-10. Parts of an ignition system.

Figure 2-11. A rotary engine. MAZDA MOTOR CORPORATION

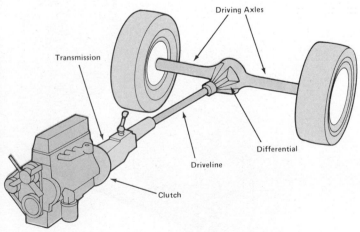

Figure 2-12. A drivetrain for a conventional rear-drive automobile.

The clutch engages or disengages engine power from the transmission. When stopping, starting, or shifting gears, the clutch must be disengaged by the driver. To disengage or engage the clutch, the driver pushes in or lets up on the clutch pedal, respectively. The clutch is located between the engine and transmission (see Figure 2-14).

Transmission and Transaxle

A *transmission* and a *transaxle* consist of gears that are shifted to obtain proper driving speeds. A transmission is used with conventional drive, and a transaxle is used with front-wheel drive. Transmissions and transaxles both come in two versions: manual or automatic.

Manual transmission. Engine power to the *manual transmission* is controlled by the clutch and the actions of the driver. The manual transmission is connected between the clutch and the driveline. The driveline is discussed later in this unit.

Manual transaxle. As with a manual transmission, the *manual transaxle* operates with a clutch. The transaxle has more parts and systems than a transmission. A transaxle assembly holds both a transmission and a differential in one assembly. Differentials are discussed later in this unit. The transmission is connected directly to the differential, so that no driveline is needed (see Figure 2-15).

Automatic transmission. No clutch is needed for an *automatic transmission*. An automatic transmission is connected directly to the engine and shifts gears automatically. The driver moves the shift lever to engage the proper drive range in the transmission (see Figure 2-16).

Automatic transaxle. The transmission portion of an *automatic transaxle* operates the same as an automatic transmission. At the differential assembly, the automatic transaxle operates the same as a manual transaxle.

Driveline

The *driveline* is used only on conventional-drive automobiles. The driveline connects the transmission at the front of the automobile to the differential at the rear. The driveline consists of a *driveshaft,* or *propeller shaft,* and *universal joints,* or *U-joints*. The driveshaft usually is a long, hollow tube. The U-joints connect the driveshaft to the transmission and to the differential. The U-joints allow the driveshaft to move up and down when the automobile moves.

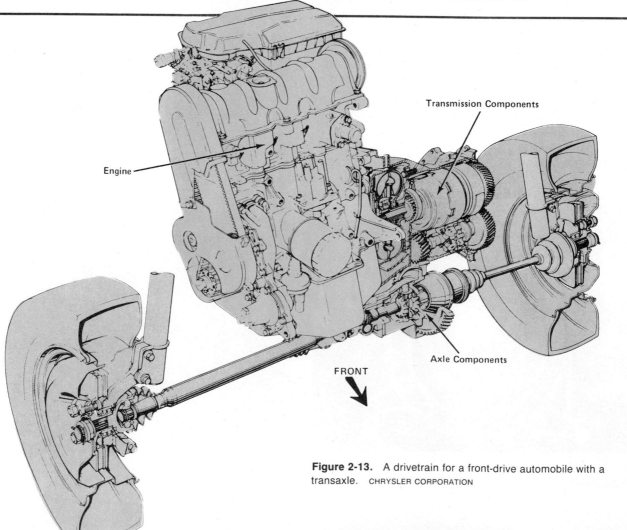

Figure 2-13. A drivetrain for a front-drive automobile with a transaxle. CHRYSLER CORPORATION

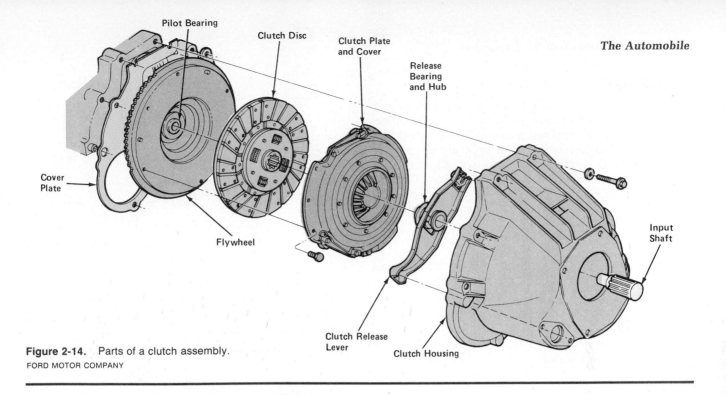

Figure 2-14. Parts of a clutch assembly.
FORD MOTOR COMPANY

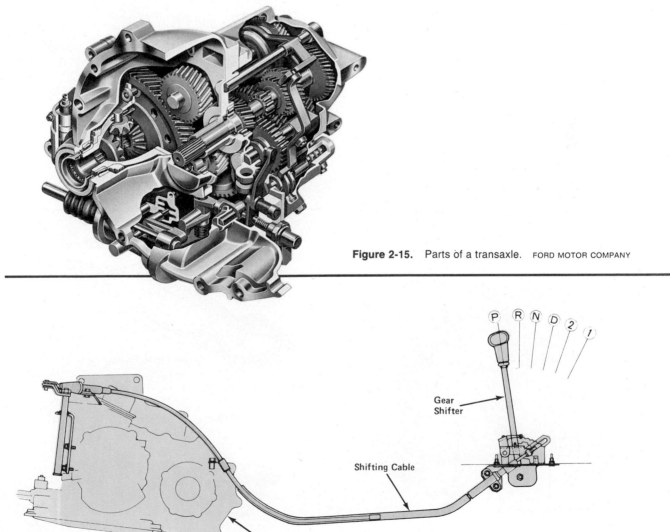

Figure 2-15. Parts of a transaxle. FORD MOTOR COMPANY

Figure 2-16. Automatic transmission shift lever and cable.
MAZDA MOTOR CORPORATION

Differential

The *differential* is a set of gears that allows the power flow to be directed to one driving wheel or the other. A driving wheel receives rotating power from the drivetrain. By differentiating, or splitting up, power, the differential allows the driving wheels to turn at different speeds when the automobile turns. This differentiating is needed to permit the outside wheel to rotate more rapidly on a curve. A conventional-drive differential is shown in Figure 2-17.

Driving Axles

Power passes from the differential to the driving wheels through the *driving axles*. The driving axles are solid shafts (see Figure 2-18).

2.4 CHASSIS

The foundation of the automobile is the *chassis*. See Figure 2-19. The chassis supports other parts of the automobile. The parts that make up the chassis are:

- Frame or unitized body
- Suspension
- Steering
- Brakes
- Wheels and tires.

Frame

A *frame* is a large supporting assembly that fits below the floor and stretches the length of an automobile. The frame is made of thick, steel members. The frame supports the engine, transmission, body, and most other assemblies of the automobile. The body is discussed in Topic 2.5. Two common frames are shown in Figure 2-20. Frames currently are used primarily on large automobiles and light-duty trucks.

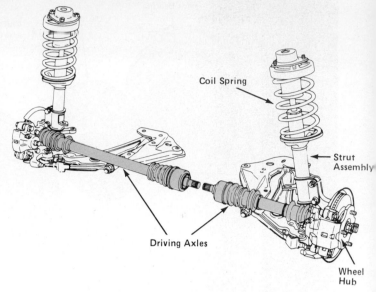

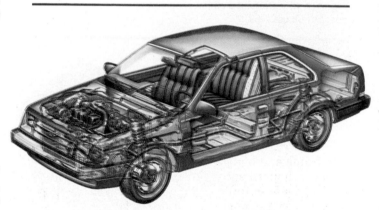

Figure 2-18. Driving axles for a front-drive automobile with transaxle. NISSAN MOTOR CORPORATION

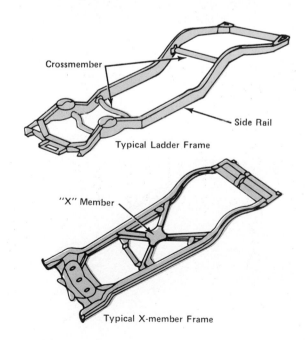

Figure 2-19. The body of an automobile is supported by the chassis. FORD MOTOR COMPANY

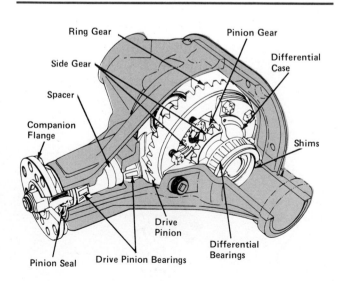

Figure 2-17. Parts of a conventional rear-drive differential.
FORD MOTOR COMPANY

Figure 2-20. Two types of full automobile frames.

Figure 2-21. Parts of a unitized body. PONTIAC MOTOR DIVISION—GMC

Unitized Body

The frame and body are combined into a single unit in many modern automobiles. This design is called a *unitized body*. A unitized body uses all of its parts for strength. The strongest part of a unitized body is the *underbody*. Metal in the underbody is thinner than metal in frames, but underbody sections are overlapped, welded, and shaped to provide strength.

Some automobiles use a partial frame, or *stub frame,* for extra support in the engine and/or rear suspension areas.

A *space frame* is another type of unitized body. A space frame has more body parts and braces built into it than most unitized bodies (see Figure 2-21).

Suspension

The ride and driving characteristics of an automobile depend upon the *suspension*. The suspension is connected to the frame or underbody and holds the wheels in proper alignment. The automobile rests on the suspension. The main parts of the suspension are the springs and shock absorbers.

Springs cushion the ride for both passengers and automobile parts. Much of the up-and-down movement from rough conditions is absorbed by the springs. The most common types of springs are coil springs and leaf springs. Figure 2-22 shows different types of springs.

The action of springs is controlled by *shock absorbers*. Shock absorbers limit spring movement and resist the continuing flexing of springs as a wheel encounters uneven surfaces (see Figure 2-23).

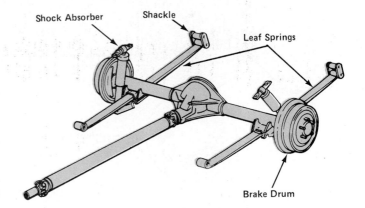

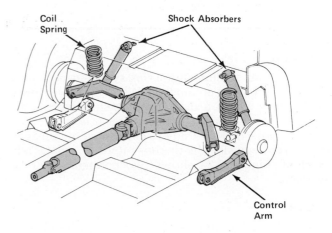

Figure 2-22. Two different types of springs are used on many automobiles. CHEVROLET MOTOR DIVISION—GMC

19

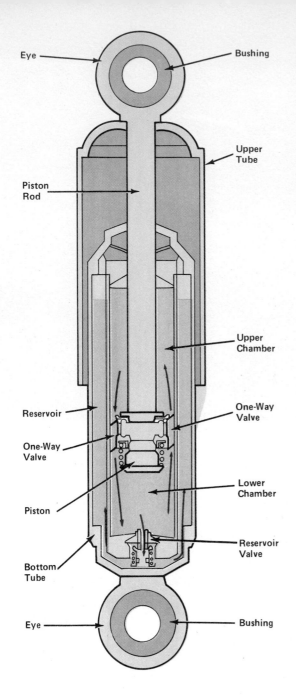

Figure 2-23. Parts of a shock absorber.

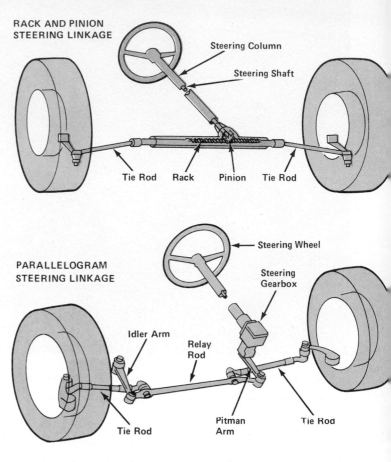

Figure 2-24. Common steering systems.

Steering

To turn an automobile, a *steering* system is built into the front end of the automobile. When the driver turns the steering wheel, a shaft from the steering column turns a steering gear. The steering gear acts on other teeth to move *tie rods* that are connected by linkages to the front wheels. The tie rods move the wheels left or right. Figure 2-24 shows two common steering systems.

Brakes

Automobiles are stopped by activating the *brakes*. Brakes are located at each wheel and operate by friction to slow and stop the automobile. A driver must push down on a brake pedal to apply the brakes.

Two types of brakes are used on automobiles: *drum brakes* and *disc brakes*. Many automobiles use a combination of the two types: disc brakes at the front wheels and drum brakes at the rear wheels.

Drum brake assemblies include a *hydraulic wheel cylinder, brake shoes* and *linings,* and the *brake drum* (see Figure 2-25). When the brake pedal is applied, the stationary brake shoe and lining is pressed against the rotating brake drum. The brake drum rotates with the wheel. Friction material (the brake lining) on the shoe grips the drum and slows it.

Disc brakes include a *rotor, caliper,* and *friction pads* (see Figure 2-26). When the brake pedal is applied, the U-shaped caliper squeezes against the rotor in a pinching fashion. Friction pads on the gripping surface of the caliper slow the rotor.

Tires and Wheels

The only contact a vehicle has with the road are its tires. Tires are made of rubber and other materials and are filled with air to cushion the ride of an automobile. Wheels are made of metal and are bolted to the axles or spindles. Wheels hold the tires in place. Wheels and tires come in many different sizes. Their sizes must be matched to one another and to the automobile.

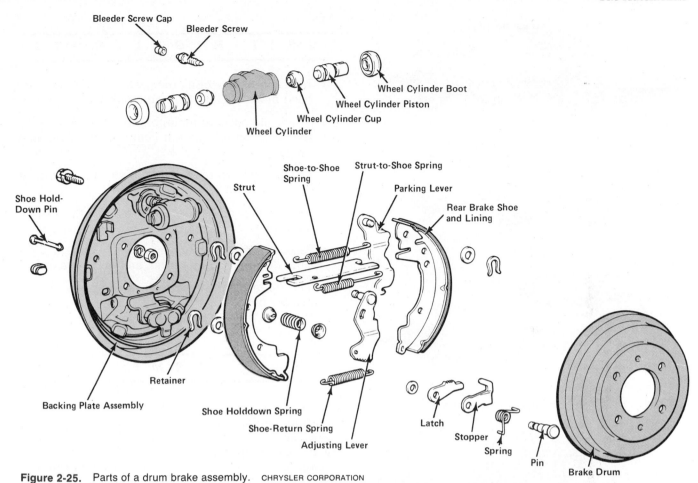

Figure 2-25. Parts of a drum brake assembly.   CHRYSLER CORPORATION

2.5 BODY

The *body* holds, carries, and protects passengers and cargo. The exterior panels of the body form a protective shell and give the automobile its shape. Interior body parts provide comfort for passengers and space for cargo.

Body Size and Styles

Automobiles and light-duty trucks come in many sizes. The smallest may be called mini-compacts. Other sizes are subcompact, compact, intermediate, and full-size. Light-duty trucks include pickup, van, and utility vehicle designs in a variety of sizes. Common automobile body styles are shown in Figure 2-27.

Aerodynamics

Aerodynamics is the science of the ability of a body to move through air. An automotive body that moves through air easily provides greater fuel economy and efficiency (see Figure 2-28).

Body Materials

Most automotive body parts and panels are made from thin steel, or sheet metal. Plastic and fiberglass are being used increasingly for body parts.

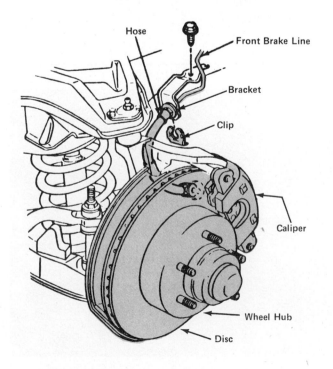

Figure 2-26. Parts of a disc brake assembly.
BUICK MOTOR DIVISION—GMC

Two-Door Sedan

Four-Door Sedan

Station Wagon

Van

Figure 2-27. Common automotive body styles.

Figure 2-28. Airflow is measured as it passes over an automobile in a wind-tunnel test. FORD MOTOR COMPANY

U N I T   H I G H L I G H T S

- Internal-combustion, reciprocating engines are used most frequently in automobiles.

- The basic parts of an automotive engine are the block, cylinder, piston, connecting rod, and crankshaft.

- For fuel to burn in an automotive engine, it must be mixed with air.

- An electrical spark is created to ignite the air-fuel mixture.

- Parts of a drivetrain may include clutch, transmission, driveline, differential, and driving axles.

- The automobile body may be attached to a frame or may have a frame built into it.

T E R M S

engine	drivetrain
internal combustion engine	power train
	transaxle
reciprocating piston engine	clutch
	manual transmission
cylinder block	transmission
cylinder	manual transaxle
cylinder head	automatic transmission
valve train	automatic transaxle
valve	driveline
piston	driveshaft
four-stroke cycle	propeller shaft
connecting rod	universal joint
crankshaft	U-joint
lubrication	differential
friction	driving axle
lubrication system	chassis
oil pan	frame
oil pump	unitized body
oil galleries	stub frame
cooling system	space frame
water-cooled	suspension
air-cooled	springs
coolant	shock absorber
radiator	steering
carburetor	brakes
fuel injection	drum brake
exhaust system	disc brake
combustion chamber	brake shoe
spark plug	brake drum
distributor	brake lining
electrical system	rotor
battery	caliper
alternator	friction pads
rotary engine	aerodynamics

R E V I E W   Q U E S T I O N S

DIRECTIONS: The following questions are similar to those used on mechanic certification tests. On a separate sheet of paper, write the letter of the correct choice.

1. Which of the following does *not* describe the most common automotive powerplant?
A. Reciprocating piston engine
B. Motor
C. Internal combustion
D. Burns air-fuel mixture

2. Which of the following statements is correct?
   I. A clutch is used with a manual transaxle.
   II. A transmission is part of a transaxle.
A. I only   B. II only   C. Both I and II   D. Neither I nor II

3. Mechanic A says that the differential can rotate one driving axle at a slow speed and the other driving axle at a fast speed.
   Mechanic B says that a frame and a unitized body are identical.
   Who is correct?
A. A only   B. B only   C. Both A and B   D. Neither A nor B

4. Which of the following parts are found in the braking system?
A. Shoes
B. Gears
C. Manifold
D. Distributor

5. All of the following are part of the suspension EXCEPT
A. coil springs.
B. calipers.
C. leaf springs.
D. shock absorbers.

S U P P L E M E N T A L   A C T I V I T I E S

1. Name several different methods that can be used to determine how many cylinders a particular engine has.
2. Look at the underside of an automobile and determine whether the driving wheels are at the front or at the rear.
3. Identify the parts of a drivetrain selected by the instructor.
4. Locate and identify the type of brake system used on a vehicle selected by the instructor.
5. Identify body styles your instructor has shown you.

3 USING SERVICE MANUALS AND SHOP FORMS

UNIT PREVIEW

Service manuals are a guide to automotive servicing and repair. Automotive manufacturers and specialized publishing companies furnish many types of manuals used by repair shops. Shop forms are another way of communicating information within the servicing business.

LEARNING OBJECTIVES

When you have completed your assignments and exercises in this unit, you should be able to:

☐ Describe how to use service manuals and service bulletins.

☐ Describe a flat rate manual and how it is used.

☐ Explain how to use specifications tables.

☐ Describe information disclosures and how they are used.

☐ Explain how a repair order is filled out.

3.1 SERVICE MANUALS

A *service manual* is a book that explains how to service and repair an automobile. Some service manuals are very complete. These manuals give the mechanic exact, step-by-step instructions on how to repair a specific part on a specific automobile. Other service publications give only the highlights on the same repair job. Some manuals even tell how much time should be required to make a repair and how much it should cost.

Mechanics use different types of service publications. The most common are:

• Manufacturers' service manuals
• Manufacturers' service bulletins
• General and specialty repair manuals
• Flat rate manuals.

Manufacturers' Service Manuals

Automotive manufacturers put out a series of service manuals each year that explain service procedures.

Manufacturers' service manuals are updated each year. New manuals are issued whenever new automobiles are introduced. One or more service manuals are produced by the manufacturer for each automotive model (see Figure 3-1).

Figure 3-1. Manufacturers publish service manuals with complete servicing information for each model they produce.

Manufacturers' service manuals provide a mechanic with step-by-step procedures on all servicing aspects of a vehicle, plus *specifications*. Specifications are measurements for tightening, fitting, and testing various parts of an automobile. Special tools and special servicing procedures also are included.

All service manuals are written in technical language. The manuals are written by manufacturers for experienced mechanics in dealerships.

Learn to use manufacturers' service manuals. The information in these manuals is important when making repairs. The use of manufacturers' service manuals is discussed in greater detail in Topic 3.2.

Manufacturers' Service Bulletins

Manufacturers' service manuals are updated by *manufacturers' service bulletins*. A manufacturer's service bulletin usually is issued as a one- or two-page description of a change. Service bulletins notify mechanics of changes or corrections in service procedures or specifications (see Figure 3-2).

General Repair Manuals

General repair manuals and *specialty repair manuals* are printed by publishing companies rather than automotive manufacturers. General repair manuals have service procedures and specifications for several automotive models and years. Information in general repair manuals is condensed, or shortened, and more general in nature. This allows the coverage of more subjects in less space. One volume of a general repair manual may contain information from 20 or more

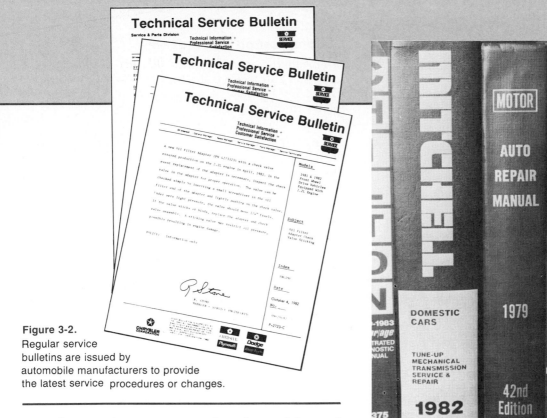

Figure 3-2.
Regular service
bulletins are issued by
automobile manufacturers to provide
the latest service procedures or changes.

Figure 3-3. General repair manuals offer service procedures for a wide variety of automobiles.

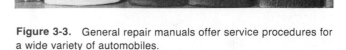

Figure 3-4. A flat-rate manual gives information on the cost of parts and labor for specific service procedures.

manufacturers' service manuals. The widely used general repair manuals are Chilton, Mitchell, and Motor's (see Figure 3-3).

In addition to manuals, information on servicing automobiles is published in many automotive service magazines. Tool manufacturers also have servicing publications showing their tools or equipment.

Flat Rate Manuals

Automotive mechanics are paid either an hourly wage, a salary, or a *flat rate* wage. A flat rate means the mechanic is paid by the job.

To operate on a flat rate scale, the business must use an up-to-date *flat rate manual*. Flat rate manuals are printed and updated regularly by automotive manufacturers and independent companies. A flat rate manual lists the cost of parts and labor for automotive repair jobs. A flat rate manual, shown in Figure 3-4, is used to provide a written estimate of repair for the customer. It also gives the mechanic a rate for the job.

3.2 USING MANUFACTURERS' SERVICE MANUALS

There are several important procedures you should understand before you attempt to use manufacturers' service manuals. These preparatory procedures are discussed below.

Choose the Correct Manual

A variety of manuals are available in most shops. Choose the correct manual based on the make, model, year, and type of work to be performed on an automobile.

TABLE OF CONTENTS

GENERAL INFORMATION A. General Information B. Maintenance and Lubrication	0.
CLIMATE CONTROL C. Electronic Climate Control D1. R-4 Compressor D2. DA-6 Compressor	1.
BODY, FRAME AND BUMPERS A. Frame and Body Mounts B. Bumpers C. Chassis Sheet Metal	2.
STEERING, SUSPENSION, WHEELS AND TIRES 3. Diagnosis A. Wheel Alignment B. Steering B1. Power Rack and Pinion B3. Power Steering Pump B4. Steering Wheel and Column C. Front Suspension D. Rear Suspension E. Wheels and Tires	3.
DRIVE AXLES	4.
BRAKES	5.
ENGINE DIESEL — 4.3 Liter V-6, Code T 6. Diagnosis A. Mechanical B. Cooling C. Fuel Injection D. Electrical E. Emission Controls F. Exhaust H. Vacuum Pump GASOLINE — HT4100 V-8, Code 8 6. Diagnosis A. Mechanical B. Cooling C. Fuel System and DFI D. Electrical E. Emission Controls F. Exhaust H. Vacuum Pump	6.
TRANSAXLE A. Maintenance and On-Car Service 440 — T4 Transaxle	7.
ELECTRICAL A. Electrical Troubleshooting B. Lighting Systems C. Instrument Panel and Gages D. Computer System Diagnosis D1. ECM Trouble Code Diagnosis D2. BCM Trouble Code Diagnosis	8.
ACCESSORIES	9.
INDEX	10.

Figure 3-5. The table of contents at the front of a service manual tells a mechanic where to look for service procedures.
CADILLAC MOTOR CAR DIVISION—GMC

Locate Desired Information

To locate the necessary information, use the table of contents and look up the proper section or sections. Check out the service procedures and specifications tables in those sections.

Using the table of contents. The table of contents is located at the front of the service manual. A table of contents is shown in Figure 3-5.

The table of contents gives a general description of service procedures for all parts of an automobile. A section listing, beside the table of contents, gives a section number where service procedures can be found.

Section guides. After locating a section in the table of contents, turn to the first page of that section. The first section page has a guide, or second table of contents, as to what that section contains. A general description of the automotive assembly in that section also is located in the section guide (see Figure 3-6).

Information within sections. Each section contains step-by-step repair procedures for one specific automotive assembly. One of these procedures is shown in Figure 3-7. Service procedures usually show the mechanic how to disassemble and reassemble a part or series of parts. Special tools, safety procedures, and precautionary notes also are included.

Specifications tables. A mechanic should use the proper specifications when reassembling and tightening parts. Making a part too tight or too loose will cause that part to fail. Specifications requirements usually are listed at the end of each section (refer to Figure 3-8).

3.3 FORMS AND RECORD-KEEPING

As in any other business, paperwork makes automotive servicing smoother. This topic discusses the forms used commonly.

Ordering Parts

A ready supply of parts should be available at all times. A good source of parts is important if servicing is to operate smoothly.

A dealership with its own parts department will keep an adequate stock of parts that are used often. A small shop will maintain close contact with a nearby parts store. Sometimes it is necessary to order special parts. Special orders must always be coordinated between the service and parts departments to ensure customer and shop satisfaction.

Parts managers fill out forms to keep an adequate number of parts in stock. New parts are ordered when the stock gets low.

440-T4 DIAGNOSIS AND ON-CAR SERVICE
CONTENTS

Figure 3-6. A section guide contains specific information about servicing procedures. CADILLAC MOTOR CAR DIVISION—GMC

Dispatch Sheet

The work schedule at a garage will be posted in the office or wherever it is handy to the service manager. A work schedule, or *dispatch sheet,* keeps track of appointments. Whenever a customer telephones, the dispatch sheet is consulted and a suitable service appointment is made.

Repair Order

After an appointment is made, the service manager, or an assistant, may fill out a *repair order.* A repair order gives information about the customer, the car (service description and parts used), and billing (see Figure 3-9).

Many states have *information disclosure* laws. Information disclosures are ways in which consumers are protected from fraud. The garage must furnish written job estimates to the customer (see Figure 3-10). Additional approval must be received if the cost will be higher than the original written estimate. Any replaced part must be returned to customer.

Work order. When the customer arrives, a service writer notes any customer complaints or labor instructions on a *work order.* These instructions are for the mechanic. A work order section, or service description, on a repair order is shown in Figure 3-9.

The repair order and the automobile are sent, or dispatched, to the mechanic assigned to do the servicing. The mechanic follows instructions on the work order to begin service.

Parts requisition. Any new parts that are needed are written in the *parts requisition* section of the repair order by the mechanic. See Figure 3-9. The mechanic takes the repair order to the parts department to receive the parts. As new parts are issued, the counter attendant writes parts prices in the parts requisition.

Labor charges. The mechanic turns in the repair order when work on the automobile is completed. The service manager, or service writer, adds the labor charges.

Billing. *Billing* is the cost of servicing. All labor charges and parts charges are totaled in the billing department. Sales tax and any extra charges are added and totaled. The customer pays the bill in the billing department.

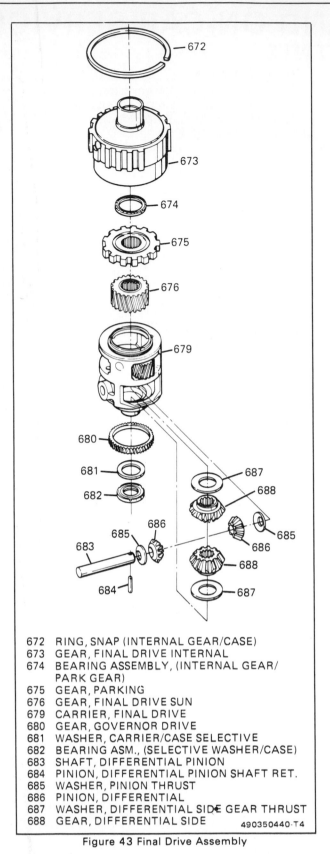

672 RING, SNAP (INTERNAL GEAR/CASE)
673 GEAR, FINAL DRIVE INTERNAL
674 BEARING ASSEMBLY, (INTERNAL GEAR/
    PARK GEAR)
675 GEAR, PARKING
676 GEAR, FINAL DRIVE SUN
679 CARRIER, FINAL DRIVE
680 GEAR, GOVERNOR DRIVE
681 WASHER, CARRIER/CASE SELECTIVE
682 BEARING ASM., (SELECTIVE WASHER/CASE)
683 SHAFT, DIFFERENTIAL PINION
684 PINION, DIFFERENTIAL PINION SHAFT RET.
685 WASHER, PINION THRUST
686 PINION, DIFFERENTIAL
687 WASHER, DIFFERENTIAL SIDE GEAR THRUST
688 GEAR, DIFFERENTIAL SIDE

490350440-T4

Figure 43 Final Drive Assembly

A FEELER GAGE
B PINION, FINAL DRIVE
679 CARRIER, FINAL DRIVE

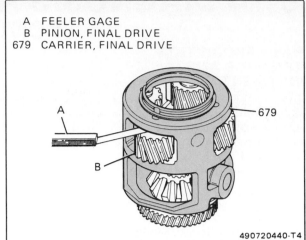

490720440-T4

Figure 44 Final Drive Pinion End Play

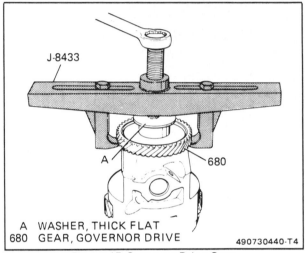

A WASHER, THICK FLAT
680 GEAR, GOVERNOR DRIVE

490730440-T4

Figure 45 Governor Drive Gear

→← Install or Connect

- Drive gear - tap into position with a soft mallet

Inspect

- Pinions (688) and side gears (686) for damage

Pinion Replacement Procedure

Disassemble (Figure 46)

- Retaining pin (684) with a pin punch
- Pinion shaft (683)
- Pinions (688), side gears (686), and washers (685 and 687)

Inspect

- Washers (685 and 687) and carrier (679) for damage.

Assemble (Figure 43)

Figure 3-7. Step-by-step service procedures give exact descriptions of the work that needs to be done.

CADILLAC MOTOR CAR DIVISION—GMC

DESCRIPTION OF USAGE	THREAD SIZE	ASM. TORQUE
CONNECTOR COOLER FITTING	1/4 - 18	41.0 N·m (30 lb.-ft.)
MODULATOR TO CASE	M8 X 1.25 X 20.0	27.0 N·m (20 lb.-ft.)
PUMP COVER TO CHANNEL PLATE	M6 X 1.0 X 94.0	14.0 N·m (10 lb.-ft.)
PUMP COVER TO PUMP BODY	M8 X 1.25 X 20.0	27.0 N·m (20 lb.-ft.)
PUMP COVER TO PUMP BODY (TORX. HD.)	M8 X 1.25 X 20.0	27.0 N·m (20 lb.-ft.)
GOVERNOR CONTROL BODY TO COVER (TORX. HD.)	M6 X 1.0 X 22.0	14.0 N·m (10 lb.-ft.)
PIPE PLUG	1/8 - 27	14.0 N·m (10 lb.-ft.)
CASE TO DRIVE SPROCKET SUPPORT	M8 X 1.25 X 23.5	27.0 N·m (20 lb.-ft.)
MANIFOLD TO VALVE BODY	M6 X 1.0 X 35.0	14.0 N·m (10 lb.-ft.)
GOVERNOR TO CASE	M8 X 1.25 X 25.0	27.0 N·m (20 lb.-ft.)
PRESSURE SWITCH	1/8 - 27	14.0 N·m (10 lb.-ft.)
SOLENOID TO VALVE BODY	M6 X 1.0 X 14.0	14.0 N·m (10 lb.-ft.)
MANUAL DETENT SPRING TO VALVE BODY	M6 X 1.0 X 16.0	14.0 N·m (10 lb.-ft.)
CASE SIDE COVER TO CHANNEL PLATE (NUT)	M6 X 1.0 X 20.0	14.0 N·m (10 lb.-ft.)
PUMP COVER TO VALVE BODY	M6 X 1.0 X 45.0	14.0 N·m (10 lb.-ft.)
PUMP COVER TO CHANNEL PLATE	M6 X 1.0 X 85.0	14.0 N·m (10 lb.-ft.)
VALVE BODY TO CASE (TORX. HD.)	M8 X 1.25 X 90.0	27.0 N·m (20 lb.-ft.)
VALVE BODY TO CASE	M8 X 1.25 X 70.0	27.0 N·m (20 lb.-ft.)
PUMP BODY TO CASE	M8 X 1.25 X 95.0	27.0 N·m (20 lb.-ft.)
VALVE BODY TO CHANNEL PLATE	M6 X 1.0 X 35.0	14.0 N·m (10 lb.-ft.)
VALVE BODY TO CHANNEL PLATE (TORX. HD.)	M6 X 1.0 X 60.0	14.0 N·m (10 lb.-ft.)
CHANNEL PLATE TO CASE (TORX. HD.)	M8 X 1.25 X 30.0	27.0 N·m (20 lb.-ft.)
CHANNEL PLATE TO DRIVEN SPROCKET SUPPORT (TORX. HD.)	M8 X 1.25 X 45.0	27.0 N·m (20 lb.-ft.)
VALVE BODY TO CASE	M8 X 1.25 X 70.0	27.0 N·m (20 lb.-ft.)
CHANNEL PLATE TO CASE (TORX. HD.)	M8 X 1.25 X 45.0	27.0 N·m (20 lb.-ft.)
VALVE BODY TO DRIVEN SPROCKET SUPPORT (TORX. HD.)	M8 X 1.25 X 90.0	27.0 N·m (20 lb.-ft.)
SIDE COVER TO CASE	M8 X 1.25 X 16.0	13.0 N·m (10 lb.-ft.)
ACCUMULATOR COVER TO CASE	M8 X 1.25 X 30.0	27.0 N·m (20 lb.-ft.)
OIL SCOOP TO CASE	M8 X 1.25 X 30.0	13.0 N·m (10 lb.-ft.)
RETAINER GOVERNOR CONTROL BODY	M8 X 1.25 X 30.0	27.0 N·m (20 lb.-ft.)
TRANSMISSION OIL PAN TO CASE	M8 X 1.25 X 16.0	13.0 N·m (10 lb.-ft.)
MANUAL SHAFT TO INSIDE DETENT LEVER (NUT)	M10 X 1.5	34.0 N·m (25 lb.-ft.)

Figure 3-8. Specifications tables give measurements and tightening requirements that must be used during service.
CADILLAC MOTOR CAR DIVISION—GMC

PARTS ____ TIRES ____ BATTERIES ____ ACCESSORIES

QTY.	PART NO.	DESCRIPTION	UNIT	ESTIMATED AMOUNT	ACTUAL AMOUNT
8	RJ12Y	spark plugs		15 60	15 60
1	RR175	condenser		1 75	1 75
1	CS786	points		5 45	5 45
		TOTAL PARTS		22 80	22 80
		OUTSIDE REPAIRS			
		TOTAL OUTSIDE REPAIRS			

TOM'S SPEEDY SERVICE
321 MAIN STREET
ANYTOWN, MICHIGAN 48910

State Registration No. F 100000

WAIVER SIGNED 1 2

NAME John Doe DATE 3/1/79
ADDRESS 104 Main, Anytown, mi. PHONE 373-9063
YEAR AND MAKE '75 Buick TYPE OF MODEL Electra 225 MOTOR NO. – SERIAL NO. 486399F110780
SPEEDOMETER 57,420 LICENSE DOS 700 PROMISED 5:00 today PHONE WHEN READY YES NO

SERVICES TO BE PERFORMED	APPROX TIME	ESTIMATED AMOUNT	ACTUAL AMOUNT
Tune Engine	1.5	30 00	30 00

NOT RESPONSIBLE FOR LOSS OR DAMAGE TO CARS OR ARTICLES LEFT IN CARS IN CASE OF FIRE, THEFT OR ANY OTHER CAUSE BEYOND OUR CONTROL

REPAIRS PERFORMED BY — SIGNATURES OF MECHANICS: 1. Joe Jones M100000 2.

YOU ARE ENTITLED BY LAW TO THE RETURN OF ALL PARTS REPLACED, EXCEPT THOSE WHICH ARE TOO HEAVY OR LARGE, AND THOSE REQUIRED TO BE SENT BACK TO THE MANUFACTURER OR DISTRIBUTOR BECAUSE OF WARRANTY WORK OR AN EXCHANGE AGREEMENT. YOU ARE ENTITLED TO INSPECT THE PARTS WHICH CANNOT BE RETURNED TO YOU.

AUTHORIZED INCREASE IN ESTIMATE BY: $ ____ APPROVED PER ____

YOU ARE ENTITLED TO A COPY OF THIS ORDER AT THE TIME OF YOUR SIGNATURE.

I hereby authorize the above repair work to be done along with the necessary material, and hereby grant you and or your employees permission to operate the car, truck or vehicle herein described on streets, highways or elsewhere for the purpose of testing and or inspection.

X John Doe

GASOLINE • OIL • GREASE	ESTIMATED AMOUNT	ACTUAL AMOUNT
GALS GAS @		
QTS OIL @		
TRANS/DIFF		
ATF @		
TOTAL		

—CERTIFICATION—
Above repairs properly performed
X G. Grant

	ESTIMATED	ACTUAL
TOTAL LABOR	30 00	30 00
TOTAL PARTS	22 80	22 80
TOTAL GAS, OIL AND GREASE		
OUTSIDE REPAIRS		
OTHER		
SUB-TOTAL	52 80	52 80
SALES TAX	91	91
TOTAL	53 71	53 71

Figure 3-9.
A repair order is filled out with information about service needed, parts replacement, and the cost of repairs.

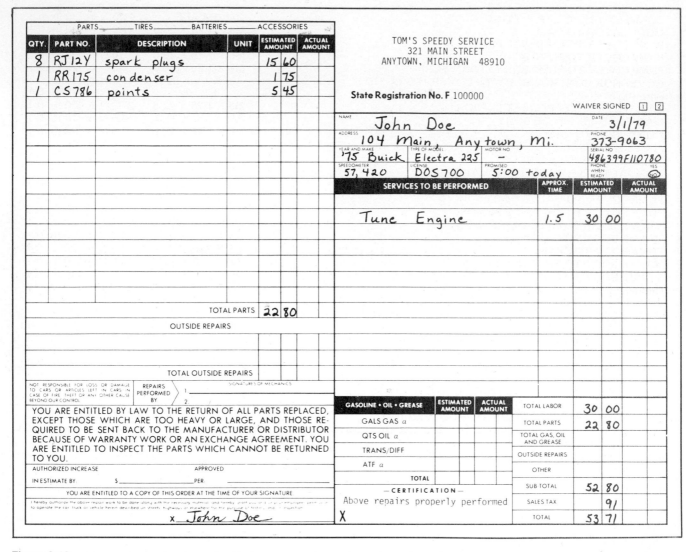

Figure 3-10. A job estimate often is required before any service work can be performed.

	UNIT HIGHLIGHTS		TERMS	

- Service manuals are a main source of information for mechanics.
- Manufacturers' service manuals have more specific service information than general repair manuals.
- Service manuals are divided into sections called tables of contents, automotive parts systems, and specifications tables.
- A repair order includes spaces for customer complaints, directions to mechanics, parts requisition, labor charges, and billing totals.

service manual	**flat rate**
manufacturer's service manual	**flat rate manual**
	dispatch sheet
specifications	**repair order**
manufacturer's service bulletin	**information disclosure**
	work order
general repair manual	**parts requisition**
specialty repair manual	**billing**

R E V I E W   Q U E S T I O N S

DIRECTIONS: The following questions are similar to those used on mechanic certification tests. On a separate sheet of paper, write the letter of the correct choice.

1. Which one of the following information sources would *not* be of help to an automotive mechanic?
A. Owner's manual
B. Manufacturer's service bulletin
C. Specialty service manual
D. Flat rate manual

2. Which of the following statements is correct?
   I. Step-by-step procedures for repairing an automobile are found in service manuals.
   II. Specifications tables in service manuals are needed to find the exact repair procedure.
A. I only   B. II only   C. Both I and II   D. Neither I nor II

3. When servicing an automobile, forms must be filled out to complete the following procedures EXCEPT
A. taking inventory.
B. making appointments.
C. giving a repair estimate.
D. moving the automobile.

4. Mechanic A says that an information disclosure provision requires that a worn-out part be returned.
   Mechanic B says that an information disclosure provision does not allow the garage to charge more than the estimate.
   Who is correct?
A. A only   B. B only   C. Both A and B   D. Neither A nor B

5. Which of the following statements is correct?
   I. A work order is a description of the servicing that is required.
   II. A work order explains what the customer wants done.
A. I only   B. II only   C. Both I and II   D. Neither I nor II

S U P P L E M E N T A L   A C T I V I T I E S

1. Select a service manual and locate the section for repairing engines.
2. Find a specifications section in a service manual and explain whether the specifications are given in the English or metric system.
3. Look in a flat rate manual of the instructor's choice and tell how many hours it takes to replace a clutch.
4. Fill out all sections of a repair order.
5. At $10 an hour, figure out the flat rate labor charge on a repair job of the instructor's choosing.

4 SAFETY AROUND THE AUTOMOBILE

UNIT PREVIEW

Safe working habits prevent accidents. Mechanics must be aware of personal safety, shop safety, and emergency procedures. No one outgrows the need for safety, regardless of experience. Shop safety is everyone's responsibility.

LEARNING OBJECTIVES

When you have completed your assignments and exercises in this unit, you should be able to:

☐ Describe using hand tools and power tools safely.

☐ Describe safety procedures to be used with compressed air.

☐ Describe the differences between jacks, hoists, and jackstands.

☐ Identify equipment misuse.

☐ Identify the different kinds of fire extinguishers.

4.1 ATTITUDE

Carelessness is caused by a poor working attitude. Your carelessness can cause injury to you or cause an accident to someone else. Be aware that only proper conduct, and a good working attitude, can prevent accidents. Thinking about safety reduces your chances of carelessness.

4.2 GOOD SAFETY HABITS

Always work in an area with proper ventilation. Running engines emit exhaust fumes that contain *carbon monoxide,* a poisonous gas. Also, fuel leakage builds up a dangerous vapor in the air, which can be set off by the slightest spark.

Keep the floor in your area clean and free of grease and oil. Grease and oil spots are slippery and cause accidents.

Keep your work area floor clear of tools and parts. Someone could trip and be injured.

4.3 SAFETY WHILE WORKING

Work carefully and give your job complete attention. Be concerned with personal safety, knowing shop layout, and knowing the location of safety devices.

Protect yourself. Wear the proper clothes and proper safety devices. Use the proper tools.

Loose clothing can catch on moving parts, and can result in serious personal injury. Dangling sleeves and shirttails should not be worn. Keep long sleeves buttoned and shirttails tucked in. Wear full leather shoes with nonskid heels and soles to protect your feet and to prevent slipping. Steel-toed safety shoes provide the best foot protection for shop work.

Long hair and jewelry also are safety hazards. Long hair should be covered with a brimless cap. A cap with a brim, as well as long hair, is caught easily in moving parts and machinery. Rings should be removed, because they can become caught.

Wear *safety glasses* or a *face shield* whenever working on parts where particles can fly around. See Figure 4-1. When using a grinding wheel or compressed air, or working around chemicals, always wear safety glasses or a face shield. If chemicals, such as cleaning solvents or battery acid, get in your eyes, wash the eyes out with water immediately. Obtain medical help as soon as possible afterward.

A good grip on tools and parts also prevents personal injury and damage. Wipe excessive oil and grease from hands and tools.

Use the proper tool for the job. The wrong tool can cause personal injury or damage the part. Do *not* place sharp tools, or other objects, in your pocket. Sharp tools will cut or stab into your skin, ruin automotive upholstery, or scratch a panel.

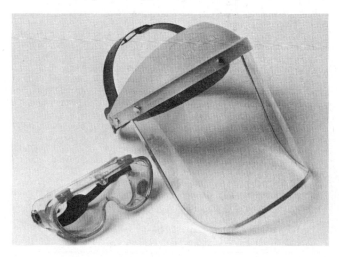

Figure 4-1. Safety glasses and face shields are worn to protect eyes and face.

Figure 4-2. A typical shop layout.

Knowing Shop Layout

A *shop layout* shows the location of work areas and equipment in a particular shop. A typical automotive repair shop is illustrated in Figure 4-2. A drawing, or layout, of a shop is shown in Figure 4-3.

In case of emergency, you should know where everything is in your shop. Locate the work areas, workbenches, lifts, and equipment. Some shops have painted lines on the floor to mark off work areas and danger areas.

Special signs may be posted throughout the shop that give safety instructions in case of emergency. There also may be instruction signs concerning the operation of specialized equipment. Become thoroughly familiar with everything in the shop.

Location of Safety Devices

Know where all exits are located. Be sure that you can locate—and know how to use—each fire extinguisher in the shop. Telephones should have emergency numbers listed beside them. Also, be aware of first-aid kits and how to use them.

Avoiding Hazards in the Shop Area

Be aware of existing hazards and how to handle them. Avoid hazards and treat them with respect. The automotive service area is no place for horseplay. Always be serious when working with tools, and treat them with respect.

Hand tools. Carelessly used hand tools account for many shop accidents that could be prevented easily. *Hand tools* are tools that are operated by hand, without power. Screwdrivers, wrenches, and hammers are typical hand tools.

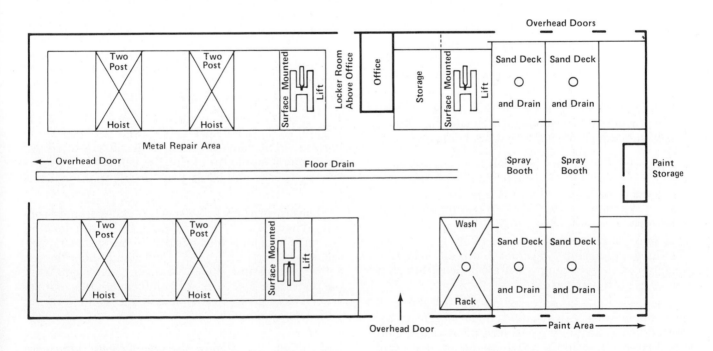

Figure 4-3. Floorplan of a shop layout.

Keep hand tools in good condition. Tools that slip can cause cuts and bruises. Should a tool fall into a moving part, it can fly out and cause serious personal injury.

Use the proper tool. Wrong tools can damage parts, the tool itself, or cause injury. Do *not* use broken or bent tools.

Be careful when using sharp or pointed tools that can slip and cause injury. If a tool is to be sharp, make sure it is sharp. Dull tools can be more dangerous than sharp tools.

Power tools. *Power tools* are operated with an outside source of power, such as electricity, compressed air, or hydraulic pressure. Safety around power tools is very important, because serious injury can result from carelessness. Always wear safety glasses when using power tools.

Do *not* use a power tool without permission from your instructor. Be sure you know how to operate the tool properly before using it. Instructions should be read carefully.

When working with larger power tools—like bench or floor equipment—check machines for signs of damage and proper adjustments. Place all *safety guards* in position (see Figure 4-4). A safety guard is a protective cover over a moving part to prevent injury. Wear safety glasses or a face shield. Make sure everyone and all parts are clear before starting the machine. Keep hands and clothing away from the moving parts.

Never leave a power tool unattended when it is running. If you leave, turn off the machine. Anyone passing an unattended machine can be hurt seriously.

If a machine does not operate properly, turn it off and notify the instructor immediately.

When finished using a power tool, turn it off and wait until it has stopped completely. Disconnect the power source of the tool, then clean, oil, and adjust it, if necessary.

Do *not* enter a work area where a power tool is being used. Obey the rules outlined by your instructor. Stay away from power tools that are being operated.

Compressed air. *Compressed air* is air that is under pressure and directed through hoses to perform work. Compressed air is used to inflate tires, to spray paint, and to drive tools. Compressed air equipment can be dangerous when not used properly.

When using compressed air, safety glasses or a face shield are needed. Particles of dirt and pieces of metal blown under high pressure can penetrate your skin or get into your eyes.

Before using a compressed air system, check all hose connections. Always hold the *air nozzle,* or air control device, securely when starting or shutting off compressed air. A loose nozzle under pressure will whip suddenly and can cause serious injury.

Figure 4-4. Safety guards on a grinder help prevent pieces from flying out and causing injury.

Do *not* point an air nozzle at anyone. Do *not* blow dirt from your clothes or hair. Do *not* use compressed air to clean the floor or a workbench. The high pressure of the compressed air will blow particles everywhere, possibly causing serious injury.

Hydraulic jacks and hoists. An automobile is raised off the ground by a hydraulic *jack* or *hoist*. A jack is a portable tool that is moved under the automobile to raise it off the ground (see Figure 4-5). A hoist is mounted permanently in a work area (see Figure 4-6). An automobile must be moved to the hoist.

Jacks and hoists allow the mechanic to work underneath the automobile. Extreme caution is necessary when using jacks and hoists. An automobile weighs more than a ton. If it falls, it will seriously injure anyone beneath it.

Before using, thoroughly understand how a jack or hoist works. Get permission from the instructor to use the jack or hoist. Have the jack or hoist inspected by the instructor to be sure it is properly prepared for raising and holding the automobile.

The doors, hood, and trunk lid of the automobile should be closed before raising the vehicle. These parts could be damaged when the vehicle is lifted. All passengers should be out of the vehicle before it is raised. *Never* jack up a vehicle when someone is underneath it.

Never use a jack or hoist that is not working properly. When the vehicle is raised, connect the locking device, if a locking device is part of the system. If you are using a floor jack, place a jackstand under the car before getting underneath. Wait for permission from the instructor before getting underneath the vehicle. Wear safety glasses or a face shield when working under an automobile.

Jackstands. *Jackstands*, also called *safety stands*, are important safety devices used in place of, or with, a

Figure 4-5. A floor jack is a portable tool used to raise an automobile.

Figure 4-6. Hoists are large, permanently installed devices that can raise an entire automobile for a mechanic to work under.

jack or a hoist. Jackstands are supports of different heights that sit on the floor. Jackstands are placed under a sturdy chassis member, such as the frame or axle housing (see Figure 4-7).

Jackstands often are used in place of jacks and as extra supports for jacks and hoists. A jack is often removed after jackstands are set in place. This eliminates a hazard, such as a jack handle sticking out. A jack handle that is bumped or kicked can cause a tripping accident or cause the vehicle to fall. Never use a jack by itself to support an automobile. Always use a jackstand with the jack, as a safety precaution.

Chain hoists and cranes. Heavy parts of the automobile, such as engines, are removed by using *chain hoists* (see Figure 4-8) or *cranes* (see Figure 4-9). Another term for chain hoist is *chain fall*. Cranes often are called cherry pickers. To prevent serious injury,

Figure 4-7. Jackstands, or safety stands, are safety supports used to support an automobile for service.

Figure 4-8. A chain hoist, mounted to an overhead pulley, is used to remove engines and other heavy assemblies.

Figure 4-9. A crane also can be used to remove an engine.
OWATONNA TOOL CO.

chain hoists and cranes must be attached properly to the parts being lifted.

Obtain permission from your instructor before attaching a hoist or crane. Attach the lifting chain or cable to the system that is to be removed. Have your instructor check the attachment.

Place the chain hoist or crane directly over the assembly that is to be removed. Make sure chain or cable is secure before lifting.

Exhaust gases from running engines. Many service procedures require that you run the engine in the shop. To do this, the exhaust should be directed outside of the shop. Many shops have an exhaust ventilation system (see Figure 4-10). In some shops, it may be required that the automobile be started and run outside.

Before starting the vehicle, get permission from the instructor. Block the wheels to prevent the vehicle from moving. Place the transmission lever in Park for automatic transmissions or in Neutral for manual transmissions. Set the emergency brake. Do *not* stand in front of or behind the automobile or let anyone else stand there.

Painting equipment. *Spray painting* is done with compressed air. Paint is flammable and toxic. Painting should be done in a spray booth with a ventilation system to remove flammable fumes. The painter should wear a respirator, or filtering mask, and safety glasses to protect against the paint spray.

Cleaning equipment. The cleaning of parts is necessary in all repair shops. Parts may be cleaned either by steam or in solvent. A *steam cleaner* uses hot water vapor, or steam, to melt dirt off parts (see Figure 4-11). *Solvent* is a chemical that acts on dirt to loosen it from parts.

When using a steam-cleaner, wear safety glasses or a face shield and gloves to protect against burns.

Some solvents are harmful chemicals that can damage clothing, skin, and eyes. When using these solvents, wear safety glasses or a face shield, gloves, and overalls or a shop coat (see Figure 4-12).

Equipment Defects and Misuse

Be on the lookout for defective and misused shop equipment.

Make sure each piece of equipment has the proper safety guard. Guards should be located over all fans, belts, pulleys, and grinders.

Electrical cords should *not* be worn or frayed. Cords should not be tacked to a wall. Poor electrical cords and connections may cause fire or even electrocute someone.

Cylinders of compressed gas, such as the kind used for welding, must *not* be stored near heat. All cylinders must be in a ventilated area. Secure all cylinders with a chain or cable. Cylinders should *not* be used to support other equipment or parts. Improper storage can cause cylinders to explode.

Do *not* use faulty welding equipment. Gas welding must be confined to a protected area with no combustibles, oil, or grease nearby to cause an explosion. Electric welding also must be done in a protected place or in a special booth. Welders should wear proper safety equipment. Fire extinguishers must be handy. Never coil welding cable during use.

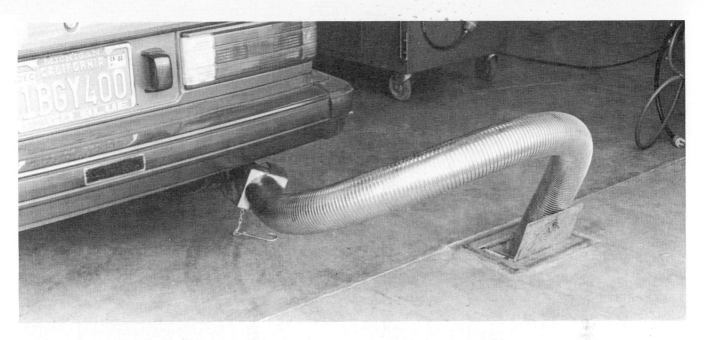

Figure 4-10. An exhaust-gas ventilation system draws exhaust fumes from an automobile tailpipe and directs it outside.

Figure 4-11. A steam cleaner removes heavy dirt from many parts of an automobile.

Figure 4-12. Parts are cleaned in a solvent tank. Safety glasses, a shop apron, gloves, and long sleeves prevent burns while cleaning in a solvent tank.

Fire Prevention and Fire Extinguishers

Gasoline, cleaning solvents, and paints are only some of the combustibles found in automotive service areas. These combustibles can catch fire or cause explosion easily if safety measures are *not* followed.

The most important sign that any mechanic should heed is the "no smoking" sign. All "no smoking" signs should be large and displayed properly. No one should smoke, or have an open flame, in a service area; that includes customers.

All combustibles must be kept in fireproof containers designed for storing. These storage containers must prevent leaking and evaporation. Improperly stored combustibles can be ignited by a spark as small as from a light switch. Never store combustibles in

Figure 4-13. Combustibles always should be kept in proper storage containers.

EXTINGUISHERS

FIRES	TYPE		USE		OPERATION
A CLASS *A* FIRES ORDINARY COMBUSTIBLE MATERIALS SUCH AS WOOD, PAPER, TEXTILES AND SO FORTH. REQUIRES. . .COOLING-QUENCHING	**FOAM** SOLUTION OF ALUMINUM SULPHATE AND BICARBONATE OF SODA		OK FOR **A B**		*FOAM:* DON'T PLAY STREAM INTO THE BURNING LIQUID. ALLOW FOAM TO FALL LIGHTLY ON FIRE
			NOT FOR **C**		
	CARBON DIOXIDE CARBON DIOXIDE GAS UNDER PRESSURE		NOT FOR **A**		*CARBON DIOXIDE:* DIRECT DISCHARGE AS CLOSE TO FIRE AS POSSIBLE. FIRST AT EDGE OF FLAMES AND GRADUALLY FORWARD AND UPWARD
B CLASS *B* FIRES FLAMMABLE LIQUIDS, GREASES, GASOLINE, OILS, PAINTS AND SO FORTH. REQUIRES. . .BLANKETING OR SMOTHERING			OK FOR **B C**		
	DRY CHEMICAL	MULTI-PURPOSE TYPE		ORDINARY BC TYPE	*DRY CHEMICAL:* DIRECT STREAM AT BASE OF FLAMES. USE RAPID LEFT-TO-RIGHT MOTION TOWARD FLAMES
		OK FOR **A B C**		NOT FOR **A**	
				OK FOR **B C**	
C CLASS *C* FIRES ELECTRICAL EQUIPMENT, MOTORS, SWITCHES AND SO FORTH. REQUIRES. . .A NONCONDUCTING AGENT	**SODA-ACID** BICARBONATE OF SODA SOLUTION AND SULPHURIC ACID		OK FOR **A**		*SODA-ACID:* DIRECT STREAM AT BASE OF FLAME
			NOT FOR **B C**		

Figure 4-14. Fire extinguisher reference chart. FORD MOTOR COMPANY

glass jugs. Glass jugs can fall, break, and explode. Examples of combustibles storage are shown in Figure 4-13.

Wipe up spilled gasoline immediately. Put gasoline-soaked rags outside to dry, away from flames and in a "No Smoking" area. All oil and paint rags should be kept in closed, fireproof containers.

When working on a leaking fuel system, catch leaking gasoline in a container or with rags. Fix the leak as quickly as possible. Do *not* touch the battery during this time, because this may cause sparks and an explosion.

Keep the shop doors open or the ventilation system operating to prevent the buildup of harmful fumes.

All shop areas should have fire extinguishers. Know the location and the specific purpose of each fire extinguisher. Only certain fire extinguishers can be used to extinguish gasoline or electrical fires. Also, know how to use fire extinguishers on all types of fires (see Figure 4-14). The sooner a fire is reached, the easier it is to control.

Do *not* play with fire extinguishers. Besides causing someone to slip or causing eye damage, empty extinguishers are useless.

Safety Rules in the Shop Area

All shops have safety rules. Follow the rules at all times. See Figure 4-15. Before beginning work, learn all of the safety rules first. Safety rules are assigned to protect you and your job.

Emergency Procedures

If an accident occurs or someone is hurt, notify your instructor immediately. Do *not* give first aid if you don't know what you are doing. Trying to help may do more harm than good.

Operating Cars Safely

Do *not* move a car in the shop or make a road test without your instructor's permission.

Special precautions. When moving a car in the work area, first test the brakes. Then, buckle up the safety belt. Use extreme care when driving a car in the shop. Make sure no one is under another car, that the way is clear, and that there are no tools or parts under the car.

When making a road test, first check the brakes. Then, fasten the safety belt. A road test is a drive to identify a specific problem or verify the repair of a problem. Observe all traffic laws. Drive only as far as is necessary to check the automobile. *Never* make jackrabbit starts, turn corners too quickly, or drive faster than conditions allow. A careless road test can damage the vehicle severely or cause an accident and injuries.

Figure 4-15. Always follow a shop's safety rules. CLIFF CREAGER

UNIT HIGHLIGHTS

- Injuries occur when you become careless and sloppy.
- Personal safety includes wearing the proper clothes, wearing the proper safety devices, and using the proper tools.
- A shop layout shows the location of work areas and equipment.
- The improper use of hand tools and power tools is a hazard in the shop area.
- Compressed air is dangerous when not used properly.
- Extreme caution is necessary when using jacks and hoists because an automobile usually weighs 3,000 pounds (1,360 kilograms) or more.
- To run an engine in the shop, the exhaust must be directed outside of the shop.
- Each piece of equipment should be inspected for defects and misuse.
- Combustibles must be stored in a special area and handled carefully to prevent fires and explosions.
- Know the location and use of all fire extinguishers in the shop area.

TERMS

carbon monoxide	jack
safety glasses	hoist
face shield	jackstand
shop layout	chain hoist
hand tools	chain fall
power tools	crane
safety guards	spray painting
compressed air	steam cleaner
air nozzle	solvent

R E V I E W   Q U E S T I O N S

DIRECTIONS: The following questions are similar to those used on mechanic certification tests. On a separate sheet of paper, write the letter of the correct choice.

1. Which of the following statements is correct?

   I. Long hair and jewelry can become caught in moving parts.

   II. Don't worry about dirty tools, because they are part of the job.

   A. I only   B. II only   C. Both I and II   D. Neither I nor II

2. Mechanic A says that screwdrivers, wrenches, and hammers are typical hand tools.

   Mechanic B says that a power tool can be kept running if the mechanic puts up a "power on" sign.

   Who is correct?

   A. A only   B. B only   C. Both A and B   D. Neither A nor B

3. All of the following statements are true EXCEPT

   A. Compressed air is used to drive tools.

   B. A jack is a portable tool that raises an automobile.

   C. A hoist is mounted permanently in a work area.

   D. Jackstands are used to keep jacks aligned properly.

4. Check servicing equipment for defects whenever there is

   A. a nail holding a cord to the wall.

   B. a separate ground wire on a machine.

   C. compressed air in a tire.

   D. a safety guard missing.

5. Which of the following statements is correct?

   I. All combustibles must be kept in a ventilated jar.

   II. A single fire extinguisher is designed to control all fires.

   A. I only   B. II only   C. Both I and II   D. Neither I nor II

S U P P L E M E N T A L   A C T I V I T I E S

1. Make a sketch of the school shop layout. Indicate any possible safety hazards. Note the locations of all exits, fire extinguishers, and water fountains.
2. List all of the ways you can think of to handle a hand tool safely.
3. Select a power tool and carefully read how to operate it. Describe the proper operation of that power tool.
4. Study the procedure for raising an automobile on the school hoist. Describe the safest way to raise and secure the automobile.
5. Describe the procedures needed to prepare an automobile before the engine is started.
6. Choose a fire extinguisher that is used in your work area. Study the instructions carefully. Describe what type of fire the extinguisher is designed to control. Explain how to control a fire with that extinguisher.

5 USING FASTENERS

UNIT PREVIEW

Fasteners attach and hold other parts together. The entire automobile is assembled and kept together with fasteners. Each fastener is used for a different purpose on an automobile. It is important to know how each fastener operates. This unit discusses the different types of fasteners and how they are used.

LEARNING OBJECTIVES

When you have completed your assignments and exercises in this unit, you should be able to:

☐ Describe the difference between screws and bolts.
☐ Explain the kinds of nuts found on automobiles and how they work.
☐ Describe the differences between the English system and the metric system in measuring thread diameters and reading designations.
☐ Describe thread pitch.
☐ Describe nonthreaded fasteners.

5.1 MEASUREMENT SYSTEMS

For automotive systems to operate properly, the parts must fit. To fit, fasteners, parts, and the tools needed to work on them, must be made to specific sizes, or measurements. Automotive manufacturers use the two most common measurement systems—the *English system* and the *metric system*.

The English System

The measurement system found most frequently in the United States is the English system. Measurements used in the English system require knowing many different combinations of numbers. For example, one foot is 12 inches, one yard is three feet, and one mile is 5,280 feet.

English measurements used in automotive service tools usually are for length. Lengths must be known for fastener sizes, tool sizes, and parts sizes. These lengths are given, almost exclusively, in inches or parts of inches. The parts of inches are expressed either as fractions or in decimals. English length and weight measurements used in automotive service are shown in Figure 5-1.

UNITS OF LENGTH MEASUREMENT

12 Inches = 1 Foot
3 Feet = 1 Yard
5½ Yards = 1 Rod
40 Rods = 1 Furlong
8 Furlongs = 1 Mile
4 Inches = 1 Hand
9 Inches = 1 Span

UNITS OF WEIGHT MEASUREMENT

16 Drams = 1 Ounce
16 Ounces = 1 Pound
14 Pounds = 1 Stone
8 Stones = 1 Hundred weight (CWT) (112 Pounds)
20 CWT = 1 Long Ton (2240 Pounds)
2000 Pounds = 1 Short Ton

Figure 5-1. English length and weight measurements.

The Metric System

The metric system is also called the international system, because it is used in most countries. The metric system is easier to use. There is no need to memorize that 12 inches make a foot, three feet make a yard, and so on. Instead, metric sizes are increased when multiplying by 10. For example, 10 millimeters equal 1 centimeter, 10 centimeters equal 1 decimeter, and 10 decimeters equal 1 meter. See Figure 5-2 for metric measurements of length.

Unlike the English system, metrics do not use fractions. Instead, units smaller than 1 meter are listed

Number of Meters	Prefix	Symbol
1,000,000,000,000	Terameter	Tm
1,000,000,000	Gigameter	Gm
1,000,000	Megameter	Mm
1,000	Kilometer	km
100	Hectometer	hm
10	Decameter	dam
1	Meter	
0.1	Decimeter	dm
0.01	Centimeter	cm
0.001	Millimeter	mm
0.000 001	Micrometer	μ m
0.000 000 001	Nanometer	nm
0.000 000 000 001	Picometer	pm
0.000 000 000 000 001	Temtometer	tm
0.000 000 000 000 000 001	Attometer	am

Figure 5-2. Metric length measurements.

as 0.1 for decimeter, 0.01 for centimeter, and 0.001 for millimeter. In this way, metric sizes also are decreased by multiplications of 10. Most metric fasteners on American cars can be identified by their blue color. This has been done to aid mechanics in identifying metric fasteners on cars.

English/Metric Conversions

Converting from English to metric, or from metric to English, is common in automotive servicing. Conversion tables or booklets usually are available in shops. A typical automotive *English/metric conversion* chart is shown in Figure 5-3.

	multiply	by	for equiv. no. of:
ACCELERATION	Foot/sec^2	0.304 8	metre/sec^2 (m/s^2)
	Inch/sec^2	0.025 4	metre/sec^2
TORQUE	Pound-inch	0.112 98	newton-metres (Nom)
	Pound-foot	1.355 8	newton-metres
POWER	horsepower	0.746	kilowatts(kw)
PRESSURE or STRESS	inches of water	0.2488	kilopascals (kPa)
	pounds/sq. in.	6.895	kilopascals (kPa)
ENERGY or WORK	BTU	1 055.	joules (J)
	foot-pound	1.355 8	joules (J)
	kilowatt-hour	3 600 000. or 3.6 x 10^6	joules (J=one W's)
LIGHT	foot candle	10.76	lumens/metre^2 (lm/m^2)
FUEL PERFORMANCE	miles/gal	0.425 1	kilometres/litre (km/l)
	gal/mile	2.352 7	litres/kilometre (l/km)
VELOCITY	miles/hour	1.609 3	kilometres/hr. (km/h)
LENGTH	inch	25.4	millimetres (mm)
	foot	0.304 8	metres (m)
	yard	0.914 4	metres (m)
	mile	1.609	kilometres (km)
AREA	inch^2	645.2	millimetres^2 (mm^2)
		6.45	centimetres^2 (cm^2)
	foot^2	0.092 9	metres^2 (m^2)
	yard^2	0.836 1	metres^2
VOLUME	inch^3	16387.	mm^3
	inch^3	16.387	cm^3
	quart	0.946 4	litres (l)
	gallon	3.785 4	litres
	yard^3	0.764 6	metres^3 (m^3)
MASS	pound	0.453 6	kilograms (kg)
	ton	907.18	kilograms (kg)
	ton	0.907 18	tonne (t)
FORCE	kilogram	9.807	newtons (N)
	ounce	0.278 0	newtons
	pound	4.448	newtons
TEMPERATURE	degree fahrenheit	0.556 ($^\circ$F −32)	degree Celsius ($^\circ$C)

Figure 5-3. English/metric conversions. FORD MOTOR COMPANY

5.2 THREADED FASTENERS

A thread is a spiral groove on the outside or inside of a fastener. This spiral groove creates, or mates with, an identical spiral groove to form a holding or sealing surface. Fasteners using threads are called *threaded fasteners*. Threaded fasteners used most frequently in automobiles are:

- Screws
- Bolts
- Studs
- Nuts.

Screws

A *screw* is a threaded fastener that turns into a threaded hole. A screw has threads on the outside, or *external threads*. A screw holds two parts together.

A *capscrew* is a common fastener. A capscrew has a six-sided, or hexagonal, head (see Figure 5-4). A capscrew, also called a *hex-head screw,* holds larger parts together.

A *machine screw* is similar to a capscrew (see Figure 5-5). A machine screw has a slotted head. The slots accommodate the head of a screwdriver. A machine screw holds smaller automotive parts.

A *hollow-head,* or *Allen head,* screw is shown in Figure 5-6. Allen head screws sometimes are used instead of slotted machine screws. Special tools called Allen wrenches are used to turn Allen head screws.

A *sheet metal screw* is used to join two pieces of sheet metal. Sheet metal is thin metal, such as body metal. The sheet metal screw is tapered and pointed at the end (see Figure 5-7). This allows it to be started easily if there is a small hole in which it can be started. Sheet metal threads are wide so that the screw will cut and hold while it is being screwed in.

Self-tapping screws cut their own threads into metal. A self-tapping screw usually is harder than the metal to which it is fastened. The external thread makes internal threads as the screw is tightened into place (see Figure 5-8).

Bolts and Nuts

A *bolt* is a fastener with external threads. A bolt fits through a hole in a part, but does *not* tighten inside the part. When a bolt is inserted into a part, the end of the bolt is exposed and extends past the part. Bolts usually have hexagonal heads (see Figure 5-9). Bolts with square heads may be used where assembly strength is not critical.

A special type of bolt is the *carriage bolt*. Carriage bolts have a raised, square section, called a *shoulder*, just below the head (see Figure 5-10). The shoulder fits into the hole with the bolt, and the bolt cannot be turned once it is tightened.

Bolts are secured with *nuts*. Nuts are fasteners with internal threads. Nuts are turned and tightened on the extended end of the installed bolt. Most automotive nuts have hexagonal heads (see Figure 5-11). Square-head nuts are used occasionally.

Figure 5-4. Capscrew.

Figure 5-5. Machine screw.

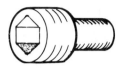

Figure 5-6. Allen head screw.

Figure 5-7. Sheet metal screw.

Figure 5-8. Self-tapping screw.

Figure 5-9. Bolt.

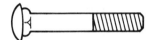

Figure 5-10. Carriage bolt.

Figure 5-11. Hex nut.

Figure 5-12. Self-locking nut.

Figure 5-13. Castellated nut and cotter pin.

Self-locking nuts, shown in Figure 5-12, have a hump, or cone, over one end of the nut. Self-locking nuts are used where extra locking action is needed. As the self-locking nut is tightened, the bolt is squeezed solidly into the cone.

A slotted nut, or *castellated nut*, is used when it is important for the nut to remain in one position. A castellated nut has slots and holes in it (see Figure 5-13). A *cotter pin* is a steel wire that is bent over. The cotter pin is fitted through the castellated nut to prevent the nut from turning.

Speed Nuts

A *speed nut*, shown in Figure 5-14, is pressed over the threads of a bolt or stud. A speed nut is used to replace conventional nuts in some automobiles.

Studs

A *stud* is a fastener with external threads on each end (see Figure 5-15). To hold parts together, a stud first is tightened into a threaded hole in a part. A second part fits over the stud. Finally, a nut fits over the exposed end of the stud and is tightened.

5.3 WASHERS

Washers are fasteners that are used between a screw or nut and the part being tightened. *Flat washers* and *lockwashers* are used frequently in automobiles.

Flat washers spread out the load of a tightened nut over a larger area (see Figure 5-16). This spreading-out action prevents damage to a part's surface.

Lockwashers have sharp edges that dig into fasteners and parts to prevent them from moving. Lockwashers, shown in Figure 5-17, are placed under a nut or screw head.

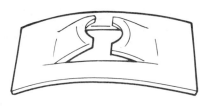

Figure 5-14. Speed nut.

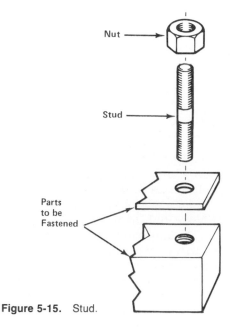

Figure 5-15. Stud.

5.4 THREAD DIAMETERS AND DESIGNATIONS

Once you have determined which type of threaded fastener is required, you must find one that works properly. Even though fasteners may look alike, they may not work together. Fasteners come in many sizes, and in both English and metric systems.

English System

Suppose the bolt shown in Figure 5-18 has an English size measurement of ½-20NF × 1. This description would tell the mechanic that the diameter of the bolt is ½ inch [12.7 mm]. There are 20 threads per inch. The bolt has a *national fine thread* (NF). A fine thread is one that has narrow spaces between threads. The length of the bolt, from the base of the head, is 1 inch [25.4 mm].

Bolt, screw, or stud diameter of ½ inch is measured from the outside thread diameter. A nut is measured from the inside thread diameter.

The figure of 20 threads per inch determines whether the bolt will fit with the threads of a part or nut. The NF also determines whether the threads will match. An NC (*national coarse thread*) designation is used, too. A coarse thread has more space between threads than a fine thread. Fine and coarse threads are based on what is called the Unified System (non-metric). The 1-inch length determines whether the bolt is short, long, or just right for the application.

Metric System

Suppose the bolt shown in Figure 5-19 has a metric size measurement of M 6.0 × 1. This description would tell the mechanic that the bolt has metric (M) threads. The diameter of this bolt is 6.0 millimeters [0.24 in.]. The *thread pitch* is indicated by the numeral 1. Thread pitch is measured in millimeters and is the distance between each thread. A bolt with a higher pitch number has a coarser thread. In the metric system, no NC or NF thread designations are used.

Figure 5-16. Flat washer.

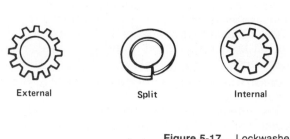

External   Split   Internal

Figure 5-17. Lockwashers.

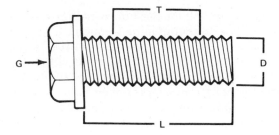

G Grade Marking (bolt strength)
L Length, (inches)
T Thread Pitch (thread/inch)
D Nominal Diameter (inches)

Figure 5-18. English system bolt measurement.
FORD MOTOR COMPANY

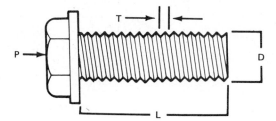

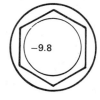

P Property Class (bolt strength)
L Length (millimeters)
T Thread Pitch (thread/millimeter)
D Nominal Diameter (millimeters)

Figure 5-19. Metric bolt measurement. FORD MOTOR COMPANY

If the metric designation is followed by a number for length, the length is given in metric units.

5.5 DETERMINING THREAD PITCH

Many manufacturers use both English and metric system fasteners on the same automobile, as well as fine and coarse thread sizes. Because different sizes of fasteners are *not* interchangeable, the mechanic must be able to determine exactly what is needed.

A *thread gauge,* either English or metric, may be needed to determine sizes. A thread gauge is a tool with a number of blades that have teeth on them (see Figure 5-20). Matching the blade teeth with the fastener threads identifies thread size.

5.6 GRADE MARKINGS

Fasteners are graded for strength. Following *grade markings* is critical for a mechanic. Always use a fastener of similar quality when a replacement is necessary, because different fasteners have different strengths. A lower grade bolt or nut probably will fail. As in thread designations, grade markings are in English and metric systems.

English systems for bolt and nut grade markings are shown in Figure 5-21. Grade markings for bolts are in slashes. An absence of slashes means the fastener is of the lowest quality. Eight slashes indicate the highest quality. Grade markings for nuts are with dots. An absence of dots means lowest quality, while six dots indicate highest quality.

Metric grade markings for bolts and nuts are shown in Figure 5-22. Grade markings for bolts are in numerals from 4.6 to 10.9. A low number indicates low quality, while 10.9 means highest quality. No marking indicates lowest quality. Grade markings for nuts also are in numerals with no numerals meaning lowest quality and 10 meaning highest quality.

Figure 5-20. Thread gauge.

5.7 TORQUE REQUIREMENTS FOR THREADED FASTENERS

Many fasteners must be tightened only a certain amount. If fasteners are made too tight or too loose, a failure of parts will result. To determine how much a fastener must be tightened, *torque specifications* are furnished by all manufacturers. Torque specifications are given as pound-inches (lb.-in.) or pound-feet (lb.-ft.) or newton-meters (Nm).

5.8 ADHESIVES AND THREAD SEALANTS

Fasteners may need sealing help on some parts of the automobile. In this case, manufacturers recommend *adhesives* and *thread sealants.* Adhesives and sealants are glues that add holding power and sealing ability

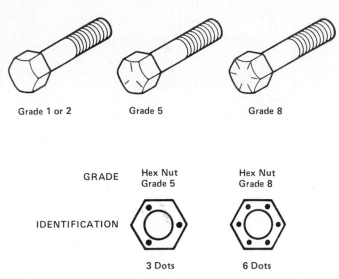

Figure 5-21. English system grade markings for bolts and nuts.
FORD MOTOR COMPANY

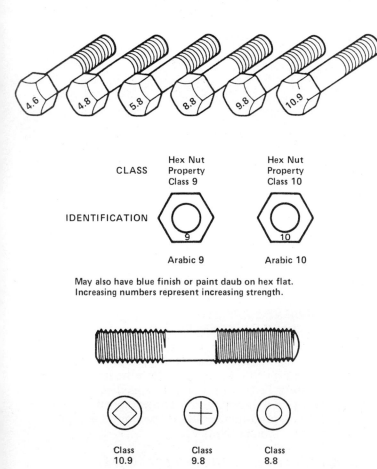

Figure 5-22. Metric grade markings for bolts, nuts, and studs.
FORD MOTOR COMPANY

where two parts are joined. Sealants usually are added to threads where fluid contact is frequent. Chemical thread retainers are either aerobic (cures in the presence of air) or anaerobic (cures in the absence of air). These chemical products can be used in place of lock washers.

Anti-seize compound is used on many fasteners, especially those used with aluminum parts (see Figure 5-23). Its use prevents dissimilar metals from reacting with one another and seizing. Be sure to follow manufacturer's recommendations on the use of this compound.

5.9 NONTHREADED FASTENERS

Several other types of fasteners are used to hold automotive parts together. Unlike bolts and screws, these fasteners do not have threads to lock them in place. The most common *nonthreaded fasteners* used on automobiles are:

- Dowel pins
- Keys
- Rivets
- Retaining rings.

Dowel Pins

Dowel pins align parts. Dowel pins are solid or hollow cylinders that fit into holes in the parts that are connected. Dowels may be straight, tapered, or have slits (called a *roll pin*). See Figure 5-24.

Keys

Figure 5-25 shows a *key* fastener. A key is a small piece of metal that locks two parts together so that they will rotate as one. Keys are positioned in slots, or *keyways*, in the connecting parts. Keys are used to connect gears to shafts.

Figure 5-23. Chemical sealants.

Rivets

A *rivet* is a soft metal pin used to attach pieces of metal permanently. When an equal-sized hole is drilled between two pieces of metal, a rivet can be inserted to hold the pieces together. The small end of the rivet is flattened to fasten the two parts (see Figure 5-26).

Retaining Rings

A *snap ring*, or *retaining ring*, fits into a groove on the inside or outside of a shaft or cylinder. See Figure 5-27. Retaining rings are used in transmissions to hold gears on shafts. A retaining ring, like a spring, is made to keep a specific shape. If a retaining ring is temporarily pushed out of shape, it will spring back to its original position.

U N I T   H I G H L I G H T S

- Measurements are made using the English system and the metric system.
- Threaded fasteners include all screws, bolts, nuts, and washers.
- Bolts have thread diameters and designations that tell the size of the thread, the width, and the length.
- Thread pitch is the distance between threads and is measured with a thread gauge.
- Grade markings tell the quality of a bolt and a nut.
- Nonthreaded fasteners are dowel pins, keys, rivets, and retaining rings.

T E R M S

English system	stud
metric system	washer
English/metric	flat washer
conversion	lockwasher
threaded fasteners	national fine thread
screw	national coarse thread
external threads	thread pitch
capscrew	thread gauge
machine screw	grade markings
hollow-head screw	torque specifications
Allen head screw	adhesive
sheet metal screw	thread sealant
self-tapping screw	anti-seize compound
bolt	nonthreaded fasteners
carriage bolt	dowel pins
nut	key
self-locking nut	keyway
castellated nut	rivet
cotter pin	snap ring
speed nut	retaining ring

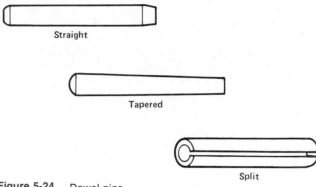

Figure 5-24. Dowel pins.

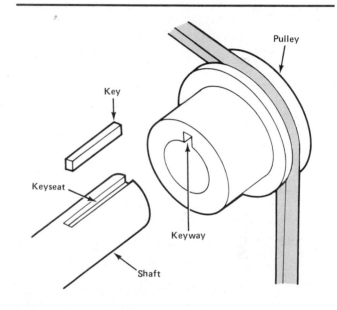

Figure 5-25. Key and keyway.

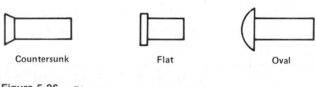

Figure 5-26. Rivets.

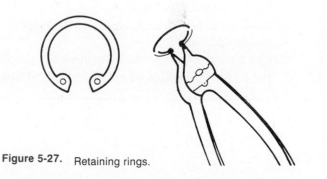

Figure 5-27. Retaining rings.

REVIEW QUESTIONS

DIRECTIONS: The following questions are similar to those used on mechanic certification tests. On a separate sheet of paper, circle the letter of the correct choice.

1. Mechanic A says that machine screws and Allen head screws are the same except for size.
   Mechanic B says that bolts and nuts can both be castellated.
   Who is correct?
   A. A only   B. B only   C. Both A and B   D. Neither A nor B

2. All of the following statements about washers are correct EXCEPT
   A. They are placed between a bolt head and a nut.
   B. They can be flat and have sharp edges.
   C. Preventing damage is one of their functions.
   D. They can lock other fasteners into position.

3. Which of the following is information a mechanic can obtain about a bolt by using the English system of threaded fastener designations?
   A. Bolt head diameter
   B. Number of threads per inch
   C. National short coarse
   D. Distance between shank and slice

4. Which of the following statements is correct?
   I. Grade markings found on bolts and nuts are marked with dots and letters.
   II. Torque specifications determine how far a bolt can be turned.
   A. I only   B. II only   C. Both I and II   D. Neither I nor II

5. Mechanic A says that dowel pins must be hollow to be called fasteners.
   Mechanic B says that a key fastener is used to connect gears and a shaft.
   Who is correct?
   A. A only   B. B only   C. Both A and B   D. Neither A nor B

SUPPLEMENTAL ACTIVITIES

1. Show the difference between capscrews, machine screws, Allen head screws, and sheetmetal screws.
2. Install a castellated nut and cotter pin on a bolt.
3. Read the threaded diameters and designations of a bolt chosen by the instructor and explain what the designation means.
4. Use a thread gauge and determine the thread pitch of a bolt furnished by the instructor.
5. Determine the grade of one English and one metric set of bolts and nuts.

6 USING HAND TOOLS

UNIT PREVIEW

Measurements are necessary to determine the proper size of a fastener or a tool. Equally important is the selection of the proper tool for a job. The basic tools that must be mastered by all mechanics are hand tools. A hand tool is one that is operated by hand, not by power. The first ability you should learn as an automotive mechanic is the proper selection and use of hand tools.

LEARNING OBJECTIVES

When you have completed your assignments and exercises in this unit, you should be able to:

☐ Describe the different types of automotive wrenches.

☐ Describe the different types of handles and accessories that can be used with a socket wrench.

☐ Explain what parts of pliers are adjustable and how they are adjusted.

☐ Explain how the cutting teeth on a file are identified.

6.1 TOOL MEASUREMENTS

Many hand tools are designed to fit only one size of fastener. These tool measurements usually are stamped into the tools (see Figure 6-1). The proper size tool should be used to prevent damage to a fastener or part. The tool measurement will be either in the English or metric system.

Common sizes for tools with English measurements include: $\frac{3}{8}$, $\frac{7}{16}$, $\frac{1}{2}$, $\frac{9}{16}$, $\frac{5}{8}$, $\frac{11}{16}$, $\frac{3}{5}$, $\frac{13}{16}$, $\frac{7}{8}$, $\frac{15}{16}$, and 1 inch. Metric tools are listed in sizes measured in millimeters. Metric tools may be listed as 8, 9, 10, 11, 12, 13, and 14mm, etc.

6.2 WRENCHES

A *wrench* is a tool used to loosen or tighten a part. One or both ends of a wrench may have an opening that is placed over a fastener. The angle of the opening is important when working conditions are tight. Plus, there must be a handle that the mechanic can grip to move the tool. To work properly, wrenches

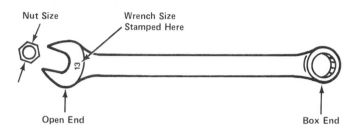

Figure 6-1. Wrench size measurements.

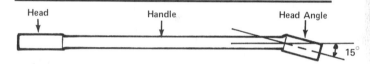

Figure 6-2. Parts of a wrench.

must be the correct size (either English or metric) and correct shape. Wrenches come in the following styles:

- Open-end
- Adjustable open-end
- Box-end
- Combination
- Socket
- Allen and Torx
- Special-purpose.

Open-End

A wrench with an opening, or *head,* at one or both ends is an *open-end wrench* (see Figure 6-2). The open end slides over a bolt or nut to tighten or loosen it. The handle is often placed at an angle to allow the wrench to be used in two different positions. Open-end wrenches come in many sizes and shapes (see Figure 6-3). Do not use an open-end wrench if a box-end can be used.

Figure 6-3. Open-end wrenches.

Adjustable Open-End

If the proper wrench size is not available, an *adjustable open-end wrench* can be used on fasteners. The adjustable wrench will fit many different sizes (see Figure 6-4). To use an adjustable open-end wrench, *always* be sure both jaws are adjusted tightly around the fastener. Adjustable wrenches should be used only when box-end or open-end wrenches will not fit.

Box-End

The heads on a *box-end wrench* are closed. The box-end, or box, wrench usually has a head of different sizes on each end. The head openings have six or 12 grooves that grip the fastener. Because of head design, a mechanic can apply more force to the box-end wrench without the wrench slipping. Box-end wrenches are shown in Figure 6-5.

Combination

When an open-end and a box-end are built into the same wrench, it is known as a *combination wrench*. See Figure 6-6. Both ends of the wrench usually have the same head sizes. The box-end may have an angled head to make it more useful.

Socket

A *socket wrench* consists of a handle and drive that holds a socket (see Figure 6-7). The socket fits over a fastener and surrounds it. Six to 12 grooves, or points, inside the socket grip the corners of the fastener. The socket has a squared hole, called a drive opening, where the socket is attached to the drive.

The handle may have a *ratchet* built in to operate the drive (see Figure 6-8). A ratchet is a mechanism inside the handle that allows drive action in either turning direction. A lever near the drive end can be positioned to switch the ratchet's operating direction to either clockwise or counterclockwise. The drive is the square peg connected to the socket.

Drive sizes. The difference in *drive size* is the best indicator of the strength of a socket wrench. Drive size refers to the diameter of the drive in the handle. A ¼-inch drive is light-duty, ⅜-inch drive is medium-duty, and ½-inch drive is heavy-duty. Socket wrench drives can be as large as 1 inch.

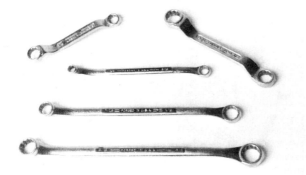

Figure 6-4. Adjustable wrenches.

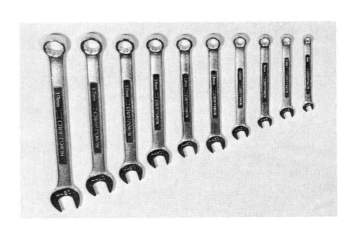

Figure 6-6. Combination wrenches.

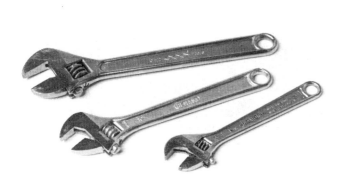

Figure 6-5. Box-end wrenches.

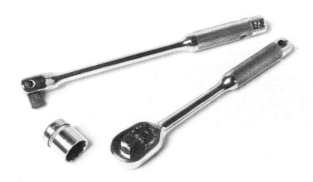

Figure 6-7. Socket wrench assembly.

Handles and accessories. A variety of handles can be used with a socket wrench. Handles and handle accessories, shown in Figure 6-8, include:

- Speed handle
- Breaker bar
- T-handle
- Extension
- Accessories.

Specialized handles allow the mechanic to use socket wrenches in places where another wrench might not fit and/or work.

A *speed handle* is a long crank with a handle that turns freely to remove loosened fasteners. A *breaker bar* is long and hinged to allow greater turning force and turning angle. A *T-handle* is flexible in tight areas and gives the mechanic more turning force when the handle is extended.

Extensions give socket wrenches greater length and versatility. Extensions of different lengths usually connect between the drive and the socket.

An adaptor, such as a *universal joint,* is used to change drive angle. Another type of adaptor can be used to change a socket for Allen head or slotted screwdriver use. Still another type of adaptor permits the use of a ½-inch-drive socket with a ⅜-inch-drive handle.

Torque. If a bolt or nut holding a part must be torqued to specifications, a *torque wrench* is required. A torque wrench indicates how much torque, or turning resistance, a fastener receives.

A torque wrench consists of a long, flexible bar and a socket drive. The proper socket is placed onto the drive and the fastener starts to be tightened. A beam torque wrench shows the torque reading on an indicator on the handle (see Figure 6-9). A micrometer type torque wrench is adjusted to proper torque and clicks when that torque is reached.

Special Wrenches

Some fasteners require special tools because of head design. Allen and Torx wrenches are tools used on fasteners with special head designs (see Figure 6-10).

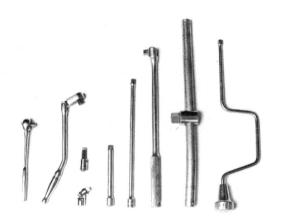

Figure 6-8. Socket wrench accessories.

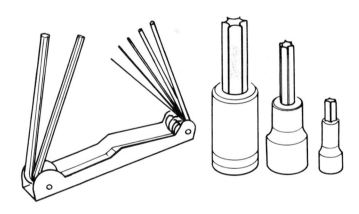

Figure 6-10. Special wrenches.

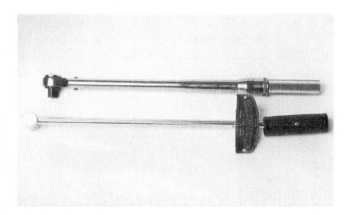

Figure 6-9. Torque wrenches.

6.3 SCREWDRIVERS

A *screwdriver* is a shaft, or shank, of metal with a handle at one end and a blade at the other end (see Figure 6-11). The shank is imbedded in a plastic, metal, or wood handle. The blade fits and turns the head of a fastener. A screwdriver blade that is too large or too small will damage the fastener and the screwdriver. Always take care to use the proper tool.

Slotted Screwdrivers

The screwdriver that many people call "common" actually is named the *slotted screwdriver*. A slotted screwdriver has a flat blade.

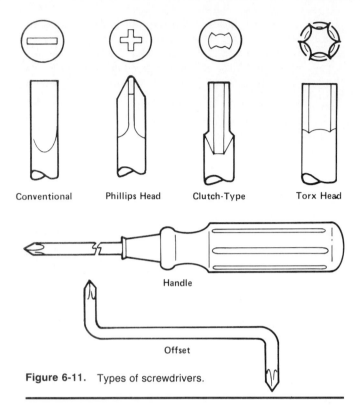

Conventional Phillips Head Clutch-Type Torx Head

Handle

Offset

Figure 6-11. Types of screwdrivers.

Special Screwdrivers

Three special screwdrivers used by automotive mechanics are the *Phillips, Torx,* and *clutch-head screwdrivers*. These screwdrivers are designed to be used only with special fasteners. Another special tool is the offset screwdriver, used in tight areas.

6.4 PLIERS

Pliers have jaws that hold, bend, rotate, or cut parts or fasteners. Pliers should *not* be used for loosening or tightening bolts or nuts. Common pliers used by mechanics are:

- Slip-joint adjustable
- Needlenose (longnose)
- Arc-joint
- Locking
- Diagonal cut
- Special-purpose.

Slip-Joint Adjustable

A slip joint holds two jaws of pliers together and allows those jaws to move. A slot on one jaw allows the slip joint to move, which changes the space between the two jaws. *Slip-joint adjustable pliers* are shown in Figure 6-12. Depending on the chosen slot adjustment, slip-joint adjustable pliers can securely hold either small or large parts. Sometimes these are called combination pliers.

Arc-Joint

A variation of slip-joint adjustables are *arc-joint pliers*. The jaws are connected by way of grooves, or channels (see Figure 6-13). The channels in the jaws are

shaped in an arc and can be adjusted to different settings.

Locking

Parts and fasteners are held in position by using *locking pliers*. The jaws of locking pliers are adjusted by turning a screw in the handle. The adjusted jaws are locked into position by pulling in on the lower handle (see Figure 6-14).

Needlenose

The jaws of *needlenose (longnose) pliers* are long and narrow to fit in tight working spaces. Length, shape, and thickness of needlenose jaws depend upon the requirements of the work to be done (see Figure 6-15).

Diagonal Cutting

Some pliers, called *diagonal cutting pliers,* or *cutters,* are used to cut electrical connections, cotter pins, and other wires on an automobile. Jaws on these pliers have extra-hard cutting edges (see Figure 6-16).

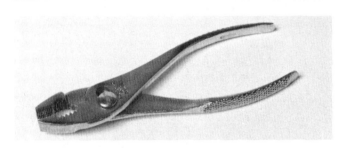

Figure 6-12. Slip-joint adjustable pliers.

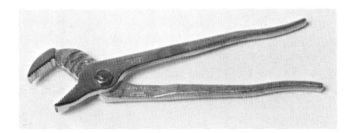

Figure 6-13. Arc-joint pliers.

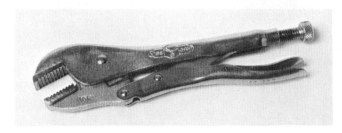

Figure 6-14. Locking pliers.

Special-Purpose

Many special pliers are used for different systems in the automobile. Pliers are made to remove snap rings, brake-shoe springs, and many other parts. Typical special-purpose pliers are shown in Figure 6-17.

6.5 HAMMERS AND MALLETS

Pounding an automotive part is not a common servicing procedure. However, *hammers* and *mallets* are used sometimes with driving punches or chisels. Some hammers and mallets have soft faces. The head of a soft-faced hammer may be made from brass, plastic, leather, or rubber. Different types of soft-faced hammers are shown in Figure 6-18. These types of hammers must be used when pounding on machined surfaces or on trim parts, such as wheel covers.

Figure 6-15. Needlenose pliers.   Figure 6-16. Diagonal pliers.

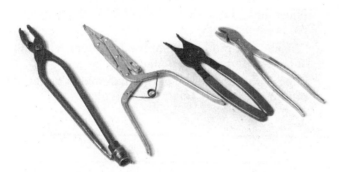

Figure 6-17.   Special-purpose pliers.

Figure 6-18.   Hammers.

6.6 CHISELS AND PUNCHES

Chisels and *punches* are used to separate or align parts during servicing (see Figure 6-19). A hammer or mallet usually is used with a chisel or punch.

Chisels are wider and heavier than punches. A flat chisel is tapered at one end and cylindrical at the opposite end where the hammer strikes. Chisels are used to cut heads off rivets or to loosen fasteners that cannot be removed normally.

Starting and aligning punches are used often in automotive service. A starting punch is used to drive out pins. An aligning punch is used to align holes in two parts that will be connected. A center punch is used to start a drill bit accurately and must be used when drilling holes.

6.7 FILES

Metal is removed, smoothed, or polished with a *file*. A file is a hardened steel tool with rows of teeth. A file also has a pointed end, or *tang*, that fits into a handle (see Figure 6-20).

The teeth of a file may be single-cut (run in one direction) or double-cut (cross each other). The distance between the cutting teeth determines how the file works. A file with teeth that are wide apart will remove more metal. A file with teeth close

Figure 6-19.   Chisels and punches.

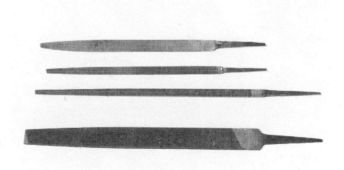

Figure 6-20.   Files.

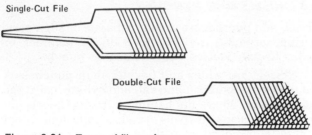

Figure 6-21. Types of file surfaces.

Figure 6-22. Taps and tap drill.

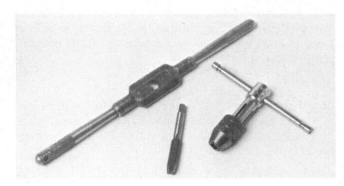

Figure 6-23. Die and die stock.

Figure 6-24. Using a pry bar to position a heavy assembly.

together is used for polishing or smoothing (see Figure 6-21).

6.8 TAPS

To repair damaged threads inside a part, a cutting tool, called a *tap*, is used (see Figure 6-22). Select the proper size tap, mount it into a tap wrench, and insert it into the hole to be threaded.

6.9 DIES

To repair external threads, another cutting tool, called a *die*, is used (see Figure 6-23). Select the proper size die and place it in a die stock. Turn the die stock to start the die.

6.10 PRY BARS

To position or break free some automotive systems, a *pry bar* is sometimes needed. A pry bar is a long, thick steel lever (see Figure 6-24).

UNIT HIGHLIGHTS

Wrenches are classified as: open-end, adjustable open-end, box-end, combination, socket, torque, and special.

Screwdrivers have blades that fit into different-shaped fastener heads.

Pliers have jaws that hold, bend, rotate, or cut parts or fasteners.

Chisels and punches remove fasteners with the aid of hammers or mallets.

Files remove, smooth, and polish metal, depending on the cutting teeth of the tools.

TERMS

wrench	Phillips screwdriver
head	Torx screwdriver
open-end wrench	clutch-head
adjustable open-end	screwdriver
wrench	slip-joint adjustable
box-end wrench	pliers
combination wrench	arc-joint pliers
socket wrench	locking pliers
ratchet	longnose pliers
drive size	diagonal cutting pliers
speed handle	hammer
breaker bar	mallet
T-handle	chisel
extension	punch
universal-joint adaptor	file
torque wrench	tap
screwdriver	die
slotted screwdriver	pry bar

R E V I E W   Q U E S T I O N S

DIRECTIONS: The following questions are similar to those used on mechanic certification tests. On a separate sheet of paper, write the letter of the correct choice.

1. The measurement systems used for automotive work include all of the following EXCEPT
A. the English System.
B. decimals.
C. barometric.
D. metric.

2. Which of the following wrenches is *not* used frequently in automotive mechanics?
A. Combination
B. Allen
C. Torx
D. Monkey

3. Mechanic A says that a socket wrench drives the T-handle.
Mechanic B says that a universal joint allows the socket and the drive to operate at different speeds.
Who is correct?
A. A only   B. B only   C. Both A and B   D. Neither A nor B

4. All of the following types of pliers can be adjusted to fit a part or fastener EXCEPT
A. arc-joint.
B. locking.
C. needlenose.
D. diagonal cutting.

5. Which of the following statements is correct?
I. Chisels and punches must *not* be struck with a hammer or mallet because they may shatter.
II. A double-cut file has cutting teeth that crisscross.
A. I only   B. II only   C. Both I and II   D. Neither I nor II

S U P P L E M E N T A L   A C T I V I T I E S

1. Identify the tools laid out by your instructor.
2. Make a list of tools that were found in the shop inventory.
3. Show how to operate a socket wrench with a ratchet handle.
4. Explain the differences among the heads of Allen, Phillips, Torx, and clutch-head fastening tools.
5. Choose the proper tool for a job that the instructor assigns.
6. Identify the size wrench needed for the fasteners laid out by your instructor.

7 USING POWER TOOLS

Power tools make a mechanic's job easier, because they operate faster and with more force than hand tools. However, power tools require greater safety measures. Power tools do *not* stop unless they are turned off. Power is furnished by either electricity, compressed air, or hydraulic fluid. Power also offers extra cleaning capability in the way of special cleaning tools.

LEARNING OBJECTIVES

When you have completed your assignments and exercises in this unit, you should be able to:

☐ Explain how electrical power tools operate.

☐ Describe the parts of a portable electric drill.

☐ Explain how to remove a bolt that has broken inside of a hole.

☐ Explain how pneumatic power tools operate.

☐ Explain how hydraulic power tools operate.

☐ Describe the different types of parts cleaning machines and how they operate.

SAFETY PRECAUTIONS

Safety is critical when using power tools. Carelessness or mishandling of power tools can cause serious injury. Always wear safety glasses when using a power tool. Do *not* use a power tool without obtaining permission from your instructor. Be sure you know how to operate the tool properly before using it. Instructions should be read carefully.

When you work with large power tools, such as bench or floor equipment, check the machines for damage. Also check for proper adjustments. Place all safety guards in position. Wear safety glasses or a face shield. Make sure the work area is clear of bystanders and parts before starting a machine. Keep hands and clothing away from moving parts.

Never leave a power tool unattended while it is running. If a machine does not operate properly, turn it off and notify your instructor.

When you finish using a power tool, turn it off. Wait until the tool has stopped completely, and then disconnect it from its power source. Clean, oil, and adjust it, if necessary.

Obey all rules outlined by your instructor. Do not enter a work area where a power tool is being used. Stay away from power tools that are in operation.

7.1 ELECTRICAL TOOLS

Different tools require different power sources. An electrical tool, for example, needs electricity to work. A plug connects to an electrical outlet, while a wire connects the plug with the tool. Electrical current flows through the wire and operates movable parts inside the tool. An on/off switch activates or stops the electrical flow. One advantage of power tools is that they work faster than hand tools. Common electrical tools used in automotive service are discussed in this section.

Trouble Light

Adequate light is necessary when working under and around automobiles. A good light is needed to help find troubles, which is where the name *trouble light* comes into use (see Figure 7-1). A trouble light is hand held and is insulated to protect the user. The bulb is surrounded by a cage to prevent accidental breaking. The light has a long cord for freedom of movement in the shop area.

Electric Impact Wrench

An *electric impact wrench* has an electric motor that drives a socket. An impact wrench gives sharp bursts of power that help to loosen parts. A switch, or trigger, on the handle starts or stops the wrench. Elsewhere on the wrench is a switch that controls the direction of operation (see Figure 7-2).

Figure 7-1. A trouble light is used when working under an automobile and in dark areas.

Figure 7-2. Electric impact wrench.

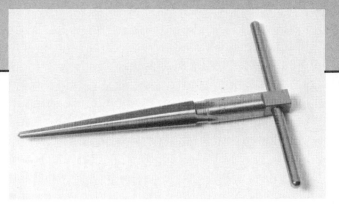

Figure 7-4. Reamer.

Figure 7-3. Portable electric drill.

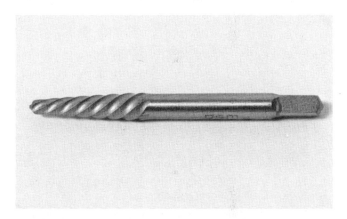

Figure 7-5. Screw extractor.

Portable Electric Drill

Many automotive tasks require the use of a *portable electric drill*. The drill must be portable so it can be moved around easily. An electric motor provides the power, and is operated by a trigger on the drill handle. An electric drill has a *chuck* and one of several different types of handles (see Figure 7-3). An electric drill drives a *drill bit* to bore holes.

The chuck is the end of the tool that holds the drill bit. The drill bit is a hardened steel shaft that has a sharp, spiral groove and cuts into metal when turned. Different handles are used to give the operating mechanic a better grip, safer handling, and more accurate control.

Drill sizes are measured when the chuck is opened to its widest setting. Common automotive drill sizes are ¼, ⅜, and ½ inch.

Reamer. Many drilled holes in automotive parts must be made accurately. A *reamer* is used for this purpose. Reamers used by automotive mechanics may be either power or hand tools. A reamer has sharp cutting edges designed to remove only small amounts of metal at a time (see Figure 7-4). Reamers are turned with a wrench.

Screw extractor. Broken bolts or studs often are removed with pliers if part of a broken fastener protrudes above the surface. If a broken fastener is below the surface, a *screw extractor* is used. A screw extractor, shown in Figure 7-5, is a hard, steel tool that grips a drilled hole in a fastener.

A hole of the proper size is drilled into the fastener. The screw extractor is driven into the drilled hole. Then the screw extractor is turned with a wrench to loosen and remove the broken fastener.

Grinders

An electric *grinder* consists of a grinding wheel and a wire wheel at the sides of the tool (see Figure 7-6). These wheels are connected by a shaft to a center-mounted electric motor. A grinding wheel is solid and is used to remove metal and to sharpen tools or parts. A wire wheel, made from several strands of wire, is used to clean tools or parts.

Sanders and Polishers

One electric-powered tool can be used as a *sander* and as a *polisher* (see Figure 7-7). This tool has interchangeable discs for a variety of jobs. A sanding disc

Figure 7-6. Electric grinder.

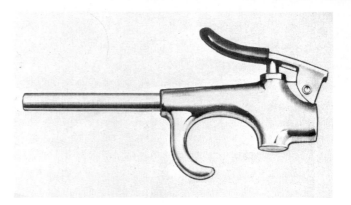

Figure 7-8. Compressed-air blowgun. SNAP-ON TOOL CORPORATION

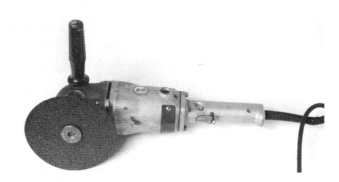

Figure 7-7. Electric sander and polisher.

Figure 7-9. Air impact wrench.
SNAP-ON TOOL CORPORATION

smooths and removes metal. A polishing disc polishes and waxes an automobile's finish.

7.2 PNEUMATIC TOOLS

Tools that are powered by compressed air are called *pneumatic tools.* Air is compressed by an electric motor and a compressor that draws air into a closed system. The air is stored in a tank.

Compressed air can be very dangerous. Always wear eye protection and direct the air *away* from others. Make sure all hoses are not leaking and that power connections are completed properly.

Blowgun

One way to use compressed air from a pneumatic hose is with a *blowgun* (see Figure 7-8). A blowgun snaps into the end of the hose and directs airflow when a button is pressed. Before using a blowgun, be sure it has *not* been modified to eliminate air-bleed holes on the side. Blowguns are used for blowing off parts during cleaning.

Air Impact Wrench

Compressed air also is used to drive pneumatic impact wrenches (see Figure 7-9). The air impact wrench

is activated by pressing a trigger in the handle. Rotational direction is controlled by a reversing switch.

Air Ratchet

An *air ratchet,* shown in Figure 7-10, is a lighter-duty impact wrench.

Air Chisel

The *air chisel* is a hammering tool often used to cut off bodywork or light, metal parts (see Figure 7-11).

Air Drill

It is necessary, during some work situations, to use a spark-resistant power tool. The *air drill* is powered by compressed air (see Figure 7-12). Thus, it eliminates the safety hazard of sparks from an electric motor. The air drill is used in much the same way as an electric drill.

7.3 HYDRAULIC TOOLS

Heavier automotive assemblies are controlled by *hydraulic tools.* Hydraulic tools operate on oil or liquid pressure. Oil is pumped into a system, where it acts on pistons that move and do work. The main hydraulically operated tools used in automotive service are discussed in this section.

Figure 7-10. Air ratchet. SNAP-ON TOOL CORPORATION

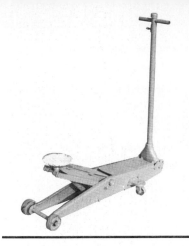

Figure 7-13. Floor jack.

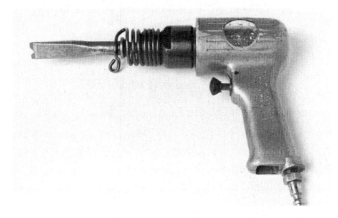

Figure 7-11. Air chisel.

Figure 7-14. Hoist.

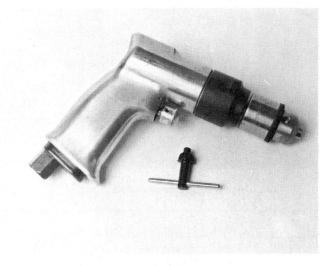

Figure 7-12. Air drill.

Floor Jack

A *floor jack* is a portable tool, mounted on wheels, that is used to raise an automobile (see Figure 7-13). A control lever at the end of the long handle directs hydraulic fluid to a cylinder, which in turn raises or lowers the *pad*. The pad is the portion of the jack that contacts the automobile. Always use jackstands to support the automobile after it is raised by a jack.

Hoist

The lift, or *hoist,* raises the entire automobile. This allows the mechanic to have extra working space

underneath. A hoist is lowered into the floor when it is not being used and is raised when an automobile is to be lifted. Most modern hoists are double-post designs (see Figure 7-14), although some single-post models remain in use. Hydraulic pressure and compressed air are used to move hoists up and down. A control lever is placed at a convenient location near the hoist.

Engine Lift

A crane, or *engine lift,* is used to remove or install an automotive engine. The engine lift operates when a hydraulic cylinder is pumped and pushes up on the long support arm. The lift is on wheels, so it can be rolled anywhere in the shop. See Figure 7-15. When ready to be installed, the lift control can lower the engine slowly to prevent serious injury or damage.

Hydraulic Press

A special platform is used to handle powerful hydraulic forces when some automotive parts are assembled. This platform is called a *hydraulic press* (see Figure 7-16). A hydraulic press forces, or presses, two tight-fitting parts together. The table portion of the press, where parts are positioned, must withstand

Figure 7-15. A crane, or engine lift.

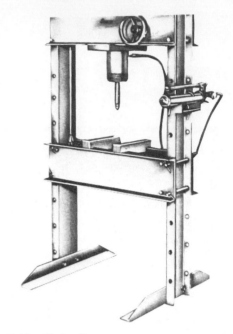

Figure 7-16. Hydraulic press. SNAP-ON TOOL CORPORATION

the tons of force applied. A handle at the side of the hydraulic press is pumped to increase pressure. A nearby lever releases pressure.

7.4 CLEANING EQUIPMENT

Cleaning parts is an important part of servicing automobiles. Improper cleaning and inspection can result in a bad repair job. All parts must be cleaned thoroughly by the mechanic with one of the systems described in this topic.

High Pressure and Steam Cleaners

High pressure and heat are effective methods for cleaning away automotive grease and grime. A high-pressure spray cleaner (Figure 7-17) forces compressed air and water through a nozzle to clean parts. A steam cleaner is used to heat water and create steam. Steam is mixed with a soap solution, and is sprayed on the parts to be cleaned.

Solvent Cleaner

Small parts are best cleaned in a *solvent cleaner*. A solvent cleaner is a tank that holds cleaning solvent (see Figure 7-18). Cleaning solvent thins grease, oil, and dirt buildups so they can be washed away. A solvent cleaner usually has different strainers or screens to keep parts from becoming lost. The solvent cleaner has an electric motor that pumps cleaning solvent through a flexible tube and flushes off the parts. Solvent returns to the tank and is filtered to remove impurities that have accumulated.

Carburetors require special cleaners to remove deposits of varnish and grime. See Topic 22.5.

Cold Tank

Certain metals, such as aluminum and brass, need to be cleaned in a *cold tank*. A cold tank is used to soak parts for long periods of time (see Figure 7-19). As its

Figure 7-17. High-pressure spray cleaner.

name implies, a cold tank is not heated. Face shields and rubber gloves are required for protection against the harsh chemicals used in a cold tank.

Hot Tank

Large iron and steel parts, such as engine blocks, are cleaned in a *hot tank*. See Figure 7-20. A hot tank is heated and contains highly caustic chemicals. Some metals, such as aluminum, will dissolve in a hot-tank solution. Wear face shields, rubber gloves, and protective clothing when working around this equipment.

Glass Bead Blaster

A final cleaning can be made with a *glass bead blaster* (see Figure 7-21). When a part is placed in a glass bead blaster, the part is enclosed and sealed. The blaster shoots small beads of glass at a part to remove any remaining dirt or residue.

Figure 7-18. Solvent cleaner. KLEER-FLOW COMPANY

Figure 7-20. Hot tank. KLEER-FLOW COMPANY

Figure 7-19. Cold tank. KLEER-FLOW COMPANY

Figure 7-21. Glass bead blaster.
INLAND RADIATOR EQUIPMENT, INC.

UNIT HIGHLIGHTS

- Electrical tools need a plug, a wire, and an electric motor to receive power.
- Power tools can help a mechanic perform tasks more easily and faster.
- Electrical power is used when turning force is needed.
- Pneumatic tools are powered by compressed air.
- Hydraulic tools operate on oil or liquid pressure.
- Jacks and hoists are used to raise automobiles.
- Proper cleaning is important to complete a good repair job.

TERMS

trouble light
electric impact wrench
portable electric drill
chuck
drill bit
reamer
screw extractor
grinder
sander
polisher
pneumatic tools
blowgun
air impact wrench
air ratchet

air chisel
air drill
hydraulic tools
floor jack
pad
hoist
engine lift
hydraulic press
steam cleaner
solvent cleaner
cold tank
hot tank
glass bead blaster

REVIEW QUESTIONS

DIRECTIONS: The following questions are similar to those used on mechanic certification tests. On a separate sheet of paper, write the letter of the correct choice.

1. Which of the following statements is correct?
   I. A chuck tightens around a drill bit.
   II. The size of a drill bit determines the size of the drill.
   A. I only   B. II only   C. Both I and II   D. Neither I nor II

2. Mechanic A says that a reamer will make a drilled hole narrower.
   Mechanic B says that a screw extractor is used to drill a hole in a broken bolt or stud.
   Who is correct?
   A. A only   B. B only   C. Both A and B   D. Neither A nor B

3. All of the following statements about pneumatic tools are correct EXCEPT
   A. They are powered by air.
   B. They are powered by oil.
   C. They connect to a hose.
   D. They do not have electrical cords.

4. Which of the following tools is *not* operated hydraulically?
   A. Floor jack
   B. Hoist
   C. Jackstand
   D. Engine lift

5. Which of the following statements is correct?
   I. A solvent cleaner is a liquid used to clean off small parts.
   II. Cold tanks are used to let engine blocks set overnight and get a thorough cleaning.
   A. I only   B. II only   C. Both I and II   D. Neither I nor II

SUPPLEMENTAL ACTIVITIES

1. Identify the different types of electrical tools.
2. Locate the safety guards on a grinder and make sure they are properly positioned.
3. Using your instructor's guidelines, raise and lower the shop hoist.
4. Show how an engine hoist is operated.
5. Identify the parts of a hydraulic press and explain how they work.
6. Use a solvent cleaner to clean off dirty parts that your instructor has selected.

8 USING MEASURING TOOLS

UNIT PREVIEW

Precise measurements are vital to proper automotive performance and reliability. A mechanic must be able to measure accurately many critical parts in an automobile to ensure proper service. A mechanic may use many measuring tools in a single day. This unit discusses different kinds of measuring tools and how they are used.

LEARNING OBJECTIVES

When you have completed your assignments and exercises in this unit, you should be able to:

☐ Explain what measurements are taken with a feeler gauge.

☐ Describe an outside micrometer and explain how it works.

☐ Describe the tools used to give measurements of hole sizes.

☐ Describe the readings that are made with a vacuum and pressure gauge.

☐ Explain how a hydrometer works.

☐ Explain what measurements are taken with a dwell-tachometer.

☐ Describe how an oscilloscope operates.

8.1 MECHANICAL MEASURING TOOLS

A tool that must be operated by hand and adjusted to take readings is called a *mechanical measuring tool.* Many different mechanical measuring tools are used by a mechanic.

Ruler

A *ruler* is a long, narrow measuring tool used for many automotive measurements. Rulers using the English system usually are divided into increments of ⅟₁₆ or ⅟₃₂ inch (see Figure 8-1). Metric rulers commonly have measurements in centimeters and millimeters (see Figure 8-2). Some rulers are known as *straightedges.* A straightedge usually is made of metal and made with straight edges along its length. Straightedges are used to check *warpage,* or the amount of bend, in metal parts. All straightedges are *not* measuring tools.

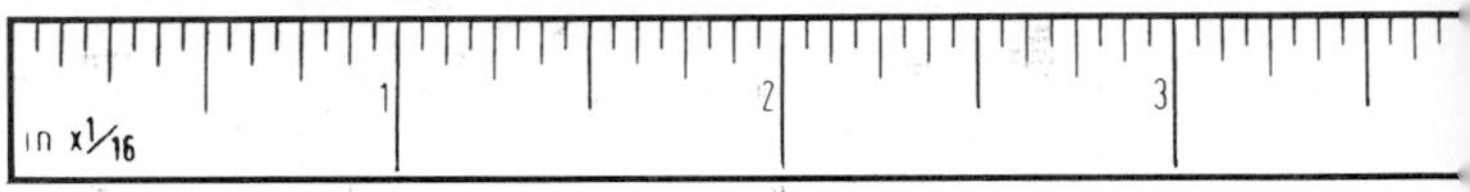

Figure 8-1. English ruler.

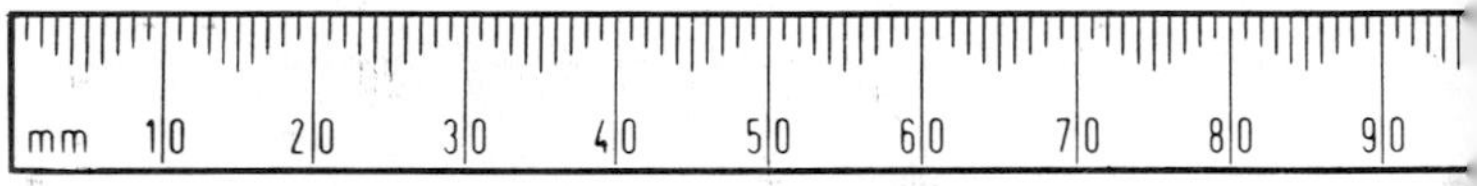

Figure 8-2. Metric ruler.

Figure 8-3. Feeler gauge set. L.S. STARRETT COMPANY

Feeler Gauge

Flat metal or plastic strips or blades are used to measure the space between two surfaces. These strips, called *feeler gauges,* usually come in sets (see Figure 8-3). Feeler gauge blades of different thicknesses are inserted into the space until the proper gauge size or setting is determined. Feeler gauges come in English and metric sizes. Thicknesses are stamped on each strip.

Wire Gauge

A round *wire gauge* is used as a feeler gauge on some automotive parts. A typical wire gauge is shown in Figure 8-4.

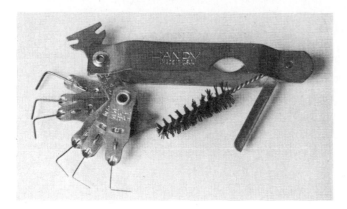

Figure 8-4. Wire gauge.

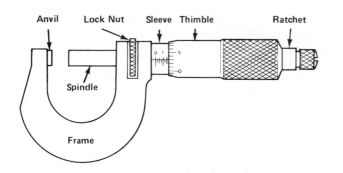

Figure 8-5. Outside micrometer.

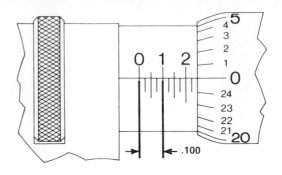

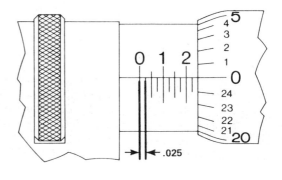

Figure 8-6. English micrometer measurement readings.
CLEVITE

Outside Micrometer

Measurements taken on the outside of a part are made with an *outside micrometer*. An outside micrometer is a measuring tool that is placed across the outside diameter of a part, tightened, and read. Figure 8-5 shows an outside micrometer. Outside micrometers have either English or metric measurements. Parts of a micrometer, often called a "mike," are:

- Frame
- Anvil
- Spindle
- Sleeve
- Thimble.

Measurements are taken between the *anvil* and the *spindle*. When a part is placed into position, the *thimble* is turned. As the thimble turns, the spindle is moved toward the stationary anvil. When spindle and anvil are snugged against the part, measurement readings are taken from the *sleeve* and from the thimble.

English system measurement. Reading an outside micrometer only requires adding sleeve and thimble numbers. Figure 8-6 shows how the two measurement scales appear on the micrometer. Each scale has slashes that indicate numbers. Measurements for an outside micrometer with the English system are read by using the following procedure.

The outside micrometer is a very accurate tool. Each rotation of the thimble, for example, moves the spindle only 0.025 in. [0.64 mm]. This rotation is recorded on the sleeve as the thimble moves in or out with the rotating spindle. The sleeve has a scale that begins with 0 and moves up to 1, 2, etc. Between those numbers are three slashes, which provide four divisions between numbers. Each division indicates one rotation of the thimble, or 0.025-in. [0.64 mm] movement by the spindle. Thus, four divisions indicate four turns, or 0.100 in. [2.54 mm], and there are four turns between the numbers on the sleeve.

An even more accurate measurement is made when reading the scale on the *beveled* end of the thimble. The edge of the thimble facing the sleeve is beveled, or tapered. The bevel scale has 25 slashes, or divisions. Each division indicates 1/25th of a turn. If a complete turn is 0.025 in. [0.64 mm], then 1/25th of a turn is 0.001 in. [0.03 mm].

Add the readings of both scales to get a measurement. From the sleeve, take the highest numbered division showing and add the unnumbered division. Sleeve readings of 1 (numbered division) and 0.050 (two unnumbered divisions) add up to 0.150. Add to this total the division on the bevel. A thimble reading of 0.006 (6 divisions) totals out to 0.156.

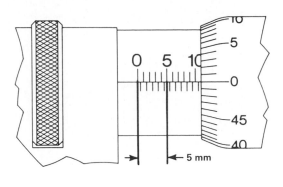

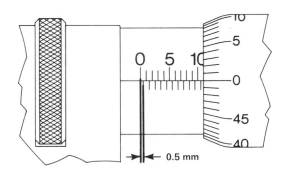

Figure 8-7. Metric micrometer measurement readings. CLEVITE

Figure 8-8. Checking a clearance with Plastigage. CLEVITE

Metric system measurement. English system and metric system outside micrometers work alike. The difference between them is the values of the measurements taken.

On a metric micrometer, the sleeve has a scale that is divided into two divisions separated by a line. See Figure 8-7 for metric system micrometer scales. The lower division indicates half, or 0.50, of a millimeter and is not numbered. The upper division indicates 1 mm, and the scale is numbered every 5 mm. One complete rotation of the thimble indicates 0.50 mm. Two complete rotations indicate 1 mm.

The bevel scale has 50 divisions. Each division indicates 1/50th of a turn. If a complete turn is 0.50 mm, then 1/50th of a turn is 0.01 mm.

Take a measurement by reading the numbers on the spindle and bevel scales. Start at the upper-division sleeve scale for a reading of 6. If the bottom scale is 0.5, the total sleeve reading is 6.50. Now add the bevel scale reading of 0.17. The total is 6.67.

Inside Micrometer

Measurements of hole sizes, or distances between parallel surfaces, are taken with an *inside micrometer.* An inside micrometer can be used to measure the diameter of a cylinder or bearing bore. Adjustments

for different sizes are made by attaching spacing collars and rods to the micrometer. English and metric measurements are taken in the same way as with outside micrometers. The use of an inside micrometer can be difficult. Care must be taken to avoid tilting the micrometer in the bore when taking a measurement.

Plastigage

A disposable tool is used to measure clearances between some parts. This tool is a plastic thread, called *Plastigage,* which flattens out when parts are clamped together (see Figure 8-8). Plastigage comes in an envelope. The envelope has measurements printed on the outside that are compared to the width of the flattened Plastigage.

Small Hole Gauge

Holes too small for use of an inside micrometer are measured with a *small hole gauge,* sometimes called a *split-ball gauge.* A small hole gauge has a split ball at the end of the handle. The split-ball end is placed in the hole, and the handle is turned. The turning handle expands the split ball until it touches the walls of the hole. The gauge is removed, and the ball is measured with an outside micrometer.

Telescoping Gauge

A *telescoping gauge* measures the inside size of a hole. Telescoping gauges are spring-loaded to make them expand to hole sizes when they are inserted. Telescoping gauges do not contain graduated markings. Instead, an outside micrometer is used to take the measurement.

Vernier Calipers

Vernier calipers often are used instead of micrometers to measure inside and outside diameters. Vernier calipers have heads that fit flat against the inner or outer edges of a part (see Figure 8-9). Measuring adjustments are made by moving the jaws closer together or farther apart.

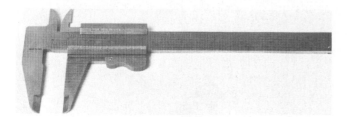

Figure 8-9. Vernier calipers.

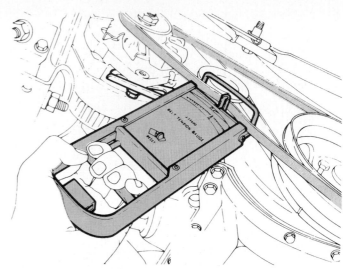

Figure 8-11. Drive-belt tension gauge.
AMERICAN MOTORS CORPORATION

Figure 8-10. Dial indicator. L.S. STARRETT COMPANY

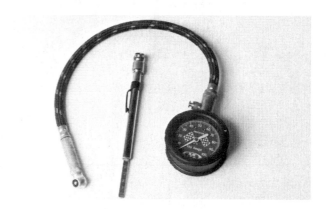

Figure 8-12. Tire pressure gauges.

Dial Indicator

Automotive parts are measured for movement, or *play,* and contour, or *runout,* with a *dial indicator.* A dial indicator is a measuring tool with a *plunger* that acts on a gauge (see Figure 8-10). The plunger touches the part that is being measured and transfers any movement from that part to the gauge. The pointer on the gauge indicates how much play or runout there is and where it is. A magnetic base, or holder, often is used when holding a dial indicator in position for measurements. Dial indicator measurements are in English (thousandths of an inch) or metric (hundredths of a millimeter).

Drive Belt Tension Gauge

A *drive belt* is a belt that operates equipment in the engine compartment. A drive belt must have the proper tension, or tightness, for it to operate properly. Tension may be measured with a *drive belt tension gauge* (see Figure 8-11). A tension gauge determines whether the belt must be tightened or loosened.

8.2 FLUID MEASURING TOOLS

Tools in this category are used to check pressures and other measurements of air and liquids.

Tire Pressure Gauge

Automotive tires are inflated with compressed air. To check inflation, a *tire pressure gauge* is used. A tire pressure gauge, shown in Figure 8-12, records how much air pressure a tire is holding. Air pressure is measured in pounds per square inch (psi) or kilopascals (kPa). Depending upon the design, pressure readings are shown on a *dial* or a *bar* indicator that extends from the gauge housing.

Compression Tester

The engine develops pressure when the piston rises and compresses the air-fuel mixture. Pressure is necessary to keep the engine operating properly. Checking this pressure is done with a *compression tester.* A compression tester, shown in Figure 8-13, is a tool that is inserted into a spark plug hole. A dial on the compression tester gives the mechanic a reading that must meet the manufacturer's specifications. Compression readings are indicated in pounds per square inch (psi) or kilopascals (kPa).

Vacuum and Pressure Gauge

Some engine operations are checked by using a *vacuum and pressure gauge.* The vacuum and pressure gauge measures engine vacuum or pressure, depending upon where the gauge is connected. The vacuum reading is obtained by connecting the gauge to the intake manifold. A pressure reading is taken when the gauge is connected to the fuel system to measure fuel pump pressure. Vacuum measurements are recorded in inches of mercury (Hg). Pressure measurements are recorded in pounds per square inch (psi). Vacuum and pressure measurements are discussed in Unit 43.

Cylinder Leakage Tester

A cylinder leakage tester is used to check piston and valve condition (see Figure 8-14). This tester directs air into a closed/sealed cylinder and measures the amount of leakage taking place. This measurement is expressed as a percent. The use of this tester is discussed in Unit 43.

Cooling System Tester

Coolant leaks are detected by using a *cooling system tester.* A cooling system tester, shown in Figure 8-15, is installed on the radiator neck after the radiator cap is removed. To check for leaks, the tester is pumped until the system reaches operating pressure. The tester also is used to check pressures on radiator caps.

Vacuum Diaphragm Tester

To check for proper operation and leaks in vacuum-operated parts, a *vacuum diaphragm tester* is used. A vacuum diaphragm tester consists of a pump, a gauge, and a rubber hose (see Figure 8-16).

Battery Hydrometer

The density of battery acid, or *electrolyte,* is tested with a *battery hydrometer.* The battery hydrometer has a suction tube, a rubber bulb that creates suction, and a clear reservoir (see Figure 8-17). The reservoir also houses a float or floating balls to record measurements. The bulb is squeezed, inserted into the battery, and released to draw electrolyte into the reservoir. The electrolyte raises the float or balls.

NOTE: Do *not* drip electrolyte on your body, clothes, or automotive finish. Electrolyte is an acid. It will eat through clothes or paint and can cause eye and skin damage.

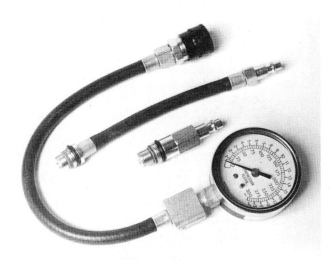

Figure 8-13. Compression tester.

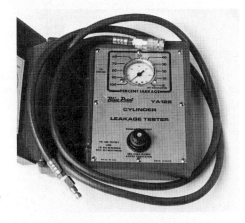

Figure 8-14.
Cylinder leakage
tester.

Figure 8-15. Cooling system tester. CLIFF CREAGER

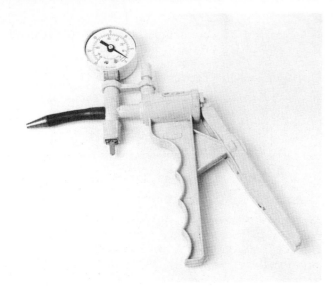

Figure 8-16. Vacuum diaphragm tester.

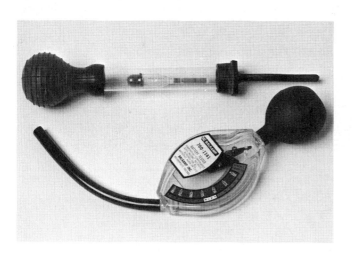

Figure 8-17. Battery hydrometers.

Coolant Hydrometer

One of the functions of coolant is to prevent liquid from freezing in the cooling system. Coolant is discussed in Unit 17. To check coolant condition, a *coolant hydrometer* is used (see Figure 8-18). A typical coolant hydrometer consists of a suction tube, a reservoir with a float, and a rubber bulb. The suction tube is placed into the radiator. The rubber bulb is squeezed, and suction draws coolant from the radiator into the reservoir. The quality of the coolant is registered by the float inside the reservoir.

8.3 ELECTRIC MEASURING TOOLS

Some measuring tools are operated off the automobile's electrical system or are plugged into a wall socket to assist in diagnosing problems. These are called electric measuring tools.

Continuity Tester

To check electrical flow in wiring, a *continuity tester* is used. A continuity tester is a tapered metal probe attached to a handle with a light bulb inside (see Figure 8-19). The bulb shines when power is flowing. This tester also may be called a *circuit tester* or a *test lamp*. Some testers, called self-powered test lights, contain their own battery.

Voltmeter

A *voltmeter,* also called a *battery tester,* is used to check the amount of voltage being delivered by the battery. A voltmeter consists of an indicator, which gives voltage measurements, and a connecting lead (see Figure 8-20).

Battery Load Tester

The battery must be able to provide and maintain a certain level of electrical current. To check electrical performance, a *battery load tester* is used. The battery

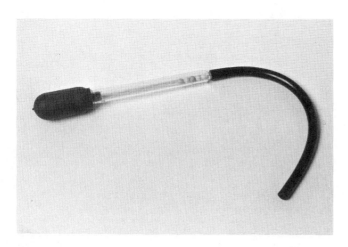

Figure 8-18. Coolant hydrometer.

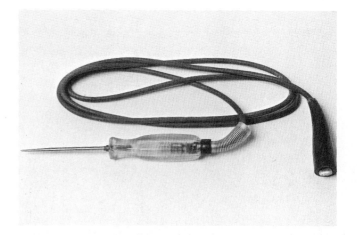

Figure 8-19. Continuity tester.

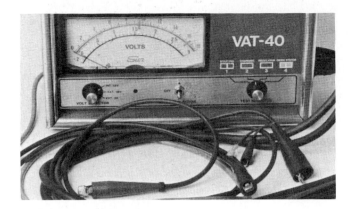

Figure 8-20. Battery voltage tester.

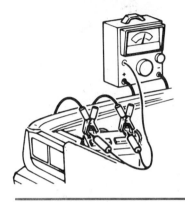

Figure 8-21. Battery load tester. AMERICAN MOTORS CORPORATION

Figure 8-22. An ammeter usually is part of a unit that also contains a voltage tester.

Figure 8-23. Dwell-tachometer.

load tester is connected to the battery (see Figure 8-21). The tester draws current from the battery quickly. Instruments on the load tester indicate the battery condition.

Ammeter

Electric current flow between the battery and the alternator is measured with an *ammeter*. Electrical flow is discussed in Unit 27. An ammeter has a pointer or a light to indicate whether the battery is being charged (see Figure 8-22).

Dwell-Tachometer

Contact-point ignition systems are adjusted with a *dwell-tachometer* (see Figure 8-23). A dwell-tachometer measures *dwell*, or how long the contact points are closed. The dwell meter also is used to test operation of electrically controlled carburetors. Ignition systems are discussed in Units 34 and 35.

The tachometer portion of the tester is used to check engine speed. The tachometer usually is connected to the ignition system and reads engine revolutions per minute (rpm).

Oscilloscope

Ignition system measurements are displayed on an *oscilloscope* screen, similar to the screen on a television set. Oscilloscopes are large (see Figure 8-24).

Figure 8-24. Oscilloscope. CLIFF CREAGER

Oscilloscope leads are clamped to various wires in the ignition system. The connected wires send signals, which are displayed on the oscilloscope screen. The pictures show the condition of the automobile's ignition system.

Exhaust Gas Analyzer

Automotive emissions are checked with an *exhaust gas analyzer*. An exhaust gas analyzer is a machine that takes readings from a probe (see Figure 8-25). The probe is placed inside the exhaust pipe to draw exhaust gases into the analyzer. This tester is used when adjusting or troubleshooting the fuel and emissions systems.

Computerized Diagnostic Tester

Some service centers use a larger machine that can furnish the mechanic with a complete printout of an automobile's condition. This machine is called a *computerized diagnostic tester* (see Figure 8-26). Wires are connected to numerous parts of the automobile. Inputs are directed to a computer. The computer controls both the oscilloscope screen and the printout from the printer.

Figure 8-25. Exhaust gas analyzer.
SUN ELECTRIC CORPORATION

Figure 8-26. Computerized diagnostic tester.
SUN ELECTRIC CORPORATION

UNIT HIGHLIGHTS

- Feeler gauges and wire gauges are used to measure the distance between two surfaces.
- An outside micrometer is very accurate. It uses both English and metric measurement systems.
- Measurements on the sleeve and thimble scales of the outside micrometer are added to obtain the proper measurement.
- An inside micrometer measures hole sizes and the distance between parallel surfaces.
- A small hole gauge, telescoping gauge, and Vernier calipers are inside measuring tools for holes.
- A dial indicator measures play and runout.
- Fluid measuring tools are used with air and liquid.
- Hydrometers measure the quality of coolant and electrolyte.
- An oscilloscope is a machine with a television-like screen that gives voltage readings of the ignition system.

TERMS

mechanical measuring tool	tire pressure gauge
straightedge	compression tester
warpage	vacuum and pressure gauge
feeler gauge	cooling system tester
wire gauge	vacuum diaphragm tester
outside micrometer	electrolyte
anvil	battery hydrometer
spindle	coolant hydrometer
thimble	continuity tester
sleeve	circuit tester
beveled	test lamp
inside micrometer	voltmeter
Plastigage	battery voltage tester
small hole gauge	battery load tester
telescoping gauge	ammeter
Vernier calipers	dwell-tachometer
play	dwell
runout	oscilloscope
dial indicator	exhaust gas analyzer
plunger	computerized
drive belt	diagnostic tester
drive belt tension gauge	

R E V I E W   Q U E S T I O N S

DIRECTIONS: The following questions are similar to those used on mechanic certification tests. On a separate sheet of paper, write the letter of the correct choice.

1. Mechanic A says that a ruler and a straightedge are exactly the same, except that one has metric measurements.
   Mechanic B says that a feeler gauge and a wire gauge measure the space between two surfaces.
   Who is correct?
   A. A only   B. B only   C. Both A and B   D. Neither A nor B

2. All of the following statements about outside micrometers are correct EXCEPT
   A. They have both English and metric measurements.
   B. Measurements are taken from the sleeve and the spindle.
   C. Each rotation of the thimble turns the spindle four times.
   D. Measurements are taken by reading the spindle and bevel scales.

3. Which of the following devices can be used to take inside measurements?
   A. Straightedge
   B. Vernier calipers
   C. Voltmeter
   D. Dwell meter

4. Which of the following statements is correct?
   I. Fluid-measuring tools are used to check vacuum and pressure.
   II. A hydrometer checks the liquid level in a battery or radiator.
   A. I only   B. II only   C. Both I and II   D. Neither I nor II

5. Mechanic A says a dwell-tachometer is used to check how long contact points remain open.
   Mechanic B says that an oscilloscope can be connected to a home television screen to get an electrical readout.
   Who is correct?
   A. A only   B. B only   C. Both A and B   D. Neither A nor B

S U P P L E M E N T A L   A C T I V I T I E S

1. Show how to use feeler gauges.
2. Use a micrometer to measure a part your instructor has furnished.
3. Demonstrate how to use an inside micrometer and explain steps that would give incorrect readings.
4. Use a dial indicator on a shop vehicle and give readings of parts outlined by your instructor.
5. Use a cooling system tester and coolant hydrometer on a vehicle selected by your instructor.
6. Check the battery condition of a vehicle selected by your instructor and give ammeter, load tester, and voltmeter readings.
7. Hook up an oscilloscope according to your instructor's directions.

9 TROUBLESHOOTING

UNIT PREVIEW

Mechanics follow specific procedures when diagnosing automotive problems. The use of diagnostic procedures is called troubleshooting. Troubleshooting charts in service manuals help to pinpoint problem areas and speed up diagnostic time for a mechanic. Troubleshooting charts also direct a mechanic in conducting the necessary tests and inspection.

LEARNING OBJECTIVES

When you have completed your assignments and exercises in this unit, you should be able to:

☐ Explain how a mechanic and car owner can work together when troubleshooting.

☐ Describe how a troubleshooting chart helps a mechanic to diagnose a problem.

☐ Describe some test driving procedures from a repair manual.

☐ Explain the procedures used for making a visual inspection.

☐ Explain the reason for repeating all troubleshooting procedures.

9.1 AUTOMOTIVE DIAGNOSTICS

Diagnosis is the investigation and analysis of the cause or nature of a condition, situation, or problem. In automotive terms, *diagnostics* is the overall analysis of automobile operation, indicating what is right and what is wrong. Diagnostic equipment is discussed throughout this text.

Mechanics frequently diagnose the nature and cause of automotive problems or complaints reported by customers. The process of locating and identifying the causes of problems is called *troubleshooting*.

9.2 TROUBLESHOOTING

Troubleshooting is a process of elimination. Using step-by-step procedures, a mechanic makes checks to eliminate certain parts or functions as the cause of a problem. Troubleshooting progresses from simple checks and inspections to more involved test procedures.

Service manuals furnish a mechanic with procedures and guides for troubleshooting the various systems on an automobile.

Defining a Problem

Begin troubleshooting by speaking with the driver. A test ride with the driver can be helpful in determining the problem. Test drives are discussed in 9.4. Using the driver's information, a mechanic may be able to find the cause of the problem more quickly. When asking questions about the complaint, concentrate on four areas:

- *What happens?* Examples: the engine stalls; the transmission shifts harshly; an exhaust smell is noticeable inside the car.

- *When does the problem occur?* Examples: when the car is cold; when the car is fully warmed up; when the car is turning.

- *Where does the problem occur?* Examples: up or down hills; on flat roads; on highways or expressways.

- *How long has the problem been noticeable?* Examples: gradually over a period of months; for a week; it just began today.

Do *not* rely on the driver's information alone. Make your own diagnosis. Although information from the driver can be helpful, the mechanic must correctly diagnose the problem and perform the repair.

9.3 TROUBLESHOOTING CHARTS

Repair manuals have *troubleshooting charts* on most automotive systems. Figure 9-1 shows a typical troubleshooting chart. Troubleshooting charts enable a mechanic to locate causes of problems quickly. This greatly reduces the amount of time a mechanic needs to spend when searching for a specific problem. Troubleshooting charts usually have three columns of information that list the condition, possible sources of the problem, and the resolution.

9.4 THE TEST DRIVE

A *test drive* is a form of troubleshooting that requires specific driving procedures and safety precautions by the mechanic. Many repair manuals outline the different driving procedures that should be followed when checking for certain problems. Figure 9-2 shows test driving procedures used in checking a driveline.

Driving safety is always important. Before you begin, buckle up the seat belt and test the brakes.

GENERAL BRAKE SYSTEM DIAGNOSIS GUIDE

CONDITION	POSSIBLE SOURCE	RESOLUTION

• Brakes grab or lock-up when applied.	• Tires worn or incorrect pressure.
	
	• Grease or fluid on linings — damaged linings.
	• Improper size or type of linings.
	• Other brake system components:
	  • Bolts for caliper attachment loose or missing.
	  • Worn, damaged or dry wheel bearings.
	  • Improperly adjusted parking brake.
		• Inflate tires to correct pressure. Replace tires with worn tread.
		• Inspect, service or replace.
		
		• Replace with correct brake in axle sets.
		
		• Inspect, service or replace as required.

• Brake warning light on.	• Hydraulic system. • Shorted light circuit. • Parking brake not returned. • Brake warning switch.	• See Master Cylinder Diagnosis Guide. • Correct short in warning circuit. • See "Parking brake will not release or fully return" below. • Replace.
• Intermittent loss of pedal.	• Loose wheel bearing.	• Adjust as required. • Perform steps under "Excessive pedal travel or pedal travel goes to floor".
• Rough engine idle or stall, brakes applied — power brakes only.	• Vacuum leak in neutral switch. • Vacuum booster.	• Check lines for leaks. Service or replace as required. • Check vacuum booster for internal leaks. Replace if required.
• Parking brake control will not latch (manual release).	• Kinked or binding release cable. • Control assembly.	• Inspect, service or replace. • Inspect, service or replace.
• Parking brake control will not latch (automatic release).	• Vacuum leak. • Vacuum switch. • Control assembly.	• Service as required. • Test. Replace if necessary. • Service or replace.
• Parking brake will not release or fully return (manual release).	• Cable disconnected. • Control assembly binding. • Parking brake linkage binding. • Rear brakes.	• Connect cable or replace. • Service or replace. • Service or replace. • Check rear brakes shoe retracting springs and parking brake levers.
• Parking brake will not release or fully return (automatic release).	• Vacuum line leakage or improper connections. • Neutral switch. • Control assembly.	• Inspect and service. • Adjust or replace. • Service or replace.

Figure 9-1. A troubleshooting chart in a service manual. FORD MOTOR COMPANY

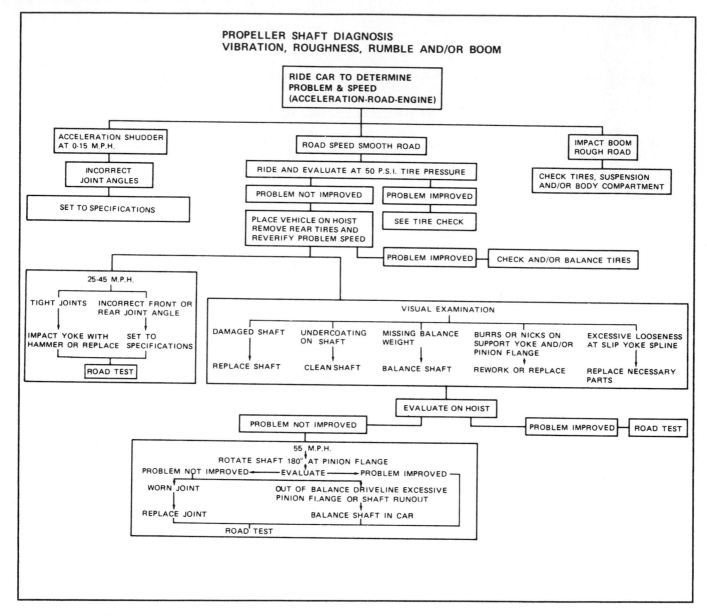

Figure 9-2. Another form of troubleshooting chart gives instructions on test driving an automobile to locate problems.
CHEVROLET MOTOR DIVISION—GMC

Jackrabbit starts, hard turning, or sudden braking should be avoided. Improper driving can make a problem worse or create a new problem. Carelessness during the test drive can result in an accident. Drive only in a manner that is required to diagnose the problem.

Consult the proper troubleshooting chart before the test drive. Test drive procedures change when different parts of the automobile are checked. Different brands of automobiles may have different test driving procedures. Procedures may call for low speeds, hard acceleration, and sudden gear changes. Follow the troubleshooting charts carefully. Using the wrong driving procedures may lead to an improper diagnosis.

9.5 PINPOINTING A PROBLEM

Following a test drive, and after checking the troubleshooting chart, the next step is to pinpoint the problem. By now, the mechanic should have a general idea of where to look. To locate the problem, two types of inspections can be made:

- Visual inspection
- Measurement inspection.

Visual Inspection

Make a visual inspection by looking around the automobile in the area where the likely problem exists. Look for leaks and loose or broken parts. Shake

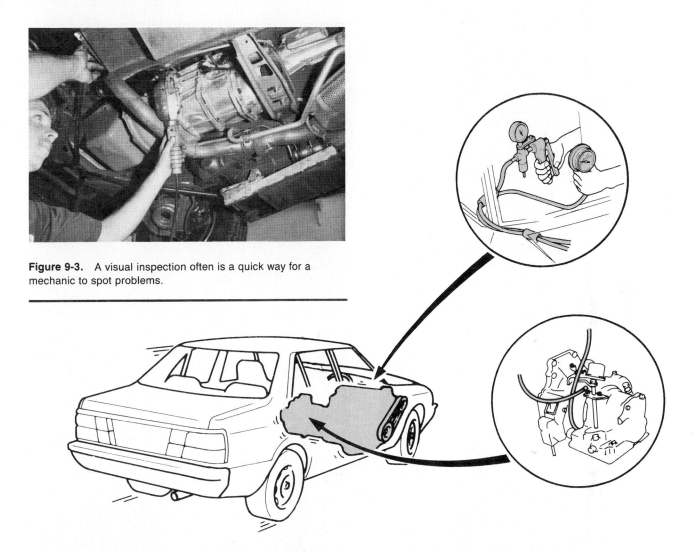

Figure 9-3. A visual inspection often is a quick way for a mechanic to spot problems.

Figure 9-4. A measurement inspection, using gauges and special tools, often is necessary to diagnose a problem.
MAZDA MOTOR CORPORATION

the parts to check for looseness, and listen for noises (see Figure 9-3).

Measurement Inspection

If visual inspection does not expose a problem, a *measurement inspection* may be needed. A measurement inspection may include one or more specific procedures. Check out the suspected problem area by using the proper measuring equipment for the job (see Figure 9-4). Specific tests are used, depending on which parts of the automobile are to be measured.

Rechecking Problem Areas

Once a problem area has been found and repaired, recheck the automobile. Two or more problems could be responsible for a complaint. Check the operation of the automobile to be sure it is satisfactory. If a problem persists, repeat all of the necessary troubleshooting procedures until a diagnosis is made.

U N I T   H I G H L I G H T S

- Troubleshooting is investigating and analyzing an automotive problem.
- Speak to the driver of an automobile to help find the cause of a problem.
- Troubleshooting charts speed up a mechanic's work by identifying the condition and locating the possible source of the problem.
- A test drive requires specific driving procedures to troubleshoot an automobile.
- Locate problems by visual and/or measurement inspection.

T E R M S

diagnostics
diagnosis
troubleshooting

troubleshooting charts
test drive
measurement inspection

R E V I E W   Q U E S T I O N S

DIRECTIONS: The following questions are similar to those used on mechanic certification tests. On a separate sheet of paper, write the letter of the correct choice.

1. All of the following statements about troubleshooting are correct EXCEPT
A. The procedure requires investigating and analyzing a problem.
B. The most accurate source of information about problems always is the driver.
C. Service manuals provide guides for troubleshooting.
D. It is necessary to know when the problem occurs.

2. Which of the following types of information is found in a troubleshooting chart?
A. Questions to ask the driver
B. How long the problem has existed
C. How to solve the problem
D. The proper lubricants to use

3. Which of the following statements is correct?
   I. Test drive procedures can change when different parts of the automobile are being checked.
   II. Test drive procedures can change when different brands of automobiles are being checked.
A. I only   B. II only   C. Both I and II   D. Neither I nor II

4. Mechanic A says that the same safety procedures are used regardless of a test drive diagnosis. Mechanic B says that driving procedures have nothing to do with safety.
   Who is correct?
A. A only   B. B only   C. Both A and B   D. Neither A nor B

5. All of the following statements about inspection are correct EXCEPT
A. It helps the mechanic pinpoint the problem.
B. The mechanic must listen carefully.
C. The mechanic must always repeat the troubleshooting procedures.
D. Specific tests are performed.

S U P P L E M E N T A L   A C T I V I T I E S

1. Locate a troubleshooting guide in a shop service manual.
2. Identify a possible problem based on an explanation furnished by your instructor.
3. Select a troubleshooting chart and explain the various test driving procedures that must be followed.
4. Make a visual inspection and locate a problem on an automobile selected by your instructor.
5. Perform a measurement inspection on a part furnished by your instructor.

THE
AUTOMOTIVE
ENGINE

10 PISTON ENGINE FUNDAMENTALS

UNIT PREVIEW

An automotive engine uses heat energy to create mechanical energy to move the vehicle. Modern automotive engines are powered by the internal burning of a fuel. Each of the parts of an automotive engine performs a specific job.

The operating principles of the engine can be divided into four basic functions. The engine must bring in fuel and air. It must heat and confine the fuel and air to a small area. The engine must burn the fuel and then, finally, it must rid itself of the burned gases.

Automotive engines consist of multiple power-producing units, and can be classified according to shape, size, fuel used, and many other characteristics.

The most common type of engine used for automobiles has been in use for over 100 years. Although other engine types have been proposed or used, the engine designed by Nikolaus Otto in 1876 remains the most practical and popular design.

LEARNING OBJECTIVES

When you have completed your assignments and exercises in this unit, you should be able to:

☐ Define and explain the terms energy, force, work, and power.

☐ Explain how an automobile engine produces power.

☐ Identify and describe the functions of the internal parts of an automotive engine.

☐ Identify and describe the operating functions of common automotive engines.

☐ Classify automobile engines according to specific characteristics.

☐ Identify alternative engine types.

10.1 ENERGY, FORCE, WORK, AND POWER

To understand how an automobile engine works, you must understand some basic terms that describe physical processes. For example, consider what happens if your car stalls in traffic. If you are strong enough by yourself, or get enough people to help you, you can push the car off to the side of the road. The ability to push a heavy car is *energy*.

When you push the car, you are applying *force* to it. Force applied to an object causes motion. If you have to push the car very far, you will have done a good bit of *work*. Basically, work is the result of *applying force* to an object and *causing it to move*. The more force applied and the more motion caused, the more work done.

Power is the rate at which work is done. *Rate* means how fast you are able to do the work of pushing.

If you have more energy, you can apply more force and do more work. The faster the work is done, the more power you are using. These concepts are summarized in Figure 10-1.

An automobile engine uses the energy present in its fuel to apply force and move the vehicle. The engine produces *torque,* a twisting force that turns the drive wheels. As the engine applies force and moves the vehicle, work is performed. The rate at which this work is done, often called engine power, is measured in *horsepower (hp), watts (W),* or *kilowatts (kw).*

Human beings and animals store energy chemically in their muscles. However, energy also can take

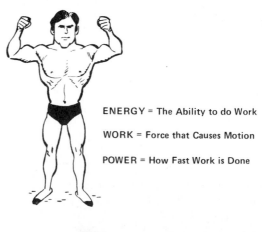

ENERGY = The Ability to do Work

WORK = Force that Causes Motion

POWER = How Fast Work is Done

Force Is Applied
To Push The Car

Figure 10-1. The concepts of power.

78

other forms. A tightly wound spring from an alarm clock stores *mechanical energy*. A fire extinguisher uses a combination of *chemical energy* and *physical energy* to spray a non-burning substance on a fire. When the flame on a gas stove is lit, *heat energy* is present for cooking.

10.2 CONVERTING HEAT ENERGY TO MOTION

Thermodynamics is the scientific study of how mechanical energy and heat energy are related. An automobile *engine* is a machine, or mechanical device, that changes heat energy into mechanical energy. Heat energy is produced by the explosion, or rapid burning, of gasoline. This heat energy is converted, or changed, into mechanical energy to turn the wheels that move the vehicle.

External Combustion Piston Engine

Two types of engines commonly have been used to convert heat energy to motion. In one type, fuel is burned outside of the engine. These engines are called *external combustion* engines. External combustion simply means "outside burning."

An old-fashioned steam locomotive is an example of an external combustion engine. The burning of fuel takes place outside of the engine areas that apply the force to move the locomotive. Fuel (wood, coal, or oil) is burned in a firebox under a boiler filled with water. The heat turns the water into steam. The steam pushes against a tight-fitting plug, called a *piston,* inside a hollow area called a *cylinder* (see Figure 10-2).

The steam exerts great *pressure* against the top, or head, of the piston. Pressure is the amount of force applied to a given area. The force pushes the piston through the cylinder. The piston is connected by a rod to the drive wheel of the locomotive. As the piston is moved in the cylinder by the steam pressure, the drive wheel of the locomotive begins to turn. This action is illustrated in Figure 10-3.

Internal Combustion Piston Engine

Another type of engine for converting heat energy to mechanical energy is called an *internal combustion* engine. Internal combustion means "inside burning." The typical automotive engine is an internal combustion engine. Fuel (gasoline or diesel fuel) is burned inside the engine, above the piston. The burning produces heat, which in turn produces pressure. The pressure forces the piston down the cylinder. This process is shown in Figure 10-4.

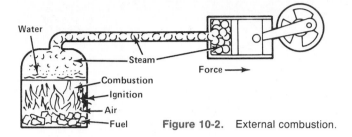

Figure 10-2. External combustion.

The piston is connected by a rod to a *crankshaft.* The crankshaft converts the downward push of the piston into a spinning, or rotary motion. The rotary motion of an engine's crankshaft is connected through a series of gears and drive mechanisms to turn the drive wheels of the vehicle. Figure 10-5 shows a cutaway view of an automotive piston engine.

10.3 HOW A PISTON ENGINE WORKS

The way an internal combustion engine works is very similar to the way an old-fashioned muzzle-loading cannon works. The cannon is made of a large piece of metal, hollowed out to form a barrel, or cylinder. The energy to shoot the cannonball comes from gunpowder that is poured down the barrel. A fuse is inserted into the gunpowder from the outside of the cannon. A cannonball, wrapped in cloth to make a tight seal, is pushed down the cannon barrel with a

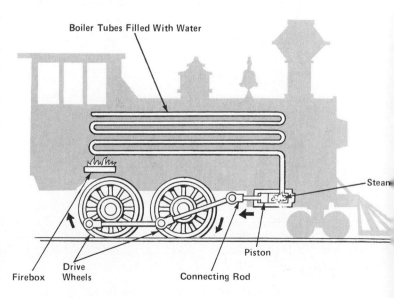

Figure 10-3. Steam pressure moves a piston that rotates the driving wheels.

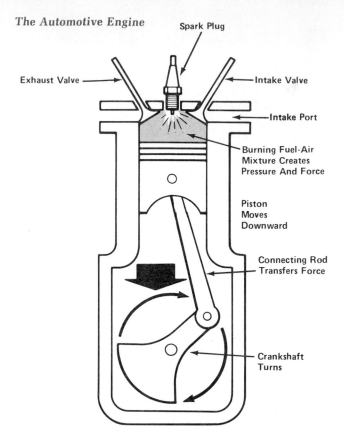

Figure 10-4. Internal combustion.

Figure 10-5. Parts of an internal combustion engine.

ramrod. A cutaway drawing of such a cannon is shown in Figure 10-6.

When the fuse is lit, the gunpowder explodes and produces hot, burning gases. The pressure produced by these gases pushes the cannonball out the barrel at high speed.

Of course, such a cannon has to be reloaded after each shot. But if you can imagine an automatically reloading cannon with the cannonball being pushed back down the barrel each time that an explosion occurs, you will have the basic idea of how a piston engine works.

10.4 PISTON ENGINE PARTS

An automotive internal combustion engine is made up of many parts. The major parts of an engine include:

- Cylinder block
- Piston and rings
- Crankshaft
- Connecting rod
- Bearings
- Cylinder head
- Valves
- Camshaft and valve train
- Flywheel
- Fuel System
- Exhaust System

Cylinder Block

Imagine starting from scratch to build an internal combustion piston engine. First you would need a large chunk, or block, of metal, similar to the body of

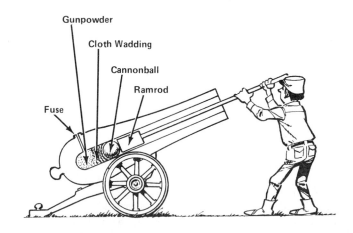

Figure 10-6. Parts of an internal combustion engine assembly work much the same as parts of a muzzle-loading cannon.

a cannon. To form the cylinder, you could drill, or bore, a large hole. See Figure 10-7. This part is called the *cylinder block*.

Piston, Rings, Crankshaft, Connecting Rod

A piece of metal could then be machined to form a piston. To make the piston fit tightly in the cylinder, springy metal *piston rings* are inserted around the piston. These act like the wadding around a cannonball, forming a tight seal for the high-pressure gases

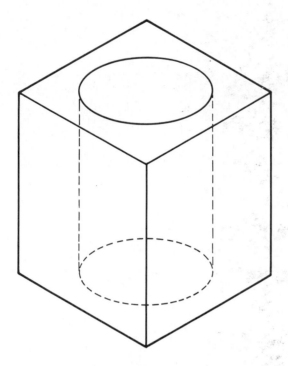

Figure 10-7. A cylinder is formed by boring a large hole in a solid piece of metal. The drilled, solid metal block is called the cylinder block.

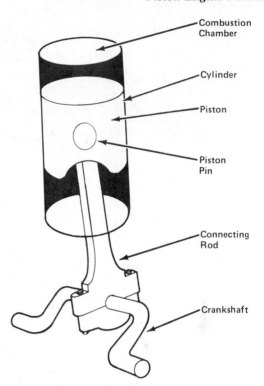

Figure 10-8. Up-and-down movement of a piston is converted into rotary motion at the crankshaft.

powering the engine. To convert the downward motion of the piston into a rotary motion, a crankshaft is attached to the bottom of the block. A rod, called a *connecting rod,* connects the piston to the crankshaft. The motion of the crankshaft is similar to the motion of the arms and shoulders of a man pushing a cannonball back down each time an explosion occurs. Figure 10-8 illustrates these parts.

Bearings

The connecting rod must be able to spin around the crankshaft. Also, the crankshaft must be able to turn freely in the engine block. To permit these motions, soft metal parts called *insert bearings* are used. These bearings also protect the connecting rod and crankshaft from rubbing against each other and wearing out. Figure 10-9 shows connecting rod bearing inserts. Many bearings are used in the engine to support and protect rotating parts, and to allow them to turn freely.

Cylinder Head and Valves

To close off the end of the cylinder above the piston, a thick piece of metal is attached. Because it is at the top of the engine and closes off the cylinder, it is called the *cylinder head.* The cylinder head is not solid, however. Hollow passages are molded, or cast, into the metal. The hollow passages, called *ports,* allow air and gasoline vapor to flow into the cylinder, and burned gases to flow out. To close the ports during the explosion of the gasoline vapor, tapered parts

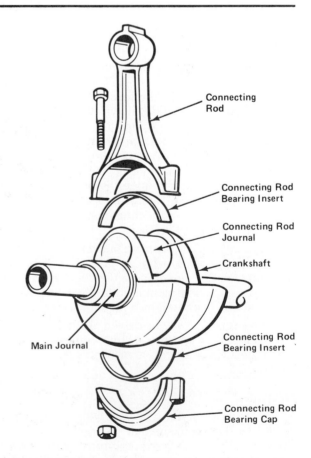

Figure 10-9. Bearings are used between the crankshaft and connecting rods.

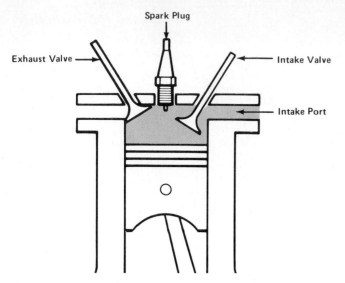

Figure 10-10. A cylinder head and valve assembly.

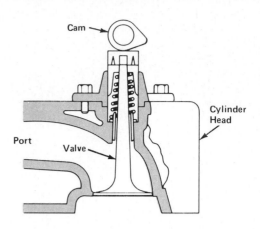

Figure 10-11. An overhead camshaft assembly.

called *valves* are fitted. A valve acts like a cork in the neck of a bottle. When the valve is closed, the cylinder is sealed. When the valve is opened, gases can flow around the valve into or out of the cylinder. Also in the head, usually close to or between the valves, is a threaded hole for a *spark plug*. The spark plug acts like the fuse in a cannon. When a spark jumps the gap at the end of the spark plug, the gasoline vapor is ignited and burns rapidly. These parts are illustrated in Figure 10-10.

Camshaft and Valve Train

Large springs are attached to the stems of the valves to pull the valves tightly shut. The valves must form a tight seal to contain the force of combustion. The parts that operate to push the valves open are known as the *valve train*. To open the valves, or ports, a rotating metal shaft with projections, called a *camshaft*, is used. A *cam* is a projection on the camshaft, with a shape similar to an egg. The projection pushes the valve downward to open the port. The camshaft can be mounted over the cylinder head, as shown in Figure 10-11. Such an arrangement is known as an *overhead camshaft (OHC)*.

Another way of opening the valves is to position the camshaft inside a hollow area of the block. Intermediate parts, shown in Figure 10-12, then are used to transfer the pushing motion to the valve stem. This arrangement is known as a *pushrod* valve train.

The camshaft may be driven, or turned, by a gear arrangement, by a chain, or by a reinforced, toothed rubber belt. Camshaft drive mechanisms are shown in Figure 10-13.

Flywheel

A heavy round metal wheel, called a *flywheel*, is attached to the crankshaft at the rear of the engine. Once the flywheel starts spinning, its momentum helps the engine to run smoothly. A flywheel is shown in Figure 10-14.

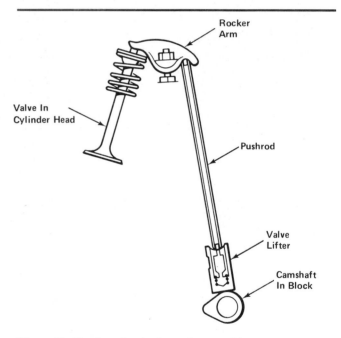

Figure 10-12. A pushrod valve train assembly.

Basic Fuel System

To supply gasoline vapor to the basic engine, a fuel system is needed. A *carburetor* mixes gasoline and air to produce a fine mist. The carburetor is connected to the *intake port* of the cylinder head by a hollow metal part called an *intake manifold*. Figure 10-15 shows a cutaway view of the carburetor, intake manifold, and engine.

Basic Exhaust System

After the air-fuel mixture is burned, the gases must be removed from the cylinder in preparation for a fresh *intake charge*, or mixture of fuel vapor and air. The *exhaust valve* is pushed open by a cam to allow the burned gases to be forced out of the cylinder. An arrangement similar to that for the intake port is used. A hollow, tubular part, called an *exhaust manifold*, is

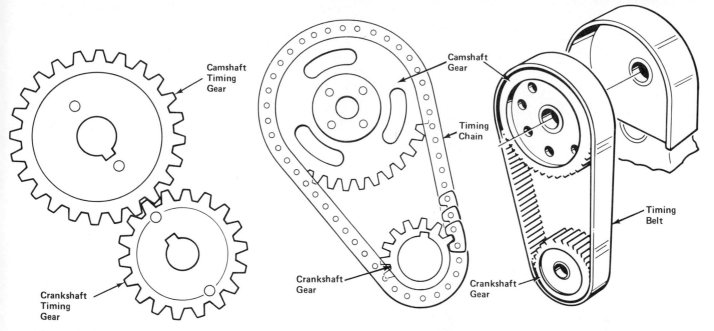

Figure 10-13. Camshafts can be operated by gears, chains, or synthetic belts.

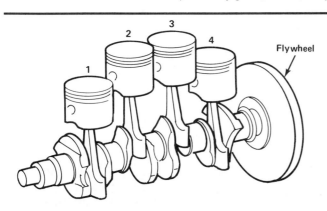

Figure 10-14. A flywheel rotates with the crankshaft to help the engine run smoothly.

bolted to the head at the exhaust port, as shown in Figure 10-16. Connecting metal tubes lead to the muffler, shown in Figure 10-17, which reduces the noise from the combustion within the engine.

10.5 THE FOUR-STROKE CYCLE

The basic engine must draw in an air-fuel mixture, compress it, burn it, and get rid of the gases. This sequence of events makes up what is known as the *four-stroke cycle*. A *stroke* is the movement of the piston in the cylinder from one end to the other. A cycle is a sequence that is repeated. The four-stroke cycle, illustrated in Figure 10-18, includes the following strokes:

- Intake
- Compression
- Power, or ignition
- Exhaust.

Follow the illustrations in Figure 10-18 as you read the following discussion.

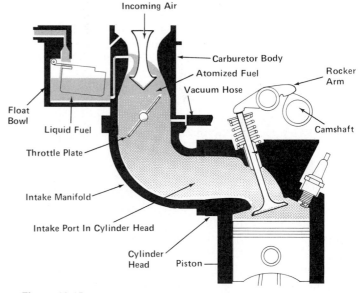

Figure 10-15. In many engines, the air-fuel mixture is introduced into the cylinders through a carburetor, intake manifold, and intake valves.

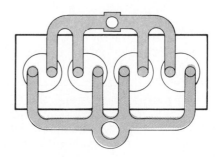

Figure 10-16. Exhaust gases are routed outward through an exhaust manifold.

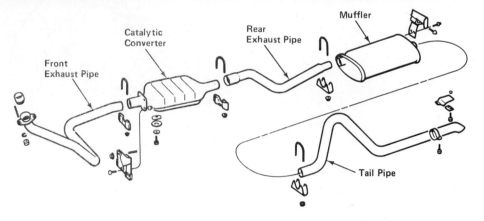

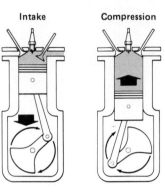

Figure 10-17. A muffler reduces noise from combustion within an engine.

Intake

The crankshaft and camshaft are both turning as intake stroke events begin. As the crankshaft turns, the connecting rod pulls the piston downward. At the same time, the intake valve leading to the intake manifold and carburetor is opened by the camshaft.

Because the piston rings seal the piston tightly in the cylinder, a low-pressure area is formed as the piston moves down. The atmospheric pressure of the outside air forces air to flow down through the carburetor. The carburetor discharges a fine mist of gasoline into the incoming air. This intake charge fills the cylinder as the piston reaches the bottom of the intake stroke. When the piston is all the way down, it is at *bottom dead center (BDC)*.

Compression

As the piston nears the bottom of its stroke and starts back up, the camshaft rotation allows the intake valve to be pulled closed by the valve spring. Both intake and exhaust valves now are closed. The air-fuel mixture is trapped as the piston continues to rise. The rising piston compresses, or squeezes the mixture. Compressing the mixture heats it for better burning, and confines it to a very small area for better combustion. The *compression ratio* is a set of numbers that expresses how much the mixture is compressed. See Figure 10-19. When the piston reaches the very top of its travel, it is at *top dead center (TDC)*. The volume of space through which the piston travels from BDC to TDC is called the *displacement* of the cylinder. In a multiple-cylinder engine, the total displacement is the sum of all the individual cylinders' displacement.

Power or Ignition

At a point near the top of the piston's travel, a high-voltage current is sent to the spark plug. The current jumps a gap to form a spark. The spark ignites the tightly compressed mixture, causing it to burn. This burning takes place within the small area above the piston, called the *combustion chamber*. The combustion causes heat, and the expanding mixture creates

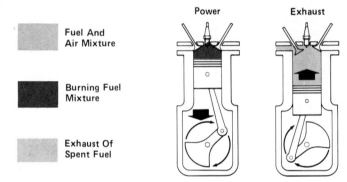

Fuel And Air Mixture	
Burning Fuel Mixture	
Exhaust Of Spent Fuel	

Figure 10-18. The four-stroke cycle.

pressure in the cylinder. Both valves are closed, and the piston is sealed by the rings against the cylinder. Therefore, the pressure pushes the piston downward. The connecting rod pushes against the crankshaft and forces it to turn.

Exhaust

Near the bottom of the power stroke, the camshaft pushes the exhaust valve open. As the piston travels up the cylinder, the piston pushes the burned gases out the exhaust port.

At this point, the piston is again near the top of the cylinder. Quickly, the camshaft allows the exhaust valve to close and opens the intake valve, and the piston begins an intake stroke immediately.

At highway speeds, the four-stroke cycle repeats itself in each cylinder thousands of times every minute.

10.6 MULTIPLE-CYLINDER ENGINES

Each cylinder is a power-producing unit. To provide the force needed to move a heavy automobile, automobile engines have several cylinders. These cylinders can be arranged differently within the cylinder block. Figure 10-20 shows the most common cylinder arrangements, or *configurations*, for passenger car engines.

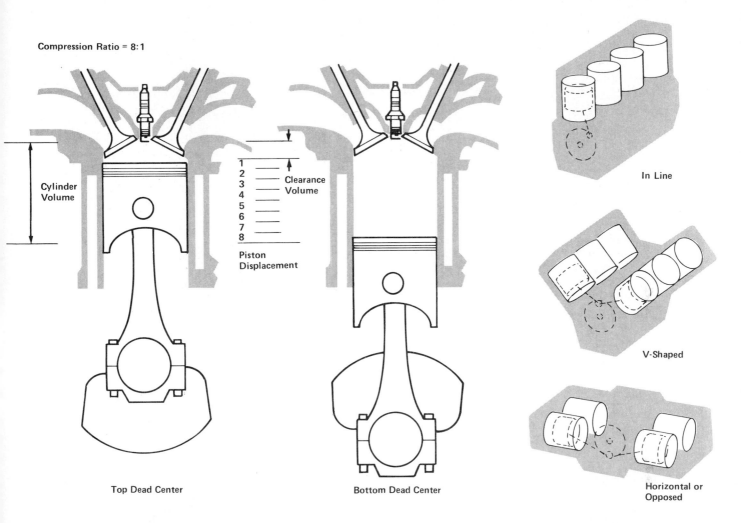

Figure 10-19. The compression ratio indicates how much the air-fuel mixture is squeezed on the compression stroke.

Figure 10-20. Typical engine cylinder configurations.

Piston Motion

In a multiple-cylinder engine, the crankshaft is made so that the movements of the pistons are staggered. That is, half of the pistons move upward as the others move downward. This arrangement helps to balance the engine so that it runs smoothly.

In a four-cylinder engine, two pistons will be moving upward at the same time that two are moving downward. One of the two moving upward will be on its compression stroke, and the other will be on its exhaust stroke. One of the two pistons moving downward will be on its intake stroke, and the other will be on its power stroke.

Cylinder Numbering

On the end of the crankshaft, opposite the flywheel, a *power pulley* is attached. Belts are stretched between the power pulley grooves and the pulleys of engine accessories. When the engine turns, the belts force the accessory device pulleys to turn. This arrangement is shown in Figure 10-21.

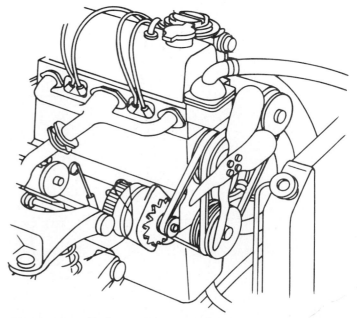

Figure 10-21. Engine accessory operation.

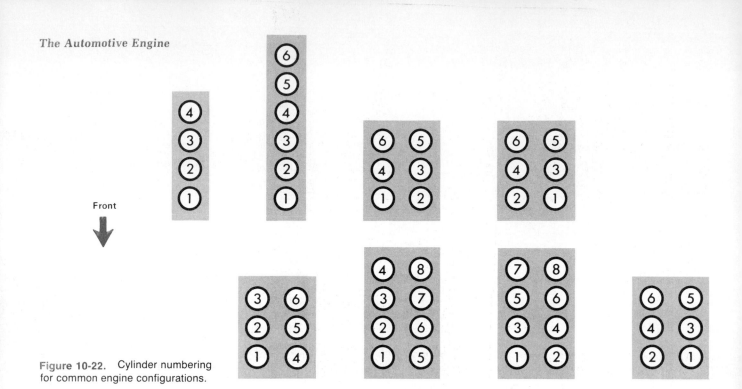

Front

Figure 10-22. Cylinder numbering for common engine configurations.

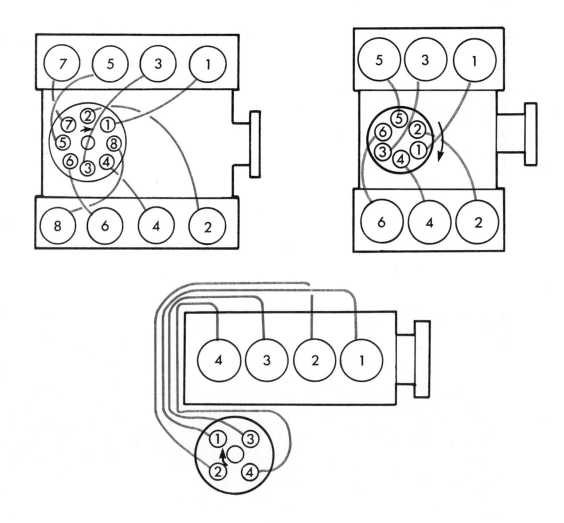

Figure 10-23. Cylinder numbering and firing order arrangements.

The engine cylinders are numbered from the power pulley end toward the flywheel end. The cylinders in an in-line engine are numbered one through four, five, or six, from the power pulley rearward.

V-type and flat engines may have different numbering systems. Figure 10-22 illustrates some cylinder numbering arrangements.

Firing Order

The order in which the power strokes occur within the cylinders usually is not the same as the cylinder numbering. Examples of cylinder numbering and firing order arrangements are shown in Figure 10-23.

Power Overlap

Two revolutions of the engine crankshaft are necessary for the four-stroke cycle to be completed in any single cylinder. The more cylinders an engine has, the more power strokes, or *power pulses,* the crankshaft receives per revolution. In engines with more than four cylinders, the power pulses overlap each other to provide a smoother application of force to the crankshaft. Thus, the more cylinders, the smoother an engine will run.

10.7 ENGINE CLASSIFICATIONS

Automobile engines can be classified according to several features. These features include:

- Number of cylinders
- Cylinder arrangement
- Valve arrangement
- Valve train type
- Combustion chamber shape
- Fuel used
- Ignition type
- Cooling system
- Lubrication system
- Strokes per cycle
- Reciprocating vs. rotary
- Use.

Number of Cylinders

Automobile engines can be classified by total number of cylinders. Current automotive engines include 3-cylinder, 4-cylinder, 5-cylinder, 6-cylinder, 8-cylinder, and 12-cylinder models.

Cylinder Arrangement

Engines can be classified according to cylinder arrangement. In other words, an engine can be of the inline, V, or flat type. Other, more complicated arrangements also have been used.

Valve Arrangement

Although the valve-in-head design is now universal for automotive engines, other valve arrangements are possible. One or both of the valves can be located within the block, instead of in the head. Automobile engines built prior to 1955 had such an arrangement, as do small engines, such as those used for lawnmowers.

Valve Train Type

As mentioned above, engine valve trains can be either pushrod type or overhead-camshaft (OHC) type. In addition, separate camshafts can be used for exhaust and intake valves. Dual overhead camshafts (DOHC) are used in some high-performance sports cars and racing cars.

Combustion Chamber Shape

Engines can be classified according to the shape of the combustion chamber used. Figure 10-24 shows the most commonly-used variations in shape for automobile engines.

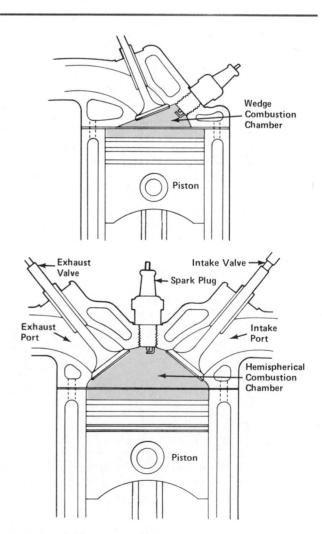

Figure 10-24. Common combustion chamber configurations.

Fuel Used

Fuels other than gasoline can be used to provide the heat energy to drive an automotive engine. Practical fuel alternatives include propane, diesel fuel, *methanol* (poisonous "wood alcohol"), and *ethanol* (grain alcohol, such as that used in liquor).

Ignition Type

The air-fuel mixture can be ignited by an electrical spark, as explained above. Such an arrangement is known as *spark* ignition. However, *diesel engines* have no spark plugs. An automotive diesel engine's compression ratio is between 20:1 and 23:1. The greater heat generated by this higher compression is sufficient to ignite the mixture for the power stroke. A diesel engine is also known as a *compression ignition* engine.

Cooling System

Heat generated by combustion of the air-fuel mixture within the combustion chamber heats the metal parts of the engine. The heat is sufficient to melt and destroy some engine parts, such as aluminum pistons. Some form of cooling system is needed to dissipate, or draw away, this excess heat.

Air cooling. Engines can be cooled by shaping the metal engine block and head into *cooling fins* and forcing air over them. *Air cooling* has been used for motorcycle and automotive engines (see Figure 10-25).

Liquid cooling. Another, more efficient way to cool the engine is to form hollow passages in the block and head, and circulate cooling liquid through them. The heat is conducted into the liquid. *Liquid cooling* allows the engine to run at a more consistent temperature in hot and cold weather. A liquid cooling system is shown in Figure 10-26.

Lubrication System

In addition to cooling requirements, the bearings and moving parts of the engine must be lubricated. An *oil pan* is fitted to the bottom of the engine to hold a supply of lubricant. Modern automotive engines are lubricated by oil flowing from an *oil pump* under pressure to moving parts (see Figure 10-27). This system is known as a *pressurized lubrication system*.

As the crankshaft rotates, it splashes some oil on the cylinder walls below the pistons. This activity is known as *splash lubrication*. Modern engines use a form of splash lubrication, called *throw-off*. Oil is allowed to "leak" from crankshaft main bearing lubrication points. The oil is thrown onto the cylinder walls as the crankshaft rotates.

Strokes per Cycle

Some engines operate on a *two-stroke cycle*. This design is used for motorcycle engines of less than 500cc displacement and for lawnmower and similar applications. In the past, small automobiles also were powered by two-stroke engines. Each time the piston in a two-stroke engine reaches TDC, the spark plug fires a compressed mixture.

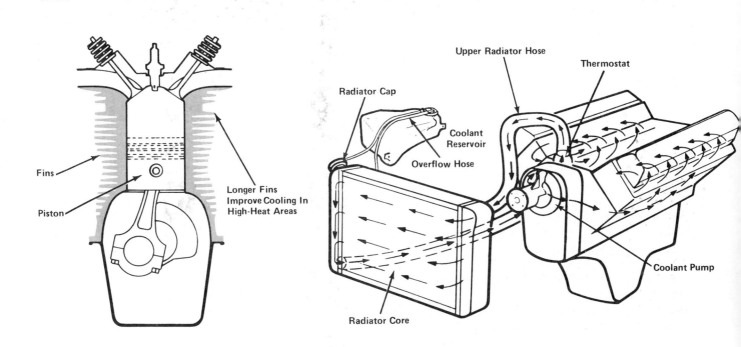

Figure 10-25. Air cooling system.

Figure 10-26. Liquid cooling system.

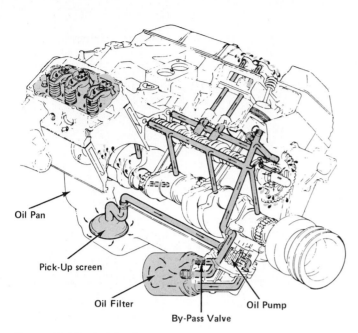

Oil Pan

Pick-Up screen

Oil Filter

By-Pass Valve

Oil Pump

Figure 10-27. Lubrication system.

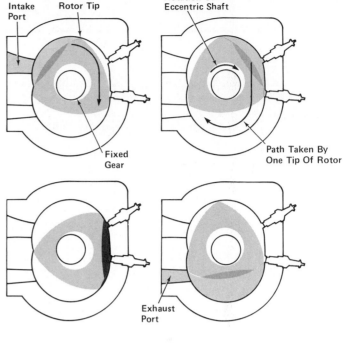

Intake Port

Rotor Tip

Rotation Of Eccentric Shaft

Fixed Gear

Path Taken By One Tip Of Rotor

Exhaust Port

Figure 10-28. Rotary engine cycle.

Reciprocating vs. Rotary

Most automobile engines are reciprocating engines. That is, their pistons travel back and forth in the cylinders. A small number of automobiles are powered by *rotary engines*. A rotary engine uses a curved, triangular rotor to perform the functions of the four-stroke cycle. A rotary engine four-stroke cycle is illustrated in Figure 10-28. In recent years, only the Mazda RX-7 sports car has been produced with a rotary engine.

Use

Engines can also be classified by use. Examples include automobile, truck, and motorcycle engines, stationary engines (for agricultural water pumps and electrical generators), airplane engines, and so on.

UNIT HIGHLIGHTS

- The terms energy, force, work, and power have specific meanings.
- An internal-combustion engine creates force to move a vehicle by burning fuel.
- The basic parts of an internal-combustion piston engine are the cylinder block, piston and rings, crankshaft, connecting rod, cylinder head, valves, camshaft, valve train, flywheel, fuel system and exhaust system.
- Engines can be classified by several characteristics of construction, operation, and use.
- The internal-combustion piston engine remains the most popular and durable of the automotive power plants.

TERMS

energy	carburetor
force	intake port
work	intake manifold
power	intake charge
torque	exhaust valve
horsepower	exhaust manifold
watt	four-stroke cycle
mechanical energy	stroke
chemical energy	bottom dead center (BDC)
physical energy	top dead center (TDC)
heat energy	compression ratio
thermodynamics	displacement
engine	combustion chamber
external combustion	configuration
piston	power pulley
cylinder	power pulse
pressure	methanol
internal combustion	ethanol
crankshaft	spark ignition
cylinder block	diesel engines
piston rings	compression ignition
connecting rod	cooling fins
bearing	air cooling
cylinder head	liquid cooling
port	oil pan
valve	oil pump
spark plug	pressurized lubrication system
valve train	splash lubrication
camshaft	throw-off lubrication
cam	two-stroke cycle
overhead camshaft	rotary engine
pushrod	
flywheel	

R E V I E W   Q U E S T I O N S

DIRECTIONS: The following questions are similar to those used on mechanic certification tests. On a separate sheet of paper, write the letter of the correct choice.

1. An internal-combustion gasoline piston engine converts
A. gasoline to torque.
B. air-fuel mixture to force.
C. heat energy to mechanical energy.
D. horsepower to watts.

2. On which strokes of the four-stroke cycle are both valves closed?
A. Intake and compression
B. Power and exhaust
C. Compression and power
D. Intake and exhaust

3. Which of the following statements is correct?
   I. Valves and piston rings form a tight seal to contain the force of the combustion that pushes the piston down.
   II. The head gasket forms a seal between the cylinder head and the block.
A. I only   B. II only   C. Both I and II   D. Neither I nor II

4. Valve adjustments are made with both the intake and exhaust valve fully closed.
   Mechanic A says both valves are closed on the intake and compression strokes.
   Mechanic B says both valves are closed on the power and exhaust strokes.
   Who is correct?
A. A only   B. B only   C. Both A and B   D. Neither A nor B

5. How many crankshaft revolutions are needed to complete all four strokes of the four-stroke cycle?
A. 4
B. 2
C. 1
D. 4, 5, 6, 8, or 12, depending on the number of cylinders

S U P P L E M E N T A L   A C T I V I T I E S

1. Define the terms energy, force, work, and power in your own words.
2. Describe how an automobile engine produces power.
3. Name the basic parts of an internal-combustion piston engine.
4. Classify the engines in your family's or friends' cars by as many characteristics as you can identify.
5. Identify engine parts on sight.

11 *ENGINE MEASUREMENTS AND PERFORMANCE*

U N I T   P R E V I E W

Engine size is a measure of the total volume of air displaced by the movement of the pistons. Displacement can be calulated from engine measurements.

Displacement and compression ratio both affect the force and power output of an engine. Engine power is the rate at which the engine can do the work of producing torque.

Engine power is lost due to friction, restrictions in the intake system, power used to drive engine accessories, and heat losses.

Overall vehicle efficiency is limited by heat and frictional losses and the resistance to movement through the air.

L E A R N I N G   O B J E C T I V E S

When you have completed your assignments and exercises in this unit, you should be able to:

☐ Make measurements and determine an engine's displacement.

☐ Determine the compression ratio of an engine.

☐ Explain the relationship of different types of horsepower ratings.

☐ Describe the types of engine power losses.

☐ Describe how the efficiency of an engine can be determined.

☐ Identify and describe factors that affect vehicle efficiency.

11.1 ENGINE SIZE

When referring to engine size, the quantity that is measured is displacement, not the physical dimensions of an engine. A "big" engine is one with a great deal of displacement. A "smaller" engine is one with less displacement.

Displacement, discussed in Unit 10, is the volume through which a piston moves from BDC to TDC on a stroke. Total engine displacement is the sum of all the individual cylinder displacements during one revolution of the crankshaft.

Two common ways of expressing measurements of all types, including displacement, are used. *Customary units* are British-based units such as inches, feet, pounds, gallons, and so on. Cylinder volume in customary units is expressed in *cubic inches*. One cubic inch is the volume contained in a cube that measures one inch on each side.

In *International System of Units (SI)*, or metric, measurements, volume is measured in *cubic centimeters (cc)*. A centimeter is 1/100 of a meter, or 10 millimeters. A cubic centimeter is the volume contained in a cube that measures one centimeter, or 10 millimeters, on each side. 1,000 cc = 1 liter = 61.0 cubic inches.

Bore and Stroke

A simplified formula for engine displacement is:

engine displacement =
0.785 × bore diameter^2 × length of stroke
× number of cylinders

The stroke can be determined by turning the crankshaft and measuring the piston's travel in the cylinder. Stroke also can be determined by measuring the crankshaft. The individual crankshaft throws, where the connecting rods are attached, are offset from the center line of the main journals. The stroke is equal to the amount of offset from the crankshaft center line multiplied by two.

For example, say a V-6 engine has a bore of 3.800 inches [9.65 cm] and a stroke of 3.400 inches [8.64 cm]. The displacement of this engine is:

$$0.785 \times (3.800)^2 \times 3.400 \times 6 = 231.24 \text{ cubic inches}$$

or

$$0.785 \times (9.65)^2 \times 8.64 \times 6 = 3,789.56 \text{ cc},$$
$$\text{or } 3.8 \text{ liters}$$

Displacement

The larger the cylinders and the longer the stroke, the greater an engine's displacement will be. Large cylinders and long strokes mean that large volumes of air-fuel mixture will be drawn into the cylinders. The more fuel that can be burned, the greater the chemical energy that can be turned into mechanical energy.

Thus, the larger an engine's displacement, the more torque will be produced.

More energy is required to move a larger mass. Larger, heavier vehicles are provided with large-displacement engines. Large-displacement engines produce more torque than smaller-displacement engines, and they also consume more fuel.

Smaller, lighter vehicles can be adequately powered by lower-displacement engines that consume less fuel.

Power, as discussed in Unit 10, is the rate at which work is done. In the case of an engine, power is the rate at which torque is produced. The faster an engine produces torque, the more powerful it is. In addition to displacement, another factor that influences engine power is compression ratio.

11.2 COMPRESSION RATIO

The more the air-fuel mixture becomes squeezed on the compression stroke, the greater the heating produced by compression. In addition, the pressure, or force per unit area, applied to the piston top is greater. Both these factors combine to produce more force on the power stroke.

The *compression ratio* is a comparison between the volume above the piston at BDC and the volume above the piston at TDC (clearance volume), as shown in Figure 11-1. The volume of the combustion chamber in the cylinder head also must be considered when determining compression ratio.

Imagine a cylinder containing 98 cubic inches with the piston at BDC and 2 cubic inches in the cylinder head. The total volume above the piston at BDC is 98 + 2 = 100 cubic inches. Now, consider the situation when the piston reached TDC. There are 8 cubic inches left in the cylinder and the same 2 cubic inches in the cylinder head. The total volume above the piston at TDC is 8 + 2 = 10 cubic inches.

If the volume is 100 cubic inches at BDC and 10 cubic inches at TDC, the compression ratio is 100 ÷ 10 = 10.0 : 1.

The formula for determining compression ratio is:

compression ratio =
volume in cylinder above piston at BDC
+ volume in cylinder head
÷ volume in cylinder above piston at TDC
+ volume in cylinder head

The higher the compression ratio, the more power an engine theoretically can produce. Also, as the compression ratio increases, the heat produced as the piston rises on the compression stroke also increases. Gasoline with a low *octane rating* can be ignited from this compressional heat, instead of from an ignition

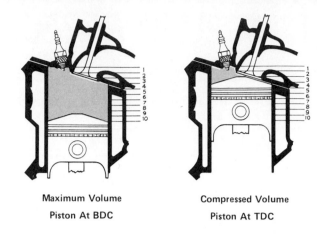

Maximum Volume
Piston At BDC

Compressed Volume
Piston At TDC

Figure 11-1. Compression ratio. BLACK & DECKER

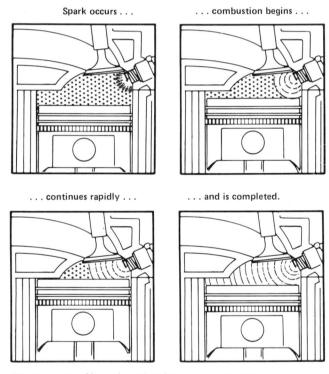

Spark occurs . . .

. . . combustion begins . . .

. . . continues rapidly . . .

. . . and is completed.

Figure 11-2. Normal combustion. CHAMPION SPARK PLUGS

spark. This can cause serious engine damage, as explained in Unit 20. The higher a gasoline's octane rating, the less likely it is to ignite through compressional heating.

Ideally, ignition should occur so that maximum pressure is produced just as the piston reaches TDC on the compression stroke. Such normal combustion is illustrated in Figure 11-2.

The compression ratio of an engine must be suited to the type of fuels available. Or, as compression ratio increases, the octane rating of the gasoline also should be increased to prevent abnormal combustion.

11.3 HORSEPOWER AND TORQUE

Torque is a turning or twisting force. The engine crankshaft applies torque that is transmitted through the drivetrain to turn the driving wheels of the vehicle.

In an engine, *horsepower* is the rate at which torque is produced.

Horsepower

In the late 1700s in England, James Watt formed a company to sell his newly-invented steam engine to coal mine operators. At that time, horses were used in the mines to lift heavy buckets of coal. In order to show the relative power of his steam engine, James Watt had to find out how powerful a horse was. Through experiments, it was found that the average horse could lift a 330-pound bucket of coal 100 feet in one minute, as shown in Figure 11-3.

The formula for determining work is:

work = force × distance

Thus, the work a horse can do equals 330 lb × 100 feet = 33,000 *foot-pounds (ft-lb)* per minute. A foot-pound is a unit of work. It is equivalent to the force that is necessary to move 1 pound through a distance of 1 foot.

In SI metric units, work is measured in *joules (J)*, after the scientist James P. Joule. A Joule is equal to one *Newton-meter (Nm)* of work per second. A Newton-meter is the force required to move 9.8 kilograms (approximately 21.6 pounds) 1 meter in 1 second. The Newton-meter is named after Sir Isaac Newton.

Torque

Engines produce power by turning a crankshaft in a circular motion. To convert terms of force applied in a straight line to force applied in a circular motion, the formula is:

torque = force × radius

A 10-pound force applied to a wrench 1 foot long will produce 10 *pounds-feet (lb-ft)* of torque. Imagine that the 1-foot-long wrench is connected to a shaft. If 1 pound of force is applied to the end of the wrench, 1 pound-foot of torque is produced. Ten pounds of force applied to a wrench 2 feet long will produce 20 pounds-feet of torque. See Figure 11-4.

Torque is measured in pounds-feet. To standardize and prevent confusion, this text specifies torque in

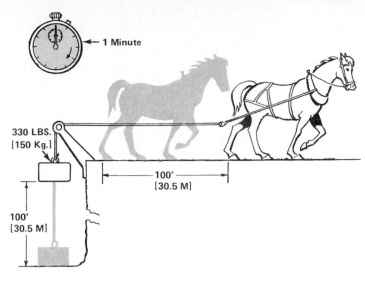

Figure 11-3. Work and horsepower.

pounds-feet and work in foot-pounds. In both cases, force causes motion through a certain distance.

In SI units, torque is specified in Newton-meters (Nm).

The Relationship of Horsepower to Torque

If torque output of an engine at a given speed (rpm) is known, horsepower can be determined by this formula:

horsepower = torque × rpm ÷ 5,252

An engine produces different amounts of torque dependent on the rotational speed of the crankshaft and other factors. A mathematical representation, or graph, of the relationship between horsepower and torque in one engine is shown in Figure 11-5.

This graph shows that torque drops off above about 1,700 rpm. Horsepower increases steadily until about 3,500 rpm, and then drops. The third line on the graph indicates horsepower needed to overcome the resistance to movement of engine internal parts against each other. This resistance is known as *friction*.

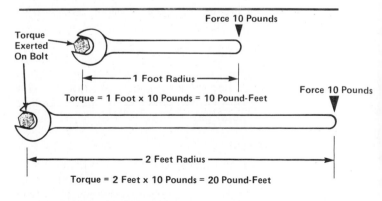

Figure 11-4. Force and torque.

93

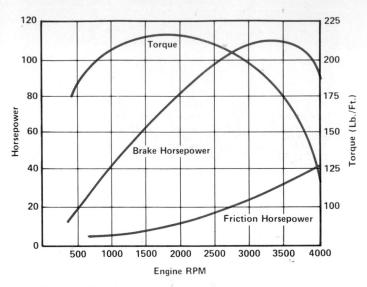

Figure 11-5. Horsepower and torque.

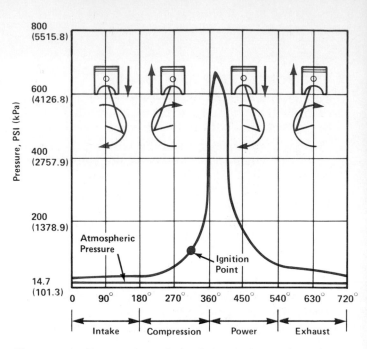

Figure 11-6. Pressure in a cylinder during the four-stroke cycle.

11.4 HORSEPOWER LOSSES

The usable power produced by an engine is known as *brake horsepower (bhp)*. To measure brake horsepower, a braking, or stopping, device is used to put a load on an engine. The more stopping force the engine can resist, the more powerful it is.

The power that an engine could theoretically produce from combustion pressure inside the cylinders is known as *indicated horsepower (ihp)*. A graph of the pressure in a cylinder during the four-stroke cycle is shown in Figure 11-6.

Indicated horsepower is less than brake horsepower because some of an engine's power is used up by friction between internal engine parts. The power necessary to overcome friction within an engine is known as *frictional horsepower (fhp)*.

The relationship between brake horsepower, indicated horsepower, and frictional horsepower is:

$$bhp = ihp - fhp$$

11.5 FRICTION

Different types of friction may be present between parts in an engine, including dry friction, greasy friction, and viscous friction.

Dry Friction

Dry friction occurs when objects directly contact each other, as metal parts rubbing against other metal parts. Dry friction causes rapid wear and heat that quickly ruins metal parts.

Greasy Friction

Greasy friction occurs when a thin film of grease or oil is present between surfaces. Within an engine, a thin film of oil remains on bearing surfaces after the engine is shut off, as shown in Figure 11-7. Greasy friction occurs before an engine starts, just as the crankshaft and other parts begin to turn.

After starting, oil is pumped between metal surfaces by the lubrication system to eliminate dry and greasy friction. Until the oil is warmed up and pumped everywhere within an engine, greasy friction does not provide adequate lubrication. Thus, parts will wear rapidly.

Viscous Friction

Viscous friction is the resistance to motion between layers of liquid, such as oil. *Viscosity* is the property of liquids that causes them to resist flowing. A highly viscous oil is thick and heavy.

The engine lubrication system pumps oil into the clearance between bearing surfaces. Within the space of the clearance, microscopic layers of oil adhere, or stick, to each other as the shaft spins. This causes a wedge-shaped film of oil to build up and support the weight of the shaft. See Figure 11-8.

With proper lubrication to prevent dry and greasy friction, bearing surfaces and other rubbing parts should last a long time.

11.6 MEASURING HORSEPOWER

A *dynamometer* is a device for measuring horsepower. A *brake dynamometer* applies a braking force to an engine. The braking force can be developed in two ways. The most common way is to force a turbine, or propeller, to turn inside a container filled with liquid. An electrical generator across which a variable load is connected can also be turned to provide braking force. See Figure 11-9.

For testing purposes, an engine can be removed from the vehicle and tested separately. In addition, all

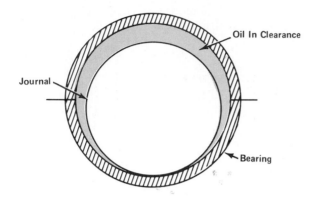

Figure 11-7. A thin film of oil remains on bearing surfaces after the engine has been turned off.

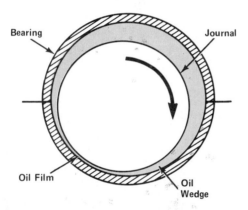

Figure 11-8. A wedge-shaped film of oil supports the weight of a shaft.

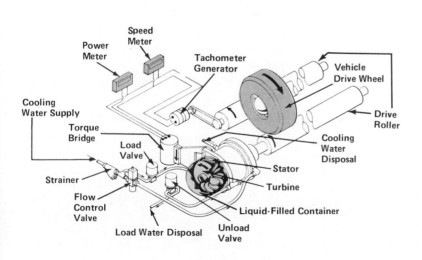

Figure 11-9. Parts of a brake dynamometer.

engine accessories, such as the waterpump, alternator, and so on, can be powered from outside sources. The rating from such a test would be an engine's *gross horsepower*. The rating with the accessories connected to the engine would be less, and is known as *net horsepower*. Power used to operate an engine accessory is known as a *parasitic loss* of horsepower.

A *chassis dynamometer* measures the power output at a vehicle's driving wheels, as illustrated in Figure 11-10.

Horsepower output is affected by atmospheric conditions, such as the barometric pressure of the air, humidity, and air temperature. The readings taken with a dynamometer are known as *observed horsepower*. Observed horsepower is corrected to a standard known as *corrected horsepower* by reference to tables listing atmospheric conditions.

The customary unit of corrected horsepower is *SAE (Society of Automotive Engineers) horsepower*.

In SI units, power is measured in *watts (W)* or *kilowatts (kw)*, named after James Watt. This unit also is used to measure electricity. One horsepower is equal to 746 watts, or 0.746 kw. A kilowatt equals 1000 watts.

11.7 ENGINE EFFICIENCY

Efficiency is a measure of how well a device can convert energy to work. To find the efficiency of a given device, the output is divided by the input, when both are stated in the same units, or terms.

Figure 11-10. Chassis dynamometer.

Mechanical Efficiency

Mechanical efficiency is a comparison of how much horsepower an engine produces at the flywheel, compared to the theoretical horsepower the engine could produce from the pressures generated in the combustion chamber. The formula for determining mechanical efficiency is:

mechanical efficiency = bhp ÷ ihp

Volumetric Efficiency

An engine can be thought of as a pump that draws gases in and forces them out. *Volumetric efficiency* is a comparison of how much fuel and air are actually drawn into an engine compared to how much could be drawn in.

At low speeds and when the carburetor throttle is fully open, atmospheric pressure has time to fill the cylinders fully. At higher speeds, and when the throttle is closed, less fuel-air mixture is drawn in. Smaller amounts of fuel-air mixture in the cylinder mean that less pressure is developed during combustion.

The formula for determining volumetric efficiency is:

volumetric efficiency =
actual air output volume
÷ maximum possible air input volume

Pumping losses are drops in volumetric efficiency due to restrictions in the intake air passages. Carburetor throttle plates, valves, and passages all may be restrictive.

A diesel engine has no throttle plate in the air intake. Instead, different amounts of fuel are introduced into the cylinder to regulate the power output. Thus, a diesel engine has fewer pumping losses.

Pumping losses can be lessened by forcing air through the intake system with a *supercharger*. A supercharger is a device that uses engine power to drive a turbine. The turbine forces air through the intake system at greater than atmospheric pressure and thus produces a higher volumetric efficiency. Superchargers are discussed in Units 19 and 20.

Thermal Efficiency

Thermal efficiency is a comparison of the energy present in the fuel used and the energy output of the engine. The customary unit of heat energy is the *British thermal unit (Btu)*. One horsepower is equivalent to 42.4 Btu/minute. Gasoline has approximately 110,000 Btu per gallon.

For a gasoline engine, the formula used to determine thermal efficiency is:

thermal efficiency =
bhp × 42.4 Btu/minute ÷ 110,000 Btu/gal
× gallons used/minute

Thermal efficiency for a typical gasoline engine is less than 25 percent. Diesel fuel contains more heat energy than gasoline, and a diesel engine has a somewhat better thermal efficiency. Part of this efficiency is due to compression ratios of between 20:1 and 23:1. As a result, vehicles with diesel engines produce better fuel mileage.

However, diesel engines have disadvantages as well. Passenger vehicle diesel engines have less horsepower and weigh more than gasoline engines of the same size (displacement). As a result, most passenger vehicles with diesel engines have slow acceleration and low top speeds. Other disadvantages are discussed in Unit 20.

Thermodynamics

Thermodynamics is the scientific study of the mechanical action or relations of heat. The first law, or principle, of thermodynamics is this: Energy can be neither created nor destroyed. In other words, energy exists or doesn't exist. However, energy may be present in different forms, such as heat energy, chemical energy, mechanical energy, and so on. Energy also can be changed from one form to another.

The second law of thermodynamics states that heat cannot be converted completely to another form of energy, e.g., mechanical energy. Heat energy, such as that present during combustion, can never be converted completely into mechanical energy, or work. Some energy always is lost, no matter how efficient the engine or device used to make the conversion.

11.8 OVERALL VEHICLE EFFICIENCY

Current gasoline piston engines waste about two-thirds of the heat energy present in gasoline. To prevent overheating, the cooling system must carry away a third of the heat that is produced during combustion. Another third of the heat energy is lost in hot exhaust gases.

Of the energy left, five percent is lost to internal engine friction. Another 10 percent is lost to friction in the drivetrain components. By the time the power reaches the driving wheels at the end of the drivetrain, about 19 percent is left.

However, *rolling resistance,* the friction between the tires and the road, uses some of this remaining power. As explained in Unit 67, radial tires offer less rolling resistance than other types of tires.

Air resistance, the result of the vehicle moving through the air, also takes its toll. Air resistance increases as speed increases. The two factors that contribute to air resistance are the vehicle's *coefficient of drag,* or C_d, and its *frontal area.* Drag is air resistance. The lower the coefficent of drag, the less air resistance the vehicle has. Frontal area is the area against which air resistance is present as the vehicle travels forward.

Since the early 1980s, vehicle manufacturers have been paying increasing attention to *streamlining,* or reducing air resistance.

As the chart in Figure 11-11 shows, only about 15 percent of the energy produced from the burning of gasoline finally goes toward moving the vehicle.

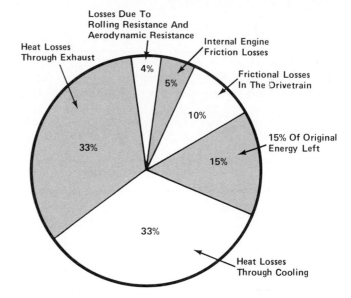

Figure 11-11. Vehicle efficiency chart.

U N I T   H I G H L I G H T S

- Engine size is a measure of displacement and can be measured in customary units (cubic inches) or SI units (cubic centimeters).

- Displacement can be calculated by using measurements of the cylinder bore and stroke in a mathematical formula.

- Larger displacements and increased compression ratios cause an engine to produce more torque and horsepower.

- Horsepower is the rate at which an engine produces torque.

- Three types of friction may be present within an engine: dry friction, greasy friction, and viscous friction.

- Engine efficiency is limited by internal friction, pumping losses, parasitic losses, and heat losses.

- Overall vehicle efficiency is limited by heat losses, frictional losses, and aerodynamic drag.

T E R M S

cubic inch
customary unit
International System
  of Units (SI)
cubic centimeter (cc)
compression ratio
octane rating
torque
horsepower
joule (J)
Newton-meter (Nm)
foot-pound (ft-lb)
pound-foot (lb-ft)
brake horsepower (bhp)
indicated horsepower
  (ihp)
friction
frictional horsepower
  (fhp)
dry friction
greasy friction
viscous friction
viscosity
dynamometer
brake dynamometer
gross horsepower

net horsepower
parasitic loss
chassis dynamometer
observed horsepower
corrected horsepower
SAE (Society of
  Automotive
  Engineers)
horsepower
watt (W)
kilowatt (kw)
mechanical efficiency
volumetric efficiency
pumping loss
supercharger
thermal efficiency
British thermal unit
  (Btu)
thermodynamics
rolling resistance
air resistance
coefficient of drag
  (C_d)
frontal area
streamlining

REVIEW QUESTIONS

DIRECTIONS: The following questions are similar to those used on mechanic certification tests. On a separate sheet of paper, write the letter of the correct choice.

1. Which of the following statements is correct?

   I. 1 liter = 1000 cc = 61.0 cubic inches.

   II. 1500 cc = 91.5 cubic inches.

   A. I only   B. II only   C. Both I and II   D. Neither I nor II

2. The volume in the cylinder above a piston at BDC is 76 cubic inches, and at TDC it is 6 cubic inches. The volume in the cylinder head is 4 cubic inches. The compression ratio is

   A. 12.66 to 1.

   B. 7.60 to 1.

   C. 8.00 to 1.

   D. none of the above.

3. Mechanic A says that work is measured in pounds-feet (lb-ft).

   Mechanic B says that torque is measured in foot-pounds (ft-lb).

   Who is correct?

   A. A only   B. B only   C. Both A and B   D. Neither A nor B

4. All of the following can be present in an engine EXCEPT

   A. viscous friction.

   B. greasy friction.

   C. lubricated friction.

   D. dry friction.

5. What quantity is found by using the equation bhp = ihp − fhp?

   A. Volumetric efficiency

   B. Thermal efficiency

   C. Brake horsepower

   D. Net horsepower

SUPPLEMENTAL ACTIVITIES

1. Make a list of engine displacement figures for engines in vehicles owned by relatives or friends. Correctly convert the displacement figures from customary units (cubic inches) to SI units (cc), or vice versa.

2. Use measuring instruments to measure the bore and stroke of a shop engine. Determine the displacement of the engine.

3. Use equipment to measure the volume of a cylinder head and of a cylinder when the piston is at TDC and BDC. Calculate the compression ratio.

4. Discussion topic: What effect does enlarging a cylinder bore (making the bore bigger) have on the compression ratio of an engine?

5. Visit several local service stations. Find the octane rating stickers on the pumps, and make a list of the octane ratings for different grades and brands of gasoline.

12 ENGINE CONSTRUCTION

UNIT PREVIEW

The cylinder block is the main engine casting. The block forms the foundation for the entire engine, with other engine components being attached at various points. Manufacturing processes used to form the block include casting and machining operations.

The crankshaft is supported under the block through the use of precision insert bearings. The crankshaft changes the reciprocating motion of the pistons into rotary motion that powers the driving wheels.

LEARNING OBJECTIVES

When you have completed your assignments and exercises in this unit, you should be able to:

□ Describe the processes used to manufacture cylinder blocks and crankshafts.

□ Explain how crankshaft design determines engine firing order.

□ Identify the main parts of the crankshaft.

□ Identify and describe the parts used to keep liquids and gases from leaking or becoming contaminated.

12.1 CYLINDER BLOCK

The cylinder block for a liquid-cooled engine includes the cylinder holes and the crankshaft attachment area, known as the *crankcase*. It also has machined surfaces to accept the attachment of other components. These include the cylinder heads, manifolds, oil and water pumps, motor mounts, transmission, and, in most cases, the camshaft. Many other smaller components also are attached to the cylinder block.

Cylinder Block Design

The number of cylinders and their configuration determines the basic shape of the engine. Figure 12-1 shows the two most common engine block shapes, the inline and the V-type.

In an inline-type cylinder block, the cylinders may be formed so that they are more or less perpendicular (at a right angle, 90 degrees) to the horizontal. The cylinders also may be at an angle, or *slant* to the horizontal.

In a V-type block the angle between the two cylinder areas, or *banks* of cylinders can vary. The angle between the cylinder banks on a V-8 engine is 90 degrees. The angle between the cylinder banks on a V-6 engine is normally 60 degrees. However, V-6 engines derived from V-8 engines (by eliminating the two rear cylinders) may have an angle of 90 degrees. The flat-type engine can be thought of as a V-type that has been spread apart to form approximately a 180-degree angle.

The casting process. The basic cylinder block is formed by a process called *casting*. A mold with the overall shape of the engine is made. Molds for cylinder blocks are made of special sand that is moistened, packed into a form, and allowed to dry. Molten, or melted, metal is poured into the mold. As the metal cools, it takes on the shape of the mold.

To form hollow areas, parts called *cores* are inserted into the mold. A core is simply a solid sand plug. The molten metal flows around the cores. When the cores are removed, the core area remains hollow. Figure 12-2 shows the type of cores used in casting cylinder blocks.

Cylinder blocks can be cast from iron or aluminum. In today's smaller cars, aluminum frequently is used to reduce vehicle weight for better fuel economy.

Machining operations. *Sand cast* surfaces are fairly rough, like the surface of the sand mold. However, sealing surfaces must be very smooth. Any nicks, scratches, or roughness will allow liquids or gases to penetrate and leak past the seal area.

To make the cylinder walls smooth, the cylinders and all other block sealing surfaces are *machined*. Machining means that a power machine is used to cut or grind a surface to the desired size, shape, or finish.

In addition to machining, holes are drilled and tapped for attaching bolts and studs.

After casting, the sand cores are removed through large holes in the side of the block. These holes are machined and fitted with soft steel plugs. These plugs sometimes are mistakenly called "freeze plugs."

Inserts and liners. Because aluminum is not as strong as cast iron, the piston rings (made of cast iron, sometimes chrome plated) would quickly wear into plain aluminum cylinders and cause deep gouges.

The most common way of solving this problem is to insert *cylinder liners* made of cast iron. A cylinder liner is a cylindrical *sleeve* that forms the cylinder

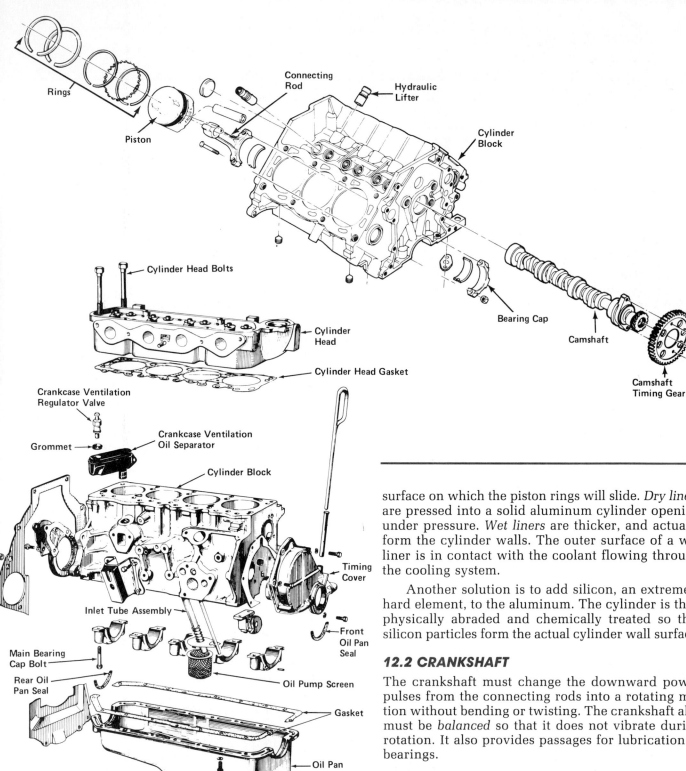

Rings

Piston

Connecting Rod

Hydraulic Lifter

Cylinder Block

Cylinder Head Bolts

Cylinder Head

Cylinder Head Gasket

Bearing Cap

Camshaft

Camshaft Timing Gear

Crankcase Ventilation Regulator Valve

Grommet

Crankcase Ventilation Oil Separator

Cylinder Block

Timing Cover

Inlet Tube Assembly

Main Bearing Cap Bolt

Rear Oil Pan Seal

Front Oil Pan Seal

Oil Pump Screen

Gasket

Oil Pan

Figure 12-1. Engine block designs. FORD MOTOR COMPANY

surface on which the piston rings will slide. *Dry liners* are pressed into a solid aluminum cylinder opening under pressure. *Wet liners* are thicker, and actually form the cylinder walls. The outer surface of a wet liner is in contact with the coolant flowing through the cooling system.

Another solution is to add silicon, an extremely hard element, to the aluminum. The cylinder is then physically abraded and chemically treated so that silicon particles form the actual cylinder wall surface.

12.2 CRANKSHAFT

The crankshaft must change the downward power pulses from the connecting rods into a rotating motion without bending or twisting. The crankshaft also must be *balanced* so that it does not vibrate during rotation. It also provides passages for lubrication of bearings.

Crankshaft Design

The areas where bearings support and protect the spinning crankshaft are called *journals*, as shown in Figure 12-3. *Rod journals* are located on the *throws*, or offset areas of the crankshaft, where the connecting rods are attached. The *main journals* are the areas where the crankshaft is attached to the crankcase at the bottom of the block.

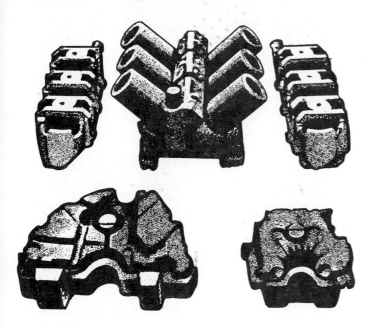

Figure 12-2. Engine block casting cores.

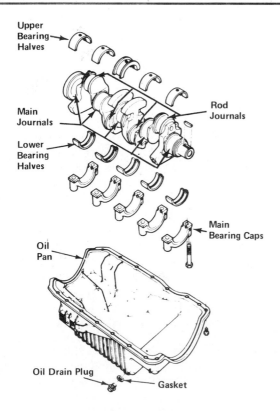

Figure 12-3. Crankshaft bearings are located at journals to support and protect the spinning crankshaft. FORD MOTOR COMPANY

The number of cylinders determines the number of throws on the crankshaft. However, in V-8 engines and some V-6 engines, two connecting rods share a single throw, as shown in Figure 12-4.

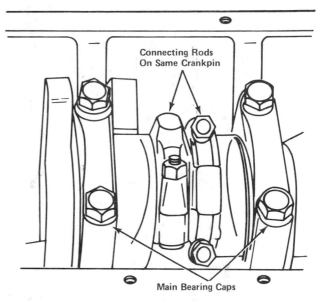

Figure 12-4. Two connecting rods can share a single throw, or offset portion of a crankshaft.

Even-firing and Uneven-firing Engines

The angle of the throws determines the firing order of the engine. To spread the power pulses out evenly, V-8 engines have a 90-degree offset between throws. Inline 6-cylinder engines have 120 degrees between throws. Inline 4-cylinder engines have 180 degrees between throws. These are known as *even firing* engines. The number of degrees of crankshaft revolution between power pulses is evenly divisible into 720 degrees. The 720 degrees represents the two full revolutions of the crankshaft necessary for the four-stroke cycle. Crankshaft designs are pictured in Figure 12-5.

V-6 engines derived from V-8s and using the 90-degree angle between throws are *uneven-firing* engines. In these engines, two connecting rods share a single *crankpin*, or attaching area. This makes it impossible to evenly space the power pulses from the two cylinders. Consequently, the engine idles roughly and unevenly.

To solve this problem, the crankpins can be individually offset, or *splayed*, on the throw, as shown in Figure 12-6. This splaying makes it possible to apply the power pulses evenly to the crankshaft.

Crankshaft Construction

Crankshafts can be cast, *forged*, or machined from a solid bar, or *billet*. Forging is a process of hammering a hot piece of metal into shape. Forged crankshafts usually are manufactured for high-performance applications.

During crankshaft manufacture, *counterweights* are formed to balance the offset throws. In addition, fine balancing is done by drilling out areas of the

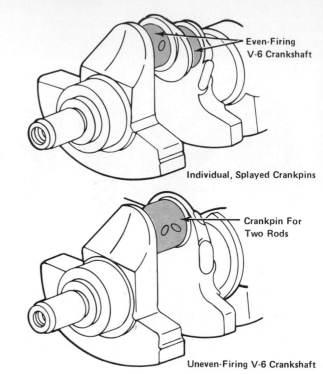

Even-Firing V-6 Crankshaft

Individual, Splayed Crankpins

Crankpin For Two Rods

Uneven-Firing V-6 Crankshaft

Figure 12-6. Crankpin offset.

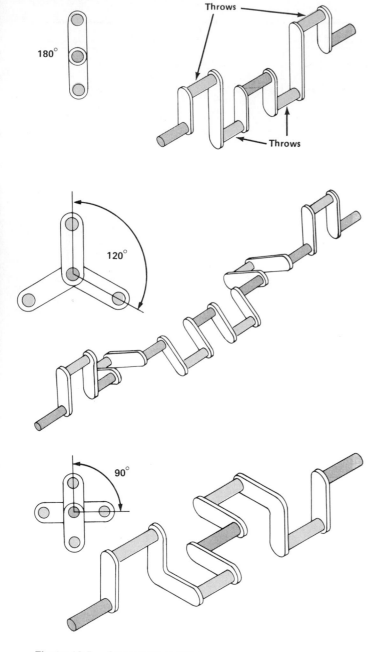

Throws

Throws

180°

120°

90°

Figure 12-5. Crankshaft designs.

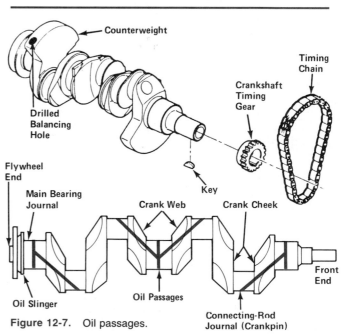

Counterweight

Timing Chain

Crankshaft Timing Gear

Drilled Balancing Hole

Key

Flywheel End

Main Bearing Journal

Crank Web

Crank Cheek

Front End

Oil Slinger

Oil Passages

Connecting-Rod Journal (Crankpin)

Figure 12-7. Oil passages.

counterweights and throws or by adding small weights.

Oil passages to supply lubricant to the connecting-rod and main-journal bearings also are drilled during manufacture. Figure 12-7 illustrates these features.

The crankshaft absorbs a great deal of force during engine operation. Therefore, care must be taken so that *stress,* or applied force, does not crack or bend the crankshaft. Stress is most likely to cause cracks at sharp edges. To relieve stress, the edges of the drilled crankshaft oil holes are *chamfered,* or beveled. In addition, the machined crankpin areas next to the counterweights are rounded by machining a small

curved area, or *fillet,* as shown in Figure 12-8. Many engines, especially high-performance gas and diesel engines, have rolled fillets.

Attaching the Flywheel and Pulley

The rear part of the crankshaft is drilled and tapped for flywheel attachment. Near the front of the crankshaft, a *timing gear,* sprocket, or pulley is attached to drive the camshaft or camshafts. A *damper pulley,* or power pulley, is attached to the outside front end of the crankshaft. In many cases, the damper, or *harmonic balancer,* is a separate unit pressed onto the front of the crankshaft. The pulley is then

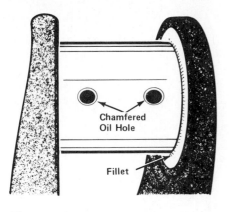

Figure 12-8. Fillets are machined in crankpin areas next to counterweights.

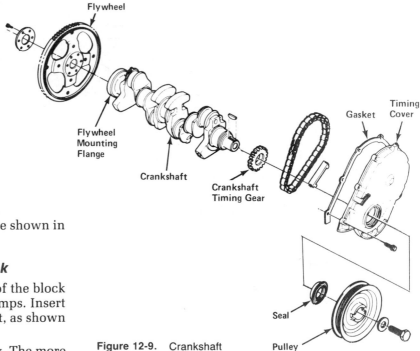

Figure 12-9. Crankshaft and flywheel assembly.

bolted on. These attachments and parts are shown in Figure 12-9.

Attaching the Crankshaft to the Block

The crankshaft is secured to the bottom of the block with *bearing caps,* or machined metal clamps. Insert bearings are placed around the crankshaft, as shown in Figure 12-10.

The number of main bearings can vary. The more main bearings, the less likely the crankshaft is to *whip,* or flex, during rotation. A well-supported crankshaft has one more main bearing than the number of throws.

12.3 ENGINE BEARINGS

One of the most important factors in engine life is the durability of engine bearings. If these bearings fail, the entire engine will be ruined. The locations of engine bearings, *bushings,* and sleeves are shown in Figure 12-11.

Bearing Design

Friction is the resistance between two rubbing or sliding materials. Excess friction eventually will wear and ruin moving parts. To reduce friction, two types of bearings can be used: *anti-friction* ball and roller bearings, and *friction,* or insert bearings. Crankshaft bearings are friction bearings and are known as *precision insert bearings,* shown in Figure 12-12.

A metal *alloy* is made of different combinations of metals. The alloy used in bearings may include babbitt material (lead or tin with small amounts of copper or anitimony). Other metals that may be included are copper-lead alloys, and aluminum with lead, copper, and/or tin. In addition, babbitt metal is sometimes used as an overplate, or outer coat, over other materials for easy bearing break-in.

Bearing Clearance and Lubrication

Under normal conditions when the engine is running, the spinning shafts should not contact the bearing surface. Rather, the shafts should ride on a microscopic

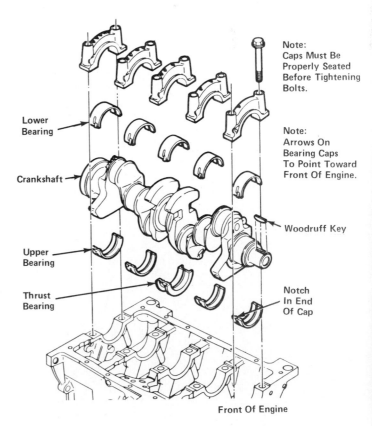

Figure 12-10. Bearing caps hold the connecting rods to the crankshaft.

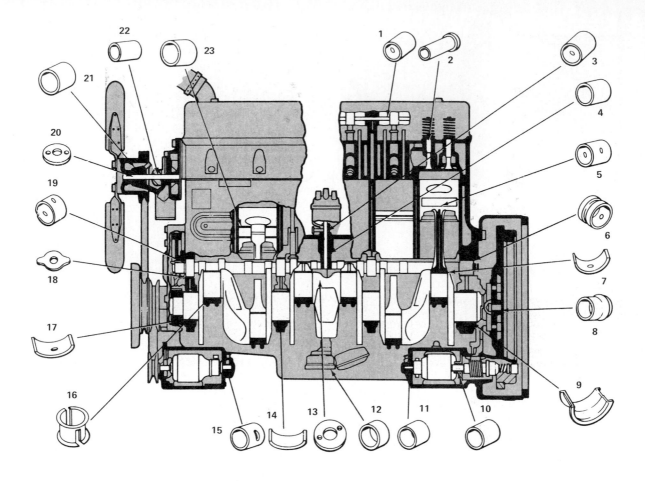

1 Rocker Arm Bushing	9 Flanged Main Bearing	17 Front Main Bearing
2 Valve Guide Bushing	10 Starting Motor Bushing, Drive End	18 Camshaft Thrust Plate
3 Distributor Bushing, Upper	11 Starting Motor Bushing, Commutator End	19 Camshaft Bushing
4 Distributor Bushing, Lower	12 Oil Pump Bushing	20 Fan Thrust Plate
5 Piston Pin Bushing	13 Distributor Thrust Plate	21 Water Pump Bushing, Front
6 Camshaft Bushing	14 Intermediate Main Bearing	22 Water Pump Bushing, Rear
7 Connecting Rod Bearing	15 Alternator Bushing	23 Piston Pin Bushing
8 Clutch Pilot Bushing	16 Connecting Rod Bearing, Floating Type	

Figure 12-11. Engine bearing, bushing, and sleeve locations.

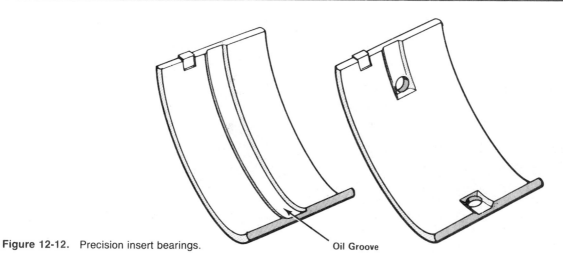

Figure 12-12. Precision insert bearings.

Oil Groove

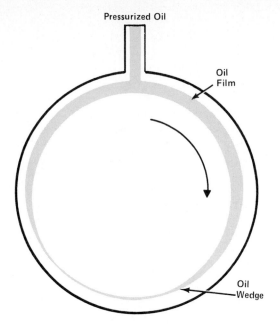

Pressurized Oil

Oil Film

Oil Wedge

Figure 12-13. Rod bearing clearance and lubrication.

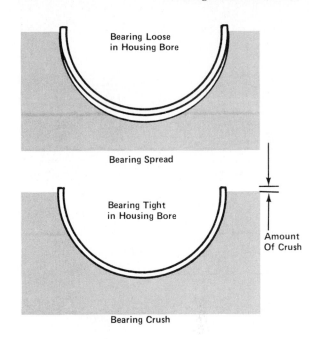

Bearing Loose in Housing Bore

Bearing Spread

Bearing Tight in Housing Bore

Amount Of Crush

Bearing Crush

Figure 12-14. Bearing spread and crush.

wedge of oil, as shown in Figure 12-13. The *clearance,* or distance, between the bearing material and the crankshaft usually ranges from 0.0005 to 0.0025 in. [0.01 to 0.06 mm]. As the clearance increases with wear, the oil flow will increase, causing a drop in oil pressure. Under these conditions, the shaft may rub against the bearing surface, causing rapid wear.

Oil for crankshaft bearing lubrication flows through a long gallery in the cylinder block. Each main bearing has its own oil supply passageway from this gallery. Passageways drilled in the crankshaft carry oil from the main-bearing journals to the adjacent rod journals. Excessive wear in one bearing will lower oil pressure to every bearing after it. Frequently, bearings will fail in progression. Bearings closest to the oil pump get adequate lubrication, but those farther away can become starved for oil.

Bearing failure puts harmful material into the oil lubrication system, further aggravating the situation.

Bearing Retaining Devices

The diameter of a precision insert bearing is slightly larger than the opening into which it fits. This *bearing spread* allows the bearing to snap into place and be held by spring tension. This makes engine reassembly much easier. In addition, the bearing halves project slightly above the openings. When the connecting rod or main bearing caps are tightened, these projections are forced together. This *bearing crush* holds the bearing in place. Bearing spread and crush are illustrated in Figure 12-14.

Two other commonly used retaining devices, the locking *tang* and the *dowel,* are illustrated in Figure 12-15. A tang is a projecting piece that fits into a matching opening. A dowel is a cylindrical part that fits in a matching opening.

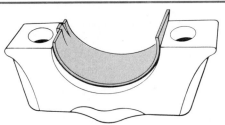

Spread Allows A Bearing To "Snap" Into Place.

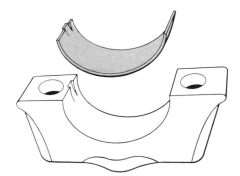

Bearing Locking Lip And Corresponding Recess In Cap.

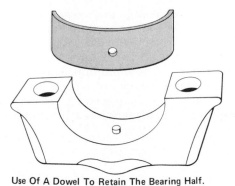

Use Of A Dowel To Retain The Bearing Half.

Figure 12-15. Main bearing retaining devices.

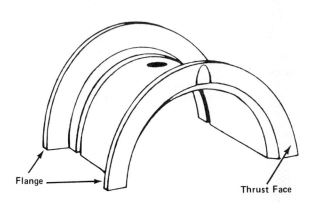

Figure 12-16. A thrust bearing has flanges on its edges to prevent front-to-back crankshaft motion.

Figure 12-17. Engine gasket set.

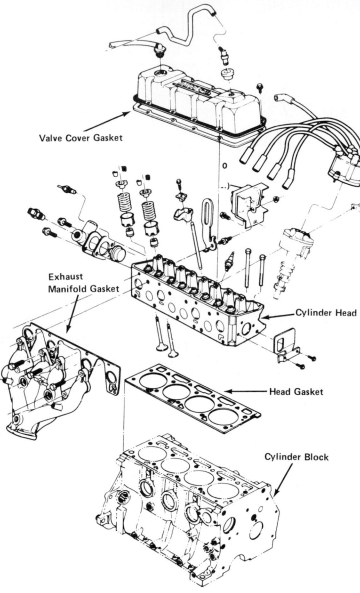

Figure 12-18. Head gasket installation.

Thrust Bearing

To prevent front-to-back motion of the crankshaft, one of the main bearings has *flanges,* or projections, on its edges, as shown in Figure 12-16. If the crankshaft moves, the sides of the throws next to the crankpin are stopped by the flanges.

12.4 GASKETS AND SEALS

A *gasket* forms a seal by being compressed between two parts. Gaskets can be made of soft materials, such as cork, rubber, paper, asbestos, or combinations of these materials. Gaskets also can be made of soft metals, such as brass, copper, aluminum, or *malleable* (soft) steel sheet metal. Gaskets are placed between stationary parts where liquids or gases could leak in or out. An engine overhaul gasket set is shown in Figure 12-17.

Head Gasket

To seal and contain the pressures of combustion within the engine, a *head gasket* is placed between the cylinder head and the block, as shown in Figure 12-18.

The head gasket also seals oil passages between the block and the head. Further, the gasket controls the flow of coolant between the block and head.

Seals

Gaskets around a rotating part would quickly wear out and leak. Instead, *seals* are used for these dynamic, or moving, applications.

Packing. *Packing* material, made from braided fabric, is often used as a rear main bearing seal.

Lip-type seal. A *lip-type seal* consists of three parts, as shown in Figure 12-19. These parts are a metal or plastic casing, a rubber sealing element, and a *garter spring*. The garter spring helps to hold the seal against a turning shaft.

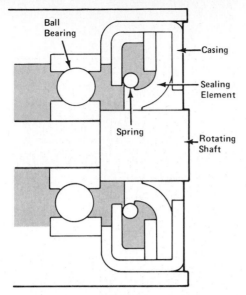

Figure 12-19. Lip-type seal installation.

Ring seals. A *ring seal* can be used both between stationary parts and around rotating shafts. A ring seal can be round, square, or half-round in section, as shown in Figure 12-20. Ring seals can be made from rubber or hollow metal tubing.

Gaskets and seals should never be reused. Use new seals and gaskets when reassembling parts.

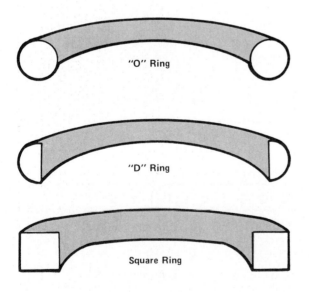

Figure 12-20. Ring seals.

UNIT HIGHLIGHTS

- The cylinder block can be of the inline-type, V-type, or flat-type.
- Casting and machining operations are used to manufacture cylinder blocks.
- The design of the crankshaft determines the firing order of the engine and how smoothly it will run.
- Rod journals and main journals are machined areas for bearing support and attachment.
- Gaskets and seals are used to keep liquids and gases from leaking or becoming contaminated.

TERMS

crankcase	timing gear
slant	damper pulley
bank	harmonic balancer
casting	bearing cap
core	whip
sand cast	bushing
machining	friction
cylinder liner	anti-friction bearing
sleeve	friction bearing
dry liner	precision insert
wet liners	bearings
balance	alloy
journal	clearance
rod journal	bearing spread
throw	bearing crush
main journal	tang
even firing	dowel
uneven firing	flange
crankpin	gasket
splay	malleable
forge	head gasket
billet	seal
counterweight	packing
stress	lip-type seal
chamfer	garter spring
fillet	ring seal

R E V I E W   Q U E S T I O N S

DIRECTIONS: The following questions are similar to those used on mechanic certification tests. On a separate sheet of paper, write the letter of the correct choice.

1. Mechanic A says that sand cores are used to form the cylinders during block manufacture. Mechanic B says that the cylinders are machined during block manufacture. Who is correct?

A. A only　　　B. B only　　　C. Both A and B　　　D. Neither A nor B

2. How many main bearings would a well-supported V-6 engine crankshaft have?

A. 7

B. 6

C. 4

D. 5

3. Which of the following statements is correct?

I. The power pulses of an uneven-firing engine are equally spaced.

II. Splayed crankpins are used to even out the application of power pulses to V-8 engine crankshafts.

A. I only　　　B. II only　　　C. Both I and II　　　D. Neither I nor II

4. All of the following are alloys used in bearings EXCEPT

A. babbit metal.

B. copper-lead alloys.

C. stainless steel.

D. aluminum with lead.

5. Mechanic A says that soft metal gaskets may be reused if they are not badly damaged. Mechanic B says that gaskets and seals should always be replaced when reassembling an engine. Who is correct?

A. A only　　　B. B only　　　C. Both A and B　　　D. Neither A nor B

S U P P L E M E N T A L   A C T I V I T I E S

1. Describe the process for producing cast metal parts.
2. Explain why some parts of cast metal parts must be machined.
3. Identify the parts of a shop crankshaft, and determine what kind of an engine it is from.
4. Explain how precision insert bearings can be held in place.
5. Identify common materials used for seals and gaskets.

13 PISTONS, RINGS, AND CONNECTING RODS

UNIT PREVIEW

The operating conditions within the engine require that pistons and connecting rods be made light yet strong. Manufacturing processes play an important role in determining how much heat and stress these parts can withstand. Pistons, connecting rods, and rings that are properly designed can operate properly under very harsh conditions. Connecting rods must be as light as possible, yet strong enough to transfer power impulses to the crankshaft.

LEARNING OBJECTIVES

When you have completed your assignments and exercises in this unit, you should be able to:

☐ Identify and describe the major parts of a piston.

☐ Explain how pistons and connecting rods are designed to solve operating problems.

☐ Describe how pistons, rings, and connecting rods are manufactured.

☐ Identify and describe the types of piston rings used.

13.1 PISTONS

The piston must be able to withstand the heat and pressures of combustion and transfer force to the connecting rod. The piston also must change direction at rates varying from about 10 times to hundreds of times each second. At the same time, the piston must remain tightly sealed within the cylinder.

To meet these requirements, the piston must be both light and strong. It also must be constructed so that heat, pressure, and the forces of movement are controlled and directed properly. Modern pistons are cast or forged from high-strength aluminum alloys.

Piston Shape

The side views of pistons that are shown in Figure 13-1 illustrate the different shapes possible for piston heads, or tops. The piston head may be flat, dished, notched, wedge-shaped, or domed, depending on the shape of the combustion chamber and on the desired compression ratio.

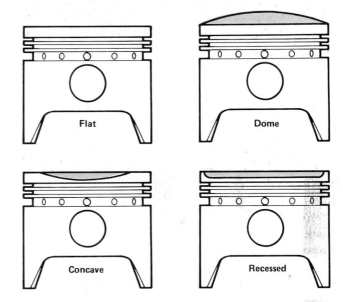

Figure 13-1. Shapes of piston heads.

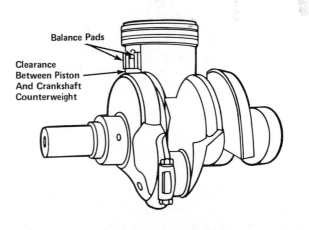

Figure 13-2. Piston skirts have a cutaway design for clearance of crankshaft counterweights. CHEVROLET MOTOR DIVISION—GMC

The cutaway shape of the piston *skirt*, or lower part, allows the piston to clear the rotating crankshaft counterweights, as shown in Figure 13-2.

Piston Parts

Figure 13-3 illustrates the major external parts of a piston, and Figure 13-4 shows a cross-sectional view of its internal construction. The thicker reinforcing area around the hole is known as a *boss*.

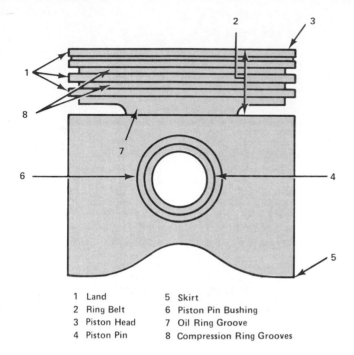

Figure 13-3. External piston construction.

1 Land	5 Skirt
2 Ring Belt	6 Piston Pin Bushing
3 Piston Head	7 Oil Ring Groove
4 Piston Pin	8 Compression Ring Grooves

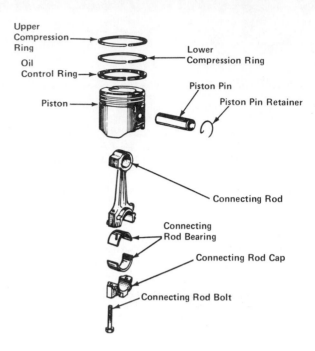

Figure 13-5. Piston, connecting rod, and piston pin assembly.
FORD MOTOR COMPANY

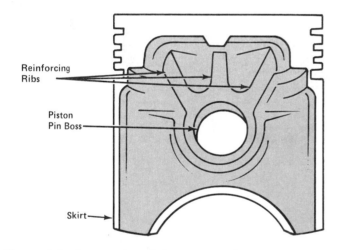

Figure 13-4. Cutaway view of piston construction.

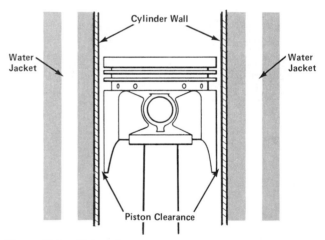

Figure 13-6. Piston clearance is the space between piston and cylinder wall.

A *piston pin,* or attaching pin, attaches the piston to the connecting rod. Figure 13-5 Shows the piston, connecting rod, and piston pin.

Piston Clearance

The piston is slightly smaller in diameter than the cylinder *bore,* or hole diameter. The distance between piston and cylinder wall, usually about 0.001 to 0.003 inch (0.03 to 0.08mm), is called *piston clearance.* Under normal circumstances, this clearance, shown in Figure 13-6, is filled with a thin film of oil.

If the pistons are badly worn, there will be too much piston clearance. As the power stroke begins,

the piston tilts sharply against the cylinder wall and makes noise, known as *piston slap.* Besides the annoying noise, piston slap can damage the piston, rings, and cylinder wall.

When an engine is rebuilt, the cylinders are rebored to a larger size. Piston slap can also result from using pistons of too small a size for the cylinder bore.

Controlling Piston Expansion

Because pistons are made of aluminum, they heat and expand more quickly than cast iron cylinder walls. If piston clearance is too small, the piston will *seize,* or become stuck, in the cylinder.

To control piston expansion, different methods can be used, including:

- Steel belts or struts
- Cam grinding
- Barrel shape.

Steel struts and belts. Steel expands less, and at a slower rate, than aluminum. Thus, steel "belts" or *struts* can be inserted inside the piston when it is cast, as shown in Figure 13-7. A *belt* is a circular band inside the piston. A strut is a flat structural piece that resists expansion.

Cam grinding. The most common way of controlling piston expansion is to machine the piston so that it is not perfectly round. The thicker area where the piston pin attaches to the piston expands less than the thinner piston skirt area. *Cam grinding* produces an oval-shaped piston, as shown in Figure 13-8. As the piston heats, it expands parallel to the piston pin and thus becomes round when hot.

Barrel shape. Pistons are ground so the lower portions of their skirts are closer to the cylinder wall than the upper parts. See Figure 13-9. Since the upper part of the piston gets hotter, it expands until the skirt is straight when hot.

Thrust Forces and Piston-Pin Offset

As the piston reaches the top of the compression stroke and begins the power stroke, two events occur. First, heated, expanding gases exert force against the piston head. Second, the connecting rod angle changes as the piston changes direction. These two events cause the piston to tilt and press against the cylinder wall. The force exerted against the piston and cylinder wall is known as *side thrust*. The side of the piston that exerts most force is known as the *major thrust face*. The opposite side of the piston tilts in the opposite direction and applies less force. This side is known as the *minor thrust face,* as shown in Figure 13-10.

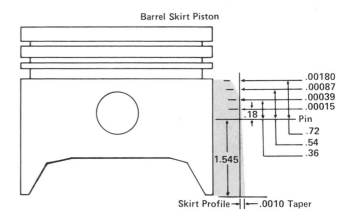

Figure 13-9. The skirt portion of a piston is made wider because it expands less than the upper portion of the piston.

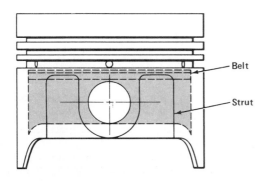

Figure 13-7. Piston struts and belts help to control piston expansion.

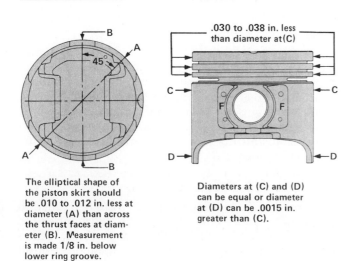

The elliptical shape of the piston skirt should be .010 to .012 in. less at diameter (A) than across the thrust faces at diameter (B). Measurement is made 1/8 in. below lower ring groove.

Diameters at (C) and (D) can be equal or diameter at (D) can be .0015 in. greater than (C).

Figure 13-8. Pistons often are cam ground to an oval configuration. Pistons become round when heated.

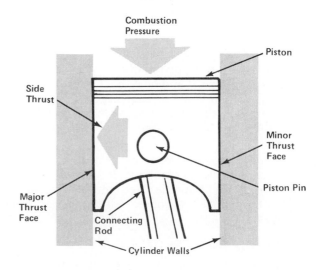

Figure 13-10. Combustion chamber pressure on the top of a piston causes it to thrust, or tilt, against the cylinder wall.

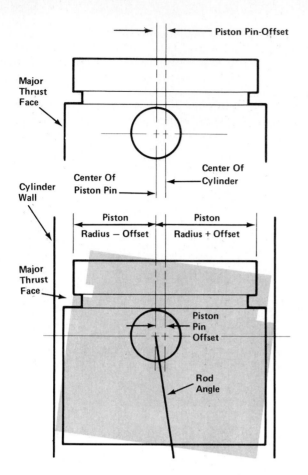

Figure 13-11. Piston pins are offset to help prevent piston slap.

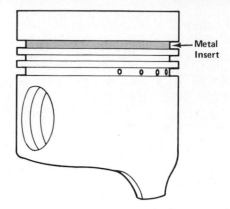

Figure 13-12. The top piston ring groove usually has a special metal insert to resist wear.

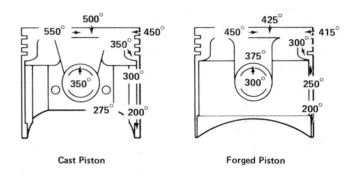

Figure 13-13. Heat concentrations in pistons differ, depending upon the materials and manufacturing techniques used.

If the piston pin is mounted exactly in the center of the piston, side thrust can help cause piston slap. However, mounting the piston pin slightly off center can reduce side thrust. When the piston pin is *offset,* or moved, in this manner, more force is exerted against the minor thrust face. This extra force tends to lessen the force against the major thrust face, as shown in Figure 13-11.

Ring-Groove Strengthening

The groove that holds the top piston ring is subjected to the most side thrust and heat of combustion. In addition, relatively little lubrication is present at the top of the cylinder. These factors move the uppermost ring against the top and bottom of its groove and cause wear.

To protect this groove, an insert of cast iron, iron alloy, or stamped steel can be added to cast pistons. See Figure 13-12. Many diesel engines use pistons of this type. Forged piston grooves can be *metal sprayed,* or sprayed with a thin coat of molten metal.

13.2 PISTON CONSTRUCTION

The piston must be able to change direction quickly at the top and bottom of the strokes. Such a change in direction is easier for a light object than a heavy one.

Aluminum is used for pistons because it is a relatively light material and conducts heat well. The heat is conducted away from the piston into the cylinder walls. Piston manufacturing processes include:

- Casting or forging
- Machining and finishing.

Casting or Forging

Pistons can be cast or forged. Casting is cheaper and quicker, and allows the insertion of separate parts. Forging produces stronger, denser parts but is more expensive. Heat is conducted better through dense materials. Figure 13-13 shows the differences in heat concentrations between cast and forged pistons. The cooler a piston operates, the less likely it is to be damaged by heat.

Machining and Finishing

After forging or casting, the pistons are machined to proper size and finish. The piston skirt under the piston pin area includes thicker portions, called *balance pads.* These balance pads can be ground down to equalize the weight of each piston. This helps balance the force transmitted during engine operation.

To prevent *scuffing,* or rubbing, the surface of the piston skirt may be machined smooth and tin plated. In other cases, a lightly grooved surface is machined onto the aluminum piston skirt to help carry oil for lubrication.

The diameter of the piston *lands,* or areas between the ring grooves, is about 0.020 inch (0.5 mm) smaller than the piston skirt.

A groove, called a *heat dam,* is often cut into the piston above the top groove. This groove prevents excess combustion heat from being transferred. The groove cut below the oil ring groove may also be called a heat dam groove.

Grinding, as mentioned above, also is a part of piston manufacture. A special machine, called a *cam grinder*, is used to machine a round cast or forged piston into the oval cam or barrel shape.

In addition, the piston pin holes are machined. In some cases bronze bushings are pressed into the openings to protect the softer aluminum from excessive wear.

13.3 RINGS

Piston ring grooves are machined deeply enough so the rings can be compressed and will not protrude past the piston skirt. The upper rings on a piston that hold the pressure generated during combustion are called *compression rings*. The lower ring that scrapes excess oil off the lower cylinder walls is called an *oil control ring*.

Compression Rings

A piston ring is not a complete circle. There is a break, or *ring gap,* in the ring to allow it to be stretched for installation around the piston. The ring gap is shown in Figure 13-14. After the piston is installed in the cylinder, the gap is reduced to a few thousandths of an inch.

The compression ring is made of cast iron. Compression rings sometimes are plated with harder metals, such as chromium, molybdenum, or aluminum oxides for longer wear. Synthetic plastic resins containing fluorine (Dupont Teflon) also have been used for ring coatings. Because of the great pressures within a cylinder (up to 1,000 psi), two rings are used. Part of the pressure of combustion gases "blows by" the top ring through the gap. The gaps on the lower rings are *staggered,* or purposely misaligned. Most of the pressure that gets by the first compression ring is trapped by the second compression ring. In this way, the pressure and wear is divided between two compression rings. Compression rings often are manufactured to provide a special ring profile. See Figure 13-15.

Oil Control Rings

The lower ring is made from grooved cast iron or separate pieces of steel sheet metal. Its function is to scrape excessive oil off the lower cylinder walls.

Figure 13-14. A piston ring gap allows the ring to be stretched during installation. HASTINGS MANUFACTURING COMPANY

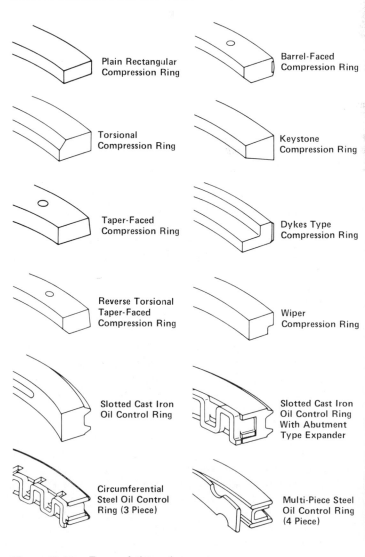

Figure 13-15. Types of piston rings.
HASTINGS MANUFACTURING COMPANY

Plain Rectangular Compression Ring

Barrel-Faced Compression Ring

Torsional Compression Ring

Keystone Compression Ring

Taper-Faced Compression Ring

Dykes Type Compression Ring

Reverse Torsional Taper-Faced Compression Ring

Wiper Compression Ring

Slotted Cast Iron Oil Control Ring

Slotted Cast Iron Oil Control Ring With Abutment Type Expander

Circumferential Steel Oil Control Ring (3 Piece)

Multi-Piece Steel Oil Control Ring (4 Piece)

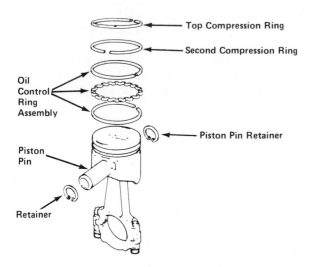

Figure 13-16. Free-floating piston pins are kept from striking cylinder walls by spring retainers. CHEVROLET MOTOR DIVISION—GMC

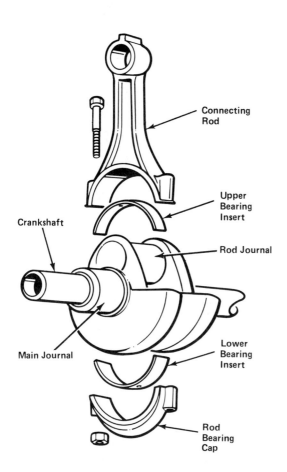

Figure 13-17. Parts of a connecting rod.

Holes cut in the oil control ring piston groove allow the oil to drain back into the oil pan.

Many different types of piston rings are made for different engines. Figure 13-15 shows a selection of the most popular types of modern piston rings.

13.4 PISTON PINS

The piston pin, also called a *wrist pin,* is inserted through the holes in the piston and connecting rod. The pin may be free to pivot in both the connecting rod and piston. The pin is held in by retaining rings in the ends of the piston pin bore. This type of attachment is known as a *free-floating piston pin.* However, it also may be fixed to either the connecting rod or to the piston. Such an attachment is known as a *semifloating piston pin.* This type of attachment does not require spring retainers to hold the pin in place.

Spring *retainers,* or clips, shown in Figure 13-16, are used to hold free-floating piston pins from moving against the cylinder walls.

13.5 CONNECTING RODS

The connecting rod must be strong enough to transfer the power impulses to the crankshaft, yet as light as possible. Connecting rods for production engines are made of cast or forged iron or steel. The long portion of the rod is partially hollowed out. In section, the shape resembles the capital letter I.

Balance pads on the rods allow material to be ground off for balancing purposes.

The top end of the rod (the small end) is connected to the piston by the piston pin. With free-floating piston pins, a bushing is pressed into the small end of the rod. The bushing helps to reduce friction and wear. The lower part of the rod that connects around the crankpin is known as the *big end.* A *rod cap* holds the rod and bearing inserts around the crankpin, as shown in Figure 13-17. The big end hole is machined after the bearing cap is bolted on. Therefore, each bearing cap can be used on only one particular connecting rod—and only in its original position.

V-6 engines often have offset connecting rods, as shown in Figure 13-18. The offset is necessary to properly align the connecting rod on the limited space available on a V-6 crankpin.

Lubricating oil is forced to the crankshaft, to the main and connecting rod bearings. Small holes, called *oil spurt holes,* sometimes are drilled into the big end or bearing cap. The spurt holes allow oil to flow through and flush out foreign material. Oil spurt holes also can be positioned to squirt oil at the underside of pistons to lubricate piston pins. This helps cool the pistons (see Figure 13-19). Some connecting rods have holes drilled from the big end through their center part to the small end. Oil flows through the connecting rod to the piston pin.

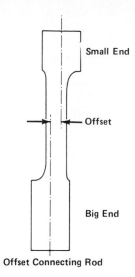

Figure 13-18. An offset connecting rod often is used in V-6 engines.

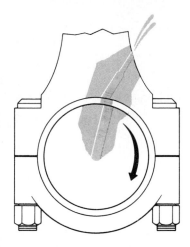

Figure 13-19. An oil spurt hole in the connecting rod directs lubricant to the crankshaft. FEDERAL-MOGUL

UNIT HIGHLIGHTS

- A piston must be strong enough to withstand the forces of combustion but light enough to be able to change directions quickly.
- The clearance between the piston and the cylinder wall is between 0.001 and 0.003 in. (0.03 to 0.08 mm).
- Pistons are made of aluminum and are either cast or forged.
- Two types of rings are used on pistons: compression rings and oil-control rings.
- The piston pin can be of either free-floating or semi-floating design.
- Production engine connecting rods are cast or forged of iron or steel.

TERMS

skirt
piston pin
boss
bore
piston clearance
piston slap
seize
struts
belt
cam grinding
piston side thrust
major thrust face
minor thrust face
offset
metal spray
balance pad

scuff
land
heat dam
cam grinder
compression ring
oil control ring
ring gap
stagger
free-floating piston pin
semi-floating piston pin
retainer
wrist pin
big end
rod cap
oil spurt hole

R E V I E W   Q U E S T I O N S

DIRECTIONS: The following questions are similar to those used on mechanic certification tests. On a separate piece of paper, write the letter of the correct choice.

1. The parts of a piston include all of the following EXCEPT
A. piston pin.
B. pin boss.
C. skirt.
D. lands.

2. Mechanic A says that wear can cause piston slap.
   Mechanic B says too small a piston can cause piston slap.
   Who is correct?
A. A only   B. B only   C. Both A and B   D. Neither A nor B

3. Which of the following statements is correct?
   I. Piston expansion can be controlled by cam-grinding the piston.
   II. Piston expansion can be controlled by casting belts or struts into the piston.
A. I only   B. II only   C. Both I and II   D. Neither I nor II

4. Why is piston pin offset used?
A. To control piston expansion
B. To lessen piston slap
C. To direct the power impulses to the crankshaft evenly
D. To hold the piston pin in the connecting rod

5. Mechanic A says that the reason the gaps on piston rings are staggered is to reduce heat transfer to the piston skirt.
   Mechanic B says that the gaps on piston rings are staggered to reduce piston slap.
   Who is correct?
A. A only   B. B only   C. Both A and B   D. Neither A nor B

S U P P L E M E N T A L   A C T I V I T I E S

1. Examine pistons and name all visible parts.
2. Explain why reinforcing the upper ring groove may be necessary.
3. Describe how piston pin offset can improve the operation of the engine.
4. Identify and describe free-floating and semi-floating piston pin designs.
5. Explain why compression rings and oil-control rings are made differently.

14 CYLINDER HEAD AND VALVE TRAIN

UNIT PREVIEW

Cylinder heads are cast and machined in much the same way as cylinder blocks. The design of the cylinder head combustion chamber affects the efficiency, power output, and production of harmful exhaust gases in an engine.

Although overhead camshaft designs are theoretically more efficient in their operation, pushrod type designs have some service advantages. The valve train can include parts that operate mechanically and/or hydraulically.

The shape of the cam lobes on a camshaft determines the opening and closing of the valves. The camshaft usually drives the distributor, and may drive oil, fuel, and water pumps.

LEARNING OBJECTIVES

When you have completed your assignments and exercises in this unit, you should be able to:

☐ Identify the processes used to manufacture cylinder heads.

☐ Explain how overhead camshaft and pushrod type valve trains operate the valves.

☐ Explain the advantages of overhead camshaft and pushrod type valve trains.

☐ Describe how valves are fitted into the cylinder head.

☐ Describe the mechanisms that can be used to make sure that the valves close fully.

☐ Identify and describe the functions and operation of the camshaft.

14.1 CYLINDER HEAD DESIGN

The cylinder head forms the combustion chamber. Combustion chamber design can vary with the intended purpose of the engine. Cylinder head designs for passenger cars must combine reasonable fuel economy with efficient and nearly complete burning of fuel. Two types of cylinder heads commonly used in passenger vehicle engines are:

• Wedge combustion chamber
• Hemispherical combustion chamber.

These shapes are shown in Figure 14-1. In a wedge head design, the valves are parallel to each other. The

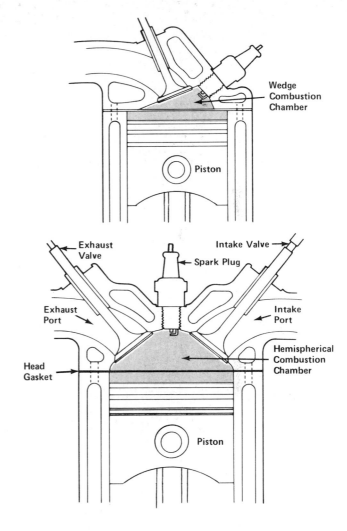

Figure 14-1. Combustion chamber designs.

valves in a hemi-head design are on opposite sides of the combustion chamber.

Cylinder Head Materials

Cylinder heads are cast from iron, iron alloy, or aluminum alloy. Aluminum is both light in weight and transfers heat more efficiently than iron or iron alloy. Efficient heat transfer allows higher compression ratios to be used for greater engine efficiency and power.

Cylinder Head Construction

Cylinder heads are manufactured in much the same way as cylinder blocks. A typical cylinder head is shown in Figure 14-2.

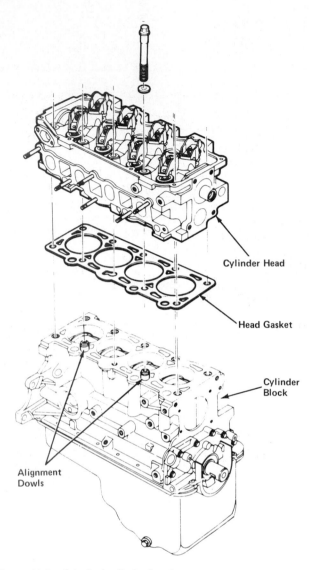

Figure 14-2. A typical cylinder head. FORD MOTOR COMPANY

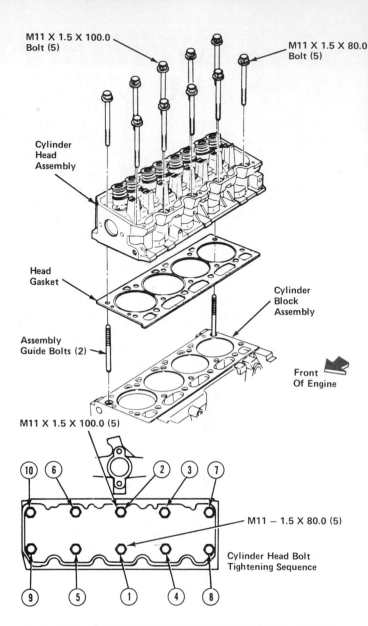

Figure 14-3. Bolts or studs hold a cylinder head to the cylinder block. FORD MOTOR COMPANY

Casting. A casting mold is made, and sand cores are inserted to form hollow areas within the cylinder head. Molten metal is poured in and allowed to cool. The cores are broken out and removed, and the cylinder head is cleaned of any remaining sand. Another casting method involves molds of expanded-bead polystyrene. When molten aluminum is poured onto it, the foam is burned away. The aluminum takes the place of the foam and solidifies. No sand is used in this process, called the "lost foam process."

Machining operations. Sealing surfaces are machined smooth. Holes are drilled and tapped for attaching bolts. In sand-cast heads, the large holes, through which sand was removed from the cores, are machined. They then are fitted with soft steel plugs.

The valve seat areas are machined from the metal of the cylinder head, or hard metal *valve seat inserts*

are pressed into machined holes. Valve seat inserts are circular metal rings with a shape that matches the shape of the valve.

In most cast-iron cylinder heads, the valve seats are machined directly into the cylinder head. The seats then are specially hardened to produce a strong, tough surface for seating the valves.

The *valve guide* area is machined from the metal of the cylinder head, or holes are drilled for pressed-in guides. Valve guides are the hollow cylindrical areas in which the stem of the valve moves.

Attaching the cylinder head to the cylinder block. The cylinder head is held to the cylinder block with bolts or studs and nuts. Holes are machined in the head for the bolts or stud shafts, as shown in Figure 14-3. During engine assembly, the bolts must be tightened and loosened in the manufacturer's specific order.

Intake and Exhaust Passages

The intake and exhaust passages and ports are made to specific sizes. These sizes are a compromise between the flow rates of gases at low engine speeds and high engine speeds. In general, smaller passages will allow more torque at low speeds. Larger passages will produce greater horsepower at high speeds.

Each intake and exhaust passage may be formed separately in the head. Alternately, the intake or exhaust passages for adjacent cylinders may be *siamesed,* or have a common, thin wall between the ports.

Cylinder head design in modern engines is of two basic types. One type has all intake and exhaust ports on one side, cast either separately or in siamese fashion. The other type is called a cross-flow head. In this design, the intake ports are on one side of the head and the exhaust ports on the other. The cross-flow design allows for straighter passageways and improved breathing. A disadvantage lies in the location of the exhaust system away from the intake passageways. The result is difficulty in preheating the incoming air-fuel charge. These configurations are illustrated in Figure 14-4.

Coolant and Oil Passages

Coolant and oil flow from the block through the head gasket into the head. To allow the removal of casting cores, coolant and oil passages are sometimes made larger than desirable. The sizes of the holes in the head gasket are used to restrict the flow of liquids to acceptable levels. See Figure 14-5.

Overhead Valve and Overhead Camshaft Designs

As explained in Unit 10, the camshaft can be located above the head or in the block. For overhead camshafts, camshaft bearing supports and cap attachment points must be cast and machined as part of the head. See Figure 14-6.

Emission Control Considerations

Emission control is the name given to techniques that reduce the level of harmful gases in the engine exhaust. Wedge-head and hemi-head designs cause the air-fuel mixture to be burned differently.

Wedge-head design. The spark plug in a wedge-head is placed near the center of the *turbulence* to ignite the mixture. Refer to Figure 14-1. The narrow areas farthest from the spark plug are known as the *quench* areas. The most tightly squeezed mixture in the

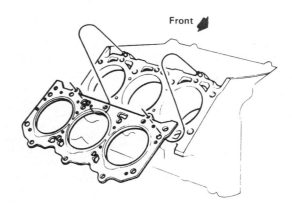

Figure 14-5. Coolant and oil flow are directed from the engine block, through a head gasket, and to the cylinder head.
CHEVROLET MOTOR DIVISION—GMC

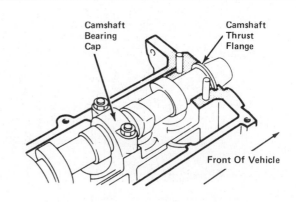

Figure 14-6. A cylinder head with an overhead camshaft is manufactured with bearing supports and cap attachment points.
FORD MOTOR COMPANY

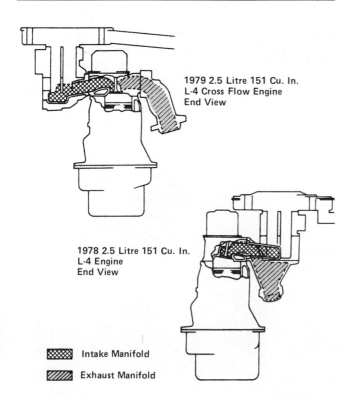

1979 2.5 Litre 151 Cu. In. L-4 Cross Flow Engine End View

1978 2.5 Litre 151 Cu. In. L-4 Engine End View

▨ Intake Manifold

▨ Exhaust Manifold

Figure 14-4. Cylinder head intake and exhaust passage designs.
PONTIAC MOTOR DIVISION—GMC

quench area is cooled by its contact with the surface of the piston and head. This contact quenches, or puts out, the *flame front,* or edge of the burning mixture. A small part of the fuel in this quench area remains unburned when the exhaust gases are forced out. This undesirable characteristic has been eliminated in the open combustion chamber.

Hemispherical-head design. The spark plug in a hemi-head is located in the center of the combustion chamber. Refer to Figure 14-1. Smaller quench areas result in more complete burning of fuel. However, there is less turbulence. Consequently, the air-fuel charge is not mixed as well as in a wedge chamber.

14.2 OVERHEAD CAMSHAFT VALVE TRAIN

Overhead camshaft (OHC) designs can use a *single overhead camshaft (SOHC)* with intake and exhaust cams on the same shaft. Another design has two separate camshafts, one each for intake and exhaust. Such an arrangement is known as a *dual overhead camshaft (DOHC)* design.

Overhead camshaft designs can use one of two methods to move the valves:

- Bucket lifters
- Rocker followers.

Bucket Lifters

The camshaft *lobes,* or individual cam shapes, shown in Figure 14-7, rotate as the camshaft is turned. A *lifter* is a part that changes the motion of the cam lobe into a *reciprocating,* or back-and-forth, motion.

A *bucket lifter* is hollow, like a bucket, as shown in Figure 14-8. As the *nose,* or high spot, of the cam lobe rotates into position over the valve, the bucket lifter moves downward and opens the valve.

A replaceable *valve adjustment shim* is part of the bucket lifter assembly.

Rocker Followers

Another way of changing the rotary motion of the cam lobes into a reciprocating motion is to use *rocker followers.* The rocker follower pivots on a supporting *rocker shaft.*

One end of the rocker is held upward by the valve spring pressure. The other end rides against a cam lobe. As the nose of the cam pushes up against the rocker, the rocker pivots down and opens the valve. A *valve adjusting screw* and *locknut* are part of the rocker assembly, as shown in Figure 14-9.

14.3 OVERHEAD CAMSHAFT DRIVE MECHANISM

Two mechanisms are used in passenger vehicles to drive overhead camshafts:

- Chain and sprockets
- Toothed belt and pulleys.

The crankshaft makes two full revolutions to complete the 4-stroke cycle in any cylinder. However, the valves open only once during the entire cycle. Thus, the camshaft must complete only one revolution for every two revolutions of the crankshaft. The camshaft must turn at one-half crankshaft speed. In addition, the motion of the camshaft must be coordinated to the action of the crankshaft.

To accomplish both the speed reduction and the coordination of motion, a form of *gear drive* can be utilized.

Gears are toothed wheels that *mesh,* or fit together, as they rotate. The meshing gear teeth are all of the same size. However, the sizes of the gears and the total number of teeth on each gear can differ. If one gear has twice as many teeth as another, it will rotate only half as many revolutions as the smaller gear rotates.

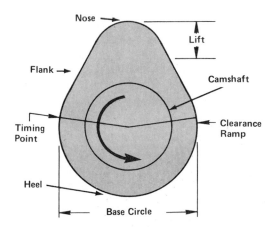

Figure 14-7. Parts of a cam lobe.

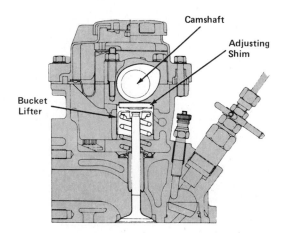

Figure 14-8. The camshaft pushes on a bucket lifter to move a valve assembly. FORD MOTOR COMPANY

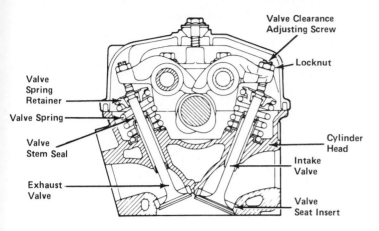

Figure 14-9. Parts of a valve assembly that uses rocker followers.
CHRYSLER CORPORATION

This principle is used to rotate the overhead camshaft at the proper speed. A sprocket or toothed pulley is attached to the front of the camshaft. A gear with half as many teeth is attached to the front of the crankshaft. As the crankshaft turns, the camshaft turns at half crankshaft speed. Such a system is shown in Figure 14-10.

The turning camshaft also can be used to drive other assemblies. The camshaft usually drives the ignition distributor. In addition, it can also drive the oil and fuel pumps. Some vehicles also use the toothed timing belt to drive a water pump.

Some overhead camshafts run in precision insert bearings similar to those used for the crankshaft. Other camshafts use fully circular *camshaft bearings,* or bushings.

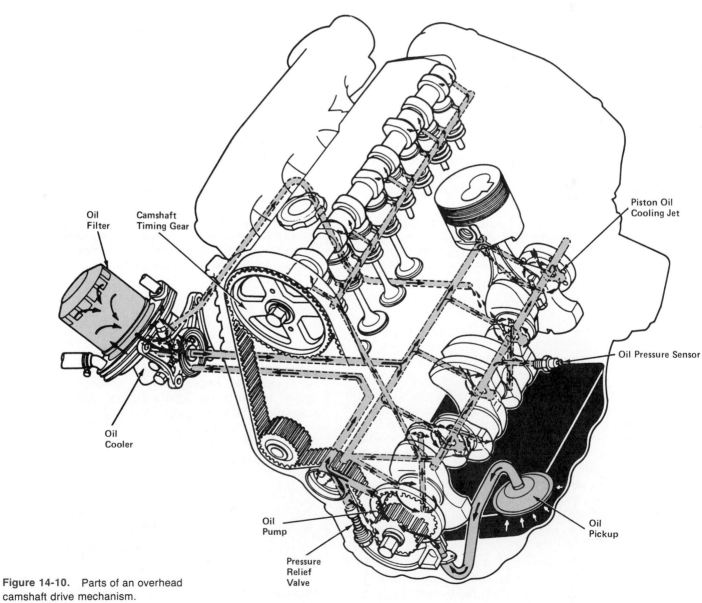

Figure 14-10. Parts of an overhead camshaft drive mechanism.
FORD MOTOR COMPANY

14.4 PUSHROD VALVE TRAINS

Remember, power is the rate at which work is done. To produce more horsepower, today's smaller engines must run faster. This extra speed can cause problems.

The intermediate parts for a pushrod valve train, shown in Figure 14-17, are larger and heavier than those for an overhead camshaft design. More weight means more momentum and the possibility of *valve float* at high engine speeds. Valve float occurs when the valve springs are unable to close the valves at the proper time in the four-stroke cycle.

The fewer and lighter the parts in the valve train, the less valve float. Thus, overhead cam designs are better for smaller engines that run faster. However, pushrod valve trains have some servicing advantages. For example, the cylinder head can be removed without disturbing the camshaft drive and timing mechanism on a pushrod engine. Pushrod valve trains also are less costly and operate more quietly than overhead cam designs.

14.5 VALVES

The valves in an automobile engine must be able to function reliably under harsh conditions for many miles. During this time, the valves may be cycled several hundred million times.

Valve Design

Suppose you drive for one hour at 55 mph [88 km/h]. During this time, each of the valves in a 4-cylinder engine open and close approximately 90,000 to 100,000 times.

The exhaust valves will be exposed to combustion temperatures of 3,800 to 4,500 degrees F [2,093 to 2,482 degrees C]. The valves will be red hot during operation, yet they must retain their hardness and shape.

Each valve weighs only about five ounces, but it must seal against pressures of up to 1,200 psi [8,274 kPa].

Valve Construction

The parts of a typical automotive *poppet valve* are shown in Figure 14-11. A poppet valve is one that moves up and down to open and close.

Intake valves usually are larger, to assure a good flow of air-fuel mixture into the cylinder under atmospheric pressure. Exhaust valves can be smaller because the hot exhaust gases are denser and under pressure as they leave the cylinder.

Exhaust valves are made of stainless steel or high-strength steel alloys. Some exhaust valves are made by welding a *Stellite* head to a steel stem. Stellite is an extremely hard alloy of cobalt, chromium, and tungsten metals.

High-performance exhaust valves sometimes are filled with metallic sodium. The sodium liquifies at high temperatures to conduct heat away from the valve head.

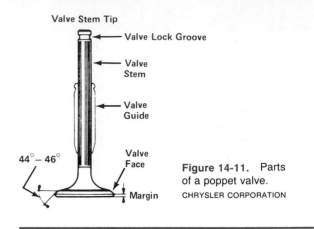

Figure 14-11. Parts of a poppet valve.
CHRYSLER CORPORATION

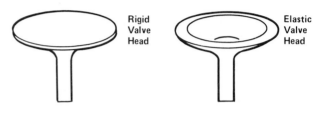

Figure 14-12. Valve head designs.

Valve heads may be formed to be either elastic (flexible) or rigid, as shown in Figure 14-12.

Valve Seats and Sealing

The valve seat is the area in the cylinder head against which the face of the valve forms a seal.

The valve face and seat may be machined to the same angle, usually 45 degrees. Alternately, the valve face and seat may be machined to different angles, usually a variance of about 1 degree. This variance forms an *interference angle* between them for better sealing, as shown in Figure 14-13.

Integral valve seat. An *integral valve seat* is one machined from the material of the cylinder head itself. Integral valve seat areas are *induction hardened,* or heat treated, to make them more resistant to wear.

Valve seat insert. A *valve seat insert* is a circular, hardened steel or Stellite ring pressed into a machined space in the head. Inserts must be used in aluminum cylinder heads.

Valve Spring Assembly

A valve spring assembly, illustrated in Figures 14-14 and 14-15, can include the following parts:

- Valve spring seat
- Valve stem seal
- Single or double valve spring
- Spring damper
- Valve spring retainer
- Valve locks
- Valve rotator.

Most valve spring assemblies use a single spring. If necessary, double valve springs or spring dampers can be used to control *valve spring surge,* or vibration.

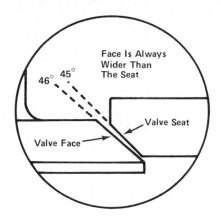

Figure 14-13. A valve face and valve seat may be machined at different angles, called an interference angle.

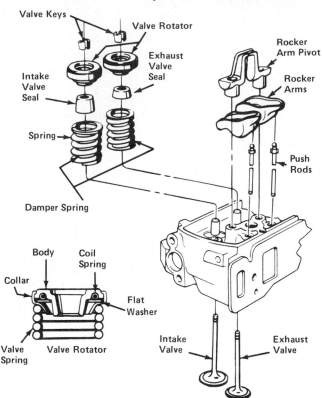

Figure 14-15. A valve rotator rotates a valve in a complete circle to help reduce heat buildup and remove deposits.
CHEVROLET MOTOR DIVISION—GMC

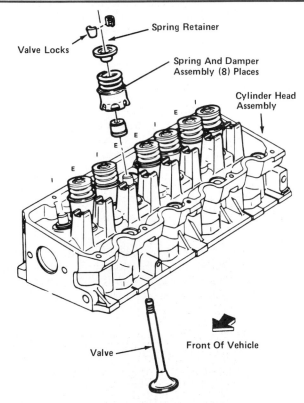

Figure 14-14. Parts of a valve spring assembly.
FORD MOTOR COMPANY

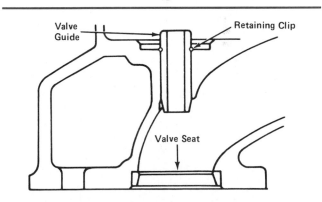

Figure 14-16. A replaceable valve guide is a bushing that supports and positions a valve stem. FORD MOTOR COMPANY

Valve springs tend to wind and unwind as they are compressed and released. This causes the valve face to turn in relation to the seat, helping even out heat buildup and remove deposits. Some engines have specially made *valve rotators* in the *valve spring retainer* to rotate the valve in a complete circle. See Figure 14-15.

14.6 VALVE GUIDES

Integral valve guides are simply machined holes in the metal of the cylinder head. *Replaceable valve guides*, shown in Figure 14-16, are bushings made of cast iron or bronze.

The guide supports and positions the valve stem in relation to the valve seat. In addition, heat is transferred from the valve stem to the guide, and from the guide to the cooling system. The guide is located near the hollow coolant passages in the cylinder head.

There must be a very small clearance between the valve stem and the inside diameter of the valve guide, usually between 0.0006 and 0.003 inch (6 ten-thousandths to 3 thousandths) [0.02 to 0.08 mm]. This clearance is necessary for lubrication. However, excessive clearance around the intake valve stem will cause oil to be drawn into the combustion chamber and burned during the intake stroke.

14.7 LIFTERS

The valve train must be able to pull the valves fully closed. To accomplish this action, either solid or hydraulic lifters may be used. Hydraulic lifters have largely replaced the older solid lifters on modern engines. Solid lifters, however, continue to be used in most overhead cam designs. Advantages of hydraulic lifters are that they do not require routine adjustment and they operate more quietly. Hydraulic lifters also compensate automatically for changes in temperature and valve train wear.

Solid Lifter

Valve clearance, or *valve lash,* must be maintained between the valve tip and the valve train when the cam is not applying pressure to open the valve. *Solid lifters,* or mechanical lifters, are made from a single piece of solid metal, as shown in Figure 14-17.

To adjust valve clearance, an adjusting screw and locknut are built into the rocker arm, as shown in Figure 14-17. *Valve clearance adjustments* must be

done at regular intervals, as specified by the vehicle manufacturer.

Hydraulic Lifter

Another way of allowing the valve to be fully closed by the valve springs is to use *hydraulic lifters.* Most pushrod valve trains use hydraulic lifters. Some manufacturers are beginning to install hydraulic lifters in overhead cam engines as well. A hydraulic lifter, shown in Figure 14-18, contains a movable plunger, springs, and other parts.

Pressurized oil from the engine lubricating system fills the inner part of the lifter whenever the engine is operating. As the cam lobe rotates to push the lifter, a *check valve* within the lifter traps the oil inside. Because liquids cannot be compressed, the hydraulic lifter acts like a solid lifter, and transfers force to open the valve.

As the cam continues to rotate, the valve spring closes the valve. Force from the valve spring pushes against the rocker arm, pushrod, and hydraulic lifter. This force causes the lifter to follow the cam lobe. As the camshaft continues to turn, the lifter reaches the *base circle,* or "flat" part of the cam lobe. At this point, the valve train is in a "relaxed" state. Any oil that has leaked or seeped out during the high-pressure portion of the operational cycle will be replaced. Replacement occurs as engine oil pressure again opens the check valve, filling the lifter body to take up any looseness.

Hydraulic lifter operation is illustrated in Figure 14-19.

Solid lifters typically cause a "tapping" noise as the valve clearance is opened and closed. Hydraulic lifters operate silently and require only an initial adjustment during engine assembly.

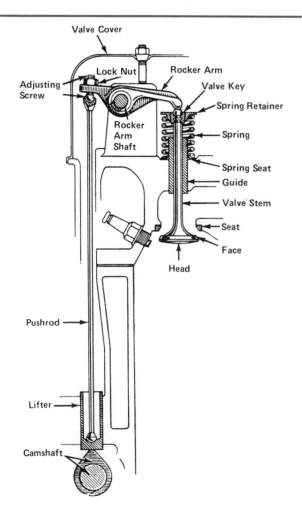

Figure 14-17. Parts of a valve train with a solid valve lifter. BLACK & DECKER

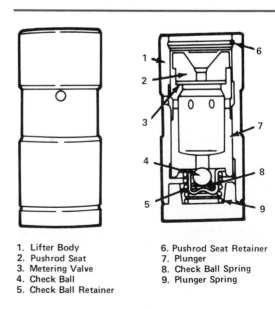

1. Lifter Body
2. Pushrod Seat
3. Metering Valve
4. Check Ball
5. Check Ball Retainer
6. Pushrod Seat Retainer
7. Plunger
8. Check Ball Spring
9. Plunger Spring

Figure 14-18. Parts of a hydraulic valve lifter.
CHEVROLET MOTOR DIVISION—GMC

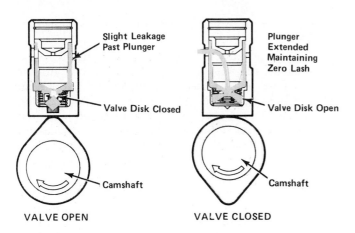

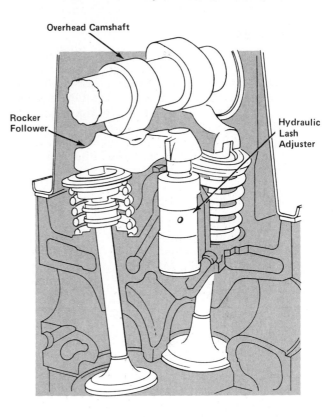

Figure 14-19. Hydraulic valve lifter operation.
FORD MOTOR COMPANY

Hydraulic lash adjuster. Some late-model vehicles use a *hydraulic lash adjuster,* similar to a hydraulic lifter, in overhead camshaft valve trains. Such an arrangement is shown in Figure 14-20.

14.8 PUSHROD

Pushrods usually are hollow for lightness. In some engines, lubricating oil is pumped up the hollow pushrod for upper valve train lubrication (refer to Figure 14-21).

Figure 14-20. A hydraulic lash adjuster often is used to maintain valve assembly clearances. FORD MOTOR COMPANY

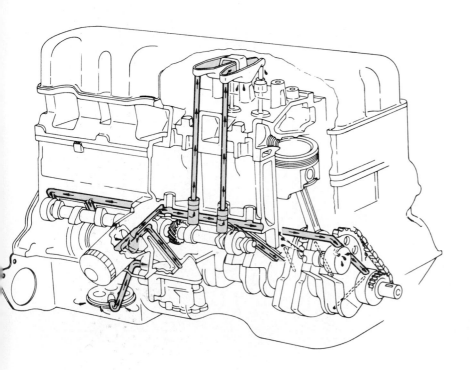

Figure 14-21. Pushrods usually are hollow and carry lubricating oil to the upper parts of the valve train. AMERICAN MOTORS CORPORATION

125

14.9 ROCKER ARM

Rocker arms can use leverage to increase the movement transmitted by the valve train. The *rocker arm ratio* is calculated by taking two measurements from the center, or pivot point, of the rocker. One measurement is the distance to the valve tip. The other measurement is the distance to the pushrod tip. See Figure 14-22. An optimum rocker arm ratio reduces lifter movement while providing adequate valve opening.

Adjustable Rocker Arms

Rocker arms for solid-lifter valve trains can be cast or forged and usually are mounted on rocker shafts. Adjusting screws and locknuts are added for valve clearance adjustments.

Nonadjustable Rocker Arms

Stamped, or pressed, sheet metal rocker arms typically are used with hydraulic valve lifters. The rocker arm is mounted on a *pivot stud,* or pivot point. During engine assembly, the rocker arm is positioned to center the hydraulic lifter plunger in its bore, as shown in Figure 14-23.

14.10 CAMSHAFT

Each cylinder in a typical engine has an intake cam lobe and an exhaust cam lobe to operate the valves. Each lobe performs three functions. It opens a valve at the proper time. It allows the valve to remain open for a sufficient period. Finally, it allows the valve to close at the proper time.

Valve Timing and Duration

Figure 14-24 shows a typical valve timing diagram. This diagram shows when the intake and exhaust valves open, how long they remain open, and when they close. Refer to Figure 14-24 as you read the following discussion.

The spiral-shaped line begins at the top, or TDC, during the engine's power stroke. The power stroke

continues until 110 degrees *after top dead center (ATDC).*

At that point, the exhaust valve opens. The exhaust gases, still very hot, begin to leave the cylinder through the open exhaust valve. After the piston reaches BDC and starts upward, the exhaust gases are pushed out by the motion of the piston. The exhaust valve remains open through 280 degrees of crankshaft rotation.

At a point 30 degrees before TDC of the exhaust stroke, the intake valve opens. The exhaust gases flowing out of the cylinder help to bring in the intake charge. Both the exhaust and intake valves are open for a total of 60 degrees of rotation. This period is from 30 degrees BTDC on the exhaust stroke to 30 degrees ATDC on the intake stroke. This situation is known as *valve overlap.*

Because of its weight and momentum, a pushrod valve train does not follow the contours of the camshaft exactly. More valve overlap becomes necessary to fully exhaust burnt gases and fully fill the cylinder with fresh air-fuel mixture. The less valve overlap, the more smoothly and efficiently an engine will idle. Because overhead camshaft valve trains follow the cam contours more exactly, less valve overlap is needed. This condition provides a smooth idle and efficient high-speed operation.

The intake valve remains open until 70 degrees ABDC on the intake stroke, or for 280 degrees of crankshaft rotation. At that point, the intake valve closes, and both valves remain closed for the compression stroke. The compression stroke lasts until TDC, a total of 110 degrees of crankshaft rotation. At TDC, the 4-stroke cycle begins again.

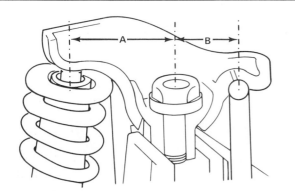

Figure 14-22. Rocker arm ratios are determined by making measurements from the pivot point to the valve tip and pushrod tip.

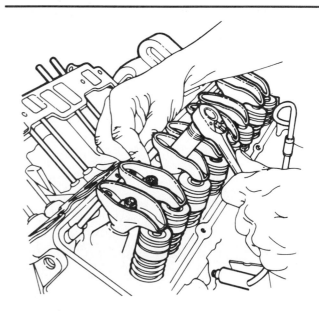

Figure 14-23. Non-adjustable rocker arms are positioned to center the hydraulic lifter plunger during assembly.
CHEVROLET MOTOR DIVISION—GMC

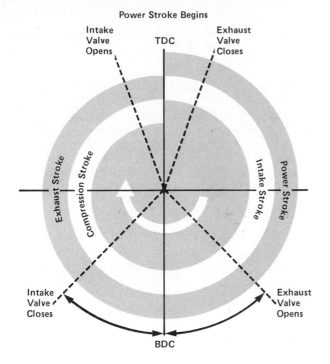

Figure 14-24. Valve timing and duration diagram.
CHEVROLET MOTOR DIVISION—GMC

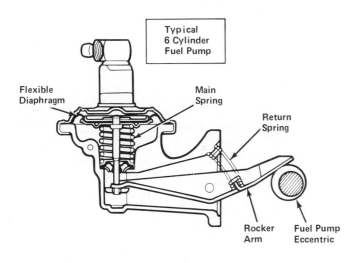

Figure 14-25. Parts of a camshaft assembly.
CHRYSLER CORPORATION

Camshaft Construction

The camshaft is cast or machined from hardenable iron alloy or steel. The cam lobes are ground to the proper shape and position in relation to one another. The bearing surfaces also are ground smooth, and the distributor drive gear is machined into the shaft. Pushrod valve train camshafts also may have an *eccentric,* or off-center, circular lobe to operate the fuel pump. See Figure 14-25.

U N I T   H I G H L I G H T S

- Cylinder heads are manufactured using the same basic processes used to make cylinder blocks.

- Wedge-head and hemispherical-head designs affect engine emissions differently.

- Overhead camshaft designs are theoretically more efficient than pushrod designs for small, fast-running engines.

- Complete valve closing can be assured by maintaining a specified valve clearance with solid lifters, or by using hydraulic lifters.

- The shape of the camshaft determines when the valves will open and close, and how much valve overlap will occur.

T E R M S

valve seat insert	poppet valve
valve guide	Stellite
siamese	interference angle
emission control	integral valve seat
quench area	induction hardening
flame front	valve spring surge
single overhead camshaft (SOHC)	valve rotator
	valve spring retainer
dual overhead camshaft (DOHC)	integral valve guide
	replaceable valve guide
lobe	valve clearance
lifter	valve lash
bucket lifter	solid lifter
nose	valve clearance adjustment
valve adjustment shim	
rocker follower	hydraulic lifter
rocker shaft	check valve
valve adjusting screw	base circle
locknut	hydraulic lash adjuster
gear drive	rocker arm ratio
mesh	pivot stud
camshaft bearing	valve overlap
valve float	eccentric

127

REVIEW QUESTIONS

DIRECTIONS: The following questions are similar to those used on mechanic certification tests. On a separate sheet of paper, write the letter of the correct choice.

1. Mechanic A says that aluminum is used for cylinder heads because it is light in weight.

   Mechanic B says that aluminum is used for cylinder heads because it transfers heat efficiently. Who is correct?

   A. A only   B. B only   C. Both A and B   D. Neither A nor B

2. Which of the following statements is correct?

   I. The more quench area in the combustion chamber, the more unburned fuel in the exhaust gases.

   II. The more quench area in the combustion chamber, the more efficiently the engine will run.

   A. I only   B. II only   C. Both I and II   D. Neither I nor II

3. The clearance between the valve stem and the valve guide should be

   A. 0.005 to 0.015 in. (0.1 to 0.4 mm).

   B. 0.0005 to 0.0015 in. (0.01 to 0.04 mm).

   C. 0.05 to 0.15 in. (1 to 4 mm).

   D. none of the above.

4. All of the following are usually found in a pushrod type valve train EXCEPT

   A. lifter.

   B. pushrod.

   C. rocker arm.

   D. bucket lifter.

5. Mechanic A says that all valve trains must have valve clearance to allow the valves to close completely.

   Mechanic B says that hydraulic lifters or lash adjusters maintain a small valve clearance automatically.

   Who is correct?

   A. A only   B. B only   C. Both A and B   D. Neither A nor B

SUPPLEMENTAL ACTIVITIES

1. Examine a cylinder head. Identify and describe the manufacturing techniques and design that were used to make the cylinder head.
2. Explain what varieties of valve guides and valve seat inserts can be found in cylinder heads.
3. Examine a cylinder head and corresponding piston and correctly identify the quench areas.
4. Using a dial indicator and a degree wheel, make a diagram of the opening and closing of the valves on an engine.
5. Explain what valve overlap is, and how it can affect engine performance.

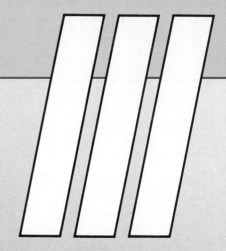

AUTOMOTIVE ENGINE SYSTEMS

15 THE LUBRICATION SYSTEM

Figure 15-1. A single-viscosity engine oil maintains one viscosity rating at operating temperatures.

UNIT PREVIEW

The engine lubrication system provides lubricating oil for all parts that move and/or contact other parts within the engine.

To provide proper lubrication, engine oil must be able to perform many tasks under difficult conditions. To help meet these requirements, petroleum-based engine oils require several additives.

Engine oil can be lost in two basic ways from the engine, by leakage and by being burned in the combustion chamber.

The lubrication system consists of several parts and components that function together to provide adequate lubrication to internal engine parts.

LEARNING OBJECTIVES

When you have completed your assignments and exercises in this unit, you should be able to:

☐ Identify and describe the functions a lubricating oil must perform within an engine.

☐ Identify and describe what additives are necessary for petroleum-based engine oils.

☐ Identify the SAE viscosity and API service ratings for gasoline and diesel engine oils.

☐ Explain how engine oil can be lost or consumed.

☐ Identify and describe the parts of an engine lubrication system.

15.1 LUBRICATION

The word *lubrication* comes from a Latin verb that means "to make slippery." *Lubricants* are materials, such as oil and grease, that reduce friction and make surfaces slippery.

A lubrication system consists of parts and components that circulate lubricant to parts that otherwise would become worn through friction. An engine lubrication system provides engine oil to all bearing surfaces and between all moving parts within the engine.

The life expectancy of major engine parts depends on proper lubrication. These major parts include bearings, crankshaft and camshaft journals, camshaft lobes, pistons and piston rings, and cylinder walls. If the engine lubrication system fails, friction can cause deep gouges and extreme heat. *Seizing*, which occurs when metal parts become hot enough to melt and stick to each other, can damage the engine beyond repair.

15.2 FUNCTIONS OF ENGINE OIL

The oil within the engine lubrication system must perform several functions, including:

* Reducing friction
* Absorbing bearing shock loads during the power stroke
* Forming a seal between the piston rings and cylinder walls
* Cooling and cleaning internal engine parts.

15.3 OIL VISCOSITY AND SERVICE RATINGS

Two groups, *Society of Automotive Engineers (SAE)* and the *American Petroleum Institute (API)*, have established standards for engine oil.

SAE Viscosity Rating

The *viscosity* ratings of engine oils are established through tests. A specified quantity of oil at a specific temperature is passed through a calibrated hole. The time required for the oil to pass through this hole establishes its viscosity rating number. For example, oil may be tested at 212 degrees F [100 degrees C] and assigned a single number rating. An example of this is SAE 30, as shown in Figure 15-1.

Single-viscosity oils commonly used for automobiles include SAE 10, 20, 30, 40, and 50. The higher the viscosity index number, the thicker the oil remains when heated. Oils with higher viscosity numbers can withstand conditions of extreme heat, such as high-speed driving in desert conditions. Oils with lower viscosity ratings are used in more moderate temperature conditions.

Multi-viscosity oils are oils that have been chemically modified to stabilize the rate of viscosity change. Thus, these oils have low viscosity when cold, yet sufficient viscosity when hot to provide adequate engine protection. A multi-viscosity oil can have a rating such as SAE 20W-50, as shown in Figure 15-2.

The "W" indicates winter, or cold weather, test conditions. "20W" indicates that the oil has been checked for viscosity at 0 degrees F [– 18 degrees C]. At that temperature, the oil has the viscosity of SAE 20 oil at 212 degrees F [100 degrees C]. "50" indicates that the oil also has been checked for viscosity at 212 degrees F [100 degrees C] and found to have a viscosity equivalent to SAE 50. Such a multi-viscosity oil can flow easily at low temperatures and allow the engine to start and run well under cold conditions. The same oil also will protect engine parts from wear even in extremely hot conditions.

The choice of a proper viscosity engine oil depends on the vehicle manufacturer's recommendations and the outside temperatures to be encountered, as shown in Figure 15-3.

API Service Rating

Engine oil also is rated for its ability to perform under a variety of engine conditions. The API ratings for increasingly severe conditions in spark-ignition engines are SA, SB, SC, SD, SE, and SF. An oil graded API SF meets the highest current standards and can be used in all automotive engines. Newer engines must use oils with the highest API ratings. In the future, oils graded SG, SH, or higher may become available.

Oils graded SA and SB are *nondetergent oils*, and are unsuitable for automotive engines. Such oils can be used in some light-duty, non-automotive engines.

The other API ratings indicate the year in which each was required to gain manufacturers' warranty approval:

SC: 1964	SE: 1972
SD: 1968	SF: 1982.

The API ratings for increasingly severe conditions in compression-ignition (diesel) engines are CA, CB, CC, and CD. Refer to Figures 15-1 and 15-2, above. Notice that, although both the single-viscosity and the multi-viscosity oils meet SF standards, one meets the CC standard and the other meets the CD standard. Some diesel engine manufacturers specify that lubricating oil must meet *both* SF and CC or SF and CD standards.

Figure 15-2. A multi-viscosity engine oil changes viscosity when it is cold and when it is hot.

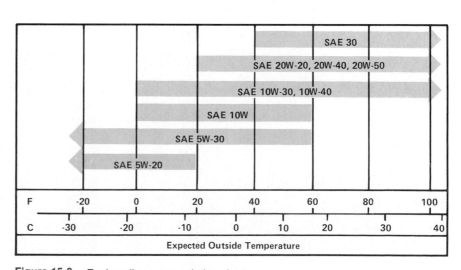

Figure 15-3. Engine oil recommendation chart.

CAUTION: Refer to the vehicle owner's manual or service manual to determine the API oil service ratings necessary for specific engines. Use of an incorrectly graded oil, especially in diesel engines, can cause engine damage and void the manufacturer's new-vehicle warranty.

15.4 NATURAL AND SYNTHETIC ENGINE OILS

The majority of engine oils are refined from petroleum, or crude oil, pumped from underground deposits. Refined petroleum oils, by themselves, cannot adequately lubricate modern engines. Chemicals, called *additives*, are blended with the oil to improve its performance.

Engine Oil Additives

Several chemical additives are used to improve the lubricating ability of petroleum engine oils. These additives include:

Detergent/dispersants keep particles of carbon and other contaminants suspended within the oil.

Viscosity index improvers allow the oil to maintain an adequately thick film as the oil is heated.

Pour point depressants allow cold oil to remain thin enough to flow to the engine parts during starting.

Extreme pressure additives help prevent the oil from being squeezed out of oil clearances when heavy loads are applied.

Anti-wear additives chemically coat bearings and other moving parts. This helps prevent wear even if the parts touch or rub slightly under heavy loads.

Corrosion inhibitors help prevent the formation of acids in the oil that can damage metal parts in the engine.

Oxidation inhibitors help prevent oil *oxidation,* the chemical breakdown of oil.

Foam inhibitors reduce the formation of *foam*, or oil mixed with air, from churning of the oil by the crankshaft. Foamy oil cannot support bearing loads and oxidizes more easily.

Oils graded API service SF contain all additives necessary for proper lubrication of automotive engines.

Synthetic Oils

Man-made, or *synthetic*, lubricating oils produced from chemicals other than petroleum generally are more "slippery" than petroleum oils. However, such oils have some disadvantages. For example, resistance to *scuffing,* or rubbing due to greasy friction, may be inferior to SF-graded petroleum oils.

Synthetic oils cost three to four times as much as high-quality petroleum oils. Manufacturers of such oils claim the higher price is offset by extended oil change intervals of 15,000 to 25,000 miles. However, vehicle manufacturers will not honor new-vehicle warranties when oil and filter changes are performed at such intervals.

Special Oils for Turbocharged Engines

In mid-1984, Valvoline Oil Company introduced an oil compounded for the special problems of turbochargers, discussed in Unit 20. This oil, Turbo V, has added detergent/dispersants and oxidation inhibitors. Other oil companies are expected to produce similar products.

15.5 OIL CONSUMPTION

Years ago, new-vehicle oil consumption up to a quart in 600 miles was considered normal. Current vehicles rarely use more than one quart of oil in 1,000 or more miles, and some vehicles use as little as one quart of oil in 3,000 miles. Oil can be lost, or consumed, in two basic ways:

* Leakage
* Burning in the combustion chamber.

Leakage

Oil can be lost by simple leakage through dried, cracked, or seeping gaskets. The most frequent source of engine oil leaks on older cars is through the valve cover gasket. This source has been minimized in recent years through the use of silicone sealer instead of gaskets. Other common sources include:

* Oil pan gasket
* Crankshaft seals
* Oil pressure sending unit
* Timing cover gasket and/or seal
* Fuel pump gasket
* Distributor drive O-ring gasket.

Burning

Oil can be consumed by being burned in the combustion chamber. Worn cylinders and piston rings can cause *oil pumping*. The suction above the piston during the intake stroke can draw oil up, past worn rings, into the combustion chamber. In addition, worn intake valve guides can allow oil to be sucked down the valve stem, into the combustion chamber. During combustion, the oil is burned.

Small amounts of oil vapors and blowby gases are burned in engines that are in good condition. The vapors and gases are drawn through the *positive crankcase ventilation (PCV) system* into the intake manifold. A PCV system keeps harmful vapors and gases from being released to the atmosphere, as discussed in Units 40–42.

In a worn engine, blowby gases carry large amounts of oil vapor into the PCV system to be burned. In addition, a clogged PCV system can cause oil to be blown up into the air filter. A clogged PCV system also can cause pressure that can rupture gaskets and cause oil leaks.

15.6 ENGINE LUBRICATION SYSTEM

An engine lubrication system, shown in Figure 15-4, consists of several parts, including:

- Oil pan
- Oil pump
- Oil filter
- Oil distribution system
- Pressure indicator
- Oil level indicator.

Oil Pan

The *oil pan,* bolted to the engine crankcase area, serves as a reservoir for oil. A *drain plug* can be removed to allow the engine oil to drain out during oil changes. An oil pump and pickup, shown in Figure 15-5, are mounted on the crankcase inside the oil pan.

Oil Pump

An oil pump, shown in Figure 15-6, consists of the following parts:

- Pickup and screen
- Housing and cover
- Gears or rotors
- Oil pressure relief valve.

Pickup and screen. The *oil pickup* is a hollow, flat cup mounted at the end of a tube. Mounted over the cup is a screen to prevent large particles from entering the pump and damaging the gears and housing. The pickup tube leads to the intake, or low pressure, side of the pump.

Housing and cover. The housing encloses the gears or rotors and contains a drive shaft for one of the gears, as shown in Figure 15-7.

Gears or rotors. Two gears or rotors are meshed in the housing. One of the gears is driven, in most cases by a shaft from the distributor drive gear. At the point where the oil pump gears unmesh, or separate, a low pressure area is created. Atmospheric pressure forces the oil up through the pickup to the low pressure area. The oil is then carried around the outside of the gear, in the chambers formed between the teeth, housing, and side plates. Refer to Figure 15-8. As the oil reaches the outlet port, it is forced out, under pressure, as the teeth go back into mesh. Thus, oil is forced out of the pump under pressure to the oil filter.

Oil pressure relief valve. To prevent excess pressure from developing, a *relief valve* is used. A spring holds a check valve or ball on a seat in the oil outlet. When oil pressure develops more force against the check valve than the spring, the valve is pushed open. This action uncovers a relief passage that allows oil to be redirected to the inlet side of the oil pump. In action, the valve acts as a controlled leak and allows only enough oil out to maintain a controlled pressure.

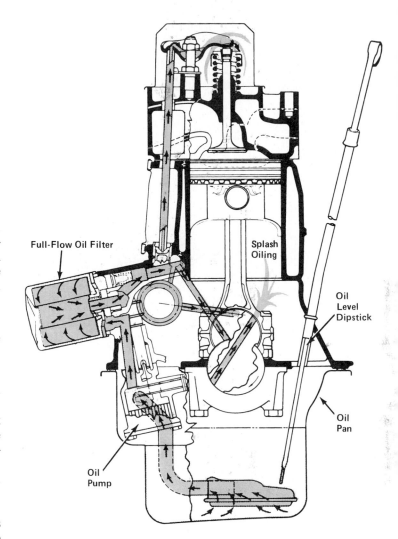

Full-Flow Oil Filter

Splash Oiling

Oil Level Dipstick

Oil Pan

Oil Pump

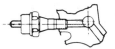

Oil Pressure Sending Unit

Figure 15-4. Engine lubrication system.
BUICK MOTOR DIVISION—GMC

Oil Filter

The *oil filter* is located in the lubrication system between the oil pump and the engine parts that require lubrication. Its purpose is to remove harmful particles from the oil. The filter usually is screwed directly onto the side of the cylinder block or mounted on an adapter. See Figure 15-9.

The oil filter itself usually consists of a pleated element made of special filtering paper inside a metal housing. See Figure 15-10.

Oil filtering systems used in current vehicles are of the *full-flow* type with bypass systems. Full-flow means that all of the oil normally passes through the

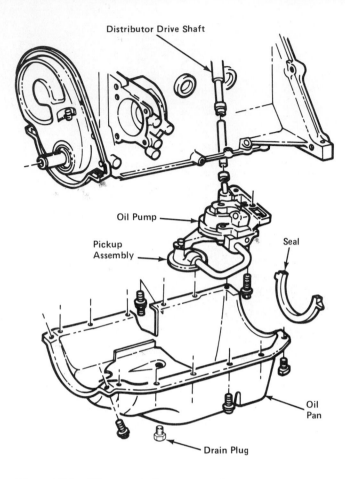

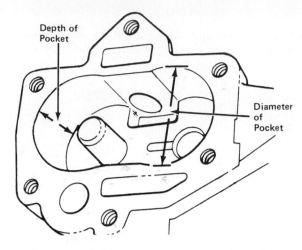

Figure 15-7. Oil pump housing. BUICK MOTOR DIVISION—GMC

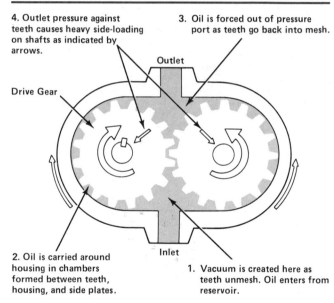

4. Outlet pressure against teeth causes heavy side-loading on shafts as indicated by arrows.

3. Oil is forced out of pressure port as teeth go back into mesh.

Outlet

Drive Gear

2. Oil is carried around housing in chambers formed between teeth, housing, and side plates.

Inlet

1. Vacuum is created here as teeth unmesh. Oil enters from reservoir.

Figure 15-8. Oil pump gear operation.

Figure 15-5. Oil pan and oil pump mountings.
BUICK MOTOR DIVISION—GMC

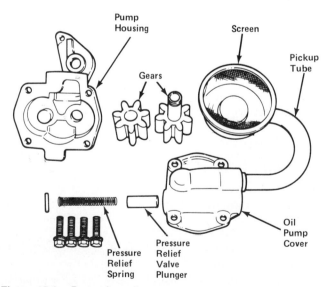

Figure 15-6. Parts of an oil pump. BUICK MOTOR DIVISION—GMC

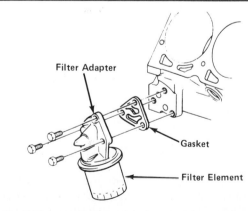

Figure 15-9. An oil filter usually is mounted on an adapter that bolts to the engine block. BUICK MOTOR DIVISION—GMC

filter before it can flow through the galleries and to the moving parts of the engine.

However, if the filter becomes excessively clogged with contaminant particles, the oil pressure could drop, causing oil starvation to moving parts. To prevent this situation, a *bypass valve* is used to redirect unfiltered oil to the engine. Dirty oil is preferable to no oil at all.

The oil bypass valve may be located in the filter mount on the engine, as shown in Figure 15-11, or within the filter itself.

Oil Distribution System

The drilled passages through which the oil passes to bearing surfaces and moving parts are called *oil galleries*.

Splash lubrication throws oil from the crankshaft to the cylinder walls, piston pins, timing chain and/or gears, and other parts, as shown in Figure 15-12.

Oil spurt holes in the connecting rods spray oil onto the lower cylinder walls. In pushrod engines, drain holes allow oil to flow from the upper valve train parts downward onto lifters and camshaft lobes.

Pressure Indicator

Low oil pressure can cause lack of lubrication and rapid engine damage. A warning system to alert the driver to low oil pressure is part of the engine lubrication system.

Warning Lamp. A simple warning system has a pressure sensor screwed into an oil gallery, wiring, and a lamp on the dash. See Figure 15-13.

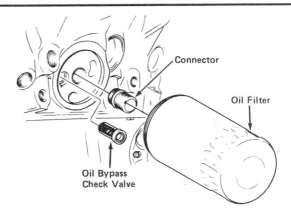

Figure 15-11. A bypass valve redirects engine oil flow if the oil filter becomes clogged. BUICK MOTOR DIVISION—GMC

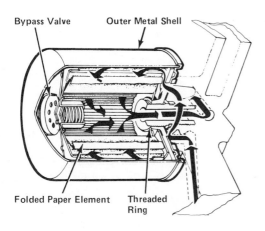

Figure 15-10. Parts of an oil filter.
CHRYSLER CORPORATION

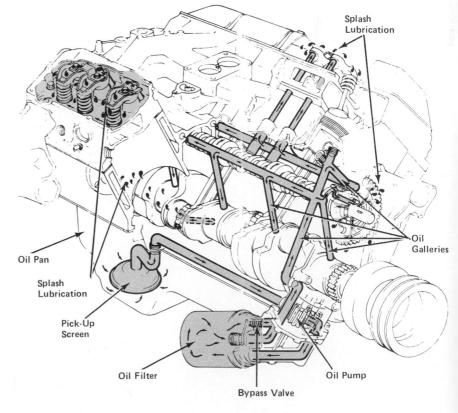

Figure 15-12. Engine lubrication system and splash lubrication.
AMERICAN MOTORS CORPORATION

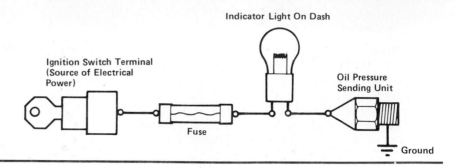

Figure 15-13. Oil pressure indicator circuit.

Oil pressure moves a *diaphragm,* or flexible metal partition, within the sensor to interrupt the electrical circuit to the lamp. See Figure 15-14. When oil pressure falls below the level necessary for safe operation, the sensor closes, completing the circuit. When the circuit is completed, electricity flows to light the warning lamp.

Electrical oil pressure gauge. Some vehicles are equipped with an oil pressure gauge, which registers the pressure developed within the lubrication system. A sensor, shown in Figure 15-15, is screwed into an oil gallery. Oil pressure moves a diaphragm connected to a variable *resistor.* A resistor lowers the amount of voltage and current passing through an electrical circuit. A gauge, or instrument, reacts to the amount of current passing through the circuit, and moves a needle over a scale to indicate the oil pressure.

Other types of oil pressure gauges operate mechanically instead of electrically. Oil travels up through a tube to the back of the gauge. A springy, flexible, hollow tube, called a *Bourdon tube,* uncoils as the pressure increases. A needle connected to the tube moves over a scale to indicate oil pressure.

Oil Level Indicator

A lack of oil will cause engine parts to become starved for oil. Friction and heat buildup will rapidly damage or destroy engine moving parts.

Dipstick. The simplest type of liquid level indicator is a *dipstick,* shown in Figure 15-16. The dipstick extends downward into the lubricant supply.

Before checking a dipstick, it is necessary to shut off the engine and wait for a few minutes. This delay allows oil to drain back to the oil pan from the upper areas of the engine. It is necessary to wipe the dipstick to remove the oil splashed on it by the spinning crankshaft before an accurate reading can be taken. The dipstick is marked to indicate a level at which oil should be added and a level beyond which no oil should be added. Too much oil in the pan can be

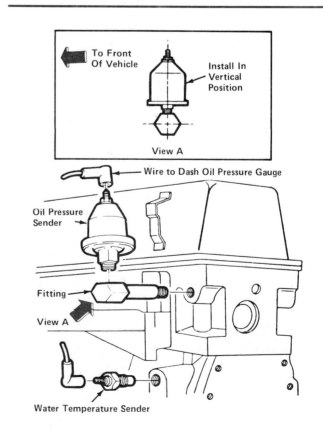

Figure 15-15. Oil pressure gauge sensor.
FORD MOTOR COMPANY

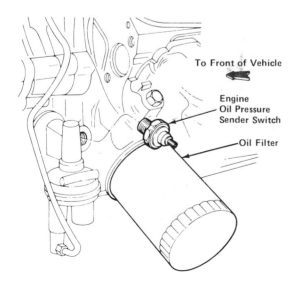

Figure 15-14. Oil pressure light sensor.
FORD MOTOR COMPANY

whipped into foam by the crankshaft, resulting in engine damage or leaks.

Electronic oil level indicator. Some vehicles built since 1980 have an electronic oil level indicator. A warning light will be activated if the amount of oil in the pan falls below a safe level. A circuit for such a warning system is shown in Figure 15-17.

U N I T   H I G H L I G H T S

- The engine lubrication system provides oil to all moving and touching internal engine parts.
- Engine oil performs several functions. These include reducing friction, absorbing shock loads, forming a seal, and cooling and cleaning internal engine parts.
- Petroleum-based engine oils require several chemical additives to help the oil provide adequate lubrication.
- Engine oils have an SAE viscosity rating and an API service rating.
- Vehicles driven mainly for short distances or in cold weather require more frequent oil and filter changes.
- Oil can be lost through leakage or by being burned in the combustion chamber.
- An engine lubrication system consists of an oil pan, oil pump, oil filter, oil distribution system, pressure indicator, and oil level indicator.

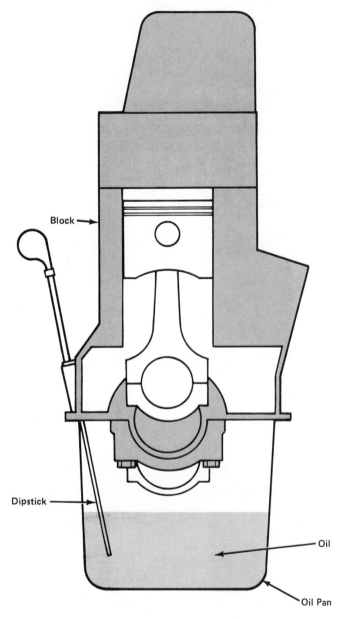

Figure 15-16. Engine oil dipstick.

T E R M S

lubrication
lubricant
seizing
Society of
  Automotive
  Engineers (SAE)
American Petroleum
  Institute (API)
viscosity
single-viscosity oil
multi-viscosity oil
nondetergent oil
additives
detergent/dispersant
viscosity index
  improver
pour point depressant
extreme pressure
  additives
anti-wear additive
corrosion inhibitor
oxidation inhibitor
oxidation

foam inhibitor
foam
synthetic oils
scuffing
oil pumping
positive crankcase
  ventilation system
  (PCV)
oil pan
drain plug
oil pickup
oil pressure relief valve
oil filter
full-flow oil filtering
  system
bypass valve
oil galleries
splash lubrication
diaphragm
resistor
Bourdon tube
dipstick

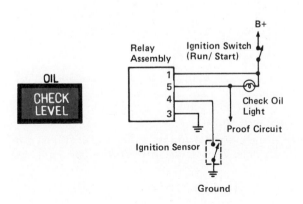

Figure 15-17. Electronic engine oil level indicator.

DIRECTIONS: The following questions are similar to those used on mechanic certification tests. On a separate sheet of paper, write the letter of the correct choice.

1. The functions of engine oil include all of the following EXCEPT

A. reducing friction and forming a seal.

B. preventing excess oil pressure.

C. absorbing shock loads.

D. cooling and cleaning engine parts.

2. Mechanic A says an engine oil rated for API service SF-CC is suitable for all modern gasoline engines.

Mechanic B says that an engine oil rated for API service SF-CC is suitable for all modern diesel engines.

Who is correct?

A. A only   B. B only   C. Both A and B   D. Neither A nor B

3. Which of the following statements is correct?

I. Oil can be lost through leakage.

II. Oil can be consumed by being burned in the combustion chamber.

A. I only   B. II only   C. Both I and II   D. Neither I nor II

4. An oil pressure relief valve is used to

A. prevent excess pressure as engine speed increases.

B. prevent oil from lubricating nonmoving parts.

C. allow a full-flow oil filtering system to bypass a clogged filter.

D. allow an oil pressure warning system to operate correctly.

5. Methods of distributing oil within the engine include all of the following EXCEPT

A. galleries.

B. splash lubrication.

C. oil spurt holes and drain holes.

D. positive crankcase ventilation (PCV) system.

S U P P L E M E N T A L   A C T I V I T I E S

1. Make a survey of the API service grades of oil for sale at an auto parts store. Make a list of the names and prices of each oil available. Report to your class on price differences between different SAE viscosities and different API service-rated oils.

2. Talk to relatives and neighbors, and check their vehicle owner's manuals for oil viscosity and oil change interval recommendations. Report to your class on any differences you find. Note differences among 4-, 6-, and 8-cylinder engines. Also note differences among types of vehicles (foreign and domestic, passenger vehicles, pickup trucks, vans, and so on).

3. Talk to a parts counter person at an auto parts store. Find out how many different oil filters are made for domestic and foreign vehicles. Report to your class how many different types are kept in stock.

4. Examine a vehicle chosen by your instructor. Locate all external physical parts of the lubrication system and check the oil level.

16 LUBRICATION SYSTEM SERVICE

UNIT PREVIEW

Regular oil and filter changes are necessary to remove by-products of normal engine operation and ensure proper engine lubrication.

In addition to scheduled maintenance, routine lubrication system service is necessary from time to time. This service includes stopping leaks from oil pan drain openings, replacing valve cover gaskets, and replacing oil pressure sender units.

Lubrication system service during an engine overhaul includes checking and/or replacing the oil pump and replacing the oil pan gasket.

LEARNING OBJECTIVES

When you have completed your assignments and exercises in this unit, you should be able to:

☐ Explain what problems make regular oil and filter changes necessary.

☐ Explain why the oil filter should be changed at every oil change.

☐ Perform an oil and filter change.

☐ Replace valve cover gaskets.

☐ Replace an oil-pressure sender unit.

☐ Identify and describe lubrication system service performed during engine overhaul.

SAFETY PRECAUTIONS

Wear eye protection at all times when in the shop area.

Oil and filter changes require that the vehicle be safely raised and supported. If using safety stands or ramps to support the vehicle, also block any wheels remaining on the ground. This will prevent the vehicle from moving forward or backward.

Use caution around hot surfaces such as exhaust manifolds, pipes, and mufflers. Hot oil draining from the oil pan or oil filter can cause burns and skin irritation.

Always refer to the vehicle manufacturer's shop manual for specific procedures.

16.1 OIL DETERIORATION

Although you may have heard that oil itself never "wears out," other problems occur that make frequent and regular oil changes necessary.

Oxidation

Oxidation is the chemical combination of oil with oxygen, which causes oil to deteriorate, or break down chemically. Oil oxidation is increased by the high temperatures common in modern engines. Oxidation causes the formation of carbon and varnish, which increase friction and can restrict (reduce the size of) oil passages. *Varnish* is a clear coating that builds up and hardens on parts.

Acid Formation

Air is drawn through the engine when it is running. The air circulates through oil return passages and above the oil in the crankcase.

Air contains moisture, or water vapor. In addition, water is formed as a by-product of the combustion of a *hydrocarbon* fuel, such as gasoline or diesel fuel. The mineral element sulfur is present in lubricating oil and gasoline. When water combines with sulfur, *sulfuric acid,* a powerfully corrosive substance, is formed. Other acids also can be formed when water vapor combines with other mineral elements in oil and motor fuels.

As the oil circulates, acid is carried to all moving parts of the engine such as bearings, crankshaft and camshaft journals, camshaft lobes, cylinder walls, and so on. Acids can rapidly corrode and etch the surfaces of these parts.

When a vehicle is driven for long distances or in hot weather, heat drives most water vapor from the oil. This lessens acid formation. However, the oil in vehicles driven mainly for short distances never gets hot enough to drive off all the moisture. Thus, moisture can remain in the oil to form more and stronger acids.

Another consideration, important in cold climates, is dilution. When a vehicle is driven in colder winter temperatures, the carburetor choke is used quite extensively during engine start-up. Short-trip driving under these conditions may never allow the engine to fully warm up. Thus, the choke stays on most of the time. This can lead to oil dilution from the gasoline in excessively rich air-fuel mixtures. Under these conditions, the oil must be changed more frequently.

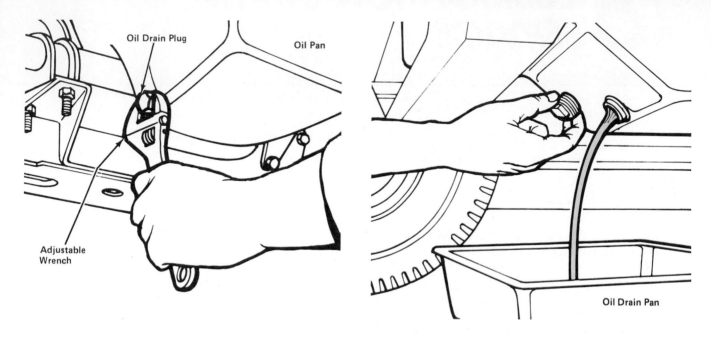

Figure 16-1. To drain engine oil, remove the drain plug. CHRYSLER CORPORATION

Sludge Formation

Enough moisture may be present to form drops of water in the crankcase. This water can be whipped by the spinning crankshaft into the oil. The combination of water and oil produces a frothy substance known as *water sludge*. Particles of carbon, acid, and other contaminants can combine to produce a thick, soft, tar-like sludge. Sludge accumulates inside the engine and can be seen inside valve covers and on upper valve train parts. In addition, sludge clogs oil screens and oil passages and can cut off oil circulation to internal engine parts.

16.2 ROUTINE LUBRICATION SYSTEM SERVICE

Routine lubrication system service consists of changing the oil and oil filter at regular intervals.

Oil Change Intervals

Vehicles driven 600 miles or less per month should have an oil and filter change every three months. Vehicles driven longer distances should have oil and filter changes as recommended by the vehicle manufacturer.

Smaller, four-cylinder engines run hotter and at higher rpm, and contain less oil, than larger, V-6 and V-8 engines. Frequent oil and filter changes for four-cylinder engines can help to prolong engine life and reliability.

Refer to the manufacturer's service manual for recommended oil and filter change intervals. However, remember that any maintenance performed more frequently than the recommended minimums

cannot cause harm. In many cases, it will lengthen engine life.

Oil Filter

On most engines, draining the engine oil does not drain the oil filter. Up to a quart of dirty oil may remain in the filter. As soon as the engine starts, clean oil is pumped to the filter, where it mixes with this dirty oil.

Oil filters should be changed at every oil change to ensure maximum engine life and service.

16.3 OIL AND FILTER CHANGE

Before beginning this service, run the engine until the oil is fully warmed up. This allows the oil to drain freely and removes a maximum amount of contaminants. When the engine has warmed up, shut it off and follow these steps:

1. Raise the vehicle and support it safely.
2. Position an oil catch pan under the drain plug.
3. Use a wrench to loosen the drain plug a few turns.
4. When the plug is loose, grasp it through a shop towel with your fingers. Press inward while unscrewing the plug.
5. When the plug comes out, pull it out of the way to allow the oil to drain, as shown in Figure 16-1.
6. While the oil is draining, clean all dirt and foreign matter from the drain plug, especially around the threads. Examine the plug and pan for stripped or damaged threads. If a gasket is

used, check it for damage. Repair of stripped drain plug and/or oil pan threads is discussed in 16.4. Allow the oil to drain for at least five minutes.

7. Install a new gasket, if needed, on the drain plug and reinstall the plug to the manufacturer's specified torque.

NOTE: **In most cases, the same catch pan cannot catch both pan oil and filter oil at the same time. Replace the drain plug before repositioning the catch pan under the filter.**

8. Position the catch pan beneath the oil filter. Filter removal and replacement are illustrated in Figure 16-2. Be sure you have the correct replacement filter. Several types of oil filter wrenches are made, as shown in Figure 16-3. Confined working spaces on some vehicles require the use of one type of wrench rather than another.

9. Be sure that the old oil filter gasket comes off with the old filter.

10. Install the new filter, tightening it three-quarters to one full turn after the gasket contacts the base.

CAUTION: **The rubber mounting gasket on the new filter must be in the same location relative to the mounting threads as the gasket on the old filter.**

11. Remove the oil filler cap. Install the correct amount of engine oil. Replace the oil filler cap.

12. Start the engine and let it idle slowly until the oil pressure light goes out or the gauge indicates proper pressure.

13. Check for leaks around the drain plug and oil filter mount and retighten if necessary.

16.4 LEAKS FROM DRAIN PLUG

Damaged drain plug and/or oil pan drain hole threads that cause leaks can be repaired. Replacement metal drain plugs, shown in Figure 16-4, are available from auto parts stores. The replacement drain plugs have a tap-like end that cuts new threads into the oil pan drain hole.

To install a replacement metal plug, align the plug perpendicular to the drain hole surface. Start the tapered end of the plug in by hand. Continue tightening with a wrench until the plug has threaded itself in and compressed the gasket.

Expandable rubber drain plugs, shown in Figure 16-5, are also available to stop leaks from badly damaged oil pan drain hole threads. A special tool, supplied with the plug, is used to stretch the plug for installation. When the tool is removed, the plug contracts and tightly seals the drain plug hole.

16.5 REPLACING VALVE COVER GASKET

Before replacing a valve cover gasket, remove belts, hoses, wires, brackets, and engine accessories blocking access to the cover. Make drawings of how each part is attached to aid in reassembly. Then proceed as follows:

1. Remove the valve cover attaching bolts as shown in Figure 16-6. Start loosening the bolts near the center of the cover and proceed outward in a crisscross pattern, as shown in Figure 16-7.

2. If the cover is stuck, tap it gently from side to side with a soft-faced mallet until it loosens.

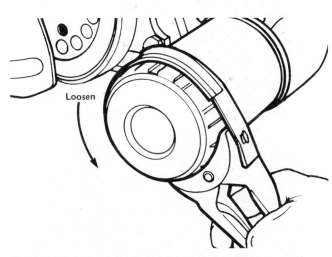

Figure 16-2. Removing the oil filter with an oil filter wrench.
CHRYSLER CORPORATION

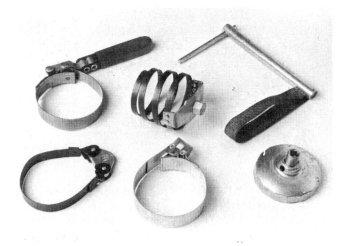

Figure 16-3. Oil filter wrenches differ in design.

Figure 16-4. Replacement drain plugs are often self-tapping.

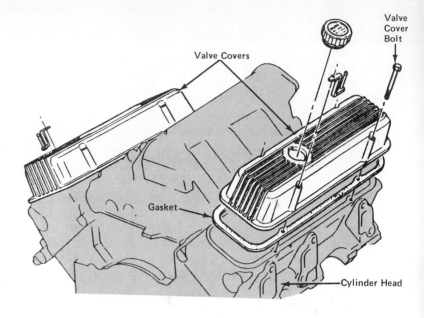

Figure 16-6. Valve cover assembly. BUICK MOTOR DIVISION

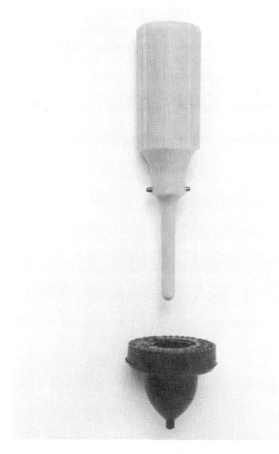

Figure 16-5. Expandable rubber drain plug.

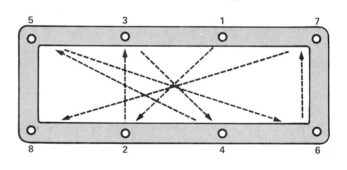

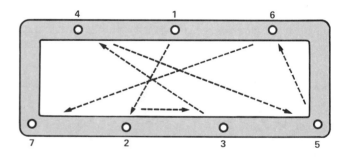

Figure 16-7. Crisscross bolt tightening and loosening patterns for valve covers.

Remove the cover. Use scrapers to remove any remains of the gasket on the cover. Do not bend the edge flanges of the cover during cleaning.

3. Check the cover for bent flanges by placing it on a flat surface. A block of wood and a hammer can be used to flatten bent flanges on pressed sheet-metal covers. Bent or badly damaged cast-aluminum covers cannot be straightened, and must be replaced.

4. Check the bolt holes for *dimples*. A dimple is a tapered depression in a thin piece of metal caused by overtightened attachment bolts. Dimples can be flattened by using the ball peen end of a hammer. Support the concave (hollow) side of the dimple against a piece of wood held in a vise. Place the ball peen of one hammer against the convex (projecting) side of the dimple. Hit the face of the first hammer with another hammer. Do not use excess force. Hit

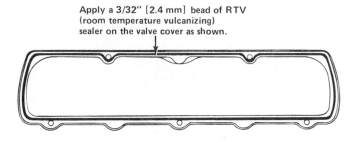

Apply a 3/32" [2.4 mm] bead of RTV (room temperature vulcanizing) sealer on the valve cover as shown.

Figure 16-8. Applying sealant on a valve cover.
BUICK MOTOR DIVISION—GMC

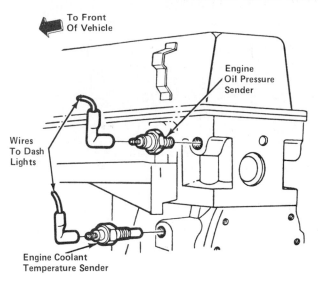

To Front Of Vehicle

Engine Oil Pressure Sender

Wires To Dash Lights

Engine Coolant Temperature Sender

Figure 16-9. Oil pressure sender replacement.
FORD MOTOR COMPANY

the dimple only hard enough to make it level with the edge flange. Recheck the flange against a flat surface.

SAFETY CAUTION: Wear eye protection at all times when hammering.

5. Use shop towels to plug oil drain holes in the cylinder head. Wrap shop towels around the upper valve train of the cylinder head. Use scrapers to remove any traces of gasket material from the valve cover sealing surfaces. Brush off any traces of crumbled gasket.

CAUTION: Gasket residue can contaminate the lubrication system. Make sure all traces of gasket material have been removed before attempting to replace the valve cover and gasket.

6. Remove all towels. Refer to the vehicle manufacturer's shop manual for recommended sealants. Apply *room temperature vulcanizing (RTV)* rubber sealant as recommended. Figure 16-8 shows a recommended sample pattern for RTV sealant on a specific valve cover.

7. If RTV is not used, press the new gasket into place around the cover. Replace the cover on the cylinder head. Start the bolts in by hand. Tighten the bolts gently to the manufacturer's recommended torque in a crisscross pattern, from the center outward. Refer to Figure 16-7.

16.6 REPLACING OIL PRESSURE SENDER

Oil pressure sender switches may develop leaks. To replace a sender, remove the wire connector from the sender, as shown in Figure 16-9.

Use a special eight-point oil sender socket to loosen lamp-type warning system senders. Unscrew and remove the sender.

Thread the new sender in by hand. Tighten with the special socket to the manufacturer's recommended torque. Replace the wire connector.

16.7 LUBRICATION SYSTEM SERVICE WITH OIL PAN REMOVED

When an engine is disassembled for repairs, the oil pump should be checked or replaced. All gaskets, including the oil pan gasket, must be replaced with new gaskets during reassembly procedures.

Oil Pump

If an engine is being disassembled, the oil pump gears or rotors can be checked for wear and clearance, as shown in Figure 16-10. If there is any doubt about the condition of the pump, install a new oil pump.

Oil Pan Gasket

Procedures for oil pan gasket replacement are similar to those for valve cover gasket replacement. All traces of the old gasket must be removed from the oil pan and cylinder block sealing surfaces. Bent flanges and dimples on pressed sheet-metal pans should be straightened before reinstallation. Bent or badly damaged cast-aluminum oil pans cannot be straightened, and must be replaced.

SAFETY CAUTION: Most engines must be raised and supported to allow removal of the oil pan. Be sure this is done carefully, to prevent damage to external engine components and connections, and to prevent personal injury.

If recommended by the manufacturer, sealant materials must be applied to the pan and/or cylinder block surfaces, as shown in Figure 16-11. Oil pan gaskets may be made in a single piece or in several pieces, as shown in Figure 16-12.

Reinstall the bolts and tighten them in the manufacturer's specified sequence to the proper torque.

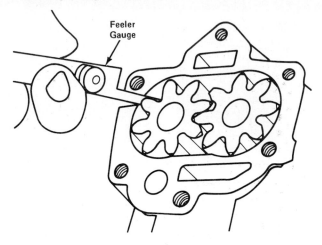

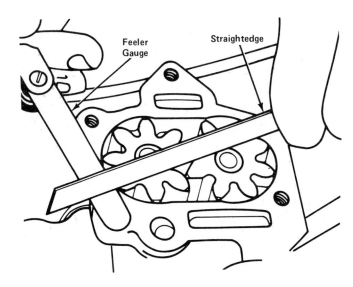

Figure 16-10. Measuring oil pump gear clearances.
BUICK MOTOR DIVISION—GMC

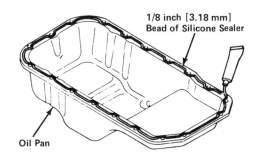

Figure 16-11. Applying sealant on an oil pan.
FORD MOTOR COMPANY

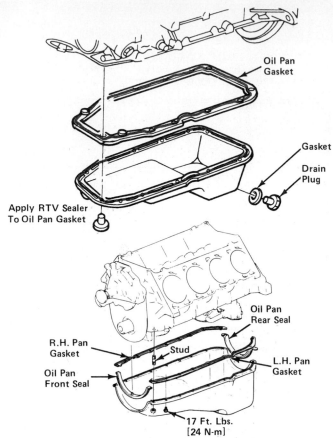

Figure 16-12. Oil pan gaskets. BUICK MOTOR DIVISION—GMC

UNIT HIGHLIGHTS

- Problems caused by oxidation, acid formation, oil dilution, and sludge require that oil and filter changes be done regularly.
- Oil filters should be changed every time an oil change is done.
- Leaks from oil drain plug openings can be repaired.
- When valve cover gaskets are replaced, no gasket residue must be allowed to enter the engine.
- Bent and dimpled flanges on pressed sheet-metal valve covers and oil pans can be repaired.
- Damaged cast-aluminum covers and oil pans must be replaced.
- Oil pressure sender replacement is a simple job.
- During engine overhaul, oil pumps must be checked or replaced.
- Gaskets should never be reused.

TERMS

varnish
hydrocarbon
sulfuric acid
water sludge

dimple
room temperature
vulcanizing (RTV)

R E V I E W   Q U E S T I O N S

DIRECTIONS: The following questions are similar to those used on mechanic certification tests. On a separate sheet of paper, write the letter of the correct choice.

1. All of the following problems make oil changes necessary EXCEPT
A. oil "wearing out" with use and age.
B. oil oxidizing, especially at high temperatures.
C. acids forming in the oil when moisture and chemical elements combine.
D. sludge forming in the oil from moisture and contaminant particles.

2. Mechanic A says vehicles driven longer distances never need oil or filter changes.
   Mechanic B says vehicles driven short distances and in cold weather need frequent oil and filter changes.
   Who is correct?
A. A only   B. B only   C. Both A and B   D. Neither A nor B

3. How should the oil filter be tightened?
A. As tight as possible by hand
B. With an oil filter wrench
C. With a torque wrench
D. Three-quarters to one turn after the gasket contacts the base

4. Which of the following statements is correct?
   I. Bent flanges on pressed sheet metal covers and oil pans can be straightened.
   II. Bent flanges on cast-aluminum covers and oil pans can be straightened.
A. I only   B. II only   C. Both I and II   D. Neither I nor II

5. All of the following conditions could cause faulty indications in a lamp-type oil-pressure warning system EXCEPT
A. a loose or disconnected electrical connector.
B. a faulty sender.
C. a burned-out bulb in the dash.
D. an oil pickup screen clogged with sludge.

S U P P L E M E N T A L   A C T I V I T I E S

1. Perform an oil and filter change on a vehicle.
2. Remove and replace a valve cover gasket on a vehicle. If the cover is made of pressed sheet metal, correct any warping and/or dimples. Report to the class on the deposits found inside the cover and on upper valve train parts. Describe the amount and nature of the deposits.
3. Remove and replace an oil pressure sender unit.

17 THE COOLING SYSTEM

UNIT PREVIEW

Heat generated during combustion is great enough to melt or damage engine parts. The cooling system must be able to remove approximately one third of the heat developed during combustion to prevent engine damage.

The parts of the cooling system work together to circulate air and liquid to transfer heat away from the engine. The pressurized cooling system of a modern vehicle allows the engine to operate at a stable temperature and provides heat for passenger comfort.

LEARNING OBJECTIVES

When you have completed your assignments and exercises in this unit, you should be able to:

☐ Explain how heat is transferred from the combustion chamber away from the vehicle.

☐ Identify and describe the parts of a vehicle's cooling system.

☐ Explain why the use of coolant is essential in modern vehicles.

☐ Explain how the radiator pressure cap helps to prevent boiling.

17.1 HEAT TRANSFER

The highest temperature within the combustion chamber can reach 4,500 degrees F [2,482 degrees C] or more. See Figure 17-1. The average combustion chamber temperature is approximately 2,000 degrees F [1,093 degrees C]. Even this is more than enough to melt aluminum pistons and warp the cylinder block and head surfaces. In addition, excess heat can ruin engine oil. An engine cooling system must transfer away enough heat to prevent engine damage. Heat energy can be transferred in three ways:

• Conduction
• Convection
• Radiation.

Conduction

When something hot contacts something cooler, heat is transferred to the cooler object. This process is known as *conduction*. For example, hot gases in the combustion chamber touch the cooler cylinder walls, which then become hot.

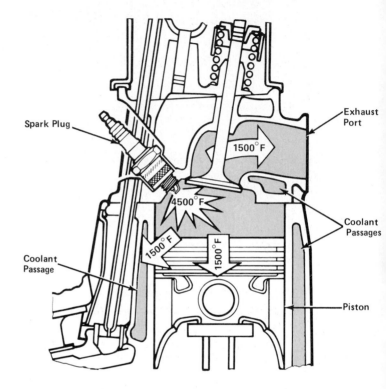

Figure 17-1. Combustion chamber temperatures.
CHRYSLER CORPORATION

Convection

The saying, "heat rises," describes *convection*. Convection operates wherever fluids (gases or liquids) and gravity are present. Heated atoms or molecules of fluid are less dense, and thus lighter, than cooler atoms or molecules. Therefore, the heated portion of the fluid rises upward, and the cooler portion sinks downward.

For example, in a room, the temperature at the ceiling is warmer than the temperature near the floor. In an automobile engine, heat rises to the uppermost parts of the engine and cooling system.

Radiation

The warmth of sunlight felt on your skin is a result of heat *radiation* from the sun. Heat energy can travel from one location to another through empty space.

Within an engine cooling system, all three forms of heat transfer take place.

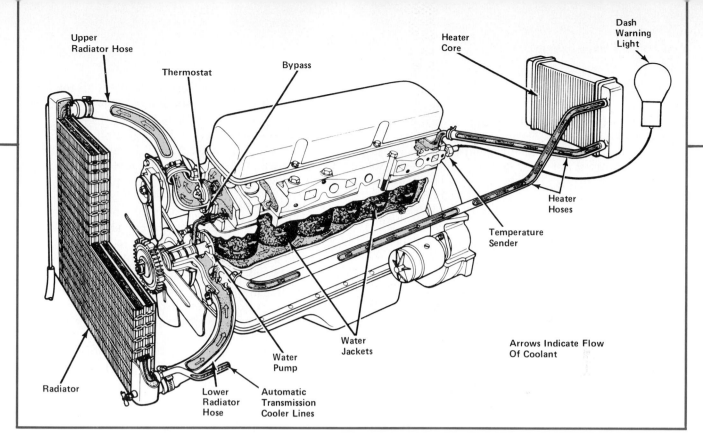

Figure 17-2. Parts of a cooling system. CHRYSLER CORPORATION

17.2 PARTS OF A LIQUID COOLING SYSTEM

A basic cooling system, shown in Figure 17-2, consists of several parts that function together to assure a stable engine operating temperature. These parts include:

- Coolant
- Radiator
- Water pump
- Fan
- Water jacket
- Thermostat
- Temperature warning system
- Radiator pressure cap
- Coolant recovery system
- Connecting hoses
- Heater core
- Oil cooler.

17.3 COOLANT

Coolant is a mixture of antifreeze and water. Antifreeze is a liquid, *ethylene glycol,* mixed with anti-corrosion chemicals. Water alone will promote rust, corrosion, and *electrolysis* in the cooling system. Electrolysis is a chemical and electrical decomposition process that occurs when two dissimilar metals are joined in the presence of moisture. Minerals and metals in the cooling system can cause water to become slightly acid. An electrical current begins to

flow that can actually cause metals in the cooling system and engine, such as brass, copper, and aluminum, to be eaten away. A fresh, proper mixture of antifreeze and water will prevent acid buildup and corrosion. Although ethylene glycol does not evaporate appreciably, the anti-corrosion chemicals in antifreeze are used up in approximately one year.

Within the engine, a hollow space filled with coolant, called a *water jacket,* surrounds the cylinders and combustion chambers. Heat is conducted into the coolant by the heated metal. If the coolant boils, liquid no longer is in contact with the heated cylinder walls and head passages. Heat conduction from the metal of the cylinder walls into the coolant stops. Excess heat builds up inside the cylinders. This can cause the pistons to scuff and seize to the cylinder walls and warp block and cylinder head surfaces.

Another function of antifreeze is to prevent freezing. When water freezes, it expands. Such expansion can exert enough pressure to crack the water jackets in blocks and cylinder heads and to rupture radiators.

A half-and-half mixture of antifreeze and water has a boiling temperature 9 degrees F [– 12.7 degrees C] higher than plain water. This provides added protection from boiling.

In summary, a high-quality antifreeze is important for several reasons: It prevents cooling system freeze-up. It prevents rust, corrosion, and acid buildup. It raises the boiling point of the coolant. Finally, it provides blended lubricants for water pump seal lubrication.

17.4 RADIATOR

The heated coolant is forced under pressure through an outlet in the cylinder head and into the upper radiator hose. The coolant then flows into the *radiator*. A radiator is made of metals, such as brass, copper, or aluminum, that conduct heat well. Hot coolant passes through hollow tubes and heats them. See Figure 17-3. Small, thin cooling fins made of copper or aluminum are in contact with the tubes to increase the surface area exposed to air.

The radiator tubes may be arranged in a vertical (downflow) or horizontal (crossflow) pattern. Crossflow radiators allow coolant to travel a longer distance, thus giving up more heat, than downflow radiators of comparable height. In addition, convection that aids cooling can occur more readily in a crossflow radiator. The flat, horizontal shape of a crossflow radiator also can fit more easily into the front of vehicles with steeply sloped hoods. Refer to Figure 17-4.

Heat is conducted from the hot tubes and fins into air passing through the radiator core. The air carries the heat away from the vehicle. The cooled liquid leaving the radiator outlet travels through the lower radiator hose to the water pump, where it is again pumped through the cooling system.

Most radiators have a drain located near the bottom, as shown in Figure 17-5, for flushing purposes. On radiators without drains, the lower radiator hose must be removed.

17.5 WATER PUMP

A *water pump,* or coolant pump, shown in Figure 17-6, is operated by a belt. The drive belt may be a V-type belt or, on OHC engines, it can be the drive belt that operates the camshaft. See Figure 17-7.

Small, fan-like blades on the *impeller,* or rotor, draw liquid into the center of the pump. The blades then force the liquid outward through centrifugal force as the shaft spins. The faster the engine turns, the faster the pump circulates coolant. Seals prevent the coolant from contacting the pump bearings.

17.6 FAN

Cooling fans can be driven by electricity or by engine power.

Electric Fan

Engines mounted *transversely,* or crossways, in front-wheel-drive vehicles have electrically driven fans. See Figure 17-8.

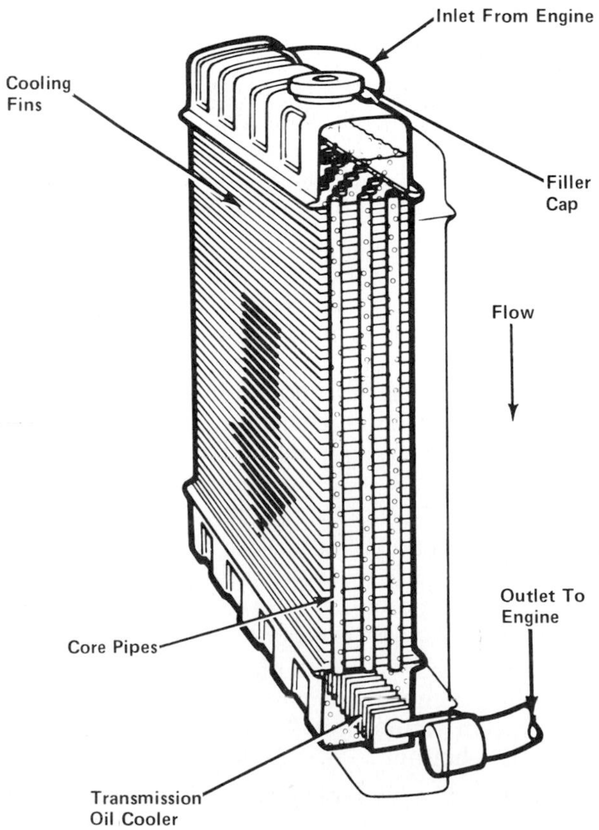

Figure 17-3. Parts of a downflow radiator.

CHRYSLER CORPORATION

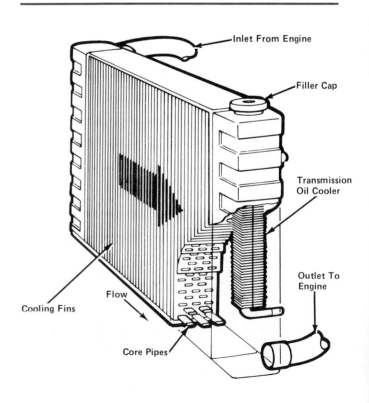

Figure 17-4. Parts of a crossflow radiator.

CHRYSLER CORPORATION

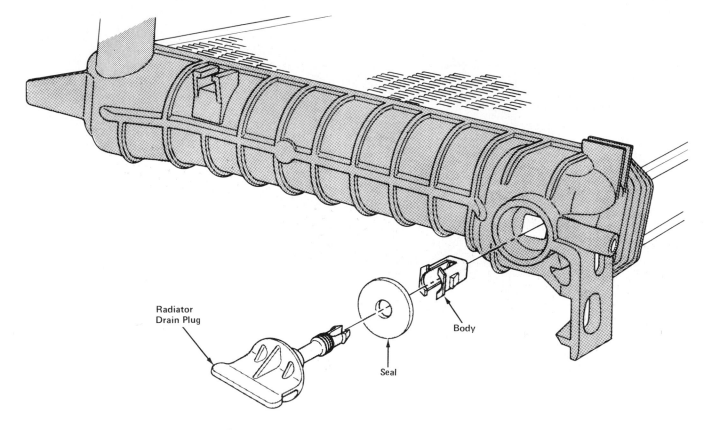

Figure 17-5. Radiator drain plug assembly. FORD MOTOR COMPANY

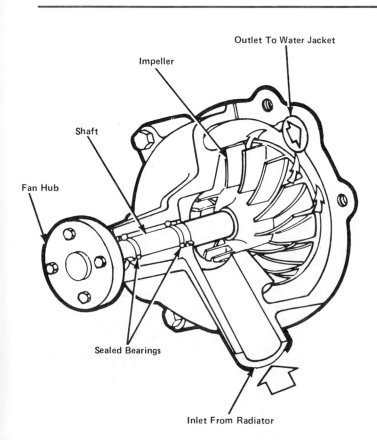

Figure 17-6. Parts of a water pump. CHRYSLER CORPORATION

An electrical switch turns the fan on and off in response to coolant temperature. The coolant switch can be located in the radiator or hoses, or screwed into the water jacket in the cylinder head as shown in Figure 17-9.

Belt-Driven Fan

Engines mounted *longitudinally,* or front-to-back, generally use a fan mounted on the water pump shaft. The fan helps to draw air through the radiator at low road speeds or when stopped. The drive belt turns both the water pump and fan, as shown in Figure 17-10. Two types of fan blades can be used: rigid or flex-blade. See Figure 17-11.

A rigid fan tends to make more noise and use more energy to turn than a flexible fan. Flexible fan blades straighten at high rpm. This straightening action moves less air, uses less energy, and makes less noise. At high road speeds, sufficient airflow is provided by the motion of the vehicle through the air.

Viscous Drive Fan Clutch

If the fan turns at full speed at all times, energy is wasted and fuel economy suffers. A *viscous drive fan clutch,* shown in Figure 17-12, is a mechanism that changes fan speed in response to engine temperature. When an engine is cold, a special silicone oil transfers less torque, allowing clutch slippage and turning the fan slower. As the engine heats up, the heated oil

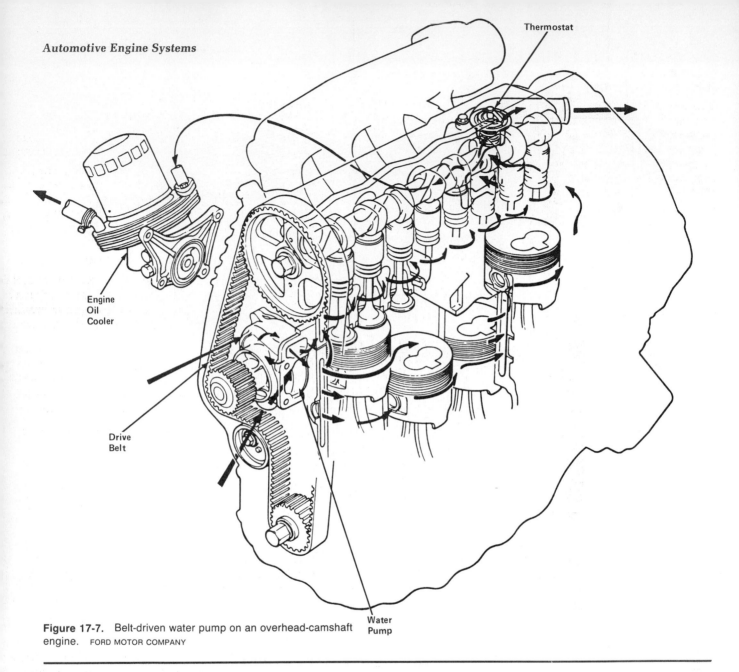

Figure 17-7. Belt-driven water pump on an overhead-camshaft engine. FORD MOTOR COMPANY

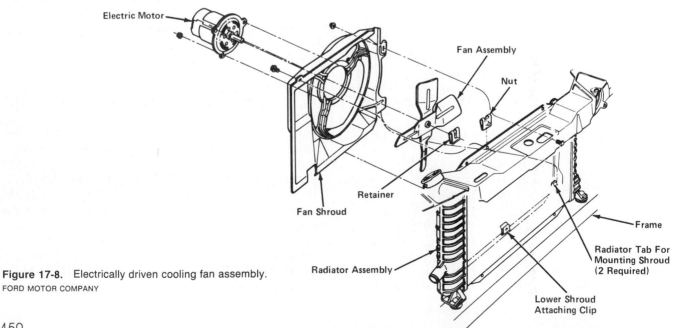

Figure 17-8. Electrically driven cooling fan assembly.
FORD MOTOR COMPANY

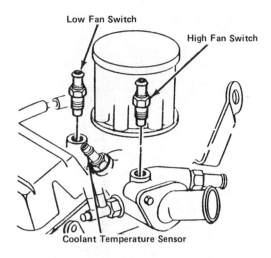

Figure 17-9. Engine fan and temperature switches.
BUICK MOTOR DIVISION—GMC

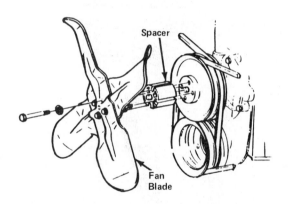

Figure 17-10. A drive belt turns both the water pump and cooling fan. BUICK MOTOR DIVISION—GMC

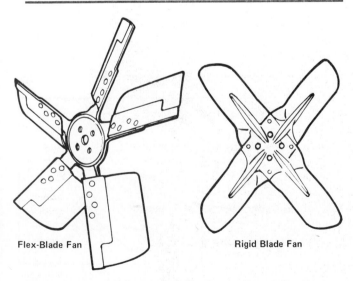

Figure 17-11. Two types of blades are used on cooling fans.
CHRYSLER CORPORATION

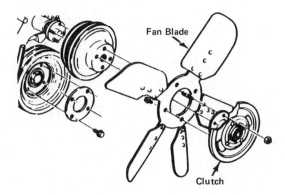

Figure 17-12. Viscous drive fan clutch assembly.
BUICK MOTOR DIVISION—GMC

transfers more torque, allowing less clutch slippage and turning the fan faster.

Such a fan clutch can be operated by a *thermostatic coil.* A thermostatic coil allows more or less silicone oil into the working chamber in response to heat.

A thermostatic coil also is known as a *bimetallic spring.* This coil or spring is made from two different metals attached back to back and wound into a coil. Different metals expand and contract at different rates, causing the coil to wind or unwind in response to underhood temperatures. See Figure 17-13.

17.7 WATER JACKET

Hollow passages in the block and cylinder head surround the areas closest to the cylinders and combustion chambers. Coolant flow through the block and head can be a *series, parallel,* or *series-parallel* flow. See Figure 17-14.

Included in the water jacket are soft plugs and a block drain plug. See Figure 17-15.

17.8 THERMOSTAT

The word *thermostat* comes from two Greek words, *therm,* meaning heat, and *stasis,* meaning stable, or steady. A thermostat is a valve that opens and closes in response to the heat of coolant to maintain a stable temperature. On nearly all vehicles, the thermostat is located under the water outlet from the cylinder head. See Figure 17-16.

A spring holds the valve closed when the coolant is cold. As the coolant heats, a special plastic, wax-like substance within the temperature sensing bulb of the thermostat expands. This expansion forces the valve to open. See Figure 17-17.

Thermostats are calibrated to open enough to maintain a stable temperature. Typical calibrations are 160 degrees F [71 degrees C], 170 degrees F [77 degrees C], and 190–195 degrees F [88–91 degrees C]. A thermostat begins opening before these temperatures are reached and is fully open about 20 degrees

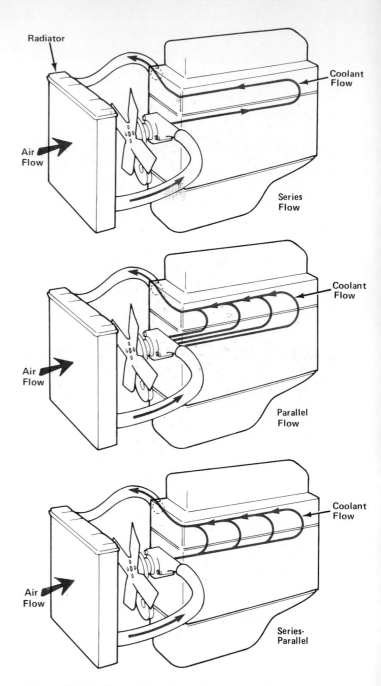

Figure 17-14. Coolant flow through the engine block and cylinder head.

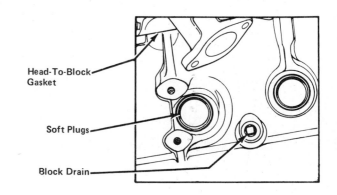

Figure 17-15. Soft plugs and a drain plug are located in the water jacket. CHRYSLER CORPORATION

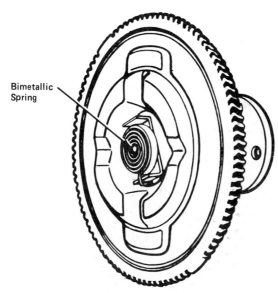

Figure 17-13. Parts of a fluid coupling fan drive.
CHRYSLER CORPORATION

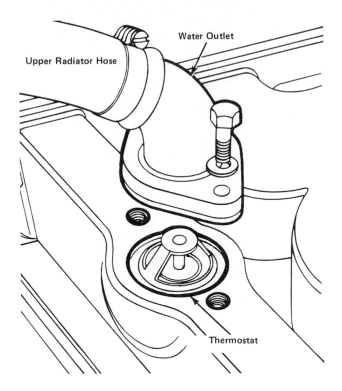

Figure 17-16. Thermostat location. CHRYSLER CORPORATION

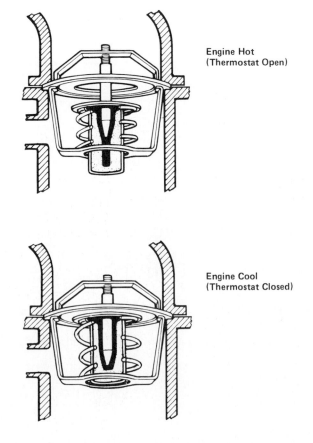

Figure 17-17. Thermostat operation. CHRYSLER CORPORATION

F [– 6.7 degrees C] above its indicated temperature. Newer vehicles come equipped with the 190–195 degrees F [88–91 degrees C] thermostats to cause their engines to run more efficiently. This greater efficiency results in better fuel economy and less unburned fuel in the exhaust gases.

When the coolant is cold, the thermostat remains shut. Coolant circulates within the block and cylinder head and through a *coolant bypass* to the water pump inlet. See Figure 17-18.

As the coolant heats, the thermostat begins to open and coolant flows through the upper radiator hose to the radiator, where it is cooled. In operation, the thermostat remains open in proportion to the amount of heat that must be transferred to the radiator. If the coolant flowing to the radiator is hotter than the preset thermostat temperature, the thermostat will remain fully open.

CAUTION: Removing the thermostat because of an overheating problem is justified only in an emergency. Without a thermostat, the engine will run cold and inefficiently. It also will waste fuel and create greater sludge and acid buildup in the oil.

17.9 TEMPERATURE WARNING SYSTEM

To alert the driver of an overheating condition, a temperature gauge and/or a lamp warning system can be installed. A temperature sensor is screwed into a threaded hole in the water jacket. See Figure 17-19.

Two types of sensors are used. One lights a warning lamp. The other type operates a temperature gauge. See Figure 17-20. Heated coolant causes the first type of sender to complete an electrical circuit to light a warning lamp. The other type of sender changes resistance to cause a gauge needle to move over a scale.

17.10 RADIATOR PRESSURE CAP

The boiling temperature of pure water is 212 degrees F [100 degrees C] at sea level. At sea level, which is the same all over the world, the weight of the atmosphere exerts a pressure of 14.7 psi [101.36 kPa].

At higher elevations, less atmospheric pressure is exerted and the boiling temperature of water decreases. At elevations below sea level (such as at Death Valley in California), added atmospheric pressure causes the boiling temperature to rise.

A spring above the relief valve of a radiator pressure cap exerts pressure over and above atmospheric pressure. See Figure 17-21. Each additional pound [0.45 kg] of pressure increases the boiling temperature of water approximately 3 degrees F [1.65 degrees C]. Thus, a 15-lb. [6.8 kg] pressure cap raises the boiling point of water to 257 degrees F [125 degrees C]. This increase, at sea level, will occur only

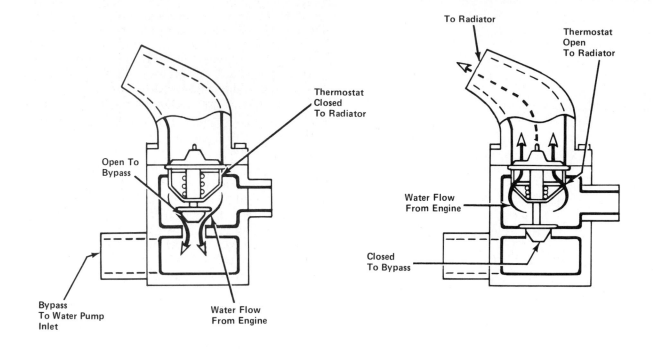

Figure 17-18. Thermostat bypass operation. CHRYSLER CORPORATION

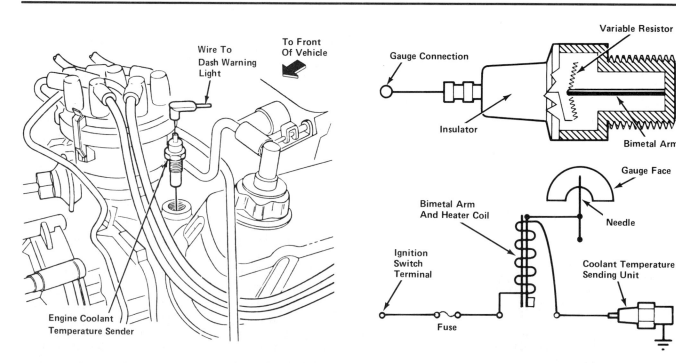

Figure 17-19. Coolant temperature sender. FORD MOTOR COMPANY

Figure 17-20. Temperature warning light and gauge circuits.

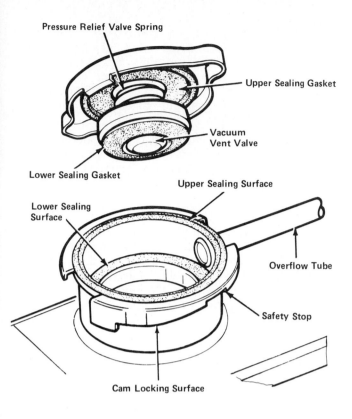

Pressure Relief Valve Spring

Upper Sealing Gasket

Vacuum Vent Valve

Lower Sealing Gasket

Upper Sealing Surface

Lower Sealing Surface

Overflow Tube

Safety Stop

Cam Locking Surface

Figure 17-21. Parts of a radiator pressure cap assembly.
CHRYSLER CORPORATION

in a tightly closed cooling system. A proper coolant mixture will further increase this by 9 degrees F [4.95 degrees C], to 266 degrees F [130 degrees C]. Some 1982 and later vehicles have 17-lb [7.71 kg] radiator pressure caps.

Driving at higher elevations, where atmospheric pressure decreases, causes the boiling temperature to be reduced. For each 1,000 feet [304.8 m] of increased elevation, the boiling temperature drops 3 degrees F [1.65 degrees C].

If the coolant overheats, pressure builds against the relief valve spring and eventually lifts the pressure seal. Hot, expanding coolant flows out of the radiator neck through an overflow tube.

As the engine cools, the coolant contracts, forming a low-pressure area within the radiator and cooling system. A vacuum vent valve allows air to be drawn in to fill the vacuum. This prevents the thin walls of the radiator from being crushed by atmospheric pressure. These actions are shown in Figure 17-22.

17.11 COOLANT RECOVERY SYSTEM

A coolant recovery system is illustrated in Figure 17-23. The system consists of a special pressure cap with an upper sealing gasket, an overflow tube, and a recovery container.

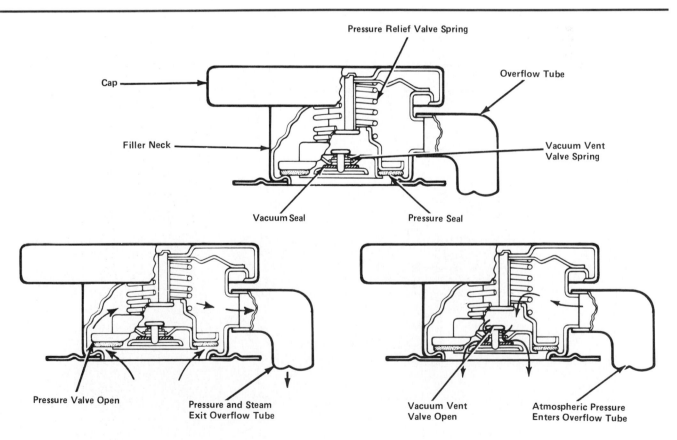

Pressure Relief Valve Spring

Overflow Tube

Cap

Filler Neck

Vacuum Vent Valve Spring

Vacuum Seal

Pressure Seal

Pressure Valve Open

Pressure and Steam Exit Overflow Tube

Vacuum Vent Valve Open

Atmospheric Pressure Enters Overflow Tube

Figure 17-22. Radiator pressure cap operation. CHRYSLER CORPORATION

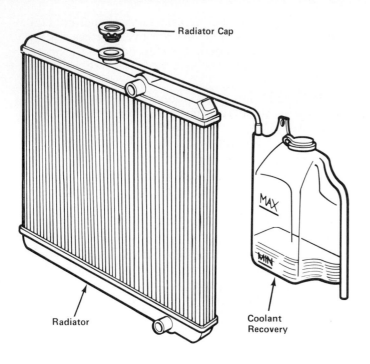

Figure 17-23. Coolant recovery system. CHRYSLER CORPORATION

Coolant recovery systems are standard equipment on almost every new vehicle. On vehicles without such systems, an air space is necessary below the radiator neck to allow space for hot coolant expansion. If coolant expands above this level, it is forced to flow out of the radiator and is lost.

In a coolant recovery system, heated coolant flows into the recovery container. When the engine cools, a low-pressure area is formed within the radiator. Thus, atmospheric pressure forces coolant back into the system, preventing loss and keeping the system full.

In this manner, coolant loss is eliminated and excess air is kept out of the system. Air contains oxygen, which combines with metals in the cooling system to form rust and corrosion.

17.12 HEATER SYSTEM

A hot-liquid heater system, shown in Figure 17-24, is part of the cooling system. Heated coolant flows through *heater hoses* to a small *heater core,* or radiator, located in a hollow container on either side of the firewall. Air is directed or blown over the hot heater core, and the heated air flows into the passenger compartment. Movable doors can be controlled to blend cool air with heated air for more or less heat. See Figure 17-25.

17.13 OIL COOLER

Radiators for vehicles with automatic transmissions have a sealed *heat exchanger,* or form of radiator, located in the coolant outlet tank. See Figure 17-26. Metal or rubber hoses carry hot automatic transmission fluid to the heat exchanger. The coolant passing over the sealed heat exchanger cools the fluid, which is then returned to the transmission.

Some diesel-engined vehicles use a similar arrangement to cool the engine oil (see Figure 17-27).

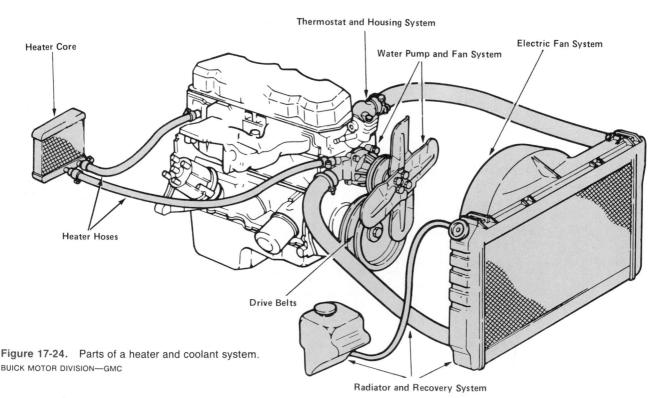

Figure 17-24. Parts of a heater and coolant system.
BUICK MOTOR DIVISION—GMC

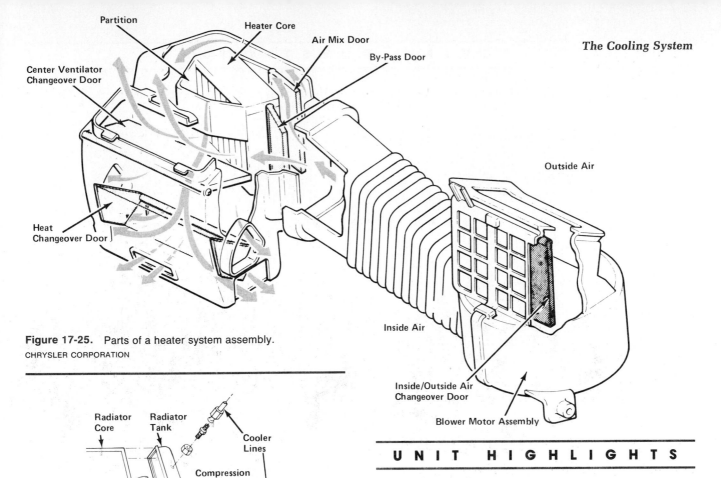

Figure 17-25. Parts of a heater system assembly.
CHRYSLER CORPORATION

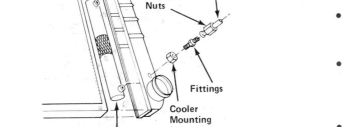

Figure 17-26. Parts of a transmission oil cooler at the engine radiator.

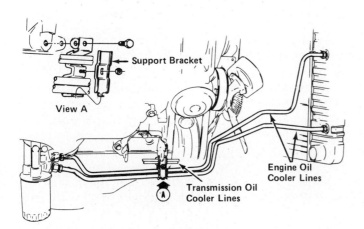

Figure 17-27. Parts of an engine oil cooler.
BUICK MOTOR DIVISION—GMC

UNIT HIGHLIGHTS

- Heat transfer within a vehicle's cooling system takes place through conduction, convection, and radiation.
- Coolant is a mixture of antifreeze and water that helps to prevent freezing, boiling, rust, corrosion, and electrolysis. Coolant should be changed yearly.
- Parts of a cooling system include coolant, radiator, water pump, fan, water jacket, thermostat, and temperature warning system. Other parts are radiator pressure cap, coolant recovery system, connecting hoses, heater core, and oil cooler.
- The radiator pressure cap helps prevent the coolant from boiling, which would prevent heat conduction from the interior of the engine.

TERMS

conduction	viscous drive fan
convection	clutch
radiation	thermostatic coil
coolant	bimetallic spring
electrolysis	series
water jacket	parallel
radiator	series-parallel
water pump	thermostat
impeller	coolant bypass
transverse	heater core
longitudinal	heat exchanger

DIRECTIONS: The following questions are similar to those used on mechanic certification tests. On a separate sheet of paper, write the letter of the correct choice.

1. Which methods of heat transfer occur within an engine?
A. Conduction
B. Convection
C. Radiation
D. All of the above

2. Mechanic A says that antifreeze is used in coolant to prevent freezing and boiling.
   Mechanic B says that antifreeze is used in coolant to prevent rust, corrosion, and electrolysis. Who is correct?
A. A only   B. B only   C. Both A and B   D. Neither A nor B

3. When checked, coolant is found in the automatic transmission fluid, and an oily substance is found in the radiator. What is the most likely cause?
A. Blown head gasket
B. Heater hoses and automatic transmission lines crossed
C. Leaking automatic transmission heat exchanger
D. Cracked block or cylinder head

4. Which of the following statements is correct?
   I. The radiator pressure cap helps to prevent the coolant from boiling.
   II. A leak in any part of the cooling system will release pressure and can cause the coolant to boil.
A. I only   B. II only   C. Both I and II   D. Neither I nor II

5. All of the following could cause insufficient heat from a heater EXCEPT
A. a clogged heater core or heater hose.
B. a jammed heater control valve.
C. a thermostat stuck in closed position.
D. a thermostat stuck in open position.

S U P P L E M E N T A L   A C T I V I T I E S

1. On a vehicle chosen by your instructor, locate all externally visible parts of the cooling system. Locate the water pump, fan, radiator and heater hoses, automatic transmission cooler lines, radiator drain, soft plugs, and block drain.
2. Examine vehicles owned by your relatives and friends. Report to your class what the pressure cap markings were and how many had coolant recovery systems.
3. Visit several auto parts stores and make a list of the ingredients listed on bottles of different brands of antifreeze. Report to your class what differences you found.
4. Ask your instructor for permission to use a voltmeter for the following experiment. Cut an orange, lemon, or other citrus fruit in half. Push a penny in one part and a dime in another part of the fruit. Set the voltmeter to the lowest DC voltage scale and connect the leads. Reverse the leads if the meter reads backwards. How much voltage do you observe? What does this experiment have to do with cooling system maintenance?
5. Before the 1950s, radiator pressure caps were rated from 3 to 7 pounds, on the average. Why do you think the pressures were so low?

18 COOLING SYSTEM SERVICE

UNIT PREVIEW

Routine cooling system maintenance consists of checking, repairing, and/or replacing cooling system parts. These parts include drive belts, hoses, gaskets, soft plugs, thermostats, and water pumps.

The coolant should be checked regularly and should be replaced approximately once a year to prevent rust, corrosion, and electrolysis.

In addition to cooling system faults, overheating can be caused by factors outside of the cooling system itself.

LEARNING OBJECTIVES

When you have completed your assignments and exercises in this unit, you should be able to:

☐ Locate, identify, and repair common cooling system leaks.

☐ Check coolant mixture strength.

☐ Detect cooling system leaks, including head gasket leaks.

☐ Replace drive belts.

☐ Replace a thermostat.

☐ Replace a water pump.

☐ Identify and describe the possible causes for overheating.

SAFETY PRECAUTIONS

Wear eye protection when working around heated cooling systems. Hot coolant can cause burns, blisters, and eye damage.

Before attempting to open a radiator cap, touch the metal of the radiator carefully to determine how hot the coolant is. Opening the radiator cap releases the pressure that prevents hot coolant from boiling. Boiling coolant can gush and spurt out of the radiator neck and cause injury. If the radiator is uncomfortably hot to the touch, do not attempt to open the radiator cap until the system cools.

Another way to check for pressure is to squeeze the upper radiator hose. If it feels tight, the system is pressurized.

Remove jewelry from hands, wrists, and around the neck. Roll up long sleeves tightly or change into a short-sleeved shirt or blouse when working around the fan and/or belts. Remember that the fan blades cannot be seen when they are spinning.

Caution: Electrically-driven fans can start at any time, including after the engine is shut off. Disconnect electrical fan power connections before attempting removal procedures.

The main ingredient in antifreeze, ethylene glycol, is poisonous if swallowed. Under some circumstances ethylene glycol is flammable. To avoid being burned, do not spill antifreeze on hot exhaust system parts when adding liquid to the cooling system.

18.1 COOLING SYSTEM PREVENTIVE MAINTENANCE

Routine preventive maintenance for the cooling system consists of the following procedures:

- Check and/or replace drive belts
- Check and/or repair leaks
- Check coolant mixture strength
- Flush old coolant and refill the system with fresh coolant
- Replace thermostat.

18.2 CHECK AND/OR REPLACE DRIVE BELTS

A drive belt, often called a *V-belt*, is so named because its cross-sectional shape resembles the letter V. A drive belt transfers force through friction between the *sides* of the belt and the pulley flanges. Refer to Figure 18-1.

Belt Condition

To transfer adequate force, drive belts must be in good condition and properly tightened. To check belt condition, twist the belt in your hands and look for defects as illustrated in Figure 18-2.

Belt Tension

A V-belt does not require extreme tightening to transmit turning force. However, an excessively loose belt will slip, cause a squealing noise, and eventually become *glazed,* or smooth. The friction surfaces of a glazed belt are too slick to transfer force properly.

Belts can be checked for proper tension with a tension gauge, or by pressing on the belt with your fingers, as shown in Figure 18-3.

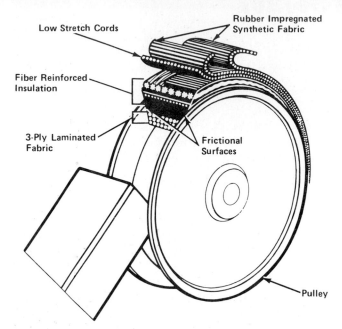

Figure 18-1. Parts of a drive belt. CHRYSLER CORPORATION

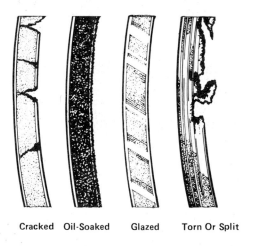

Cracked   Oil-Soaked   Glazed   Torn Or Split

Figure 18-2. Drive belt defects. CHRYSLER CORPORATION

Belts can be replaced or belt tension adjusted by moving an idler pulley toward or away from the power pulley. In most cases, the idler pulley is the alternator drive pulley. A bottom pivot bolt and top adjustment bolt on the alternator unit must be loosened. The alternator must be pushed inward or outward. See Figure 18-4. Any other belts in front of the belt to be replaced must be removed first.

A loosened belt to be replaced must be worked off from the pulleys and from around the fan. A new belt is replaced in the proper pulley grooves. The pivoting idler unit then is pulled away from the engine to tighten the belt. When the belt tension is correct, the adjustment bolt and pivot bolt are tightened.

After approximately 200 miles of use, new belts will stretch. They should be checked and retightened if necessary.

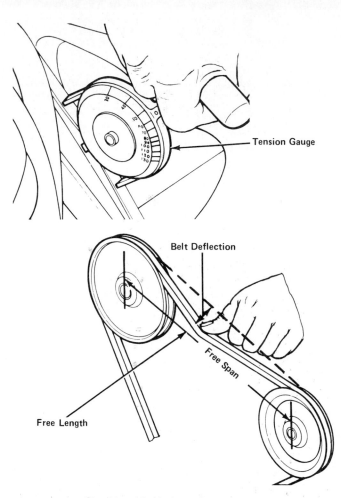

Figure 18-3. Checking drive belt tension. CHRYSLER CORPORATION

18.3 CHECK FOR AND/OR REPAIR LEAKS

Loss of pressure and/or leaks can occur at many locations within the cooling system. Some leaks occur when the system is cold and parts are contracted to form gaps. Other leaks occur when the system is hot and under pressure. The following areas are the most common sources of leaks:

- Hoses
- Gaskets
- Radiator
- Heater core and heater control valve
- Water pump
- Soft plugs.

Pressure Checks

Even small leaks will allow pressure to be lost from the cooling system. Loss of pressure will cause the coolant to boil at a lower temperature. A *cooling system pressure tester,* shown in Figure 18-5, can be used to check cooling system pressure up to the limit held by the radiator cap. A cooling system pressure tester consists of an air pump and a gauge. Pressure

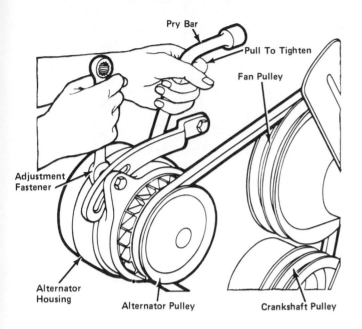

Figure 18-4. Drive belt replacement. CHRYSLER CORPORATION

is created by pumping the handle. If leakage occurs, the gauge pressure reading will drop.

The pressure tester can be used to check both the cooling system and the radiator cap. If the pressure reading drops when connected to the radiator, look for external leaks. Check hoses, soft plugs, the water pump, and so forth. If the radiator cap will not hold its rated pressure, replace the cap.

If no external leaks are found, check for internal leaks. Remove the oil dipstick and check for water—which shows up as a milky color.

Head gasket leakage, explained below, may be detected by connecting the pressure tester to the radiator neck, applying low pressure, and running the engine at slow speeds. Excessive pressure buildup indicates that combustion chamber gases are entering the cooling system.

Hoses

Hoses are made of layers of rubber and cloth. Rubber is subject to deterioration from heat, vibration, and from oil and fuel vapors. Hoses are manufactured as either molded or flexible types. See Figure 18-6.

Check hoses for leakage, hardening, swelling, or *chafing,* as shown in Figure 18-7.

Several types of hose clamps are used, as shown in Figure 18-8. The *worm-drive clamp* can be reused and tightened without loss of holding power, unlike the other types shown. When replacing hoses, a good policy is to replace wire or banded clamps with worm-drive clamps. Hose replacement is illustrated in Figure 18-9.

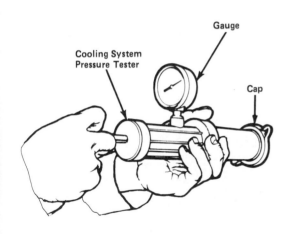

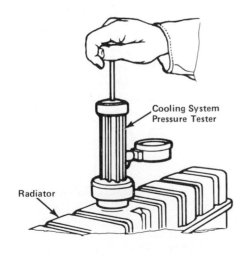

Figure 18-5. Pressure testing a cooling system.
CHRYSLER CORPORATION

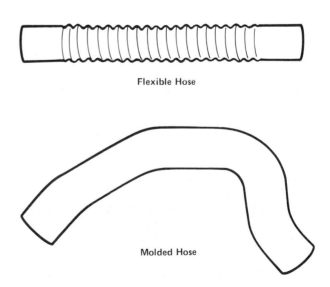

Figure 18-6. Cooling system hoses. CHRYSLER CORPORATION

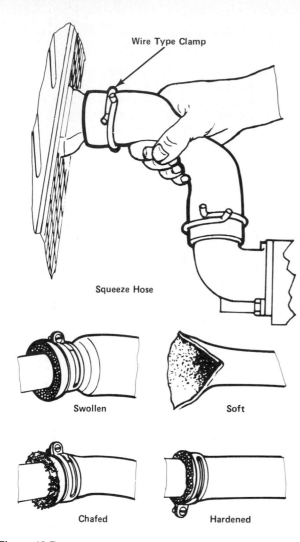

Wire Type Clamp

Squeeze Hose

Swollen

Soft

Chafed

Hardened

Figure 18-7. Defects in cooling system hoses.
CHRYSLER CORPORATION

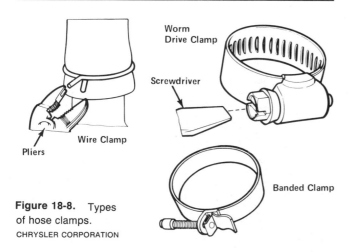

Worm
Drive Clamp

Screwdriver

Wire Clamp

Pliers

Banded Clamp

Figure 18-8. Types
of hose clamps.
CHRYSLER CORPORATION

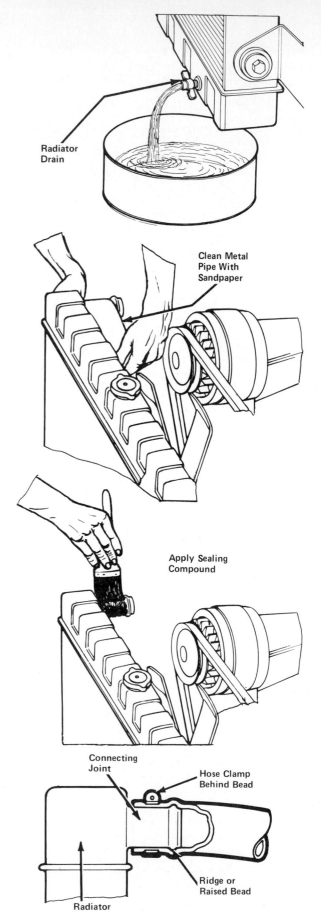

Radiator
Drain

Clean Metal
Pipe With
Sandpaper

Apply Sealing
Compound

Connecting
Joint

Hose Clamp
Behind Bead

Ridge or
Raised Bead

Radiator

Figure 18-9. Cooling system hose replacement.
CHRYSLER CORPORATION

CAUTION: Be careful when removing hoses, especially radiator hoses, to avoid damaging the hose sealing surface. Do not use a screwdriver or excessive force on the new radiators with "plastic" tanks. They are quite fragile and easily damaged.

Gaskets

Gaskets that can cause cooling system leaks and problems include the following:

- Radiator pressure cap
- Water outlet (thermostat gasket)
- Water pump gasket
- Cylinder head gasket.

Radiator pressure cap. Inspect the radiator pressure cap rubber seals and vacuum relief valve as shown in Figure 18-10. If the seals are cracked, stiff, or brittle, or the vacuum valve is sticky or broken, replace the cap. Check the radiator neck for bent, broken, or otherwise damaged flanges. If not badly damaged, radiator necks can be repaired.

Other gaskets. If thermostat, water pump, and/or cylinder head gaskets are leaking, the units themselves are replaced or reconditioned before replacement.

Thermostat and water pump gasket replacement are explained below. Head gasket replacement is covered in Unit 44, Cylinder Head Service.

Leakage around the thermostat and water pump gaskets can be found by visual inspection during a cooling system pressure test.

Head gasket. Indications of a blown head gasket include:

- Coolant on the engine oil dipstick
- Oily deposits inside the radiator neck
- Coolant on the spark plug firing tips after the engine has cooled overnight.

Suspected head gasket leaks can be verified by use of a *combustion leak detector,* shown in Figure 18-11. Enough coolant is drained from the radiator to leave at least a 1-inch space above the fluid. Then, the engine is started. Special test fluid is poured into the tester. The bulb then is squeezed to draw gases from above the coolant through the test fluid. If combustion chamber gases are present, indicating a blown head gasket, the fluid will change color.

Another method for detecting head gasket leakage is to use the probe of an *exhaust gas analyzer* over the radiator neck to detect combustion chamber gases. An exhaust gas analyzer is an electronic diagnostic instrument used to determine amounts of harmful gases in engine exhaust fumes. This is discussed in Unit 43.

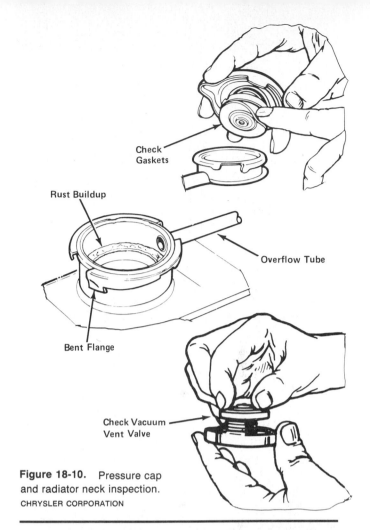

Figure 18-10. Pressure cap and radiator neck inspection.
CHRYSLER CORPORATION

Figure 18-11. Combustion leak detector for checking head gasket leaks.

Radiator

Most radiator leak repairs require the removal of the radiator from the vehicle. The coolant must be drained and all hoses and oil cooler lines disconnected. Bolts holding the radiator are loosened and removed.

The radiator inlet and outlet tanks and core are joined together. At the *seams,* or lines of contact, leaks can occur. In the past, most radiators were made of metals, such as brass and copper, that can be *soldered,* or joined, to prevent leaks, replace tanks, or replace radiator cores.

Soldering is a process of using heat, a cleaning substance called *flux,* and *solder* to join parts. Solder is an alloy, or mixture, of lead and tin. When cleaned metal parts are heated sufficiently, applied solder will melt and join the parts together.

However, the aluminum radiators used on many modern automobiles cannot be soldered. In addition, plastic inlet and outlet tanks are used on newer vehicles with brass or aluminum cores. On such radiators, metals tabs on the core are *crimped,* or tightly bent, to join the tanks to the core. A rubber O-ring seal prevents leaks, as shown in Figure 18-12.

Figure 18-13 shows one type of crimping operation used to join the core to a radiator tank.

If the metal is sound and sufficiently thick, radiator core tube leaks can be repaired. Radiator cores with badly corroded tubes must be replaced.

Brass or copper tubes can be soldered. Aluminum cores can be patched with an *epoxy resin* plastic cement. Epoxy resin is a hardening agent that forms a strong, hard bond when it sets. An epoxy repair is illustrated in Figure 18-14.

Oil coolers in the outlet tank can be replaced or repaired when the tank is removed from the core.

Heater Core and Heater Control Valve

Heater core repairs are performed in the same way as radiator repairs. Leaks from heater cores usually show up inside the vehicle, on the front passenger floor space under the dash.

Heater control valve. Stuck heater control valves often can be lubricated with light oil and manually moved to allow them to operate freely. Removing a leaking control valve simply involves loosening clamps, removing hoses, and unfastening the old valve. Replacement is essentially the reverse of this procedure. A typical heater control valve is shown in Figure 18-15.

Water Pump

The water pump shaft turns on anti-friction ball bearings that are lubricated by a sealed lubricant supply. If the seals fail, coolant will wash the lubricant from the bearings and cause them to become ruined. In addition, coolant can leak from around the front of the shaft and from the *weep hole.* The weep hole is the ventilation hole located at the bottom of the shaft housing.

On a running engine, ruined, noisy water pump bearings can be heard through a mechanic's stethoscope or rubber tubing.

SAFETY CAUTION: Whenever you work near a running engine, keep your hands and clothing away from the moving fan, belts, and pulleys. Do not

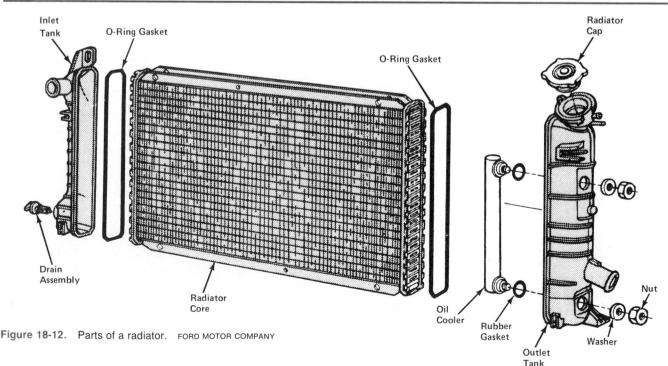

Figure 18-12. Parts of a radiator. FORD MOTOR COMPANY

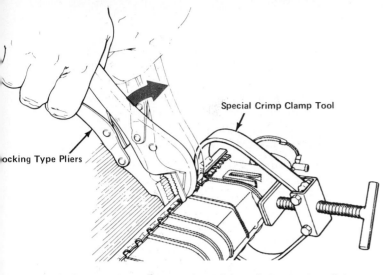

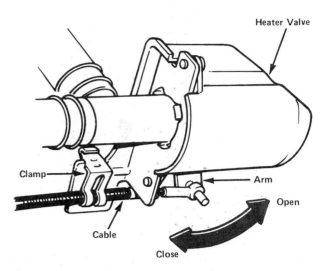

Figure 18-13. Crimping operation to join radiator core to radiator tank. FORD MOTOR COMPANY

Figure 18-15. Heater control valve assembly.
HONDA MOTOR COMPANY

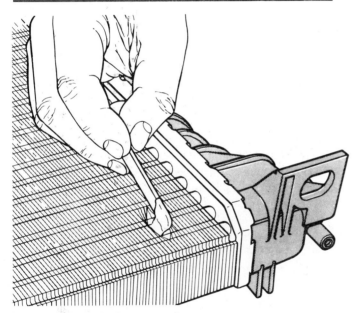

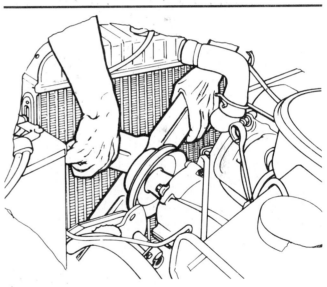

Figure 18-14. Applying epoxy repair material to seal a radiator core. FORD MOTOR COMPANY

Figure 18-16. Checking water pump bearings.
CHRYSLER CORPORATION

allow the stethoscope or rubber tubing to be caught by moving parts.

There is another test that can be performed with the engine off and the fan belt removed. This involves grasping the fan and attempting to move it in and out and up and down. See Figure 18-16. More than $\frac{1}{16}$ inch (1.6 mm) of movement indicates worn bearings that require water pump replacement.

Special tools are available to loosen bolts that attach fan blades and viscous drive units with the radiator in place. Water pump removal with the radiator in place requires that the fan and spacer or viscous drive unit be removed first. Use caution to avoid damaging the radiator.

Soft Plugs

Insufficient fresh coolant can cause soft plugs in the block and/or cylinder head to rust or corrode through. This will cause leaks, as shown in Figure 18-17.

Gaining access to soft plugs may require removing engine accessories and/or intake or exhaust manifolds. In difficult cases, it may be necessary to remove the entire engine.

Rusted or corroded soft plugs can be removed by driving a punch through the metal plug. The punch then is used as a lever to remove the old plugs. The cooling system should be drained before this procedure is begun.

Special tools and drivers are available to help the mechanic drive in soft plugs in difficult locations.

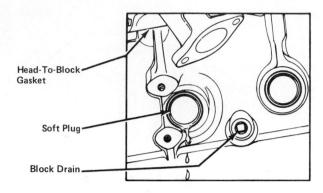

Head-To-Block Gasket

Soft Plug

Block Drain

Figure 18-17. Engine block soft plugs. CHRYSLER CORPORATION

18.4 CHECK COOLANT MIXTURE

Coolant mixtures can be checked with a *coolant hydrometer,* shown in Figure 18-18. A coolant hydrometer measures the freezing point of the mixture of antifreeze and water. For example, a half-and-half mixture has a freezing point of – 34 degrees F [– 36.6 degrees C].

A higher freezing temperature would indicate more than 50% water, because pure water has a freezing point of + 32 degrees F [0 degrees C].

Different percentages of antifreeze can be mixed with water to prevent freezing at varying temperatures. Refer to the charts printed on antifreeze containers. However, never use 100% antifreeze in a cooling system. In severely cold temperatures, pure antifreeze will gel, or thicken, and will not flow through the system. In addition, the use of 100% antifreeze can cause boiling in hot weather.

To change the proportion of antifreeze to water in the coolant mixture, liquid must be drained from the system so that additional antifreeze can be added. Coolant mixtures more than one year old should be flushed and replaced with fresh coolant.

18.5 FLUSH COOLING SYSTEM

Before flushing is done, chemical cleaners can be added to the cooling system to help dissolve rust and scale deposits. Two types of cleaners are commonly used for this purpose.

Heavy-duty cooling system cleaners consist of powdered phosphoric acid. The thermostat must be removed to prevent damage before heavy-duty cleaners are used. After use, a chemical neutralizer (baking soda) is put into the system to neutralize any remaining phosphoric acid before flushing.

SAFETY CAUTION: **Be careful not to inhale fumes when pouring the powdered cleaner into the radiator. If powder gets on skin, wash the area right away. Wear safety glasses.**

Liquid cooling system cleaners consist of a milder solution of phosphoric acid dissolved in water and mixed with detergent. Liquid cleaners can be used without removing the thermostat. The flushing procedure removes the cleaning solution.

Reverse flushing is a procedure of forcing clean liquid backwards through the cooling system. This carries away rust, scale, corrosion, and other contaminants. A *flushing gun* that operates on compressed air is used to force clean water and air through the system. See Figure 18-19.

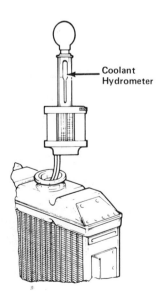

Coolant Hydrometer

Figure 18-18. Checking coolant mixture with a coolant hydrometer. CHRYSLER CORPORATION

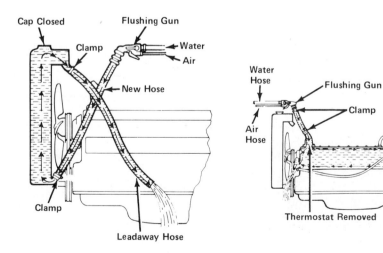

Cap Closed   Flushing Gun

Clamp   Water

Air

New Hose

Clamp

Clamp

Leadaway Hose

Water Hose

Flushing Gun

Air Hose

Clamp

Thermostat Removed

Figure 18-19. Reverse flushing a cooling system. CHRYSLER CORPORATION

18.6 REPLACE THERMOSTAT

Thermostats should be replaced, as illustrated in Figure 18-20, approximately every two years. Markings on the thermostat indicate which end should face toward the radiator. The sensored end always must be installed toward the engine.

If a thermostat is more than two years old, or there is any doubt about its operation, replace the thermostat.

18.7 REPLACE WATER PUMP

The cooling system must be drained before water pump removal. Vehicles with belt-driven fans have components that must be removed to permit access to the water pump. These components include belts, the fan and spacer or viscous drive clutch, and other engine accessories. In many cases, the radiator and *shroud,* shown in Figure 18-21, must be removed to gain access to the water pump. A shroud is a hollow duct that helps to direct air toward the fan for better cooling.

The water pump is attached to the cylinder block as shown in Figure 18-22. Loosen and remove the bolts in a crisscross pattern from the center outward.

Insert a rag into the block opening and scrape off any remains of the old gasket. Apply the vehicle manufacturer's recommended sealant to the new gasket and sealing surfaces. Insert the bolts by hand, then tighten in a crisscross pattern, from the center outward, to the manufacturer's recommended torque.

18.8 OVERHEATING PROBLEMS

Overheating can be caused by many factors. Typical causes include:

- Cooling system clogged by rust, corrosion, or scale deposits
- Loose or slipping fan belt
- Improper operation of a viscous fan drive clutch
- Pressure loss through leaks (including defective radiator cap)
- Thermostat installed incorrectly
- Airflow through radiator blocked
- Incorrect mixture of coolant
- Heavy loads imposed by using the air conditioner, carrying excess weight, or towing trailers
- Incorrect ignition timing and/or carburetor adjustment
- Engine vacuum leaks
- Automatic transmission overheating.

Only the first seven causes involve the cooling system itself. The remaining causes involve other systems or parts of the automobile. The mechanic must be prepared to look past the obvious causes in diagnosing overheating problems.

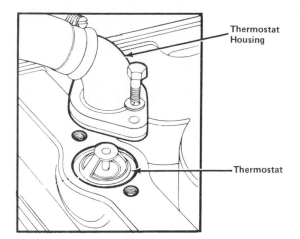

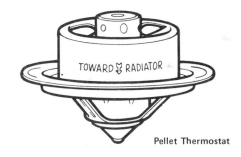

Pellet Thermostat

Figure 18-20. Thermostat installation. CHRYSLER CORPORATION

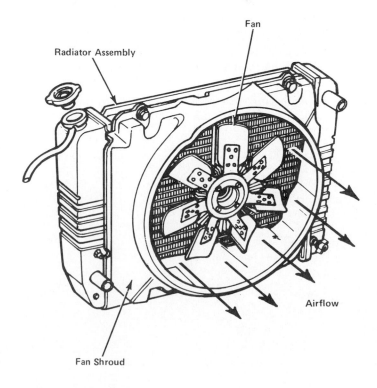

Figure 18-21. Radiator, shroud, and cooling fan assembly.
CHRYSLER CORPORATION

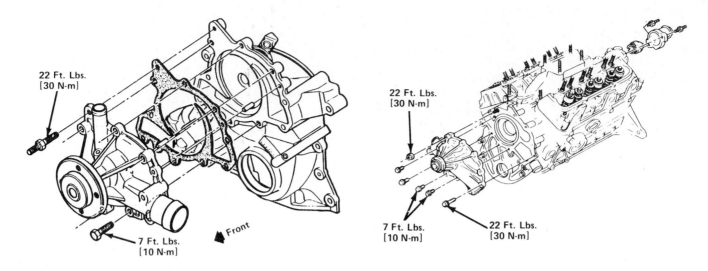

Figure 18-22. Water pump mounting assembly. BUICK MOTOR DIVISION—GMC

U N I T H I G H L I G H T S	T E R M S

- Routine cooling system maintenance includes checking and/or replacing of drive belts, and checking and/or repairing leaks. Other routine maintenance procedures include: determining coolant mixture strength, replacing thermostats, replacing the antifreeze, and flushing the cooling system.

- Leaks can be detected by visual inspection or by using a cooling system pressure tester.

- Leaking thermostat, water pump, and cylinder head gaskets usually indicate more than the need to replace the gaskets. Replacing or reconditioning of the affected units also may be required.

- Overheating can be caused by many problems, some of which are not directly related to the cooling system.

TERMS

V-belt
glazed
cooling system pressure
  tester
chafing
worm-drive clamp
combustion leak
  detector
exhaust gas analyzer
seam
solder

crimp
epoxy resin
weep hole
coolant hydrometer
heavy-duty cooling
  system cleaner
liquid cooling system
  cleaner
reverse flushing
flushing gun
shroud

R E V I E W   Q U E S T I O N S

DIRECTIONS: The following questions are similar to those used on mechanic certification tests. On a separate sheet of paper, write the letter of the correct choice.

1. Mechanic A says drive belts can become glazed if they are installed too loosely.
   Mechanic B says drive belts can become glazed if they are installed too tightly.
   Who is correct?
   A. A only   B. B only   C. Both A and B   D. Neither A nor B

2. Which of the following statements is correct?
   I. When tested, a radiator pressure cap should open at its indicated limit and release pressure.
   II. When tested, a radiator pressure cap should hold pressure up to its indicated limit.
   A. I only   B. II only   C. Both I and II   D. Neither I nor II

3. All of the following can be used to detect a blown head gasket EXCEPT
   A. visual inspection and/or cooling system pressure tester.
   B. combustion leak detector or exhaust gas analyzer.
   C. cylinder compression or leak-down test.
   D. oil pressure tester.

4. All of the following indicate water pump seal and/or bearing problems EXCEPT
   A. excessive movement of water pump shaft.
   B. leakage from a water pump weep hole.
   C. excessive noise from water pump bearings when the engine is running.
   D. free spinning of a viscous fan drive clutch when warm.

5. Which of the following could cause overheating?
   A. Automatic transmission problems
   B. Use of radial tires
   C. Manual transmission problems
   D. Weak battery

S U P P L E M E N T A L   A C T I V I T I E S

1. Inspect a vehicle's cooling system and use a pressure tester to diagnose possible problems. Report to your class what problems were found during inspection.
2. Check drive belts on a vehicle for proper tension. Remove and replace all belts and tighten them to the proper tension.
3. Perform visual inspection on a vehicle to detect head gasket problems. With the equipment available in your shop, make tests to verify whether the vehicle has a blown or leaky head gasket.
4. Clean, flush, and replace the thermostat and radiator hoses on a vehicle.
5. Check for damaged water pump seals and/or bearings. Report the results of each test to your class.
6. Replace the water pump on a vehicle.

19 FUEL SYSTEM FUNDAMENTALS

UNIT PREVIEW

To provide proper performance, automotive fuels must have several characteristics. Gasoline and diesel fuel are the most widely used petroleum-based motor fuels.

A basic fuel system includes a fuel tank, fuel pump, filters, and parts to meter liquid fuel properly. Devices can be used to pressurize the intake manifold to produce a denser intake charge and more powerful combustion pressures. These devices are being used increasingly on smaller-displacement engines to produce better horsepower and torque output.

LEARNING OBJECTIVES

When you have completed your assignments and exercises in this unit, you should be able to:

☐ Identify and describe the characteristics of gasoline and diesel motor fuels.

☐ Explain the causes of abnormal combustion in gasoline and diesel engines.

☐ Visually identify and describe the parts of a basic fuel system on a vehicle.

☐ Explain the difference between different types of gasoline fuel injection and diesel fuel injection.

☐ Identify and describe the main parts of a turbocharger, and explain its function.

19.1 AUTOMOTIVE FUELS

Fuels used in automotive engines include petroleum fuels such as gasoline, diesel fuel, propane, and butane. Alcohol-type fuels, such as methanol and ethanol, also can be used. In addition, approximately 10% alcohol can be mixed with 90% gasoline to produce a *gasohol* blend.

CAUTION: **Some fuel system components designed for use exclusively with gasoline may not be compatible with alcohol or gasohol fuels. These include rubber, plastic, and some metal parts. Use of alcohol or gasohol fuels may damage or destroy such parts, causing fuel system failure.**

19.2 GASOLINE

Gasoline is the most widely used motor fuel. Gasoline, like other petroleum fuels, is a compound of hydrogen and carbon atoms, known as *hydrocarbon (HC)* molecules. To perform well as a motor fuel, gasoline must have several properties, including:

- Correct volatility and resistance to ice formation
- Resistance to abnormal combustion
- Chemical stability
- Low sulfur content.

Volatility

A gasoline engine runs on a vapor composed of gasoline and air. Gasoline molecules become atomized and mixed with air molecules in the carburetor and/or intake manifold to form this vapor. A liquid that evaporates easily is said to be *volatile*. Liquids, including gasoline, become more volatile as they are heated.

Petroleum refineries anticipate the air temperatures to be encountered and blend gasolines for the correct volatility for engine performance. In cold weather, gasoline must have greater volatility to vaporize more easily at low temperatures for easy starting and running. In warm temperatures, too volatile a gasoline blend produces combustion problems.

Gasoline must be delivered in a liquid form to the parts of the fuel system that atomize it. If the fuel vaporizes before it reaches the carburetor or fuel injection system, *vapor lock* will stop the engine. Vapor lock is the formation of bubbles of vaporized fuel, blocking the flow of liquid fuel in the fuel system.

Gasoline also will vaporize more easily at lower atmospheric pressures, such as at high altitudes. Gasoline refineries produce different blends of gasoline for different geographical and temperature regions and altitudes to prevent as many problems as possible. Blends are changed three times a year.

De-icers. Water vapor from the air condenses on the inside of the gasoline tank. Water eventually will settle at the bottom of the fuel tank, fuel lines, fuel pump, and carburetor or fuel injection pump.

When the temperature drops low enough, ice crystals can form, blocking the flow of gasoline, especially where atomization takes place. To prevent this problem, chemical *de-icers* are added to prevent ice particles from forming and adhering to cold metal surfaces.

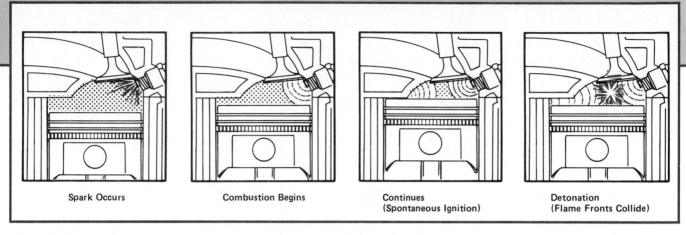

Figure 19-1. Combustion chamber detonation. CHAMPION SPARK PLUG COMPANY

Spark Occurs   Combustion Begins   Continues (Spontaneous Ignition)   Detonation (Flame Fronts Collide)

Resistance to Abnormal Combustion

Normal combustion begins with a spark from a spark plug. The combustion continues evenly until nearly all of the fuel in the combustion chamber is burned. Combustion is discussed in Unit 10.

Detonation. Increased heat and pressure are created as the flame front from combustion moves across the combustion chamber from the spark plug. This heat and pressure can cause the remaining gases to explode, or *detonate*, after the spark plug fires. See Figure 19-1.

For maximum power output, maximum combustion pressure should be produced just after the piston reaches TDC. Detonation interferes with this controlled combustion process. Detonation also causes excess heat and pressure on the piston crown at the wrong time.

When detonation occurs, a knocking or hammering sound is heard. However, detonation that occurs at high speeds generally cannot be heard because of engine and road noise.

Severe detonation can lead to holes melted and blown through the top of the piston crown. Even mild detonation decreases fuel economy because the combustion pressures build and peak erratically.

Automotive engineers design engines so that, under normal conditions, detonation is prevented while engine efficiency is maintained. Key elements include shapes of combustion chambers and pistons, compression ratios, intake charge flow patterns, ignition timing, and fuel specifications. Such designs promote *swirl*, a circular or whirlpool-shaped flow, that helps fuel mix with air more completely, and *turbulence*. Turbulence is an irregular pattern of flow. Swirl and turbulence are used to promote better vaporization and combustion and reduce detonation. See Figure 19-2.

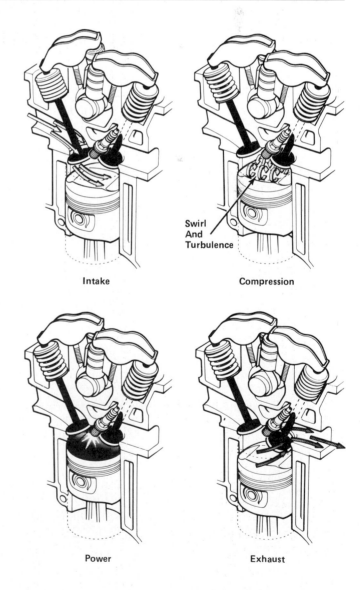

Intake   Compression

Swirl And Turbulence

Power   Exhaust

Figure 19-2. Combustion chambers are designed to encourage swirl and turbulence and reduce detonation. FORD MOTOR COMPANY

An engine's tendency to detonate is increased by the following factors:

- High compression ratios
- Ignition spark that occurs too soon
- Lean air-fuel mixtures
- Low humidity
- Overheating.

Octane rating. *Octane rating* is a measure of a motor fuel's ability to resist ignition through heat and pressure (anti-knock quality). *Iso-octane* is a hydrocarbon fuel that is assigned an octane rating of 100. Gasoline octane ratings are related to this standard. The higher the octane rating, the more the gasoline matches (or in the case of aviation gasoline for airplanes, exceeds) iso-octane's resistance to ignition through heat and pressure.

Two methods are used to determine octane ratings, the Research method and the Motor method. Both methods use a standardized variable-compression, single-cylinder, fuel research engine. The Research method, which produces the Research Octane Number (RON), operates at relatively low speed and low inlet air temperatures. The Motor method, which produces the Motor Octane Number (MON), operates at higher speeds and higher air inlet temperatures. The Research method rating numbers usually are 4 to 6 points higher than those for the Motor method.

The octane ratings on EPA (Environmental Protection Agency) required stickers on gasoline pumps reflect an average of the two methods: R(Research) + M(Motor) ÷ 2.

Chemicals can be added to gasoline to increase octane rating. Beginning in 1915, *tetraethyl lead* was added to gasoline. Such *leaded gasolines* in the late 1960s achieved octane ratings as high as 102, measured by the Research method.

However, lead poisons the air and causes health problems. Although currently still available, leaded fuels ("regular" and "premium leaded") will no longer be produced after 1990.

Beginning in the mid-1970s, engines and emission (smog) control systems were redesigned to run on lower-octane unleaded fuel. Different methods of refining and different chemical additives produce unleaded gasoline with averaged octane ratings of from 87 to 92.

If no detonation problems occur, higher-octane fuel will neither cause the engine to run better nor improve fuel economy.

Preignition. Deposits in the combustion chamber can cause *preignition*, or "ping" or "knock." Preignition occurs when a glowing deposit or metal part becomes heated enough to begin ignition *before* a spark plug fires. See Figure 19-3.

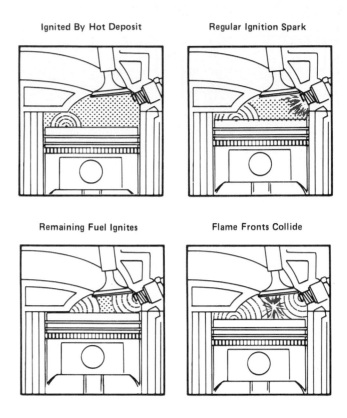

Figure 19-3. Combustion chamber pre-ignition.
CHAMPION SPARK PLUG COMPANY

Preignition can be caused by any of the following:

- Low-octane fuel used in an engine with a high compression ratio
- Hot carbon deposits in the combustion chamber from burned gasoline or oil
- An overheated sharp metal edge.

Preignition can cause holes to be melted and blown through piston crowns and lead to other physical damage. The symptoms and results of preignition and detonation are very similar and often are confused.

As an engine is used, deposits form on the piston crown and within the combustion chamber. Deposits on older engines that used leaded gasoline were relatively soft and would flake off beyond a certain depth. In addition, lead in gasoline served as a "lubricant" to cushion the impact of valve faces against valve seats. Newer vehicles, using unleaded gasoline, must employ harder materials, such as Stellite and stainless steel, for valve heads and seats. Cast-iron heads use induction-hardened valve seats. Deposits in engines that use unleaded gasoline are much harder and do not flake off as easily.

Combustion chamber deposit buildup of any kind causes an increase in compression ratio. The more deposits in the combustion chamber, the higher octane fuel the engine requires to prevent preignition and detonation. Combustion chamber designs with greater quench areas reduce tendencies toward detonation and preignition.

Dieseling. *Dieseling,* or *run-on,* in gasoline engines is caused by excessive heat within the combusion chamber and/or excessive rpm. Dieseling occurs when combustion chamber parts or deposits are hot enough to provide ignition after spark ignition stops. Cooling the combustion chamber, slowing the engine, and using a higher-octane gasoline all can help prevent dieseling.

Chemical Stability

Gasoline molecules tend to degrade, or break down, and form heavy, gummy deposits. These deposits can coat valve stems, valve lifters, carburetor parts, and piston rings. Improved chemical processes have increased gasoline's chemical stability and reduced its tendency to form deposits.

Low Sulfur Content

As discussed under Topic 16.1, sulfur in combination with water forms sulfuric acid. Sulfur levels in gasoline and lubricating oil depend upon geographic areas from which petroleum comes and the refining processes used. Excessive sulfur also can reduce the effectiveness of additives that are used to raise the octane rating.

19.3 BASIC FUEL SYSTEM

A basic fuel system, illustrated in Figure 19-4, consists of the following components:

- Fuel tank
- Connecting lines
- Fuel pump
- Fuel filter
- Air filter
- Fuel metering and atomization system.

Fuel Tank

The fuel tank is made either of pressed sheet metal with welded seams or of a reinforced plastic material. A filler neck with a cap allows fuel to be added, as shown in Figure 19-5.

An electrical fuel gauge sender is located in the tank and operates in basically the same way as an oil-pressure or water-temperature gauge sender. A diagram of such a unit is shown in Figure 19-6.

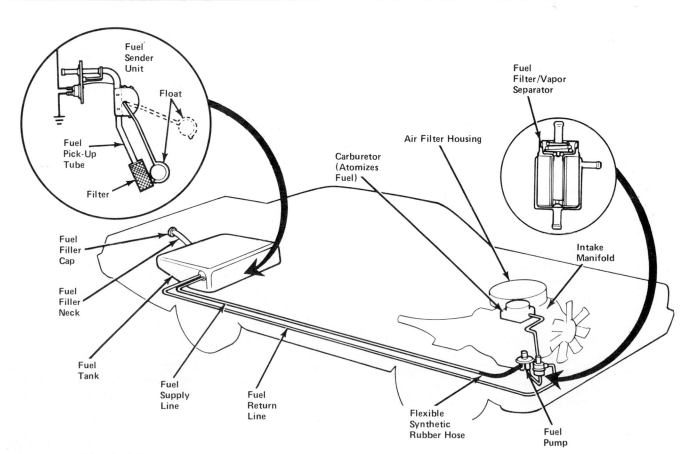

Figure 19-4. Parts of a fuel system. CHRYSLER CORPORATION

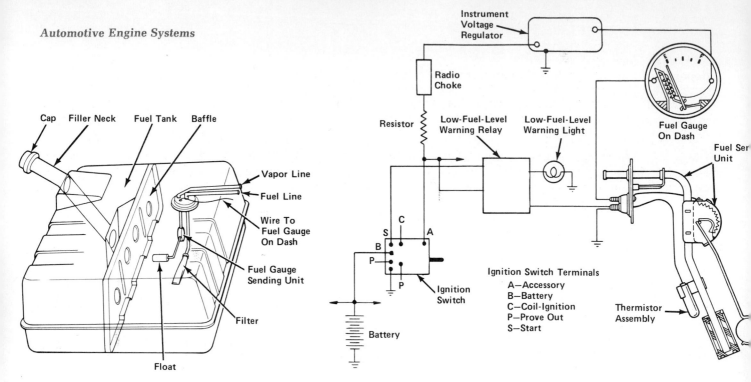

Figure 19-5. Parts of a fuel tank.

Figure 19-6. Fuel gauge system.

Connecting Lines

Small-diameter metal tubing and synthetic rubber hoses connect the fuel tank to the fuel pump. Synthetic rubber hoses are used where vibration might crack or bend metal lines.

Fuel Pump

The fuel metering and atomization system is located higher in the vehicle than the fuel tank. A mechanical or electrical pump is used to draw the fuel from the tank and deliver it to the carburetor or fuel injection system.

Mechanical pump. A *mechanical fuel pump* is driven by engine power, usually from the camshaft. The power is transmitted either through an eccentric lobe or a lobe, pushrod, and rocker arm arrangement. See Figure 19-7.

Mechanical pumps produce suction by moving a synthetic rubber diaphragm against a spring inside a closed housing. This action produces a low-pressure area and draws fuel into the housing through a one-way valve. As the camshaft turns, the spring expands. This forces the diaphragm in the opposite direction, pushing the fuel out of the pump through another one-way valve.

Mechanical pumps in the engine compartment are subject to heat. In addition, during fuel intake, a low-pressure area is created in the fuel line. Both conditions can lead to vapor lock. Many modern mechanical fuel pumps include a *fuel vapor separator* and vapor return line to the fuel tank. These components reduce the tendency toward vapor lock.

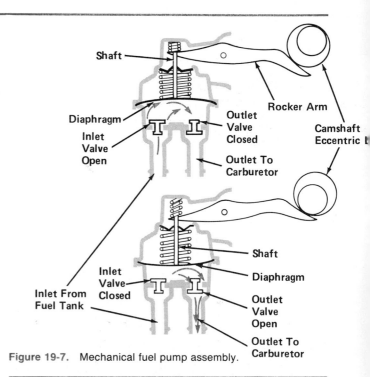

Figure 19-7. Mechanical fuel pump assembly.

Electrical pump. There are two types of electrical pumps, shown in Figure 19-8. One type is an *impeller pump* that operates like a water pump. The second type operates like a mechanical fuel pump, except that a magnetic field is used to produce the force to compress a spring and move a synthetic rubber diaphragm.

Electrical pumps often are mounted at or in the fuel tank to protect them from heat. In addition, impeller-type pumps keep the fuel line pressurized at

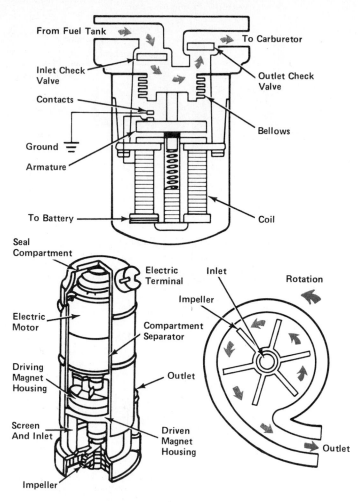

Figure 19-8. Parts of an electrical fuel pump.
FORD MOTOR COMPANY

all times to reduce vapor formation that can lead to vapor lock.

Fuel Filter

Moisture and contaminants can collect in the fuel tank. Particles of rust from the tank can clog fuel lines and small passages in the fuel metering and atomization system. A screen is located in the fuel tank over the fuel outlet. One or more *fuel filters* in the system trap sediment, rust particles, and other contaminants that leave the tank.

Fuel filters can be located anywhere between the fuel in the tank and the carburetor or fuel-injection system intake. See Figure 19-9.

Air Filter

Air contains dust and dirt particles and other contaminants. To prevent contaminants from entering the engine with the air-fuel mixture, an *air filter* is mounted in a housing. See Figure 19-10. Air drawn in on the intake stroke passes through the housing and filter, to a carburetor or fuel-injection system. The resulting air-fuel mixture then passes through an intake manifold into the cylinders.

Fuel Atomization and Vaporization Systems

The fuel system should provide the correct air-fuel mixture to operate the engine efficiently at varying speeds and loads. This mixture is expressed as a number of parts of air to one part of gasoline. At sea level, the chemically correct mixture is 14.7 parts of air to 1 part of gasoline, measured by weight. This

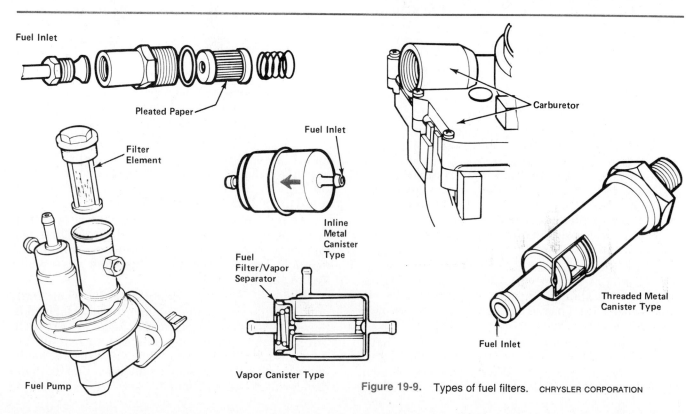

Figure 19-9. Types of fuel filters. CHRYSLER CORPORATION

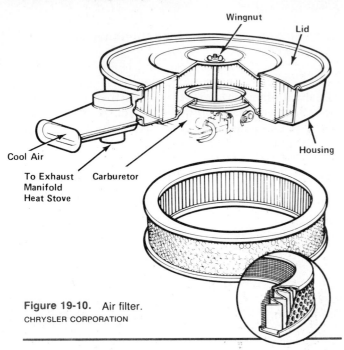

Figure 19-10. Air filter.
CHRYSLER CORPORATION

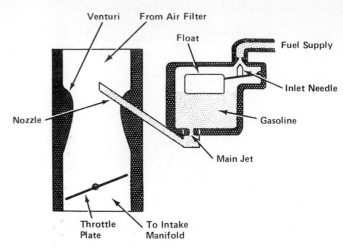

Figure 19-11. Basic carburetor assembly.
CHEVROLET MOTOR DIVISION—GMC

may be expressed by the ratio 14.7:1. A chemically correct air-fuel mixture is called *stoichiometric.* At higher elevations, air contains less oxygen. Thus, more parts of air are required for complete combustion.

Air-fuel ratios with higher concentrations of air, such as 16:1, 18:1, or 20:1, are called *lean mixtures.* Air-fuel ratios with fewer parts of air to gasoline, such as 12:1, 10:1, or 8:1, are called *rich mixtures.* Beyond these lean and rich limits, the engine will not run properly.

During warm-up and on heavy acceleration, the engine requires a mixture as rich as 11.5:1. After warm-up and during low-load cruising, mixtures as lean as 18:1 can be used. However, the most power for the amount of fuel consumed occurs at an air-fuel ratio of 14.7:1 (at sea level).

Carburetor

A *carburetor* is a vacuum-operated device that supplies a fine spray of gasoline into the incoming air stream. The amount of gasoline drawn in by vacuum is proportional to the amount of air drawn through the *barrel* of the carburetor. The barrel is the throat opening or *throttle bore.* The amount of air that passes through the carburetor can be controlled by operating a movable valve called a *throttle plate* in an opening at the bottom of the carburetor bore.

A low-pressure area can be created by narrowing the opening at a point within the bore. See Figure 19-11. To maintain a constant volume of flow, air must speed up as it passes through this *venturi,* or narrow restriction.

A tube end placed within the venturi will have suction, or vacuum, applied to it. If the opposite end is in a supply of gasoline, the gasoline is drawn through the tube, into the venturi. See Figure 19-12.

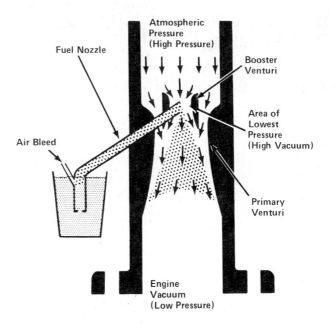

Figure 19-12. Carburetor venturi principle.
CHEVROLET MOTOR DIVISION—GMC

The end of the tube is designed and placed so the fuel is drawn out in a finely atomized spray. Some carburetors have multiple venturis, known as *booster venturis,* one within the other, further increasing the speed of air flow. Refer to Figure 19-12.

After the fuel is atomized into the intake manifold, three factors combine to vaporize the fuel. These factors are the flow of the mixture, low pressure in the manifold, and heat within the manifold as shown in Figure 19-13.

The basic carburetor described above would function correctly only at high engine speeds. Many additional fuel passages, parts, and linkages are required. Together, they provide the range of correct air-fuel mixtures necessary at different engine speeds, loads, and temperatures. These parts and their operation are discussed in Units 21 and 22.

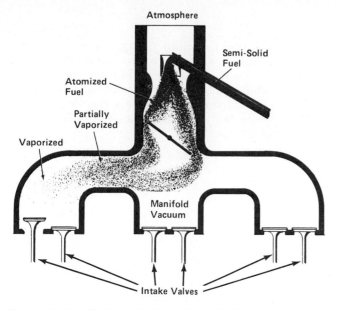

Figure 19-13. Fuel atomization and vaporization.
CHEVROLET MOTOR DIVISION—GMC

Electronic Fuel Injection Systems

Electronic fuel injection performs exactly the same function as a carburetor: It provides a range of air-fuel mixtures. This range of mixtures allows the engine to run properly and efficiently at widely varying speeds, loads, and temperatures.

However, a carburetor operates on mechanical and hydraulic principles. Pushing down or letting up suddenly on the accelerator pedal does not cause an immediate change in air-fuel mixture. As a result, fuel economy, performance, and exhaust emission control suffer.

Electronic fuel injection (EFI) systems spray fuel under pressure through *injectors,* or small nozzles, into the intake manifold. The amount of fuel sprayed is regulated by an electronic computer that receives signals from many sensors on the engine.

A list of the *input* and *output* electrical signals for one EFI system is shown in Figure 19-14. Input

---

PARAMETERS SENSED	PARAMETERS CONTROLLED
• A/C SYSTEM ENABLE	• AIR CONTROL VALVE SIGNAL
• BAROMETRIC PRESSURE	• AIR SWITCHING VALVE SIGNAL
• BRAKE PEDAL ENGAGEMENT	• CANISTER PURGE CONTROL SIGNAL
• ENGINE COOLANT TEMPERATURE	• EGR CONTROL SIGNAL
• ENGINE CRANKSHAFT POSITION	• ELECTRONIC SPARK TIMING SIGNAL
• ENGINE CRANK MODE	• IDLE CONTROL SIGNAL
• ENGINE DETONATION	• THROTTLE BODY INJECTION CONTROL SIGNAL
• EXHAUST OXYGEN CONCENTRATION	• TRANSMISSION TORQUE CONVERTER CLUTCH SIGNAL
• INJECTOR VOLTAGE	• A/C CLUTCH CONTROL SIGNAL
• MANIFOLD ABSOLUTE PRESSURE	• AIR DOOR CONTROL SIGNAL
• PARK/NEUTRAL MODE	• COOLING FAN CONTROL
• THROTTLE POSITION	
• TIME (INTERNALLY GENERATED WITHIN ECM)	
• TRANSMISSION GEAR INDICATION	
• VEHICLE SPEED	

ELECTRONIC CONTROL MODULE (ECM)

Figure 19-14. Input and output signals for an electronic fuel injection system. BUICK MOTOR DIVISION—GMC

signals are electrical currents from temperature and other sensors that indicate information, or facts, such as coolant temperature. Output signals are electrical currents to units that can modify engine operation, such as turning on an electrical cooling fan.

EFI systems operate much more rapidly and efficiently than carburetors. Such systems can provide better fuel economy, performance, and less harmful exhaust gases.

Two general forms of fuel injection are currently in use: *Single-point* and *multi-point* fuel injection.

Single-point fuel injection. Single-point fuel injection sprays fuel at a device, a *throttle body,* that contains a throttle plate like a carburetor. See Figure 19-15. Another name for such a system is *throttle body injection (TBI).* One or two injectors may be used in a single throttle body. In addition, multiple throttle bodies may be used.

A simplified diagram of TBI operation is shown in Figure 19-16. Fuel is atomized and mixed within the intake manifold in the same way as in a carbureted fuel system.

Multi-point fuel injection. In carbureted or TBI fuel systems the amount of fuel distributed to the cylinders through the intake manifold can vary. This is illustrated in Figure 19-17.

A manifold's design and shape, and its distance from the carburetor or throttle body, influence how equally fuel is distributed.

A fuel injection system can be designed with separate, individual injectors for each cylinder. This design supplies each cylinder with an equal mixture of air and fuel. Each injector is positioned in an intake manifold runner. The injector is located just in front of the cylinder head intake port, behind the intake

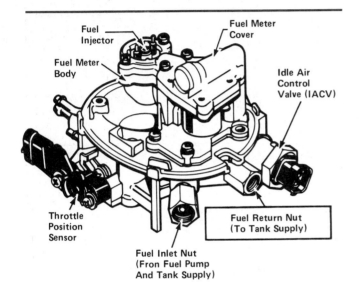

Figure 19-15. Throttle body fuel injection system.
BUICK MOTOR DIVISION—GMC

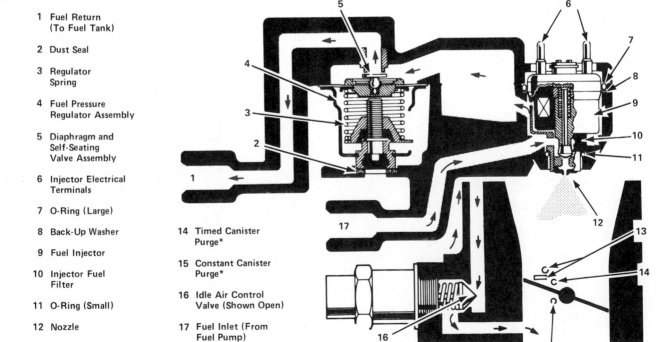

1 Fuel Return
   (To Fuel Tank)

2 Dust Seal

3 Regulator
   Spring

4 Fuel Pressure
   Regulator Assembly

5 Diaphragm and
   Self-Seating
   Valve Assembly

6 Injector Electrical
   Terminals

7 O-Ring (Large)

8 Back-Up Washer

9 Fuel Injector

10 Injector Fuel
   Filter

11 O-Ring (Small)

12 Nozzle

13 Typical Vacuum
   Ports* (For EGR
   and Spark)

14 Timed Canister
   Purge*

15 Constant Canister
   Purge*

16 Idle Air Control
   Valve (Shown Open)

17 Fuel Inlet (From
   Fuel Pump)

*Not On All Models.

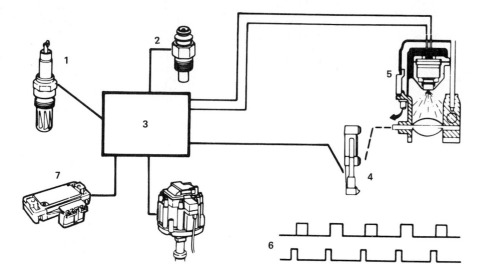

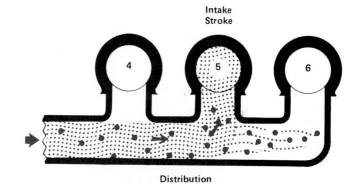

1	O$_2$
2	Coolant Temperature
3	ECM
4	Throttle Position Sensor
5	Injector
6	Distributor Pulses
7	MAP

Figure 19-16. Throttle body fuel injection operation. BUICK MOTOR DIVISION—GMC

valve. A line called a *fuel rail* supplies fuel to each injector.

Electrical signals to the injectors cause them to open to spray fuel. The longer the electrical signal opens the injectors, the more fuel is sprayed. When the electrical signal is shut off, springs close the injector.

The spraying of the fuel from all injectors can occur independently of the opening of the intake valves. Such a system is known as *continuous fuel injection*. In a continuous fuel injection system, the amount of air allowed through the throttle valve determines the air-fuel ratio.

Fuel injectors also may be grouped so that half of them spray at one time and half at another time. See Figure 19-18. Some fuel remains in the intake manifold until a cylinder begins its intake stroke. Such a system is known as *non-sequential fuel injection*, or *pulsed fuel injection*.

Alternately, fuel can be sprayed from individual injectors, in sequence, just before their respective intake valves open. This system is known as *sequential fuel injection (SFI)*. An SFI system is shown in Figure 19-19. Fuel injection systems are discussed in more detail in Unit 23.

19.4 HEATED INTAKE MANIFOLD

To help vaporize fuel, heat from the exhaust manifold can be routed under or near the intake manifold. See Figure 19-20.

Exhaust Manifold Valve

A valve can be used in the exhaust manifold to increase heat within the intake manifold. This valve, sometimes called a *heat riser valve*, is similar to a throttle plate in a carburetor. See Figure 19-21. The

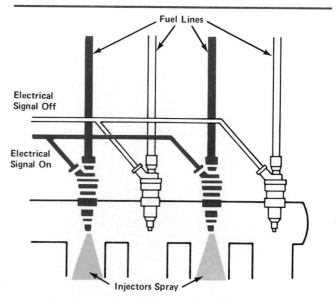

Figure 19-17. Fuel distribution in the intake manifold.
CHEVROLET MOTOR DIVISION—GMC

Figure 19-18. Nonsequential fuel injection operation.
ROBERT BOSCH CORPORATION

179

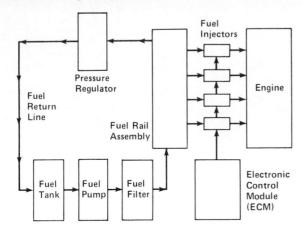

Figure 19-19. Sequential fuel injection system.
BUICK MOTOR DIVISION—GMC

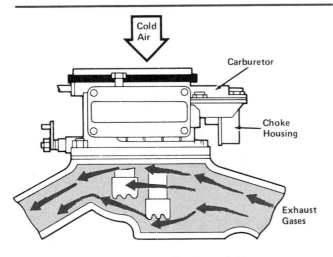

Figure 19-20. Heat from the exhaust manifold is routed near the intake manifold.

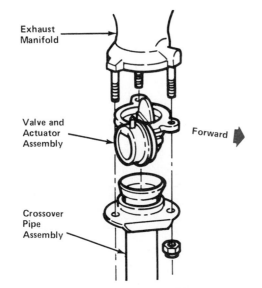

Figure 19-21. Exhaust manifold valve assembly.
CHEVROLET MOTOR DIVISION—GMC

valve can be operated by a thermostatic spring and/or a vacuum motor.

When the engine is cold and idling slowly, a thermostatically controlled vacuum motor closes the flap almost completely. Exhaust gases pass out of the exhaust manifold more slowly and cause the engine and intake manifold to heat up more quickly. The result is better fuel vaporization. This system is known as *early fuel evaporation (EFE)* on General Motors vehicles.

Hot coolant also can be routed through the intake manifold to accomplish the same purpose.

19.5 DIESEL FUEL

Diesel fuel, unlike gasoline, is composed of heavier, more viscous hydrocarbon molecules. Because of this composition, diesel fuel contains more potential heat energy than gasoline.

Volatility Rating

Diesel fuel is graded for volatility as Number 1 (more volatile, for colder temperatures) or Number 2 (less volatile, for more moderate temperatures). Most passenger car diesel engines use Number 2 diesel fuel.

Cetane Rating

A diesel engine depends on compressional heat to ignite the fuel. A *cetane rating* measures the ease with which diesel fuel will ignite under the heat and pressure of compression. A cetane rating measures ignition quality.

Pure cetane is a hydrocarbon compound that has an octane rating of 0. Diesel fuel cetane ratings measure how closely a fuel matches the ignitability of cetane.

A higher cetane rating means the fuel will ignite easily. Diesel fuel with too low a cetane rating has a long ignition delay period, followed by rapid combustion. This causes *diesel knocking,* a condition similar to detonation in a gasoline engine.

19.6 DIESEL FUEL SYSTEM

A schematic diagram of a diesel fuel injection system is shown in Figure 19-22. Refer to this illustration as you read the following discussion.

In a diesel engine, only air is compressed by the piston. Diesel fuel is sprayed into the cylinder under high pressure through a *mechanical fuel injection nozzle,* shown in Figure 19-23. A mechanical fuel injection nozzle is an assembly similar to a pressure relief valve. Diesel fuel pumped under high pressure forces a spring to open and the nozzle to spray fuel. Diesel fuel will not vaporize at the lower temperatures in the intake manifold. Therefore, all diesel injection systems are multi-point injection systems that inject fuel into each cylinder.

Diesels have no throttle plate in the air induction system. The speed of the engine is controlled by the

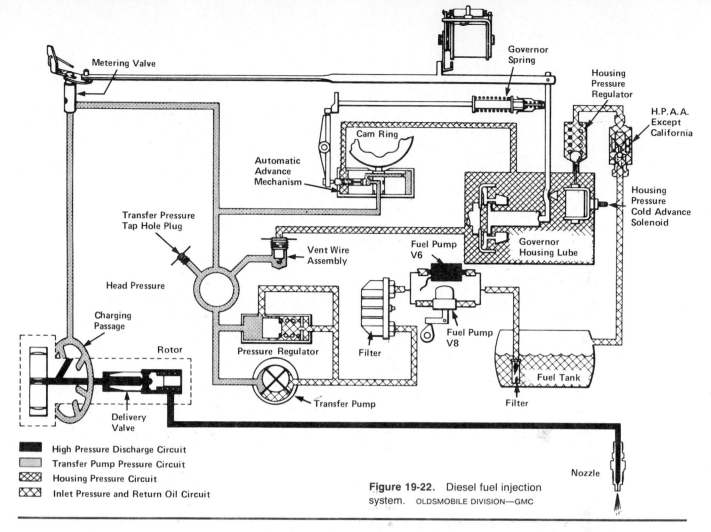

Figure 19-22. Diesel fuel injection system. OLDSMOBILE DIVISION—GMC

Labels in figure:
- Metering Valve
- Governor Spring
- Housing Pressure Regulator
- H.P.A.A. Except California
- Cam Ring
- Automatic Advance Mechanism
- Housing Pressure Cold Advance Solenoid
- Transfer Pressure Tap Hole Plug
- Governor Housing Lube
- Vent Wire Assembly
- Fuel Pump V6
- Head Pressure
- Charging Passage
- Rotor
- Pressure Regulator
- Filter
- Fuel Pump V8
- Fuel Tank
- Delivery Valve
- Transfer Pump
- Filter
- Nozzle

Legend:
- High Pressure Discharge Circuit
- Transfer Pump Pressure Circuit
- Housing Pressure Circuit
- Inlet Pressure and Return Oil Circuit

amount of diesel fuel injected and the time at which it is injected.

A *diesel injection pump,* shown in Figure 19-24, creates fuel pressures of approximately 840 to 1,225 psi [5,791 to 8,446 kPa] to force open the injection nozzle. Injection timing is controlled mechanically.

Electronic controls also are being applied to diesel injection pumps, as shown in Figure 19-25.

Stepping motors move parts to control the amount of fuel injected and the injection timing. A stepping motor is an electrical device that can move a plunger a precise distance in or out.

19.7 TURBOCHARGING

In the past, several methods were used to gain more engine performance:

- Increased engine displacement
- Increased compression ratio
- Higher-lift and longer-duration camshafts
- Rich air-fuel mixtures.

Because of the need for reasonable fuel economy and lower emissions, most of these methods no longer can be used. To produce horsepower and torque more efficiently from today's smaller engines, and from diesel engines, *turbocharging* is being used increasingly.

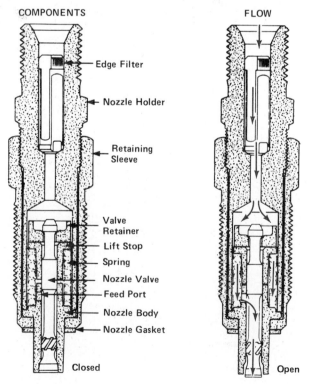

COMPONENTS — FLOW

Labels:
- Edge Filter
- Nozzle Holder
- Retaining Sleeve
- Valve Retainer
- Lift Stop
- Spring
- Nozzle Valve
- Feed Port
- Nozzle Body
- Nozzle Gasket
- Closed
- Open

Figure 19-23. Diesel mechanical fuel injection nozzle. OLDSMOBILE DIVISION—GMC

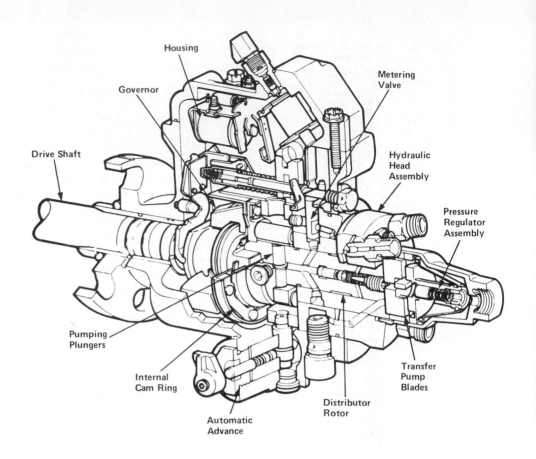

Figure 19-24. Parts of a diesel fuel injection pump. OLDSMOBILE DIVISION—GMC

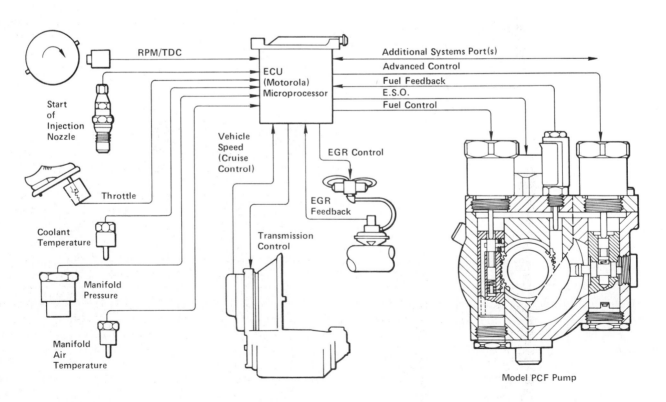

Figure 19-25. Computer-controlled diesel fuel injection pump. DIESEL SYSTEMS GROUP—STANADYNE, INC.

Turbocharging is a method of *supercharging.* Supercharging is forcing more air-fuel mixture into a cylinder than can be drawn in by atmospheric pressure alone. A type of compressor, or pump, forces air and fuel, under pressure, into the intake manifold.

Turbochargers on gasoline engines can be used with carburetors or with fuel injection systems. When used with a carburetor, a turbocharger can either force or draw air through the carburetor. Mechanics call such systems "blow-through" and "suck-through" designs, respectively. An example of a turbocharger that draws air through a carburetor is shown in Figure 19-26.

The denser mixture produced by compressing the air-fuel mixture creates more force during combustion. This force enables a smaller displacement engine to produce greater torque and horsepower.

A *supercharger* is a compressor driven by the engine crankshaft or camshaft. Since it works off engine power, a supercharger produces *parasitic*

losses of horsepower. The Mercedes-Benz W196 racing car engine of the 1930s developed more than 640 horsepower. However, almost 120 horsepower was needed just to drive the supercharger!

A *turbocharger* uses the wasted heat energy of the exhaust gases flowing from the engine to drive a compressor. A schematic view of a turbocharging system is shown in Figure 19-27.

The turbocharger unit consists of two separate impellers, or *turbines,* mounted on a shaft within a housing (see Figure 19-27). As the hot exhaust gases are forced into the turbine wheel, they give up their heat and kinetic energy. This heat and energy cause the turbine, turbine shaft, and compressor to spin at very high speeds, approximately 100,000 rpm. The

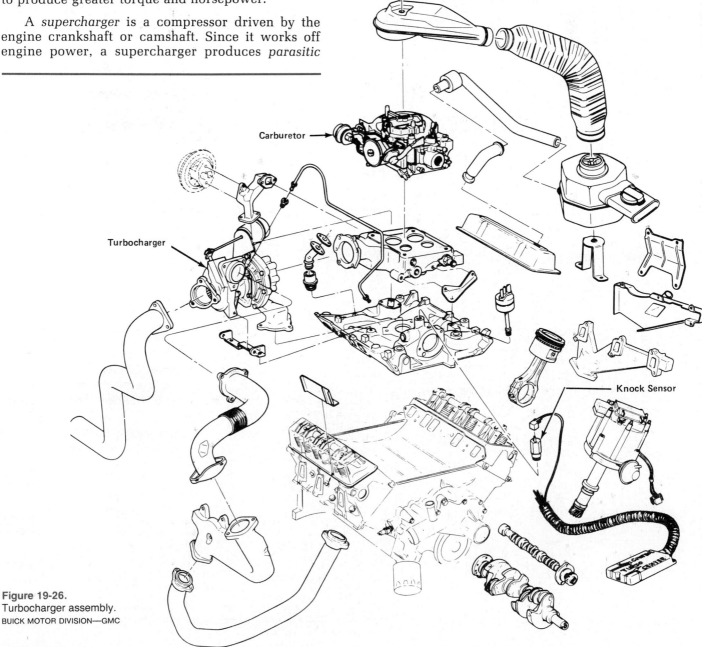

Figure 19-26.
Turbocharger assembly.
BUICK MOTOR DIVISION—GMC

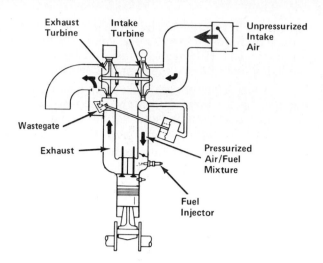

Figure 19-27. Turbocharger air-fuel and exhaust flow.
FORD MOTOR COMPANY

spinning compressor draws in the air-fuel mixture, compressing it and pressurizing it into the intake manifold.

To prevent excessive pressure from building up, a *wastegate,* or pressure relief valve, is part of the turbocharger system. See Figure 19-28. The wastegate operates like a pressure relief valve in a lubrication system. Pressures in turbocharged passenger car intake manifolds generally are limited to 15 psi [103 kPa] or less above atmospheric pressure.

Turbocharging has some drawbacks. The exhaust turbine creates a restriction within the exhaust manifold. Excessive *backpressure* from such a restriction can reduce engine efficiency.

As the intake air is compressed, it is heated, making it less dense (less oxygen). This loss of density reduces combustion efficiency. An *intercooler,* a type of radiator heat exchanger, can be mounted in the airstream to cool the intake air charge. This restores most of the lost efficiency. Figure 19-29 indicates the location of an intercooler on a Ford Mustang SVO.

Most turbochargers do not begin to function well until engine rpm builds enough to force exhaust gases out rapidly. This delay in function is called *turbo lag.* At low rpm, the engine power output is comparable to a nonturbocharged, or *normally aspirated* engine.

The turbocharger shaft, spinning at speeds of up to 100,000 rpm, is lubricated by oil from the engine lubrication system. Clean oil is critical to the life of the turbocharger. Special oils formulated for use with turbochargers can be used to help prevent damage to turbocharger and engine bearings.

In addition, some special driving precautions must be observed with turbocharged engines. The engine and turbocharger should be warmed up gently and fully before high power output is demanded. Also, a hot turbocharged engine should be allowed to idle for a few minutes. This permits slow cooling before shutoff.

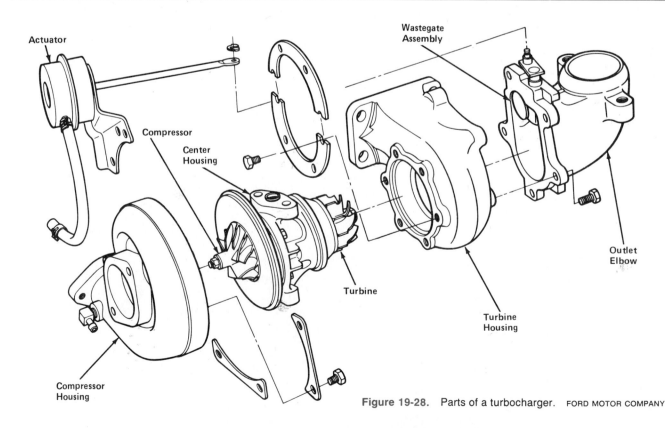

Figure 19-28. Parts of a turbocharger. FORD MOTOR COMPANY

Intercooler
Inside
Air Intake
Housing

Figure 19-29. Turbocharger installation with intercooler.
FORD MOTOR COMPANY

- Diesel fuel contains more heat energy per unit volume than gasoline and vaporizes less easily.

- Cetane rating is a way of measuring a motor fuel's ease of ignition through applied heat and pressure.

- Turbocharging is a way of using an engine's exhaust gases to drive a compressor to pressurize the air-fuel mixture into the intake manifold.

UNIT HIGHLIGHTS

- Gasoline and diesel fuel are the most common hydrocarbon engine motor fuels.

- Gasoline must vaporize properly, resist the formation of ice crystals, resist abnormal combustion, and have low sulfur content.

- Octane rating is a way of measuring a motor fuel's resistance to ignition through applied heat and pressure.

- Detonation is an uncontrolled explosion of remaining air-fuel mixture *after* the spark plug fires. Preignition is the ignition of the air-fuel mixture *before* the spark plug fires.

- A basic fuel system consists of a fuel tank, connecting lines, fuel pump, fuel filter, air filter, and fuel atomization system.

- A fuel metering and atomization system can be either a carburetor or a fuel injection system.

- Fuel is vaporized in the intake manifold by swirl, turbulence, heat, and low pressure, or vacuum.

TERMS

gasohol	single-point fuel
gasoline	injection
hydrocarbon (HC)	multi-point fuel
atomize	injection
volatile	throttle body
vapor lock	throttle body injection
de-icer	(TBI)
detonate	fuel rail
swirl	continuous fuel
turbulence	injection
octane rating	non-sequential fuel
iso-octane	injection
tetraethyl lead	pulsed fuel injection
leaded gasoline	sequential fuel
preignition	injection (SFI)
dieseling	heat riser valve
fuel-vapor separator	early fuel evaporation
mechanical fuel pump	(EFE)
impeller pump	cetane rating
fuel filter	diesel knocking
air filter	mechanical fuel
stoichiometric	injection nozzle
lean mixture	diesel injection pump
rich mixture	stepping motor
carburetor	turbocharging
barrel	supercharging
throttle bore	supercharger
throttle plate	turbocharger
venturi	parasitic losses
booster venturis	turbine
electronic fuel injection	wastegate
(EFI)	backpressure
injectors	intercooler
input signals	turbo lag
output signals	normally aspirated

REVIEW QUESTIONS

DIRECTIONS: The following questions are similar to those used on mechanic certification tests. On a separate sheet of paper, write the letter of the correct choice.

1. All of the following will promote detonation EXCEPT
A. high compression ratio.
B. lean fuel mixture.
C. ignition spark occurring too soon.
D. high humidity in the air.

2. Mechanic A says that multi-point fuel injection can be used on a gasoline engine.
   Mechanic B says that throttle-body fuel injection can be used on a diesel engine.
   Who is correct?
A. A only   B. B only   C. Both A and B   D. Neither A nor B

3. All of the following statements about a venturi are correct EXCEPT
A. It is also known as a carburetor bore.
B. It is a restriction within a carburetor bore.
C. It causes the airflow through a carburetor bore to speed up.
D. It helps to cause a low-pressure area to draw fuel up a tube immersed in a supply of gasoline.

4. Which of the following gasoline air-fuel ratios theoretically would be best for engine performance at altitudes above sea level?
A. 13.7:1
B. 14.7:1
C. 15.7:1
D. 30:1

5. Which of the following statements is correct?
   I. A turbocharged small-displacement engine can produce as much horsepower as a normally aspirated larger-displacement engine.
   II. A turbocharged small-displacement engine can produce as much torque as a normally aspirated larger-displacement engine.
A. I only   B. II only   C. Both I and II   D. Neither I nor II

SUPPLEMENTAL ACTIVITIES

1. Examine a vehicle and identify all visible fuel system components. Determine what type of fuel and fuel atomization system the vehicle uses.
2. Examine all flexible rubber fuel and vapor lines on a vehicle chosen by your instructor. Can you locate any leaks or cracks? Make a simple drawing of the fuel and vapor lines and report on their location and condition to your class.
3. Survey your relatives and friends. How many have vehicles with carburetors? How many have vehicles with fuel injection? How many have diesel engines? How many have vehicles with turbocharged engines? Report the results of the survey to your class.
4. Visit new-car dealerships and obtain advertising booklets on vehicles with turbocharged and non-turbocharged engines. Make a table of horsepower-to-displacement ratios by dividing the number of rated horsepower by the number of cubic inches or liters of displacement for each engine. Include EPA estimated mileage figures for all engines. Report the results of the survey to your class.
5. Discussion question: Would turbocharging be more or less effective at higher altitudes? Why?

20 FUEL SYSTEM SERVICE

UNIT PREVIEW

Fuel system maintenance helps to ensure reliable and efficient engine operation at all speeds, loads, and temperatures. Basic maintenance consists of filter replacement, checking for and repairing fuel leaks, and cleaning exterior carburetor linkages.

Diesel fuel systems are quite different and contain many specialized parts and components. However, many of the basic maintenance procedures are much the same.

Fuel system service procedures may require the replacement of individual parts or entire components.

Before turbochargers are removed for service or replacement, basic engine performance factors must be checked. A visual inspection of the turbocharger also must be performed.

LEARNING OBJECTIVES

When you have completed your assignments and exercises in this unit, you should be able to:

☐ Check for the presence of fuel.
☐ Identify and describe sources of fuel leaks.
☐ Replace damaged metal and synthetic rubber fuel lines.
☐ Perform basic tests on gasoline fuel pumps.
☐ Replace a gasoline fuel pump.
☐ Identify and describe specific differences between gasoline and diesel filtering systems.

SAFETY PRECAUTIONS

Perform fuel system work only in well-ventilated areas. Familiarize yourself with the location and operation of shop fire extinguishers before beginning such work.

Working around fuel systems can be hazardous. One gallon of gasoline, totally vaporized, has the explosive power of 14 sticks of dynamite—enough to destroy a large building and injure many people. Diesel fuel, although not as volatile, is flammable and can cause serious fires.

Be aware of sources of ignition for gasoline vapors. These include:

- Lighted cigarettes
- Ignition sparks
- Electrical switches
- Electric drills and other tools
- Air compressor motors
- Heat from exhaust pipes
- Flames from gas or oil heaters
- Welding equipment.

Wear eye protection when working with motor fuels or using compressed air to clean parts. Fuel explosions can hurl objects into the eyes. Liquid fuel can cause serious eye and skin burns. Compressed air can hurl particles and liquids into the eyes.

Protective gloves should be worn to avoid prolonged skin contact with motor fuels and cleaning solvents.

Fuel should be drained into and stored only in approved metal containers with caps that can be tightly closed. Glass or plastic containers should not be used. They can break or leak and cause a fire and/or explosion hazard.

Before disconnecting fuel lines, prepare proper metal containers to catch fuel and use pinch-off clamps on flexible fuel lines to prevent uncontrolled fuel flow.

Fuel-soaked rags should be placed in tightly closed, approved, fireproof metal containers. Spontaneous combustion of oily or fuel-soaked rags can cause fires and explosions.

20.1 CHECKING FOR FUEL

Before assuming any fuel system problem, check for fuel. Determine if fuel is present in the tank and at the carburetor or fuel injection system. Also check for the presence of ignition spark, as discussed in Unit 36.

To check for fuel in a carburetor, first be sure that the engine is not running. Open the *choke plate,* as shown in Figure 20-1. Shine a flashlight down the carburetor bore, and pump the accelerator linkage quickly two or three times. Look, listen, and/or smell for a strong squirt of fuel each time. If fuel is present, it should be ejected in a strong stream down the carburetor bore each time. Carburetors are covered in more detail in Unit 22.

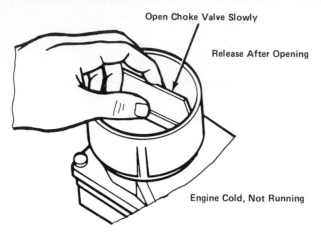

Figure 20-1. Checking for fuel in the carburetor by opening the choke plate. CHRYSLER CORPORATION

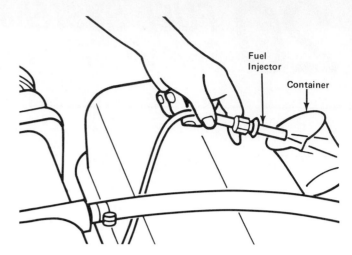

Figure 20-2. Checking for fuel in injection system by removing an injector and placing it in a container to catch fuel spray.

Checking for fuel in a fuel injection system can generally be done at a fuel rail connection or an individual injector. Refer to the manufacturer's service manual for detailed procedures. Disable the ignition system and have a metal container ready to catch fuel pumped through the rail or injector. See Figure 20-2.

20.2 FUEL SYSTEM PREVENTIVE MAINTENANCE

Preventive maintenance for basic fuel system components consists of the following items:

Checking for and/or repairing leaks

Inspecting and/or replacing filters.

20.3 CHECKING FOR LEAKS

Leaks can occur at any point in the fuel system. This includes everything from the filler cap and filler neck of the fuel tank forward to the intake manifold. Liquid fuel, especially gasoline, can cause fires that could result in personal injury and damage to the vehicle. Check for leaks at the following points, shown in Figure 20-3:

- Filler cap
- Filler neck connection to tank
- Fuel tank seams
- Fuel and vapor line connections
- Metal and synthetic rubber fuel and vapor lines
- Fuel filter
- Fuel pump
- Vapor canister
- Carburetor
- Fuel injection pump
- Fuel injection lines and injectors
- Carburetor gaskets or fuel injection pump seals
- Intake manifold gasket.

Make a thorough visual inspection. Intermittent leaks often leave stains on parts. Some leaks occur only when the system is pressurized. Run your hand gently over lines and connections. Wetness can indicate fuel leakage. Smell the wetness to determine if it is fuel.

SAFETY CAUTION: **Be extremely careful when checking for leaks when the engine is running. Hot exhaust system components can cause fuel to vaporize and/or explode. Ignition sparks can ignite fuel vapors. Keep a fire extinguisher capable of extinguishing class B flammable materials fully charged and readily available.**

Start the engine and let it run slowly at idle. Check for leaks between the fuel pump and the carburetor or fuel injection system.

SAFETY CAUTION: **Stay away from moving fans, belts, and pulleys when the engine is running. Roll up long sleeves, remove all jewelry, and tie long hair back when working on a running engine.**

20.4 REPAIRING LEAKS

Most leaks are repaired by replacing gaskets, fuel lines, and fuel line fittings. If a part without a replaceable gasket leaks, the entire unit must be replaced.

Fuel Tank and Related Parts

In general, fuel tank caps, if defective, are replaced. Rubber sleeves or couplings connecting fuel tank filler necks to tanks can be replaced separately. Metal fuel tanks can be repaired by special welding techniques. In addition, epoxy compounds can be used to patch small leaks.

SAFETY CAUTION: **Do not attempt any fuel tank repair requiring heat, welding, or hammering. Welding of metal fuel tanks is a specialized technique. Fuel vapors, even in an empty and thoroughly washed tank, can explode violently if the tank is heated or crushed.**

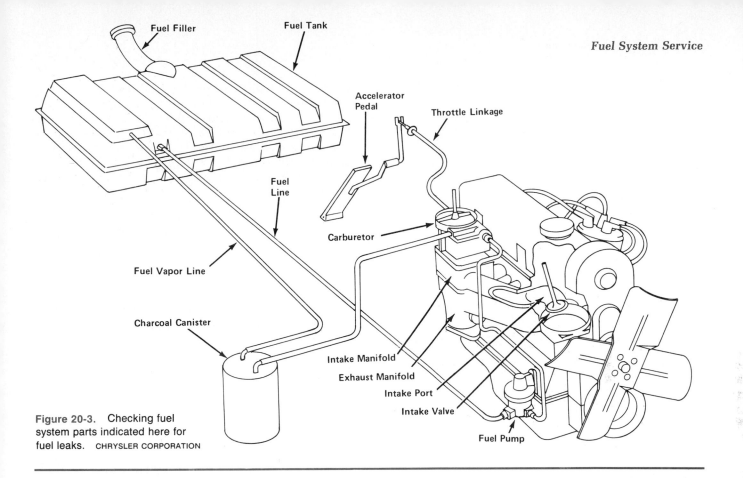

Figure 20-3. Checking fuel system parts indicated here for fuel leaks. CHRYSLER CORPORATION

Fuel and Vapor Lines

Leaks caused by loose clamps on synthetic rubber lines in good condition can be repaired by tightening or replacing the clamp. Fuel or vapor lines that are cracked or leaking should be replaced immediately.

SAFETY CAUTION: The fuel tank should be drained before attempting to replace synthetic rubber or metal fuel lines. Store the fuel in a clean, tightly sealed, approved metal container away from any sources of vapor ignition.

In addition to wire, banded, and worm-drive clamps, *crimp-type clamps* may be used on rubber fuel lines. See Figure 20-4.

Used crimp-type clamps must be spread or cut off with wire cutters. Replacement of crimp-type clamps with worm-drive clamps of the correct diameter is recommended during replacement.

Fuel line replacement. Metal lines can become closed, abraded (worn through rubbing), or rusted through. A special type of *flare,* or end shape, is used on metal fuel lines and brake lines. This is called a double lap flare. Preparation of a new metal fuel line is illustrated in Figure 20-5.

Short sections (12 inches or less) of damaged tubing can be replaced. Cut out the defective section and replace it with approved fuel line hose. Overlap each end approximately 2 inches to allow for proper clamping and sealing.

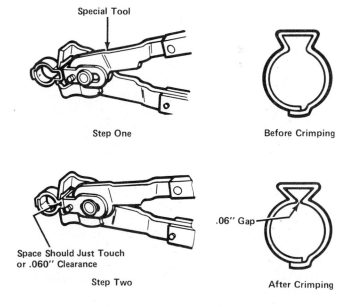

Figure 20-4. Crimp-type clamps often are used on fuel lines. CHRYSLER CORPORATION

Sections longer than 12 inches should be replaced with steel tubing. The steel tubing should be connected at each end with approved fuel line hose and clamps. Be sure to properly secure any new line or hose to prevent damage from vibration.

Any damaged or leaking fuel line hose must be replaced with a complete new hose.

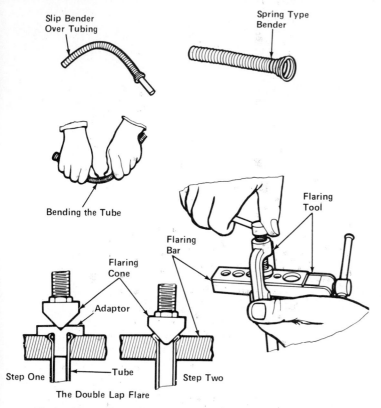

Figure 20-5. Preparing a new fuel line. CHRYSLER CORPORATION

Leakage from Fuel System Parts

If a part such as a fuel pump or fuel filter is leaking, the entire unit must be replaced. Leakage from carburetor sections can be repaired during carburetor overhaul, discussed in Unit 22. Leakage from fuel injection system components may be repairable, or may require replacement, as discussed in Unit 24.

Gaskets

Leaks around fuel pump, carburetor, or other fuel system gaskets generally require partial disassembly or removal of the unit. In some cases, sealants can be used to stop leakage. In other cases, entire gaskets must be replaced.

CAUTION: Use only sealants compatible with the fuel used. Refer to the manufacturer's service manual for recommended procedures and sealants. In some cases, sealants are not to be used on gaskets.

If a molded plastic or rubber fuel system part is cracked or broken, the entire unit should be replaced.

Carburetor service is discussed in Unit 22, and fuel injection service is covered in Unit 24. Fuel pump replacement is discussed under Topic 20.7.

Carburetor and intake manifold gaskets. In addition to fuel leaks, air leakage past carburetor and intake manifold gaskets can cause fuel system problems.

NOTE: Air leaks can be detected by the following procedure: Run the engine slowly at idle and spray carburetor spray cleaner briefly at the suspected carburetor or intake manifold gasket. Any change in rpm indicates an air leak. The carburetor spray cleaner momentarily changes the lean mixture caused by the air leak and causes the engine speed to change.

CAUTION: Some fuel injection components may be harmed by carburetor spray cleaner. Refer to the manufacturer's service manual for recommended testing procedures for fuel injection units.

Replacement of carburetor, fuel injection system, or intake manifold gaskets requires component removal. Refer to the manufacturer's service manual for correct removal and replacement procedures.

20.5 REPLACING FUEL AND AIR FILTERS

Fuel filters may be installed in a fuel line or inside a fuel system component. PCV filters always should be checked and/or replaced when air filters are replaced.

Inline Fuel Filter

Fuel filters may be installed between sections of synthetic rubber fuel lines. This type of filter is removed by loosening the clamps and pulling the filter from the lines. Replace the rubber fuel line sections and reinstall the new filter with the arrow pointing *toward* the carburetor or fuel-injection system. Refer to Figure 20-6.

Screw-On Fuel Filter

Fuel filters are removed from screw-on housings by loosening the housing cover and removing the filter. New gaskets generally are supplied with the filter. Tighten the housing cover as recommended by the vehicle manufacturer. See Figure 20-7.

Fuel Filter in Carburetor Housing

Replacement of fuel filters within carburetor housings requires special care. An open-end and a *flare-nut wrench* must be used together to prevent the metal fuel line from becoming bent, twisted, or crimped. Hold the open-end wrench tightly as the flare-nut wrench is turned to loosen the fitting. See Figure 20-8.

Unscrew the fitting. Then, unscrew and remove the large housing nut. Note the position of the filter and spring as it is removed and replace the new filter in the same position.

Replace Air and PCV Filter

Replacing most air filters requires removing the top of an air cleaner housing. Wipe the inner surfaces of the housing with a lightly oiled rag to remove dust and other contaminants.

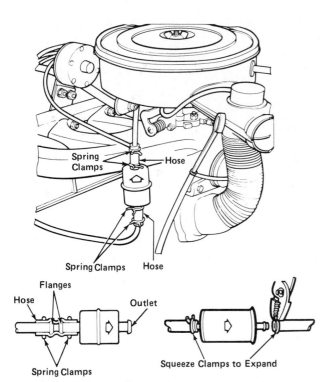

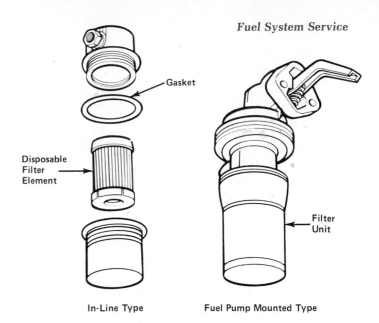

Figure 20-7. Screw-on fuel filter assembly. CHRYSLER CORPORATION

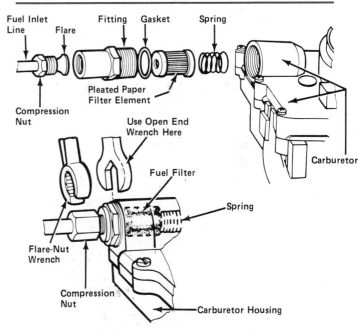

Figure 20-8. Removing parts of a carburetor fuel filter.
CHRYSLER CORPORATION

Figure 20-6. Inline fuel filter replacement.
CHRYSLER CORPORATION

Pleated-paper air cleaner elements cannot be effectively cleaned. Replace the element if thick dust is evident on the surface of the paper or if it has been in service more than one year or 12,000 miles.

Check that the air-cleaner-to-carburetor gasket, shown in Figure 20-9, is in good condition. Replace the gasket if torn or broken.

Also check and/or replace the PCV filter, shown in Figure 20-10, if fitted. PCV systems are explained in Unit 42.

20.6 TESTING A FUEL PUMP

Three tests may be made to determine if a fuel pump is defective and needs to be replaced:

- Pressure test
- Output volume and aeration test
- Inlet vacuum test.

SAFETY CAUTION: Have a properly charged fire extinguisher capable of extinguishing class B fires readily available during fuel pump testing. Diesel injection fuel pump testing requires special high-pressure test instruments and procedures. Do not attempt diesel fuel injection pump testing without the manufacturer's specific instructions and test equipment.

Pressure Test

A pressure test is conducted by connecting a pressure/vacuum gauge to a T-fitting in the fuel line, as

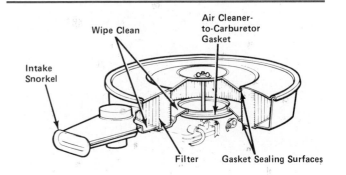

Figure 20-9. Air cleaner element replacement.
CHRYSLER CORPORATION

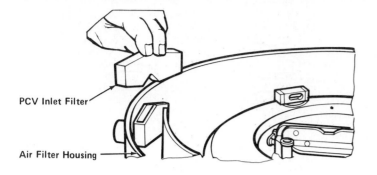

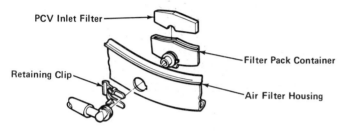

Figure 20-10. Replacing PCV filter. CHRYSLER CORPORATION

shown in Figure 20-11. Refer to the manufacturer's specifications for correct pressure output and test procedures.

If the pump has a vapor return to the fuel tank, disconnect and plug the line tightly. After your pressure reading has been recorded, note the time necessary for the pressure to dissipate. A serviceable diaphragm-type pump should hold pressure for at least 30 seconds. This check does not apply to impeller-type pumps.

Output Volume and Aeration Test

Perform the following test to determine whether a diaphragm-type pump can provide a sufficient volume of gasoline and is not leaking. Disconnect the output side of the fuel line from the carburetor. Disable the ignition system as described in Unit 15. Connect a length of hose to the end of the line. Direct the hose into a metal container away from the engine. This procedure is shown in Figure 20-12.

Start the engine and let it idle. Hold the hose down in the bucket. Check for *aeration*, the presence of air bubbles, as the fuel covers the end of the hose. Let the engine run 30 seconds. Aeration and/or less than 16 ounces [0.5 liter] of fuel produced usually indicates a leaking fuel pump diaphragm. Check manufacturer's specifications for exact volumes.

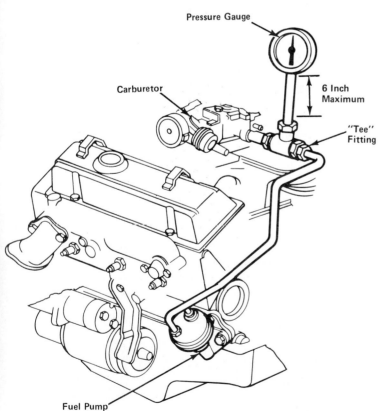

Figure 20-11. Fuel pump pressure test. CHRYSLER CORPORATION

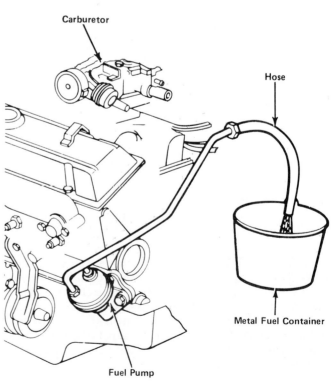

Figure 20-12. Fuel pump output test. CHRYSLER CORPORATION

Similar problems in an electrical pump can be caused by a number of other factors, including:

- Dirty or corroded electrical ground or power connections
- Weak battery
- Faulty fuel pump relay (switch) unit
- Faulty safety relay unit.

Refer to the manufacturer's service manual to check and repair these problems.

Blocked fuel lines, especially in cold weather, may also cause insufficient pump output from electrical or mechanical pumps.

Inlet Vacuum Test

To check inlet vacuum, remove the fuel supply line from the fuel pump. Connect a vacuum gauge to the inlet connection. Crank the engine and compare the reading to manufacturer's specifications. If the pressure, volume, and vacuum tests meet specifications, the fuel line may be blocked or plugged.

Checking for fuel line blockage. To check for blockage, remove the fuel supply line from the fuel pump and apply low-pressure compressed air to the line. See Figure 20-13. Be sure to remove the filler cap.

SAFETY CAUTION: To prevent fuel from pouring down the line, this test is best performed when the tank is one-fourth or less full. Raise the front of the vehicle so that the fuel lines tilt toward the tank.

Have a helper listen for bubbles at the filler neck. If ice formation is suspected, rags soaked in boiling water or heat lamps can be used to heat the fuel lines. This will melt the ice.

SAFETY CAUTION: Never use a torch of any kind to attempt to melt ice in fuel lines. Immediate explosions and fire can occur.

20.7 REPLACING THE FUEL PUMP

Modern fuel pumps are not repairable. They must be replaced if faulty.

SAFETY CAUTION: Before starting, disconnect the battery ground terminal to prevent electrical sparks that could ignite fuel vapors during fuel pump replacement.

Mechanical Fuel Pump

To replace a mechanical fuel pump, first loosen and remove the fuel lines, shown in Figure 20-14. Then, loosen the mounting bolts and gently remove the

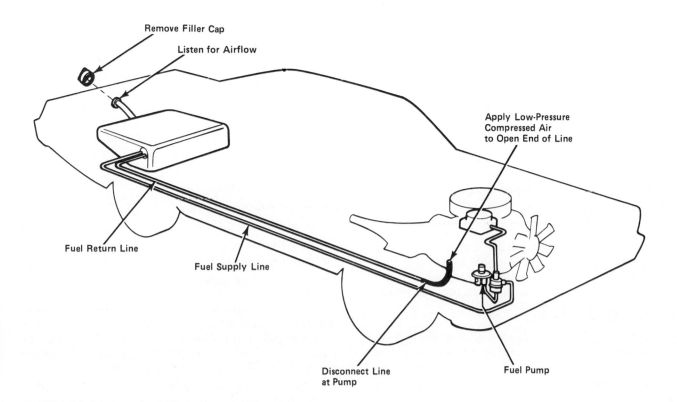

Figure 20-13. Check fuel lines for blockage at these points. CHRYSLER CORPORATION

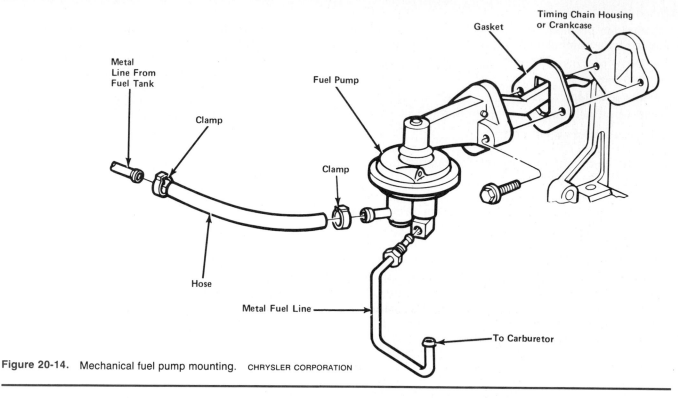

Figure 20-14. Mechanical fuel pump mounting. CHRYSLER CORPORATION

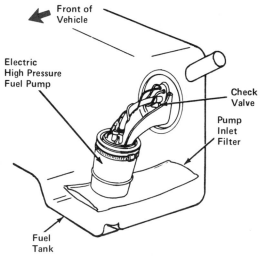

Figure 20-15. Electrical fuel pump mounting.
FORD MOTOR COMPANY

pump. Clean the gasket mounting surface and install a new gasket and pump. If the position of the camshaft eccentric prevents pump replacement, turn the engine slightly by hand to reposition the eccentric.

Electrical In-Tank Pump

Electrical fuel pumps mounted within the fuel tank, as illustrated in Figure 20-15, must be removed from the tank.

Clean the mounting surface and install a new gasket and the pump. Clean and reconnect the electrical connections. Double check all connections and

allow fuel vapors to dissipate. Reconnect the battery ground terminal when finished.

20.8 DIESEL FUEL FILTERS AND WATER SEPARATORS

Fuel injection systems, in general, can be damaged severely by small contaminant particles and water that might pass through a carbureted gasoline fuel system without problem.

Diesel fuel injection systems are particularly subject to water and particle contamination. Electronic systems that warn of water in the fuel can be part of a diesel fuel tank sender unit.

The most modern diesel fuel filter combination units, shown in Figure 20-16, can include several elements:

- Water separator
- Water sensor sender
- Water drain
- Fuel heater
- Hand primer pump
- Filter change indicator sender.

Diesel fuel systems have a number of fuel conditioning components, which differ among manufacturers. However, all systems have fuel filters, which must be replaced routinely according to prescribed maintenance schedules. Refer to Topic 24.6.

Many systems have water sensors located either in the fuel tank or in a separate water separator. When the water sensor light is lit, the system must

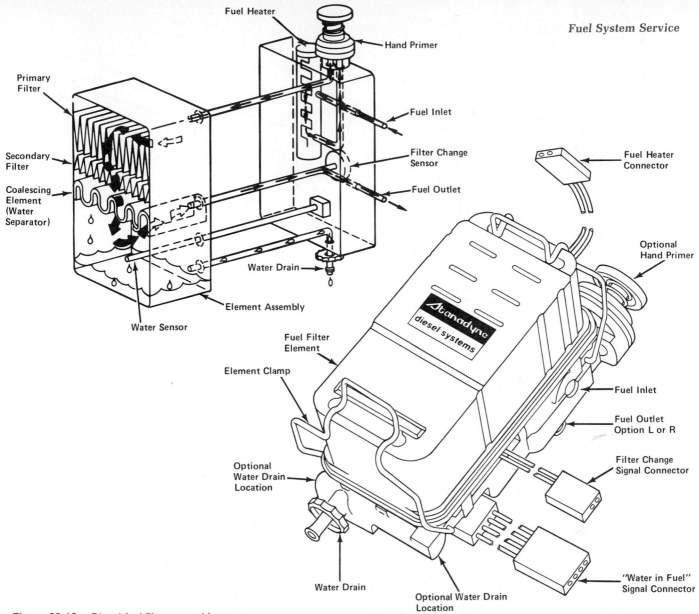

Figure 20-16. Diesel fuel filter assembly. DIESEL SYSTEMS GROUP—STANADYNE, INC.

have the water drained as soon as possible. Refer to Topic 24.6.

Another feature common to diesels is a fuel heater. Warming the fuel prevents *clouding* (formation of small wax particles) and plugging of the fuel filter during cold-temperature operation.

A fuel filter change signal, available on some systems, warns of an excessive pressure drop, which indicates filter plugging.

All these features are included in the unit shown in Figure 20-16.

20.9 TURBOCHARGER SERVICE

Most passenger car turbocharger service needs are caused by lubrication problems. Oil *coking,* or the formation of gum, varnish, and carbon through heat, can damage or destroy bearings and shafts. Excess clearance on such parts then can cause rubbing damage to the compressor wheels and housings.

CAUTION: Care must be exercised whenever a basic engine bearing or internal part is damaged or changed on a turbocharged engine. The oil and oil filter should be changed to remove possible contaminants. In addition, the turbocharger should be flushed with clean engine oil to remove contaminants before reuse. Special oils (for example, Valvoline Turbo V), formulated for use with turbochargers, will help prevent oil coking and resultant damage.

A turbocharger may not be the cause of an engine running problem. Refer to Unit 43 for basic engine troubleshooting procedures.

To inspect for turbocharger damage, remove intake and exhaust tubing and use a light to inspect the compressor blades. See Figure 20-17.

Rotate the compressor wheel by hand and check for binding or rubbing. Lift both the compressor and

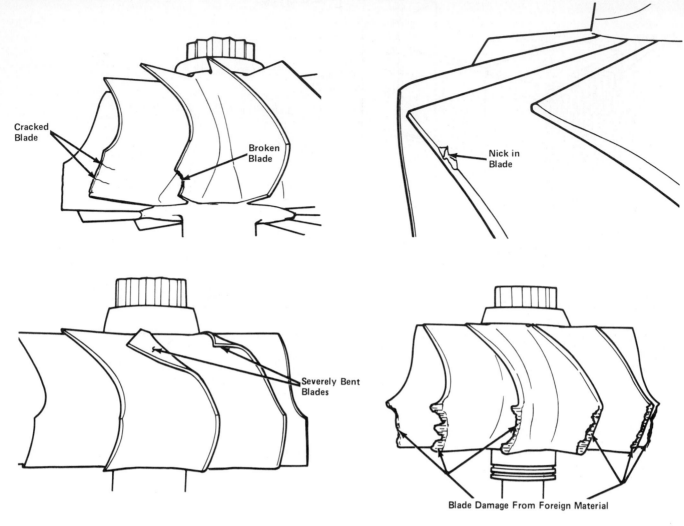

Figure 20-17. Turbocharger blade defects. BUICK MOTOR DIVISION—GMC

turbine wheels and check the shaft and bearings for excessive clearance play. Refer to the manufacturer's service manual for specific checking procedures.

Some manufacturers require that turbochargers be replaced as complete units. Other manufacturers recommend field servicing for minor damage or wear. Refer to the vehicle manufacturer's service manuals for correct procedures.

U N I T   H I G H L I G H T S

- Before assuming that a fuel system part must be defective, check for the presence of fuel in the tank. Also check for fuel at the fuel metering and atomization system.

- Basic fuel system maintenance consists of checking for leaks and replacing filters.

- Most leaks are repaired by replacing gaskets, fuel lines, and fuel line fittings. If a part without a replaceable gasket leaks, the entire unit must be replaced.

- Diesel fuel system filter combination units can include fuel heaters, water separators and drains, warning light systems, and hand-operated primer pumps.

- Basic fuel pump tests include pressure, output volume, and inlet vacuum tests.

- Diesel fuel injection pumps require special testing procedures and test equipment.

- The main cause of turbocharger damage is related to lubrication problems. Turbocharger compressor vanes can be inspected visually for damage.

T E R M S

choke plate	aeration
crimp-type clamps	clouding
flare	coking
flare-nut wrench	

R E V I E W   Q U E S T I O N S

DIRECTIONS: The following questions are similar to those used on mechanic certification tests. On a separate sheet of paper, write the letter of the correct choice.

1. Which of the following statements is correct?

   I. Basic fuel system checks include looking for the presence of fuel and fuel leaks.

   II. Basic fuel system service includes replacing fuel and air filters.

   A. I only   B. II only   C. Both I and II   D. Neither I nor II

2. All of the following should be done when conducting a gasoline fuel pump output volume test EXCEPT

   A. disconnecting the battery ground cable.

   B. disabling the ignition system.

   C. using a metal container to catch fuel.

   D. having a class B fire extinguisher ready.

3. Mechanic A says that ice crystals can block a gasoline fuel line in cold weather.

   Mechanic B says that diesel fuel wax particles can block a diesel fuel filter in cold weather.

   Who is correct?

   A. A only   B. B only   C. Both A and B   D. Neither A nor B

4. When replacing a mechanical fuel pump, the pump does not seem to fit close enough to the engine to fasten the bolts. What is the most likely cause?

   A. Wrong fuel pump

   B. Fuel pump arm jammed inside pump

   C. Fuel pump arm too long

   D. None of the above

5. Why is a hand primer pump included in some diesel fuel systems?

   A. To remove water from contaminated diesel fuel

   B. To pump water from the filtering unit

   C. To remove air bubbles from the system

   D. To pump fuel in case the diesel fuel injection pump is defective

S U P P L E M E N T A L   A C T I V I T I E S

1. Locate all fire extinguishers in the shop area.
2. Safely perform a check for fuel on a carbureted fuel system.
3. Replace fuel, air, and PCV filters on a vehicle chosen by your instructor.
4. Safely perform fuel pump pressure and output volume tests on a vehicle chosen by your instructor. Report the results of the tests to your class.
5. Safely remove and replace a mechanical or electrical fuel pump on a gasoline fuel system chosen by your instructor. Report to your class about specific procedures recommended in the vehicle manufacturer's service manual.
6. If available, perform an inspection on a turbocharger according to the manufacturer's instructions. Report on any defects found to your class.

21 THE CARBURETOR

UNIT PREVIEW

An engine should operate efficiently and smoothly, with low exhaust emissions, under all loads, speeds, and temperatures. To perform this way, an engine must be provided a proper mixture of air and gasoline. This is the function of the carburetor.

The carburetor provides a precisely metered amount of gasoline to be atomized into the incoming air stream. Separate circuits within the carburetor provide a varying air-fuel ratio for good driveability under many different conditions.

Different types and numbers of carburetors may be used to meet specific vehicle requirements.

LEARNING OBJECTIVES

When you have completed your assignments and exercises in this unit, you should be able to:

☐ Explain the basic processes that are involved in carburetion.

☐ Identify and describe the six basic carburetor circuits.

☐ Visually identify carburetor parts and accessories.

☐ Explain why different types and numbers of carburetors may be used on specific vehicles.

21.1 CARBURETION

Carburetion means enriching a gas (usually air) by combining it with a carbon-containing compound (a hydrocarbon fuel, usually gasoline). Three general stages, or steps, are involved in carburetion:

- Metering
- Atomization
- Vaporization.

21.2 METERING

Metering means measuring. In the case of carburetion, fuel is metered into the airstream passing through the barrel of the carburetor. The amount of fuel is varied according to the amount of air passing through the carburetor. Other factors also influence the amount of fuel metered into the air. These factors include engine temperature, load and speed requirements, and the amount of harmful gases in the exhaust fumes.

The amount of fuel metered into the airflow is controlled by *jets*. Jets are precisely sized, calibrated holes in a hollow passage for fuel or air. Three basic types of jets are used:

- Fixed restriction
- Variable restriction
- Air-bleed.

Fixed Restriction

Jets may be formed by drilling in the metal at the end of a fuel passage within the carburetor. However, in most cases, jets are small metal fittings with holes that are screwed or pressed into the fuel passages. See Figure 21-1.

Such a jet can control the amount of fuel delivered to the carburetor venturi, as shown in Figure 21-2.

Variable Restriction

In some carburetors, a tapered or stepped needle moves within the jet *orifice*, or hole. This allows different amounts of fuel to flow through the hole. The larger the step or needle diameter positioned within the hole, the less fuel can flow through the jet. See Figure 21-3. Needle movement can be controlled by mechanical linkage, vacuum, or the movement of an electrical solenoid or stepping motor.

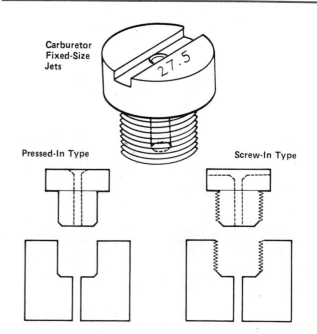

Figure 21-1. Jets control fuel flow in a carburetor.

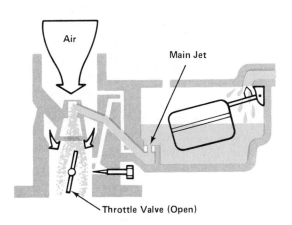

Figure 21-2. Main metering circuit.

Some carburetors use a screw with a needle-shaped end to perform the same function. The needle end of the screw fits into a conical (cone-shaped) passage. Turning the screw inward or outward decreases or increases the fuel flow in proportion to the space left open. Such an arrangement, known as a *needle valve,* is shown in Figure 21-4. Most *idle mixture control screws* are needle valves. On many carburetors built since the late 1970s, the mixture control screws have been capped or sealed. This is done to prevent readjustment, which might increase exhaust gas emissions.

Air-Bleed Jet

Because a basic carburetor provides fuel in proportion to air flow, the mixture could become over-rich at high engine rpm. This condition would result in poor fuel economy. To lean the mixture during high-rpm operation, special jets called *air-bleed jets* can be used. See Figure 21-5.

As fuel is consumed more quickly at high engine speeds, the fuel level drops, uncovering a perforated tube. Air enters this tube from the top. The air mixes progressively with the fuel passing out the sides of the jet as the fuel level drops. This action provides a leaner, more correct mixture at low-load high cruising speeds. Air-bleed jets are also known as *emulsion tubes.*

To make the air-fuel mixture leaner or richer, additional air or fuel passages can be opened or closed. These methods are discussed in the following topics.

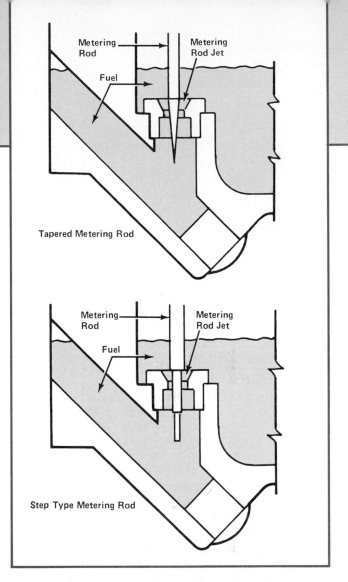

Figure 21-3. Metering rods move within a carburetor to vary fuel flow.

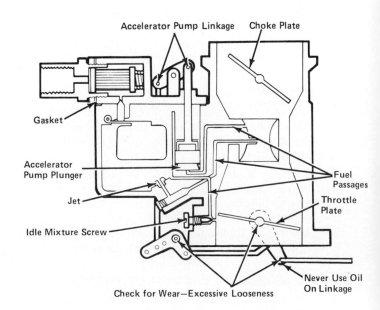

Figure 21-4. Parts of a carburetor. CHRYSLER CORPORATION

199

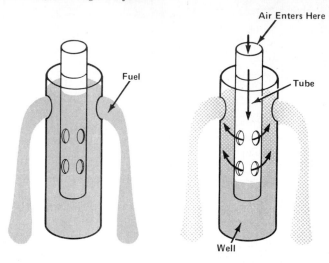

Figure 21-5. Air-bleed jets lean the air-fuel mixture at high rpm.

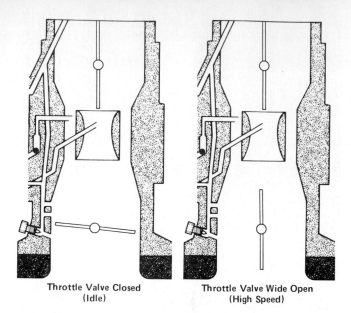

Throttle Valve Closed
(Idle)

Throttle Valve Wide Open
(High Speed)

Figure 21-6. A throttle valve controls airflow into the carburetor.

21.3 ATOMIZATION

The metered air-fuel emulsion is drawn into the air-stream in the form of tiny droplets. Despite the name of this process, *atomization,* fuel particles are not reduced to the size of atoms. Very small droplets of fuel are drawn out of passages, called *discharge ports.* From these ports, the droplets enter the airstream that flows into the intake manifold.

21.4 VAPORIZATION

Because an atomized droplet is small, its surface area is in contact with a relatively large amount of surrounding air. In addition, the venturi is a low-pressure area. These factors—emulsification, vaporization, low pressure—combine to create a fine mist of fuel below the venturi in the bore.

Vaporization takes place below the venturi, in the intake manifold, and within the cylinder. As discussed in Unit 19, swirl, turbulence, and heat within the intake manifold and cylinder also help to vaporize fuel.

21.5 CONTROL OF AIR FLOW

The amount of air that flows through a carburetor is controlled by the throttle valve, or throttle plate. The throttle valve is located at the bottom of the carburetor (see Figure 21-6).

The throttle plate is linked to the accelerator pedal within the passenger compartment by metal rods or a cable mechanism. The throttle plate can be opened the correct distance to produce a uniform and correct idle speed. This adjustment is made with an electrical and/or mechanical device on the carburetor.

21.6 CARBURETOR VACUUM OPERATION

The vacuum developed within the intake manifold varies according to throttle position. As the throttle is opened suddenly, vacuum drops. Without such

a mechanism to compensate for this problem, the mixture would become too lean.

When the throttle is closed suddenly after it has been open, a high vacuum exists within the intake manifold. This high vacuum causes excess fuel to be drawn into the cylinders, causing an overly rich mixture. In addition, exhaust gases may be drawn into the cylinder during valve overlap by the high intake manifold vacuum. This excess amount of exhaust gas takes the place of oxygen in the intake charge, causing poor combustion.

To compensate for these and other operating conditions, several *circuits,* or systems of mechanisms, are included within the carburetor. These circuits provide the proper air-fuel mixture for widely varying engine speed, load, and temperature conditions.

21.7 BASIC CARBURETOR CIRCUITS

The basic circuits within a carburetor are:

- Float
- Idle and low-speed
- Accelerator pump
- Main metering
- Enrichment
- Choke.

Float Circuit

A constant level of gasoline within the carburetor is needed to supply the engine during various operating conditions. This fuel level is maintained within the *float bowl,* a miniature fuel reservoir within the carburetor.

A lightweight part called a *float* rests on the surface of the fuel, as shown in Figure 21-7. A needle valve controls the flow of fuel into the float bowl.

As fuel is consumed, the fuel level drops and the float descends. This action opens the needle valve farther. Fuel from the fuel pump enters the float bowl and raises the float, cutting down the needle valve opening and the flow of fuel.

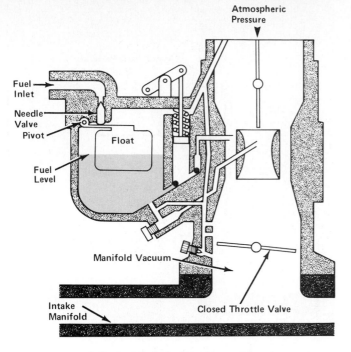

Figure 21-7. A float controls fuel level in a carburetor.

During normal vehicle operation, the needle valve remains open just enough to maintain a constant level of fuel within the float bowl. A cutaway view of a carburetor float circuit is shown in Figure 21-8.

Idle and Low-Speed Circuit

Idling is engine operation without the accelerator pedal depressed. During idling, only a small gap exists between the almost-closed throttle plate and the carburetor bore. The flow of air through the venturi is not sufficient to draw fuel into the carburetor bore.

The pistons are still moving on their intake strokes, attempting to draw in an intake charge. However, the supply of air is restricted, or throttled, so a high vacuum exists below the throttle plate.

An opening called the *idle discharge port* is positioned just below the edge of the throttle plate. See Figure 21-9. The high vacuum draws fuel to allow the engine to run at idle.

Because of the relatively small amount of air, air-fuel mixture at idle is rich, approximately 12:1.

Low-speed operation. As the throttle plate is opened for acceleration, the amount of vacuum applied to the idle discharge port drops. The amount of fuel flowing through the port is not sufficient for the vehicle to run smoothly at low speeds.

Another port, known as the *off-idle, transitional,* or *transfer* port, is located just above the idle discharge port. Refer to Figure 21-9. During idle conditions, this port acts as an air bleed to provide extra air and assist atomization.

As the throttle begins to open, however, vacuum is applied to the off-idle port. Both the idle discharge port and the off-idle port supply fuel to allow smooth engine operation at low speeds. See Figure 21-10. The air-fuel ratio at constant low speeds with light engine loads is approximately 14.7:1.

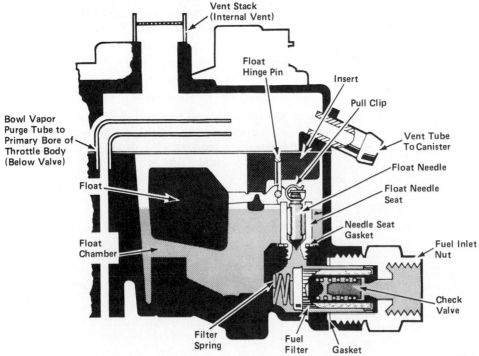

Figure 21-8. Float system circuit.
BUICK MOTOR DIVISION—GMC

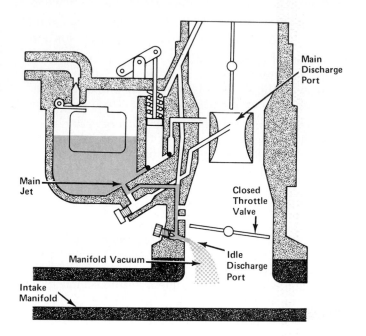

Figure 21-9. An idle discharge port draws fuel from the carburetor to allow the engine to run at idle.

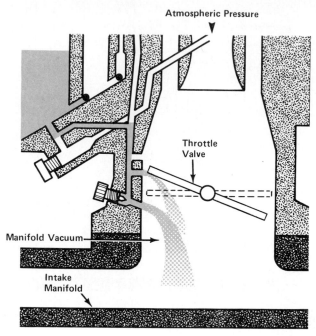

Figure 21-10. The idle discharge port and off-idle port supply fuel to the carburetor at low speeds.

Accelerator Pump Circuit

When the driver presses the accelerator down suddenly to accelerate, the vacuum in the intake manifold drops momentarily. This occurs because the restriction caused by the throttle plate is almost completely removed. Atmospheric pressure forces air into the intake manifold, and the vacuum drops. The discharge of fuel from the idle and off-idle ports slows while a transition, or change, takes place. Fuel had been discharging from the idle circuit. Now, the fuel begins to discharge from the main metering discharge port in the venturi area. This brief period of change results in a lean mixture that can cause the engine to cough or stall.

To richen the mixture quickly, an *accelerator pump,* shown in Figure 21-11, is used. An accelerator pump can consist of a synthetic rubber plunger within a well, or cylinder, filled with fuel. Or, it may be a flexible diaphragm next to a small container of fuel. A check ball and spring usually prevent fuel from flowing through the passage to the carburetor bore. The exception is when the accelerator pedal is depressed quickly.

The plunger or diaphragm may be operated by mechanical linkage and/or by vacuum. When the accelerator is depressed suddenly, the plunger or diaphragm moves. This forces fuel to flow past the check ball and through a discharge port or nozzle into the carburetor bore. This momentary "shot" of fuel enriches the mixture. This allows the engine to pick up speed smoothly as the air flow speeds up in the venturi. The accelerator pump fuel supply refills with fuel from the float bowl.

The air-fuel mixture during acceleration ranges from 10 to 12:1.

Main Metering Circuit

At cruising speeds, engine rpm is higher. Air flow through the carburetor bore and venturi can draw fuel directly from the float bowl through the *main metering circuit.* The main metering circuit, as discussed in Unit 21, operates by drawing fuel through a tube inserted into the float bowl. The *discharge nozzle,* or end of the tube, is placed within the low-pressure area at the venturi for maximum suction. See Figure 21-12.

The main jet determines the amount of fuel drawn through the tube, as shown in Figure 21-13.

At moderate cruising speeds, the air-fuel mixture is approximately 14.7:1 or leaner. Some vehicles operate as lean as 18:1 during extremely light-load cruising. Heavy engine loads combined with low speeds can produce mixtures as rich as 12 or 13:1.

Enrichment Circuit

For full-power, heavy-throttle operation, the fuel mixture must be made richer. An *enrichment circuit,* shown in Figure 21-14, moves a *metering rod,* or tapered needle, within the main jet to allow more fuel to be drawn through the main metering circuit.

The needle is tapered or stepped and can be operated by mechanical means, vacuum, or electrical solenoid or stepper motor. See Figure 21-15.

During enrichment for full-power operation, the air-fuel mixture is approximately 13:1.

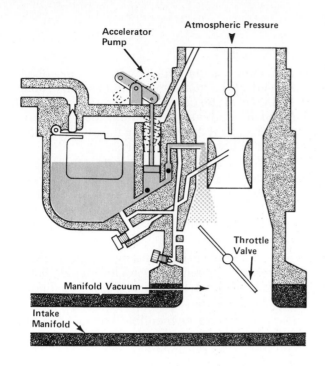

Figure 21-11. Accelerator pump operation.

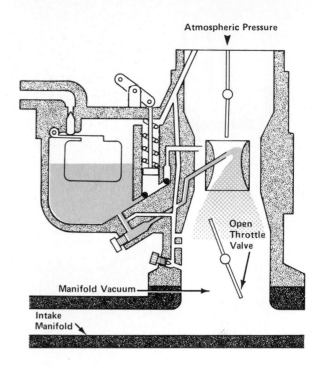

Figure 21-12. At high speeds, fuel flows through a jet and out the discharge nozzle.

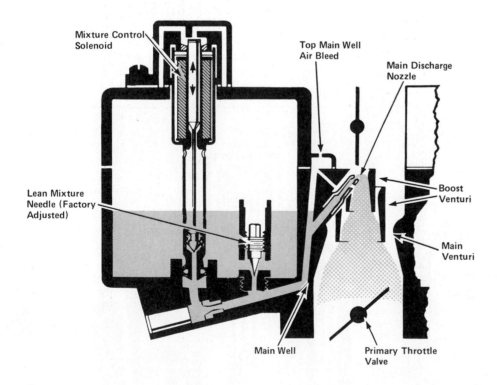

Figure 21-13. Main metering system. BUICK MOTOR DIVISION—GMC

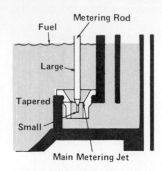

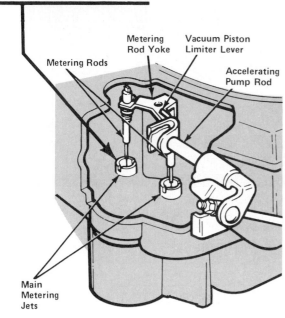

Figure 21-14. An enrichment circuit moves a metering rod to allow more fuel through the main metering circuit.

Choke Circuit

When an engine is cold, fuel condenses, or collects, on the inside of the intake manifold in small droplets. This is similar to the condensation on a glass of cold liquid. When condensation occurs, fuel is removed from the air-fuel mixture, making it lean. In addition, cold fuel does not vaporize easily.

To supply enough vaporized fuel for starting and warm-up purposes, another valve is placed at the top of the carburetor bore. Similar to the throttle plate, this valve is called the *choke plate*. On most vehicles, it is operated automatically by a thermostatic spring, as shown in Figure 21-16.

Cold makes the spring wind more tightly, closing the choke plate. When the vehicle is cold, the accelerator pedal must be depressed to the floor to unlock the mechanism.

Heat from the intake manifold, exhaust manifold, or circulating coolant is used to operate the thermostatic spring. As the engine warms up, heat causes the spring to unwind and open the choke plate. The choke coil spring can be located in a well, or depression, in the intake manifold. Or, it can be located on the side of the carburetor.

When the choke plate is closed, only a small gap exists between the edge of the choke plate and the *air horn*. The air horn is the top of the carburetor bore.

As the starting system begins to turn the crankshaft, the pistons move up and down, producing a

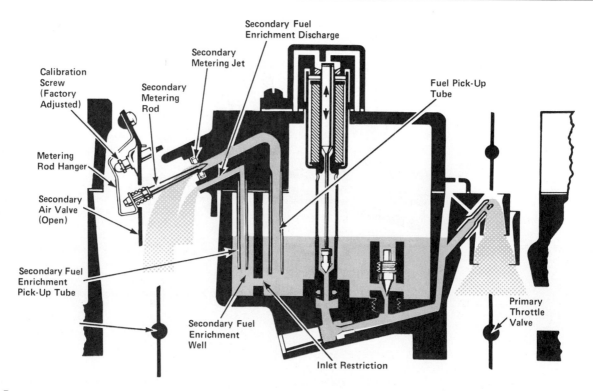

Figure 21-15. Power system. BUICK MOTOR DIVISION—GMC

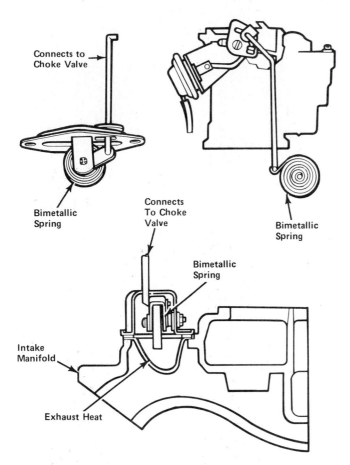

Figure 21-16. Bimetallic choke spring assemblies.
CHRYSLER CORPORATION

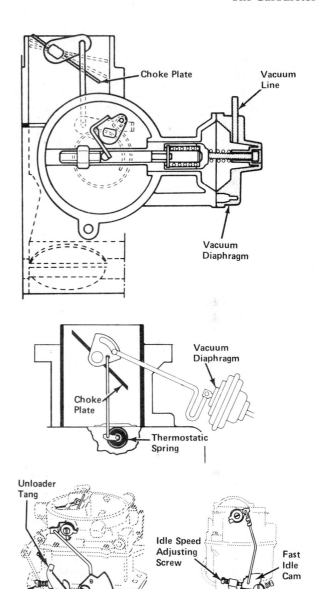

Figure 21-17. Choke pull-off and choke break mechanisms.
CHRYSLER CORPORATION.

vacuum in the carburetor bore. This vacuum causes fuel to be drawn from the idle, off-idle, and main discharge ports. This action causes a very rich mixture to be drawn into the intake manifold.

As the engine starts, the choke plate must immediately open a slight amount. This allows enough air in to mix with the fuel, preventing flooding. As the engine warms up, the choke coil automatically opens the choke plate to the fully open position. This leans the mixture in response to temperature and engine requirements.

Several methods are used to open the choke plate slightly after starting. The choke plate shaft is offset to one side. The heavier side of the choke plate is positioned so the air flow will help force the choke open slightly.

A *choke pull-off* or *choke break* mechanism uses engine vacuum to open the choke slightly after start-up. These mechanisms are pictured in Figure 21-17.

Another mechanism, called a *fast-idle cam,* is used to help the engine run faster during warm-up. A fast-idle cam is connected by small metal rods or levers to the choke plate, as shown in Figure 21-18. This

linkage opens the throttle plate to make the engine run faster.

When the choke is closed, an extremely rich mixture passes through the engine. This rich mixture produces poor fuel economy and large amounts of harmful exhaust gases.

To help the choke open more quickly, electrical heating elements can be used inside a choke coil housing. See Figure 21-19.

When the key switch is on, electrical current can flow to warm the heating element and force the choke plate to open faster.

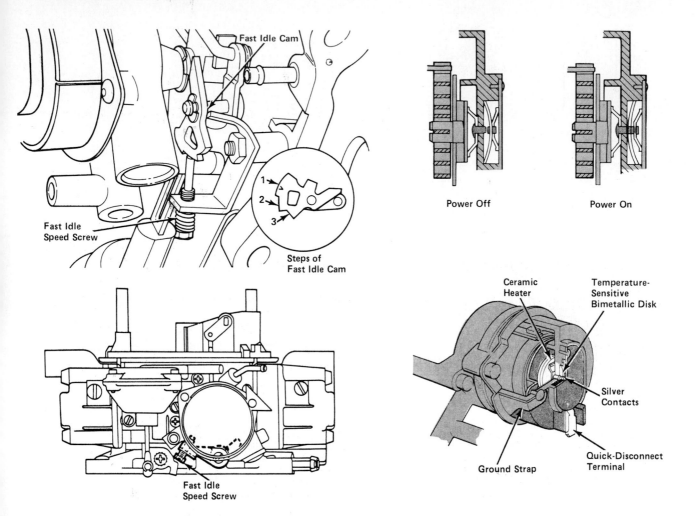

Figure 21-18. Fast-idle cam assembly. FORD MOTOR COMPANY

Figure 21-19. Electrically heated choke assembly.

21.8 ADDITIONAL CARBURETOR EQUIPMENT

To meet complex and stringent fuel economy, driveability, and emission control requirements, modern carburetors have additional equipment, including:

- Temperature-controlled devices
- Fuel-bowl vent
- Altitude-compensation valve
- Throttle-return dashpot
- Vacuum vents
- Throttle positioner solenoid
- Electronic control devices.

Temperature-Controlled Devices

When the engine and carburetor are cold, fuel vaporizes less easily. Fuel is wasted, and high exhaust emissions occur. When the engine and carburetor are hot, fuel may vaporize too easily, possibly causing the engine to stall. To prevent temperature-related problems, devices that respond to temperature are used on current carburetors.

Hot-idle compensator. When the engine is over-heated, a *hot-idle compensator* opens an air passage to lean the mixture slightly. This increases idle speed to help cool the engine and also helps to prevent too rich a mixture from excess fuel vaporization within the carburetor. See Figure 21-20.

Temperature-compensated accelerator pump. A temperature-sensitive device on the accelerator pump can allow more fuel to be pumped when the engine is cold. This helps the engine accelerate well when cold. The device also causes less fuel to be pumped when the engine is hot. An example of such an accelerator pump is shown in Figure 21-21.

Other temperature-controlled devices can be used for carburetion problems on specific vehicles.

Fuel-Bowl Vent

Vapors from within the fuel bowl that escape into the air cause air pollution. To trap the vapors, a vapor recovery system, discussed in Unit 42, is used. A large, pipe-like vent is attached to the top of the fuel

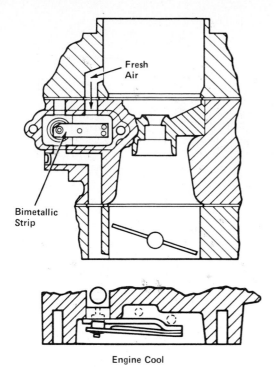

Engine Cool

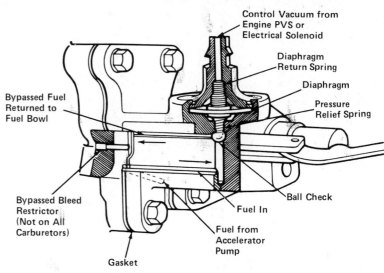

Figure 21-21. Parts of a temperature-compensated accelerator pump. FORD MOTOR COMPANY

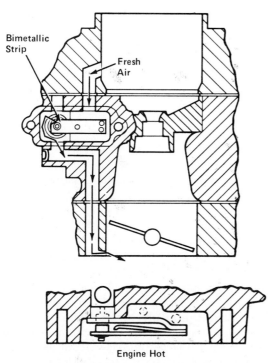

Engine Hot

Figure 21-20. Hot-idle compensator operation.

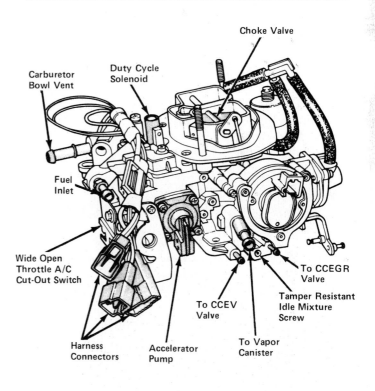

Figure 21-22. Fuel bowl vent locations. CHRYSLER CORPORATION

bowl, as shown in Figure 21-22. This vent allows the vapors to be trapped and later drawn into the intake manifold.

Some manufacturers place an electrically controlled vent valve in this fitting.

Altitude Compensation Valve

At higher altitudes, leaner fuel mixtures are required. An *aneroid bellows* can be used to move a metering needle within a jet to automatically compensate for altitude changes. The bellows responds to atmospheric pressure. An example of such a device is shown in Figure 21-23.

Throttle-Return Dashpot

If the throttle is suddenly released, fuel continues to dribble in large droplets from the main discharge nozzle and produce inefficient atomization. The rapid

207

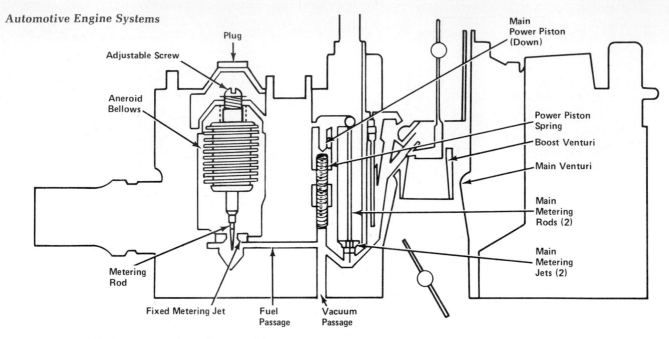

Figure 21-23. Altitude compensation valve assembly. CHEVROLET MOTOR DIVISION—GMC

cutoff of the air-fuel mixture also might cause the engine to stall.

To slow the closing of the throttle plate, a *dashpot* can be attached to the throttle linkage. A dashpot is a partially sealed, flexible diaphragm attached to a pushrod. When the accelerator is suddenly released, the throttle linkage hits the pushrod, which slowly moves inward. Some dashpots also use vacuum to control the rate at which the throttle closes. See Figure 21-24.

Vacuum Vents

Vacuum developed in the venturi and elsewhere in the carburetor bore can be used with vacuum-operated devices to perform work. Ports within the carburetor bore are connected to vacuum motors and other devices by small-diameter metal pipes and tubes. Uses of vacuum developed within the carburetor bore can include:

- Making ignition spark occur sooner or later (see Unit 34)
- Operating emission-control mechanisms (refer to Unit 41).

Ported vacuum. *Ported vacuum* is vacuum from a port placed slightly above the position of the throttle plate at idle. As the throttle plate opens, more of the port is exposed to the flow of air through the barrel. This causes a higher vacuum. If the throttle is opened wide suddenly, vacuum drops. Ported vacuum can be used to operate ignition distributor advance and/or retard mechanisms, as discussed in Unit 34.

Throttle-Positioner Solenoid

The position of the throttle plate for idle speed operation can be controlled by a simple screw mechanism on the throttle linkage. However, an *electrical solenoid* also can be used to set the correct idle speed when the engine is running. An electrical solenoid is a device that uses electricity to create a magnetic force to push, pull, or hold mechanical linkage.

Some engines tend to diesel badly when the ignition is shut off. On other engines, turning on accessory units such as an air conditioner will slow engine idle speed. Idle speed may be slowed to a point at which the engine will shake badly. To prevent both conditions, idle speed can be set by use of an *idle-speed solenoid.*

An idle positioner solenoid is shown in Figure 21-24. When electricity is applied to the solenoid, its plunger extends. The plunger holds the throttle plate open enough to produce the correct idle speed, often called *curb idle speed.* When electricity is shut off, the plunger retracts, and the throttle plate closes further. This cuts off the fuel supply to prevent run-on.

This movement is used to decrease engine idle speed sufficiently when the ignition is shut off to prevent dieseling. Alternately, turning on the solenoid can increase engine idle speed. This will make up for the slowing effect of parasitic losses from use of engine accessories, such as an air conditioner compressor.

Electronic Control Devices

Control devices can be either input information senders or output control *actuator* mechanisms. An actuator is a device that responds to a signal by producing an action, such as moving a mechanical device.

Throttle-position sensor. A *throttle-position sensor* relays information to a control system about how far the throttle plate of the carburetor is opened. See Figure 21-25. Depending on this information, signals

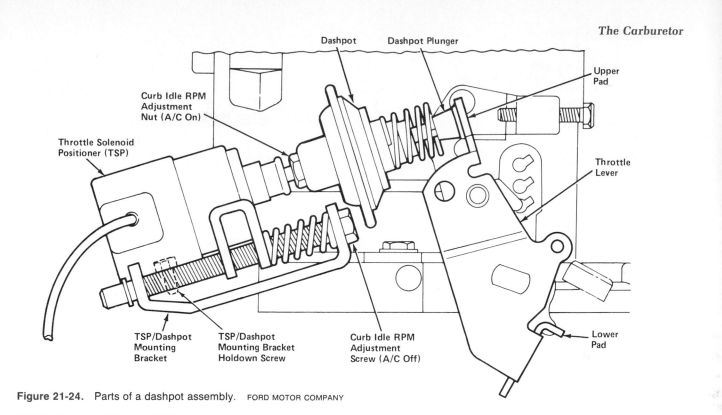

Figure 21-24. Parts of a dashpot assembly. FORD MOTOR COMPANY

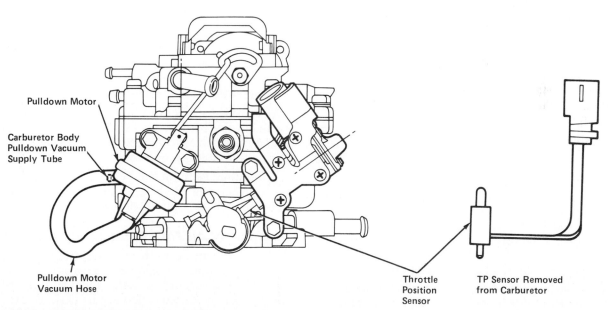

Figure 21-25. Throttle position sensor assembly. FORD MOTOR COMPANY

might be sent to other units within the vehicle to modify their operation.

Mixture-control solenoid. To maintain an optimum air-fuel ratio, a tapered or stepped needle can be positioned in one or more carburetor jets. This needle is similar to that used in a mixture-enrichment system. The control unit can send a signal to a solenoid to lower or raise the needle. Lowering the needle cuts off fuel flow, while raising the needle permits fuel flow. The control unit responds to other signals from the engine about air-fuel ratio, as discussed in Unit 38. A solenoid-operated mixture-control unit is shown in Figure 21-26. Such systems are used in *feedback carburetors,* which vary mixture ratio in relation to information provided by sensing units. The raw information is processed by an *electronic control unit* and "fed back" as control signals to the *mixture-control solenoid.*

In operation, the needle continuously closes and opens the fuel passage. This provides as close to a stoichiometric (14.7:1) air-fuel ratio as possible. When

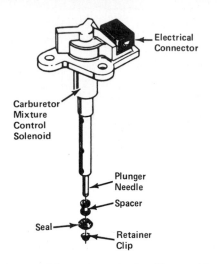

Figure 21-26. Mixture control solenoid assembly.
BUICK MOTOR DIVISION—GMC

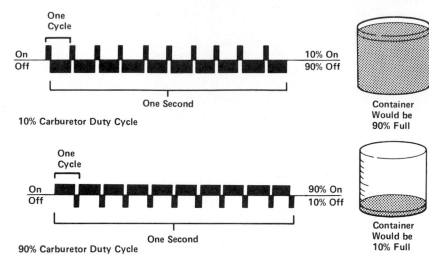

Figure 21-27. Duty cycles. CHRYSLER CORPORATION

electricity flows to the mixture-control solenoid, the needle is held in the closed position.

The relative amount of time that the mixture-control solenoid closes the fuel passage is called the *duty cycle*. Figure 21-27 illustrates the results of different duty cycles.

21.9 ALTERNATE TYPES OF CARBURETORS

In addition to the single-bore carburetor with a fixed venturi size discussed above, other types of carburetion may be used. These types include:

- Multiple-venturi carburetors
- Variable-venturi carburetors.

Multiple-Venturi Carburetors

The more carburetor bores, the more air-fuel mixture can be drawn into the engine to increase power output. Two- and four-venturi (2V and 4V) carburetors are common. Three-venturi carburetors are produced for Honda vehicles. The third bore provides a rich mixture for a stratified-charge engine design.

On 2V carburetors, both bores may operate at all times in the ways discussed above. Or, one bore may operate only when extra power is demanded by the driver's pressure on the accelerator. The action and synchronization of the throttle plates can be controlled by vacuum and/or mechanical linkage.

When one bore is used for additional engine power, it may open *progressively* in relation to the *primary,* or first, throttle plate. Such a *secondary progression system* is illustrated in Figure 21-28.

Carburetors come in many different sizes and configurations. One-venturi carburetors generally are used with inline engines. Two-venturi carburetors are used mostly on V-type engines.

Two-venturi primary/secondary and four-venturi primary/secondary carburetors were developed to gain a compromise of economy and power. They are "middle-of-the-road" carburetors.

These units have a primary side developed for high economy and a secondary side for additional power. Understand, of course, that both economy and power cannot be attained at the same time. An example of a four-venturi carburetor is the General Motors Rochester model known as the Quadrajet, illustrated in Figure 21-29.

Variable-Venturi Carburetors

The venturi (restriction) in a carburetor bore can be varied in size by moving a *slide valve* within an opening. A slide valve is a device that slides back and forth to open or close an opening.

Manifold vacuum can be used to position the slide valve to change the size of the venturi. A cutaway view of such a system is shown in Figure 21-30.

Direction of Air Flow Through the Carburetor

Note that the air flows through the slide valve venturi sideways, or horizontally. Such a carburetor is known as a *sidedraft carburetor*. Late-model Honda Preludes use two sidedraft variable-venturi carburetors.

Ford used variable venturi carburetors for one year. As can be seen from Figure 21-31, Ford's sliding valves and venturis were positioned horizontally, rather than vertically.

When air flows vertically downward, as in most passenger vehicle carburetors, the design is known as a *downdraft carburetor*. Early vehicles also had *updraft carburetors,* in which the air flowed upward through the barrel.

Multiple Carburetors

More than one carburetor can be used on specially designed intake manifolds. Multiple carburetors are often used on racing and high-performance vehicles.

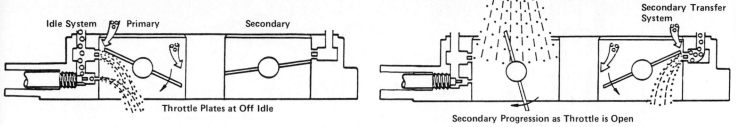

Idle System   Primary   Secondary

Throttle Plates at Off Idle

Secondary Transfer System

Secondary Progression as Throttle is Open

Figure 21-28. Secondary progression system operation.   FORD MOTOR COMPANY

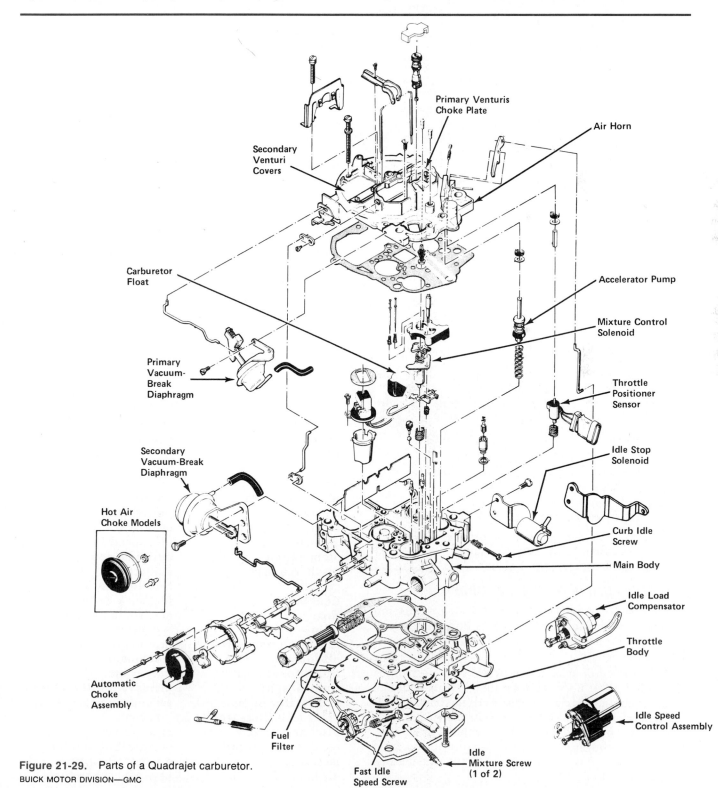

Primary Venturis
Choke Plate

Air Horn

Secondary
Venturi
Covers

Carburetor
Float

Accelerator Pump

Mixture Control
Solenoid

Primary
Vacuum-
Break
Diaphragm

Throttle
Positioner
Sensor

Secondary
Vacuum-Break
Diaphragm

Idle Stop
Solenoid

Hot Air
Choke Models

Curb Idle
Screw

Main Body

Idle Load
Compensator

Throttle
Body

Automatic
Choke
Assembly

Idle Speed
Control Assembly

Fuel
Filter

Idle
Mixture Screw
(1 of 2)

Fast Idle
Speed Screw

Figure 21-29.   Parts of a Quadrajet carburetor.
BUICK MOTOR DIVISION—GMC

211

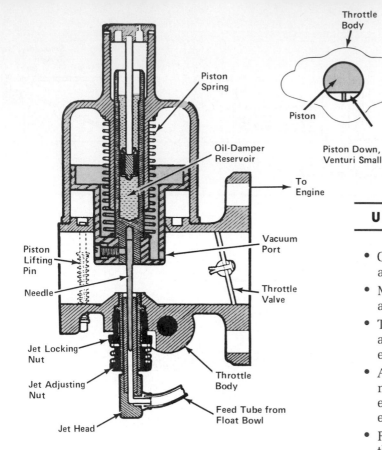

Figure 21-30. Variable-venturi carburetor assembly.

Piston Spring

Oil-Damper Reservoir

To Engine

Piston Lifting Pin

Needle

Vacuum Port

Throttle Valve

Jet Locking Nut

Jet Adjusting Nut

Jet Head

Throttle Body

Feed Tube from Float Bowl

Throttle Body

Piston

Piston Down, Venturi Small

Tapered Needle

Piston Half-Way Up, Venturi Larger

Venturi

Piston Up, Venturi Maximum Size

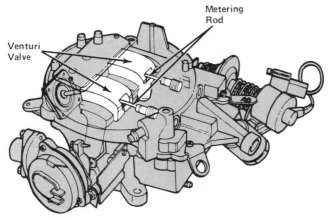

Figure 21-31. Ford carburetor with horizontal venturi valves.
FORD MOTOR COMPANY

Metering Rod

Venturi Valve

21.10 THE FUTURE OF THE CARBURETOR

To meet increasingly complex and strict emission control, performance, and fuel economy requirements, carburetors have become more complicated and expensive.

Fuel injection systems controlled by electronics can perform the necessary air-fuel mixture change functions more quickly, reliably, and inexpensively. It is expected that, by 1990, all production passenger vehicles will be equipped with fuel injection systems. However, carburetor service will continue to be a necessary and well-paid job skill for auto mechanics for many years.

UNIT HIGHLIGHTS

- Carburetion consists of metering, atomization, and vaporization.
- Metering is accomplished by fixed, variable, and air-bleed jets.
- The basic carburetor circuits are the float, idle and low-speed, accelerator pump, main metering, enrichment, and choke circuits.
- Additional equipment is added to carburetors to modify their operation for temperature, altitude, emission control requirements, and operation of external devices.
- Feedback carburetors modify air-fuel ratios through information provided by sensors. This information is "fed back" through an electronic control unit to move a mixture-control solenoid.
- Alternate systems of carburetion include multiple-barrel, variable-venturi, and multiple-carburetor systems.

TERMS

carburetion	choke pull-off
metering	choke break
jet	fast-idle cam
orifice	hot-idle compensator
needle valve	aneroid bellows
idle mixture control screw	dashpot
air-bleed jet	ported vacuum
emulsion tube	electrical solenoid
atomization	idle-speed solenoid
discharge port	curb idle speed
circuit	actuator
float bowl	throttle-position sensor
float	feedback carburetors
idling	electronic mixture control
idle discharge port	mixture-control solenoid
off-idle port	
transitional port	duty cycle
transfer port	primary throttle plate
accelerator pump	secondary progression system
main metering circuit	
discharge nozzle	slide valve
enrichment circuit	sidedraft carburetor
metering rod	downdraft carburetor
air horn	updraft carburetor

DIRECTIONS: The following questions are similar to those used on mechanic certification tests. On a separate sheet of paper, write the letter of the correct choice.

1. All of the following stages are involved in the carburetion process EXCEPT

A. condensation.

B. metering.

C. atomization.

D. vaporization.

2. Two mechanics are discussing what happens when a throttle plate is closed suddenly during cruising.

Mechanic A says that large amounts of fuel can be drawn into the cylinders and cause increased power output.

Mechanic B says that exhaust gases can be drawn into the cylinders during valve overlap and cause increased fuel economy.

Who is correct?

A. A only   B. B only   C. Both A and B   D. Neither A nor B

3. Which of the following statements is correct?

I. Many carburetor circuits are necessary to provide varying air-fuel mixture ratios for different engine temperature, load, and speed conditions.

II. Many carburetor circuits are necessary to achieve a constant stoichiometric (14.7:1) air-fuel mixture at all times.

A. I only   B. II only   C. Both I and II   D. Neither I nor II

4. Which of the following is an essential part of a feedback carburetor?

A. Throttle position sensor

B. Engine information sending units

C. Mixture-control solenoid

D. Electronic control unit

5. Mechanic A says that ported vacuum can be used to operate ignition distributor mechanisms.

Mechanic B says that intake manifold vacuum can be used to draw blow-by gases and oil vapors from a PCV system into the cylinders.

Who is correct?

A. A only   B. B only   C. Both A and B   D. Neither A nor B

SUPPLEMENTAL ACTIVITIES

1. Examine a carburetor on a vehicle chosen by your instructor. Refer to the vehicle manufacturer's service manual and identify and describe as many parts as possible.

2. Refer to the proper vehicle manufacturer's service manual and locate all adjustments on a shop carburetor. Make a list of the adjustments possible on that particular carburetor.

3. Make a drawing on the classroom blackboard of a needle valve and explain how it could be adjusted to provide more or less fluid flow.

4. Imagine starting a car that has been sitting overnight. Describe the operation of each of the basic carburetor circuits as the vehicle is started, warmed up, and driven from low to highway speeds, including passing other vehicles.

5. Explain the duty-cycle of a mixture-control solenoid in a feedback carburetor.

22 CARBURETOR SERVICE

UNIT PREVIEW

Carburetor preventive maintenance consists of replacing filters, checking for leaks, and adjusting automatic choke operation.

Common carburetor problems include lack of fuel at carburetor, stuck or gummy automatic choke, flooding, and driveability problems.

Driveability problems include dieseling, detonation, stalling, rough idle, missing, hesitation, surging, sponginess, poor gas mileage and cutting out.

Carburetor overhaul involves several steps. The first stage includes carburetor identification, disconnection of attachments, and carburetor removal. The next stage includes carburetor disassembly, cleaning and inspection, replacement of parts and gaskets, bench adjustments, and reassembly. The last stage includes carburetor replacement, replacement of all linkage and other connections, and carburetor adjustments.

On modern carburetors, idle mixture adjustments must be done with the aid of an exhaust gas analyzer. This is done to meet federal and state air standards.

LEARNING OBJECTIVES

When you have completed your assignments and exercises in this unit, you should be able to:

☐ Perform routine carburetor maintenance.

☐ Adjust an automatic choke.

☐ Adjust idle speed.

☐ Replace carburetor and intake manifold vacuum lines.

☐ Identify and describe some possible causes for driveability problems.

☐ Correctly adjust a carburetor float.

SAFETY PRECAUTIONS

Have a class B (flammable liquids) fire extinguisher fully charged and readily available when attempting any type of carburetor or fuel system service.

Make sure no sources of possible ignition are present in the area where carburetor or fuel system service is being performed. These sources include lighted cigarettes, electrical switches or tools, and open flames of any kind.

Avoid looking directly down the bore of a carburetor still installed on a vehicle. Wear eye protection at all times in the shop area. If the engine is cranked or started, flames from a backfire can shoot out of the carburetor bore. This can cause serious burns and/or blindness.

Overhauling carburetors involves working with powerful solvents that can cause skin and eye irritation and damage. Always wear rubber gloves to avoid prolonged skin contact with carburetor cleaning chemicals.

Wear eye protection when using compressed air to dry carburetor parts.

After carburetor service, crank the engine to allow the fuel pump to deliver fuel to the carburetor for starting. Do not attempt to pour liquid gasoline down the throat of the carburetor. Severe explosions and fires can result.

On vehicles with automatic transmissions, some adjustments are done with the engine running and the selector in drive. Set the emergency brake tightly and block the driving wheels before attempting any carburetor adjustment procedures.

Never stand directly in front of a running vehicle while carburetor adjustments are being done. If the throttle is opened suddenly, the vehicle may jump forward over wheel blocks. It can run over or crush anyone standing in front.

Modern carburetors are extremely complicated. They vary greatly among manufacturers and models. Even the same basic carburetor installed on different engines can vary considerably. Do not attempt carburetor maintenance, repairs, or adjustments without the proper manufacturer's service manual.

22.1 CARBURETOR PREVENTIVE MAINTENANCE

Carburetor preventive maintenance consists of the following items:

- Replacing air and PCV filters
- Replacing fuel filter
- Checking for fuel and air leaks
- Cleaning external carburetor linkages
- Checking and/or adjusting automatic choke operation.

Filter Replacement

Refer to Topic 20.5 for fuel, air, and PCV filter replacement. Check the proper shop manual for filter identification.

Fuel and Air Leaks

Refer to Topic 20.4 for procedures to check for leaks. A carburetor is divided into three major sections:

- The *air horn,* or top
- The *main body,* which contains the float bowl and most passages and discharge ports
- The *throttle body,* or lower portion, which contains the throttle plates.

These sections and other attachments are shown in Figure 22-1. Leakage can occur between sections or where fittings or external parts are attached.

In some cases, external leakage from parts of the carburetor can be stopped by tightening fittings or attaching fasteners.

Refer to the manufacturer's service manual for correct torque specifications. Carburetors are made of metal that can crack or distort. This can occur if a fitting is overtightened or if covers are tightened in an improper sequence. One example of an air horn tightening sequence is shown in Figure 22-2.

Checking an Automatic Choke

In time, fuel varnish and deposits can build on choke plates, cross-shafts and bearing points, and external linkage. Carburetor spray cleaner can be used, as shown in Figure 22-3, to remove these deposits. The choke plate can be moved by hand to work the cleaner into tiny crevices and free sticky, gummy linkage.

SAFETY CAUTION: Wear eye protection whenever using spray cans of any kind. Carburetor spray cleaner can cause severe skin and eye irritation, and can lead to blindness.

Carburetor spray cleaner also can be used to clean the external parts of the carburetor.

CAUTION: Carburetor spray cleaner can damage or destroy some rubber and plastic parts used in carburetors. Avoid spraying such parts. Cleaning the exterior of the carburetor will not cure problems caused by internal gum and varnish buildup.

Internal carburetor problems caused by fuel varnish and deposits require carburetor disassembly and cleaning, as described below.

Adjusting an Automatic Choke

Automatic choke maintenance consists of three basic adjustments:

- Richness
- Choke pull-off
- Fast idle speed.

Richness adjustment.   The amount of fuel delivered during engine cranking depends upon how far the choke plate is closed. An adjustment can be made to make the choke plate close the correct amount. This is done when the engine is cold and the accelerator pedal or linkage has been depressed to unlock the choke. In some cases, a drill bit or other gauge of a specific size is used to measure a specific opening distance. This measurement is made between the top edge of the choke plate and the air horn wall.

One method of adjustment is to physically bend metal parts until they hold the choke plate in the desired position. There should be no pressure on the drill bit or gauge (see Figure 22-4).

Modern methods include the use of a choke *protractor,* or angle gauge, that attaches to the choke plate with a magnet. See Figure 22-5. Several adjustments can be made accurately with such a protractor. These include fast-idle cam adjustment, vacuum break adjustments, and unloader adjustments.

Adjustments can be made to automatic choke thermostatic spring mechanisms mounted on the carburetor. Loosen three holding screws and rotate a cover attached to the spring (see Figure 22-6).

Choke mechanisms on 1978 and later vehicles may be riveted so that no minor adjustments can be made. The rivets can be drilled out for major carburetor service, as shown in Figure 22-7.

CAUTION: Removal of riveted choke covers and adjustment to specifications other than those of the vehicle manufacturer will change exhaust emissions. This is a violation of federal and/or state air-pollution laws.

Choke pull-off adjustment.   Several types of choke pull-off mechanisms can be used. Vacuum-operated pull-off devices may require using a hand vacuum tester. This tool is used to apply vacuum, plug vent

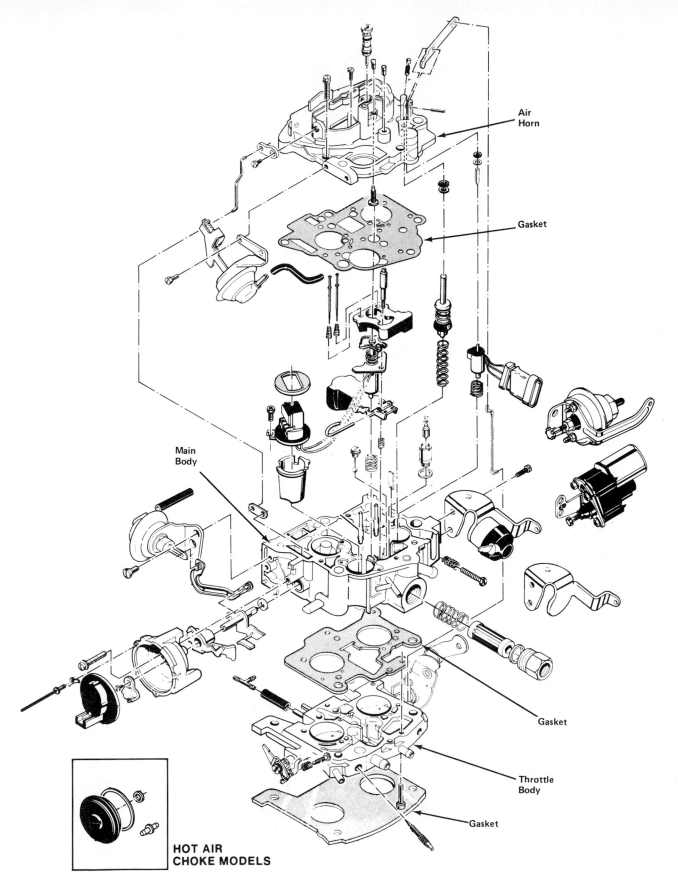

Air Horn

Gasket

Main Body

Gasket

Throttle Body

Gasket

HOT AIR CHOKE MODELS

Figure 22-1. Parts of a carburetor. BUICK MOTOR DIVISION—GMC

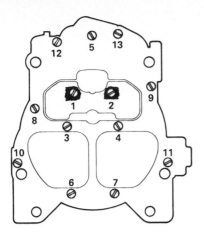

Figure 22-2. Air horn tightening sequence.
BUICK MOTOR DIVISION—GMC

Figure 22-3. Cleaning an automatic choke mechanism.
CHRYSLER CORPORATION

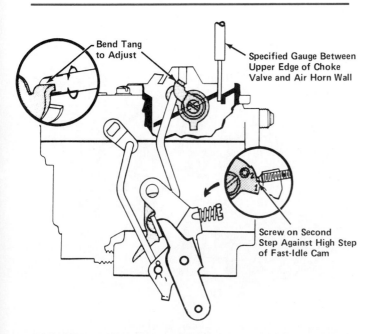

Figure 22-4. Choke rod adjustment. BUICK MOTOR DIVISION—GMC

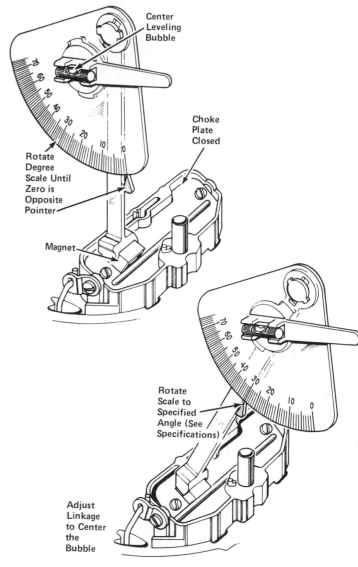

Figure 22-5. Choke valve angle gauge.
BUICK MOTOR DIVISION—GMC

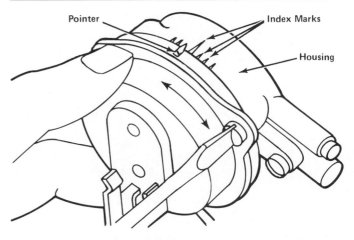

Figure 22-6. Choke spring adjustment.

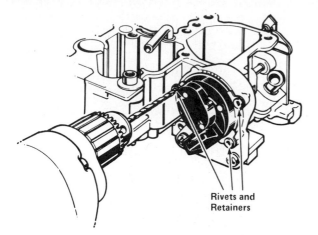

Figure 22-7. Choke cover removal. BUICK MOTOR DIVISION—GMC

Plugging Air Bleed Holes

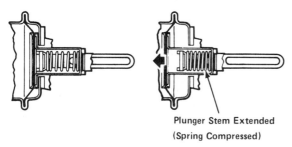

Pump Cup or Valve Stem Seal

Tape Hole in Tube

Tape End of Cover

BUCKING SPRINGS

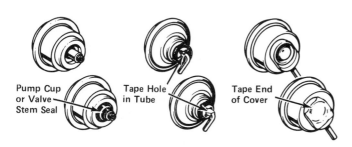

Plunger Stem Extended
(Spring Compressed)

Plunger Bucking Spring

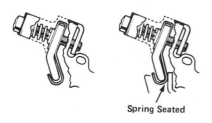

Spring Seated

Leaf Type Bucking Spring

Figure 22-8. Vacuum break adjustment information.
BUICK MOTOR DIVISION—GMC

holes, and/or extend plungers and spring mechanisms, as shown in Figure 22-8.

Refer to the manufacturer's service manual for correct adjustment procedures. One example of a pull-off adjustment is shown in Figure 22-9.

Fast-idle speed adjustment. Adjustments for fast-idle speed are made with the adjusting screw resting on a specified step of the fast-idle cam. To position the fast-idle screw correctly, the throttle must be opened and the choke plate manually closed. This permits moving the fast-idle cam. The correct adjustment is obtained by connecting a tachometer to the engine and adjusting the screw until specified rpm is reached. Refer to Figure 22-9. This adjustment is made while the engine is at normal operating temperature.

22.2 CARBURETOR PROBLEMS

Common carburetor problems include the following:

- Lack of fuel at carburetor
- Stuck or gummy automatic choke
- Flooding
- Driveability problems.

1 Attach rubber band to green tang of intermediate choke shaft.

2 Open throttle to allow choke valve to close.

3 Set up angle guage and set angle to specification.

4 Retract vacuum break plunger, using vacuum source, at least 18″ Hg. plug air bleed holes where applicable

4a On Quadrajets, air valve rod must not restrict plunger from retracting fully. If necessary, bend rod here to permit full plunger travel. Where applicable, plunger stem must be extended fully to compress plunger bucking spring.

5 To center bubble, either:
A Adjust with 1/8″ hex wrench (vacuum still applied) —or—
B Support at "S" and bend vacuum break rod (vacuum still applied)

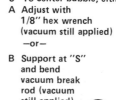

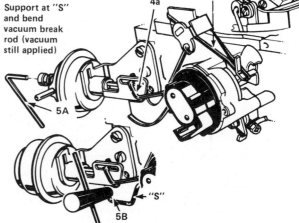

Figure 22-9. Rear vacuum break adjustment.
BUICK MOTOR DIVISION—GMC

Lack of Fuel at Carburetor

Refer to Unit 20 for a discussion of diagnosing fuel-delivery system problems. The following symptom may indicate that a needle valve is stuck closed: A check indicates no discharge from the accelerator pump nozzles as the throttle is opened quickly.

You may be able to free the needle valve by gently tapping on the fuel inlet fitting. Use a small metal hammer or part. This must be done gently, and only briefly, to avoid cracking or breaking the metal of the carburetor. See Figure 22-10.

After tapping, crank the engine to activate the fuel pump. Move the throttle linkage and check for fuel. If tapping does not solve the problem, follow these steps:

1. Remove the air horn.
2. Inspect and clean or replace the needle valve, float parts, and accelerator pump.
3. Properly reinstall the air horn.

Stuck Automatic Choke

It is possible for the automatic choke to become stuck fully open, fully closed, or at any point in between. Cleaning a stuck automatic choke is discussed in Topic 22.1.

Flooding

Flooding is excess unvaporized fuel in the intake manifold. Flooding can be caused by heating of fuel in the float bowl after the engine is shut off. (The cooling system is no longer operating.) Flooding occurs most commonly in hot weather or after prolonged stop-and-go driving. Flooding also can occur during unsuccessful attempts at starting in cold weather.

Percolation. *Percolation* is the name given to the boiling of fuel within the float bowl. Boiling fuel can travel through discharge and vent tubes to the barrel of the carburetor and into the intake manifold.

To start a flooded engine, depress the accelerator pedal all the way to the floor and hold it down. This action opens the throttle plates fully for maximum air flow, which will vaporize the excess gasoline. Turn the key and crank the engine until it starts. Crank for 15-second intervals, not longer. This will prevent the starter from overheating.

Float and fuel pump problems. Flooding also can be caused by a needle valve that fails to close, or by excess fuel pump pressure. These problems can be detected by observing the fuel bowl vent as the engine is cranked. Fuel will gush out of the vent, as shown in Figure 22-11.

A contaminant particle may lodge between the needle valve and its seat and prevent the valve from closing. Tapping the fuel inlet fitting gently, and briefly, as described above, may free the valve. If not, the air horn must be removed and the needle valve serviced.

The same problem can be caused by excess fuel pressure. Excess pressure may result from a defective pressure-regulation valve within the fuel pump or a blocked vapor-return line. It also may be caused by a saturated float that has sunk to the bottom of the bowl.

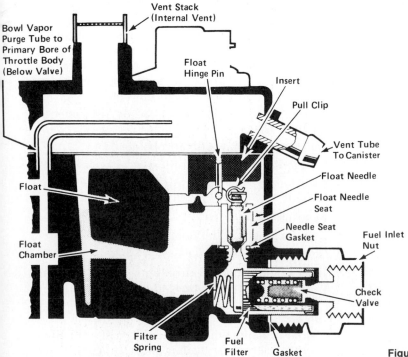

Figure 22-10. Float system assembly. BUICK MOTOR DIVISION—GMC

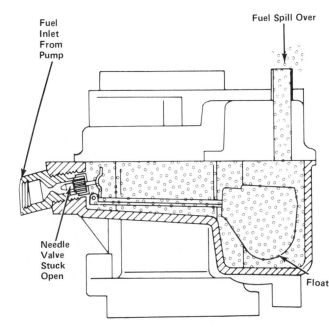

Figure 22-11. Flooding caused by excess fuel or fuel pressure. CHRYSLER CORPORATION

Checking for correct fuel-pump pressure output is discussed in Unit 20.

22.3 DRIVEABILITY PROBLEMS

Driveability describes the proper operation of a vehicle. The vehicle starts easily, does not stall or die, accelerates well, runs smoothly, and delivers reasonable gas mileage. Driveability problems include:

- Dieseling
- Detonation
- Stalling
- Rough idle
- Missing
- Hesitation
- Surging
- Sluggishness
- Sponginess
- Poor gas mileage
- Cutting out.

Dieseling and Detonation

Dieseling and detonation are discussed in Unit 19. Fuel system problems contributing to dieseling are lean fuel mixtures, excessive idle speed, and sticking linkages.

Lean air-fuel mixtures also can contribute to detonation. An example of a visual flowchart for diagnosis and repair of detonation is illustrated in Figure 22-12.

Stalling and/or Rough Idle

Stalling, when the engine dies after starting, and/or rough idle can occur when the engine is cold or hot.

Cold stalling or rough idle. Cold stalling can be caused by ignition problems, discussed in Unit 35. Fuel system problems that cause too lean a fuel mixture also can produce stalling and rough idle. These problems include:

- Loose, broken, cracked, kinked, or disconnected vacuum hoses
- Leaking carburetor or intake manifold gaskets
- Sticky carburetor throttle or choke linkage
- Stuck needle valve (flooding)
- Defective or misadjusted vacuum pull-off units
- Incorrect choke richness or fast idle speed
- Defective thermostatic air cleaner (see Unit 42)
- Defective EGR (opening too early).

Hot stalling or rough idle. Hot stalling or a rough idle can be caused by ignition problems, discussed in Unit 35. Fuel system problems that can produce stalling or a rough idle when the engine is hot include:

- Loose, broken, cracked, kinked, or disconnected vacuum hoses
- Leaking carburetor or intake manifold gaskets
- Incorrect curb-idle speed
- Flooding
- Defective thermostatic air cleaner (see Unit 42)

- Clogged PCV valve (see Unit 42)
- Defective EGR valve (see Unit 42)
- Carburetor idle mixture screws set too rich
- Excessive carbon buildup on piston crowns (see Unit 45)
- Clogged oil filter element.

Missing

Missing is a lack of power from one or more cylinders. Missing can be caused by ignition system and engine mechanical problems, discussed in Unit 43. Fuel system problems that can cause missing include:

- Loose, broken, cracked, kinked, or disconnected vacuum hoses
- Leaking carburetor or intake manifold gaskets.

Hesitation

Hesitation is a momentary lack of response as the accelerator is pressed down, such as when moving away from a stop. Severe hesitation can cause the engine to stall and die. Hesitation can be caused by ignition system problems, discussed in Unit 35. Fuel system-related problems that can cause hesitation include:

- Loose, broken, cracked, kinked, or disconnected vacuum hoses
- Leaking carburetor or intake manifold gaskets
- Sticky carburetor throttle or choke linkage
- Defective accelerator pump linkage or parts
- Incorrect float level
- Defective thermostatic air cleaner.

Surging

Surging occurs when the engine speeds up and/or slows down with the throttle held steady. Surging can occur at any road speed. Surging can be caused by ignition system problems. In addition, fuel system problems contributing to surging include:

- Loose, broken, cracked, kinked or disconnected vacuum hoses
- Defective thermostatic air cleaner
- Clogged carburetor fuel filter
- Insufficient fuel pump pressure and/or volume output
- Restricted fuel lines
- Low fuel level in the float bowl
- Contaminants or water in fuel tank
- Internal carburetor problems (contaminants, water, defective or damaged parts, and so on).

Sluggishness or Sponginess

Sluggishness occurs when the engine will not deliver sufficient power under load or at high speed. It does not accelerate as quickly as normal, loses too much

Step/Sequence

Result

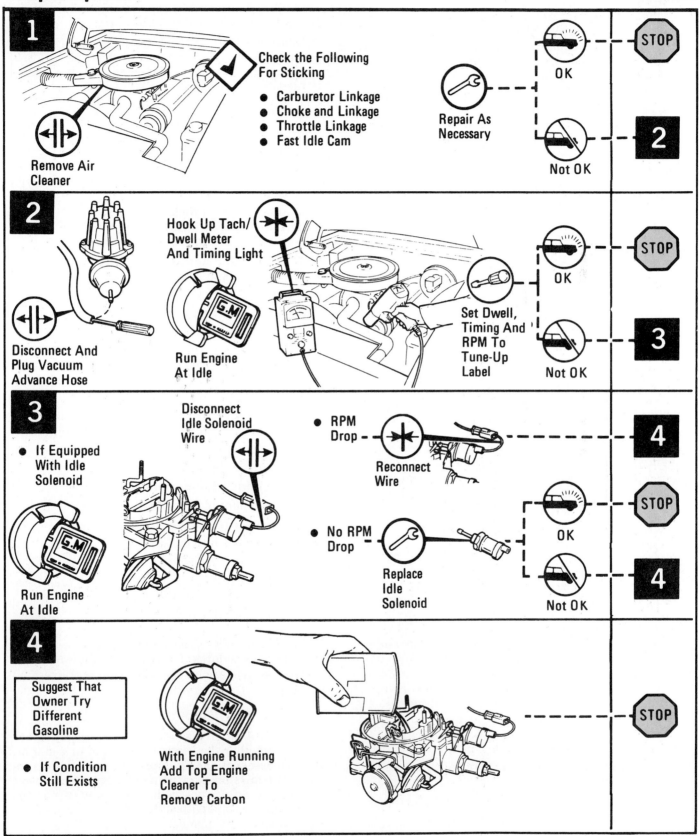

Figure 22-12. Dieseling diagnosis and repair. GENERAL MOTORS CORPORATION

speed going up hills, and cannot reach normal top speed.

Sponginess occurs when the engine does not speed up as much as expected when the accelerator is depressed, especially during cruising. Pushing the pedal down farther than normal produces an increase in speed.

Sluggishness or sponginess can be the result of engine problems, as discussed in Unit 43. Incorrect ignition system operation or specifications also can cause these problems, as discussed in Unit 35. Fuel system problems related to sponginess include:

- Dirty air filter
- Throttle and/or carburetor linkage preventing throttle plates from opening fully
- Defective thermostatic air cleaner (see Unit 42)
- Internal carburetor problems (sticky enrichment circuit parts, contaminants in jets, incorrect float adjustment, or bent, damaged, or inoperative metering rods and power valves)
- Defective EGR valve (see Unit 42)
- Low fuel pressure.

Poor Gas Mileage

Before assuming that something mechanical is wrong when a vehicle owner complains of poor gas mileage, ask about driving habits. Vehicles driven less than 10 miles before being shut off do not warm up fully. A cold engine will deliver only about half of its gas mileage capability. Best mileage occurs when the engine is fully warmed up and running at constant speeds on the highway. Other factors that lower gas mileage include:

- Extra weight in the vehicle
- Driving on steep mountain grades
- Driving in cold weather
- Underinflated tires
- Poor wheel alignment
- Driving against the wind.

The EPA (Environmental Protection Agency) new-vehicle car mileage ratings are derived in a laboratory on a chassis dynamometer. The ratings are not achieved by driving vehicles under real-world conditions. The EPA ratings include a disclaimer, or warning, that driving conditions affect gas mileage.

Mechanical conditions that can affect gas mileage include engine problems, discussed in Unit 43, and ignition system problems, Unit 35. Fuel system problems that can cause lowered gas mileage include:

- Dirty air filter
- Fuel leaks
- Loose, broken, cracked, kinked, or disconnected vacuum lines
- Carburetor or intake manifold gasket leaks

- Improper thermostatic air-cleaner operation
- Stuck heat riser valve
- Choke richness and fast-idle settings
- Internal carburetor problems (sticky enrichment circuit parts, contaminants in jets, incorrect float adjustment, or bent, damaged, or inoperative metering rods and power valves).

Cutting Out

Cutting out occurs when the engine stops entirely at irregular intervals and produces no power. The engine usually does not die completely, but the loss of power occurs repeatedly and intermittently. Cutting out is usually worse under heavy acceleration.

Ignition system problems, discussed in Unit 35, are strongly associated with cutting out. Fuel system problems that can cause cutting out include:

- Clogged carburetor fuel filter
- Insufficient fuel pump pressure and/or output volume
- Clogged or leaking fuel lines
- Contaminants or water in fuel tank.

22.4 CARBURETOR OVERHAUL

Carburetor overhaul consists of these general steps:

1. Carburetor identification
2. Disconnecting attachments to the carburetor
3. Carburetor removal
4. Carburetor disassembly
5. Carburetor cleaning and inspection
6. Replacement of parts and gaskets
7. Carburetor bench adjustments
8. Carburetor reassembly
9. Carburetor replacement
10. Replacing linkage, hoses and tubes, fuel lines, and electrical connections
11. Carburetor adjustments.

The manufacturer's service manual must be consulted for specific procedures. The outline below covers the general steps that are involved in carburetor overhaul operations.

Carburetor Identification

Vehicle manufacturers use different carburetors based on whether the vehicle is a sedan or a station wagon, whether it has air conditioning and an automatic transmission or a manual transmission, and other factors. Before proceeding with any carburetor adjustments or repairs, positive identification of the carburetor must be made.

Removable metal identification tags are attached to carburetors (see Figure 22-13). In some cases, an

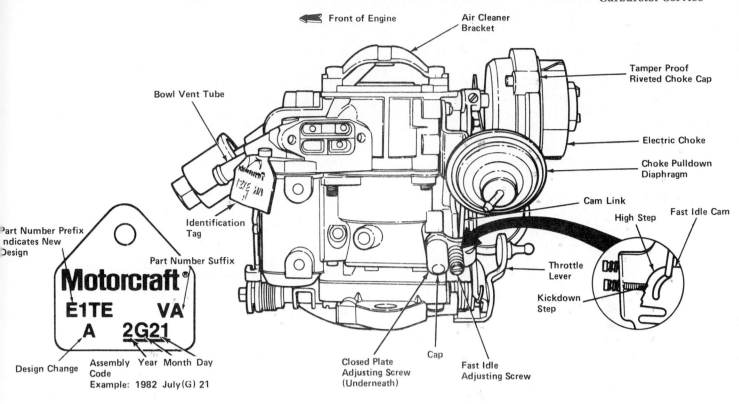

Figure 22-13. Carburetor identification tag location. FORD MOTOR COMPANY

alphanumeric identification will be stamped some-where on the unit.

Proper identification is impossible without the metal tag or stamped identification. Do not lose the tag during overhaul operations.

Disconnecting Carburetor Attachments

To remove the carburetor, all items attached to it must be removed.

SAFETY CAUTION: **Disconnect the battery ground terminal before attempting carburetor service to prevent electrical sparks that could cause an explosion or fire.**

These attachments include throttle linkage, (Figure 22-14), vapor lines, electrical wiring connections, fuel lines, and well-type choke linkage. Make sketches or notes of how each part comes off for aid in reassembly.

Carburetor Removal

Carburetors are removed by unbolting fasteners connecting the carburetor to the intake manifold. Note the position of any gaskets and/or metal plates during removal. Gaskets and/or metal plates must be reinstalled or replaced exactly as found.

Carburetor Disassembly

Refer to the manufacturer's service manual for the correct sequence of carburetor disassembly.

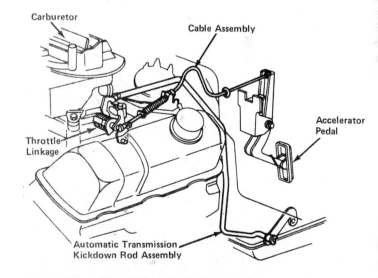

Figure 22-14. Throttle linkage attachment points.
FORD MOTOR COMPANY

External linkage. Generally, all external links must be disconnected before dividing the carburetor into its main sections: air horn, main body, and throttle body. In some cases, the throttle body actually forms the lower part of the main body.

Make drawings or notes of links before they are removed, as shown in Figure 22-15. It is extremely easy to replace links upside down or facing in the wrong direction.

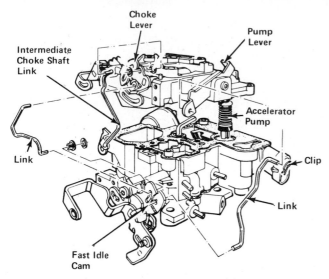

Figure 22-15. Air horn and main body disassembled.
BUICK MOTOR DIVISION—GMC

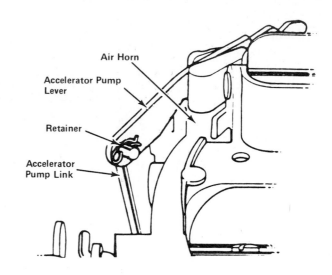

Figure 22-16. Pump link retainer. BUICK MOTOR DIVISION—GMC

Also make drawings of the holes or slots into which the links attach. Moving the links from one hole or slot to another will change the distance that a part will move. Examples are an accelerator pump plunger and a diaphragm. Such a change will alter the amount of fuel discharged, probably causing running problems.

Be especially careful to save and label the small attaching clips that may hold the links on the carburetor, as shown in Figure 22-16.

Main body disassembly. Remove the screws holding the air horn to the main body and the throttle body to the main body. Removal must be done in the sequence recommended by the manufacturer to prevent warping the parts.

Lift the air horn gently, straight up from the main body, as shown in Figure 22-17. Be careful not to bend or damage emulsion tubes and float linkage.

Make drawings or notes of all parts as they are removed, especially the position and size markings of jets, as shown in Figure 22-18.

Be especially careful of the positioning of weights and check valve balls (see Figure 22-19). These small parts must not be intermixed and must be replaced in the correct holes.

Remove all electrically operated devices such as solenoids, stepping motors, and choke heaters. These parts should not be cleaned with any type of solvent.

Remove all parts made of rubber or plastic, such as the float and accelerator pump parts, as shown in Figure 22-20. These parts would be destroyed by the carburetor cleaner solvent. They should always be replaced during carburetor overhaul.

CAUTION: **Do not attempt to remove the throttle plates from the throttle shaft. These are mated parts.**

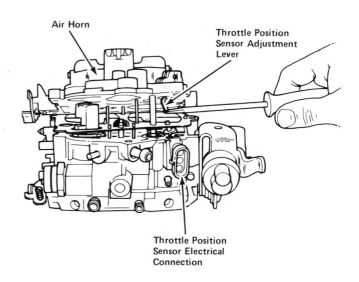

Figure 22-17. Air horn removal. BUICK MOTOR DIVISION—GMC

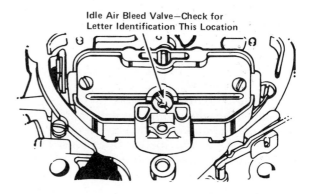

Figure 22-18. Jet identification location.
BUICK MOTOR DIVISION—GMC

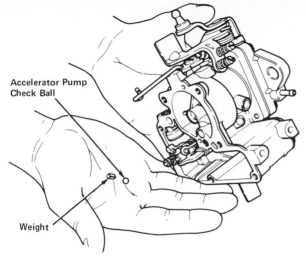

Accelerator Pump
Check Ball

Weight

Figure 22-19. Accelerator pump checkball and weight.
FORD MOTOR COMPANY

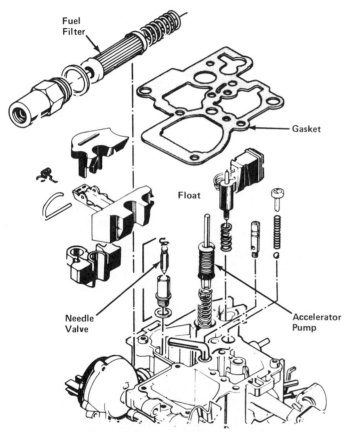

Fuel
Filter

Gasket

Float

Needle
Valve

Accelerator
Pump

Figure 22-20. Parts in the float bowl.
BUICK MOTOR DIVISION—GMC

Carburetor Cleaning and Inspection

Place small carburetor parts in a fine-mesh parts basket before immersion in cleaning solvent.

SAFETY CAUTION: Carburetor cleaning solvent is extremely irritating to skin and can cause permanent blindness if splashed in the eyes. Wear eye protection and rubber gloves when placing carburetor parts in cleaning solvent. Toxic chemicals can be

absorbed through the skin. If heated solvent is being used, make sure adequate ventilation exists and no sources of ignition are present. Carburetor solvent can explode or burn when vaporized by heat.

Main carburetor sections can be placed in larger parts baskets or within the cleaning container. Allow sufficient time for the solvent to dissolve built-up fuel and dirt deposits.

After cleaning, rinse carburetor solvent from parts with water and use compressed air to blow out all ports and passages.

SAFETY CAUTION: Wear eye protection at all times when using compressed air.

CAUTION: Do *not* use any type of metal tool or wire in an attempt to clean carburetor passages or orifices. Such tools or wire will enlarge, scratch, and damage the passages and orifices, causing poor carburetor operation.

Inspect all of the parts for damage, such as cracks, scratches, or deformed metal. Small scratches on mating surfaces between main carburetor sections can be removed by careful filing with a mill file. Care must be taken to maintain flatness and parallelness of such surfaces. Only the amount of metal necessary to eliminate the scratches must be removed. Clean off all traces of metal filings.

Inspect the throttle plates and bores for evidence of gouges or scratches. Check the throttle plate and choke plate shafts for excessive looseness within the throttle body and air horn sections. Air leaks from around these shafts can cause driveability problems. In some cases, the shaft holes can be fitted with bushings to remove excessive clearance.

Badly damaged main carburetor sections usually require the replacement of the entire carburetor.

Replacement of Parts and Gaskets

Carburetor overhaul kits contain necessary replacement parts and gaskets (see Figure 22-21). When replacing accelerator pump plunger cups, it may be necessary to use a thin feeler gauge as a tool. The feeler gauge is used to help fit the edges of the cup into the well. Do this carefully so that the feeler gauge does not cut the cup. Carefully follow the reassembly procedures outlined in the instructions provided with the kit or contained in the manufacturer's service manual.

Carburetor Bench Adjustments

A *bench adjustment* is an adjustment performed while a part or assembly is removed from the vehicle, such as on a workbench. One such important adjustment is float adjustment (Figure 22-22). Other bench adjustments are performed as recommended by the manufacturer's service manual.

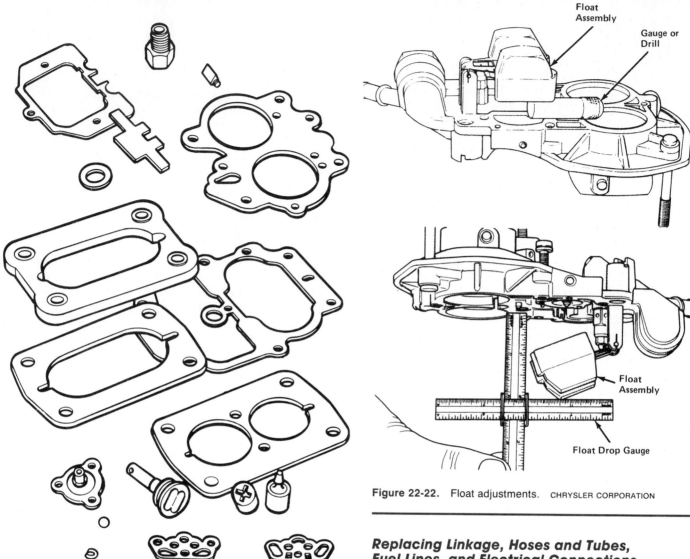

Figure 22-21.   Carburetor overhaul kit.   CHRYSLER CORPORATION

**Float
Assembly**

**Gauge or
Drill**

**Float
Assembly**

Float Drop Gauge

Figure 22-22.   Float adjustments.   CHRYSLER CORPORATION

Carburetor Reassembly

Be especially careful when replacing the carburetor float and air horn assemblies. If parts do not seem to fit together, do not use force. Disassemble and inspect carefully for misplaced or bent parts that prevent reassembly.

Refer to the manufacturer's service manual for correct reassembly sequence. Tighten all screws and attaching parts to the manufacturer's specified torque in the proper pattern, or sequence. Reconnect all external linkage and make bench adjustments as required.

Carburetor Replacement

Carburetor replacement is essentially the reverse of removal. Use all new carburetor base gaskets, properly positioned.

Replacing Linkage, Hoses and Tubes, Fuel Lines, and Electrical Connections

Refer to your drawings or notes made before disconnection. Reconnect all throttle, choke, and other mechanical linkages correctly. Replace all disconnected wires, hoses, and tubes.

Reconnect the battery. Disable the ignition system and crank the engine to allow the fuel pump to supply fuel to the carburetor. Check for fuel leaks.

SAFETY CAUTION: Have a fire extinguisher capable of extinguishing class B fires fully charged and readily available if an explosion or fire should occur. Wear eye protection during starting procedures.

Correct any fuel leakage problems. Make any further external adjustments and checks, such as the external float level check on some General Motors vehicles (see Figure 22-23).

Idle mixture screw adjustment. When possible, make preliminary idle mixture screw adjustments. Gently bottom the idle mixture screws by hand.

226

Unscrew the screws two full turns outward. This should provide a relatively rich mixture adequate for starting.

Carburetor Adjustments

Make preliminary automatic choke and fast idle cam speed adjustments, where possible.

Start the vehicle and let it warm to normal operating temperature. Check for proper choke operation during warm-up.

Adjust curb idle speed by turning idle speed adjustment screws or *solenoid* adjustments (Figure 22-24). A solenoid uses electricity to provide force to hold the throttle open during normal running.

Carburetors may include both an electrically operated solenoid adjustment and a secondary curb idle speed screw adjustment. A secondary curb idle speed screw allows the throttle plate to close more fully, aiding in shutting off the engine quickly.

Solenoids can be used to provide a normally higher curb idle speed. When the ignition key is turned off, electricity no longer provides force to hold the throttle open. The throttle closes farther to slow and shut the engine down. Solenoids can also be used to increase curb idle speed when accessories such as air conditioners are turned on. When accessories are shut off, curb idle speed is controlled by the shutdown idle speed screw.

Secondary curb idle speed screws are a "backup" system for solenoids. If the solenoid fails, the secondary curb idle speed screw prevents the engine from dying.

A specified faster engine speed can be obtained by moving an adjustment on a solenoid when electricity powers the solenoid. To do this, other electrical switches—for example, the air conditioner controls—must be switched on.

To set a specified slower engine speed, wiring connections to the solenoid are disconnected. The secondary curb idle speed screw is then turned to position the throttle plate.

Vehicles without solenoid idle speed adjustments have a single curb-idle speed screw adjustment. Idle

1 With engine running at idle, choke wide-open, carefully insert gauge in vent slot or vent hole (next to air cleaner mounting stud) in air horn. Release gauge and allow it to float freely.

CAUTION: Do not press down on gauge to cause flooding or damage to float.

2 Reading at eye level, observe mark on gauge that lines up with top of casting at the vent slot or vent hole. Setting should be within ±1/16" from specified float level setting.

Remove float gauge from air horn.

3 If the mechanical setting (step 2) varies over ±1/16" from specifications, remove air horn and adjust float level to specifications following normal adjustment procedures.

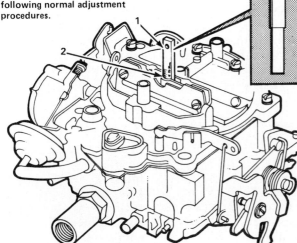

Figure 22-23. External float level adjustment.
CHEVROLET MOTOR DIVISION—GMC

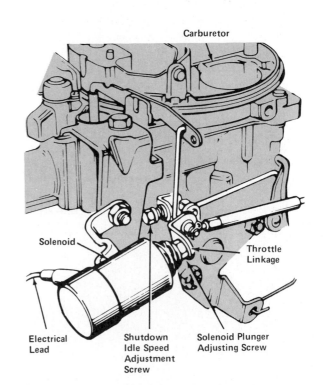

Figure 22-24. Solenoid and secondary curb idle speed screw locations.

Figure 22-25. Exhaust gas analyzer.

speed adjustment procedures are specified in the manufacturer's service manuals.

Idle mixture screws control air-fuel mixture at idle. To conform to clean-air standards, most idle mixture adjustments require a propane adjustment procedure and an exhaust gas analyzer. Connect the analyzer probe to the tailpipe (refer to Figure 22-25). This is discussed in Unit 42. Follow the vehicle manufacturer's instructions to prepare the vehicle properly for testing. This may include ignition system maintenance, explained in Unit 35.

Turn adjustable mixture screws to obtain the proper readings for hydrocarbons (HC) and carbon monoxide (CO).

On a carburetor with a plugged mixture screw access hole, it may be necessary to remove the plug first. See Figure 22-26. Then, adjust mixture screws to obtain correct readings.

With your instructor's permission, perform a road test and check for proper carburetor operation.

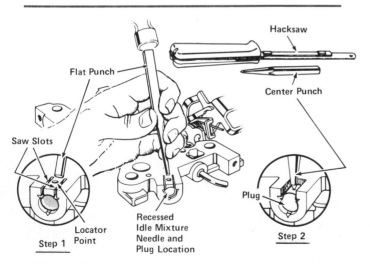

Figure 22-26. Removing idle mixture caps.
BUICK MOTOR DIVISION—GMC

SAFETY CAUTION: Drive in a safe manner. Driving conditions other than normal can create new vehicle performance problems. Carelessness during the test drive can result in an accident. Remember, you are responsible for someone else's vehicle. Drive only in the manner that is required to check or diagnose proper vehicle operation. Observe all speed limits and obey all traffic laws.

UNIT HIGHLIGHTS

- Many safety precautions must be observed when performing fuel system or carburetor service.
- Carburetor preventive maintenance includes replacing air, PCV, and fuel filters. It also involves checking for fuel and air leaks, and checking and/or adjusting automatic choke operation.
- Automatic choke adjustment concerns richness, fast idle speed, and choke pull-off operation.
- Common carburetor problems include lack of fuel at carburetor, stuck or gummy automatic choke, flooding, and driveability problems.
- In addition to engine mechanical and ignition system problems, driveability problems can be caused by carburetor and fuel system defects.
- Driveability problems include dieseling, detonation, stalling, rough idle, missing, hesitation, surging, sluggishness, sponginess, poor gas mileage, and cutting out.
- Carburetor overhaul includes several steps. The first steps include carburetor identification, disconnection of attachments, and carburetor removal. The next steps include carburetor disassembly, cleaning and inspection, replacement of parts and gaskets, bench adjustments, and reassembly. The last steps include carburetor replacement, replacement of all linkage and other connections, and carburetor adjustments.
- On modern carburetors, most idle mixture adjustments include a propane idle adjustment. Also, the adjustments must be done with the aid of an exhaust gas analyzer to meet clean-air standards.

TERMS

air horn	missing
main body	hesitation
throttle body	surging
protractor	sluggishness
flooding	sponginess
percolation	cutting out
driveability	bench adjustment
stalling	solenoid

R E V I E W   Q U E S T I O N S

DIRECTIONS: The following questions are similar to those used on mechanic certification tests. On a separate sheet of paper, write the letter of the correct choice.

1. Carburetor preventive maintenance includes all of the following EXCEPT
A. replacing filters.
B. resetting the float level.
C. checking for fuel and air leaks.
D. checking and/or adjusting automatic choke operation.

2. Mechanic A says that the choke pull-off closes the choke plate during starting.
   Mechanic B says that the fast-idle cam opens the choke plate during starting.
   Who is correct?
A. A only   B. B only   C. Both A and B   D. Neither A nor B

3. A car will not start, and a heavy odor of gasoline is present in the engine compartment. When the air cleaner is removed and the engine is cranked, fuel spurts out of the float bowl vent tube. What is the most likely cause?
A. Defective fuel pump diaphragm
B. Needle valve stuck closed
C. Needle valve stuck open
D. Automatic choke plate stuck closed

4. Which of the following statements is correct?
   I. Loose, broken, cracked, kinked, or disconnected vacuum lines can cause many driveability problems.
   II. Ignition system defects can cause many driveability problems.
A. I only   B. II only   C. Both I and II   D. Neither I nor II

5. All of the following are parts of a carburetor overhaul EXCEPT
A. identification of the carburetor.
B. cleaning, inspection, and replacement of parts.
C. replacement of main carburetor sections.
D. bench and running adjustments.

S U P P L E M E N T A L   A C T I V I T I E S

1. On a vehicle chosen by your instructor, replace air, PCV, and fuel filters, and check for fuel and air leaks.
2. On a vehicle chosen by your instructor, refer to the manufacturer's service manual and adjust choke richness, fast idle, and choke pull-off operation.
3. On a vehicle chosen by your instructor, check and/or replace any defective vacuum lines.
4. Ask at least two relatives or friends about driveability problems with their vehicles. Refer to the text, and make a list of possible causes for each of the driveability problems mentioned.
5. On a disassembled shop carburetor, check and/or make float level adjustments.

23 FUEL INJECTION

UNIT PREVIEW

A fuel injection system can provide more efficient engine operation than a carbureted fuel system.

Many modern passenger car gasoline engines have electronically controlled fuel injection systems that use sensor information fed to a computer. The computer determines how much fuel is to be injected.

In a gasoline engine, fuel may be injected before the opening of an intake valve, into the intake manifold. Depending on the system, gasoline can be injected twice per crankshaft revolution, once per revolution, or once every two revolutions. Injecting gasoline immediately before the opening of the intake valves is the most advanced form of gasoline fuel injection in production.

In a diesel engine, fuel must be injected near the end of the compression stroke, directly into the cylinder.

LEARNING OBJECTIVES

When you have completed your assignments and exercises in this unit, you should be able to:

☐ Explain the advantages of fuel injection.
☐ Explain the operation of a diesel fuel injection system.
☐ Identify and describe the two main types of diesel fuel injection pumps.
☐ Explain why electronically controlled fuel injection is used for gasoline engines.
☐ Identify and describe the basic parts of a gasoline fuel injection system.
☐ Identify all visible parts of a fuel injection system.
☐ Identify and describe the physical and operating differences possible among fuel injection systems.

23.1 ADVANTAGES OF FUEL INJECTION

In a gasoline engine, fuel injection performs the same functions as a carburetor. That is, fuel injection atomizes fuel in the amount necessary to provide the correct air-fuel ratio for efficient engine operation. However, fuel injection systems have several advantages over carburetors.

A fuel injection system does not need a venturi in the air intake. This means that air can pass through more easily to increase engine volumetric efficiency (its ability to "breathe").

The intake air charge in a fuel injection system does not need to be heated to help vaporize the fuel. When air is heated within a carburetor, the air becomes less dense and thus contains less oxygen. Less oxygen in the air results in less efficient combustion. A cooler, denser intake air charge in a fuel injection system results in better combustion.

Better combustion results in better fuel economy, more power, and less harmful exhaust gases. Thus, a fuel injection system can provide:

- Increased volumetric efficiency
- More efficient combustion
- Better fuel economy
- More power than a carbureted fuel system
- Less harmful exhaust gases

The first gasoline fuel injection control mechanisms were extremely complicated and expensive mechanical units. For passenger vehicles, carburetors were less efficient but much cheaper. For many years, the only vehicles that used mechanical fuel injection systems were airplanes, racing and sports cars, and vehicles with diesel engines.

23.2 GASOLINE ELECTRONIC FUEL INJECTION

Electronic controls, like those used in radios and televisions, can also be applied to control mechanical devices. Simple electrical devices, such as solenoids and stepper motors, can be operated by electronic controls.

As early as 1932, crude electronic controls were used for fuel injection on diesel truck engines.

In 1961, the Bendix Corporation was granted patents for all forms of gasoline *electronic fuel injection (EFI)* systems. A gasoline EFI system operates by

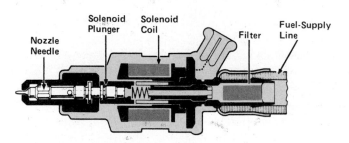

Figure 23-1. Solenoid-operated fuel injector.
ROBERT BOSCH CORPORATION

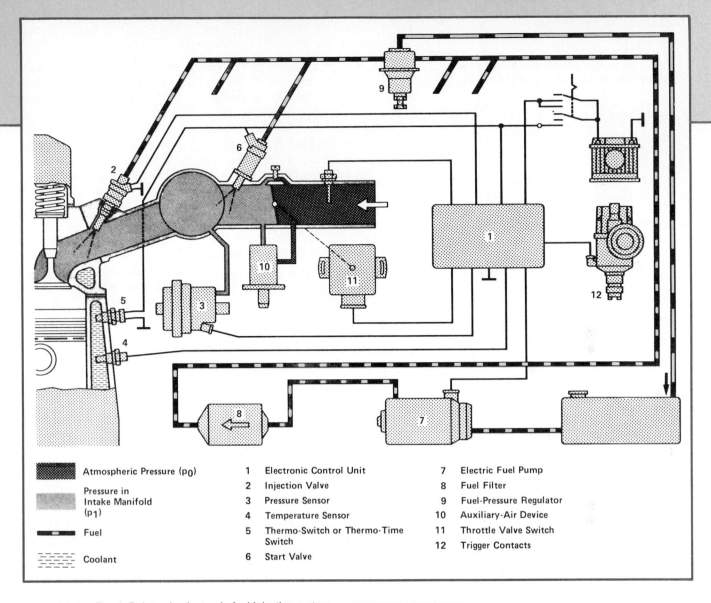

Figure 23-2. Bosch D-Jetronic electronic fuel injection system. ROBERT BOSCH CORPORATION

■ Atmospheric Pressure (p_0)	1	Electronic Control Unit	7	Electric Fuel Pump
	2	Injection Valve	8	Fuel Filter
Pressure in Intake Manifold (p_1)	3	Pressure Sensor	9	Fuel-Pressure Regulator
	4	Temperature Sensor	10	Auxiliary-Air Device
■ Fuel	5	Thermo-Switch or Thermo-Time Switch	11	Throttle Valve Switch
			12	Trigger Contacts
Coolant	6	Start Valve		

creating an electromagnetic field to move a solenoid connected to a fuel-injector nozzle. The nozzle (Figure 23-1) is held closed by the force of a spring. Pressurized fuel is supplied behind the nozzle from one or more pumps, and fuel is sprayed when the nozzle opens. When electricity to the solenoid is shut off, the spring closes the nozzle, stopping fuel flow.

The first production vehicles with electronic fuel injection were produced by Volkswagen in 1968. This system, shown in Figure 23-2, was known as *D-Jetronic* (D for the German word, *druck*, meaning pressure). Other systems are discussed in Topics 23.4 and 23.5.

Microprocessors, or computer chips, have lowered the cost of control systems. Thus, the cost of modern electronic fuel injection systems is very close to that of modern carbureted fuel systems. It is expected that by the year 1990, all new gasoline-powered vehicles will be equipped with EFI systems.

Basic Parts of an Electronic Fuel Injection System

A fuel injection system must provide the correct air-fuel ratio for all engine load, speed, and temperature conditions. Unlike a carburetor, a fuel injection system uses the same basic single system to provide different air-fuel ratios. This basic system includes:

- Fuel tank and connecting lines
- Fuel pumps
- Fuel pressure regulator
- Fuel filters
- Electronic control unit
- Input information sensors
- Fuel injectors.

Fuel Tank and Connecting Lines

The fuel tank and connecting lines are like those of a carbureted system. One difference is that excess fuel

231

is returned to the tank from a fuel-pressure regulator. This return line is indicated in Figure 23-3.

Fuel Pumps

Fuel pressures for EFI systems range from a low of 10 psi [69 kPa] to 79 psi [545 kPa]. A transfer, or supply, pump can be used to help bring fuel from the tank to another high-pressure pump. In other cases, a single pump brings fuel from the tank and supplies the system with sufficient pressure to operate the injectors. Three types of pumps are used for gasoline EFI systems:

- Diaphragm pump
- Rotary roller pump
- Turbine-type pump.

Diaphragm pump. A diaphragm pump is the same type of mechanical pump used on many carbureted fuel systems. Such a pump is used only as a transfer pump to supply fuel to a high-pressure pump.

Rotary roller pump. A *rotary roller pump* consists of rollers on a centrally mounted eccentric that rotates within a housing (see Figure 23-4).

Springs push the rollers outward against the inside of the housing. As the rollers push against the housing, fuel flows in behind them. The eccentric

continues to rotate, compressing the rollers and creating pressure on the fuel behind them. As the eccentric rotates past a discharge port, fuel is squeezed out under pressure.

Turbine-type pump. A *turbine-type pump* (Figure 23-5) is a centrifugal pump similar to a water pump or turbocharger compressor wheel. Fuel is drawn in at the center of the wheel and forced outward through centrifugal force. The centrifugal force creates pressure.

Fuel Pressure Regulator

A fuel pressure regulator is similar to an oil-pressure regulator. A fuel pressure regulator is used to maintain a constant pressure for a uniform spray from the injectors.

A diaphragm and spring hold a relief opening closed. When fuel pressure exceeds a preset limit, the diaphragm moves upward, uncovering the relief passage to the fuel tank. Excess fuel is returned to the tank.

In normal operation, the regulator acts as a controlled leak, maintaining a constant fuel pressure.

Fuel Filters

Small contaminant particles can lodge in an injection nozzle, blocking it partially open or closed. Water also can corrode the closely machined parts of the injectors. One or more fuel filters are mounted in the system to remove contaminants and small amounts of water. These filters are similar to those used on carbureted engines.

Electronic Control Unit

The heart of the system is the *electronic control unit (ECU),* a small computer mounted *on-board,* elsewhere on the vehicle. The ECU also may be called an *electronic control module (ECM),* or *combustion control computer (CCC).* It usually is mounted within the passenger compartment, away from the heat and vibration of the engine.

The ECU receives signals from sensors on the engine and determines the amount of fuel to be injected (see Figure 23-6). On current vehicles, this computer also determines the timing of the ignition spark, as discussed in Unit 35.

The amount of fuel injected is determined by how long the injector nozzle remains open. The nozzle opens and closes in response to signals from the ECU. The time during which the signal is on to open the injector is known as the *pulse width* (Figure 23-7).

Input Information Sensors

Input information on which the computer determines the amount of fuel to be injected can be based on

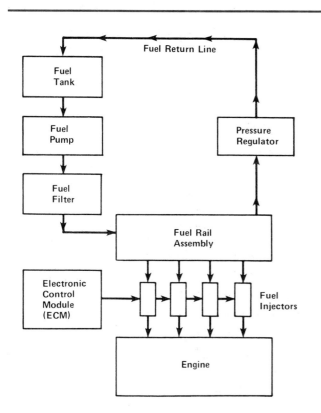

Figure 23-3. Fuel supply system. BUICK MOTOR DIVISION—GMC

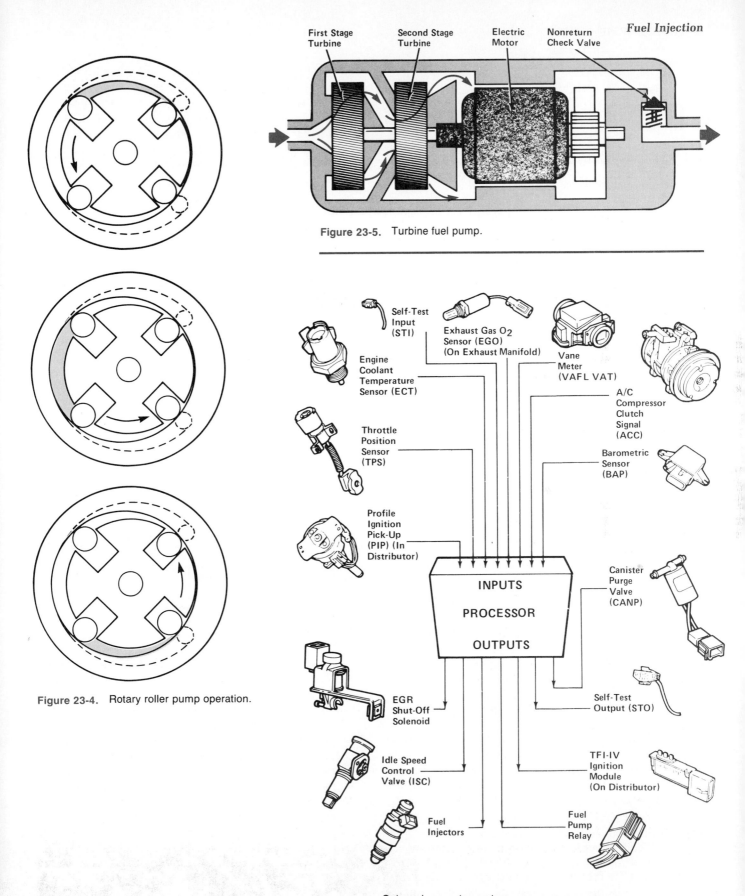

Figure 23-5. Turbine fuel pump.

Figure 23-4. Rotary roller pump operation.

Self-Test Input (STI)

Exhaust Gas O₂ Sensor (EGO) (On Exhaust Manifold)

Engine Coolant Temperature Sensor (ECT)

Vane Meter (VAFL VAT)

A/C Compressor Clutch Signal (ACC)

Throttle Position Sensor (TPS)

Barometric Sensor (BAP)

Profile Ignition Pick-Up (PIP) (In Distributor)

Canister Purge Valve (CANP)

INPUTS

PROCESSOR

OUTPUTS

EGR Shut-Off Solenoid

Self-Test Output (STO)

Idle Speed Control Valve (ISC)

TFI-IV Ignition Module (On Distributor)

Fuel Injectors

Fuel Pump Relay

Figure 23-6. Onboard computer system. FORD MOTOR COMPANY

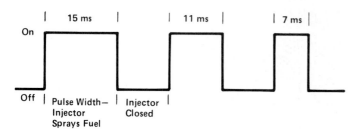

Figure 23-7.   Pulse width.

signals from many sensors. These sensors provide information on engine conditions that can include:

- Engine rpm
- Throttle position
- Coolant temperature
- Crankshaft position
- Camshaft position
- Intake airflow
- Timing of ignition spark
- Air conditioner operation
- Gearshift lever position
- Battery voltage
- Amount of oxygen in exhaust gases
- Emission control device operation.

Signals to the computer can be in either *analog* or *digital* form.

Analog signals change with changing conditions. For example, a coolant temperature sensor will have more electrical resistance when it is cold and less when hot.

Digital signals are presented as a series of on-off pulses. The pulses are counted by a computer to determine a condition. For example, a sensor on a crankshaft can produce an electrical signal each time the crankshaft revolves. By counting the number of pulses that occur in a given time, the computer can determine engine rpm.

Some sensor information to and/or control commands from the computer may be in the form of vacuum, rather than electrical, signals. Vacuum hoses, connectors, and other devices are used to transmit, relay, and receive these signals.

Sensors provide information to the computer about engine load, speed, temperature, and other conditions affecting vehicle operation. The computer is *programmed,* or provided with instructions, to produce correct air-fuel mixtures and throttle openings for given conditions. A solenoid or stepper motor is used to open the throttle for fast idle conditions.

For example, starting a cold engine produces signals that provide relatively long pulse widths. This results in a rich air-fuel mixture and a fast idle. Cruising on level roads at moderate speeds would produce shorter pulse widths and a leaner air-fuel mixture.

For less harmful exhaust gases, a stoichiometric (14.7:1) air-fuel mixture is required to allow emission control devices to operate properly. Emission control and other electronic devices are discussed in Units 38 and 39.

Current ECU units include what is known as a "limp-in" or "fail-safe" mode. If the ECU should fail, the vehicle will still run, though poorly. The vehicle will run well enough to be driven to a service garage.

Fuel Injectors

An electronically controlled fuel injector can open or close within one millisecond (1/1,000 second). In operation, the opening pulse width may vary from 7 to 15 milliseconds. The pulse width depends on the leanness or richness of the air-fuel mixture needed.

Some confusion may arise regarding the idea of *duty cycle.* A duty cycle is a period of time when power is applied to do work, divided by a period of time when power is off, as shown in Figure 23-8.

In a feedback carburetor, power is applied to *close* a fuel metering jet and *shut off* the flow of fuel.

In an EFI system, power is applied to *open* a fuel injector nozzle and *turn on* the flow of fuel.

Therefore, the term duty cycle has opposite meanings as applied to feedback carburetors and EFI systems.

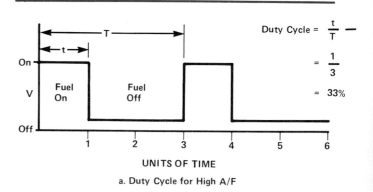

a. Duty Cycle for High A/F

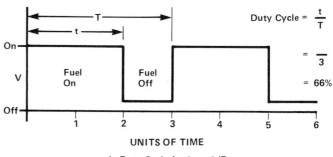

b. Duty Cycle for Low A/F

Figure 23-8.   Electronic fuel injection duty cycle.

Basic Types of EFI Systems

Fuel can be injected either at a single point, or at each intake port. The following discussions contain examples of both types.

Single-point injection. Throttle-body (TBI), or single-point, injection can be thought of as a compromise between a carburetor and a complete EFI system. Throttle-body injection (Figure 23-9) provides a more correct air-fuel ratio than a carburetor. TBI is simpler and less expensive than multi-point injection, but less efficient. Like a carburetor system, fuel is not distributed equally to all cylinders.

Chrysler system. Chrysler Corporation uses a different type of single-point injection. Fuel is sprayed continuously from *fuel bars,* or hollow tubes, above the throttle body assembly (see Figure 23-10). Varying the fuel pressure changes the amount of fuel sprayed. The Chrysler system combines the functions of fuel injection and ignition spark timing in a single ECU.

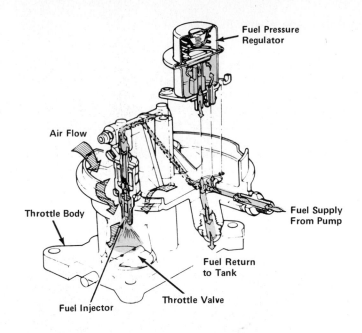

Figure 23-9. Throttle body injection system. FORD MOTOR COMPANY

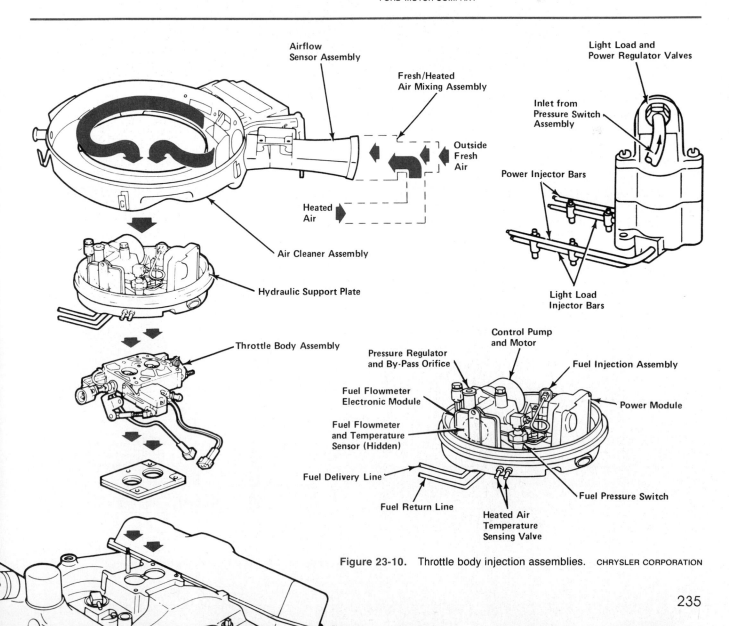

Figure 23-10. Throttle body injection assemblies. CHRYSLER CORPORATION

235

Multi-point injection. A multi-point, or *port-type*, injection system provides a more accurate and efficient delivery of fuel. However, multi-point systems are more expensive and complicated. Because fuel is injected behind each intake valve, as shown in Figure 23-11, *fuel wetting* of the manifold is minimized. Fuel wetting is the accumulation of excess fuel on the walls and floors of the intake manifold and ports. Fuel wetting results in unequal fuel distribution.

Injection grouping. On most EFI systems, the injectors spray fuel in groups. Half the injectors spray once each crankshaft revolution, and the other half spray on the next crankshaft revolution (see Figure 23-12).

Injection timing. Because the 4-stroke cycle requires two complete revolutions to occur, the air-fuel mixture is not drawn into the cylinders immediately. Consequently, some of the mixture "waits" in the manifold until an individual intake valve opens.

Sequential fuel injection (SFI). On systems such as the Buick *SFI (Sequential Fuel Injection)* Turbo engine,

fuel is sprayed just before the opening of each individual intake valve. Thus, each injector sprays once every two crankshaft revolutions (see Figure 23-13). The mixture is drawn into the cylinder immediately.

Sequential fuel injection ECUs can be programmed to provide a more precise air-fuel mixture than systems that pulse alternate injector groups.

Currently, sequential fuel injection is the most highly developed form of fuel injection. Such a system provides increased performance, better fuel economy, and improved exhaust emissions over a grouped injection system.

Top-feed and bottom-feed injectors. Two types of injectors currently are in use (see Figure 23-14). In a *top-feed injector,* fuel is fed in under higher pressure,

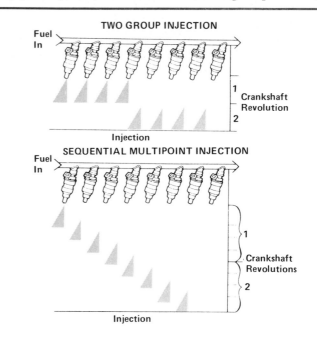

Figure 23-13. Grouped and sequential fuel injection.

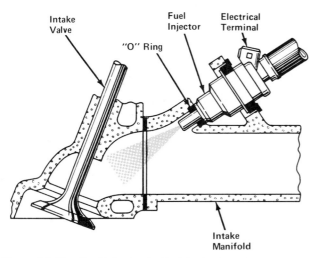

Figure 23-11. Fuel injection behind the intake valve.
BUICK MOTOR DIVISION—GMC

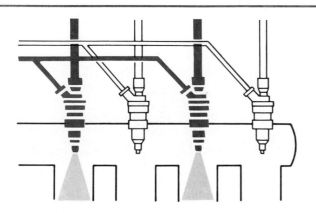

Figure 23-12. Injector grouping.

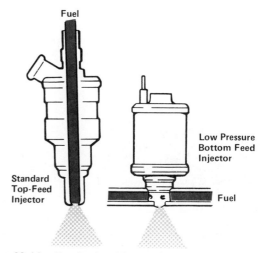

Figure 23-14. Top-feed and bottom-feed injectors.

up to 79 psi [545 kPa] to help prevent vaporization. This higher pressure requires a more expensive fuel pump. In addition, fuel vapors tend to rise into the stream of incoming fuel and may prevent fuel delivery.

Bottom-feed injectors are able to use fuel pressures as low as 10 psi [69 kPa]. Fuel vapors flow upward through the injector to a return line to the tank. With bottom-feed injectors, a less expensive pump can be used, and fuel vapors do not tend to block fuel flow.

23.3 COMMON FUEL INJECTION SYSTEMS

There are several common types of fuel injection systems, introduced on European and Japanese vehicles. These include:

- D-Jetronic
- K-Jetronic
- L-Jetronic and its variations
- Motronic.

D-Jetronic

The Robert Bosch D-Jetronic system (see Figure 23-2) measures airflow by using a sensor to measure the pressure of the air in the intake manifold. This measurement is known as *manifold absolute pressure (MAP)*.

When a higher pressure (less vacuum) exists, a denser air charge will flow relatively slowly into the cylinder. The system responds by injecting more fuel to maintain a correct air-fuel ratio.

However, this system does not allow for the presence of increased amounts of exhaust gases in the cylinder for modern smog controls. The presence of exhaust gases lowers the combustion temperature, reducing one type (oxides of nitrogen, NO_X) of harmful gas.

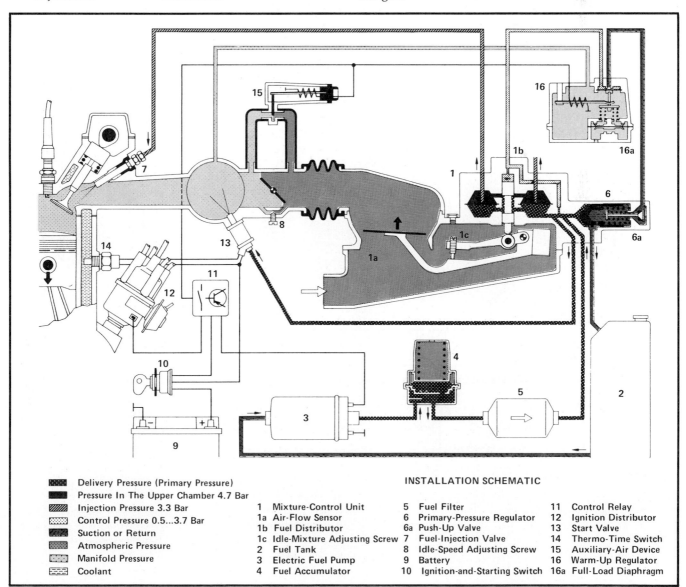

INSTALLATION SCHEMATIC

Delivery Pressure (Primary Pressure)
Pressure In The Upper Chamber 4.7 Bar
Injection Pressure 3.3 Bar
Control Pressure 0.5...3.7 Bar
Suction or Return
Atmospheric Pressure
Manifold Pressure
Coolant

1 Mixture-Control Unit	5 Fuel Filter	11 Control Relay
1a Air-Flow Sensor	6 Primary-Pressure Regulator	12 Ignition Distributor
1b Fuel Distributor	6a Push-Up Valve	13 Start Valve
1c Idle-Mixture Adjusting Screw	7 Fuel-Injection Valve	14 Thermo-Time Switch
2 Fuel Tank	8 Idle-Speed Adjusting Screw	15 Auxiliary-Air Device
3 Electric Fuel Pump	9 Battery	16 Warm-Up Regulator
4 Fuel Accumulator	10 Ignition-and-Starting Switch	16a Full-Load Diaphragm

Figure 23-15. Bosch K-Jetronic fuel injection system. ROBERT BOSCH CORPORATION

K-Jetronic

A different type of fuel injection system allows fuel to be sprayed constantly from all injectors. This type is called *K-Jetronic* (K from the German word *konstanter*, constant). The amount of fuel sprayed is controlled by changing the pressure of the fuel going to the injectors.

The volume of air entering the engine is sensed by the movement of a flat plate within a tapered, venturi-like opening. See Figure 23-15. The more air that flows into the engine, the more the plate moves. The movement of an arm connected to the plate operates a fuel-pressure regulator. More fuel is injected to maintain the correct air-fuel ratio.

L-Jetronic

The *L-Jetronic* (L from the German word *luft* meaning *air*) system (Figure 23-16) measures airflow with a pivoting flap in the airstream. Fuel is injected in proportion to the fresh air entering the intake manifold. All of the injectors squirt half the fuel required *twice* each crankshaft revolution.

Except for these differences, the L-Jetronic system is very similar to the D-Jetronic.

LH-Jetronic. The *LH-Jetronic* EFI system is a variation of the L-Jetronic. LH-Jetronic uses microprocessors (integrated circuit computer chips) instead of transistors to control the injector timing and duration.

Motronic

The Bosch *Motronic* system combines electronic ignition timing control with fuel injection control in a single ECU. Motronic is the most advanced and sophisticated of all Bosch systems. It is particularly efficient in controlling emissions levels.

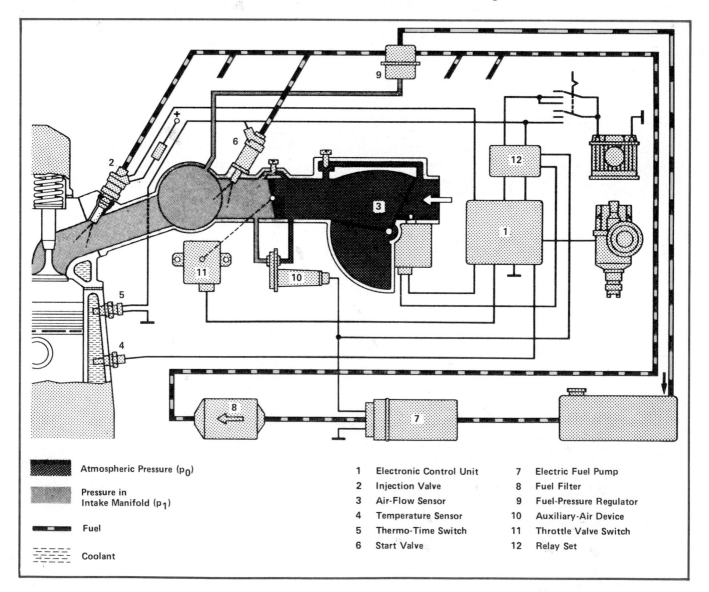

1	Electronic Control Unit	7	Electric Fuel Pump
2	Injection Valve	8	Fuel Filter
3	Air-Flow Sensor	9	Fuel-Pressure Regulator
4	Temperature Sensor	10	Auxiliary-Air Device
5	Thermo-Time Switch	11	Throttle Valve Switch
6	Start Valve	12	Relay Set

Legend:
- Atmospheric Pressure (p_0)
- Pressure in Intake Manifold (p_1)
- Fuel
- Coolant

Figure 23-16. Bosch L-Jetronic fuel injection system. ROBERT BOSCH CORPORATION

23.4 EFI AIR MEASUREMENT

Possibly the largest difference in EFI systems concerns how the intake air charge is measured. Most current systems measure air volume. The latest designs, such as the LN-Jetronic and the 84 Buick SFI Turbo engine, measure air mass. LN-Jetronic and Buick SFI systems are discussed below. These air-measuring systems include:

- Manifold absolute pressure (MAP) sensor
- Movable plate in a tapered opening
- Movable flap
- Vortex flow
- Heated film
- Heated wire.

The MAP, movable plate, and flap are discussed above.

Vortex Flow

Chrysler Corporation uses a principle called *vortex flow* to determine the volume of air entering the intake manifold. Vortex flow means a swirling, twisting motion.

Air entering the airflow sensor assembly passes through vanes arranged around the inside of a tube. As the air flows through the vanes, it begins to swirl (see Figure 23-17). The outer part of the swirling air exerts high pressure against the outside of the housing. There is a low-pressure area in the center.

The low-pressure area moves in a circular motion as the air swirls through the intake tube. Two pressure-sensing tubes near the end of the tube sense the low-pressure area as it moves around. An electronic sensor counts how many times the low-pressure area is sensed.

The faster the airflow, the more times the low-pressure area will be sensed. This is translated into a signal that indicates to the combustion control computer how much air is flowing into the intake manifold. The computer then adjusts the pressure of the fuel flowing through the fuel bars to maintain the correct air-fuel ratio.

Mass Airflow Sensor

In the mid-1980s, Buick introduced a new type of sensor called a *mass airflow sensor.* This sensor measures the *mass,* not the volume, of the air flowing into the intake manifold. Mass means the quantity, or amount, in absolute terms.

Remember, the ideal 14.7:1 ratio is based on the weight of air and gasoline. Weight, in scientific terms, is the gravitational attraction of the Earth for a given mass.

The volume of air may be misleading, because air can be more or less dense, depending upon temperature and atmospheric pressure. However, being able to measure the mass of air directly means that the stoichiometric air-fuel ratio can be maintained much more accurately.

Buick S.F.I Turbo. The Buick mass airflow sensor (Figure 23-18) uses a heated, electrically conductive metal foil film placed in the intake airstream. The amount of electricity required to keep the film at a constant 167 degrees F [75 degrees C] is measured. This information indicates how much air mass is flowing over the heated film to cool it.

LN-Jetronic. A variation of the L-Jetronic is the *LN-Jetronic* system that uses low-pressure bottom-feed fuel injectors. A different type of air flow sensor, called a *hot-wire sensor,* is used (see Figure 23-19).

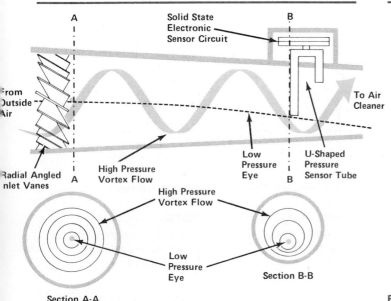

Figure 23-17. Vortex flow.

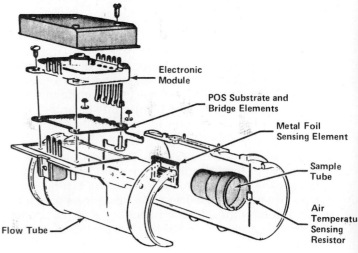

Figure 23-18. Mass airflow sensor assembly.
GENERAL MOTORS CORPORATION

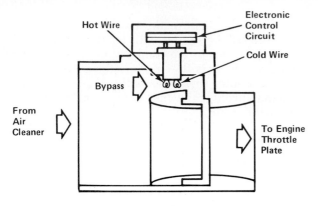

Figure 23-19. Hot-wire sensor operation.

Electricity is used to heat one wire in the intake airstream. Another wire is unheated. A comparison of the amount of electrical resistance in the heated and unheated wires indicates the mass of air flowing over the heated wire.

23.5 DIESEL MECHANICAL FUEL INJECTION

Diesel fuel systems may be divided into two categories: *direct injection* and *indirect injection*. In direct injection systems, the fuel is injected directly into the combustion chamber, on top of the piston. Indirect injection systems are those in which fuel is injected into a *precombustion chamber,* also called a *prechamber.* The combustion process begins in the prechamber and blows through a port to the top of the piston. See Figure 23-20.

Ignition in a diesel engine is dependent upon the heat of the compressed air charge. For starting when the cylinder is cold, the cylinder or prechamber contains a *glow plug,* or electrical heating element. Before the engine is cranked, the glow plug preheats the air to a temperature sufficient to ignite the fuel. The relative positions of a glow plug and an injection nozzle can be seen in Figure 23-21.

A diagram of an automotive diesel fuel injection system is shown in Figure 23-22.

Most modern diesel engines have no throttle plates in the air intake. Thus, there is no venturi to restrict air flow. This increases diesel engine volumetric efficiency. Diesel engine power output is determined by the amount of fuel injected. The more fuel injected, the faster the engine runs.

A supply pump brings fuel under relatively low pressure to the injection pump. The injection pump boosts the pressure to overcome the strong spring pressure holding the diesel fuel injector nozzle closed. Automotive diesel fuel injection pumps produce operating pressures of 800 to 3,000 psi [5,516 to 20,685 kPa]. Diesel injection pressures also are measured in *bars*. One bar equals 14.5 psi [99.98 kPa].

Two types of injection pumps are used on automotive diesel engines: *inline pumps* and *rotary*

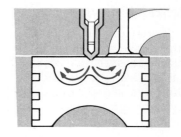

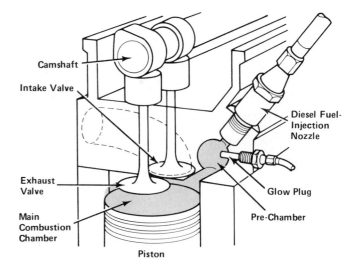

Figure 23-20. Diesel mechanical fuel injection systems.

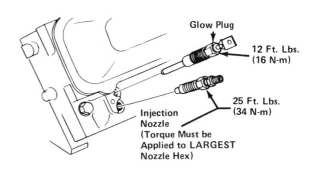

Figure 23-21. Glow plug and injection nozzle locations.
BUICK MOTOR DIVISION—GMC

pumps. Inline pumps have a separate pumping plunger for each cylinder. Rotary pumps have a common pumping chamber for all cylinders.

Inline Diesel Injection Pump

An *inline diesel injection pump* is powered mechanically by the engine, which drives a camshaft in the bottom of the pump. Each cam lobe operates a roller lifter and a plunger.

The plunger is closely fitted into a cylinder called a *barrel*. As the camshaft rotates, the plunger moves

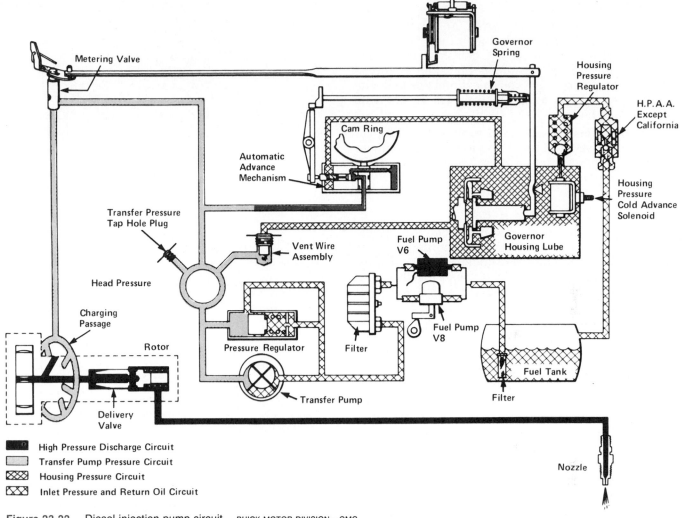

High Pressure Discharge Circuit

Transfer Pump Pressure Circuit

Housing Pressure Circuit

Inlet Pressure and Return Oil Circuit

Figure 23-22. Diesel injection pump circuit. BUICK MOTOR DIVISION—GMC

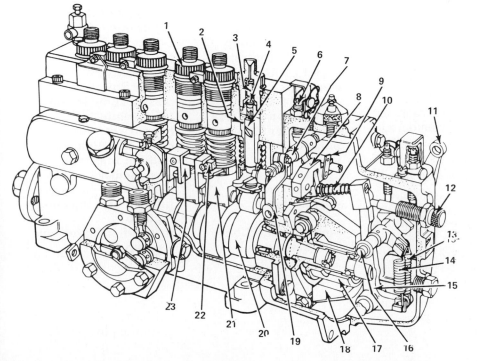

1 Delivery-Valve Holder
2 Barrel
3 Volume Reducer
4 Delivery Valve
5 Plunger
6 Maximum-Fuel-Stop Screw
7 Excess-Fuel Device
8 Bridge Link
9 Trip Lever
10 Telescopic Link
11 Speed Control Lever
12 Damper
13 Governor Idling Spring
14 Governor Main Spring
15 Crank Lever
16 Speed Lever Shaft
17 Governor Sleeve
18 Governor Flywheel
19 Stop Control Lever
20 Camshaft Lobe
21 Tappet Assembly
22 Control Rod
23 Control Fork

Figure 23-23. Inline diesel injection pump assembly. CAV LTD.

up and down within the barrel. At the bottom of the stroke, the barrel is filled with fuel. This fuel is trapped in the barrel as the camshaft forces the plunger upward. The trapped fuel then is forced through a delivery valve and injection lines to the injection nozzle. The nozzle then sprays the fuel into the prechamber.

As the camshaft continues to rotate, the plunger and roller lifter are forced downward by a plunger return spring. An inline diesel injection pump is shown in Figure 23-23.

Rotary Distributor Type Pump

In a *rotary distributor type pump,* fuel enters a circular fuel charging passage and travels into the pumping chamber between plungers. Rollers rotating against an internal cam ring force the plungers together. This action pushes the fuel out of alternate discharge ports under high pressure, as shown in Figure 23-24.

Fuel metering and delivery timing are determined by complicated mechanical and hydraulic devices. These parts must be machined precisely to tolerances sometimes measured in millionths of an inch [hundreds of thousandths of a millimeter]. Thus, a mechanical fuel injection pump is complicated and very expensive. Pump repairs are best left to trained experts.

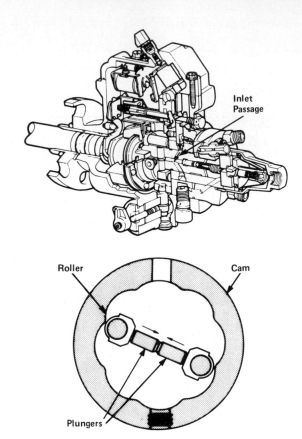

Figure 23-24. Diesel charging ports and pressurizing fuel.
OLDSMOBILE DIVISION—GMC

UNIT HIGHLIGHTS

- Fuel injection can provide increased volumetric efficiency, more efficient combustion, better fuel economy, and more power than a carbureted fuel system. Fuel injection also can produce less harmful exhaust gases.
- Mechanical fuel injection pumps are complicated and expensive.
- Electronic fuel injection systems are comparable in cost to modern carbureted fuel systems.
- An EFI system uses information from sensors fed through a computer to determine the amount of fuel injected.
- The amount of fuel injected in most EFI systems depends on how long an injector nozzle is held open by a solenoid.
- On the K-Jetronic and Chrysler TBI systems, the amount of fuel injected is determined by varying the fuel pressure.
- Depending on the system, EFI can inject fuel twice per crankshaft revolution, once per revolution, or once every two revolutions.
- Sequential fuel injection provides fuel just before individual intake valves open, and is more precise and accurate than other systems.

TERMS

electronic fuel injection (EFI)
D-Jetronic
microprocessor
rotary roller pump
turbine-type pump
electronic control unit (ECU)
electronic control module (ECM)
combustion control computer (CCC)
pulse width
analog
digital
programmed
duty cycle
fuel bars
port-type injection
fuel wetting
sequential fuel injection (SFI)

top-feed injector
bottom-feed injector
manifold absolute pressure (MAP)
K-Jetronic
L-Jetronic
LH-Jetronic
Motronic
vortex flow
mass airflow sensor
LN-Jetronic
hot-wire sensor
direct injection
indirect injection
prechamber
glow plug
inline diesel injection pump
rotary distributor type pump
barrel

REVIEW QUESTIONS

DIRECTIONS: The following questions are similar to those used on mechanic certification tests. On a separate sheet of paper, write the letter of the correct choice.

1. Which of the following statements is correct?
   I. Fuel injection can provide more power and better fuel economy than a carbureted fuel system.
   II. The cost of EFI makes it suitable only for racing cars and expensive vehicles.
   A. I only   B. II only   C. Both I and II   D. Neither I nor II

2. The purpose of a glow plug in a diesel engine is to
   A. heat the air in a cold cylinder.
   B. inject fuel directly into the cylinder.
   C. inject fuel into a prechamber.
   D. heat the surrounding metal in a combustion area.

3. Mechanic A says that gasoline EFI systems can operate with fuel pressures of 10 psi [69 kPa]. Mechanic B says diesel fuel injection systems operate with pressures of up to 3,000 psi [20,685 kPa]. Who is correct?
   A. A only   B. B only   C. Both A and B   D. Neither A nor B

4. What determines the air-fuel ratio produced by an EFI system?
   A. Sensors
   B. ECU
   C. Fuel pressure
   D. Either B or C

5. All of the following are advantages of sequential fuel injection EXCEPT
   A. more precise control of air-fuel ratio.
   B. less fuel wetting.
   C. less harmful exhaust emissions.
   D. single fuel injector.

SUPPLEMENTAL ACTIVITIES

1. Visit several local new-car dealers and obtain information on the base prices of vehicles available with and without diesel engines. Which are more expensive, and by how much? Why is one type of engine more expensive than another? What are the EPA fuel mileage ratings for both types?
2. Visit local gas stations and compare the prices of diesel fuel and gasoline fuels. Try to figure out how much money could be saved in one year by driving a diesel-engined vehicle. (Use the mileage information from the first activity to calculate your cost projections.)
3. Visit the parts department of a vehicle dealer who sells vehicles with diesel engines. Find out the repair or replacement cost of a diesel injection pump and report to your class.
4. Visit new-car dealers and examine the engine compartments of vehicles with fuel injection. Identify and sketch as many fuel injection parts as possible.
5. Explain the differences between sensing mass airflow and the volume of airflow, and which is preferable for maintaining correct air-fuel ratios.
6. Explain why EFI systems can maintain a more correct air-fuel ratio than a carburetor.
7. Visit the parts department of a new-car dealer who sells vehicles with EFI. Find out the replacement cost of an EFI electronic control unit.

24 FUEL INJECTION SERVICE

UNIT PREVIEW

Gasoline fuel injection systems are not a common cause of running problems.

Preventive maintenance for fuel injection systems consists of checks and adjustments, where possible. A fuel injection system is among the least likely causes of starting and/or running problems.

Manufacturers' service manuals must be used to find the correct cause of fuel injection problems.

Fuel injection service includes identification, reference to manufacturers' service manuals, and replacement and/or repair of fuel pumps, sensors, injectors, and ECUs.

Diesel fuel injection service is performed at two different levels. Injection nozzle and line service usually is performed in a garage. However, pump service and overhaul usually are performed at an injection pump shop.

LEARNING OBJECTIVES

When you have completed your assignments and exercises in this unit, you should be able to:

☐ Perform fuel injection preventive maintenance.

☐ Check for fuel delivery on a fuel injection system.

☐ Identify and describe sounds of a correctly operating fuel injector.

☐ Perform a multi-point fuel injection balance test.

☐ Correctly identify a TBI system.

SAFETY PRECAUTIONS

Have a fire extinguisher capable of extinguishing class B fires (flammable liquids) fully charged and readily available. This type of extinguisher should be nearby whenever you attempt any type of fuel injection or fuel system service.

Make sure no sources of possible ignition are present in the area where fuel injection or fuel service is being performed. These sources include lighted cigarettes, electrical switches and tools, and open flames of any kind.

Wear eye protection at all times when working on fuel injection or fuel system parts.

Fuel injection systems are extremely complicated and vary greatly between manufacturers, models, and even between similar systems installed on different engines. Do not attempt any fuel injection maintenance, repairs, or adjustments without the proper manufacturer's service manual.

After fuel injection service, crank the engine to allow the system to deliver fuel for starting. Do not attempt to pour liquid gasoline down the throat of the air intake. Severe explosions and fires can result.

In many cases, air must be removed from injection lines after service procedures. "Bleeding," or air removal procedures, will allow fuel to leak onto and around the engine. Wipe up excess fuel with a shop towel and place the towel in a safety container. Allow all fuel to dry before attempting to start the vehicle.

On vehicles with automatic transmissions, some adjustments are done with the engine running and the selector in drive. Set the emergency brake tightly and block the driving wheels before attempting any engine speed or mixture adjustment procedure. Never stand directly in front of a running vehicle while adjustments are being made. If the throttle should be opened suddenly, the vehicle could jump forward over wheel blocks and run over or crush anyone standing in front of the vehicle.

24.1 PRELIMINARY CHECKS

Before assuming that a fuel injection system is the cause of starting and/or running problems, all other systems should be checked. In most cases, the fuel injection system is one of the least likely causes of problems.

First, check the battery and starting system (see Units 29 and 31). Then, check the charging system (see Unit 33), ignition system (see Unit 35), and engine mechanical operation (see Unit 43).

24.2 FUEL INJECTION PREVENTIVE MAINTENANCE

Preventive maintenance for fuel injection systems includes checking and repairing or replacing the following:

* Fuel and air leaks
* Loose, broken, cracked, kinked, or disconnected vacuum hoses
* Loose, corroded, or grounded electrical connections

- Loose or improperly supported fuel rails, lines, and injectors
- Dirty fuel and air filters
- Incorrect idle speed and/or mixture.

Fuel and Air Leaks

Fuel and air leaks are corrected in basically the same manner as in carbureted systems, described in Topics 20.4 and 22.1. However, fuel lines for multi-point fuel injection on many cars are steel or plastic tubing with flare-type fittings. A loose connection that leaks fuel can also allow air into the lines, which will cause erratic running problems.

CAUTION: Extremely small amounts of contaminants in a fuel injection system can cause expensive damage. Care must be taken to make sure that all parts to be replaced are extremely clean. Clean fuel lines and other parts thoroughly before removal and again before reassembly. Make sure that tools and hands are clean during reassembly procedures.

Bleeding fuel lines. If lines must be replaced, some fuel injection systems require that air be bled from the fuel lines. A fuel line is loosened and fuel is pumped. At first, both fuel and air bubbles will spurt out. When fuel appears without air bubbles, the line can be tightened. Fittings must be tightened to the manufacturer's specified torque (see Figure 24-1).

SAFETY CAUTION: Because liquid fuel and fuel vapors will be present during bleeding, make sure that no possible ignition sources are present. If

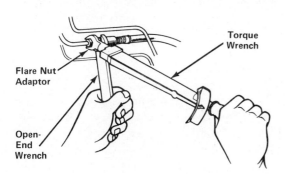

Figure 24-1. Tightening fuel line fittings.
TOYOTA MOTOR SALES, U.S.A.

necessary, push the vehicle away from electrical switches and tools, heaters, and so on. Perform bleeding only in a well-ventilated area. Have a fully-charged fire extinguisher capable of extinguishing class B fires available.

Some diesel vehicles include a hand-priming pump for bleeding purposes. Electrical connections to the fuel pump on vehicles with gasoline engines can be made to pump fuel through the lines.

Air leaks. Carefully inspect all rubber hoses and connections in the air-induction system. A length of rubber tubing can be used to listen for the hissing of an intake manifold air leak. Even a small air leak will result in a lean air-fuel mixture. Air leaks around metal parts, such as throttle-body shafts, can be detected by listening. Another method is to spray carburetor cleaner at the suspected leak. Refer to Topics 20.4 and 22.1 for procedures.

Loose, Broken, Cracked, Kinked, or Disconnected Vacuum Hoses

Rubber and plastic vacuum hoses are subject to heat and vapors from fuel and oil. These elements tend to dry, deteriorate, and crack the hoses. The ends of the hoses become expanded where they have been pushed onto small-diameter metal or plastic tube connections.

Vacuum hoses can become kinked or pulled loose during other service procedures. Because many signals for some fuel injection systems are in vacuum form, disconnected or switched hoses can cause confusing problems. A typical vacuum hose routing diagram is shown in Figure 24-2. Some vehicles have numbered or color-coded hoses to aid in correct replacement. Inspect and/or replace hoses one end at a time to avoid incorrect connections.

Loose, Corroded, or Grounded Electrical Connections

Shake, wiggle, and twist electrical connectors to make sure they are tightly connected (Figure 24-3).

Loose and/or corroded connections. The connections for electrical sensors and fuel injectors can become loose and/or corroded in time. If not properly supported, wires can rub against metal parts and wear through insulation. Any of these conditions can cause a lack of signals or improper signals to be sent to or from the computer control unit.

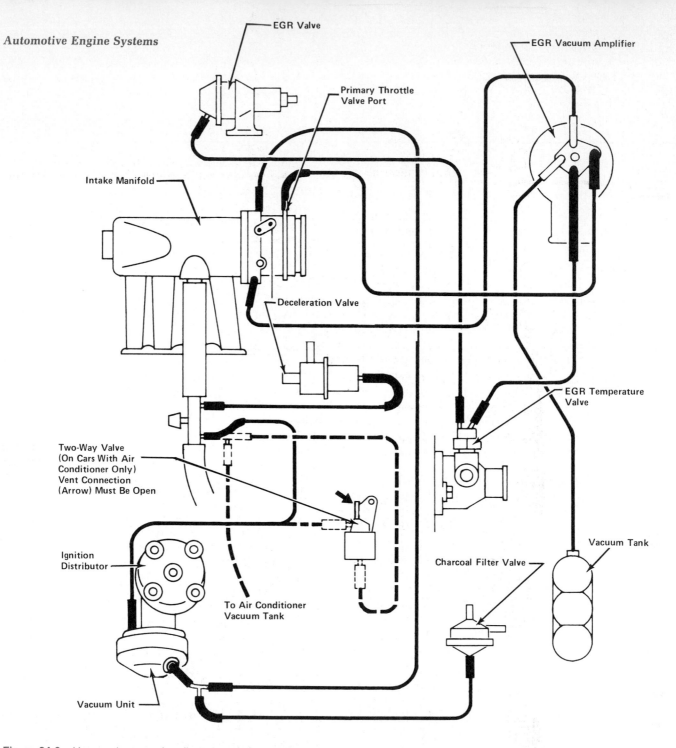

EGR Valve

EGR Vacuum Amplifier

Primary Throttle Valve Port

Intake Manifold

Deceleration Valve

EGR Temperature Valve

Two-Way Valve (On Cars With Air Conditioner Only) Vent Connection (Arrow) Must Be Open

Ignition Distributor

To Air Conditioner Vacuum Tank

Charcoal Filter Valve

Vacuum Tank

Vacuum Unit

Figure 24-2. Vacuum hose routing diagram. VOLKSWAGEN OF AMERICA

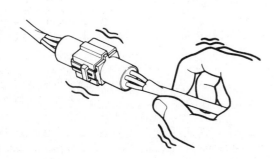

Figure 24-3. Checking electrical connectors for looseness.
TOYOTA MOTOR SALES, U.S.A.

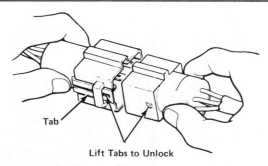

Tab

Lift Tabs to Unlock

Figure 24-4. Disconnecting electrical connectors.
TOYOTA MOTOR SALES, U.S.A.

Connections on sensors and actuators should be removed and checked for corrosion. Clean connectors have shiny metal male and female plug parts.

Some manufacturers use special conductive fluids or greases to help prevent corrosion. Refer to the manufacturer's service manual to determine if the connector pins or tabs should be coated with any special material.

Connectors can be pulled apart to check the condition of metal tabs and pins (see Figure 24-4).

CAUTION: **Make sure the ignition switch is in the OFF position before making disconnections, connections, or checks for looseness. In some cases, the battery ground connection also must be removed. The manufacturer's instructions regarding electrical connector service must be followed exactly. Accidentally touching a screwdriver or other metal tool from one terminal to another can damage or destroy electronic components. Water or other liquids in connectors can cause grounding and short-circuiting. Permanent damage to expensive ECU units can result from improper procedures.**

Fuel injector connectors. Some injectors for multipoint fuel injection have metal wire clips to hold the electrical connector securely. Gently pry the wire open while pulling on the connector to remove it (Figure 24-5). Grasp the connector and pull gently. Never pull on a wire; instead, always pull on the connector itself.

Grounded or shorted wiring. Check along the length of wires for rubbing or fraying. If the metal conductor of the wire is visible, wrap it with electrical tape or replace the wire.

An ohmmeter also can be used to check for grounded wires. Refer to the manufacturer's instructions for specific directions.

CAUTION: **Disconnect the battery ground cable before using an ohmmeter to check electrical wires. If battery power is present in any wire being checked, the ohmmeter will be damaged.**

Loose or Improperly Supported Fuel Rails, Lines, and Injectors

Fuel rails and metal or plastic lines should be properly supported to protect them from engine vibration. Vibration can loosen or *fatigue* such parts. Fatigue is cracking or breaking damage that results from repeated flexing and bending. Metal or plastic mounting clips and ties should be in place and securely fastened.

On some vehicles, individual fuel injectors are attached by being pushed into a tight-fitting rubber grommet. In other cases, a bolt or nut holds the injector in a mounting bracket (see Figure 24-6).

Check the injector by attempting to move it forward and backward and up and down. Excessive movement can indicate a worn-out rubber grommet or a loose bolt or nut. These problems can result in a lean air-fuel mixture.

Dirty Fuel and Air Filters

Refer to 20.5 for replacement of fuel and air filters. Replacement of PCV filters also is important and is discussed in Topic 20.5.

Adjusting Idle Speed and/or Mixture

Some vehicles equipped with electronic controls also control idle speed and mixture electronically. Periodic adjustment is not required. Adjustment, if possible, is made only during major service. Other vehicles have easily adjustable idle speed controls. Idle mixture controls, however, are usually hidden and require special tools for adjustment to prevent tampering (see Figure 24-7). Provision for fast idle is usually made with an electronically controlled solenoid to open the throttle farther when the engine is cold.

Correct mixture-control adjustment requires the use of an exhaust gas analyzer, as discussed in Unit 22.

CAUTION: **Idle speed and mixture adjustments to other than the federal and/or state standards will change the exhaust emissions and may result in violation of federal and/or state laws. In some states,**

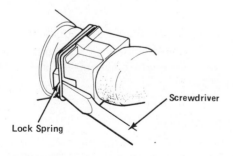

Figure 24-5. Removing the fuel injector connector.
TOYOTA MOTOR SALES, U.S.A.

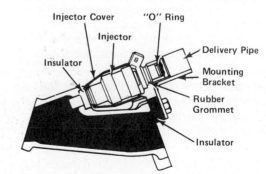

Figure 24-6. Injector mounting. TOYOTA MOTOR SALES, U.S.A.

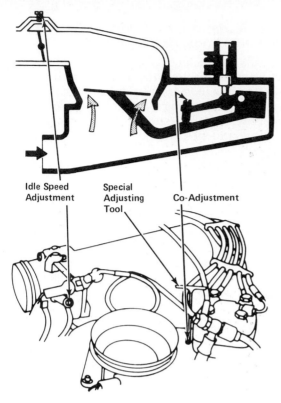

Figure 24-7. Idle speed and CO adjustments.
VOLKSWAGEN OF AMERICA

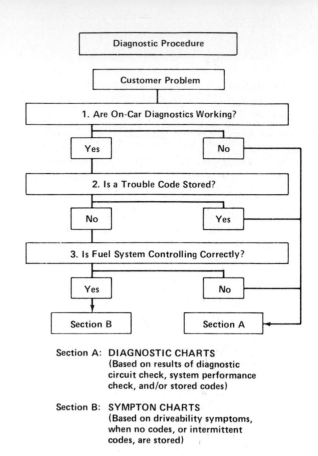

Figure 24-8. Diagnostic procedure for electronically controlled fuel injection. BUICK MOTOR DIVISION—GMC

such procedures may result in fines and/or loss of a mechanic's license or certification.

24.3 TROUBLESHOOTING FUEL INJECTION SYSTEMS

A general procedure for troubleshooting modern vehicles with electronic controls is shown in Figure 24-8. *Trouble codes* are numbers that the on-board computer stores to indicate specific problems. The electronic control unit can indicate to the mechanic what specific problems exist, as discussed in Unit 39. The mechanic can activate the ECU to display problem codes by making temporary electrical connections between certain connectors. Refer to the manufacturer's service manual for specific procedures.

If all these systems are operating correctly, refer to the manufacturer's service manual for troubleshooting charts. A troubleshooting chart is similar to a map with different directions at crossroads. Start at the top and follow the directions downward.

After following the beginning instructions, there will be two or more choices. Find the condition that matches your problem. Then follow the chart downward again for further checks, explanations, or instructions for performing repairs (see Figure 24-9).

Manufacturers' service manuals for modern vehicles contain literally hundreds of such charts. Different charts are needed for specific vehicles, varying

engine and transmission combinations, and so on. The service manuals list the meanings for abbreviations such as CKT (circuit) and ECM (electronic control module).

No mechanic can memorize all of these charts, so it is necessary to find and use the correct chart in the proper service manual. To obtain and hold a job, today's mechanic must be able to read, understand, and correctly follow these charts.

Driveability Problems

Driveability problems, similar to those of carbureted fuel systems, can occur with fuel injection systems. However, manufacturers' service manuals must be consulted to determine the general or specific causes for particular systems and vehicles. An example of such a chart is shown in Figure 24-10.

24.4 CHECKING FOR FUEL DELIVERY

If all other basic systems appear to be working properly, the fuel injection system should be checked for fuel delivery.

Simple Checks

On single-point fuel injection, fuel should be seen spraying down the throat of the throttle-body during cranking.

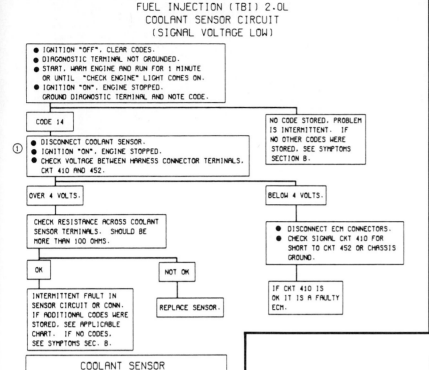

1984
CODE 14
FUEL INJECTION (TBI) 2.0L
COOLANT SENSOR CIRCUIT
(SIGNAL VOLTAGE LOW)

- IGNITION "OFF", CLEAR CODES.
- DIAGONOSTIC TERMINAL NOT GROUNDED.
- START, WARM ENGINE AND RUN FOR 1 MINUTE OR UNTIL "CHECK ENGINE" LIGHT COMES ON.
- IGNITION "ON", ENGINE STOPPED. GROUND DIAGNOSTIC TERMINAL AND NOTE CODE.

CODE 14 / NO CODE STORED. PROBLEM IS INTERMITTENT. IF NO OTHER CODES WERE STORED, SEE SYMPTOMS SECTION B.

①
- DISCONNECT COOLANT SENSOR.
- IGNITION "ON", ENGINE STOPPED.
- CHECK VOLTAGE BETWEEN HARNESS CONNECTOR TERMINALS, CKT 410 AND 452.

OVER 4 VOLTS. / BELOW 4 VOLTS.

CHECK RESISTANCE ACROSS COOLANT SENSOR TERMINALS. SHOULD BE MORE THAN 100 OHMS.

- DISCONNECT ECM CONNECTORS.
- CHECK SIGNAL CKT 410 FOR SHORT TO CKT 452 OR CHASSIS GROUND.

OK / NOT OK

IF CKT 410 IS OK IT IS A FAULTY ECM.

INTERMITTENT FAULT IN SENSOR CIRCUIT OR CONN. IF ADDITIONAL CODES WERE STORED, SEE APPLICABLE CHART. IF NO CODES, SEE SYMPTOMS SEC. B.

REPLACE SENSOR.

COOLANT SENSOR		
TEMPERATURE TO RESISTANCE VALUES (APPROXIMATE)		
°F	°C	OHMS
210	100	185
160	70	450
100	38	1,600
70	20	3,400
40	-4	7,500
20	-7	13,500
0	-18	25,000
-40	-40	100,700

Figure 24-9. Coolant sensor signal troubleshooting chart.
BUICK MOTOR DIVISION—GMC

HARD START

Definition: Engine cranks OK, but does not start for a long time. Does eventually run. If the engine starts but immediately dies (as soon as key is released from "start" position), see "Cranks But Won't Run", **CHART A-3**, page 6E:3-39.

- Perform careful visual check as described at start of Section B.
- Make sure driver is using correct starting procedure.
- Check fuel pump relay: Probe fuel pump test terminal with a test light to ground. Turn ignition off for 10 seconds, then turn ignition on. Test light should light for 2 seconds. If not OK, see CHART A-5 TEST POINT 1.
- Check TPS for sticking or binding.
- Check injectors for leaking. See **CHART A-7.**
- Check for high resistance in coolant sensor circuit or sensor itself. See **CODE 15 CHART,** page 6E:3-55.

- A faulty in-tank fuel pump check valve will allow the fuel in the lines to drain back to the tank after the engine is stopped. See **CHART A-7.**
- Check ignition system - Section 6D. Check distributor for:
  - Proper Output with ST-125.
  - Worn shaft.
  - Bare and shorted wires.
  - Pickup coil resistance and connections.
  - Loose ignition coil ground.
  - Moisture in distributor cap.
  - Check fuel pressure. See **CHART A-7.**
- Remove spark plugs. Check for wet plugs, cracks, wear, improper gap, burned electrodes, or heavy deposits. Repair or replace as necessary.

STALL AFTER START

Definition: The engine starts OK, but 1) dies after brief idle; 2) dies as soon as any load is placed on engine (such as A/C turned on or transmission engaged); or 3) dies on initial driveaway.

- Perform careful visual check as described at start of Section B.
- Check for proper operation of IAC System. See **CHART C-2C,** page 6E:3-187.
- Check PCV valve for proper operation by placing finger over inlet hole in valve end several times. Valve should snap back. If not, replace valve.

- Check for overcharged A/C system.
- Check for high A/C head pressure - could be caused by inoperative engine cooling fan.
- Check for plugged or restricted fuel lines. See **CHART A-5.**
- Check for weak spark from faulty ignition coil (see Section 6D).

HESITATION, SAG, STUMBLE

Definition: Momentary lack of response as the accelerator is pushed down. Can occur at all car speeds. Usually most severe when first trying to make the car move, as from a stop sign. May cause the engine to stall if severe enough.

- Perform careful visual check as described at start of Section B.
- Check fuel pressure. See **CHART A-7.** Also check for water contaminated fuel.
- Check vacuum hose to MAP sensor for leaks or restrictions.
- Check for fouled spark plugs.

- Check for correct PROM number. Also check Service Bulletins for latest PROM.
- Check TPS for binding or sticking.
- Check ignition timing. See Emission Control Information label.
- Check ECM controlled idle speed. See "Fuel Control" system.
- Check generator output voltage. Repair if less than 9 or more than 16 volts.
- Check canister purge system for proper operation.

Figure 24-10. Driveability troubleshooting chart.
BUICK MOTOR DIVISION—GMC

SAFETY CAUTION: Wear eye protection, and never look directly down the throat of the throttle body. If the engine begins to start, a backfire explosion can cause severe burns or other injury. Have a fire extinguisher capable of extinguishing class B fires fully charged and readily available.

On a multi-point injection system, a mechanic's stethoscope can be used to listen for the pulsing of the injector solenoid. In some cases, it is possible to feel the pulsing by placing a finger on the injector.

After disabling the ignition, multi-point injectors can be removed and the spray observed for proper size and shape (see Figure 24-11).

The volume of fuel delivered in a given amount of time also can be checked by spraying the fuel into a graduated container. Refer to the manufacturer's service manual for correct fuel delivery volume.

Instrument Checks

Special tools are needed for accurate diagnosis of fuel injection system problems. Examples of such tools are shown in Figure 24-12.

Multi-point injector balance test. A pressure test can be performed on some EFI systems (see Figure 24-13). Fuel pressure changes should be almost identical on all injectors. Too low or too high a reading indicates a defective injector.

24.5 FUEL INJECTION SYSTEM REPAIRS

Fuel injection system repairs include the following:

- Identification of system and components
- Reference to manufacturer's troubleshooting charts
- Reference to manufacturer's repair procedures
- Replacement or repair of fuel pumps
- Replacement of sensors
- Replacement of injectors
- Replacement of electronic control units.

System Identification

Identification codes for fuel injection system parts may be attached to a tag or plate. In other cases, numbers may be stamped or cast into the parts themselves (see Figure 24-14).

Troubleshooting Charts

Reference always should be made to the proper diagnostic, or troubleshooting, charts (see Figure 24-9). Fuel injection systems are too complicated for "guesswork."

Manufacturer's Service Procedures

Follow the manufacturer's instructions on fuel injection system repairs. Do not attempt to bypass or alter

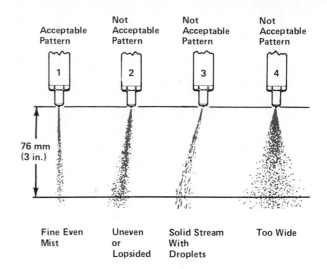

Figure 24-11. Injection nozzle spray pattern.
FORD MOTOR COMPANY

the system in any way. Such repairs may result in changed exhaust emissions and violations of federal and/or state laws.

Fuel Pump Service

Diaphragm-type fuel transfer pumps and electrical pumps for gasoline fuel injection systems are replaced as described in Unit 20.

Repairs to, or replacement of, diesel fuel injection pumps is an automotive specialty. Diesel pump repair requires specialized training, tools, and reference materials.

CAUTION: Diesel fuel injection pumps are highly precise, expensive components. Do not attempt any adjustments or repairs to diesel fuel injection pumps without proper training, tools, reference materials, and calibration equipment. Improper adjustments or repairs may result in failure of the pump.

Sensor Replacement

Sensors are replaced as discussed in Units 16, 17, and 42.

CAUTION: Before attempting to replace any electrical components of a fuel injection system, be sure the ignition switch is in the OFF position. Some vehicles also require that the battery ground cable be disconnected. Simply disconnecting or connecting a wire when the switch is on may damage or destroy expensive electronic equipment.

Injector Replacement

Whenever a fuel injector (single- or multi-point) is replaced, new rubber O-rings and grommets must be used (see Figure 24-15).

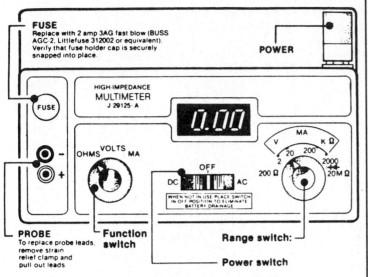

FUSE
Replace with 2 amp 3AG fast blow (BUSS AGC-2, Littlefuse 312002 or equivalent). Verify that fuse holder cap is securely snapped into place.

POWER

HIGH-IMPEDANCE
MULTIMETER
J 29125-A

MA
V   K Ω
20   200
2   2000
200 Ω   20M Ω

OHMS VOLTS MA

OFF
DC   AC
WHEN NOT IN USE PLACE SWITCH IN OFF POSITION TO ELIMINATE BATTERY DRAINAGE

PROBE
To replace probe leads, remove strain relief clamp and pull out leads.

Function switch

Range switch:

Power switch

HIGH IMPEDANCE MULTIMETER
J29125-A

VOLTMETER—Voltage Position Measures amount of voltage. Connected parallel to exiting circuit. A digital high impedance voltmeter is used because some circuits require accurate low voltage readings, and some circuits have a very high resistance in the ECM. This meter also accurately measures extremely low current flow. Refer to meter for more information.

- Both function and range switch must be set properly, and the DC or AC position selected. DC is used for most measurements.

OHMMETER—Resistance Position Measures resistance of circuit directly in ohms. Refer to meter for more information.

- $\boxed{1.}$ display in all ranges indicates open circuit.
- Zero display in all ranges indicates a short circuit.
- Intermittent connection in circuit may be indicated by digital reading that will not stabilize on circuit.
- Range Switch.

J23738/BT7517	**VACUUM PUMP (20 IN. HG. MINIMUM)** Use gage to monitor manifold engine vacuum. Check vacuum sensors, solenoids and valves with hand pump.
J28742/BT8234-A	**WEATHER PACK TERMINAL REMOVER** Used to remove terminals from Weather Pack connectors. Refer to wiring harness service for removal procedure.
J33095/BT8234-A	**ECM CONNECTOR TERMINAL REMOVER** Use to extract a terminal from connectors at the ECM.
	UNPOWERED TEST LIGHT Used to check wiring for complete circuit. Connect lead wire to good ground. Probe with test prod to connector or component terminal. Bulb will light if voltage is present.
	JUMPER WIRES (#16, 18 OR 20 GAGE WIRE) • Clip jumper wire used to complete a circuit by bypassing an open. • Set of jumper wires used to insert between Weather Pack connectors to permit access to the connector terminals for circuit checking. Six wires approximately 6'' long. Use terminals 12014836 and 12014837. One set - female terminals both ends, one set - male at both ends and four sets - male terminals at one end and female terminals at the opposite end.
	TACHOMETER Use either a crankshaft harmonic balance pickup type or electronic coil trigger signal pickup type
J28698-A/BT8251	**FUEL LINE WRENCH** Used to connect or disconnect fuel lines at TBI unit by holding fuel nut at throttle body.
J33031/BT8130	**IDLE AIR CONTROL WRENCH** Used to remove or install IAC valve on TBI unit throttle body.
J28687-A/BT8220	**OIL PRESSURE SWITCH WRENCH** Used to remove or install oil pressure gage switch on engine.

J29658/BT8205	**FUEL PRESSURE GAGE** Used to check and monitor fuel line pressure of fuel system.
J33047/BT8207-A	**IDLE AIR PASSAGE PLUGS** Used to block idle air passages when adjusting minimum idle speed on TBI unit. Also may be used to check ECM idle control.
J33179-20	**MINIMUM AIR RATE ADJUSTING WRENCH** Used to adjust minimum air rate screw on TBI unit.

Figure 24-12. Electronic fuel injection diagnostic tools. BUICK MOTOR DIVISION—GMC

1984
CHART C-2A
PORT FUEL INJECTION—INJECTOR BALANCE TEST
Before performing this test, the items listed below must be done.

- Check spark plugs and wires.
- Check compression.
- Check fuel injection harness for being open or shorted.

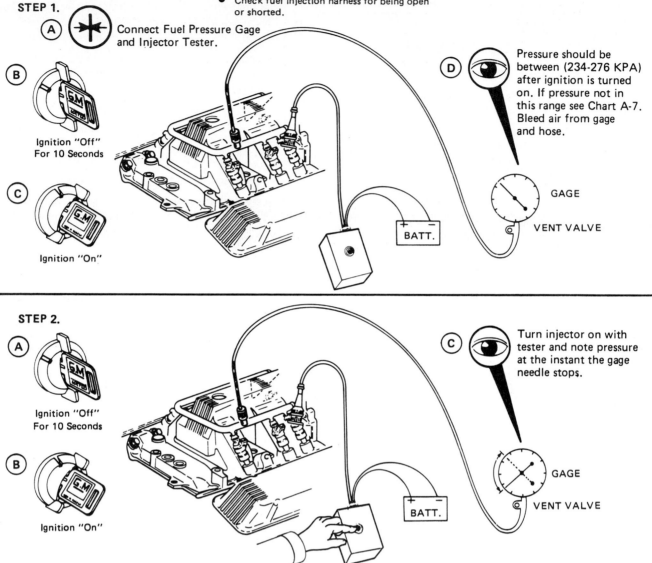

STEP 1.

(A) Connect Fuel Pressure Gage and Injector Tester.

(B) Ignition "Off" For 10 Seconds

(C) Ignition "On"

(D) Pressure should be between (234-276 KPA) after ignition is turned on. If pressure not in this range see Chart A-7. Bleed air from gage and hose.

GAGE
VENT VALVE
BATT.

STEP 2.

(A) Ignition "Off" For 10 Seconds

(B) Ignition "On"

(C) Turn injector on with tester and note pressure at the instant the gage needle stops.

GAGE
VENT VALVE
BATT.

STEP 3.

Repeat test as in step 2 on all injectors and record pressure drop on each.

Retest injectors that appear faulty. Replace any injectors that have a 10 KPA difference either (more or less) in pressure.

— EXAMPLE —

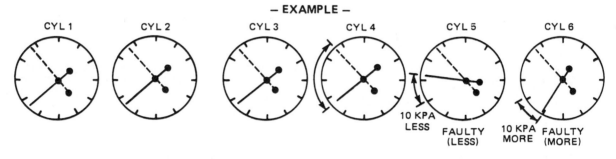

CYL 1   CYL 2   CYL 3   CYL 4   CYL 5   CYL 6

10 KPA LESS   FAULTY (LESS)   10 KPA MORE   FAULTY (MORE)

Figure 24-13. Injector balance test. BUICK MOTOR DIVISION—GMC

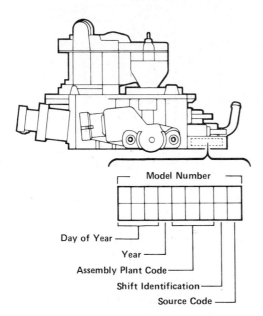

Model Number

Day of Year
Year
Assembly Plant Code
Shift Identification
Source Code

Figure 24-14. Throttle body fuel injection identification.
BUICK MOTOR DIVISION—GMC

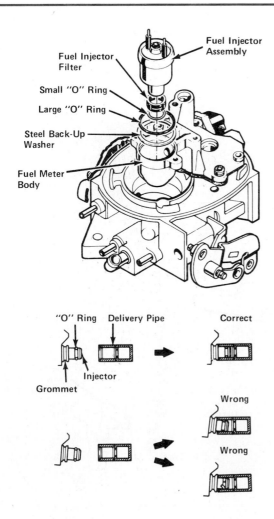

Fuel Injector Filter
Fuel Injector Assembly
Small "O" Ring
Large "O" Ring
Steel Back-Up Washer
Fuel Meter Body

"O" Ring   Delivery Pipe   Correct

Injector
Grommet

Wrong

Wrong

Figure 24-15. Fuel injector grommet and O-ring locations.
BUICK MOTOR DIVISION—GMC/TOYOTA MOTOR SALES, U.S.A.

CAUTION: When refitting O-rings, make sure the injector is aligned correctly, seats squarely, and does not pinch or damage the O-ring.

Electronic Control Unit Replacement

Refer to Unit 39 for a discussion of ECU replacement procedures. Replacement of electronic control units may require making specialized wiring connection repairs, as shown in Figure 24-16.

CAUTION: Before attempting to replace any electrical components of a fuel injection system, the ignition switch must be in the OFF position. Some vehicles also require that the battery ground cable be disconnected. Simply disconnecting or connecting a wire when the switch is on may damage or destroy expensive electronic equipment.

Refer to the vehicle or injection system manufacturer's service manual for all major repairs to gasoline fuel injection systems.

24.6 DIESEL FUEL SYSTEM SERVICE

Diesel fuel system service is somewhat more specialized than gasoline system service. However, there are several preventive and/or corrective diesel fuel service procedures that can be performed, including:

* Removing water from the system
* Replacing fuel filters
* Testing injection nozzles.

Removing Water From the System

Most diesel-powered vehicles have a provision for dealing with a common diesel problem: water in the fuel. Some vehicles have a special water separator in the fuel system. These units are discussed in Topic 20.8. Water separators usually are drained by opening a drain on the bottom of the separator (see Figure 24-17). Follow manufacturer's service recommendations for these procedures.

Water separators often are installed as aftermarket equipment on vehicles that are not so equipped. Some diesel systems are equipped with a combination fuel pickup/fuel level indicator/water sensor in the fuel tank. See Figure 24-18. This unit will detect the presence of water when it reaches a level of 1 to 1½ gallons in the tank. The unit will light a dashboard light to warn the driver.

The vehicle can be driven some distance under this condition before water is drawn into the fuel system. However, it is advisable to drain water from the tank as soon as possible. This can be done by removing the fuel return hose located at the front of the engine (see Figure 24-19). After removing the fuel tank filler cap, the water may be removed by pumping or siphoning from the previously disconnected

WEATHER PACK CONNECTORS REPAIR PROCEDURE

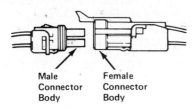

Male Connector Body

Female Connector Body

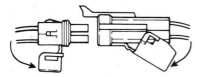

1. Open secondary lock hinge on connector

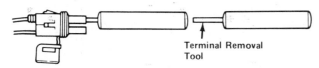

Terminal Removal Tool

2. Remove terminals using special tool

3. Cut wire immediately behind cable seal

   A. Slip new seal onto wire

   B. Strip 5.0 mm (0.2'') on insulation from wire

   C. Crimp terminal over wire and seal

Wire

Seal

Seal

TWISTED/SHIELDED CABLE

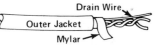

Drain Wire

Outer Jacket

Mylar

1. Remove outer jacket.

2. Unwrap aluminum/mylar tape. Do not remove mylar.

3. Untwist conductors, strip insulation as necessary.

Drain Wire

4. Splice wires using splice clips and rosin core solder. Wrap each splice to insulate.

5. Wrap with mylar and drain (uninsulated) wire.

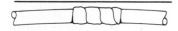

6. Tape over whole bundle to secure as before.

TWISTED LEADS

1. Locate damaged wire.

2. Remove insulation as required.

Splice and Solder

3. Splice two wires together using splice clips and rosin core solder.

4. Cover splice with tape to insulate from other wires.

5. Retwist as before and tape with electrical tape and hold in place.

Figure 24-16. Electronic control unit replacement and wiring diagram. BUICK MOTOR DIVISION—GMC

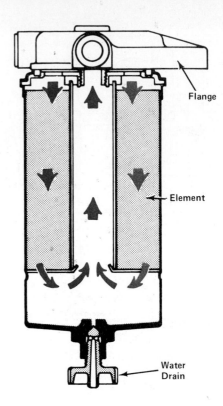

Flange

Element

Water Drain

Figure 24-17. Diesel fuel filter/water separator assembly. VOLKSWAGEN OF AMERICA

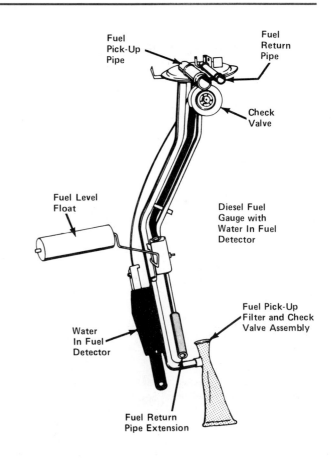

Fuel Pick-Up Pipe

Fuel Return Pipe

Check Valve

Diesel Fuel Gauge with Water In Fuel Detector

Fuel Level Float

Fuel Pick-Up Filter and Check Valve Assembly

Water In Fuel Detector

Fuel Return Pipe Extension

Figure 24-18. Combination fuel pickup/fuel level indicator/water sensor. GENERAL MOTORS CORPORATION

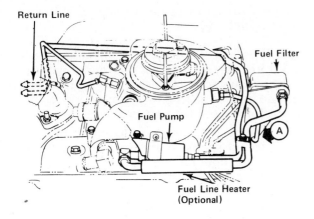

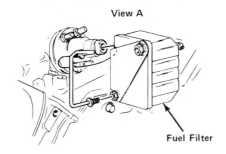

View A

Figure 24-19. Diesel fuel line locations.
OLDSMOBILE DIVISION—GMC/CHEVROLET MOTOR DIVISION—GMC

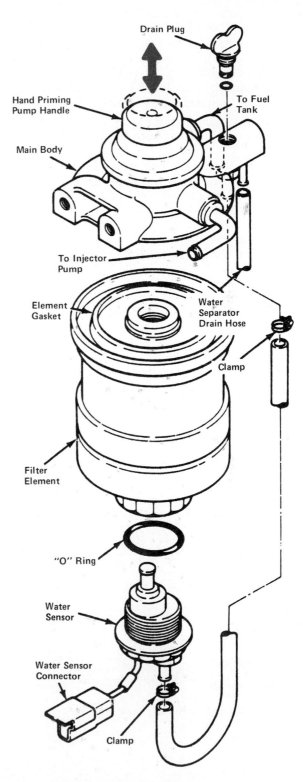

Figure 24-20. Diesel fuel filter assembly.
CHEVROLET MOTOR DIVISION—GMC

line. Use a clear plastic line to determine when uncontaminated fuel begins to flow. Replace the filler cap and return hose when finished.

SAFETY CAUTION: Be extremely careful when working with open fuel lines. Hot exhaust system parts, sparks, or open flames can cause fires. Keep a fire extinguisher capable of extinguishing class B fires fully charged and readily available.

Replacing Fuel Filters

All diesel fuel systems are fitted with fuel filters that have very fine filtering elements. These filters can remove particles that measure 10 microns in diameter. A *micron* is a very small metric dimensional measurement, equal to 39 millionths (0.000039) of an inch. These filters must be changed routinely to prevent erratic engine operation or fuel system damage.

Diesel fuel filters may be either self-contained units (see Figure 24-19) or separate spin-on units (see Figure 24-17). Always follow the manufacturer's service instructions for correct replacement procedures. These instructions usually provide detailed information on bleeding the fuel system to eliminate air. In some cases, a hand priming pump is provided for this purpose (see Figure 24-20).

Injection Nozzle Testing

The injection nozzle is an important part of the diesel fuel system. The injection pump develops very high pressures (800 to 3,000 psi [5,516 to 20,685 kPa]). These pressures are routed through thick steel injection lines to the nozzles (see Figure 24-21).

Check the manufacturer's service manual before proceeding with nozzle removal.

CAUTION: Be sure the nozzles and lines are clean before proceeding with nozzle removal. Any contaminants or foreign material in the fuel system can cause problems.

Once the injection nozzles have been removed, they can be checked for the following:

• Correct spray pattern
• Noise
• Correct opening pressure
• Leakage.

A nozzle or "pop" tester is used to evaluate nozzle condition (see Figure 24-22).

SAFETY CAUTION: Always follow nozzle tester manufacturer's test procedures and safety cautions. Never pass your hands near the nozzle when testing.

The high-pressure spray can penetrate the skin and cause blood poisoning.

Carefully follow the equipment manufacturer's test procedures to check for proper spray pattern. Figure 24-23 shows acceptable and unacceptable patterns for one type of nozzle. Refer to service recommendations for the correct pattern.

While moving the operating handle rapidly, a "creaking" sound should be heard if the nozzle is clean and in good condition. Refer to service recommendations for correct noise.

Open the gauge handle a small amount. Observe the gauge while slowly operating the lever to determine the opening pressure of the nozzle. Refer to service specifications for the correct pressure.

Again, slowly operate the lever, carefully bringing the pressure to 200 psi [1,379 kPa] and observe the nozzle tip.

SAFETY CAUTION: Do not touch the tip or place your hand near it. The pressure from the spray can cause the fluid to penetrate the skin and cause blood poisoning.

Figure 24-24 shows acceptable and unacceptable amounts of leakage for one type of nozzle. Refer to service recommendations for proper specifications.

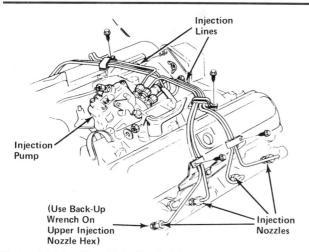

Figure 24-21. Diesel injection fuel lines.
CHEVROLET MOTOR DIVISION—GMC

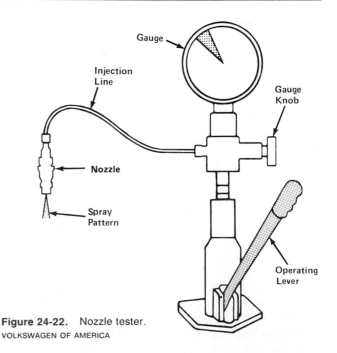

Figure 24-22. Nozzle tester.
VOLKSWAGEN OF AMERICA

ACCEPTABLE NOZZLE SPRAY PATTERNS

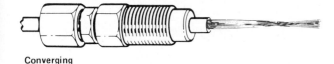

Converging

Straight

Narrow Cone

UNACCEPTABLE NOZZLE SPRAY PATTERNS

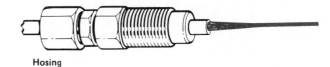

Hosing

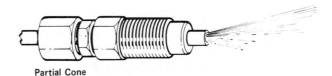

Partial Cone

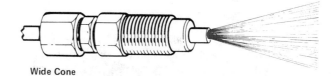

Wide Cone

Figure 24-23. Diesel fuel injector nozzle spray patterns.

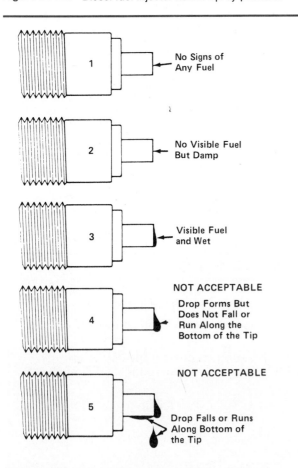

1 — No Signs of Any Fuel

2 — No Visible Fuel But Damp

3 — Visible Fuel and Wet

NOT ACCEPTABLE

4 — Drop Forms But Does Not Fall or Run Along the Bottom of the Tip

NOT ACCEPTABLE

5 — Drop Falls or Runs Along Bottom of the Tip

Figure 24-24. Checking poppet nozzle seat tightness.

U N I T   H I G H L I G H T S

- A fuel injection system is among the least likely causes of starting and/or running problems.
- Fuel injection preventive maintenance consists of checking for several types of problems. These include leaks, vacuum hose defects, poor electrical connections, dirty filters, incorrect idle specifications, and loose fuel rails, lines, or injectors.
- Troubleshooting fuel injection systems and driveability problems requires reference to the manufacturer's service manuals.
- Simple checks can be made for fuel delivery.
- A multi-point fuel injector balance test can be conducted with a pressure gauge of the proper range.
- Diesel fuel injection pressures are extremely high and can cause physical injury.
- Fuel injection service includes identification, reference to manufacturer's service manuals, and replacement and/or repair of fuel pumps, sensors, injectors, and ECUs.

T E R M S

fatigue
micron

trouble code

DIRECTIONS: The following questions are similar to those used on mechanic certification tests. On a separate sheet of paper, write the letter of the correct choice.

1. Mechanic A says that fuel injection systems are complicated and cause many starting and running problems on newer vehicles.

   Mechanic B says that fuel injection system problems are about the least likely causes of starting and running problems.

   Who is correct?

   A. A only   B. B only   C. Both A and B   D. Neither A nor B

2. Fuel injection system preventive maintenance includes checking, replacing, and/or repairing all of the following EXCEPT

   A. leaks, vacuum hose defects, and poor electrical connections.

   B. loose or improperly supported fuel rails, lines, and injectors.

   C. air and fuel filters.

   D. diesel fuel injection pump delivery volume and timing.

3. Which of the following statements is correct?

   I. The ignition switch must be in the ON position before any electrical components of a fuel injection system are disconnected or connected.

   II. Electronic parts are not easily damaged by grounding or shorting.

   A. I only   B. II only   C. Both I and II   D. Neither I nor II

4. After removing and replacing a diesel fuel line, which of the following procedures must be done before starting the engine?

   A. Change the fuel filters.

   B. Drain water from the water separator.

   C. Check injection timing.

   D. Bleed the fuel lines to remove air.

5. Before attempting work on any fuel injection system, what should the mechanic do?

   A. Talk to the owner about running problems.

   B. Test drive the vehicle.

   C. Check for fuel delivery.

   D. Refer to the manufacturer's service manual for troubleshooting procedures and charts.

1. Perform fuel injection preventive maintenance on a vehicle chosen by your instructor.
2. Check for fuel delivery on a fuel injected vehicle chosen by your instructor. Report to your class what method you used.
3. Listen to a fuel injector with a mechanic's stethoscope on a running engine. Describe the sounds you hear to your class in terms of loudness and frequency. What happens to the sounds if the engine is run at higher or lower rpm?
4. If suitable equipment and a vehicle are available, perform a fuel injector balance test on a multi-point fuel injection system.
5. Refer to the manufacturer's service manual and identify a TBI system. Report to your class where the numbers were found and what they indicate about the system.

25 THE EXHAUST SYSTEM

UNIT PREVIEW

The exhaust system consists of many separate parts. Together, these parts direct harmful gases and heat away from the vehicle and reduce noise and exhaust air pollution.

Exhaust noise is caused by pressure waves leaving the exhaust port. Almost one-third of the energy in gasoline is converted into unwanted heat, which is routed away safely through the exhaust system.

Exhaust systems on current vehicles include several common systems that reduce harmful exhaust pollution.

LEARNING OBJECTIVES

When you have completed your assignments and exercises in this unit, you should be able to:

☐ Identify and describe modern exhaust system parts and their functions.

☐ Explain what devices are used to lessen harmful exhaust gas emissions.

☐ Describe how a muffler cuts down the noise of the exhaust.

☐ Identify and describe the internal parts of a muffler.

☐ Identify and describe the basic types of catalytic converters.

25.1 BASIC EXHAUST SYSTEM

The basic purpose of the exhaust system is to direct harmful exhaust gases and heat away from the engine and underside of the vehicle. Exhaust gases contain carbon monoxide (CO). Carbon monoxide poisoning, caused by the accidental venting of exhaust gases into the passenger compartment, results in many deaths each year.

The exhaust system also reduces noise caused by the combustion process within the cylinders.

On current vehicles, the exhaust system also helps to change harmful exhaust gases chemically to relatively harmless compounds.

A typical modern exhaust system, as shown in Figure 25-1, consists of the following parts:

• Exhaust manifold and gasket
• Exhaust pipe and seal
• Connector pipe
• Catalytic converter
• Intermediate pipes
• Muffler
• Resonator
• Tail pipe
• Heat shields
• Clamps and hangers.

Exhaust Manifold and Gasket

Near the end of the power stroke, the exhaust valve opens and exhaust gases begin to leave the cylinder.

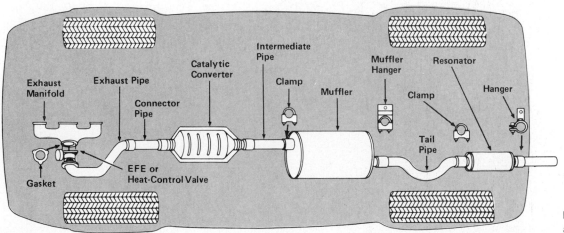

Figure 25-1. Parts of an exhaust system.

The piston continues on its exhaust stroke, pushing the burned gases into the exhaust manifold.

Every time the exhaust valve opens, waves of high pressure gases are forced into the exhaust manifold. Sound, or noise, is produced by pressure waves.

One exhaust manifold design factor is the length of passages within the manifold. If an exhaust manifold is designed correctly, pulses from the cylinders do not interfere with one another. Thus, exhaust gases can flow easily through the manifold.

To assure a good flow of gases with minimum backpressure, the exhaust manifold has large tubular sections. In addition, engineers try to avoid sharp bends that can slow the passage of gases.

However, the exhaust manifold often has to fit into narrow, cramped spaces between the engine and the body of the vehicle. Access to spark plugs and other parts also helps to determine the shape of the exhaust manifold.

Thus, exhaust manifold shapes are often compromises between good gas flow and limited mounting areas.

Exhaust manifolds for higher-performance versions of an engine often are noticeably different in shape for better gas flow (see Figure 25-2).

Exhaust manifolds for most passenger vehicles are made of cast iron. An exhaust manifold gasket is inserted between the manifold and the cylinder head to prevent exhaust leakage (refer to Figure 25-2). Some newer vehicles have stamped, heavy-gauge sheet metal exhaust manifolds.

Air injection. To make exhaust gases less harmful, fresh air can be injected into the exhaust manifold. This helps to oxidize the unburned fuel still remaining in the exhaust gases. Metal connector pipes and fittings to carry and distribute fresh air are screwed into the exhaust manifold (see Figure 25-3). Air injection systems are discussed in Unit 41.

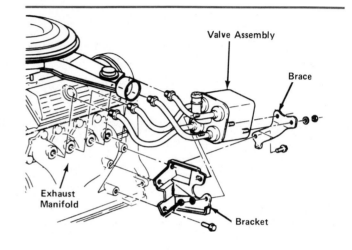

Figure 25-3. Air injection mountings.
CHEVROLET MOTOR DIVISION—GMC

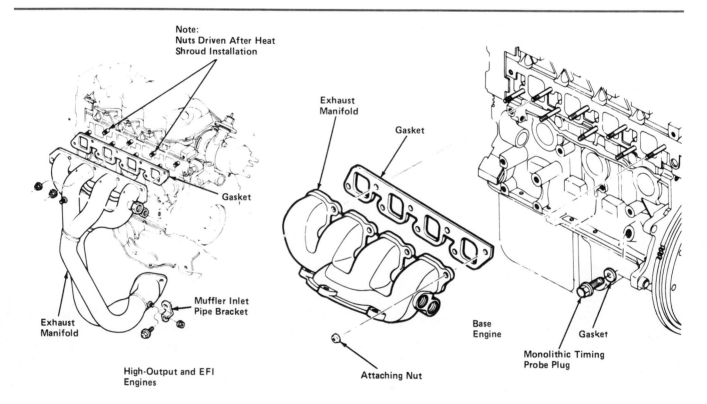

Figure 25-2. Normal and high-performance exhaust manifolds. FORD MOTOR COMPANY

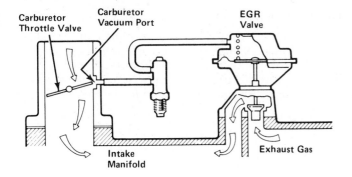

Figure 25-4. Exhaust gas recirculation (EGR) operation.

1 Exhaust Pipe
2 Right Manifold
3 Crossover Pipe
4 22 Ft. Lbs. (30 N·m)
5 Spring
6 Left Manifold
7 EFE Valve

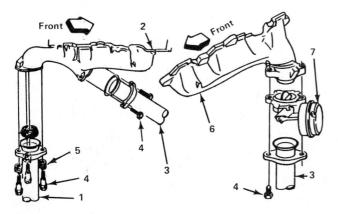

Figure 25-5. Early fuel evaporation (EFE) mounting.
BUICK MOTOR DIVISION—GMC

EGR. A process called *exhaust gas recirculation (EGR)* is used to lower combustion temperatures for control of NO_x (oxides of nitrogen). The EGR process routes small amounts of exhaust gas into the intake air-fuel charge (see Figure 25-4). EGR is discussed in Unit 41.

Exhaust Pipe and Seal

The *exhaust pipe* is connected to the exhaust manifold. A beveled seal, made of wire-reinforced asbestos or a solid steel ring, is inserted between the exhaust pipe and manifold. If an EFE (early fuel evaporation) system is used, it usually is mounted between exhaust manifold and exhaust pipe (refer to Figure 25-5).

V-type engine exhaust connections. The exhaust gases from most current V-type engines are routed into a single collector pipe. Either a Y-shaped pipe or a *crossover pipe* connects the two sides of the engine (see Figure 25-6). A crossover pipe can be routed behind or below the engine.

High-performance vehicles with V-type engines sometimes have two separate exhaust systems, one for each bank of the engine.

Turbocharged engine exhaust connections. Exhaust gases that drive a turbocharger must be routed from the exhaust pipe into and out of the exhaust turbine housing. Examples of exhaust pipe configurations, or shapes, to accomplish this routing are shown in Figure 25-7.

A high-performance *header* is a combination of an exhaust manifold and an exhaust pipe, custom-formed from thin steel tubing.

1 Right Hand Manifold
2 Seal (Engine Code "N")
3 EFE Valve
4 Spring (Engine Code "N")
5 22 Ft. Lbs. (30 N·m)
6 Crossover Pipe
7 Left Pipe
8 40 Ft. Lbs. (55 N·m)
9 Spring
10 Seal
11 Left Hand Manifold
12 Right Pipe

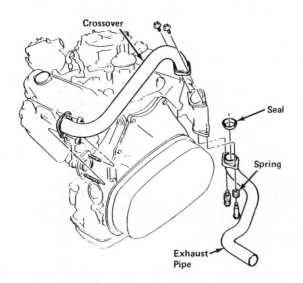

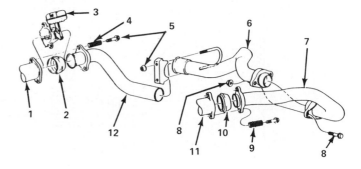

Figure 25-6. Exhaust pipe connections for V-type engines. BUICK MOTOR DIVISION—GMC

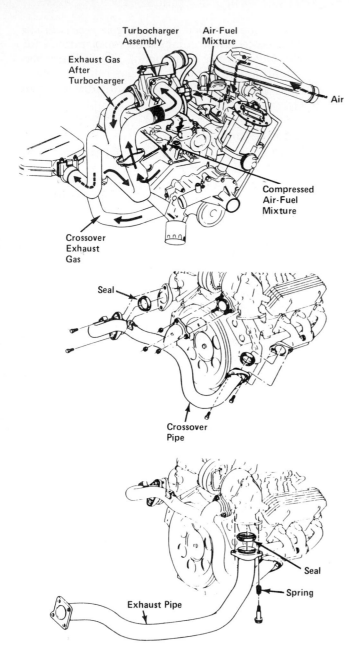

Figure 25-7. Exhaust pipe configurations.
BUICK MOTOR DIVISION—GMC

Catalytic Converter

Catalytic converters have been included in exhaust systems since 1975. A *catalytic converter* is a part that converts, or changes, harmful exhaust gases into less harmful gases through chemical action. The operation of catalytic converters is explained in Unit 41.

One or two catalytic converters may be used in an exhaust system. In a system using two converters, one may be a "light-off" converter that operates during warm-up. Such a converter pretreats and heats the exhaust gases for treatment by the main converter, as shown in Figure 25-8.

In other systems, one of the converters changes CO (carbon monoxide) and HC (unburned hydrocarbons) into carbon dioxide and water. Mechanics refer to this catalytic converter (CO and HC) as a "two-way cat." Another, separate converter changes NO_x (oxides of nitrogen) into nitrogen and oxygen.

Newer vehicles combine the functions of both converters into a single unit, called a *three-way catalytic converter* (CO, HC, and NO_x). This type of catalytic converter also is called a "three-way cat" or a *dual-bed converter*. Some three-way catalytic converters have dual beds, or sections, where gases are treated (see Figure 25-9).

Other three-way catalytic converters combine all exhaust gas treatment functions into a single unit (see Figure 25-10).

The catalytic converter is enclosed within a shell, usually made of stainless steel, to prevent corrosion and resist heat.

Intermediate Pipes

Intermediate, or connecting pipes, can be used at any point past the exhaust pipe to join exhaust system components. These intermediate pipes can be shaped to fit around axles and suspension components, away from shock absorbers and fuel tanks, and so on.

Pipe connections. Gaskets and seals are used to join the exhaust manifold and exhaust pipe to the cylinder

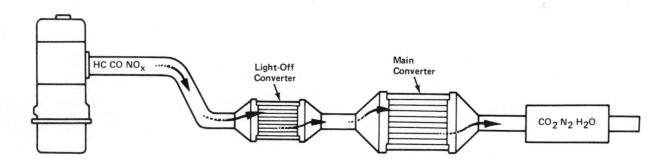

Figure 25-8. Separate catalytic converters. TOYOTA MOTOR SALES, U.S.A.

head and to each other. In most other parts of the exhaust system, pipes usually are either clamped or welded together. See Figure 25-11.

Welding is a process in which heat is used to melt metal and allow the molten portions to flow together. When cooled, a welded joint is as strong as, or sometimes stronger than, a single piece of metal.

Clamps can be used when the two connecting pipes are formed in such a way that one slips inside the other. This design makes a close fit. The clamp then holds this connection tight.

Another type of pipe connection is a *ball joint* (see Figure 25-12). A ball joint is a type of connection with a rounded, ball-shaped part that fits into a matching rounded, hollow socket. Ball joints are used where connections cannot be made in a straight line. Nuts and bolts are used to hold the ball joint together. Ball joints are used extensively in front-wheel-drive vehicles to join the exhaust pipe to the manifold.

Muffler

The *muffler* muffles, or softens, noise. The exhaust gases, which travel in pulses, would produce a loud roar without a muffler in the system.

A muffler consists of a series of chambers, holes, and *baffles* through which the exhaust gases must pass (see Figure 25-13). A baffle is a wall, plate, or screen to control the flow of fluids, such as liquids, or gases.

Passing through the muffler, the gases and pressure waves are slowed down, and much of their energy is absorbed. This process reduces the intensity of exhaust gas pressure waves and resultant noise.

Even a well-designed muffler will produce some backpressure in the system. Backpressure reduces an engine's volumetric efficiency, or ability to "breathe." Excessive backpressure caused by defects in a muffler or other exhaust system part can slow or stop the engine.

However, a small amount of backpressure can be used intentionally to allow a slower passage of exhaust gases through the catalytic converter. This slower passage results in more complete conversion to less harmful gases.

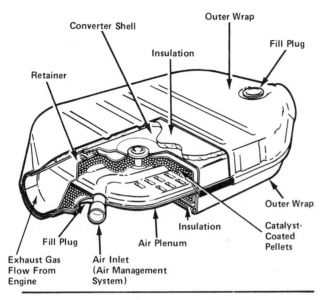

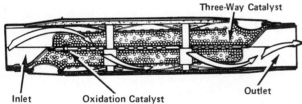

Figure 25-9. Dual-bed catalytic converter.
CHEVROLET MOTOR DIVISION—GMC

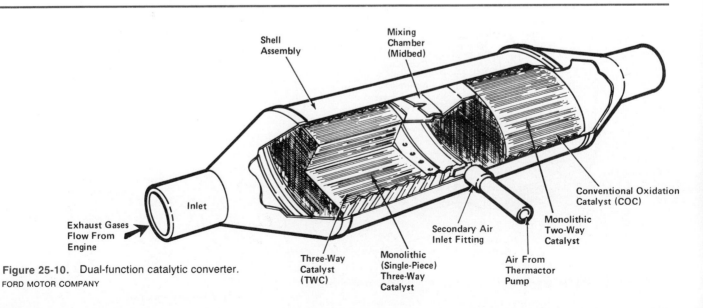

Figure 25-10. Dual-function catalytic converter.
FORD MOTOR COMPANY

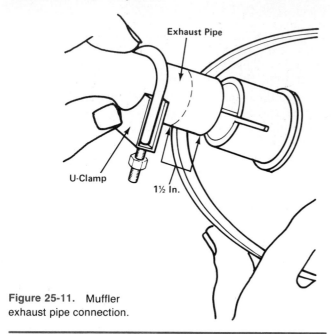

Figure 25-11. Muffler exhaust pipe connection.

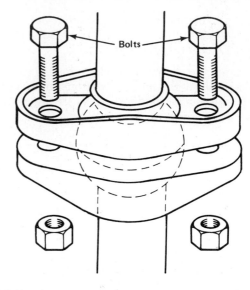

Figure 25-12. Ball joint exhaust pipe manifold connection.

Resonator

Another muffler-like device, a *resonator,* is added to some exhaust systems to absorb additional sound frequencies. The resonator helps to cut down objectionable noise.

Tail Pipe

The *tail pipe* is the endmost part of the exhaust system. Exhaust gases pass out of the tail pipe into the atmosphere.

Heat Shields

Heat shields are made of pressed or perforated sheet metal. They are used to protect vehicle parts from the heat of the exhaust system and catalytic converter (see Figure 25-14).

Clamps and Hangers

Clamps and hangers, shown in Figure 25-13, serve two purposes. Clamps help to secure exhaust system parts to one another as well as to the bottom of the vehicle. Clamps are bolts formed into a half-circular shape, with a bar that bolts across the open "U."

Hangers help to isolate noise, thereby preventing its transfer through the frame or body to the passenger compartment. Hangers are made from rubber, which is sometimes reinforced with fabric. One type of hanger resembles a large, thick rubber band stretched between hooks on the underbody and exhaust system. See Figure 25-15.

Together, clamps and hangers correctly support and position exhaust system components.

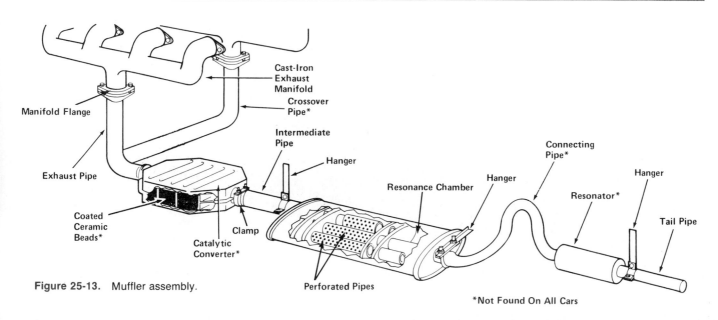

Figure 25-13. Muffler assembly.

*Not Found On All Cars

264

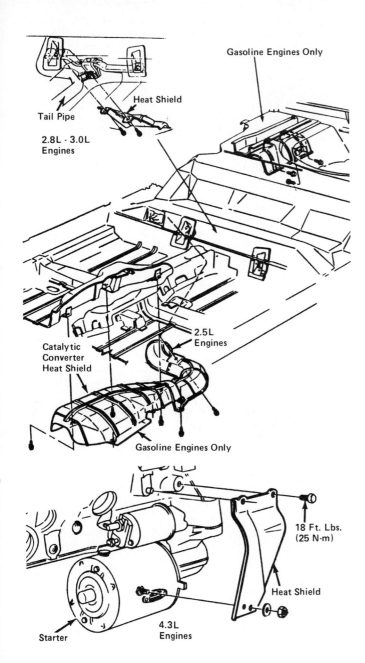

Gasoline Engines Only

Heat Shield

Tail Pipe

2.8L - 3.0L
Engines

Catalytic
Converter
Heat Shield

2.5L
Engines

Gasoline Engines Only

18 Ft. Lbs.
(25 N-m)

Heat Shield

Starter

4.3L
Engines

Figure 25-14. Heat shields. BUICK MOTOR DIVISION—GMC

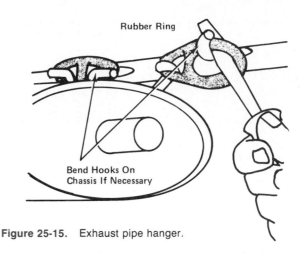

Rubber Ring

Bend Hooks On
Chassis If Necessary

Figure 25-15. Exhaust pipe hanger.

U N I T   H I G H L I G H T S

- Exhaust systems on current vehicles direct harmful gases and heat away from the engine and underside of the vehicle. They also reduce noise and harmful exhaust gases.

- Exhaust systems consist of many parts, extending from the engine to the rear of the vehicle.

- Exhaust noise is caused by pressure waves leaving the exhaust port.

- The muffler reduces the intensity and pressure of exhaust gases, thus reducing noise.

- Methods used to reduce harmful gases in the exhaust system include air injection, EGR, and catalytic conversion.

T E R M S

exhaust gas recirculation (EGR)	dual bed converter
exhaust pipe	welding
crossover pipe	ball joint
header	muffler
catalytic converter	baffle
three-way catalytic converter	resonator
	tail pipe
	heat shield

R E V I E W   Q U E S T I O N S

DIRECTIONS: The following questions are similar to those used on mechanic certification tests. On a separate sheet of paper, write the letter of the correct choice.

1. Mechanic A says that exhaust systems direct exhaust gases away from the underside of the vehicle.

   Mechanic B says that late-model exhaust systems change carbon dioxide and nitrogen into CO, HC, and NO$_X$.

   Who is correct?

   A. A only   B. B only   C. Both A and B   D. Neither A nor B

2. What causes exhaust noise?

   A. Ignition spark

   B. Pressure waves formed as the exhaust valve opens

   C. Backpressure in the muffler and catalytic converter

   D. HC, CO, and NO$_X$

3. Which of the following statements is correct?

   I. EGR introduces fresh air into the exhaust manifold.

   II. Air injection introduces exhaust gases into the intake manifold.

   A. I only   B. II only   C. Both I and II   D. Neither I nor II

4. All of the following are parts of a muffler EXCEPT

   A. perforated pipe.

   B. a resonating chamber.

   C. baffles.

   D. stainless steel shell.

5. All of the following are types of catalytic converters EXCEPT

   A. "light-off."

   B. dual-bed.

   C. "three-way cat."

   D. "one-way cat."

S U P P L E M E N T A L   A C T I V I T I E S

1. Identify and describe the parts and functions of modern exhaust system.
2. Examine relatives' or friends' vehicles. How many have catalytic converters in the exhaust systems?
3. Examine several V-type engines' exhaust systems. Sketch the location and type of pipes that connect from one side of the engine to the other.
4. Identify and describe the basic types of catalytic converters.
5. Explain why engineers might design a muffler assembly that produces more backpressure than absolutely necessary.

26 EXHAUST SYSTEM SERVICE

Exhaust system parts are subject to chemical and physical damage. Leaks from a damaged exhaust system can cause asphyxiation and death.

Physical damage to exhaust system connector pipes or other components can cause inefficient engine operation and increased air pollution and noise.

Preventive maintenance for the exhaust system consists of inspections and minor repairs. Muffler and connector pipe replacement may require the use of special tools and/or welding equipment.

As with mufflers, catalytic converters can be replaced. Some bead-type converters can be serviced to restore chemical efficiency.

LEARNING OBJECTIVES

When you have completed your assignments and exercises in this unit, you should be able to:

☐ Explain why exhaust leaks are dangerous.

☐ Perform an inspection of an exhaust system from the engine to the tail pipe and identify any defects.

☐ Use a vacuum gauge to check engine operation for evidence of an exhaust restriction.

☐ Replace exhaust manifold gaskets, seals, hanger brackets and/or clamps.

☐ Free a stuck heat riser valve or replace an EFE valve.

☐ Replace a muffler and/or connector pipe.

SAFETY PRECAUTIONS

Exhaust gases are harmful. Work on running vehicles only in well-ventilated areas outdoors, or in indoor areas with exhaust hose connections to remove fumes.

Whenever possible, wait until the vehicle has cooled down before attempting exhaust system inspection, preventive maintenance, or repairs. Hot exhaust system parts can cause severe burns.

Working on the exhaust system requires that the entire underside of the vehicle be accessible. Safely raise and support the vehicle before attempting inspection or repair procedures.

Wear eye protection at all times when working under the vehicle. Because they are heated during operation, exhaust system parts rust quickly. Loose rust particles can cause pain and/or permanent blindness if they become lodged in the eyes.

Removal and/or replacement of some exhaust system components may require heating, cutting, or welding. Do not attempt any of these procedures without proper training, safety equipment, and permission from your instructor.

Refer to the manufacturer's service manual for correct replacement procedures, parts, clearances between parts, and recommended sealants.

26.1 EXHAUST SYSTEM PROBLEMS

Exhaust system parts are subject to rust, corrosion, and physical damage. Gas leaks can cause harm to the vehicle's passengers and parts. Exhaust restrictions can cause the engine to run inefficiently, stall, and/or die.

Gas Leaks

Heat speeds up the chemical processes of rust and corrosion. In addition, acid forms within the pipes. As the exhaust system cools after the engine is off, cool air from the atmosphere is drawn up the pipe. This cool air contains moisture.

Moisture combines with sulfur and other minerals deposited in the exhaust system by the flowing exhaust gases. Sulfuric and nitric acids are formed. These acids eat away pipes and other components from the inside.

If a vehicle is driven longer distances, the moisture that collects inside the system is turned to vapor and evaporates. This vapor, or "steam," can be seen at the tail pipe when the vehicle is started after being parked overnight.

Vehicles driven only short distances retain large amounts of moisture and produce large amounts of acid. Thus, exhaust system components on such vehicles are rusted and eaten through very quickly.

The underbody of the vehicle is not gas-tight. Exhaust gases from damaged pipes and other components can enter the passenger compartment through openings and seams in the floor pan.

In cold climates, people sometimes become trapped in snow drifts in their vehicles. They close all the windows and leave the engines running to obtain heat from the heater. If the exhaust system has holes in it, exhaust gases can enter the passenger compartment. Every year, many people are asphyxiated and die from exhaust gases in this way.

Exhaust Restrictions

A *restricted exhaust* will reduce engine efficiency and/or cause the engine to stall or stop.

Exhaust pipes can become bent, flattened, or kinked. In some cases, an inner pipe within an outer shell can collapse. Baffles within a muffler can become loose and partially block the passage of gases.

A restricted exhaust can be detected by using a vacuum gauge connected to a source of engine intake manifold vacuum. Refer to Unit 43. Check for a vacuum reading that drops almost to zero as the engine is accelerated, then slowly climbs back to normal. This usually indicates a restricted exhaust system part.

26.2 EXHAUST SYSTEM PREVENTIVE MAINTENANCE

Preventive maintenance for the exhaust system consists of the following items:

- Inspecting the system for leaks, holes, and physical damage
- Inspecting the hangers and brackets for damage
- Replacing leaking gaskets and seals
- Replacing broken or weak hangers and brackets
- Checking heat riser/EFE valves for sticking
- Servicing stuck heat riser/EFE valves.

Inspecting for Leaks, Holes, and Physical Damage

The vehicle should be safely raised and supported. After the exhaust system has cooled thoroughly, the entire system should be inspected from the tail pipe to the cylinder head. Figure 26-1 illustrates some of the checks discussed below.

Visual inspection. Mufflers, resonators, and connector pipes should be inspected for evidence of rusted, jagged holes. Rust spots may be only surface rust. Suspected deep rust should be jabbed with a screwdriver. If the screwdriver penetrates the rusty spot, the part is defective and would fail soon.

A wooden block or even your knuckles can be used to knock and pound on pipes and mufflers to detect weak spots. A good part will be solid and firm. A defective part has a tinny, thin sound and feel. Loose baffles within a muffler can sometimes be heard moving around when knocked or shaken.

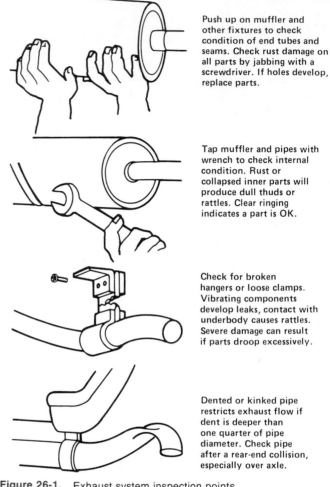

Push up on muffler and other fixtures to check condition of end tubes and seams. Check rust damage on all parts by jabbing with a screwdriver. If holes develop, replace parts.

Tap muffler and pipes with wrench to check internal condition. Rust or collapsed inner parts will produce dull thuds or rattles. Clear ringing indicates a part is OK.

Check for broken hangers or loose clamps. Vibrating components develop leaks, contact with underbody causes rattles. Severe damage can result if parts droop excessively.

Dented or kinked pipe restricts exhaust flow if dent is deeper than one quarter of pipe diameter. Check pipe after a rear-end collision, especially over axle.

Figure 26-1. Exhaust system inspection points.

The exhaust manifold and exhaust pipe connections should be checked for any loose or missing bolts or nuts.

Catalytic converters can overheat. This may be seen in a bluish or brownish discoloration of the outer stainless steel shell. In addition, undercoating or paint above and near the converter may appear blistered or burned.

Pipes and mufflers should be checked for signs of bending, scraping, or other physical damage. Flattened pipes and mufflers should be replaced.

Leaks at connections sometimes can be spotted by the presence of exhaust deposits (dark or grayish soot). If such a leak is suspected, a check should be made with the engine running.

Noise checks. Exhaust leaks often can be heard as an intermittent hissing or blowing sound when the engine is running. To locate the source, use a length of rubber tubing held to your ear to magnify the sound. Move the rubber tubing near and around the suspected leak. When found, the sound will be loud and clearly defined. In some cases, simply replacing a missing bolt or nut or tightening a loose clamp can stop the leakage.

SAFETY CAUTION: Have a helper in the car to start and stop the engine. Make sure the emergency brake is set tightly and the transmission is in park (automatic transmission) or neutral (manual transmission). Keep hands, arms, and other body parts away from heated exhaust system parts and drivetrain parts that could move during testing.

Inspecting Hangers and Brackets for Damage

Rubber hangers should be inspected for deep cracking or tearing. Small cracks are normal after a few years in service. The tail pipe and connector pipes should be grasped and vigorously wiggled. More than 1 inch [25.4 mm] of motion usually indicates a loose, broken, or disconnected hanger or support.

Pipes and other components should be inspected for shiny or rubbed spots. Such areas can indicate defective straps or hangers, or improper positioning between or near moving suspension parts.

Replacing Leaking Gaskets and Seals

The most likely spots for leaking gaskets and seals are between the exhaust manifold and the cylinder head, and between the exhaust pipe and the exhaust manifold.

Exhaust system nuts and bolts are usually rusty and difficult to unscrew. *Penetrating solvent* should be used before attempting to unscrew such fasteners. Penetrating solvent is a thin, oily solvent that flows between threads and helps to lubricate parts for removal. The solvent should be sprayed or squirted on

the fasteners. The fasteners then should be tapped sharply with a small hammer on the ends or sides (not on the threads). After a few minutes, the solvent will penetrate and make removal easier.

Room must be obtained to move the exhaust manifold away from the engine or the exhaust pipe away from the manifold. This usually makes it necessary to disconnect brackets and hangers. The exhaust system then can be lowered gently and supported during service (see Figure 26-2).

Old gaskets should be discarded and replaced with new gaskets during reassembly (see Figure 26-3). In some locations, the manufacturer's service manual may recommend the use of special high-temperature sealants to prevent gas leaks.

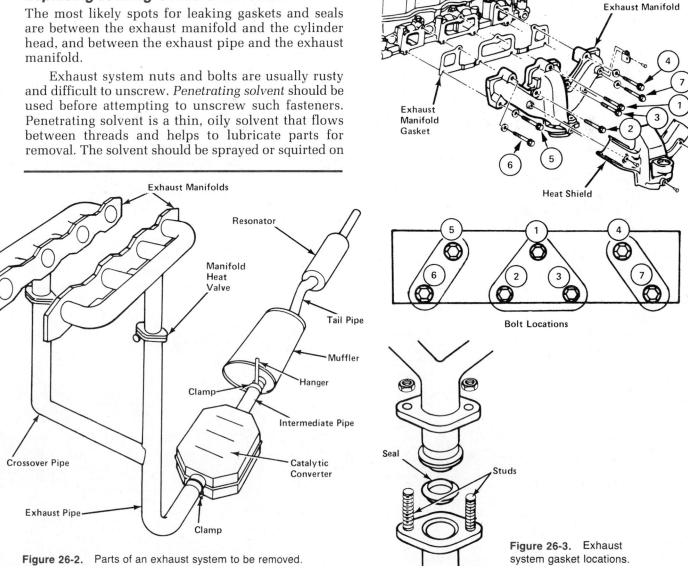

Figure 26-2. Parts of an exhaust system to be removed.

Figure 26-3. Exhaust system gasket locations.

Checking for manifold warp   The exhaust manifold sometimes warps because of heat. Use a straightedge and feeler gauges to check the machined surface of the manifold, across the surfaces indicated in Figure 26-4. If the manifold is warped beyond manufacturer's specifications, replace the manifold.

Replacing Hangers and Clamps

Hangers and clamps should be replaced if deeply cracked or broken (see Figure 26-5). Clearance around suspension parts and fuel tanks should be maintained as indicated in manufacturers' service manuals. Penetrating solvent should be used on bolt and nut connections before removal is attempted.

Checking Heat Riser/EFE Valves

Heat riser and EFE valves (see Figure 26-6) mounted between the exhaust manifold and exhaust pipe should operate freely. Vacuum-type valves are tested by connecting a vacuum pump to the diaphragm connection. As vacuum is applied, the shaft should move. Mechanically operated valves can be checked by moving the balance weight. It should move easily.

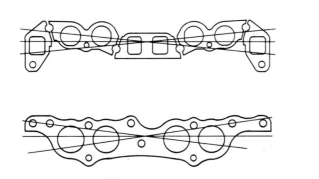

Figure 26-4.   Exhaust manifold surfaces are checked for warpage. TOYOTA MOTOR SALES, U.S.A.

When rusted, these parts may be frozen, or stuck, in position.

SAFETY CAUTION: Allow the exhaust system to cool before attempting to check or service heat riser or EFE valves.

Servicing Heat Riser/EFE Valves

A stuck vacuum-operated valve must be replaced.

A mechanical heat riser valve often can be serviced by spraying it with *graphited oil* and physically moving the balance weight. Graphited oil is a thin lubricant containing graphite particles. After the engine starts, the oil will burn off, but the graphite, an excellent dry lubricant, will remain.

Pliers are used to move the balance weight and valve shaft slowly and carefully. Graphited oil is applied liberally during this process until the shaft moves freely and easily.

26.3 MUFFLER AND CONNECTOR PIPE REPLACEMENT

Replacing exhaust system parts requires the use of tools to cut, shape, and expand the steel tubing used (see Figure 26-7).

To remove a rusted-on muffler, the ends must be slit with a hand or power cutter (see Figure 26-8).

Exhaust and intermediate pipes can be cut with a special tool for replacement (see Figure 26-9).

An expander tool is used to enlarge the size of pipes made smaller by cutting (see Figure 26-10).

Small sections of damaged pipe can be replaced, or pipes can be joined with couplings, as shown in Figure 26-11.

SAFETY CAUTION: Do not attempt to use welding equipment without proper training, safety equipment, and your instructor's permission. The light

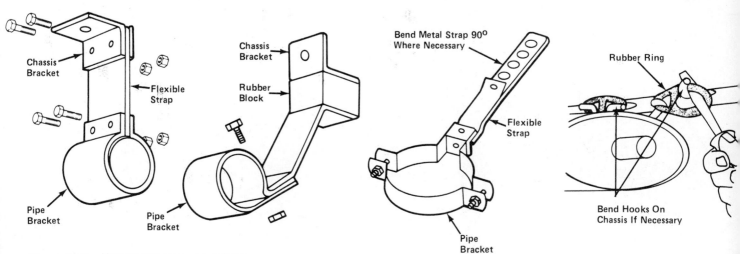

Figure 26-5.   Hanger and clamp assemblies.

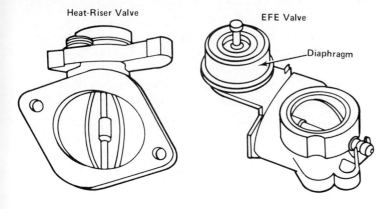

Figure 26-6. Heat riser and EFE valves.

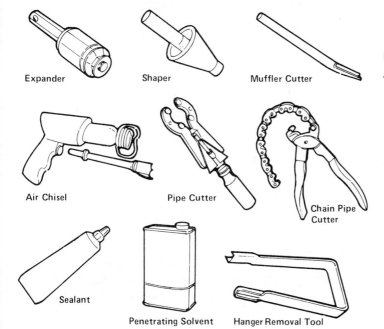

Figure 26-7. Exhaust system tools.

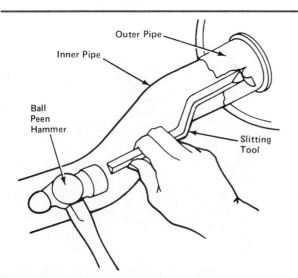

Figure 26-8. Removing a rusted-on muffler.

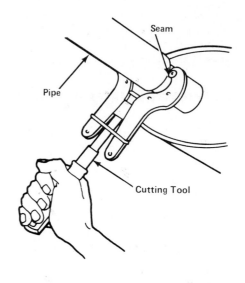

Figure 26-9. Cutting an exhaust pipe.

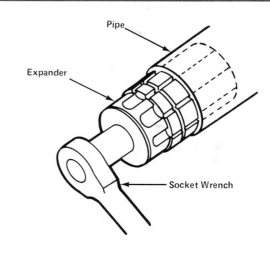

Figure 26-10. Expanding an exhaust pipe.

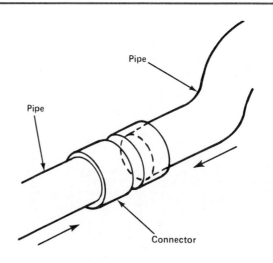

Figure 26-11. Exhaust pipe coupling.

from gas or electric-arc welding can cause permanent eye damage or blindness. In addition, the heat from welding can ignite fuel vapors or damage parts such as shock absorbers and carpets.

26.4 CATALYTIC CONVERTER PROBLEMS

Catalytic converters can become damaged from being bumped or scraped. In addition, illegal use of leaded fuel can lead to clogging, overheating, and melting of catalyst inside the converter.

Physical Damage

External physical damage to the outer shell of the converter may indicate internal damage. The outer shell of the converter is cut apart to inspect the inner converter (see Figure 26-12). If damaged, the entire converter must be replaced. If only the outer shell has sustained damage, it must be replaced.

CAUTION: Care must be used when cutting dual-bed converters to avoid damaging or puncturing the air inlet.

If no inner physical damage is evident, a special high-temperature sealant is applied. The outer shell is clamped on with channels and retaining clamps (see Figure 26-13).

Bead Replacement

Some older catalytic converters were filled with chemically coated beads or pellets. These pellets can be replaced if they are coated with lead or are otherwise not functioning. A plug is removed from such converters. A vibrator is attached to the catalytic converter to vibrate and shake the pellets loose and into a container.

To refill the converter, new beads are placed in the can. See Figure 26-14. The air hose is then attached to the vibrator unit, and a vacuum pump is attached to the tail pipe. New beads will be drawn into the converter. When full, the tools are removed and the converter plug is coated with nickel-based anti-seize compound and replaced.

NOTE: If beads come out through the tail pipe during this procedure, the entire converter must be replaced.

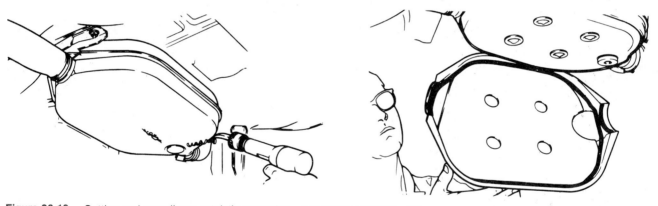

Figure 26-12. Cutting and resealing a catalytic converter. BUICK MOTOR DIVISION—GMC

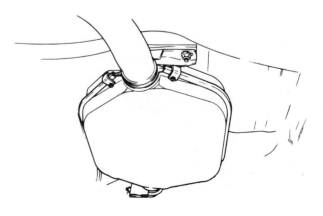

Figure 26-13. Catalytic converter with channel clamps.
BUICK MOTOR DIVISION—GMC

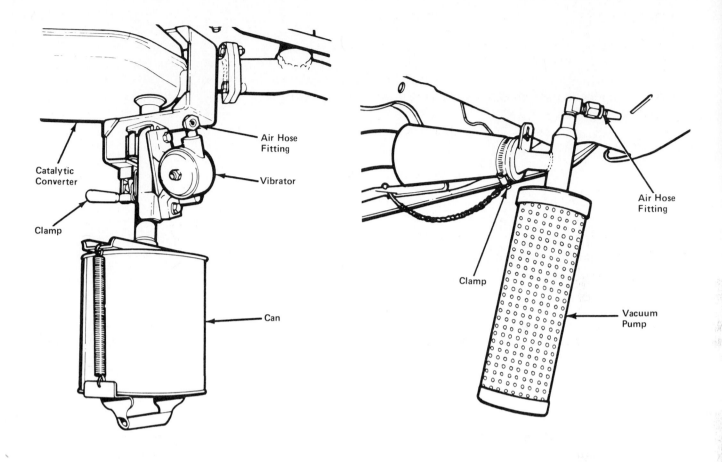

Figure 26-14. Catalytic converter bead replacement. BUICK MOTOR DIVISION—GMC

U N I T H I G H L I G H T S	T E R M S

- Exhaust system parts are subject to rust, corrosion, and physical damage.
- Exhaust gas leaks can be fatal to vehicle passengers.
- Exhaust system restrictions can cause inefficient and erratic vehicle operation.
- Exhaust system preventive maintenance includes inspections for leaks, holes, physical damage, and freeing stuck heat riser/EFE valves.
- Exhaust system part connections may be sealed with gaskets, seals, or ball joints, or by welding. In addition, special high-temperature sealants may be used.
- Muffler and connector pipe replacement may require cutting, expanding pipe sections, or welding.
- Some catalytic converter covers may be removed to inspect the converter. On older vehicles, chemically coated beads can be replaced.

restricted exhaust   **graphited oil**
penetrating solvent

DIRECTIONS: The following questions are similar to those used on mechanic certification tests. On a separate sheet of paper, write the letter of the correct choice.

1. A vehicle used in a humid climate had an entire exhaust system replaced one year ago. Inspection reveals small spots rusted through on the bottom of the muffler and at the bottom of bends in connector pipes. What is the most likely cause?

A. Wrong muffler installed

B. Catalytic converter overheating

C. Vehicle driven only short distances

D. Improper installation procedures

2. A restricted exhaust could cause all of the following EXCEPT

A. loss of power during acceleration.

B. stalling and dying.

C. poor gas mileage.

D. excessive noise.

3. Mechanic A says that the use of leaded gasoline in a system with a catalytic converter is illegal.

Mechanic B says that the use of leaded gasoline in a vehicle with a catalytic converter will lead to converter damage.

Who is correct?

A. A only   B. B only   C. Both A and B   D. Neither A nor B

4. Which of the following statements is correct?

I. The most important function of the exhaust system is to vent gases away from the engine.

II. The most important function of the exhaust system is to vent gases away from the passenger compartment.

A. I only   B. II only   C. Both I and II   D. Neither I nor II

5. All of the following could occur if a heat riser or EFE valve is stuck in the closed position EXCEPT

A. slow engine warmup.

B. exhaust restriction.

C. engine overheating.

D. boiling and percolation of fuel in carburetor.

S U P P L E M E N T A L   A C T I V I T I E S

1. Perform a visual inspection of an exhaust system on a vehicle chosen by your instructor. Talk to the driver of the vehicle to determine what type of use the vehicle receives. Report to your class on the condition of the exhaust system and possible causes for defects. Which part of the system seemed most solid, toward the engine or toward the tail pipe? Why?

2. On a vehicle chosen by your instructor, use a vacuum gauge to check for possible exhaust restrictions.

3. Replace an exhaust manifold gasket and/or exhaust pipe seal on a vehicle chosen by your instructor.

4. On a vehicle chosen by your instructor, replace hanger brackets and/or clamps.

5. Lubricate a heat riser valve or replace an EFE valve on a vehicle chosen by your instructor.

6. Replace a muffler and/or connector pipe on a vehicle chosen by your instructor.

IV

AUTOMOBILE ELECTRICAL AND ELECTRONIC SYSTEMS

27 ELECTRICAL AND ELECTRONIC FUNDAMENTALS

All matter is composed of atoms. Electricity is the flow of tiny atomic particles through a conductor. Electricity is a form of energy that can be used to create light, heat, or motion.

Electricity can be used to produce magnetism, and magnetism can produce electricity, depending upon how electrical devices are connected.

Some materials make good electrical conductors, while others act as good insulators. Still others will pass current easily under certain conditions, yet will act as insulators, blocking current flow, under other conditions.

When properly connected, a single source can supply electrical energy to many units and systems on an automobile.

As an aid to problem diagnosis, electrical diagrams, or schematics, are used. Schematics help the troubleshooter trace electrical connections between components.

The study of electronics differs from that of electricity. Electronics deals with small amounts of current as they operate semiconductor circuits.

L E A R N I N G   O B J E C T I V E S

When you have completed your assignments and exercises in this unit, you should be able to:

☐ Identify and describe the elements of a typical automotive electrical circuit.

☐ Explain what causes a flow of electricity.

☐ Explain how magnetism and electricity can be related.

☐ Identify common electrical conductors, insulators, and semiconductor materials.

☐ Explain the difference between the conventional and electron theories of electrical flow.

☐ Identify and describe series, parallel, and series-parallel circuits.

☐ Explain the difference between direct current and alternating current.

☐ Use basic electrical symbols to draw a simple electrical circuit.

☐ Use basic equations to figure out electrical values.

☐ Conduct basic electrical experiments with an un-powered test light.

27.1 BASIC AUTOMOTIVE ELECTRICAL CIRCUITS

Electricity is a form of energy. Electricity can be used to create light, heat, or force to cause motion. In an automobile, electricity is used for all these purposes. For example, electricity provides the power to operate lights, heating elements, and electrical motors. Electricity also powers other accessories, such as radios, instruments, and computer control units.

Sources, Circuits, and Conductors

A source of electricity, such as a car battery, produces electricity through chemical action. You may already know that batteries have two *terminals,* or connection points, labeled Positive (+) and Negative (–).

Electricity provides energy to do work when it can flow to an electrical *load,* through the load, and back to the source. A load is a device that uses electricity. Electricity flows from one terminal of a source, through conductors and a load, and back to the other terminal.

This circular pattern of movement is called an electrical *circuit* (see Figure 27-1). Electricity travels through *conductors.* A conductor is a material that allows the passage of electricity. Common conductive materials include most metals (copper, silver, gold, iron, and so forth) and some liquids (including water that contains minerals). Copper is the most commonly used metal for wires.

A *switch* can be used to form a complete circuit or to interrupt the flow of electricity, thus shutting off power to the load. The switch can be in an open (off) position or a closed (on) position (see Figure 27-2).

Ground Terminal

In a vehicle, one battery terminal is connected to the metal of the vehicle body. Since metal is a conductor, the entire vehicle can be used as part of an electrical circuit. This common electrical path back to the source of electricity is known as a *ground.*

Using a common ground connection eliminates the need for two separate wires to every electrical load. Thus, vehicles can be cheaper and simpler to build and service. This way of wiring a vehicle is known as a *single-wire circuit.*

Before 1956, some vehicles had ground connections made to positive battery terminals, although most were made to negative terminals. In 1956, it was decided to standardize automotive electrical systems by connecting the negative battery terminal to a ground. This standard is known as *negative ground.*

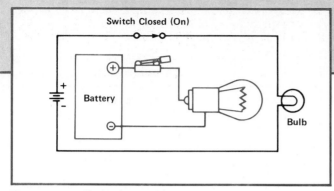

Figure 27-1. Basic electrical circuit: schematic (black) and pictorial (red).

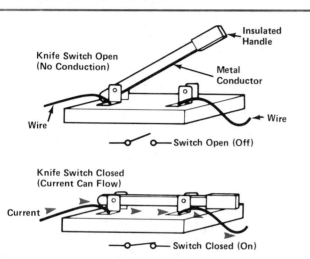

Figure 27-2. Electrical switch positions.

Pre-1956 vehicles (especially British-made) may have *positive ground.*

In addition, since 1967, all passenger vehicles have used 12-volt batteries. Some older vehicles had 6-volt batteries.

Schematic Drawings

A special form of drawing, known as an *electrical schematic,* is used to indicate electrical circuits. A table of symbols for commonly used automotive components is shown in Figure 27-3.

The use of a common ground for an electrical circuit is shown in Figure 27-4.

Insulators

Electricity will not pass through an *insulator.* Common insulating materials include most plastics, enamel, paper, rubber, and *ceramics.* Ceramics are materials like most household dishes, made from clay baked in special high-temperature ovens.

Electrical conductors in a vehicle, such as copper wires, are covered with an insulator to prevent electricity from flowing to any other conductor. (See Figure 27-5.)

If the wires were not insulated, electricity could flow through any conductor and back to its source. If one conductor touches another conductor or ground, electrical energy can be misused or wasted, or can create heat and fire.

27.2 MATTER AND ATOMS

Everything physical is *matter.* Metal, stone, glass, plastic—even air—are all matter. Matter is made of *atoms.* An atom is the smallest portion of a given type of matter that still retains its unique set of characteristics.

Individual atoms are so small that they cannot be seen even with the most powerful microscope. Knowledge about atoms comes from scientific experiments and mathematical calculations.

Matter can be composed entirely of the same type of atoms. Such matter is said to be an *element,* or specific type of material, for example, iron or copper. There are 92 naturally occurring elements. These range from the simplest, hydrogen, to the most complex, uranium. Other elements have been made in scientific laboratories.

The smallest physical unit of a substance that contains the properties of that substance is called a *molecule.* A molecule may contain a single atom, two or more atoms of the same element, or two or more different atoms. Different elements or molecules can be combined as compounds or mixtures.

A *compound* is a substance containing two or more elements that are joined chemically. The elements in a compound give up their individual properties to form the different properties of the compound. Being united chemically means that the elements in a compound cannot be separated by mechanical means. Water is an example of a chemical compound. Each molecule of pure water is exactly the same as every other molecule. Each contains 11.11% hydrogen and 88.89% oxygen, by weight.

A *mixture* is a substance containing two or more elements or compounds, each of which retains its individual properties. There are three characteristics of mixtures that distinguish them from compounds:

1. The proportions in which the components of a mixture are put together are not fixed.

2. The properties of a mixture combine the properties of its components.

3. The components of a mixture can be separated by mechanical means, based upon the differing

ELECTRICAL SYMBOLS				
SYMBOL	**REPRESENTS**	**SYMBOL**	**REPRESENTS**	
(Alt)	Alternator	HORN	Horn	
(A)	Ammeter		Lamp or Bulb (Preferred)	
—||—	Battery - One Cell		Lamp or Bulb (Acceptable)	
—|||—	Battery - Multicell	(MOT)	Motor-Electric	
12V +—|||—	Where required, battery voltage and/or polarity may be indicated as shown. The long line is always positive polarity.	—	Negative	
Bat	Battery-Voltage Box	+	Positive	
Ⅲ	Bi-Metal Strip		Relay	
—•—	Cable-Connected	—\/\/\/—	Resistor	
—|—	Cable-Not Connected		Resistor-Variable	
—)|—	Capacitor	IDLE STOP	Solenoid-Idle Stop	
	Circuit Breaker	B SOL Starting Motor	Starting Motor	
—<	Connector-Female Contact			
—>	Connector-Male Contact			
—»—	Connectors-Separable-Engaged			
—▶|—	Diode	—o͟ o—	Switch-Single Throw	
HEI	Distributor	—o o o—	Switch-Double Throw	
—◡◠—	Fuse	(TACH)	Tachometer	
(FUEL)	Gauge-Fuel	—•—	Termination	
(TEMP)	Gauge-Temperature	(V)	Voltmeter	
—E	Ground-Chassis Frame (Preferred)	⦶⦶⦶⦶ or ⌒⌒⌒	Winding-Inductor	
—|ı	Ground-Chassis Frame (Acceptable)			

Figure 27-3. Electrical symbols. GENERAL MOTORS CORPORATION

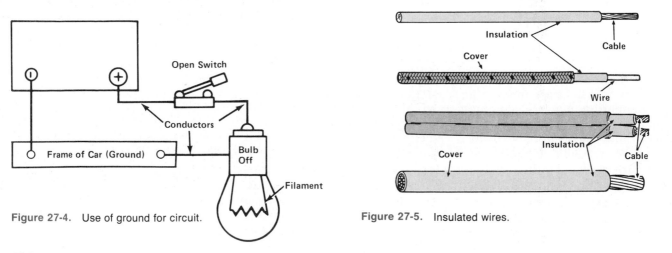

Figure 27-4. Use of ground for circuit.

Figure 27-5. Insulated wires.

278

physical qualities of each component. These differences include weight, size, volatility, and so forth.

Air is a mixture. In relation to the first characteristic above, air contains less oxygen as altitude (height above sea level) increases. In automotive terms, an internal combustion engine burns an air-fuel mixture.

A compound that contains carbon is referred to as an *organic compound*. Gasoline, which contains carbon and hydrogen atoms, is an organic compound.

Atoms

Atoms consist of several parts, as illustrated in Figure 27-6. The center, or *nucleus*, of the atom consists of parts called *protons* and *neutrons*. Protons have a positive *charge*, or quality. Neutrons are neutral and have no charge. Spinning around the nucleus in a spherical fashion are layers, or *shells*, of tiny *electrons*. A single electron weighs only about about 1/1,800 as much as a proton or a neutron. Electrons have a negative charge. All these parts can also exist separately from an atom.

Attraction and Repulsion

In electrical and magnetic applications, electrical charges can attract (pull toward) or repel (push away from) one another. Like charges repel. Unlike charges attract one another.

Two negative or two positively charged particles will exert a force against each other. Two particles, one negatively charged and the other positively charged, will attract each other.

This can be demonstrated with two bar magnets. The ends of the bar magnets are coded N and S, for north (positive) and south (negative). Trying to push two north or two south ends together results in a repulsive force you can feel (see Figure 27-7).

However, opposite charges will attract and pull toward one another (see Figure 27-8).

Electrons are negatively charged. They are attracted to the positively charged protons in the atom's nucleus. Normally, the positive and negative charges are in balance, creating a *binding force* that literally holds matter together.

Bound and Free Electrons

The element hydrogen, normally a gas, is the simplest atom (see Figure 27-9). Only one electron spins around the nucleus.

An atom of copper is much more complicated (see Figure 27-10). Four distinct electron shells orbit spherically around the nucleus.

Each shell can contain a certain maximum number of electrons. The closer to the nucleus, the more tightly bound, or held, the electrons are to the atom. The fourth shell of an atom could contain a

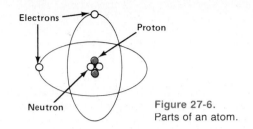
Figure 27-6. Parts of an atom.

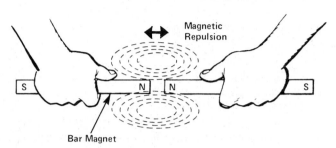
Figure 27-7. Magnetic repulsion.

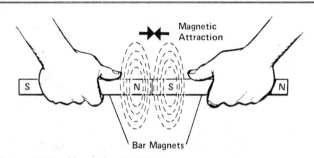
Figure 27-8. Magnetic attraction.

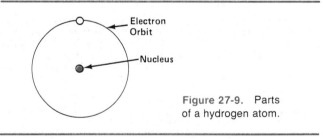
Figure 27-9. Parts of a hydrogen atom.

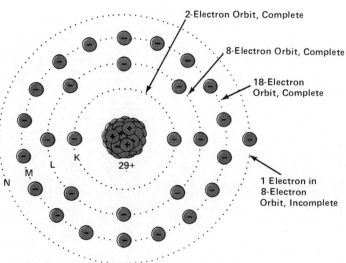
Figure 27-10. Parts of a copper atom.

maximum of 8, 18, or 32 electrons, depending on the element.

Because the fourth, outer shell of copper contains only one electron, the electron is relatively "free," or unbound. Such an electron can be dislodged easily from its orbit. This outer electron can travel to another copper atom and "bump" the electron in its outer shell. This bumping can continue from atom to atom (see Figure 27-11).

Such a movement of electrons constitutes an *electrical current,* or flow.

When an element loses or gains an electron, the number of electrons no longer balances the number of protons in the nucleus. Such an unbalanced element is known as an *ion.* When an atom or a portion of an atom gains an electron, it is said to be positively *ionized,* or charged. When an electron is lost, the atom is said to be negatively ionized.

Electrons that nearly fill the outer shell of a particular element cannot be dislodged easily. These electrons are known as *bound electrons.*

Elements whose outer electron shells are relatively full-form insulators or *semiconductors,* discussed in 27.9. Such electron shells are composed of bound electrons that cannot be dislodged easily to create an electrical flow.

27.3 DIRECTION OF ELECTRICAL FLOW

You will encounter two opposite ways of thinking about the direction in which electricity flows. These views on electricity are called:

1. Conventional theory
2. Electron theory.

Conventional Theory

Before the existence and properties of atoms were known, early scientists tried to determine how the world and the universe worked.

In 1752 Benjamin Franklin, the American statesman/scientist/journalist, conducted an experiment with lightning to determine if it was a form of electricity. On a rainy day, he flew a kite with a metal key attached to the string. Lightning struck the kite and traveled down the string to the key, where it jumped

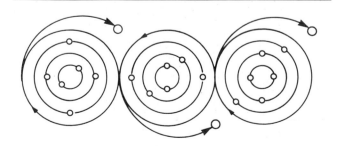

Figure 27-11. Electron flow through atoms.

toward the ground. Like other forms of electricity, the lightning flowed through a conductor (the wet string). Had the lightning struck Franklin instead, we might not have a source of confusion over the direction of electrical flow.

Franklin reasoned that electricity was a form of force and, as such, was positive in its nature. Thus, he believed that electricity must always travel from a positive source to something that lacked such force. He called the lack of force negative. Thus, Franklin believed that electricity always flowed from positive to negative, or ground.

Thus, the *conventional electrical theory* states that electricity flows from positive to negative. Mechanics often speak of the positive terminal of a vehicle battery as the source of electricity.

The ground connection, through the vehicle frame, thus is considered the return path for electricity to return to the battery.

Electron Theory

When atomic theory was first introduced, the conventional electrical theory seemed backwards. Electrons have a negative charge, and are attracted to a positive charge.

Thus, the *electron electrical theory* states that electricity flows from the negative terminal of a battery to a load, and returns to the positive terminal. Thus, the chassis ground connection is seen as the source of electrical power, and the conductor to the positive battery post as the return line.

Electrical Flow and Vehicle Service

Neither the conventional theory nor the electron theory has been proven conclusively to be right or wrong. If you go on to take further courses in automotive electrical service, you will find books that use either one theory or the other exclusively.

For the purposes of vehicle service and troubleshooting, neither theory has an advantage. The main problem you will encounter in working on the electrical system of a vehicle is finding out whether a proper circuit exists.

There may be an *open,* or break in electrical flow at some point in a circuit.

In some cases, a conductor accidentally may touch another conductor and produces a *short circuit.* Electricity flows to a different load than the one intended and completes a circuit.

In other cases, a conductor accidentally may touch a ground connection, thereby producing an *accidental ground.* The accidental ground can overheat a wire or can cause a fuse or circuit breaker to interrupt the electrical flow.

Batteries and electrical testers have a positive connection (usually red) and a negative connection (usually black). As long as a circuit exists among an electrical source, conductors, and a load, electricity will flow.

CAUTION: **It is important to retain the polarity (direction of electrical flow) of the electrical system intended by the vehicle manufacturer. Switching the battery terminals will result in damage to vehicle components, especially motors and electronic equipment.**

Fuses

A *fuse* is a safety device that conducts electricity. A fuse is made of special metal that melts when a certain amount of current flows through it. When the fuse blows, or melts, the circuit is incomplete, or open, and no current can flow. Without protective fuses in an electrical circuit, wires could overheat, burn off insulation, and cause a fire (see Figure 27-12).

Typical fuses are shown in Figure 27-13.

27.4 DC AND AC

Electrons will move when they are attracted more strongly by an electrical charge than they are bound to atoms of a conductor. This process occurs in any complete circuit. Electrical current flows from a location with an excess of electrons to a location with a shortage of electrons.

The connection from an electrical source, through conductors and a load, and back to the source, creates such a flow. Thus, electrical current flows when all the elements of a circuit are properly connected:

- Electrical source
- Conductors
- Load
- Switch (optional).

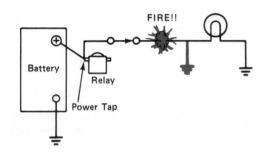

Figure 27-12. Accidentally grounded circuit causing fire.

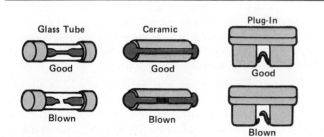

Figure 27-13. Types of fuses.

Direct and Alternating Current

Two types of electrical current are used:

1. Direct current
2. Alternating current.

Direct current. *Direct current (DC)* flows in one direction from one terminal of an electrical source to the other terminal. Batteries produce direct current. The electricity flows in one direction only. The direction of current flow can be reversed by switching conductor connections at a battery.

A simple device, such as a light bulb, will operate with the connections made either way. Motors and other more complicated devices may be damaged or may not operate with *reversed polarity,* or switched connections.

Alternating current. *Alternating current (AC)* is the type of electricity used in homes, shops, and factories. Alternating current changes direction, or switches polarity, several times per second. In some countries, it changes directions 50 or more times per second. In the United States, it changes directions 60 times per second. These direction changes are called *cycles per second (cps)*. In the metric system, this is stated as 60 hertz (Hz), named after a German scientist.

Some electrical devices will work on either DC or AC. Other units are designed specifically to work on only DC or only AC current.

27.5 ELECTRICAL MEASUREMENTS

The electrical qualities of conductors, circuits, insulators, and other equipment can be measured. There are several basic measurements whose meanings you will need to know:

- Amperes (amps)
- Ohms
- Volts
- Watts.

All of these terms come from the names of scientists who conducted early experiments with electricity. A basic analogy, or comparison, can be made between the flow of water through pipes and the flow of electricity through wires. Thus, these terms and their relationships can be understood as relatively simple concepts.

Amperes

The *ampere*, or *amp,* is named after Andre M. Ampere (1775–1836), a French scientist. An ampere is a certain number of electrons flowing each second past a given point. An ampere is similar to the amount of water, measured in drops, flowing each second past a point in a pipe.

Because electrons are so extremely small, a tremendous number of electrons must flow to make one ampere. One ampere of current equals

6,280,000,000,000,000,000 (six quintillion 280 quadrillion) electrons flowing past a given point each second.

Electricity travels at the speed of light, approximately 186,000 miles in one second. Obviously, no one can count electrons one by one as they pass by. A measuring instrument, called an *ammeter,* is used to measure current flow.

Ohms

Electricity flows easily through materials that are good conductors, such as silver, copper, and aluminum. Electrical flow through other materials is more difficult. Think of water flow, which is more difficult through a small pipe than through a large one. A material through which current flow is difficult is said to have high *resistance*. For example, different sizes of wire have different amounts of resistance. A large, thick wire, like a large pipe, has little resistance. A small, thin wire, like a tiny pipe, has more resistance. Materials with extremely high resistance are used as insulators (see Figure 27-14).

Resistance is measured in *ohms*, symbolized by Ω (the Greek letter *omega*). George S. Ohm (1787–1854) was a German scientist who studied electrical resistance.

If electricity can flow through either a high resistance or a lower resistance, it will flow through the lower resistance. The saying is, "Electricity always follows the path of least resistance."

Volts

Voltage, named after Alessandro Volta (1745–1827), an Italian scientist, is similar to the pressure pushing water through a pipe. The higher the pressure, the greater the flow of water. Thus, more voltage will push greater amounts of current through a circuit.

One *volt* is defined as the electrical pressure necessary to make one ampere of electricity flow through one ohm of resistance.

Ohm's Law

The relationship among amps, ohms, and volts can be summarized in an equation or a drawing (see Figure 27-15). The symbol for voltage is E, short for EMF (electromotive force). The symbol for amperage (current) is I. The symbol for resistance is R. This equation can be stated in several ways, as shown in Figure 27-15.

Thus, Ohm's Law allows you to find an unknown value by manipulating known values.

NOTE: Ohm's Law, as stated above, applies to DC circuits only. More complicated equations are needed for circuits with AC current. In addition, the resistance of a device, such as a light bulb, changes with temperature. A light bulb might have very little resistance when measured with an ohmmeter.

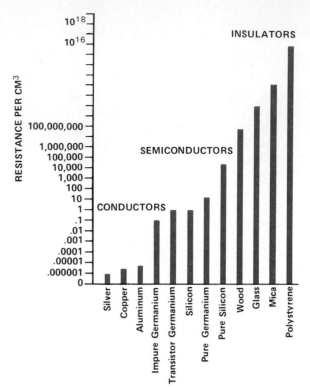

Figure 27-14. Properties of conductors.

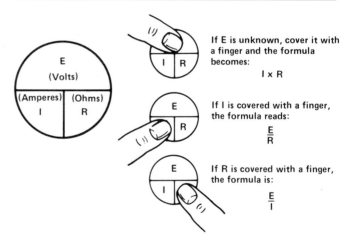

Figure 27-15. Diagrams illustrate Ohm's Law equations.

However, when the filament is hot enough to produce light, the resistance may be thousands of times greater.

Electrical Power

Power, as in an engine, is the rate at which work can be done. Forcing a current to flow through a resistance is work. Power is measured in *watts*, named after James Watt (1736–1819), the Scottish scientist who devised the horsepower rating.

Electrical power, or the rate of work, is determined by multiplying the amount of voltage by the amount of amperes flowing. The symbol for power (watts) is P. The symbol for voltage is E. The symbol for amperage is I. Thus, the equation to determine electrical power is P = E × I. One horsepower equals 746 watts.

27.6 ELECTRICAL CIRCUITS

Electrical circuits fall into three general categories:

1. Series
2. Parallel
3. Series-parallel.

Series Circuits

In a *series circuit,* electrical current passes through loads one at a time, in order, or in series (see Figure 27-16). Electrical current is shared among all loads in a series circuit. Each separate load forms part of the conductive path of the circuit.

To illustrate, strings of inexpensive Christmas tree lights often are wired in series. If one bulb fails, the entire string goes out. To find the burned-out bulb, each bulb must be checked or replaced one at a time.

Series Circuit Laws

There are three laws that apply to series circuits:

1. Current Law: Current in a series circuit is the same value in all parts of the circuit.
2. Resistance Law: Total resistance (ohms) in a series circuit is equal to the sum of all individual resistances.
3. Voltage Law: Source voltage in a series circuit is equal to the sum of the individual voltage drops.

Voltage drop. Each separate bulb has resistance. A brighter or more powerful bulb has more resistance than a smaller bulb. The more resistance a load has, the greater the voltage required to push current through it.

Thus, the *voltage drop,* or voltage measurement across a higher-resistance load, is greater (see Figure 27-17). The voltage drop can be determined by using Ohm's Law, above, if the resistance is known. Alternately, the resistance can be determined by measuring the voltage drop and applying Ohm's Law.

Parallel Circuits

In a parallel circuit, electricity takes several paths through separate loads to complete a circuit (see Figure 27-18).

Consider a string of Christmas tree lights wired in parallel. If one of the bulbs is burned out, the other bulbs will still burn. The voltage drop across each load is the same. However, the total resistance of the circuit is *less* than the resistance of any single load.

Each load in a parallel circuit provides an additional path for electrical current, making it easier for

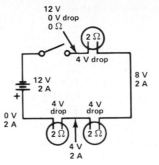

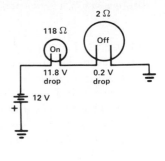

Figure 27-16. Series circuit.

Figure 27-17. Voltage drops.

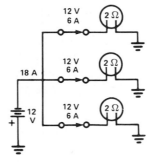

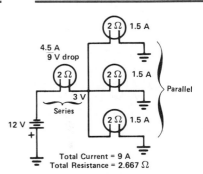

Figure 27-18. Parallel circuit.

Figure 27-19. Series-parallel circuit.

current to complete a circuit. This effect produces less resistance than any individual load.

However, the amount of current flowing does increase according to the number of loads added. Too many loads can create excessive current flow that can cause heat and fire, or blow a fuse.

Parallel Circuit Laws

There are three laws that apply to parallel circuits:

1. Current Law: Total current flow in a series circuit is equal to the sum of the individual branch current flows.
2. Resistance Law: Total resistance in a parallel circuit is less than the lowest individual resistance.
3. Voltage Law: Voltage in a parallel circuit is the same in each individual branch.

Series-Parallel Circuits

It is possible to combine series and parallel circuits into a single circuit (see Figure 27-19).

Most circuits in an automobile are series-parallel circuits. Ohm's Law is used to work out the values for current, voltage drops, and overall resistance values shown, although the process is complicated.

27.7 MAGNETISM

Electricity and magnetism are related. No one really knows what causes certain materials to function as magnets. One theory is that the alignment of molecules allows a natural flow of electrons through and around the magnet (see Figure 27-20).

Ferrous, or iron-containing, materials are attracted to this flow. To demonstrate, a sheet of paper can be placed over a magnet. Small iron filings then are sprinkled lightly onto the surface. A pattern of the continuous force fields of magnetism will be formed (see Figure 27-21).

Electromagnetism

The flow of electrons in an electrical circuit can be demonstrated in a similar manner. Iron filings on paper at right angles to a conductor will arrange themselves in a circular pattern around the wire. A compass near the wire will indicate the direction of flow (see Figure 27-22).

The direction of current flow can be changed in such a circuit by reversing the wiring connections (see Figure 27-23). This process is also known as reversing the polarity of the circuit. Polarity describes how the ends of a circuit are connected to the electrical source connections. One end is connected to the positive connection, and the other end is connected to the negative connection. The polarity of the circuit determines the direction in which the compass needle will point.

As current flow is shut off, the magnetic field around the conductor collapses, or moves, rapidly inward until it no longer exists.

Coil

To produce a strong magnetic field, conductors can be arranged parallel and next to each other. If the current in the conductors flows in the same direction, the magnetic fields of force will combine and become stronger. If the current in the conductors flows in opposite directions, the magnetic fields will repulse each other and tend to cancel out (Figure 27-24).

The shape of the magnetic field surrounding the loops in a coil is shown in Figure 27-25.

Electromagnet

A simple way to construct a device that will produce a strong magnetic field is to wrap wire in a coil

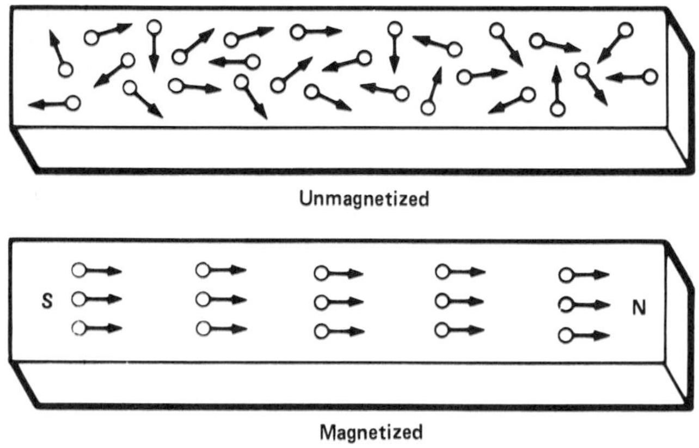

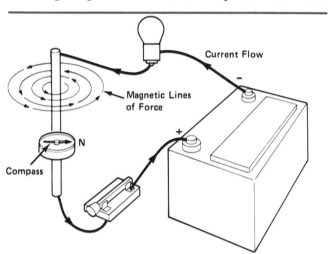

Figure 27-22. Magnetic field surrounding a conductor.

Figure 27-20. Unmagnetized and magnetized steel.

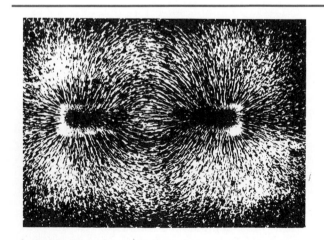

Figure 27-21. Magnetic force fields.

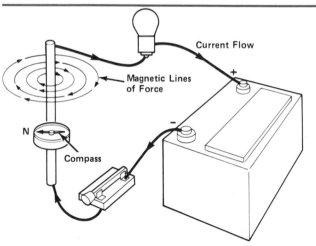

Figure 27-23. Reversed magnetic field surrounding a conductor.

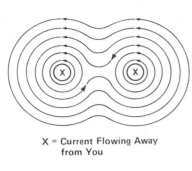

X = Current Flowing Away
from You

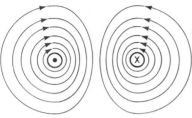

⊙ Current Flowing Toward You.

Ⓧ Current Flowing Away From You.

Figure 27-24. Magnetic fields of force.

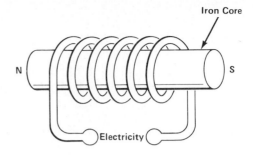

Figure 27-26. Electromagnet.

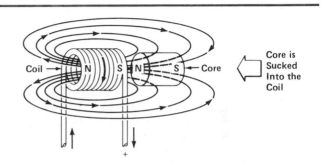

Figure 27-27. Magnetic fields around a solenoid.

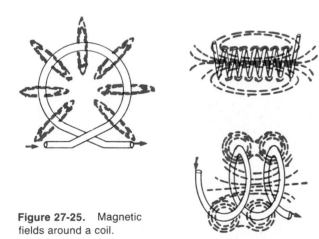

Figure 27-25. Magnetic fields around a coil.

around a *reluctor*. A reluctor is a material, such as iron, that conducts magnetic force fields well. An electrical source then can be connected to the ends of the wire. Such a device is known as an *electromagnet* (see Figure 27-26).

Solenoid

If an iron bar is placed next to a coil in which current is flowing, the bar will be pulled into the coil. A device that produces such a mechanical effect is known as a *solenoid* (see Figure 27-27).

Solenoids are used in several applications in modern vehicles, including fuel injectors and starter circuits. Starter circuits are discussed in Unit 30.

27.8 MAGNETIC INDUCTION

A flow of electrons in a conductor can produce magnetism. Magnetism also can produce electrical flow in a conductor (see Figure 27-28).

An ammeter can be connected across the ends of a conductor. Wrapping the conductor in a coil shape will make the process of creating electricity more efficient.

A magnet moved next to the coil of wire will produce a flow of electrons within the conductor. The meter will register how much electrical current is *induced,* or created by magnetic force. The stronger the magnet and the faster it is moved, the more electrical current will be produced.

Transformers

The magnetic field produced in one conductor can be used to induce current in a second conductor placed close to, and parallel to, the first. Such an arrangement that uses two parallel coils is known as a *transformer.*

If two coils are close together, and the magnetic field of one is moved, an electrical current will flow through the other.

Shutting off the current in the first coil will cause the magnetic field to collapse and move. This will induce a momentary pulse of current in the second coil (see Figure 27-29).

Wrapping both coils around a reluctor, or iron core, will increase the efficiency of this process. Typical transformer construction is shown in Figure 27-30.

285

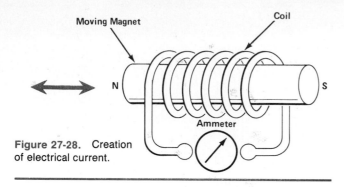

Figure 27-28. Creation of electrical current.

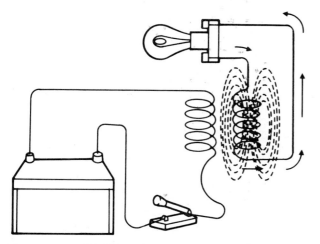

Figure 27-29. Principles of a transformer.

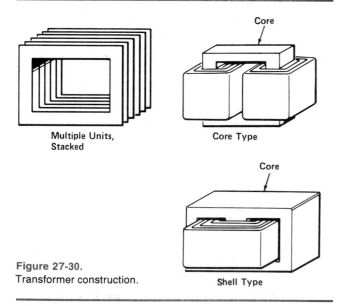

Multiple Units, Stacked

Core Type

Shell Type

Figure 27-30. Transformer construction.

The voltage induced in the second coil is proportional to the number of turns of wire in each coil.

If the second coil has more turns of wire, the induced voltage will be greater than that in the first coil. Thus, voltage can be increased through the use of a transformer. This type of transformer is known as a *step-up transformer.*

If the second coil has fewer turns of wire than the first, the voltage induced will be lower. Thus, voltage can be decreased through the use of a transformer.

This type of transformer is known as a *step-down transformer.*

27.9 ELECTRONICS AND SEMICONDUCTORS

Electronics is a branch of physics that deals with the behavior and effects of small amounts of electrons in semiconductor circuits. Electrical equipment uses larger amounts of current.

Thus, a television or a computer is considered to be an electronic device, whereas a light bulb or a motor is an electrical device.

Semiconductors

You may have noticed that, in Figure 27-14, some materials were classified as *semiconductors.* Semiconductors are materials that partially conduct electricity. Semiconductors can act either as conductors or as insulators, depending upon the circumstances.

Silicon, the ingredient in ordinary sand, can be used as a semiconductor when mixed with *trace,* or small, amounts of other minerals.

Doping

Mixing minerals with a semiconductor material is known as *doping.* Minerals used for doping include antimony, arsenic, phosphorus, aluminum, boron, gallium, and indium. Depending upon the type of mineral used, the semiconductor can have a positive (P) or negative (N) characteristic.

Diode

Electrons will flow from a negatively doped semiconductor material (N) toward a positively doped material (P). Joining N and P semiconductor materials will create a junction. Such a junction creates a simple form of electrical device called a *diode* (see Figure 27-31). A diode is a device with two (from the Greek *di-*) poles, or a cathode and an anode.

Electricity will flow through a diode in one direction only. Both positive and negative diodes are used in automobiles. Diodes can be used to change alternating current into pulsating DC, as in an automotive alternator.

Transistor

A *transistor* is made of three pieces of semiconductor material in a "sandwich," either NPN or PNP (see Figure 27-32). Transistors can be used to control or amplify current flow (see Figure 27-33).

A transistor is capable of conducting relatively large amounts of current from the *emitter* to the *collector.* The emitter discharges, or emits, electrons. These electrons flow to the collector. However, a transistor will perform in this manner only if a small amount of electricity passes from the emitter to the base. This, in effect, "turns on" the transistor.

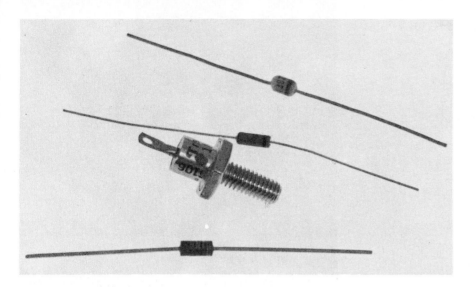

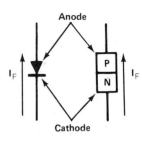

Figure 27-31. Diode junction.

Figure 27-32. Transistors.

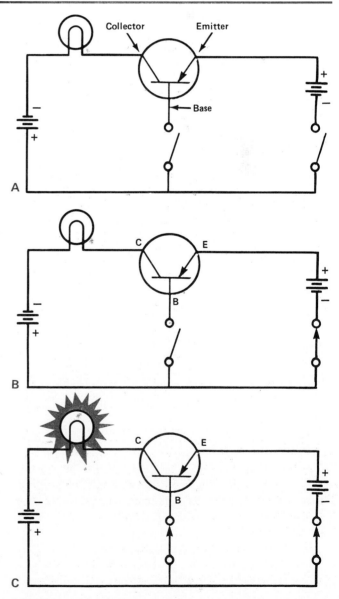

Figure 27-33. Diagrams of a transistor in a circuit:
A. No current is applied to base or emitter. **B.** Current
is applied to emitter (transistor off). **C.** Current is
applied to emitter and base (transistor on).

A transistor can be used as a switch to turn current flow on or off. It also can act as an amplifier to increase and magnify a given current flow.

Integrated Circuit

Transistors, resistors, and other electrical components can be combined into circuits to perform complicated functions. These components can be greatly miniaturized into what is known as an *integrated circuit*. Figure 27-34 shows such an integrated circuit, or computer chip, so small that it can pass through the eye of a needle. Such integrated circuits also are known as microchips.

Integrated circuits are made of thin wafers of silicon, on which materials have been deposited. These deposited materials form conductors, resistors, diodes, transistors, and other types of electrical components to form circuits.

Integrated circuits are used as regulators for alternator voltage output, electronic control units (ECUs), radio circuits, and other electronic devices.

Automotive servicing does not require detailed knowledge of electronics. In general, all a mechanic is required to do is determine whether an electronic device is operating. If not, it is replaced. Electronic devices and servicing procedures are discussed in Units 38 and 39.

Figure 27-34. Integrated circuit.

U N I T   H I G H L I G H T S

- Electricity is a form of energy that can be used to create heat, light, or force to cause motion.

- A typical electrical circuit includes an electrical source, conductors, and a load.

- Modern vehicles all have negative ground.

- Electrical schematics are like maps that use symbols to indicate the position of electrical sources, conductors, loads, and other devices.

- Conductors allow the passage of electricity; insulators prevent the passage of electricity.

- Electrical current is caused by the movement of electrons from one atom of a conductor to another atom of a conductor.

- Electrical circuits can be hooked up in series, parallel, or series-parallel.

- Magnetism can be used to produce electricity, and electricity can be used to produce magnetism.

- Magnetic induction can produce magnetism or electrical current in a conductor.

- Semiconductors are materials that can be made to conduct electricity. Diodes conduct electricity in one direction only. Transistors can act as switches or as amplifiers.

T E R M S

electricity	electron electrical
terminal	theory
load	open
circuit	short circuit
conductor	fuse
switch	direct current (DC)
ground	alternating current (AC)
single-wire circuit	cycles per second (cps)
negative ground	reversed polarity
positive ground	ampere
electrical schematic	resistance
insulator	ohms
matter	voltage
atom	watts
element	series circuit
molecule	voltage drop
compound	ferrous
mixture	reluctor
organic compound	electromagnet
nucleus	solenoid
proton	induce
neutron	transformer
charge	electronics
shell	trace
electrons	doping
binding force	diode
electrical current	transistor
ion	emitter
semiconductor	collector
conventional electrical	integrated circuit
theory	

DIRECTIONS: The following questions are similar to those used on mechanic certification tests. On a separate sheet of paper, write the letter of the correct choice.

1. A normal electrical circuit contains all of the following EXCEPT

A. an electrical source.

B. an open.

C. a load.

D. conductors.

2. Mechanic A says that electrical current consists of a flow of electrons from one atom of a conductor to another.
   Mechanic B says that electrical current flows from one pole of an electrical source to the other pole.
   Who is correct?

A. A only   B. B only   C. Both A and B   D. Neither A nor B

3. Which of the following statements is correct?
   I. The conventional theory states that electrical current flows from negative to positive.
   II. The electron theory states that electrical current flows from positive to negative.

A. I only   B. II only   C. Both I and II   D. Neither I nor II

4. Each time a fuse is replaced, it immediately blows. What is the most likely cause?

A. Open

B. Short circuit

C. Accidental ground

D. Reversed polarity

5. In a new car, a current of 10 amperes is measured in a circuit. Using Ohm's Law, what is the resistance of the load?

A. 0.833 Ω

B. 120 Ω

C. 1.2 Ω

D. Cannot be determined from information given.

S U P P L E M E N T A L   A C T I V I T I E S

1. Trace the battery cable connections on a vehicle. Report to your class where the positive and negative cables are connected.

2. Discussion topic: From what you have learned in this unit, can you figure out how turning an alternator with a drive belt could produce electricity? (Hint: When a vehicle is running, a small amount of electricity from the battery flows through coils in the alternator.)

3. Using the symbols in Figure 27-3, draw a schematic of a circuit with two headlight bulbs, four side marker lights, and two tail lights. Include a battery and a switch. Use the symbol for ground and draw a parallel circuit.

4. Under the supervision of your instructor, connect an unpowered test light to the positive terminal of the battery. Scratch through paint and touch the probe to metal objects in the engine compartment. What does this experiment demonstrate?

5. Under the supervision of your instructor, connect an unpowered test light to a metal part of a vehicle near the fuse box. Touch the probe to each end of the fuses. What does this experiment demonstrate? Why doesn't the test light light on both ends of all fuses?

28 BATTERIES

UNIT PREVIEW

The battery provides current to start the engine, provides a reserve electrical capacity, and aids in electrical system regulation.

A basic battery consists of two dissimilar metals immersed in an acid. A chemical reaction within the battery produces the potential for electrical flow. Automotive batteries are classified as lead-acid batteries.

Battery construction may be classified as either conventional or maintenance-free, or wet or dry charged.

Battery rating procedures generally are designed to reflect battery capacity.

To provide long periods of dependable service, the battery and electrical system must be maintained routinely.

LEARNING OBJECTIVES

When you have completed your assignments and exercises in this unit, you should be able to:

☐ Describe the function, construction, and operation of a vehicle battery.

☐ Identify and describe problems that can shorten battery life.

☐ Explain the different ratings for battery capacity and their significance.

☐ Determine the coded group number of a sample battery.

☐ Determine what differences exist between available models of the same group size battery.

28.1 BATTERY FUNCTION

The battery is one of the two electrical sources in a vehicle. The other source is the alternator, explained in Unit 32. The battery provides current to turn the starter motor and power the ignition system during starting.

After the vehicle starts, the alternator provides the current needed by the electrical system. The alternator also replaces electricity used by the battery during starting.

If the electrical load exceeds alternator output, the battery supplies the rest of the current needed.

The battery can also act as a load or a source to help even out voltage *spikes*. Spikes are surges of voltage that occur when loads are switched on or off.

28.2 ELECTROCHEMICAL ACTION

A battery does not store electricity. It provides the opportunity, or potential, for electrons to flow. Current flows only when a load is connected across the battery terminals. This process is an example of *electrochemical action*.

A battery uses chemicals to produce electrical potential. A method of constructing a small battery was described in the Supplemental Activities of Unit 17. A penny and a dime were placed in a slice of citrus fruit. A small voltage was created between the two coins.

To create a battery, different metals are placed side by side in an acid solution. A voltmeter (a small electrical load) is connected between the metals. Electrical potential can be measured between the metals. See Figure 28-1.

Electrolyte

Electrolyte is a material whose atoms become *ionized* in solution. As in a conductor, electrons can flow easily through electrolyte.

Electrolyte used in automotive batteries is a mixture of 36 percent water and 64 percent sulfuric acid,

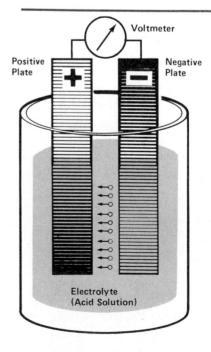

Figure 28-1.
A simple battery.

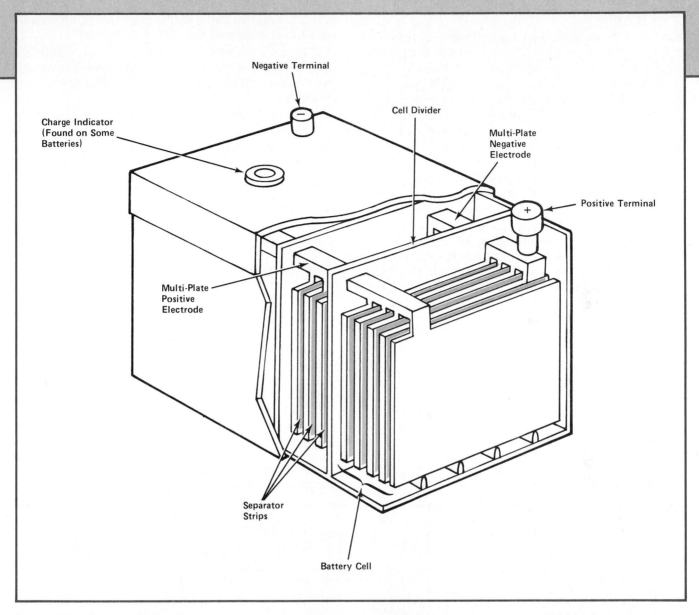

Figure 28-2. Battery cell construction.

Labels in figure: Negative Terminal; Cell Divider; Charge Indicator (Found on Some Batteries); Multi-Plate Negative Electrode; Positive Terminal; Multi-Plate Positive Electrode; Separator Strips; Battery Cell

---

by weight. By volume, sulfuric acid is approximately 25 percent of the electrolyte.

SAFETY CAUTION: Battery electrolyte is extremely corrosive and can cause skin burns, blindness, and damage to parts. Be very careful when working with electrolyte. Always wear safety glasses.

Battery Elements and Cells

A *battery element* consists of two dissimilar metal plates separated by a porous *separator strip*, or insulator, and immersed in electrolyte. Several battery elements are connected to form a single *battery cell* (see Figure 28-2).

Lead paste is spread on grids and baked to form battery plates (see Figure 28-3).

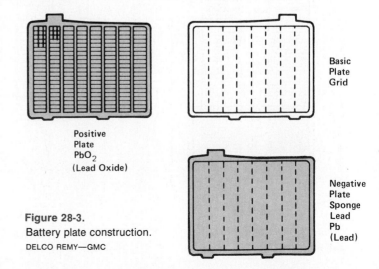

Labels in figure: Positive Plate PbO_2 (Lead Oxide); Basic Plate Grid; Negative Plate Sponge Lead Pb (Lead)

Figure 28-3.
Battery plate construction.
DELCO REMY—GMC

Positive Plate

One of the two grids in a battery element is coated with *lead peroxide (PbO₂)*. Lead peroxide is a porous, chocolate-brown, crystalline substance.

Electrons (negatively charged) leave the porous lead peroxide plate and enter the electrolyte. This leaves the lead peroxide with a positive charge, and this grid forms the positive plate of a battery element.

Negative Plate

The other grid in a battery element is coated with porous *sponge lead (Pb)*. Electrons travel through the electrolyte and into the sponge lead, causing it to have a negative charge.

When a load is connected across the terminals, electrons flow from the negative terminal, through the load, and back to the positive terminal. Electricity flows to do work, as shown in Figure 28-4.

Battery Construction

Each battery cell can produce approximately 2.1 volts. When connected in series, six cells produce approximately 12.6 volts. Construction of an individual cell (called an element before electrolyte is added) is illustrated in Figure 28-5.

Each of the cells has an individual supply of electrolyte. The cells are enclosed in a polyethylene battery case. A top encloses the cells. Openings to the cells may be permanently sealed or openable. Small spaces, or vents, are designed into the top to allow gases to be released. See Figure 28-6.

If a negative and positive plate touch, an *internal short* is created and the battery is ruined.

In time, material from the plates flakes and falls off. A space at the bottom of the case allows this material to collect. This space is called a sediment chamber.

Connections to the positive and negative plates are made through internally threaded *side terminals* or *battery posts* (see Figures 28-6 and 28-7). The battery is sealed around the posts or side terminals to prevent electrolyte from leaking. Batteries with top posts have different-sized posts. The positive post is always larger than the negative post (see Figure 28-7).

Flanges or *recesses* can be molded into the outer plastic case to aid in holding the battery securely in the vehicle. A flange is a projecting lip or edge. A recess is a shaped hollow space (see Figure 28-8 and refer to Figure 28-6).

28.3 BATTERY CHEMISTRY

The supply of electrons in the negative plate of the battery is not unlimited. As electricity discharges, or flows out of the battery, the electrons return to the ions of the positive and negative plates.

Discharging and Sulfation

The positive plate loses oxygen (O₂) to the electrolyte. At the same time, sulfate (SO₄) from the electrolyte combines with the lead of both the positive and negative plates. This chemical process, known as *sulfation*, forms *lead sulfate (PbSO₄)*.

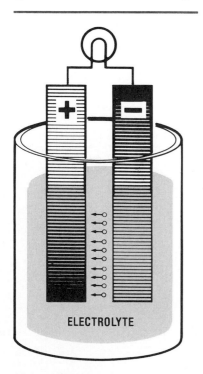

Figure 28-4. Electrical battery current flow.

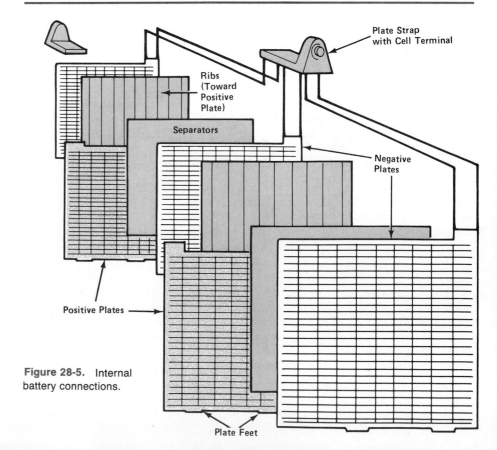

Figure 28-5. Internal battery connections.

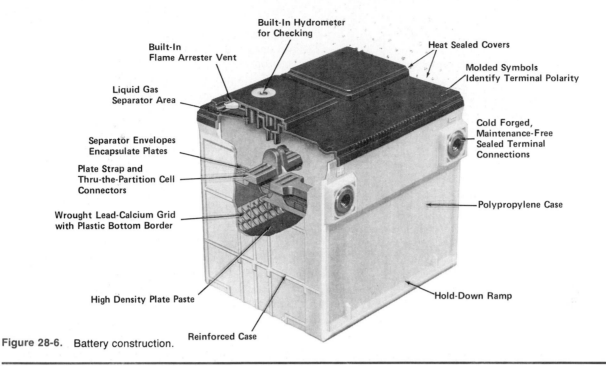

Figure 28-6. Battery construction.

Eventually, both the positive and negative plates become coated with lead sulfate, and the percentage of water in the electrolyte increases. See Figure 28-9.

Charging

In normal operation, the process of discharging and temporary sulfation is reversed by *charging*. Charging is done by connecting a source of DC (direct current) electricity to the battery terminals. Charging can be done at a high current input (fast charging) or a low current input (slow charging).

During charging, electrons combine with the ions of the positive plate to create atoms of lead.

Charging causes oxygen and hydrogen gases to be formed from the watery electrolyte during charging. Oxygen from the weak electrolyte combines with the lead on the positive plate to form lead peroxide again.

Charging also causes sulfate to leave the positive and negative plates and to turn into liquid. The electrolyte becomes strong sulfuric acid again.

When the battery is fully charged, electrons again are present in the negative plates (refer to Figure 28-9). The battery plates return to being lead peroxide and sponge lead.

SAFETY CAUTION: During charging, an explosive mixture of hydrogen and oxygen gases is released into the atmosphere. If a source of ignition is present, the battery can explode. Battery explosions splatter sulfuric acid and can lead to blindness, skin burns, and damage to automotive parts.

Battery Life

With proper maintenance, discussed in Unit 29, batteries should give at least three to four years of good

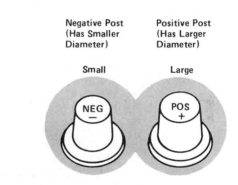

Figure 28-7. Battery posts.

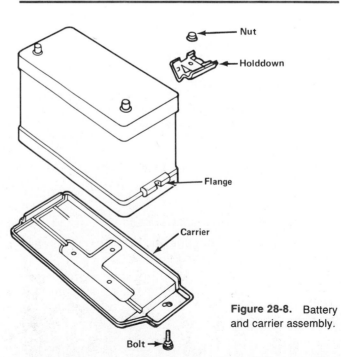

Figure 28-8. Battery and carrier assembly.

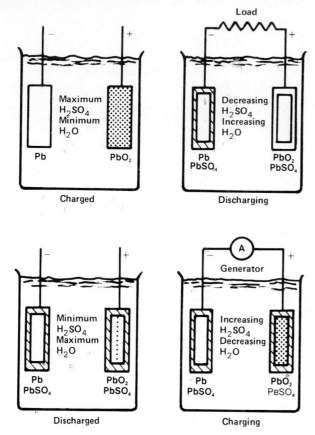

Figure 28-9. Charge and discharge cycles.

service. No battery lasts forever, however. In time, hard sulfation, loss of material from plates, and internal shorts can render a battery unserviceable.

Other than problems of age, several factors can shorten battery life:

- Remaining in a discharged state over a long period of time
- Deep discharging and charging cycles
- Dirt and acid buildup
- Inadequate charging
- Overcharging
- Vibration and movement
- Physical damage
- Extremely cold or hot temperatures
- Improper proportions of acid and water in electrolyte
- Corroded terminal connections
- Loose battery connections.

When a battery is left discharged over a long period of time, sulfation can coat the plates permanently. Hard sulfation prevents electrolyte from penetrating the plates properly.

Deep discharging, such as that caused by prolonged cranking when the engine does not start, can shorten battery life.

Dirt and acid buildup on the outer surface of the battery can form a path between the terminals. This electrical flow can discharge the battery.

Inadequate charging can result in early battery failure. Inadequate charging can be caused by a loose alternator belt, a faulty voltage regulator, or limited driving.

High-current "fast" charging can cause too high an electrolyte temperature and *gassing*. Gassing is the discharge of large amounts of hydrogen gas and loss of water and acid during charging.

If a battery is not held down securely, the internal connections between plates can be broken or separated. In addition, material can be shaken loose from the grids to cause an internal short at the bottom of the plates.

Physical damage, such as a cracked, bulged, or leaking case, will shorten battery life. Such damage can be caused by vibration or loose holding devices, or by overtightening the holding devices.

Chemical reactions occur more readily when the chemicals are heated. Because battery operation depends on chemical reactions, cold temperatures reduce the flow of electricity. In addition, engine lubricants are more viscous, or thick, at cold temperatures. Thus, it is more difficult to turn the engine crankshaft for starting. The combination of these two factors results in difficult starting in cold weather (see Figure 28-10).

Severely hot weather conditions or overcharging can result in evaporation and loss of water and electrolyte, resulting in high acid concentrations.

Too much sulfuric acid in the electrolyte can damage the metal plates and grids of the battery and shorten their life.

Corroded battery connections can cause improper charging and hard starting. Electricity cannot pass easily, in or out, through corroded connections.

Loose battery connections can result in sparks that can cause a battery explosion.

28.4 BATTERY RATINGS

Each cell of a battery is designed to produce approximately 2.1 volts. Before 1967, vehicles had batteries with three cells, making approximately six volts. All passenger vehicles built since 1967 have 12 volt batteries. Battery size does not change the battery voltage. However, size does affect the capacity of the battery.

Electrical Capacity

A given battery has a specific *electrical capacity*. More and larger plates increase battery capacity. There are

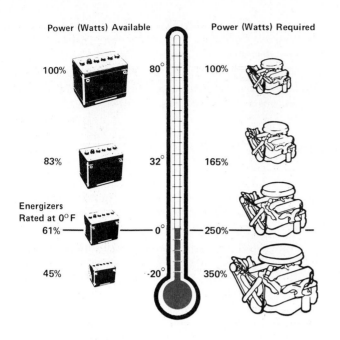

Power (Watts) Available   Power (Watts) Required

100%   80°   100%

83%   32°   165%

Energizers
Rated at 0°F
61%   0°   250%

45%   -20°   350%

Figure 28-10. Battery power availability and requirements.
DELCO REMY—GMC

several ways to measure and indicate battery electrical capacity:

- Cold cranking performance
- Reserve capacity
- Ampere-hour rating
- Watt-hour rating.

Three of these four ratings were introduced by the Battery Council International and Society of Automotive Engineers (SAE) in 1977.

Cold cranking performance is measured with a fully charged 12-volt battery that has been cooled to 0 degrees F [– 17.8 degrees C]. The battery is tested for 30 seconds to determine maximum current flow. The *cold cranking amperes* rating is the number of amperes that can be drawn from the battery before the voltage drops below 7.2 volts.

Replacement batteries should have at least as many cold cranking amps as the number of cubic inches of engine displacement. For additional starting power, a battery with more cold cranking amps can be used.

Reserve capacity is the length of time a 25-ampere current can be maintained before voltage falls to 10.5 volts. This test is conducted with a fully charged battery at 80 degrees F [27 degrees C].

This test approximates how many minutes a vehicle could continue running satisfactorily if the alternator did not produce electricity. A typical rating for a battery might be 90 minutes of reserve capacity.

Ampere-hour rating refers to a test performed with a fully charged battery at a constant 80 degrees F [27 degrees C]. The battery is discharged at a constant rate. At the end of the test, the voltage remaining should be 10.5 volts.

A battery that can supply 4 amperes for 20 hours is rated as an 80 ampere-hour battery. Amperes × hours = ampere-hours. An ampere-hour rating is useful knowledge for some service operations, such as slow charging and battery testing.

Watt-hour is a useful rating of battery power. The number of ampere-hours × voltage = watt hours. Thus, a 12-volt battery rated at 80 amp-hours would be rated at 960 watt-hours. The equation: 80 × 12 = 960.

28.5 MAINTENANCE-FREE BATTERIES

Virtually all new passenger vehicles come equipped with *maintenance-free batteries*. In normal operation, it should not be necessary to add water to the cells of a maintenance-free battery. Older, conventional batteries required periodic addition of water to the cells to keep the plates covered with electrolyte.

Lead-Calcium Grid

The grids on modern long-life batteries are made of lead and calcium rather than the lead antimony used in conventional batteries. The antimony in the negative plates prevents the flow of electricity and contributes to gassing during charging.

Lead-calcium grids allow lower current flows to be used for charging, which reduces electrolyte temperature. Lower temperatures mean that less water is lost from the electrolyte during charging.

Envelope-Type Separator

The separators used on maintenance-free batteries wrap around the bottom of the plates, preventing loss of plate material. Plate material on older batteries could fall to the bottom of the case and eventually build up to cause an internal short.

Amount of Electrolyte Above Plate

If battery plates become dry because of lack of electrolyte, the battery can be damaged or ruined. Maintenance-free batteries have a larger space above the plates for electrolyte (refer to Figure 28-6). Thus, the plates can remain submerged in the electrolyte. Also, because the plates are enclosed in envelopes, the sediment chamber has been eliminated. This space is used for extra plate area, allowing higher output.

28.6 PHYSICAL SIZE

Batteries are classified as to physical size by *group numbers*. Typical group numbers for top-terminal batteries are 22, 24, 24F, 27, and 27F.

Grp. Size	Vlt.	Cold cranking power— amps for 30 secs. at 0°F*	No. of mo. warranted	Size of battery container in inches (incl. terminals)		
				Lgth.	Wd.	Ht.
17HF	6	400	24	7¼	6¾	9
21	12	450	60	8	6¾	8½
22F	12	430	60	9	6⅞	8⅛
22F	12	380	55	9	6⅞	8⅛
22F	12	330	40	9	6⅞	8⅛
22NF	12	330	24	9½	5½	8⅞
24	12	525	60	10¼	6⅞	8⅝
24	12	450	55	10¼	6⅞	8⅝
24	12	410	48	10¼	6⅞	8⅝
24	12	380	40	10¼	6⅞	8⅝
24	12	325	36	10¼	6⅞	8⅝
24	12	290	30	10¼	6⅞	8⅝
24F	12	525	60	10¼	6⅞	8⅝
24F	12	450	55	10¼	6⅞	8⅝
24F	12	410	48	10¼	6⅞	8⅝
24F	12	380	40	10¼	6⅞	8⅝
24F	12	325	36	10¼	6⅞	8⅝
24F	12	290	30	10¼	6⅞	8⅝
27	12	560	60	12	6⅞	8⅝
27F	12	560	60	12	6⅞	9
41	12	525	60	11 9/16	6 13/16	6 15/16
42	12	450	60	9⅝	6⅞	6¾
42	12	340	40	9⅝	6⅞	6¾
45	12	420	60	9½	5½	8⅞
46	12	460	60	10¼	6⅞	8⅝
48	12	440	60	12	6⅞	7½
49	12	600	60	14½	6⅞	7½
56	12	450	60	10	6	8⅜
56	12	380	48	10	6	8⅜
58	12	425	60	9¼	7¼	6⅞
71	12	450	60	8	7¼	8½
71	12	395	55	8	7¼	8½
71	12	330	36	8	7¼	8½
72	12	490	60	9	7¼	8¼
72	12	380	48	9	7¼	8¼
74	12	585	60	10¼	7¼	8¾
74	12	525	60	10¼	7¼	8¾
74	12	505	60	10¼	7¼	8¾
74	12	450	55	10¼	7¼	8¾
74	12	410	48	10¼	7¼	8¾
74	12	380	40	10¼	7¼	8¾
74	12	325	36	10¼	7¼	8¾

*Meets or exceeds Battery Council International rating standards.

Figure 28-11. Battery size chart.

Side-terminal batteries of the same dimensions would be 72, 74, 74F, 77, and 77F. The initial "7" indicates side-terminal design (see Figure 28-11).

The F designation indicates batteries for Ford vehicles. These batteries have positive and negative terminal posts in reverse position from other batteries.

UNIT HIGHLIGHTS

- The battery provides current to operate the starter motor and to power the ignition system during starting.
- After starting, the alternator produces current to run the vehicle. The battery supplies current when the electrical demand exceeds the alternator's output.
- Electrochemical action within the battery produces the potential for electrical flow. Electrical flow does not occur until a load is connected to a battery.
- A basic battery consists of two different metals immersed in electrolyte, an acid material that becomes ionized in solution.
- The materials in a vehicle battery are lead peroxide (PbO_2), sulfuric acid (H_2SO_4) electrolyte, and sponge lead (Pb).
- In a discharged battery, the plates become lead sulfate ($PbSO_4$) and the electrolyte becomes mostly water.
- In normal operation, charging restores the battery's potential for producing electricity.
- Many problems can shorten battery life.
- The basic ratings for battery capacity are cold cranking amperes, reserve capacity, and watt-hours. One battery capacity rating useful for service procedures is ampere-hours.
- Battery physical size and terminal type are indicated by group numbers.

TERMS

spike	flange
electrochemical action	recess
electrolyte	lead sulfate ($PbSO_4$)
separator strip	sulfation
battery element	charging
battery cell	gassing
lead peroxide (PbO_2)	electrical capacity
sponge lead (Pb)	cold cranking amperes
internal short	maintenance-free
side terminals	battery
battery post	group number

R E V I E W   Q U E S T I O N S

DIRECTIONS: The following questions are similar to those used on mechanic certification tests. On a separate sheet of paper, write the letter of the correct choice.

1. Mechanic A says that the battery is a source of electrical power in a vehicle.
   Mechanic B says that the alternator is a source of electrical power in a vehicle.
   Who is correct?
   A. A only   B. B only   C. Both A and B   D. Neither A nor B

2. Which of the following statements is correct?
   I. A battery stores electricity.
   II. When a load is connected, a battery produces electricity.
   A. I only   B. II only   C. Both I and II   D. Neither I nor II

3. All of the following are parts of a battery EXCEPT
   A. positive and negative plates.
   B. electrolyte.
   C. cables.
   D. case and terminals.

4. The most important difference between most maintenance-free batteries and conventional batteries is that
   A. a different material is used in the battery plate grids.
   B. a different type of electrolyte is used.
   C. a different type of separator is used.
   D. the top of the battery is sealed and cannot be opened.

5. Mechanic A says that battery electrolyte can explode if ignited.
   Mechanic B says that the gases produced during charging can explode if ignited.
   Who is correct?
   A. A only   B. B only   C. Both A and B   D. Neither A nor B

S U P P L E M E N T A L   A C T I V I T I E S

1. Inspect the battery on a vehicle owned by a relative or a friend. Note any problems evident in visual inspection and make a report to your class.
2. Measure the physical dimensions of a battery with a plastic ruler and determine its group number. Refer to the chart in Figure 28-11.
3. Examine the battery on a vehicle chosen by your instructor. Report to your class its group number and all other information that can be found on the battery.
4. Visit an auto parts store or battery shop. What physical difference can be noticed between a group 24 and a group 24F battery? Between a group 27 and a group 27F battery?
5. Visit a department store or auto parts store that sells batteries. Ask the prices, warranty periods, cold cranking amps, and reserve capacities of different models of the same group size battery. Make a chart of this information and report to your class what differences are found.

29 BATTERY SERVICE

Automotive batteries properly sized for the vehicles in which they are installed should provide many years of dependable service. However, the engine and charging system must be maintained in good operating order to allow long battery life.

The battery and its connections also must be serviced routinely to ensure long battery life. An important part of battery service is safety. The electrolyte can cause serious burns and blindness. Explosive gases, produced during battery operation, can explode if safety considerations are not followed carefully.

Engine starting problems should be diagnosed carefully before replacing the battery. The problems may be caused by the state of engine tune or the condition of the charging system. Proper test procedures will help pinpoint the problem.

A discharged battery may be recharged and restored to serviceable condition if it has not been damaged or worn out.

There are no magic potions or chemicals that can restore a damaged or worn-out battery to serviceable condition. Damaged or worn-out batteries must be replaced.

LEARNING OBJECTIVES

When you have completed your assignments and exercises in this unit, you should be able to:

☐ Describe safety precautions necessary when working around batteries.

☐ Correctly and safely use jumper cables.

☐ Perform battery maintenance.

☐ Correctly and safely use a battery hydrometer.

☐ Correctly and safely perform load tests on batteries.

☐ Correctly and safely charge a battery.

SAFETY PRECAUTIONS

Always wear eye protection when working around batteries. Batteries contain sulfuric acid electrolyte that can cause blindness, skin burns, and metal corrosion. Wear protective rubber or plastic gloves to protect your hands.

Always have a source of fresh, clean water nearby to wash acid off.

Do not tip the battery over or on its side when performing battery service. Electrolyte will flow through the gas vents.

Remove all metal jewelry such as rings, watches, and neck chains when working around batteries. Metal objects conduct electricity and can lead to burns or sparks that cause battery explosions.

The hydrogen and oxygen gases created during battery operation are highly explosive. When a battery explodes, sulfuric acid is splattered over everything nearby.

Work in a well-ventilated area when performing battery service and avoid breathing fumes from charging batteries. These fumes contain sulfuric acid that can cause lung and breathing problems. Also be careful not to breathe in battery acid particles when cleaning the terminals and tray.

To prevent battery explosions, shocks, burns, and blown fuses, remove the battery ground terminal before service.

When removing a battery, take off the ground terminal first. When replacing a battery, put the ground terminal on last.

29.1 JUMP-STARTING PROCEDURES

Jump starting is a process of starting a vehicle with a weak or dead battery. *Jumper cables* are connected between the electrical system of the vehicle with a weak battery and a good battery. Jumper cables are heavy electrical cables with color-coded ends.

SAFETY CAUTION: **Always wear eye and skin protection when jump starting. A battery explosion caused by improper connections can cause blindness or severe skin burns. Keep all jumper cables and clamps away from the fan, belts, and pulleys of both engines.**

The correct hookup sequence for safe jump starting is shown in Figure 29-1. Notice especially that the last negative connection (to the vehicle with the weak battery) is *not* made to the battery terminal. Rather, it is made only to the engine or to an engine bracket.

When a connection is completed to a good battery, a spark will occur. If the connection is made at the battery, there will be a spark at the battery. This spark could ignite residual gas in the area.

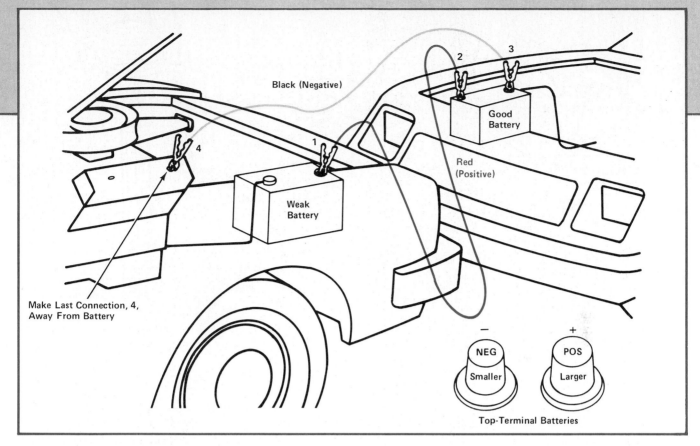

Figure 29-1. Battery jumper cable hookup.

Therefore, the last negative connection always is made away from the battery. A spark there will not cause a battery explosion.

After the connections have been safely made, the vehicle with the good battery is started. The vehicle with the weak battery then is started. Both vehicles are run at a moderately high idle. The cables are removed carefully in the exact reverse order of connection. The last connection, the negative connection on the engine, always is the first to be removed after the engine has started.

SAFETY CAUTION: **Roll up long sleeves and keep hands and arms away from moving fans, belts, and pulleys when removing jumper cables.**

The charging system of the vehicle with the weak battery then should be checked to find the problem (see Unit 33).

29.2 BATTERY PREVENTIVE MAINTENANCE

Basic battery preventive maintenance consists of the following four areas:

1. Visual inspection
2. Instrument testing
3. Removal and cleaning
4. Replacement, reconnection, and protection of terminals.

29.3 VISUAL INSPECTION

Check the battery for obvious problems. Such problems include:

- Bulging or cracked case or cover
- Physically damaged case or cover
- Leakage
- Corrosion on battery terminals and clamps
- Terminal tightness
- Holding device tightness
- Battery cable insulation condition
- Proper electrolyte level (if openable).

Make a list of all problems found during visual inspection. Parts that are badly damaged require servicing or replacing (see Figure 29-2).

29.4 INSTRUMENT TESTING

Instrument testing includes using hydrometers (where possible), test lights, and electrical test instruments.

Hydrometer

A hydrometer is illustrated in Figure 29-3. The hydrometer measures the relative *specific gravity*, or density, of a liquid, compared to pure water. A good-quality hydrometer also includes a thermometer to measure electrolyte temperature.

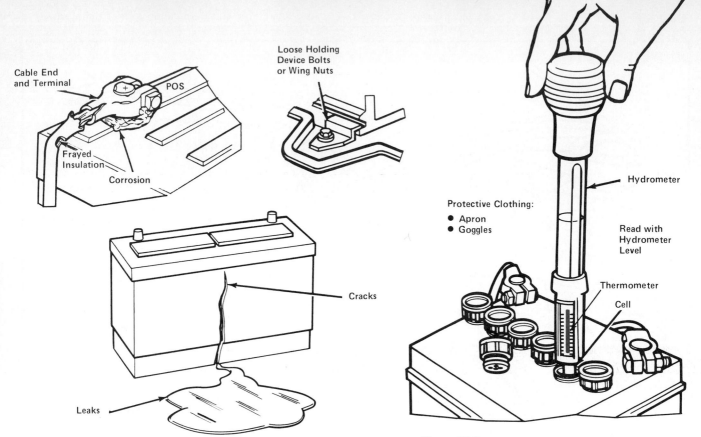

Figure 29-2. Battery inspection. CHRYSLER CORPORATION

Figure 29-3. Battery testing with a hydrometer.
CHRYSLER CORPORATION

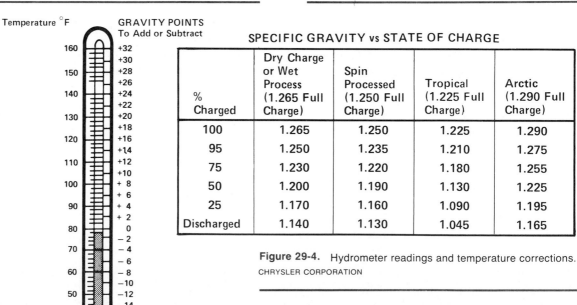

SPECIFIC GRAVITY vs STATE OF CHARGE

% Charged	Dry Charge or Wet Process (1.265 Full Charge)	Spin Processed (1.250 Full Charge)	Tropical (1.225 Full Charge)	Arctic (1.290 Full Charge)
100	1.265	1.250	1.225	1.290
95	1.250	1.235	1.210	1.275
75	1.230	1.220	1.180	1.255
50	1.200	1.190	1.130	1.225
25	1.170	1.160	1.090	1.195
Discharged	1.140	1.130	1.045	1.165

Figure 29-4. Hydrometer readings and temperature corrections.
CHRYSLER CORPORATION

A table of specific gravity readings and necessary temperature compensations is shown in Figure 29-4.

Hydrometer tests must be made of each individual cell. If water recently has been added to the cells, the test is invalid. The battery should be charged before testing (see Topic 29.7).

A charged battery with more than 0.050 specific gravity variance between cells probably should be replaced.

Maintenance-free batteries have permanently sealed tops. However, a built-in hydrometer allows a visual

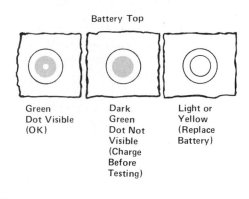

Green
Dot Visible
(OK)

Dark
Green
Dot Not
Visible
(Charge
Before
Testing)

Light or
Yellow
(Replace
Battery)

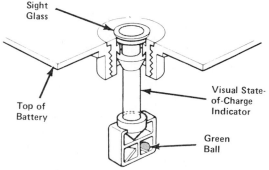

Figure 29-5. Battery condition indicator.
CHRYSLER CORPORATION

CHART FOR LOAD SETTING

Battery Group Size	Test Load (Amps)
22	200
72	215
24	250
74	250
27	280
77	280

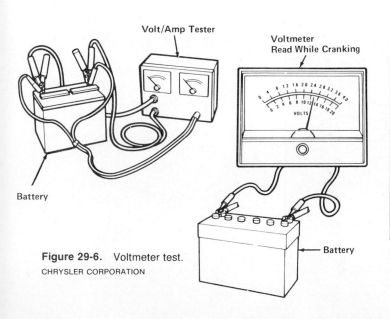

Figure 29-6. Voltmeter test.
CHRYSLER CORPORATION

check of battery condition (see Figure 29-5). When the battery is more than 65 percent charged, a green ball is visible in the plastic window.

Electrical Testing

If the battery electrolyte specific gravity is above 1.220 or the indicator is green, electrical testing can be performed.

Two types of instruments can be used to test batteries:

1. Voltmeter
2. Battery load tester.

Voltmeter. A voltmeter can be used to test the battery while still in the vehicle (see Figure 29-6).

The ignition system must be disabled, as discussed in Unit 43. The engine is cranked, without starting, for 15 seconds continuously.

At 70 degrees F [21 degrees C] or more, the voltage should not drop below 9.6 volts during the test. Figure 29-7 shows temperature corrections necessary for colder temperatures.

Battery-starter tester. A *battery-starter tester* can be used for a more accurate check of battery condition (see Figure 29-8). A battery-starter tester has a voltmeter, an ammeter, and a variable electrical resistance load.

To perform this test accurately, the ampere-hour rating of the battery must be known. If the watt-hour rating is known, the ampere-hour rating can be determined by the following equation:

Ampere-hour rating =
watt-hour rating ÷ 12 (for a 12-volt battery).

Temperature (F °)	Minimum Voltage Acceptable	
	12-Volt	6-Volt
70 (or more)	9.6	4.8
60	9.5	4.75
50	9.4	4.7
40	9.3	4.65
30	9.1	4.55
20	8.9	4.45
10	8.7	4.35
0	8.5	4.25

Figure 29-7. Temperature correction table.
FORD MOTOR COMPANY

The positive (red) and negative (black) leads are connected to the battery. The load is adjusted to three times the ampere-hour rating. The battery is loaded for 15 seconds continuously. During the test, the voltage should not drop below 9.6 volts. Apply the temperature corrections shown in Figure 29-7.

29.5 BATTERY REMOVAL AND CLEANING

The battery should be removed and cleaned once per year, or whenever corrosion and acid buildup are noticed.

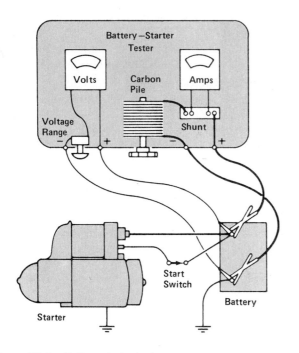

Figure 29-8. Battery-starter tester.

Removing the Battery

In removing the battery, first disconnect the grounded terminal (see Figure 29-9). Position the grounded cable well away from the battery.

SAFETY CAUTION: Always disconnect the grounded terminal from the vehicle first. Otherwise, a wrench or other tool can connect positive to negative, causing a direct short and sparks. Sparks can produce battery explosions.

Disconnect the battery positive terminal last. Then remove the holding devices (clamps, bars, or frames). Use a battery carrier to lift and remove the battery from the vehicle (see Figure 29-10).

Cleaning the Battery

Before cleaning, the battery caps (where used) must be tightened securely. A mild cleaning solution of 1 tablespoon baking soda mixed with one quart of water is used to clean and neutralize acid. Brush the solution over the battery and flush with water (see Figure 29-11). Dry the battery with paper towels and throw the towels away.

Cleaning the Battery Tray and Holding Devices

Corrosion and rust on the battery tray, holding clamps, and nearby metal parts must be removed by scraping and brushing.

Use scrapers, putty knives, and wire brushes to clean metal parts, down to bare metal.

After physically removing all corrosion, use a mild solution of baking soda and water to neutralize acid (see Figure 29-12). Flush with water and dry with paper towels. Throw the towels away.

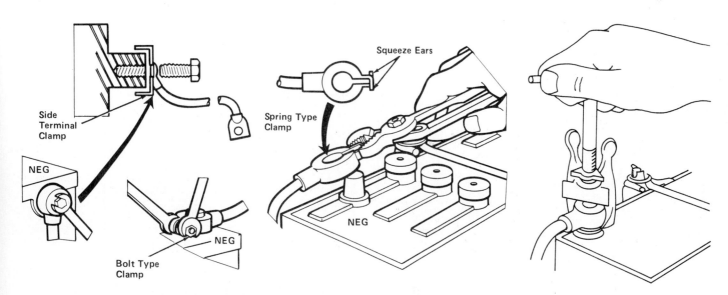

Figure 29-9. Battery cable removal. CHRYSLER CORPORATION

Use a special grease- or silicone-base spray to protect the cleaned tray and associated parts that may be exposed to battery acid.

Cleaning Clamps and Cable Ends

Clean battery clamps, terminal ends, and battery connections with a wire brush cleaner (refer to Figure 29-13). After proper cleaning, the metal should be clean and shiny.

If a cable end is badly corroded or physically damaged, cable ends or entire cables should be replaced.

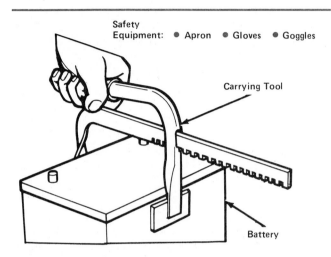

Figure 29-10. Battery carrier is used to lift and remove the battery. CHRYSLER CORPORATION

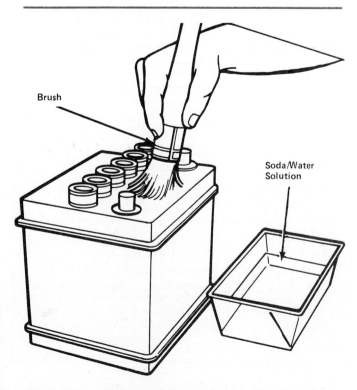

Figure 29-11. Cleaning the battery. CHRYSLER CORPORATION

29.6 BATTERY REPLACEMENT

After all cleaning operations are complete, the battery is replaced in its tray. Holding devices are tightened.

CAUTION: Tighten battery holding devices securely, but do not overtighten. Overtightening can lead to distortion and bulging of the battery case, and battery case leaks.

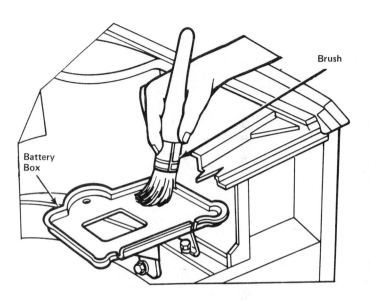

Figure 29-12. Servicing the battery tray. CHRYSLER CORPORATION

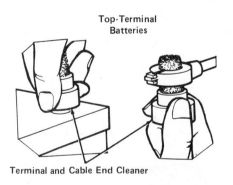
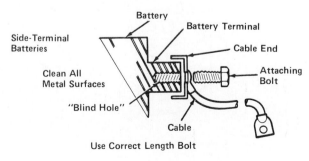

Figure 29-13. Cleaning battery posts and cables. CHRYSLER CORPORATION

303

Replacing Cables

Always replace the positive cable first. Replace the grounded (negative) cable last.

SAFETY CAUTION: The grounded (negative) cable must be replaced last to prevent shocks, sparks, and possible battery explosions.

Protective Sprays and Liquids

After replacing the clamps, special battery protective spray or liquids may be used on the outer parts of the connections.

CAUTION: Avoid getting battery protective materials between the cable and the battery terminal. Such materials are insulators, and prevent the flow of electricity.

29.7 BATTERY CHARGERS

A vehicle's own charging system should keep the battery properly charged. However, if the vehicle is started frequently and driven only short distances, the battery can become discharged. A faulty charging system also can cause problems (refer to Unit 32).

Batteries can be charged with a *battery charger* machine. A battery charger is a device that changes line current (110V AC) to low-voltage DC. Charging can be done with the battery in or out of the vehicle. However, if the battery is left in the vehicle, remove the battery cables before charging.

SAFETY CAUTION: Under no circumstances should a frozen battery be charged. Be sure the battery is thawed out before charging.

Fast Charging

Fast charging (at high current) can be done to "boost" a weak battery. This procedure may be necessary to get a vehicle started (see Figure 29-14). If the vehicle's charging system is operating properly, normal driving should bring the battery up to full charge.

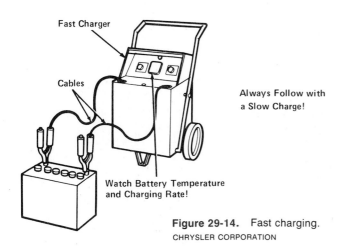

Figure 29-14. Fast charging.
CHRYSLER CORPORATION

CAUTION: Battery electrolyte temperature must not exceed 125 degrees F [52 degrees C], and excessive gassing must not occur during fast charging. In addition, distilled or clean tap water must be added if the electrolyte level drops below the proper level. Be sure not to overfill when adding water (see Figure 29-15).

Refer to the manufacturer's service manual for recommended fast charging rates and times. In general, 12-volt batteries should not be charged at a rate over 35 amperes. One manufacturer's recommendations are shown in Figure 29-16.

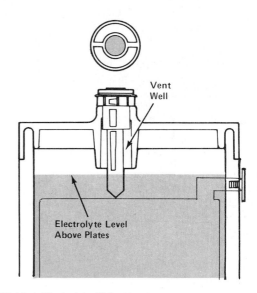

Figure 29-15. Electrolyte fill level.

Specific Gravity Reading	Charge Rate Amperes	Battery Capacity—Amp Hours			
		45	55	70	80
		High Rate Charging Time			
1.125* to 1.150	35	65 min.	80 min.	100 min.	115 min.
1.150 to 1.175	35	50 min.	65 min.	80 min.	95 min.
1.175 to 1.200	35	40 min.	50 min.	60 min.	70 min.
1.200 to 1.225	35	30 min.	35 min.	45 min.	50 min.
Above 1.225	5	Note: Charge at Low Rate Only Until Specific Gravity Reaches 1.250 at 80°F.			

*If Specific Gravity is Below 1.125, Use Indicated High Rate, Then Follow with Low Rate of Charge (5 Amperes) Until Specific Gravity Reaches 1.250 at 80°F.

Figure 29-16. Fast charging guidelines. FORD MOTOR COMPANY

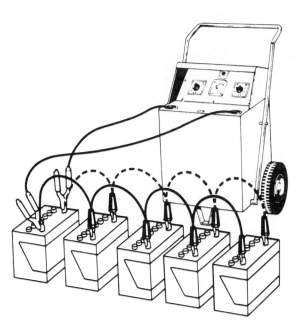

Figure 29-17. Multiple-battery charging hookup.
FORD MOTOR COMPANY

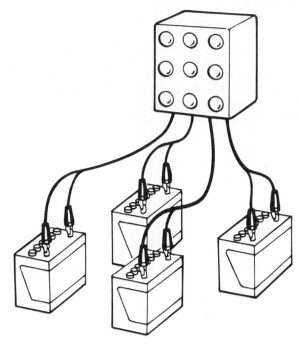

Figure 29-18. Slow charging hookup. FORD MOTOR COMPANY

Multiple batteries can be connected in parallel for charging (see Figure 29-17).

Slow Charging

Slow charging, or charging at rates less than 3 amperes, can be used to bring a battery to full charge (see Figure 29-18). One definition of "fully charged" is proper specific gravity reading after 24 hours of slow charging.

Periodic slow charging also can be used to keep stored batteries charged before sale or installation.

CAUTION: Continuous overcharging, even with a slow charger, can cause positive plate damage.

29.8 'MAGIC' BATTERY CHEMICALS

Chemical products that are claimed to bring old batteries back to life "magically" are available on the market. However, these chemicals do nothing but increase battery electrolyte temperature temporarily. This causes a temporary increase in electrical output.

The battery will appear to be "rejuvenated" for a short time but then will fail again.

SAFETY CAUTION: Sulfuric acid added to weak electrolyte can cause an explosion. Weak electrolyte is caused by internal battery chemistry that cannot be corrected by addition of sulfuric acid.

No permanent, magic cure exists for a badly sulfated, internally shorted, or physically damaged old battery. Batteries that fail hydrometer and load test procedures should be replaced.

U N I T   H I G H L I G H T S

- Jumper cable starting hookups must be made in sequential order to prevent battery explosions. The last connection is to an engine ground.
- Basic battery preventive maintenance consists of visual inspection, instrument testing, removal, cleaning, replacement, and terminal protection.
- Hydrometer readings must be adjusted for electrolyte temperature.
- Load testing can be done by cranking the engine, or by using a battery-starter tester.
- Battery electrolyte level and temperature must be checked during fast charging. Fast charging must be followed by slow charging to bring the battery to a fully charged state.
- "Magic" battery chemicals are a waste of money.

T E R M S

jump starting	battery-starter tester
jumper cables	battery charger
specific gravity	slow charging

R E V I E W   Q U E S T I O N S

DIRECTIONS: The following questions are similar to those used on mechanic certification tests. On a separate sheet of paper, write the letter of the correct choice.

1. Mechanic A says that jumper cables are connected battery-to-battery only.
   Mechanic B says that the last connection is made to a ground away from the weak battery.
   Who is correct?
   A. A only   B. B only   C. Both A and B   D. Neither A nor B

2. Basic battery preventive maintenance includes all of the following EXCEPT
   A. visual inspection and instrument testing.
   B. removal and cleaning.
   C. charging.
   D. replacing, reconnecting, and protecting terminals.

3. How much variance is acceptable in battery cell readings with a hydrometer?
   A. 0.050
   B. 0.500
   C. 5.00
   D. 0.005

4. Which of the following statements is correct?
   I. The maximum load on a 720 watt-hour 12V battery during a load test should be 65 amps.
   II. The maximum load on a 600 watt-hour 12V battery during a load test should be 50 amps.
   A. I only   B. II only   C. Both I and II   D. Neither I nor II

5. After fast charging a 12-volt battery at 75 amps, the battery will not hold a charge. Which of the following is the most likely cause?
   A. Battery has died due to old age.
   B. Electrolyte contains too much water.
   C. Battery damaged during charging.
   D. Excess sulfation prevented full charging.

S U P P L E M E N T A L   A C T I V I T I E S

1. Correctly and safely connect and disconnect jumper cables on two vehicles for jump starting.
2. Use a hydrometer and perform a check of battery electrolyte. Compensate properly for temperature. Make notes and report to your class on the readings noted.
3. Correctly and safely perform a load test using the starter of the vehicle as a load. Compensate properly for temperature. What was the final voltage reading, and what does it indicate?
4. Correctly and safely perform a load test on a battery using a battery-starter tester. Compensate properly for temperature. What was the final voltage reading, and what does it indicate?
5. Charge a discharged battery by either fast or slow charging. Perform a load test and/or a hydrometer test on the charged battery. What readings are obtained, and what do they indicate?

30 THE STARTING SYSTEM

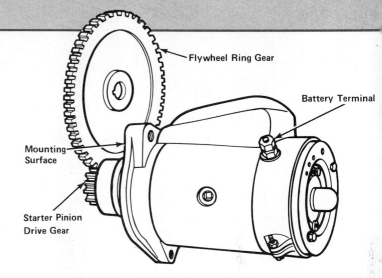

Figure 30-1. Starter and flywheel connection.
CHRYSLER CORPORATION

UNIT PREVIEW

The battery supplies electrical power to a motor to crank the engine for starting. The starting motor uses electromagnetism to produce motion.

A basic starting system consists of several elements. These parts are used to control and protect the starting motor, engine, and vehicle.

Different types of starter and control mechanisms can be used on passenger vehicles.

LEARNING OBJECTIVES

When you have completed your assignments and exercises in this unit, you should be able to:

☐ Explain how an electric motor operates.

☐ Identify and describe the basic parts of a starter motor.

☐ Identify and describe the parts of a basic starting system.

☐ Explain how magnetic switches operate.

☐ Explain how vehicles with automatic transmissions are prevented from starting in gear.

☐ Locate visible parts of a vehicle's starting system.

30.1 STARTING AN ENGINE

To start an engine, the crankshaft must be turned. The pistons and valves begin to move and the fuel system supplies fuel. The cylinders draw in an air-fuel mixture. The ignition system (see Unit 34) ignites the mixture, and the engine begins to run on its own. On early vehicles, the crankshaft was turned by hand, using a metal cranking rod.

In 1912, an engineer named Charles F. Kettering invented the self-starter. The self-starter uses a battery, a switch, and a powerful electric motor to turn the crankshaft. The flywheel, attached to the end of the engine crankshaft, has gear teeth. The gear teeth may be cut into the flywheel, or may be a separate, attached ring gear. The starter motor has a pinion, or small drive gear. The pinion gear meshes with the flywheel gear teeth to turn the crankshaft (see Figure 30-1). The gear teeth mesh only during starting, then are disengaged.

30.2 ELECTRIC MOTOR OPERATION

Electromagnetism supplies the turning power in an electric motor. Magnetic fields oppose each other to produce a turning force. This turning force, or torque, is used to turn a starter pinion gear.

Electromagnetic Fields

Figure 30-2 shows a conductor within a horseshoe, or U-shaped, magnet. The continuous lines of magnetic force from the magnet move from the north to the south poles.

When electrical current flows through the conductor, concentric circles of magnetic force are produced around the conductor. However, the flow of magnetic force on one side of the conductor is opposite to that of the magnet. The opposing magnetic forces cause the conductor to be unbalanced, in relation to the magnetic field of the magnet. This unbalanced condition causes the conductor to move (see Figure 30-3).

Simple Electric Motor

The conductor is shaped like a loop, or simple coil, and placed within a magnet. When electricity flows through the loop, one side will be pushed upward, and the other side downward. This action causes rotational, or circular, movement (Figure 30-4).

Armature

The ends of the loop can be connected to semicircular *segments,* or partial rings, that rotate. Together, the segments form a *'commutator. Brushes* that ride against the segments can conduct electricity to the

307

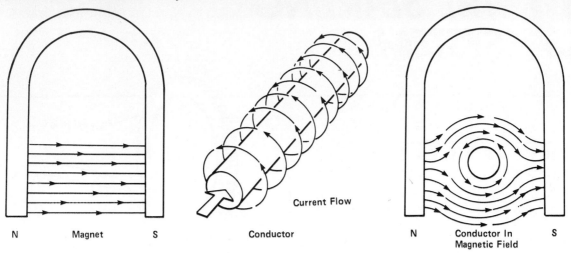

Current Flow

N   Magnet   S   Conductor   N   Conductor In   S
                                              Magnetic Field

Figure 30-2. Electromagnetic starter fields.

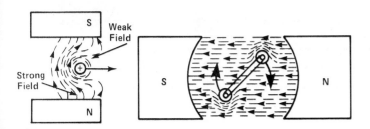

S

Weak
Field

Strong
Field

N   S   N

Figure 30-3. Unbalanced electromagnetic field.

S   N

Figure 30-4. Simple electric motor principle.

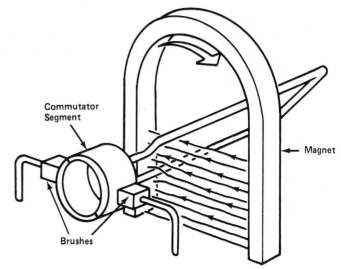

Commutator
Segment

Magnet

Brushes

Figure 30-5. Commutator and starter brushes.

segments as they rotate (see Figure 30-5). Brushes can be made of carbon or soft copper. Starter motor brushes are usually solid copper impregnated with graphite. The graphite serves as a lubricant.

As the loops move parallel to the magnetic field, the magnetic effect is weaker. When the loops are farthest away (at center position) from the magnet ends, the magnetic effect is nonexistent.

30.3 STARTER MOTOR

The simple motor described above would not actually run. The loop would stop turning at the center position.

A real motor often has hundreds of loops of wire to create a constant turning force. A starter motor is a specialized form of electrical motor that produces high torque to turn the flywheel ring gear.

To maintain a constant turning force, many *windings,* or coils of wire, and segments are used (see Figure 30-6). To increase magnetic force, the windings are looped around a laminated, or layered, core made of iron discs. Such an arrangement is known as an *armature.*

Field Coils

Magnets are not used in a motor. Instead, coils of wire, called *field coils,* create magnetic fields for the armature (Figure 30-7). The field coils are wrapped around metal cores called *pole pieces* or *pole shoes.*

Frame Assembly

The field coils are mounted within a heavy metal frame. Figure 30-8 shows a frame and field coil assembly.

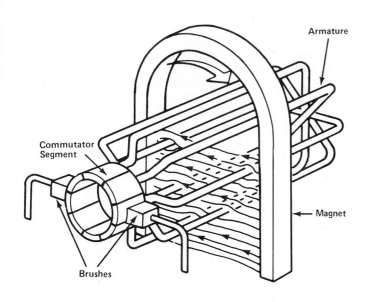

Figure 30-6. Multiple armature windings.

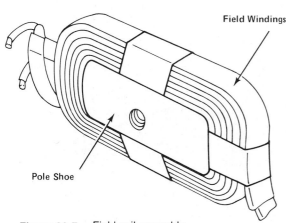

Figure 30-7. Field coil assembly.

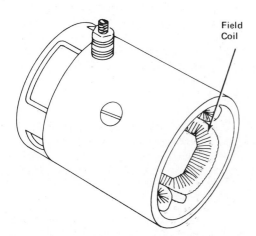

Figure 30-8. Field coil frame.

30.4 STARTING SYSTEM

In addition to the starter motor, a basic starting system consists of the following elements (see Figure 30-9):

- Battery
- Ignition switch
- Battery cables
- Magnetic switch
- Overrunning clutch
- Pinion drive gear.

Battery

The battery supplies current for the starter motor. In cold weather, required starting current for a large engine can approach 300 amperes.

Ignition Switch

The ignition switch is operated with the use of an ignition key (see Figure 30-10).

Battery Cables

Large, heavy-duty copper cables are used to conduct the high amounts of electrical current needed for cranking the engine. Refer to Figure 30-10.

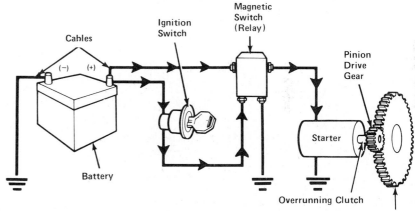

Figure 30-9. Basic starting system. CHRYSLER CORPORATION

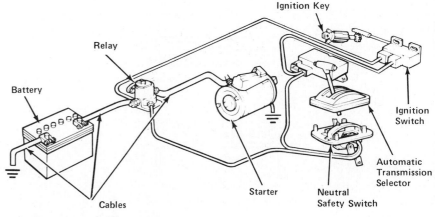

Figure 30-10. Ignition switch and starting system assemblies.
CHRYSLER CORPORATION

Magnetic Switch

Because turning the engine crankshaft is hard work, the starter uses more current than any other component. To connect the battery to the starter, a heavy-duty magnetic switch, called a *relay,* is used.

Relay. A small amount of electricity passes through the ignition switch to a coil within the relay. A spring then pushes the movable plunger toward one end of the relay.

The coil pulls the plunger and holds it in place. Connected to the plunger is a thick copper *contact disk,* or washer (see Figure 30-11).

When pulled in and held, the contact disk connects two terminals. One of the terminals is attached to the battery positive cable. The other terminal is attached to the starter motor positive terminal. The starter is grounded through its connection to the engine block. Electricity is supplied to the field coils and the armature, forcing the armature to turn.

Some vehicles use starter relays, and others use a combination of a relay and a *solenoid.* Still others use only a solenoid (see Figure 30-12).

Solenoid. Instead of an in-line relay, a solenoid can be mounted on the starter motor. A solenoid is similar to a starter relay. However, the motion of the plunger also moves the starter pinion gear to mesh with the flywheel gear. A *shift lever* transfers motion to the starter pinion (see Figure 30-13).

A diagram of a starting system using a solenoid is shown in Figure 30-14. Most vehicles use such a starting system.

Overrunning Clutch

A starting system in good condition can crank an engine at up to 300 rpm. Once the engine starts, it can run up to 2,500 rpm on fast idle. To prevent starter motor damage, an *overrunning clutch* is used to drive the starter pinion gear.

An overrunning clutch allows the starter gear to run over, or faster than, the speed of the armature driveshaft (see Figure 30-15). This action prevents the armature from being turned too rapidly. If the pinion

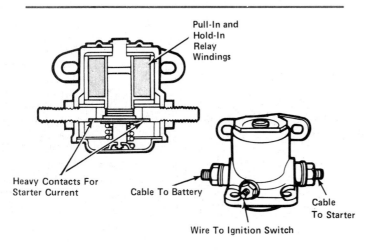

Figure 30-11. Starter solenoid assembly.
CHRYSLER CORPORATION

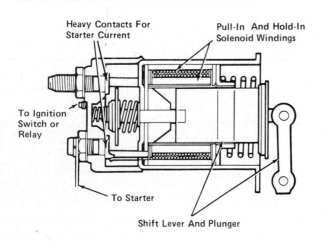

Figure 30-12. Starter relay systems.
CHRYSLER CORPORATION/FORD MOTOR COMPANY

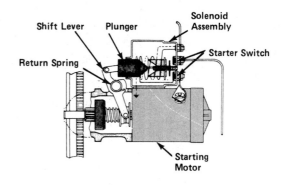

Disengaged

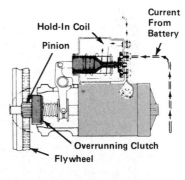

Pinion Fully Engaged And
Starting Motor Cranking

Figure 30-13. Solenoid and overrunning clutch operation.
DELCO REMY—GMC

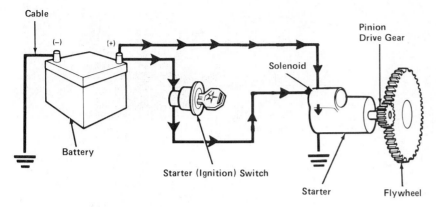

Figure 30-14. Solenoid starting system. CHRYSLER CORPORATION

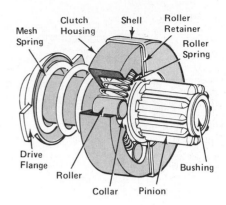

Figure 30-15. Overrunning clutch assembly.

shifts but fails to mesh, the *meshing spring* keeps constant pressure on the pinion. This forces the pinion to snap into mesh as it begins to rotate. This action prevents excessive damage to gear teeth during engagement.

Drive Pinion Gear

The drive pinion gear meshes with and drives the ring gear. The overrunning clutch and the drive pinion gear are combined into a single unit called a *starter drive*. The starter drive is mounted on the armature shaft (see Figure 30-15).

A cutaway view of a complete starter and solenoid is shown in Figure 30-16.

30.5 TYPICAL STARTER MOTORS

Three types of starters are in general use:

1. Solenoid direct drive
2. Movable pole
3. Solenoid gear reduction.

Solenoid Direct Drive

The most common type of starter is the solenoid direct drive. Such starters are used on most General Motors products, late-model Ford products, and most foreign vehicles (see Figure 30-17).

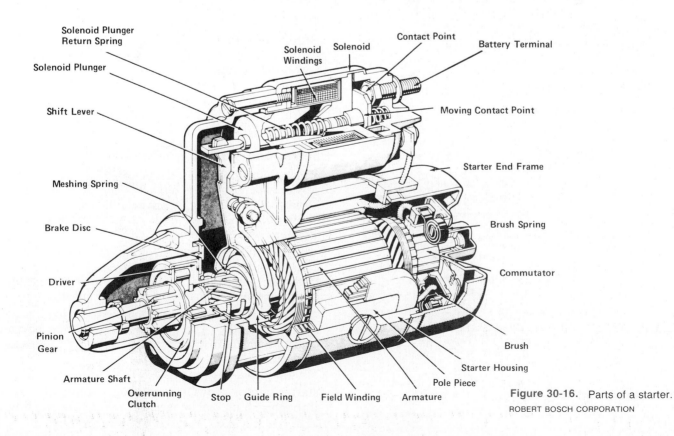

Figure 30-16. Parts of a starter.
ROBERT BOSCH CORPORATION

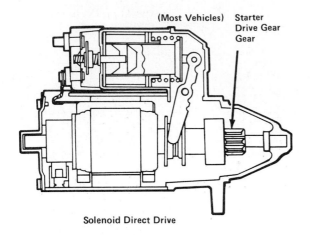

Solenoid Direct Drive

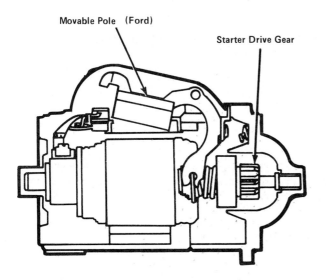

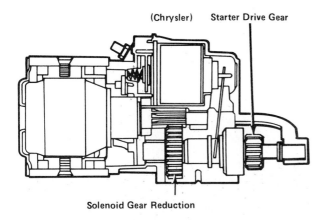

Figure 30-17. Typical starter motors. CHRYSLER CORPORATION

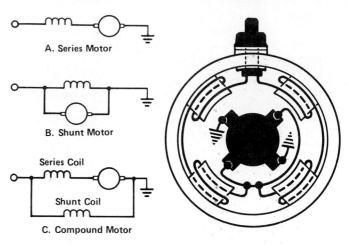

Figure 30-18. Starter circuits.

Movable Pole

Older domestically produced Ford vehicles use a movable pole piece to engage the starter drive. A shift lever attached to the pole moves the starter gear into mesh with the flywheel gear (see Figure 30-17).

Solenoid Gear Reduction

Domestically produced larger Chrysler vehicles, and some General Motors vehicles, use a system of gears to increase starter torque. See Unit 49 for a discussion of torque increase.

This set of gears produces a distinctive, high-pitched sound when starting (see Figure 30-17).

30.6 STARTER MOTOR WIRING

Different combinations of series, series-parallel, and parallel circuits can be used within a starter. The circuit design depends on many factors. These factors include the engine cranking speed and torque requirements, battery cable size, battery capacity, and motor brush and switch capacity. These circuits are shown in Figure 30-18.

Series and Shunt Field Coils

Two types of field coils can be used: series and shunt. A *shunt* is an electrical bypass (refer to Figure 30-18). Series-wound field coils are wound with heavy, flat copper ribbon. Shunt coils contain more turns of smaller wire.

Current that flows through series-wound field coils also flows through armature windings. The faster the motor turns, the more magnetic force is produced, causing a further increase in speed.

When the motor turns freely, without load, it can spin too rapidly. Too great a rotational speed can cause the armature windings to be thrown outward from their slots.

Shunt-wound field coils are used to prevent the starter motor from turning too rapidly. Current through a shunt coil bypasses the armature and flows

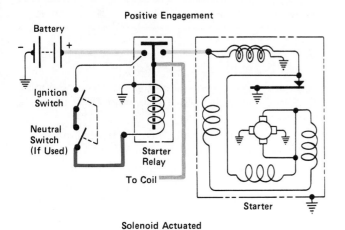

Positive Engagement

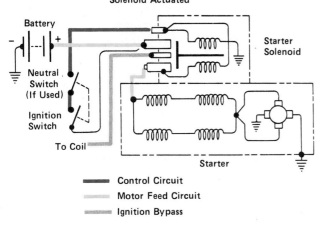

Solenoid Actuated

— Control Circuit
— Motor Feed Circuit
— Ignition Bypass

Figure 30-19. Starting system wiring. FORD MOTOR COMPANY

30.7 STARTER MOTOR CIRCUITS

Diagrams of common starter motor circuits are shown in Figure 30-19.

Vehicles with automatic transmissions must have some way to prevent the vehicle from being started in gear. As explained above, a *neutral safety switch* can be used. The neutral safety switch is located in the starter control circuit (see Figure 30-20). It will complete the starter control circuit only if the automatic

back to the battery. The speed of the motor is determined and limited by battery voltage.

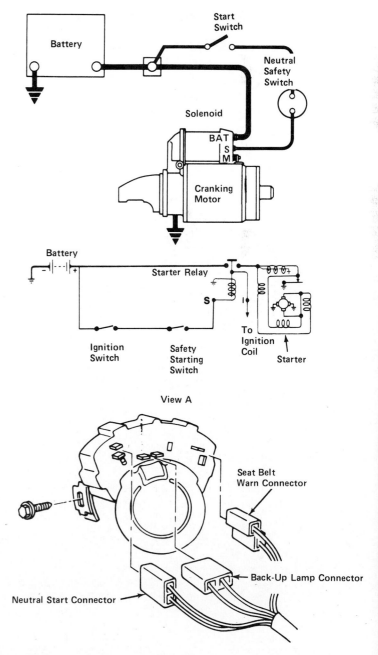

View A

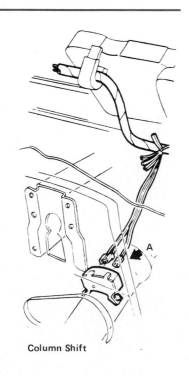

Column Shift

Figure 30-20. Neutral safety switch assemblies. GENERAL MOTORS CORPORATION

transmission is in park or neutral. If the vehicle is equipped with a standard transmission, the safety switch is placed on the clutch. The switch allows the starter to operate only if the clutch pedal is depressed.

Many newer vehicles use an *ignition interlock* to prevent the key from being turned except in park (refer to Figure 30-21). An ignition interlock is a theft-prevention device. It also locks the steering wheel if the key is not inserted and turned.

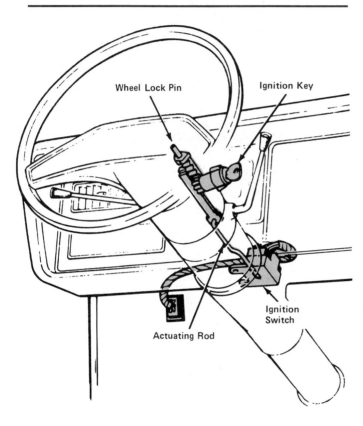

Figure 30-21. Ignition switch assembly.

UNIT HIGHLIGHTS

- A battery supplies electrical power to a motor to crank the engine for starting.
- A motor uses electromagnetism to produce opposing lines of magnetic force, and thus produce motion.
- In a motor, an armature turns in the magnetic lines of force produced by field coils.
- A basic starting system consists of several elements. These include the battery, ignition switch, magnetic switch, starter motor, and overrunning clutch.
- A magnetic switch can be a relay or a solenoid.
- An overrunning clutch prevents the starter from being turned too rapidly by the flywheel when the engine starts.
- Three types of starters are commonly used. These are direct drive solenoid, gear drive solenoid, and movable pole.
- Shunt-wound field coils prevent the starter from turning too rapidly when disengaged.
- A neutral safety switch or an ignition interlock can be used to prevent a vehicle with an automatic transmission from starting.

TERMS

segments	contact disk
commutator	solenoid
brush	shift lever
winding	overrunning clutch
armature	meshing spring
field coil	starter drive
pole piece	shunt
pole shoe	neutral safety switch
relay	ignition interlock

R E V I E W Q U E S T I O N S

DIRECTIONS: The following questions are similar to those used on mechanic certification tests. On a separate sheet of paper, write the letter of the correct choice.

1. Electrical motor operation is being discussed.
   Mechanic A says that the magnetic lines of force oppose each other to produce motion.
   Mechanic B says that separate armature windings are used to increase magnetic force.
   Who is correct?
   A. A only   B. B only   C. Both A and B   D. Neither A nor B

2. All of the following are part of a starting system EXCEPT
   A. ignition interlock.
   B. solenoid.
   C. overrunning clutch.
   D. alternator armature.

3. Which of the following statements about magnetic switches is correct?
   I. A coil produces electromagnetic force to pull a plunger.
   II. A coil produces electromagnetic force to hold a plunger.
   A. I only   B. II only   C. Both I and II   D. Neither I nor II

4. Shunt-wound field coils are used to
   A. prevent the starter motor from turning too rapidly.
   B. save money when manufacturing starters.
   C. prevent the engine from turning too rapidly during cranking.
   D. all of the above.

5. All of the following are types of starters EXCEPT
   A. solenoid and movable pole.
   B. solenoid gear reduction.
   C. movable pole.
   D. solenoid direct drive.

S U P P L E M E N T A L A C T I V I T I E S

1. Trace battery positive cables on several different vehicles. To what are they attached?
2. Examine a vehicle's starting system. Note the make and year of the vehicle. Report to your class what type, or combination, of magnetic switch or switches is used.
3. Identify and describe the three types of starters commonly used.
4. Explain how a starter relay works, and how a solenoid differs from a starter relay.
5. Examine a vehicle's starter. Report what difficulties would be encountered in removing the starter from the vehicle.

31 STARTING SYSTEM SERVICE

UNIT PREVIEW

Starter preventive maintenance consists of checking and cleaning connections and terminals.

On-car and off-car tests may be necessary to diagnose starting problems. These tests include electrical tests, visual inspection, and simple physical manipulation.

Faulty solenoids or starter relays are replaced. Faulty starters can be repaired, or an exchange starter can be installed.

LEARNING OBJECTIVES

When you have completed your assignments and exercises in this unit, you should be able to:

☐ Safely remove, clean, and replace battery and starter cables and clean connections.

☐ Perform on-car electrical tests.

☐ Check the pull-in and hold-in windings of a solenoid.

☐ Remove, disassemble, test, and replace a starter.

SAFETY PRECAUTIONS

Remove all rings, watches, neck chains, and any other metal objects when servicing starting system parts. Be sure that no metal tools connect from grounded metal to parts connected to the positive battery terminal.

The battery must be fully charged and in good condition before starter tests can be made. Refer to Unit 29.

Before attempting to remove starter motors or connecting cables and wires, disconnect the grounded battery terminal. Secure the cable end away from the battery. Injury can result from sparks and red-hot metal caused by grounded positive leads if the negative terminal is not removed.

Starter motors are heavy. Plan how to get the starter around obstructions before starting removal procedures. During removal, support the starter as the last mounting bolt is taken out. If the starter falls, it can crush fingers, hands, or other parts of your body. If the starter falls to the floor, it can be damaged.

31.1 STARTER PREVENTIVE MAINTENANCE

Starter motors are reasonably durable. Preventive maintenance consists of the following items:

- Checking and cleaning connections and wiring
- Replacing all damaged or frayed cables or terminal ends.

Checking and Cleaning Connections and Wiring

Loose, corroded, or damaged connections at the battery, solenoid, or starter motor may cause starting problems.

Battery terminals. Check the battery connections for corrosion and, if necessary, clean as discussed in Unit 29.

SAFETY CAUTION: Remove the grounded battery terminal first. Remove the positive terminal last. Replace the positive terminal first. As the last step, replace the grounded battery terminal. Battery explosions, sparks, and burns may result if the terminals are not removed and replaced in this order.

Cables. Check cables for proper size, broken wires, loose or frayed insulation, and corrosion. Proper cable sizes for 12-volt batteries are shown in Figure 31-1. An undersize cable can overheat, resulting in insufficient current flow.

Cable ends. Battery cable connections at the battery, relay or solenoid, starter, and engine or frame ground must be checked. Check cables both visually and

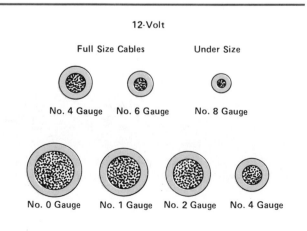

Figure 31-1. Battery cable sizes.

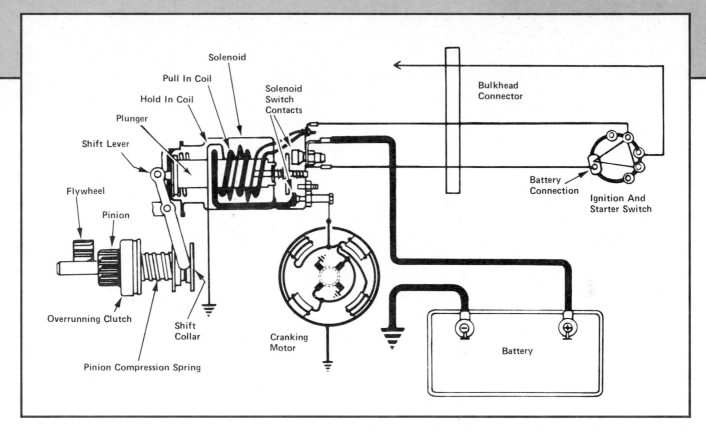

Figure 31-2. Potential trouble spot locations. CHEVROLET MOTOR DIVISION—GMC

manually for looseness and corrosion. Attempt to rotate and wiggle the connections. Tighten loose cables.

SAFETY CAUTION: Remove the grounded battery terminal before attempting to tighten the positive battery cable at either end. A metal tool will conduct electricity from ground to any metal part of a positive battery terminal. Battery explosions, sparks, and physical injury can result.

Corrosion is removed by scraping and using a wire brush on the connections until they are clean and shiny.

Starter mounting bolts. Attempt to wiggle and move the starter motor itself. If the mounting bolts are loose, a poor or intermittent ground will cause starter problems.

Replacing Damaged or Frayed Cables

Broken wires in a cable will effectively reduce cable size and increase resistance. Cables with broken wires should be replaced.

SAFETY CAUTION: Remove the grounded battery terminal before attempting to replace the positive battery cable. Metal tools can ground the positive cable at any point. Such grounding can result in sparks, battery explosions, burns, or damage to metal parts.

Loose or frayed insulation on the positive cable can cause grounding. If near the battery, battery explosions can result. Damage to parts can result from grounding the positive cable at other points.

Frayed or missing insulation on either the positive or the grounded cable can lead to corrosion under the insulation. Corrosion hampers electrical current flow. Visible corrosion under loose or missing insulation necessitates cable replacement.

If cable wires are clean and unbroken, electrical tape can be used to insulate cable wires. Wrap several layers around and past the damaged portion.

31.2 STARTING SYSTEM TROUBLESHOOTING

A failure to crank may originate at any point in the starting system circuit. Refer to Figure 31-2 for potential trouble spots. Cranking problems generally fall into four distinct categories:

1. No cranking
2. Engine cranks slowly, does not start
3. Starter spins, does not crank engine
4. Excessive noise during cranking.

No cranking and slow cranking can be diagnosed with the starter installed on the vehicle. An operating starter that fails to engage the flywheel gear teeth may require testing on and off the vehicle. Excessive noise during cranking can be caused by gear misalignment, incorrect gear tooth clearance, or starter internal problems. Gear tooth clearance can be checked with a wire gauge between starter pinion and flywheel gear teeth (see Figure 31-3).

Internal starter problems include worn bearings, a bent armature shaft, dragging pole shoes, worn brushes and bushings, and electrical problems.

Troubleshooting procedures for basic cranking problems on Ford Motor Company vehicles are summarized in Figure 31-4. Refer to the manufacturer's service manual for troubleshooting procedures for specific vehicles.

31.3 ON-CAR SERVICE

Several tests can be made with the starter installed in the vehicle. Other problems, discussed below, require starter removal and repair.

No Cranking

Starter system troubleshooting generally proceeds from the most accessible parts to the least accessible. The items to be checked, shown in Figure 31-5, are:

1. Start switch
2. Neutral safety switch or clutch start switch
3. Starter relay or solenoid
4. Starter motor.

Troubleshooting a no-cranking situation is illustrated in Figure 31-6.

Slow Cranking, Failure to Start

In Unit 27, it was explained that a voltage drop can be measured across a given load, or resistance. Excessive resistance in battery cables can be determined with a *voltage drop test.*

A voltage drop test measures the amount of voltage drop, or loss, across a conductor while current is flowing. The higher the voltage reading, the greater the resistance.

Battery cables in good condition should have very low resistance. Thus, the voltage drop across cables during cranking should be less than 0.2 volt.

Two things always must be done to perform a voltage drop test. First, the voltmeter must be connected on each side of the circuit, or component, to be measured. Second, electrical current must be flowing through the circuit or component being measured. The fact that the voltmeter may read a voltage immediately upon being connected does *not* mean that current is flowing.

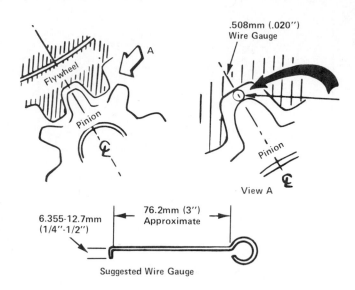

Figure 31-3. Meshing starter and flywheel teeth.
CHEVROLET MOTOR DIVISION—GMC

To perform a voltage drop test, a voltmeter is connected to the ends of a cable. The ignition system is disabled so that the vehicle cannot start. The starter is operated, and the voltage drop across the cable is measured (see Figure 31-7).

CAUTION: **Catalytic converters may receive an overrich air-fuel mixture during prolonged cranking. Electronic ignition systems also may be damaged by incorrect starting system test procedures. Refer to the manufacturer's service manual for specific starting system troubleshooting procedures.**

Starter Spins, Does Not Crank Engine

This condition can be caused by a faulty starter drive mechanism or a gear mesh problem. Some manufacturers' service manuals recommend an on-car check for testing starter drive mechanisms. Other manufacturers require that the starter be removed from the vehicle for testing. Refer to specific service manuals for proper testing procedures.

However, if the starter makes an electric motor sound, rather than a gear-grinding sound, the starter drive probably is at fault.

31.4 STARTER SOLENOID TESTING AND REPLACEMENT

A typical solenoid wiring diagram and connections are shown in Figure 31-8. A solenoid can be tested by connecting a battery, a switch, and an ammeter to the two solenoid windings.

Test connections are made to the solenoid switch terminal and to the ground, or second switch terminal, if present (see Figure 31-9). This check tests the

STARTING SYSTEM TROUBLESHOOTING CHART

Complaint Condition	Perform Test*	Results Indicate	Corrective Action
A. Starter spins, but does not crank engine.	Starter drive test.	Slipping starter drive.	Replace starter drive.
	Inspect starter drive components.	Worn or broken starter drive components.	Replace starter drive.
	Inspect flywheel ring gear.	Worn or broken ring gear teeth.	Replace ring gear.
B. Engine cranks slowly.	Starter cranking circuit test.	Excessive resistance in cranking circuit.	Clean and tighten connections; repair or replace components as necessary.
	Starting motor load (current draw) test.	Out-of-spec readings indicate internal starter motor problems.	Make bench tests. Repair or replace starter motor.
C. Engine won't crank.	Starting control circuit test.	Excessive resistance in starter control circuit.	Clean and tighten connections; repair, replace or adjust wires or switches as necessary.
	Relay bypass test. (Positive engagement only)	Inoperative starter relay.	Replace starter relay.
	Starter solenoid test. (Solenoid starter only)	If no pull-in or over 10 volts required, solenoid is damaged, or not operating properly.	Replace solenoid.
	Starter no-load tests.	Internal starter problems.	Disassemble and perform further bench tests.
	Armature open circuit test Armature and field grounded test.	Specific starter problems.	Repair or replace starter motor.
D. Noisy starter cranking.	Inspect starter mounting and drive components.	Improper mounting or misalignment condition.	Replace worn components; correct alignment problems. If problem persists, repair or replace starter motor.

*See manual for description of test.

Figure 31-4. Starting system troubleshooting chart. FORD MOTOR COMPANY

hold-in winding. The hold-in winding should hold the contact disk firmly across the battery and motor contacts.

Refer to the manufacturer's service manual for specific solenoid testing procedures and test result interpretation.

During testing, the ammeter reading is compared with the manufacturer's specifications. A high amperage reading indicates a shorted or grounded hold-in winding. A low amperage reading indicates excessive resistance.

To check the pull-in winding, connections are made from the solenoid switch terminal to the motor terminal.

CAUTION: To prevent solenoid coil overheating, do not leave test leads connected for more than 15 seconds.

NOTE: To reduce battery voltage to the correct value, a carbon pile can be connected between the battery and motor terminals. This hookup is indicated by dashed lines in Figure 31-9. If not needed, connect a lead directly from the battery to the motor terminal. Refer to the manufacturer's service manual for specific test procedures and test result interpretation.

If defective, solenoids or starter relays are replaced. Refer to the manufacturer's service manual for specific procedures.

31.5 STARTER REMOVAL

The greatest problem in removing starters is gaining access to the starter and mounting fasteners. On some vehicles, the starter can be removed only from the bottom of the engine compartment (see Figure 31-10). In

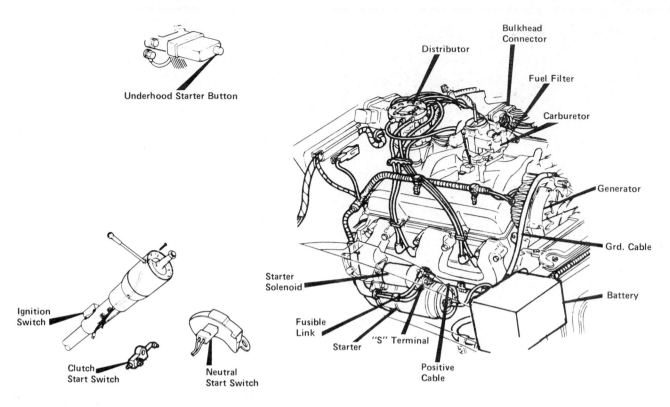

Figure 31-5. A typical locator chart that indicates a no-cranking situation. GENERAL MOTORS CORPORATION

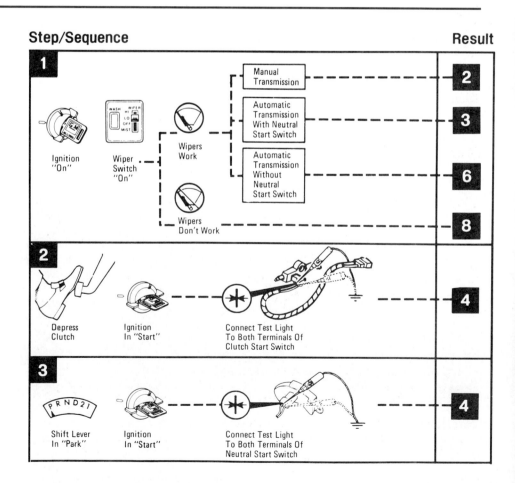

Figure 31-6. Troubleshooting a no-cranking situation.

GENERAL MOTORS CORPORATION

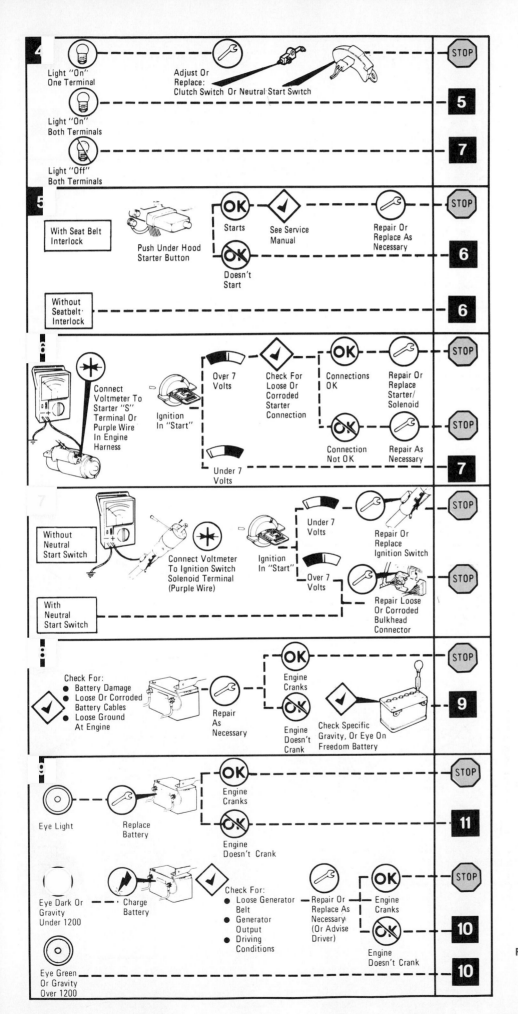

Figure 31-6. Continued.

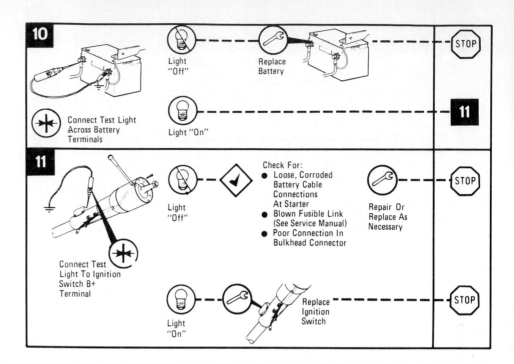

Figure 31-6. Concluded.

Tests

1. Positive lead to battery "+" terminal;
   Negative lead to solenoid "Starter" terminal.
   Reading should be no more than 0.5 volts.

2. Positive lead to solenoid "Bat" terminal;
   Negative lead to solenoid "Starter" terminal.
   Reading should be no more than 0.3 volts.

3. Positive lead to battery "+" terminal;
   Negative lead to solenoid "Bat" terminal.
   Reading should be no more than 0.2 volts.

4. Negative lead to battery "−" terminal.
   Positive lead to engine ground.
   Reading should be no more than 0.1 volt.

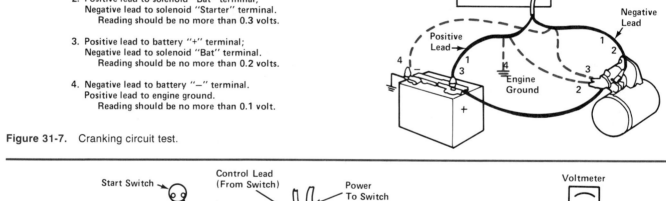

Figure 31-7. Cranking circuit test.

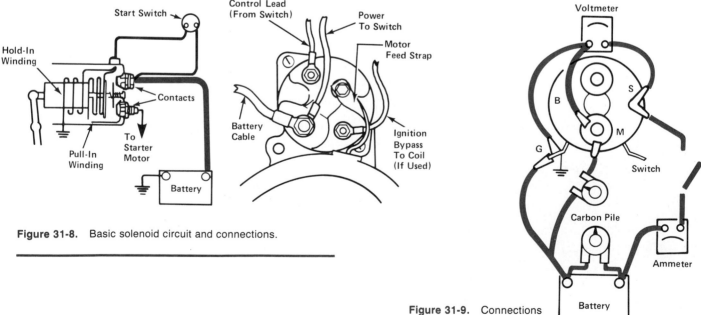

Figure 31-8. Basic solenoid circuit and connections.

Figure 31-9. Connections for checking a solenoid.

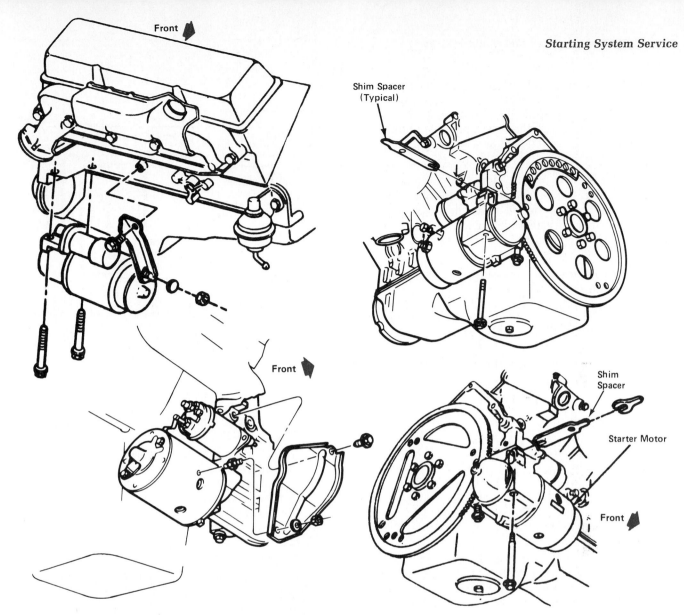

Figure 31-10. Starter mountings. CHEVROLET MOTOR DIVISION—GMC

some cases, suspension components, exhaust manifolds, and other parts must be removed first.

SAFETY CAUTION: **Remove the grounded battery terminal before any starter or cable removal procedure. Place the cable in a position where it cannot accidentally touch the negative battery terminal.**

31.6 STARTER INSPECTION

If a starter engagement problem was noted, inspect the starter pinion gear and flywheel ring gear teeth (see Figure 31-11).

A damaged starter pinion gear can be replaced. Major damage to flywheel gear teeth requires that the flywheel or flexplate be removed for ring gear replacement.

Simple Checks

The starter pinion gear should turn freely in one direction only. The armature should turn freely when

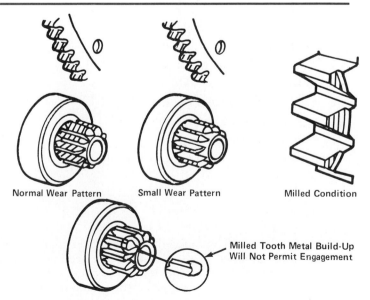

Normal Wear Pattern Small Wear Pattern Milled Condition

Milled Tooth Metal Build-Up
Will Not Permit Engagement

Figure 31-11. Gear tooth wear patterns.

the pinion gear is pried with a screwdriver in the opposite direction. Tight bearings, a bent shaft, or a loose pole shoe will bind the armature. If the armature does turn freely, a no-load rpm test should be performed.

No-Load RPM Test

A *no-load rpm test* checks the free rotational speed of the armature with a special tachometer (see Figure 31-12). The variable resistance shown in the figure adjusts battery voltage to the same value as during actual cranking.

Many problems can be diagnosed using a no-load rpm test. Such problems include:

- Excess friction
- Shorted armature
- Grounded armature
- Direct ground in terminal or field coils
- Open field circuit
- Open armature coils
- Poor connections between the brushes and commutator
- High internal resistance
- Shorted field coils.

Refer to the manufacturer's service manual for specific tests and interpretation of results.

31.7 STARTER REPAIR

Some service facilities simply exchange a faulty starter for a new or rebuilt unit. Other shops rebuild starters. The major steps in rebuilding a starter include:

1. Disassembly
2. Replacing starter drive
3. Replacing bushings or bearings
4. Testing armature and field coils
5. Resurfacing commutator
6. Replacing defective field coils
7. Checking brush spring tension
8. Replacing brushes
9. Checking and/or replacing solenoid
10. Reassembly
11. Testing
12. Replacement.

Before a starter is disassembled, punch marks to aid in reassembly must be made. Punch marks are made at each end of the starter end housings and frame. These marks identify the proper locations and orientation of each end housing in relation to the frame. Starter end housings and frames must be reassembled

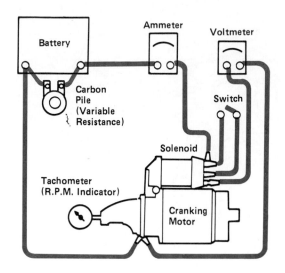

Figure 31-12. No-load rpm test hookup. DELCO REMY—GMC

in the same positions as found during disassembly (see Figure 31-13).

Special tools may be required for starter repair. For example, an electrical tester called a *growler* can be used to detect shorts in armature windings. A growler produces strong magnetic lines of force. This strong magnetic field can induce current flow and magnetism in a conductor. The growler "hums" with 60-cycle AC current and produces a "growling" noise.

A hacksaw blade is placed parallel to the armature, and the armature is rotated. If the armature is shorted, the hacksaw blade will vibrate, indicating the location of the short. See Figure 31-14.

Most growlers include a powered 110-volt AC continuity test light. When connected to a conductor, the test light will burn. An armature can be checked for grounds by placing the leads between a commutator segment and the laminated core segments. See Figure 31-15.

SAFETY CAUTION: The powered 110-volt continuity tester leads will produce a dangerous shock if touched. Hold the test probes only by the insulated handles during continuity checking.

Commutators become out-of-round and worn as the brushes ride against them. The commutator can be cut in a lathe, as illustrated in Figure 31-16.

Brush wires may be soldered to coil leads or screwed to ground or positive terminals (see Figure 31-17). Ford starters also may include a set of *contact points,* also shown in Figure 31-17. Refer to the manufacturer's service manuals for special testing procedures for such starters.

To replace soldered brushes, the old leads must be cut. New brush leads must be soldered to the coil

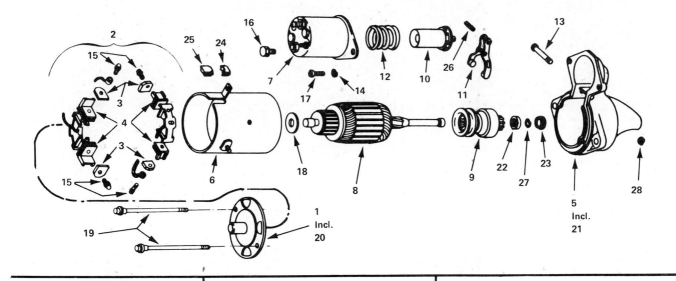

1. Frame—Commutator End	10. Plunger	19. Thru Bolt
2. Brush And Holder Pkg.	11. Shift Lever	20. Bushing—Commutator End
3. Brush	12. Plunger Return Springer	21. Bushing—Drive End
4. Brush Holder	13. Shift Lever Shaft	22. Pinion Stop Collar
5. Housing—Drive End	14. Lock Washer	23. Thrust Collar
6. Frame And Field Asm.	15. Screw—Brush Attaching	24. Grommet
7. Solenoid Switch	16. Screw—Field Lead To Switch	25. Grommet
8. Armature	17. Screw—Switch Attaching	26. Plunger Pin
9. Drive Asm.	18. Leather Washer—Brake	27. Pinion Stop Retainer Ring
		28. Lever Shaft Retaining Ring

Figure 31-13. Parts of a starting motor. CHEVROLET MOTOR DIVISION—GMC

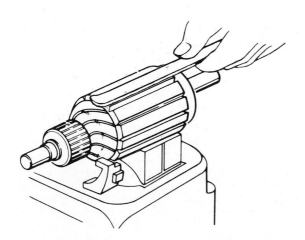

Figure 31-14. Using a growler to check an armature for short circuits. DELCO REMY—GMC

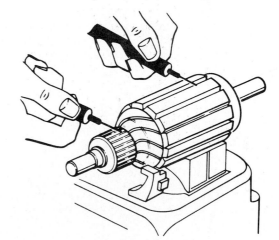

Figure 31-15. Testing an armature for grounds. DELCO REMY—GMC

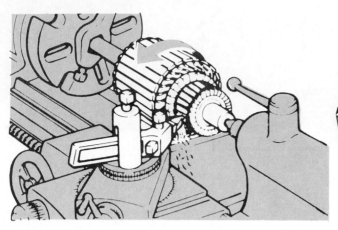

Figure 31-16. Turning an armature on a lathe.

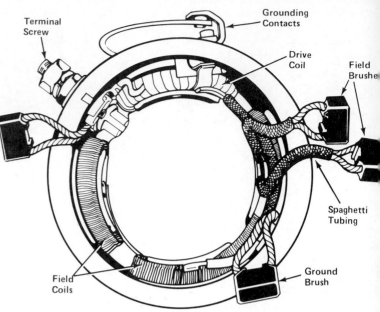

Figure 31-17. Armature field coils, contacts, and terminal assembly.

leads and insulated with *spaghetti tubing*. Spaghetti tubing is a hollow, straw-shaped flexible insulating material that is slipped over wires before solder connections are made. After soldering, the spaghetti tubing is positioned to cover the solder joint.

Reassembly of the end housings and frame must be performed according to the previously made punch marks.

The starter must be tested, as discussed above, before installation.

When tests indicate that the starter is working properly, it is reinstalled in the vehicle. After installation, the last steps are to reconnect the battery ground terminal and check starter operation in the vehicle.

U N I T   H I G H L I G H T S

- The battery must be fully charged and in good condition before on-car starter tests are made.
- Starter preventive maintenance consists of checking and cleaning connections and terminals.
- Cranking problems include no cranking, slow cranking without starting, starter spinning without cranking, and excessively noisy cranking.
- On-car and off-car tests may be necessary to diagnose some starting problems.
- Faulty solenoids or starter relays are replaced.
- Faulty starters can be repaired, or an exchange starter can be installed.

T E R M S

voltage drop test   growler
remote starter switch   spaghetti tubing
no-load rpm test   contact points

R E V I E W   Q U E S T I O N S

DIRECTIONS: The following questions are similar to those used on mechanic certification tests. On a separate sheet of paper, write the letter of the correct choice.

1. Which of the following statements is correct?

   I. The battery must be fully charged and in good condition before on-car starter tests are made.

   II. The grounded battery terminal must be disconnected before attempting starter removal.

   A. I only   B. II only   C. Both I and II   D. Neither I nor II

2. After replacing faulty battery cables with new No. 8 gauge cables, a vehicle fails to start in cold weather. What is the most likely cause?

   A. Insufficiently charged or low-capacity battery

   B. Battery damaged or shorted during cable replacement

   C. Defective starter solenoid, relay, or starter

   D. Wrong size cables installed

3. Mechanic A says that a rotating starter motor that does not crank an engine can have a defective drive mechanism.

   Mechanic B says that the problem may be in the starter pinion and flywheel gear mesh.

   Who is correct?

   A. A only   B. B only   C. Both A and B   D. Neither A nor B

4. Common starter problems can include all of the following EXCEPT

   A. no cranking.

   B. engine cranks slowly, does not start.

   C. engine cranks quickly, does not start.

   D. excessive noise during cranking.

5. A voltage drop test checks for

   A. insufficient resistance in a conductor.

   B. excessive resistance in a conductor.

   C. correct battery voltage.

   D. correct cranking voltage.

S U P P L E M E N T A L   A C T I V I T I E S

1. Safely clean and replace battery and starter cables and connections.
2. Demonstrate to your class how to conduct voltage drop tests on both battery cables.
3. Refer to the manufacturer's service manual for a vehicle. Demonstrate to your class how to conduct tests on the pull-in and hold-in windings of a solenoid.
4. Remove a starter from a vehicle. Refer to the manufacturer's service manual and perform a no-load rpm test on the starter. Report test findings to your class.
5. Refer to the manufacturer's service manual and disassemble the starter removed in Supplemental Activity 4, above. Perform inspection and tests on the armature and field coils. Report test results to your class. Reassemble and replace the starter.

32 THE CHARGING SYSTEM

UNIT PREVIEW

The charging system provides for the electrical needs of the vehicle when the engine is running. The battery provides additional current as needed.

A charging system includes several parts to produce, control, and monitor electrical current.

Alternating electrical current can be produced by magnetic induction and is changed to DC by the use of diodes.

The output of the alternator is controlled by a switching device. The switching device can be controlled either electromechanically or electronically.

Warning lights, ammeters, or voltmeters can be used to monitor charging system operation.

LEARNING OBJECTIVES

When you have completed your assignments and exercises in this unit, you should be able to:

☐ Identify and describe the parts of a charging system.

☐ Explain how AC current is produced and changed to DC current in an alternator.

☐ Explain the basic operation of a voltage regulator.

☐ Identify and describe the types, functions, and basic circuits used for charging indicators.

32.1 CHARGING SYSTEM FUNCTION

The charging system supplies the vehicle's electrical needs when the engine is running. In addition, the alternator supplies electrical current to recharge the battery. The battery supplies electrical current beyond the capacity of the charging system (see Figure 32-1).

In addition to the battery, a typical charging system, illustrated in Figure 32-2, includes the following components:

- Alternator
- Voltage regulator
- Charging indicator
- Wiring connections.

32.2 ALTERNATOR

An *alternator* produces alternating electrical current (AC) when driven by a belt turned by engine power. The AC is *rectified,* or changed, to direct current (DC) for use in vehicle systems and for recharging the battery. Aluminum is used for the alternator case

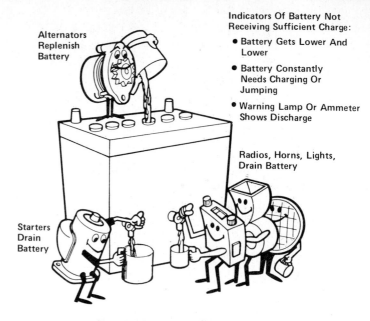

Figure 32-1. Charging system function. CHRYSLER CORPORATION

because it is nonmagnetic, light in weight, and dissipates heat well. See Figure 32-3. Most alternators use a fan to pull cooling air through the alternator.

Generating Current

A simplified alternator consists of a rotating magnet within a coil (see Figure 32-4). As the magnet is rotated, its lines of magnetic force pass through the coil, inducing electrical current flow. The rotating magnet is called a *rotor*. The stationary coil in which current is produced is called a *stator*.

When the rotor is midway through its revolution (perpendicular to the coil), the induced current drops to zero. However, as the magnet continues to rotate, the opposite pole approaches the coil. This produces electrical flow in the opposite direction. A graph, or picture, of such a current flow shows what is called a *sine wave*. See Figure 32-5.

In an alternator, the rotor consists of a *field coil* with many turns of wire. Magnetism is produced by connecting the ends of the coil to battery voltage. Smooth rings, called *slip rings,* and brushes are used to form the moving connection.

Coils of wire with many turns also form the stator, shown in Figure 32-6.

Electrical Output

For maximum utility, the electrical output of the alternator must be high enough at low speeds to satisfy the

328

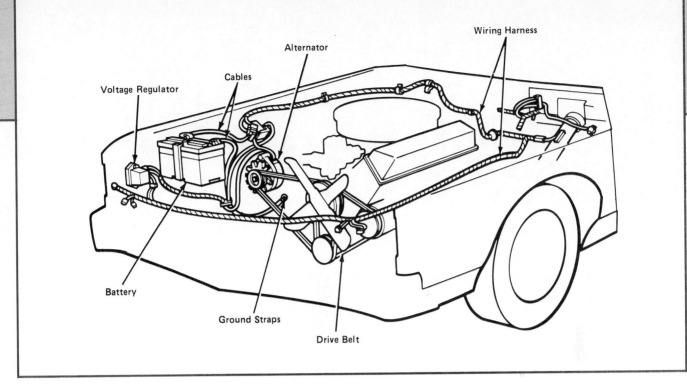

Figure 32-2. Charging system operation. CHRYSLER CORPORATION

electrical requirements of the vehicle. Also, the electrical output must be smooth, not pulsing.

Too low an output would result in an undercharged battery and poor starting and electrical consumer performance. Irregular output could damage sensitive electronic components of the vehicle.

Increasing electrical output. An alternator can produce more electrical output if the strength of the rotor's magnetic field is increased. Magnetic field strength is increased by raising the current flow passing through the rotor field coil.

Increasing alternator efficiency. To increase alternator efficiency, the rotor has several "fingers," or poles, that form alternating north and south magnetic poles. As the rotor turns, these separate poles form separate continuous lines of magnetic force. The more poles, the more even is the voltage output.

Three-Phase Current

To further increase alternator output, the stator can consist of more than one coil. Thus, each time the rotor's magnetic force lines pass through a separate

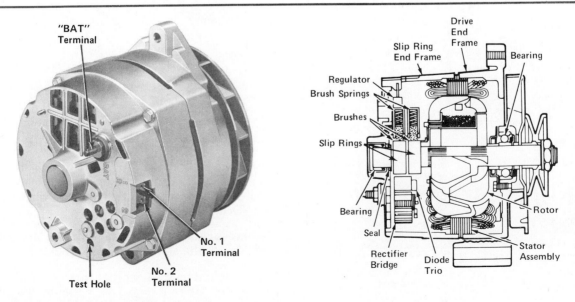

Figure 32-3. Alternator assembly. CHEVROLET MOTOR DIVISION—GMC

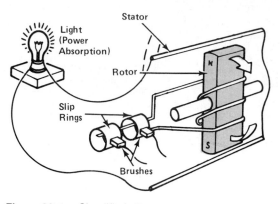

Figure 32-4. Simplified alternator.

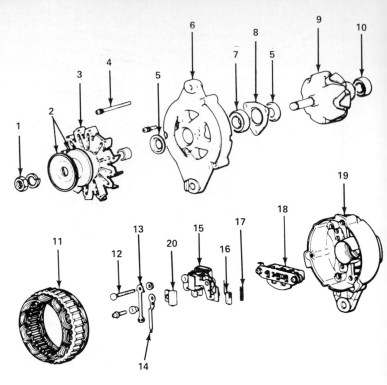

1 Pulley Nut	12 Terminal "B" Bolt
2 Pulley	13 Plate "B"
3 Fan	14 Plate "L"
4 Through Bolt	15 Electronic Voltage Regulator
5 Seal	And Brush Holder
6 Front Bracket	16 Brush
7 Ball Bearing	17 Brush Spring
8 Bearing Retainer	18 Rectifier Assembly
9 Rotor Assembly	19 Rear Bracket
10 Ball Bearing	20 Condenser
11 Stator Assembly	

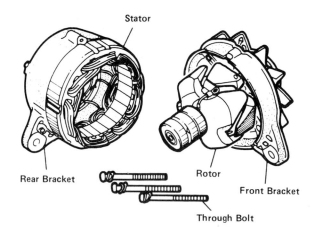

Figure 32-6. Alternator assembly. CHRYSLER CORPORATION

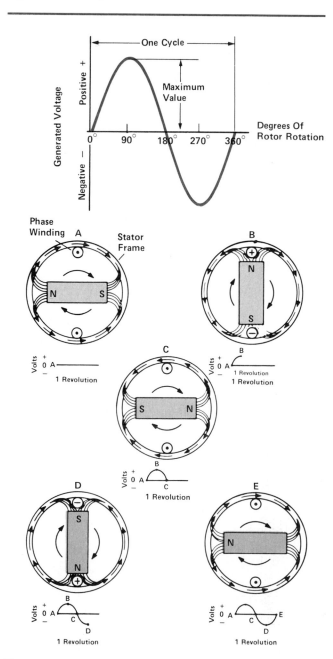

Figure 32-5. Alternating current.

coil, electricity is produced. An automotive stator has three separate windings, each consisting of many coils in series. The three windings can be connected in a "Y" or a "Delta" connection, as shown in Figure 32-7.

The three windings overlap within the laminated core sections of the stator (see Figure 32-8).

Voltage is induced in each of three overlapping coils at slightly different times, or *phases*, by the rotor poles (Figure 32-9).

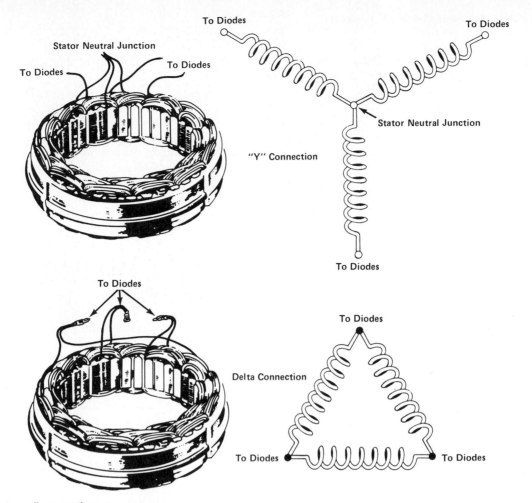

"Y" Connection

Delta Connection

Figure 32-7. Stator coil connections.

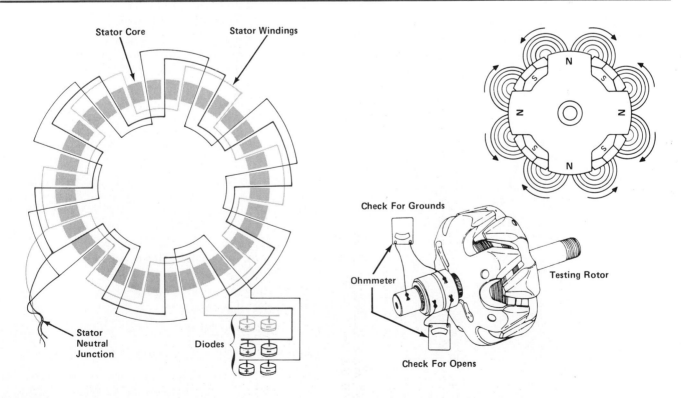

Figure 32-8. Stator windings and diodes.

Figure 32-9. Rotor poles and coils. FORD MOTOR COMPANY

A graph of the overlapping phases, or sine waves, produced by this arrangement is shown in Figure 32-10. Each sine wave is at a slightly different point, or phase, of its cycle at a given time. Thus, such alternating current produced by the three coils is known as *three-phase AC current*.

Rectifying AC Current

AC must be rectified to DC to charge the battery and to operate vehicular electrical systems. The shape of AC and DC current graphs indicate that DC flows

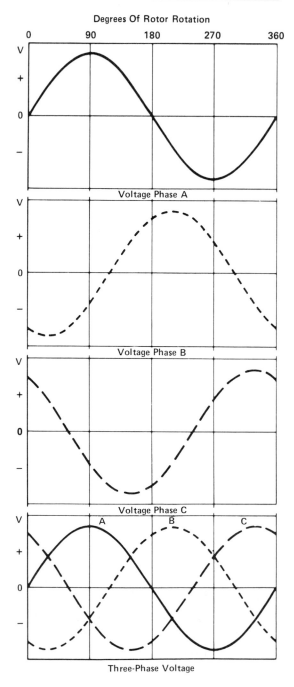

Figure 32-10. Electrical current sine waves.

only in one direction, at a given voltage. Refer to Figure 32-11.

To change AC current into DC current, diodes can be used. A diode, as discussed in Unit 27, allows current to pass in one direction only (refer to Figure 32-12). This principle can be used to prevent current from flowing in the opposite direction. In a three-phase alternator, a *bridge rectifier circuit* is used to provide reasonably constant DC voltage (see Figure 32-13).

An alternator bridge rectifier circuit has two diodes for each phase winding. Thus, six diodes are used to allow current flow in only one direction.

As can be seen from the illustrations, although rectified alternator output is DC, it does have an insignificant, slight pulsation. This "ripple," or pulsation, can be further "smoothed" by using a *capacitor*.

A capacitor is an electronic device that can hold an electrical charge, then release it. A capacitor can thus act as a "surge tank" to smooth out electrical pulses. In practice, these slight pulsations do not interfere with battery charging.

During rectification of AC to DC, the diodes produce heat. Thus, rectifier bridges are mounted on finned aluminum *heat sinks* to dissipate heat (see Figure 32-14).

32.3 ALTERNATOR REGULATION

If the voltage applied to the rotor coil was unregulated, the alternator output would be uncontrolled. This situation could result in battery and other electrical system problems. To regulate alternator output, a *voltage regulator* is used.

A voltage regulator is a device that monitors electrical system voltage levels. A voltage regulator switches current on and off to the rotor field to regulate current output.

Voltage regulators and alternators include devices to prevent battery voltage from draining back to the ground and discharging the battery. In most modern systems, diodes provide for this anti-drain-back feature.

Alternator regulators also include temperature-sensitive devices. These devices provide higher charging rates during cold weather and lower charging rates during hot weather.

Figure 32-15 shows the basic types of regulators in use on modern cars. These regulators can be divided into three basic categories:

• Separate electromechanical
• Separate electronic
• Integral electronic.

Separate Electromechanical Regulator

Electromechanical regulators use *relays* (refer to Figure 32-16). A relay is a specialized form of switch. A relay uses electromagnetic force created by small

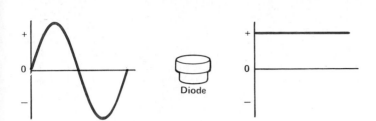

AC   Rectified   DC

Figure 32-11. AC/DC waveforms. CHRYSLER CORPORATION

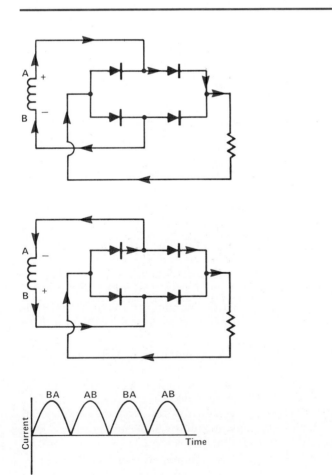

Alternator

Current Flows

Connections Reversed- No Current Flows

Figure 32-12. Diode current flow.

Bridge rectifier circuit images

Figure 32-13. Bridge rectifier circuit.

TESTING RECTIFIER BRIDGE

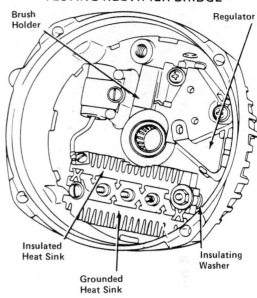

Brush Holder

Regulator

Insulated Heat Sink

Grounded Heat Sink

Insulating Washer

Figure 32-14. Alternator bridge.
CHEVROLET MOTOR DIVISION—GMC

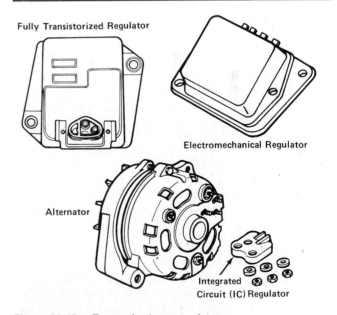

Fully Transistorized Regulator

Electromechanical Regulator

Alternator

Integrated Circuit (IC) Regulator

Figure 32-15. Types of voltage regulators.
CHRYSLER CORPORATION

current flows to close heavy-duty contacts for large current flows.

A relay consists of a coil, a flat spring, a movable plate, and a set of electrical contacts. Spring tension can hold the electrical contacts open or closed. When sufficient current is applied to the coil, a magnetic field moves the plate against the spring. This opens or closes electrical contacts, depending on the design of the relay.

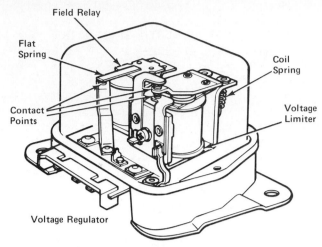

Figure 32-16. Electromechanical voltage regulator.
CHRYSLER CORPORATION

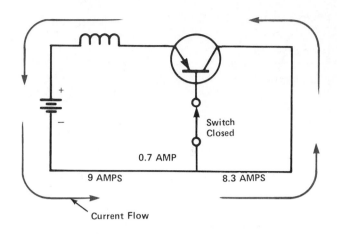

Figure 32-17. Basic transistor circuit.

Voltage limiter relay. A small amount of current flows through a set of contacts to provide an initial magnetic field when the key is switched on. This action provides a small magnetic field to "prime" the rotor coil for current generation. Voltage also flows through an indicator lamp on the dash to warn the driver that the charging system is not operating properly.

The voltage limiter relay is connected to the field circuit of the charging system. During operation, when system voltage falls below approximately 14 volts, the voltage limiter contacts close to supply additional current to the rotor field, boosting alternator output.

As system voltage rises, the voltage limiter, sensing this rise, moves the contacts open to reduce the amount of current flowing to the rotor field. The cycle of connecting and disconnecting battery current to the rotor field may occur as often as 100 times per second.

Field relay. When the engine is not running, a spring holds the rotor field relay contacts open. As the engine begins to start, voltage is applied to the field relay. The contacts close. This action allows voltage to travel from the voltage relay to the rotor field coil. When the engine stops, a spring pulls the field relay contacts open and prevents battery discharge through the rotor coil.

Separate Electronic Regulator

As discussed in Unit 27, transistors can be used to control large current flows. Small amounts of current across the emitter-base connections will cause the transistor to conduct. Large amounts of current can be conducted across the emitter-collector connections (see Figure 32-17).

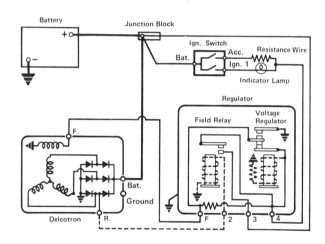

Figure 32-18. Field relays and voltage regulator.
BUICK MOTOR DIVISION—GMC

The small amount of current used to make the transistor conduct is known as *bias current*. Transistors can thus be *forward-biased* (conducting across emitter and collector), when bias current is in the correct direction.

Transistors can also be *reverse-biased* (nonconducting), when bias current is in the opposite direction.

Thus, transistors can be used to perform the functions of both the field and voltage regulator relays. However, transistors operate much more rapidly than relays. Thus, the rotor field coil can be energized, on and off, up to several hundred times a second. An electronic voltage regulator can be mounted separately from the alternator.

Some voltage regulators combine an electromechanical field relay with a transistorized voltage regulator (see Figures 32-18 and 32-19). However, most current voltage regulators are fully transistorized.

Integral Electronic Regulator

An *integrated circuit (IC)* can contain hundreds or thousands of transistors, resistors, capacitors, and other circuit parts. IC "chips" can be extremely small (see Figure 32-20). All the functions of the regulator can be performed by an extremely small integrated circuit.

In most present-day vehicles, an IC regulator is built into the alternator housing (see Figure 32-21).

Some alternators use a *diode trio*. A diode trio consists of three diodes connected in parallel (refer to

Figures 32-13 and 32-14). Diode trios supply the rotor field coil with rectified DC current from the stator. In addition, diode trios are used to apply bias current to regulator transistors.

32.4 CHARGING INDICATOR

Three types of charging indicators currently are used:

1. Indicator light
2. Ammeter
3. Voltmeter.

Indicator Light

An indicator light for a charging system is shown in Figure 32-22. When the charging system is operating properly, battery and alternator output voltage should be equal. Electrical flow occurs only from a source with a surplus of electrons to a source with a lack of electrons. When equal electrical potential is present at both sides of the bulb, current does not flow.

When alternator output falls below battery voltage, current flows from the battery toward the alternator. The indicator light bulb lights, warning the driver that the charging system is not operating properly.

Ammeter

An ammeter can be connected in series in the alternator output circuit. The ammeter usually is calibrated to 60 amperes, plus or minus. Because of its location, starter current draw does not pass through the ammeter. Starter current draw would damage the ammeter.

The ammeter reflects the amount of current flowing into (+) or out of (–) the battery. Thus, after starting, the ammeter should indicate a relatively high charging rate to replace the energy used by the starter.

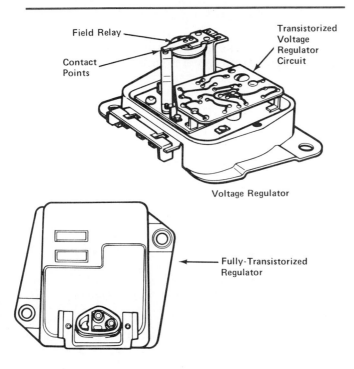

Figure 32-19. Transistorized voltage regulator.

CHRYSLER CORPORATION

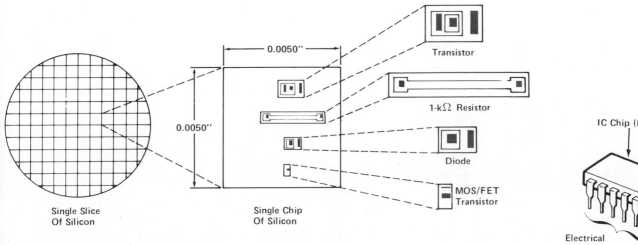
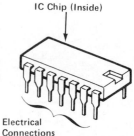

Figure 32-20. Integrated circuit.

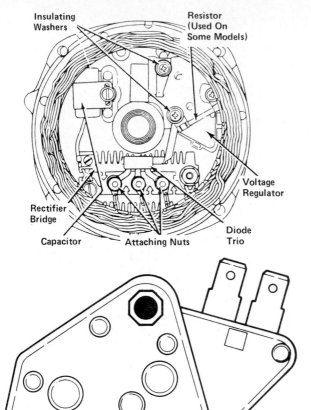

Figure 32-21. Integrated circuit regulator. DELCO REMY—GMC

As the battery becomes recharged, the charging rate should taper off. If current is flowing out of the battery, the ammeter will show a discharge. A discharge is normal if, for example, the headlights are turned on while the engine is not running.

Normal alternator charging system operation is indicated by a slight charging rate when the engine is running above idle.

Voltmeter

Many current vehicles use a voltmeter to measure charging system operation. After starting and running, battery voltage should remain between 13.5 and 15.0 volts.

A voltmeter is connected between the battery terminals and ground (see Figure 32-23).

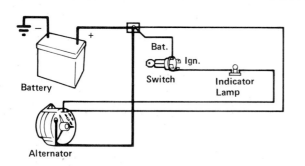

Figure 32-22. Indicator lamp circuit.

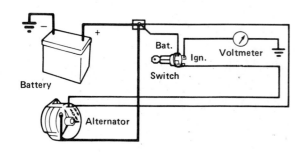

Figure 32-23. Voltmeter circuit.

UNIT HIGHLIGHTS

- The charging system provides for the electrical needs of the vehicle when the engine is running. The battery provides additional current as needed.

- A charging system includes a battery, alternator, voltage regulator, wiring connections, and charging indicator.

- DC passing through the rotor creates a moving magnetic field. AC is produced in the stator coils by this magnetic field.

- AC produced in the stator coils is rectified by a rectifier bridge that consists of six diodes.

- A voltage regulator turns rotor field current on and off to control alternator output.

- Mechanical relays or transistors can be used to switch current on and off in a voltage regulator.

- Lights, ammeters, or voltmeters can be used to monitor charging system operation.

TERMS

alternator	capacitor
rectify	heat sink
rotor	voltage regulator
stator	relays
sine wave	bias current
field coil	forward-biased
slip ring	reverse-biased
phase	integrated circuit (IC)
three-phase AC current	diode trio
bridge rectifier circuit	

R E V I E W   Q U E S T I O N S

DIRECTIONS: The following questions are similar to those used on mechanic certification tests. On a separate sheet of paper, write the letter of the correct choice.

1. Alternator operation is being discussed.
   Mechanic A says an alternator produces AC current in the rotor coil.
   Mechanic B says DC current is induced in the stator coils.
   Who is correct?
   A. A only   B. B only   C. Both A and B   D. Neither A nor B

2. Which of the following controls alternator output?
   A. Rectifier bridge
   B. Diode trio
   C. Voltage regulator
   D. Brushes

3. All of the following statements about charging systems are correct EXCEPT
   A. Batteries can be charged only by direct current (DC).
   B. Alternators produce pulsating DC.
   C. Rectifier bridges change AC into pulsating DC.
   D. Voltage regulators regulate alternator output by periodically energizing the stator field coil.

4. Which of the following statements is correct?
   I. Most current vehicles use electromagnetic voltage regulators.
   II. Most current vehicles use transistorized IC voltage regulators.
   A. I only   B. II only   C. Both I and II   D. Neither I nor II

5. All of the following can be used to monitor charging system operation EXCEPT
   A. a voltmeter.
   B. an indicator light.
   C. an ohmmeter.
   D. an ammeter.

S U P P L E M E N T A L   A C T I V I T I E S

1. Examine a vehicle's charging system and identify all visible parts. Does the vehicle have a separate or integrated voltage regulator? Does the alternator have a fan? What type of circuit indicator does the system have? Report to your class the locations of charging system parts.
2. Explain how the rotor of an alternator is similar to the field coils of an electrical motor, and how it is different.
3. Identify and describe the basic internal parts of an alternator.
4. Explain the purpose of a rectifier bridge.
5. Explain how a field relay and a voltage regulator relay operate to control and protect the charging system.
6. Draw basic charging system indicator circuits, and explain how such indicators can report problems.

33 CHARGING SYSTEM SERVICE

UNIT PREVIEW

Most charging systems are designed to give years of trouble-free operation. Preventive maintenance for the charging system is quite minimal.

However, because it is more electronic than mechanical, many mechanics are somewhat reluctant to service charging systems. There are no mysterious components or magical procedures associated with charging system service.

Undercharging or overcharging may be caused by something as simple as a loose drive belt or a defective regulator. On the other hand, a problem may involve extensive bench testing and repair. However, simple and accurate step-by-step troubleshooting and diagnosis, followed by careful servicing, will result in quality repair work.

LEARNING OBJECTIVES

When you have completed your assignments and exercises in this unit, you should be able to:

☐ Identify and describe causes of undercharging and overcharging.

☐ Perform charging system preventive maintenance.

☐ Perform a charging voltage/alternator output test.

☐ Perform a circuit-resistance test on a charging system.

☐ Safely and correctly remove, disassemble, reassemble, and replace an alternator.

SAFETY PRECAUTIONS

When working on a running engine, roll up long sleeves and remove watches, rings, and all other jewelry or neck chains. Wrap or tie long hair in a ponytail and tuck it down the back of your shirt or blouse. Be especially careful to keep fingers, hands, and arms away from moving parts.

Before attempting to remove an alternator or voltage regulator, disconnect the grounded battery terminal. Place the cable in a position where it cannot accidentally contact the battery terminal.

After alternator or voltage regulator service or replacement procedures, double-check all wiring connections. Reconnect the grounded battery cable only after you are sure all wiring connections are correct.

33.1 CHARGING SYSTEM PREVENTIVE MAINTENANCE

Routine charging system preventive maintenance includes the following procedures:

- Checking charging system indicators and battery charge
- Checking, adjusting, and/or replacing alternator drive belts
- Checking, inspecting, and/or cleaning wiring connections
- Visually inspecting the alternator and voltage regulator
- Checking for alternator bearing noise.

Undercharging and Overcharging

Warning lights, ammeters, or voltmeters can indicate charging system problems. Charging or a normal voltage reading (approximately 14–15 volts) should be indicated when the engine is running. However, problems in indicator circuits can be misleading. A burnt-out warning light bulb or non-functioning meter will not indicate a discharge condition. Bulbs and/or meters are replaced if defective (see Unit 37). Indicator circuit wiring connections should be checked as described below.

If indicators are functioning properly and indicating discharge or insufficient charging with the engine idling, engine idle speed should be checked. Engine idle speed below the manufacturer's specifications can cause an indicator to show undercharging.

Before damage to charging system components is suspected, engine idle speed should be checked and/or adjusted. In some cases, a complete tune-up may be required (see Unit 35). In other cases, idle speed readjustment may be all that is required.

If idle speed is correct, battery checks are made (see Unit 29). Undercharging can be caused by alternator or voltage regulator problems. Overcharging is usually the result of a faulty voltage regulator. Causes of undercharging include:

- Frequent starting and short-trip driving
- Faulty starters
- Loose alternator drive belts
- Alternator problems
- Voltage regulator problems.

Frequent starting and short-trip driving may not allow the charging system to operate sufficiently to fully charge a battery.

Faulty starters may draw excessive amounts of current. This may show up as a discharged battery, especially during frequent short-trip driving. In such a case, a starter overhaul may solve the undercharged/discharged battery problem.

Loose alternator drive belts also can cause undercharging. A loose belt slips and does not transmit turning power properly. Belts should be inspected and replaced if worn or damaged (see Figure 33-1). However, properly tightening a belt in good condition may correct an undercharging condition.

CAUTION: Do not overtighten a drive belt. Check for proper tension (see Unit 18) after tightening. Overtightened belts will cause bearing failure in driven units.

Alternator problems include worn or dirty brushes; shorted, open, or grounded rotor or stator windings; shorted or open diodes; and bearing problems. These also can cause undercharging. Alternator service is discussed in Topic 33.4.

Voltage regulator problems can cause undercharging. After long service, electromechanical regulator contact points can become burned, pitted, or "welded" together. In addition, spring tension can decrease with heat and time. Any of these problems can cause improper alternator output.

Some electromechanical regulators are adjustable to increase or decrease alternator output to specifications. Partially transistorized voltage regulators also may be adjustable. However, such service requires specialized tools and training.

In general, fully transistorized IC regulators are not adjustable. If faulty, the entire unit is replaced. Alternators with integral IC regulators may require disassembly for such replacement.

A voltage regulator also can cause overcharging. Overcharging symptoms include rapid loss of electrolyte, excessive corrosion near the battery, and frequent burned-out bulbs from excessive voltage.

A faulty field relay can cause battery discharge when the engine is not running. Voltage regulator checks are discussed in Topic 33.2.

Alternator and Regulator Wiring Connection Checks

Alternator and regulator connections are checked in a manner similar to that for starter connections.

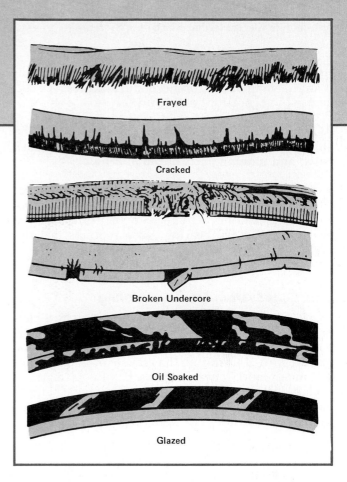

Figure 33-1. Drive belt damage. FORD MOTOR COMPANY

However, caution must be taken not to damage small wires or plastic connectors. Connectors are gently shaken, twisted, and pulled. Corroded connections can be cleaned and coated with a light lubricant spray. Loose screws, nuts, or bolts can be tightened.

SAFETY CAUTION: Remove the battery ground cable before using metal tools on alternator or regulator connection fasteners.

Slightly cracked plastic connectors or frayed wiring can be wrapped with electrical tape. If badly damaged, plastic connectors and/or wiring must be replaced.

Visual Checks of Alternator and Voltage Regulator

Alternators and voltage regulators should be inspected for physical damage. Burn marks or traces of carbon can indicate shorting or grounding. Cracked housings can indicate physical abuse that can cause internal problems.

Wiring and/or insulating parts can be wrapped with electrical tape or replaced. However, damage that appears to come from inside a unit requires unit disassembly or replacement.

Checking for Alternator Bearing Noise

A short length of hose or mechanic's stethoscope can be used to check for bearing noise.

SAFETY CAUTION: Noise checks are made with the engine running. Use caution around the fan, other belts, and moving parts of the alternator.

The end of the hose is placed carefully near the alternator pulley. The probe of a mechanic's stethoscope is placed on the alternator housing near the bearing. Excessive bearing noise requires that the alternator be disassembled and the bearing replaced. Refer to Topic 33.4.

Charging System Troubleshooting

Charging system problems may include a single unit or a combination of units. The alternator, regulator, battery, indicator, and wiring all may need to be checked to determine the cause of a problem. Troubleshooting charts can be helpful in logically tracking down a charging system problem. Figure 33-2 shows a troubleshooting chart for Ford Motor Company vehicles.

33.2 CHARGING SYSTEM ELECTRICAL TESTS

Charging system electrical tests can include the following:

- Charging voltage/alternator output
- Oscilloscope trace
- Circuit resistance (voltage drop).

Before charging system electrical tests are made, obvious problems are corrected. Loose or damaged belts are tightened or replaced. Corroded battery connections are cleaned. Engine idle speed is adjusted. In addition, the battery is tested and recharged (see Unit 29).

Charging Voltage and Alternator Output Tests

To isolate the cause of undercharging, two tests are performed: charging voltage and alternator output.

Charging voltage test. A charging voltage test is used to indicate whether the charging system will boost battery voltage. With the engine off, a voltmeter is connected across the battery terminals. The voltage reading is noted for later use. The engine is then

BASIC TYPES OF TROUBLE	PROBABLE CAUSES	SERVICE PROCEDURES
Alternator noise Note: Water pump noise is sometimes confused with alternator noise. A sound detecting device, such as a stethoscope, will eliminate indecision in this respect.	Alternator drive belt (Squealing noise).	Adjust or replace belt, as required. (An application of belt dressing may eliminate noise caused by minor surface irregularities.)
	Alternator bearing (Squealing noise).	Replace bearing if found to be out-of-round, worn, or causing shaft scoring.
	Alternator diode (Whining noise).	Test alternator output. (A shorted diode causes a magnetic whine and a reduction in output.) Test diodes and replace, as required. Replacing rectifier assembly may be most feasible fix.
Indicator gauge fluctuates —or— Indicator light flickers.	Charging system wiring.	Tighten loose connections. Repair or replace wiring, as required.
	Regulator contacts	Oxidized or dirty regulator contacts. Replace regulator, if necessary.
	Brushes	Check for tightness and wear. Replace, if necessary.

Figure 33-2. Troubleshooting chart. FORD MOTOR COMPANY

BASIC TYPES OF TROUBLE	PROBABLE CAUSES	SERVICE PROCEDURES
Indicator light stays on.	Broken, loose, or slipping drive belt.	Adjust or replace, as required.
	Battery cables, charging system wiring.	Clean battery cables and terminals. Tighten loose connections. Repair or replace as required.
Ammeter registers constant discharge.	Battery specific gravity.	If unsatisfactory, replace battery.
Battery will not hold charge.	Alternator output low, or no alternator output.	Perform the voltage output tests to determine if trouble is in the regulator, wiring harness or the alternator itself.
	Alternator drive belt.	Adjust or replace belt, as required.
	Battery cables, charging system wiring	Clean battery cables and terminals. Tighten loose connection. Repair or replace, as required.
Battery low in charge. Headlights dim at idle. Note: A history of recurring discharge of the battery, which cannot be explained, suggests the need for checking and testing the complete charging system.	Electrolyte (specific gravity)	Test each cell and evaluate condition: All readings even at 1.225 or above — Battery OK. All readings even, but less than 1.225 — Recharge and retest. High-low variation between cells less than 50 gravity points — Recharge and retest. High-low variation between cells exceeds 50 gravity points — Replace battery.
	Battery (capacity)	Test capacity and evaluate condition: Minimum voltage 9.6 for 12 volt battery or 4.8 for 6 volt battery. (Both values under specified test load conditions.) If capacity is under minimum specifications, perform 3 minute charge test. If below maximum (15.5 volts for 12 volt battery or 7.75 volts for 6 volt battery at 40 and 75 amps, charge rate, respectively) battery is OK — recharge. If above maximum, battery is sulfated. Slow charge at 1 amp./positive plate. Replace battery if it doesn't respond to slow charge.
Lights and fuses fail prematurely. Short battery life. Battery uses excessive water. Burning of distributor points. Burning of resistor wire. Coil damage. High charging rate.	Charging system wiring, including regulator ground wire.	Tighten loose connections. Repair or replace wiring, as required.
	Voltage limiter setting.	Perform the voltage output tests to verify the condition of the regulator.

Figure 33-2. Concluded.

started and run at fast idle (1,500 to 2,000 rpm) for three minutes. The voltage should increase by approximately two volts over the original reading (see Figure 33-3). Such an increase indicates normal charging system operation. If the voltage increase is not approximately two volts, an alternator output test should be made.

Alternator output test. Alternator output is the ability of an unregulated alternator to produce electricity. Different methods, depending on the charging system, are used to *full field* the alternator. Full-fielding means fully, or constantly, energizing the alternator field windings with full battery current to produce maximum output. Alternator current output then is checked.

An *inductive ammeter* that clamps around a battery cable should be used. An inductive ammeter does not require disconnection of wires that can cause *voltage spikes,* or pulses. Voltage spikes can damage or destroy sensitive electronic equipment on the vehicle.

Two types of circuits are used: A and B circuits (see Figure 33-4).

On Delco alternators, a screwdriver is used to ground a test tab inside the rear of the alternator (see Figure 33-5). This grounding bypasses the internal regulator. At the same time, the voltmeter and ammeter readings are noted.

CAUTION: Do not force the screwdriver farther than 1 in. [25.4 mm] into the test hole. Damage to internal components can result. The tab is kept grounded less than 10 seconds, just long enough to complete the test.

If the battery voltage increases to between 14 and 16 volts, the problem is in the regulator. If battery voltage does not increase to this level, the problem is in the alternator. Alternator current output should come to within 5 amps of the manufacturer's ratings.

Typical full alternator output varies according to alternator design. Generally, it ranges from 55 to 70 amps.

Full-fielding some charging systems requires momentarily connecting a jumper wire to a disconnected regulator plug. The other end of the jumper is connected to ground or to the battery positive terminal (see Figure 33-6).

CAUTION: Refer to the manufacturer's service manual to determine the correct test locations and connections. Improper connections can instantly damage or ruin internal alternator components.

A complete test sequence for General Motors Corporation vehicles is shown in Figure 33-7.

Oscilloscope Trace Test

An *oscilloscope* is a device that resembles a television set. Different electrical signals will produce characteristic *traces,* or patterns, on a screen.

Oscilloscope test leads usually are connected to ignition system primary terminals (see Unit 34). When the engine is running, the characteristic pattern of slightly pulsing DC current should be seen (see Figure 33-8).

Any other pattern indicates problems that require the alternator be removed from the vehicle and

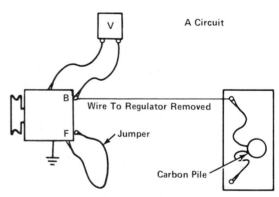

Alternator With External Solid State Regulator

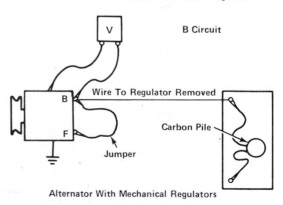

Alternator With Mechanical Regulators

Figure 33-4. Connections for testing internal field ground B-circuit and external ground A-circuit alternators.

Figure 33-3.
Charging voltage test.
CHRYSLER CORPORATION

Read Voltage With Engine Off (Lower Scale)

Start Engine And Read Voltage

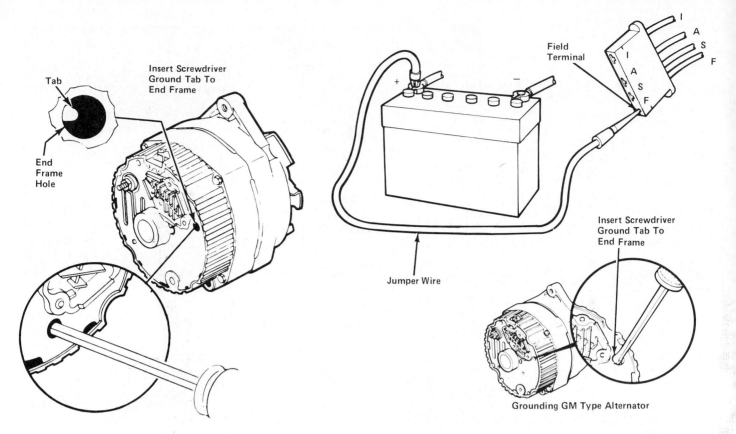

Figure 33-5. Generator test hole. BUICK MOTOR DIVISION—GMC

Figure 33-6. Testing field system. CHRYSLER CORPORATION

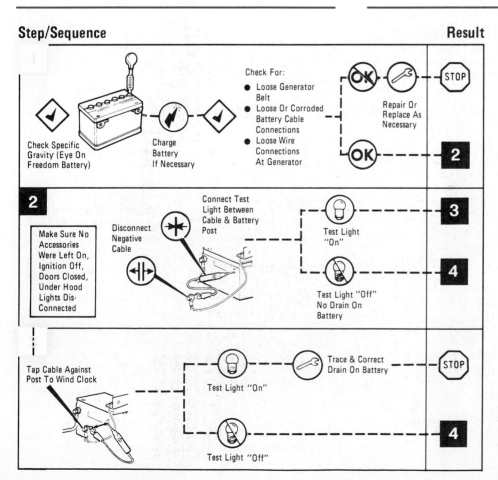

Figure 33-7.
Battery charging
problem diagnosis.
GENERAL MOTORS CORPORATION

343

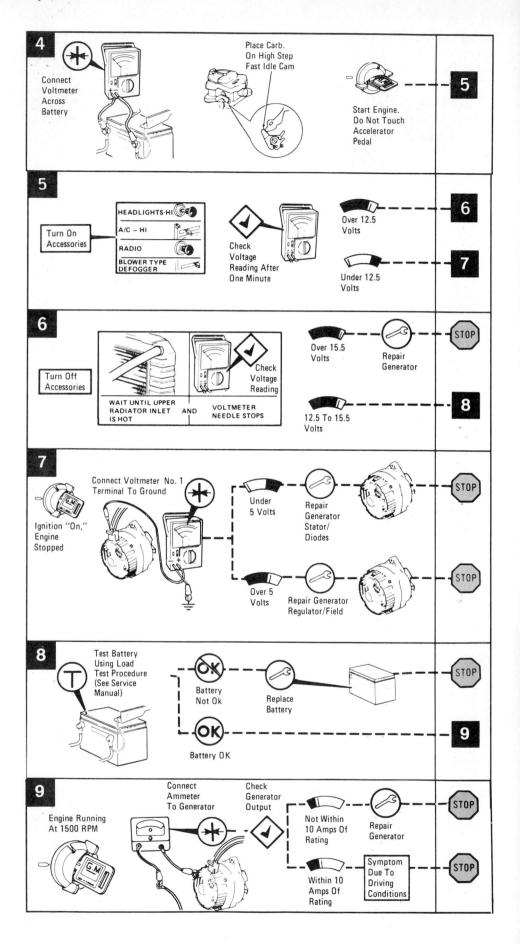

Figure 33-7. Concluded.

repaired. Oscilloscope traces are the quickest way to determine alternator problems, although simpler instruments can be used.

Circuit Resistance (Voltage Drop) Test

This test is similar to that performed on the battery cables during starter problem diagnosis. A voltmeter is connected across the ends of alternator wiring connections. A carbon pile is used to load the alternator to create a current output of 20 amps.

The insulated charging circuit should have less than 0.7 volt (ammeter indicator) or 0.3 volt drop (warning light indicator). Figure 33-9 shows the correct connections for a circuit resistance test.

33.3 FUSIBLE LINK SERVICE

A *fusible link* is a wire smaller in diameter than the wire used in the circuit it is to protect. Like a fuse, excessive current will cause a fusible link to burn out and open the circuit. Fusible links can be used at several locations on a vehicle to protect circuits, including the charging system circuit. See Figure 33-10.

Fusible links usually are identified by color and/or by a molded tag in the insulation. A burned-out fusible link may have bare wire ends protruding from the insulation, or expanded or bubbled insulation.

If excessive current flows, such as during incorrect booster cable hookup, the fusible link will burn out to protect the alternator or wiring. Fusible link replacement is illustrated in Figure 33-11.

Figure 33-8. Normal alternator oscilloscope trace pattern.

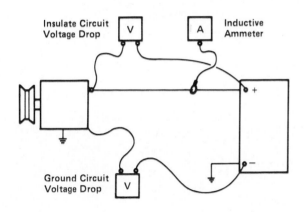

Figure 33-9. Charging system voltage drop test.

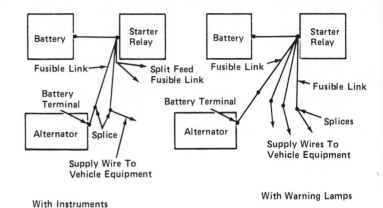

With Instruments

With Warning Lamps

Figure 33-10. Fusible link locations. FORD MOTOR COMPANY

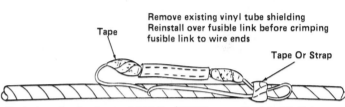

Typical repair using the special 17 Ga. (9.00" long - yellow) fusible link required for the Air/Cond. circuits (2) #687E and #261A located in engine compartment

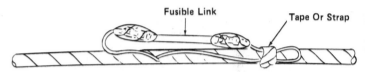

Typical repair for any inline fusible link using the specified gauge fusible link for the specified circuit

Typical repair using the eyelet terminal fusible link of the specified gauge for attachment to a circuit wire end

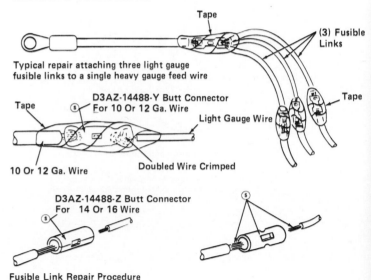

Typical repair attaching three light gauge fusible links to a single heavy gauge feed wire

Fusible Link Repair Procedure

Figure 33-11. Fusible link service procedure. FORD MOTOR COMPANY

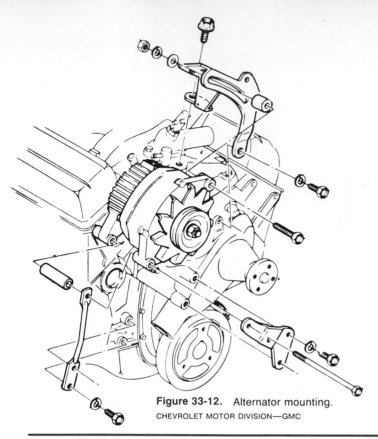

Figure 33-12. Alternator mounting.
CHEVROLET MOTOR DIVISION—GMC

33.4 ALTERNATOR OFF-CAR SERVICE

If tests indicate alternator and/or internal regulator problems, the alternator must be removed from the vehicle for service.

SAFETY CAUTION: Remove the grounded battery cable from the battery before you begin alternator removal procedures.

The alternator is mounted with brackets to the engine, as shown in Figure 33-12. Wiring connections and the alternator belt are removed. Then the pivot and adjusting bolts are removed. Other fasteners may need to be loosened or removed if the alternator cannot be lifted from the vehicle.

Alternator bench tests can be performed with appropriate test equipment. An electric motor is used to drive the alternator during testing.

Basic repair steps for General Motors Corporation alternators are illustrated in Figure 33-13. After service procedures are performed, the alternator should be bench tested before reinstallation.

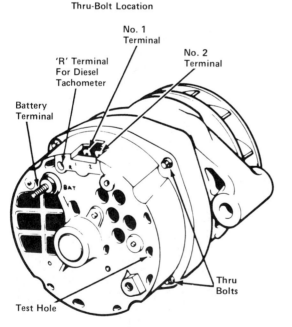

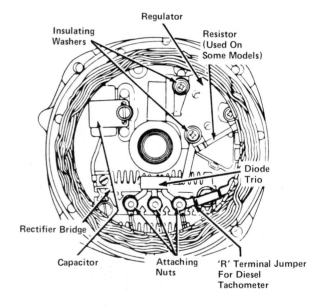

1. Make scribe marks on end frames to facilitate reassembly.

2. Remove four thru-bolts and separate drive end frame assembly from rectifier end frame assembly.

3. Remove three attaching nuts and three regulator attaching screws.

4. Separate stator, diode trio and regulator from end frame. The regulator cannot be tested on the work bench except with a regulator tester.

Figure 33-13. Alternator disassembly. BUICK MOTOR DIVISION—GMC

Testing Stator

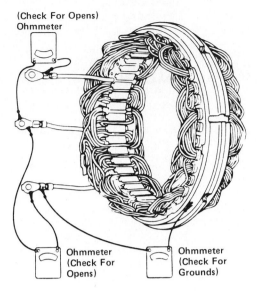

(Check For Opens)
Ohmmeter

Ohmmeter
(Check For
Opens)

Ohmmeter
(Check For
Grounds)

5. Check stator for opens with ohmmeter (two checks). If either reading is high (infinite), replace stator.

6. On all series, check stator for grounds. If reading is low, replace stator.

Testing Trio

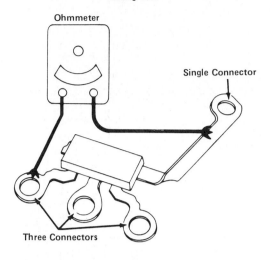

Ohmmeter

Single Connector

Three Connectors

9. To check diode trio, connect ohmmeter as shown, then reverse lead connections. Should read high and low. If not, replace diode trio.

10. Repeat same test between single connector and each of other connectors.

Testing Rotor

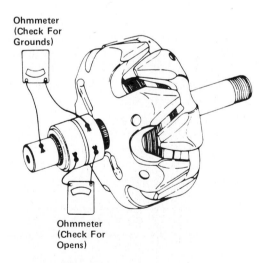

Ohmmeter
(Check For
Grounds)

Ohmmeter
(Check For
Opens)

7. Check rotor for grounds with ohmmeter. Reading should be very high (infinite). If not, replace rotor.

8. Check rotor for opens. Should read 2.4 — 3.5 ohms. If not, replace rotor.

Figure 33-13.   Continued.

Testing Rectifier Bridge

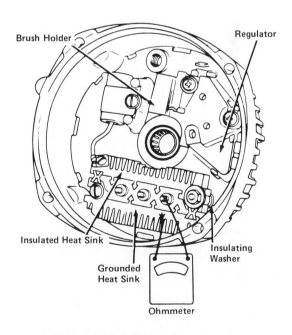

Brush Holder

Regulator

Insulated Heat Sink

Grounded
Heat Sink

Insulating
Washer

Ohmmeter

11. Check rectifier bridge with ohmmeter connected from grounded heat sink to flat metal on terminal, not the stud. Reverse leads. If both readings are the same, replace rectifier bridge.

12. Repeat test between grounded heat sink and other two flat metal clips.

13. Repeat test between insulated heat sink and three flat metal clips, not the stud. To replace bridge, remove attaching screws.

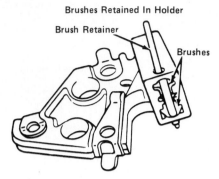

Brushes Retained In Holder

Brush Retainer

Brushes

14. Clean brushes with soft, dry cloth.
15. Put brushes in holder and hold with brush retainer wire.

Drive End Bearing

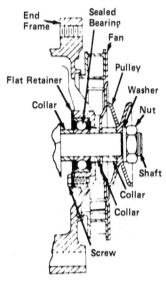

End Frame
Sealed Bearing
Fan
Pulley
Flat Retainer
Washer
Collar
Nut
Shaft
Collar
Collar
Screw

16. Observe stack-up of parts in both illustrations. To remove rotor and drive end bearing, remove shaft nut, washer and pulley, fan and collar. Push rotor from housing.
17. Remove retainer plate inside drive end frame and push bearing out. Clean all parts with soft cloth.
18. Press against outer race to push bearing in. The 12SI uses a sealed bearing — no lubricant is required. Assemble retainer plate.
19. Press rotor into end frame. Assemble collar, fan pulley, washer and nut. Torque shaft nut to 54 - 82 N·m (40 - 60 ft. lbs.).

Figure 33-13. Concluded.

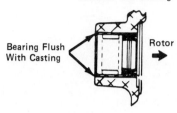

Rectifier End Bearing

Bearing Flush With Casting
Rotor

20. Push slip ring end bearing out from outside toward inside of end frame.
21. Place flat plate over new bearing, press from outside toward inside until bearing is flush with end frame.
22. Assemble brush holder, regulator, resistor, diode trio, rectifier bridge and stator to slip ring end frame.
23. Assemble end frames together with thru-bolts. Remove brush retainer wire.

U N I T   H I G H L I G H T S

- Routine charging system preventive maintenance includes checking charging indicators, alternator drive belts and wiring connections. In addition, visual checks for physical damage are made.
- Undercharging can be caused by low engine idle rpm, by loose belts, or by alternator or regulator problems.
- Charging system troubleshooting includes checking the battery, alternator, regulator, and wiring connections.
- Charging system electrical tests include charging voltage/alternator output tests, oscilloscope trace tests, and circuit resistance tests.
- Fusible links may be used to protect a charging system alternator and/or wiring.
- Alternator off-car service includes removal, disassembly, checking and/or replacing parts, replacement, reassembly, and final testing before reinstallation.

T E R M S

full field
inductive ammeter
voltage spike

oscilloscope
trace
fusible link

R E V I E W   Q U E S T I O N S

DIRECTIONS: The following questions are similar to those used on mechanic certification tests. On a separate sheet of paper, write the letter of the correct choice.

1. Undercharging can be caused by all of the following EXCEPT
A. excessively tight alternator belt or excessively high engine rpm.
B. frequent starting or defective starter.
C. low idle speed or loose alternator belt.
D. alternator or regulator problems.

2. Which of the following statements is correct?
I. Fully transistorized IC regulators usually can be adjusted.
II. Electromechanical regulators usually cannot be adjusted.
A. I only   B. II only   C. Both I and II   D. Neither I nor II

3. Mechanic A says that an oscilloscope trace pattern can be used to check for normal alternator operation.
Mechanic B says that a charging voltage/alternator output test can determine whether the alternator or regulator causes undercharging.
Who is correct?
A. A only   B. B only   C. Both A and B   D. Neither A nor B

4. A charging voltage test indicates less than 1.2 volts rise above battery voltage. An alternator output test indicates rated alternator current output.
What is the most likely cause of undercharging?
A. Shorted alternator field windings
B. Shorted diode in rectifier bridge
C. Defective regulator
D. Defective diode trio

5. Mechanic A says that fusible links are located only in a vehicle's charging system.
Mechanic B says that the conductor in a fusible link is smaller in diameter than the circuit it is to protect.
Who is correct?
A. A only   B. B only   C. Both A and B   D. Neither A nor B

S U P P L E M E N T A L   A C T I V I T I E S

1. Perform charging system preventive maintenance on a vehicle. Report to your class what problems, if any, were found.
2. Perform a charging voltage test on a vehicle. Report to your class what readings are obtained.
3. Perform an alternator output test on the same vehicle used in Supplemental Activity 2, above. Report to your class on the readings obtained.
4. Perform a circuit-resistance (voltage-drop) test on a vehicle. Report the readings obtained to your class.
5. Demonstrate to your class how to correctly connect and perform an oscilloscope trace test, if available, on a charging system.
6. Referring to the manufacturer's service manual, correctly remove and disassemble an alternator. Perform tests and replace parts as necessary. Correctly reassemble, install, and replace the alternator in the vehicle.

34 THE IGNITION SYSTEM

UNIT PREVIEW

The purpose of the ignition system is to ignite the air-fuel mixture in the combustion chambers of the engine.

Ignition systems are much alike. The relatively low voltage of the battery is increased to thousands of volts by the ignition coil. This high voltage is timed and directed to the individual cylinders by the distributor.

Proper engine operation depends upon accurate ignition system adjustment and service. Ignition timing is very important, affecting both engine performance and emissions.

LEARNING OBJECTIVES

When you have completed your assignments and exercises in this unit, you should be able to:

☐ Explain how an ignition system operates and identify what factors influence correct ignition timing.

☐ Identify and describe ignition system parts on a vehicle.

☐ Determine what type of switching device is used on a vehicle.

☐ Perform basic checks of the ignition system operation.

34.1 PURPOSE OF THE IGNITION SYSTEM

The ignition system produces a spark in a cylinder at the proper point in a gasoline engine 4-stroke cycle. The spark must be sufficiently strong to jump the spark plug air gap and ignite the air-fuel mixture, beginning combustion.

Lean mixtures and/or high compression pressures require higher-voltage, or stronger, sparks. Richer mixtures and/or lower compression pressures can be ignited with lower-voltage sparks.

34.2 IGNITION SYSTEM PARTS

An ignition system includes a low-voltage *primary circuit* and a high-voltage *secondary circuit*. Mechanical and/or vacuum controls can be used to make the spark occur sooner or later than an initial setting. In addition, many current vehicles use sensors and computers (see Unit 38) to control the ignition system.

However, the basic operation of all spark-ignition systems is the same. In 1908, Charles F. Kettering, who also invented the electric starter, designed a basic spark ignition system. A basic system, shown in Figure 34-1, consists of a battery, ignition coil, switch, primary and secondary wiring connections, and a spark plug.

The following discussion of modern automotive ignition systems includes several key components:

- Ignition coil
- Distributor
- Primary circuit
- Secondary circuit.

34.3 IGNITION COIL

An ignition coil is a *pulse transformer*. A pulse transformer produces periodic surges of high voltage. A transformer, as discussed in Unit 27, consists of two coils wrapped around an iron core. Magnetic lines of force formed by current flow in one coil will induce current flow in the second coil. The voltage output of the second coil is proportional to the number of turns in the first and second coils.

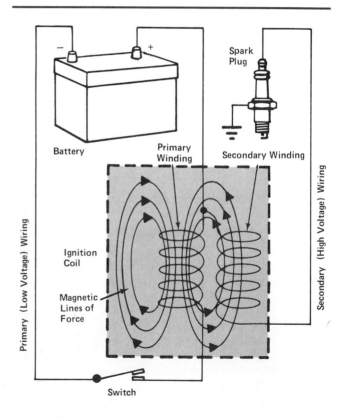

Figure 34-1. Basic ignition system.

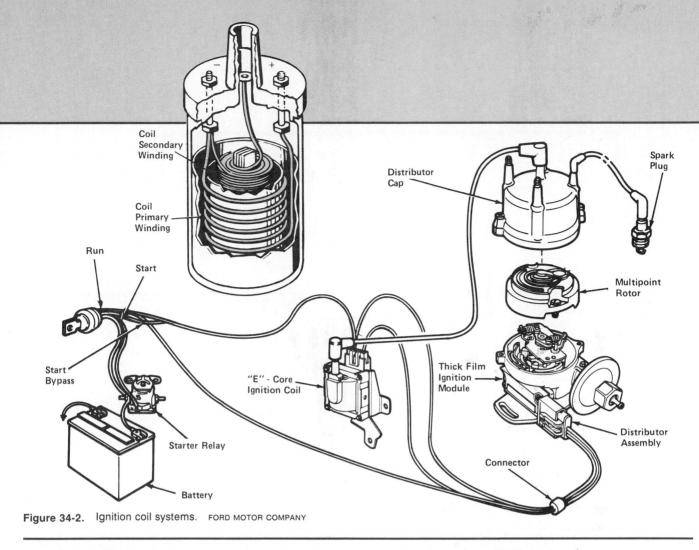

Figure 34-2. Ignition coil systems. FORD MOTOR COMPANY

Both coils in an ignition coil are wrapped around a laminated iron core. The first, or primary, outer coil consists of from 100 to 150 turns of 20-gauge wire. This wire is approximately 0.05 in. [1.27 mm] thick. The inner, or secondary, coil is made of 15,000–20,000 turns of fine copper wire thinner than human hair. Windings are separated by paper or plastic insulation and can be enclosed in an oil-filled cannister or exposed. See Figure 34-2.

When a switch is turned on, battery current energizes the primary coil to form magnetic lines of force. When the switch is turned off, the magnetic field collapses, or moves inward toward the laminated iron core. As they collapse, the magnetic lines of force move across the secondary coil. This action induces a magnetic field in the secondary coil and produces a current flow. In modern ignition systems, secondary voltage can reach 40,000 volts. High voltage is required to cause a spark to jump across an *air gap* at the end of a spark plug. An air gap is a measured space between two objects.

34.4 DISTRIBUTOR

An ignition system must produce a spark for each cylinder every time a piston completes a compression stroke. Typical passenger vehicle ignition systems must be capable of producing and distributing up to 350 sparks per second. To accomplish this task, a *distributor* can be used.

A distributor, shown in Figure 34-3, controls primary current and distributes secondary current. A distributor includes the following parts:

- Housing
- Shaft and drive mechanism
- Switching device
- Rotor
- Cap.

The outer housing of a distributor is made of aluminum. The shaft is turned by a drive mechanism attached to the camshaft. Thus, the distributor shaft turns with the camshaft at one-half crankshaft speed.

The lower part of the distributor contains a switching device and wiring connections for the primary circuit. The switching device controls current flow to the primary winding in the ignition coil.

The upper part of the distributor contains a *rotor* and a cap with metal terminals for the secondary circuit. A rotor conducts secondary current from a central, carbon coil terminal to metal terminals outside the distributor cap. The rotor is attached to the distributor shaft, which is turned by the crankshaft.

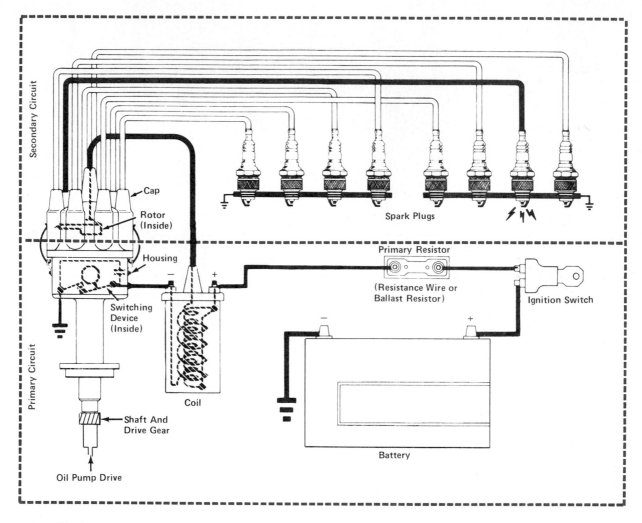

Figure 34-3. Distributor system. PRESTOLITE

A *coil wire* connects the ignition coil to the carbon terminal in the center of the distributor. Spark plug cables attach from the metal cap terminals to spark plugs screwed into the cylinder head (refer to Figure 34-4).

The action of the rotor is coordinated with that of the switching device in the distributor. Each time the rotor nears a metal terminal, the switch opens the primary circuit and secondary voltage is produced (see Figure 34-5).

The high voltage travels from the coil to the central terminal of the distributor cap, then to the rotor. A spark jumps an air gap between the tip of the rotor and the outside metal cap terminals. The high voltage continues through the spark plug cables to the center electrode of the spark plug. The high voltage again produces a spark at the spark plug's air gap to ignite an air-fuel mixture.

The switching device then closes the primary circuit in preparation for production of another spark.

This action is repeated as many as 350 times per second in passenger vehicles.

Each cylinder must receive an ignition spark at the proper time for the engine to run efficiently.

34.5 PRIMARY CIRCUIT

A basic primary circuit consists of a current source, a primary ignition coil, and a switching device that controls current flow. Two types of switching devices are common:

- Breaker points
- Electronic switching circuits.

Mechanical Switching Circuit

A set of *breaker points,* or ignition points, is a mechanically operated switch. Two electrical contacts are held together by spring tension. One of the contacts can move against the spring. The other contact is stationary, or fixed. A *rubbing block* is attached to the movable contact point. A rubbing block rubs, or is held, against a *distributor cam* attached to the

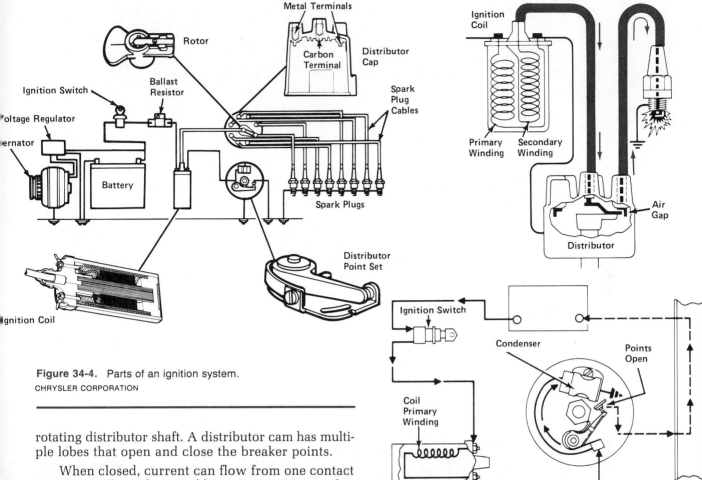

Figure 34-4. Parts of an ignition system.

CHRYSLER CORPORATION

rotating distributor shaft. A distributor cam has multiple lobes that open and close the breaker points.

When closed, current can flow from one contact point to another. The movable contact is connected to one of the primary coil terminals. Thus, when the points are closed, the primary coil is energized (see Figure 34-6).

The lobes, or high points, of the distributor cam push the breaker points open momentarily. A 4-cylinder engine's distributor would have four lobes, a 6-cylinder would have six, and so on.

Each time the points are opened, a high-voltage pulse is produced in the secondary coil. High voltage from the secondary coil flows, in order, to:

1. Coil cable
2. Distributor cap center terminal
3. Rotor
4. Distributor cap outside terminals
5. Spark plug cable
6. Spark plug.

A flat spring in the breaker point assembly closes the points as the distributor cam rotates. A *condenser*, or capacitor, prevents excessive arcing across the breaker points as they open.

The points must remain closed long enough to *saturate*, or fully develop, the primary coil's magnetic

Figure 34-5. Spark ignition circuit.

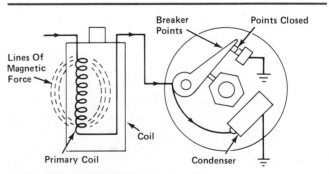

Figure 34-6. Breaker points.

lines of force. The amount of rotation through which the distributor points remain *closed* determines magnetic saturation. This rotation is known as the *dwell angle* (see Figure 34-7).

Breaker points eventually wear and may burn. This deterioration changes the dwell angle, reduces primary coil current, and changes the point at which ignition spark occurs. In addition, incorrect spring

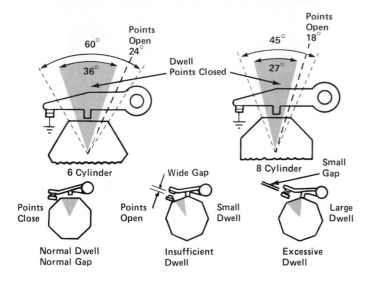

Figure 34-7. Dwell angle.

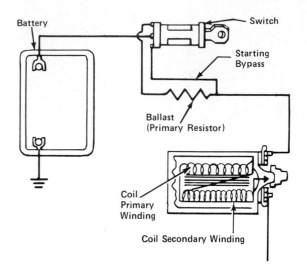

Figure 34-8. Ballast resistor circuits.

tension and/or high distributor rpm can cause problems.

Current available to energize the primary coil is limited by the contact points. Thus, secondary voltage in a conventional breaker-point ignition is limited to approximately 20,000 volts.

A *ballast resistor* can be used to protect the primary circuit from excessive voltage. A ballast resistor changes resistance in response to dwell angle and engine rpm. At relatively slow engine speeds, less current is needed to ignite the mixture. At high rpm, more current is used to prevent the spark from being "blown out" by high combustion pressures.

During starting, a ballast resistor is bypassed to provide maximum current flow to the primary coil (see Figure 34-8). A ballast resistor may be a separate unit or a specially made wire.

Since 1973, mechanical breaker point systems have been phased out by automobile manufacturers in search of improved fuel economy and reduced emissions. However, many vehicles with breaker-point ignitions are still being driven and need periodic servicing.

Electronic Switching Circuit

To eliminate breaker-point problems, non-wearing electronic sensors and transistorized *electronic ignition control units* can be used. An electronic ignition control unit switches current to the ignition primary coil on and off with transistorized circuits. Two types of electronic sensors are found on current vehicles:

- Magnetic position sensor
- Hall-effect sensor.

Magnetic position sensors consist of a central *reluctor,* or *armature,* and a *pickup coil assembly*. A reluctor, or armature, is a device that conducts lines of

magnetic force easily. A pickup coil assembly consists of a permanent magnet and a small coil, as illustrated in Figure 34-9.

The reluctor is attached to the rotating distributor shaft with an air gap between the reluctor and the pickup coil. The number of "teeth," or pole pieces, of the reluctor correspond to the number of cylinders. When a tooth becomes aligned with the core of the pickup coil, magnetic lines of force travel a path indicated by the arrows. This magnetic field induces a signal current in the pickup coil. The ends of the pickup coil are connected to a transistorized IC control unit.

General Motors products use parts similar in function to the above description. However, General Motors' High-Energy Ignition (HEI) parts are slightly different in appearance (see Figure 34-10).

The control unit shuts off battery current to the ignition coil and creates a high-voltage pulse.

Magnetic position sensors and electronic ignition control units eliminate the physical wear and deterioration problems of breaker points. However, magnetic position sensors can cause ignition timing to vary slightly at high rpm.

Hall-effect sensors use sophisticated electronic principles to create a signal voltage for a transistorized control unit.

A source of constant voltage is applied in one direction across a flat piece of semiconductor material. A magnet brought close to the semiconductor will cause current to flow at right angles to the applied voltage. See Figure 34-11.

In a distributor, a U-shaped magnet faces a similar steel or iron core. A Hall-effect semiconductor element is placed between one end of the facing "U"'s. A steel disc passes between the lower ends of

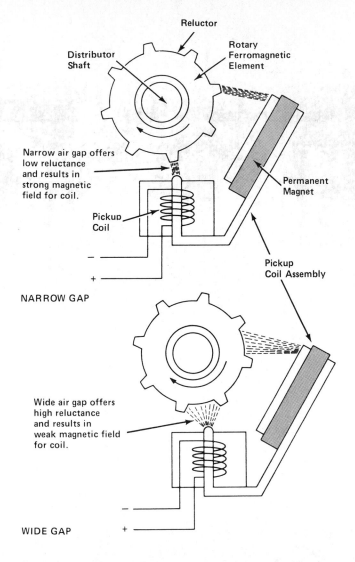

Figure 34-9. Magnetic position sensor.

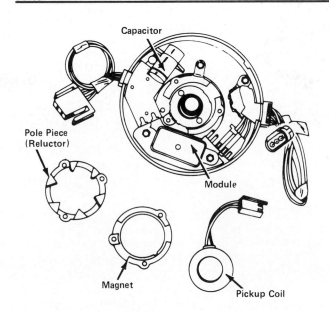

Figure 34-10. Pickup coil. CHEVROLET MOTOR DIVISION—GMC

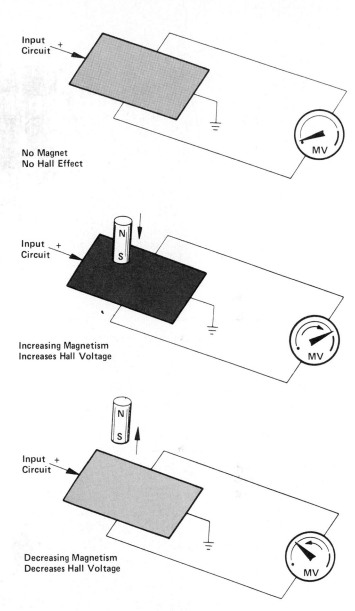

Figure 34-11. Hall-effect principles.

the "U"s, without touching them. As in the magnetic position sensor, magnetic lines of force flow in a circular path. The magnetic lines of force cause voltage to be created across the Hall element (see Figure 34-12). This voltage is used as a signal by a transistorized control unit, which shuts off primary current to produce high voltage.

Hall-effect sensors, unlike magnetic position sensors, are not affected adversely by rotational speed. Thus, ignition timing can remain more constant as engine speed increases.

Control modules, or control units, may be enclosed in housings separate from the distributor. In other cases, control modules may be located within, or attached to, a distributor (see Figure 34-13).

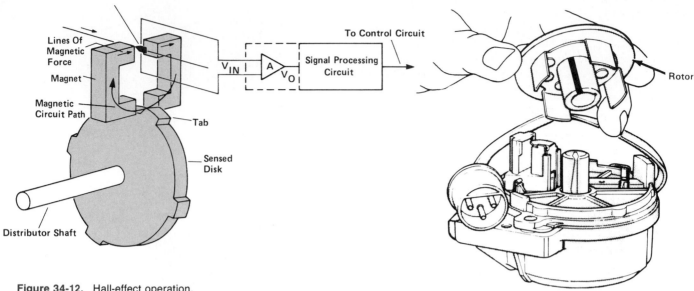

Figure 34-12. Hall-effect operation.

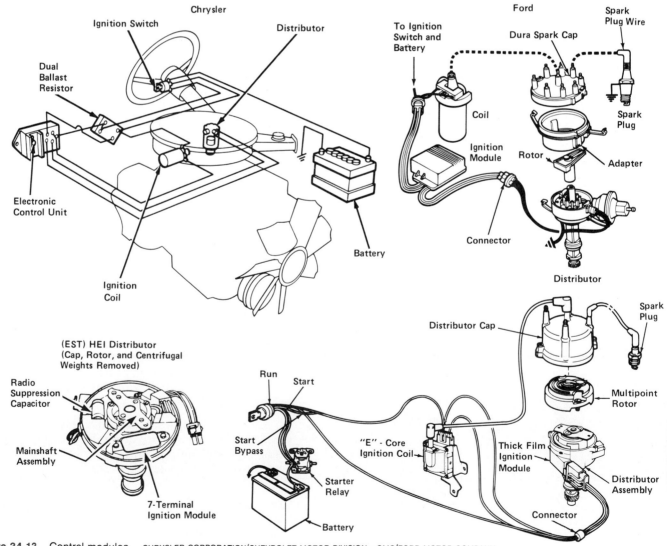

Figure 34-13. Control modules. CHRYSLER CORPORATION/CHEVROLET MOTOR DIVISION—GMC/FORD MOTOR COMPANY

Control modules contain transistors to open and close the primary circuit. A simplified diagram of such a circuit is pictured in Figure 34-14. The use of transistors allows higher current flows to be used to produce greater magnetic saturation. Secondary voltages of nearly 50,000 volts can be produced by late-model electronic ignition systems and ignition coils.

Dwell time is controlled by additional circuits within the control unit and is not totally dependent on distributor shaft rotation. In addition, ballast resistor functions are controlled by current-limiting circuits within the control unit.

34.6 SECONDARY CIRCUIT

The secondary circuit consists of the secondary coil winding, coil cable, distributor rotor, spark plug cables, and spark plugs.

Distributor Rotor and Cap

Many different sizes and shapes of distributor caps and rotors are common (see Figure 34-15). Plastic used for rotors and caps must be able to insulate against high voltage and prevent it from reaching ground.

Coil Cable and Spark Plug Cables

Spark plug cables and the coil cable are made of strands of carbon-impregnated fiberglass. The strands are surrounded by layers of insulation and an outer jacket (see Figure 34-16).

Electronic ignition coil cable and spark plug cable insulation must be able to insulate against higher voltages than a breaker-point system. Wires for electronic ignition systems are 8 mm in diameter. Cables for breaker-point ignitions are slightly smaller, 7 mm in diameter.

General Motors was the first to incorporate the ignition coil within the plastic distributor cap (see

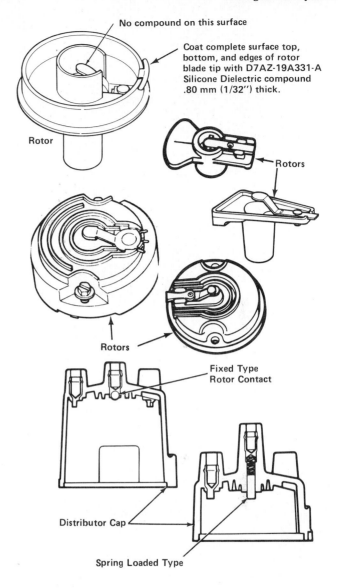

Figure 34-15. Rotors and caps. CHRYSLER CORPORATION/ FORD MOTOR COMPANY/GENERAL MOTORS CORPORATION

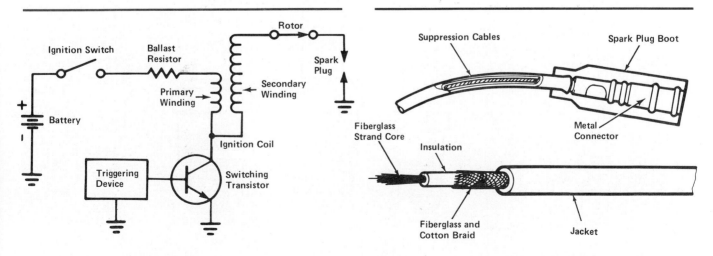

Figure 34-14. Modified control module.

Figure 34-16. Spark plug cables. CHRYSLER CORPORATION

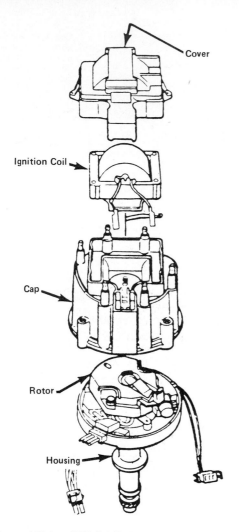

Figure 34-17). The ignition secondary contact is directly below the coil and eliminates the need for a separate coil wire.

Spark Plugs

Spark plugs are made up of several separate parts (see Figure 34-18). High-voltage current from the secondary coil completes a circuit across the air gap between the center and side electrodes.

To fit properly, spark plugs must be of the proper size and *reach*. Reach refers to the length of the threaded part of the spark plug (see Figure 34-19).

The center electrode tip of the spark plug must reach a temperature hot enough to burn off deposits. Yet the firing tip must remain cool enough to prevent rapid oxidation and electrode wear. The optimum firing tip temperature is between 650 and 1,500 degrees F [344 and 816 degrees C].

Spark plugs are available in different *heat ranges*. A heat range indicates how well a spark plug can conduct heat away from the tip. A "colder" plug will transfer heat away from the tip rapidly, resulting in lower tip temperatures. A "hotter" plug will transfer heat away slowly, resulting in higher tip temperatures (see Figure 34-20). The shape of the porcelain insulator and its contact with the outer metal shell determines spark plug heat range. The heat range is indicated by a code imprinted on the side of the plug, usually on the porcelain insulator.

A "normal" heat range plug is specified for a mixture of stop-and-go and highway driving. Hotter or colder plugs are available in steps for specialized driving conditions.

Figure 34-17. General Motors HEI distributor.
BUICK MOTOR DIVISION—GMC

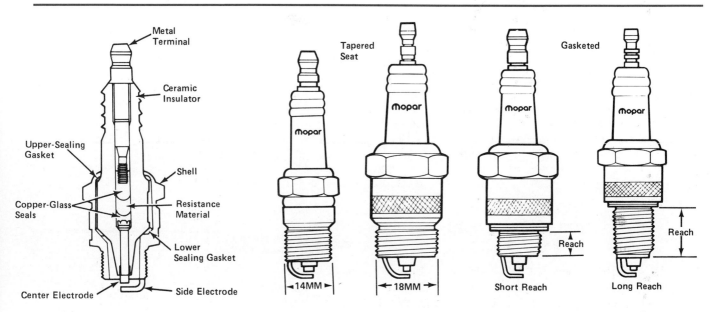

Figure 34-18. Parts of a spark plug.
AC SPARK PLUG DIVISION—GMC

Figure 34-19. Types of spark plugs. CHRYSLER CORPORATION

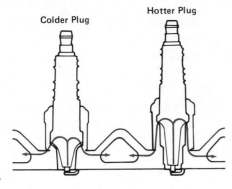

Figure 34-20. Heat transfer through a spark plug. CHAMPION SPARK PLUG COMPANY

34.7 COMBUSTION AND ENGINE POWER OUTPUT

Combustion of the mixture requires a short period of time, usually measured in thousandths of a second.

Higher compression pressures tend to speed up combustion. Higher-octane gasolines and lower-cetane diesel fuels ignite less easily and require increased burning times. Increased vaporization and turbulence tend to decrease combustion times. Other factors, including intake air temperature, humidity, and barometric pressure, also affect combustion.

Just as combustion is completed, maximum pressure is exerted against the piston top. For most efficient engine operation, maximum pressure should occur 10 degrees ATDC on the power stroke.

Ignition Timing

Ignition timing refers to the precise time when spark occurs. Ignition timing is specified by referring to a piston position in relation to crankshaft rotation. External *ignition timing marks* can be located on engine parts and on a pulley or flywheel to indicate piston position (see Figure 34-21). Vehicle manufacturers specify initial, or basic, ignition timing.

When the marks are aligned at TDC, or 0, the piston in the No. 1 cylinder is at TDC (compression stroke). Additional numbers on a scale indicate the number of degrees of crankshaft rotation *before TDC (BTDC)* or *after TDC (ATDC)*. In a majority of engines, initial timing is specified at a point between TDC and 20 degrees BTDC. A few manufacturers specified initial timing at from 1 to 5 degrees ATDC for vehicles built during the 1970s.

Two major engine factors influence operational ignition timing:

- Speed (rpm)
- Load.

Engine RPM and Ignition Timing

At higher rpm, the crankshaft turns through more degrees in a given period of time. If the combustion is to be completed by 10 degrees ATDC (power stroke), ignition timing must vary according to rpm.

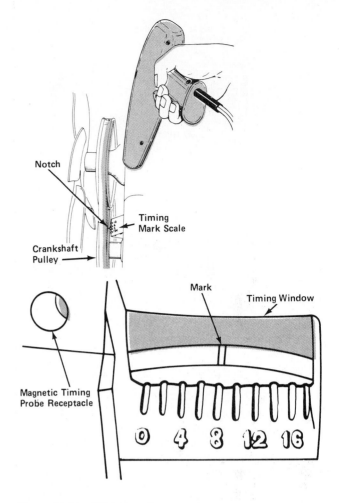

Figure 34-21. Timing mark.

Higher rpm requires that ignition spark must occur sooner, or be *advanced*.

However, air-fuel mixture turbulence (swirling) increases with rpm. Increased turbulence causes the mixture to burn faster. Increased turbulence requires that ignition must occur slightly later, or be slightly *retarded*.

These two factors must be balanced for best engine performance. Thus, increasing engine speed requires ignition advance that varies with engine speed. A mechanical device can be used to move the rotor tip and switching mechanism ahead as rpm increases (see Figure 34-22). This *centrifugal advance mechanism* causes ignition spark to occur sooner.

Engine Load and Ignition Timing

The load on an engine is the work it must do. Driving up hills or pulling extra weight increases vehicle engine load. Under load, the engine operates more slowly and less efficiently. A good indication of engine load is intake manifold vacuum.

Under light loads, when the throttle is opened only partially, a low vacuum exists in the intake

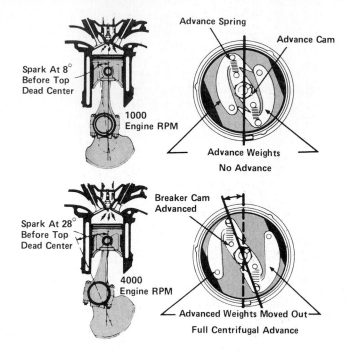

Figure 34-22. Centrifugal advance. DELCO REMY—GMC

manifold. The amount of air-fuel mixture drawn into the manifold and cylinders is small. On compression, this "thin" mixture will produce less combustion pressure and combustion time will be slow. To complete combustion by 10 degrees ATDC, ignition timing must be advanced.

Under heavy loads, when the throttle is opened fully, a larger mass of air-fuel mixture can be drawn in. High combustion pressure and rapid burning will result. In such a case, the ignition timing must be retarded to accomplish complete burning by 10 degrees ATDC.

A *vacuum advance mechanism* can advance and retard ignition timing in response to engine load and throttle position. A vacuum advance unit consists of a flexible diaphragm within a metal housing. The diaphragm is connected to the metal plate of the distributor on which the switching device is located (see Figure 34-23). A spring pushes the diaphragm toward the switching device.

The other side of the diaphragm is connected to a source of *ported vacuum*. Ported vacuum is a vacuum source on the carburetor slightly above the throttle plate.

When the throttle plate is closed during idle or deceleration, no vacuum can reach the vacuum diaphragm. No ignition advance due to vacuum occurs.

When the throttle is partially open, manifold vacuum acts on the diaphragm. The switching device is pulled in a direction opposite to distributor shaft

rotation. That action causes the ignition timing to advance.

When the throttle is fully open, low manifold vacuum allows the spring to push the diaphragm back. The effect of this action is to retard total ignition advance.

Vacuum advance operates together with centrifugal advance. The portion of total ignition advance due to vacuum is shown in Figure 34-24.

A *vacuum retard mechanism* applies vacuum to the opposite side of a sealed diaphragm. Such devices are used to retard ignition timing for emission control requirements. See Unit 41.

Electronic Controls and Spark Advance

Engineers have found that the optimum spark advance for a given engine is not a simple curve. A more correct way of picturing optimum spark advance for a particular engine is a *map* (see Figure 34-25). A map is a three-dimensional graph that resembles a mountain range.

For any given combination of engine vacuum and speed, a point can be found on the map that corresponds to best ignition advance. A computerized control unit can vary spark advance according to the coordinates of a map stored in the computer. Sensors are used to monitor engine vacuum, speed, and other factors to determine the ignition advance necessary (see Figure 34-26). Engines equipped with electronic spark advance do not have centrifugal or vacuum advance units.

34.8 CYLINDER NUMBERING AND FIRING ORDER

Cylinders receive ignition spark in firing order, not cylinder number order. Examples of firing orders are shown in Figure 34-27.

34.9 DETONATION CONTROL

Abnormal combustion, or detonation, can damage pistons and other engine parts. Extreme detonation, or "knocking," can be heard. However, inaudible, or high-speed, detonation is more damaging to engine parts than knocking.

Knocking can be reduced by retarding ignition timing slightly. However, retarded ignition timing reduces engine efficiency. For most efficient operation, an engine should operate at maximum possible advance before detonation occurs.

To prevent detonation, a *detonation sensor* can be part of an electronic ignition control circuit. A detonation, or knock, sensor acts like a phonograph cartridge. It picks up high-intensity sound wave vibrations in an engine and converts them to an electrical signal. This signal is sent to a control unit that retards ignition timing just enough to eliminate detonation (see Figure 34-28).

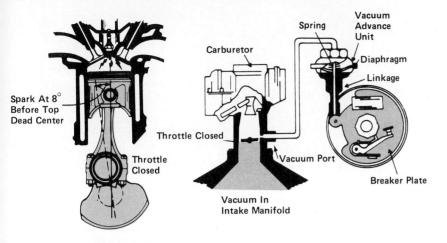

Spark At 8° Before Top Dead Center

Throttle Closed

Spring

Carburetor

Vacuum Advance Unit

Diaphragm

Linkage

Throttle Closed

Vacuum Port

Breaker Plate

Vacuum In Intake Manifold

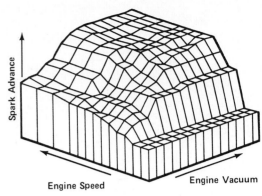

Figure 34-25. Spark advance map.
BUICK MOTOR DIVISION—GMC

Spark Advance

Engine Speed

Engine Vacuum

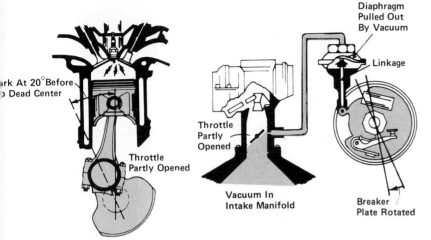

Spark At 20° Before Dead Center

Throttle Partly Opened

Diaphragm Pulled Out By Vacuum

Linkage

Throttle Partly Opened

Vacuum In Intake Manifold

Breaker Plate Rotated

Figure 34-23. Vacuum advance. DELCO REMY—GMC

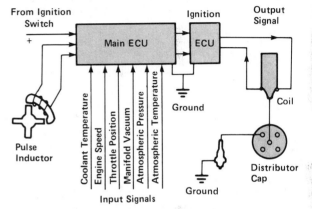

From Ignition Switch

Main ECU

Ignition ECU

Output Signal

Pulse Inductor

Coolant Temperature
Engine Speed
Throttle Position
Manifold Vacuum
Atmospheric Pressure
Atmospheric Temperature

Ground

Ground

Coil

Distributor Cap

Input Signals

Figure 34-26. Computer-controlled ignition advance system.

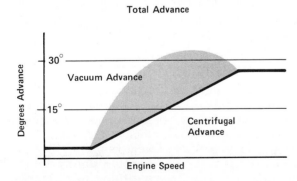

Total Advance

30°

Vacuum Advance

15°

Centrifugal Advance

Degrees Advance

Engine Speed

Figure 34-24. Vacuum and centrifugal advance curves.
DELCO REMY—GMC

Turbocharged engines, because of the higher pressures developed in the cylinders, are more likely to experience detonation. However, nonturbocharged engines also benefit from maximum possible spark advance. Thus, many new vehicles include detonation sensors as part of an electronically controlled ignition system.

Electronic controls also can be used to monitor and adjust air-fuel ratio. Thus, very precise control of

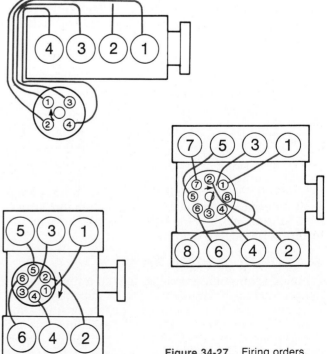

Figure 34-27. Firing orders.

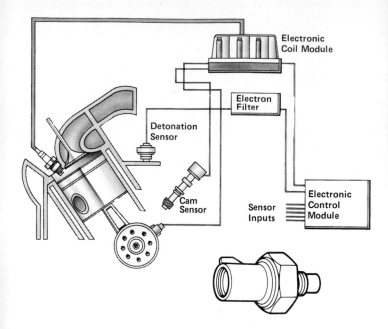

Figure 34-28. Knock and detonation sensors.
FORD MOTOR COMPANY/BUICK MOTOR DIVISION—GMC

Figure 34-29. Computer-controlled coil ignition.
BUICK MOTOR DIVISION—GMC

many engine functions can be included in an electronic control device. Electronic controls are discussed in Units 38 and 39.

34.10 DISTRIBUTORLESS IGNITION

The plastic materials used for distributor caps and rotors can break down under the high voltage produced by electronic ignitions. In severe cases, no ignition spark reaches the spark plugs, and the engine cannot run.

Several manufacturers, including Ford and General Motors, have produced larger distributor caps to increase separation between terminals. However, the distributor cap and rotor still remain the weak spots of electronic ignition.

Buick was among the first of vehicle manufacturers to introduce a production version of an ignition system without a distributor (see Figure 34-29). The Buick Computer Controlled Coil Ignition [C^{3}I] uses a control unit and three special ignition coils. Each of the coils has *two* secondary windings attached to *two* spark plug cables, one at each end of a coil.

When a primary coil field collapses, high voltage is sent to both spark plugs. One of the plugs is in a cylinder on its compression stroke. The other plug is in an alternate-firing cylinder on its exhaust stroke. The ignition spark on an exhaust stroke does not interfere with engine operation.

34.11 DIESEL IGNITION TIMING

Diesel ignition timing is called injection timing and is determined by the moment at which injection occurs. It is specified by reference to piston position and degrees of crankshaft rotation. Diesel injection advance may be provided either hydraulically or electronically in the injection pump.

REVIEW QUESTIONS

DIRECTIONS: The following questions are similar to those used on mechanic certification tests. On a separate sheet of paper, write the letter of the correct choice.

1. Mechanic A says that an ignition spark is produced when the switching device turns on current to the primary coil.
   Mechanic B says that an ignition spark is produced when the switching device turns off current to the primary coil.
   Who is correct?

   A. A only   B. B only   C. Both A and B   D. Neither A nor B

2. All of the following can be used as a switching device EXCEPT

   A. breaker points.

   B. detonation sensor.

   C. Hall-effect switch.

   D. magnetic position sensor.

3. A vehicle will not start. The coil wire is removed from the distributor cap and held 0.25 in. (6.3 mm) from the engine block. When the engine is cranked, ignition spark will jump from the coil cable to ground. The coil wire is replaced and spark plug cables checked in the same manner. No sparks will jump from any spark plug cable to ground.
   Which of the following defective components is the most likely cause?

   A. Coil

   B. Switching mechanism

   C. Rotor

   D. Spark plug cables

4. What does an ignition advance map indicate?

   A. Ignition advance for maximum performance

   B. Ignition advance necessary at different rpm

   C. Ignition advance necessary at different vacuum (load) conditions

   D. All of the above

5. Which of the following will prevent detonation?

   A. Advancing ignition timing

   B. Retarding ignition timing

   C. Detonation sensor

   D. Distributorless ignition

SUPPLEMENTAL ACTIVITIES

1. Explain how an ignition system operates and what factors influence correct ignition timing.
2. Locate and identify ignition system parts on a vehicle to your class.
3. Remove the distributor cap from a vehicle and determine what type of switching device is present. If electronic ignition, determine which type of switching device is used and try to locate the ignition control module.
4. Remove a separate coil cable from a distributor cap and hold the metal end 0.25 in. [6.3 mm] from the engine block. Have another student crank the engine. What results are obtained?

35 IGNITION SYSTEM SERVICE

UNIT PREVIEW

The ignition system has a great influence on engine performance, economy, emissions, and drive-ability. The ignition system must deliver high-voltage electrical current to the correct cylinder at the proper instant.

Such a system requires careful maintenance and service. A tune-up includes checks and maintenance of the charging, fuel, ignition, and emission control systems.

Ignition system preventive maintenance includes troubleshooting, replacement of defective parts, and adjustments on ignition timing. Basic checks to determine why an engine won't start include checks for fuel and for ignition spark. Commonly used ignition system diagnostic instruments include engine analyzers, timing lights, hand-operated vacuum pumps, and oscilloscopes.

Setting ignition timing properly may involve following carefully detailed procedures as listed on emission control specification stickers.

LEARNING OBJECTIVES

When you have completed your assignments and exercises in this unit, you should be able to:

☐ Check for the presence of spark.
☐ Perform a visual inspection of ignition system parts and identify problems found.
☐ Correctly use a remote starter, engine analyzer, timing light, hand vacuum pump, and oscilloscope to diagnose ignition system problems.
☐ Remove, color read, and replace spark plugs and set ignition timing properly.
☐ Remove a distributor and dead time an engine.

SAFETY PRECAUTIONS

Keep hands, arms, and other body parts away from moving fans, belts, and pulleys when the engine is cranking or running. Roll up long sleeves and remove all jewelry from your hands, arms, and around your neck. Wrap long hair in a ponytail and place it inside your shirt or blouse.

Ignition timing specifications are checked and adjusted with the engine running. Keep hands, arms, and other body parts away from hot engine exhaust manifolds, radiator hoses and other parts.

Ignition systems produce up to 50,000 volts. This high voltage can produce painful electrical shocks. When testing for spark, hold spark plug and coil cables with insulated pliers.

Wear eye protection when using compressed air to clean debris from spark plug wells.

When replacing breaker points, make sure the ignition switch is in the off position.

35.1 CHECKING FOR SPARK

Basic tests to determine why a vehicle won't start include checks for fuel (see Unit 20) and for ignition spark. To check for ignition spark, any spark plug cable is grasped by the boot, twisted, pulled, and removed.

CAUTION: Pull the cable from a spark plug only by the boot end. Pulling on the cable itself can cause a fracture in the inner conductive core that can result in a misfire.

After removal, a metal object, such as an insulated screwdriver, is inserted into the spark plug boot. The metal shank is placed approximately ¼ inch [6.3 mm] from the engine block or cylinder head. When the engine is cranked, a spark should jump the gap (see Figure 35-1).

The spark should continue to jump the gap as the cable is moved up to ½ inch [12.7 mm] away. If not, inspect the cables, distributor cap, and rotor as described below.

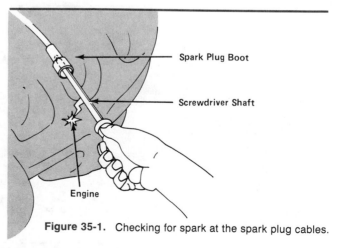

Figure 35-1. Checking for spark at the spark plug cables.

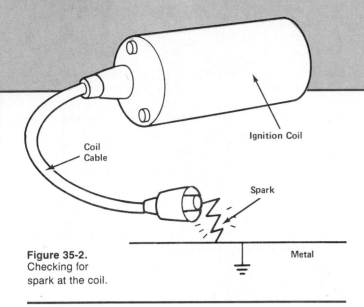

Figure 35-2.
Checking for
spark at the coil.

If no spark is observed, replace the spark plug cable and try other cables. Ignition spark should be present at all cables.

If no spark is observed from spark plug cables, remove the coil cable (if present) from the distributor cap. Check for spark from the coil cable when the engine is cranked (see Figure 35-2).

SAFETY CAUTION: On high-energy ignitions, do not hold the cable. General Motors HEI (High Energy Ignition) units and those of some other manufacturers do not have coil cables.

Spark output from the coil but not from the spark plug cables indicates a distributor rotor or cap problem. No spark output from the coil cable indicates a primary system problem, bad coil cable, or bad coil. Too-slow engine cranking that speeds up as the coil cable is removed indicates overadvanced initial ignition timing.

Breaker point primary ignition systems are subject to wear and burning. In many cases, primary system problems are due to worn rubbing blocks and/or burned contact points. Breaker point replacement is covered in 35.7. For primary electronic ignition circuits, consult the manufacturer's service manual for correct diagnostic and service procedures.

35.2 IGNITION SYSTEM SERVICE

Ignition system service usually is performed as part of a tune-up. A tune-up includes checks and maintenance of:

- Battery and charging systems
- Fuel system
- Ignition system
- Automotive emissions-related equipment.

Maintenance of the first three items in this list has always formed the basis for a tune-up. Ignition system service aims at providing most efficient ignition system operation. In former years, maximum engine power and/or economy was the goal of a tune-up.

However, the need to control automotive emissions has changed the emphasis of tune-up procedures. Federal and state laws require that harmful automotive exhaust emissions be reduced. Emission controls are discussed in Unit 41. Proper ignition system operation is necessary for both efficient engine operation and minimal emissions. The following items form the basis for ignition system service:

- Diagnostic procedures to locate defective parts
- Removal and replacement of defective parts
- Adjustments to ignition timing.

Troubleshooting procedures include inspections, basic tests for ignition spark, and diagnostic procedures done during tune-ups. Advanced diagnostic techniques include the use of electronic instruments.

35.3 VISUAL INSPECTION

If an engine runs, but poorly, the ignition system is functioning well enough to provide high-voltage sparks. Before making basic or advanced tests, the ignition system is checked for obvious problems. Such problems can include:

- Disconnected, loose, or damaged secondary cables
- Disconnected, loose, or dirty primary wiring
- Loose distributor cap
- Damaged distributor cap and/or rotor
- Worn and/or damaged primary system switching mechanism
- Improperly mounted electronic control unit.

Secondary and Primary Wiring Connections

Spark plug and coil cables should be pushed tightly into the distributor cap and coil, and onto spark plugs. Loose primary coil connections should be tightened. Frayed or cracked primary wires or secondary cables are replaced. Replacement of distributor spark plug cables on Chrysler products may require the use of long-nose pliers (see Figure 35-3).

Secondary cables must be connected in correct *firing order*. Firing order is the sequence in which ignition occurs in the numbered cylinders of an engine. Many firing orders are common (see Figure 35-4). Reference to the manufacturer's service manual must be made to determine correct firing order.

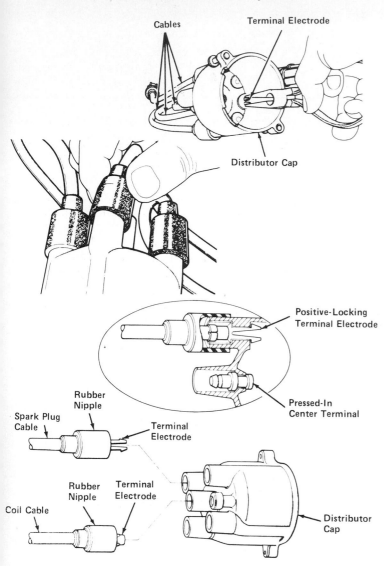

Figure 35-3. Removing and installing distributor cap wires.
CHRYSLER CORPORATION

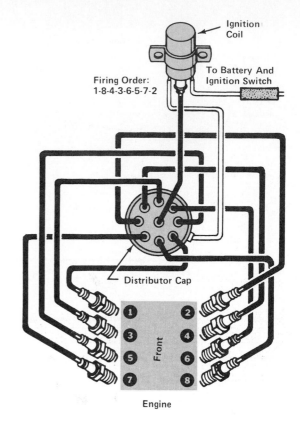

Figure 35-4. Firing order and spark plug routing.

White or grayish powdery deposits on secondary cables where they cross or near metal parts indicate faulty insulation. High-voltage electricity has "burned" collected dust. Such faulty insulation may produce a spark that sometimes can be heard and seen in the dark. An occasional glow around the spark plug cables, known as a *corona effect,* is not harmful. To test for faulty insulation, a grounded test lead is moved along a spark plug wire. A spark jumping to the test lead indicates a faulty wire.

Spark plug cables from consecutively firing cylinders should cross rather than run parallel to one another (see Figure 35-5). Parallel secondary cables can induce firing voltage in one another and cause spark plugs to fire at the wrong time.

Primary ignition system wiring should be checked for tight connections, especially on vehicles with electronic ignitions. Electronic circuits operate on very low voltage. Resistance caused by corrosion or dirt can cause running problems. Separate connectors and check them for dirt and corrosion. Clean the connectors according to the manufacturer's service manual recommendations. Some late-model vehicles require the use of a special silicone dielectric grease on connector terminals. This is done to seal the connections from outside elements.

Distributor Cap

The distributor cap should be properly indexed and firmly seated on its base. All clips or screws should be tightened securely (see Figure 35-6).

The distributor cap and rotor also should be removed for visual inspection. Physical or electrical damage is easily recognizable.

Electrical damage from high voltage can include corroded or burned metal terminals and *carbon tracking* inside distributor caps. Carbon tracking is the formation of a line of carbonized dust between distributor cap terminals, or between a terminal and the distributor housing. Carbon tracking indicates that high-voltage electricity has found an improper, low-resistance conductive path over or through the plastic. The result is a cylinder that fires at the wrong time, or a misfire. Damaged and/or carbon-tracked distributor caps and/or rotors are replaced (see Figure 35-7). Carbon tracking frequently takes on the appearance of a crack.

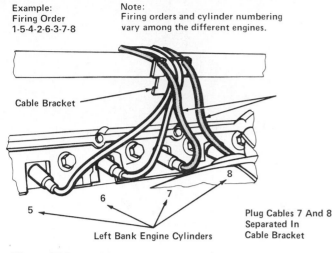

Example:
Firing Order
1-5-4-2-6-3-7-8

Note:
Firing orders and cylinder numbering vary among the different engines.

Cable Bracket

8

6 7

5

Left Bank Engine Cylinders

Plug Cables 7 And 8 Separated In Cable Bracket

Figure 35-5. Routing of spark plug cables.
CHRYSLER CORPORATION

Check the outer cap towers and metal terminals for defects. Cracked plastic requires replacement of the unit. Lightly corroded outer metal contacts sometimes can be cleaned with a special wire brush (see Figure 35-8).

The rotor plastic should be inspected carefully for discoloration, especially on vehicles with electronic ignition. Inspect the top and bottom of the rotor carefully for grayish, whitish, or rainbow-hued discolored spots. Such discoloration indicates that the rotor plastic has lost its insulating qualities. High-voltage electricity is being conducted to ground through the plastic (see Figure 35-9).

Check separate ignition coils for damage around the center tower. Cracks or burned spots require coil replacement (see Figure 35-10).

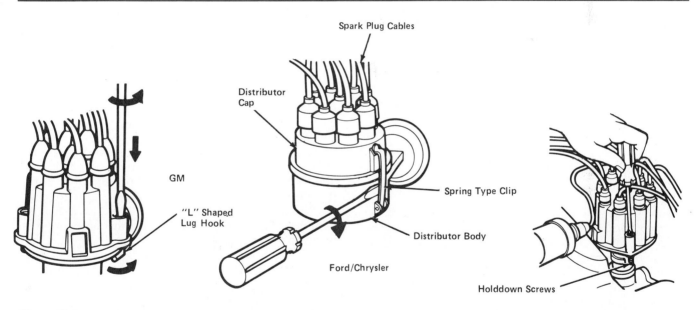

Spark Plug Cables

Distributor Cap

GM

"L" Shaped Lug Hook

Spring Type Clip

Distributor Body

Ford/Chrysler

Holddown Screws

Figure 35-6. Distributor bolting devices. CHRYSLER CORPORATION

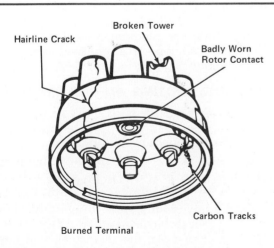

Hairline Crack

Broken Tower

Badly Worn Rotor Contact

Burned Terminal

Carbon Tracks

Figure 35-7. Distributor cap and rotor damage.
CHRYSLER CORPORATION

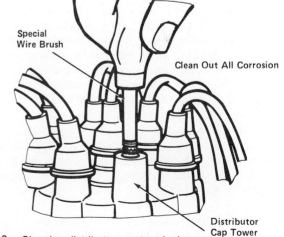

Special Wire Brush

Clean Out All Corrosion

Distributor Cap Tower

Figure 35-8. Cleaning distributor cap terminals.
CHRYSLER CORPORATION

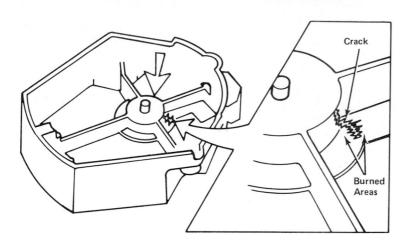

Figure 35-9. General Motors HEI distributor/rotor inspection.

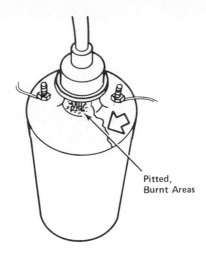

Figure 35-10. Cracked coil tower.

Primary System Switching Mechanisms

With the distributor cap and rotor off, inspect the switching mechanism inside the distributor base. Primary system problems are most common in vehicles equipped with breaker point ignitions. The points and condenser or the electronic switch component is checked for secure fastening. Loose components can cause erratic ignition system operation.

Vacuum advance mechanism linkage should be attached securely. Disconnected linkage can cause stalling and dying.

Breaker points should be pushed open with a screwdriver to check the condition of the contact surfaces (see Figure 35-11). Badly oxidized (blackened) or pitted points should be replaced. Badly pitted surfaces indicate a mismatched condenser.

Magnetic pulse generators are relatively trouble-free. The reluctor or pole piece is replaced only if broken or cracked.

Pickup coil wire leads can become grounded if insulation rubs off when vacuum advance and/or retard mechanisms operate. Inspect these leads carefully (see Figure 35-12). If worn insulation is found, a temporary repair can be made by wrapping the wire with electrical tape. The wires also should be placed so that they do not rub the switch plate as it moves.

Hall-effect switch problems are similar to those of magnetic pulse generators. Connecting wires that can move and rub as the vacuum advance/retard mechanisms move the switch plate should be inspected. See Figure 35-13.

Electronically controlled advance mechanisms eliminate centrifugal and vacuum advance/retard mechanisms within the distributor. However, all

wiring connections and parts should be thoroughly inspected for damage.

Distributorless ignitions are controlled by an electronic circuit within the coil/control unit. Refer to the manufacturer's service manual for detailed diagnosis and service procedures.

Centrifugal advance mechanisms can be checked for free motion. The rotor on the distributor shaft is rotated clockwise and counterclockwise. The rotor should rotate in one direction approximately ¼ inch [6.3 mm], then spring back. If not, the centrifugal advance mechanism may be binding or rusty. A lubricant may be necessary on advance mechanism pivots and rubbing surfaces.

Electronic Control Units

Heat can damage or destroy sensitive electronic control units. Control units should be tightly mounted to clean surfaces.

Loose mounting can cause a heat buildup that can destroy transistors and other electronic components. Some manufacturers recommend use of a special heat-conductive silicone grease between the control unit and its mounting (see Figure 35-14).

35.4 TROUBLESHOOTING WITH INSTRUMENTS

Instruments can be used to diagnose running problems and the need for tune-up procedures. The instruments most commonly used include:

- Engine analyzer
- Timing light
- Hand vacuum pump
- Oscilloscope.

Specialized instruments, including ignition coil testers, condenser testers, and others, can be used for specific tests. However, the instruments discussed here can be used to diagnose almost all ignition system problems.

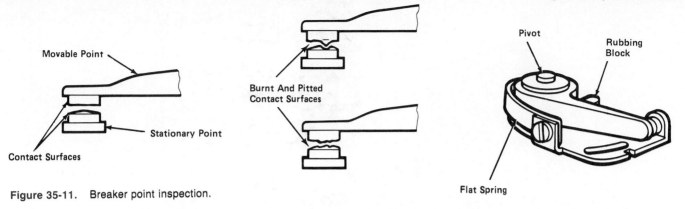

Figure 35-11. Breaker point inspection.

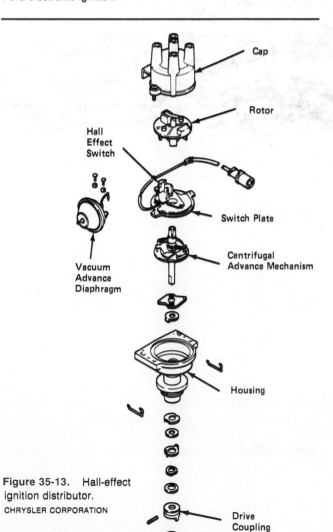

Figure 35-12.
Ford electronic ignition.

Figure 35-13. Hall-effect
ignition distributor.
CHRYSLER CORPORATION

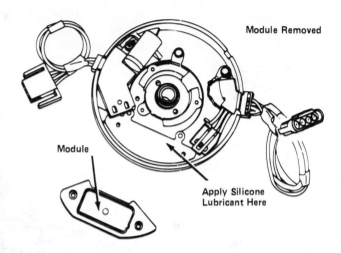

Figure 35-14. Module replacement.
CHEVROLET MOTOR DIVISION—GMC

Engine Analyzer

An engine analyzer (see Figure 35-15) includes several test functions. These functions can include:

- Low and high rpm
- Dwell
- Voltage
- Resistance
- Amperage
- Pickup coil output
- Alternator ripple current check.

Instruments may require batteries or may have cables to use battery voltage to power certain test functions. Ohmmeter functions require a separate battery.

The instrument shown in Figure 35-15 has an *inductive pickup* for rpm functions. An inductive pickup is a device that contains a pickup coil which clamps around a wire or cable. A current passing through the conductor induces a signal voltage. The signal voltage can be modified and interpreted by the instrument to

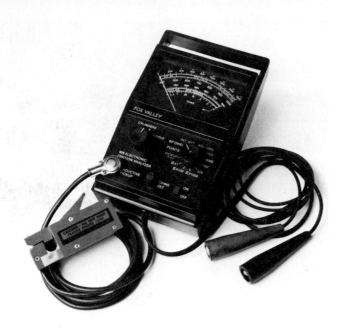

Figure 35-15. Engine analyzer.

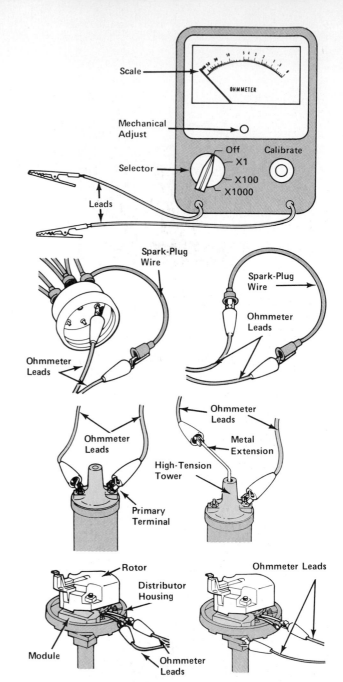

Figure 35-16. Ohmmeter checks.

produce a specified reading, such as rpm. An inductive pickup for rpm can be clamped around any spark plug cable.

Other instruments require connections to an ignition coil primary terminal and ground to pick up coil pulses. Such instruments require setting a dial for the number of cylinders or reading a separate scale for correct rpm figures.

Diagnostic meters can have an *analog* or *digital* readout. A meter is a form of analog readout. In response to higher rpm, for example, the needle moves up the scale farther. A digital readout would be in the form of numbers. Instead of a scale, the meter simply displays a number, such as 650. As rpm changes, the number changes.

Many ignition system problems can be found by using the ohmmeter function (see Figure 35-16). High resistance will lower current flow. Low resistance will increase the current flow. Manufacturers' service manuals list proper resistance specifications for given components. Resistance in some units, such as electronic ignition pickup coils, can change greatly with temperature. In such cases, temperature compensations must be made when taking resistance readings.

CAUTION: Ohmmeters can be ruined instantly by attaching test leads to powered circuits. Disconnect the grounded battery terminal to prevent damage to ohmmeters during resistance tests.

Secondary cable resistance can increase over time and thus decrease firing current. A general recommendation is that no cable, regardless of length, should have more than 50,000 Ω (ohms) resistance.

Engine analyzers can have many test leads and cords for various functions. Refer to the instrument manufacturer's instructions for proper test hookups.

Timing Light

A *timing light* is an instrument that produces a brief (1/1000 second), repeated flash of light that appears to "freeze" a moving pulley or flywheel. The flash is triggered by current flowing to the No. 1 spark plug. Thus, timing marks on the engine can be seen for checking and/or adjustment.

An *inductive timing light* has an inductive pickup to be clamped around the No. 1 spark plug cable. Two other connections to the battery terminals power the flash and sensing circuitry inside the timing light (see Figure 35-17).

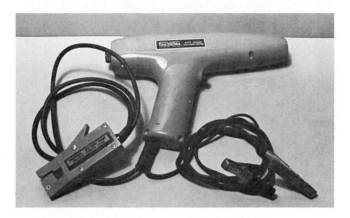

Figure 35-17. Timing light.

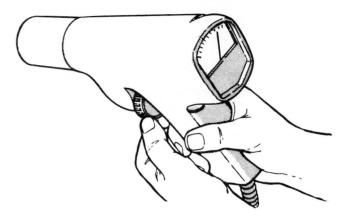

Figure 35-18. Advance timing light.

SAFETY CAUTION: On most vehicles, timing marks are located on and near the power pulley, near the fan and moving belts. The fan becomes almost invisible as it spins. Be extremely careful to avoid the spinning fan, belts, and pulleys as the timing light is aimed at timing marks. Personal injury or damage to the timing light can result if it is caught by moving parts.

Vacuum and centrifugal advance mechanisms can be checked with an *advance timing light* (see Figure 35-18). A calibrated dial on the instrument can be set to, in effect, "move" the timing marks to initial timing. This function allows a mechanic to determine ignition advance by reading a number scale.

Manufacturers' service manuals specify vacuum and centrifugal advance at different engine rpm. By removing and plugging the vacuum advance and/or retard hoses, centrifugal advance alone can be determined. Subtracting the centrifugal advance from the total advance with hoses connected will indicate vacuum advance alone.

Magnetic probe timing adapters are meant for use with special instruments. A probe inserted into the hole can detect the presence of a notch on a crankshaft balancer pulley. Some vehicles have provision for using either a timing light or a magnetic probe timing instrument (see Figure 35-19).

Hand Vacuum Pump

A *hand vacuum pump* is useful for checking vacuum-diaphragm operated devices for proper operation and/or leakage (see Figure 35-20). After securely attaching a rubber tube, the hand vacuum pump is squeezed until the gauge registers vacuum. At least 15 inches [381 mm] of vacuum should be used for testing. At the same time, the mechanical linkage is checked for movement.

If the linkage moves, the vacuum is held for at least 30 seconds. A loss of vacuum indicates a leaking diaphragm assembly that must be replaced. A leaking

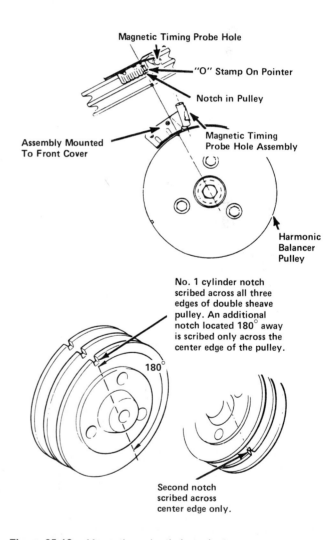

Figure 35-19. Magnetic probe timing adapter.
BUICK MOTOR DIVISION—GMC

or broken vacuum advance diaphragm can cause hesitation, stalling, and dying on acceleration.

To check for internal breakage in primary switching mechanism wires, such a test can be performed with the engine running. If the engine dies or stalls, the primary switching mechanism and leads should be double-checked with an ohmmeter while repeating the vacuum test.

Oscilloscope Tests

An *oscilloscope* is a sophisticated electronic testing instrument. An oscilloscope displays changing levels of voltage in an electrical system. Characteristic patterns, or traces, are recognizable on the face of a screen similar to that of a television set (see Figure 35-21). Patterns for both the primary and secondary systems can be displayed.

A typical firing trace for a single spark plug in a breaker point ignition system is shown in Figure 35-22. Deviations from the typical pattern shown can pinpoint ignition system problems.

Spark plug firings can be displayed in several ways (see Figure 35-23). For example, all firing patterns can be displayed one on top of the other, or *superimposed*. A *raster* pattern displays all firing order

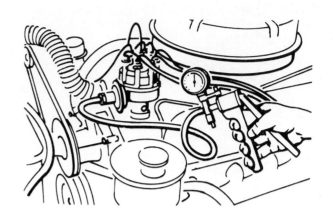

Figure 35-20. Using a hand vacuum pump.

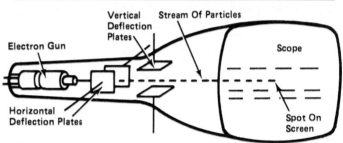

Figure 35-21. Oscilloscope tube.

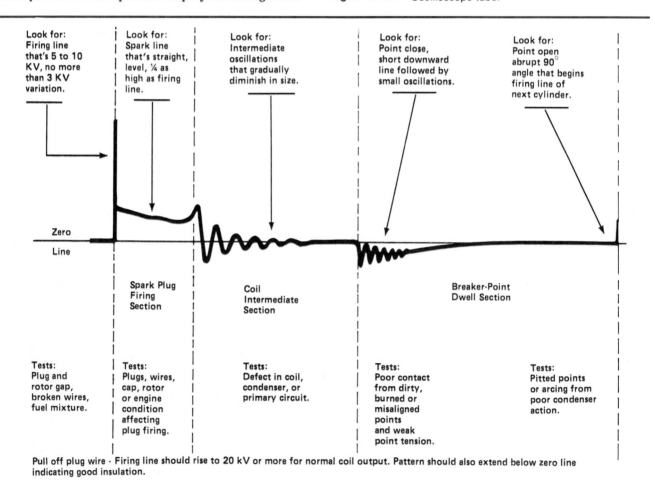

Look for:
Firing line that's 5 to 10 KV, no more than 3 KV variation.

Look for:
Spark line that's straight, level, ¼ as high as firing line.

Look for:
Intermediate oscillations that gradually diminish in size.

Look for:
Point close, short downward line followed by small oscillations.

Look for:
Point open abrupt 90° angle that begins firing line of next cylinder.

Zero Line

Spark Plug Firing Section

Coil Intermediate Section

Breaker-Point Dwell Section

Tests:
Plug and rotor gap, broken wires, fuel mixture.

Tests:
Plugs, wires, cap, rotor or engine condition affecting plug firing.

Tests:
Defect in coil, condenser, or primary circuit.

Tests:
Poor contact from dirty, burned or misaligned points and weak point tension.

Tests:
Pitted points or arcing from poor condenser action.

Pull off plug wire - Firing line should rise to 20 kV or more for normal coil output. Pattern should also extend below zero line indicating good insulation.

Figure 35-22. Sun scope pattern. SUN ELECTRIC CORPORATION

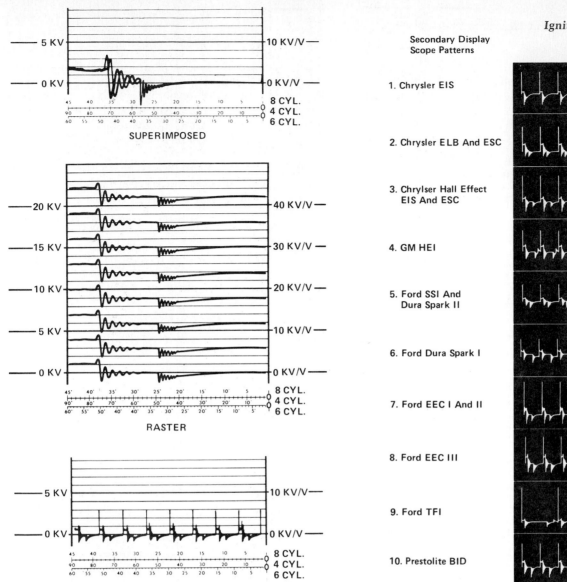

Figure 35-23. Superimposed, raster, and display patterns.
SUN ELECTRIC CORPORATION

Secondary Display
Scope Patterns

1. Chrysler EIS

2. Chrysler ELB And ESC

3. Chrylser Hall Effect
EIS And ESC

4. GM HEI

5. Ford SSI And
Dura Spark II

6. Ford Dura Spark I

7. Ford EEC I And II

8. Ford EEC III

9. Ford TFI

10. Prestolite BID

Figure 35-24. Secondary display patterns.
SUN ELECTRIC CORPORATION

traces separately, in a stack. A *normal display* shows the firings one after the other, in firing order.

Patterns for electronic ignition systems differ. Typical patterns for a variety of these systems are shown in Figure 35-24.

Problems can be spotted on a display (see Figure 35-25). Single cylinder firings then can be displayed for more detailed analysis.

Properly used, an oscilloscope can be an important tool in determining the cause of engine operation problems. Experience in recognizing ignition system problems from oscilloscope patterns is a valuable job skill for a mechanic.

35.5 TESTING ELECTRONIC IGNITION CONTROL UNITS

Test procedures for electronic ignition control units may involve multiple steps and measurements with voltmeters and ohmmeters. Manufacturers also may specify the use of special testers for electronic ignition modules. *Testing by substitution* may be the recommended procedure.

Testing by substitution means substituting a part that is known to be good for a suspected bad part. If the good part functions properly, the problem is in the old part.

Refer to the vehicle manufacturer's service manual for correct servicing procedures. Improper servicing procedures can result in damage to sensitive electronic components.

35.6 SPARK PLUG REPLACEMENT

On older models, spark plugs were replaced at intervals of 10,000–12,000 miles [16,093–19,312 km], or approximately once a year. However, high-voltage electronic ignition systems and the use of unleaded gasoline allow spark plugs to continue firing longer. On current vehicles, spark plug replacement intervals of 15,000–45,000 miles [24,140–72,418 km] are recommended.

Removing Spark Plugs

Before attempting spark plug removal, mark the spark plug wires for correct replacement. Compressed air

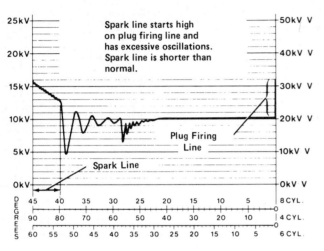

POSSIBLE CAUSES

A. Higher than normal.
  1. Worn spark plug.
  2. Open plug wire.
  3. Distributor cap.
  4. Unbalanced (lean) fuel mixture.

B. Lower than normal.
  1. Closely-gapped or fouled spark plugs.
  2. Shorted or broken spark plug.
  3. Cylinder compression low.

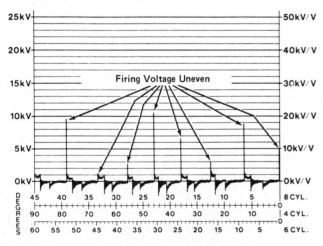

POSSIBLE CAUSES

A. Present on all cylinders.
  1. Coil tower.
  2. Coil tower wire.
  3. Corroded coil terminals.
  4. Distributor cap.
  5. Rotor.

B. Present on one or more cylinders, but not all.
  1. Open plug wire.
  2. Distributor cap.
  3. All plug wire connections corroded.

Figure 35-25. Firing problems. HEATH COMPANY

can be used to blow out dirt and debris from around spark plugs before removal (see Figure 35-26). Such materials could fall into the cylinder through the spark plug hole and cause internal damage. Small chips of rock also can lodge between the valve face and seat, preventing valve closure.

SAFETY CAUTION: **Wear eye protection whenever working with compressed air. Pain or blindness can result from debris or liquids blown into the eyes.**

Obstructions often cause problems in spark plug replacement. Different combinations of extensions and universal joints may be necessary to reach some spark plugs. On some vehicles, spark plugs can be removed from below the engine through wheel wells when the vehicle is raised.

Use a ratchet or breaker bar to loosen the spark plug, then turn it out by hand. Keep the spark plugs in order as they are removed. Inspect the spark plug for damage, wear, and indications of engine problems (see Figure 35-27).

Spark Plug Color Reading

An engine that is operating properly with the specified spark plugs will produce characteristic colored deposits on the spark plugs. Color reading is done at the firing tip and insulator nose only. Correct colors are medium grays, browns, and tans.

Extremely light deposits (white, yellow, pink) indicate combustion temperatures that are too high. Possible causes include vacuum leaks, lean mixtures, cooling system problems, and spark plugs of incorrect (too hot) heat range.

Extremely dark deposits (dark brown or sooty black) indicate combustion temperatures that are too

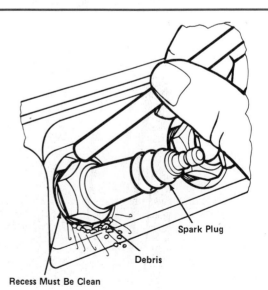

Figure 35-26. Cleaning spark plug wells. CHRYSLER CORPORATION

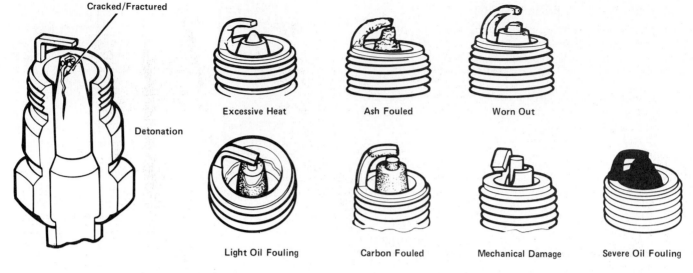

Cracked/Fractured

Detonation

Excessive Heat

Ash Fouled

Worn Out

Light Oil Fouling

Carbon Fouled

Mechanical Damage

Severe Oil Fouling

Figure 35-27. Inspecting spark plugs. CHRYSLER CORPORATION

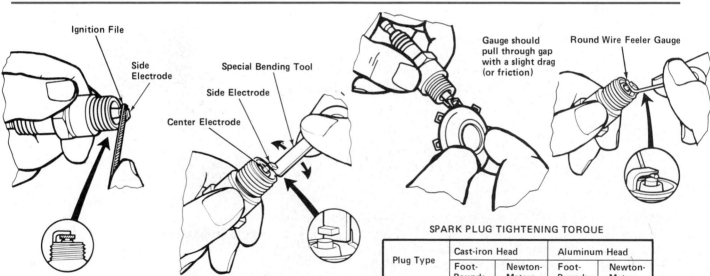

Ignition File

Side Electrode

Special Bending Tool

Side Electrode

Center Electrode

Gauge should pull through gap with a slight drag (or friction)

Round Wire Feeler Gauge

Plug Type	SPARK PLUG TIGHTENING TORQUE			
	Cast-iron Head		Aluminum Head	
	Foot-Pounds	Newton-Meters	Foot-Pounds	Newton-Meters
14-mm Gasketed	25-30	34-40	15-22	20-30
14-mm Tapered Seat	7-15	9-20	7-15	9-20
18-mm Tapered Seat	15-20	20-27	15-20	20-27

low. Possible causes include rich mixtures, short trip/cold weather operation, cooling system problems, and spark plugs of incorrect (too cold) heat range. Spark plug color reading can be done accurately only on plugs from an engine that has been brought to normal operating temperature.

Replacing Spark Plugs

The plugs found installed in an engine may not have the correct heat range or reach. Always refer to the manufacturer's service manual for correct replacement spark plug numbers.

New plugs must be checked for a correct air gap. If incorrect, the plug must be regapped. To install, start the plug by hand, then tighten to the manufacturer's torque specification (see Figure 35-28). As a final step, the correct spark plug cable is pushed firmly onto the spark plug.

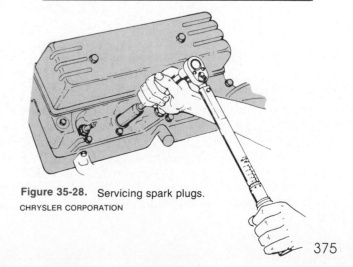

Figure 35-28. Servicing spark plugs.
CHRYSLER CORPORATION

35.7 REPLACING BREAKER POINTS

Breaker points require regular replacement at intervals of 10,000–12,000 miles [16,093–19,312 km]. If no pitting of the contact point surfaces is evident, the condenser need not be replaced.

Leads from the coil primary terminal and condenser may be screwed on or held behind the point spring. Screws holding the point set must be loosened and/or removed (see Figure 35-29).

To adjust a replacement set of points, the point rubbing block must rest on a corner of the distributor cam. To position the distributor cam, the engine must be rotated. If the crankshaft pulley nut is accessible, the engine can be turned by hand with the proper-sized wrench. Another method of positioning the crankshaft is to connect a *remote starter* to the starter relay or solenoid (see Figure 35-30).

A remote starter is a simple electrical switch with leads. Either lead is connected to battery power. The other end is connected to the key switch terminal. When the button is pushed, the starter cranks the engine. A remote starter switch also can be used to position the engine for other service operations.

When the points are fully opened, the breaker point air gap must be set correctly (see Figure 35-31). Point and condenser holding screws are tightened and the point gap checked again. Tightening point holding screws may change the adjustment. Connecting wires from the coil and condenser are tightened securely.

CAUTION: **Air gaps on electronic ignition systems normally do not need adjustment or checking. Electronic ignition systems require the use of non-magnetic brass feeler gauges. Use of steel gauges can cause a pickup coil or reluctor to become magnetized and no longer function properly.**

After setting points, a dwell reading is taken with an engine analyzer. If the dwell angle is incorrect, ignition timing will be affected. Too wide a gap will produce a low dwell angle and advanced timing. Too narrow a gap will produce a high dwell angle and retarded timing.

35.8 SETTING IGNITION TIMING

Ignition timing is dependent upon many factors. These factors include:

- Spark plug air gap
- Dwell
- Engine rpm
- Emission control devices.

Both spark plug gap and dwell must be correct before ignition timing is set. Also, the engine must be at full operating temperature. On electronic ignitions, dwell is determined electronically and is not adjustable.

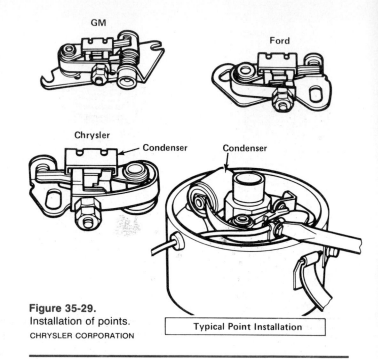

Figure 35-29.
Installation of points.
CHRYSLER CORPORATION

Typical Point Installation

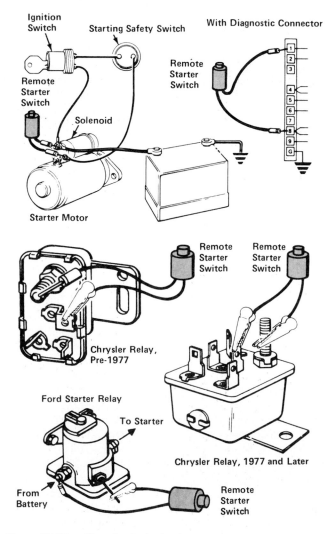

Figure 35-30. Remote starter hookup.

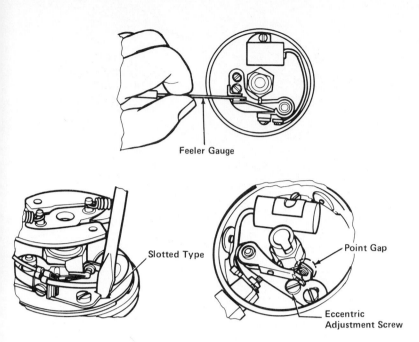

Feeler Gauge

Slotted Type

Point Gap

Eccentric
Adjustment Screw

Figure 35-31. Adjustment of points. CHRYSLER CORPORATION

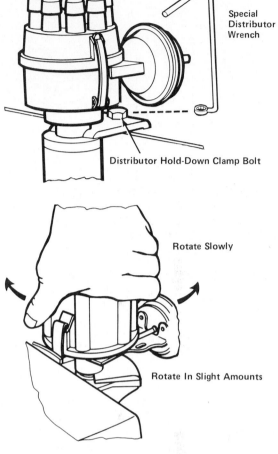

Special
Distributor
Wrench

Distributor Hold-Down Clamp Bolt

Rotate Slowly

Rotate In Slight Amounts

Figure 35-32. Turning distributor to set timing.
CHRYSLER CORPORATION

In some cases, engine rpm must be adjusted slower or faster than normal for ignition timing purposes. Engine rpm is changed by turning fuel-system idle speed adjustments.

Most vehicles built since 1969 include emissions control instructions on a sticker or decal in the engine compartment. Step-by-step instructions must be followed to tune an engine correctly. It may be necessary to disconnect and plug several vacuum hoses before ignition timing can be set properly. Emission control systems are discussed in Unit 41.

Refer to the underhood sticker or manufacturer's service manual for proper ignition timing procedures.

To check ignition timing, timing light leads are attached to the battery and the No. 1 cylinder spark plug cable. All instrument leads are positioned away from moving parts at the front of the engine. The vacuum advance hose is disconnected and plugged. Clean and mark the timing mark and plate with white chalk before checking timing.

The engine is started and the timing checked. Be sure the idle speed is correct. If it is necessary to correct timing, the hold-down clamp beneath the distributor is loosened. The distributor is rotated slightly until the marks are aligned correctly (see Figure 35-32). Rotating the distributor changes the relationship of the rotor and switching mechanism to the distributor shaft. After the hold-down clamp bolt is tightened, timing is rechecked. Tightening the clamp may cause the timing to shift slightly. All disconnected vacuum hoses are replaced.

The timing mark on some late-model vehicles appears not as a single notch, but as a wide pattern (see Figure 35-33). Refer to the manufacturer's service manual for correct ignition timing procedures.

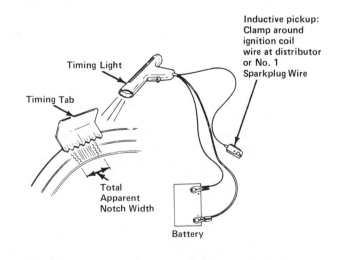

Timing Light

Timing Tab

Inductive pickup:
Clamp around
ignition coil
wire at distributor
or No. 1
Sparkplug Wire

Total
Apparent
Notch Width

Battery

Figure 35-33. Timing notch width. BUICK MOTOR DIVISION—GMC

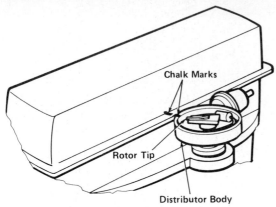

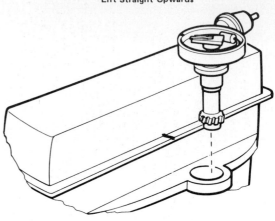

Lift Straight Upwards

Figure 35-34. Removing and replacing distributor. CHRYSLER CORPORATION

Do Not Crank Engine When Distributor Is Removed

35.9 DISTRIBUTOR REMOVAL AND REPLACEMENT

For some service operations, the distributor must be removed. Most distributors are driven by a helical gear that meshes with another gear on the camshaft. If the distributor is removed, the relationship between ignition timing and valve timing is changed.

The distributor rotor must be properly positioned in relationship to crankshaft and camshaft position when the distributor is replaced. Misalignment by only one gear tooth will change ignition timing enough to keep the engine from starting or running.

Reference marks are made when the rotor is pointing toward the engine (see Figure 35-34). Because the gear is curved, the rotor will rotate as the distributor is removed and replaced. When the distributor is reinstalled, the reference marks must be realigned by correctly positioning the gear. The engine must not be cranked while or after the distributor is removed.

Dead Timing

Dead timing can be done if the engine is accidentally cranked, or when reinstalling a distributor on an overhauled engine. Dead timing is a process of replacing a distributor correctly in an engine for starting purposes. After starting, ignition timing can be reset properly. Dead timing consists of two steps:

1. Position the engine crankshaft at the No. 1 cylinder's firing position. This can be determined from ignition timing marks and pressure from the No. 1 cylinder's spark plug hole. As the piston moves on its compression stroke, pressure is created. Placing a thumb *over* the spark plug hole will help you to feel compression. Then align the timing marks to initial timing.

2. Place the distributor back in its mounting hole. The rotor must be aligned with the metal cap terminal leading to the No. 1 spark plug wire.

Refer to the manufacturer's service manual for firing order and approximate distributor positioning.

UNIT HIGHLIGHTS

- Basic checks to determine why an engine won't start include checks for the presence of fuel and ignition spark.

- A tune-up includes checks and maintenance of the charging, fuel, ignition, and emission control systems.

- Visual inspection can locate the causes of many ignition system faults. Diagnostic instruments can be used to help locate other ignition system problems.

- Ignition system service includes diagnostic procedures, removal and replacement of defective parts, and adjustments to ignition timing.

- Commonly used ignition system diagnostic instruments include the engine analyzer, timing light, hand vacuum pump, and oscilloscope.

- Experience in recognizing proper and improper oscilloscope patterns is a valuable job skill for mechanics.

- Ignition timing is set at a specified rpm. The engine must be at full operating temperature, and spark plug gap and dwell must be correct. Emission control vacuum lines may need to be disconnected and plugged before timing is set.

TERMS

firing order	hand vacuum pump
corona effect	oscilloscope
carbon tracking	superimposed
inductive pickup	raster
analog	normal display
digital	testing by substitution
timing light	remote starter
inductive timing light	dead timing
advance timing light	

REVIEW QUESTIONS

DIRECTIONS: The following questions are similar to those used on mechanic certification tests. On a separate sheet of paper, write the letter of the correct choice.

1. An ignition system is being checked for spark. With the coil cable attached to the distributor, the engine barely cranks over. With the coil cable removed, the engine cranks easily.

   The most likely cause is
   A. worn or fouled spark plugs.
   B. defective rotor or cap.
   C. ignition timing too far advanced.
   D. ignition timing too far retarded.

2. All of the following are checked and/or adjusted during a tune-up EXCEPT
   A. belts, hoses, and tire pressures.
   B. battery and charging system.
   C. fuel and ignition systems.
   D. emission control systems.

3. Mechanic A says that ignition system problems can be found during visual inspections. Mechanic B says that diagnostic instruments can be used to find ignition system problems. Who is correct?
   A. A only　　　B. B only　　　C. Both A and B　　　D. Neither A nor B

4. Which of the following statements is correct?
   I. Ignition timing procedures may require changing idle speed.
   II. Ignition timing procedures may require disconnecting and plugging vacuum hoses.
   A. I only　　　B. II only　　　C. Both I and II　　　D. Neither I nor II

5. When is dead timing necessary?
   A. During every tune-up
   B. When ignition timing is reset
   C. Every time the distributor is removed from the engine
   D. When the crankshaft has been moved while the distributor is out

SUPPLEMENTAL ACTIVITIES

1. Check a vehicle for spark at both the spark plug and coil cables. Demonstrate to your class proper operation and/or any problems found.
2. Perform a visual inspection of all ignition system parts. Make notes and report any problems found to your class.
3. Form small groups. Choose one diagnostic instrument and read the instrument manufacturer's instructions for use. Demonstrate to the rest of the class, one group at a time, how to connect and use diagnostic instruments. Choose either the remote starter, engine analyzer, timing light, hand vacuum pump, or oscilloscope.
4. Remove, color read, and replace spark plugs and set ignition timing properly on a vehicle. Report to your class on problems found and conditions necessary for setting ignition timing.
5. Remove a distributor and crank the engine of a vehicle. Perform dead timing, start the engine, and set ignition timing properly.

36 ELECTRICAL DEVICES

UNIT PREVIEW

Wires for vehicle circuits are grouped together in harnesses, or bundles. Individual wires are color-coded to aid in identification. Several wires may be connected to a common source of power or ground.

Circuit protection devices include fuses, fusible links, and circuit breakers. Relays are used in place of heavy-duty switches to conduct large current flows.

A wiring diagram is like a road map to indicate the path of current flow for individual circuits.

Warning devices and instruments are used to alert the driver to problem conditions. Sending units are used with either lights or gauges. Some indicating devices operate mechanically, rather than electrically.

Electrical devices include lighting, warning or indicating devices, and comfort accessories.

LEARNING OBJECTIVES

When you have completed your assignments and exercises in this unit, you should be able to:

☐ Describe how wiring connections are made in a vehicle.

☐ Identify and describe parts on vehicle wiring diagrams.

☐ Trace wires and locate connectors on a vehicle.

☐ Locate fuse blocks and turn-signal flashers on a vehicle.

☐ Locate warning light or gauge sending units on a vehicle.

☐ Check and replace burned-out bulbs on a vehicle.

36.1 WIRING CIRCUITS

As discussed in Unit 27, electricity flows from a source, through conductors to an electrical load, and back to the source. The roughly circular path through which electricity flows is called a circuit. In addition to charging and starting systems, electrical system circuits include circuits for lighting, indicating, and accessory circuits. A simplified diagram of an automotive electrical system is shown in Figure 36-1.

Each electrical unit on a vehicle is part of a specific circuit. Lights, radios, windshield wiper motors, blower motors, and other units each may have a

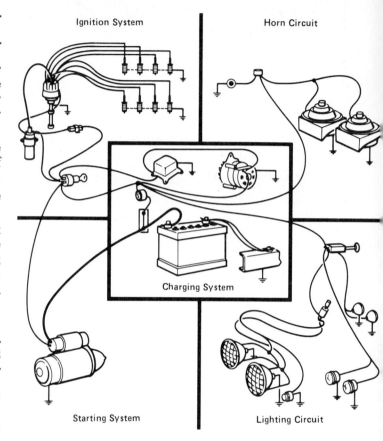

Figure 36-1. Simplified electrical system.

separate circuit. Even though physically far apart, series, parallel, and series-parallel circuits may be electrically interconnected (see Figure 36-2).

Common Connections

A shared source of power or a common ground can be used to decrease separate connections. (See Figure 36-3.) Wherever several units are physically close, such as instruments and lights in an instrument panel, common connections can be used.

Wiring Harness

Wires of different sizes run throughout a vehicle (see Figure 36-4). Wires are grouped together in *harnesses*. A harness is a bundled group of wires. At specific points, wires lead from a harness to electrical units.

Wiring harnesses can contain many wires, especially in the areas of the dash and firewall (see Figure 36-5).

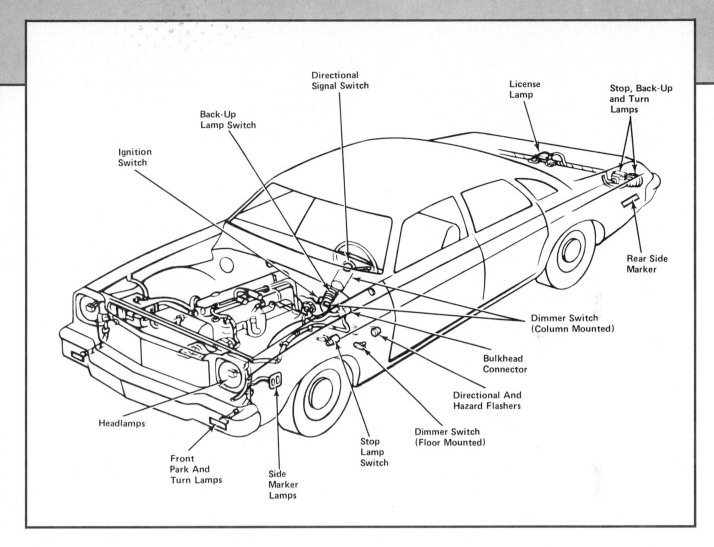

Figure 36-2. Typical locator. GENERAL MOTORS CORPORATION

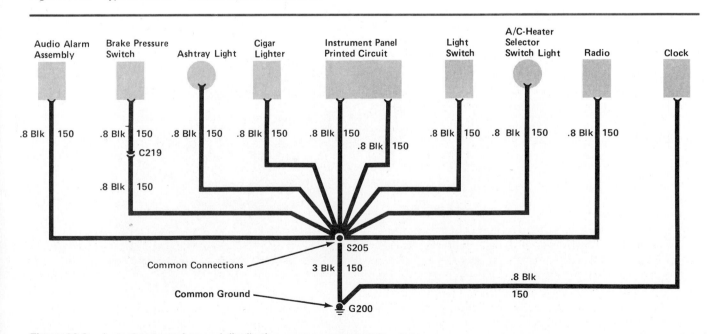

Figure 36-3. Instrument panel ground distribution. BUICK MOTOR DIVISION—GMC

Color Coding of Wires

Colored plastic insulation on wires helps a mechanic to trace wires through connections. The plastic insulation may be a solid color or may have a small *tracer,* or stripe, of another color. Wires often run to connectors that can be disassembled for checking and/or replacement of electrical units (see Figure 36-6). Finding the same color wire on both sides of a connector helps to trace a wire if a problem occurs.

Printed Circuits

A *printed circuit* is a thin sheet of nonconductive plastic material on which conductive metal has been deposited. Parts of the metal are etched, or eaten

away, by acid. The remaining metal lines form conductors for separate circuits (see Figure 36-7).

A wiring connector can be plugged into a common point (see the numbered areas in Figure 36-7). Power or ground circuits are completed through connected wires.

Wiring Diagram

A *wiring diagram* is a drawing similar to a road map. Wiring diagrams show how wires are connected in circuits (see Figure 36-8). Insulation colors may be reproduced on a diagram. In other cases, black lines are used to indicate all wires. In such cases, insulation colors may be written next to lines indicating wires,

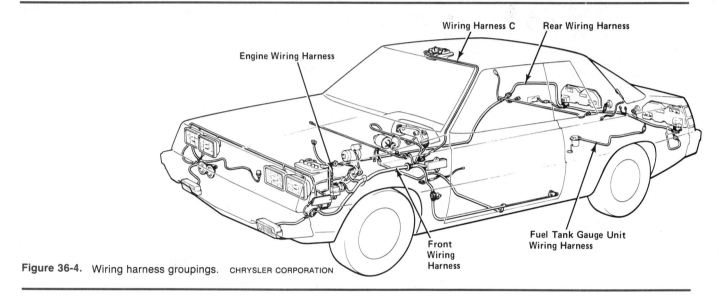

Figure 36-4. Wiring harness groupings. CHRYSLER CORPORATION

1. Flood Lamp Feed
2. Low Fuel Lamp
3. Low Brake Vacuum Conn.
4. Dash Interconnect
5. Courtesy Lamps
6. A/C Connectors
7. Ash Tray Feed
8. Power Antenna Feed
9. C.C.C. Connectors
10. Twilight Sentinel Conn.
11. Convenience Center
12. Radio
13. A/C Heater Control
14. ALDL

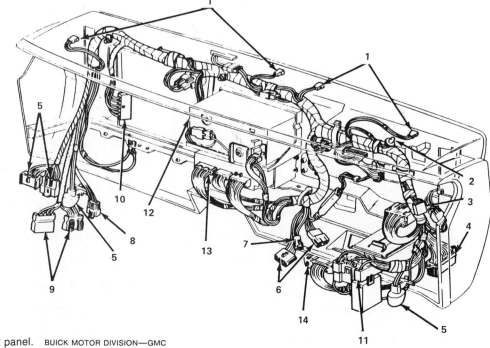

Figure 36-5. Back side of instrument panel. BUICK MOTOR DIVISION—GMC

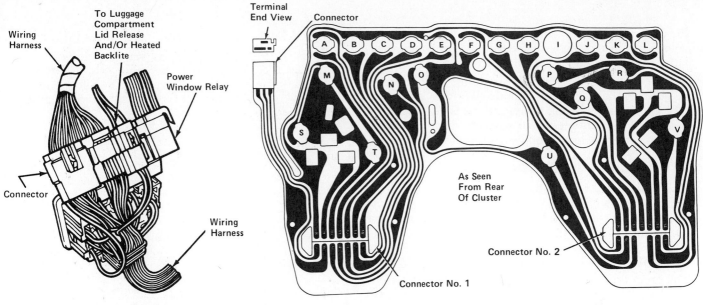

Figure 36-6. Connections from instrument panel to fuse panel. FORD MOTOR COMPANY

Figure 36-7. Printed circuit. BUICK MOTOR DIVISION—GMC

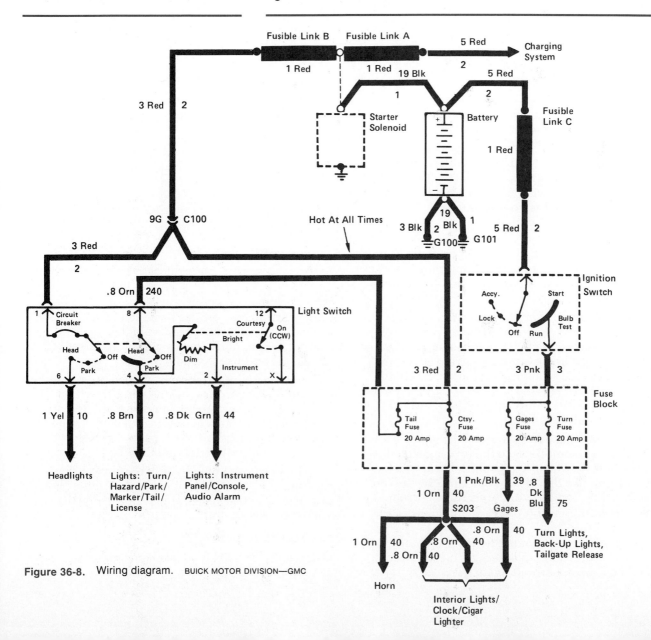

Figure 36-8. Wiring diagram. BUICK MOTOR DIVISION—GMC

for example: "pink with black stripe." Insulation colors may also be abbreviated (pnk/blk) or coded with letters (p/b). When coded with letters, a guide is included with a wiring diagram (p = pink, b = black).

Wiring diagrams may include all or only a portion of a vehicle's electrical system. Because of the complexity of vehicle electrical systems, partial wiring diagrams are easier to follow and understand.

36.2 CIRCUIT PROTECTION

The vehicle must be protected from fire hazards that occur if a powered circuit is accidentally shorted or grounded. Fuses, fusible links, and *circuit breakers* can be used to protect circuits.

Fuses and Fusible Links

The functioning of fuses and fusible links is discussed in Unit 27. Fuses and fusible links are rated by current-carrying capacity. For example, a fuse for a given circuit might be rated at 5, 10, 15, or 20 or more amperes. When more than the rated current attempts to flow, the fuse or fusible link conductor melts to open the circuit. Burned-out fuses and fusible links must be replaced. Fusible links are usually located in the engine compartment near the battery, alternator, or separate voltage regulator.

Although separate fuses also are used, main circuit fuses are usually grouped together in *fuse blocks*. Fuse blocks contain fuses, circuit breakers, *turn signal flashers,* and relays (see Figure 36-9).

Fuse blocks often are located under the dash near the headlight switch. However, fuse blocks also can be located elsewhere under the dash, in the glove compartment, or in the engine compartment.

Circuit Breaker

A circuit breaker also is a device that interrupts, or opens, a circuit when too much current flows. However, a circuit breaker does not need replacement like a fuse or fusible link.

A simple form of circuit breaker contains only a bimetallic spring and a set of contact points (see Figure 36-10). The bimetallic spring heats as current passes through it. When excessive current flows, the spring bends upward to interrupt the circuit. While the circuit is interrupted, the spring cools. When the spring has cooled sufficiently, it bends downward to complete the circuit again.

A turn signal flasher is a specialized form of circuit breaker. Current flows to the turn signal bulbs through the flasher. The turn signal flasher uses a flat bimetallic spring like that shown in Figure 36-10. The flasher alternately conducts and interrupts current to the turn signal bulbs when the turn signal switch is turned on.

Some circuit breakers must be reset by hand. A locking device must be released to close contact points and complete a circuit again.

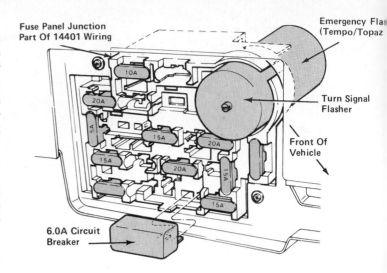

Fuse Value Amps	Color Code
4	Pink
5	Tan
10	Red
15	Light Blue
20	Yellow
25	Natural
30	Light Green

Figure 36-9. Fuse block and fuse locations.

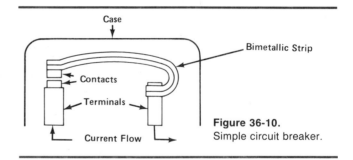

Figure 36-10. Simple circuit breaker.

36.3 RELAYS

A large current flow can be switched by a heavy-duty switch. For example, older vehicles used a foot-operated headlight dimmer switch to go from low to high beams and back.

Newer vehicles may use a small switch mounted on a *stalk,* or lever, next to the steering wheel. The small switch is connected to a relay that operates like a starter relay or solenoid (see Figure 36-11). When the small switch is operated, relay contacts close to direct a large current flow to the headlights.

Relays are used wherever high current flows are necessary. Other examples of such circuits include the starter motor, horns, and electrically operated window defroster units.

36.4 WARNING DEVICES

To alert a driver quickly to problem conditions, warning lights or sound warning devices can be used.

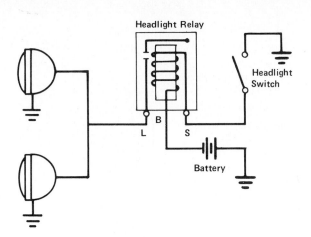

Figure 36-11. Headlight relay system.

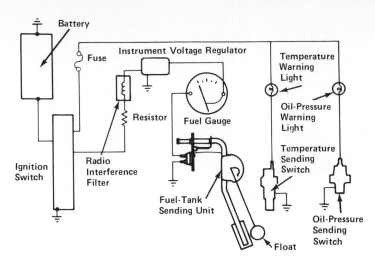

Figure 36-12. Instrument warning lights.

These devices operate only when a problem condition occurs.

Warning Lights

Warning lights are located on the dash to indicate problem conditions to a driver. Standard warning lights include:

- Overheating
- Charging
- Low oil pressure
- Brake system failure/handbrake applied
- Turn signal operation
- High-beam headlight operation.

When all monitored systems are operating normally, lights remain off. Circuits that include warning light bulbs and/or sensors are incomplete until a problem condition occurs. When a monitored system is malfunctioning, a power or ground connection is made to complete a circuit (see Figure 36-12).

Lights also may be used to warn of other problem conditions, such as burned-out bulbs and low fluid levels (Figure 36-13).

Sound Warning Devices

Buzzers or chimes are used to alert a driver to certain conditions. These can include doors that are ajar, keys left in an ignition switch, and lights left on. Figure 36-14 illustrates a tone generator system schematic and a typical location of a warning device.

Graphic Displays

Graphic displays are translucent drawings or pictures of a vehicle. Lights operate to indicate problem locations. Figure 36-15 illustrates examples of graphic warning displays.

36.5 INSTRUMENTS

Instruments, or gauges, are used to monitor vehicle systems. Instruments can indicate a relative position within a scale of values or an exact number. Those

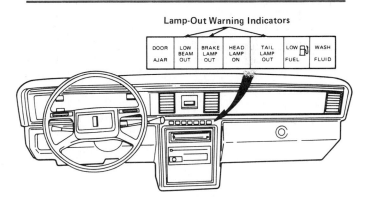

Figure 36-13. Lamp-out warning indicators.
FORD MOTOR COMPANY

that indicate a relative scale of values are known as analog instruments. Those that indicate an exact number for a measured quantity are known as digital instruments.

Gauges

Common electrical analog instruments include gauges used for:

- Fuel level
- Engine oil pressure
- Coolant temperature
- Charging system operation
- Tachometer.

Instrument Voltage Regulator

The fuel, oil pressure, and coolant temperature gauges require a stable voltage source for proper operation. An *instrument voltage regulator* is used to stabilize and limit voltage for accurate instrument operation (see Figure 36-16).

Sending Units

Sending units are devices with variable electrical resistance based on physical movement. Movement may be caused by pressure against a diaphragm, heat,

385

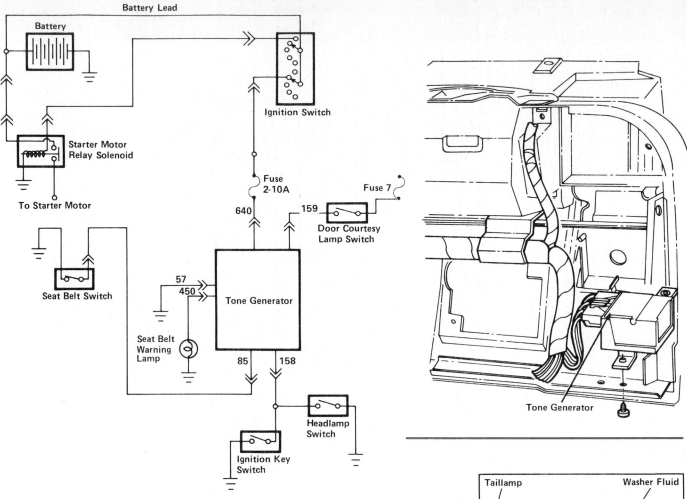

Figure 36-14. Tone generator warning system. FORD MOTOR COMPANY/GMC

or motion of a float as liquid fills a fuel tank. Two types of electrical analog gauges commonly are used with sending units:

- Magnetic
- Thermal.

Magnetic Gauges

The simplest form of a magnetic gauge is a simple ammeter. A permanent magnet attracts a ferrous indicator needle connected to a pivot point and holds it centered. An armature, or coil of wire, is wrapped around the base of the needle, near the pivot point. Current can flow through a conductor beneath the armature. (See Figure 36-17.)

When current flows, a magnetic field around the conductor induces magnetism in the armature. This magnetism opposes that of the permanent magnet. Attractive or repulsive magnetic forces cause the needle to swing left or right. The direction in which the needle swings depends on the direction of current flow in the conductor.

Balancing Coil Gauge

A *balancing coil gauge* also operates on principles of magnetic attraction and repulsion. However, no permanent magnet is used. The base of an indicating arm

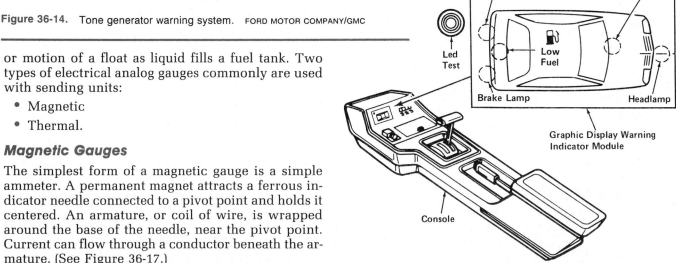

Figure 36-15. Graphic display warning system.
FORD MOTOR COMPANY

is pivoted and includes an armature. Two coils are used to create magnetic fields (see Figure 36-18).

A sending unit has a variable resistance. Electricity always follows the path of least resistance. The two coils are connected so that electricity can flow through either one. When the resistance of a sending unit is low, the right-hand coil receives more current than the left-hand coil. More magnetism is created in

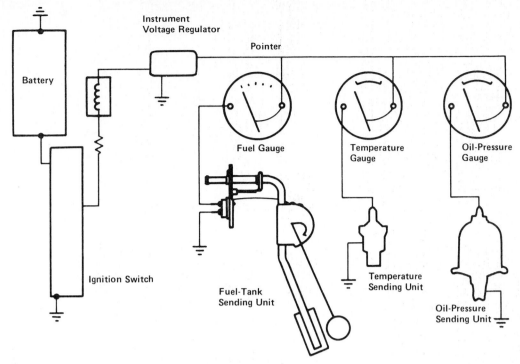

Figure 36-16. Instrument voltage regulator and gauges.

the right-hand coil, attracting the armature. Thus, a gauge needle moves to the right.

When resistance of a sending unit is high, the left-hand coil receives more current. More magnetic force is created in the left-hand coil, and a gauge needle swings to the left.

Thermal Gauge

A *thermal gauge* operates through heat created by an electrical flow (see Figure 36-19). A variable-resistance sending unit causes different amounts of current to flow through a heating coil within a gauge. The heat acts on a bimetallic spring attached to a gauge needle. When more heat is created, the needle swings farther up the scale. When less heat is created, the needle moves down the scale.

Nonelectrical Gauges

Not all instruments on a vehicle are electrical. Some gauges operate mechanically, without electrical power. Examples include:

- Speedometers
- Odometers
- Vacuum pressure gauges.

Speedometer

On most vehicles, speedometers are mechanical, not electrical, instruments. A drive cable attached to a gear in the transmission turns a magnet inside a cup-shaped metal piece (see Figure 36-20). The cup is attached to a speedometer needle and held at zero by a *hairspring,* a fine wire spring. As the cable rotates faster with increasing speed, magnetic forces act on

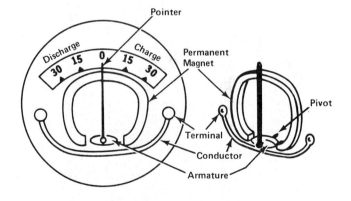

Figure 36-17. Simple ammeter.

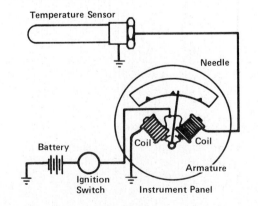

Figure 36-18. Balancing coil gauge.

387

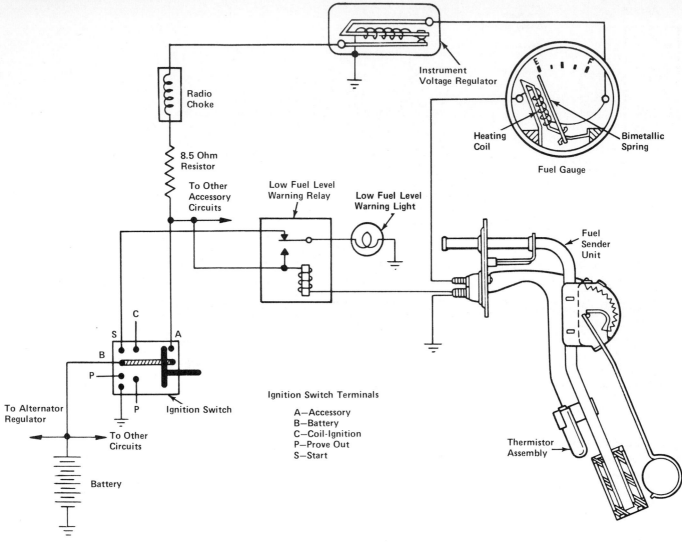

Figure 36-19. Thermal gauge.

the cup and force it to rotate. The speedometer needle, attached to the cup, moves up the speed scale.

Odometer

An *odometer* is a digital instrument that records how far a vehicle has traveled. An odometer displays numbers that indicate distance in miles or kilometers. Odometer number drums are turned by a gear arrangement driven off a speedometer cable, as shown in Figure 36-21.

Vacuum/Pressure Gauge

A vacuum/pressure gauge can be used to indicate how much manifold vacuum is present as an engine runs. Such gauges often are used as a rough indicator of fuel mileage because engine load is reflected in manifold vacuum readings.

For turbocharged engines, *boost,* or manifold pressure, can indicate when a turbocharger operates.

A vacuum/pressure gauge is operated by a *Bourdon tube.* A Bourdon tube is a flat, hollow, coiled tube.

A gauge needle is attached to the tube. A source of vacuum or pressure is connected to one end of the tube. The other end is sealed. A Bourdon tube coils or uncoils in response to vacuum or pressure, thus moving a gauge needle (see Figure 36-22).

36.6 LIGHTS

Lighting systems to improve visibility at night and to make a vehicle visible to other drivers include:

- Headlights, parking lights, and taillights
- Turn signal, cornering, and side marker lights
- Stop lights
- License plate lights
- Courtesy and convenience lights.

Headlights

Headlights are usually large, *sealed-beam bulbs* with single or double *filaments.* A sealed beam bulb is a large, *evacuated* glass lens and reflector assembly that contains a filament. Evacuated means that a vacuum

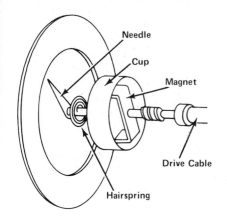

Figure 36-20. Speedometer.

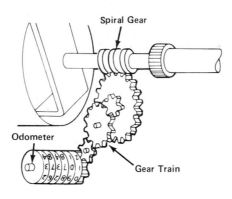

Figure 36-21. Odometer.

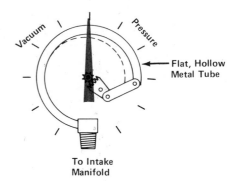

Figure 36-22. Bourdon tube gauge.

exists within a closed chamber. A filament is a metal element within a light bulb. When electricity passes through a filament, the filament becomes white-hot and thus produces light. Headlights may have one or two filaments, depending upon their use. A headlight with two filaments is used for both bright and dim operation. A single-filament lamp is used only for one mode or the other.

Halogen lights also may be used as headlights. A halogen light contains a small quartz-glass bulb, inside of which is a filament surrounded by halogen gas. The small, gas-filled bulb fits within a larger reflector and lens element. Halogen lights produce a whiter, brighter light than conventional sealed-beam headlights (see Figure 36-23).

When burned out, covers and *bezels* must be removed to replace headlight bulbs (see Figure 36-24). A bezel is a retainer around a light or instrument. Bezels may be decorative or functional. Screws or springs are used to fasten a metal retainer ring that holds a bulb.

Headlight adjusting screws are located near lights. One screw tilts the bulb upward and downward. The other tilts the bulb left and right. When bulbs are removed, care must be taken not to mistake headlight aiming screws for retaining screws. Misadjusted headlights can create poor visibility at night and/or temporarily blind drivers of oncoming vehicles.

Taillights, Turn Signal, Side Marker, and Cornering Lights

Taillights burn when the headlights are on. Taillights have replaceable bulbs that may be reached from inside the trunk or by removing a plastic lens (see Figure 36-25).

Turn signals and *side marker lights* may be separate units or combined in wrap-around plastic lenses (refer to Figure 36-24). Side marker lights are located on the sides of a vehicle so that it can be seen more easily at night. Taillights, parking lights, side marker

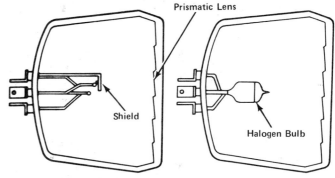

Figure 36-23. Headlights.

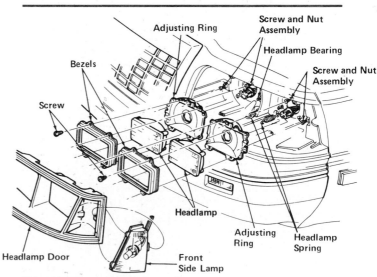

Figure 36-24. Headlamp removal.
FORD MOTOR COMPANY

lights, and license plate lights operate when headlights are turned on. *Cornering lights* burn steadily, when turn signals operate, to light up an area in the direction of a turn.

A typical parking light, side marker light, and cornering light circuit is shown in Figure 36-26.

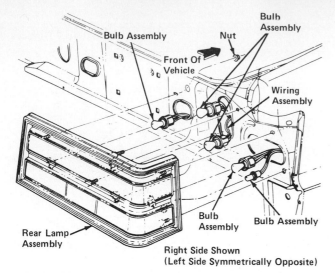

Figure 36-25. Taillights. FORD MOTOR COMPANY

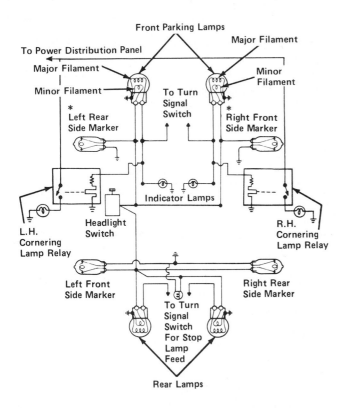

* Add cornering lamps into circuit to function with park and turn lamps when turn signal is activated.

Note: If parking lamp or taillamp has a three-wire socket, the black wire is the ground. If parking lamp or taillamp has a two-wire socket, the bulb is grounded through the lamp assembly.

Figure 36-26. Side marker circuit. FORD MOTOR COMPANY

Stop Lights

Stop lights operate when a brake pedal is pushed downward. Most late-model vehicles have motion-operated switches attached to a brake pedal (Figure 36-27). Older vehicles may have pressure-operated switches operated by brake master cylinder pressure.

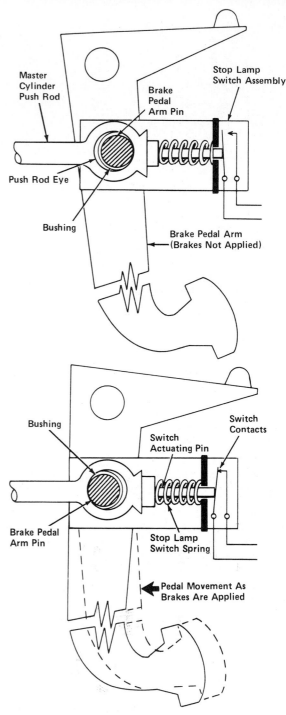

Figure 36-27. Brake pedal switch. FORD MOTOR COMPANY

Courtesy and Convenience Lights

Courtesy and convenience lights include dome and courtesy lights that light when a door is opened. A switch is held in the open position by a closed door. When the door is opened, a spring pushes the switch closed to complete the circuit to dome or courtesy lights.

Underhood and trunk lights may be operated by a *mercury switch*. A mercury switch consists of two

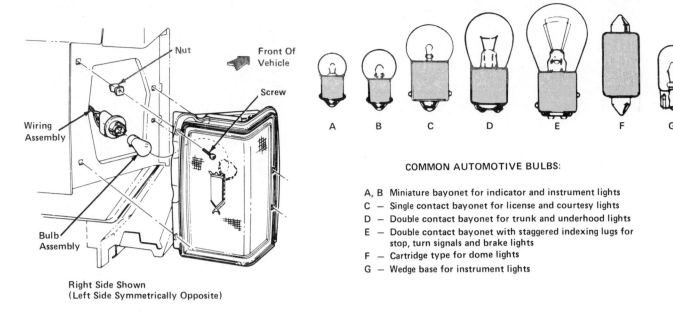

Right Side Shown
(Left Side Symmetrically Opposite)

COMMON AUTOMOTIVE BULBS:

A, B Miniature bayonet for indicator and instrument lights
C — Single contact bayonet for license and courtesy lights
D — Double contact bayonet for trunk and underhood lights
E — Double contact bayonet with staggered indexing lugs for
       stop, turn signals and brake lights
F — Cartridge type for dome lights
G — Wedge base for instrument lights

Figure 36-28. Types of bulbs and installations.

separated contacts within a glass tube that also contains liquid metal mercury. When the glass tube is tilted, mercury flows to contacts and completes a circuit. When the tube is tilted in the opposite direction, mercury flows away from the contacts and opens a circuit.

Bulbs

Bulbs fit into sockets and are held by spring tension or mechanical force (see Figure 36-28). Bulbs are coded with numbers for replacement purposes. Bulbs with different code numbers may appear physically similar but have different wattage ratings. Smaller bulbs may simply push into a socket. Most bulbs must be pushed inward and turned counterclockwise to be removed. Replacement is accomplished by pushing in and turning clockwise.

36.7 WINDSHIELD WIPER AND WASHER

Windshield wipers are powered by a small single- or multi-speed electric motor. A switch on a stalk or on the dash activates the motor. A separate plastic reservoir, motor, and pump force liquid through tubing to adjustable nozzles (see Figure 36-29). The nozzles spray liquid on the windshield to wash it. The wash and wiper functions often are combined, so that both occur when the washer is activated.

36.8 HORN

Horn switches are mounted in the steering wheels of most vehicles. Some Ford Motor Company vehicles have the horn switch mounted on a stalk (see Figure 36-30). A horn relay is part of the circuit and is usually mounted in a small, metal box in the engine compartment.

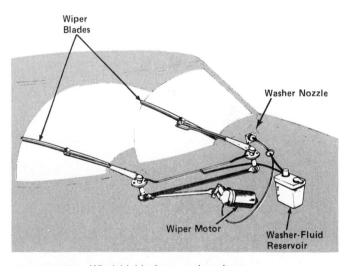

Figure 36-29. Windshield wipers and washers.
TRICO PRODUCTS CORPORATION

36.9 COMFORT ACCESSORIES

Comfort accessories are provided for the comfort and convenience of vehicle occupants. Such accessories can include:

- Power seats
- Power windows
- Electrically positioned outside mirrors
- Automatic leveling devices
- Cruise control
- Automatic headlight dimmers.

Power seats are operated by small electric motors (see Figure 36-31). Power window motor switches are

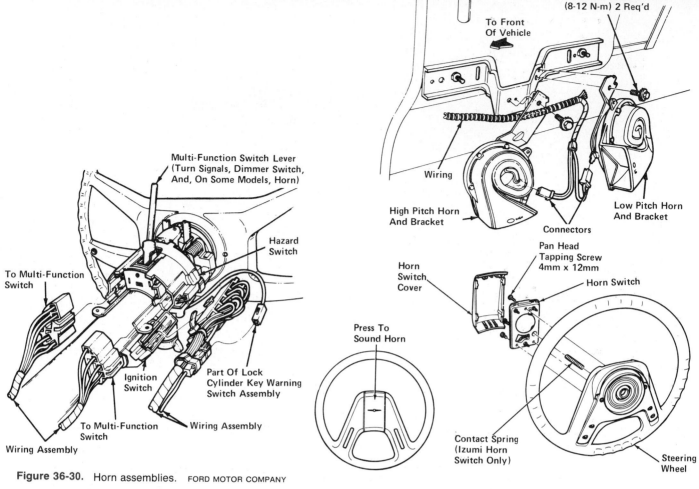

Figure 36-30. Horn assemblies. FORD MOTOR COMPANY

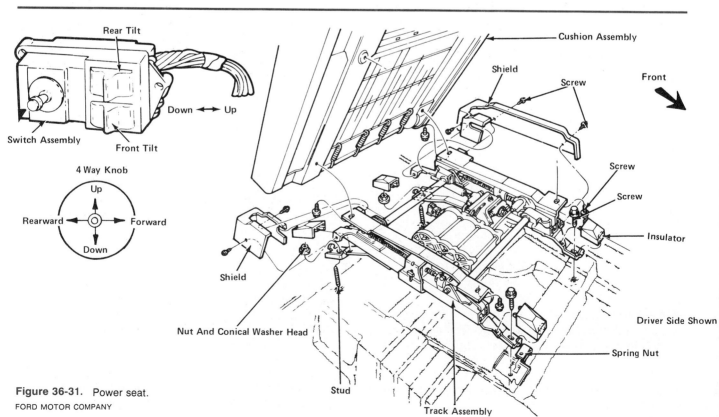

Figure 36-31. Power seat.

FORD MOTOR COMPANY

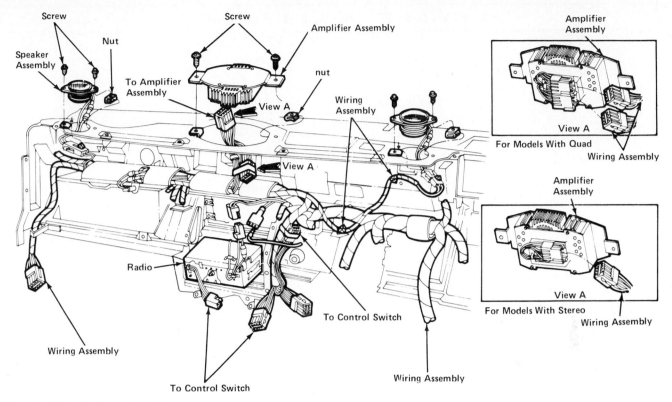

Figure 36-32. Radio and speakers. FORD MOTOR COMPANY

located at each window, with a master control near the driver.

Some devices, such as cruise control, may be electronically controlled by computer units on a vehicle. Unit 38 discusses functions of electronic devices.

Vehicle manufacturers offer many comfort accessory options. Refer to the manufacturer's service manual for information on specific vehicle systems.

36.10 AUDIO SYSTEMS

Audio systems include radios, cassette tape players, amplifiers, and speaker systems. Radios are installed in the dash, with wiring harnesses to door and rear shelf speakers (see Figure 36-32).

- Warning devices include lights, buzzers, chimes, and graphic displays.

- Most common electrical gauges are analog instruments. Sending units vary resistance to change the amount of current in a gauge circuit. Gauges can be permanent-magnet, balancing-coil, or thermal-type.

- Speedometers, odometers, and vacuum/pressure gauges are usually operated mechanically rather than electrically.

- Lights, horns, windshield wipers and washers, and many comfort and convenience accessories operate electrically.

UNIT HIGHLIGHTS

- Wiring harnesses are necessary to complete circuits in all parts of the vehicle. Wires are color-coded for identification purposes. Several units may share a common connection for power or ground.

- Circuits can be protected with fuses, fusible links, or circuit breakers. Relays are used in place of heavy-duty switches to conduct large current flows.

- A wiring diagram indicates color coding of wires and circuit connections.

TERMS

harness	**thermal gauge**
tracer	**hairspring**
printed circuit	**odometer**
wiring diagram	**boost**
circuit breaker	**Bourdon tube**
fuse block	**sealed-beam bulb**
turn signal flasher	**filament**
stalk	**evacuated**
graphic displays	**halogen light**
instrument voltage	**bezel**
regulator	**side marker light**
sending unit	**cornering light**
balancing coil gauge	**mercury switch**

DIRECTIONS: The following questions are similar to those used on mechanic certification tests. On a separate sheet of paper, write the letter of the correct choice.

1. Mechanic A says colored stripes or tracers on wire insulation indicate the size of wires.

   Mechanic B says stripes or tracers on wire insulation indicate a specific conductor.

   Who is correct?

   A. A only   B. B only   C. Both A and B   D. Neither A nor B

2. All of the following are used in vehicle electrical circuits to protect the vehicle and electrical components EXCEPT

   A. flashers.

   B. circuit breakers.

   C. fuses.

   D. fusible links.

3. All of the following are types of electrical analog instruments EXCEPT

   A. permanent-magnet ammeter.

   B. warning light.

   C. balancing-coil meter.

   D. thermal meter.

4. Which of the following statements is correct?

   I. Headlight adjusting screws are located near headlight retaining screws.

   II. Every time a headlight is replaced, it must be readjusted for correct road illumination.

   A. I only   B. II only   C. Both I and II   D. Neither I nor II

5. A vehicle's taillights are operating properly, but stop lights do not work when the brake pedal is pushed.

   What is the most likely cause?

   A. Defective headlight switch

   B. Dead battery

   C. Defective brake-light switch

   D. Ignition switch off

SUPPLEMENTAL ACTIVITIES

1. Examine and follow wiring harnesses in a vehicle. Make a simple diagram of where connectors are located. Check for color coding of wires on both sides of connectors.

2. Locate fuse blocks and turn-signal flashers on a vehicle.

3. Refer to a manufacturer's service manual for wiring diagrams of a vehicle. Trace wiring connections for headlights, taillights, radio, turn signals, horn, cigarette lighter, and windshield wipers. Make a list of the types and sizes of protective devices used for each item.

4. Locate sending units on a vehicle for warning devices or gauges for coolant temperature, oil pressure, and fuel. Make a simple diagram showing their locations and indicate color codings of connecting wires.

5. Check all exterior and interior lights, horn, and windshield wipers and washers for proper operation. Remove any burned-out bulbs and make a list of the code numbers on the bulbs.

37 ELECTRICAL SERVICE

UNIT PREVIEW

Regular checks are performed to make sure that all electrical equipment is working properly. Basic checks include visual and manual inspections of the battery, electrical units, circuit protection devices, and wiring connections.

Electrical system service includes both troubleshooting and repair procedures. Troubleshooting requires a thorough understanding of basic principles, logic, and common sense. Troubleshooting procedures can include visual inspections, use of wiring diagrams and test instruments, and testing by substitution.

The most difficult part of electrical troubleshooting or service can be gaining access to wiring and to electrical units. Wires may be run under carpeting, seats, and through body panels.

Breaks or shorts in wires can be found with special test equipment, and wires can be bypassed to make repairs.

In general, defective electrical units are replaced, not repaired.

LEARNING OBJECTIVES

When you have completed your assignments and exercises in this unit, you should be able to:

☐ Explain which electrical checks are done on a regular basis.

☐ Identify and describe techniques used in electrical troubleshooting and service.

☐ Safely remove, clean, and replace exterior light bulbs and clean bulb sockets.

☐ Safely make and solder electrical wire joints.

☐ Safely and correctly use solderless connectors and quick-splice connectors for terminating and joining wires.

☐ Remove and replace dash warning light bulbs and/or a radio unit.

SAFETY PRECAUTIONS

Accidental shorting or grounding of powered circuits can cause sparks, fires, and/or personal injury. In addition, expensive electrical or electronic components can be damaged or destroyed.

Remove and replace electrical units when no power is connected to the circuit. Make sure all switches are off before replacing electrical units.

For unfused circuits, disconnect the grounded battery terminal from the battery. After repair or replacement procedures, double-check all wiring connections before replacing the grounded terminal on the battery.

Testing procedures may require working with "live," or powered, electrical circuits. Use extreme care when working with jumper leads or test wires connected to sources of electrical power and ground. Make sure such leads do not touch each other and do not cause an accidental short or ground.

Use extreme care when working in cramped, crowded areas with many connections. Conductive metal tools can cause an accidental electrical short or ground when you are working near fuse blocks and connectors. Therefore, be sure to remove all jewelry before doing any electrical work.

37.1 PREVENTIVE MAINTENANCE

No specific preventive maintenance is done to electrical wiring and circuit protective devices. However, the battery and charging system affect the operation of all other parts of the electrical system. Battery and charging system preventive maintenance are discussed in Units 29 and 33.

Regular checks are performed to make sure that safety, lighting, and other electrical equipment are functioning properly. Common electrical units include such items as:

- Light bulbs
- Turn signal flasher units
- Electrical motors
- Horns
- Radios and audio systems
- Electrical heating elements.

Electrical units and circuit protective devices are replaced when defective.

37.2 BASIC ELECTRICAL CHECKS

To find the cause of a nonfunctioning or malfunctioning electrical unit, basic checks are done first. Basic checks include inspection of:

- Battery connections
- Battery voltage
- Electrical bulbs and units
- Circuit protection devices
- Wiring connections.

Battery Connections

The "heart" of the electrical system is the battery. If no electrical units operate, turn on headlights to check if they operate. If the headlights do not operate, attempt to wiggle and move the battery cable connections. On top terminal batteries, a thin screwdriver can be inserted between the battery terminal and the clamp. If lights and other electrical units work when these checks are done, the terminals must be removed and cleaned. Refer to Unit 29. Battery connections must be clean and fit securely for maximum current to flow in or out of the battery.

Battery Voltage

Battery voltage checks are done next to determine if sufficient battery power is available to power electrical units. Even a new battery may become discharged or damaged. Battery voltage checks are discussed in Unit 29.

Electrical Bulbs and Units

Electrical bulbs, motors, and other units can become defective. For example, a single nonworking bulb in a circuit may need replacing. An example of a single circuit with multiple bulbs is the taillight, parking light, and side-marker light circuit.

If only one bulb is not burning, remove the bulb and inspect it. Check for broken filaments. Check the brass base and bottom contacts for corrosion. Gently attempt to turn the glass element in the brass base. Replace bulbs with broken filaments or loose glass elements. Clean corrosion from the base and/or contacts, or obtain a new bulb.

Also check and/or clean the socket by scraping or using a small wire brush (see Figure 37-1). Apply a light film of grease to the connector to help reduce corrosion.

CAUTION: Make sure all light switches are off before attempting to clean a socket. Cleaning a socket with power present can ground the circuit and blow a fuse.

Circuit Protection Devices

Depending on the vehicle, several devices may be protected by one fuse, fusible link, or circuit breaker. If no devices operate in a common circuit, the most

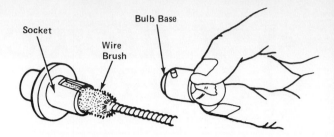

Figure 37-1. Cleaning a light socket.

likely cause is a nonconductive circuit protection device. Special tools are available for removing and replacing fuses (see Figure 37-2).

If fuses or fusible links burn out again when a switch is closed, the circuit is grounded or shorted. A grounded circuit will cause a circuit breaker to click rapidly and constantly. A grounded conductor must be repaired or bypassed, as discussed in Topic 37.5.

Wiring Connections

Inspect accessible wiring for bare spots or frayed insulation. Electrical tape can be wrapped around wires with worn insulation to insulate them. Gently push and pull on terminals and connections to see if wires are loose or disconnected.

37.3 ELECTRICAL SYSTEM SERVICE

If basic checks and repairs do not solve a problem, electrical system service is necessary. Electrical system service consists of:

- Troubleshooting
- Service and/or repair procedures.

37.4 ELECTRICAL TROUBLESHOOTING

Electrical problems can occur at any point in an electrical circuit. For example, consider the simple oil pressure warning light circuit shown in Figure 37-3. Suppose that the light fails to operate when the key switch is in the "on" position, engine off. The problem could be at any of the following points in the circuit:

- Battery plates or internal connections
- Battery positive connection or cable
- Wire from battery positive to junction block
- Junction block
- Wire from junction block to ignition switch
- Ignition switch
- Wire from ignition switch to indicator lamp
- Indicator lamp socket
- Indicator bulb
- Wire to oil pressure switch
- Connector terminal on wire
- Oil pressure switch
- Engine ground
- Battery ground connection or cable.

Troubleshooting involves thinking and checking until a trouble source is found. The more knowledge and

Figure 37-2. Fuse puller and replacer.

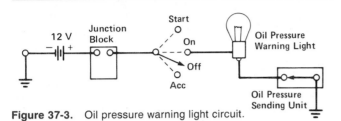

Figure 37-3. Oil pressure warning light circuit.

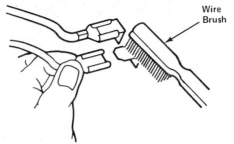

Figure 37-4. Cleaning a terminal and connection.

experience a mechanic has, the more rapidly and easily a problem can be found and fixed. Electrical system troubleshooting can involve:

- Thorough basic knowledge of electricity
- Visual inspection
- Use of wiring diagrams
- Logical approach
- Use of test instruments
- Testing by substitution.

Basic Knowledge of Electricity

Electrical and electronic fundamentals are discussed in Unit 27. Knowledge of how series, parallel, and series-parallel circuits operate is necessary to troubleshoot interconnected circuits.

Basic causes of electrical problems include opens, shorts, and grounds. Opens can be caused by circuit protection devices, burned-out electrical units, or disconnected wiring. Shorts and grounds can be caused by physical damage to wires or incorrect connections.

Inspection

Before proceeding to more complicated troubleshooting, make a thorough inspection for obvious problems. Burned-out bulbs and disconnected wires are obvious when found.

It is estimated that more than 90 percent of all "electrical problems" are not electrical, but mechanical. That is, most of these problems involve loose or dirty connections, not defects in electrical parts.

In some cases, pulling a connector apart and reconnecting it may restore an electrical circuit. Light scraping and/or polishing of electrical contacts may be necessary to restore a corroded connection (see Figure 37-4). Use your eyes and hands to find simple problems. If wires are bundled into harnesses, it may be necessary to trace them with the help of an electrical diagram.

Use of Wiring Diagrams

The use and importance of wiring diagrams are discussed in Unit 36. When attempting troubleshooting, such wiring diagrams can be a valuable help in tracing circuit conductors and interconnections. Small diagrams may require the use of a magnifying glass and a ruler to trace specific circuits. In some cases, a wire of one color may be connected to another color of wire at a *junction block* or plug-in connector.

A junction block is an area where common wire connections are made. A junction block usually consists of a plastic base with metal terminals and connectors. Wires run from remote locations to common junction block connections, then continue. A fuse block is a junction block that includes circuit protection devices in addition to common connections.

Common connections can be confusing when you are trying to find defects. A wiring diagram may be necessary to find the ultimate source of a problem.

Logical Approach

In order to find the cause of a problem, it is necessary to approach the problem logically. As mentioned above, if only one bulb in a common circuit is out, the cause is most likely in the bulb itself. If all bulbs are out, the problem is most likely in a circuit protection device.

However, it is necessary to separate problems and the reasons for those problems. In the following example, the problem is that the vehicle's parking lights are not working. The chart is an example of cause-and-effect diagnosis in a step-by-step format:

Problem (effect)	Reason (cause)
No parking lights	Burned-out fuse
Burned-out fuse	Grounded wire
Grounded wire	Physical damage to wire in trunk
Physical damage to wire in trunk	Loose jack in trunk

Cause-and-effect diagnosis thus identified an unlikely cause to the parking light failure: A jack had not been secured after a tire was changed. To fix electrical or other problems, it often is necessary to find the underlying cause.

Consider the circuit example in Figure 37-3. A logical approach to determining why the light does not work would be to eliminate the least likely possibilities.

If other electrical parts of the vehicle function properly, the battery and its connections can be eliminated. The next check would be to find if other circuits with a common power connection operate. That is, are other circuits that draw power from the same terminal of the ignition switch operating? If such circuits work properly, all connections up to and including the switch terminal can be eliminated.

Another logical step is to consider the probability of failure for given parts. For example, it is well known that oil-pressure sending units fail more often than light bulbs used for warning systems. Thus, it would be more logical to look for a problem at the sending unit than at the dash light.

The next step would be to check the most accessible parts of the system. In the warning-light system above, these parts would be the oil-pressure sender and connecting wire on the engine. Parts most difficult to access are checked and/or repaired last. Removal of dash and/or instrument panel parts for dash light access would be done last. Thus, logic and common sense are used to find and fix the problem in the quickest, easiest way.

Use of Test Instruments

Most electrical problems can be found with a simple *unpowered test light* and *jumper wires* (see Figure 37-5). An unpowered test light contains a small bulb that will light when connected to power and ground. Jumper wires are wires used to "jump over" existing wiring and make connections.

Other electrical instruments such as voltmeters and ohmmeters can be used to measure voltage drops and resistance.

Unpowered test lights can be used to check for power or ground. One contact of the test light bulb is connected to a wire and a clip. The other contact of the

bulb is connected to a sharp, ice pick-like probe. The probe can be used to scratch through corrosion or paint to make a good connection. If sharp enough, the probe can also be lightly pushed through insulation to make contact with a wire conductor.

If the clip is attached to ground and the probe touched to a source of power, the bulb will light. If the connections are reversed, the bulb will light when ground is touched. Thus, the test light can be used to find or confirm a source of power or a good ground (see Figure 37-6).

If an electrical unit has a source of both adequate power and ground, it should operate. If not, the unit itself may be defective.

Jumper wires can be used to connect a unit to a known source of power and/or ground. This is done to determine whether the problem lies in the unit itself (see Figure 37-7). In some cases, wiring or connectors may be faulty. If a unit operates when connected with jumper wires, the problem is in a connection, not in the unit.

Voltmeters and ohmmeters can be used to determine resistance in conductors and/or electrical units. Excessive voltage drops indicate excessive resistance. Excessive resistance can be checked directly with an ohmmeter.

CAUTION: Using an ohmmeter on a powered circuit will destroy the ohmmeter. Disconnect the grounded battery terminal to prevent damage when performing resistance checks with an ohmmeter.

Testing by Substitution

After simple checks have been made, testing by substitution can be used to determine if an electrical unit is defective. A unit that works can be substituted for one that does not. If the substitute unit functions properly, the problem is in the old unit. This approach often works when other checks indicate connections are all correct but a unit still does not function.

Testing by substitution can have drawbacks. Electrical parts are not returnable. If a substitute unit does

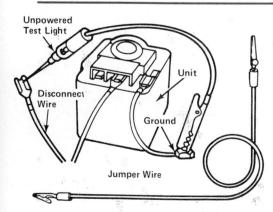

Figure 37-5. Unpowered test light and jumper wires.

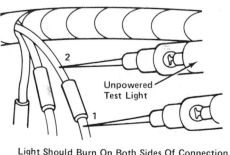

Light Should Burn On Both Sides Of Connection

Figure 37-6. Using a test light.

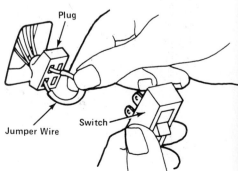

Figure 37-7. Using a small jumper.

not function, money is wasted. In addition, an improper connection that damaged an existing unit can also damage a substitute unit.

However, if other methods fail, testing by substitution may be the simplest and quickest way to determine if a unit is defective.

37.5 ELECTRICAL SERVICE

The main difficulty in performing electrical service is gaining access to wiring and electrical units. During assembly, wiring harnesses and many electrical units are installed before the dash, seats, carpeting, headliner, and upholstery are fitted. Thus, wiring harnesses, connectors, and electrical units may be in areas that are accessible only if many parts are removed. Such removal can increase the cost of a simple repair greatly. For wiring under carpets and panels, other service techniques are available.

Gaining Access to Wiring and Electrical Units

It may be necessary to remove air conditioning units, radios, dash pads, and many other parts to locate problems. Such work is often more difficult than the actual troubleshooting or electrical repair necessary.

Wiring harnesses in the area of the fuse block contain many tightly bundled wires. On older vehicles, wiring harnesses were formed by wrapping wires with electrical tape. Newer vehicles also may use removable plastic sleeves to contain, protect, and bundle wires (see Figure 37-8).

Replacement Wiring

In many cases, it is not practical to inspect nonconductive wiring that runs beneath carpeting and inside body panels. Special test instruments, called *short finders,* are available to pinpoint the location of shorted or grounded wires in such locations.

Short finders induce current in a wire through induction. A powered coil within the short finder can induce current in a conductor. An inductive ammeter detects this current. At a point where a wire is broken or shorted, no electrical energy is present. The short finder indicates this point with a meter and/or buzzer (see Figure 37-9).

The quickest and simplest way to replace a wire in an inaccessible location is to physically bypass the wire. *Bypass wiring,* or jumper wiring, is used to replace physically inaccessible defective wires.

A defective wire is cut at both ends. A jumper, or replacement, wire of the correct size is *spliced* on the cut ends. Splicing means joining. There are three common types of joints: pigtail, T-type, and Western Union (see Figure 37-10).

Splicing and Terminating Wires

The most permanent way of joining electrical wires is by soldering. A heated soldering iron is used to apply heat to wires. The heated wires melt solder, which flows to form an electrically conductive and physically secure joint (see Figure 37-11). After soldering,

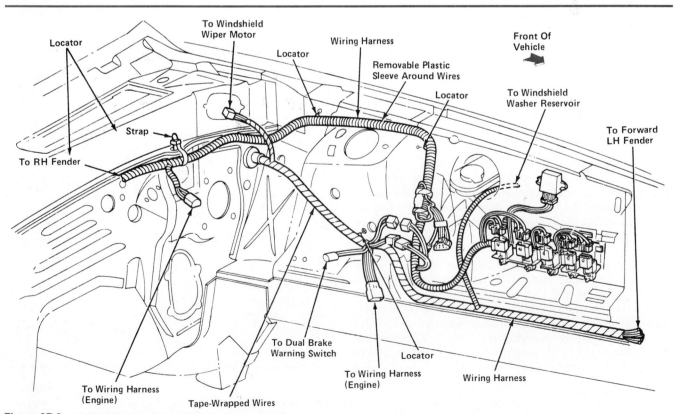

Figure 37-8. Engine compartment wiring. FORD MOTOR COMPANY

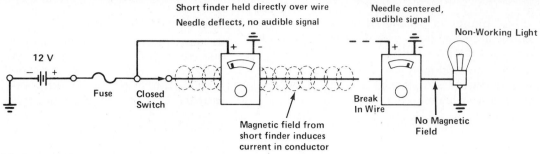

Figure 37-9. Short finder operation.

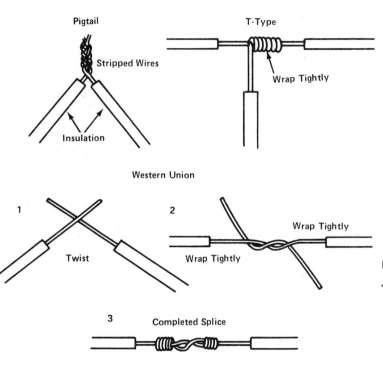

Figure 37-10. Types of wire joints.

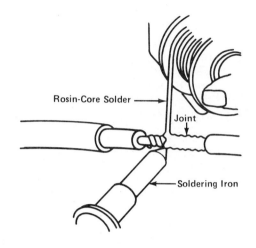

Figure 37-11. Soldering procedure.

joints are insulated by wrapping them securely with electrical tape.

SAFETY CAUTION: **Soldering irons in use and molten solder are extremely hot, and can cause serious burns. In addition, the solder may contain harmful acid. Wear eye and face protection when soldering.**

Solderless connectors are hollow, tubular metal parts covered with insulating plastic. The terminals may be at the end of a wire, or in a splice. *Stripped,* or bare, wire conductors are inserted into a connector. The connector is then *crimped,* or deformed, to hold the wire securely (see Figure 37-12). *Quick-splice connectors* also can be used to quickly splice or tap into wires. A quick-splice connector is a device specifically intended for making quick, easy splices.

Electrical current bypasses the nonconductive wire and flows through the new wire (see Figure

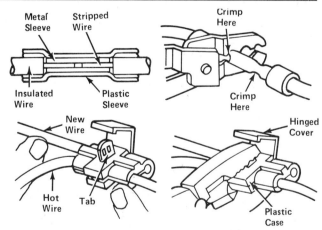

Figure 37-12. Crimped connectors.

37-13). Such replacement may involve running a jumper wire under the floor of the vehicle. Replacement wiring must be of sufficient size to carry current expected in a circuit, as illustrated in Figure 37-14.

Removing and Replacing Defective Units

Although some electrical units can be repaired, in most cases replacement is recommended. For service procedures, any electrical device can be considered as

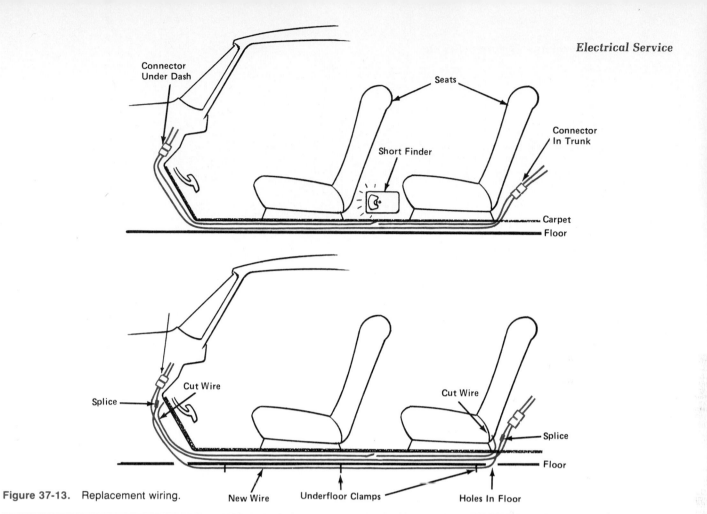

Figure 37-13. Replacement wiring.

Suggested AWG Cable Size 12 V				METRIC SIZE	AWG SIZE
Ammeter to Fuse Block	12	Heater to Fuse Block	16	.22	24
Ammeter to Switch	14	Horn Button Circuit	16	.35	22
Back Up Lights	18	Horn to Relay and Battery	12	.5	20
Battery to Ammeter	12	Ignition Switch Feed	12	.8	18
Battery to Fender Ground	14	Instrument Lamps/Sending		1.0	16
Cigar Lighter	14	Units	18	2.0	14
Coil Wire (Low Tension)	16	Interior Lights	18	3.0	12
Dome Light	16	Light Switch to Relay		5.0	10
Directional Signals	16	or Fuse	18	8.0	8
Fuel Gauge	18	Marker (Fender) Lights	18	13.0	6
Fuse Lights	See Note	Parking Lights	18	19.0	4
Generator/Alternator		Radio to Ammeter or Fuse	18	32.0	2
to Regulator	16	Taillights	18		
Generator/Alternator		Stop Lights	18		
to Starter Relay	12	Windshield Wiper and Washer	16		
Headlight Circuit	16	High Tension Spark Plug			
Headlight Relay	12	and Coil Wire	7 mm		
			Suppression Cable		

Note: For fuse links
    Where circuit is 10 gauge, use 14 gauge for fuse link.
    Where circuit is 14 gauge, use 18 gauge for fuse link.
  Fuse links are usually 4 gauges smaller than circuit in which they are found.

Figure 37-14. Replacement wiring sizes. BUICK MOTOR DIVISION—GMC

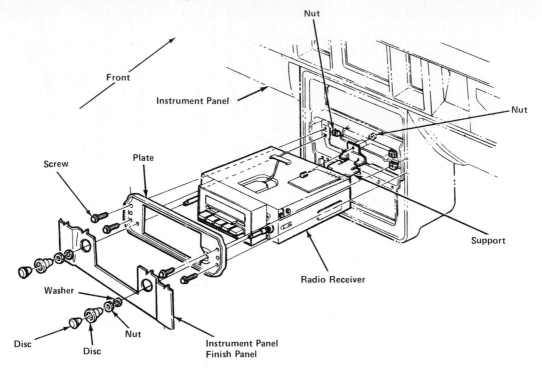

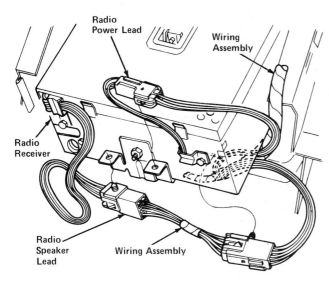

Figure 37-15. Radio replacement. FORD MOTOR COMPANY

a replaceable unit, regardless of function. Unit replacement of a radio is illustrated in Figure 37-15.

Electrical power to the unit is shut off. If battery power is not controlled by a switch, a fuse or circuit breaker can often be removed. If a circuit is not fused, as some safety systems are not, the battery must be disconnected.

SAFETY CAUTION: Disconnect the grounded battery cable to avoid sparks, shocks, and damage to electrical units. Reconnect the battery grounded cable after all wiring connections have been made and double-checked.

UNIT HIGHLIGHTS

- Regular checks are done to make sure that lighting, safety, and other electrical equipment are working properly.
- Basic checks include inspection of the battery, electrical units, circuit protection devices, and wiring connections.
- Electrical system service includes troubleshooting and repair procedures. Troubleshooting requires a thorough understanding of basic principles, logic, and common sense.
- Electrical system troubleshooting procedures can include visual inspections, use of wiring diagrams and test instruments, and testing by substitution.
- Gaining access to wiring and to electrical units can be the most difficult part of electrical system repair procedures. Breaks or shorts in wires can be found with special test equipment, and wires can be bypassed.
- In most cases, electrical units are replaced, not repaired.

TERMS

junction block

unpowered test light

jumper wire

short finder

bypass wiring

splice

solderless connector

strip

crimp

quick-splice connector

DIRECTIONS: The following questions are similar to those used on mechanic certification tests. On a separate sheet of paper, write the letter of the correct choice.

1. Basic checks to determine the cause of electrical problems include checks of all the following EXCEPT
A. voltage drop across an electrical unit.
B. battery and connections.
C. wiring connections and electrical units.
D. circuit protection devices.

2. Two taillight bulbs do not burn in a common circuit with a total of eight bulbs. What should be checked first?
A. Fuse
B. Bulbs
C. Sockets
D. Wiring

3. A fuse appears to be good, but a circuit has no power. A test light's wire is connected to a good ground. The probe of the test light is touched alternately to one end of the fuse and the other. The test light burns when touched to one end of the fuse but not when touched to the other end.
   What is wrong?
A. Resistance of bulb in test light too high
B. Nonconductive fuse
C. Defective wiring from fuse to circuit
D. Dead battery

4. Which of the following should be done last?
A. Check battery
B. Replace bulb
C. Replace fuse
D. Replace wiring

5. Which of the following statements is correct?
   I. Electrical troubleshooting requires knowledge, logic, and common sense.
   II. Electrical troubleshooting is done when simple checks do not locate the cause of a problem.
A. A only   B. B only   C. Both A and B   D. Neither A nor B

S U P P L E M E N T A L   A C T I V I T I E S

1. Remove all exterior light bulbs from a vehicle, one at a time. Inspect and clean bulb contacts and safely clean all socket connections.
2. Locate the fuse block of a vehicle. Use a test light to check both ends of all fuses for power. Replace any defective fuses found.
3. Strip lengths of wire and make neat examples of T-type, pigtail, and Western Union joints. Safely and correctly solder the joints.
4. Strip lengths of wire and use solderless connectors and quick-splice connectors to terminate and splice wires.
5. Refer to the manufacturer's service manual for procedures to remove and replace dash light bulbs and a radio unit. Safely and properly perform the procedures on a vehicle.

38 ELECTRONIC DEVICES

UNIT PREVIEW

Electronic devices can monitor and/or control virtually all of an automobile's major parts and systems. Display devices alert the driver to problems. Electronic computers can operate mechanisms and devices that control vehicle functions. Because they operate so quickly and precisely, electronic devices are the best and least expensive way to control complicated vehicle functions.

LEARNING OBJECTIVES

When you have completed your assignments and exercises in this unit, you should be able to:

☐ Describe how electronic displays can be used in warning systems.

☐ Identify parts of a speed-control system.

☐ Explain how a basic feedback-control system operates.

☐ Describe the difference between closed-loop and open-loop computer modes.

☐ Identify vehicle systems that use electronic controls.

38.1 AUTOMOTIVE ELECTRONICS

Many electronic devices are used on modern automobiles. They can be broken down into two general groups: those that present information and those that control vehicle functions.

Warning and Indication Systems

Electronic circuits and *display devices* can be used in place of conventional gauges to present information (see Figure 38-1). When information is presented as digits, or numbers, it is known as *digital* information.

A conventional fuel gauge needle moves up or down a scale, from E to F. A sending unit, or *sensor,* sends an electrical signal to the gauge based upon the amount of fuel in the tank. Such a conventional type of instrument is an *analog* display device.

More complicated information can be presented in other forms. For example, a warning device that plays or creates a message in human language can be used. Such a *voice warning device* is shown at the bottom left of Figure 38-2. When a door is ajar or the ignition key is left in the lock, a message is played to

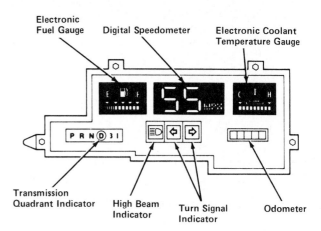

Figure 38-1. Digital dashboard display. FORD MOTOR COMPANY

alert the driver. More sophisticated units have *voice simulators* that produce language sounds to form sentences and warnings.

Parts for display and voice warning devices are not available separately. If defective, the device must be replaced as a unit.

Computers

Facts, or *data,* gathered by sensors also can be added to other data, used in mathematical calculations, or used as is. A *computer* is a device that *processes,* or changes, raw data into useful information. The processing is directed by a set of instructions in the computer known as a *program.* Computers receive and process data, and deliver information in the form of electrical signals, or discharges of electrical current.

The human brain can be thought of as an extremely complicated and sophisticated form of computer. It processes many types of data rapidly.

When you are driving down the street and see a red light at an intersection, you step on the brakes and bring the vehicle to a safe stop. Information (red light ahead) is gathered by your eyes and sent to your brain. Your brain then processes this data, based on your memory (your "programming"). The result is a signal to the muscles in your legs and feet to push down on the brake pedal.

An automotive example of this is an electronic engine control system that uses a microprocessor or computer. As the automobile is driven at a steady speed, the ignition timing also is fairly steady. As the accelerator is depressed, the manifold pressure

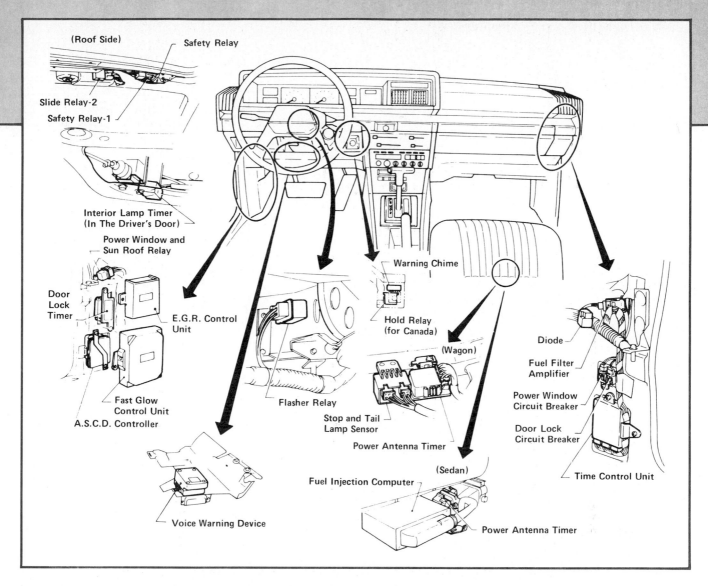

Figure 38-2. Electronic devices. NISSAN MOTOR COMPANY

sensor detects a drop in vacuum. The sensor sends an electrical signal to the computer, telling the computer that the vacuum is dropping. The computer is programmed to respond to this message by sending a signal to retard the ignition.

An automotive trip computer can receive data about fuel level, fuel usage, vehicle speed, and distance to a destination. The trip computer processes these *inputs*, or data units. The results, or *outputs* of the processing are displayed for driver use. For example, a trip computer can compute and display a fuel consumption figure in miles per gallon, or an estimated time of arrival. Using such information, the driver can determine how to drive for best fuel economy or an early arrival time. Figure 38-3 shows a trip computer and related parts.

38.2 CONTROL SYSTEMS

Computers can also be used to control vehicle functions. The data from various sensors is processed to produce an output signal. The output signal is used to operate switches, motors, solenoids or other *output devices* to control vehicle functions. The main parts of a basic computer control system are:

- Input sensors
- Computer processing unit
- Output devices
- Wiring connections.

The computer receives inputs from sensors located at various parts of the vehicle. One type of sensor is shown in Figure 38-4. The computer output operates devices to control various functions. An *output device*, or actuator, for a cruise control system is shown in Figure 38-5.

An automotive computer can be thought of as a *"black box,"* as shown in Figure 38-6. If a given input signal is presented to the computer, it should produce a certain output. The "black box" simply processes the input and produces an output. It is not necessary for a mechanic to fully understand the inner parts and

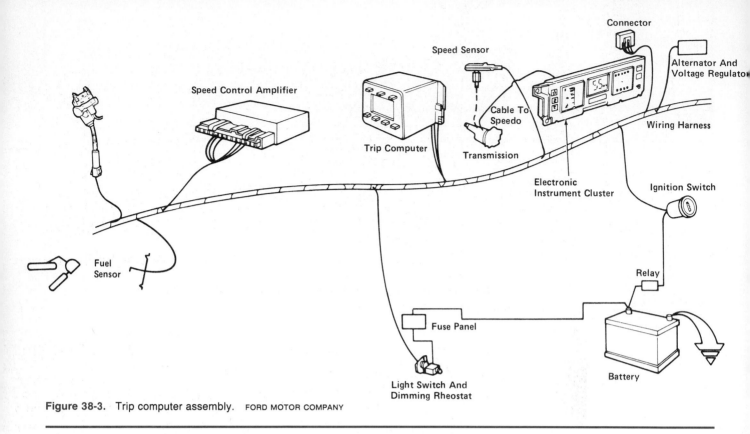

Figure 38-3. Trip computer assembly. FORD MOTOR COMPANY

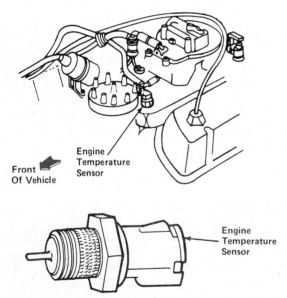

Figure 38-4. Engine temperature sensor. FORD MOTOR COMPANY

functions of the computer. The mechanic needs only to be able to determine if the unit is working properly.

Test procedures for particular computer processing units, or *modules,* are given in manufacturers' service manuals. With a given input signal, the computer should produce a certain output signal. If not, the unit is defective.

In most cases, computer modules are not serviceable. If a computer module is defective, it must be replaced as a unit. A typical computer module is shown in Figure 38-7.

Feedback Control

Computers, sensors, and output devices can be connected to monitor and adjust vehicle functions continuously. For example, a cruise control unit can maintain a set speed. When vehicle speed falls below the set speed, the computer output signal operates a *servomechanism,* or output device, to move the throttle linkage. The servo, or servomechanism, opens the throttle to increase vehicle speed. When the set speed is reached, the servo eases off the throttle. The speed control unit continuously monitors and adjusts vehicle speed.

A block diagram of such an arrangement, known as *feedback control,* is shown in Figure 38-8. Feedback control means that data concerning the effects of the computer's output are fed back into the computer as input signals.

These input data are compared to a set value, such as the speed selected on a cruise control. If the input data do not match the selected speed, the computer changes the output signal. The servo moves the throttle linkage. The sensor reports the new speed. The input data are compared again to the set speed. The output signal is changed until vehicle speed matches the selected speed.

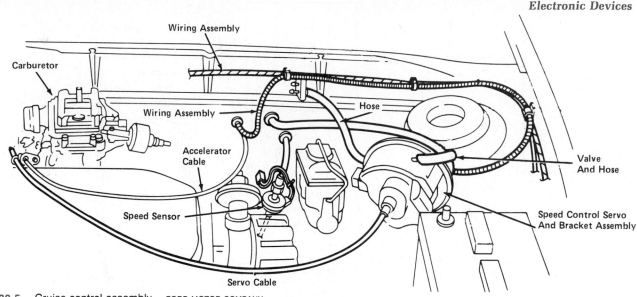

Figure 38-5. Cruise control assembly. FORD MOTOR COMPANY

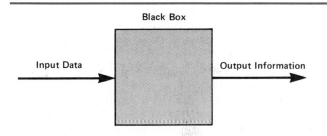

Figure 38-6. A black box, or computer, receives inputs, processes them, and produces usable outputs.

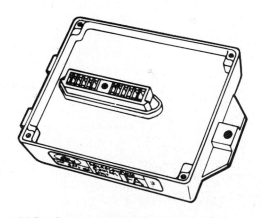

Figure 38-7. Computer processing control unit. FORD MOTOR COMPANY

The computer receives a constant flow of data about the process being controlled. The computer compares the input data to a set figure in its memory. The computer then changes its output. Whenever the process being controlled changes, the computer changes the output to bring everything back into line. This type of feedback control is also known as a *closed-loop* mode of operation. In Figure 38-8, the line starting at 1 and returning at 4 forms a closed, or continuous, loop.

Engine Controls

A more important and necessary use of electronic controls is for engine operation. Automobiles must offer better fuel economy and improved emissions controls in each new model year. Electronic controls react quicker and more precisely than the mechanical controls used in the past. Another significant advantage of electronic controls is that they do not wear out.

Since electricity travels at the speed of light (approximately 186,000 miles [299,330 km] per second), electronic controls operate rapidly. In addition, the mass production of *integrated circuits* has brought the cost of electronic controls to a reasonable level. An integrated circuit, or IC, contains many thousands of miniaturized electronic components, such as resistors, capacitors, and transistors. Using sensors, computer modules, and output devices in feedback-controlled circuits, it is possible to accurately control an engine's operation.

Closed-loop systems. The two main areas of engine control at present are ignition timing and air-fuel ratio. Figure 38-9 shows the parts of a closed-loop system for adjusting carburetor air-fuel ratio. An electronic ignition control system is in Figure 38-10.

By adjusting ignition timing and air-fuel ratio precisely for running conditions, the vehicle can be made to run very efficiently. The vehicle will start easily, run well, have good power and acceleration, and deliver good fuel economy. In addition, the combustion process can be adjusted so that the vehicle's exhaust gases are less harmful.

Open-loop systems. For starting, warm-up, and hard acceleration, the engine needs a steady air-fuel ratio richer than 14.7:1. The closed-loop system that continually adjusts air-fuel mixture is not needed. For warm-up and hard acceleration, the computer can be directed to provide *open-loop* operation. In open-loop

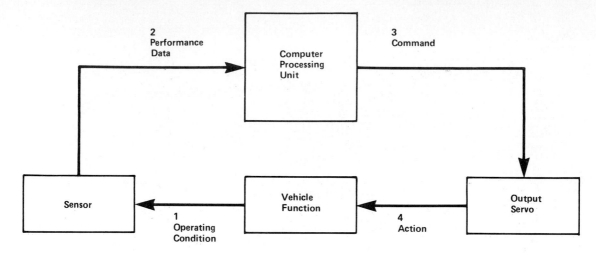

Figure 38-8. Closed-loop feedback control.

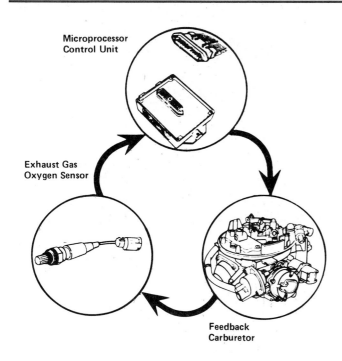

Figure 38-9. Closed-loop fuel control. FORD MOTOR COMPANY

operation, the computer does not continually monitor and adjust the air-fuel ratio. It simply provides a constant, rich mixture for smooth engine operation during warm-up and hard acceleration. After the engine warms up or the driver stops pushing hard on the accelerator pedal, the system returns to closed-loop operation. An open-loop mode for a fuel supply system is shown in Figure 38-11. The line connecting the oxygen sensor, control module, and feedback carburetor does not form a closed loop. The loop is open.

Emission Controls

The ideal, or *stoichiometric,* air-fuel ratio of 14.7 to 1 is also ideal for reducing harmful exhaust gas emissions. By using electronic controls, the exhaust gases, or emissions, can be made less harmful.

To monitor the air after the engine is warmed up, an exhaust gas *oxygen sensor* is used. An oxygen sensor is a device that detects the amount of oxygen in the exhaust gases. The oxygen sensor, illustrated in Figure 38-12, is screwed into the exhaust manifold or header pipe.

Carbon monoxide results from incomplete burning of fuel. Exhaust gases containing high amounts of carbon monoxide also contain much unburned fuel. The unburned fuel is a major cause of air pollution. The oxygen sensor sends an input signal to the computer module based upon how much oxygen is present.

The computer output signal is sent to a special feedback carburetor. After the engine warms up, the exhaust gases are sampled continuously, and the carburetor air-fuel mixture is adjusted continuously. The air-fuel mixture stays at, or very near, 14.7:1.

Several emission control devices directly affect the amount of other harmful gases in vehicle exhausts. Typical locations for these devices are shown in Figure 38-13. Some of these devices are used to provide input data or affect the combustion process. Electronic controls are used to monitor or control these emission control devices. Emission control devices are covered in more detail in Unit 42.

38.3 SELF DIAGNOSTICS

Computers located in, or on board, the vehicle also can be used to store data or information about vehicle operation. For example, the computer can store information codes about vehicle malfunctions. When proper electrical test connections are made, the computer will flash the dashboard "CHECK ENGINE" light in a coded sequence. See Figure 38-14. Flashes separated by pauses indicate numbers. One flash, followed by a pause, and then two more flashes, indicate a code 12 malfunction. Manufacturer's service manuals list the problems indicated by the code numbers. Vehicles with trip computers often use the trip computer display to show trouble code numbers during test procedures.

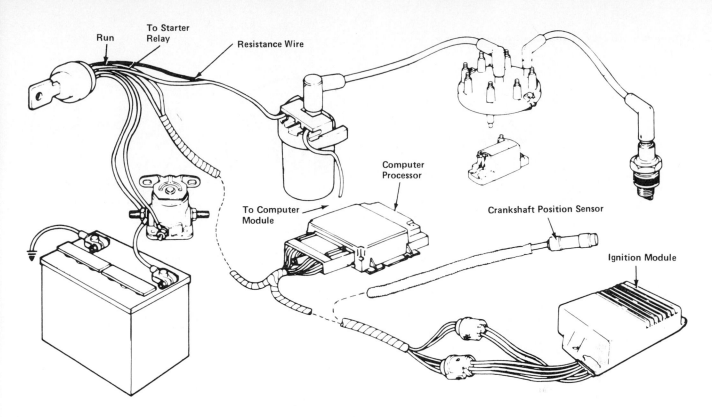

Figure 38-10. Solid-state ignition system. FORD MOTOR COMPANY

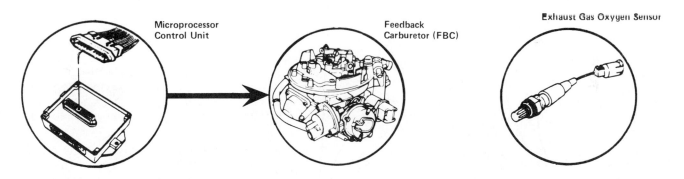

Figure 38-11. Open-loop fuel control. FORD MOTOR COMPANY

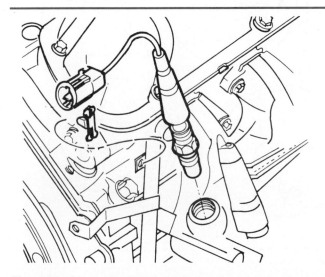

Figure 38-12. Oxygen sensor assembly. FORD MOTOR COMPANY

38.4 OTHER USES OF ELECTRONIC CONTROLS

Electronic controls can be used to control virtually every area of vehicle operation. Beginning in the early 1980s, computer controls were applied to shift automatic transmissions for better mileage and lower exhaust emissions.

Late-model Lincoln Continentals use a computer-controlled suspension system to control vehicle ride height. At low speeds, the vehicle rides at a normal height. At higher speeds, the vehicle lowers automatically to provide better aerodynamics and handling, and to increase fuel economy.

In the mid-1980s, Buick introduced computer-controlled systems for fuel injection and distributorless ignition to provide better performance with low exhaust emissions.

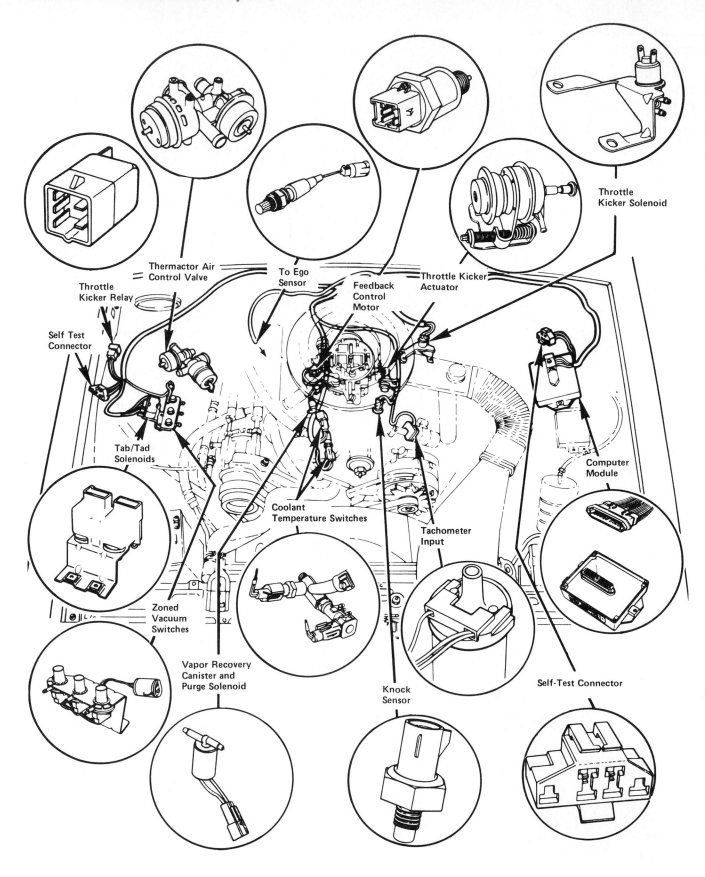

Figure 38-13. Emission control device locations. FORD MOTOR COMPANY

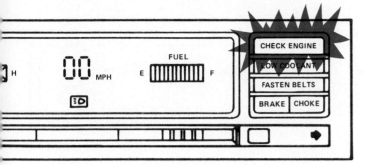

Figure 38-14. Dashboard computer code readout.

The Conquest, first imported for Plymouth and Dodge dealers in 1984, has an electronically controlled anti-skid braking system. See Figure 38-15. The computer monitors the rotation of the wheels and reduces braking force when skidding is detected.

Computer controls have been used by Toyota and Nissan of Japan to control shock absorber stiffness. Other companies have experimented with computer-controlled power steering systems.

The future uses of electronic controls are unlimited. For example, Porsche of Germany has experimented with electronically controlled accelerator linkage. The accelerator pedal in such a system is connected to an electrical sensor unit. The computer processes the input signal and sends an output signal to a solenoid or stepper motor on the fuel-injection system. Since 1982, Rolls-Royce of England has produced vehicles with a similar system for brake-pedal operation.

U N I T   H I G H L I G H T S

- Automotive electronics can be used to display data or information or control vehicle functions.
- A computer is a device that processes data, or facts, into usable information.
- A computer can be thought of as a "black box" that produces a certain output from a given input.
- A basic computer control system consists of input sensors, a computer processing unit, and output devices.
- Computers can store data and/or information about vehicle malfunctions.
- Electronic controls can be used to monitor or control virtually all vehicle functions.

T E R M S

display device	output
digital	output device
sensor	black box
analog	module
voice warning device	servomechanism
voice simulator	feedback control
data	closed-loop
computer	integrated circuit
process	open-loop
program	stoichiometric
input	oxygen sensor

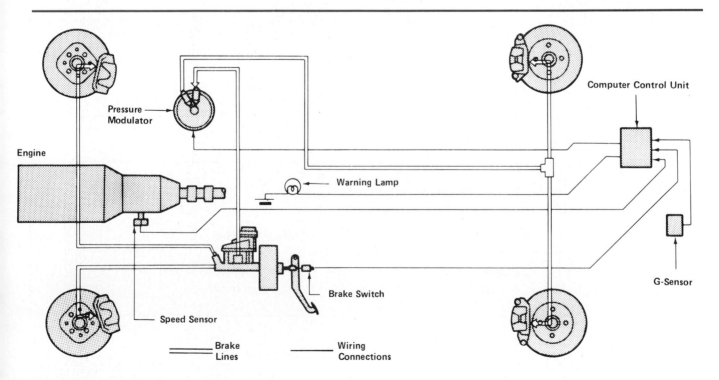

Figure 38-15. Anti-skid braking system. CHRYSLER CORPORATION

R E V I E W   Q U E S T I O N S

DIRECTIONS: The following questions are similar to those used on mechanic certification tests. On a separate sheet of paper, write the letter of the correct choice.

1. Which of the following statements is correct?

   I. Automotive electronics can be used to operate gauges or warning devices.

   II. Automotive electronics can be used to control vehicle operation.

   A. I only   B. II only   C. Both I and II   D. Neither I nor II

2. A computer is capable of doing all of the following EXCEPT

   A. receiving input data.

   B. processing input data according to a program, and producing output information.

   C. moving linkage to affect vehicle operation.

   D. storing data and/or information.

3. Mechanic A says that a mechanic needs to know how a computer operates internally to correct automotive electronics problems.

   Mechanic B says that a mechanic needs to know how to determine if a computer is working.

   Who is correct?

   A. A only   B. B only   C. Both A and B   D. Neither A nor B

4. All of the following statements about feedback control are correct EXCEPT

   A. Sensor input data are sent to the computer.

   B. Computer output is used to operate servos.

   C. The computer changes output in response to input data.

   D. Computer output signals are fed back into the computer as input data.

5. Which of the following statements is correct?

   I. For starting and warm-up, the computer that operates ignition timing and the fuel delivery system operates in closed-loop mode.

   II. After warm-up, the computer that operates ignition timing and the fuel delivery system operates in open-loop mode.

   A. I only   B. II only   C. Both I and II   D. Neither I nor II

S U P P L E M E N T A L   A C T I V I T I E S

1. Name the basic parts of a computer control system.
2. List at least two vehicle systems that can use computer control systems.
3. Describe and explain closed-loop and open-loop modes.
4. Describe how an oxygen sensor is used in an air/fuel computer control system.
5. Describe how onboard vehicle computers can be used to diagnose problems.

39 ELECTRONIC DEVICE SERVICE

UNIT PREVIEW

Service of electronic devices is somewhat limited. Typical tasks include checking for proper wiring connections and operation, replacing defective units, and making adjustments on mechanical output devices. Many vehicles built since 1980 include self-diagnostic features to aid the mechanic in finding problems. Test procedures and equipment vary among manufacturers, and from model to model. Therefore, specific procedures from manufacturers' service manuals must be followed.

LEARNING OBJECTIVES

When you have completed your assignments and exercises in this unit, you should be able to:

- [ ] Explain the precautions necessary when checking and replacing electronic systems components or modules.
- [ ] Inspect and clean electrical connector plugs.
- [ ] Check electronic indicating devices for proper operation before attempting service procedures.
- [ ] Activate self-diagnostic functions on computer-controlled systems.
- [ ] Determine whether a vehicle is operating in the open-loop or closed-loop mode.
- [ ] Replace defective sensors or computer modules, and adjust mechanical output devices.

SAFETY PRECAUTIONS

Personal injury and unnecessary damage to electronic components can be avoided by observing the following precautions.

Do not attempt to check or replace electronic parts without the manufacturer's specific test or replacement procedures. These procedures change from year to year and from model to model. Make sure you have the correct service manual for the vehicle being checked.

Expensive damage to electronic systems can result from common checking procedures that are used for checking simpler systems. For example, to check a simple warning light system, a mechanic might normally connect battery voltage to the bulb. However, on some vehicles with a low-fuel warning light for an electronic fuel gauge, this procedure will destroy the gauge.

Use the manufacturer's special test equipment when necessary. Use of other than the correct test equipment may result in false readings.

If necessary, remove the battery negative terminal to disconnect electrical power from the vehicle. Remove rings, watches, and any other metal jewelry items before working on electrical or electronic components.

When procedures call for connecting test leads, or wires, to electrical connections, use extreme care and follow the manufacturer's instructions. Identify the correct test terminals before attempting to connect test leads.

Accidentally touching a metal clip lead or test probe between metal terminals can cause a short circuit. Expensive computer modules or sensors can be destroyed instantly, without warning, by incorrect test wiring hookups.

Many test procedures require that electrical power or ground be supplied to the circuit being tested. Do not ground powered circuits with metal tools. Avoid touching live electrical leads to grounded metal parts of the automobile. Personal injury from sparks may result, or the unit being tested may be damaged or destroyed.

39.1 PREVENTIVE MAINTENANCE

In most circumstances, no preventive maintenance is required for electronic sensors or modules. However, in areas of extreme humidity or dust, electrical connections can become degraded by oxidation or contaminated by dust. These poor connections can cause erratic operation and/or damage to sensitive electronic components. Preventive maintenance in such areas might consist of periodically cleaning electrical terminals. Mechanical output units operated by electronic devices may require periodic lubrication, adjustment, and/or other maintenance. The following procedures are provided as a general guide to the maintenance of electronic systems components.

Cleaning Electrical Connector Plugs

It has been estimated that more than 90% of the problems with electrical or electronic units are caused by poor electrical connections. In most cases, electrical connections between vehicle electronic units are made with the use of *electrical connector plugs*. Figure 39-1 shows several types of connectors.

Plastic locking tabs on some connector bodies must be released before the connector can be pulled apart. Some tabs are released by pressing inward. Other types of tabs must be lifted to release. Release the tabs and pull the connector apart, as shown in Figure 39-2.

Simply pulling the connector apart and reconnecting it may restore an electrical connection. However, the terminals may need to be cleaned or replaced.

Clean the terminals as recommended by the manufacturer. Never use metal tools, such as screwdrivers, to scrape the terminals. Metal tools can cause a short circuit between the terminals.

After cleaning, protect the terminals as the manufacturer recommends to prevent further corrosion or oxidation. Some manufacturers recommend using a *dielectric compound*, such as silicone grease. Line up any alignment tabs, and push the connector plug back together firmly. Seat the locking tabs firmly into position so that the connector cannot pull apart from vibration.

39.2 INDICATING DEVICES

If a problem is suspected with an electronic indicating device, preliminary checks can be made to isolate the source or cause. Refer to the manufacturer's service manual for the correct checking procedures.

Figure 39-3 shows what is known as a check-out sequence, or *prove-out sequence,* for an electronic speedometer. A prove-out sequence is a display of information showing that the basic operation of an indicating device is correct. When the key switch of this vehicle is turned on, all *segments,* or lighted areas, of the display come on. The display reads "188 km/h MPH." This proves that none of the segments are burned out. Next, all segments go off, proving that none of them remain lit incorrectly. Finally, the speedometer displays "0 MPH," and the display remains on. This proves that the speedometer reads accurately when the vehicle is stopped. Each manufacturer may have a different check-out or prove-out sequence for each instrument. If an electronic indicating device is defective, the unit must be removed and replaced with a new unit. No repairs are possible on electronic indicating devices.

39.3 SELF DIAGNOSTICS

Most vehicles with electronic controls built since 1980 include features to help the mechanic locate malfunctions. The control modules have *memory* features that can store, or save, information about problems. To activate these *self-diagnostic* features, jumper wires are connected to special connector plugs located under the dash or hood. Connecting the jumper wires correctly will cause the control module to display a *trouble code.*

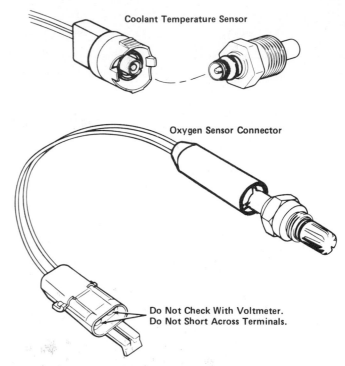

Coolant Temperature Sensor

Oxygen Sensor Connector

Do Not Check With Voltmeter.
Do Not Short Across Terminals.

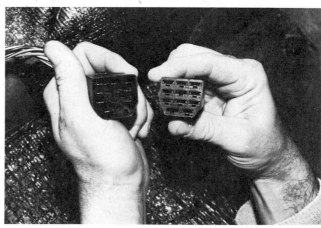

Figure 39-1. Electrical wire connectors.

Activating Self-Diagnostic Functions

Figure 39-4 shows how jumper wires and a voltmeter probe should be attached to a self-diagnostic connector. This illustration applies to 1980 Ford and American Motors MCU (Microprocessor Control Unit) systems.

The simplest display is a dash light that blinks on and off in coded sequence. Some vehicle manufacturers require that a voltmeter be connected to certain terminals. Others require that a vacuum/pressure gauge be inserted in certain hoses. The movement of the meter needle or gauge then indicates code numbers. Figure 39-5 shows how to read a typical light code, used on General Motors vehicles.

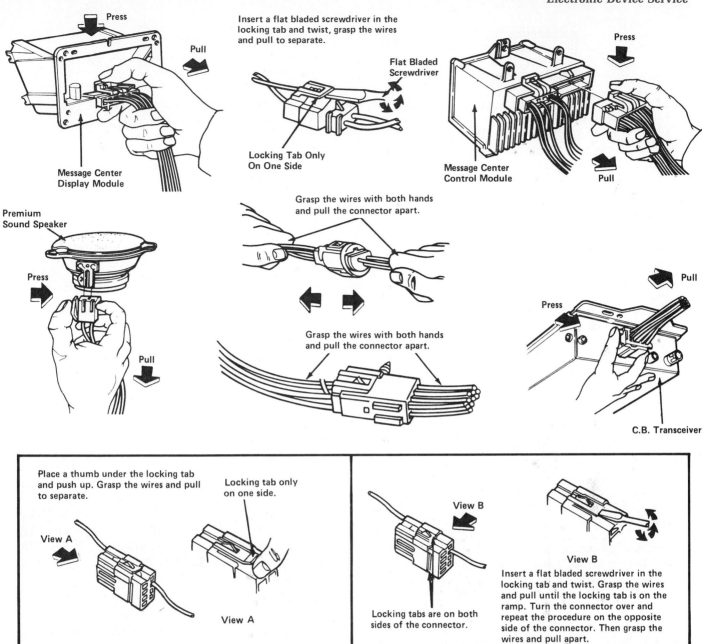

Press

Pull

Insert a flat bladed screwdriver in the locking tab and twist, grasp the wires and pull to separate.

Flat Bladed Screwdriver

Locking Tab Only On One Side

Press

Pull

Message Center Display Module

Message Center Control Module

Premium Sound Speaker

Press

Pull

Grasp the wires with both hands and pull the connector apart.

Grasp the wires with both hands and pull the connector apart.

Press

Pull

C.B. Transceiver

Place a thumb under the locking tab and push up. Grasp the wires and pull to separate.

Locking tab only on one side.

View A

View A

View B

View B

Insert a flat bladed screwdriver in the locking tab and twist. Grasp the wires and pull until the locking tab is on the ramp. Turn the connector over and repeat the procedure on the opposite side of the connector. Then grasp the wires and pull apart.

Locking tabs are on both sides of the connector.

Figure 39-2. Disconnecting electrical connectors. FORD MOTOR COMPANY

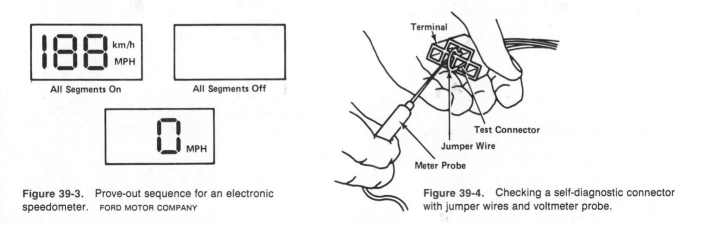

All Segments On

All Segments Off

0 MPH

Terminal

Test Connector

Jumper Wire

Meter Probe

Figure 39-3. Prove-out sequence for an electronic speedometer. FORD MOTOR COMPANY

Figure 39-4. Checking a self-diagnostic connector with jumper wires and voltmeter probe.

415

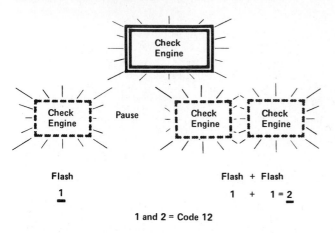

Figure 39-5. Diagnostic code display.
GENERAL MOTORS CORPORATION

GENERAL MOTORS TROUBLE CODES

Code	Problem
12	Computer not receiving rpm signal
13	Defect in oxygen sensor's wiring
14	Short circuit in coolant-temperature sensor's wiring
15	Open circuit to coolant temperature sensor
21	Defect in throttle-position sensor
23	Defect in carburetor solenoid wiring
24	Defect in vehicle-speed sensor
32	Defect in barometric-pressure sensor
35	Short circuit in idle-speed control switch
42	Ground in ignition timing bypass circuit
44	Defect in oxygen sensor
51	Defects in computer module
54	Defect in carburetor mixture-control solenoid and/or computer module
55	Defect in throttle-position sensor, oxygen sensor, or computer module (depending on engine model)

Figure 39-6. Trouble code identification.
GENERAL MOTORS CORPORATION

Figure 39-6 shows a table of codes to be used for problems with General Motors vehicles. A code 12 would indicate that no rpm signal is being received from the distributor when the engine is off. This checking code is used to confirm that the diagnostic system is operating properly before other tests are performed. Each vehicle manufacturer uses a different set of codes.

39.4 OPEN-LOOP AND CLOSED-LOOP OPERATION

As explained in Unit 38, engine control systems can operate in either an open-loop or a closed-loop mode. A dwell meter can be used to determine if the engine is operating in the proper mode.

Determining Open-Loop and Closed-Loop Operation

Connect the dwell meter leads to the mixture control solenoid on the feedback carburetor, as shown in Figure 39-7.

NOTE: This procedure requires that the dwell meter be set to the six-cylinder scale, even if the engine being checked is a 4- or 8-cylinder engine. Some dwell meters may not work properly for these procedures. Do not use a dwell meter that causes engine speed to change when connected.

In the open-loop mode, an on-off signal of fixed length is sent to the carburetor mixture control solenoid. This action provides a steady, rich mixture to the engine. In the open-loop mode, the dwell meter will indicate a steady reading of between 21 and 35 degrees.

At idle, after warm-up, the engine control system should be in the closed-loop mode. The control module constantly modifies the signal to the carburetor mixture control solenoid in response to exhaust emissions. In the closed-loop mode, the dwell meter indicates a dwell reading that varies constantly

between 5 and 55 degrees. Figure 39-8 shows the range of dwell change during closed-loop operation.

To double-check that the system is in closed-loop operation, momentarily "choke" the carburetor air horn with your hand. The dwell meter should indicate a slightly higher reading if the system is in closed-loop operation.

39.5 SENSORS

Many types of sensors are used with electronic engine controls. Examples of sensors can include:

- Engine coolant temperature
- Exhaust gas oxygen
- Throttle position
- Barometric pressure
- Manifold absolute pressure
- Vacuum
- Intake air mass
- Intake air temperature
- Transmission gear
- Ambient temperature.

These sensors provide information to the control module about engine and vehicle functions and atmospheric conditions. Based on this information, the control module sends output signals. These signals

The "CHECK ENGINE" light will only be "ON" if the malfunction exists under the conditions listed below. It takes up to five seconds minimum for the light to come on when a problem occurs. If the malfunction clears, the light will go out and a trouble code will be set in the ECM. Code 12 does not store in memory. If the light comes "ON" intermittently, but no code is stored, go to the "Driver Comments section. Any codes stored will be erased if no problem reoccurs within 50 engine starts.

THE TROUBLE CODES INDICATE PROBLEMS AS FOLLOWS:

Code	Problem	Code	Problem
12	No distributor reference pulses to the ECM. This code is not stored in memory and will only flash while the fault is present.	32	Barometric pressure sensor (BARO) circuit low, or altitude compensator low on J-car.
13	Oxygen sensor circuit — The engine must run up to five minutes at part throttle, under road load, before this code will set.	35	Idle speed control (ISC) switch circuit shorted. (Over 50% throttle for over 2 sec.)
14	Shorted coolant sensor circuit — The engine must run up to five minutes before this code will set.	42	Electronic spark timing (EST) bypass circuit or EST circuit grounded or open.
15	Open coolant sensor circuit — The engine must run up to five minutes before this code will set.	44	Lean exhaust indication — The engine must run up to five minutes, in closed loop, at part throttle and road load before this code will set.
21	Throttle position sensor circuit — The engine must run up to 25 seconds, at specified curb idle speed, before this code will set.	44 & 55	(At same time) — Faulty oxygen sensor circuit.
		51	Faulty calibration unit (PROM) or installation. It takes up to 30 seconds before this code will set.
23	Open or grounded M/C solenoid circuit.	54	Shorted M/C solenoid circuit and/or faulty ECM.
24	Vehicle speed sensor (VSS) circuit — The car must operate up to five minutes at road speed before this code will set.	55	Grounded V ref. (terminal "21", faulty oxygen sensor or ECM.

Figure 39-6. Concluded.

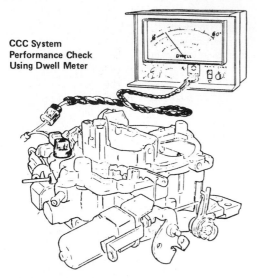

Figure 39-7. Dwell meter connection.
GENERAL MOTORS CORPORATION

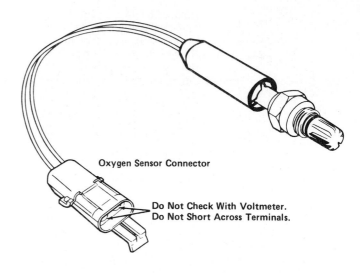

Figure 39-9. Oxygen sensor. GENERAL MOTORS CORPORATION

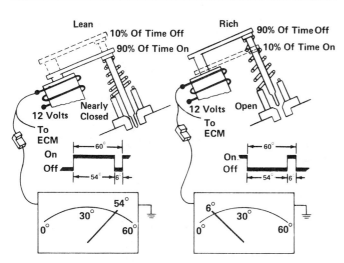

Figure 39-8. Dwell range during closed-loop operation.
GENERAL MOTORS CORPORATION

control air-fuel mixture, spark advance, some emissions control devices, and (in some cases) gear selection.

Each manufacturer provides specific test and replacement information for each type of sensor used on its vehicles. The following information is provided as a general guide to the replacement of the exhaust gas oxygen sensor used on General Motors vehicles.

Oxygen Sensor Replacement

An oxygen sensor is shown in Figure 39-9.

SAFETY CAUTION: The exhaust gas oxygen sensor is located in the exhaust manifold. Make sure the exhaust system is cool before attempting to check or replace the sensor. Severe burns can result from touching a hot exhaust manifold.

CAUTION: If an oxygen sensor is handled roughly or dropped, it will no longer provide accurate input information to the control module. Handle the oxygen sensor carefully. Do not allow grease, lubricants, or cleaning solvents of any kind to touch the sensor end or the electrical connector plug. Apply the manufacturer's special anti-seize compound to the threads before installing the sensor.

Disconnect the electrical connector plug. Unscrew the sensor with the manufacturer's special wrench or a flare-nut wrench. Coat the threads of the new sensor with the manufacturer's special anti-seize compound. Thread it in by hand. Tighten the sensor to the manufacturer's specified torque. Make sure that the silicone rubber boot on the connector wire does not touch the exhaust manifold after tightening.

39.6 CONTROL MODULES

Some manufacturers provide special diagnostic test equipment for their own electronic engine control systems. In other cases, normally used shop testers are used to check the operation of electronic control modules. Figure 39-10 shows the types of tools needed to check a late-model General Motors CCC (Computer Command Control) system.

Vehicles can be equipped with a variety of engines, transmissions, differential ratios, and wheel and tire sizes. Because of these variations, one control module will not work for all vehicles. Some manufacturers provide separate modules with programs for each individual vehicle. Other manufacturers provide a separate, smaller module that plugs into the main control module. This smaller module is known as an *engine calibration unit* or *programmable read-only memory (PROM)*. See Figure 39-11.

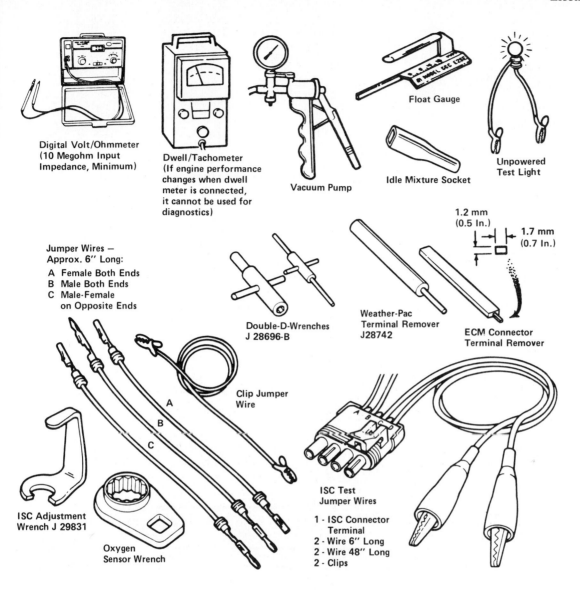

Digital Volt/Ohmmeter (10 Megohm Input Impedance, Minimum)

Dwell/Tachometer (If engine performance changes when dwell meter is connected, it cannot be used for diagnostics)

Vacuum Pump

Float Gauge

Idle Mixture Socket

Unpowered Test Light

Jumper Wires — Approx. 6'' Long:
A Female Both Ends
B Male Both Ends
C Male-Female on Opposite Ends

Double-D-Wrenches J 28696-B

Weather-Pac Terminal Remover J28742

1.2 mm (0.5 In.)
1.7 mm (0.7 In.)

ECM Connector Terminal Remover

Clip Jumper Wire

ISC Adjustment Wrench J 29831

Oxygen Sensor Wrench

ISC Test Jumper Wires

1 - ISC Connector Terminal
2 - Wire 6'' Long
2 - Wire 48'' Long
2 - Clips

Figure 39-10. Control module diagnostic tools. GENERAL MOTORS CORPORATION

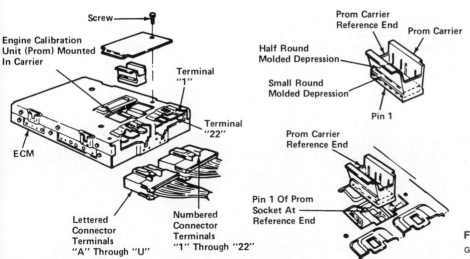

Screw

Engine Calibration Unit (Prom) Mounted In Carrier

ECM

Terminal "1"

Terminal "22"

Lettered Connector Terminals "A" Through "U"

Numbered Connector Terminals "1" Through "22"

Prom Carrier Reference End

Prom Carrier

Half Round Molded Depression

Small Round Molded Depression

Pin 1

Prom Carrier Reference End

Pin 1 Of Prom Socket At Reference End

Figure 39-11. Electronic control module.
GENERAL MOTORS CORPORATION

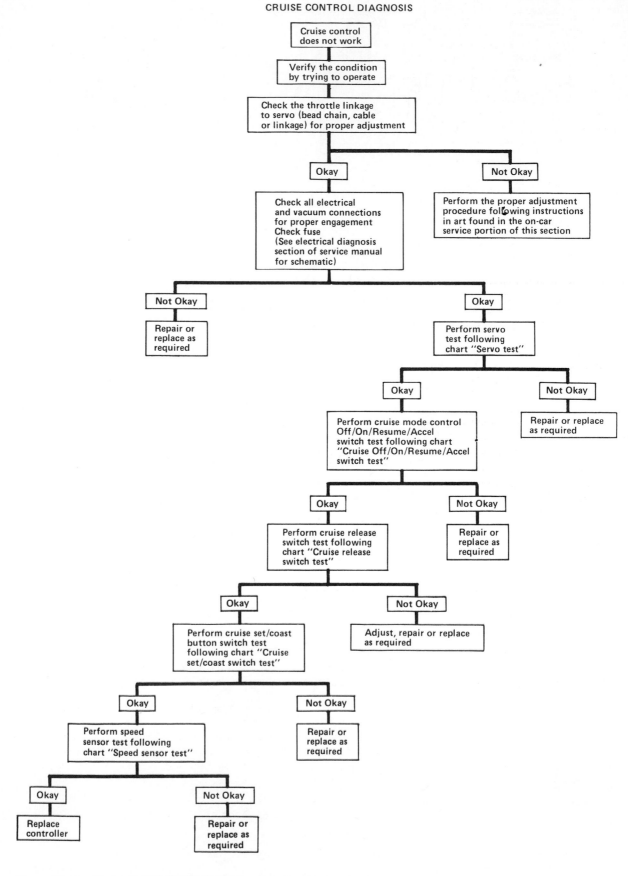

Figure 39-12. Cruise control diagnostic chart. PONTIAC MOTOR DIVISION—GMC

ADJUSTMENT PROCEDURE

Assemble chain to be taut with carburetor in
the hot idle position, and with the idle control
solenoid de-energized. Place ball of chain into
coupling cavity which permits chain to have
slight slack. Cut off excess chain hanging
outside of coupling. Chain slack not to exceed
one ball diameter, (ref. No. 10 ball diameter),
when measured at hot idle position, with the
idle control solenoid de-energized.

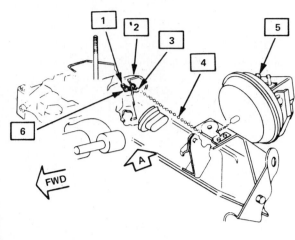

1—Retainer
2—Lever (Carburetor)
3—Stud
4—Chain (Servo Unit)
5—Servo Assembly
6—Pin

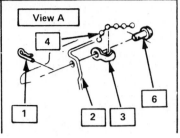

Figure 39-13. Throttle linkage adjustment procedure. PONTIAC MOTOR DIVISION—GMC

Replacing a Control Module

To replace the main control module, lift the locking
tabs and gently rock the connectors to unplug them.
Remove the main control module. Remove the access
cover over the PROM. Unplug the connector terminals and gently rock the PROM to remove it. Note
the alignment tabs and depressions. Check the stock
numbers on the new main control module to make
sure they match the numbers on the old module.
Carefully replace the PROM and seat it in the new
module. Replace the access cover and main control
module. Plug the connectors into the module and
make sure that the locking tabs seat properly.

39.7 MECHANICAL OUTPUT DEVICES

Mechanical output devices are operated by engine
vacuum, electrical solenoids, or electrical motors. A
typical flowchart showing the diagnosis procedure for
a cruise-control unit is shown in Figure 39-12.

Adjusting a Mechanical Output Device

Some mechanical output devices require adjustment.
The adjustment procedure for a cruise-control servo
that operates throttle linkage is shown in Figure 39-13.

U N I T   H I G H L I G H T S

- There are many differences in servicing procedures for electronic devices. Therefore, the
  mechanic must always refer to the proper manufacturer's service manual for correct checking
  and/or replacement procedures.
- Many electronic system problems are caused by
  poor connections.
- Self-diagnostic functions can help the mechanic to
  find problems.
- A dwell meter can be used to determine if an
  engine control system is operating in open-loop or
  closed-loop mode.
- Service procedures for electronic devices consist
  of cleaning connections; replacing modules, sensors, and indicating devices; and maintaining
  mechanical output devices.

T E R M S

electrical connector
  plug
dielectric compound
prove-out sequence
display segment
memory

self-diagnostics
trouble code
engine calibration unit
programmable read-
  only memory (PROM)

R E V I E W   Q U E S T I O N S

DIRECTIONS: The following questions are similar to those used on mechanic certification tests. On a separate sheet of paper, write the letter of the correct choice.

1. Mechanic A says that the procedures for repairing electronic devices are the same as for electrical devices.

   Mechanic B says that special precautions and specific instructions from the manufacturer's service manual are necessary for servicing electronic devices.

   Who is correct?

   A. A only   B. B only   C. Both A and B   D. Neither A nor B

2. Which of the following statements is correct?

   I. A prove-out sequence shows how accurate an indicating device is throughout its range of measurement.

   II. A prove-out sequence checks the basic operation of an indicating device.

   A. I only   B. II only   C. Both I and II   D. Neither I nor II

3. During self-diagnostic functions of an electronic control module, two flashes or pulses followed by one flash or pulse indicate

   A. no rpm signal being received (engine off).

   B. exhaust gas oxygen sensor faulty.

   C. a code 21.

   D. a code 12.

4. When checking for open- or closed-loop operation, a dwell reading that constantly *varies* between 5 and 55 degrees indicates

   A. open-loop operation.

   B. closed-loop operation.

   C. dwell meter not set to 6-cylinder scale.

   D. dwell meter is changing engine speed when connected.

5. When replacing an exhaust gas oxygen sensor, all of the following must be done EXCEPT

   A. making sure the exhaust system is cool.

   B. checking the old sensor by connecting a voltmeter across its terminals.

   C. coating the threads of the replacement sensor with the manufacturer's special anti-seize compound.

   D. making sure the silicone rubber boot does not touch the exhaust manifold.

S U P P L E M E N T A L   A C T I V I T I E S

1. Locate, disconnect, clean, and reconnect connector plugs on a shop vehicle.
2. Read the proper section in a manufacturer's service manual for an instructor-chosen vehicle and check if indicating devices are operating correctly.
3. Read the proper section in a manufacturer's service manual for an instructor-chosen vehicle and activate the computer's self-diagnostic functions.
4. Use a dwell meter to determine whether a shop vehicle's engine control system is operating in open-loop or closed-loop mode.
5. Locate and identify sensors and mechanical output devices on an instructor-chosen vehicle.

V

EMISSIONS SYSTEMS

40 EMISSION CONTROL FUNDAMENTALS

UNIT PREVIEW

Unhealthful air can result from natural or man-made causes. Incomplete burning of fuels to produce heat and energy can produce chemicals that pollute the air. Air pollution can cause irritation or diseases in living things and damage to objects.

Atmospheric conditions can trap and concentrate polluted air. Smog, or polluted air, may be visible or invisible. Invisible pollution can be more harmful to health than visible pollution.

Major sources of air contaminants from automobiles include the exhaust, fuel system, and crankcase. U.S. government regulations limit the amount of certain pollutants produced by new vehicles.

The combination of clean-air and fuel-economy regulations has stimulated vehicle manufacturers to use advanced technology. This technology includes feedback carburetors, fuel injection, electronic ignition, catalytic converters, and computer controls.

The technology of emission controls is not simple. However, mechanics who have a good attitude and are willing to learn new knowledge and skills always are in demand. This is true especially in the area of emission control service.

LEARNING OBJECTIVES

When you have completed your assignments and exercises in this unit, you should be able to:

☐ Identify and describe sources and effects of air pollution.

☐ Identify and describe the products of complete and incomplete combustion of a hydrocarbon fuel.

☐ Locate emission control information labels on late-model vehicles and describe specific tune-up procedures required for limiting emissions.

☐ Identify and describe trends over a period of years in engine size, horsepower output, and ignition timing of vehicles.

☐ Describe the type of training necessary for mechanics who wish to perform emission control service.

☐ Describe the problems encountered in servicing emission controls.

40.1 AIR POLLUTION

Pollution means a process of contamination. *Air pollution* is the contamination of air by harmful substances. Air pollution may occur through natural processes or through the contamination of air by man-made substances and gases. Air pollution is a problem because it damages and harms plants, animals, people, and objects.

Air is made up of nitrogen (N_2), oxygen (O_2), and a very small proportion of other natural gases (see Figure 40-1). Air pollution occurs when harmful gases and particles are added to air.

Natural Pollution

Natural pollution comes from sources in nature. These pollutants include:

• Smoke from naturally caused forest and grass fires

• Gases given off by growing and decomposing vegetation

• Dust and dirt blown by the wind

• Smoke, ashes, dust, and gases from volcanic eruptions.

Natural pollution was present in the atmosphere before humans appeared on Earth. However, natural forces such as wind and rain tend to dilute and spread pollutants. The "balance of nature" tends to maintain an atmosphere that allows plants and animals to grow and live in a healthful manner.

Man-Made Air Pollution

Man-made air pollution is caused mainly by the burning of fuel to produce heat and power. Refineries and

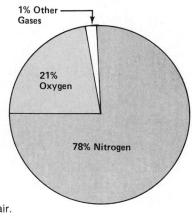

Figure 40-1.
Composition of air.

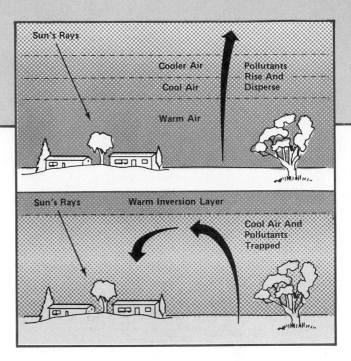

Figure 40-2. Inversion layer.

other industrial operations also produce chemicals and gases that pollute the air. Under certain conditions, the concentration of automobiles and factories in cities can produce air pollution that causes serious health problems.

Air pollution can irritate and damage breathing passages in the nose, throat, and lungs. Acids are formed from a combination of water vapor and sulfur, nitrogen, and other chemical pollutants.

Taking a deep breath can be painful because of the acids' effect on the lungs. Coughing is another symptom noticed during periods of high pollution. Eyes become watery from irritating particles and acids. Air pollution has been linked to many health problems, including:

- Asthma
- Cancer of the lungs and stomach
- Emphysema
- Heart and circulatory system problems
- Skin problems.

Smog

Smog is a combination of the words "smoke" and "fog." However, air pollution is not always caused by a combination of *particulate* matter and fog. Particulates are extremely small particles of solid material, like bits of burned material in smoke. However, the slang term "smog" is widely used to mean "air pollution" of all sorts.

Hundreds of years ago, the burning of soft coal in European and British cities caused foul-smelling, dirty air. As recently as a few decades ago, many people in London died because of a "killer fog." This deadly fog was caused by a combination of stagnant air, carbon monoxide gas, coal dust, and sulfuric acid from the smoke.

Smog became a health and visibility problem in Los Angeles as early as the late 1930s. Hundreds of years before, native Indians in Southern California called the area "valley of smokes." They had noticed that smoke from campfires would rise to a certain level, then spread out in a flat layer.

This atmospheric phenomenon is known as an *inversion layer,* a condition in which normally cooler upper air becomes warmer. This warmer air acts as a "lid" to trap and concentrate air pollution (see Figure 40-2). When geographic conditions combine with a lack of wind, stagnant air can intensify air pollution.

Photochemical Smog

The action of sunlight can change contaminants into more harmful pollution. *Photochemical smog* is air pollution produced through the action of sunlight on chemicals and moisture in still air.

Incomplete Combustion and Air Pollution

If combustion of a hydrocarbon fuel is 100 percent efficient, the products are water vapor (H_2O) and *carbon dioxide (CO_2)*. Both of these harmless chemicals are part of the natural environment. Carbon dioxide is one of the colorless, odorless gases exhaled when you breathe.

As discussed in Unit 10, 100 percent combustion is never achieved in an internal combustion engine. Quench areas within the combustion chamber put out the flame, and some fuel remains unburned. Thus, even in a new, perfectly tuned vehicle, internal combustion engine exhaust gases always contain some unburned *hydrocarbon (HC)* fuel. In addition, incomplete combustion produces *carbon monoxide (CO)*, a toxic gas. Both of these pollutants usually are colorless.

Bluish-white smoke from a tail pipe indicates that engine oil, a hydrocarbon, is being burned. Thus, unburned petroleum hydrocarbons are being released into the air. Black smoke indicates an air-fuel mixture too rich to burn completely. Again, hydrocarbons are released into the air. However, even vehicles that produce no smoke at all are releasing pollutants into the air.

Invisible Pollution

Small amounts of hydrocarbon pollutants and carbon monoxide are not visible. *Invisible pollution* takes the

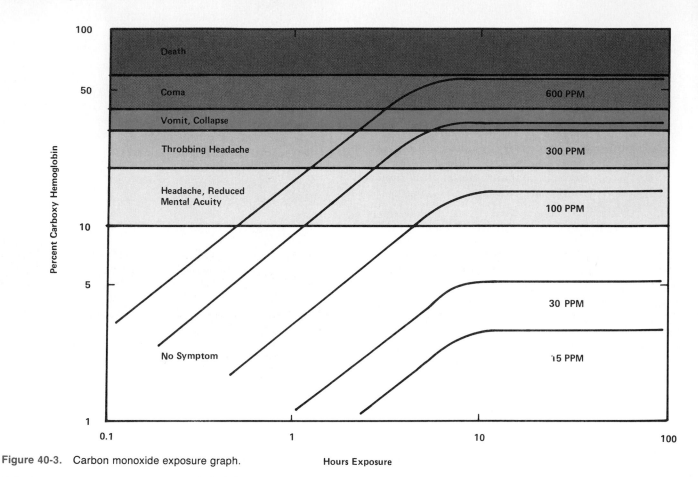

Figure 40-3. Carbon monoxide exposure graph.

form of invisible gases and vapors that cause health problems.

For example, carbon monoxide (CO) gas from auto exhausts can displace oxygen in the bloodstream, resulting in *carbon monoxide poisoning.*

The concentration of a gas or particulate in air can be measured in *parts per million (ppm).* That is, in one million parts of air, a certain number of the parts are composed of a certain gas or particulate.

Below 50 ppm of CO in the air, no symptoms are noticeable. Mild CO poisoning is noticeable as a headachy, drowsy feeling. Increasingly severe stages of CO poisoning include throbbing headaches, vomiting and collapse, and coma. At a concentration of 600 ppm, death occurs (see Figure 40-3).

Thus, even though it cannot be seen, invisible air pollution can cause serious health problems. Mechanics must be especially aware of the dangers of carbon monoxide poisoning when working on vehicles in an enclosed garage. See Figure 40-4.

SAFETY CAUTION: Always have an adequate source of ventilation when operating an engine indoors. Open the garage doors or turn on ventilating fans whenever engines are running inside an enclosed area. Carbon monoxide poisoning can cause serious health problems.

Carbon Monoxide Is A Toxic Gas

Figure 40-4. Carbon monoxide warning sign.

40.2 AUTOMOTIVE EMISSIONS

Sources of air pollution from vehicles are illustrated in Figure 40-5. These sources include:

- Exhaust emissions
- Fuel system vapors
- Crankcase fumes.

Exhaust Emissions

Emissions, or pollutants, in the exhausts of internal-combustion engines account for a large percentage

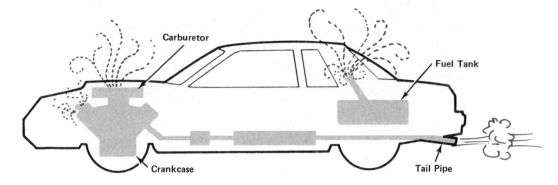

Figure 40-5. Sources of automotive pollution.

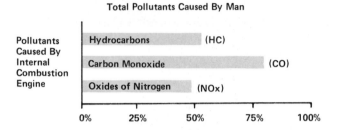

Figure 40-6. Internal combustion pollutants.

of pollutants caused by man. Refer to Figure 40-6. Automotive exhaust emissions include:

- Hydrocarbons (HC)
- Carbon monoxide (CO)
- Oxides of nitrogen (NO_X)
- Oxides of sulfur (SO_X)
- Ozone (O_3)
- Particulate matter.

Hydrocarbons are molecules that contain hydrogen and carbon atoms, such as petroleum fuels and lubricating oils. Unburned hydrocarbons are the major source of automotive air pollution.

Carbon monoxide is a colorless, odorless, toxic gas produced by incomplete combustion. As discussed in Topic 40.1, carbon monoxide can be deadly.

Oxides of nitrogen are produced when combustion temperatures and pressures are raised. To reduce HC and CO emissions, engines can be designed to run on leaner mixtures and at higher combustion temperatures. Higher combustion temperatures, however, result in the combination of nitrogen and oxygen to form NO_X. NO_X contributes to the formation of nitric acid, a powerfully corrosive substance.

Oxides of sulfur are produced by the chemical reaction in a catalytic converter. Sulfur combines with water vapor to form sulfuric acid.

Ozone can be produced by sunlight acting on oxygen in the air, or by an electrical discharge, or spark. Thus, the secondary ignition system is a source of ozone. Ozone has a sharp, pungent smell. It is harmful to the lungs and can cause rubber to deteriorate.

Particulates in exhaust gases can include carbon soot and lead particles (in older vehicles using leaded fuel). Diesel engines produce large amounts of soot, which is believed to be a *carcinogen*. A carcinogen is a substance that causes cancer.

Fuel System Emissions

Petroleum-based motor fuels are pure hydrocarbons. When fuel is allowed to evaporate, massive amounts of HC are released into the air. When temperatures rise, fuel in vehicle tanks expands and vaporizes. In addition, fuel in the carburetor float bowl also can evaporate.

On earlier vehicles, neither of these sources of pollution was controlled. It was known that fuel that became heated in a fuel tank produced vapors and pressure. Vented gas caps allowed pressure buildup and vapors to be vented to the atmosphere to prevent rupturing the fuel tank.

Before pollution controls, fuel within the carburetor float bowl was allowed to evaporate and produce HC vapors (see Figure 40-7).

Crankcase Emissions

Crankcase emissions include *blowby gases* and fumes from heated oil. Blowby gases are gases that leak past piston rings during combustion. Blowby gases contain water vapor (H_2O), HC, CO, and sulfur (S). These pollutants combine to form acids and sludge in lubricating oil. To prevent pressure buildup from blowing out oil pan and valve cover gaskets, blowby gases must be controlled.

Before emission controls, blowby gases were vented directly to the atmosphere through a *road draft tube*. A road draft tube is simply an open tube leading from the crankcase. Blowby gases and crankcase vapors leave the crankcase area through this tube and are vented to the atmosphere.

Positive crankcase ventilation (PCV) systems were tried as early as the 1920s to prevent contamination of lubricating oil. A PCV system uses intake manifold vacuum to draw in crankcase emissions with the intake charge. Crankcase emissions are thus "recycled" for further combustion (see Figure 40-8).

40.3 GOVERNMENT REGULATION AND AIR POLLUTION

In 1959, California became the first state to enact automobile emission regulations. A state Air Resources Board (ARB) was formed to set standards for automotive emissions and testing procedures.

In 1968, based on the work of California's ARB, the U.S. Congress passed the Clean Air Act, mandating emission controls for all vehicles. As a result, allowable levels of the three pollutants considered most harmful were to be controlled. Those three pollutants are:

- Hydrocarbons (HC)
- Carbon monoxide (CO)
- Oxides of nitrogen (NO_x).

Federal standards for reduction of these pollutants, measured in *grams per mile (gpm)* were established (see Figure 40-9). A gram is a metric measurement of mass, equivalent to 0.035 ounce. Grams per mile is a way of measuring a mass of pollutant emitted over a distance traveled.

Other states, primarily high-altitude western states, passed their own laws and applied for waivers of the federal standards. As a result, during the 1970s

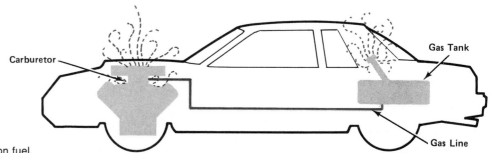

Figure 40-7.   Evaporation of hydrocarbon fuel.

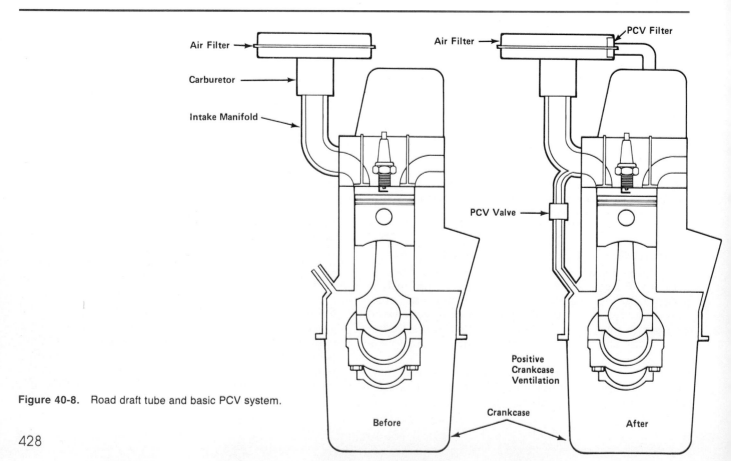

Figure 40-8.   Road draft tube and basic PCV system.

Federal Standards—New Vehicle Summary

Passenger Cars

The following standards, up to 1975, apply only to gasoline-fueled light-duty vehicles. Standards for 1975 and later apply to both gasoline-fueled and diesel light-duty vehicles.

Year	Test Procedure [2]	Hydrocarbons	Carbon Monoxide	Oxides Of Nitrogen	Particulates [3]	Evaporative [4] Hydrocarbon
Prior	7-mode	850 ppm	3.4%	1000 ppm	—	—
to	7-mode	11gpm	80 gpm	4 gpm	—	—
controls	CVS-75	8.8 gpm	87.0 gpm	3.6 gpm	—	—
1968-69	7-mode					
	50-100 CID	410 ppm	2.3%	—	—	—
	101-140 CID	350 ppm	2.0%	—	—	—
	over 140 CID	275 ppm	1.5%	—	—	—
1970	7-mode	2.2 gpm	23 gpm	—	—	—
1971	7-mode	2.2 gpm	23 hpm	—	—	6 g/test [5]
1972	CVS-72	3.4 gpm	39 gpm	—	—	2 g/test
1973-74	CVS-72	3.4 gpm	39 gpm	3.0 gpm	—	2 g/test
1975-76	CVS-75	1.5 gpm	15 gpm [6]	3.1 gpm	—	2 g/test
1977 [7]	CVS-75	1.5 gpm	15 gpm	2.0 gpm	—	2.0 g/test
1978-79	CVS-75	1.5 gpm	15 gpm	2.0 gpm	—	6.0 g/test
1980	CVS-75	0.41 gpm	7.0 gpm	2.0 gpm	—	6.0 g/test
1981	CVS-75	0.41 gpm	3.4 gpm [8]	1.0 gpm [9][10]	—	2.0 g/test
1982 [11]	CVS-75	0.41 gpm	3.4 gpm [8]	1.0 gpm [9][10]	0.6 gpm	2.0 gTtest
		(0.57)	(7.8)	(1.0) [9]	—	(2.6)
1983 [11]	CVS-75	0.41 gpm	3.4 gpm	1.0 gpm [9]	0.6 gpm	2.0 g/test
		(0.57)	(7.8)	(1.0) [9]	—	(2.6)
1984	CVS-75	0.41 gpm	3.4 gpm	1.0 gpm [9]	0.6 gpm	2.0 g/test
1985 and later	CVS-75	0.41 gpm	3.4 gpm	1.0 gpm	0.2 gpm	2.0 g/test

Light Duty Vehicles:

1 Standards do not apply to vehicles with engines less than 60 CID from 1968 through 1974.

2 Different test procedures have been used since the early years of emission control which vary in stringency. The appearance that the standards were relaxed from 1971 to 1972 is incorrect. The 1972 standards are actually more stringent because of the greater stringency of the 1972 test procedure.

3 Applies only to diesels.

4 Evaporative emissions determined by carbon trap method through 1977, SHED procedure beginning in 1978. Applies only to gasoline-fueled vehicles.

5 Evaporative standard does not apply to off-road utility vehicles for 1971.

6 Carbon monoxide standard for vehicles sold in the State of California is 9.0 gpm.

7 Cars sold in specified high altitude counties required to meet standards at high altitude.

8 Carbon monoxide standard can be waived to 7.0 gpm for 1981-82 by the EPA Administrator.

9 Oxides of nitrogen standard can be waived to 1.5 gpm for innovative technology or diesel.

10 Oxides of nitrogen standard can be waived to 2.0 gpm for American Motors Corporation.

11 Standards in parentheses apply to vehicles sold in specified high altitude counties. Vehicles eligible for a carbon monoxide waiver for 7.0 gpm at low altitude are eligible for a waiver to 11 gpm at high altitude.

gpm—grams per mile
CID—cubic inch displacement
CVS-72—constant volume sample cold start test
CVS-75—constant volume sample test which includes cold and hot starts
7-mode—137 second driving cycle test
ppm—parts per million

Figure 40-9. Federal standards for new automobiles.

and early 1980s, gasoline vehicles were built to three different emission standards:

- California vehicles
- Federal (49-state) vehicles
- High-altitude vehicles.

California's standards allowed less pollution than federal standards. Federal controls were less stringent. Because there is less oxygen at high altitudes to promote combustion, high-altitude standards were almost as strict as California's. To identify the vehicle and to aid mechanics, emission control information labels were affixed in the underhood area (see Figure 40-10).

Diesel engines must meet additional regulations. Diesel soot is a problem. Also, because of high combustion pressures and temperatures, diesel engines produce large amounts of NO_x. In recent years, a partial or total ban on the sale of diesels has been considered by California's ARB. Appropriate technology

for trapping particulates without restricting exhaust flow has been difficult to achieve.

In 1977, the federal Clean Air Act was amended to require vehicle emission control inspection and maintenance (I/M) programs. Dec. 31, 1987, was the date chosen by which all states would be required to meet national air quality standards.

The Environmental Protection Agency (EPA) was given broad powers to enforce the Clean Air Act. The EPA can limit federal grants or cancel federal projects, such as highways, until states comply with clean air standards.

The EPA also has established a pollutant standards warning system (see Figure 40-11). Health warnings are broadcast on television and radio station weather reports.

The technology for achieving a constant reduction in levels of pollutants was not specified by the Clean Air Act. Manufacturers are free to choose methods and devices for achieving these reductions.

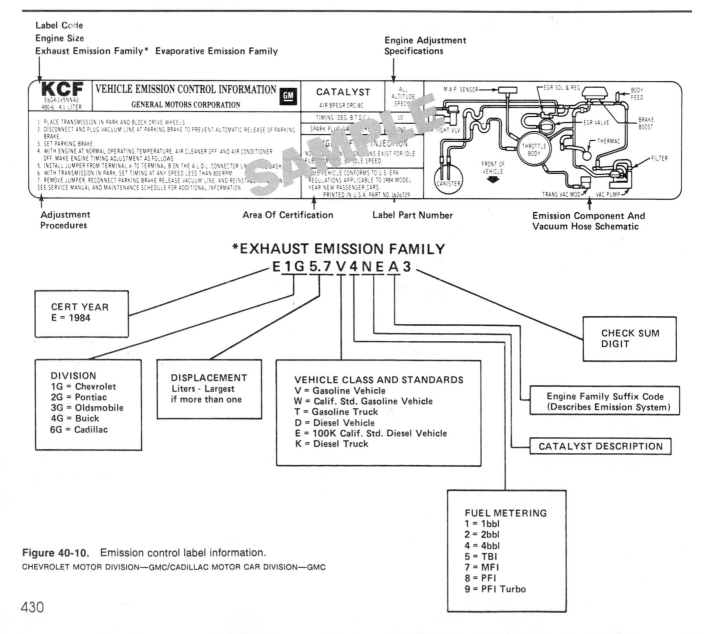

Figure 40-10. Emission control label information.
CHEVROLET MOTOR DIVISION—GMC/CADILLAC MOTOR CAR DIVISION—GMC

	Stages	Health Effects	Health Warnings
0-50	Good	None	None
50-100	Moderate	None	None
100-200	Air Quality Goal Unhealthful	Mild aggravation of symptoms in susceptible persons, with irritation symptoms in the healthy population.	Persons with existing heart or respiratory ailments should reduce physical exertion and outdoor activity.
200-300	1st Stage Alert Very Unhealthful	Significant aggravation of symptoms and decreased exercise tolerance in persons with heart or lung disease, with widespread symptoms in the healthy population.	Elderly and persons with existing heart or lung disease should stay indoors and reduce physical activity.
300-400	2nd Stage Alert Hazardous	Premature onset of certain diseases in addition to significant aggravation of symptoms and decreased exercise tolerance in healthy persons.	Elderly and persons with existing diseases should stay indoors and avoid physical exertion. General population should avoid outdoor activity.
400-500	3rd Stage Alert Hazardous	Premature death of ill and elderly. Healthy people will experience adverse symptoms that affect their normal activity.	All persons should remain indoors, keeping windows and doors closed. All persons should minimize physical exertion and avoid traffic.

Figure 40-11. Pollutant standards index.

As a result, general similarities exist among different manufacturers' methods, but there are many variations in hardware and devices.

To correctly diagnose and find problems on literally hundreds of different pollution control systems is a problem for mechanics. As a result, mechanics must refer to specific manufacturers' service manuals for correct inspection and test procedures of pollution controls.

40.4 GOVERNMENT REGULATION AND FUEL MILEAGE

During late 1973 and early 1974, the oil-producing countries of the Middle East refused to ship petroleum products. Motorists waited in gasoline lines for hours or days, and the price of gasoline and diesel fuel doubled. In mid-1973, premium (leaded) gasoline cost approximately 30 to 36 cents per gallon. Diesel fuel cost approximately 24 cents per gallon. Since that time, fuel prices have risen and fallen dramatically to present levels.

To encourage a reduction in fuel usage, Congress enacted the Energy Policy and Conservation Act. This act set standards for *corporate average fuel economy (CAFE)*. Overall average fuel mileage requirements were part of this legislation (see Figure 40-12).

Technology, Air Pollution, and Performance

Prior to the CAFE regulations, emissions control technology tended to lessen fuel mileage. To meet

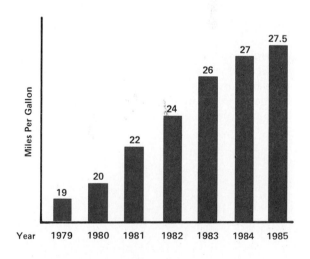

Figure 40-12. CAFE standards.

both clean air and CAFE regulations, vehicle manufacturers applied advanced technology to vehicle controls. Sensors, computer modules, and actuator devices became standard equipment on vehicles.

Several late-model vehicles produce a combination of good fuel mileage, driveability, low exhaust emissions, and brisk acceleration. These improvements have been brought about by several

431

relatively recent applications of technology to automotive developments:

- Feedback carburetors and electronic fuel injection
- Electronic ignition
- Catalytic converters
- Computer controls
- Lockup torque converters for automatic transmissions (see Unit 53)
- Turbocharging (see Unit 19).

Computer-controlled fuel injection, ignition, and automatic transmissions have increased performance while lowering automotive exhaust pollutants. Fuel system controls, including catalytic converters, have allowed engines to be tuned for performance without sacrificing air quality. Turbocharging permits a smaller engine to have as much, or more, horsepower than a normally aspirated larger engine.

In addition to these devices, specific pollution control equipment has been developed. Emission control systems are discussed in Unit 41.

All these approaches and devices have benefitted each of us, in terms of improved air quality and automotive performance. However, for the mechanic they have meant the necessity of learning much new technology. Some mechanics still have not accepted the inevitability of electronic controls and modern approaches to automotive performance and emission control.

In the future, automotive technology will continue to change and improve. As a mechanic, you must be ready and able to learn new skills and approaches. In any field of work, as in life, a good attitude and a willingness to learn are important. With such an attitude and outlook, you can satisfy yourself, your employer, and the customer whose car you service.

UNIT HIGHLIGHTS

- Air pollution can be caused by natural or man-made pollutants. Man-made pollutants result from the burning of fuels to produce heat and energy. Air pollution causes health problems for living things and damage to objects. Atmospheric conditions can trap and concentrate air pollution in geographical areas.

- Complete combustion of a hydrocarbon fuel results in the formation of water vapor and carbon dioxide. Incomplete combustion releases unburned hydrocarbons and carbon monoxide.

- Air pollution can be visible as "smog" or invisible. Invisible pollution can be more harmful to health than visible pollution.

- Major sources of automotive pollutants include the exhaust, fuel system, and crankcase.

- Exhaust emissions include HC, CO, NO_X, SO_X, O_3, and particulates. U.S. government regulations govern new-car emissions of HC, CO, and NO_X.

- Older models of vehicles included different regulations for California, federal (49-state), and high-altitude vehicles.

- The combination of CAFE regulations and Clean Air Act requirements stimulated vehicle manufacturers to use advanced technology. This technology includes feedback carburetors, fuel injection, electronic ignition, catalytic converters, and computer controls.

- Mechanics who have a good attitude and are willing to learn new knowledge and skills will always be in demand.

TERMS

pollution	parts per million
air pollution	(ppm)
smog	emissions
particulate	carcinogen
inversion layer	blowby gases
photochemical smog	road draft tube
carbon dioxide (CO_2)	positive crankcase
hydrocarbon (HC)	ventilation (PCV)
carbon monoxide (CO)	grams per mile (gpm)
invisible pollution	corporate average
carbon monoxide	fuel economy (CAFE)
poisoning	

DIRECTIONS: The following questions are similar to those used on mechanic certification tests. On a separate sheet of paper, write the letter of the correct choice.

1. Which of the following statements is correct?

   I. Complete combustion of a hydrocarbon fuel produces HC and CO.

   II. Incomplete combustion of a hydrocarbon fuel produces H_2O and CO_2.

   A. I only   B. II only   C. Both I and II   D. Neither I nor II

2. Major sources of automotive pollutants include all of the following EXCEPT

   A. crankcase.

   B. fuel system.

   C. exhaust.

   D. transmission.

3. Mechanic A says that ozone, sulfur, and particulate emissions levels are controlled by federal and state laws.

   Mechanic B says that HC, CO, and NO_x emissions levels are controlled by federal and state laws.

   Who is correct?

   A. A only   B. B only   C. Both A and B   D. Neither A nor B

4. Different U.S. emission control requirements and equipment were applied to all of the following EXCEPT

   A. vehicles sold in Alaska and Hawaii.

   B. high-altitude vehicles.

   C. 49-state vehicles.

   D. California vehicles.

5. Which of the following mandates fuel-economy standards?

   A. Clean Air Act

   B. CAFE requirements

   C. California Air Resources Board

   D. Environmental Protection Agency

S U P P L E M E N T A L   A C T I V I T I E S

1. Inspect several vehicles and locate their emission control information labels. Make up a table that indicates the locations of different manufacturers' labels.

2. Copy all information from a vehicle's emission control information label. Report to your class what adjustments and conditions must be met to correctly tune up the vehicle.

3. Refer to general repair manuals for tune-up specifications for a given make and model of vehicle. Note engine size, horsepower output, and ignition timing specifications from 1967 to the present. Report to your class what general trend can be noticed.

4. Visit a local auto dealership and talk to the service manager. Ask him or her what training is provided for mechanics in emission control servicing. Report to your class on what training is done, and how often mechanics must attend training sessions.

5. Visit an independent garage and talk to a mechanic or shop owner. Ask about problems in servicing different manufacturers' vehicles and emission control systems. Report to your class about problems mentioned.

41 EMISSION CONTROL SYSTEMS

UNIT PREVIEW

Virtually every part or system that changes vehicle performance and driveability also changes vehicle exhaust emissions. Emission control measures are not only add-on devices but integral parts of total vehicle systems.

Vacuum and/or electricity are used to control many engine and emissions control parts and systems. Vacuum-operated devices can be used to control other mechanical or electrical devices.

Electronically controlled functions operate in either an open-loop or closed-loop mode. Electronic control is more precise than vacuum control.

Specific emission control equipment includes devices to control fuel evaporation, crankcase emissions, and exhaust emissions. These devices include vapor recovery, positive crankcase ventilation, air injection, exhaust gas recirculation, and catalytic converters.

Catalytic converters permit engines to have both relatively clean exhaust emissions and improved performance and driveability.

LEARNING OBJECTIVES

When you have completed your assignments and exercises in this unit, you should be able to:
- ☐ Identify and describe parts and systems that affect exhaust emissions.
- ☐ Explain how vacuum controls operate and what sources of vacuum may be used.
- ☐ Explain what specific systems are used for emission control purposes.
- ☐ Locate and identify vacuum-operated control mechanisms on a vehicle.
- ☐ Locate and identify PCV, air injection, EGR, and catalytic converter system parts.

41.1 FACTORS THAT AFFECT EMISSIONS

An automobile is a complex group of interrelated systems and parts, like a human body. A single change can affect many other parts and systems.

For example, a change in idle speed can affect idle air-fuel mixture and ignition timing, and thus affect engine performance. Decreased engine performance can change automatic transmission shift points, thus decreasing acceleration, overall performance, and economy. These factors, in turn, can change the amount of pollutants emitted by a vehicle.

Vehicle Parts and Systems

Virtually every vehicle part and system that affects performance and driveability also influences automotive exhaust emissions. Thus, emission control measures are not merely add-on parts or systems but are inseparable from total vehicle operation. These parts and systems include:
- Internal engine parts (crankshaft, pistons, valves)
- Engine systems (cooling, lubrication, fuel, ignition, exhaust, electrical, and electronic control)
- Combustion chamber shape
- Camshaft profile
- Emissions control equipment
- Transmission gear ratios and shift points
- Final drive gear ratios
- Tire and wheel size.

Vehicle Operating Mode

Automotive emissions also vary according to vehicle *operating mode*. An operating mode is a specific way in which a vehicle might operate, including:
- Warm-up
- Idling
- Acceleration
- Wide-open throttle (WOT)
- Cruising
- Deceleration.

41.2 ENGINE CONTROLS

Controlling an engine during different operating modes requires both a source of force and a method of control. The most commonly used sources of force for emissions control purposes are:
- Vacuum
- Electricity.

Vacuum

Vacuum can be used as a signal or as an actuating force. That is, vacuum can be used to signal another device to operate, or to operate a mechanical device directly. Valves that block or open vacuum passages can be operated mechanically and/or electrically. For example, a temperature-operated valve can direct or block vacuum to a given device.

Electricity

Electricity can be used to operate solenoids and stepper motors to push, pull, or hold mechanical devices. For example, a solenoid valve can open or block a vacuum passage for different engine operating modes. Electricity may be controlled by mechanical switches or by electronic control units.

Figure 41-1 shows the interrelationship among vacuum, electricity, and electronic controls for one type of emission control.

41.3 VACUUM-OPERATED CONTROLS

Vacuum-operated controls use one of three sources of vacuum (see Figure 41-2):

- Manifold vacuum
- Ported vacuum
- Venturi vacuum.

Manifold Vacuum

Manifold vacuum, as described in Unit 10, is created in an intake manifold when an engine cranks or runs. Manifold vacuum is high when a throttle plate is closed or partially closed during idling and deceleration. Manifold vacuum drops when a throttle plate is opened wide during acceleration and high-speed operation.

Thus, manifold vacuum is related to throttle position, engine load, and engine volumetric efficiency.

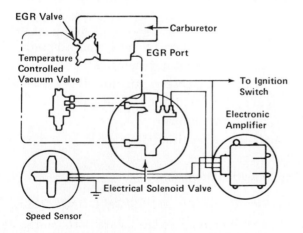

Figure 41-1. Emission control system using temperature, electronics, and manual actuation.

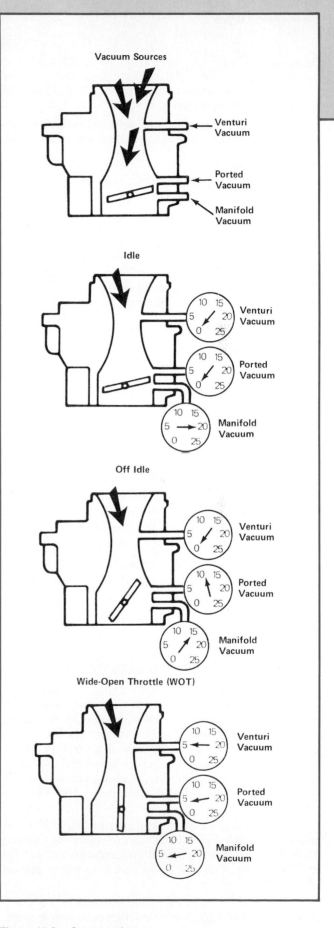

Figure 41-2. Sources of vacuum.

435

Manifold vacuum will vary from 15 to 22 in. [38.1 to 55.88 cm] Hg at idle. When a throttle plate is momentarily opened to *wide-open throttle (WOT),* manifold vacuum will drop to zero.

Manifold vacuum can be applied to control devices through *taps,* or openings, in an intake manifold.

Ported Vacuum

Ported vacuum, as discussed in Unit 21, is created in a throttle body barrel. When a throttle plate is moved to increase engine speed above idle, the vacuum port is exposed to manifold vacuum. Ported vacuum does not exist at idle, and it drops as a throttle plate opens wide. Ported vacuum will vary between zero and 22 in. [55.88 cm] Hg. Ported vacuum, as explained in Topic 34.7, can be used to operate devices such as distributor vacuum advance mechanisms.

Venturi Vacuum

Venturi vacuum is created at a venturi, or restriction, in a carburetor barrel. At idle and when a throttle plate is only partially open, air velocity is too low to develop vacuum. However, when a throttle plate is fully open and air flow increases, venturi vacuum is present. Venturi vacuum varies from zero to 4 in. [10.16 cm] Hg.

Mechanically Operated Valves

Mechanically operated controls can take many forms. Distributor centrifugal advance mechanisms are mechanical controls. A heat-operated valve also can direct or block vacuum to vacuum-operated controls (see Figure 41-3).

Electrically Operated Controls

Electrically operated controls, such as solenoid valves, can be used to direct or block vacuum to vacuum-operated controls. The unit shown in Figure 41-4 uses mechanical actuation and/or a solenoid to direct vacuum to a distributor vacuum advance unit.

41.4 VACUUM-OPERATED CONTROL SYSTEMS

The use of vacuum-operated engine and emissions control equipment may require the use of multiple vacuum hoses. Such a system is shown in Figure 41-5. If a single vacuum hose becomes loose, disconnected, or broken, elements of a total emissions control system will not function properly. Manufacturers' service manuals contain vacuum hose diagrams for specific models, years, engines, and optional equipment.

Vacuum-operated systems operate on basic mechanical principles and thus are relatively durable. However, vacuum-operated controls do not act immediately. In addition, leaks and accidental disconnections can occur.

The need for controls that respond rapidly and reliably has led vehicle manufacturers to develop electronically operated systems.

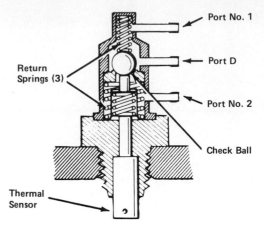

Figure 41-3. Typical ported vacuum switch.
HONDA MOTOR COMPANY

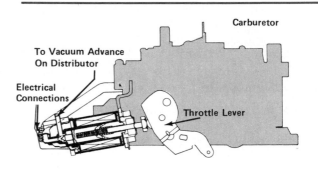

Figure 41-4. Vacuum-electric solenoid assembly.

41.5 ELECTRONICALLY OPERATED CONTROL SYSTEMS

Sensors, electronic control units, and actuator units can be used to adjust air-fuel ratios, exhaust gas recirculation, and ignition timing. This is discussed in Unit 38. As necessary, other actuator-operated devices can be combined with basic systems to form overall electronic control systems. A diagram of inputs and outputs that include emissions control devices is shown in Figure 41-6.

41.6 EMISSION CONTROL EQUIPMENT

Specific emission control equipment (see Figure 41-7) is included as part of an overall group of vehicle systems. Emission control subsystems include:

- Evaporative emission controls
- Positive crankcase ventilation (PCV) system
- Fuel system modifications and controls
- Combustion control
- Exhaust gas recirculation (EGR)
- Air injection
- Catalytic converters.

41.7 EVAPORATIVE EMISSION CONTROLS

Evaporative emission controls are parts and systems designed to prevent fuel vapors from escaping directly into the air. *Vapor recovery systems* trap and

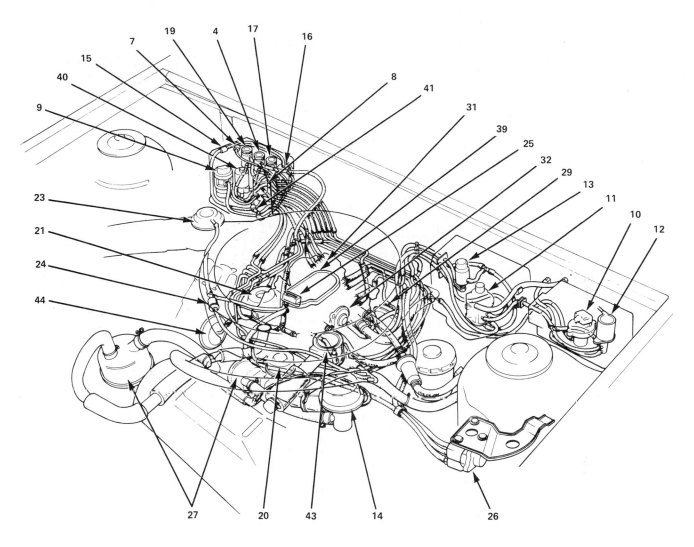

(See page 438 for complete system)

4	PJ Cut Solenoid Valve	21	EGR Valve
7	Dashpot Check Valve (except 1300 49 ST 5-speed)	23	Intake Air Control Diaphragm
8	Control Switch Solenoid Valve	24	Check Valve for Intake Air Temperature Control
9	Control Switch	25	Air Bleed Valve
10	Vacuum Switch	26	Air Jet Controller (California and high altitude only)
11	EGR Control Valve A and B		
12	EGR Control Solenoid Valve B	27	Air Chambers A and B
13	EGR Control Solenoid Valve A	29	Throttle Controller
14	Anti-Afterburn Valve	31	Fast Idle Unloader
15	Throttle Controller Check Valve	32	Air Vent Cut-Off Diaphragm
16	Cranking Solenoid Valve	39	Idle Controller
17	Cranking Leak Solenoid Valve	40	Vacuum Holding Solenoid Valve
19	Idle Control Solenoid Valve A (manual transmission only)	41	Power Valve Check Valve
		43	Condensation Chamber
20	Air Suction Valve and Air Suction Cut-Off Diaphragm Valve	44	Distributor Vacuum Advance

Figure 41-5. Vacuum hose and electrical connections. HONDA MOTOR COMPANY (Continued on next page.)

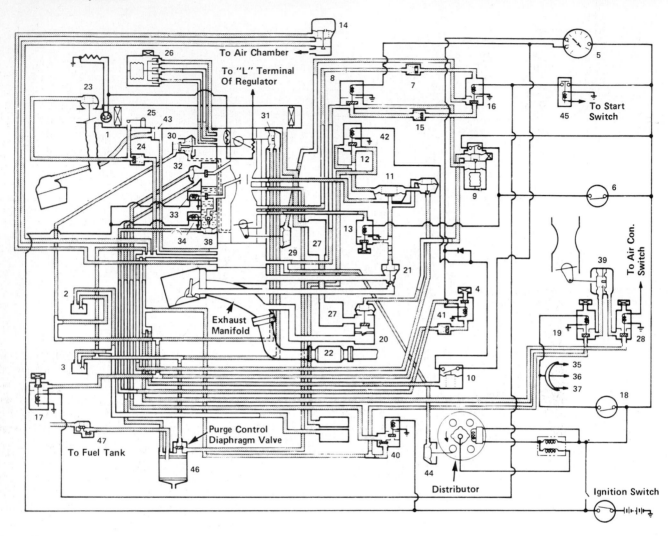

1	Intake Air Temp. Sensor	
2	Thermovalve A	
3	Thermovalve B	
4	PJ Cut Solenoid Valve	
5	Speed Sensor	
6	Thermosensor A	
7	Dashpot Check Valve (except 1300 49 ST 5-speed)	
8	Control Switch Solenoid Valve	
9	Control Switch	
10	Vacuum Switch	
11	EGR Control Valve A and B	
12	EGR Control Solenoid Valve B	
13	EGR Control Solenoid Valve A	
14	Anti-Afterburn Valve	
15	Throttle Controller Check Valve	
16	Cranking Solenoid Valve	
17	Cranking Leak Solenoid Valve	
18	Thermosensor B (manual transmission only)	
19	Idle Control Solenoid Valve A (manual transmission only)	
20	Air Suction Valve and Air Suction Cut-Off Diaphragm Valve	
21	EGR Valve	
22	Catalytic Converter	
23	Intake Air Control Diaphragm	
24	Check Valve for Intake Air Temperature Control	
25	Air Bleed Valve	
26	Air Jet Controller (California and high altitude only)	
27	Air Chambers A and B	
28	Idle Control Solenoid Valve B (car with air conditioner only)	
29	Throttle Controller	
30	Choke Opener	
31	Fast Idle Unloader	
32	Air Vent Cut-Off Diaphragm	
33	Primary Main Fuel Cut-Off Solenoid Valve	
34	Primary Slow Mixture Cut-Off Solenoid Valve	
35	Rear Window Defroster Switch (manual transmission only)	
36	Heater Blower Switch (manual transmission only)	
37	Headlight Switch (manual transmission only)	
38	Power Valve	
39	Idle Controller	
40	Vacuum Holding Solenoid Valve	
41	Power Valve Check Valve	
42	EGR Air Filter	
43	Condensation Chamber	
44	Distributor Vacuum Advance	
45	Starter Relay	
46	Canister	
47	Two-Way Valve	

Figure 41-5. Concluded.

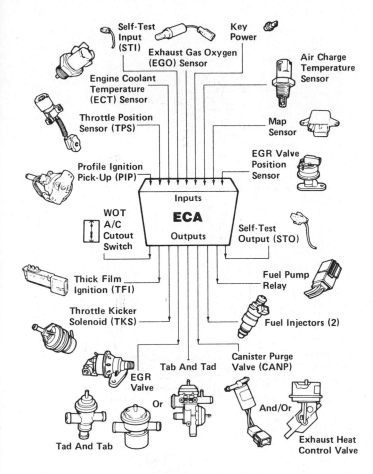

Figure 41-6. Emissions system parts. FORD MOTOR COMPANY

hold fuel vapors until they can be drawn into the engine with an intake charge. A vapor recovery system (see Figure 41-8) can include:

- Nonvented fuel tank filler cap
- Domed fuel tank
- Vapor/fuel separator
- Connecting hoses and tubes
- Vapor recovery canister
- Check valves
- Source of manifold vacuum.

Nonvented Fuel Tank Filler Cap

Filler caps on late-model vehicles are sealed to prevent escape of fuel vapors (see Figure 41-9). These caps include vacuum and pressure relief valves to prevent damage to a fuel tank from excessive pressure or vacuum.

As fuel cools, it contracts. A partial vacuum is formed in the tank. Atmospheric pressure acting on the walls of a tank could collapse it. A *vacuum relief valve* opens to allow outside air into the tank. This action balances pressure against inside and outside surfaces of a tank.

When a fuel tank is heated by outside temperatures, fuel and vapors expand, producing pressure that could rupture fuel tank seams. Normally, this pressure buildup is slight, and pressure is dissipated throughout a vapor recovery system. However, if

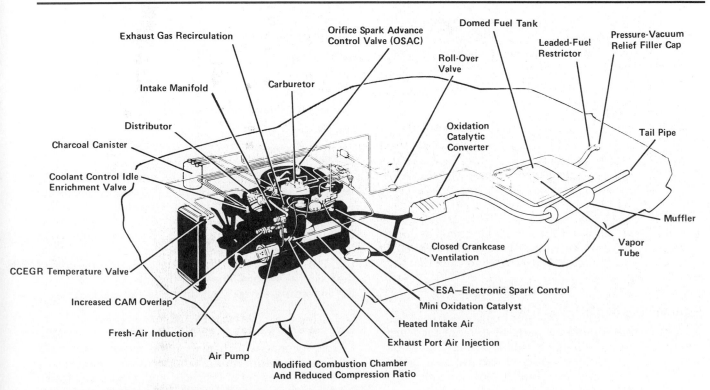

Figure 41-7. Emissions system parts locations. CHRYSLER CORPORATION

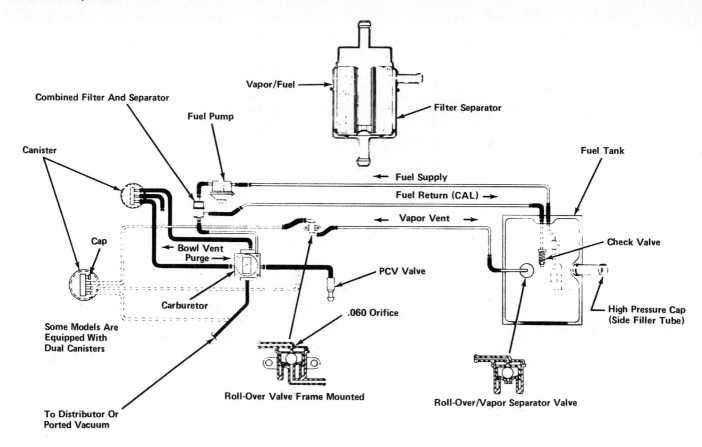

Figure 41-8. Vapor recovery system. CHRYSLER CORPORATION

hoses or tubes become clogged or accidentally pinched, pressure could damage a tank. A *pressure relief valve* opens to allow excessive pressure to escape. Normally, up to 1 psi [6.895 kPa] of pressure can exist in a tank and vapor recovery system. Pressure over that limit will open the pressure relief valve. (See Figure 41-9.)

Domed Fuel Tank

Fuel vapors rise to the upper portion of a tank. An *expansion dome* collects fuel vapors from the tank (see Figure 41-10). An expansion dome is a raised portion of an upper fuel tank wall.

Vapor/Fuel Separator

A *vapor/fuel separator* allows fuel vapors to pass into connecting hoses. The vapor/fuel separator collects droplets of liquid fuel and directs them back into the tank (see Figure 41-10).

Connecting Hoses and Tubes

Hoses and tubes connect parts of a vapor-recovery system. Special fuel/vapor rubber tubing must be used. Ordinary rubber hoses would rot and crack quickly from the effects of fuel. Metal tubing is used under a vehicle.

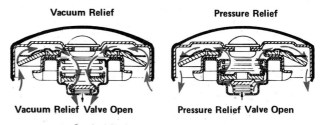

Figure 41-9. Sealed fuel tank cap.

Vapor Recovery Canister

A *vapor recovery canister* is a container that stores fuel vapors. The vapor recovery canister is filled with *activated charcoal*. Activated charcoal is a highly porous substance that can store large amounts of vapors. During engine operation, fresh air is drawn in through the charcoal by means of intake manifold vacuum. This air flow purges or strips the charcoal of the gasoline vapors. These vapors then are mixed with the incoming air-fuel mixture (see Figure 41-11).

Check Valves

Check, or one-way, valves keep vapors confined. When an engine runs, vacuum and/or electrically operated valves open. Fresh air and vapors are drawn into the intake manifold. See Figure 41-11.

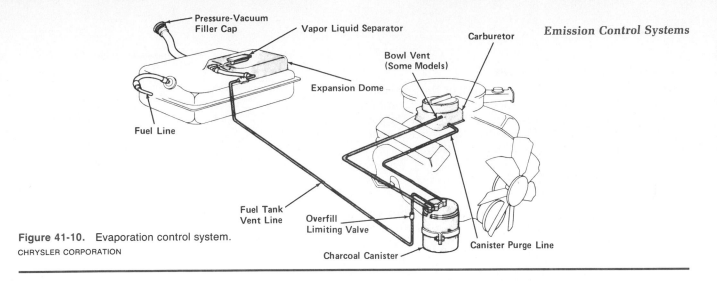

Figure 41-10. Evaporation control system.

CHRYSLER CORPORATION

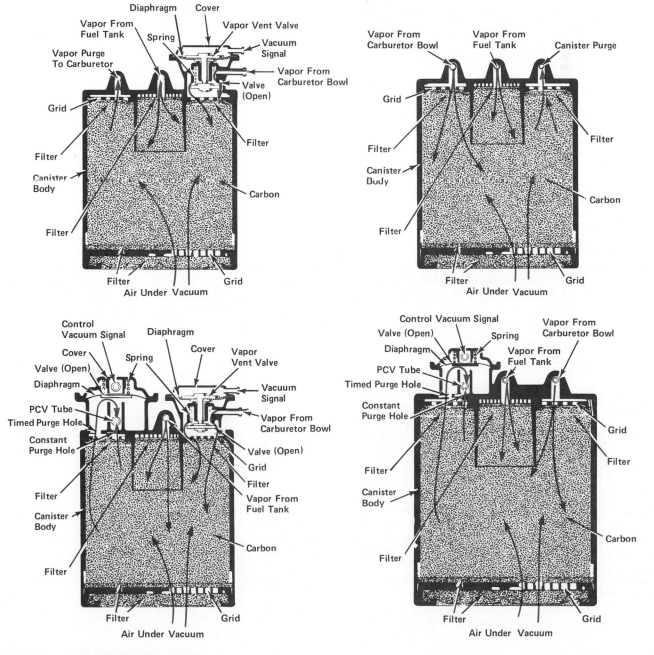

Figure 41-11. Vapor recovery canisters.

Source of Manifold Vacuum

Ported vacuum often is used to control the canister purge circuit. This is done to prevent purge operation during idle. If vapors were drawn in during idle, a rough idle could result along with excessive exhaust emissions, especially during hot operation.

41.8 POSITIVE CRANKCASE VENTILATION SYSTEM

A positive crankcase ventilation (PCV) system removes blowby gases and oil vapors from crankcase and air passages within an engine. A typical closed PCV system is shown in Figure 41-12.

A PCV, or check, valve meters flow of blowby gases and fresh air through a PCV system. The PCV valve also prevents backfire explosions in an intake manifold from travelling back to internal engine spaces. Operation of a PCV valve during different engine modes is shown in Figure 41-13.

41.9 FUEL SYSTEM MODIFICATIONS

The first approach to reducing HC and CO exhaust emissions was to create a leaner than stoichiometric mixture. A lean mixture increases combustion temperatures. In this way, HC and CO emissions can be reduced. However, as can be seen from the graph in Figure 41-14, NO_x emissions climb sharply as the air-fuel mixture becomes leaner.

Stoichiometric Mixtures

A stoichiometric mixture is best for both engine efficiency and smog control. A catalytic converter operates most efficiently with a stoichiometric (14.7:1) air-fuel mixture (see Figure 41-15).

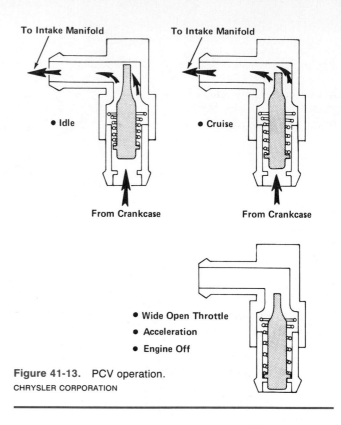

Figure 41-13. PCV operation.
CHRYSLER CORPORATION

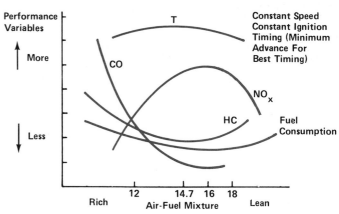

Figure 41-14. Air-fuel ratio and emissions variations.

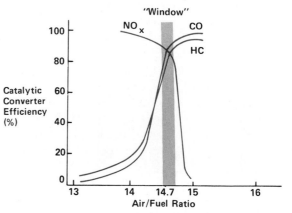

Figure 41-15. Conversion efficiency of a three-way catalyst.

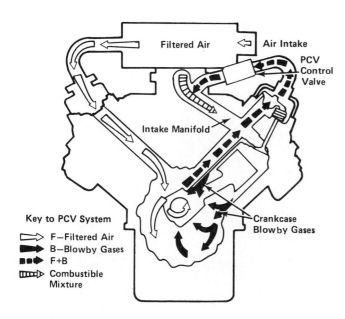

Figure 41-12. PCV system.

As discussed in Topic 21.8, computer-operated feedback carburetors can vary jet openings to provide a nearly stoichiometric mixture. Electronic fuel-injection systems operate in a similar way. Thus, computer controls can help reduce exhaust emissions when the system operates in the closed-loop mode.

Tamper-Proof Adjustments

To prevent tampering, idle mixture screws may be factory-preset and plugged. On late-model vehicles, mechanics can make only base idle speed adjustments.

Thermostatically Controlled Air Cleaner

A *thermostatically controlled air cleaner* can be used to promote fuel vaporization. Depending on underhood air temperature, a thermostatically controlled air cleaner can provide hot, warm, or *ambient* air. Ambient air is air at the surrounding, or ambient, temperature. Heated air aids in fuel vaporization. The source of heated air is a *heat stove*. A heat stove is a sheet metal enclosure around an exhaust manifold, through which air can flow and be heated.

The mixing of heated and cold air is controlled by a temperature sensor inside an air cleaner. Heated air maximizes vaporization and minimizes unburned HC exhaust emissions. After warm-up, cool, denser air is provided for maximum engine power output (see Figure 41-16).

A temperature sensor with a bimetallic spring opens and closes a vacuum valve. The valve bleeds off or passes manifold vacuum to a *vacuum motor* on an air cleaner intake. A vacuum motor consists of a vacuum diaphragm attached to a pull rod.

The pull rod is attached to an air control valve, or damper door, in an air intake. A spring pulls the door closed. When vacuum is applied to the vacuum motor, intake manifold vacuum pulls the damper open (see Figure 41-17).

When underhood temperature is low, heated air is directed into an air cleaner to promote fuel vaporization. As underhood temperature rises, part heated and part cool air are mixed for proper vaporization. After warm-up and during hard acceleration, the damper closes to provide cool, dense air (see Figure 41-18).

Throttle Positioners

When a throttle plate is closed suddenly during deceleration, a high vacuum is created underneath. This high vacuum draws in a rich mixture from idle discharge ports. It also will cause any liquid fuel in the manifold to flash off into a vapor. A sudden "spike," or high reading, of high HC and CO emissions is created.

To prevent this problem, some carburetors use *deceleration valves* and *throttle positioners*. A deceleration valve is a valve that operates for a specific length

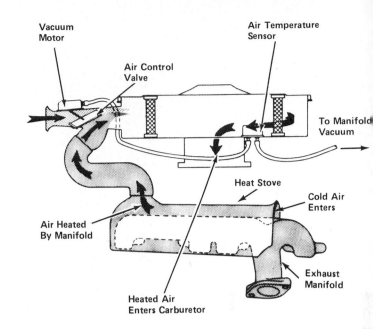

Figure 41-16. Thermostatic air cleaner. CHRYSLER CORPORATION

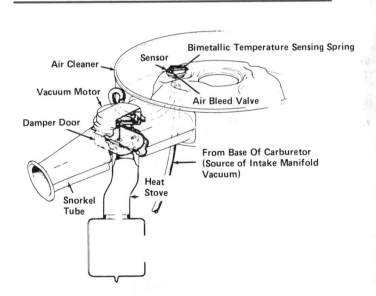

Figure 41-17. Parts of a thermostatically controlled air cleaner. CHEVROLET MOTOR DIVISION—GMC

of time on deceleration. A throttle positioner holds a throttle open. Throttle positioners use a small vacuum diaphragm and an air bleed to gradually reduce throttle position to idle. These actions eliminate temporary high readings of HC and CO.

41.10 COMBUSTION CONTROL

The quality of combustion within an engine directly affects engine performance and exhaust emissions. If combustion is efficient, maximum power is produced from minimum fuel. In addition, efficient combustion means that less unburned HC and CO emissions are

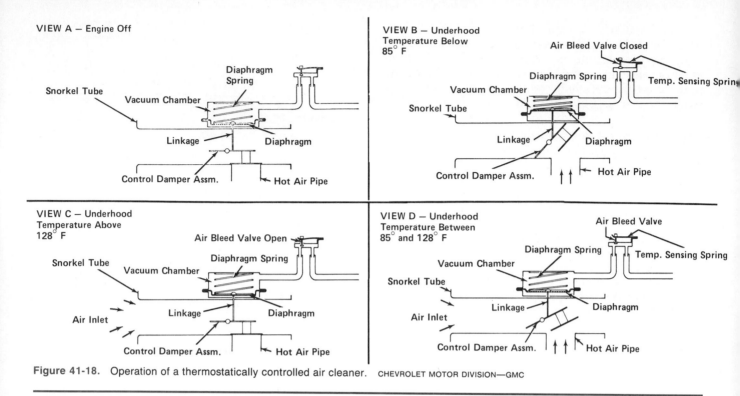

VIEW A — Engine Off

Snorkel Tube — Vacuum Chamber — Diaphragm Spring — Diaphragm — Linkage — Control Damper Assm. — Hot Air Pipe

VIEW B — Underhood Temperature Below 85° F

Air Bleed Valve Closed — Diaphragm Spring — Temp. Sensing Spring — Vacuum Chamber — Snorkel Tube — Linkage — Diaphragm — Control Damper Assm. — Hot Air Pipe

VIEW C — Underhood Temperature Above 128° F

Snorkel Tube — Vacuum Chamber — Air Bleed Valve Open — Diaphragm Spring — Air Inlet — Linkage — Diaphragm — Control Damper Assm. — Hot Air Pipe

VIEW D — Underhood Temperature Between 85° and 128° F

Air Bleed Valve — Diaphragm Spring — Temp. Sensing Spring — Vacuum Chamber — Snorkel Tube — Air Inlet — Linkage — Diaphragm — Control Damper Assm. — Hot Air Pipe

Figure 41-18. Operation of a thermostatically controlled air cleaner. CHEVROLET MOTOR DIVISION—GMC

produced. Controlling the temperature of the combustion process can help reduce NO_X emissions. Methods of controlling the combustion process include:

- Engine and intake manifold modifications
- Ignition timing modifications
- Exhaust gas recirculation.

41.11 ENGINE AND INTAKE MANIFOLD MODIFICATIONS

Engine and intake manifold modifications are made to improve fuel vaporization, intake gas flow and turbulence, and exhaust gas flow. In addition, exhaust gases can be mixed with an intake charge to decrease burning temperatures.

Combustion Chamber Shape

Combustion chamber shape can be changed to decrease quench areas. Spark plug holes can be placed so that a combustion flame front travels rapidly and evenly to combustion chamber areas. Modifications to combustion chamber shape can help increase gas flow and promote vaporization, as discussed in Topic 14.1. Increasing intake valve size and repositioning intake and exhaust valves can result in reduced exhaust emissions. Intake and exhaust valves also can be made to operate at steeper angles to each other, which increases turbulence.

Late-model vehicles may use a *pentroof* combustion chamber, as shown in Figure 41-19. A pentroof combustion chamber is shaped like the roof of a house. It is an angular version of a hemispherical combustion chamber.

Figure 41-19. Pentroof combustion chamber.
TOYOTA MOTOR SALES, U.S.A.

Additional Intake and/or Exhaust Valves

Two intake and/or two exhaust valves can be used in each cylinder to improve both turbulence and volumetric efficiency. See Figure 41-20. Two smaller valves are better than one large valve because gas flow rate must increase through smaller openings. Higher flow rates increase turbulence and promote smoother operation. Thus, engine efficiency increases, providing better power output and lower exhaust emissions.

Stratified Charge

Stratified charge engines, such as those used in Honda automobiles, have a special, smaller intake valve. A rich mixture from a third carburetor barrel is drawn in directly below a spark plug. Below this, a lean mixture is drawn in through a normal, larger intake valve (see Figure 41-21). Thus, the charge is layered, or stratified, with a rich mixture on top and a leaner mixture on the bottom. When the spark plug fires, the rich upper mixture ignites easily, thus igniting the lean mixture beneath.

Cylinder Head and Intake Manifold Design

Redesigned cylinder head intake ports and intake manifolds can increase turbulence. Late-model vehicles from Toyota have a variable induction system that opens additional intake ports at high rpm (see Figure 41-22). This allows high rates of gas flow at both low and high rpm, for increased volumetric efficiency, torque, and turbulence.

Increased Valve Overlap

Valve overlap, as discussed in Topic 14.10, occurs when both intake and exhaust valves are open on an intake stroke. Camshafts are designed differently for emission control purposes. Intake and exhaust camshaft lobes are repositioned relative to each other and reshaped to provide increased valve overlap (see Figure 41-23). This allows more exhaust gases to mix with an intake charge.

Because exhaust gases contain little oxygen, the mixed intake charge and exhaust gases do not burn rapidly. A slower, lower-temperature burning takes place, thus reducing NO_x exhaust emissions.

41.12 IGNITION TIMING MODIFICATIONS

Ignition timing directly affects engine efficiency and emissions. However, the dual goals of efficient engine operation and low HC and CO emissions are not always compatible.

Figure 41-20. Four-valves-per-cylinder cylinder head.
TOYOTA MOTOR SALES, U.S.A.

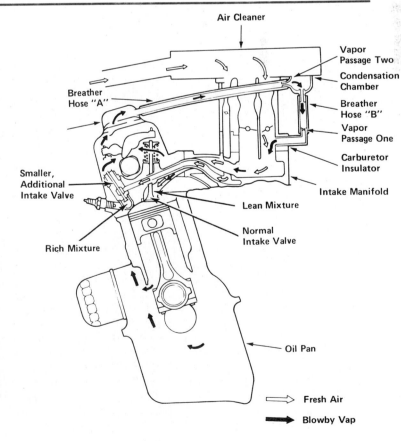

Figure 41-21. Stratified charge engine.
HONDA MOTOR COMPANY

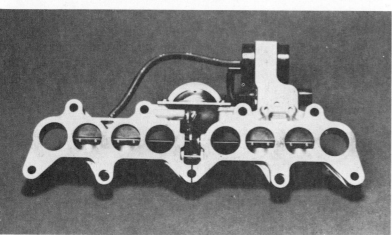

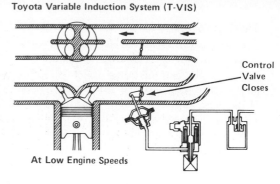

Toyota Variable Induction System (T-VIS)

Control Valve Closes

At Low Engine Speeds

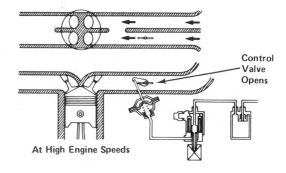

Control Valve Opens

At High Engine Speeds

T-VIS Torque Curves

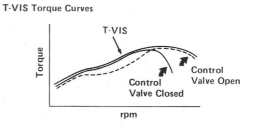

Figure 41-22. Variable induction system. TOYOTA MOTOR SALES, U.S.A.

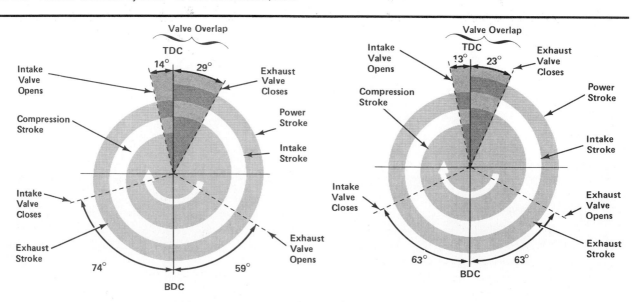

Figure 41-23. Valve overlap changes.

Timing for Engine Power and Emissions

For maximum performance, ignition timing should occur so that maximum pressure is produced at a point approximately 10 degrees ATDC. This normally requires that initial timing be set some degrees BTDC. Retarding spark so that ignition occurs ATDC will lower pressure, engine torque, and power. However, as pressure decreases, a more thorough, slow burning occurs.

A thorough, slow burning increases the amount of fuel burned in an intake charge. Retarded timing can help to burn a rich air-fuel mixture more completely. Such a mixture is produced during deceleration.

The graph shown in Figure 41-24 illustrates a basic problem with ignition timing. Timing that produces maximum engine torque output and lowest fuel consumption increases HC and NO_x exhaust emissions. If ignition timing remained constant, an engine would produce either low emissions or good torque, but not both. Thus, ignition timing must be changeable as required for power output or emissions considerations.

Vacuum-Operated Ignition Advance/Retard Controls

Mechanical devices can be used to control vacuum advance/retard diaphragm operation (see Figure 41-25). Such devices can include:

- Thermo-vacuum valves
- Vacuum delay valves
- Vacuum check valves.

Thermo-vacuum valves can be used to block or direct ported or manifold vacuum. In this way, vacuum can control distributor advance and/or retard mechanisms for maximum power or more complete combustion.

Vacuum delay valves are small plastic units in a vacuum line that contain a calibrated restriction. Vacuum delay valves slow the application of vacuum buildup that operates a device. A vacuum delay valve can be used to slow spark advance until an engine reaches higher rpm.

Vacuum check valves allow vacuum to travel in only one direction through a tube or hose. Vacuum check valves can be used to isolate a vacuum-operated unit from specific sources of vacuum.

Computer-Controlled Ignition

Computer-controlled ignition timing, as discussed in Unit 34, can control ignition timing according to a "spark map." A computer program thus can select the best ignition timing compromise for good power and low exhaust emissions.

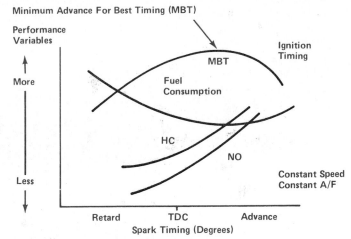

Figure 41-24. Variation of performance with spark timing.

41.13 EXHAUST GAS RECIRCULATION

As discussed in Topic 41.11, dilution of an intake charge with exhaust gases can lower NO_x emissions. *Exhaust gas recirculation (EGR)* is a method of reusing exhaust gases in an intake charge to reduce NO_x.

An *EGR valve* is a vacuum-operated valve that can open a passage between exhaust and intake manifold areas. Many types and combinations of EGR control are possible (see Figure 41-26).

Temperature-Controlled EGR

Exhaust gas recirculation reduces power output and would cause a vehicle to stall during warmup or at idle. Temperature-sensitive vacuum control valves can be used to prevent EGR until an engine warms up. Refer to Figure 41-26.

Backpressure Transducer

In previous years, EGR operated only in an on or off way. Late-model vehicles' EGR systems are *modulated*, or controlled. Thus, an EGR valve can be closed, partially opened, or fully opened.

A *backpressure transducer* can be used to modulate, or change, the amount an EGR valve opens (see Figure 41-26). A backpressure transducer is a device that senses exhaust gas pressure and regulates a vacuum-control valve. Exhaust gas pressure is dependent on engine rpm. The EGR valve may be closed or partially opened at different engine speeds.

Electronically Controlled Solenoid Valve

A computer-controlled solenoid can open or close an EGR valve in relation to any sensor-provided information (see Figure 41-27). Thus, many engine operating conditions can influence EGR.

41.14 AIR INJECTION

Air injection is an introduction of fresh air into an exhaust manifold. In previous years, air injection was done to promote additional burning, or oxidation, of

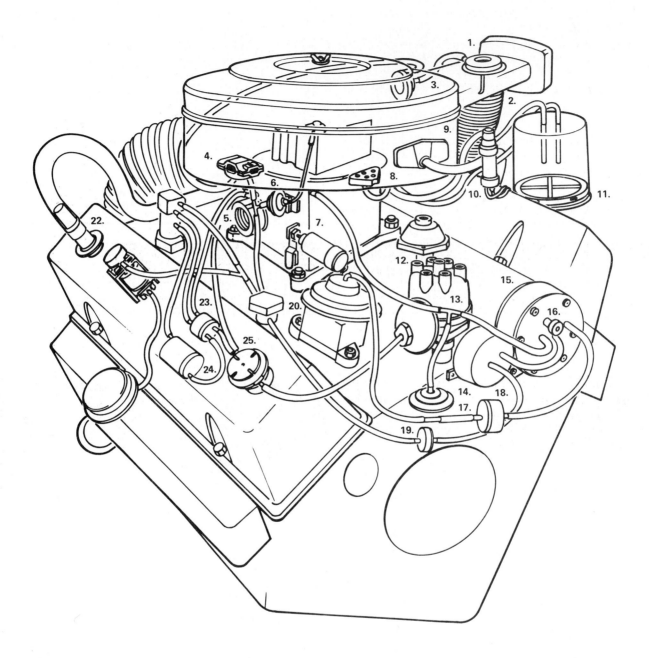

1	Vacuum Motor	9	Breather Filter (Inside Housing)	17	Wide-Open Throttle (WOT) Valve
2	Thermostatically-Controlled Air Cleaner Manifold Stove Heater Duct	10	Carburetor Float Bowl Solenoid Valve	18	Thermal Control Valve
3	Temperature Control Valve	11	Vapor Recovery Canister Replacement Filter	19	Distributor Check Valve
4	Temperature Sensor	12	Deceleration Valve	20	EGR Valve
5	Automatic Choke Thermostat	13	Vacuum Hose Tee Connector	21	PCV Valve
6	Choke Pull-Off	14	Vacuum Reservoir	22	Spark Delay Valve
7	Idle Speed Solenoid	15	Vacuum Amplifier	23	Fuel/Vapor Separator
8	Choke Air	16	EGR Air Bleed Filter	24	Vacuum Regulator
				25	Three-Way Spark Control

Figure 41-25. Vacuum control system.

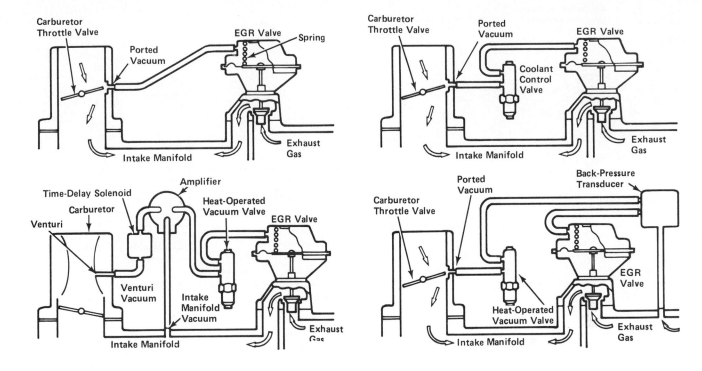

Figure 41-26. EGR variations.

HC within the exhaust manifold itself. For a burning process to occur, there must be fuel, heat, and oxygen. Small amounts of fuel (HC) and heat are present in exhaust gases. Introducing air into an exhaust manifold provides oxygen, and additional burning occurs.

Late-model vehicles use air injection to provide additional air for an oxidizing catalytic converter. An oxidizing catalytic converter, described in 41.15, promotes the combination of CO and NO_x with oxygen. Relatively less-harmful carbon dioxide (CO_2), nitrogen (N_2), water (H_2O), and oxygen (O_2) are formed. Two types of air injection are common:

- Engine-driven pump system
- Exhaust gas pulse system.

Engine-Driven Pump

An engine-driven pump air injection system is illustrated in Figure 41-28. This type of system can include the following parts:

- Air pump
- Diverter valve
- Air-switching valve
- Check valves
- Distribution manifold
- Temperature-sensitive vacuum valves
- Vacuum source
- Connecting tubes and hoses.

An air pump draws air in and forces pressurized air out. A diverter valve diverts, or detours, air during

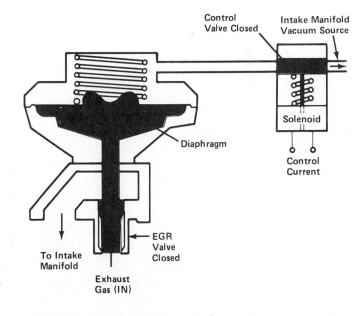

Figure 41-27. EGR actuator control.

deceleration. Excess air in exhaust rich with fuel can produce a backfire or explosion in a muffler. A vacuum signal operates the diverter valve during deceleration. Compressed air is diverted to the atmosphere.

Late-model vehicles include diverter/bypass valves that can direct air to an exhaust manifold and/or a catalytic converter. See Figure 41-29.

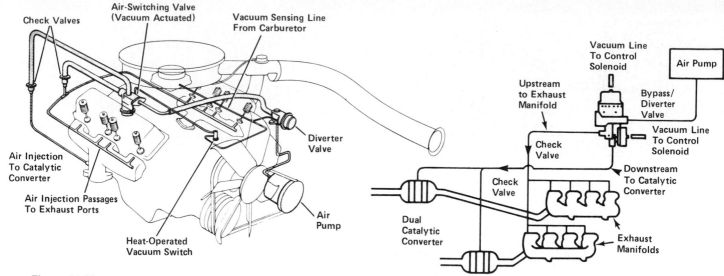

Figure 41-28. Engine-driven air pump.
CHRYSLER CORPORATION

Figure 41-29. Parts of an air injection system.
FORD MOTOR COMPANY

Catalytic converter air can be injected into the exhaust pipe before the catalytic converter or between elements of the converter.

An air-switching valve switches the location of injected air to lessen formation of NO_X after warm-up. Check valves prevent exhaust gases from reaching a diverter valve or air pump.

Exhaust Gas Pulse System

Exhaust gases leave an engine in pulses, as explained in Unit 25. These pulses produce noise, which is lessened by a muffler. However, these pulses also can be used to provide force to draw fresh air into an exhaust manifold.

A *pulse air valve* directs air into the distribution manifold pipes (see Figure 41-30). A pulse air valve is a container with *reed valves*. A reed valve is a device with a flexible diaphragm covering an opening. After an exhaust pulse has passed the valve, a low pressure is developed, which pulls a reed valve open. Air is then drawn in through the reed valve to an exhaust manifold port.

41.15 CATALYTIC CONVERTER

Catalytic converters have been part of new vehicles' exhaust systems since 1975, as discussed in Unit 25. Vehicles that are designed to use only unleaded fuels have catalytic converters. A catalytic converter contains a chemical *catalyst*. A catalyst is a chemical that promotes a chemical reaction between other chemicals, without being consumed itself.

The complete combustion of HC fuel in air produces water and carbon dioxide. However, as discussed in Unit 40, internal combustion engines do not completely burn all the fuel in an intake charge. The result of incomplete combustion is HC and CO pollutants. In addition, high combustion temperatures produce NO_X.

Early attempts to reduce hydrocarbons involved raising combustion temperatures, using lean mixtures, and retarding ignition timing. Such practices produced vehicles that stalled and died repeatedly when cold, ran poorly, and returned poor gas mileage. In addition, high amounts of NO_X were produced.

The use of catalytic converters allows richer mixtures and advanced ignition timing for improved driveability, performance, and fuel mileage. Thus, catalytic converters promote both cleaner air and reasonable performance.

Catalytic converters convert harmful pollutants into relatively harmless products through two processes:

- Oxidation
- Reduction.

Oxidation

If HC and CO could be combined with extra oxygen (O_2), the result would be H_2O and CO_2. The catalyst in a catalytic converter promotes a combining action of oxygen with both HC and CO. This action is known as chemical *oxidation,* or combination with oxygen.

Such a *two-way catalyst* was used in catalytic converters in 1975 and subsequent years. The chemicals used for two-way catalysts are *platinum* and *palladium*. Platinum and palladium are both expensive, rare metals. Ceramic beads or a ceramic *substrate* are coated with a thin layer of catalyst. A substrate is a honeycomb grid structure as shown in Figure 41-31.

Exhaust gases pass through beads or a substrate, and oxidation occurs. Thus, HC and CO are combined with oxygen from excess air provided by an air-injection system. The resulting compounds are H_2O and CO_2, both part of the natural environment (see Figure 41-32).

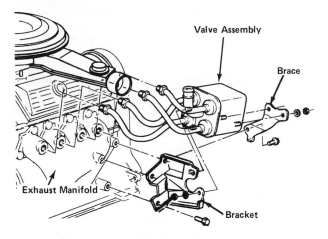

Figure 41-30. Pulse air system. CHEVROLET MOTOR DIVISION—GMC

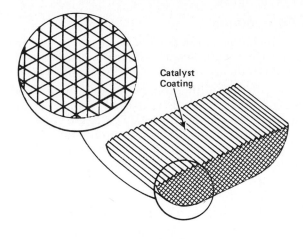

Figure 41-31. Substrate structures.

Reduction

Another chemical reaction that can be promoted by a catalyst is *reduction*. Reduction is the removal of oxygen from a compound. If oxygen can be removed from NO_X, nitrogen (N_2) and oxygen (O_2), both parts of air, will be formed.

Chemical reduction of NO_X is accomplished with catalysts of platinum and *rhodium*. Rhodium is another rare metal that is often used for plating jewelry. Platinum and rhodium also are effective for oxidizing HC and CO. A *three-way catalyst* thus changes HC, CO, and NO_X into H_2O, CO_2, N, and O_2 (refer to Figure 41-33).

Catalytic converters may contain *dual beds*, or two areas where catalytic reactions occur. Dual beds may be used in two-way or three-way catalytic converters. A three-way (HC, CO, NO_X) catalytic converter is shown in Figure 41-34.

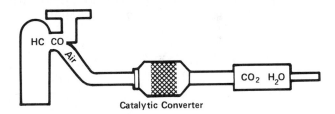

Figure 41-32. Exhaust conversion from a two-way catalytic converter.

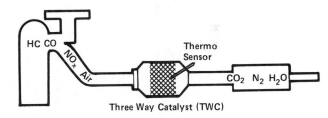

Figure 41-33. Exhaust conversion from a three-way catalytic converter.

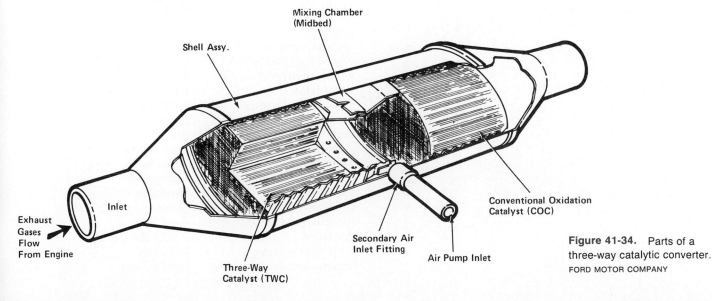

Figure 41-34. Parts of a three-way catalytic converter. FORD MOTOR COMPANY

SO$_x$ Compounds

During oxidation, sulfur (S) that is present in fuel and lubricating oil combines with oxygen (O). The resulting compounds are known as oxides of sulfur (SO$_x$).

In addition, sulfur dioxide gas (SO$_2$) is formed. Some vehicles' catalytic converters produce an unpleasant, "rotten egg" smell. SO$_2$ is the same gas formed in rotting eggs. Although unpleasant, SO$_2$ is not considered a major pollutant at present.

Oxides of sulfur also combine with water vapor (H$_2$O) to produce small amounts of sulfuric acid (H$_2$SO$_4$). The long-term effects of adding small amounts of sulfuric acid to air are not known.

However, *acid rain* and *acid fog* are caused by large amounts of sulfur added to air through industrial processes. Acid rain and acid fog contain large amounts of sulfuric acid, which pollutes rivers and streams, kills fish, and harms vegetation.

Misfueling

Misfueling is adding leaded gasoline to vehicles with catalytic converters. Exhaust fumes containing lead will coat catalyst beads or substrate, "poisoning" a converter. Exhaust emissions rise dramatically, although a vehicle's driver may notice no change in performance.

More than one tankful of leaded gasoline will poison a converter and make converter replacement necessary.

U N I T   H I G H L I G H T S

- Virtually every part and system that affects vehicle performance and driveability also influences vehicle exhaust emissions. Thus, emission control measures are not merely add-on devices but integral parts of total vehicle systems.

- Vehicle operating mode also influences exhaust emissions.

- Vacuum and/or electricity are used to control many engine and emission control functions. Three types of vacuum are used: manifold, ported, and venturi. Vacuum controls are relatively durable but do not respond quickly.

- Electronically controlled functions operate in either an open-loop or closed-loop mode. Electronic control is more precise than vacuum control.

- Specific emission control equipment includes devices to control fuel evaporation, crankcase emissions, and exhaust emissions. These devices include vapor recovery, PCV, air injection, EGR, and catalytic converters.

- Catalytic converters permit engines to use richer fuel mixtures and advanced ignition timing for improved performance.

T E R M S

operating mode	vacuum delay valves
wide-open throttle (WOT)	vacuum check valves
evaporative emission controls	exhaust gas recirculation (EGR)
vapor recovery system	EGR valve
vacuum relief valve	modulate
pressure relief valve	backpressure transducer
expansion dome	air injection
vapor/fuel separator	pulse air valve
vapor recovery canister	reed valve
activated charcoal	catalyst
tap	oxidation
thermostatically controlled air cleaner	two-way catalyst
ambient air	platinum
heat stove	palladium
vacuum motor	substrate
deceleration valve	reduction
throttle positioner	rhodium
pentroof	three-way catalyst
stratified charge	dual bed
thermo-vacuum valves	acid rain
	acid fog
	misfueling

R E V I E W   Q U E S T I O N S

DIRECTIONS: The following questions are similar to those used on mechanic certification tests. On a separate sheet of paper, write the letter of the correct choice.

1. Which of the following statements is correct?

   I. Specific emission control devices influence vehicle emissions.

   II. Virtually any part or system that affects vehicle operation also affects vehicle emissions.

   A. I only   B. II only   C. Both I and II   D. Neither I nor II

2. Mechanic A says that vacuum can be used to control engine parts that affect vehicle operation and emissions.

   Mechanic B says that electricity can be used to control vehicle parts that affect vehicle operation and emissions.

   Who is correct?

   A. A only   B. B only   C. Both A and B   D. Neither A nor B

3. EGR stands for
   A. exhaust gas recombination.
   B. exhaust gas recirculation.
   C. exhaust gas reduction.
   D. exhaust gas restriction.

4. All of the following statements about air injection systems are true EXCEPT
   A. They can use an air pump.
   B. They can use a pulse-air valve.
   C. They can prevent additional burning of HC in the exhaust manifold.
   D. They can provide oxygen for an oxidation catalyst.

5. A three-way catalyst
   A. treats HC, CO, and SO_x emissions.
   B. has two areas for oxidation reactions.
   C. treats HC, CO, and NO_x emissions.
   D. has three areas for reduction reactions.

S U P P L E M E N T A L   A C T I V I T I E S

1. Refer to the manufacturer's service manual. Locate and identify vacuum-operated control mechanisms and individual parts on a vehicle.
2. Locate and identify electrically operated solenoid valves on a vehicle's vacuum control system.
3. Locate vacuum taps on a carburetor and/or intake manifold. Mark vacuum tubing for reconnection, and test each tap with a vacuum gauge. Test each tap at idle, during acceleration, WOT-operation, and deceleration. Make notes of the readings for each tap during tests.
4. Locate and trace vacuum and vapor lines and components for PCV, air injection, EGR, and catalytic converter systems. Demonstrate to your class where components are located on a vehicle.
5. Refer to manufacturers' shop manuals and determine where exhaust gases are to be sampled during air-fuel mixture adjustment. Report to your class on what differences are found.

42 EMISSION CONTROL SYSTEMS SERVICE

UNIT PREVIEW

Late-model vehicles are designed and built to deliver good economy and reasonable performance while greatly reducing harmful exhaust emissions. They do this best when all systems are tuned and adjusted to manufacturers' specifications.

Recommended maintenance and service often include careful inspection, testing, and diagnostic procedures as outlined by the manufacturer. Any shortcuts or attempts to memorize testing procedures for all models of vehicles will only cause problems and further frustration. Choose the proper service manual and follow it step by step.

Intentionally disconnecting, bypassing, or disabling emission control devices will result not only in lost performance and economy, but also in customer dissatisfaction. These practices also are prohibited by law and can result in fines and/or loss of licenses or certifications.

LEARNING OBJECTIVES

When you have completed your assignments and exercises in this unit, you should be able to:

☐ Explain what problems are caused by tampering with emission control devices.

☐ Describe what systems must be maintained to reduce exhaust emissions to legal levels.

☐ Inspect and replace defective vacuum control lines.

☐ Perform checks on heat and solenoid-operated vacuum valves and vacuum delay valves.

☐ Check PCV valves, thermostatically operated air cleaners, air pumps, diverter valves, and EGR valves for proper operation.

☐ Correctly connect and use an exhaust gas analyzer to determine exhaust emission levels and diagnose the causes of emission problems.

SAFETY PRECAUTIONS

Many ignition, fuel system, and emission checks and adjustments are done with the engine running. Clothing, jewelry, or hair can be caught in moving fans, belts, and pulleys and cause serious personal injury.

Remove all watches, rings, neck chains, and other jewelry. Roll up long sleeves or wear a short-sleeved shirt or blouse. Tie long hair in a ponytail and stuff down the back of your shirt or blouse. Keep hands, arms, and face away from moving parts.

Hot exhaust manifolds and other parts can cause serious burns. Avoid touching exhaust manifolds, radiator surfaces, and other heated metal parts. Allow the vehicle to cool fully before attempting service procedures on exhaust or engine system parts.

Exhaust gas analysis is performed with the engine running. Make sure there is proper ventilation before working on a running engine in an enclosed area. Carbon monoxide poisoning can cause serious health problems or death.

42.1 EMISSION CONTROL DEVICES AND TAMPERING

Federal and/or state laws prohibit intentional *tampering* with equipment that can change vehicle emissions levels. Tampering means removing, modifying, disconnecting, or disabling such devices.

Legal Sanctions

Licensed or certified mechanics can lose licenses or certifications and/or be fined for tampering with emission control devices. Additional penalties may be imposed by specific states.

In many states, vehicles that cannot pass a strictly monitored emissions equipment inspection and test cannot be registered.

In California, tests and inspections are done on a regular basis to detect tampering and/or high emissions levels. Emission control equipment that has been tampered with must be returned to original condition. No matter what the replacement cost, vehicles must be equipped with all original, manufacturer-supplied emission control equipment.

Emission Control and Performance

Tampering with emission control equipment on late-model vehicles usually is counterproductive. That is, performance and durability of engines and other parts of a vehicle may decrease, rather than increase.

For example, disconnecting an EGR valve increases engine power output and thus increases manifold vacuum. However, such tampering can cause detonation and piston damage. In addition, vacuum controls on automatic transmissions respond to increased vacuum by reducing hydraulic pressures.

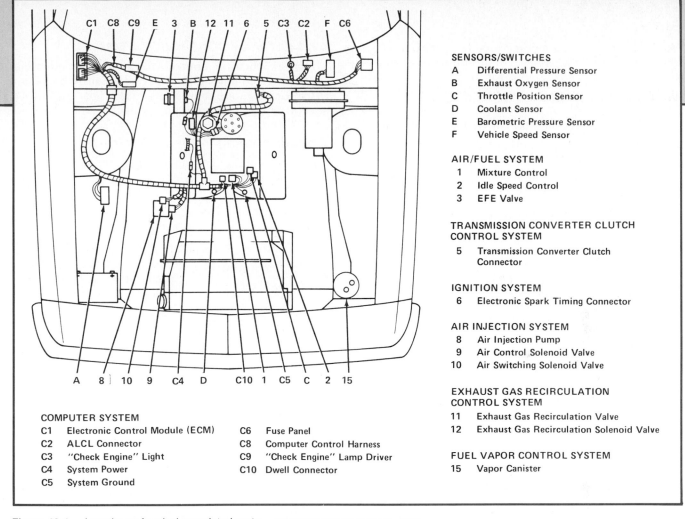

SENSORS/SWITCHES

A   Differential Pressure Sensor
B   Exhaust Oxygen Sensor
C   Throttle Position Sensor
D   Coolant Sensor
E   Barometric Pressure Sensor
F   Vehicle Speed Sensor

AIR/FUEL SYSTEM

1   Mixture Control
2   Idle Speed Control
3   EFE Valve

TRANSMISSION CONVERTER CLUTCH CONTROL SYSTEM

5   Transmission Converter Clutch Connector

IGNITION SYSTEM

6   Electronic Spark Timing Connector

AIR INJECTION SYSTEM

8   Air Injection Pump
9   Air Control Solenoid Valve
10 Air Switching Solenoid Valve

EXHAUST GAS RECIRCULATION CONTROL SYSTEM

11 Exhaust Gas Recirculation Valve
12 Exhaust Gas Recirculation Solenoid Valve

FUEL VAPOR CONTROL SYSTEM

15 Vapor Canister

COMPUTER SYSTEM

C1	Electronic Control Module (ECM)	C6	Fuse Panel
C2	ALCL Connector	C8	Computer Control Harness
C3	"Check Engine" Light	C9	"Check Engine" Lamp Driver
C4	System Power	C10	Dwell Connector
C5	System Ground		

Figure 42-1. Locations of emissions-related parts. CHEVROLET MOTOR DIVISION—GMC

Lowered hydraulic pressures can cause component failures within automatic transmissions.

Late-model engines and vehicles are built for proper operation with all emission control equipment in place and functioning. Tampering often can cause serious and expensive damage.

Health and Environmental Pollution

Even if no legal, performance, or engine durability problems were created by tampering, health and environmental problems still exist. Everyone, including mechanics, breathes the same air and eventually can suffer health problems from air pollution.

As a mechanic, you may gain the knowledge and skill necessary to tamper with emission controls. However, as a human being, you will know that such tampering is wrong and contributes to health and environmental problems.

42.2 EMISSION CONTROLS PREVENTIVE MAINTENANCE

As discussed in Unit 35, the main purpose of a modern tune-up is to reduce exhaust emissions and maximize fuel economy. An emissions-legal tune-up includes checks and maintenance of the following systems:

- Fuel
- Charging
- Ignition
- Emission control.

Refer to the manufacturer's emission control information label in the engine compartment for proper tune-up procedures. Refer to the manufacturer's service manual for location of emissions-related parts and systems (see Figure 42-1).

Federal laws require that vehicle manufacturers warranty emissions-related equipment for the first 50,000 miles of vehicle use. Electronic ignition, fuel injection, and electronic controls all contribute to reliable and durable emission control measures.

Refer to Units 20, 22, 24, 29, 33, and 35 for preventive maintenance for the fuel, charging, and ignition systems. Refer to Unit 39 for electronic device service.

Checking Emission Control Devices

Checks for proper operation can be performed with simple test equipment for some systems, such as vapor-recovery and PCV systems. However, for some devices, such as a catalytic converter, an *exhaust gas analyzer* may be necessary to determine proper operation. An exhaust gas analyzer is an electronic instrument that samples exhaust gases for the presence of HC, CO, and CO_2.

Specific emission control devices that can be checked include:

- Vacuum, vapor, and fuel lines
- Vacuum control systems
- Thermostatically controlled air cleaner
- Vapor recovery system
- PCV system
- Air injection system
- EGR system
- Catalytic converter.

Integrated Control Systems

Electronic controls on late-model vehicles may operate several parts of an emission control system. In addition, information about emission control device operation can be "fed back" into a computer control module. Thus, *integrated control systems* can monitor and adjust almost every aspect of vehicle performance and emissions. An integrated control system combines many functions into a single electronic control unit.

42.3 VACUUM, VAPOR, AND FUEL LINES

Carefully examine all vacuum and vapor hoses and fuel lines for hardening, cracks, breaks, kinks, and loose or disconnected connections. Rubber hoses should be flexible, not stiff and hard. Typical vacuum line defects are shown in Figure 42-2. Replace defective lines one at a time to avoid misrouting. Refer to the manufacturer's service manual for correct vacuum hose routing if more than one hose is disconnected (see Figure 42-3).

Replace vapor lines and fuel lines with special fuel/vapor hose. Use of heater hose or vacuum tubing will result in rapid cracking, leaks, and breakage.

42.4 VACUUM CONTROL SYSTEMS

To check vacuum controls, refer to the manufacturer's service manual for correct location and identification of components. As discussed in Unit 41, several types of vacuum control valves may be used.

Troubleshooting Vacuum Controls

Vacuum control troubleshooting is similar to all other troubleshooting. Troubleshooting procedures can include:

- Visual inspection
- Thorough basic knowledge of operating principles
- Use of vacuum hose diagrams
- Logical approach
- Use of test instruments.

Faulty operation can be caused by any part of the system or connecting lines. Check all parts thoroughly.

Checking Vacuum Valves

When a vacuum valve is closed, vacuum will be blocked from passing through the valve. When a valve opens, vacuum will pass through. Refer to the manufacturer's service manual for correct valve operating conditions and test procedures.

A hand-held vacuum pump and vacuum gauge can be used to check for proper opening and closing. Use at least 15 in. [38.1 cm] Hg of vacuum for checking purposes (see Figure 42-4).

Vacuum control valves that do not operate properly are replaced.

On-Car and Off-Car Checks

Checks can be done on or off the vehicle. Checking vacuum control devices on the vehicle may require watching for movement of an operated device with the engine off. In other cases, movement or a change in an instrument reading may be checked when the engine is running.

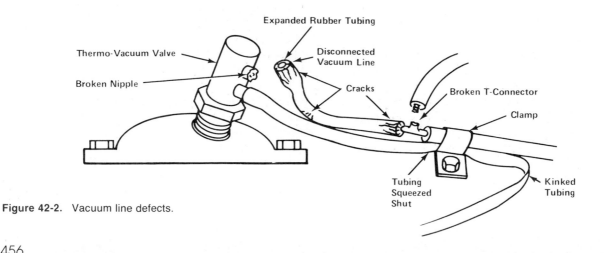

Figure 42-2. Vacuum line defects.

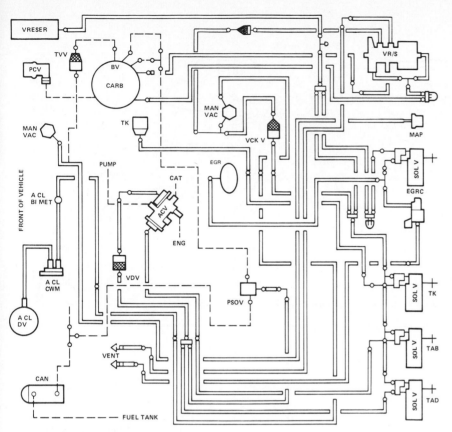

Figure 42-3. Vacuum schematic drawing. FORD MOTOR COMPANY

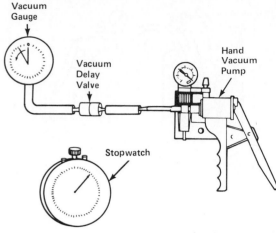

Figure 42-4. Checking the vacuum delay valve.

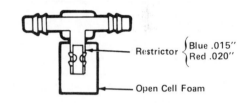

Figure 42-5. Vacuum vent air bleed with filter assembly. FORD MOTOR COMPANY

To check vacuum control valves removed from a vehicle, use a vacuum gauge and a hand vacuum pump (see Figure 42-4).

Air Bleeds

Some vacuum-operated devices include a calibrated *air bleed* to limit vacuum actuation (see Figure 42-5). An air bleed is a calibrated *orifice,* or opening, through which air is drawn into a vacuum line. An air bleed limits the amount of vacuum applied to a device.

When testing vacuum-operated units, check for air bleeds in lines. Air bleeds will cause vacuum readings and/or actuation to decrease as air enters through the orifice.

Vacuum Delay Valve

To check a vacuum delay valve, connect a vacuum gauge on the output side of the delay valve. Vacuum is applied on the vacuum supply side of the delay valve. Use a watch to determine how many seconds are required for full vacuum to appear (see Figure 42-4). Refer to the manufacturer's service manual for correct delay times.

Heat-Operated Vacuum Valves

Heat-operated controls include heat-operated vacuum valves and bimetallic temperature sensors. A heat-operated vacuum valve screws into a water jacket

passage in the cylinder head. Checking a removed valve is illustrated in Figure 42-6.

Solenoid Vacuum Valves

Electrically operated solenoid vacuum valves can be checked with a test light or voltmeter for power. Jumper wires can be used to provide electrical power to actuate a solenoid. Hand vacuum pumps and vacuum gauges are used to verify proper valve operation.

42.5 THERMOSTATICALLY CONTROLLED AIR CLEANER

Thermostatically controlled air cleaners are checked for proper hose and vacuum line connections. Replace missing or torn hot-air and/or cool-air ducts.

Checking Bimetallic Temperature Sensors

Bimetallic temperature sensors in air cleaner housings can be checked by applying heat or cold. Such sensors should allow vacuum to pass through when cold, and will bleed vacuum off when hot. A hair dryer or heat gun can be used to heat the sensor. An ice cube wrapped in a shop rag can be used to cool the sensor. Connect a hand vacuum pump to the vacuum source tube and check the operation of the damper door. If the damper door does not operate, check the vacuum motor (see Figure 42-7).

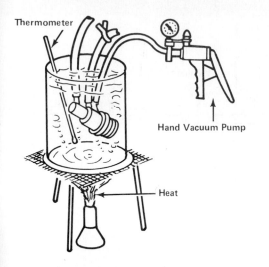

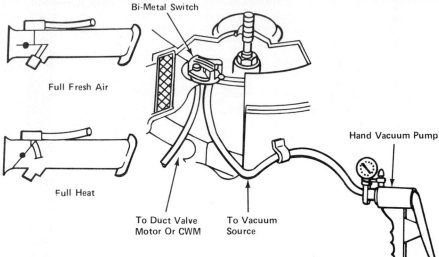

Figure 42-6. Checking a TVS valve.

Figure 42-7. Checking a vacuum motor.

Checking Vacuum Motor Operation

Apply vacuum directly to the vacuum motor and watch the damper door to check its operation. If the motor is defective, spot welds can be drilled out and the vacuum motor replaced (see Figure 42-8). *Blind rivets* are used to hold the new vacuum motor in place. Blind rivets are special metal rivets inserted with a special riveting tool. When inserted and tightened, these rivets make a "popping" sound that indicates they are fully expanded.

If the vacuum motor operates properly when checked directly, the bimetallic temperature sensor is at fault. Replace the sensor.

42.6 VAPOR RECOVERY SYSTEM

Check vapor recovery systems for proper hose connections and hose conditions. Replaceable fiberglass air filters may be incorporated in vapor recovery canisters (see Figure 42-9).

Filter Replacement

To replace vapor recovery canister filters, pull out the old filter and carefully insert the new filter under the bar. Replaceable filters should be replaced when the fuel system air filter is replaced.

Late-model canisters may not have replaceable filters. The entire canister must be replaced if defective. Canisters are held in place by sheet metal straps and screws. Loosen the screws, mark vapor and vacuum lines for replacement, and remove the canister. Install a new canister and reconnect vapor and vacuum lines correctly.

Vapor Recovery System Problems

Plugged vapor recovery canisters, faulty purge valves, and/or clogged and pinched lines can produce excessive pressure in fuel tanks. When the filler cap is opened, a strong hiss can be heard as vapors are released.

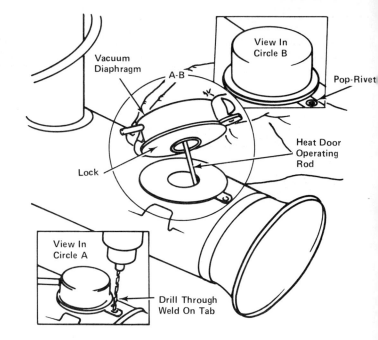

Figure 42-8. Vacuum motor replacement.

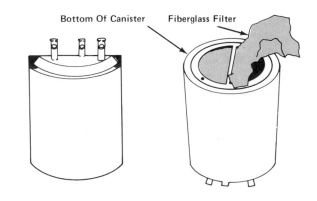

Figure 42-9. Vacuum recovery canister replacement.

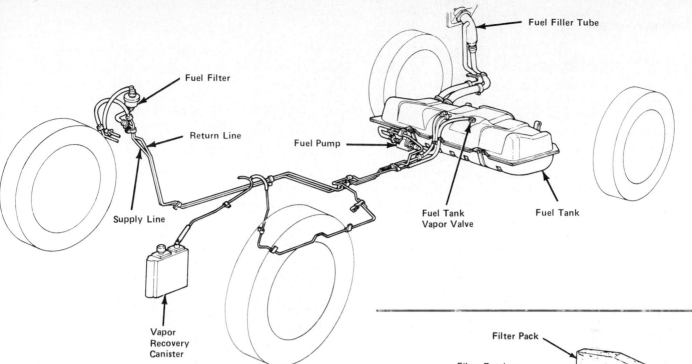

Figure 42-10. Fuel pump and fuel lines. FORD MOTOR COMPANY

Refer to the manufacturer's service manual for proper checking procedures for vapor recovery canisters and purge valves.

Lines to the fuel tank can be checked by applying compressed air at the vapor recovery canister end (see Figure 42-10). A strong hissing should be heard through the fuel tank filler opening. Be sure that the filler cap has been removed.

SAFETY CAUTION: Always wear eye protection when working with compressed air. Eye injury or permanent blindness can result from liquid or solid contaminants blown into the eyes.

Fuel odors in the passenger compartment can be caused by broken, leaking, or disconnected vapor and/or fuel lines. Gasoline vapors noticeable during hard cornering may indicate faulty operation of a vapor/fuel separator in the fuel tank.

42.7 PCV SYSTEM

Check PCV systems for proper hose connections, clogged filters, and proper PCV valve operation. When an engine is running, vacuum should be present at oil filler openings on the valve cover. A PCV filter, if used, is fitted into the air cleaner housing (see Figure 42-11).

PCV System Problems

PCV filters should be changed when the air filter is changed. Liquid oil in the air cleaner housing and an oily PCV filter can indicate problems. Even a light film of oil on the air cleaner will decrease air flow and result in a richer mixture, which will waste fuel.

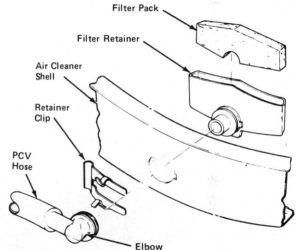

Figure 42-11. PCV filter installation. FORD MOTOR COMPANY

Oil from a PCV system can be caused by two problems. First, the PCV valve or hose may be clogged, allowing oil fumes to back up into the air filter housing. Second, excessive blowby from worn piston rings and cylinders can force oily vapors through the PCV breather filter tube.

Checking PCV Valves

To check a PCV valve, remove it from its rubber grommet and shake it. A valve that is not clogged will rattle, indicating that the check valve is free. To check for proper operation, start the engine and block the engine end of the PCV valve with your thumb. A strong suction should be felt, and engine speed should drop at least 50 rpm (see Figure 42-12). If not, the valve or line is clogged.

A defective PCV valve can cause rough idling, stalling, and the introduction of oil to the air cleaner. PCV valves should be replaced approximately every two years or 24,000 miles, or as recommended by the manufacturer.

42.8 AIR INJECTION SYSTEM

Air injection system checks include vacuum hose, air hose, and distribution manifold conditions, drive operation, and diverter valve operation. Damaged or defective parts are replaced. Loose drive belts are tightened.

NOTE: **Air pumps on some late-model Chrysler products are driven off the camshaft. Refer to specific Chrysler Corporation service manuals for proper servicing procedures.**

Exhaust gas pulse air injection systems are relatively trouble-free. Check for evidence of scorched paint and/or burned-through metal pipes and valve units. Replace exhaust pulse valves and manifolds if defects are found.

Checking Air Pump Output

Air pump output can be checked by removing output hoses and holding your hand over the ends. A strong, continuous gush of air should be felt from either or both outlets. If not, the pump may need replacement. Air pumps are *vane-type pumps,* as illustrated in Figure 42-13. A vane-type pump uses vanes, or blades, to compress air. A fanlike assembly behind the drive pulley uses centrifugal force to remove contaminant particles from intake air (see Figure 42-14).

Most shops install a new or rebuilt air pump rather than servicing defective pumps. If an air pump is defective, loosen and remove the drive belt. Mark hoses for proper reassembly. Loosen and remove pivot and adjusting bolts, braces, and hoses. Remove and replace the air pump (see Figure 42-15).

Checking Diverter Valve Operation

Diverter valve operation can be checked by starting the engine and holding the throttle at a high idle (1,500–2,000 rpm). When the throttle is released suddenly, air should be forced out of diverter/bypass valve outlets (see Figure 42-16). This rush of air can be heard as well as felt with the fingers.

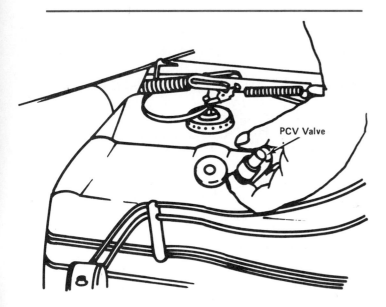

Figure 42-12. Checking a PCV valve.

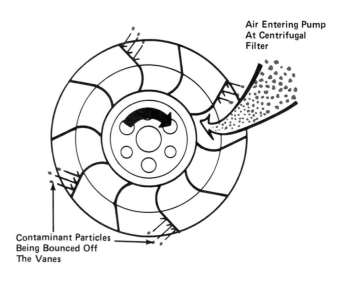

Figure 42-14. Centrifugal filter operation.

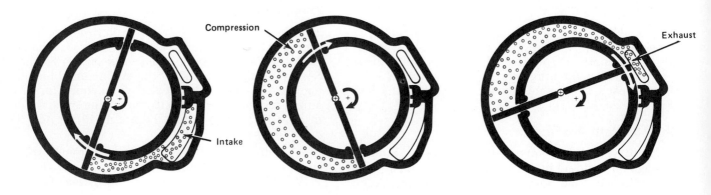

Figure 42-13. Vane-type air pump operation. CHEVROLET MOTOR DIVISION—GMC

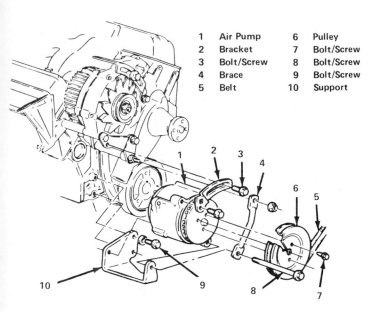

1	Air Pump	6	Pulley
2	Bracket	7	Bolt/Screw
3	Bolt/Screw	8	Bolt/Screw
4	Brace	9	Bolt/Screw
5	Belt	10	Support

Figure 42-15. Air pump mounting.
CHEVROLET MOTOR DIVISION—GMC

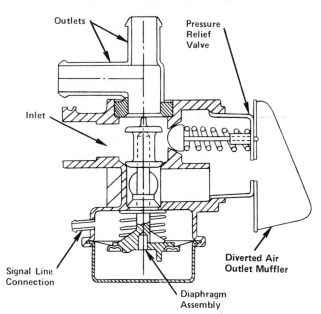

Figure 42-16. Parts of an EGR valve.
CHEVROLET MOTOR DIVISION—GMC

The diverter valve also can be checked with a hand vacuum pump. Apply vacuum to the control diaphragm at the signal line connection and check for diverted air from the bypass holes. If a diverter valve fails these tests, it must be replaced.

42.9 EGR SYSTEM

EGR systems are checked for vacuum hose condition and valve operation. EGR valves may be checked visually and/or with a hand vacuum pump.

EGR Valve Checks

Start the engine and let it warm up to normal operating temperature. Increase engine speed to approximately 2,500 rpm and watch the EGR valve stem (see Figure 42-17). It should move upward.

Allow the engine to return to idle. Apply vacuum to the diaphragm. The stem should move upward, and the engine should die. If the EGR valve fails these tests, remove the valve (see Figure 42-18). Clean passages in the intake/exhaust manifolds as recommended by the manufacturer.

Replacing and/or Cleaning EGR Valves

Some vehicle manufacturers recommend a cleaning procedure if exhaust deposits have jammed an EGR valve (see Figure 42-19). Other manufacturers recommend replacement of the valve if it does not operate.

CAUTION: Do not wash EGR valve assemblies in solvents or degreaser. Permanent damage to the diaphragm will result. Also, sandblasting may cause defective valve operation. Refer to the manufacturer's service manual for the proper cleaning procedures.

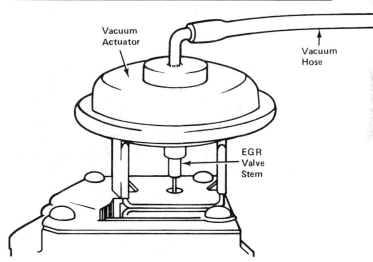

Figure 42-17. Checking an EGR valve.

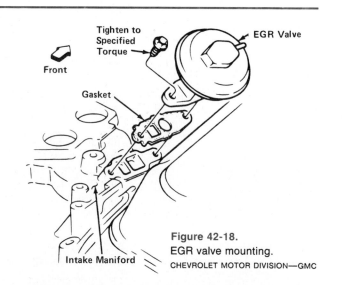

Figure 42-18.
EGR valve mounting.
CHEVROLET MOTOR DIVISION—GMC

461

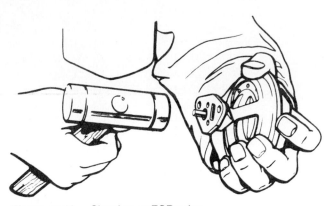

Figure 42-19. Cleaning an EGR valve.
CHEVROLET MOTOR DIVISION—GMC

42.10 CATALYTIC CONVERTER

Catalytic converters do not require maintenance. However, if an engine is poorly tuned or has fuel system problems, a catalytic converter can be damaged or destroyed. Excess unburned fuel from a misadjusted carburetor or misfiring spark plug can cause heat buildup within the converter. The heat generated can melt substrate or pellet bed retainers and destroy the catalyst.

"Rotten egg smell" is not harmful in terms of vehicle function or emissions. A thorough tune-up will restore the efficiency of the engine and may reduce or eliminate this smell.

Heat shields around the catalytic converter should be tightly secured in their proper location.

SAFETY CAUTION: **Allow all exhaust system components to cool completely before attempting work on catalytic converters. Heat in excess of 1,800 degrees F [982.2 degrees C] is generated by the catalytic converter. Severe burns can result from touching or brushing against a hot catalytic converter.**

Check heat shield and catalytic converter fasteners. Tighten or replace fasteners and/or shields as required.

Exhaust Gas Analyzer

After all other tune-up and emissions control service has been performed, exhaust emissions can be checked with an exhaust gas analyzer. A *sampling*

DIAGNOSIS OF EXHAUST GAS ANALYZER READINGS AT IDLE

HC	CO	SYMPTOMS	POSSIBLE CAUSES

High	Normal	Rough Idle	1. Faulty ignition:
			  a. Incorrect timing
			  b. Defective condenser or points
			  c. Fouled, shorted or improperly gapped plugs
			  d. Open or crossed ignition wires
			  e. Cracked distributor cap
			2. Leaking exhaust valves
			3. Leaking cylinder

High	Low	Rough Idle
		
		Fluctuating HC reading
			1. Vacuum leak:
			  a. Vacuum hose
			  b. Intake manifold
			  c. Head gasket
			2. Lean mixture

High	High	Rough Idle
		
		Black smoke fron exhaust
			1. Restricted air filter
			2. Plugged PCV Valve
			3. Faulty carburetion:
			  a. Idle mixture too rich
			  b. Faulty choke action
			  c. Incorrect float setting
			  d. Leaking needles or seats
			  e. Leaking power valve

Figure 42-20. Diagnosis of exhaust gas analyzer readings.

probe is inserted into the tail pipe of the vehicle. A sampling probe is a tube device that allows small amounts of exhaust gas to enter an exhaust gas analyzer. A sampling probe also can be used to find fuel vapor and exhaust gas leaks by moving the probe in the area of a suspected leak.

Refer to the vehicle manufacturer's service manual for correct placement of the sampling probe. Probes may be inserted directly into a tail pipe. In other cases, a plug may need to be removed from the exhaust system to insert the probe. Sampling locations may be in the exhaust pipe before a catalytic converter.

With the sampling probe inserted in the proper location, readings are taken at idle and under cruise (2,500 rpm) conditions for HC, CO, and CO_2. A table of analyzer readings and possible causes is shown in Figure 42-20.

Late-model computerized exhaust gas analyzers have memories that store data on allowable levels of emissions. These emissions levels can be compared with sampled gases for different vehicle makes, models, and years.

Figure 42-21. Exhaust gas analysis on a computer screen.

Figure 42-22. Technician removes analysis printout from computerized engine analyzer.

The mechanic enters the year, make, and model of the vehicle on a keyboard. The entered information is displayed on a screen (see Figure 42-21). After sampling, results appear on the screen and on a slip of paper printed by the analyzer (see Figure 42-22).

If a vehicle's exhaust has higher levels of pollutants than allowed by law, some analyzers will indicate probable causes and recommended servicing.

Catalytic converters that have failed due to heat buildup must be serviced or replaced. Bead-type converters may be refilled. Substrate-type converters must be replaced as a unit. Catalytic converter service and bead replacement are covered in Unit 26.

U N I T   H I G H L I G H T S

- Intentional tampering with parts and/or systems that affect emissions is prohibited by federal and state laws. Mechanics can lose their licenses and/or certifications and be fined for tampering.

- Late-model vehicles are built to operate properly with all manufacturer-supplied emission control equipment. Tampering with emission control devices can cause expensive damage.

- An emissions-legal tune-up includes checks and maintenance of fuel, charging, ignition, and emission control devices.

- Vacuum, vapor, and fuel lines are checked for proper connections and hose conditions. Vapor canisters, PCV valves, air pumps and diverter valves, and EGR valves can be replaced if defective.

- A hand vacuum pump can be a useful tool to check vacuum controls and to operate many emissions-related parts. Many checks consist of simple manipulations and visual observation. Other checks may require the use of instruments.

- After all other tune-up and emission control checks have been performed, exhaust emissions are checked. Late-model computerized exhaust gas analyzers can produce visual and printed records of test results and of recommended maintenance.

T E R M S

tampering
exhaust gas analyzer
integrated control
  system
air bleed

orifice
blind rivet
vane-type pump
sampling probe

DIRECTIONS: The following questions are similar to those used on mechanic certification tests. On a separate sheet of paper, write the letter of the correct choice.

1. Which of the following statements is correct?

   I. It is both illegal and counterproductive to tamper with emission control devices.

   II. Emission control devices on late-model vehicles contribute to cleaner, healthier air.

   A. I only   B. II only   C. Both I and II   D. Neither I nor II

2. Vehicle manufacturers are required to warrant emission control equipment for

   A. 5,000 miles

   B. 15,000 miles

   C. 50,000 miles

   D. 500,000 miles.

3. Mechanic A says plugging an EGR vacuum control line will increase engine power.

   Mechanic B says plugging an EGR vacuum control line can result in engine and automatic transmission damage.

   Who is correct?

   A. A only   B. B only   C. Both A and B   D. Neither A nor B

4. Defects in vacuum controls for emissions-related devices can include all of the following EXCEPT

   A. excessive manifold vacuum.

   B. vacuum lines connected at incorrect locations.

   C. cracked, loose, leaking, disconnected, or pinched vacuum lines.

   D. defective heat or solenoid-operated vacuum valves.

5. Mechanic A says that a diverter valve can be checked by watching for movement as the engine is speeded up.

   Mechanic B says a diverter valve can be checked by listening or feeling for air output as the throttle is released to slow down the engine.

   Who is correct?

   A. A only   B. B only   C. Both A and B   D. Neither A nor B

1. Inspect a vehicle's vacuum lines for defects. Replace lines, one at a time, if defects are found.
2. Check a vehicle's PCV valve for proper operation both by shaking it and by checking rpm drop.
3. Refer to the manufacturer's service manual and perform vacuum checks on heat and solenoid-operated vacuum valves and vacuum delay valves.
4. Check an air pump for proper output.
5. Use a hand-operated vacuum pump and check a thermostatically controlled air cleaner, diverter valve, and EGR valve for proper operation.
6. Refer to the instrument manufacturer's instructions and set up an exhaust gas analyzer correctly for sampling. Refer to the emission control information label and check for proper emission levels. Make notes of high emission levels, and write your recommendations for service of any problems found.

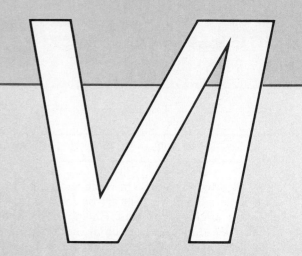

AUTOMOTIVE ENGINE SERVICE

43 ENGINE PROBLEM DIAGNOSIS

UNIT PREVIEW

Before work is done to replace or repair mechanical engine parts, tests are performed to determine specific engine problems. Checks can be made for intake vacuum, cylinder compression pressure and leakage, engine lubricating oil pressure, and engine noise sources.

Some tests are more specific than others. The combination of results from several tests can confirm suspected engine problems. Once the problem has been diagnosed carefully, repair procedures can be performed.

Engine repair and service procedures are discussed in Units 44 through 46.

LEARNING OBJECTIVES

When you have completed your assignments and exercises in this unit, you should be able to:

☐ Explain how engine tests can be used to locate specific engine problems.

☐ Identify and describe the most common types of tests used to diagnose engine mechanical problems.

☐ Perform engine tests and make a diagnosis of engine problems.

SAFETY PRECAUTIONS

Almost all engine diagnostic procedures involve working on engines that are at normal operating temperatures. Hot exhaust and cooling system parts can cause severe burns. Avoid touching such areas.

Some testing procedures involve cranking, or turning over, the engine using the starter motor. Keep hands, arms, long hair, and loose clothing away from moving belts, pulleys, and fan blades.

Remove all rings, watches, neck chains, and other jewelry.

Wear short-sleeved clothing or roll up long sleeves when working near moving belts and pulleys.

Wear safety goggles or safety glasses at all times in the shop area. Avoid pointing compressed air nozzles and blowguns at the face. Serious injury from metal or dirt particles or sprayed liquids can result.

Do not attempt to use any power machinery until you have received proper safety instructions and operating directions from your instructor. Obtain your instructor's permission before operating any power tools or equipment.

43.1 DIAGNOSTIC PROCEDURES

To diagnose engine mechanical problems, several tests can be made. Some tests are better than others for locating specific problems. In addition, two or more tests may be used to confirm a problem diagnosis. Engine tests generally include:

- Vacuum tests
- Cylinder leakage test
- Compression tests
- Engine oil pressure test.

43.2 VACUUM TESTS

When an engine in good condition is running, the low pressure created by the pistons on their intake stroke produces a steady vacuum, or suction, in the intake manifold. During cranking, less vacuum is produced. Vacuum readings during cranking and at idle can be compared to determine problems. A vacuum reading taken while the engine is running can locate many engine problems including leaking piston rings, leaking valves, worn valve guides, weak valve springs, and engine tuning problems.

Cranking Vacuum Test

To perform a cranking vacuum test, first run the engine until it has reached normal operating temperature. Connect the vacuum gauge hose securely to a source of engine *manifold vacuum*, as shown in Figure 43-1.

Disable the ignition system so that the engine will not start. To do this on vehicles with a separate ignition coil, remove the coil wire from the distributor cap. Connect an electrical jumper lead from the coil wire to a *grounded,* unpainted metal part of the engine or frame. Grounded means connected to the negative battery terminal. In modern automobiles, all metal parts of the vehicle are grounded, or connected, to the battery negative terminal.

To disable electronic ignition systems without a separate ignition coil, disconnect the electrical connector that supplies battery voltage to the system. Figure 43-2 shows the connector for the General Motors High Energy Ignition disconnected.

SAFETY CAUTION: Make sure the vacuum gauge hose is well away from the belts, pulley, and fan before cranking or running the engine.

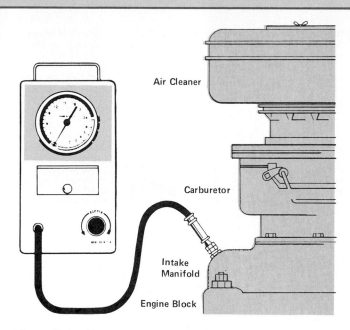

Figure 43-1. Vacuum gauge connection.

Using the key switch or a remote starter switch, crank the engine and watch the vacuum gauge. (Do not depress the accelerator pedal.) Make a note of the vacuum reading produced and the steadiness of the reading. In general, engines in good condition should produce cranking vacuum readings of 5 in. [127 mm] of vacuum or more.

Less than 5 inches of cranking vacuum indicates leakage. Leakage could be external, such as from an intake manifold or carburetor gasket, or a broken or disconnected vacuum line.

Inspect external engine components for signs of leakage or disconnection. If everything appears correct, the leakage may be from internal engine components. To locate internal engine vacuum problems, perform a vacuum test with the engine running.

Running Vacuum Test

Reconnect the ignition system so that the engine can be started.

SAFETY CAUTION: **Hot exhaust, cooling system, and other engine parts can cause severe burns. Avoid touching hot surfaces during test procedures. Also be careful to avoid moving engine parts.**

Start the engine and let it warm up. After the engine has reached normal operating temperature, note the vacuum reading produced while the engine is idling. Also, observe the steadiness of the reading.

Figure 43-2. Disconnecting High Energy Ignition (HEI) system.

Figure 43-3 illustrates vacuum readings for several engine problems.

NOTE: **Late model engines with high-lift camshafts and increased valve overlap may have lower and more uneven readings than illustrated in Figure 43-3. Emission control systems may also lower intake manifold vacuum readings.**

43.3 COMPRESSION TESTS

To confirm a problem, such as worn piston rings, indicated by vacuum test results, other tests can be done. A *compression test* measures compression pressure directly and can be used to determine piston ring or valve problems. A compression tester is shown in Figure 43-4.

To conduct a compression test, run the engine until it is at normal operating temperature.

Make sure the battery is fully charged so that the engine will crank quickly and easily.

The spark plugs must be removed to perform the compression test. Remove all spark plug cables, properly identifying them for replacement in correct

Steady reading
between 15 and 22 in.-Hg with the engine warmed up and idling is normal (left, top). Snap the throttle plate suddenly. The needle should drop to 5 in.-Hg or lower before stabilizing at the normal reading between 15 and 22 in.-Hg (left, bottom).

Fluctuating reading
that periodically drops 2 to 6 in.-Hg below normal indicates worn points or low compression.

Needle floats over a range of about 14 to 16 in.-Hg. Suggests that spark plugs may be gapped too close after incorrect servicing. Adjust gap.

Regular fluctuation
between a low reading of about 5 in.-Hg and a slightly lower-than-normal reading means the head gasket is leaking. See a mechanic.

Needle that swings erratically between about 10 and 20 in.-Hg when the engine is accelerated smoothly may indicate weak valve springs. See a mechanic.

Low reading that holds steady around 5 in.-Hg indicates a vacuum leak at intake manifold or carburetor gaskets, or a disconnected or leaking vacuum hose.

Reading drifts back and forth over a range of 4 to 5 in.-Hg within the normal range to indicate incorrect carburetor adjustment.

Steady high reading that holds above 21 in.-Hg indicates restricted air intake. Check for clogged air filter or a stuck choke.

Low reading that holds steady between 8 and 14 in.-Hg suggests that ignition timing is off or that piston rings are leaking. Check timing and compression.

Rapid needle vibration between 14 and 19 in.-Hg indicates that worn valve guides are letting intake valves chatter as they seat. See a mechanic.

Needle drops to near zero when the engine is accelerated, then climbs back almost to normal level. Exhaust system may be blocked or kinked.

Figure 43-3. Analyzing vacuum readings.

order. Next, loosen the spark plugs several turns before blowing any loose dirt from around the base of each plug. This will prevent dirt from falling into the cylinders when the plugs are removed.

Remove all spark plugs from the engine. Disable the ignition system, as discussed in Topic 43.2, to prevent high-voltage sparks at the spark plug wires. Make sure that the carburetor choke plate is fully open. Block the accelerator pedal or throttle linkage fully open to allow air to be drawn easily into the engine.

Screw the compression tester into cylinder No. 1. Crank the engine through the same number of revolutions for each cylinder, at least four full revolutions for each. Note how the pressure reading rises in steps, and note the final pressure reading obtained. Repeat the test for each cylinder.

Normal Compression Reading

Pressure readings for a cylinder in good condition will be built up in large jumps at first, and then smaller jumps. The final compression reading will be within the manufacturer's specifications. In general, all cylinder readings should be between 100 and 180 psi (690 and 1240 kPa). The lowest acceptable reading in an engine can be found by multiplying the highest recorded reading by 0.75. Excessive pressure readings can indicate carbon buildup in the cylinders.

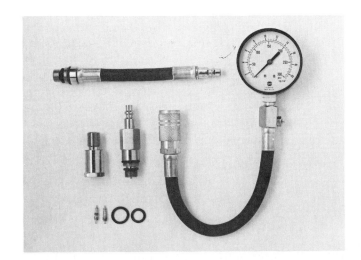

Figure 43-4. Compression gauge.

Piston Ring Problems

Pressure readings for a cylinder with leaking piston rings will build up in smaller jumps and not reach the manufacturer's specified reading. To check for piston ring problems, perform a *wet compression test*. Remove the compression gauge and squirt one tablespoon of engine oil through the spark plug hole.

Replace the gauge and repeat the test. If the readings for this test rise to nearly normal, the piston rings are defective. The added engine oil temporarily forms a seal around the piston.

NOTE: One broken compression ring on a piston will result in a low compression reading for that cylinder. In this case, a wet compression test will not greatly improve the compression reading.

Valve Problems

Compression readings for an engine with leaking valves will build up in nearly equal, small jumps. The final reading will be below the manufacturer's specification. A wet compression test will indicate readings still below manufacturer's specifications. The compression tester will indicate only that valve problems exist. A compression test will not specify whether the problem is due to an intake or an exhaust valve problem.

Head Gasket Problems

The small areas of a head gasket between cylinders can rupture, or be *blown,* by combustion pressure. A blown head gasket between cylinders will result in those two cylinders having very low, but equal final readings. As one piston moves up on the compression stroke, pressure leaks into the adjacent cylinder. On that cylinder's compression stroke, pressure leaks into the first cylinder. Both cylinders produce similar low readings.

A blown head gasket or a crack in a combustion chamber also can be detected by using an exhaust gas analyzer. Remove the radiator cap and place the analyzer probe in the radiator neck. If the analyzer records the presence of exhaust gases, a blown head gasket or a combustion chamber leak or crack is indicated.

43.4 CYLINDER LEAKAGE TEST

To perform a cylinder leakage test, a special instrument called a *leak-down tester* is used with an air compressor. A leak-down tester is shown in Figure 43-5. A leak-down tester can determine piston ring, intake or exhaust valve, and head gasket problems quickly and specifically.

To perform a cylinder leak-down test, first remove the radiator pressure cap. Then, run the engine until it has reached normal operating temperature.

SAFETY CAUTION: Do not touch hot surfaces during test procedures. Hot engine, exhaust, and cooling system parts can cause severe burns. Also, keep your hands, arms, hair and clothing away from moving engine parts.

Remove the spark plug from cylinder No. 1. Disable the ignition system. Crank the engine until the piston in cylinder number one is at TDC on its compression stroke. The timing marks should be on zero. Remove the air cleaner and oil filler covers.

Connect air pressure to the leak-down tester and zero the tester dial. Screw the *air-hold adapter* into the spark plug hole and connect the hose from the tester to the adapter. An air-hold adapter is a hollow metal fitting of the same size as a spark plug, as shown in Figure 43-6.

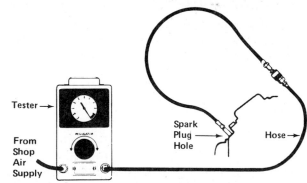

Figure 43-5. Leak-down tester. SUN ELECTRIC CORPORATION

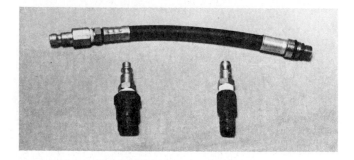

Figure 43-6. Air-hold adapter.

Note the reading on the leak-down tester. The tester reads the amount of air leaking from the cylinder, expressed as a percentage. No leakage at all would result in a reading of zero. A cylinder in normal condition will have up to 10 percent leakage. More than 10 percent leakage indicates problems.

To determine the source of the problem, use a short length of rubber tubing held to your ear as a primitive "stethoscope."

Hissing heard through the carburetor indicates a leaking intake valve. Hissing from the oil filler opening indicates leaking piston rings. Bubbling heard or seen in the radiator indicates a blown head gasket. Hissing from the exhaust pipe indicates a leaking exhaust valve.

43.5 ENGINE OIL PRESSURE TEST

The lubricating system of an engine in good condition supplies pressurized oil to the critical moving parts and bearing surfaces within the engine. Oil is supplied to the main and connecting rod bearings on the crankshaft, the valve train, and the lower cylinder walls. The faster the engine turns, the more pressure is produced. At a preset pressure, a relief valve in the lubrication system opens to release excess pressure.

Worn engine main and connecting rod bearings, as explained in Unit 10, will cause a loss of oil pressure. With good maintenance, engine bearing wear should not be excessive until the vehicle has traveled at least 100,000 miles [160,930 km].

If high-mileage wear problems are suspected, a check of engine oil pressure at idle and at higher rpm can help determine lubrication system and bearing wear problems.

To conduct an engine oil pressure test, first check that the engine oil level is correct. Add oil if necessary. Then locate the oil pressure sensor, shown in Figure 43-7, on the engine block.

NOTE: Gasoline from a leaking fuel pump diaphragm can contaminate engine oil and make it thinner. Thin oil will cause false oil pressure readings. Check for gasoline contamination by smelling and feeling the oil on the dipstick.

Remove the wiring connection. Using a special socket, shown in Figure 43-8, remove the sensor.

Thread the end of an oil pressure gauge hose into the engine block, as shown in Figure 43-9. Start the engine and let it run at idle until normal operating temperature is reached.

SAFETY CAUTION: Avoid touching hot exhaust, cooling system, and other engine parts during test procedures. They can cause severe burns. Also be careful to stay away from moving engine parts.

In general, idle oil pressure should be at least 20 to 25 psi [138 to 172 kPa]. Slowly depress the throttle

Figure 43-7. Oil pressure sensor.

Figure 43-8. Oil pressure sensor socket.

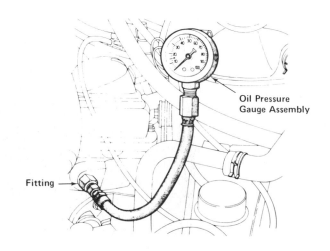

Oil Pressure Gauge Assembly

Fitting

Figure 43-9. Oil pressure gauge. CHRYSLER CORPORATION

linkage until the engine is running at approximately 2,000 rpm. At 2,000 rpm, engine oil pressure should be approximately 45 to 60 psi [310 to 414 kPa]. Refer to the manufacturer's service manual for correct oil pressure readings.

Oil pressures below specifications can indicate any of several problems, including worn bearings or a worn oil pump. Other possible problems include leaking seals, a clogged oil pump screen, or a defective oil pump pressure relief valve. To determine the exact cause, it is necessary to remove the oil pan. Then, inspect the main and connecting rod bearings, rear main bearing seal, and oil pump.

Quick Check of Main Bearing Clearance

While the oil pressure gauge is connected, a quick check of main bearing clearance may be performed. While watching the pressure gauge, quickly snap the throttle open briefly and then let it snap shut. The high vacuum during idle tends to "pull" or "hold" the crankshaft up against the main bearing oil discharge holes. This tendency keeps oil pressure artificially high. The quick throttle opening will drop intake manifold vacuum. This will allow the crankshaft to drop down, if bearing clearance is excessive, producing a momentary drop in oil pressure.

43.6 LOCATING ENGINE NOISES

A length of rubber tubing or a *mechanic's stethoscope* can be used to find engine noise sources. Hold one end of the rubber hose to your ear and move the other end of the hose close to suspected noise sources. Touch the metal probe of the stethoscope to stationary metal parts.

SAFETY CAUTION: Be extremely careful when listening for noises around moving belts and pulleys at the front of the engine. Keep the end of the hose or stethoscope probe away from moving parts. Physical injury can result if the hose or stethoscope is pulled inward or flung outward by moving parts.

Start the engine and begin checking for noise sources. Some noises are more pronounced on a cold engine because clearances are greater when parts are not expanded by heat.

Open the oil filler cover and listen through the opening. A tapping noise indicates either a clogged hydraulic lifter or excess valve clearance. Tapping that stops after the engine warms up indicates a partially closed oil passage on a hydraulic lifter.

Touch the stethoscope to each intake and exhaust manifold *runner,* or hollow tube, near the cylinder head. The tapping noise will be loud and distinct at the affected valve.

Engine noises that seem to occur at a rate slower than crankshaft rotation are related to camshaft rotation. Distributors, fuel pumps, and oil pumps are accessories usually driven by the camshaft.

Engine accessories such as alternators, water pumps, power-steering pumps, air-conditioning compressors, and air pumps all can cause noise. Noises from the extreme ends of these units are usually caused by bad bearings or bushings.

Listen at several locations on the block for noises that seem to occur at the same speed as the crankshaft revolution. Noises heard from the block can be caused by piston slap, by loose piston pins, or by a *rod bearing knock.*

Listen at the oil pan near the crankshaft front pulley and at the extreme rear of the oil pan. Noises heard from these locations are usually caused by main bearing problems.

Remember that aluminum and iron expand at different rates as temperatures rise. For example, a cold knock that disappears as the engine warms up probably is piston slap or knock. An aluminum piston expands more than the iron block, allowing the piston to fit more closely as engine temperature rises.

U N I T   H I G H L I G H T S

- More than one engine test can be performed to confirm suspected engine problems.
- Vacuum tests can indicate many engine problems, but are not as specific as compression and cylinder leakage tests.
- A compression test can determine leaking or broken piston rings, leaking valves, or a blown head gasket.
- A cylinder leakage test determines problems more specifically than a compression test.
- Engine oil pressure tests can indicate engine bearing wear problems, oil pump and lubrication system problems, and leaking seals.
- Simple procedures can be used to locate the source of engine noises.

T E R M S

manifold vacuum	leak-down tester
ground	air-hold adapter
compression test	mechanic's stethoscope
wet compression test	runner
blown	rod bearing knock

R E V I E W   Q U E S T I O N S

DIRECTIONS: The following questions are similar to those used on mechanic certification tests. On a separate sheet of paper, write the letter of the correct choice.

1. Vacuum tests can determine all of the following EXCEPT
A. blown head gasket.
B. worn valve guides.
C. restricted exhaust system.
D. worn main bearings.

2. Mechanic A says that a wet compression test can determine whether piston rings or valves are leaking.
Mechanic B says that a wet compression test can determine whether the intake or the exhaust valve is leaking.
Who is correct?
A. A only   B. B only   C. Both A and B   D. Neither A nor B

3. Which of the following statements is correct?
I. A cylinder leakage test can locate specific engine problems more quickly than a compression test.
II. A cylinder leakage test can provide more information than a compression test.
A. I only   B. II only   C. Both I and II   D. Neither I nor II

4. An oil pressure test can indicate problems with all of the following items EXCEPT
A. main and connecting rod bearings.
B. oil pump.
C. oil intake screen.
D. piston rings.

5. Which of the following can be diagnosed with a mechanic's stethoscope or length of rubber tubing?
A. Worn piston rings
B. Plugged hydraulic lifter
C. Leaking intake valve
D. Weak valve springs

S U P P L E M E N T A L   A C T I V I T I E S

1. Perform vacuum tests on a vehicle chosen by your instructor. Report your findings to the class.
2. Perform a compression test on the same vehicle tested in Activity 1. Report your findings to the class.
3. Perform a cylinder leakage test on the same vehicle tested in Activity 1. Report your findings to the class.
4. Perform an engine oil pressure test on the same vehicle tested in Activity 1. Report your findings to the class.
5. Locate engine noises on the same vehicle tested in Activity 1. Report your findings to the class.
6. Based on your own tests and on the reports of your classmates, list problems found in the vehicle tested.

44 CYLINDER HEAD SERVICE

UNIT PREVIEW

Some service procedures for the engine cylinder head do not require removing the head from the engine. These service procedures include valve clearance adjustment and the replacement of valve springs, valve stem seals, and retaining parts. Measurements of critical dimensions also can be done with the cylinder head in place.

Most overhead camshaft engines require removal of the camshaft for cylinder head repair procedures. Cylinder head repair procedures for most pushrod engines can be performed without major engine disassembly.

After the head has been removed, major resurfacing and machining operations usually are done by an automotive machinist.

LEARNING OBJECTIVES

When you have completed your assignments and exercises in this unit, you should be able to:

☐ Safely and correctly perform cylinder head service procedures.

☐ Explain what steps must be followed to perform valve clearance checks and adjustments.

☐ Perform a valve adjustment.

☐ Remove and replace valve retainers, springs, and valve stem seals.

☐ Check for proper valve guide clearance and camshaft lobe lift.

☐ Explain the problems involved in resurfacing and machining operations on the cylinder head.

SAFETY PRECAUTIONS

Always refer to the manufacturer's service publications for correct service procedures. Incorrect procedures may result in damage to expensive parts.

Some procedures require working on engines at normal operating temperatures. Avoid touching hot exhaust and cooling system parts.

Sharp metal edges on parts can inflict serious cuts. When inspecting parts, move your hands and fingers slowly around the edges. Use a shop rag when lifting or moving parts.

Remove all rings, watches, neck chains, and other jewelry before beginning work.

Wear short-sleeved clothing or roll up long sleeves when working near a running engine.

Wear safety goggles or safety glasses at all times in the shop area.

Use caution when working with compressed air. Do not point blowguns or other air tools at other persons.

Do not attempt to use any power machinery until you have received proper instruction and training from your instructor. Obtain your instructor's permission before operating any power tools or equipment.

44.1 ON-CAR CYLINDER HEAD SERVICE

Service procedures that can be performed with the cylinder head still attached to the cylinder block include:

- Inspection for worn valve train parts
- Valve adjustment
- Checking for valve guide wear
- Checking camshaft lobe lift
- Checking for valve spring damage
- Replacing the valve springs, retainers, and valve stem seals.

Before on-car service procedures can be performed, the engine and cylinder head must be cleaned. Dirt and grease can fall through oil drain holes in the cylinder head and contaminate the engine's lubrication system.

Cleaning the Engine

Scrape heavy grease and dirt deposits from the engine with a putty knife or dull scraper. Use solvent and a parts brush to dissolve grease in hard-to-reach areas. Use a steam-cleaning machine or high-pressure spray to wash the engine.

SAFETY CAUTION: Hot steam from the steam-cleaning machine can cause severe burns. Wear protective clothing, gloves, and safety goggles during steam cleaning.

Thoroughly and carefully clean around such areas as valve, timing gear, and other covers and the oil pan. Rinse the engine with cool water and dry off with compressed air. Dry the spark plug wires and ignition distributor thoroughly.

SAFETY CAUTION: Wear eye protection whenever compressed air is used. Severe eye injury or permanent blindness can result from particles or liquids blown into the eyes.

44.2 INSPECTING THE CYLINDER HEAD

To aid in reassembly, make drawings of parts that are removed to allow access to the valve cover or covers. Remove parts to allow access to the cylinder head cover. Tag and number disconnected wires and hoses with masking tape. Identify and save attaching fasteners and brackets.

Remove the valve cover bolts or nuts in a criss-cross pattern, from the ends toward the center (see Figure 44-1). Identify and save the attaching bolts or nuts.

Inspect the cylinder head for cracks and leaks. (Final inspection for cracks and leaks should be performed after the head has been removed.) Cracked heads require removal from the engine for service or replacement.

Inspect *soft plugs* for leaking. Soft plugs are cup-shaped, stamped metal plugs inserted into cast-metal parts to fill holes. As shown in Figure 44-2, a soft plug can be either a *cup plug* or an *expansion plug*.

If accessible, replacement soft plugs can be installed with the cylinder head attached to the block.

To replace soft plugs, drive a center punch or small chisel through the plug. Pull the old plug out with pliers. Coat the new soft plug with sealant and drive it in with a special tool, as shown in Figure 44-2.

44.3 INSPECTING THE VALVE TRAIN

Visually inspect all visible parts of the valve train for looseness, wear, or damage. Check for the following problems:

- Loose mounting bolts, studs, and nuts
- Worn or pitted OHC lobes (see Figure 44-3)
- Damaged OHC valve train parts
- Worn rocker arms or rocker followers
- Broken valve springs
- Bent pushrods
- Improperly seated valve locks and retainers
- Missing or damaged valve stem seals.

Tighten loose mounting bolts, studs, and nuts. Refer to the manufacturer's service manual for OHC removal procedures. On pushrod engines and some OHC engines a number of parts can be replaced without removing the cylinder head. These parts include damaged rocker arms or followers, valve springs, retainers, valve stem seals, and pushrods.

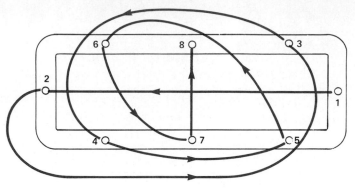

Figure 44-1. Valve cover bolt removal pattern.

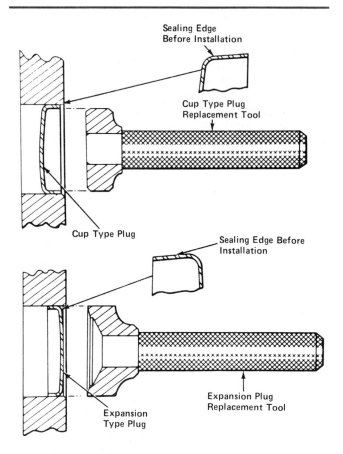

Figure 44-2. Soft plug and cup installation.
FORD MOTOR COMPANY

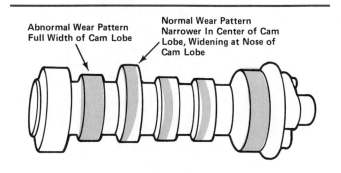

Figure 44-3. Even and uneven wear on camshaft lobes.

See Topic 44.4. Check for bent pushrods by rolling each pushrod across a flat surface.

Check for plugged oil drain holes in the cylinder head by inserting a wire or thin metal probe into the holes. Be sure that gasket sealing surfaces are not damaged or deeply scratched.

Oil drain holes can be unplugged by cleaning with screwdrivers, metal rods, and wire brushes. Minor damage to gasket sealing surfaces can be carefully dressed with mill files or fine emery cloth. Make sure that abrasive particles do not get into the engine.

44.4 VALVE CLEARANCE ADJUSTMENT

Valve clearance adjustments are required at specified intervals on engines with solid or mechanical lifters. Engines with hydraulic valve lifters or hydraulic lash adjusters normally require adjustment (if possible) only when an engine is being reassembled. Hydraulic lifters also can be collapsed, or compressed, to check for proper positioning and functioning.

Valve clearance for mechanical lifters must be checked as specified by the vehicle manufacturer, with the engine hot or cold. Refer to the manufacturer's service manual for correct adjustment procedures. The following is intended as a general guide to performing valve clearance adjustment.

Positioning the Engine

Valve clearance on a cylinder is checked when both valves are in their fully closed positions. To achieve this condition, position the engine as close as possible to TDC on the compression stroke.

The piston in a given cylinder can be positioned by cranking the engine with the starter motor. Another method is to turn the crankshaft pulley nut manually, using a breaker bar and socket.

The ignition distributor rotor can be used to indicate which cylinder is near TDC on its compression stroke. When the distributor rotor is aligned under one of the distributor cap terminals, the piston in that cylinder is very near its *firing position*. The firing position is the point at which the spark ignites the air-fuel mixture. This point is near TDC on the compression stroke.

Crank or position the engine until the pulley timing marks indicate TDC. Remove the distributor cap. Find the terminal on the cap with which the distributor rotor tip is aligned. Follow that spark plug wire to its cylinder. Valve clearance can be checked and/or adjusted at that cylinder. See Figure 44-4. To adjust any other cylinder's valves, reposition the engine to align the distributor rotor with that cylinder's spark plug wire terminal.

Checking and Adjusting Valve Clearance

Valve clearance may be different for intake and exhaust valves. Valves aligned with intake manifold runners are intake valves; valves aligned with exhaust manifold runners are exhaust valves, as shown in Figure 44-5.

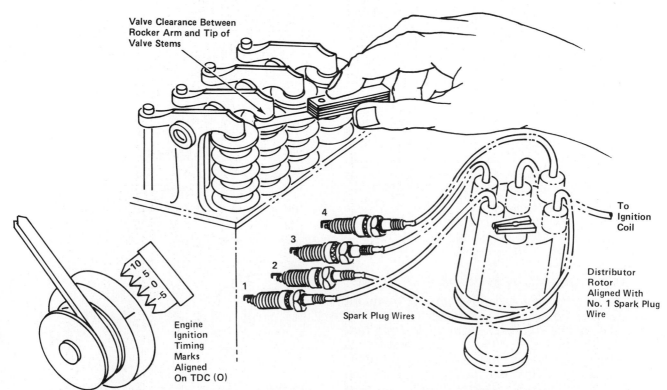

Figure 44-4. Engine and distributor positions.

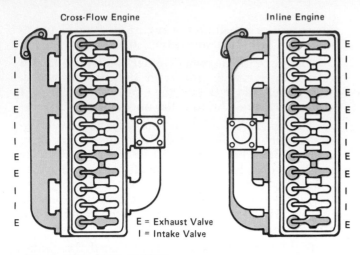

Figure 44-5. Valve positions.

E = Exhaust Valve
I = Intake Valve

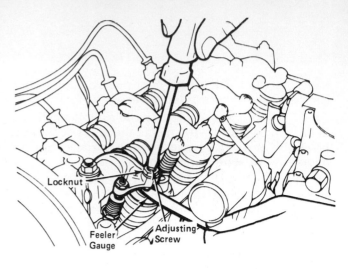

Figure 44-6. Valve clearance adjustment.
CHRYSLER CORPORATION

Rocker arm or follower. Valve clearance on an engine with rocker arms or followers is checked between the valve stem tip and the end of the rocker. Slide a feeler gauge of the proper size between the valve tip and the rocker. A light drag should be felt if the clearance is correct. If not, an adjustment is necessary. Loosen the locknut with a wrench. Turn the adjusting screw to adjust the clearance, as shown in Figure 44-6. When the clearance is correct, tighten the locknut. Tightening the locknut can change the clearance, so recheck the clearance and readjust if necessary.

Bucket lifter. Valve clearance on overhead camshaft engines with bucket lifters is checked between the camshaft lobe base circle and the adjustment shim, as shown in Figure 44-7.

If adjustment is necessary, the shim must be removed with special tools, as shown in Figure 44-8.

Replacement shims of different thicknesses, as shown in Figure 44-9, are available to reduce or increase the valve clearance to specifications.

To check hydraulic valve lifter assembly clearance, collapse the lifter according to instructions in the manufacturer's service manual. Measure the clearance between the valve stem and the tip of the rocker arm, as shown in Figure 44-10.

If the valve clearance is incorrect, adjust it by turning the pivot point adjusting nut, as shown in Figure 44-11.

44.5 REMOVING VALVE SPRINGS

On most engines, damaged valve springs, retainers, and valve stem seals can be replaced without removing the cylinder head from the engine. Overhead camshaft engines require that the camshaft and timing belt or chain be removed and replaced. Refer to the manufacturer's service manual for correct service procedures.

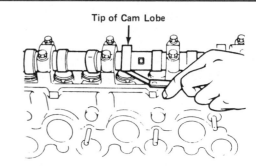

Tip of Cam Lobe

Figure 44-7. Checking valve clearance. FORD MOTOR COMPANY

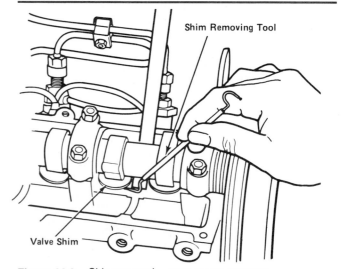

Shim Removing Tool

Valve Shim

Figure 44-8. Shim removal. FORD MOTOR COMPANY

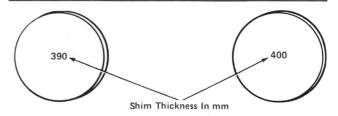

390   400

Shim Thickness In mm

Figure 44-9. Valve shim sizes. FORD MOTOR COMPANY

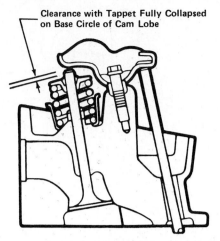

Figure 44-10. Checking collapsed valve lifter clearance.
FORD MOTOR COMPANY

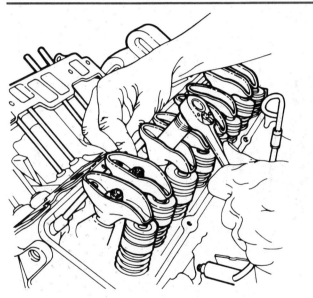

Figure 44-11. Valve adjustment. FORD MOTOR COMPANY

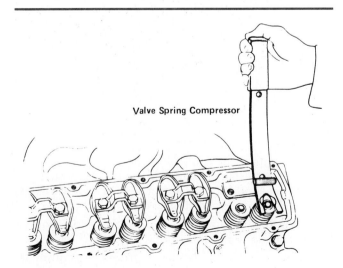

Figure 44-12. Removing valve springs.
CHEVROLET MOTOR DIVISION—GMC

Engines with rocker arms or followers require that the rockers be removed. The rocker shaft and rockers or individual rocker pivots must be unbolted and removed.

To remove valve springs and related parts, position the cylinder at TDC on its compression stroke, as described in Topic 44.4. Remove the spark plug and screw in an air-hold adapter. Connect an air hose to supply air pressure of at least 75 psi [517 kPa]. The air pressure will keep the valves in their closed positions so that they cannot drop down into the cylinder.

Use the special tool shown in Figure 44-12 to compress the valve springs. Have a helper ready to help remove the valve locks, retainer, and springs.

The valve stem seals should be removed as shown in Figure 44-13.

44.6 CHECKING FOR VALVE SPRING DAMAGE

Bent valve springs can cause uneven valve seating. To check a spring, place it on a *surface plate* or a flat surface. A surface plate is a steel plate that has been accurately machined until it is almost perfectly flat. Rotate the spring on the plate, next to a metal square. The clearance between the end of the spring and the square should be ⅟₁₆ inch [1.6 mm] or less as the valve is turned, as shown in Figure 44-14.

Valve springs can weaken and lose spring tension, causing the engine to run poorly at higher rpm—perhaps even causing engine damage. Valve springs can be checked for proper tension with a special fixture and a torque wrench, as shown in

44.7 MEASURING VALVE GUIDE CLEARANCE

Before valve stem seals are replaced, valve guide clearance should be checked with a dial indicator, as shown in Figure 44-16.

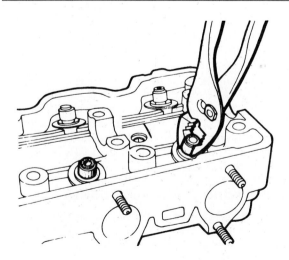

Figure 44-13. Removing valve stem seals.
CHRYSLER CORPORATION

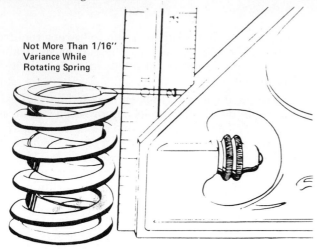

Figure 44-14. Checking a valve spring.
CHEVROLET MOTOR DIVISION—GMC

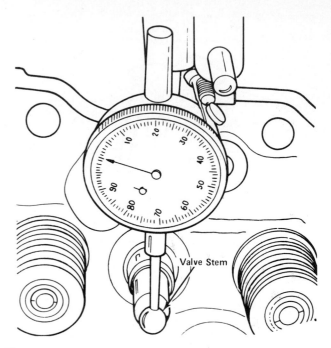

Figure 44-16. Measuring valve guide clearance.
FORD MOTOR COMPANY

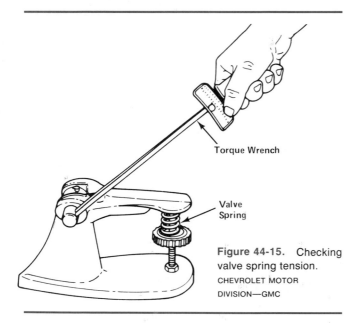

Figure 44-15. Checking valve spring tension.
CHEVROLET MOTOR DIVISION—GMC

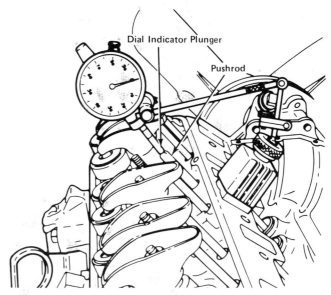

Figure 44-17. Measuring camshaft lobe lift.
CHEVROLET MOTOR DIVISION—GMC

Wrap tape around the mid-part of the valve stems so that the valves cannot drop into the cylinder. Release the air pressure so that the valve is free to move. Position the dial indicator so that the plunger is resting against the end of the valve stem. Move the valve down about 1/16 in. [1.6 mm] off its seat. Move the valve stem back and forth toward the dial indicator plunger and note the readings. Subtract the lower reading from the higher. The difference indicates the valve guide clearance. If clearance is greater than specifications, the cylinder head and valves must be removed from the engine for servicing.

44.8 MEASURING CAMSHAFT LOBE LIFT

Pushrod engine camshaft lobes can be checked for wear and correct lift by using a dial indicator mounted on the cylinder head. See Figure 44-17.

Position the dial indicator plunger against the pushrod tip. Hold the pushrod in position. Using a breaker bar and socket on the crankshaft pulley nut,

slowly rotate the engine. Note the highest and lowest readings recorded. The difference indicates camshaft lift. If camshaft lobe lift is not within specifications, the camshaft must be replaced.

Overhead camshaft lobe lift can be determined by measuring the lobes directly. See Figure 44-18.

If no other cylinder head problems require the removal of the cylinder head, reinstall the air-hold adapter. The adapter is screwed into the spark plug hole, as described in Topic 44.5. Then, install new

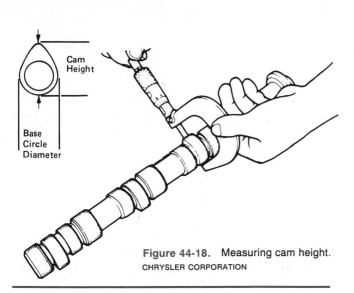

Cam Height

Base Circle Diameter

Figure 44-18. Measuring cam height.
CHRYSLER CORPORATION

valve stem seals and/or other needed parts. Compress the springs and replace the retainers and valve locks. Replace the rockers and/or camshaft. Adjust valve clearance.

44.9 OFF-CAR CYLINDER HEAD SERVICE

Off-car cylinder head service includes:

- Removal of the cylinder head
- Cleaning and visual inspection
- Checking for physical damage
- Measuring valve and head parts for wear
- Machining and repair operations.

Before attempting to remove a cylinder head from an engine, drain the cooling system and engine oil. Disconnect the grounded battery terminal to prevent electric shock. Disconnect electrical wires to sensors, spark plugs, or other devices attached to the head.

All parts that would interfere with head removal must be moved or disconnected. Make simple drawings of how parts are to be replaced. Tag and identify all removed parts and fasteners.

44.10 CYLINDER HEAD REMOVAL

Before removing the cylinder head(s), follow the procedures described in 44.8 to determine if the camshaft meets manufacturer's specifications. If it does not, the camshaft and lifters (followers) must be replaced.

Unbolt and remove the exhaust manifold, which is shown in Figure 44-19, or the exhaust pipe from the manifold.

Disconnect the fuel lines and throttle linkage and remove the carburetor or fuel injection throttle body. Unbolt and remove the intake manifold, shown in Figure 44-20. Unbolt and remove the intake manifold with the carburetor attached, if possible.

A V-type engine's intake manifold must be unbolted from both heads before the cylinder heads can be removed, as shown in Figure 44-21.

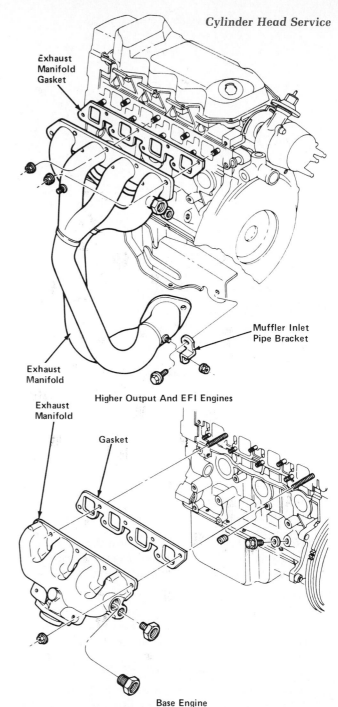

Exhaust Manifold Gasket

Muffler Inlet Pipe Bracket

Exhaust Manifold

Higher Output And EFI Engines

Exhaust Manifold

Gasket

Base Engine

Figure 44-19. Exhaust manifold removal. FORD MOTOR COMPANY

On overhead camshaft engines, align the timing marks, loosen the belt or chain tensioner, and remove the timing belt. Timing marks for a belt-driven overhead camshaft are shown in Figure 44-22.

Remove the rocker shaft or individual rockers. Remove pushrods, in order, from their openings. Tag and identify the pushrods so that they can be reinstalled in the same order.

Remove the spark plugs from the cylinder head.

Unbolt the cylinder head attaching bolts in the pattern recommended by the manufacturer. Be sure

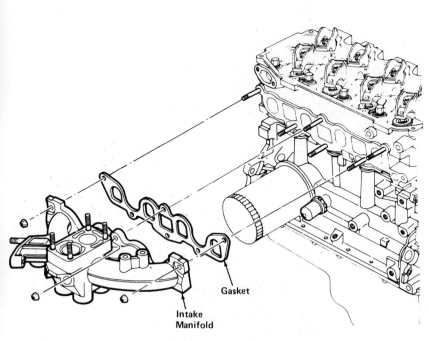

Figure 44-20. Intake manifold removal. FORD MOTOR COMPANY

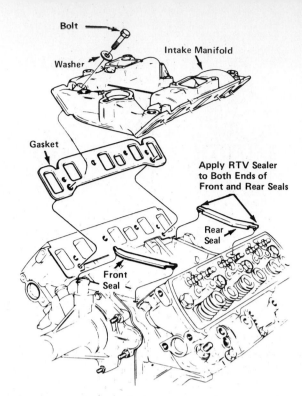

Figure 44-21. Removing a V-type intake manifold and gasket. CHEVROLET MOTOR DIVISION—GMC

that all head bolts have been removed. On some engines, head bolts are located under plugs in the intake manifold.

If the cylinder head is stuck, pry gently against the edges of the head until it becomes loose. Remove the cylinder head.

CAUTION: Do not insert tools into the intake or exhaust ports or other head openings. Prying against the ports can crack the cylinder head.

Use a special tool to remove the valve lifters, shown in Figure 44-23. Place the lifters in separate clean plastic bags, and identify them so that they can be reinstalled in the same locations.

44.11 CLEANING AND VISUAL INSPECTION

After the head has been removed, look for evidence of leakage or damage around the block sealing surface, intake and exhaust ports, and valve seats, as shown in Figure 44-24.

Scrape the sealing surfaces of the head with a flat scraper. Clean the combustion chamber walls with a scraper and a wire brush. Use a wire brush and drill motor to remove heavy deposits.

CAUTION: Use a special brush with brass bristles on aluminum heads.

Remove the valves, springs, and retainers. Check for heavy carbon deposits and pitting on the valve head and fillet area. Remove any threaded plugs or other covers. Remove all soft plugs.

Place the head in a *hot tank* or a *jet spray booth* to remove rust, corrosion, and deposits. A hot tank is a

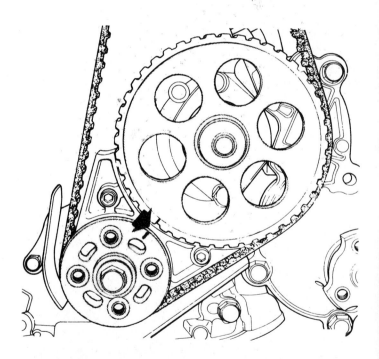

Figure 44-22. Timing marks. CHRYSLER CORPORATION

metal tank filled with corrosive solvent, used to clean ferrous (iron or steel) parts. A jet spray booth is a closed container in which large parts are cleaned with multiple high-pressure spray jets. See Figure 44-25.

CAUTION: Do not place aluminum heads, or iron heads with aluminum attachments, into a hot tank.

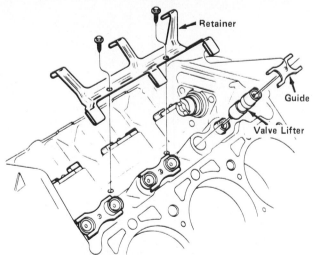

Figure 44-23. Removing valve lifters, guides, and retainers.
CHEVROLET MOTOR DIVISION—GMC

Figure 44-25. High-pressure spray cleaner booth.
STORM VULCAN

Figure 44-24. Inspecting for corrosion and wear.
BLACK & DECKER

Steam clean the head after removing it from the hot tank. Rinse in cool water and dry with compressed air.

Use a drill motor, or manual valve guide cleaner to remove *varnish* deposits from the valve guides, as shown in Figure 44-26.

Check the cylinder head carefully for cracks, especially around the valve seats. Small cracks may be repairable.

44.12 CHECKING FOR PHYSICAL DAMAGE

Cracks that may not be visually apparent can be detected by spraying special liquids onto the metal surface of the block. This may involve using more than one liquid, one after another. Chemical reactions between the chemicals cause the cracks to stand out in color. Alternately, special chemicals that fluoresce, or glow, under ultraviolet (black) light can be used to detect hairline cracks. Special attention must be paid to areas around valve seats and ports.

Warpage, or bending, of the cylinder block sealing surface can be detected by using a *straightedge* and feeler gauges. A straightedge is a heavy metal bar that has been machined so that its edges are straight and parallel. Lay the straightedge across the head in seven

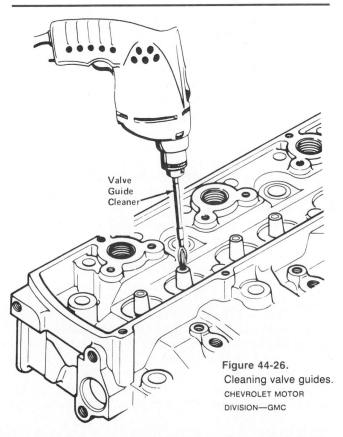

Figure 44-26.
Cleaning valve guides.
CHEVROLET MOTOR
DIVISION—GMC

Valve Guide Cleaner

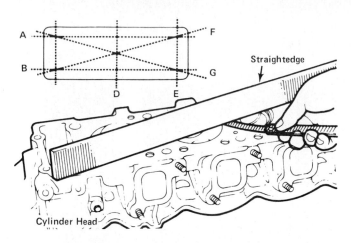

Figure 44-27. Distortion checkpoints. CHRYSLER CORPORATION

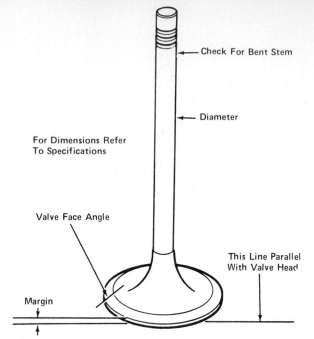

Figure 44-28. Valve measurement points.
FORD MOTOR COMPANY

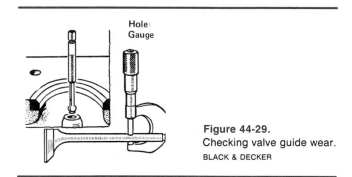

Figure 44-29.
Checking valve guide wear.
BLACK & DECKER

places, as indicated in Figure 44-27, and slide increasingly larger feeler gauges under the bar. The largest feeler gauge that will slide under the bar with a light drag indicates the amount of warpage. In general, no more than 0.004 in. (0.1 mm) of warpage is allowable.

If the cylinder head is warped more than 0.004 in. (0.1 mm), it must be machined flat or replaced.

44.13 MEASURING VALVES AND VALVE GUIDES

Valves are measured with a micrometer and precision rulers at the points indicated in Figure 44-28.

If a valve is not badly worn or damaged, the valve stem tip and valve face can be ground smooth, as discussed in Topic 44.14.

Valve guides can be checked for wear with a small hole gauge and micrometer, as shown in Figure 44-29.

Worn valve guide inserts can be pressed or driven out and new guides inserted with a hydraulic press. Worn integral valve guides can be reamed to a larger size, as shown in Figure 44-30, and valves with larger stems can be installed. Damaged guides can be completely drilled or reamed out and new guides pressed in, if necessary.

44.14 MACHINING AND REPAIR OPERATIONS

Machining and repair operations are usually done by an *automotive machinist*. An automotive machinist specializes in precision machining of automotive parts, and must have a good background in auto mechanics, machine shop practices, mathematics, and geometry.

When material is machined or ground away, other parts may not fit properly. An automotive machinist must know how to machine other affected parts so that everything fits together properly again. For example, when one head from a V-type engine is refinished, the other cylinder head also must be machined the same amount. At that point, the intake manifold will not line up properly with the intake ports and bolt holes. The machinist must be able to

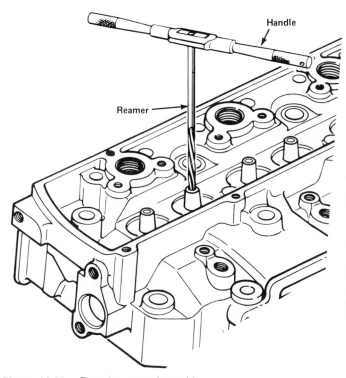

Figure 44-30. Reaming out valve guides.
CHEVROLET MOTOR DIVISION—GMC

figure out where to remove material from the intake manifold and how much to remove to restore proper alignment.

Slightly worn valve seats can be machined smooth with an electric grinder, as shown in Figure 44-31. Badly worn valve seat inserts must be replaced. If an integral valve seat is badly damaged, the entire head must be replaced. Or, the seat may be machined to accept a valve seat insert.

After the valve seats have been machined, the seat width must be checked, as shown in Figure 44-32.

If the resurfaced seat is too wide, it must be narrowed by grinding, as shown in Figure 44-33.

After the valve seats have been ground, the valve will protrude farther through the head than previously. The valve spring installed height must be checked, as shown in Figure 44-34, and corrected. The valve stem height must be checked, and the valve

stem ground down. In addition, shims must be added under the valve springs to keep them under proper tension.

If a cylinder head is not badly cracked, it usually can be repaired by drilling, threading, and screwing in metal rods. The rods are then ground off flush and welded to the head. This process is repeated several times to repair larger cracks.

After all machining operations are completed, the cylinder head is scrubbed with hot water and detergent. Bottle brushes are used to clean ports and head passages. All traces of metal chips and dust, abrasives, or other contaminants must be removed before reassembly. Rinse the head with clean water and dry with compressed air.

After cleaning, the ports and valve guides are swabbed with engine oil applied to a lint-free cloth. Valves, springs, and retainers are installed. Rocker shafts or pivots, and lifters or hydraulic lash adjusters are replaced. New soft plugs are coated with the manufacturer's recommended sealant and installed. Check the valve lifters for excessive wear. If a lifter is noticeably *concave* (dished or curved inward) on the bottom (cam) side, it should be replaced.

Use a tap of the correct size to clean block attaching bolt holes.

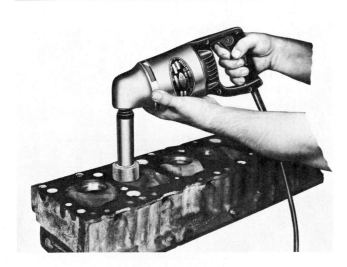

Figure 44-31. Machining valve guides smooth.
SIOUX TOOLS INCORPORATED

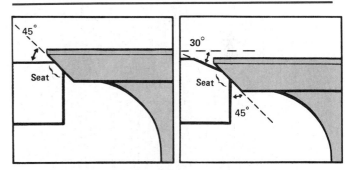

Figure 44-33. Valve seat machining. SIOUX TOOLS INCORPORATED

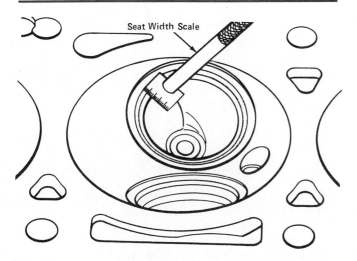

Figure 44-32. Checking valve seat width. FORD MOTOR COMPANY

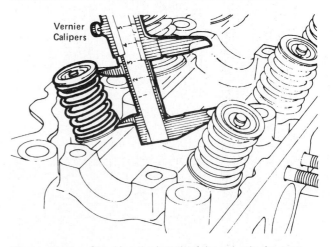

Figure 44-34. Checking the length of the valve in the seat.
CHRYSLER CORPORATION

44.15 CYLINDER HEAD REASSEMBLY AND INSTALLATION

When the head is ready for reinstallation, install reusable numbered valve lifters in lifter bores. Install reusable pushrods in their original locations. Reassemble all upper valve-train parts as specified by the manufacturer.

Dowels or *pilots* are used to align the head to the block. A pilot is a shaft or other part that guides two attaching parts into correct alignment.

Place a new head gasket between the head and the block. Do not apply gasket sealers to the head gasket unless recommended by the gasket manufacturer. Tighten the head bolts, in the manufacturer's specified order, to the correct torque. A typical cylinder head bolt tightening sequence is illustrated in Figure 44-35.

CAUTION: Head bolts must be oiled before installation, and partially tightened by stages, in the correct sequence, to the proper torque.

After the head is in place, adjust the valve clearance and replace the rocker cover. Align crankshaft and overhead camshaft timing marks and install the timing chain or belt. Tighten the chain or belt tensioner as recommended by the manufacturer.

Replace the exhaust and intake manifolds, the carburetor or fuel injection throttle body, all hoses, brackets, and all other removed parts.

Refill the cooling system. Change the oil filter and add the recommended amount of oil to the engine.

Reconnect the battery and start the engine. Let it run until it has reached normal operating temperature. On diesels and on some import gasoline engines, the following procedures are necessary. Shut the engine off and follow the procedure discussed in Topic 44.2 to remove the valve cover. Tighten the cylinder head bolts, in sequence, to the proper torque again. Readjust the valves. Reinstall the valve cover and connect all parts that were removed. This completes cylinder head service.

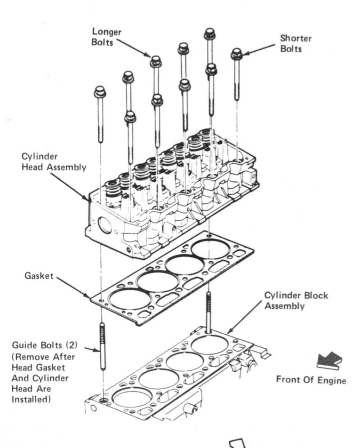

Longer Bolts

Shorter Bolts

Cylinder Head Assembly

Gasket

Cylinder Block Assembly

Front Of Engine

Guide Bolts (2) (Remove After Head Gasket And Cylinder Head Are Installed)

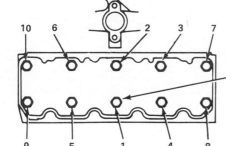

Figure 44-35. Cylinder head bolt tightening sequence.
FORD MOTOR COMPANY

U N I T   H I G H L I G H T S

- Specific procedures in the vehicle manufacturer's service publications must be followed to correctly perform cylinder head service.

- All of the following can be done without removing the cylinder head from the engine: valve clearance adjustment; replacement of valve springs, retainers, and valve stem seals; checking valve guide clearance; and checking camshaft lobe lift.

- Most overhead-camshaft engines require that the camshaft be correctly removed and replaced for some service procedures.

- An automotive machinist specializes in precision machining operations, such as valve seat and cylinder head resurfacing.

T E R M S

soft plug	jet spray booth
cup plug	warpage
expansion plug	straightedge
firing position	automotive machinist
surface plate	concave
hot tank	pilot

REVIEW QUESTIONS

DIRECTIONS: The following questions are similar to those used on mechanic certification tests. On a separate sheet of paper, write the letter of the correct choice.

1. What must be done before proceeding with any cylinder head service?
A. Observe all safety precautions and refer to the manufacturer's service manual for correct procedures.
B. Remove parts that would interfere with cylinder head removal.
C. Diagnose the problem.
D. Adjust valve clearance.

2. All of the following require cylinder head removal for repair EXCEPT
A. visible cracks in the head.
B. excessive valve guide clearance.
C. broken, damaged, or missing valve stem seals.
D. damaged valve guide inserts.

3. Mechanic A says that valve clearance can be adjusted when the piston in a cylinder is exactly at TDC of its compression stroke.
   Mechanic B says that valve clearance can be adjusted when the piston in a cylinder is at its firing position.
   Who is correct?
A. A only   B. B only   C. Both A and B   D. Neither A nor B

4. Which of the following statements is correct?
   I. The cylinder head must be removed to check valve guide clearance.
   II. The cylinder head must be removed to check camshaft lobe lift.
A. I only   B. II only   C. Both I and II   D. Neither I nor II

5. Which of the following is usually done by an automotive mechanic?
A. Machining cylinder head sealing surfaces
B. Adjusting valve clearance
C. Machining intake manifolds
D. Checking valve spring installed height

SUPPLEMENTAL ACTIVITIES

1. Perform a valve adjustment on a vehicle chosen by your instructor.
2. Remove valve retainers, springs, and valve stem seals from a vehicle chosen by your instructor.
3. Measure valve guide clearance and camshaft lobe lift on a vehicle chosen by your instructor.
4. Explain what other machining must be done if one cylinder head on a V-type engine must be resurfaced.
5. Make a report to the class on the shop equipment available for major cylinder head machining operations.

45 PISTON, RING, AND ROD SERVICE

UNIT PREVIEW

Before pistons, rings, and rods can be serviced, the engine should be removed from the vehicle. The oil pan and cylinder head must be removed to allow access to cylinders and connecting rod bolts.

Ridges in the upper cylinder area, formed through wear, must be removed before the pistons can be pushed out the top. Pistons, connecting rods, and rod bearing caps must be marked for proper reinstallation.

Pistons are removed from connecting rods by forcing out the piston pins under pressure.

Piston service includes cleaning, inspection, measurement, and machining operations. Connecting rod service includes cleaning, inspection, measurement, and surface finishing. Connecting rod bearings are inspected for problems and wear.

Before reinstallation, cylinder block and lower engine services are performed.

LEARNING OBJECTIVES

When you have completed your assignments and exercises in this unit, you should be able to:
- [ ] Safely and properly remove ridges from engine cylinders.
- [ ] Remove and replace piston rings.
- [ ] Measure pistons for wear.
- [ ] Safely and properly clean pistons.
- [ ] Safely and properly remove pistons from connecting rods.

SAFETY PRECAUTIONS

Always refer to the manufacturer's service publications for correct service procedures. Incorrect procedures may result in damage to expensive parts.

Engine removal procedures require that heavy assemblies and parts be securely fastened before removal. Loosened assemblies, such as transmissions and engines, must be safely and properly supported.

Sharp metal edges on piston rings can inflict serious cuts. When inspecting rings and other parts,

move your hands and fingers slowly around the edges.

Wear safety goggles or safety glasses at all times in the shop area.

Do not attempt to use any power machinery until you have received proper instruction and training from your instructor. Obtain your instructor's permission before operating any power tools or equipment.

45.1 ENGINE REMOVAL

Before attempting to service pistons, rings, and connecting rods, the engine should be removed from the vehicle. Engine removal can include the following procedures:

- Disconnecting the battery
- Steam cleaning or power spraying the exterior of the engine
- Draining the cooling and lubrication systems
- Removing the fan and radiator
- Removing all external engine system accessories
- Disconnecting exhaust pipes
- Disconnecting hoses and other plumbing connections
- Disconnecting and/or removing linkage
- Disconnecting and/or removing instrument wiring and cables
- Removing intake and exhaust manifolds
- Supporting the transmission and removing transmission mounting bolts
- Disconnecting the driveline
- Supporting the engine and loosening motor mounts
- Lifting the engine from the vehicle with an engine hoist.

Refer to the manufacturer's service manual for specific procedures.

SAFETY CAUTION: Do not attempt engine removal procedures without safety instruction, specific training, and permission from your instructor.

45.2 PREPARING FOR PISTON REMOVAL

Before pistons and connecting rods can be removed, the cylinder head must be removed from the engine, as discussed in Unit 44. Other procedures necessary before piston removal include:

- Marking connecting rods and bearing caps
- Removing connecting rod bearing caps
- Inspecting connecting rod bearings and crankshaft journals
- Measuring connecting rod bearing clearance
- Removing cylinder ridges.

Marking Connecting Rods and Bearing Caps

The connecting rod and rod bearing cap must be replaced in their proper locations. If the rods and bearing caps are not marked by the manufacturer for reinstallation, the mechanic must make numbering and alignment marks. Use a centerpunch, small chisel, or numbering die to number the rods and bearing caps. Mark the rods and bearing caps as shown in Figure 45-1 to indicate which part should face the front of the engine.

Removing Connecting Rod Bearing Caps

Remove the oil pan and oil pump from the cylinder block. Remove the connecting rod nuts. Remove the connecting rod bearing caps and inspect the insert bearings for defects, as shown in Figure 45-2.

Inspecting Connecting Rod Bearings and Crankshaft Journals

Inspect the crankshaft rod journals for corresponding defects and *scoring*. Scoring consists of grooves worn around the inside or outside circumference of a part.

Figure 45-2. Bearing defects. FORD MOTOR COMPANY

A rough check for unacceptable scoring is to run the tip of your fingernail across the journal. Be sure your fingernail is clean before performing this test. If your fingernail drops into the grooves, they are unacceptably deep.

Measuring Connecting Rod Bearing Clearance

To measure connecting rod bearing clearance, lay a strip of *Plastigage* across the bearing surface, parallel to the crankshaft. See Figure 45-3. Perfect Circle Plastigage is a thin strip of wax-like material that flattens when it is compressed. The amount of flattening indicates the clearance between two parts.

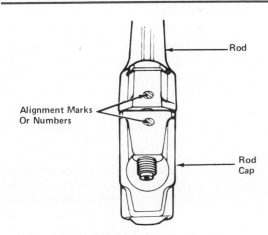

Figure 45-1. Connecting rod alignment marks.
FORD MOTOR COMPANY

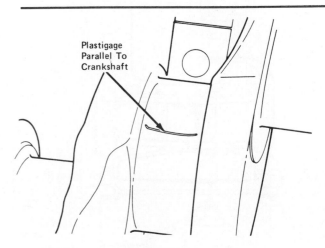

Figure 45-3. Using Plastigage on a journal.
CHEVROLET MOTOR DIVISION—GMC

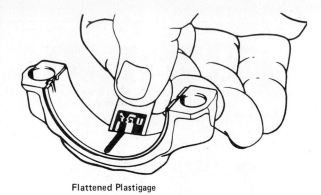

Flattened Plastigage

Figure 45-4. Measuring bearing clearance with Plastigage.
CHEVROLET MOTOR DIVISION

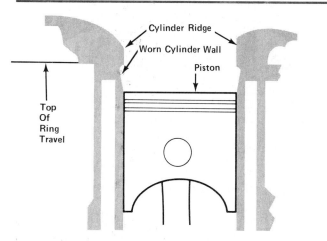

Figure 45-5. Cylinder ridges are caused by cylinder wear.

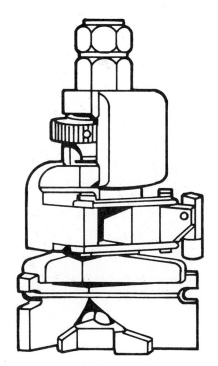

Figure 45-6. Cylinder ridge remover.

Replace the bearing cap and lower insert bearing. Tighten the connecting rod nuts to the manufacturer's specified torque. Loosen and remove the nuts and bearing cap. Use the gauge supplied with the Plastigage to find the bearing clearance, as shown in Figure 45-4.

Refer to the manufacturer's service manual for acceptable bearing clearance. Different readings at the ends of the Plastigage indicate one of three conditions. The first is a tapered journal, larger at one end than the other. Another is a spool-shaped crankshaft journal (smaller in the middle than at the ends). The last is a barrel-shaped journal (larger in the middle than at the ends).

Removing Cylinder Ridges

After many thousands of miles of operation, the cylinders become worn by the friction of the piston rings. One aspect of this wear is the formation of *cylinder ridges,* as shown in Figure 45-5.

Cylinder ridges must be removed before the piston can be pushed out from the bottom of the cylinder. A *cylinder ridge remover,* or ridge reamer, shown in Figure 45-6, is used to remove the ridge. Turn the crankshaft until the piston in the cylinder is at BDC. Insert a clean shop rag to catch metal shavings.

CAUTION: Refer to the cylinder ridge remover manufacturer's service literature to correctly adjust and use the tool. Improper use can damage the cylinder beyond repair.

Cover the other cylinders to protect them from shavings. Insert the ridge remover and adjust the cutting bit. Rotate the tool by hand. After the ridge has been cut, remove the tool and clean the shavings from the cylinder. Repeat this procedure for all cylinders.

45.3 REMOVING PISTONS AND CONNECTING RODS

Rotate the crankshaft so that the piston/rod to be removed is at the bottom of its stroke. Unbolt and remove the rod bearing caps. Place short lengths of rubber hose over the connecting rod bolts, as shown in Figure 45-7, to protect the crankshaft journals and cylinder walls.

If the piston is to be removed from the connecting rod, mark the piston top for cylinder number and proper mounting on the connecting rod, so that correct piston pin offset is maintained. Pistons are often notched or otherwise marked to indicate which part is to face toward the front of the engine, as shown in Figure 45-8.

Place a length of wooden dowel or broomstick against the bottom of the piston. Carefully drive out the piston with a mallet.

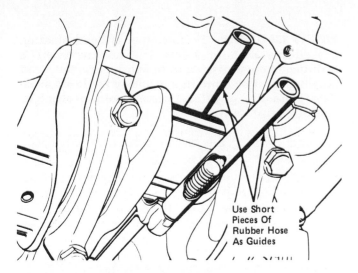

Figure 45-7. Connecting rod-bolt guide.
CHEVROLET MOTOR DIVISON—GMC

Use Short
Pieces Of
Rubber Hose
As Guides

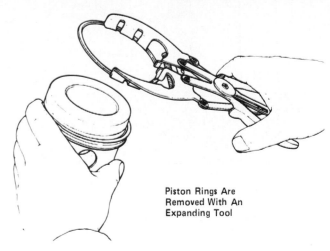

Piston Rings Are
Removed With An
Expanding Tool

Figure 45-9. Piston ring expander.
CHRYSLER CORPORATION

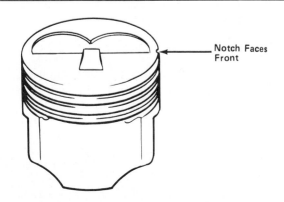

Notch Faces
Front

Figure 45-8. Piston identification.
CHEVROLET MOTOR DIVISION—GMC

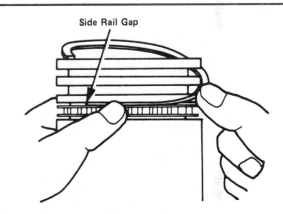

Side Rail Gap

Figure 45-10. Removing oil control piston ring.
CHRYSLER CORPORATION

Removing Piston Rings

A *piston ring expander,* shown in Figure 45-9, is used to remove cast rings, such as compression rings and some oil-control rings, from the piston without breakage.

Oil control rings made up of expanders and side rails can be removed carefully by hand, as shown in Figure 45-10.

45.4 REMOVING PISTONS FROM CONNECTING RODS

To remove piston pins that are press-fitted to connecting rods or pistons, a *hydraulic press* is used to press them out. A hydraulic press is an assembly that uses the pressure of a hydraulic jacking unit or hydraulic cylinder to produce pushing force.

SAFETY CAUTION: Do not attempt to use the hydraulic press without safety instruction, specific training, and permission from your instructor. The force generated by the press can cause metal to shatter suddenly and throw sharp metal parts outward.

Remove pin retaining clips, if used, before attempting to press out the piston pin. During the pressing operation, the piston pin boss area of the piston must be supported. A press setup for removing piston pins is shown in Figure 45-11.

45.5 PISTON SERVICE

If not badly damaged or worn, pistons can be reused. Piston service can include:

* Cleaning
* Inspection
* Measurement
* Machining operations.

Cleaning Pistons

Carbon, varnish, and deposits are removed from pistons by soaking the pistons in carburetor cleaner or by *bead blasting.* Bead blasting is a process that uses compressed air to blow small glass beads at metal parts. The glass beads gently abrade, or wear off, deposits.

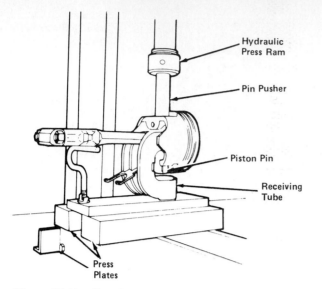

Figure 45-11. Pressing out piston pin. FORD MOTOR COMPANY

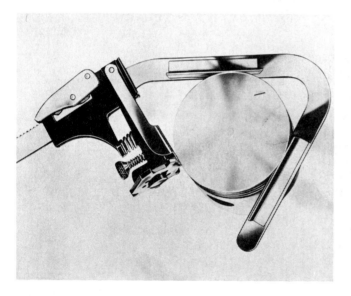

Figure 45-12. Cleaning piston ring groove. AMMCO TOOLS, INC.

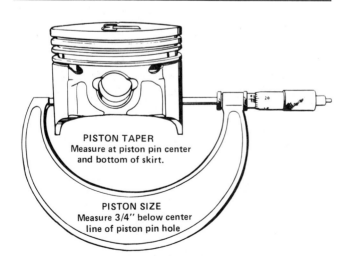

Figure 45-13. Measuring a piston.
CHEVROLET MOTOR DIVISION—GMC

SAFETY CAUTION: Do not attempt bead blasting procedures without safety instruction, specific training, and permission from your instructor. Bead blasting must be done in a properly enclosed area. Safety hoods, goggles, gloves, and protective clothing must be worn.

After cleaning, the piston ring grooves are cleaned with a groove cleaner (see Figure 45-12).

Oil return holes in the oil ring groove can be cleaned with a small drill.

During cleaning operations, no metal is to be removed from the piston. Deposits and varnish must be cleaned off without damage to the piston.

Inspecting and Measuring Pistons

Measure the piston as shown in Figure 45-13. Compare this reading with the bore size of the cylinder block. Refer to the manufacturer's service manual for recommended piston-to-bore clearance.

Piston taper. Pistons can become *tapered*, or narrower at one end. When measuring taper, the largest reading must be at the bottom of the skirt. Refer to the manufacturer's service manual for allowable piston taper. Pistons can be expanded, or made slightly larger, by machining operations described below.

CAUTION: Handle pistons with care. Do not attempt to force pistons into or through cylinders until the cylinders have been machined to the correct size. Pistons can be damaged through careless handling.

Ring groove wear. The ring grooves can become enlarged through wear. To check ring groove clearance, use feeler gauges inserted between a new ring and the piston groove (see Figure 45-14).

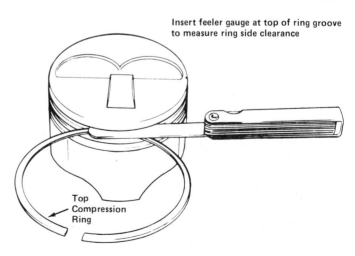

Figure 45-14. Piston ring side clearance.
CHEVROLET MOTOR DIVISION—GMC

Refer to the manufacturer's service manual for allowable clearance measurements. If clearance on the top compression ring groove is excessive, the groove can be machined approximately 0.025 in. [0.64 mm] larger. A flat steel groove spacer can then be inserted above the ring to reduce the clearance to specifications (see Figure 45-15).

Piston pin bore wear. If the piston pin hole, or bore, is worn, the pin can move excessively within the piston. Such wear generally requires that the piston and pin both be replaced. Alternately, the piston and connecting rod small end can be rebored and a new, larger pin installed.

Knurling Pistons

A piston skirt may be slightly expanded by *knurling*, as shown in Figure 45-16.

Knurling is a machining process. The piston is mounted in a lathe. A knurling bit is slowly forced into the spinning skirt. The bit produces a raised pattern, or knurl. This raised pattern enlarges the diameter of the skirt.

45.6 CONNECTING ROD SERVICE

Connecting rods that are not badly twisted or worn can be reconditioned and reused. Connecting rod service can include:

- Cleaning
- Inspection
- Measurement.

Cleaning

Connecting rods can be cleaned after removal from the piston and pin by soaking them in a hot tank of cleaning solution. Blow compressed air through the oil squirt hole to make sure it is open.

SAFETY CAUTION: Wear eye protection whenever you use compressed air. Liquids or particles can be blown into the eyes with great force and cause injury or blindness.

Inspection

Connecting rods can become bent or twisted because of the forces exerted against them by the piston pin and the crankshaft journal (see Figure 45-17).

Special measurement tools and fixtures are available to check the rod for bending and twisting.

If only slightly twisted, connecting rods can be straightened by inserting a bar and twisting. The limits for correctable connecting rod twist are shown in Figure 45-18.

The connecting rod big end bore can become enlarged through stretching, as shown in Figure 45-19. Connecting rods with enlarged bores should be remachined by an automotive machine shop or be replaced.

Figure 45-16. Knurling a piston. PERFECT CIRCLE

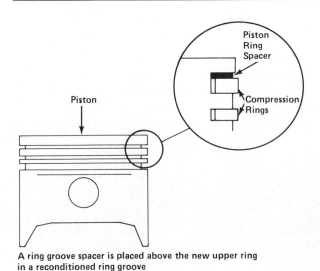

A ring groove spacer is placed above the new upper ring in a reconditioned ring groove

Figure 45-15. Ring groove spacer.

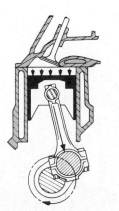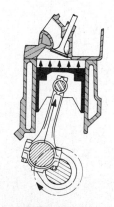

POWER STROKE
(Downward Force)
"Piston driving the crankshaft"

COMPRESSION STROKE
(Upward Force)
"Crankshaft driving the piston"

Figure 45-17. Connecting rod forces.

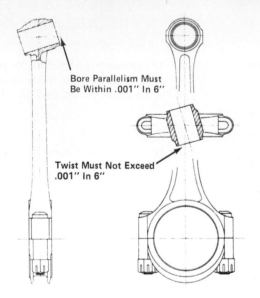

Figure 45-18. Connecting rod twist. FEDERAL-MOGUL

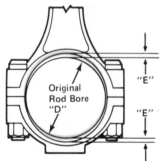

Figure 45-19. Stretched connecting rod bore.

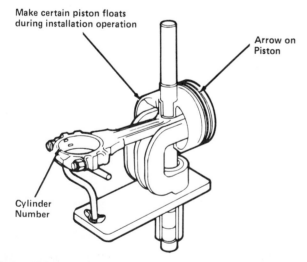

Figure 45-20. Piston pin installation. FORD MOTOR COMPANY

45.7 CONNECTING ROD BEARING INSPECTION

Connecting rod bearings are subject to several forces from: power stroke combustion, spinning (centrifugal force), and the weight being moved.

Bearing damage from these forces can take many forms. Refer to Figure 45-2.

The most frequent cause of damaged bearings is contaminated engine oil. Small particles of dirt or sand, metals, sludge, or other contaminants left in the engine can destroy new bearings quickly.

There are four major factors that contribute to rapid bearing failures in newly rebuilt engines. These factors are: improper fit, excess or insufficient crush, lack of lubrication, and contamination. Be sure to have clean work habits—especially clean hands. Always use good quality engine oils with the proper API service ratings.

45.8 INSTALLING PISTONS ON CONNECTING RODS

After piston and connecting rod service, piston pins are pressed into the connecting rods. The press setup for this operation is shown in Figure 45-20.

45.9 INSTALLING PISTON RINGS

Refer to the manufacturer's specifications for proper types of compression and oil control rings to be fitted. However, before rings are installed on the piston, the rings must be checked in the cylinder for proper fit. Other procedures, such as refinishing crankshaft journals, are necessary before installing the piston and connecting rod assembly in its cylinder. These procedures are discussed in Unit 46.

UNIT HIGHLIGHTS

- The engine should be removed from the vehicle before pistons, rings, and connecting rods are serviced.
- Cylinder ridges must be machined from the cylinders before the pistons can be removed.
- Connecting rods, bearing caps, and pistons must be marked for proper reinstallation.
- Piston rings are removed before piston pins are pressed out.
- Piston machining operations include enlarging the top compression ring groove for spacer installation and knurling the piston skirt.
- Small amounts of twist in connecting rods can be corrected.
- Before new piston rings are fitted and the piston and connecting rod assembly reinstalled, other machining and fitting operations are necessary.

TERMS

scoring	hydraulic press
Plastigage	bead blasting
cylinder ridge	taper
cylinder ridge remover	knurling
piston ring expander	

R E V I E W   Q U E S T I O N S

DIRECTIONS: The following questions are similar to those used on mechanic certification tests. On a separate sheet of paper, write the letter of the correct choice.

1. Mechanic A says that the connecting rods must be marked to indicate in which cylinder they are to be reinstalled.
   Mechanic B says that the connecting rods must be marked to indicate which way they must face in their cylinders.
   Who is correct?
   A. A only   B. B only   C. Both A and B   D. Neither A nor B

2. Which of the following is not done before pistons are removed?
   A. Mark the connecting rods for reassembly.
   B. Remove cylinder ridges.
   C. Mark the cylinder number on the piston.
   D. Remove the main bearing caps.

3. All of the following must be done to remove or replace a piston on a connecting rod EXCEPT
   A. receive safety instruction and specific training from your instructor.
   B. wear eye protection.
   C. support the piston pin boss.
   D. use a piston pin of the same diameter to drive out the old piston pin.

4. Which of the following statements is correct?
   I. Knurling produces a better gripping surface for the piston against the cylinder wall.
   II. Knurling expands the piston skirt diameter.
   A. I only   B. II only   C. Both I and II   D. Neither I nor II

5. All of the following contribute to early bearing failures EXCEPT
   A. improper fit.
   B. excessive or insufficient crush.
   C. lack of lubrication.
   D. cleanliness during reassembly.

S U P P L E M E N T A L   A C T I V I T I E S

1. Read the instruction manual for your shop's cylinder ridge remover. Ask your instructor about safety precautions and correct use of the tool. Demonstrate to your class how to avoid cutting too much material from the cylinder wall.
2. Ask your instructor about safety precautions and correct use of your shop's bead blaster or other compressed air cleaning device. Demonstrate to your class proper piston cleaning procedures.
3. Inspect and measure a shop piston for taper with an outside micrometer. Refer to the manufacturer's service manual and report to your class why the piston can or cannot be reused.
4. Demonstrate to the class the correct removal and replacement procedures for cast compression and oil-control rings.
5. Ask your instructor about the safe and proper use of your shop's hydraulic press. Demonstrate for your class proper safety precautions and usage of the press to remove piston pins.

UNIT PREVIEW

Before block and crankshaft service can be completed, the components must be cleaned. After a thorough cleaning, measurements are taken. Then, a careful inspection of all parts and components must be performed.

Following the cleaning, measuring, and inspection, it will be possible to make accurate service recommendations. These may include replacement, remachining, and/or reconditioning of components.

When the serviceable parts and components have been staged, the reassembly process can be started.

After engine reassembly, special procedures are followed for initial start-up, break-in, and during the first 100 miles of driving.

LEARNING OBJECTIVES

When you have completed your assignments and exercises in this unit, you should be able to:
☐ Measure main bearing clearance and crankshaft end play.
☐ Determine if a cylinder is misshaped or worn.
☐ Determine the condition of crankshaft and camshaft journals and lobes.
☐ Fit piston rings correctly to a piston.
☐ Explain the importance of correctly tightening cylinder heads and other parts in sequence to the manufacturer's specified torque.

SAFETY PRECAUTIONS

Always refer to the manufacturer's service publications for correct service procedures. Incorrect procedures may result in damage to expensive parts.

Wear safety goggles or safety glasses at all times in the shop area.

Parts to be reused must be identified as to location and positioning. Handle parts, especially precision bearing inserts, carefully. Store such parts wrapped in soft cloths.

Do not attempt to use any power machinery until you have received proper safety training and operating instructions from your instructor. Obtain your instructor's permission before operating any power tools or equipment.

New gaskets and sealants recommended by the manufacturer must be used when parts are reinstalled.

46.1 PRE-DISASSEMBLY MEASUREMENTS

Before proceeding with cylinder block and crankshaft service, crankshaft end play and main bearing clearances are checked.

Measuring Crankshaft End Play

End play is the movement of a shaft in a back-and-forth direction parallel to its length. *Crankshaft end play* is the movement of the crankshaft forward or rearward in the block. Excessive end play usually indicates worn flanges on the crankshaft thrust bearing.

To measure crankshaft end play, use a screwdriver to pry carefully between the crankcase and a crankshaft counterweight. Pry the crankshaft toward the front of the engine. Measure the clearance between the crankshaft flange surface and the rear main bearing with a feeler gauge, as shown in Figure 46-1.

If the clearance is not to the manufacturer's specifications, remove and examine the thrust bearing. If worn, replace all engine bearings when you reassemble the engine. Reinstallation of the engine is discussed in Topic 46.9.

NOTE: In most engines, the thrust bearing and main bearing are parts of a set. The thrust bearing cannot be replaced separately.

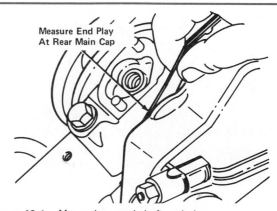

Figure 46-1. Measuring crankshaft end play.
CHEVROLET MOTOR DIVISION—GMC

Measuring Main Bearing Clearance

To check main bearing clearance, mark the main bearing caps for location and alignment with punch marks and/or numbering dies. Unbolt the main bearing caps. Position Plastigage on the lower main bearing insert, parallel to the crankshaft.

CAUTION: The crankshaft must not rotate during the gauging operation. If the crankshaft rotates, the plastic material will be damaged and will not indicate correct clearance measurements.

Replace the main bearing caps and bearing inserts. Tighten the cap nuts or bolts to the manufacturer's specified torque. Loosen the bolts, carefully remove the main bearing caps and bearing inserts. Use the width gauge supplied with the Plastigage to judge main bearing clearance, as shown in Figure 46-2. The plastic measuring material may be stuck to the journal or to the bearing insert.

Different readings at the ends and/or middle of a journal can indicate defects. The journal may be tapered, spool-shaped, or barrel-shaped. These defects can be corrected by regrinding the crankshaft journals to a smaller size. Oversize, or thicker, main bearings then are used to return the clearance to specifications.

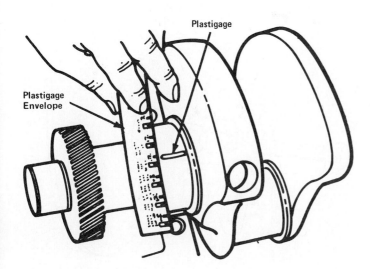

Figure 46-2. Checking main bearing clearance.
FORD MOTOR COMPANY

Inspect the crankshaft main journals for signs of damage or scoring. In most cases, the crankshaft can be reused if the following conditions apply:

- The main journals are not severely damaged.
- The crankshaft clearance is within specifications.
- The engine was removed for repairs other than main bearings.

46.2 CYLINDER BLOCK SERVICE

Engine overhaul procedures generally include refinishing cylinders and cleaning the cylinder head sealing surfaces and bearing surfaces. Cylinder block service and repair procedures can include:

- Cleaning and inspection
- Measuring cylinders and bearing surfaces
- Reboring and honing cylinders
- Replacing cylinder sleeves
- Reboring and refinishing camshaft and main bearing housings
- Replacing soft plugs
- Repairing cracks
- Repairing damaged threads.

46.3 CYLINDER BLOCK CLEANING AND INSPECTION

All major attached and inserted parts must be removed from the cylinder block before the block can be thoroughly cleaned.

SAFETY CAUTION: The crankshaft is heavy. Have a helper ready to assist you in lifting the crankshaft from the crankcase area. If the crankshaft drops, it will be damaged. Physical injury also can result.

Parts Removal

The crankshaft must be removed from the cylinder block prior to cleaning operations. If main bearing caps are not marked, use a punch and/or numbering dies to make identification and alignment marks. Remove the main bearing caps and lower bearing inserts, as shown in Figure 46-3.

Unbolt and remove the water pump.

Unbolt and remove the engine flywheel and any cover plates, as shown in Figure 46-4.

The crankshaft pulley or damper is removed with a special puller, as shown in Figure 46-5.

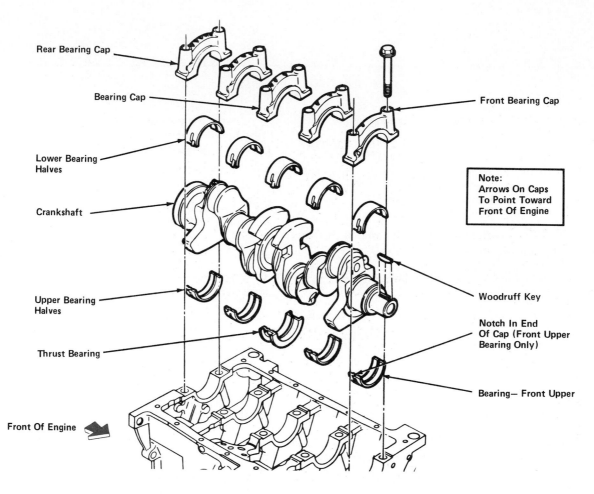

Figure 46-3. Removing main bearing caps. FORD MOTOR COMPANY

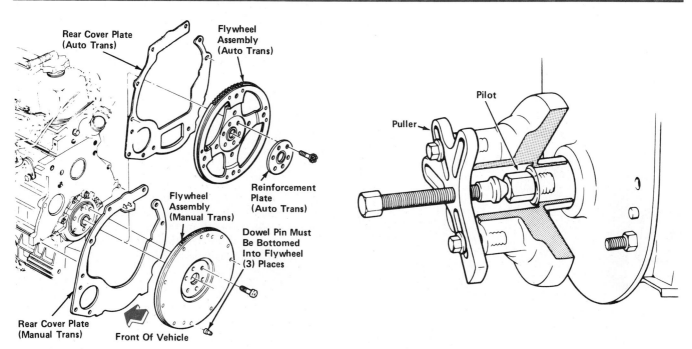

Figure 46-4. Flywheel removal. FORD MOTOR COMPANY

Figure 46-5. Damper removal. CHEVROLET MOTOR DIVISION—GMC

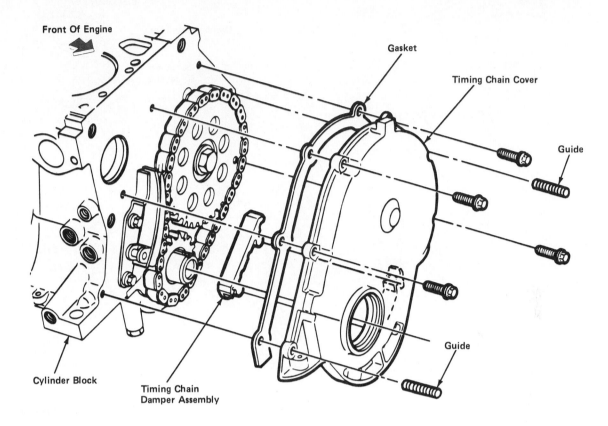

Figure 46-6. Timing cover removal. FORD MOTOR COMPANY

On pushrod-type engines, the timing cover (see Figure 46-6) is removed to expose the timing chain and/or gears.

The timing chain, shown in Figure 46-7, and/or gears are disconnected and removed. Pushrod-type valve lifters are removed as discussed in Unit 44.

The camshaft then is removed carefully from the block, as shown in Figure 46-8. Camshaft removal on some engines may require the use of special puller tools. Special camshaft retainers or thrust plates must be removed on some engines.

Camshaft bearings on pushrod engines are removed with a special puller, shown in Figure 46-9. As the nut is tightened, the camshaft bearing is pulled from its bore. If the camshaft bearings are to be reused, number them and make alignment marks for reinstallation.

The thermostat housing and all other covers and attachments then are removed from the cylinder block. All soft plugs are removed so that the interior passages of the block can be cleaned.

Cleaning

After all attached parts have been removed, the cylinder block is put into a hot tank for several hours or cleaned in a high-pressure or jet spray booth. This removes sludge, rust, and other deposits. After removal from the hot tank, the block is steam cleaned.

Circular wire brushes are used to clean oil and coolant passages, as shown in Figure 46-10.

A tap is used to clean the threads of the cylinder block attaching bolt holes. Dirt in the holes can cause false torque readings when head bolts are tightened during cylinder head replacement.

Inspection

After cleaning, the block is thoroughly inspected for evidence of cracks and other damage. The cylinder head sealing surfaces are checked for warpage. This check is performed by using a straightedge and feeler gauges (refer to Topic 44.12) across the surfaces. See Figure 46-11.

Refer to Topic 44.12 for a guide to checking for cracks in metal surfaces. Small cracks in non-sealing external surfaces may be repairable by welding. Large cracks in sealing surfaces or cylinder walls usually require that the block be discarded. Small cracks in cylinder walls may be repaired by *sleeving*, or machining the cylinder to accept a sleeve. See Topic 46.6.

Porosity, or tiny holes caused by air bubbles during casting, can be patched with *epoxy cement*. Epoxy cement is a plastic resin that hardens to form a patch. The porous areas, shown in Figure 46-12, are ground down and filled with epoxy. Heat is applied to dry the epoxy. After repair, the epoxy is sanded and painted.

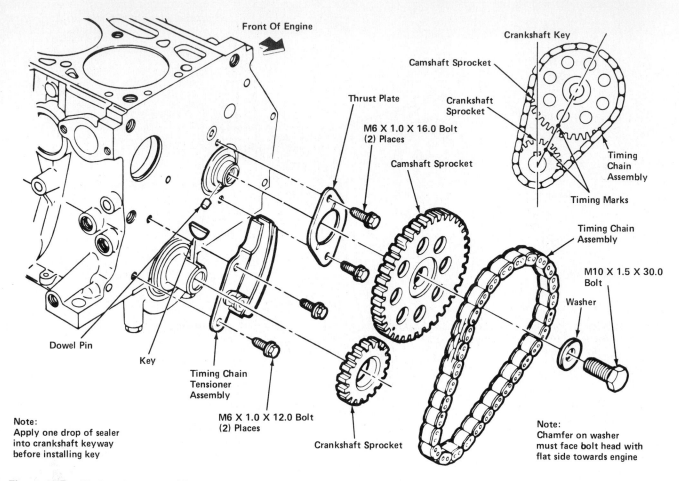

Figure 46-7. Timing chain assembly. FORD MOTOR COMPANY

Front Of Engine

Thrust Plate

M6 X 1.0 X 16.0 Bolt (2) Places

Camshaft Sprocket

Dowel Pin

Key

Timing Chain Tensioner Assembly

M6 X 1.0 X 12.0 Bolt (2) Places

Crankshaft Sprocket

Crankshaft Key

Camshaft Sprocket

Crankshaft Sprocket

Timing Chain Assembly

Timing Marks

Timing Chain Assembly

M10 X 1.5 X 30.0 Bolt

Washer

Note:
Apply one drop of sealer into crankshaft keyway before installing key

Note:
Chamfer on washer must face bolt head with flat side towards engine

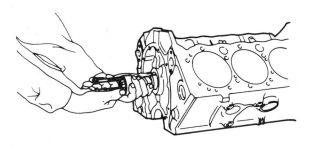

Figure 46-8. Camshaft removal.
CHEVROLET MOTOR DIVISION—GMC

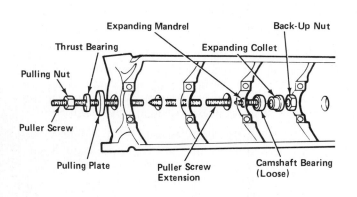

Expanding Mandrel

Thrust Bearing

Back-Up Nut

Expanding Collet

Pulling Nut

Puller Screw

Pulling Plate

Puller Screw Extension

Camshaft Bearing (Loose)

Figure 46-9. Camshaft bearing removal. FORD MOTOR COMPANY

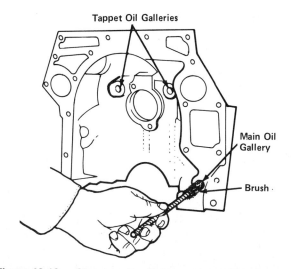

Tappet Oil Galleries

Main Oil Gallery

Brush

Figure 46-10. Cleaning oil galleries. FORD MOTOR COMPANY

46.4 CYLINDER MEASUREMENT

Use a cylinder bore gauge to measure the cylinders at three points. These points are the top, middle, and bottom of the areas contacted by the piston rings. Measure the cylinder at points parallel and perpendicular (at 90 degrees) to the crankshaft, as shown in Figure 46-13.

Different measurements between points A and B indicate an out-of-round, or oval, cylinder. Increasingly smaller measurements at the top, middle, and bottom of the ring travel indicate *cylinder taper*. Refer to the manufacturer's service manual for allowable cylinder dimensions.

46.5 BEARING SURFACE MEASUREMENT

To measure the main bearing housing bore, the main bearing caps are replaced in the correct order and position. The caps then are tightened to the manufacturer's torque specification. A telescoping gauge and outside micrometer are used to measure the bore.

The bores can become misaligned, as shown in Figure 46-14, due to crankcase warpage or a bent crankshaft.

To check for main bearing housing misalignment, a specially ground *arbor,* or bar, is placed in the crankcase bore. See Figure 46-15. Feeler gauges are used to check for clearance under the bar at any bearing housing. Clearance indicates misaligned bearing housings.

Such misalignment can be corrected by *align boring* the housings. The bearing caps are installed and torqued to specifications. A special machine is

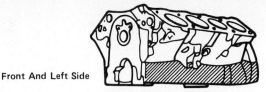

Front And Left Side

Note — Portions of the front surface that are not machined or not part of the water jacket are repairable. Shaded areas may be repaired with epoxy.

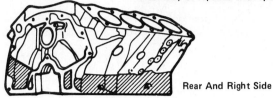

Rear And Right Side

Shaded areas may be repaired with epoxy.

Figure 46-12. Repairable block areas. FORD MOTOR COMPANY

A — At right angle to center line of engine.

B — Parallel to center line of engine.

Top Measurement:	Make 12.70mm (½") below top of block deck.
Bottom Measurement:	Make within 12.70mm (½") above top of piston—where piston is at BDC.
Bore Service Limit:	Equals the average of "A" and "B" when measured at the center of the piston travel.
Taper:	Equals difference between "A" top and "A" bottom.
Out-of-Round:	Equals difference between "A" and "B" when measured at the center of piston travel.

Refer to manufacturer's specification tables.

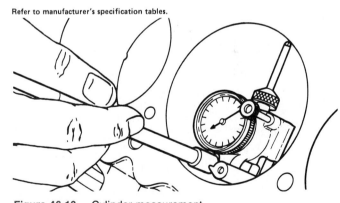

Figure 46-13. Cylinder measurement.
BUICK MOTOR DIVISION—GMC/FORD MOTOR COMPANY

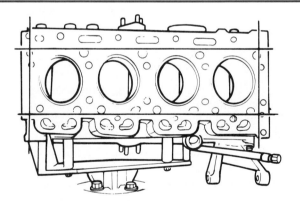

Figure 46-11. Checking cylinder block sealing surface distortion.
FORD MOTOR COMPANY

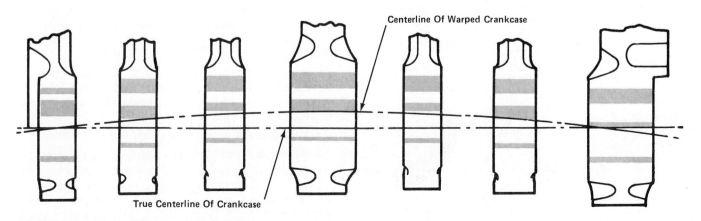

Centerline Of Warped Crankcase

True Centerline Of Crankcase

Figure 46-14. Bearing surface measurements.

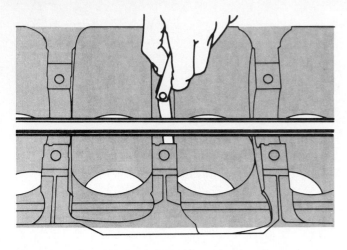

Figure 46-15. Checking crankcase alignment.

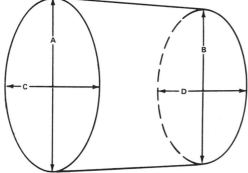

Figure 46-16. Cylinder honing tool.

A vs B = Vertical Taper
C vs D = Horizontal Taper
A vs C
B vs D = Out of Round

Check for Out-of-Round at each end of journal

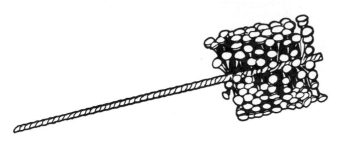

Figure 46-17. Crankshaft journal measurement.
FORD MOTOR COMPANY

Note that the difference in insert thickness is made up in the flexible steel backing itself, while the thin alloy lining layer remains constant.

Figure 46-18. Bearing insert measurements.

used to bore new, larger holes in the housings. Oversize bearings are fitted to the bored housings. Align boring is done by an automotive machinist.

Camshaft bearing bores are measured with a telescoping gauge and outside micrometer. Out-of-round or oversize conditions can be corrected by machining operations.

46.6 CYLINDER BORING AND REFINISHING

Cylinders can be rebored *oversize,* usually in steps of 0.010 inch [0.25mm] up to 0.060 inch [1.52mm]. Larger pistons and piston rings, available in matching oversize steps, are installed. Cylinder reboring usually is done by an automotive machinist.

After boring, the cylinders must be honed, or finished, to the proper size and finished with a honing tool, shown in Figure 46-16.

Cylinder Sleeves

In some cases, it is possible to repair cylinder wall cracks or excessive wear in cast-iron cylinder blocks. This can be done by boring the cylinder to accept a dry liner. The *overbore,* or larger bore diameter, is usually 0.125 inch [3.18 mm] or more. The dry liner is then pressed or driven into the block, bored to the correct size, and honed.

Wet cylinder sleeves are removed from blocks and replaced when worn past the manufacturer's limits.

46.7 CRANKSHAFT AND CAMSHAFT JOURNAL MEASUREMENT

If crankshaft journals have not been badly scored or damaged, the crankshaft can be reused. Use an outside micrometer to measure the crankshaft journals as indicated in Figure 46-17.

Inspect and measure camshaft lobes as discussed in Topic 44.8. Measure camshaft bearing journals and compare the measurements to the manufacturer's specifications.

Crankshaft and camshaft journals can be *reground,* or refinished, to a smaller size. Camshaft lobes, if worn but not damaged, also can be reground.

Thicker bearings, shown in Figure 46-18, are used on undersize crankshaft and camshaft journals.

46.8 CYLINDER BLOCK REASSEMBLY

After all machining procedures on the cylinder block have been performed correctly, the engine is ready for reassembly. Cylinder block reassembly can include the following procedures:

- Preparing the cylinder block for reassembly
- Replacing camshaft bearings
- Replacing soft plugs
- Replacing crankshaft seals
- Replacing main bearings
- Checking crankshaft end play

- Fitting piston rings
- Replacing piston/connecting rod assemblies
- Replacing connecting rod bearings
- Replacing the cylinder head
- Replacing timing gears and/or chains on pushrod engines
- Replacing the flywheel
- Replacing the oil pump and oil pan
- Replacing parts and covers.

Preparing the Cylinder Block for Reassembly

The cylinder block is cleaned by scrubbing it with hot water and detergent. A stiff bristle brush and bottle brushes are used to throughly scrub the cylinders, crankcase, camshaft bore, and all other openings.

CAUTION: **The cylinder block must be thoroughly cleaned. Any traces of abrasives or metal chips will quickly wear cylinder bores, crankshaft and camshaft journals, and bearings. Do not use gasoline or kerosene to clean the cylinder block.**

After washing, swab the bores repeatedly with clean engine oil on a lint-free cloth. Do this until no trace of iron or abrasive particles is left.

Replacing Camshaft Bearings and Camshaft

Camshaft bearings for pushrod engines are available for standard and undersize journals. Undersize journals are the result of machining operations to remove scoring and other problems from the camshaft.

In some cases, the removal tool also can be used to pull or press the camshaft bearings into the block. In other cases, special tools are used to push the camshaft bearings into place.

The camshaft bearing oil holes are aligned with the cylinder block oil galleries before insertion. After bearing installation, check for oil hole alignment as shown in Figure 46-19.

NOTE: **Manufacturers do not recommend any special break-in oil. However, new cams usually are coated with a special lubricant.**

The camshaft timing gear is attached to the camshaft, and the shaft is inserted through the bore. Retaining devices are connected and tightened to the manufacturer's specified torque.

Replacing Soft Plugs

Cylinder block soft plugs are replaced in the same manner as cylinder head soft plugs. Refer to Topic 44.2 for replacement procedures.

Replacing Crankshaft Seals

Several types of rear main bearing oil seals are used in modern automobiles. A *rope-type seal* is used on many engines. After being coated with oil, this type of seal is pressed or rolled into a groove behind the rear main bearing, as shown in Figure 46-20. The corresponding half of this seal is rolled into the rear main bearing cap. A razor blade cutting tool is used to cut off excess seal material flush with the housing.

Replacing Main Bearings

Replacement precision bearing inserts are available for standard or undersize crankshaft main journals. Before installation, the bearing inserts and crankshaft journals are coated with the recommended oil for lubrication when the engine is first started. The tangs and oil holes are aligned correctly, and the upper bearing insert is snapped into place. The crankshaft then is lowered carefully, making sure this is done evenly. The lower main bearing inserts are then installed in the main bearing caps. Finally, the main bearing caps are installed in their proper location and alignment.

The main bearing cap bolts or nuts are installed finger-tight. A block of wood is used to align the thrust bearing flanges, as shown in Figure 46-21. The bolts or nuts are then tightened to the manufacturer's specified torque.

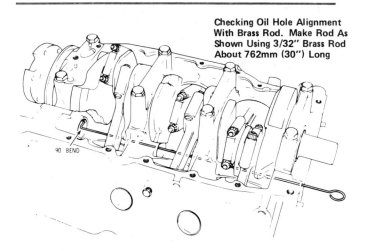

Checking Oil Hole Alignment With Brass Rod. Make Rod As Shown Using 3/32" Brass Rod About 762mm (30") Long

90 BEND

Figure 46-19. Checking oil hole alignment.
CHEVROLET MOTOR DIVISION—GMC

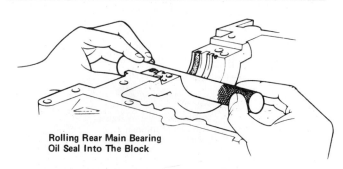

Rolling Rear Main Bearing Oil Seal Into The Block

Figure 46-20. Installing rear main bearing seal.
CHEVROLET MOTOR DIVISION—GMC

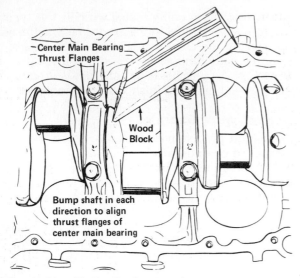

Figure 46-21. Aligning the thrust washer.
CHEVROLET MOTOR DIVISION—GMC

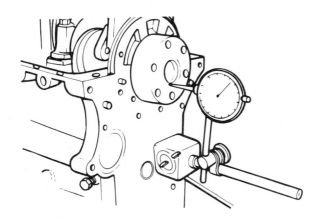

Figure 46-22. Checking crankshaft end play.
FORD MOTOR COMPANY

Checking Crankshaft End Play

After main bearing installation, check for proper crankshaft end play, as explained in Topic 46.1. End play also can be checked by using a dial indicator (see Figure 46-22).

Fitting Piston Rings

Before installation on the pistons, an important check is performed on the piston compression rings and oil-control ring rails. These are inserted squarely in the cylinder at the bottom of the ring travel area. The end gap of the rings is checked for the proper dimension (see Figure 46-23).

The piston rings also are checked in the piston ring grooves for proper ring side clearance. See Figure 46-24.

Replacing Piston/Connecting Rod Assemblies

The piston ring end gaps are positioned so that they are staggered, as shown in Figure 46-25, to lessen blowby.

The pistons and rings are coated with engine oil. Lengths of rubber hose are inserted over the connecting rod bolts to protect the cylinder walls and the crankshaft journals. A *piston ring compressor,* shown in Figure 46-26, is used to squeeze the rings tightly for insertion into the cylinder. The upper connecting rod bearing insert is placed in the connecting rod and coated with lubricant. The numbered piston/connecting rod assembly is properly aligned over the crankshaft throw and inserted into the cylinder. Offset connecting rods are properly positioned. The wooden handle of a hammer or mallet is used to tap the top of the piston until it is inserted in the cylinder.

Replacing Connecting Rod Bearings

The lower connecting rod bearing insert is placed in the connecting rod cap. The numbered bearing cap is

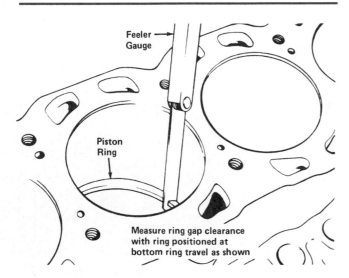

Figure 46-23. Measuring piston ring gap.
CHEVROLET MOTOR DIVISION—GMC

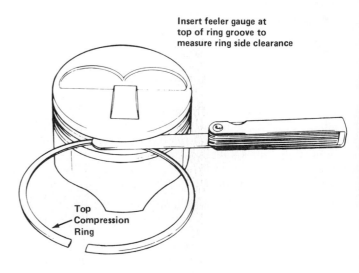

Figure 46-24. Checking ring side clearance.
CHEVROLET MOTOR DIVISION—GMC

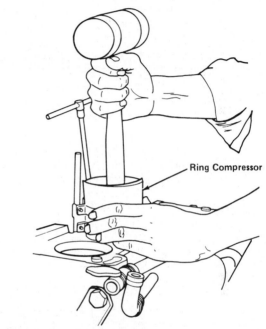

Oil Ring Gap 90° from Compression Ring Gaps and on Camshaft Side of Piston

Notch Toward Front of Engine (Left Bank Piston Shown)

Top Compression Ring Gap Opposite Notch on Piston

Second Compression Ring Gap Below Notch on Piston

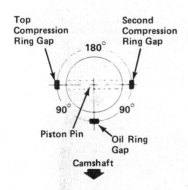

TOP VIEW OF PISTON

Top Compression Ring Gap

Second Compression Ring Gap

180°

90°   90°

Piston Pin

Oil Ring Gap

Camshaft

Figure 46-25. Piston ring gap positioning.
CHEVROLET MOTOR DIVISION—GMC

properly aligned and positioned, and the nuts are screwed on by hand. The nuts are left hand-tight until all piston/connecting rod assemblies are installed.

Checking Connecting Rod Side Clearance

When two connecting rod assemblies are mounted on a single crankpin, the side clearance between the rods must be checked, as shown in Figure 46-27. Improper clearance can indicate incorrectly installed offset connecting rods.

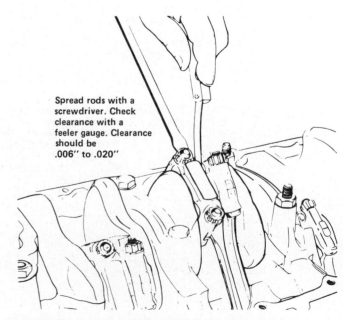

Ring Compressor

Figure 46-26. Piston ring compressor. FORD MOTOR COMPANY

Spread rods with a screwdriver. Check clearance with a feeler gauge. Clearance should be .006″ to .020″

Figure 46-27. Checking connecting rod side clearance.
CHEVROLET MOTOR DIVISION—GMC

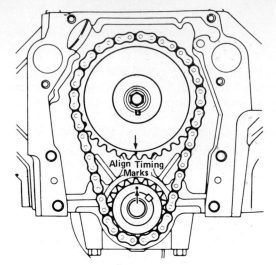

Figure 46-28. Aligning timing gear marks.
CHEVROLET MOTOR DIVISION—GMC

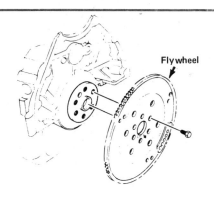

Figure 46-29. Flywheel installation.
CHEVROLET MOTOR DIVISION—GMC

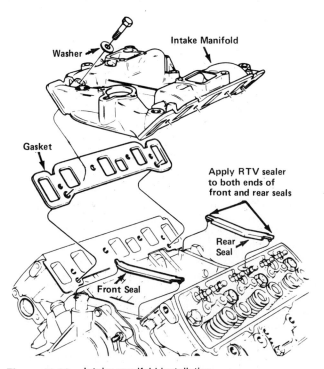

Figure 46-30. Intake manifold installation.
CHEVROLET MOTOR DIVISION—GMC

When all connecting rods have been assembled and checked for proper side clearance, the nuts are torqued to the manufacturer's specification.

Replacing the Cylinder Head

The cylinder head and upper valve train parts are replaced. The attaching bolts or nuts are tightened, in the specified order, to the manufacturer's specified torque. Valve adjustment is performed when the engine is cold. Refer to Topics 44.4 and 44.15 for correct procedures.

Replacing Timing Gear and/or Chain

The crankshaft timing gear is attached to the crankshaft. The crankshaft and camshaft are rotated until the timing gear marks are aligned, as shown in Figure 46-28. The timing chain then is installed.

Replacing the Flywheel

The flywheel is installed as shown in Figure 46-29, and the attaching bolts are tightened to the specified torque.

Replacing the Oil Pump and Oil Pan

A new oil pump and gasket are installed. A new oil pan gasket and/or sealant is installed, as recommended by the manufacturer. Then, the oil pan is bolted into place. The oil pan bolts are torqued, in the proper sequence, to the manufacturer's specification.

Replacing Parts and Covers

New gaskets and the manufacturer's recommended sealants are used when removed parts are replaced.

All parts that do not interfere with engine reinstallation, such as water and fuel pumps, are installed.

The intake manifold and seals are installed (see Figure 46-30).

The intake manifold bolts must be torqued in the proper sequence (refer to Figure 46-31). The exhaust manifold is installed in a similar manner.

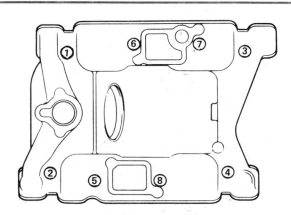

Figure 46-31. Intake manifold torque sequence.
CHEVROLET MOTOR DIVISION—GMC

The manufacturer's recommended sealants are applied to seals and threaded plugs. Covers are tightened, in the proper sequence, to the manufacturer's recommended torque specifications.

46.9 ENGINE REINSTALLATION

Engine reinstallation is essentially the reverse of removal. The engine is lowered carefully into place. The motor mounts are connected and tightened to the manufacturer's recommended torque specification.

SAFETY CAUTION: Do not attempt the engine reinstallation procedures without proper safety instruction and training from your instructor. The engine is heavy enough to injure you or another person fatally if it falls. Refer to the manufacturer's service manual for correct installation procedures.

All remaining engine accessories, such as alternators, power steering pumps, and air conditioning compressors, are installed.

Hoses and other plumbing parts are reconnected. Electrical wiring and instrument connections are reinstalled.

The engine is filled with the correct amount of oil, and a new oil filter is installed. The cooling system is refilled to the proper level. Belts are installed on engine accessories and tightened to their proper tension.

New spark plugs are installed and the spark plug wires are reconnected. The ignition timing is set (dead timing) as accurately as possible, as explained in Topic 35.9.

After a final check to make sure that everything has been reconnected and installed properly, the battery ground terminal is reconnected.

Starting Procedure

Before attempting to start the engine, the ignition system is disabled and all spark plugs removed. The oil pump is turned with a drill motor until the oil pressure warning light goes out. The ignition system then is reconnected.

The engine is started and allowed to run at fast idle until it reaches normal operating temperature. The engine then is shut off.

The cylinder head attaching bolts or nuts may have to be tightened again to the correct torque specification. Check the manufacturer's service manual for information.

Valve clearance is checked and readjusted if necessary.

The engine is started again, and final ignition timing and carburetor or fuel injection adjustments are made.

46.10 ENGINE BREAK-IN PROCEDURE

To properly *seat* piston rings against the cylinder walls, a break-in procedure must be followed. Seating is a process in which parts that *mate,* or fit together, rub against each other until their mating surfaces match almost perfectly. Until the piston rings seat against the cylinder walls, the seal formed will have greater leakage.

To correctly break in the engine, the vehicle is accelerated gently to 30 mph [48 km/hr]. The vehicle then is accelerated until a speed of approximately 50 mph [80 km/hr] is reached, then allowed to coast down to 30 mph [48 km/hr] again. The acceleration procedure from 30 to 50 mph [48 to 80 km/hr] is repeated at least 10 times.

This procedure applies a load rapidly to the engine for short periods after the engine has reached operating temperature. The procedure pushes the piston rings against the cylinder walls and speeds the break-in process. In addition, the deceleration creates a vacuum above the piston that draws oil up to the rings.

After the break-in procedure, the vehicle can be driven at normal speeds. However, sustained high speeds must be avoided for the first 100 miles [160 km]. After the first 100 miles, the vehicle can be driven normally. The oil and oil filter should be changed after about 500 miles.

UNIT HIGHLIGHTS

- Before the cylinder block is disassembled, main bearing clearance and crankshaft end play are checked.
- Before cleaning, all attached and inserted parts are removed from the cylinder block.
- Crankshafts and camshafts may be reground to undersize measurements. Thicker bearings are used to make up for removed material.
- The manufacturer's service manual procedures must be followed to correctly reinstall engines.
- After overhaul, specific procedures must be followed during initial start-up, after warm-up, and during the first 100 miles of driving.

TERMS

end play	oversize (cylinder reboring)
crankshaft end play	
sleeve	overbore
porosity	regrind
epoxy cement	rope-type seal
cylinder taper	piston ring compressor
arbor	seat
align boring	mate

DIRECTIONS: The following questions are similar to those used on mechanic certification tests. On a separate sheet of paper, write the letter of the correct choice.

1. All of the following must be done before the cylinder block is cleaned EXCEPT
A. checking main bearing clearances.
B. checking crankshaft end play.
C. measuring cylinder block warpage.
D. removing all attached and inserted parts from the cylinder block.

2. Mechanic A says that main bearing clearances that are smaller in the middle than at either end indicate tapered crankshaft journals.
   Mechanic B says that main bearing clearances that are smaller at one end than another indicate barrel-shaped or spool-shaped journals.
   Who is correct?
A. A only   B. B only   C. Both A and B   D. Neither A nor B

3. Which of the following statements is correct?
   I. Different cylinder bore measurements at the top and bottom of the ring travel indicate cylinder taper.
   II. Different cylinder bore measurements at 90 degrees to each other at the top of the ring travel indicate an out-of-round condition.
A. I only   B. II only   C. Both I and II   D. Neither I nor II

4. How is residue from honing and cylinder machining operations removed from the cylinder block?
A. By washing with gasoline
B. By washing with kerosene
C. By washing with solvent
D. By washing with water and detergent, then swabbing with clean cloths and motor oil

5. Mechanic A says that the valve adjustment must be corrected after a newly rebuilt engine is allowed to warm up.
   Mechanic B says that the main and connecting rod bearings must be retorqued after a newly rebuilt engine is allowed to warm up.
   Who is correct?
A. A only   B. B only   C. Both A and B   D. Neither A nor B

S U P P L E M E N T A L   A C T I V I T I E S

1. Measure main bearing clearances on a shop engine and inspect the bearings and crankshaft journals. Compare your readings with the manufacturer's specifications. What, if anything, must be done to the crankshaft and/or bearings?

2. Measure end play on a shop engine by using both feeler gauges and a dial indicator. Make a report on what differences, if any, you find between the two methods.

3. Measure cylinder dimensions on a disassembled shop engine. Check for out-of-round and cylinder taper conditions. Compare your readings to the manufacturer's service manual specifications. Make a report to your class about the condition of the cylinders and what needs to be or has been done.

4. Measure a shop engine's crankshaft journals. Make a report to your class on the condition of the journals and what needs to be done, or has been done, to the crankshaft.

5. Measure the clearance between rings and the ring grooves on a shop piston. Determine what, if anything, must be done for proper fit.

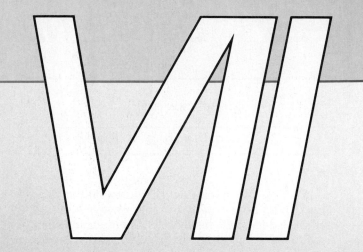

VII

AUTOMOTIVE DRIVETRAINS

47 DRIVELINES

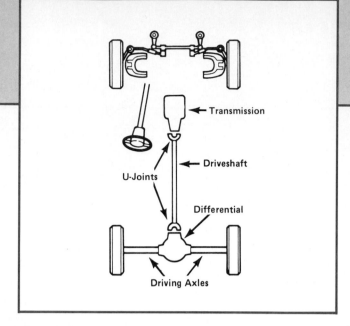

Figure 47-1. Conventional rear drivetrain.
CHEVROLET MOTOR DIVISION—GMC

UNIT PREVIEW

The torque generated by the engine must be transmitted to the driving wheels to move the vehicle. This can be done in any of several ways, depending upon the design of the vehicle. Engine torque can be used to drive, or rotate, the front wheels, rear wheels, or all four wheels.

Rear-wheel-drive and four-wheel-drive vehicles must transmit power from the transmission to a differential at the rear of the vehicle. There are two basic rear-wheel-drive systems, each consisting of several parts, used to transfer power to the differential.

One system uses a solid steel shaft inside a hollow tube to transfer torque to move the vehicle. The other system uses a hollow metal tube and flexible joints to provide the "push" that moves the vehicle.

Parts are used to connect, align, and transmit torque. Different types of flexible joints can be used in a driveline to connect, align, and transmit torque.

LEARNING OBJECTIVES

When you have completed your assignments and exercises in this unit, you should be able to:

☐ Explain how the driveline operates.

☐ Identify and describe the parts of the driveline.

☐ Explain the purpose of universal joints.

☐ Describe the operation of a conventional universal joint.

☐ Explain how a constant-velocity universal joint operates.

☐ Describe the operation and purpose of a slip joint.

47.1 DRIVELINE DESIGN

The parts of a rear-wheel *drivetrain* are the clutch or torque converter, manual or automatic transmission, *driveline*, differential, and driving axles. A basic rear-wheel drivetrain is shown in Figure 47-1.

The purpose of the driveline is to transfer torque, or turning force, from the transmission to the differential. The driveline consists of a hollow tube or solid metal shaft with one or more flexible joints, as shown in Figure 47-2.

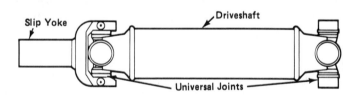

Figure 47-2. Driveline. OLDSMOBILE DIVISION—GMC

Driveshaft

The *driveshaft*, also called the *propeller shaft*, usually is a hollow tube. However, solid metal shafts are used on some foreign vehicles, such as the current German Porsche 944. (Pontiac used a similar system for the Tempest in the early 1960s.)

As the vehicle moves down the road, the driveline must be able to transfer torque smoothly and continuously. However, the wheels and suspension of the vehicle must move up and down with the contours of the road surface. As the rear suspension moves, the differential also moves up and down. The differential allows the inner and outer driving wheels to rotate at different speeds as the vehicle turns corners. Differentials are discussed in Unit 55. The upward and downward movement of the differential with the suspension causes both the distance and the angle between the transmission and the differential to change.

To transfer torque smoothly and continuously, the driveline must perform these three functions:

• Rotate

• Move up and down

• Compensate for varying distances between the transmission and differential.

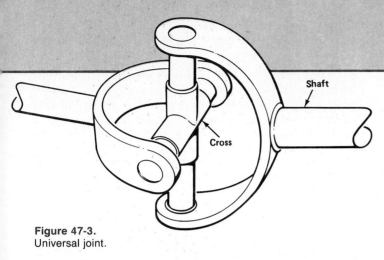

Figure 47-3.
Universal joint.

Universal Joint

The driveline must be able to perform all of these tasks at the same time. However, the driveshaft tube itself can only transmit power in a straight line. To transfer torque as the angle between the transmission and the differential changes, *universal joints*, or U-joints, are used. A simple universal joint is shown in Figure 47-3.

A U-joint can transfer torque at an angle while rotating. The front U-joint accepts torque from the transmission and transmits the torque to the driveshaft. The rear U-joint accepts torque from the driveshaft and transmits the torque to the differential. Thus, the driveline can move as required by road and driving conditions without interrupting torque transfer.

Slip Joint

The distance between the transmission and the differential changes as the angle between them varies. However, the driveshaft and universal joints cannot stretch or shrink to make up for this changing distance. To allow the driveline to maintain a connection as the distance changes, a *slip joint* is used. A slip joint is formed of two parts. One part is the *splined* end of the transmission output shaft. Splines are machined ridges around or inside a part. The other part of a slip joint is called the *slip yoke*. The slip yoke consists of a hollow, splined metal tube at one end. The other end is the yoke, which connects to the front U-joint. The splined end of the transmission output shaft fits inside the hollow end of the slip yoke (see Figure 47-4).

Splines act much like gears. When the transmission output shaft rotates, the two sets of splines mesh, or connect. This causes the slip yoke to rotate. At the same time, the slip yoke can slide, or slip, back and forth on the transmission shaft. This sliding action maintains the connection as the distance between the transmission and the differential changes. Slip joints also may be found at connecting points in split driveshafts.

47.2 THE EFFECTS OF TORQUE

As torque is applied by the driveline to the differential, the entire differential and driving axle housing twists. This effect is known as *rear-end torque*. This torque presents certain problems in the operation of the driveline, differential, and driving axles.

The axle housing moves in a direction that is opposite to rear-wheel rotation.

As the vehicle begins to move forward, the front of the differential moves upward. This upward motion, shown in Figure 47-5, can cause the U-joints to bind, or stick, and be damaged.

To prevent excessive movement of the differential and axle housing, some form of bracing must be used. Common methods of bracing used on modern vehicles are:

- Torque-tube drive
- Hotchkiss drive.

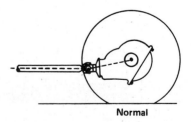

Normal

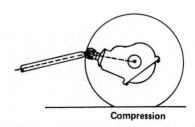

Compression

Figure 47-5. Rear-end torque.

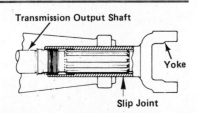

Transmission Output Shaft

Yoke

Figure 47-4. Slip joint.

Slip Joint

47.3 TORQUE-TUBE DRIVE

The idea of the *torque tube* is to keep the driveshaft in perfect alignment with the differential at all times. To do this, a driveshaft housing, or torque tube, is bolted between the differential housing and the transmission or vehicle frame. This direct, rigid connection helps to control rear-end torque. A typical torque-tube system is shown in Figure 47-6.

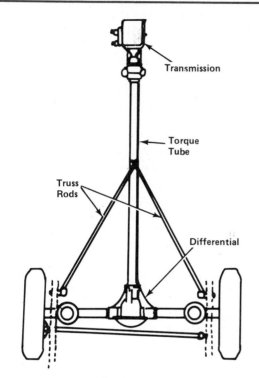

Figure 47-6. Torque-tube drive.

A solid steel driveshaft runs inside the torque tube. This driveshaft attaches to the differential drive pinion by way of a flexible drive coupling, as shown in Figure 47-7.

Only one U-joint is used with a torque-tube drive. This U-joint is mounted at the front of the driveshaft, with a slip joint that connects it to the rear of the transmission. In addition, a support bearing is often mounted near the front of the torque tube. The support bearing helps to control whip, or uneven rotation of the driveshaft. Additional braces, or *truss rods*, are sometimes used to locate further and to hold the torque tube.

A torque-tube driveline is extremely heavy. In addition, the entire torque tube, differential, and rear-axle assembly must be removed for servicing the transmission.

Because of its disadvantages, torque-tube drive is used infrequently on modern vehicles. Recent examples of torque-tube drive systems include the Chevrolet Chevette and some Japanese-made vehicles.

47.4 HOTCHKISS DRIVE

Hotchkiss drive uses an open driveshaft. It eliminates the disadvantages of torque-tube drive and uses the vehicle's rear suspension to control rear-end torque. In a Hotchkiss drive system, the differential and driving axle housing can twist slightly because of rear-end torque. However, this motion is kept within safe limits by the rear suspension of the vehicle.

Driveshafts used with Hotchkiss drive are usually hollow tubes. To help reduce vibration, the hollow driveshaft may have cardboard or rubber elements within them.

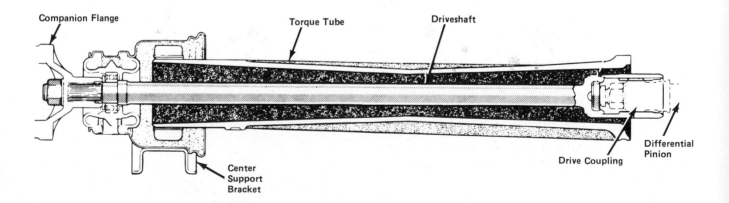

Figure 47-7. Torque-tube assembly. PONTIAC MOTOR DIVISION—GMC

The driveshaft and differential on a vehicle with Hotchkiss drive are not in perfect alignment. However, the universal joints allow torque to be transferred smoothly.

Hotchkiss drive is more adaptable than torque-tube drive. A Hotchkiss drive system can use longer driveshafts. In addition, Hotchkiss-drive driveshafts can be made in separate sections, connected by additional universal joints.

Hotchkiss drive can be used either with leaf springs, shown in Figure 47-8, or with coil springs. When Hotchkiss drive is used with coil springs, additional braces, called *control arms*, must be used (see Figure 47-9).

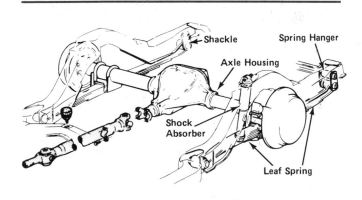

Figure 47-8. Hotchkiss drive. CHEVROLET MOTOR DIVISION—GMC

Leaf springs are attached to the frame or sub-frame by brackets located ahead of and behind the rear axle housings. The leaf springs also attach to the rear axle housings with U-shaped bolts.

When rear-end torque begins, the axle housings twist and move upward. This action squeezes, or compresses, the fronts of the leaf springs. When the springs are compressed to their limits, rear axle movement stops, and rear-end torque is controlled. Torque is transferred from the housings to the vehicle's frame through the leaf spring mounts or control arms. This, in effect, pushes the vehicle forward.

47.5 DRIVESHAFT

The lengths and diameters of driveshafts vary, simply because all vehicles are not alike. Many factors determine what type of driveshaft system is used. The physical size and *wheelbase* of the vehicle are prime considerations. Wheelbase is the distance from the axle center of the front wheel to the axle center of the rear wheel.

While most vehicles have one-piece driveshafts, some vehicles have *split driveshafts* that consist of two connected shorter shafts. A split driveshaft can be angled upward or downward from the transmission to reduce the size of the hump that runs down the middle of the vehicle floor. Larger vehicles, such as trucks, use split driveshafts because of greater distances between their transmissions and differentials. A split driveshaft is shown in Figure 47-10.

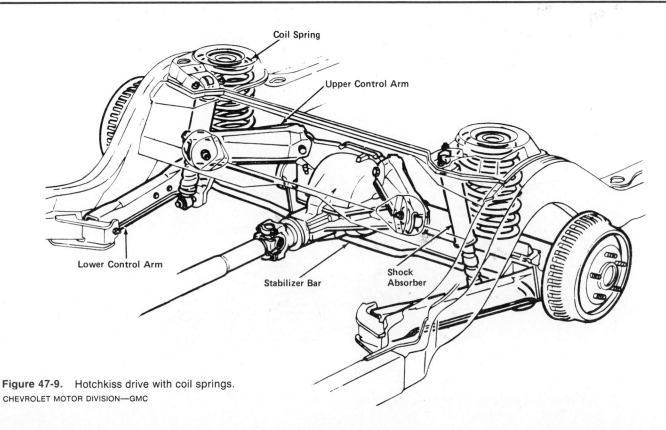

Figure 47-9. Hotchkiss drive with coil springs.
CHEVROLET MOTOR DIVISION—GMC

511

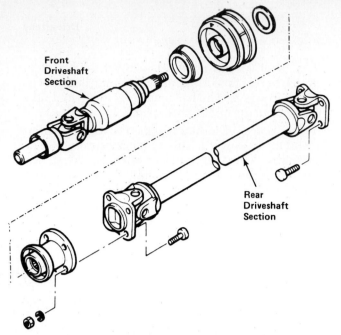

Figure 47-10. Split driveshaft. NISSAN MOTOR CORPORATION

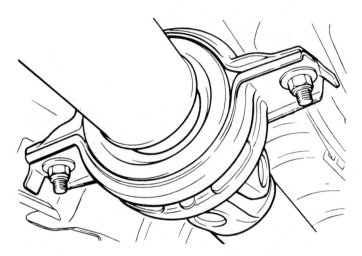

Figure 47-11. Center bearing support. CHRYSLER CORPORATION

A driveshaft must have high strength and must be well balanced. The driveshaft receives and transfers great twisting forces from the transmission to the differential. Because the driveshaft spins rapidly, it must be in balance.

Small pieces of metal are welded to the driveshaft to correct imbalances. An unbalanced driveshaft will vibrate, cause noise, and wear out the other drivetrain parts.

47.6 CENTER SUPPORT BEARING

Vehicles with split driveshafts must use a center support bearing to support and align the sections of the driveshaft.

A center support bearing also may be used with a one-piece driveshaft. The bearing minimizes whip and vibration and allows the driveshaft to rotate smoothly. Center support bearings are used on a variety of vehicles, from expensive luxury sedans to imported economy cars.

A typical center support bearing is shown in Figure 47-11.

47.7 UNIVERSAL JOINT

The conventional universal joint is a double-hinged joint. This means that the U-joint can swivel in two different directions. A U-joint consists of two metal *yokes* and a cross, or spider. A yoke is a U-shaped piece used to attach one part to another. Figure 47-12 shows a U-joint, also known as a *Cardan joint.*

Two *trunnions*, or arms, of the cross-shaped spider connect to the driving yoke. The other two trunnions connect to the driven yoke. The driving yoke applies torque. The driven yoke accepts torque.

Small, lubricated roller bearings, called needle bearings, allow the joint to swivel and transfer power smoothly. A seal between the bearings and the spider, shown in Figure 47-13, helps to keep contaminants out and lubricant in.

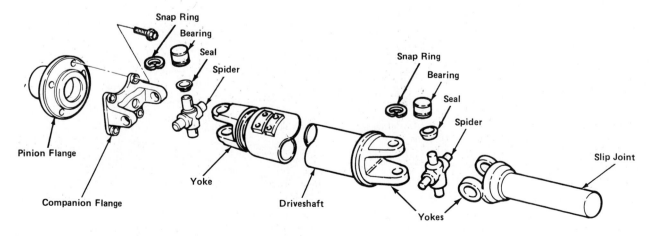

Figure 47-12. Universal joint assembly. CHRYSLER CORPORATION

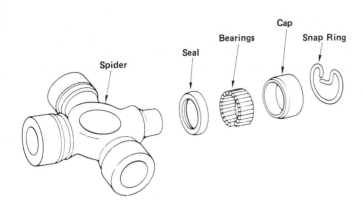

Figure 47-13. Parts of a universal joint.
CHEVROLET MOTOR DIVISION—GMC

Ball Support Yoke
Link Yoke
Ball Tube Yoke

Figure 47-14. Double Cardan universal joint assembly.
CADILLAC MOTOR CAR DIVISION—GMC

Conventional Universal Joint

As the universal joint changes angle during rotation, the torque applied to the driven yoke fluctuates, or changes. The driving yoke rotates at a constant speed. However, the driven yoke speeds up and slows down twice during each rotation.

This fluctuation could cause pulsing and vibration in the driveline. As the angle of the yokes increases, the fluctuation increases. However, the second U-joint at the differential end of the driveshaft cancels out the uneven rotation. The rear U-joint produces a reaction that is opposite to the reaction produced at the front U-joint. That is, the rear U-joint slows down as the speed increases in the front U-joint. Also, the rear U-joint will speed up when the front U-joint slows down. The final result is a fairly constant rate of driveshaft rotation.

Double Cardan (Constant Velocity) Joint

As U-joint angles increase, driveline speed fluctuation and vibration increase. In addition, conventional U-joints are limited as to the angle at which they can operate.

When driveshaft angles become too great for conventional U-joints, a *constant-velocity U-joint* is used. A constant-velocity U-joint maintains a relatively constant speed during rotation, unlike a conventional U-joint. One or more constant-velocity U-joints may be used anywhere along the driveshaft. The type of constant-velocity U-joint used on rear-drive vehicles is called a *double Cardan joint*.

The double Cardan joint is actually two conventional U-joints that are closely connected. Figure 47-14 shows a double Cardan joint. In a double Cardan joint, each U-joint bends only half as much to create the same angle.

Since the constant-velocity U-joint has a driving yoke and a driven yoke, a fluctuation in rotating speed still exists. However, because it contains two conventional U-joints, this fluctuation cancels itself out.

UNIT HIGHLIGHTS

- Engine torque is transferred by the drivetrain to the driving wheels.
- Engine torque can be used to drive, or rotate, the front, rear, or all four wheels, depending on the design of the vehicle.
- The drivetrain accepts and controls the engine torque, and transfers it to the driving wheels.
- Drivetrains are classified according to which wheels are driven by engine torque.
- The driveline consists of the driveshaft and universal joints, or a torque-tube assembly.
- A universal joint transfers torque at an angle while rotating.
- Some drivelines use a center support bearing for support, alignment, and reduction of vibration.
- A double Cardan joint is used when the angle between the differential and transmission is too great for conventional universal joints.
- A slip joint allows two rotating parts to remain connected as the distance between them changes.

TERMS

drivetrain	Hotchkiss drive
driveline	control arms
driveshaft	wheelbase
propeller shaft	split driveshaft
universal joint	yoke
slip joint	Cardan joint
slip yoke	trunnion
spline	constant velocity
rear-end torque	U-joint
torque-tube drive	double Cardan joint
truss rods	

R E V I E W   Q U E S T I O N S

DIRECTIONS: The following questions are similar to those used on mechanic certification tests. On a separate sheet of paper, write the letter of the correct choice.

1. All of the following statements are true EXCEPT
A. The function of the driveline is to transfer torque.
B. Driveshafts are found only on front-engine, rear-drive vehicles.
C. The driveshaft is either a solid steel shaft or a hollow tube.
D. Although the length of the driveshaft may vary, all driveshafts have the same diameter.

2. Hotchkiss drive
A. uses the vehicle's rear suspension to control rear-end torque.
B. uses a driveshaft inside a rigid tube.
C. never uses more than two U-joints.
D. is never used with long or split driveshafts.

3. All of the following statements about torque-tube drive are true EXCEPT
A. The torque tube is bolted directly to the differential.
B. A torque-tube drive system is extremely heavy.
C. A hollow steel driveshaft runs inside the torque tube.
D. Only one U-joint is used with a torque-tube drive.

4. All of the following statements are true EXCEPT
A. The driveshaft rotates.
B. The driveshaft moves up and down.
C. The driveshaft remains connected as the distance between the transmission and the differential changes.
D. The driveshaft transfers power at an angle.

5. Two conventional U-joints are used on most drivelines because
A. all drivelines have two U-joints.
B. two U-joints reduce fluctuating, or uneven, rotation.
C. no driveline has more than two U-joints.
D. two U-joints have to bend only half as much as a single U-joint.

S U P P L E M E N T A L   A C T I V I T I E S

1. Identify the parts of the drivetrain on a vehicle in the shop.
2. Explain why two universal joints are used on Hotchkiss drive systems.
3. Examine a driveline on a vehicle in the shop. Identify the parts of the driveline, including any balancing weights.
4. Name the parts of a universal joint.
5. Explain why a double Cardan joint is used.

48 DRIVELINE SERVICE

UNIT PREVIEW

Preventive maintenance and service are important to the safe and reliable operation of the drivetrain. The driveline is a relatively simple and rugged part of the drivetrain. However, its parts are subject to wear and damage.

The driveline must be maintained at regular intervals to spot defects and prevent potential problems. Driveline preventive maintenance includes cleaning, inspection, and lubrication. Simple driveline service includes universal joint replacement and rebalancing.

LEARNING OBJECTIVES

When you have completed your assignments and exercises in this unit, you should be able to:

☐ Explain the precautions necessary when servicing the driveline.

☐ Clean, inspect, and lubricate a driveline.

☐ Check driveshaft inclination and runout.

☐ Remove and replace a driveline.

☐ Balance a driveshaft.

SAFETY PRECAUTIONS

Personal injury and unnecessary damage to parts can be avoided by following the precautionary steps discussed here.

Driveshaft preventive maintenance and service require that the vehicle be raised and supported safely. *Never* work under a vehicle unless you are absolutely sure that it cannot move or fall. No type of jack is meant to support the weight of a vehicle safely. Safety stands, or jack stands, must be used if the vehicle is not on a hoist.

The underside of the vehicle is dirty. Dirt, grime, or foreign objects can fall into the eyes during service procedures. Safety glasses or goggles must be worn to protect the eyes from injury.

Hot exhaust system parts on vehicles can cause severe burns. Be careful when working near exhaust system parts, and let the vehicle cool off, whenever possible, before servicing.

The driveline is heavy. If it drops, it can cause personal injury or damage to the parts. Have a helper ready to assist in removing or replacing the driveline.

Some driveline service procedures involve working under a running vehicle, near the spinning driveline. Loose clothing or long hair can be caught by the moving driveline, causing serious injury. Use extreme caution near the spinning driveline and/or wheels.

48.1 PREVENTIVE MAINTENANCE

Driveline preventive maintenance includes:

- Cleaning
- Inspection
- Lubrication.

SAFETY CAUTION: When working under a vehicle, the vehicle must be supported properly by jackstands or on a hoist. *Never* work under a vehicle supported only by a jack.

Cleaning the Driveline

Shift the transmission of the car into neutral, and release the emergency brake so that the driveline can be rotated by hand during inspection and service. Safely raise and support the vehicle.

SAFETY CAUTION: Be sure the vehicle to be inspected or serviced is cooled down. Hot exhaust system parts can cause severe burns. Driveline parts can have sharp edges that will cut. Move your hands slowly and carefully over the driveline during inspection to prevent cuts and scrapes.

Remove any dirt, mud, undercoating, or other foreign material from the driveline with a putty knife or scraper. Turn the shaft by hand to clean all areas of the driveline.

Driveline Inspection

Use a droplight to inspect the driveline. Grasp the driveshaft near the front universal joint, or U-joint, as shown in Figure 48-1. Try to move the U-joint and slip joint up and down. Excess movement indicates a bad transmission bushing or U-joint. No motion at all may indicate a stiffened transmission rear oil seal.

Shake and twist the driveshaft at both ends. Check for erratic, binding rotation and/or clicking as you try to move the U-joint.

Figure 48-1. Twisting and shaking the front universal joint to check it for looseness.

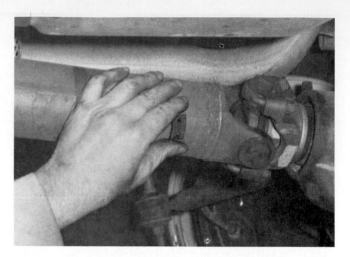

Figure 48-2. Checking to make sure driveshaft balancing weight is still attached.

Look for evidence of powdery red rust around the U-joint trunnion grease seals. Rust indicates that the seals have failed and that the bearing surfaces have become rusted.

Carefully examine the seal in the transmission around the slip joint. Check for leaks, cracks, or other signs of seal damage.

Check that the driveshaft balancing weight, shown in Figure 48-2, is not loose or missing. The balancing weight usually is located at the rear of the driveshaft.

Check visually and manually for dents, wrinkles, or cracks in the driveshaft tube. Very shallow dents are not necessarily serious. However, deep dents, wrinkles, or cracks in the driveshaft are signs of serious damage. Finally, check the rear universal joint for looseness, cracks, or damage.

Lubricating Universal Joints

Factory-installed U-joints on passenger vehicles usually are sealed, and cannot be lubricated with a grease gun. Grease fittings, shown in Figure 48-3, are included on most replacement U-joints.

Look for grease fittings on the front U-joint, behind the transmission, and on the rear U-joint, ahead of the differential. Some vehicles may have a third U-joint, shown in Figure 48-4, in the middle of the driveshaft.

Inspect each universal joint for grease fittings. Some U-joints may have plugs that can be removed to insert a nozzle for greasing. Sealed U-joints are lubricated before installation and cannot be serviced. Lack of lubrication in a sealed U-joint requires that the U-joint be replaced. Refer to a lubrication chart or the proper service manual for specific lubrication procedures.

Use a grease gun to pump grease slowly into grease fittings on the universal joints. When grease begins to appear at all four bearing cups, stop pumping. Too much pressure can damage the U-joint seal. No grease at one or more bearing cups may indicate

Figure 48-3. A universal joint with grease fittings.

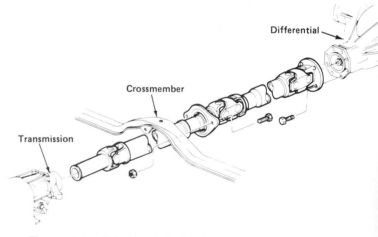

Figure 48-4. Split driveshaft with three universal joints.
CADILLAC MOTOR CAR DIVISION—GMC

that there are clogged grease passages within the trunnions. (Clogged passages cannot be cleared without removing the U-joint. The removal and replacement of U-joints is discussed in 48.3.) Wipe off any excess grease with a rag.

Grease all of the fittings in the driveline in the same manner.

If grease cannot be pumped through a fitting, the fitting may be clogged with dirt or other foreign material. Replace clogged fittings and attempt to grease the unit again. If no grease can be pumped through a unit, the unit must be replaced.

Make a thorough inspection for grease fittings. Lack of lubrication can cause U-joint and/or driveline failure.

48.2 DIAGNOSING DRIVELINE PROBLEMS

The mechanic is responsible for properly diagnosing problems before expensive work is begun. Driveshaft mechanical problems include:

- Incorrect U-joint angles
- Excessive driveshaft runout.

U-Joint Angle

U-joints transmit power through a limited range of angles. Manufacturers specify the correct driveshaft angles, or inclinations, for each vehicle. To check front or rear U-joint angles, a special tool, called an *inclinometer*, shown in Figure 48-5, is used.

Clean all surfaces where the inclinometer will be placed. Hold the inclinometer on the driveshaft near the U-joint to be checked and read the angle indicated.

If the angle is incorrect, shims, or thin spacers, can be added to or removed from transmission and rear axle housing mounts. See the vehicle manufacturer's service manual for specific procedures.

CAUTION: Do *not* use force when positioning the inclinometer. Hold the instrument firmly but gently to obtain correct readings.

Driveshaft Runout

A bent or damaged driveshaft can cause vibration and noise. A driveshaft in good condition will have very little *runout* during rotation. Runout is the distance that an edge or surface of a rotating part moves in or out during rotation. Excessive runout can cause vibration and noise.

Figure 48-6 shows a setup for measuring the driveshaft runout. Runout readings are taken at the center, and near both ends, of the driveshaft.

Before attempting to measure driveshaft runout, clean all dirt and/or foreign material from the areas where the plunger of the dial indicator will ride. Mount the dial indicator base on the frame or underbody of the vehicle, according to the vehicle manufacturer's specifications. Position the dial indicator so that the plunger contacts a smooth and clean area of the driveshaft. Rotate the driveshaft slowly by hand.

The plunger of the dial indicator will move in or out as the driveshaft moves toward, or away from, the indicator. As the plunger is moved, the dial indicator will record how much runout is present. An acceptably true, or straight, driveshaft will move a few thousandths of an inch [hundredths of a millimeter] toward or away from the dial indicator.

Refer to the vehicle manufacturer's service manual for specific runout limits. If the readings are greater than the manufacturer's allowed runout specifications, the driveshaft must be replaced.

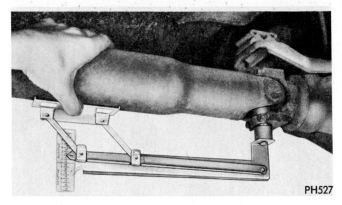

Figure 48-5. Driveshaft angles (inclinations) are checked with an inclinometer. CHRYSLER CORPORATION

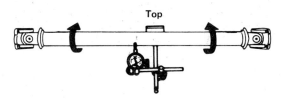

Figure 48-6. Driveshaft runout is checked with a dial indicator. NISSAN MOTOR CORPORATION

48.3 DRIVELINE SERVICE

The most frequent driveline service is replacement of universal joints, which requires that the driveline be removed from the vehicle.

SAFETY CAUTION: Driveline assemblies are heavy and awkward to carry. Use proper care—and a helper, if necessary—to remove and replace the driveline. Place an oil catch pan at the rear of the transmission to prevent lubricant from dripping on the shop floor.

Raise and support the vehicle safely on a hoist. Mark the parts for reassembly. If the driveline parts are not reassembled in the same positions relative to each other and to the transmission and differential, vibration can occur. Use paint or chalk to mark the parts of the driveline for reassembly, as shown in Figure 48-7.

Remove Center Bearing Support Bolts

To remove the driveshaft of a vehicle equipped with a center bearing, the bearing support assembly must be removed. See Figure 48-8.

CAUTION: Make matchmarks on the separate parts of a split driveline for reassembly.

Support the driveline as the center support bolts are removed. Use a jackstand to support the driveline, or have a helper hold it.

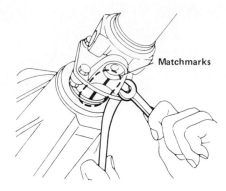

Figure 48-7. Matchmarks on the driveshaft assembly indicate how it is to be reassembled. NISSAN MOTOR CORPORATION

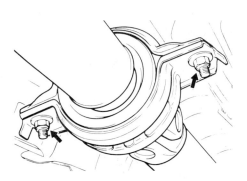

Figure 48-8. Remove the center bearing by unfastening the nuts and bracket. CHRYSLER CORPORATION

SAFETY CAUTION: Support the front of a split driveline to prevent it from separating and falling. If the driveline falls, it can be damaged or cause injury.

Remove Driveline

The rear universal joint is held to the differential companion flange by U-bolts or straps. Loosen the nuts or bolts and slide the driveline forward toward the transmission. Then lower the driveline and pull it off the transmission output shaft.

Place a plug, shown in Figure 48-9, on the transmission output shaft to prevent the lubricant from leaking.

Remove and Replace Center Bearing/Support Assembly

Some center support bearings are made in one piece with the rubber support assembly, and must be replaced as a unit. Other center support bearings are separate from the support assembly, and can be replaced. A hydraulic press is used to push out the old bearing and push in the new bearing. See Figure 48-10.

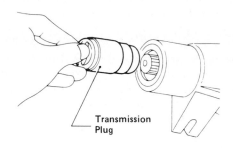

Figure 48-9. Installing a plug at the rear of the transmission extension housing to prevent fluid from leaking out. NISSAN MOTOR CORPORATION

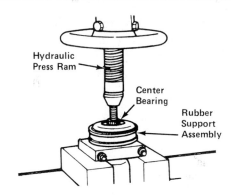

Figure 48-10. A support fixture holds the center bearing assembly while a press is used to remove and install the bearing. NISSAN MOTOR CORPORATION

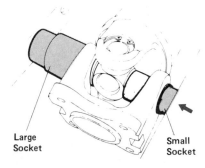

Figure 48-11. A vise and different size sockets are used to press universal joints out of the yoke. CHRYSLER CORPORATION

Remove and Replace Universal Joint

Scratch or paint matchmarks on the U-joint bearing caps, the trunnions, and the driveshaft yoke for reassembly.

Press out the U-joints from the driveshaft yokes, using a vise and sockets. Using a small socket, push the bearing cups through the yoke, into a larger socket, as the vise is tightened. See Figure 48-11.

The vise and sockets also are used to push the new U-joint into the yoke. After reassembly, check to see that each U-joint swivels easily in all directions.

A driveline with a double Cardan joint requires special tools and procedures for disassembly and reassembly. In addition, whenever a double Cardan joint is disassembled, the U-joints must be replaced. Consult the vehicle manufacturer's shop manual for required tools and specific procedures.

Replace Driveline

After both U-joints have been installed, the driveline can be replaced in the vehicle. Align matchmarks on split driveshafts and slide the sections together.

Support split driveshafts to prevent them from bending during installation. Slide the slip joint yoke into the transmission end. Align the matchmarks on the differential companion flange and the rear driveshaft yoke. Thread the fasteners a few turns to hold the parts loosely.

Support the driveline, and thread the center bearing support bolts a few turns to hold the support loosely. Tighten the differential companion flange bolts to the vehicle manufacturer's torque specification. Finally, tighten the center bearing support bolts to the vehicle manufacturer's torque specification.

48.4 DRIVELINE BALANCING

During driveline manufacture, small variations in thickness of parts can occur. These variations can cause one side of the driveline to be heavier than the other side. During rotation, centrifugal force will cause the heavy side to be pulled outward and create vibration.

Driveshafts are balanced during manufacture by the welding of small balancing weights to the lighter side of the driveshaft. However, balancing weights can come off, causing the driveshaft to become unbalanced.

An unbalanced driveshaft will cause vibration and noise in the driveline. If a mechanic notices that a balancing weight is missing, the driveshaft must be rebalanced. Driveshafts can usually be rebalanced in the shop, without removing the driveshaft from the vehicle.

Check the driveshaft for proper runout, as explained in Topic 48.2, before attempting balancing procedures.

To balance a driveshaft, first safely raise and support the vehicle on a hoist. Support the rear-axle housings on jackstands. The driving wheels and driveshaft must be free to rotate, as shown in Figure 48-12.

SAFETY CAUTION: You need a helper in the car to start the engine, engage the transmission, and apply the brakes as needed. Instruct your helper to use low gear—first gear on a manual transmission, or

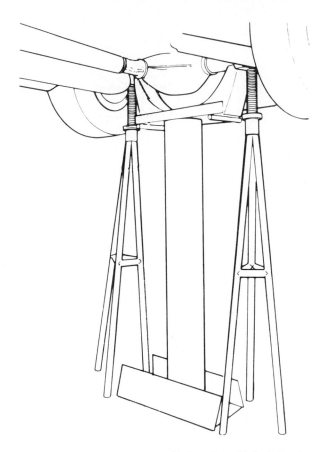

Figure 48-12. Support the rear axle housing with jackstands to allow the wheels and driveshaft to rotate freely.
CHEVROLET MOTOR DIVISION—GMC

low range on an automatic. This is no time for horseplay. Be sure that your helper will follow your instructions exactly.

Remove the rear wheels. Replace and tighten the lug nuts with the flat edge against the brake drums. The rear wheels are removed so that wheel balance problems will not affect driveshaft rebalancing procedures. Clean the driveshaft thoroughly to remove any undercoating and accumulated dirt.

SAFETY CAUTION: The balancing procedure involves working next to the rotating driveshaft. Use extreme care. Serious injury could result from clothing, hair, jewelry, or body parts being caught or abraded by the rotating parts.

Locate the heavy spot on the driveshaft by slowly and carefully moving a piece of chalk or crayon close to the spinning driveshaft. As the heavy spot moves away from the center of rotation, the chalk will touch it, leaving a mark. See Figure 48-13.

SAFETY CAUTION: Keep the chalk or crayon away from the balancing weights on the driveshaft. Touching the balancing weights could cause serious injury.

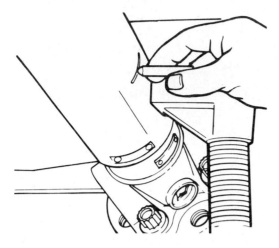

Figure 48-13. Supporting hand on a steady rest while using chalk to mark heavy spot on a rotating driveshaft. FORD MOTOR COMPANY

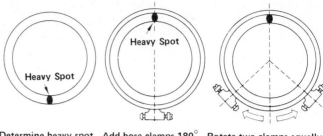

Determine heavy spot   Add hose clamps 180° from heavy spot   Rotate two clamps equally away from each other until best balance is achieved

Figure 48-14. Positioning hose clamps on a driveshaft to achieve the best balance. CHEVROLET MOTOR DIVISION—GMC

After the heavy spot on the driveshaft has been located, two hose clamps are clamped around the driveshaft, at the rear. The screw heads are located 180 degrees from, or directly opposite, the position of the heavy spot. See Figure 48-14. The weight of the hose clamp screw heads will help to counterbalance the weight of the heavy spot.

If the imbalance still exists when tested again, shift the position of the hose clamp screw heads. Move each of them, 45 degrees at a time, in opposite directions from the first location, as illustrated in Figure 48-14.

The balancing procedure can also be tried at the front of the driveshaft, if results are unsatisfactory at the rear. If the driveshaft cannot be satisfactorily balanced in the shop, driveshaft removal and professional rebalancing are necessary.

Some vehicle manufacturers recommend using an electronic wheel balancer with a flashing strobe light to locate the heavy spot. See the vehicle manufacturer's service manual for specific procedures.

UNIT HIGHLIGHTS

- Visual inspection can reveal driveline problems, such as worn or damaged universal joints and driveshafts, and missing balance weights.
- Regular lubrication can prevent universal joint failure.
- The angle of the front and rear U-joints is important for reliability and smooth operation of the driveline.
- Driveline vibration can be caused by damage, imbalance, or excessive runout.
- Driveshafts can usually be rebalanced in the shop by adding weight opposite the heavy spot on the driveshaft.

TERMS

inclinometer

runout

R E V I E W   Q U E S T I O N S

DIRECTIONS: The following questions are similar to those used on mechanic certification tests. On a separate sheet of paper, write the letter of the correct choice.

1. To find a driveline problem, all the following might have to be done EXCEPT

A. a lubrication.

B. a visual inspection.

C. checking U-joint angles.

D. measuring driveshaft runout.

2. Which of the following statements is correct?

   I. Damage to the driveshaft can result in vibration.

   II. A lost balancing weight can result in vibration.

A. I only   B. II only   C. Both I and II   D. Neither I nor II

3. Mechanic A says that center bearings are replaced as a unit with their rubber support assemblies.

   Mechanic B says that center bearings can be pressed out from rubber support assemblies and replaced separately.

   Who is correct?

A. A only   B. B only   C. Both A and B   D. Neither A nor B

4. When marking a driveshaft for balancing, the chalk will mark

A. the light spot on the driveshaft.

B. the heavy spot on the driveshaft.

C. a point 180 degrees from the heavy spot.

D. a point 48 degrees from the heavy spot.

5. Driveline preventive maintenance includes all of the following EXCEPT

A. cleaning.

B. inspection.

C. U-joint replacement.

D. lubrication.

S U P P L E M E N T A L   A C T I V I T I E S

1. Perform a visual inspection and lubrication of a vehicle's driveline.
2. Measure front and rear U-joint angles on a vehicle.
3. Measure driveshaft runout on a vehicle.
4. Under the supervision of your instructor, remove and replace a driveline.
5. Under the supervision of your instructor, balance the driveshaft of a vehicle.

49 THE MANUAL TRANSMISSION

UNIT PREVIEW

A transmission allows the driver to increase or decrease engine torque for different road speeds and load conditions. Torque control is accomplished by meshing, or connecting, different sizes of gears.

In a manual transmission, the driver controls the meshing of gears by hand. This unit discusses manual transmissions for rear-wheel drivetrains. Manual drivetrains for front-wheel-drive vehicles are covered in Unit 57.

LEARNING OBJECTIVES

When you have completed your reading assignments and exercises in this unit, you should be able to:

☐ Explain how gears are used to increase or decrease torque and speed.

☐ Identify and describe the main parts of a transmission.

☐ Describe the operation of a manual transmission.

☐ Explain how gears are shifted inside a transmission.

☐ Follow the flow of power through the transmission gears.

49.1 TRANSMISSION DESIGN

An automobile must be able to perform well under many different conditions. Automobiles must be able to move away from rest, or a stopped position, smoothly and easily, and accelerate well. They also must be able to carry extra weight or passengers when necessary. Automobiles must be able to go up or down steep grades and to travel in reverse.

To allow the vehicle to do all these jobs, varying amounts of engine torque must be applied to the drivetrain. A transmission allows engine torque to be increased or decreased before it is transmitted to the rest of the drivetrain.

A manual transmission is an arrangement of shafts and gears inside a case, which usually is made of aluminum or cast iron. A cutaway view of a transmission is shown in Figure 49-1.

Torque

To move a vehicle, sufficient engine torque, or twisting force, must be transmitted through the drivetrain to the driving wheels. However, the torque produced by an engine at low rpm is not enough to move the vehicle easily.

If the engine were coupled directly to the driveline, it would be difficult to move the vehicle from rest. As power was engaged to move the vehicle, the engine would tend to stall and die. High crankshaft rpm would be necessary to provide enough torque to move the vehicle away from a stop easily.

Acceleration would be jerky and poor, and the vehicle would perform well at only one speed. The vehicle would not go up steep hills or grades. In addition, there would be no way to make the vehicle move in reverse.

To eliminate these problems and make the vehicle perform well under many speed and load conditions, a transmission is used. A transmission allows the driver to increase or decrease engine torque, obtain different road speeds, and move a vehicle in reverse.

Gear Ratios

A *gear*, shown in Figure 49-2, is a toothed wheel that fits into another toothed wheel. Suppose two gears with the same number of teeth are meshed, or connected. If one gear (the driving gear) is turned, the other gear (the driven gear) will rotate at the same speed. For each revolution of the driving gear, the driven gear will rotate one revolution, as shown in Figure 49-3.

The comparison between the relative number of turns and turning speeds of two gears is known as the *gear ratio*. For two gears that have equal numbers of teeth, the gear ratio is 1:1 (read: one to one). For each turn of one gear, the other gear will make one turn. In addition, both gears will turn at the same speed.

However, suppose that two gears with different numbers of teeth are meshed. These gears do *not* rotate at the same speed, or through an equal number of rotations. In Figure 49-4, a smaller driving gear of 10 teeth is meshed with a larger driven gear of 20 teeth. The smaller driving gear must make two revolutions to turn the larger gear through a single revolution. The smaller gear must turn twice as fast as the larger gear. The gear ratio of such a set of gears is 2:1.

To determine the gear ratio of any set of gears, first count the number of teeth on each gear. Then divide the number of teeth on the driving gear into the

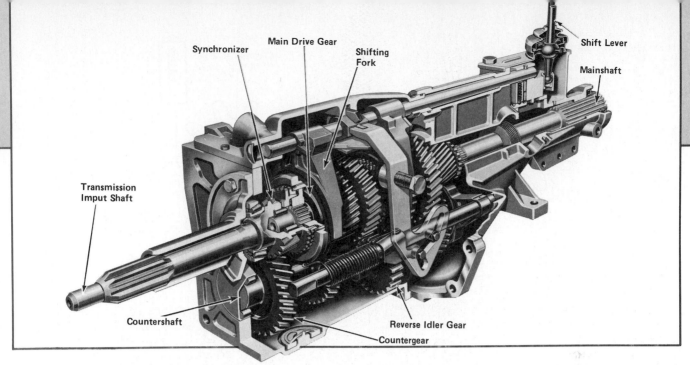

Figure 49-1. Parts of a transmission.

number of teeth on the driven gear. The answer tells you the gear ratio. For example, say the driving gear of a meshed set has 10 teeth and the driven gear has 25 teeth. Divide 10 into 25, which gives a quotient of 2.5 (25 ÷ 10 = 2.5). Thus, the gear ratio is 2.5:1. The smaller (driving) gear will rotate 2.5 times to turn the larger gear around once.

Notice that the value of the driving gear in a gear ratio is expressed as the first number. A ratio simply is another form for expressing a fraction. The ratio 2.5:1 has the same value as the fraction 2.5/1, or 25/10.

Torque on Gears

Torque on a gear is measured in a straight line from the center of a tooth to the gear *axis*. The axis is the center of the gear, around which the gear rotates. Say that 10 pounds of force is exerted on a gear tooth one foot from the axis of the gear. In this case, 10 pounds-feet (lb.-ft.) of torque is exerted at the axis of the gear. More precisely, 10 lb.-ft. of torque is exerted at the axis of the shaft holding the gear. See Figure 49-5.

There is an easy method for finding the torque on a shaft in customary units. Simply multiply the pounds of force on a gear tooth by the distance from the tooth to the shaft axis. If the distance is measured in feet, the torque is expressed in pounds-feet. If the distance is measured in inches, the torque is expressed in pounds-inches (lb.-in.)

Similarly, force can be applied to the teeth of a gear mounted on a shaft by turning the shaft. Say that 10 lb.-ft. of torque are applied to such a shaft. Also say that the distance from the axis of the shaft to the gear teeth is one foot. In this case, 10 pounds of force will be exerted on each gear tooth (see Figure 49-6).

Meshing another gear with this driving gear results in 10 pounds of force being exerted on each

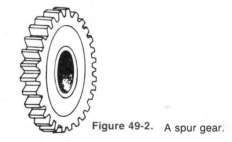

Figure 49-2. A spur gear.

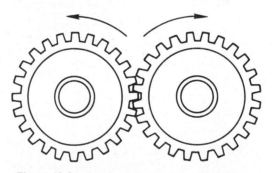

Figure 49-3. Meshing gears of the same size.

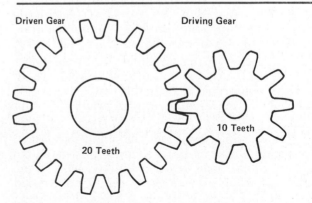

Driven Gear   Driving Gear

20 Teeth   10 Teeth

Figure 49-4. Meshing gears of different sizes.

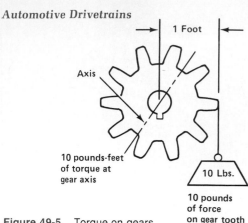

Figure 49-5. Torque on gears.

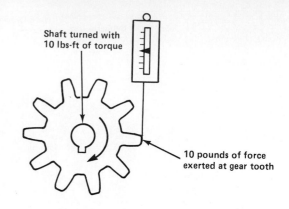

Figure 49-6. Torque applied on a single gear.

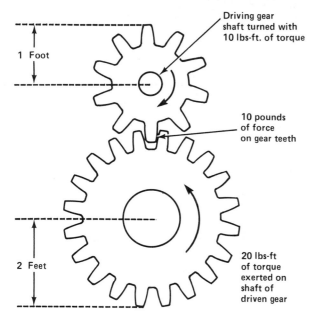

Figure 49-7. Smaller gear driving a larger gear.

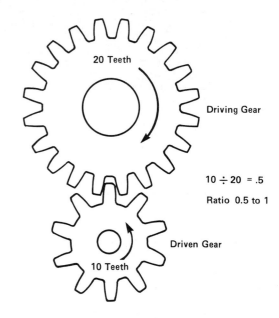

Figure 49-8. Larger gear driving a smaller gear.

tooth of the second gear. If both gears are of the same size, the torque on each gear shaft is the same.

However, if a driving gear is meshed with a larger driven gear, torque on the driven gear shaft is greater. Suppose that the distance from the teeth to the axis of the larger driven gear is 2 feet. The resulting torque on the driven gear shaft is 20 lb.-ft. To determine torque exerted on a shaft, multiply the force on the gear teeth by the distance to the axis. See Figure 49-7.

In this example, the torque on the larger gear's shaft is twice the torque on the smaller gear's shaft. By using larger driven gears in this way, it is possible to multiply, or increase, greatly an original amount of torque.

In this example, the larger gear and its shaft turn at one-half the speed of the smaller gear. However, the shaft of the larger gear is turned with twice the torque of the smaller gear. Remember: A reduction in speed from a smaller driving gear to a larger driven gear increases torque.

Overdrive Ratios

It is also possible to make the larger of two gears the driving gear instead of the smaller. For example, in Figure 49-8 the larger driving gear has 20 teeth, and the smaller driven gear has 10 teeth. Dividing 20 into 10 gives the gear ratio: 0.5:1. This is known as an *overdrive* gear ratio. Overdrive means that the speed of the driven gear is greater than, or over, the speed of the driving gear.

In an overdrive gearset, the torque on the driven gear is reduced, or divided, rather than increased, or multiplied. The torque on the driven gear shaft in the example discussed above is only half the torque on the driving gear.

However, the speed of the driven gear is twice that of the driving gear. Overdrive gearing is used to increase the speed of the driven gear and shaft. An increase in speed from a larger driving gear to a smaller driven gear reduces torque.

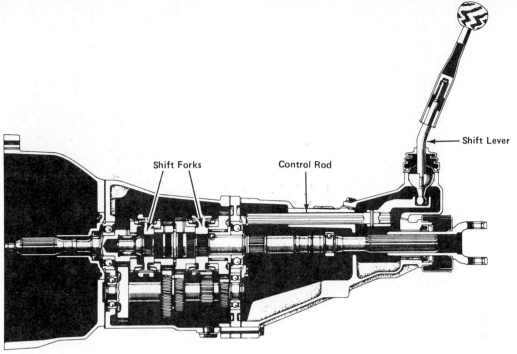

Figure 49-9. Transmission assembly. CHRYSLER CORPORATION

49.2 MANUAL TRANSMISSION CONSTRUCTION

A manual transmission consists of parallel sets of metal shafts on which meshing gearsets of different ratios are mounted. By moving the shift lever, gear ratios can be selected to produce different amounts of torque multiplication. The shafts and gears are mounted inside a metal case made of aluminum or cast iron, shown in Figure 49-9. The case contains lubricant to reduce friction between the meshing gears and between shaft bearing surfaces.

Engine torque is connected to, or disconnected from, the transmission by engaging, or disengaging, the clutch. The construction and operation of the clutch are discussed in Unit 51. When the clutch is engaged, engine torque turns the *transmission input shaft,* shown in Figure 49-10.

A *main drive gear* is attached to the rear of the input shaft. The main drive gear meshes with and drives a larger *countergear.* A countergear is one of four gears on the *countershaft* of the simplified sliding-gear transmission shown in Figure 49-11. Three shafts can be seen: the input shaft, the countershaft (the lower shaft), and the *mainshaft* (the upper shaft). The mainshaft, sometimes called the output shaft, is connected at the rear to the driveline.

When the clutch gear turns, the countergear rotates. From the front of the transmission to the rear, the gears on the countershaft become smaller. From front to rear, these gears are: countergear, intermediate (second) gear, low (first) gear, and reverse gear.

Figure 49-10. Transmission input shaft.

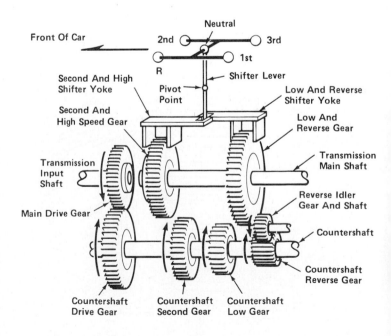

Figure 49-11. Simplified transmission.

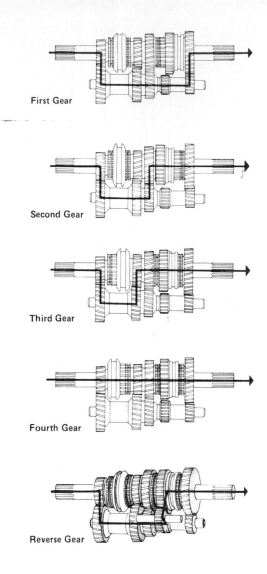

First Gear

Second Gear

Third Gear

Fourth Gear

Reverse Gear

Figure 49-12. Transmission power flow diagram.
VOLVO CAR CORPORATION

Constant-Mesh Gears

Modern manual transmissions are of the *constant-mesh* type. Constant mesh means that all countershaft gears and mainshaft gears are constantly in mesh with each other. During operation, however, only one of the gears on the mainshaft is engaged, or locked, to the mainshaft. The other gears turn freely on the mainshaft and are not engaged to it.

Study the power flow diagram in Figure 49-12. All the gears on the mainshaft and countershaft are meshed. Because each gearset has a different gear ratio, only one gearset can be engaged at a time to turn the mainshaft.

The gears in a modern transmission are helical-cut gears, which transfer power more quietly and smoothly than spur gears. See Figure 49-13.

Approximate gear ratios in a typical four-speed manual transmission are: first, 2.5:1; second, 1.9:1; third, 1.5:1; and fourth, 1:1. The numerically higher the gear ratio, the greater the torque multiplication.

In fourth (high) gear, which has a 1:1 gear ratio, there is no torque multiplication. That is why fourth gear is not used to get the vehicle rolling. Fourth gear is used for high speeds and light loads.

Shifting Arms

On the outside of a four-speed transmission case, there are three *shifting arms,* shown in Figure 49-14. These shifting arms are attached to short shafts, called *shifting shafts,* that go through the side of the transmission case. The upper two shifting shafts are attached to two *shifting forks* for the forward gears inside the transmission. The lower shifting shaft is attached to the reverse shifting fork. The shifting forks, shown in Figure 49-15, determine which gearset drives the mainshaft.

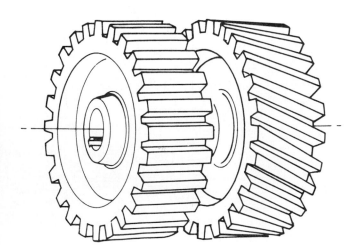

Figure 49-13. Comparing a helical gear (right) with a spur gear.

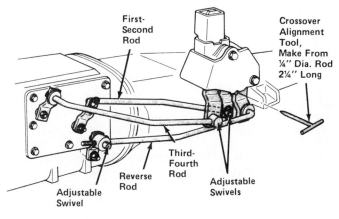

First-Second Rod

Crossover Alignment Tool, Make From ¼" Dia. Rod 2¼" Long

Reverse Rod

Third-Fourth Rod

Adjustable Swivels

Adjustable Swivel

Figure 49-14. Shift linkage assembly. CHRYSLER CORPORATION

Synchronizers

The action of the shifting forks moves the *synchronizers*. A synchronizer is a metal assembly that can lock a selected gear to the mainshaft. Two synchronizers, or synchros, are used in a four-speed transmission.

When the driver selects a gear, the linkage rods move the shifting arms on the transmission case. The shifting arms move the forks inside the case, and the forks move parts of the synchronizers back and forth.

When the synchronizer moves toward a gear, it locks, or engages, the gear to the mainshaft. The gear then turns the mainshaft. The synchronizer can move forward or backward to engage either of two gears.

Between these two positions, the synchronizer does not engage either gear in its *neutral position*. When both synchronizers are in their neutral positions, the countershaft and mainshaft gears mesh and turn. However, no mainshaft gear is engaged to turn the mainshaft.

The parts of a synchronizer assembly are shown in Figure 49-16. Synchronizer parts include:

- Inner hub
- Detent springs
- Inserts, or detents
- Outer sleeve
- Blocker rings.

Refer to Figure 49-17, which shows a disassembled manual transmission, while reading the following discussion of synchronizer operation. The synchronizer hub has splines inside that mate with splines on the mainshaft to make both parts rotate together. The outside of the synchronizer hub also is splined to the outer sleeve.

The synchronizer assemblies allow gears to engage without clashing, or grinding. Clashing occurs when two gears are forced to engage as they rotate at different speeds. Clashing can chip or break the gear teeth or gears. To eliminate clashing, the gears must rotate at the same speed as they mesh. When the gears rotate at the same speed, they are synchronized. This is how synchronizers get their name.

Synchronizing begins when the shift fork moves the synchronizer sleeve toward the selected gear. The inserts force the blocker ring toward the gear. A cone-shaped clutch surface on each gear creates friction against the cone-shaped clutch part of the blocker ring. The friction slows or speeds up the clutch gear/input shaft and clutch disc.

When the speeds are matched, the sleeve slips over the small teeth on both the blocker ring and the gear. Until the hub and gear rotate at the same speed, the blocker ring acts as its name implies. It blocks, or prevents, the small mainshaft gear teeth from fully engaging the inner teeth of the sleeve. When hub and

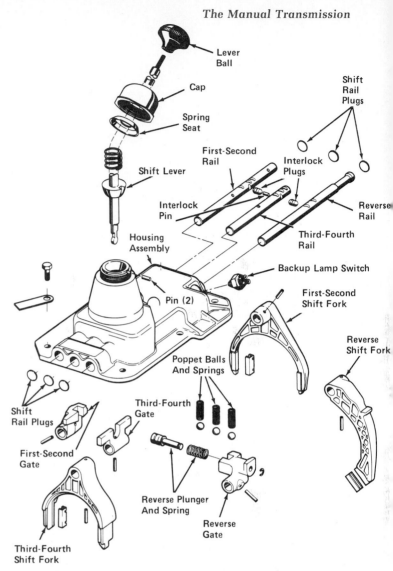

Figure 49-15. Shifting forks and shafts. CHRYSLER CORPORATION

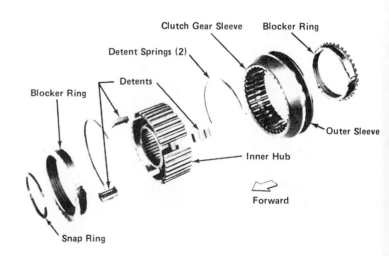

Figure 49-16. Parts of a synchronizer. CHRYSLER CORPORATION

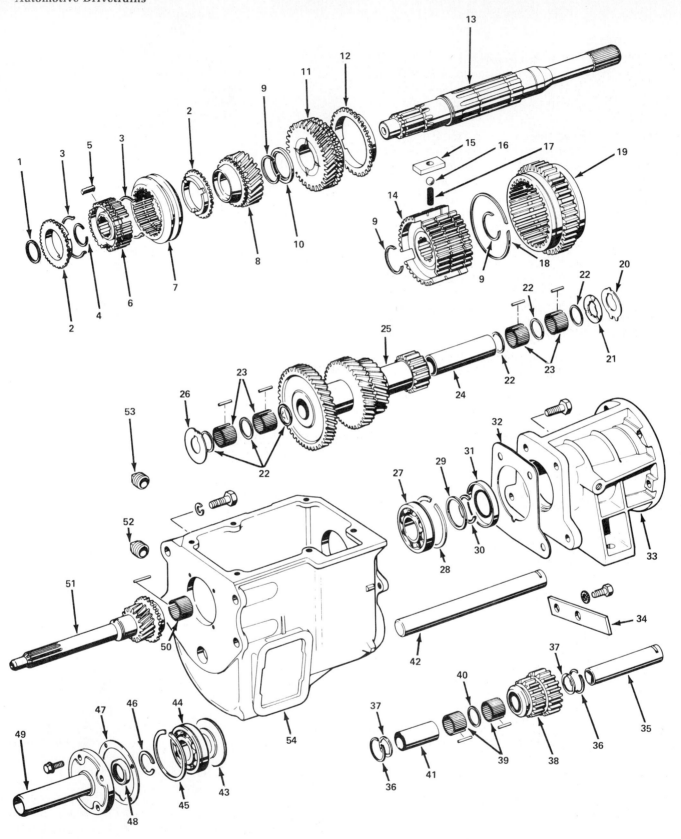

Figure 49-17. Parts of a four-speed transmission. CHRYSLER CORPORATION

1	Mainshaft Pilot Bearing Roller Spacer	20	Countershaft Gear Thrust Washer (Steel) (Rear)	37	Reverse Idler Gear Thrust Washer
2	Third-Fourth Blocking Ring	21	Countershaft Gear Thrust Washer (Steel Backed Bronze) (Rear)	38	Reverse Idler Gear
3	Third-Fourth Retaining Ring	22	Countershaft Gear Bearing Washer	39	Reverse Idler Gear Bearing Rollers (74)
4	Third-Fourth Synchronizer Snap Ring	23	Countershaft Gear Bearing Rollers (88)	40	Reverse Idler Gear Bearing Washer
5	Third-Fourth Shifting Plate (3)	24	Countershaft Gear Bearing Spacer	41	Reverse Idler Shaft Sleeve
6	Third-Fourth Clutch Hub	25	Countershaft Gear	42	Countershaft
7	Third-Fourth Clutch Sleeve	26	Countershaft Gear Thrust Washer (Front)	43	Front Bearing Retainer Washer
8	Third Gear	27	Rear Bearing	44	Front Bearing
9	Mainshaft Snap Ring	28	Rear Bearing Locating Snap Ring	45	Front Bearing Locating Snap Ring
10	Second Gear Thrust Washer	29	Rear Bearing Spacer Ring	46	Front Bearing Lock Ring
11	Second Gear	30	Rear Bearing Snap Ring	47	Front Bearing Cap Gasket
12	Second Gear Blocking Ring	31	Adapter Plate Seal	48	Front Bearing Cap Seal
13	Mainshaft	32	Adapter Plate to Transmission Gasket	49	Front Bearing Cap
14	First-Second Clutch Hub	33	Adapter to Transmission	50	Mainshaft Pilot Bearing Rollers (22)
15	First—Second Shifting Plate (3)	34	Countershaft - Reverse Idler Shaft Lockplate	51	Clutch Shaft
16	Poppet Ball	35	Reverse Idler Gear Shaft	52	Drain Plug
17	Poppet Spring	36	Reverse Idler Gear Snap Ring	53	Filler Plug
18	First-Second Insert Ring			54	Transmission Case
19	First-Second Clutch Sleeve				

Figure 49-17. Concluded.

---

gear rotation speeds are the same, the gear is forced to turn with the synchronizer and mainshaft.

When the driver selects reverse, both forward gear synchronizer sleeves are moved to their neutral positions. Reverse gear has no synchronizer. The reverse-gear linkage rod from the shifter moves the reverse-gear shifting arm. This slides reverse gear forward until it engages the reverse idler gear. To shift the transmission into reverse, the vehicle must be brought to a complete stop.

Gearshift Linkage

Three types of manual transmission shift linkage are commonly used on automobiles. These include two types of floor-shift linkages and one type of column-shift linkage.

The two types of floor-shift linkages are those mounted outside the transmission case and those mounted inside the transmission case. Floor shifts are found in three-, four-, and five-speed manual transmissions. See Figures 49-18 and 49-19.

Column-shift linkage is mounted outside the transmission case. It is found primarily on older vehicles with three-speed manual transmissions. See Figure 49-20.

49.3 FOUR-SPEED TRANSMISSION POWER FLOW

The movement of the synchronizers controls the flow of power through the transmission gears. Refer to Figure 49-21 to follow the power flow through the transmission as you read the following discussion.

When the driver selects first gear, the shifting fork moves the first/second synchronizer sleeve to engage first gear.

When the driver selects second gear, the fork moves the first/second synchronizer sleeve away from first and toward second. When the synchronizer sleeve engages second gear, second gear rotates the mainshaft.

When the driver selects third gear, two movements occur inside the transmission. As the shift lever begins to move, the first/second synchronizer sleeve is moved away from second gear. The sleeve is moved into the neutral position between first and second gears. As the driver continues to move the lever, the second movement occurs in the transmission. The other shifting fork moves the third/fourth synchronizer sleeve toward third gear until it is engaged with the mainshaft.

When the driver selects fourth (high) gear, the forward shifting fork moves the forward synchronizer sleeve away from third gear. The synchronizer sleeve moves toward the clutch gear on the input shaft. When the clutch gear is engaged, the input shaft and the mainshaft are locked to rotate at the same speed. The countergear continues to turn but no longer transmits any torque. In fourth gear, there is no speed change or torque multiplication. The transmission is in direct drive.

Many modern transmissions use what is known as "all-indirect" gearing. In such a transmission, power always flows through the countergear and countershaft gears to the mainshaft gears. A 1:1 gear

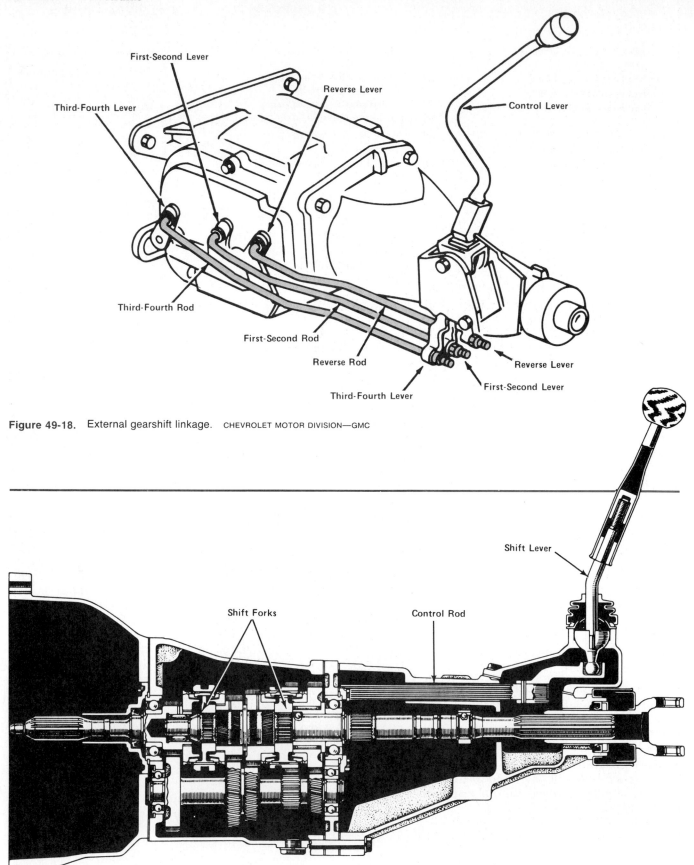

Figure 49-18. External gearshift linkage. CHEVROLET MOTOR DIVISION—GMC

Figure 49-19. Internal gearshift linkage. TOYOTA MOTOR SALES, U.S.A.

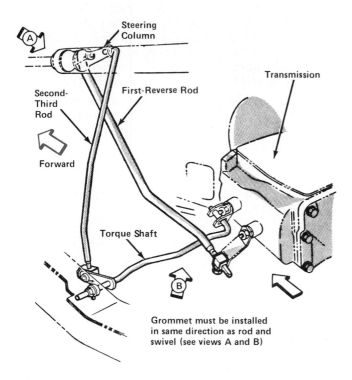

Figure 49-20. Column-shift linkage.
CHRYSLER CORPORATION

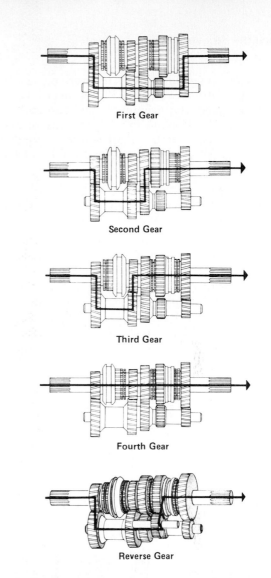

First Gear

Second Gear

Third Gear

Fourth Gear

Reverse Gear

Figure 49-21. Four-speed transmission power flow.
VOLVO CAR CORPORATION

ratio is not obtained by coupling the input shaft and mainshaft. Rather, gear ratio is obtained by selecting countershaft and mainshaft gears with the same number of teeth.

Some four-speed transmissions have an overdrive-ratio fourth gear. This overdrive ratio allows the mainshaft of the transmission to turn faster than engine speed for highway driving. The engine turns slower for better gas mileage.

When the driver selects reverse gear, both synchronizer sleeves are moved to their neutral positions. The reverse-gear linkage rod from the shifter moves the reverse-gear shifting arm. The shifting arm slides the reverse gear forward until it engages the reverse idler gear. Reverse gear is different from other gears because it doesn't mesh directly with a gear on the countershaft. Between the rearmost countershaft gear and reverse gear is an *idler gear,* shown in Figure 49-22. The idler gear rides on a separate, short shaft. The idler gear makes the reverse gear rotate in the opposite direction. When reverse is engaged and the clutch pedal is released, the mainshaft rotates backwards and the vehicle moves in reverse.

The gear to be used depends upon load and speed requirements. Lower gears are used when the load is

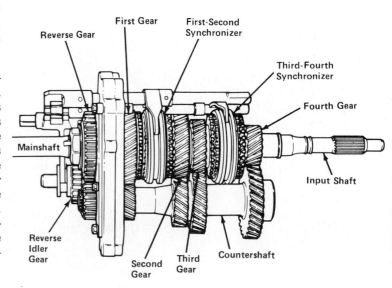

Figure 49-22. Gear locations. FORD MOTOR COMPANY

531

heavy or when speed is low. The more gears a transmission has, the more easily it can meet a vehicle's load and speed requirements. On automobiles, a manual transmission may have three, four, or five forward speeds. The number of speeds refers to forward speeds only. All automotive transmissions also have a reverse gear.

In a normal start from a standstill, shifting progresses from first gear through second and third and on into fourth. This process is called upshifting.

If the driver encounters an increased load, such as a hill, or slow traffic, a lower gear must be used. When climbing a hill, the driver may shift from fourth down to third, second, or even first gear. This process is called downshifting.

49.4 FIVE-SPEED TRANSMISSION

Five-speed transmissions are found most often in small, economy vehicles and in sports cars. The extra gearset makes the smaller engines more flexible in handling different loads and road conditions. Some five-speed transmissions have overdrive gearing for both fourth and fifth gears to improve fuel economy.

Most five-speed transmission cases in smaller vehicles are constructed of aluminum to save weight. In these designs, the shift linkage is built into the transmission.

Some five-speeds have cases that are constructed in two halves. These cases are split down the middle. An example of this construction is pictured in Figure 49-23.

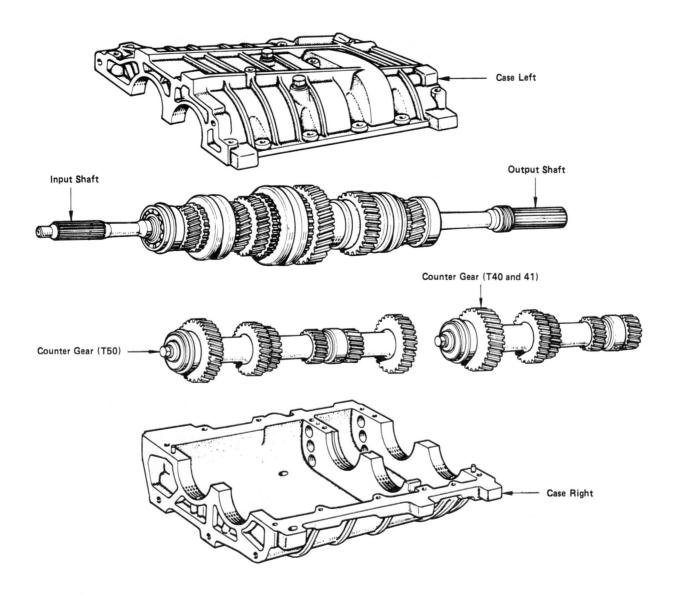

Figure 49-23. Split-case, five-speed transmission assembly. NISSAN MOTOR CORPORATION

49.5 OTHER TRANSMISSION PARTS

Other parts and devices found in manual transmissions include:

- Ball and needle roller bearings
- A gear arrangement to drive the speedometer cable (see Figure 49-24)
- A switch to turn on backup lights when the vehicle is shifted into reverse (see Figure 49-25)
- Sensors that indicate to control mechanisms which gear is engaged (see Figure 49-26).

Figure 49-25. Removing the backup light switch.

Figure 49-24. Removing the speedometer drive gear.

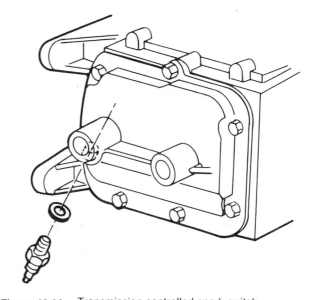

Figure 49-26. Transmission-controlled spark switch.
PONTIAC MOTOR DIVISION—GMC

UNIT HIGHLIGHTS

- Gearsets can be used to increase or decrease torque or speed.
- A transmission uses gearsets to control and multiply engine torque.
- The three shafts of a manual transmission are the input shaft, countershaft, and mainshaft.
- Although all the gearsets on the mainshaft and countershaft are meshed at the same time, only one gearset drives the mainshaft at any one time.
- Synchronizers engage the gears to the mainshaft to select and engage a chosen gear.
- Automobile transmissions commonly have three, four, or five forward speeds, plus reverse.

TERMS

gear	mainshaft
gear ratio	constant-mesh gears
axis	shifting arms
overdrive	shifting shafts
transmission input shaft	shifting forks
main drive gear	synchronizer
countergear	neutral position
countershaft	idler gear

R E V I E W   Q U E S T I O N S

DIRECTIONS: The following questions are similar to those used on mechanic certification tests. On a separate sheet of paper, write the letter of the correct choice.

1. Twenty-five lb.-ft. of torque is applied to a gear with a radius of 6 inches. That gear is meshed with a gear with a radius of 3 feet. What is the torque on the shaft of the larger gear?
A. 75 lb.-ft.
B. 450 lb.-ft.
C. 37.5 lb.-ft.
D. 25 lb.-ft.

2. A driving gear with nine teeth is meshed with a driven gear of 37 teeth. Which of the following numbers represents the gear ratio?
A. 4.11:1
B. 0.24:1
C. 333:1
D. 49:1

3. Mechanic A says that the driving gear of an overdrive gearset is larger than the driven gear. Mechanic B says that the driving gear of any gearset is always the smaller gear. Who is correct?
A. A only   B. B only   C. Both A and B   D. Neither A nor B

4. All of the following statements about a manual transmission are true EXCEPT
A. The main drive gear is on the input shaft.
B. The countershaft is driven by the countergear.
C. The synchronizers engage the gears to the mainshaft and the countershaft.
D. Only one forward gearset drives the mainshaft at any one time.

5. Which of the following statements are correct?
I. Going up a hill always requires the driver to upshift.
II. Going down a hill always requires the driver to downshift.
A. I only   B. II only   C. Both I and II   D. Neither I nor II

S U P P L E M E N T A L   A C T I V I T I E S

1. List the main parts of a manual transmission.
2. Describe how gearing affects rotational speed and torque in a gearset.
3. Locate and identify the shift linkage rods on a shop vehicle.
4. Describe how you might be able to figure out the gear ratios on a manual transmission removed from a vehicle, without disassembling it.
5. Explain how a synchronizer matches the speed of a mainshaft gear to the speed of the mainshaft during upshifting.
6. Explain the difference between a 1:1 ratio in a direct-drive transmission and in a transmission with all-indirect drive.
7. Synchronizers are not used on the transmissions of large tractor-trailer rigs. Try to figure out how the drivers manage to shift gears without clashing.

UNIT PREVIEW

Most service performed on manual transmissions is preventive maintenance. Inspection of transmission problems usually requires removing and reinstalling the transmission. This unit discusses preventive maintenance, diagnosis, and servicing of manual transmissions.

LEARNING OBJECTIVES

When you have completed your assignments and exercises in this unit, you should be able to:

☐ Describe how preventive maintenance is performed on a manual transmission.

☐ Identify problems often found in manual transmissions during diagnosis, and describe the causes of those problems.

☐ Identify the parts that must be removed before a transmission can be lowered from the automobile.

☐ Describe the cleaning and inspection steps performed after disassembly of a transmission.

SAFETY PRECAUTIONS

The transmission is one of the heaviest assemblies that may be removed from an automobile. Most transmission service tasks require that the automobile be raised and supported safely. Proper jacks and supporting tools are essential when servicing transmissions. If a transmission is to be removed from a vehicle, the engine also must be supported. Failure to support the engine and transmission can lead to serious personal injury and damage to the vehicle. It is also essential to have a helper assist in these procedures.

Hot transmission oil and transmission and exhaust system parts can cause severe burns. When possible, let the vehicle cool before work is begun.

The underside of the vehicle is dirty. Dirt and foreign objects can fall into your eyes during service procedures. Always wear safety glasses or goggles when working under a vehicle.

When reassembling parts of the transmission, be sure all parts are lubricated before they are reinstalled. Do *not* spin-dry bearings with compressed air. This can damage the bearings.

50.1 PREVENTIVE MAINTENANCE

Preventive maintenance includes checking and draining the oil and lubricating the gearshift linkage.

Check Transmission Lubricant Level

Transmission lubricant level should be checked at regular intervals, usually during chassis lubrications. Raise the automobile on a hoist to check the transmission lubricant level. The vehicle must be level to obtain an accurate reading.

Two plugs usually are located on one side of the transmission, as shown in Figure 50-1. The *fill plug* is removed to check lubricant level. The *drain plug,* or drain bolt, is removed to drain the lubricant.

Wipe away road dirt with a shop towel. Loosen and remove the fill plug. Look inside the fill-plug hole to see if lubricant is visible. If lubricant is not visible, insert a finger or a bent rod into the fill hole. Lubricant should be level with, or not more than ½ inch below, the bottom of the fill hole. If lubricant level is low, add the proper gear lubrication oil. Transmission lubricant is added with a pressurized gun, a bulb-type syringe, or a suction gun. See Figure 50-2. Replace and tighten the fill plug.

CAUTION: All manual transmissions do not use the same type of lubricant. Check the proper service manual to determine the correct lubricant for the vehicle.

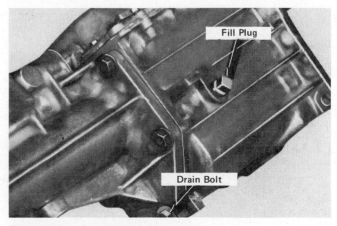

Figure 50-1. Transmission plugs.
AMERICAN MOTORS CORPORATION

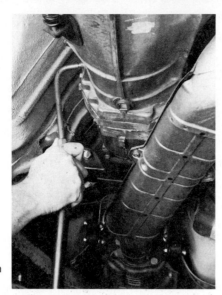

Figure 50-2.
Refilling transmission with fluid.

Figure 50-3. Draining transmission fluid.

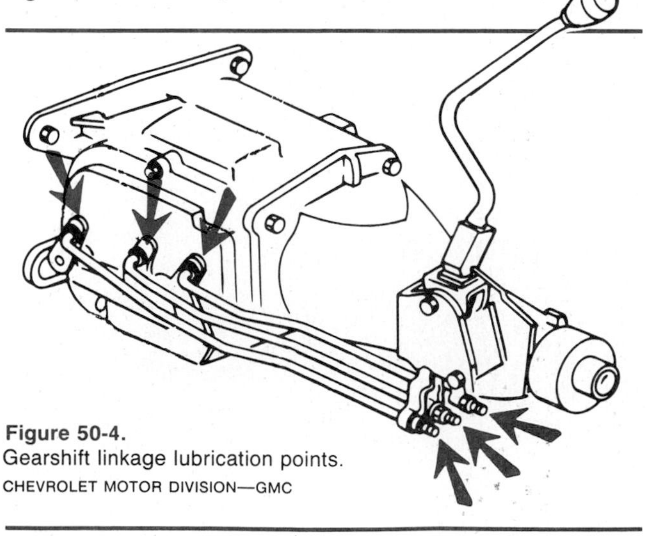

Replace Transmission Lubricant

Manual transmission lubricant should be changed periodically according to the manufacturer's recommendations. Some manufacturers do not specify any recommended interval for changing the lubricant. In such cases, a good rule is to change the lubricant every two years or 24,000 miles. If a vehicle is used for trailer towing or other heavy-duty service, the lubricant should be changed more frequently. Replacing transmission lubricant involves raising the vehicle on a hoist, draining the old lubricant, and adding new lubricant.

The lubricant should be warm when it is drained. Impurities are held in suspension by the lubricant during operation. If the lubricant is allowed to cool, the impurities will settle at the bottom of the transmission case. Many of these harmful impurities will remain in the transmission if the lubricant is cold.

Wipe off the fill plug and the drain plug. Place a catch pan under the transmission to catch the old lubricant (see Figure 50-3). Remove the fill plug to allow air to enter the transmission. This helps the draining process. Remove the drain plug, or drain bolt, thereby allowing the lubricant to flow into the catch pan.

When the lubricant has drained, apply the proper sealant to the threads on the drain plug or bolt. Tighten the drain plug or bolt in place.

Fill the transmission with the proper lubricant, using a pressurized gun or a lubricant dispenser. Fill until the lubricant begins to spill out of the hole. Replace and tighten the fill plug.

Lubricate Gearshift Linkage

Gearshift linkages usually are lubricated as part of chassis lubrication service. A lubricating oil or grease is used, depending on the manufacturer's requirements. The number of *grease points,* or lubrication areas, depends on the type of gearshift linkage used. Typical gearshift linkage grease points are shown in Figure 50-4.

50.2 DIAGNOSING TRANSMISSION PROBLEMS

Diagnosing a transmission problem involves troubleshooting, or locating the source of the condition. A reported transmission problem actually might be a problem in the clutch, driveline, or differential. The most common transmission problems are discussed here.

Transmission Noises

Most manual transmission complaints involve noises. However, many of these noises are caused by other drivetrain parts and only seem to be coming from the transmission. A mechanic's first job is to make a thorough diagnosis to determine if the problem is caused by the transmission.

Figure 50-4.
Gearshift linkage lubrication points.
CHEVROLET MOTOR DIVISION—GMC

Make a visual inspection and check for loose bolts and loose or damaged gearshift linkage. Check the level and condition of the transmission lubricant. If the level is low, check for leaks. Metal in the lubricant may indicate broken parts. Some metal usually will be present due to normal wear.

Transmission noises also may indicate worn or damaged bearings, gear teeth, or synchronizers.

Determining the location of the noise is important. This can be done simply by listening. (On transaxle-equipped cars, determining the source of a noise can be difficult. This is because the transmission and differential share the same housing.) Listening under the car with a stethoscope while a helper operates the transmission in different gears can be helpful. A noise that changes or disappears in different gears is a transmission noise.

The type of noise also is important. For example, a loud clicking or knocking sound indicates the possibility of a missing gear tooth.

Gear Clash

Gear clash is a noise made when the transmission is shifted from one gear to another. Externally, gear clash can be caused by incorrect clutch adjustment or binding of clutch or gearshift linkage. Inside the transmission, gear clash usually is caused by a damaged, worn, or defective synchronizer blocker ring. Use of the wrong lubricant will cause gear clashing.

Hard Shifting

If the transmission shift lever is hard to move from one gear to another, check clutch adjustment and clutch linkage. Clutch service is discussed in Unit 52. Also check gearshift linkage for binding and damage. Hard shifting also may be caused by damage inside the transmission. Common hard-shifting problems include badly worn bearings and damaged clutch gear, shift rails, shift forks, or synchronizers.

Jumping Out of Gear

A manual transmission sometimes jumps out of gear into neutral. Check the gearshift linkage for adjustment or damage. Excessive play in the gears or excessive end play in the input shaft also can cause jumping out of gear. Still another cause is badly worn bearings. Other transmission parts to inspect are the clutch pilot bearing, gear teeth, shift forks, shift rails, and springs or detents.

Locked in Gear

A transmission is locked when it cannot be shifted out of a gear. Check the gearshift linkage for adjustment or damage. Low lubricant level can cause needle bearings, gears, and synchronizers to seize and lock up the transmission. Inspect the countershaft gear, clutch shaft, reverse idler, shift rails, shift forks, and springs or detents for damage.

50.3 MANUAL TRANSMISSION SERVICE

If a visual inspection does not identify a problem, the transmission must be removed from the vehicle. This allows the mechanic to disassemble, clean, and inspect all parts for damage and excessive wear.

SAFETY CAUTION: **Raise and support the vehicle safely on a hoist. Manual transmissions are large and heavy. Use proper care, and a helper, to remove and replace the transmission.**

Place an oil catch pan under the transmission and drain the lubricant.

Remove Driveline

Refer to Topic 48.3 for driveline removal.

Remove Linkage

Several parts are removed at the same time as the gearshift linkage. Parts to be removed are:

* Speedometer cable
* Backup light switch
* Shift linkage
* Exhaust system.

Remove speedometer cable. The speedometer is operated by a *speedometer cable* that is connected to the transmission. The speedometer cable may be screwed or bolted to the transmission extension housing. See Figure 50-5. Disconnect the speedometer cable from the transmission.

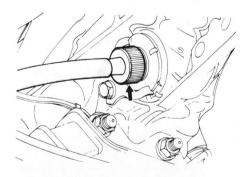

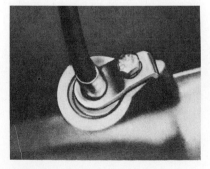

Figure 50-5. Speedometer cables screwed (top), bolted (bottom) to transmission case. CHRYLSER CORPORATION/ FORD MOTOR COMPANY

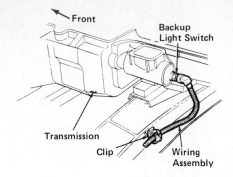

Figure 50-6. Backup light switch. FORD MOTOR COMPANY

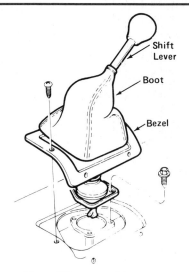

Figure 50-7. Floor shifter assembly.
AMERICAN MOTORS CORPORATION

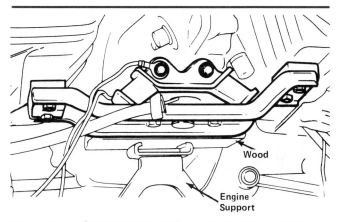

Figure 50-8. Supporting the engine. CHRYSLER CORPORATION

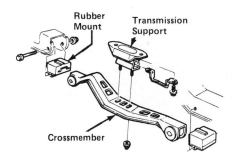

Figure 50-9. Removing the crossmember.
FORD MOTOR COMPANY

Remove backup light switch. A backup light switch usually is located near, and activated by, the shift lever (see Figure 50-6). Disconnect the switch by pulling out a wire connector.

Remove shift linkage. When removing the transmission, it is necessary only to disconnect the linkage at the transmission end on vehicles with column shift. On vehicles with floor-shift linkage, the shift-lever assembly and the shift linkage usually are removed. This means working inside and under the vehicle. A floor-shift assembly is shown in Figure 50-7.

Remove exhaust system. Some automobile exhaust systems must be disconnected before a transmission can be removed.

Remove Crossmember and Transmission

Much weight is supported by the *transmission crossmember*. The transmission crossmember is a steel frame that usually supports the transmission and the engine. Before unbolting the crossmember from the chassis, the engine should be held in place by a jack or other support. See Figure 50-8.

SAFETY CAUTION: **Failure to support the engine before transmission removal can result in serious injury and vehicle damage.**

Remove the bolts that hold the transmission support to the crossmember (see Figure 50-9). Raise the engine support to take tension off the crossmember. Remove the crossmember and any part of the emergency brake system that may be attached to the crossmember. Secure the transmission with a transmission jack before proceeding (see Figure 50-10).

SAFETY CAUTION: **The manual transmission is very heavy. Have a helper assist.**

Remove the top two bolts holding the transmission to the bellhousing. Screw in two dowels, or alignment pins. The dowels will help to hold the weight of the transmission during removal and again during installation. Remove the lower transmission bolts. Pull the transmission straight back until it clears the

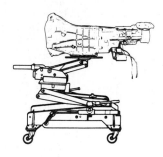

Figure 50-10. Transmission jack. CHRYSLER CORPORATION

clutch. Lower the transmission jack and place the transmission on a workbench.

If the transmission is separate from the bellhousing, it is not necessary to remove the bellhousing. With the transmission supported safely, remove the bolts (usually four) holding the transmission to the bellhousing. Then remove the transmission, pulling straight back.

Disassemble Transmission

Disassembling a manual transmission can vary considerably among manufacturers and models. A mechanic should have the proper service manual and a cutaway drawing of the transmission being serviced. Use Figure 50-11 as a cutaway guide to the disassembly and assembly procedures discussed here for a Chevrolet four-speed transmission.

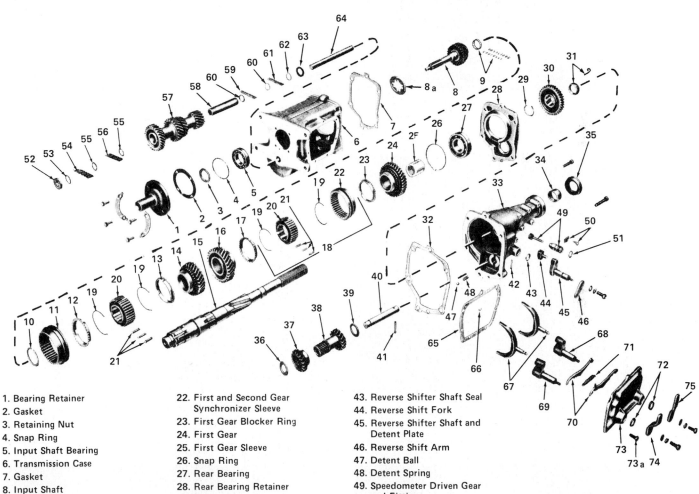

1. Bearing Retainer
2. Gasket
3. Retaining Nut
4. Snap Ring
5. Input Shaft Bearing
6. Transmission Case
7. Gasket
8. Input Shaft
8a. Oil Slinger
9. Bearing Rollers (17) and Cage
10. Snap Ring
11. Third and Fourth Synchronizer Sleeve
12. Fourth Gear Blocker Ring
13. Third Gear Blocker Ring
14. Third Gear
15. Mainshaft
16. Second Gear
17. Second Gear Blocker Ring
18. First and Second Gear Synchronizer Assembly
19. Detent Spring
20. Synchronizer Inner Hub
21. Synchronizer Detents

22. First and Second Gear Synchronizer Sleeve
23. First Gear Blocker Ring
24. First Gear
25. First Gear Sleeve
26. Snap Ring
27. Rear Bearing
28. Rear Bearing Retainer
29. Selective Fit Snap Ring
30. Reverse Gear
31. Speedometer Drive and Clip
32. Gasket
33. Rear Extension Housing
34. Bushing
35. Rear Oil Seal
36. Reverse Idler Front Thrust Washer (Tanged)
37. Reverse Idler Gear (Front)
38. Reverse Idler Gear (Rear)
39. Flat Thrust Washer
40. Reverse Idler Shaft
41. Roll Pin
42. Lock Pin

43. Reverse Shifter Shaft Seal
44. Reverse Shift Fork
45. Reverse Shifter Shaft and Detent Plate
46. Reverse Shift Arm
47. Detent Ball
48. Detent Spring
49. Speedometer Driven Gear and Fitting
50. Retainer and Bolt
51. O-Ring
52. Tanged Washer
53. Spacer
54. Bearing Rollers (28)
55. Spacer
56. Bearing Rollers (28)
57. Countergear
58. Spacer
59. Bearing Rollers (28)
60. Spacer
61. Bearing Rollers (28)
62. Spacer
63. Tanged Washer
64. Countershaft
65. Gasket

66. Detent Retainer Spring
67. Forward Shift Forks
68. First and Second Shifter Shaft and Detent Plate
69. Third and Fourth Shifter Shaft and Detent Plate
70. Detent Cams
71. Detent Cam Spring
72. Lip Seals
73. Side Cover
73a. Headed Cam Pin
74. Third and Fourth Shift Arm
75. First and Second Shift Arm

Figure 50-11. Parts of a four-speed transmission. CHEVROLET MOTOR DIVISION—GMC

Figure 50-12. Removing shift forks.

Figure 50-13. Removing the front bearing.

Figure 50-14. Removing the extension housing.

Disassembly is begun by removing the transmission cover, gasket, and shifting forks, as shown in Figure 50-12.

Unbolt and remove the front bearing retainer (see Figure 50-13). Loosen the front bearing retainer nut. Pull forward on the input shaft to loosen the front bearing.

Unbolt and remove the extension housing (see Figure 50-14).

Remove reverse idler gear, speedometer drive gear, and reverse gear. Slide the third/fourth synchronizer sleeve toward fourth gear. Tap the rear bearing retainer with a mallet. Remove mainshaft and gear assembly from the rear of the transmission case as shown in Figure 50-15.

Drive the countergear shaft to the rear of the transmission case with a hammer and soft drift punch. Needle bearings will fall into the case as the countergear shaft comes out of the countergear assembly. See Figure 50-16. Remove the countergear assembly.

A hydraulic press is used to remove second gear and the first/second synchronizer assembly from the mainshaft (see Figure 50-17).

Clean and Inspect Parts

Clean all parts thoroughly in clean solvent. Remove all traces of old gaskets.

Wash roller bearings in solvent and dry. Do *not* spin-dry bearings with compressed air.

Rotate the outer race against the inner race. Listen carefully for noise, and feel for tightness or roughness. Visually check the rollers and races for wear. Lubricate bearings according to the manufacturer's specifications before reassembly.

Figure 50-15. Removing the mainshaft and gears.

Check all needle bearings and needle-bearing bushings for signs of wear or roughness.

Synchronizer blocker rings should remain with the gears they mate with. Do *not* mix the blocker rings between gears. Check blocker rings for fit and wear according to the manufacturer's service manual.

Check all parts of the transmission, including brass bushings (for the output shaft, countergear, etc.), for wear or damage. Replace parts as necessary.

Lubricate each transmission part after inspection, following manufacturer's specifications.

Replace oil seals with new ones, and lubricate the lips of new seals.

Replace all damaged snap rings with new ones.

Reassemble Transmission

Press second gear and the first/second synchronizer assembly onto the mainshaft with a hydraulic press. Seat second gear on the mainshaft. Replace the first-gear block ring (see Figure 50-18) and first gear.

Slide the rear bearing and bearing retainer over the mainshaft. Install the snap ring onto the mainshaft. Measure end play. Slide reverse gear onto the mainshaft and against the rear bearing retainer (see Figure 50-19).

Install third gear, the third-gear blocker ring, and the third/fourth synchronizer hub. Slide the fourth-gear synchronizer blocker ring against the third/fourth synchronizer assembly (see Figure 50-20). Set the mainshaft and gear assembly aside.

Lower the countergear assembly into place between two thrust washers. Tap the countergear shaft into its place with the countershaft assembly using a soft-faced hammer. Install the front reverse-idler gear

Figure 50-17. Pressing off gears.

Figure 50-18. Replacing the blocker ring.

Figure 50-16. Removing the countershaft.

Figure 50-19. Replacing reverse gear.

Figure 50-20. Replacing the synchronizer assembly.

Figure 50-22. Installing the mainshaft and gears.

Figure 50-21. Installing the reverse idler gear.

Figure 50-23. Installing the side cover.

against the thrust washer from the inside of the case (see Figure 50-21).

Slide the third/fourth sychronizer sleeve forward to engage fourth gear. Install a new gasket on the rear bearing retainer. Install the mainshaft and geartrain assembly into the case from the rear, as shown in Figure 50-22.

Bolt the extension housing to the transmission case. Push the input shaft and snap ring into the case. Install the front bearing retainer and a new gasket. Move the third/fourth synchronizer assembly to the neutral position. Move the first/second synchronizer assembly and the side-cover shifting forks to engage second gear. Move the rearward fork into second-gear position. Install the side cover and a new gasket. Tighten the side-cover bolts, and the transmission is ready to be installed (see Figure 50-23).

Replace Transmission

The steps for installing a manual transmission are in almost the exact reverse order from those used in removal. The automobile should be on a hoist with the engine or bellhousing supported. Be sure the alignment pins are in place in the upper bolt holes.

Lift the transmission with a jack. Align the dowels, which will carry the weight of the transmission before the input-shaft splines are aligned.

Rock the transmission and push it forward until the input shaft splines engage with the clutch hub. Tighten the lower transmission bolts, remove the dowels, and insert and tighten the upper bolts.

Install and tighten the transmission crossmember. Hook up the emergency brake linkage. Install the gearshift linkage, exhaust parts, backup light switch, and speedometer cable. Install the driveline, as discussed in Topic 48.3.

The vehicle now is ready for road testing to check the repair.

SAFETY CAUTION: Before beginning a road test, buckle your safety belt and test the brakes to be sure they are functioning properly. Drive carefully and only in a manner required to determine if the problem has been corrected. Obey all traffic laws.

UNIT HIGHLIGHTS

- Transmission lubrication and preventive maintenance are conducted at regular intervals.
- Diagnosis first is conducted to determine whether the problem is being caused by the transmission or another drivetrain assembly.
- A series of cables and linkages need to be removed before the transmission can be disconnected.
- Transmission removal requires special jacks and supporting tools.
- A manual transmission is placed on a workbench and disassembled in a specific order.
- Cleaning and inspection of transmission parts are keys to proper diagnosis.
- Transmission reassembly is performed in a specific order.
- A road test will determine if the problem has been corrected.

TERMS

fill plug
drain plug
grease points
gear clash

speedometer cable
transmission
crossmember

R E V I E W   Q U E S T I O N S

DIRECTIONS: The following questions are similar to those used on mechanic certification tests. On a separate sheet of paper, write the letter of the correct choice.

1. Preventive maintenance procedures for manual transmissions include
A. adding lubricant when the dipstick reads low.
B. adjusting shift lever travel.
C. lubricating synchronizer assemblies.
D. lubricating shift lever assemblies.

2. Which of the following statements is correct?
   I. Transmission noises also are called driveline or differential noises.
   II. Gear clash is a noise created when the driver shifts too quickly from one gear to another.
A. I only   B. II only   C. Both I and II   D. Neither I nor II

3. The following procedures are performed when removing a manual transmission EXCEPT
A. draining the transmission oil.
B. cleaning the torque converter.
C. unplugging the backup light.
D. removing bolts that hold the transmission support to the crossmember.

4. Mechanic A says that alignment pins hold the transmission to the bellhousing.
   Mechanic B says that the speedometer drive gear and the reverse idler gear are pressed off using a hydraulic press.
   Who is correct?
A. A only   B. B only   C. Both A and B   D. Neither A nor B

5. After disassembling a manual transmission, the next important step of servicing is
A. spinning the bearings with compressed air.
B. cleaning and inspecting parts.
C. bolting the extension housing to the bellhousing.
D. aligning the input shaft splines.

S U P P L E M E N T A L   A C T I V I T I E S

1. Check the lubricant level of a manual transmission.
2. Drain and fill the transmission on a vehicle selected by your instructor.
3. Check a designated shop vehicle and identify which parts of the gearshift linkage are to be lubricated.
4. Identify the type of transmission noise and possible cause of that noise on a vehicle selected by your instructor.
5. On an automobile that is to have the linkage removed, locate the backup light switch and speedometer cable.
6. Remove a transmission from a shop vehicle.
7. Disassemble a transmission.
8. Clean and inspect the parts of a transmission.
9. Reassemble a transmission and place it back in the automobile.

51 THE CLUTCH

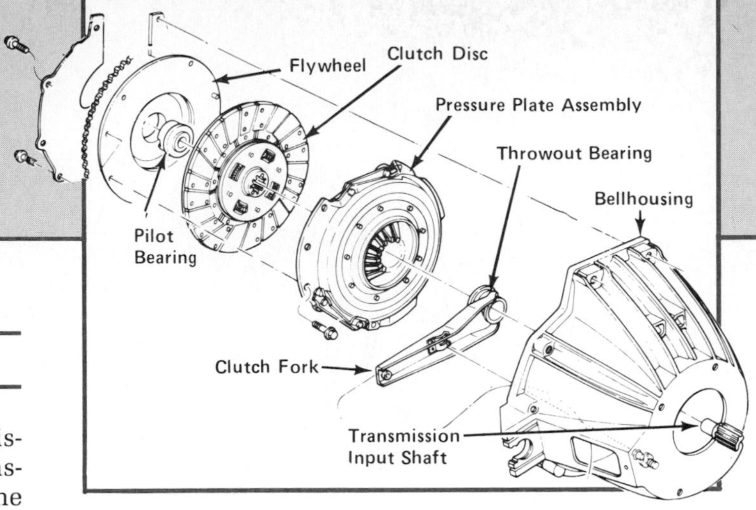

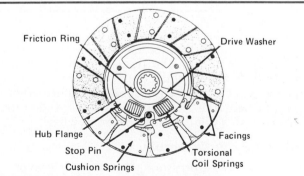

Figure 51-1. Clutch assembly. FORD MOTOR COMPANY

UNIT PREVIEW

A dry clutch, used only with a manual transmission, is located between the engine and transmission. The clutch couples and uncouples engine power from the transmission. The driver operates the clutch by using a foot pedal in the passenger compartment. This unit discusses the parts of a clutch and how those parts transmit engine power to the transmission.

LEARNING OBJECTIVES

When you have completed your assignments and exercises in this unit, you should be able to:

☐ Explain how engine power is transferred by the clutch disc to the transmission.

☐ Describe the parts of a pressure plate assembly.

☐ Describe coil-spring and diaphragm-spring pressure plate assemblies.

☐ Describe the operation of the throwout bearing and clutch fork.

☐ Identify the three different types of clutch linkages: rod and lever, cable, and hydraulic.

51.1 CLUTCH DESIGN

The clutch is located between the transmission and the engine. The clutch allows the driver to connect or disconnect power from the engine to the transmission. The clutch also allows the driver to shift smoothly and to start the engine. A clutch assembly contains several parts:

- Flywheel
- Clutch disc
- Pressure plate assembly
- Throwout bearing
- Clutch fork.

A clutch assembly is shown in Figure 51-1. All parts of the clutch, except linkage and pedal, are enclosed in a *bellhousing*. A bellhousing is a protective metal case shaped like a bell. The large end of the case is connected to the engine block. The small end is connected to the transmission housing.

Flywheel

The flywheel is an important part of the engine. See Unit 10. The flywheel also is the main driving member of the clutch. The rear surface of the flywheel is smooth and provides a good gripping surface for proper clutch operation. Holes are drilled into the flywheel surface where other parts of the clutch are attached.

Clutch Disc

A *clutch disc*, also called a *clutch plate*, is a driven member that receives engine power from the flywheel. The clutch disc transfers engine power to the transmission. The clutch disc is a thin, steel disc that is covered with a friction material. The friction material grips the flywheel when the clutch is coupled, or engaged. The flywheel and clutch disc separate when the clutch is uncoupled, or disengaged.

The friction facing on the clutch disc is riveted or *bonded*. Bonded material is held in place with an adhesive. Separate metal parts under the friction material, called *cushioning springs,* absorb shock when the clutch is engaged. *Torsional coil springs* around the hub absorb torsional vibrations and help the clutch disc rotate smoothly. Stop pins limit this torsional movement. A clutch disc and its parts are shown in Figure 51-2.

Figure 51-2. Parts of a clutch disc assembly.
CHEVROLET MOTOR DIVISION—GMC

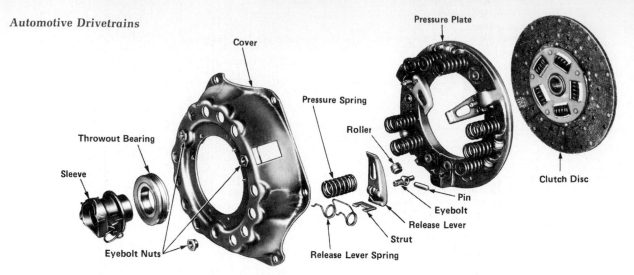

Figure 51-3. Pressure plate assembly. CHRYSLER CORPORATION

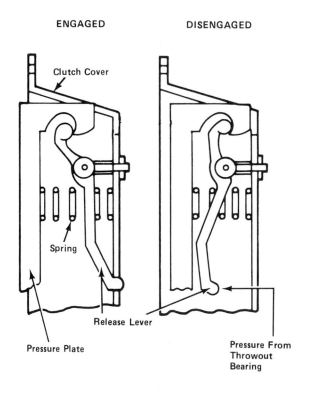

Figure 51-4. Coil-spring clutch assembly release lever action.

The clutch disc is aligned with the flywheel by the transmission input shaft and a pilot bearing. The input shaft comes from the transmission and passes through the center, or *hub,* of the clutch disc. The input shaft and clutch disc are splined together. After it passes through the clutch disc, the end of the input shaft fits into a pilot bearing in the flywheel.

Pressure Plate Assembly

The purpose of the *pressure plate assembly* is to press the clutch disc tightly against the flywheel. The pressure plate assembly also must be able to release,

or disengage, the clutch disc so that it can stop rotating. To do this job, the pressure plate assembly, shown in Figure 51-3, has the following parts:

- Cover
- Pressure plate
- Release levers
- Spring, or springs.

The steel cover bolts to the flywheel and acts as a housing to hold the parts together.

The *pressure plate* is a heavy, flat ring made of *nodular iron.* Nodular iron contains graphite, which acts as a lubricating agent. The surface of the pressure plate, where it contacts the clutch disc, is smooth. The smooth surface gives the clutch disc a good area for gripping.

Release levers are positioned around the cover. Three release levers usually are used. Release levers "release" the holding power of the springs.

Two types of springs are used in pressure plate assemblies: coil springs and diaphragm springs.

Coil spring pressure plate assembly. Helical springs, or *coil springs,* are made of wire that is wound into rings or spirals. Coil springs in a pressure plate assembly are spaced evenly around the inside of the cover. As the springs contract and expand, the pressure plate moves in and out. Release levers direct the action of the springs. (See Figure 51-4.)

The springs are extended when the clutch is engaged. The pressure plate is squeezed against the clutch disc. This forces the clutch disc against the flywheel. The springs are released when the clutch is disengaged. The release levers are moved, the springs are compressed, and the pressure plate is pulled away from the clutch disc and flywheel.

Diaphragm spring pressure plate assembly. A *diaphragm spring* is a single, thin sheet of metal that works much the same as the bottom of an oil can.

When pressure is applied to the bottom of the oil can, the metal yields to the pressure. When pressure is released, the bottom of the oil can returns to its original position.

On a pressure plate assembly, the diaphragm spring is placed between the cover and the pressure plate. The center portion of the diaphragm is slit into numerous fingers that act as release levers. Figure 51-5 shows a diaphragm pressure plate assembly.

When the clutch is engaged, the diaphragm spring is almost flat at the center. At the outer rim, the spring is moved outward and the pressure plate is forced against the clutch disc.

When the clutch is disengaged, the fingers are moved against the diaphragm spring and force the outer rim inward. This action pulls the pressure plate from the clutch disc.

Throwout Bearing Assembly

The release bearing, or *throwout bearing,* is a prelubricated ball bearing. The throwout bearing is pressed onto a sleeve, or collar, that fits into the yoke of the clutch fork. The relationship of the throwout bearing and clutch fork is shown in Figures 51-6 and 51-7.

The throwout bearing rotates when the release levers rotate. To engage and disengage, the throwout bearing is moved in and out. When the clutch is engaged, the throwout bearing does not touch the release levers. When the clutch is disengaged, the throwout bearing is pushed against the release levers. Throwout bearing movement is controlled by the clutch fork.

Clutch Fork

The *clutch fork* is a lever that pivots in an opening in the bellhousing. The small end of the clutch fork protrudes from the bellhousing and is connected to the clutch linkage. The linkage acts on the clutch fork to move the throwout bearing into or away from the pressure plate assembly.

51.2 CLUTCH VARIATIONS

Two other types of clutches are found in some automobiles. These variations are the semi-centrifugal clutch and the double-disc clutch. Double-disc clutches, used primarily in heavy-duty trucks, are not discussed here.

Semi-Centrifugal Clutch

A *semi-centrifugal clutch* assembly uses *centrifugal force* to increase force against the pressure plate. Centrifugal force is an outward pull from the center of a rotating axis.

Lighter spring pressures can make clutch pedal operation easier. The centrifugal force also produces greater spring pressure as clutch speed increases.

The release levers on a semi-centrifugal clutch are reshaped. Weights are added to the outer ends of the

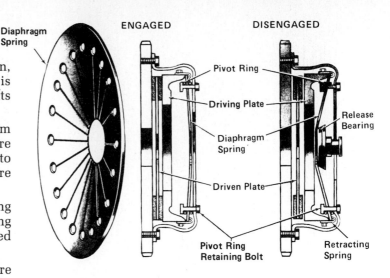

Figure 51-5. Diaphragm-spring clutch assembly.
CHEVROLET MOTOR DIVISION—GMC

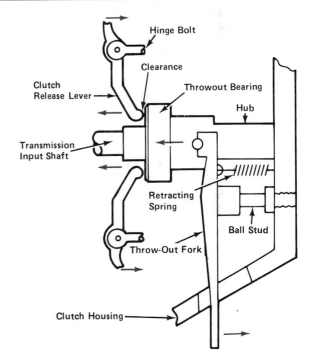

Figure 51-6. Throwout bearing assembly action. Arrows indicate clutch assembly movement.

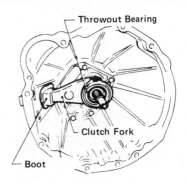

Figure 51-7. Clutch fork and throwout bearing location in bellhousing. NISSAN MOTOR CORPORATION

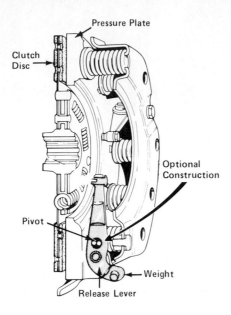

Figure 51-8. Semi-centrifugal clutch pressure plate assembly.
FORD MOTOR COMPANY

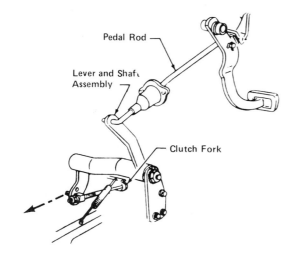

Figure 51-9. Rod and lever linkage. BUICK MOTOR DIVISION—GMC

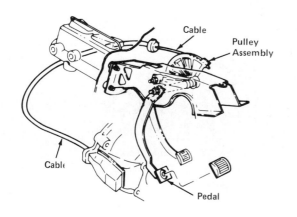

Figure 51-10. Cable linkage. FORD MOTOR COMPANY

release levers. As clutch speed increases, the weights are forced outward by centrifugal force and act against the pressure plate. This force is added to that of the springs. A semi-centrifugal clutch is shown in Figure 51-8.

51.3 CLUTCH LINKAGE

Through a series of parts, the *clutch linkage* is connected from the clutch pedal to the clutch fork. In addition to operating the clutch fork, the linkage provides leverage to help compress the pressure plate springs.

Clutch linkage may be mechanical or hydraulic. The basic types of clutch linkage are:

- Rod and lever
- Cable
- Hydraulic.

Rod and Lever Linkage

Rod and lever linkage is a series of rods and levers that are connected to operate the clutch. Figure 51-9 shows a typical rod and lever linkage system.

A pedal rod connects the clutch pedal to a lever on the *lever and shaft assembly*. The lever and shaft assembly has two levers connected to one shaft. When one lever is moved, the shaft moves the second lever. The bottom lever in Figure 51-9 is connected to a pushrod. When the bottom lever is moved, the pushrod is moved against the clutch fork. The lever and shaft assembly is located between the chassis and the engine block, at the left rear of the block.

Cable Linkage

Cable linkage has a flexible, protective housing that covers a wire cable. At one end, the wire cable is connected to the clutch pedal. At the other end, the wire cable is connected to the clutch fork, as shown in Figure 51-10.

The clutch pedal action determines whether the clutch cable is pulled or pushed to operate the clutch fork.

Hydraulic Linkage

Movement from the clutch pedal to the clutch fork can be determined by *hydraulic linkage*. In hydraulic linkage, hydraulic pressure transmits motion from one cylinder to another through a connecting tube, or hydraulic line. See Figure 51-11.

When the clutch pedal is depressed, the piston inside the master cylinder is moved forward by the pushrod. Hydraulic fluid, under pressure, is pushed through the hydraulic line and into the slave cylinder. When fluid enters the slave cylinder, it is pressed against the slave cylinder piston. The piston is moved against a pushrod connected to the clutch fork.

When the clutch pedal is released, hydraulic fluid is directed back to the master cylinder reservoir.

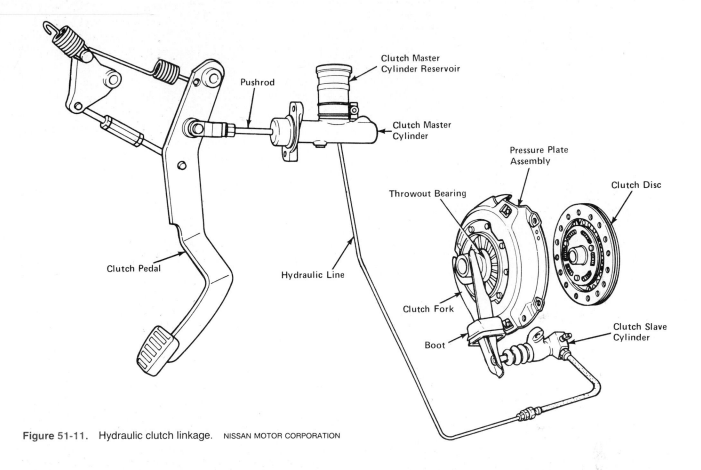

Figure 51-11. Hydraulic clutch linkage. NISSAN MOTOR CORPORATION

U N I T   H I G H L I G H T S

- A clutch allows the driver to start and stop the automobile, and to shift the automobile easily.
- The main parts of the clutch are contained in a bellhousing.
- A clutch disc takes power from the flywheel and furnishes power to the transmission.
- A pressure plate assembly squeezes the clutch disc against the flywheel.
- Coil springs and diaphragm springs are used for pressure plate assemblies.
- A throwout bearing and clutch fork control spring action inside a pressure plate assembly.
- Clutch linkage is connected from the clutch pedal to the clutch fork.
- Rod and lever, cable, and hydraulic clutch linkages are used.

T E R M S

bellhousing
clutch disc
clutch plate
bonded
cushioning springs
torsional coil springs
hub
pressure plate assembly
pressure plate
nodular iron
release levers
coil springs

diaphragm spring
throwout bearing
clutch fork
semi-centrifugal clutch
centrifugal force
clutch linkage
rod and lever linkage
lever and shaft
    assembly
cable linkage
hydraulic linkage

R E V I E W   Q U E S T I O N S

DIRECTIONS: The following questions are similar to those used on mechanic certification tests. On a separate sheet of paper, write the letter of the correct choice.

1. A clutch disc is made up of all of the following parts EXCEPT
A. a splined hub.
B. a throwout bearing.
C. torsional coil springs.
D. facing.

2. A pressure plate assembly comes in contact with the
A. intermediate flywheel.
B. throwout bearing.
C. clutch plate.
D. flywheel.

3. Mechanic A says a diaphragm-spring pressure plate squirts the clutch with oil, just like an oil can. Mechanic B says that a throwout bearing rides inside of a sleeve. Who is right?
A. A only   B. B only   C. Both A and B   D. Neither A nor B

4. Which of the following statements is correct?
   I. A semi-centrifugal clutch uses reshaped weights on the release levers.
   II. Double-disc clutches are used in large trucks.
A. I only   B. II only   C. Both I and II   D. Neither I nor II

5. All of the following statements about clutch linkages are true EXCEPT
A. They connect the clutch pedal to the clutch fork.
B. A lever and shaft assembly is one of the parts.
C. Hydraulic pressure can operate the linkage.
D. Rods and levers hold the cable housing.

S U P P L E M E N T A L   A C T I V I T I E S

1. List the parts of the clutch located inside the bellhousing.
2. Identify the parts of a clutch disc.
3. Identify coil-spring and diaphragm-spring pressure plate assemblies and describe how they operate.
4. Describe how a throwout bearing operates when it is engaged and disengaged.
5. Explain the differences between a conventional clutch and a semi-centrifugal clutch.
6. Identify the three types of clutch linkages.

52 CLUTCH SERVICE

The clutch may take more abuse than any other drivetrain assembly. For this reason, the clutch should be checked frequently.

Preventive maintenance for the clutch consists of periodic clutch linkage checks, lubrication, and adjustment.

Clutch service is a simple, but demanding, task that requires removing the transmission and other drivetrain parts. This unit discusses preventive maintenance and overhaul of the clutch.

LEARNING OBJECTIVES

When you have completed your assignments and exercises in this unit, you should be able to:
- ☐ Describe free travel and how it is measured.
- ☐ Explain how to adjust a clutch with cable linkage.
- ☐ Explain the diagnosis procedures for pedal pulsation, slipping, drag, and chatter.
- ☐ Describe procedures for inspecting all clutch parts.
- ☐ Disassemble and reassemble a clutch assembly.

SAFETY PRECAUTIONS

Clutch service involves two major hazards: asbestos fibers and the removal of several very heavy assemblies. The dust and dirt inside the bellhousing and on the clutch assembly contain asbestos fibers that are a health hazard. Do *not* blow this dust off with compressed air. Any dust should be removed with a special vacuum cleaner designed for use with asbestos fibers. When emptying the vacuum cleaner, do it in such a way that the dust does not escape into the air. Use proper ventilation equipment when servicing clutch parts.

Clutch preventive maintenance and service require that the vehicle be raised and supported safely. *Never* work under a vehicle unless you are absolutely sure that it cannot move or fall. No type of jack is meant to support the weight of a vehicle safely. Safety stands, or jackstands, must be used if the vehicle is not raised on a hoist.

Jackstands and special jacks are used to support the engine and transmission. These parts are very heavy, so it is necessary to have a helper assist in their removal. Use extra care during removal. These parts have many sharp edges that can cut easily.

The underside of an automobile is dirty. Dirt or foreign objects can fall into your eyes during service procedures. Safety glasses or goggles must be worn to protect the eyes from injury.

Many troubleshooting procedures require that the automobile be operated in the shop area. Always place *wheel chocks* against the wheels. Wheel chocks are blocks designed to be wedged against wheels to prevent accidental movement of a vehicle. Be sure the work area is properly ventilated, or attach a ventilating hose to the vehicle's exhaust system whenever operating an automobile indoors. Do *not* allow anyone to stand in front of or behind the automobile while its engine is running.

Exhaust systems become very hot. Working around the transmission and clutch may put you in contact with these parts. Let the vehicle cool down to avoid the danger of serious burns.

52.1 PREVENTIVE MAINTENANCE

Clutch preventive maintenance includes lubrication and linkage adjustment.

Lubricating Clutch Linkage

Clutch linkage is lubricated with grease or oil on a regular basis, usually during a chassis lubrication. The same grease used for U-joints is acceptable for many clutch linkages. Always consult an owner's manual, service manual, or lubrication chart to determine the proper lubricant.

Lubricate clutch linkage at all sliding surfaces and pivot points in the linkage. After lubrication, the linkage should move freely. Some linkages, or linkage parts, may need only a lubricating oil. This lubricating oil is applied with a squirt can. Typical lubrication points are shown in Figure 52-1.

On automobiles with hydraulic linkages, always check the hydraulic fluid level. It should be approximately ¼ in. [6.35 mm] from the top. If the fluid is low, check for leaks. Follow manufacturer's recommendations if fluid must be added.

Clutch Linkage Adjustment

Clutch linkage adjustment (clutch adjustment) is required as the clutch linkage or clutch disc wears.

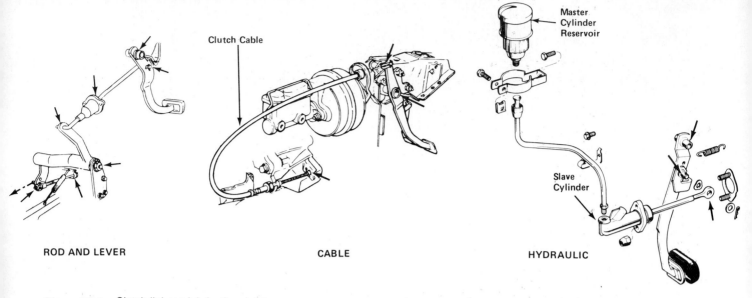

Figure 52-1. Clutch linkage lubrication points. BUICK MOTOR DIVISION—GMC/FORD MOTOR COMPANY/AMERICAN MOTORS CORPORATION

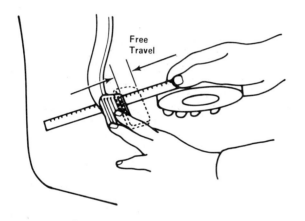

Figure 52-2. Measuring free travel.

Clutch adjustment is performed to maintain a specified clearance between the throwout bearing and the pressure plate assembly. This distance is not included in service manual specifications. However, correct clearance can be ensured if the clutch pedal has the correct amount of free play, or *free travel*. Free travel is the distance a clutch pedal moves when depressed, before slack is taken up in the clutch linkage. When the clutch pedal is depressed, there should be some free movement before resistance is felt. Free travel measure may not be required for automobiles with hydraulic linkages. Always check the manufacturer's service recommendations.

To measure free travel, use a tape measure or ruler. Place one end of the tape measure or ruler on the floor of the automobile, as shown in Figure 52-2. Note the reading. This reading is the height of the fully extended clutch.

Next, hold the tape measure or ruler and push down with one finger until resistance is felt. Note the reading on the tape measure or ruler. The difference between the two measurements is the amount of free travel.

A clutch adjustment may not be part of a scheduled maintenance program. However, free travel should be checked on a regular basis. Adjustment should be performed when free travel is not correct, or when the clutch does not engage or disengage properly.

Clutch adjustments may be similar among rod and lever, cable, and hydraulic linkage systems. However, variations do exist, so check the proper service manual before you proceed. Cable linkage is used extensively in modern automobiles. See Figure 52-3 for a typical cable assembly.

Clutch adjustments are made either from under the automobile or from under the hood. Follow the necessary safety practices when raising and working under the automobile.

Clean the linkage with a shop towel. A cleaning solvent may be necessary. Check the linkage and replace any damaged or missing parts. On automobiles with hydraulic linkage systems, check for leaks. Adjust the linkage according to the manufacturer's specifications.

52.2 DIAGNOSING CLUTCH PROBLEMS

Before you plunge into diagnosing a clutch problem, check clutch pedal free travel. If free travel is not within specifications, adjust the clutch before proceeding. Many clutch problems simply involve improper adjustment. Also, check the clutch linkage for damage or missing parts.

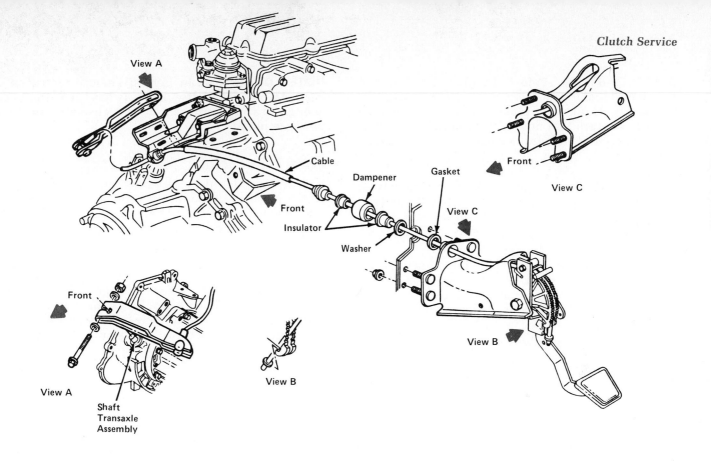

View A

View C

Cable

Dampener

Gasket

Front

View C

Front

Insulator

Washer

View B

Front

View A

Shaft
Transaxle
Assembly

View B

Figure 52-3. Parts of cable linkage used during adjustment. CHEVROLET MOTOR DIVISION—GMC

The most common clutch problems are found in the following categories:

- Slippage
- Drag
- Chatter
- Pedal pulsation
- Vibration
- Noises.

Slippage

When the speed of the car does not match the speed of the engine, *clutch slippage* is indicated. Slippage occurs during acceleration, upshifts, and/or downshifts.

The clutch can be checked for slippage during a test drive.

SAFETY CAUTION: Before beginning a test drive, buckle safety belt and check brake operation. Drive only enough to determine the problem. Drive safely and obey all traffic laws.

First, drive the automobile enough to warm up the clutch. Acceleration from a stop and several gear changes will indicate whether the clutch is slipping.

Slippage also can be checked in the shop.

SAFETY CAUTION: Block the front wheels with wheel chocks. Set the parking brake and place the gearshift lever in neutral. Be sure that no one is standing in front of the automobile during this test because the vehicle could move.

Start the engine and let it run until the temperature indicator on the dashboard indicates a normal operating temperature. Manufacturers differ in the procedures they recommend to test for clutch slippage. For all tests, use procedures from the proper service manual. An example follows:

Shift the transmission into high gear and increase engine speed to about 2,000 rpm. Release the clutch pedal slowly until the clutch is fully engaged. The engine should stall immediately. Do *not* keep the clutch engaged for more than five seconds at a time. Clutch parts could become overheated and damaged.

If the engine does *not* stall within a few seconds, raise the automobile on a hoist. Check the clutch linkage. If no clutch linkage problems are found, the clutch must be disassembled.

Clutch slippage is caused by an oil-soaked or worn disc facing, warped pressure plate, or weak diaphragm spring. Both the clutch disc and pressure plate should be replaced. It is general practice also to replace the throwout bearing whenever replacing major internal clutch components.

Drag

Clutch drag occurs when the clutch disc and input shaft do not completely stop when the clutch pedal is depressed fully. Clutch drag can cause gear clash when shifting into reverse. Clutch drag also can cause hard starting.

SAFETY CAUTION: Before checking clutch drag in the shop, block the wheels with wheel chocks. Set the parking brake and place the gearshift lever in neutral. Be sure that no one is standing in front of the automobile during this test because the vehicle could move.

The clutch disc, input shaft, and transmission gears should require no more than five seconds to come to a complete stop after disengagement. This is known as clutch *spindown time*. It is normal and should not be mistaken for clutch drag.

Start the engine. Depress the clutch pedal completely. Shift the transmission into first gear. Do *not* release the clutch. Now, shift the transmission into neutral and wait 5–10 seconds. Shift the transmission into reverse.

If the shift into reverse causes gear clash, raise the vehicle on a hoist and check clutch linkage. If no defects are found, the clutch must be disassembled.

Clutch drag can be caused by a loose disc facing or by a warped disc or pressure plate. Binding can occur in the disc hub and in the release levers.

Chatter

Clutch chatter is a shaking or shuddering that is felt in the vehicle. Chatter usually occurs when the pressure plate first makes contact with the clutch disc. Chatter will stop when the clutch is fully engaged.

SAFETY CAUTION: If the clutch is being tested in the shop area, be sure no one stands in front of or behind the automobile. The automobile could move. Place chocks under the wheels. Set the emergency brake and place the gearshift lever in neutral.

Start the engine. Depress the clutch completely. Shift the transmission into first gear. Increase engine speed to about 1,500 rpm. Slowly release the clutch pedal. When the pressure plate first makes contact with the clutch disc, make a note of any clutch chatter. Then, depress the clutch pedal and reduce the engine speed.

SAFETY CAUTION: Do not release the clutch pedal, or the automobile might jump and cause serious injury. As soon as the clutch is partially engaged, depress the clutch pedal immediately.

Clutch chatter usually is caused by oil on the disc facing. A defective rear main oil seal in the engine often is the reason for this. Also look for broken engine mounts, loose bellhousing bolts, and damaged clutch linkage. During disassembly, check for a burned or glazed disc facing, warped pressure plate or flywheel, and worn input shaft splines. If the chattering is caused by an oil-soaked clutch disc, only the disc need be replaced.

NOTE: Determine how long this condition has existed. An oil-soaked disc probably has been slipping enough to cause grooves or heat checking on the pressure plate.

Pedal Pulsation

A rapid up-and-down pumping movement of the clutch pedal is called *clutch pedal pulsation*. Pedal movement usually is slight but can be seen in some cases. Clutch pedal pulsation occurs when the throwout bearing first touches, or is in contact with, the release levers or fingers.

SAFETY CAUTION: Before checking for clutch pedal pulsation in the shop, block the wheels with wheel chocks. Set the parking brake and place the gearshift lever in neutral. Make sure that no one stands in front of or behind the automobile because the vehicle could move.

Start the engine. Depress the clutch pedal slowly until the clutch just begins to disengage. Stop briefly. Then, continue depressing the clutch pedal slowly, and check for pulsation as the pedal is depressed to a full stop.

If any pulsation is felt, the clutch must be disassembled. Minor pulsation is considered normal on many automobiles.

Pedal pulsation is caused by misalignment of parts. Broken, bent, or warped release levers or fingers create misalignment. Check for a misaligned bellhousing, bent flywheel, and warped disc, pressure plate, or clutch cover.

Vibration

Clutch vibration can occur at any clutch pedal position. Usually, vibration occurs at normal engine operating speeds—over 1,500 rpm. Clutch-related vibrations are different from pedal pulsations. Clutch-pedal vibrations are not as rapid as pedal pulsations and can be felt throughout the automobile.

To check for clutch vibration, raise the automobile on a hoist. Check the engine mounts and look for any indication that engine parts are rubbing against the body or frame. Look for a damaged crankshaft vibration damper. Lower the automobile.

Remove the drive belts one at a time. Place the transmission in neutral, set the emergency brake, and follow all safety precautions. Start the engine after each belt is removed to see if accessories may be the cause. Do *not* run the engine for more than one minute when checking for vibrations with the belts removed.

The transmission will have to be removed before other clutch parts can be examined. Check for loose flywheel bolts, excessive flywheel runout, and pressure plate cover balance.

Noises

Many clutch noises are caused by bearing and bushing problems.

Throwout bearing noise is a whirring, grating, or grinding sound. It happens when the clutch pedal is depressed. Throwout bearing noise stops when the pedal is fully released.

Transmission input shaft or countershaft bearing noises also create whirring, grating, or grinding sounds. These noises are heard when the clutch is engaged or when the transmission is in gear. The noises are most noticeable in neutral with the clutch engaged.

Pilot bushing noises are squealing, howling, or trumpeting sounds. The noises are most noticeable in cold weather. They usually occur when the pedal is being depressed and the transmission is in neutral.

52.3 CLUTCH SERVICE

Removing and replacing the clutch in an automobile also requires the removal of the driveline and the transmission.

SAFETY CAUTION: Extreme caution must be used when working with any heavy parts. Special jacks are used to support the engine and transmission. These parts are very heavy, so you must have a helper to assist in their removal. Exhaust systems become very hot. Let the vehicle cool down before starting work. Always wear safety goggles or a face mask when working under an automobile.

Removing the Clutch

Raise the vehicle on a hoist. Clean excessive dirt, grease, or foreign material from around the clutch. Disconnect and remove the clutch linkage.

On rear-drive automobiles, remove the driveline (see Topic 48.3) and remove the transmission (see Topic 50.3). Depending on the automobile, the bellhousing is removed either with the transmission or after the transmission is removed.

On automobiles with transaxles, parts of the body and suspension must be removed, along with some exterior engine parts.

A variety of tools and procedures must be used when removing a clutch. Always refer to the proper service manual.

Once the bellhousing is off, the clutch assembly will remain bolted to the flywheel. Remove asbestos dust and dirt from the clutch assembly with a special vacuum cleaner. Mark the flywheel and clutch plate for proper reassembly (see Figure 52-4). Unbolt and remove the clutch assembly.

Inspection

Before disassembly, be sure all asbestos dust has been removed properly. Look for evidence of oil leaks on the clutch assembly, flywheel, and bellhousing.

After disassembly, examine the flywheel surface closely for discoloration, a mirror-like surface, scoring, cracks, or uneven wear.

The pilot bearing or bushing usually is replaced when the clutch has been disassembled. Pilot bearings or bushings should be smooth, with no signs of wear.

Do *not* touch the friction surface of the clutch disc. Grease from hands can contaminate the clutch lining. The friction facings must be uniform over the entire contact area. Check the splined hub for wear. Check for loose or broken hub springs, rivets, and cushioning plates.

The clutch disc wears more rapidly than any other part of the clutch assembly. Measure the thickness of the lining above the rivet heads for wear. See Figure 52-5. Bonded facing is measured for total thickness. Check the proper service manual for acceptable lining thickness. Always replace discs that are in questionable condition.

The clutch disc and pressure plate are replaced together. If one is damaged, both should be replaced.

Inspect the pressure plate surface for grooving, discoloration, mirror-like shine, cracks, and warping. To check a pressure plate for warping, set a straightedge across the surface, as shown in Figure 52-6. Use a feeler gauge to determine the largest gap, and compare this gap to specifications.

Release levers should be worn evenly where they contact the throwout bearing.

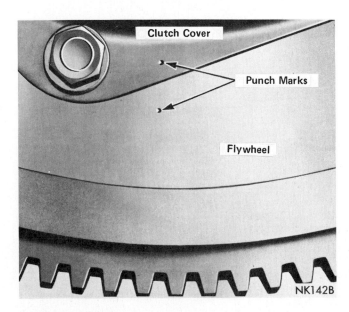

Figure 52-4. Clutch cover and flywheel matchmarks.
CHRYSLER CORPORATION

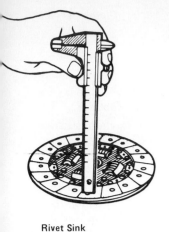

Rivet Sink

Figure 52-5.
Measuring clutch lining.
CHRYSLER CORPORATION

Figure 52-6.
Checking for pressure plate warpage.
FORD MOTOR COMPANY

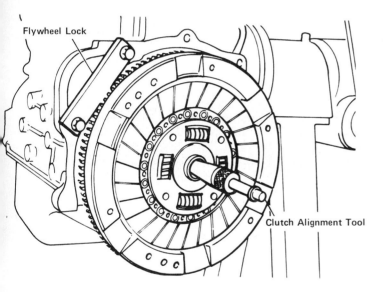

Flywheel Lock

Clutch Alignment Tool

Figure 52-7. Clutch alignment tool. MAZDA MOTOR CORPORATION

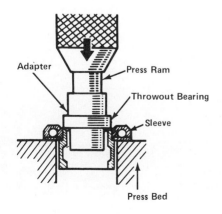

Adapter

Press Ram

Throwout Bearing

Sleeve

Press Bed

Figure 52-8. Installing a throwout bearing.
TOYOTA MOTOR SALES, U.S.A.

The throwout bearing usually is replaced whenever the transmission is disassembled. To check a throwout bearing, check for smooth operation and damage.

Inspect the clutch fork for wear on the throwout-bearing mount and on the linkage pivot. Also look for warping or bending.

Assembling and Replacing the Clutch

Grease the pilot bearing or bushing and tap it into the center of the flywheel. Place the clutch disc against the flywheel. Be sure the correct side of the clutch disc is against the flywheel. Insert an alignment tool, shown in Figure 52-7, to support the disc.

Line up the marks on the clutch cover and flywheel. Bolt the two parts together.

Throwout bearings usually are mounted in a sleeve. Clip the throwout bearing into the clutch fork. Some throwout bearings are driven or pressed out of a sleeve. Install a new bearing by pressing it into the sleeve as shown in Figure 52-8. Place small amounts of lubricant inside the hub and on the surface that contacts the release levers, or fingers.

Put a small amount of lubricant on the clutch fork pivot points. Install the clutch fork.

Install the bellhousing if it has been removed. Install the transmission (see Unit 50) or transaxle (see Unit 58), driveline (see Unit 48), and linkage systems.

U N I T   H I G H L I G H T S

- Parts of the clutch linkage are lubricated with grease or oil.

- Free travel is the measurement from the top of the clutch pedal until the pedal begins to have resistance.

- Clutch adjustments are made in the clutch linkage.

- Clutch problem diagnosis is made in the shop by operating the automobile under strict safety precautions.

- To remove the clutch, the transmission and driveline must be removed.

- Inspection requires that the mechanic check for discoloration, damage, and wear of all parts.

- It is important to lubricate some parts—but not all—during clutch reassembly and installation.

T E R M S

wheel chocks	spindown time
free travel	clutch chatter
clutch slippage	clutch pedal pulsation
clutch drag	clutch vibration

R E V I E W   Q U E S T I O N S

DIRECTIONS: The following questions are similar to those used on mechanic certification tests. On a separate sheet of paper, write the letter of the correct choice.

1. When making a clutch adjustment, it is necessary to
A. measure clutch pedal free travel.
B. lubricate the clutch linkage.
C. check hydraulic fluid level.
D. place the transmission in reverse.

2. Which of the following statements is true?
   I. Clutch slippage is most noticeable during acceleration and gear shifts.
   II. Clutch drag eliminates spindown time.
A. I only   B. II only   C. Both I and II   D. Neither I nor II

3. Mechanic A says that the bellhousing always must be removed after the transmission is removed.
   Mechanic B says that the pilot bearing or bushing and the throwout bearing usually are replaced when the clutch is disassembled.
   Who is correct?
A. A only   B. B only   C. Both A and B   D. Neither A nor B

4. Clutch inspection requires the following procedures EXCEPT
A. inspecting clutch disc springs.
B. measuring the depth of friction material.
C. looking for a mirror-like shine on the flywheel and pressure plate.
D. placing a straightedge across the clutch disc.

5. During reassembly and clutch replacement, the mechanic must
A. lubricate the pilot bearing.
B. align marks on the clutch cover and clutch disc.
C. support the clutch disc with one of the mounting bolts.
D. replace the pressure plate only if the clutch disc is undamaged.

S U P P L E M E N T A L   A C T I V I T I E S

1. Demonstrate how to use a special vacuum cleaner used for removing asbestos fibers from a clutch.
2. Explain where to lubricate the clutch linkage on a vehicle chosen by your instructor.
3. Measure free travel on a vehicle chosen by your instructor.
4. Explain the clutch noise that occurs on a vehicle chosen by your instructor, and how to diagnose the noise.
5. Describe the steps that are necessary to remove a clutch from a vehicle chosen by your instructor.
6. Explain what parts were found to be bad after inspection, and why.
7. Describe how to replace a throwout bearing in a sleeve, or collar.

53 THE AUTOMATIC TRANSMISSION

UNIT PREVIEW

An automatic transmission shifts gears automatically. To do this, it is designed to function both mechanically and hydraulically. The automatic transmission transfers power from the engine to the rest of the drivetrain by using a fluid coupling. This unit discusses how many different parts work together to accomplish "automatic" shifting.

LEARNING OBJECTIVES

When you have completed your assignments and exercises in this unit, you should be able to:

☐ Describe how a torque converter operates and improves simple fluid coupling.

☐ Explain how the various parts of a planetary gearset work together.

☐ Describe the function of apply devices and holding and driving members.

☐ Explain the function of a valve body.

☐ Describe the operation of a transmission cooling system.

☐ Describe the power flow through a transmission.

53.1 AUTOMATIC TRANSMISSION DESIGN

An automatic transmission receives signals from the engine output shaft and from the driver to shift into forward gears "automatically." An automatic transmission engages and disengages engine power without a manually operated clutch. Unlike a manual transmission, it also affects torque, or twisting force, from the engine. To perform all of these functions, an automatic transmission uses four main assemblies:

1. Torque converter (fluid coupling)
2. Planetary gearset
3. Apply devices
4. Hydraulic controls

The parts of an automatic transmission differ considerably from parts used in a manual transmission.

53.2 FLUID COUPLING

An automatic transmission accepts power from the engine through a fluid connection, or coupling. A simple *fluid coupling* consists of an *impeller* and a *turbine*.

See Figure 53-1. The impeller is bolted to the engine flywheel. The turbine is placed closely behind the impeller.

The impeller and turbine resemble two fans with blades, or vanes, that face each other. When one fan (impeller) is turned, it pushes fluid through the vanes of the second fan (turbine). The fluid passing through the vanes of the second fan force it to turn.

The impeller turns at engine speed. The turbine turns in response to fluid flow. Some power is lost, because the impeller can turn faster than the turbine. This slower action by the turbine is called *slippage*, or *slip*. To reduce slip in automatic transmissions, a torque converter is used.

53.3 TORQUE CONVERTER

A *torque converter* is a series of parts that reduce slip and multiply torque. A torque converter, shown in Figure 53-2, may have six separate parts:

1. Torque converter housing
2. Impeller
3. Turbine
4. Stator
5. Overrunning clutch
6. Lockup clutch assembly.

Torque Converter Housing

All parts of a torque converter are enclosed and sealed in a *torque converter housing*. The torque converter housing bolts to a *flexplate,* which bolts to the crankshaft. A flexplate/torque converter combination serves as the flywheel on cars with automatic transmissions. A flexplate is shown in Figure 53-3.

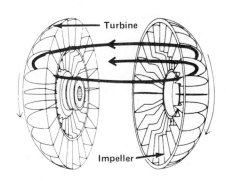

Figure 53-1. Fluid coupling.

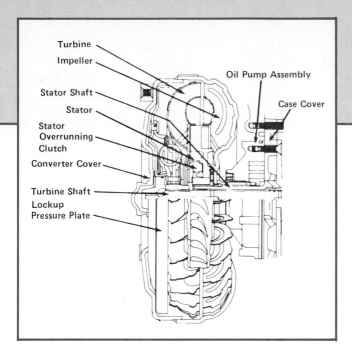

Figure 53-2. Parts of a torque converter assembly.
OLDSMOBILE DIVISION—GMC

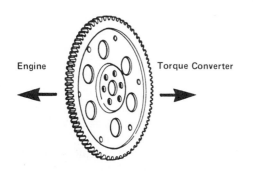

Figure 53-3. Flexplate. TOYOTA MOTOR SALES, U.S.A.

Impeller

In a torque converter, the impeller is mounted differently than in a simple fluid coupling. The impeller is part of the *rear* half of the torque converter housing. The torque converter housing is bolted to the flexplate and the flexplate to the crankshaft. Thus, the impeller still turns at engine speed.

The impeller is often called "the pump" because it pushes, or pumps, fluid inside the torque converter housing. The fluid is directed forward and toward the turbine. The impeller, however, is *not* "the oil pump." The oil pump is a separate part that builds up hydraulic pressure in an automatic transmission.

Turbine

The turbine spins inside the front half of the torque converter housing. Fluid from the impeller is pumped into the curved vanes on the outside of the turbine. The moving fluid strikes the turbine, causing the turbine to rotate (see Figure 53-4). The input shaft also

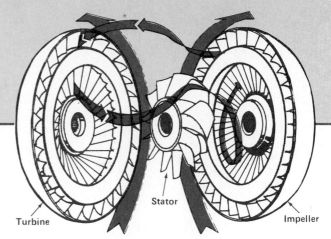

Figure 53-4. Turbine, stator, and impeller operation.
AMERICAN MOTORS CORPORATION

rotates because it is splined to the turbine hub. The rear of the input shaft is connected to the gears.

As the turbine rotates, the fluid that caused it to rotate falls to the center of the turbine. At the center of the turbine, the fluid passes through the stator.

Stator

When fluid is directed from the impeller to the turbine, the fluid flow is reversed. To correct the flow, a *stator* is placed between the impeller and turbine. A stator is shown in Figure 53-5. The vanes on the stator redirect fluid from the turbine to the impeller's direction of rotation. This change in fluid flow direction to match that of the impeller creates torque multiplication.

Overrunning Clutch

An *overrunning clutch*, or one-way clutch, allows the stator to rotate in only one direction. This assures that the stator will redirect fluid flow during low-speed operation. During higher-speed operation, the returning fluid from the turbine strikes the back side of the stator vanes. This causes the stator to rotate in a clockwise direction. The overrunning clutch is built into the hub of the stator.

Lockup System

Even during high-speed operation, the torque converter has a certain amount of slippage. To eliminate slip and improve efficiency, a *lockup system* may be used. A lockup system locks the turbine and the torque converter housing together.

The parts of a lockup system are a clutch friction material, a sliding clutch piston, and torsion springs. See Figure 53-6.

A typical converter lockup occurs when fluid is channeled through the input shaft and between the clutch piston and turbine. The fluid pressure forces the piston against the clutch friction material to lock the turbine to the impeller.

Some transmission systems use a thick silicone fluid to create lockup.

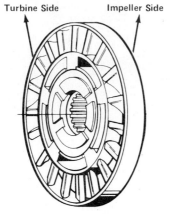

Figure 53-5. Stator. HYDRA-MATIC DIVISION—GMC

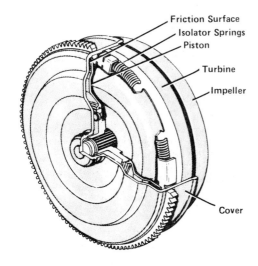

Figure 53-6. Lockup torque converter. CHRYSLER CORPORATION

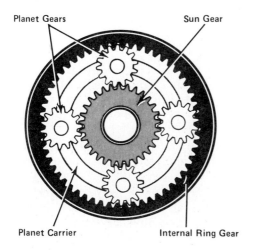

Figure 53-7. Simple planetary gearset.

53.4 PLANETARY GEARSET

An automatic transmission is shifted without disconnecting engine power from the transmission. To do this, an automatic transmission is equipped with one or more *planetary gearsets*. A gearset is a series of gears. A simple planetary gearset, shown in Figure 53-7, has the following parts:

- Sun gear
- Ring gear with internal teeth
- Planet gears
- Planet carrier.

A planetary gearset resembles the solar system. Planet gears orbit, or circle, the sun gear. Planet gears are held in place by the planet carrier and the ring gear. The ring gear surrounds, and meshes with, the planet gears.

In a planetary gearset, the teeth of each gear are meshed at all times with the teeth of another gear. This is known as a constant-mesh gearset. Whenever one gear, or part, is turned, all other gears and parts in the system are affected.

To transmit power through a planetary gearset, one gear, or part, turns as the *drive member*. Another part, called the *reaction member,* is held and prevented from moving. A third part becomes the *driven member,* or output member. The driven member transmits torque to the driveline.

All modern automatic transmissions have either two or three planetary gearsets linked together. These gearsets are called compound planetaries. A three-speed automatic has two planetary gearsets. A four-speed overdrive automatic transmission has three planetary gearsets. Each gearset is controlled by a common or separate sun gear. Figure 53-8 shows a sun gear that actually is a long tube splined to accept planetaries at both ends.

Planetary Gearset Power Flow

Planetary gears are used to change torque, change speed, and reverse direction of rotation. Planetary gears also provide a neutral and act as a coupling for direct drive. Direct drive is a 1:1 ratio between the transmission input and output shafts. This means that the two shafts are turning at the same speed.

Multiplying torque generally is known as *reduction*, because there is always a decrease in the speed of the output member. With a constant input speed, the output torque increases as the output speed decreases.

The following discussions describe the common forms of planetary gearset power flow.

Simple reduction. Simple reduction occurs when the sun gear is held and torque is applied to the ring gear in a clockwise direction. See Figure 53-9. In this case, the planetary pinions rotate in a clockwise direction and "walk" around the stationary sun gear. This causes the carrier assembly to rotate clockwise, in reduction.

Direct drive. Direct drive occurs when any two members of the planetary gearset rotate in the same direction at the same speed. This forces the third member to turn at the same speed. See Figure 53-10. In this condition, the pinions do not rotate on their axles. The pinions lock the entire unit together to form one rotating part.

Reverse. Reverse occurs whenever the carrier is held and power is applied to either the sun gear or the ring gear. This causes the planet pinions to drive the output member in the opposite direction. See Figure 53-11.

53.5 APPLY DEVICES

A planetary gearset is controlled by apply devices. An *apply device* applies force that actuates, holds, or drives other parts. Depending upon which apply device is activated, one member of a planetary gearset is held and another is driven.

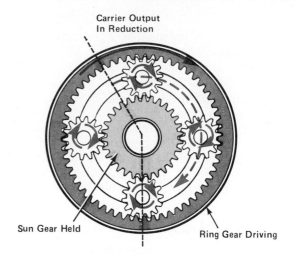

Carrier Output In Reduction

Sun Gear Held

Ring Gear Driving

Figure 53-9. Simple reduction.

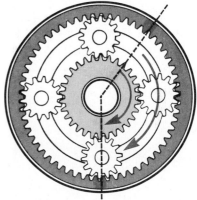

Sun Gear, Internal Gear, and Carrier Revolving in the Same Direction at the Same Speed. Pinions Do Not Revolve.

Figure 53-10. Direct drive.

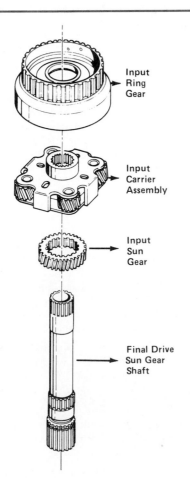

Input Ring Gear

Input Carrier Assembly

Input Sun Gear

Final Drive Sun Gear Shaft

Figure 53-8. Compound planetary sun gear.

HYDRA-MATIC DIVISION—GMC

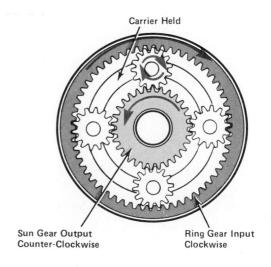

Carrier Held

Sun Gear Output Counter-Clockwise

Ring Gear Input Clockwise

Figure 53-11. Reverse gear.

Apply devices for planetary gearsets can be separated into two categories:

1. Hydraulic actuators
2. Holding and driving devices.

Hydraulic actuators, such as servos, and piston clutches, apply hydraulic pressure to activate holding and driving devices. The holding and driving devices, such as multiple-disc clutches, transmission bands, and overrunning clutches, apply mechanical force to gearsets.

Multiple-Disc Clutch

A *multiple-disc clutch* consists of a series of friction discs, or plates, sandwiched between steel discs (see Figure 53-12). Friction discs have rough gripping surfaces. Steel discs have smooth surfaces.

To lock a multiple-disc clutch, fluid pressure pushes a piston to compress a return spring. This forces the clutch plates against the pressure plate. When friction and steel discs are compressed against the pressure plate, the discs, input shaft, and drum rotate as a unit.

The clutch pack is released when fluid flow is stopped.

Transmission Band

A *transmission band,* also called a *brake band,* is a holding member. A transmission band is a flexible piece of metal wrapped around a clutch drum (see Figure 53-13). The inside of a transmission band has a friction surface that grips the clutch drum. The band is tightened to stop a clutch drum and is released to allow the drum to rotate freely.

Servo

A *servo* is an actuating device. It consists of a piston and rod in a hydraulic cylinder (see Figure 53-14). A servo activates a transmission band.

A transmission band has two lips, or flanges, at its open end. One flange fits into a slot in the transmission. The other flange is forced inward, toward the stationary flange, by a servo. The servo is operated by hydraulic pressure to control the action of the transmission band.

Piston Clutch

A *piston clutch* is an actuating device. It has a large cylinder fitted with a large flat piston. When pressure is applied to the piston, force from the piston is applied directly to the piston pressure plate (see Figure 53-15).

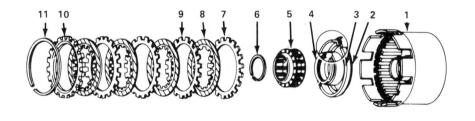

1. Reverse Input Housing
2. Reverse Input Outer Seal
3. Reverse Input Piston
4. Reverse Input Inner Seal
5. Reverse Input Spring Assembly
6. Reverse Input Spring Snap Ring
7. Reverse Input Plate (Waved)
8. Reverse Input Plate (Composition)
9. Reverse Input Plate (Steel)
10. Reverse Input Backing Plate
11. Reverse Input Snap Ring

Figure 53-12. Multiple-disc clutch assembly. CHEVROLET MOTOR DIVISION—GMC

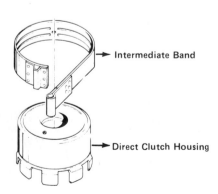

Figure 53-13. Transmission band assembly.
HYDRA-MATIC DIVISION—GMC

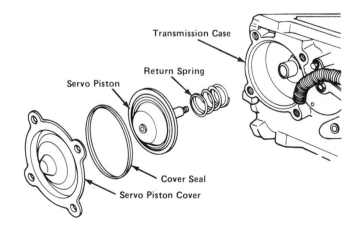

Figure 53-14. Servo assembly. FORD MOTOR COMPANY

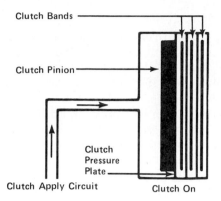

Figure 53-15. A piston clutch.

Figure 53-16. Accumulator assembly.

Accumulator

An *accumulator* is not, strictly speaking, an apply device. Rather, an accumulator acts as a shock absorber when a clutch, piston, or band is applied. When pressure enters a servo, the pressure also enters the accumulator, which cushions the application of clutches and bands. Parts of an accumulator are shown in Figure 53-16.

Overrunning Clutches

An overrunning clutch is used with a planetary gearset system. Its function is to prevent counter, or backward, rotation. An overrunning clutch has small, spring-loaded rollers. When the clutch is applied, these rollers are wedged between the drum and the hub to prevent counterclockwise rotation (see Figure 53-17).

53.6 HYDRAULIC PRINCIPLES

Liquids cannot be compressed, or squeezed into a smaller volume. For example, place a plunger into a tightly sealed cylinder filled with water (see Figure 53-18). When force is applied to the plunger, the plunger cannot squeeze the liquid into a smaller volume. The plunger pushes against the liquid, causing *pressure* to build up. Pressure is the amount of force pushing on each unit of the liquid's surface area. Pressure also is applied to all inner surfaces of the container.

Pressure is measured by dividing the force pushing on a liquid by the amount of surface area to which the force is applied. If the force on the plunger is 100 pounds, and the surface area of the plunger is 10 square inches, the pressure on the liquid is 100 pounds divided by 10 square inches, or 10 pounds per square inch (psi). To find pressure, divide the force by the area of the plunger, or piston, face.

Pressure is applied equally to every surface touched by the liquid. This relationship is known as Pascal's Law. This law states: Pressure applied on a confined liquid is transmitted equally in all directions and acts with equal force on equal areas.

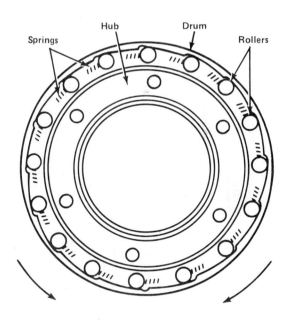

Figure 53-17. An overrunning clutch.

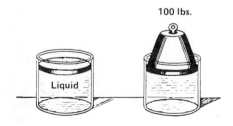

Figure 53-18. Liquid cannot be compressed, even when adding weight. PONTIAC MOTOR DIVISION—GMC

563

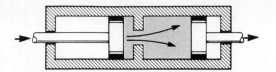

Figure 53-19. Liquid under pressure can be pushed from one cylinder to another by the use of pistons.

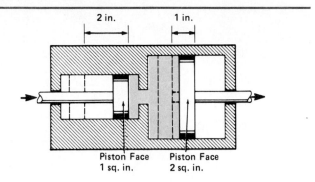

Figure 53-20. If the area between two cylinders and pistons is different, the larger piston will move less distance.

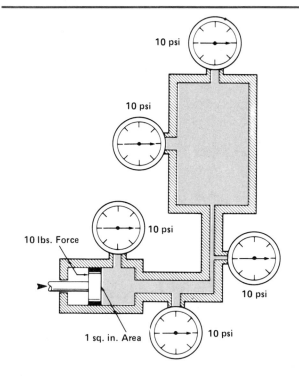

Figure 53-21. Pressure is the same throughout a sealed system.

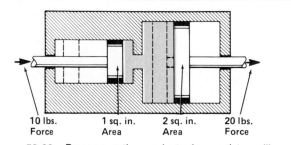

Figure 53-22. Pressure acting against a larger piston will increase the amount of force transferred.

Motion Transfer

Liquid under pressure can be made to do work. Connecting two piston and cylinder units together will allow liquid pressure to push against the second piston, causing it to move. See Figure 53-19. This is called *motion transfer*.

Moving one piston will push liquid into the second cylinder. If both pistons and cylinders are the same size, moving one piston will cause the other piston to move the same distance.

However, if one piston and cylinder have half the area of a connected piston and cylinder, the motion of the second piston will be less. Moving the smaller piston 2 inches will cause the larger piston to move only 1 inch (see Figure 53-20).

Pushing on a larger piston would transfer more liquid to the smaller cylinder. If the larger piston is pushed 2 inches, the smaller piston will move twice as far, or 4 inches.

The distance between cylinders has no effect. If the connecting tube and both cylinders are filled with fluid, both fluid and motion will be transferred.

Pressure Transfer

Pressure transfer occurs in a fluid-filled system. The pressure in a closed, sealed system is the same everywhere. If pressure gauges are attached at various points, they will all register the same pressure, as shown in Figure 53-21.

Force Transfer

Pressure in connected cylinders is the same. However, if the cylinders in a hydraulic system are of different sizes, different amounts of force will be exerted on the pistons. This is called *force transfer*.

Remember, pressure is measured in force per unit area, commonly in pounds per square inch (psi) or, in metric terms, kilopascals (kPa). Pounds per square inch are converted to kilopascals by multiplying psi by 6.895. Thus, a pressure of 10 psi is equal to 68.95 kPa in metric terms.

Suppose a 1-square-inch piston is connected by a passage or a tube to a 2-square-inch piston. The smaller piston has a 10-pound force acting on it. The pressure acting against the larger piston is 10 pounds per square inch. However, because the larger piston has 2 square inches of area, the pushing force is doubled. The total force pushing the larger piston is 10 pounds × 2, or 20 pounds (see Figure 53-22).

Pressure and Flow

Pressure can be generated only if there is some resistance to the flow of liquid. In a closed container, pressure is generated by the resistance of the walls of the container to the movement of the fluid. If a leak develops, pressure within the container drops.

In a system with separate cylinders connected by tubes or passages, the resistance of the cylinder pistons to movement and leakage causes pressure to build up.

53.7 HYDRAULIC CONTROLS

The hydraulic system controls all of the operations of an automatic transmission. The following discussions describe the various parts, components, and functions of the hydraulic control system.

Gearshift Controls

The gearshift lever for an automatic transmission may be located on the steering column or on the floor. An indicator near the gearshift lever always points to one of the shift positions, which may include:

Park (P)	Drive (D)
Reverse (R)	Second gear (2)
Neutral (N)	First gear
Overdrive (O)	(marked either 1 or L).

This series of letters, P-R-N-O-D-2-L, is called the *shift quadrant*. This type of quadrant would be found in an automobile equipped with a four-speed overdrive transmission. Variations of shift quadrants are shown in Figure 53-23.

Gearshift linkage for an automatic transmission is connected from the gearshift lever to a lever arm on the transmission. Either rod and lever or cable linkage is used with an automatic transmission, as shown in Figure 53-24.

A separate linkage system, called *kickdown linkage,* is used for downshifting the transmission without moving the gearshift lever. Kickdown linkage, or *throttle valve cable,* is connected with the throttle, or throttle pedal, and the transmission. Kickdown linkage can be mechanical (see Figure 53-25), cable (see Figure 53-26), or electric (see Figure 53-27). Kickdown occurs when the throttle pedal is depressed to the floor, such as in highway passing situations.

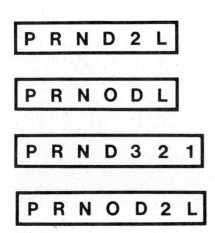

Figure 53-23. Shift quadrant variations.

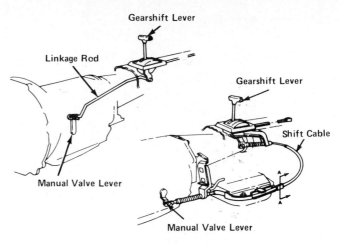

Figure 53-24. Shift linkage systems. FORD MOTOR COMPANY

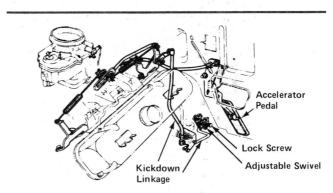

Figure 53-25. Mechanical kickdown linkage.
CHRYSLER CORPORATION

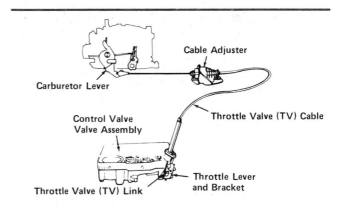

Figure 53-26. Cable kickdown linkage.
CHEVROLET MOTOR DIVISION—GMC

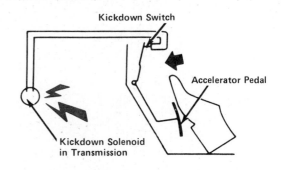

Figure 53-27. Electronic kickdown linkage.
NISSAN MOTOR CORPORATION

Automatic Transmission Fluids

The liquid used to operate hydraulic controls should have certain qualities. It must be able to transmit pressure, lubricate, cool, and have the proper *viscosity* to flow through the narrow orifices. Viscosity is the thickness or thinness of a fluid, its ability to resist flowing.

Automatic transmission fluid is a petroleum-based oil, similar to motor oil. Additives are mixed with the fluid to maintain viscosity and to help resist foaming, sludge and varnish buildup, and corrosion. The three common types of automatic transmission fluid, or ATF, are:

- DEXRON II
- Type F
- Ford Type CJ.

Each of these transmission fluids is quite different. They must not be interchanged. Follow manufacturer's specifications.

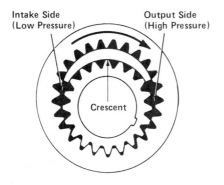

Figure 53-28. Gear and crescent oil pump operation.
CHEVROLET MOTOR DIVISION—GMC

Oil Pump

One of the most important components, or parts, of an automatic transmission is the *oil pump*. The oil pump creates pressure to operate apply devices and to circulate fluid throughout the system.

One oil pump is used. It is located just behind the torque converter and is driven by the torque converter. The pump will not operate unless the engine is running.

An oil pump is made up of a drive member, a driven member, and two pump body halves. The pump body halves contain passages that direct fluid to various parts of the transmission. Some oil pumps have other controls built into them.

All transmission oil pumps draw fluid from a reservoir and distribute the fluid throughout the hydraulic system. The three common types of oil pumps are:

1. Gear and crescent (see Figure 53-28)
2. Rotor (see Figure 53-29)
3. Vane type (see Figure 53-30).

Control Valves

A *valve body* is a housing that contains a maze of passages with valves to direct hydraulic pressures to the proper locations. A valve body is located inside the transmission oil pan (see Figure 53-31). A *separator plate,* or transfer plate, is placed between the two parts of the valve body. The separator plate helps to direct and connect fluid pressure (see Figure 53-32).

Control valving consists of pressure-regulating, balancing, and shifting valves located inside machined bores in the valve body. Hydraulic pressure is regulated for use in a particular hydraulic circuit.

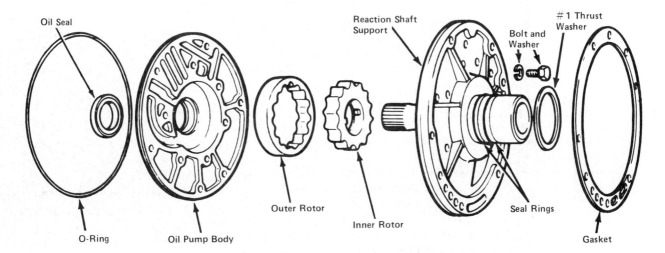

Figure 53-29. Rotor oil pump. AMERICAN MOTORS CORPORATION

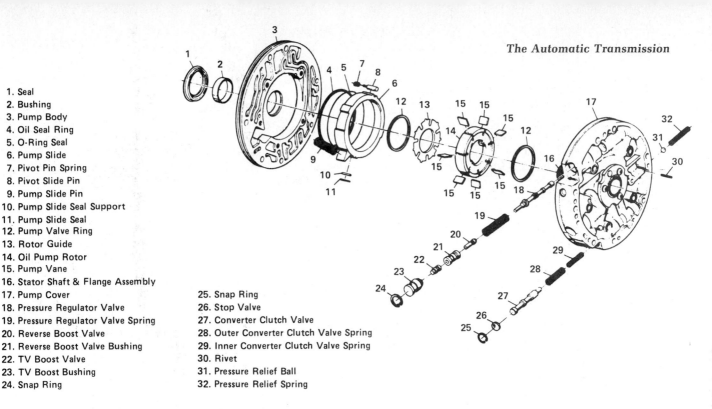

1. Seal
2. Bushing
3. Pump Body
4. Oil Seal Ring
5. O-Ring Seal
6. Pump Slide
7. Pivot Pin Spring
8. Pivot Slide Pin
9. Pump Slide Pin
10. Pump Slide Seal Support
11. Pump Slide Seal
12. Pump Valve Ring
13. Rotor Guide
14. Oil Pump Rotor
15. Pump Vane
16. Stator Shaft & Flange Assembly
17. Pump Cover
18. Pressure Regulator Valve
19. Pressure Regulator Valve Spring
20. Reverse Boost Valve
21. Reverse Boost Valve Bushing
22. TV Boost Valve
23. TV Boost Bushing
24. Snap Ring

25. Snap Ring
26. Stop Valve
27. Converter Clutch Valve
28. Outer Converter Clutch Valve Spring
29. Inner Converter Clutch Valve Spring
30. Rivet
31. Pressure Relief Ball
32. Pressure Relief Spring

Figure 53-30. Vane-type oil pump. CHEVROLET MOTOR DIVISION—GMC

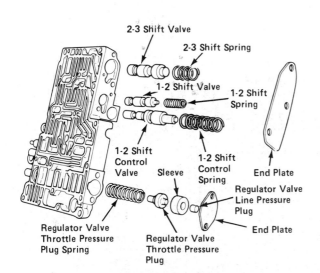

Figure 53-31. Valve body. AMERICAN MOTORS CORPORATION

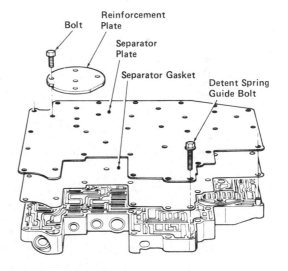

Figure 53-32. Separator plate. FORD MOTOR COMPANY

Four main types of fluid pressure are used in automatic transmissions:

1. Mainline pressure
2. Throttle pressure
3. Modulator pressure
4. Governor pressure.

Mainline pressure. Hydraulic pressure from the oil pump is regulated to prevent damage. This regulated pressure is called *mainline pressure.*

A *pressure regulator valve* controls pressure from the oil pump. The valve balances between a force exerted by a spring and a hydraulic force against the piston (see Figure 53-33).

When the gearshift lever is moved, it moves a *manual control valve.* A manual control valve is a directional control. See Figure 53-34. It directs fluid to other shifting and pressure-regulating valves and to apply devices.

An extra load on the engine requires higher hydraulic pressure for clutches and bands to ensure

The Automatic Transmission

567

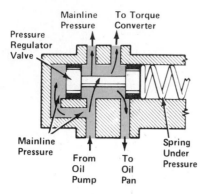

Figure 53-33. Pressure regulator valve assembly.

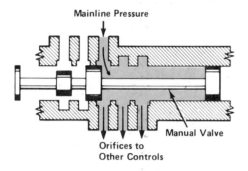

Figure 53-34. Manual control valve assembly.

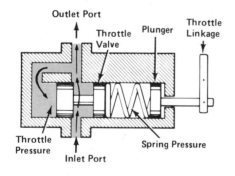

Figure 53-35. Throttle valve assembly.

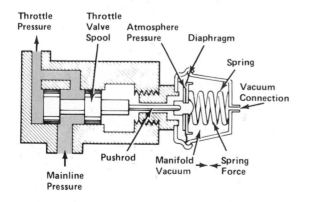

Figure 53-36. Vacuum modulator.

a stronger grip. A *booster valve* is used to raise mainline pressure during these circumstances. A booster valve is a balancing valve with a pressure-regulating spring.

Shifting valves route oil pressure to apply devices to engage the correct gear ratio for driving conditions. Shifting valves are operated by a combination of throttle pressure and governor pressure.

Throttle pressure. *Throttle pressure* is used to increase mainline pressure and to help control shifting. Throttle pressure increases and decreases with movement of the throttle.

Throttle pressure is regulated by a *throttle valve* (see Figure 53-35). A throttle valve is a balancing valve with a lever-regulated spring. A throttle valve can be either connected to the throttle linkage or operated by engine vacuum.

Vacuum modulator pressure. Engine vacuum also is used to exert pressure on the throttle valve spring. A vacuum-controlled diaphragm, or *vacuum modulator,* is controlled by vacuum from the engine intake manifold (see Figure 53-36). As the throttle is opened and closed, the vacuum modulator modulates, or changes, throttle pressure in response to engine load. High vacuum results in lower modulator pressure. Low vacuum results in higher modulator pressure.

Other valves also are used to control pressure. These valves may be called *downshift, dent,* or *kickdown valves.*

Governor pressure. *Governor pressure* is used to help upshift the transmission into the proper gear. Governor pressure and throttle or modulator pressure work against each other to produce upshifts or downshifts at the correct time.

A governor, illustrated in Figure 53-37, reduces mainline pressure in response to output shaft speed. Higher output shaft speed results in higher governor pressure and vice versa.

53.8 TRANSMISSION OIL COOLING

The actions of the torque converter, shafts, and gears heat the automatic transmission fluid. Excessive heat and friction will quickly damage an automatic transmission. A special cooling system is used with automatic transmissions. The system may have an internal or external cooler. Some vehicles are equipped with both types of coolers.

Internal Transmission Cooler

The engine radiator contains a small, sealed cooler that operates as an *internal transmission cooler.* Heated transmission fluid is pumped into that portion of the radiator, cooled, and returned to the transmission. The routing of internal cooler lines is shown in Figure 53-38.

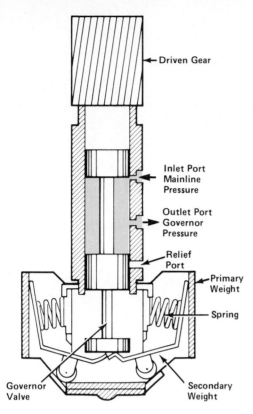

Figure 53-37.　Governor assembly.

Labels on Figure 53-37: Driven Gear; Inlet Port Mainline Pressure; Outlet Port Governor Pressure; Relief Port; Primary Weight; Spring; Governor Valve; Secondary Weight

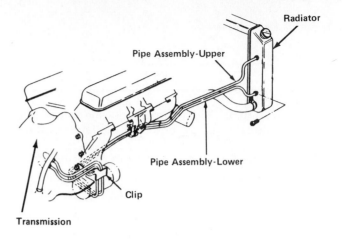

Figure 53-38.　Internal transmission cooler routing lines.
BUICK MOTOR DIVISION—GMC

Labels on Figure 53-38: Radiator; Pipe Assembly-Upper; Pipe Assembly-Lower; Clip; Transmission

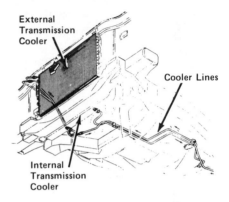

Figure 53-39.　External transmission cooler assembly.
CHRYSLER CORPORATION

Labels on Figure 53-39: External Transmission Cooler; Cooler Lines; Internal Transmission Cooler

External Transmission Cooler

A separate radiator may be used for an *external transmission cooler*. This cooling system is common on trucks and other vehicles that are subjected to heavy loads, such as towing. The transmission radiator is mounted outside the engine radiator, frequently just in front of it. Heated fluid usually runs through the internal cooler first and then through the external cooler before returning to the transmission. An external cooler is shown in Figure 53-39.

UNIT HIGHLIGHTS

- A fluid coupling transfers engine power to the transmission.
- A torque converter reduces slip and increases performance in an automatic transmission.
- A planetary gearset can change gear ratios and shift while it is meshed.
- Apply devices are holding and driving assemblies.
- Hydraulics can be controlled by changing the sizes of different valves.
- A valve body is a housing that contains a maze of passages and valves to direct hydraulic pressure.
- Four main types of fluid pressures are used in automatic transmissions.
- A transmission is cooled by circulating its fluid through a radiator.

TERMS

fluid coupling
impeller
turbine
slip
torque converter
torque converter
  housing
flexplate
stator
overrunning clutch
lockup system
planetary gearset
drive member
reaction member
driven member
apply device
multiple-disc clutch
transmission band
servo
piston clutch
accumulator
motion transfer
pressure transfer

force transfer
shift quadrant
kickdown linkage
throttle valve cable
automatic transmission
  fluid
oil pump
valve body
separator plate
mainline pressure
pressure regulator
  valve
manual control valve
booster valve
shifting valve
throttle pressure
throttle valve
vacuum modulator
governor pressure
internal transmission
  cooler
external transmission
  cooler

REVIEW QUESTIONS

DIRECTIONS: The following questions are similar to those used on mechanic certification tests. On a separate sheet of paper, write the letter of the correct choice.

1. All of the following statements are true EXCEPT
A. A fluid coupling consists of a torque converter and a flexplate.
B. A stator is placed between the impeller and the turbine.
C. An overrunning clutch turns in only one direction.
D. A lockup system locks the turbine and torque converter housing together.

2. A planetary gearset
A. operates the solar system.
B. is meshed when all gears are holding.
C. must have its own sun gear.
D. engages in direct drive when all three members are rotating.

3. Which of the following statements is correct?
   I. Multiple-disc clutches operate mechanically and hydraulically.
   II. A servo is a shock-absorbing component.
A. I only   B. II only   C. Both I and II   D. Neither I nor II

4. Mechanic A says that, according to hydraulic principles, pushing on a larger piston transfers more liquid to a smaller cylinder.
   Mechanic B says that pressure can be generated whenever there is a resistance to the flow of liquid. Who is correct?
A. A only   B. B only   C. Both A and B   D. Neither A nor B

5. All of the following statements about hydraulic pressure controls are correct EXCEPT
A. Mainline pressure is regulated.
B. A manual control valve operates only when the gearshift lever is moved.
C. A throttle valve is activated by vacuum.
D. A governor slows fluid flow.

SUPPLEMENTAL ACTIVITIES

1. Identify the parts of a torque converter.
2. Demonstrate how a lockup system operates.
3. Describe the parts of a planetary gearset.
4. Show how a transmission band and servo work together.
5. Explain one transfer of power described in Topic 53-6, Hydraulic Principles.
6. Describe the different types of shift quadrants.
7. Explain mainline pressure.
8. Identify a type of transmission cooling system chosen by your instructor.

54 AUTOMATIC TRANSMISSION SERVICE

UNIT PREVIEW

There are many different kinds of automatic transmissions. Each model has a slightly different way of working, and each is affected by other parts of the automobile. Because of the many different servicing procedures, a mechanic must rely on the proper service manual for guidance. Proper diagnosis of automatic transmission problems requires that many different tests be performed. This unit discusses procedures for both routine and more complicated transmission service.

LEARNING OBJECTIVES

When you have completed your assignments and exercises in this unit, you should be able to:

☐ Check for proper fluid level.
☐ Diagnose the condition of transmission fluid.
☐ Perform a filter or screen change.
☐ Perform a pressure test and explain how it helps in diagnosing transmission problems.
☐ Change a vacuum modulator.
☐ Describe adjustments that can be made to linkage systems.
☐ Adjust transmission bands.
☐ Describe the procedures used for inspecting automatic transmission parts.

SAFETY PRECAUTIONS

Many service aspects of the transmission require that the automobile be raised and supported safely. *Never* work under a vehicle unless you are absolutely sure that the automobile or any of its heavy assemblies cannot move or fall. Proper jacks and supporting tools, as well as a helper, are essential when servicing transmissions. The transmission is a very heavy assembly.

Transmission fluid, transmission parts, engines, and exhaust systems that are hot can cause serious burns. Let the automobile cool before starting to do any servicing.

The underside of the automobile is dirty. Always wear safety glasses or a face shield to prevent dirt and foreign objects from falling into your eyes.

A road test usually is necessary when checking an automatic transmission. Drive in a safe manner. Jackrabbit starts, hard cornering, and sudden braking should be avoided. Extreme driving conditions can worsen a problem or create a new one. Carelessness during a test drive can result in an accident. Drive only in a manner that is required to check or diagnose transmission operation. Always fasten your seat belt and test the vehicle's brakes before beginning a road test.

A number of electrical systems are connected to an automatic transmission. Remove rings or jewelry before working on an electrical part. Avoid touching grounded tools to powered electrical leads or connections, which can result in severe burns or dangerous sparks. Sparks can cause an explosion if fumes from gasoline or volatile solvents are present. Manufacturers recommend disconnecting the battery when working on an automatic transmission.

Many automatic transmission diagnostic tests require that the engine be running. Be sure that proper ventilation equipment is used to remove dangerous exhaust fumes from an enclosed shop area. Do *not* allow anyone to stand in front of, or behind, the automobile during these tests. Block the wheels. Set the parking brake and apply the service brakes if possible. Carelessness or defective parts can allow the automobile to move, possibly causing serious injury.

If a procedure requires that you be under the automobile while the test is being performed, be extremely careful. The driveline and rear wheels will be turning during most tests. Contact with a spinning driveline or wheel can cause serious injury.

Many torque converters are inspected by removing an inspection cover. This exposes part of the torque converter. Do *not* put your fingers near the moving torque converter while the engine is operating.

Always wear eye and face protection when using compressed air. Particles can be blown into the eyes and can injure your skin. Do *not* point any compressed air tool at another person.

54.1 PREVENTIVE MAINTENANCE

Automatic transmission preventive maintenance includes lubricating the gearshift linkage, checking automatic transmission fluid level and condition, and replacing filter and screen.

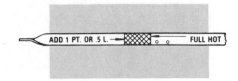

Figure 54-1. Typical automatic transmission dipstick.
PONTIAC MOTOR DIVISION—GMC

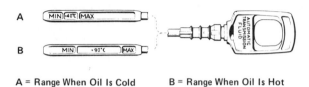

A = Range When Oil Is Cold   B = Range When Oil Is Hot

Figure 54-2. Dipstick with readings on both sides.
VOLVO OF AMERICA CORPORATION

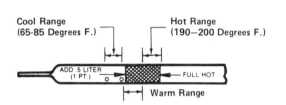

Figure 54-3. Hot and cold dipstick readings on one side.
CHEVROLET MOTOR DIVISION—GMC

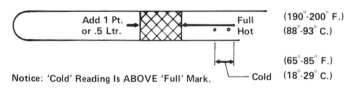

Figure 54-4. Transaxle dipstick with cold reading above hot reading. CHEVROLET MOTOR DIVISION—GMC

Figure 54-5. Adding automatic transmission fluid.

Lubricating and Checking Gearshift Linkage

Gearshift linkage usually is lubricated during chassis lubrication service. Clean the linkage with a shop towel. Check for missing or damaged parts. The linkage is lubricated where parts pivot or slide.

Checking Transmission Fluid Level

Automatic transmission fluid (ATF) level should be checked at regular mileage or time intervals. Fluid level is checked with a dipstick. The dipstick usually is located near the firewall in the right rear section of the engine compartment.

On many automobiles, the fluid level can be checked accurately only when the transmission is at operating temperature. A dipstick, shown in Figure 54-1, indicates full, safe, and low fluid levels. The engine must be running and the shift lever placed in park (P) or neutral (N) with the parking brake applied.

Some dipsticks have readings on both sides (see Figure 54-2). Others have readings on only one side (see Figure 54-3). On some newer vehicles with automatic transaxles, the cold fluid level will be higher than the hot fluid level (see Figure 54-4).

To check fluid level, start the engine and bring it to operating temperature. Remove the dipstick and wipe it clean with a lint-free cloth or paper towel. Reinsert the dipstick. Remove it again and note the reading.

Before adding fluid, always be sure the proper ATF is used. A special spout is inserted into the transmission dipstick hole to add fluid (see Figure 54-5). *Never* add too much transmission fluid. Remove excess fluid with a suction gun.

Diagnosing Transmission Fluid

The condition of ATF always should be noted when fluid level is checked. The condition of the fluid can indicate a transmission problem.

ATF usually is red. A dark brown color, accompanied by an odor of burning indicates overheating. In this case, the ATF and the filter must be changed. A pink or milky color can indicate that engine coolant is leaking in from the transmission cooler.

Bubbles on the dipstick indicate the presence of air. The bubbles usually are caused by a high-pressure leak.

Wipe the dipstick on absorbent white paper. Look at the fluid stain. Dark particles in the fluid indicate band or clutch material. Silvery particles are bits of metal that may indicate excessive wear. If varnish or gum remains on the cleaned dipstick, the ATF and the filter should be replaced.

Changing Transmission Fluid

Try to change the fluid while the transmission is warm. Contaminants flow out more completely when the fluid is warm. Raise and support the automobile properly on a hoist. Place a catch pan under the transmission.

Fluid can be drained by removing a drain plug or by loosening the oil pan bolts. A typical drain plug location is shown in Figure 54-6.

If oil pan bolts are to be loosened to drain the ATF, start at the front of the transmission. Loosen one or two bolts on each side of the oil pan. Be sure the catch pan is in position. When the bolts are loosened, the oil pan will tilt forward to allow draining.

On some oil pans, all but two of the bolts are removed. The two remaining bolts are shown in Figure 54-7. One bolt is replaced with a special bolt, and the second bolt is loosened. Use a rubber-faced mallet to strike the oil pan and break the seal to allow draining.

Remove the oil pan and check the bottom for signs of damaged parts. Some accumulation of small metal parts is a fairly normal condition. Clean the inside of the pan with solvent and a lint-free shop towel.

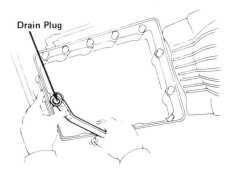

Figure 54-6. Automatic transmission fluid drain plug.
TOYOTA MOTOR SALES, U.S.A.

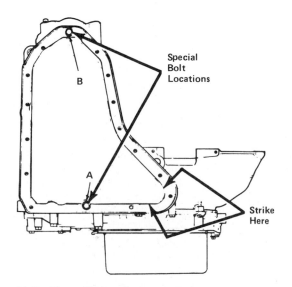

Figure 54-7. Transmission oil pan removal.
BUICK MOTOR DIVISION—GMC

Draining the torque converter. Some fluid remains in the torque converter during draining. This remaining transmission fluid must be removed if the ATF is badly contaminated.

Most newer automobiles do *not* have a torque converter drain plug. Instead, the transmission is refilled, the car driven to circulate ATF through the torque converter, and the ATF drained again. This procedure is repeated until most of the contaminants have been removed from the torque converter.

If a drain plug is used, place a catch pan under the torque converter. The drain plug is located behind an access-hole plate at the bottom of the transmission housing (see Figure 54-8). Loosen the plug to drain the fluid.

Replacing the filter and screen. A disposable filter or reusable screen is used to remove particles from the ATF. A filter is replaced, or a screen is cleaned, according to manufacturer's recommendations. Some manufacturers do not recommend periodic service for filters or screens.

A filter or screen usually is attached to the bottom of the valve body (see Figure 54-9).

Filters are made of paper or fabric (see Figure 54-10). A filter may be held in place by screws, clips, or bolts. Remove the fasteners and O-ring or gasket from the filter, and discard them. A filter kit contains new parts. Install the filter.

Screens are removed in the same way as filters. Some transmissions have valves and springs between the valve body and screen. Do *not* loosen these parts. Clean the screen with fresh solvent and a stiff brush. A screen is shown in Figure 54-11. Replace the screen.

Remove any traces of the old gasket on the transmission and oil pan by scraping with a gasket scraper or putty knife. Install the oil pan and gasket.

Lower the vehicle and refill with new ATF. Be careful not to overfill. When ATF has been added to manufacturer's specifications, move the shift lever through all the shift positions. Then recheck the automatic transmission fluid level.

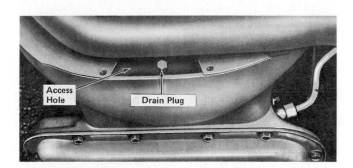

Figure 54-8. Access cover drain plug location.
CHRYSLER CORPORATION

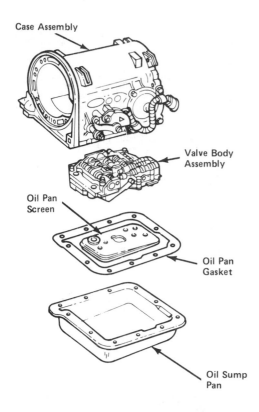

Figure 54-9. Oil screen location. FORD MOTOR COMPANY

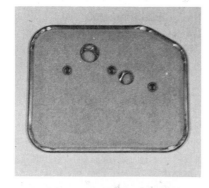

Figure 54-10.
Transmission fluid filter.

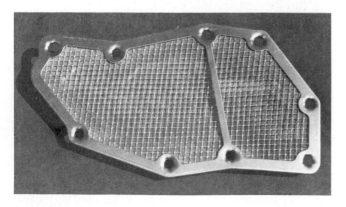

Figure 54-11. Transmission fluid screen.

54.2 AUTOMATIC TRANSMISSION DIAGNOSIS

There are many different models of automatic transmissions. Identification numbers are stamped into the transmission case or on an attached metal identification tag. To identify a transmission, refer to the proper service manual for the vehicle. Different automatic transmissions are diagnosed in different ways.

Troubleshooting charts are extremely important for diagnosing automatic transmission problems. One type of transmission problem may have 15 or more possible causes. It is important to follow each of the step-by-step procedures outlined in these troubleshooting charts. More than one problem may be found when troubleshooting.

Transmission problems can be caused by engine malfunctions. A poorly tuned or worn-out engine that does not produce enough vacuum can cause shifting problems. A clogged engine cooling system can cause the transmission fluid to overheat. Worn-out engine bearings can cause downward pressure on the input shaft, damaging or destroying internal transmission parts. Any problem that affects engine power can affect transmission operation.

Make a visual inspection of the transmission and transmission cooler lines for damage. Check fluid level and condition. Look for leaks, broken lines, and misadjusted linkage. Check electrical connections and look for damaged wiring. Be sure all vacuum lines are connected.

A properly conducted road test can indicate how the apply devices are operating. The mechanic also can check for slippage, harsh or delayed shifting, or shifts at incorrect road speeds.

54.3 TESTING

Much of the diagnosis performed on automatic transmissions requires test equipment. Many different tests can be made on an automatic transmission. Two of the more common tests are the pressure test and the air pressure test.

Pressure Test

Procedures for a *pressure test* vary considerably. Therefore, check the proper service manual for exact procedures. A pressure test checks hydraulic pressures inside the transmission. Gauges are attached to the transmission. The transmission is shifted into a specific gear, and the engine is run at a recommended speed. Pressure readings are recorded during the test procedures.

Pressure test openings, or ports, are located on the transmission case. See Figure 54-12. Pressure fittings are screwed into the ports. A tachometer and vacuum gauge, or a combination tester, are used to make a pressure test (see Figure 54-13). In some cases, a tester with long hoses is located inside the car and pressures are recorded during a road test.

Air Pressure Test

The source of a transmission hydraulic problem can be difficult to locate. An *air pressure test* can be conducted to pinpoint the problem. An air pressure test checks the operation of apply devices. A blowgun with a rubber nozzle is used to apply the air pressure (see Figure 54-14).

After the valve body has been removed, air pressure is applied to the case holes and passages leading to the apply devices. Correct operation of servos and clutches can be heard and/or felt. Refer to the manufacturer's service manual for the correct location of the passages.

Some manufacturers recommend the use of special metal plates that are bolted to the transmission to seal the apply passages. See Figure 54-15.

54.4 AUTOMATIC TRANSMISSION ADJUSTMENT AND LIGHT SERVICE

Servicing an automatic transmission may involve only on-car service, such as an adjustment. Off-car service, such as an overhaul, is defined as a major job. This section covers on-car adjustments and light service.

Linkage Adjustment

There are three types of linkage adjustments. These are quadrant adjustment, gearshift adjustment, and kickdown adjustment.

The quadrant adjustment is made to center the pointer (see Figure 54-16).

Gearshift linkage adjustment varies between manufacturers. Usually, the manual valve lever is positioned in a specific location. Adjustments are made to linkage that is connected to this lever (see Figure 54-17). Always check the proper service manual.

Several types of linkage systems can be controlled by the accelerator pedal. These include: accelerator linkage, kickdown rod linkage, and throttle valve linkage. Many automobiles use more than one of these linkage systems. Figure 54-18 shows a typical kickdown linkage system. Linkage systems vary considerably, so it is important always to check the appropriate service manual.

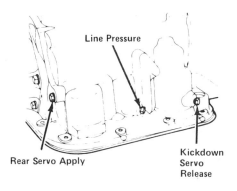

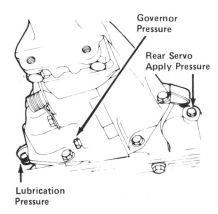

Figure 54-12. Pressure test locations. CHRYSLER CORPORATION

Figure 54-14. Compressed air blow gun with rubber nozzle.

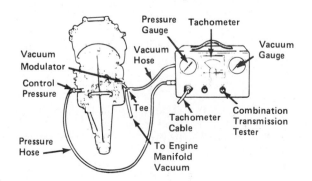

Figure 54-13. Pressure combination tester.
FORD MOTOR COMPANY

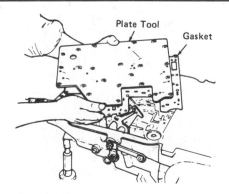

Figure 54-15. Air pressure plate. FORD MOTOR COMPANY

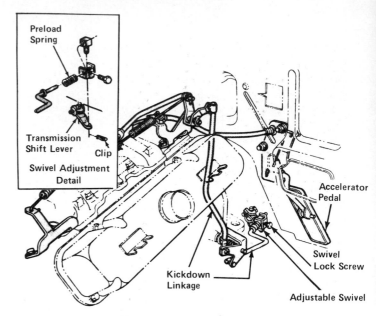

Figure 54-18. Kickdown linkage system. CHRYSLER CORPORATION

Band Adjustment

Adjusting transmission bands may or may not be part of a scheduled maintenance program. Some transmissions have no provision for band adjustments. Some band adjustments may require draining the ATF and removing the oil pan.

Figure 54-19 shows an external intermediate band adjustment on a Ford transmission. To adjust the band, discard the old locknut. Tighten the adjusting nut to specifications with a special tool. Install a new locknut.

Vacuum Modulator Service

The vacuum modulator usually is screwed or clamped into place at the side or rear of the transmission. See Figure 54-20.

Improper shifting may be caused by a defective vacuum modulator or by defective or missing modulator connections (see Figure 54-21). Follow the diagnostic procedure outlined in the manufacturer's service manual to determine the exact cause.

A repeated low fluid level in the transmission with no visible external leaks may indicate a ruptured diaphragm in the modulator. To check for this condition, pull the vacuum hose off the modulator connection. If ATF is present in the hose, the vacuum modulator must be replaced.

Replacement generally involves a good cleaning of the modulator area. Then, disconnect the modulator vacuum hose. The modulator itself is either unscrewed or unclamped from the transmission housing and removed carefully. Take care that the modulator valve does not fall out during this removal. The new replacement then is installed.

Refer to a service manual for more complete replacement procedures.

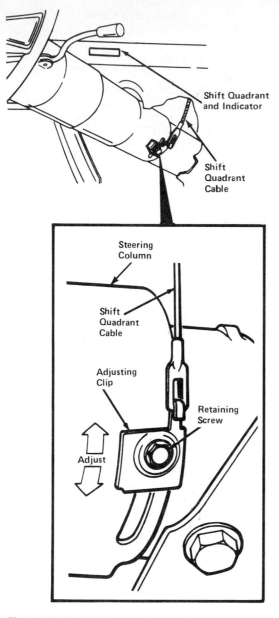

Figure 54-16. Shift quadrant adjustment.
AMERICAN MOTORS CORPORATION

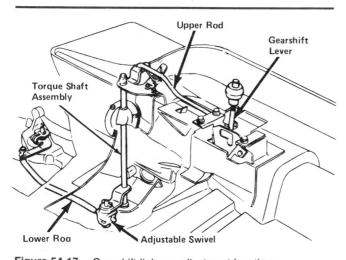

Figure 54-17. Gearshift linkage adjustment locations.
CHRYSLER CORPORATION

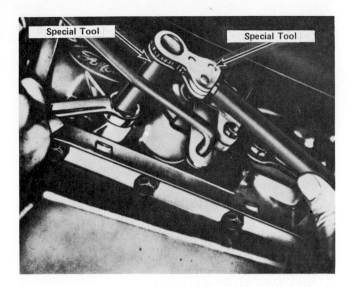

Figure 54-19. Band adjustment. FORD MOTOR COMPANY

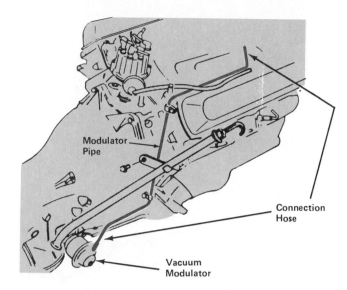

Figure 54-20. Vacuum modulator and connections.

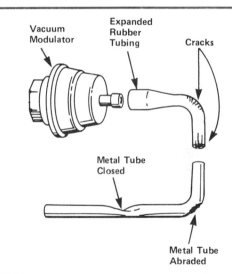

Figure 54-21. Damaged vacuum line can cause improper shifting.

Governor Service

Improper shift points may be caused by a malfunction in the governor. Governor operation is discussed in Topic 53.7.

Although all governors are mounted internally, some require removal of the extension housing or oil pan for access. Figure 54-22 shows such a governor. This unit can be serviced only after the extension housing has been removed.

Another type of governor is a complete unit. This type may be serviced by removing a retaining clamp (see Figure 54-23) and then removing the governor.

Regardless of the type of governor, always follow the manufacturer's recommended diagnostic and service procedures.

Oil Leaks

A frequent cause for concern with automatic transmissions is oil leaks, especially as miles of service accumulate on the unit. There are many possible sources for the leakage of ATF. One of these, the pump seal, can be replaced only if the transmission is removed from the vehicle.

Case porosity occurs during the casting process, causing small holes in the metal, through which the ATF seeps. These holes may be repaired using an epoxy-type sealer. All traces of oil must be removed before attempting this repair, which also requires transmission removal.

The other types of leaks, caused by worn or defective gaskets or seals, are stopped by replacing the defective part. The transmission need not be removed for this service. Follow the replacement recommendations of the manufacturer. Figure 54-24 shows possible sources of leaks on an automatic transmission.

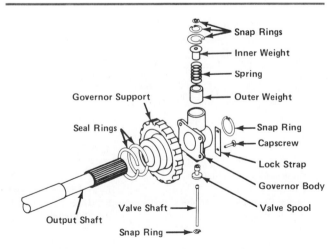

Figure 54-22. Governor valve assembly.
AMERICAN MOTORS CORPORATION

577

Governor
Cover
Governor
Seal
Cover
Retainer

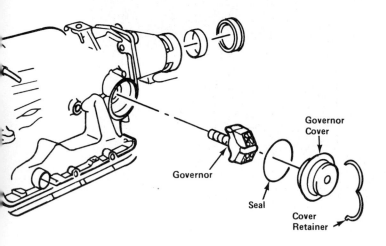

Figure 54-23. Governor held in place by retaining clamp.

UNIT HIGHLIGHTS

- Transmission fluid level is checked with a dipstick when the fluid is at operating temperature.
- Some dipsticks have different temperature readings on each side.
- The condition of an automatic transmission can be determined by fluid color and residue.
- Transmission fluid usually is drained by loosening the oil pan bolts.
- An automatic transmission filter or screen is located beneath the valve body.
- Much of the diagnosis that is done on automatic transmissions requires test equipment.
- Several linkage systems on an automatic transmission may need adjustment.
- Never wipe transmission parts with a cloth, because lint could cause poor transmission operation.

TERMS

pressure test

air pressure test

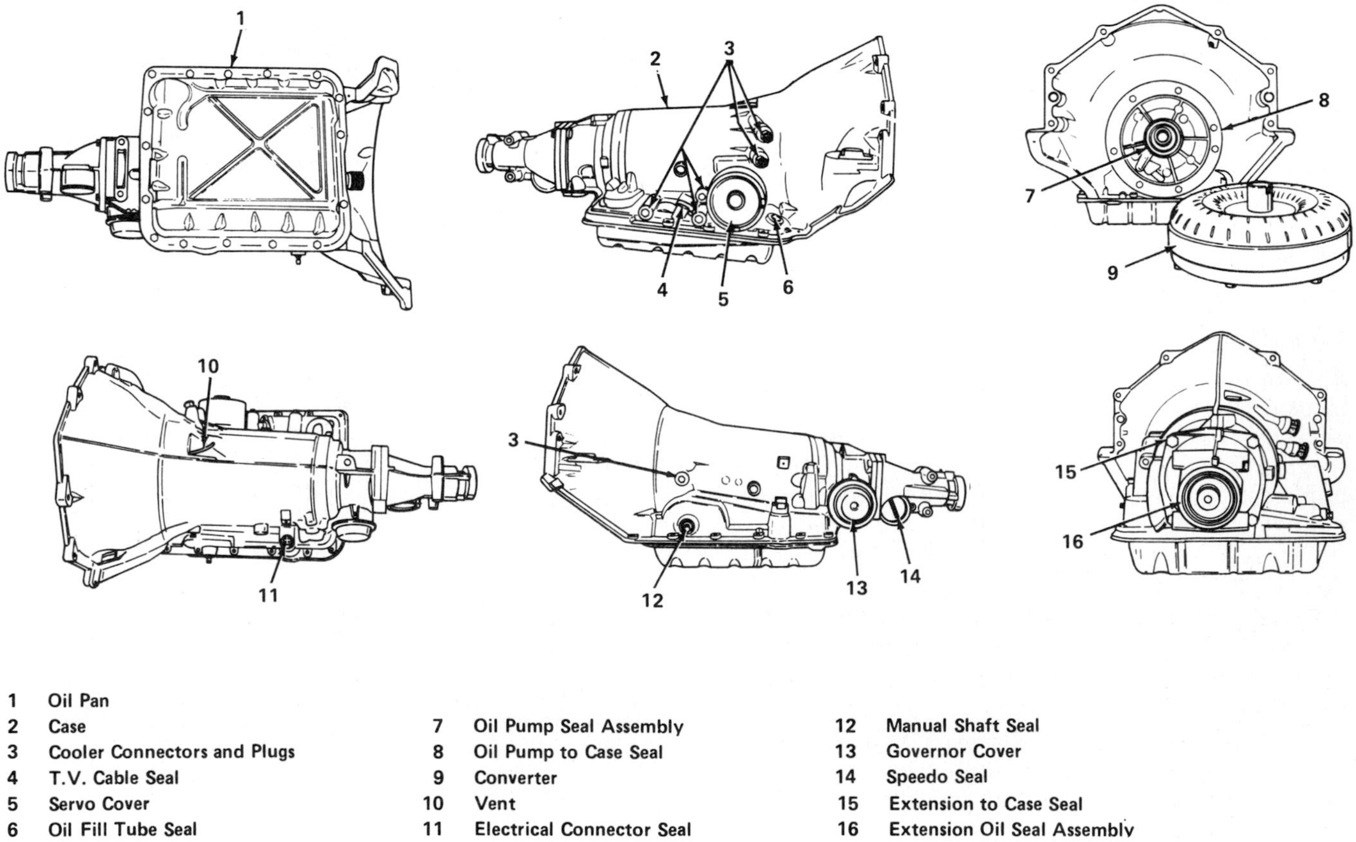

1
2
3
4
5
6
7
8
9
10
11
3
12
13
14
15
16
1 Oil Pan
2 Case
3 Cooler Connectors and Plugs
4 T.V. Cable Seal
5 Servo Cover
6 Oil Fill Tube Seal
7 Oil Pump Seal Assembly
8 Oil Pump to Case Seal
9 Converter
10 Vent
11 Electrical Connector Seal
12 Manual Shaft Seal
13 Governor Cover
14 Speedo Seal
15 Extension to Case Seal
16 Extension Oil Seal Assembly

Figure 54-24. Possible sources of transmission fluid leaks. PONTIAC MOTOR DIVISION—GMC

R E V I E W Q U E S T I O N S

DIRECTIONS: The following questions are similar to those used on mechanic certification tests. On a separate sheet of paper, write the letter of the correct choice.

1. Mechanic A says both cold and hot fluid levels are marked on all automatic transmission dipsticks.
   Mechanic B says ATF color and condition can be checked with a white paper towel.
   Who is correct?
   A. A only   B. B only   C. Both A and B   D. Neither A nor B

2. All of the following statements are true EXCEPT
   A. A mallet can be used to loosen the oil pan.
   B. All automatic transmissions have drain plugs.
   C. A disposable paper filter is used in automatic transmissions.
   D. A screen can be cleaned in solvent.

3. Which of the following statements is correct?
   I. A pressure test is used to check hydraulic pressure.
   II. An air pressure test is used to check vacuum lines.
   A. I only   B. II only   C. Both I and II   D. Neither I nor II

4. Which of the following statements is correct?
   A. A quadrant adjustment centers the gearshift lever.
   B. Gearshift linkage adjustments are made to linkage that is connected to the manual valve lever.
   C. The accelerator pedal may control as many as five linkage systems.
   D. Shop towels should not be used to clean off kickdown linkage.

5. Mechanic A says that transmission bearings should be lubricated with petroleum jelly.
   Mechanic B says that scraping off old gaskets can damage sealing surfaces.
   Who is correct?
   A. A only   B. B only   C. Both A and B   D. Neither A nor B

S U P P L E M E N T A L A C T I V I T I E S

1. Describe precautionary safety measures that should be followed when making tests for automatic transmission diagnosis.
2. Locate the quadrant adjustment linkage on an automobile the instructor selects.
3. Check the transmission fluid level in a vehicle.
4. Diagnose the condition of transmission fluid in a vehicle selected by the instructor.
5. Describe the procedure for draining a torque converter.
6. Describe how a filter and a screen differ.
7. Make a visual inspection of a transmission in a vehicle and describe any defects that are found.
8. Describe the procedure for performing a pressure test.
9. Describe procedures for inspecting automatic transmission parts.

55 DIFFERENTIALS AND DRIVING AXLES

UNIT PREVIEW

The differential is a combination of gears that performs two major functions. First, it changes the direction of engine power to turn the driving wheels. Second, it allows the rear wheels to rotate at different speeds when the vehicle is turning.

The driving axles transfer the proper power from the differential to the driving wheels.

LEARNING OBJECTIVES

When you have completed your assignments and exercises in this unit, you should be able to:
- ☐ Explain the different types of gears used in a differential.
- ☐ Describe the operation of a differential as an automobile rounds a corner.
- ☐ Explain the operation of a limited-slip differential.
- ☐ Describe how a driving wheel is connected to a driving axle.
- ☐ Describe the three common types of driving axles.
- ☐ Identify the rear axle parts that are involved in power flow.

55.1 DIFFERENTIAL DESIGN

The differential is an assembly of gears located between the two driving axles. Commonly called a rear end or rear axle, the differential accommodates the differing speed requirements of the two driving wheels.

The differential has two jobs. First, it changes the angle of power flow. Second, it provides varying amounts of torque to the driving axles. When the vehicle is moving in a straight line, the differential delivers equal torque to the two driving axles. When the driving wheels go around a turn, the differential provides unequal torque to the driving axles.

Torque enters the differential at the *drive pinion gear* (see Figure 55-1). A pinion gear is the smaller of two meshing gears. The drive pinion gear is connected to the driveline at the rear U-joint yoke.

The drive pinion gear meshes with a larger *ring gear* inside the differential housing. The ring gear is set on end and transfers torque, through a series of parts, to the driving wheels.

When driveline rotation reaches the differential, it must be redirected to allow the driving wheels to rotate forward or backward. To get the proper direction of rotation, the driveline axis of rotation is turned at right angles, or 90 degrees.

The drive pinion gear and ring gear are *hypoid gears* that resemble beveled gears. A hypoid gear contacts more than one tooth at a time and makes contact with a sliding motion. Also, the center lines of the ring and pinion gears do not match. The drive pinion meshes with the ring gear at a point below its center line. A hypoid ring and pinion assembly is shown in Figure 55-2.

To allow a different rotation for each driving wheel, the differential contains four other assemblies:

1. Differential case
2. Pinion shaft
3. Differential pinion gears
4. Differential side gears.

The ring gear is bolted to the *differential case*, or *carrier*. As the ring gear rotates, the case rotates. The remaining differential parts are located inside the case.

The *pinion shaft* is mounted in holes in the case. *Differential pinion gears* are mounted on the pinion shaft to mesh with the *side gears*. This relationship is illustrated in Figure 55-3.

When driving in a straight line, the pinion shaft does not rotate. The pinion shaft is mounted rigidly to the differential case. The case rotates, carrying the pinion shaft around with it. At this time, the differential pinion gears do not rotate on the pinion shaft. The pinion gears remain stationary. As the pinion shaft moves with the case, the gears are meshed with, and exert pressure on, the side gears. The side gears now turn at the same speed as the ring gear, driving both wheels at the same speed.

When the automobile rounds a corner, or curve, the outer wheels turn faster than the inner wheels. To allow this difference between the two driving wheels, the two pinion gears rotate on the pinion shaft. As the pinion gears rotate, they transmit more speed to the outer side. This extra speed allows the outside axle to turn faster than the inside axle.

55.2 DIFFERENTIAL CONSTRUCTION

The differential can be constructed in either of two ways: as an integral-carrier differential or as a removable-carrier differential.

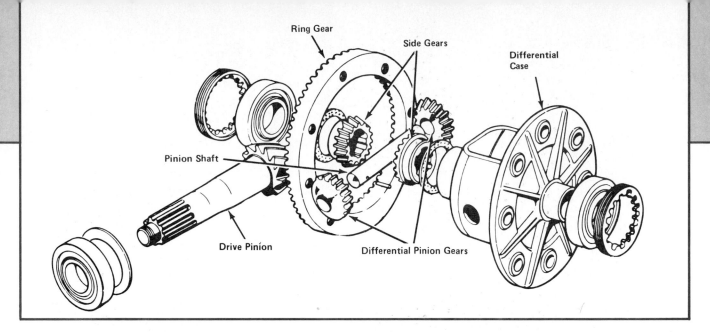

Figure 55-1. Parts of a differential. MAZDA MOTOR CORPORATION

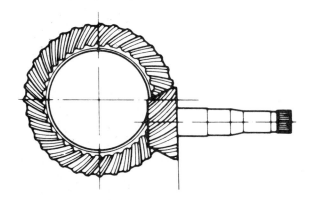

Figure 55-2. Hypoid gearset. NISSAN MOTOR CORPORATION

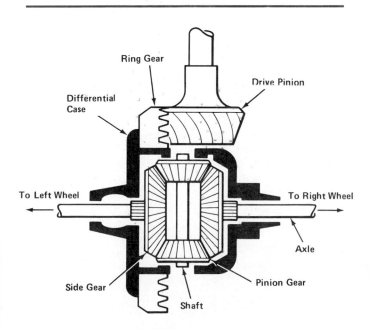

Figure 55-3. Relationship among pinion shaft, pinion gears, and side gears in a typical differential.

Integral-Carrier Differential

An *integral-carrier differential* assembly is part of the rear axle housing (see Figure 55-4). The differential must be serviced through the rear of the housing. The differential bearings must be disassembled before the differential can be removed from the automobile.

Removable-Carrier Differential

A *removable-carrier differential* can be unbolted and removed, intact, from the rear axle housing (see Figure 55-5). The entire differential can be set on a workbench and serviced as a unit.

55.3 LIMITED-SLIP DIFFERENTIAL

A *limited-slip differential* operates much as a standard differential when the vehicle is moving straight or turning. However, both driving axles can be locked together through clutches in the differential. In this way, both wheels will deliver power, even if one wheel is on ice and tends to spin.

The biggest difference between a standard differential and a limited-slip differential is the addition of a clutch assembly to the limited-slip. The clutch assembly applies pressure to the side gears to eliminate wheel spin under conditions in which one wheel may not have good traction. The clutch assembly is located inside the differential case, between the side gears and the inside walls of the carrier.

Two types of limited-slip differentials are common: the clutch plate type and the cone type.

Clutch Plate Limited-Slip

The *clutch plate limited-slip* differential consists of a series of clutch plates, called a *clutch pack*. Two clutch packs usually are located inside the differential case—one at each side gear. A clutch pack has steel plates and friction plates that are stacked alternately. A clutch pack assembly is shown in Figure 55-6.

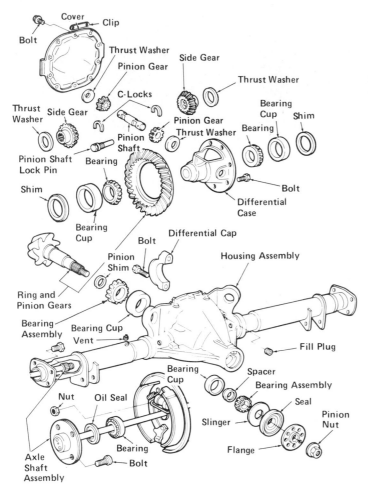

During normal operation, there is enough slippage in the clutch pack to prevent lockup. When one wheel begins to spin, the side gear at the spinning wheel is moved inward. This inward movement is called *side thrust*. The side gear applies an added force against the clutch pack at the opposite side gear. This locks up the axles to the differential case so that they can rotate at the same speed.

Cone Limited-Slip

Many of the newer automobiles use *cone limited-slip* assemblies at each side gear (refer to Figure 55-7). The cones have friction surfaces that grab against the differential case when limited-slip operation is necessary. The cones are splined to the side gear hubs.

The cone-type system operates in essentially the same way as the clutch plate design. The cones are forced against the case and squeezed. At this point, the cone rotates with the carrier and locks up both axles.

55.4 DRIVING AXLES

Driving axles are solid steel shafts that transfer differential torque to the driving wheels. A separate axle shaft is used for each driving wheel. The driving axles, and part of the differential, are enclosed in an axle housing that protects and supports these parts. Figure 55-8 shows a housing and axle assembly.

Each driving axle is connected to a side gear in the differential. As the side gears are turned, the axles to which the gears are connected turn at the same speed.

Figure 55-4. Parts of an integral-carrier differential assembly.
FORD MOTOR COMPANY

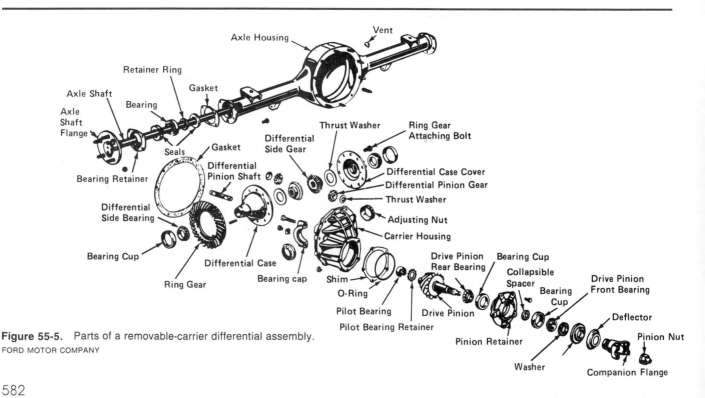

Figure 55-5. Parts of a removable-carrier differential assembly.
FORD MOTOR COMPANY

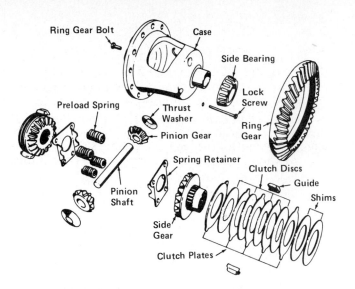

Figure 55-6. Limited-slip clutch plate assembly.
CHEVROLET MOTOR DIVISION—GMC

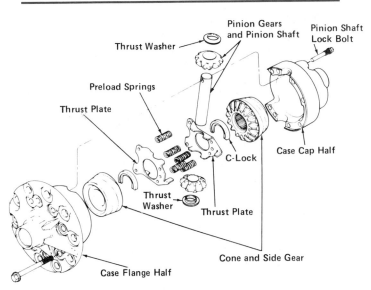

Figure 55-7. Limited-slip cone assembly. FORD MOTOR COMPANY

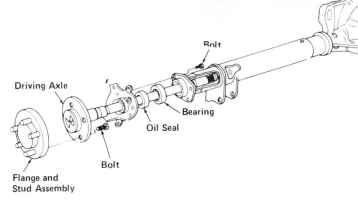

Figure 55-8. Differential housing and drive axle assembly.
FORD MOTOR COMPANY

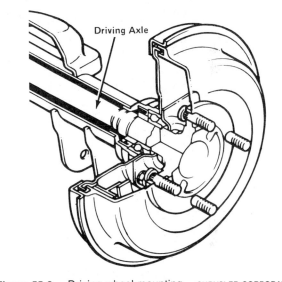

Figure 55-9. Driving wheel mounting. CHRYSLER CORPORATION

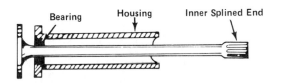

Figure 55-10. Semi-floating axle assembly.
CHEVROLET MOTOR DIVISION—GMC

The outer ends of the axles are attached to the driving wheels. For attachment to a wheel, the outer end of each axle has a flange. Studs are used to hold the wheel in place against the flange. The wheel fits over the studs, and a lug nut is tightened over the open end of the stud. This holds the wheel in place, as shown in Figure 55-9.

The inner end of each axle shaft is supported by the differential carrier. The outer end of the axle shaft is supported by a bearing inside the axle housing. This bearing, called an *axle bearing,* allows the axle to rotate smoothly inside the axle housing.

Two types of driving axles are common on automobiles with drivelines:

1. Semi-floating axles
2. Independently suspended axles.

Semi-Floating Axle

The most common rear-drive axle is the *semi-floating axle.* A semi-floating axle (Figure 55-10) helps to support the weight of the vehicle. One end of the axle shaft is splined to a side gear. The wheel end of the axle shaft has a flange that is bolted to the hub of the wheel.

Another method of securing the wheel is to run the end of the axle through the wheel hub. The end of the axle has a key, or spline, to hold the axle to the hub (see Figure 55-11).

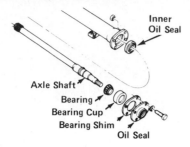

Figure 55-11. Key and spline axle assembly.
AMERICAN MOTORS CORPORATION

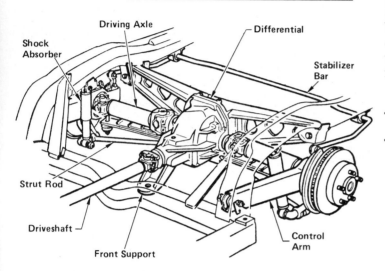

Figure 55-12. De Dion axle assembly.
CHEVROLET MOTOR DIVISION—GMC

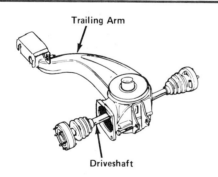

Figure 55-13. Swing axle assembly. VOLKSWAGEN OF AMERICA

One roller or ball bearing is used in a semi-floating axle. The bearing is located inside the outer end of the axle housing. The end of the axle shaft supports the weight of the automobile.

Independently Suspended Axles

This type of rear-driving axle system is found mostly on European automobiles and on the American Corvette. The driving axles usually are open instead of being enclosed in an axle housing.

Two types of independently suspended rear-driving axles are common: the De Dion system and the swing axle.

The *De Dion axle* system resembles a miniature driveline (see Figure 55-12). The driving axle resembles a driveshaft, with U-joints at each end of the axle. A slip joint is attached to the inboard, or innermost, U-joint. The outboard, or outermost, U-joint is connected to the driving wheel. This allows the driving axle to move up and down as it rotates.

On automobiles with *swing axles,* the driving axles may be open or enclosed. An axle fits into the differential by way of a ball-and-socket system. The ball-and-socket system allows the axle to pivot up and down. As the axle pivots, the driving wheel "swings" up and down. A typical swing-axle assembly is shown in Figure 55-13.

U N I T   H I G H L I G H T S

- Power from the driveline passes through the drive pinion gear and is redirected by the ring gear.
- Hypoid gears mesh with a sweeping action and make contact below the ring gear center line.
- The ring gear bolts to the differential case, which houses most of the differential parts.
- The differential can have an integral or a removable carrier.
- A limited-slip clutch assembly locks up both driving axles in the differential.
- Driving axles transfer power from the differential to the driving wheels.
- Some driving axles, like the De Dion system, are open and rely on U-joints.

T E R M S

drive pinion gear	removable-carrier
ring gear	differential
hypoid gears	limited-slip differential
differential case	clutch plate limited-slip
carrier	clutch pack
pinion shaft	side thrust
differential pinion	cone limited-slip
gears	axle bearing
side gears	semi-floating axle
integral-carrier	De Dion axle
differential	swing axle

R E V I E W   Q U E S T I O N S

DIRECTIONS: The following questions are similar to those used on mechanic certification tests. On a separate sheet of paper, write the letter of the correct choice.

1. Which of the following statements is correct?

   I. The drive pinion gear meshes with the differential pinion gear.

   II. The differential pinion gear meshes with a side gear.

   A. I only   B. II only   C. Both I and II   D. Neither I nor II

2. Mechanic A says that the differential case houses all of the differential parts.

   Mechanic B says that the pinion shaft rotates with the differential pinion gears.

   Who is correct?

   A. A only   B. B only   C. Both A and B   D. Neither A nor B

3. All of the following statements are true EXCEPT

   A. A limited-slip clutch assembly locks the driving axles together.

   B. A clutch pack is made up of steel discs.

   C. The inward movement of a side gear is called side thrust.

   D. Cones are keyed to the side gear splines.

4. Driving axle parts include

   A. flanges.

   B. studs.

   C. needle bearings.

   D. wheel wells.

5. Driving axles do all of the following EXCEPT

   A. float in differential lubricant.

   B. help support the weight of the automobile.

   C. transfer torque to the driving wheels.

   D. rotate inside the differential.

S U P P L E M E N T A L   A C T I V I T I E S

1. Show how a ring and pinion mesh on a hypoid gearset.
2. Describe the operation of the differential parts when the automobile is rounding a corner.
3. Identify the type of differential construction shown on a vehicle chosen by your instructor.
4. Explain how a clutch plate limited-slip locks both driving axles.
5. Identify the parts of a driving axle assembly.
6. Describe the operation of a De Dion system.
7. List the parts in a rear axle in the order in which they transmit power from the drive pinion to the wheel.

56 DIFFERENTIAL AND DRIVING AXLE SERVICE

UNIT PREVIEW

Different types of differentials and driving axles are used. The mechanic must know the type of system before servicing. Using the proper testing procedures and making the proper adjustments are as important as the disassembly and reassembly of parts. This unit describes service variations among different types of assemblies.

LEARNING OBJECTIVES

When you have completed your assignments and exercises in this unit, you should be able to:

- ☐ Describe the operation of C-lock and retainer-type axles.
- ☐ Disassemble the integral-carrier and removable-carrier differentials.
- ☐ Remove a differential drive pinion assembly.
- ☐ Make differential bearing preload and backlash adjustments.
- ☐ Perform a gear tooth contact pattern test.

SAFETY PRECAUTIONS

Differential and driving axle preventive maintenance and service require that the automobile be raised and supported safely. *Never* work under an automobile unless you are sure that it cannot move or fall. Safety stands, or jackstands, must be used if the vehicle is not on a hoist.

The underside of the vehicle is dirty. Dirt, grime, or foreign objects can fall into the eyes during service procedures. Always wear safety glasses or goggles to protect your eyes from injury.

Hot exhaust system parts on vehicles can cause severe burns. Be careful when working near exhaust system parts. Allow the vehicle to cool off before servicing.

The differential is heavy. If it falls, it can cause injury or damage to parts. Have a helper ready to assist in removing and replacing the differential.

Diagnosing differential and driving axle problems may require a test drive. Always check differential lubricant level before making a test drive. Buckle the seat belt and check the brakes before starting. Obey the law. Do *not* make jackrabbit starts or unnecessary, sudden stops. Follow the proper driving procedures for troubleshooting the problem.

When disassembling, handle the parts carefully. Many differential and driving axle parts have sharp edges that can cut.

Remove brake assemblies with extreme caution. Brake linings contain asbestos, which is harmful if inhaled. To remove asbestos from the brake assemblies, use a special vacuum cleaner. Do *not* use compressed air to blow out a brake assembly.

Lead compounds are sometimes used for marking ring and pinion gearsets. Lead is poisonous. Extreme care must be used when working with a lead compound. Use a nonlead compound if possible.

An arbor press often is used to press on bearings and other driving axle parts. A press operates under very high pressures. Use the proper adapters. Always check with your instructor to make sure the press is set up for proper operation.

56.1 PREVENTIVE MAINTENANCE

A visual inspection of the differential and driving axles should be made whenever the automobile is on a hoist. Many new automobiles do *not* require a differential lubricant change. However, the differential oil level should be checked during chassis lubrication.

Checking for Leaks

Inspect the differential housing for leaks, cracks, or damage. Locate the filler plug and make sure it is tight and not leaking. Check for leaks around the differential housing and at the drive pinion. Leaks caused by *casting porosity*, an imperfection involving tiny holes created during manufacture, can be sealed with special glues.

Look at the inside of each rear wheel. Any wetness could be differential lubricant. Check the viscosity of the leaking fluid. Brake fluid is thin; differential lubricant is thick.

Checking and Adding Correct Lubricant

The differential has a fill plug similar to that on a manual transmission. The fill plug may be located at either the back or the front side of the differential (see Figure 56-1).

To check differential lubricant level, wipe off the fill plug. Use the proper wrench to remove the plug. Place a finger or a bent rod into the hole.

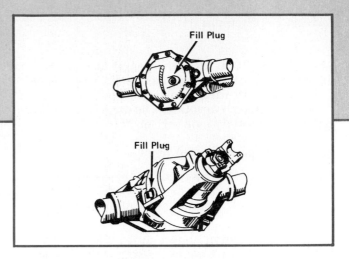

Figure 56-1.   Fill plug locations.

SAFETY CAUTION: Do not rotate the tires or the driveshaft. Differential gears are sharp and can cause serious cuts.

Lubricant level should be no more than ½ inch below the fill hole.

To add lubricant, use a pressurized gun, syringe, or suction gun. After lubricant has been added, replace and tighten the fill plug.

CAUTION: The differential may not be filled with the same oil that is used in the transmission. Different types of lubricants may be recommended. Conventional gear oil cannot be used with limited-slip differentials. Always follow the manufacturer's recommendations.

Draining and Refilling

Remove a drain plug from beneath the differential housing or use a suction gun to drain the differential (see Figure 56-2). The rear cover may have to be removed to drain some differentials. Fill with the proper lubricant.

56.2 DIAGNOSING DIFFERENTIAL PROBLEMS

Noises are the best indication that something is going wrong in the differential. Consult the proper troubleshooting chart to analyze each noise during the test drive. Noises that seem to come from the differential may be caused elsewhere in the drivetrain.

Gear Noises

Two types of gear problems cause unusual noises: a damaged gear, and gears that do not mesh properly.

Noises from a damaged gear are heard over the entire speed range. Noises caused by gears that don't mesh properly usually are heard at specific speeds. The noise may be different during acceleration and deceleration. Worn or damaged side gears and differential pinion gears rarely make noise during normal driving. These noises may be more noticeable when the vehicle is turning.

Bearing Noises

Differential bearings usually make a growling or scraping noise. The noise remains constant but will vary in intensity with vehicle speed. Bearing noise also should be louder when the vehicle is turning.

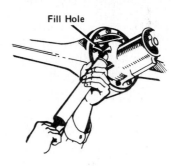

Figure 56-2.   Removing differential lubricant with a suction gun.

Limited-Slip Diagnosis

Improper limited-slip operation can be heard, felt, or both. The noise is a chatter or whirring, snapping sound, usually heard when rounding a corner.

Another sign of limited-slip problems is when the vehicle swerves during acceleration.

To make sure the limited-slip is operating properly, place the transmission in neutral. Block the front wheels so that the vehicle won't move. Raise one rear wheel off the ground. Place a jackstand under the vehicle. Block the front of the opposite wheel. Remove the wheel that has been raised off the ground.

Place a special tool over the wheel lugs, as shown in Figure 56-3. Tighten the lug nuts. Attach a torque wrench to the special tool. Rotate the torque wrench slowly until the wheel begins to turn. The point at which the wheel begins to rotate is known as *breakaway torque*. Take a torque reading just as the wheel begins to rotate. The torque should *not* be less than the manufacturer's specification. Continue rotating the torque wrench slowly. The axle shaft should turn with even pressure without binding.

If torque is less than the specification, or the axle shaft does not rotate with even pressure, check the limited-slip differential.

SAFETY CAUTION: Never attempt to start or run the engine when making this check. A limited-slip differential will direct power to the wheel on the ground, causing it to rotate. The car can run off the jackstand, possibly causing serious injury.

56.3 DIFFERENTIAL SERVICE

Before servicing, the size and type of differential, plus the rear-axle ratio, must be identified. To locate this information, look for an identification code (refer to Figure 56-4).

An identification code may be stamped on the front side of the rear-axle housing. Sometimes the code is stamped on a metal tag that is attached to the differential cover retaining bolts. On some automobiles, the code is included with the vehicle identification number on the driver's-side door jamb.

Gearset Contact

The *differential gearset* consists of the ring gear and drive pinion gear. Teeth on the drive pinion can contact the ring gear at either the same or different places

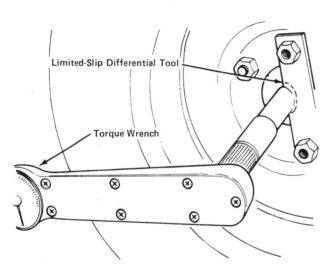

Figure 56-3. Checking limited-slip operation.
FORD MOTOR COMPANY

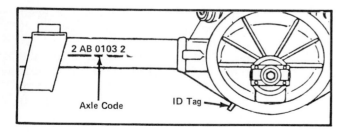

Figure 56-4. Differential identification code.
OLDSMOBILE DIVISION—GMC

after several revolutions. Three terms describe gearset contact:

1. Hunting gearset
2. Nonhunting gearset
3. Partial nonhunting gearset.

The number of teeth on the ring gear and drive pinion gear determine the type of gearset. Knowing the type of gearset is important during reassembly. A nonhunting or partial nonhunting gearset will be marked with special timing marks to ensure correct assembly.

Hunting gearset. When one drive pinion gear tooth contacts every ring gear tooth after several revolutions, it is a *hunting gearset*.

Nonhunting gearset. When one drive pinion gear tooth contacts only certain ring gear teeth, it is a *nonhunting gearset*.

Partial nonhunting gearset. On a *partial nonhunting gearset*, one pinion gear tooth contacts twice as many teeth as a nonhunting gearset. On the first revolution, it may contact three ring gear teeth. On the second ring gear revolution, it will contact three different ring gear teeth.

Removing Axles

The driving axles must be removed before the differential can be taken out. Two different driving-axle assemblies are found in modern automobiles: the C-lock type and the retainer-plate type.

The *C-lock axle assembly* is held in place by a C-lock that is located inside the differential housing. This assembly has the axle bearing pressed into the axle housing. Whenever the axle is removed, the axle seal should be replaced.

On a *retainer-plate axle assembly*, the axle shaft is held in place by a retaining plate. The retaining plate is bolted to the end of the axle. This assembly has the axle bearing pressed onto the axle shaft.

Whenever the axle assembly is removed, all gaskets and oil seals should be replaced.

C-lock axle removal. Raise the automobile on a hoist to a comfortable working height. Remove the rear wheels (see Topic 66.3) and brake drums (see Topic 68.1). Be sure the parking brake is disengaged. Otherwise, the brake shoes will be expanded and will hold the brake drum firmly in place.

NOTE: It is not necessary to remove the entire brake assembly with C-lock driving axle assemblies.

Use a wire brush and a rag to clean all dirt from the differential rear cover. Place an oil catch pan under the differential. To drain the differential, remove the drain plug or the rear cover.

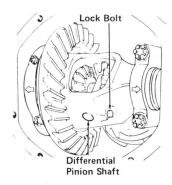

Figure 56-5. Drive pinion lockscrew locations.
FORD MOTOR COMPANY

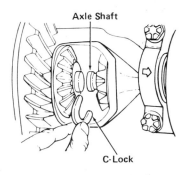

Figure 56-6. Removing C-locks. FORD MOTOR COMPANY

Rotate the differential carrier by hand to expose the differential pinion lockscrew or lock bolt, shown in Figure 56-5. Remove the lockscrew or bolt and pull out the pinion shaft.

CAUTION: **Do not rotate the axle shafts while the pinion shaft is out. The differential pinion gears may fall out.**

Push each axle shaft inward. Remove the C-locks from the grooves in the ends of the axle shaft. See Figure 56-6.

Remove the axle shaft by pulling on the flanged end of the shaft. See Figure 56-7. Pull slowly, being careful not to damage the oil seal and bearing, which will remain in the housing.

Remove the oil seal by using a slide hammer, shown in Figure 56-8. The axle bearing also is removed with a slide hammer.

Retainer-type axle removal. Raise the vehicle on a hoist to a comfortable working height. Remove the rear wheels (see Topic 66.3) and brake drums (see Topic 68.1). A retainer-type axle assembly is shown in Figure 56-9.

NOTE: **Be sure the parking brake is off. Otherwise, the brake shoes will expand and hold the brake drum firmly in place.**

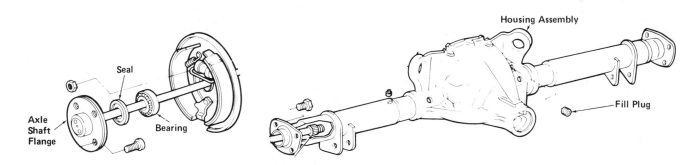

Figure 56-7. Parts of a C-lock axle assembly. FORD MOTOR COMPANY

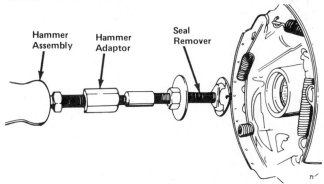

Figure 56-8. Removing an oil seal with a slide hammer.
BUICK MOTOR DIVISION—GMC

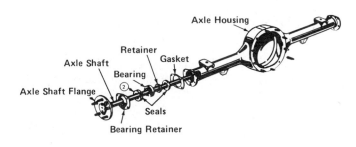

Figure 56-9. Parts of a retainer-type axle assembly.
FORD MOTOR COMPANY

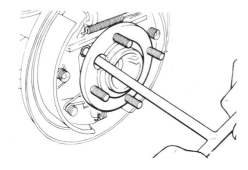

Figure 56-10. Removing a retainer plate assembly.
CHRYSLER CORPORATION

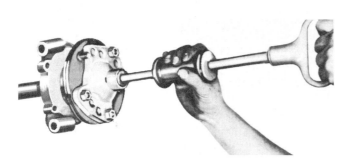

Figure 56-11. Removing an axle shaft with an axle puller.
FORD MOTOR COMPANY

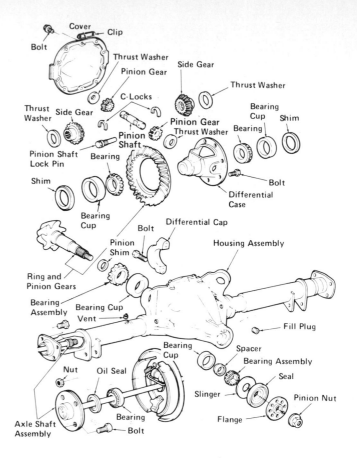

Figure 56-12. Parts of an integral-carrier differential assembly.
FORD MOTOR COMPANY

The flange on the axle shaft has one or more access holes. Rotate the flange by hand to align the access holes with the nuts on the retainer plate. Place the appropriate socket wrench through the access hole, as shown in Figure 56-10. Remove the retainer plate nuts. If no access holes are provided, the nuts are removed from the backside of the retainer plate.

Sometimes the axle shaft can be pulled out by hand. Pull out the shaft slowly and carefully. More often, a special axle puller must be used (see Figure 56-11). Remove the bearing and seal.

Use a piece of mechanic's wire to attach the brake backing plate to the frame of the vehicle. Do not let the brake assembly hang loosely from the brake lines. This can cause brake line damage.

Removing the Differential

Two differential assemblies are used: integral carrier and removable carrier.

Integral carrier. The *integral-carrier differential* is removed, part by part, from the rear of the axle housing. An integral-carrier differential is illustrated in Figure 56-12.

First, remove the driveline (Topic 48.3), wheels (Topic 66.3), brake drums (Topic 68.1), pinion shaft, and axle shafts. Roll out the differential pinion gears and thrust washers by turning the side gears.

Check the bearing caps to make sure they are marked "R" and "L" for right and left. If not, mark them. Loosen the bearing cap bolts until only a few threads hold them in place. Place a pry bar behind the differential case, as shown in Figure 56-13. Pry out the case until it falls free against the bearing caps.

Hold the differential assembly with one hand. Remove the bolts and other differential parts. Remove the case and place it on a workbench.

Drive pinion removal. Measure pinion bearing preload, if specified by the manufacturer, before removing the drive pinion assembly. Place a pound-inch [Nm] torque wrench on the drive pinion nut (see Figure 56-14). Rotate the wrench and record the torque that is required to maintain rotation.

Mark the positions of the pinion nut, companion flange, and drive pinion shaft for reassembly (see Figure 56-15).

Place a special holding tool on the companion flange, as shown in Figure 56-16. Hold the special tool and, with a socket wrench, remove the drive pinion nut and companion flange.

Remove the oil seal with an oil seal remover. Place shop towels in the differential housing and replace the rear cover. Tap out the drive pinion with a soft-faced mallet (see Figure 56-17). Remove the rear cover, drive pinion assembly, and all differential parts.

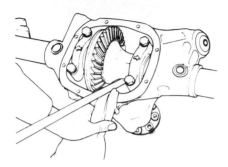

Figure 56-13. Prying out a carrier assembly.
FORD MOTOR COMPANY

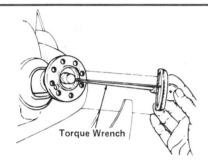

Torque Wrench

Figure 56-14. Measuring pinion shaft preload.
FORD MOTOR COMPANY

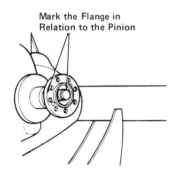

Mark the Flange in
Relation to the Pinion

Figure 56-15. Marking the pinion flange for reassembly.
FORD MOTOR COMPANY

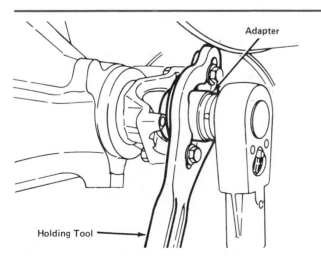

Adapter

Holding Tool

Figure 56-16. Companion flange holding tool.
AMERICAN MOTORS CORPORATION

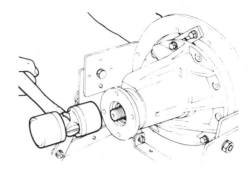

Figure 56-17. Driving out drive pinion with a soft-faced mallet.
CHRYSLER CORPORATION

Removing the removable carrier. A *removable-carrier differential* is taken off the axle housing as an assembly and disassembled on a workbench. A typical removable-carrier differential is shown in Figure 56-18.

Clean the differential thoroughly, using a wire brush. Drain the lubricant. Remove the rear wheels (see Topic 66.3), brake drums (see Topic 68.1), axle shafts, and driveline (see Topic 48.3).

Support the removable-carrier housing on a jack-stand or transmission jack. Have a helper hold the carrier housing while the nuts or bolts and washers are removed. Remove the carrier housing from the axle housing. Place the carrier housing in a holding fixture on a workbench. Figure 56-19 shows a holding fixture.

SAFETY CAUTION: The carrier housing is extremely heavy and difficult to handle.

Removable carrier disassembly. Disassembling the removable carrier is similar to disassembling the integral carrier.

Mark each bearing cap. Remove the bearing caps and bearing cups. Lift the differential assembly out of the carrier housing. Use extreme care; the differential is very heavy. Place the differential assembly on a clean bench.

Make an alignment mark on the differential case and ring gear. Remove the bolts that hold the ring gear and case together. Be sure the ring gear will not fall and be damaged.

Drive out the differential lockpin with a drift. Separate the halves of the differential case. Drive out the pinion shaft with a brass drift. Remove the differential pinion gears. Then, remove the differential side gears.

Two different drive pinion assemblies are used with removable carriers. These are the *retainer-type drive pinion* (see Figure 56-20) and the *nonretainer-type drive pinion* (refer to Figure 56-21). Drive pinions are disassembled in much the same way as integral-carrier assemblies.

Retainer drive pinion disassembly. Remove the bolts that hold the pinion retainer and remove the drive pinion assembly from the carrier housing. Take

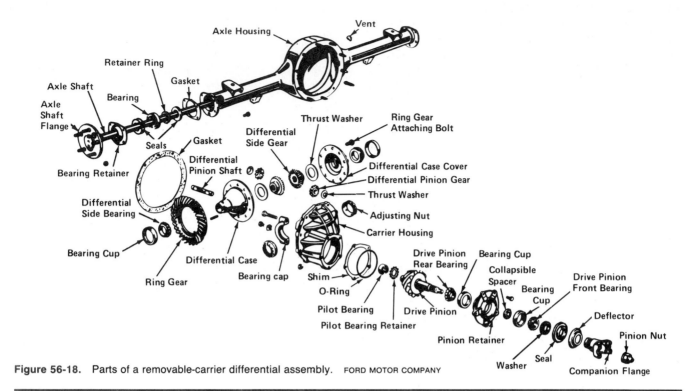

Figure 56-18. Parts of a removable-carrier differential assembly. FORD MOTOR COMPANY

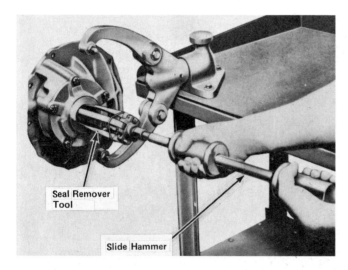

Figure 56-19. Removable-carrier holding fixture.
FORD MOTOR COMPANY

care not to lose the retainer shims that are between the retainer and the housing. Remove the companion flange using a holding tool and socket wrench. Remove the drive pinion gear and oil seal with a slide hammer, shown in Figure 56-19. Remove the front and rear pinion bearings.

Nonretainer drive pinion disassembly. A nonretainer drive pinion is disassembled in two steps. First, the companion flange, front oil seal, and front bearing assembly are removed. The second step is performed after the differential has been disassembled: The drive pinion and rear bearing assembly are removed from the rear of the differential housing.

Limited-slip removal and disassembly. Follow the same procedures used for removing a standard differential. When removing the driving axles, do *not* rotate either axle shaft unless both axle shafts are in position. Rotating one axle shaft could cause a misalignment of the clutches that can be difficult to correct.

Cleaning and Inspection

Improper cleaning of differential parts can lead to early failure. Use the following guidelines.

Bearings can be cleaned in a suitable solvent. Lubricate the bearings immediately after cleaning. *Never* spin a bearing or blow a bearing dry with compressed air.

The remaining parts, including the bores, can be cleaned with solvent. These parts can be blow-dried with compressed air.

If the ring and pinion are scored with grooves or are chipped, the axle housing must be thoroughly cleaned.

Limited-slip clutch packs are cleaned best with fast-evaporating mineral spirits or a dry-cleaning solvent. Clutch packs can be blow-dried with compressed air.

SAFETY CAUTION: Safety glasses or goggles should always be worn when working with compressed air. Compressed air is under high pressure and will blow metal chips, dirt, and liquids in all directions. Serious injury can result.

Inspect all parts. Look for signs of damage or wear. Check the carrier and housing for cracks, nicks, burrs, or scoring. Scoring may occur where the bearing is pressed onto the carrier. Scoring is caused by the bearing race spinning on the carrier.

Replace any parts that are worn or damaged. The ring and pinion gearset must be replaced as an assembly, even though only one may be damaged. Oil seals and drive pinion nuts are always replaced. Check the proper service manual for parts that must be replaced after disassembly.

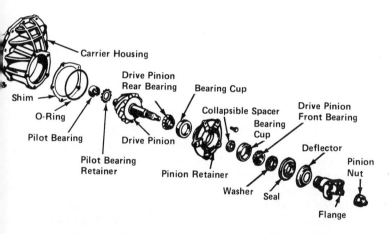

Figure 56-20. Parts of a retainer-type drive pinion assembly. FORD MOTOR COMPANY

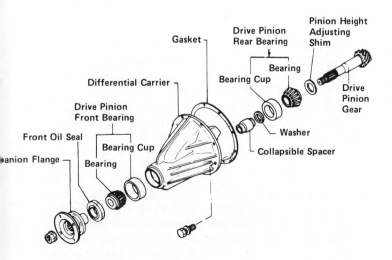

Figure 56-21. Parts of a nonretainer-type drive pinion assembly. FORD MOTOR COMPANY

Reassembly and Adjustment

Many checks and adjustments are necessary when reassembling any differential. The drive pinion and ring gear are always replaced as a set. If any of these checks or adjustments are *not* made, differential noise or early failure can occur. Reassembling the differential requires the following procedures:

- Drive pinion depth setting
- Drive pinion reassembly
- Differential reassembly
- Differential installation.

Drive pinion depth setting. The center of the drive pinion gear teeth must mesh with the centerline of the ring gear teeth. This adjustment is made by moving the drive pinion in or out of the drive pinion bore in the housing. See Figure 56-22. The in-and-out adjustment, or *pinion depth setting,* is controlled by a shim. See Figure 56-23.

A special installation tool is used to replace any bearings (see Figure 56-24).

Several different tools are used to check pinion depth. Always refer to the proper service manual. A pinion depth tool is shown in Figure 56-25. The pinion depth tool provides an important measurement. The measurement helps determine the correct thickness of the shim to be used to ensure proper pinion depth during installation.

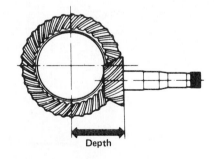

Figure 56-22. Drive pinion depth. NISSAN MOTOR CORPORATION

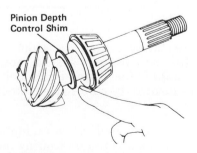

Figure 56-23. Depth-control shim location. NISSAN MOTOR CORPORATION

593

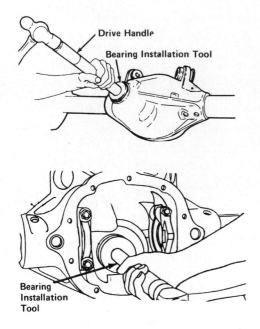

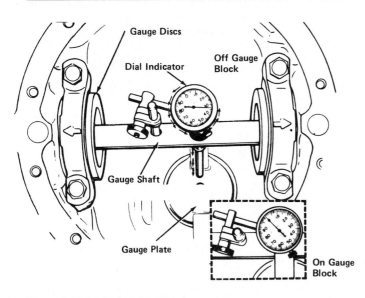

Figure 56-24. Pinion bearing installations.
OLDSMOBILE DIVISION—GMC/CHEVROLET MOTOR DIVISION—GMC

Figure 56-25. Pinion depth tool.
CHEVROLET MOTOR DIVISION—GMC

Integral-carrier drive pinion reassembly. Use all new shims, spacers, washers, gaskets, and oil seals when reassembling the differential. Refer to the proper service manual. Be sure all parts are lubricated properly.

Reassembly begins with drive pinion assembly. Use an arbor press and a pinion bearing installation tool to press on the correct shim and bearing. See Figure 56-26. Place the front bearing cone in the

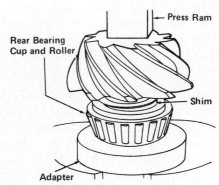

Figure 56-26. Press on new pinion bearing.
FORD MOTOR COMPANY

housing. Install the pinion oil seal with a seal installation tool. Insert the drive pinion, and install the companion flange, using the same special tool that was used to remove it. Measure pinion bearing preload with a torque wrench.

Removable-carrier drive pinion reassembly. The nonretainer drive pinion assembly is reassembled and adjusted in the same manner as the integral-carrier drive pinion assembly.

On the retainer drive pinion assembly, pinion bearing preload adjustment is made before pinion depth setting. Use Figure 56-27 as a guide.

Press the rear and front bearing cones and rollers into place. Be sure the collapsible spacer is against the rear bearing. Place the drive pinion assembly into the carrier. Install the oil deflector and oil seal. Install the companion flange and washer. Torque the pinion nut according to manufacturer's specifications, checking pinion bearing preload several times as you tighten the drive pinion nut. Avoid tightening the nut so far that the bearing preload is excessive. If this happens, you must obtain a new collapsible spacer and pinion nut and try again.

Integral-carrier differential reassembly. Install thrust washers and side gears. Install the differential pinion gears between the side gears. Install the pinion shaft and the lockscrew or bolt.

Position the ring gear on the carrier. Pilot studs may be needed to align the bolt holes. Refer to Figure 56-28. Thread *new* bolts into the ring gear and torque the bolts to specifications. Press side-bearing cones in place.

Removable-carrier differential reassembly. Procedures for reassembling the removable-carrier differential are similar to the procedures for reassembling an integral-carrier differential. The main difference is that removable-carrier reassembly is done on a workbench. Reassembly of an integral-carrier differential is done on the vehicle. Follow service manual procedures carefully.

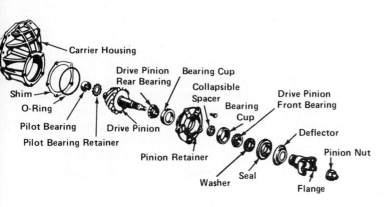

Figure 56-27. Parts of a retainer-type drive pinion assembly.
FORD MOTOR COMPANY

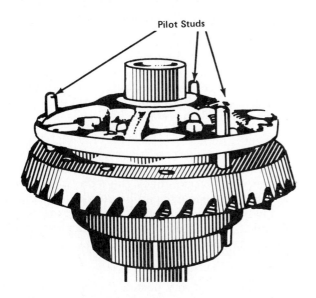

Figure 56-28. Pilot bolts are used to position the ring gear correctly on the differential case.

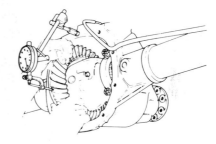

Figure 56-29. Using shims to adjust bearing preload.
FORD MOTOR COMPANY

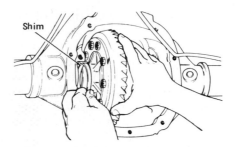

Figure 56-30. Checking backlash with a dial indicator.
FORD MOTOR COMPANY

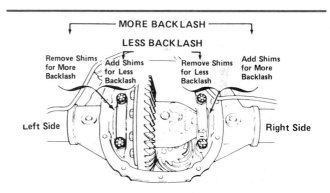

Figure 56-31. Backlash adjustments. FORD MOTOR COMPANY

Limited-slip differential reassembly. The only difference in reassembling a limited-slip differential is when the clutch packs or cones are installed. Check the proper service manual for these procedures.

Final Checks and Adjustments

After reassembly, three checks are made to determine whether the differential is operating within specifications:

1. Differential bearing preload
2. Backlash
3. Gear tooth contact pattern test.

Differential bearing preload and backlash. Adjustments for *differential bearing preload* and *backlash* usually are done at the same time. Differential bearing preload refers to the load or pressure the bearings

are under when installed. Backlash is the proper meshing of free play of the ring and pinion gear teeth.

Differential bearing preload adjustment varies considerably from automobile to automobile. It is important to consult the proper service manual. Adjusting bearing preload often involves using shims or adjusting nuts at each side of the carrier (refer to Figure 56-29).

Backlash on the ring gear is checked with a dial indicator (see Figure 56-30). Backlash is corrected by changing the shims or adjusting nuts on each side of the carrier (see Figure 56-31).

Gear tooth contact pattern test. A *gear tooth contact pattern test* indicates how ring and pinion gears mesh. Proper mesh will eliminate differential noise and help prevent gear damage. Gear tooth contact pattern tests are made after reassembling the differential and often before disassembly. Drive pinion depth and backlash adjustments can be made from the results of a gear tooth contact pattern test.

Before this test is performed, the differential must be assembled and installed in the housing or removable carrier. Each tooth of the ring and pinion must be cleaned. A stiff brush is used to apply a gear marking compound, as shown in Figure 56-32.

SAFETY CAUTION: If a lead marking compound is used, be extremely careful. Lead is poisonous. In some states, lead compounds cannot be purchased. Use of lead marking compounds should be avoided if possible.

After the gear teeth have been coated with compound, the drive pinion is rotated with a torque wrench. This rotation creates a pattern on the gear teeth. The shape and position of the contact pattern is analyzed. See Figure 56-33 for typical contact

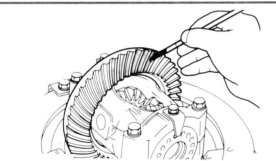

Figure 56-32. Applying a coat of gear marking compound.
FORD MOTOR COMPANY

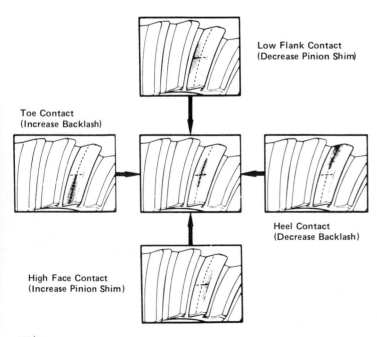

Low Flank Contact
(Decrease Pinion Shim)

Toe Contact
(Increase Backlash)

Heel Contact
(Decrease Backlash)

High Face Contact
(Increase Pinion Shim)

Figure 56-33. Gear tooth contact patterns.
CHEVROLET MOTOR DIVISION—GMC

patterns. The drive pinion can be rotated in both directions to give both drive and coast patterns. Sometimes, inserting a block of hard wood against the differential case to retard it will give a clearer pattern.

Differential Installation

An integral-carrier differential is installed during reassembly. The driving axles (see Topic 56.4) and rear cover are installed. Replace the rear cover using a new gasket or sealant. Refill the differential with lubricant according to manufacturer's specifications.

Install the removable-carrier assembly using a gasket and a jackstand to support the carrier. The carrier is heavy, so a helper will be needed. Tighten the carrier bolts to specifications. Install the driving axles (see Topic 56.4), brake assemblies (see Topics 68.5 and 68.6), and wheels (see Topic 66.3).

56.4 DRIVING AXLE SERVICE

Premature failure of an oil seal or axle bearing frequently is caused by poor inspection or reassembly. Inspect the inside of the axle housing, where the seal is mounted, for rough spots, burrs, rust, and corrosion. Axle shaft splines should be free of burrs, wear, and damage. Check the retainer and studs for damage.

Oil seals usually are replaced with new ones.

Unsealed bearings can be cleaned in solvent. Look for signs of pitting, wear, and other damage (refer to Figure 56-34). Also check the axle shaft bearing surface. Sealed bearings can be checked by rotating them slowly by hand. Listen for noise and feel for any roughness. If anything appears wrong—no matter how slight—replace the bearing.

Driving Axle Runout

Improper runout at any part of the driving axle can cause vibration. Runout is checked with a dial indicator at three different areas of the driving axle assembly:

    1. Pilot   2. Flange face   3. Axle shaft.

The pilot is a machined area at the outside end of the axle shaft on C-lock axle assemblies. Remove the axle and chuck it in a lathe. Place a dial indicator on the pilot, and rotate the shaft (Figure 56-35).

On retainer axle assemblies, check the flange and wheel lugs for runout (see Figure 56-36).

C-Lock Bearing and Seal Installation

Lubricate the new bearing. Use a special bearing installation tool to install the bearing in the housing bore (see Figure 56-37).

CAUTION: Do not use the oil seal to straighten the bearing in the bore. Never apply heat to the bearing or journals. Never beat the bearing with a hammer to install it.

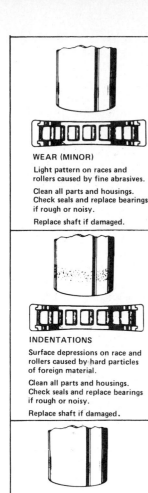

WEAR (MINOR)

Light pattern on races and rollers caused by fine abrasives.

Clean all parts and housings. Check seals and replace bearings if rough or noisy.

Replace shaft if damaged.

WEAR (MAJOR)

Heavy pattern on races and rollers caused by fine abrasives.

Clean all parts and housings. Check seals and replace bearings if rough or noisy.

Replace shaft if damaged.

BRINELLING

Surface indentations in raceway caused by impact loading or vibration while the bearing is not rotating.

Replace bearing if rough or noisy.

Replace shaft if damaged.

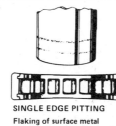

INDENTATIONS

Surface depressions on race and rollers caused by hard particles of foreign material.

Clean all parts and housings. Check seals and replace bearings if rough or noisy.

Replace shaft if damaged.

SINGLE EDGE PITTING

Flaking of surface metal resulting from fatigue, usually at one edge of race and rollers.

Replace bearing — clean all related parts.

Replace shaft if damaged.

DOUBLE EDGE PITTING

Flaking of surface metal resulting from fatigue, usually at both edges of race and rollers.

Replace bearing — clean all related parts.

Replace shaft if damaged.

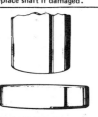

MISALIGNMENT

Replace bearing and make sure races are properly seated.

Replace shaft if bearing operating surface damaged.

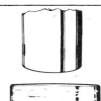

FRETTAGE

Corrosion set up by small relative movement of parts with no lubrication.

Replace bearing. Clean related parts. Check seals and check for proper fit and lubrication.

Replace shaft if damaged.

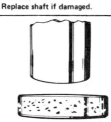

SMEARS

Smearing of metal due to slippage. Slippage can be caused by poor fits, lubrication, overheating, overloads or handling damage.

Replace bearings, clean related parts and check for proper fits and lubrication.

Figure 56-34. Driving axle bearing diagnosis. CHEVROLET MOTOR DIVISION—GMC

Figure 56-35.
Checking pilot runout.
CHRYSLER CORPORATION

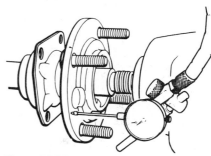
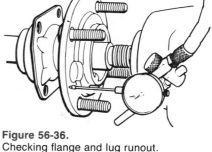

Figure 56-36.
Checking flange and lug runout.
CHRYSLER CORPORATION

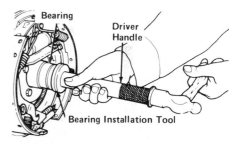

Figure 56-37.
Bearing installation tool.
CHEVROLET MOTOR DIVISION—GMC

Use an oil seal drive, or the recommended special tool, to install the oil seal. See Figure 56-38. Spread grease on the seal after installation.

Retainer-Type Bearing and Seal Installation

There are many variations on installing a bearing and seal on different automobiles. Always check the proper service manual for the correct procedure.

Lubricate the bearing and seal. Install the bearing and retaining collar on an arbor press or with special tools. Press the new bearing onto the axle shaft, as shown in Figure 56-39. Press the new seal in place with a seal installation tool.

C-Lock Axle Reassembly

Remove the lockscrew and pinion shaft. Slide the axle shaft into the housing. Be careful not to damage the oil seal and axle bearing. Start the splines into the side gears. Push the axle shaft in until the button end of the shaft can be seen in the differential case. Install the C-locks and pull out on the axle. Replace the pinion shaft and lockscrew.

C-lock end-play adjustment. End play is controlled by the C-locks and is checked at the outer axle end. *End play* is the in-and-out movement of the axle shaft inside the axle housing.

Strike the ends of both axle shafts with a soft-faced mallet. Install an end-play tool and dial indicator. See Figure 56-40. Push and pull on the axle shaft and read the movement on the dial indicator. Shims are used at the C-locks to correct end play.

Retainer-Type Axle Reassembly

Position the gaskets, brake backing plate, and brake assembly over the axle housing. Lubricate the axle

597

splines. Slide the axle shaft into the housing. Push the axle splines into the side gears. Install retainer plate nuts and torque to specifications.

Retainer-type end-play adjustment. End-play adjustment is done in much the same way as C-lock adjustment. On retainer-type assemblies, end play usually is adjusted at the left axle shaft only. Adjustments are made to shims located behind the retainer plate.

Complete reassembly by installing the brake drums (see Topic 68.6), retainer clips, and wheel assembly.

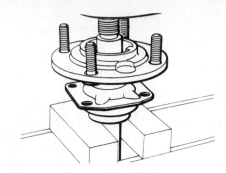

Figure 56-39. Pressing on the axle bearing.
CHRYSLER CORPORATION

Figure 56-38. Oil seal installation tool.
CHEVROLET MOTOR DIVISION—GMC

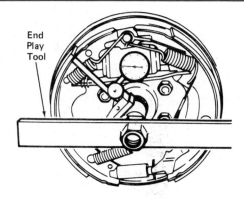

Figure 56-40. End play tool. AMERICAN MOTORS CORPORATION

UNIT HIGHLIGHTS

- Preventive maintenance includes a visual inspection and checking of differential lubricant level.
- Noises are the best indication that something is going wrong in the differential.
- The ring and pinion gears make contact in three different ways.
- Driving axles are held in place by C-locks or retainer plates.
- An integral carrier is serviced from the rear of the differential and is removed part by part.
- A removable carrier is bolted to the front of the differential and is removed as a unit before disassembly.
- Drive pinion depth setting is the in-and-out movement of the drive pinion gear.
- Differential bearing preload is the load or the pressure on bearings after installation.
- A gear tooth contact pattern test indicates how the ring and pinion gears mesh.
- Runout is checked at three different places on a driving axle.
- Axle bearings and seals are installed with special tools specified for these purposes.
- End play is the in-and-out movement of the axle shaft in the axle housing.

TERMS

casting porosity
breakaway torque
differential gearset
hunting gearset
nonhunting gearset
partial nonhunting
   gearset
C-lock axle assembly
retainer-plate axle
   assembly
integral-carrier
   differential

removable-carrier
   differential
retainer-type drive pinion
nonretainer-type drive
   pinion
pinion depth setting
differential bearing
   preload
backlash
gear tooth contact
   pattern test
end play

R E V I E W   Q U E S T I O N S

DIRECTIONS: The following questions are similar to those used on mechanic certification tests. On a separate sheet of paper, write the letter of the correct choice.

1. When diagnosing a differential problem, all of the following are correct EXCEPT
A. The proper troubleshooting chart should be consulted.
B. Worn or damaged bearings rarely make noise.
C. Noises from a damaged gear are heard over the entire speed range.
D. When the vehicle swerves during acceleration, it may indicate a limited-slip problem.

2. A C-lock and a retainer-plate driving axle both are
A. splined to the side gears.
B. pressed into the axle housing.
C. loosened through access holes in the flange.
D. locked to the driving wheel by a collar.

3. Which of the following statements is correct?
   I. An integral carrier case is bolted to the rear of the axle housing and is removed in one piece.
   II. Pinion bearing preload can be measured before removing the drive pinion gear.
A. I only   B. II only   C. Both I and II   D. Neither I nor II

4. Mechanic A says drive pinion depth setting adjusts in-and-out movement of the drive pinion gear. Mechanic B says that differential bearing preload is the in-and-out movement of the axle shaft. Who is correct?
A. A only   B. B only   C. Both A and B   D. Neither A nor B

5. Which of the following driving axle service procedures is correct?
A. The pilot must match flange face runout.
B. A seal must be lubricated during bearing installation.
C. End play is controlled by shims.
D. A gear tooth contact pattern test should be made.

S U P P L E M E N T A L   A C T I V I T I E S

1. Peform a visual inspection of the differential and driving axles, and check differential fluid level.
2. Drain and refill a differential.
3. Remove C-lock and retainer-type driving axles.
4. Remove a differential drive pinion chosen by your instructor.
5. Clean and inspect a differential.
6. Adjust differential bearing preload and backlash.
7. Perform a gear tooth contact pattern test.
8. Replace a differential.
9. Measure axle shaft runout.
10. Demonstrate how an axle bearing and an oil seal are installed with a slide hammer.

57 MANUAL TRANSAXLES

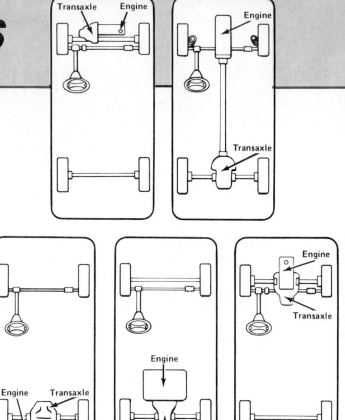

Figure 57-1. Transaxle locations.

Front-engine, front-wheel-drive automobiles with transaxles have begun to dominate the new-car market. A transaxle replaces the separate transmission and differential assemblies used in rear-drive automobiles. The transaxle and engine usually are located together, under the hood of the automobile. No driveline is used with modern transaxles. This unit discusses the operation of the manual transaxle and the differences between conventional-drive and transaxle-equipped automobiles.

LEARNING OBJECTIVES

When you have completed your assignments and exercises in this unit, you should be able to:

☐ Describe the operation of transaxles and front-wheel-drive systems.

☐ Identify the drivetrain parts of a transaxle.

☐ Explain how torquing-over affects power train operation.

☐ Describe how torque steer can be corrected.

☐ Describe the different types of constant-velocity joints.

57.1 TRANSAXLE DESIGN

A manual transaxle is a combination of two drivetrain units: a transmission and a differential. The transmission and differential parts are combined in one unit, inside the same housing.

There are advantages to combining these two drivetrain systems. The weight of a transaxle is less than the combined weight of a separate transmission and differential. The transaxle also is smaller than a separate transmission and differential.

The engine and transaxle can be mounted together at the front or rear of the vehicle (refer to Figure 57-1).

Most transaxle automobiles have front-wheel drive (FWD). In a FWD automobile, the engine and drivetrain are combined at the front to drive the front wheels. The power train usually is mounted transversely, or sideways (see Figure 57-2). In longitudinal, front-to-back, mounting, the engine is mounted in a line from front to back of the automobile.

NOTE: Not all FWD vehicles use transaxles. Some use a transmission with a separate differential unit (see Figure 57-3 and Topic 59.3).

Passenger room and trunk space are increased when the engine and drivetrain are mounted in the front. The large transmission hump and driveline tunnel in the floorpan are eliminated. Front-wheel-drive automobiles have smaller humps and tunnels, which are designed to stiffen the floorpan. A stiffened floorpan strengthens the body.

57.2 TRANSAXLE DRIVETRAIN

Fewer drivetrain parts are used with a transaxle. Manual transaxle drivetrain parts include:

• Clutch   • Transaxle   • Driving axles.

No driveline or driveshaft is used with modern transaxle drivetrains.

Clutch

The same type of clutch is used with manual transaxles as with manual transmissions (see Figure 57-4). The clutch is located between the engine and the transmission part of the transaxle. The clutch is discussed in Unit 51.

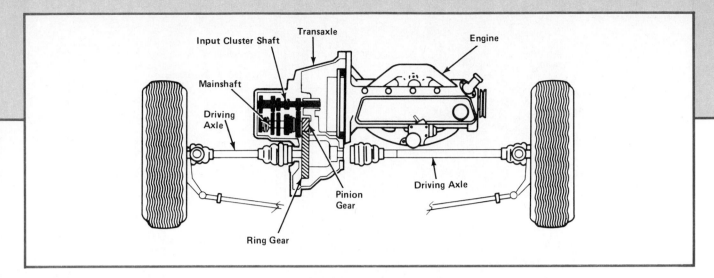

Figure 57-2. Transverse-mounted transaxle.

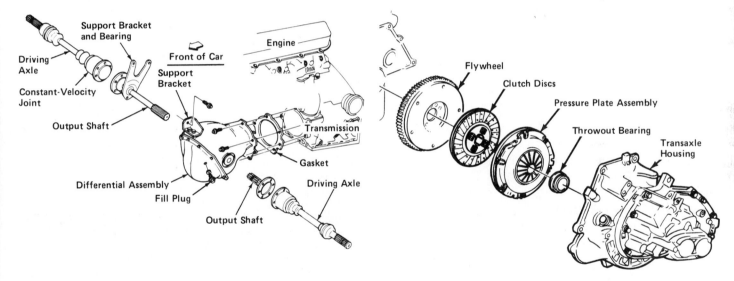

Figure 57-3. Front-wheel-drive transmission.
OLDSMOBILE DIVISION—GMC

Figure 57-4. Clutch assembly.
PONTIAC MOTOR DIVISION—GMC

Transaxle

The main difference between transaxle and conventional drive is that the differential and transmission are inside the same housing in a transaxle. The differential ring gear is driven directly off the output shaft of the transmission. Parts of a transaxle are shown in Figure 57-5.

The entire transaxle power train is located under the hood of the automobile. The engine, transaxle, and driving axles are in a relatively small space, which can make servicing difficult.

A transaxle also can be affected noticeably when engine rpm increases. The engine will twist slightly in the engine mounts, in a direction opposite to crankshaft rotation. This twisting is called *torquing-over*.

Torquing-over can twist the shift linkage. This twisting could cause the transaxle to shift into another gear or damage the linkage. To prevent this, braces or struts often are connected between the body and the power train, parallel to the shift linkage. Refer to Figure 57-6.

Power flow and all-indirect gearing. In a rear-drive automobile, power flows to the transmission through the input shaft. Power then flows from the transmission through the output shaft. Power flows in at one end and out the opposite end.

In a typical FWD automobile with a transverse-mounted power train, the flow is different. Power flows into the transaxle, is turned around, and goes

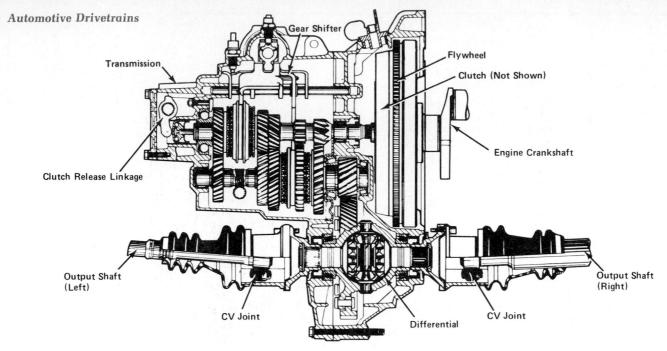

Figure 57-5. Transaxle assembly. CHRYSLER CORPORATION

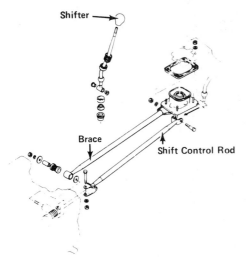

Figure 57-6. Gearshift linkage bracing.
MAZDA MOTOR CORPORATION

out the same end to the driving axles. Figure 57-7 is an exploded view of the parts of a transaxle. The driving axles are positioned lower than the other shafts in the transaxle.

In a four- or five-speed transaxle, the gearing is referred to as all indirect. This means that power flow through the input shaft always passes through the countershaft gear cluster. From the countershaft gear cluster, power is coupled to the main, or output, shaft. Power flow through a transaxle never directly couples the input shaft and the mainshaft.

Gear ratios for economy. In transaxles on economy automobiles, the final transmission gear ratios are less than 1:1. That is, they are overdrive ratios. Modern five-speed transaxles may have overdrive ratios in

both fourth and fifth gears. A typical fourth-gear ratio might be 0.87:1, while a fifth-gear ratio might be 0.78:1 or less.

Shift and clutch linkages. In transversely mounted power trains, the transaxle is *not* parallel to the front-to-back line of the automobile. It is perpendicular, or at a 90-degree angle, to the front-to-back line. This means that the shift linkage must change the normal front-to-back motions of the shift pattern into side-to-side motions. The simplest solution is to use flexible cables (see Figure 57-8). Rod-and-lever linkage systems, with braces, also are used.

Cable also is used in most transaxle clutch linkage systems.

Driving Axles

The driving axles on a FWD automobile are *not* enclosed in a housing, as they would be in a conventional differential. The inner parts of the driving axles are connected to the differential. The outer parts of the axles are connected to a wheel hub.

When the power train is mounted transversely, the differential is not always located at the center of the automobile. The transaxle usually is set to one side of the engine compartment. Because of this offset, one of the driving axles must be longer.

When torque from the transaxle begins to turn the driving axles, the axles begin to twist before they turn. The longer axle shaft will twist more than the shorter shaft before it begins turning. This added twisting, or torquing, of the longer axle makes it begin to turn slightly later than the shorter axle. Thus, the wheel connected to the longer axle begins to turn slightly later than the opposite driving wheel. When this happens, the vehicle will pull toward the side with the

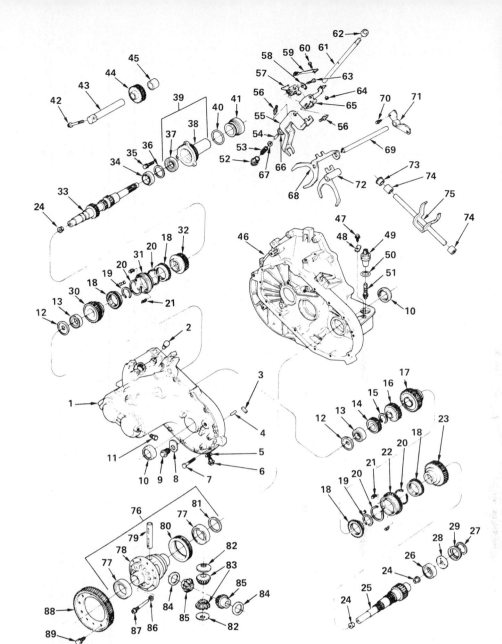

1. Case Assembly
2. Vent Assembly
3. Magnet
4. Pin
5. Washer, Drain Screw
6. Screw, Drain
7. Bolt
8. Washer, Fill Plug
9. Plug, Fill
10. Seal Assembly, Axle Shaft
11. Plug
12. Shield, Oil
13. Bearing Assembly
14. Gear, 4th Speed Output
15. Ring, 3rd Speed Output Gear Retaining
16. Gear, 3rd Speed Output
17. Gear, 2nd Speed Output
18. Ring, Synchronizer Blocking
19. Ring, Synchronizer Retaining
20. Spring, Synchronizer Key Retaining
21. Key, Synchronizer
22. Synchronizer Assembly
23. Gear, 1st Speed Output
24. Sleeve, Oil Shield
25. Gear, Output
26. Bearing Assembly, Output
27. Shim, Output Gear Bearing Adjustment
28. Shield, Output Bearing Oil
29. Retainer, Output Gear Bearing Oil Shield
30. Gear, 4th Speed Input
31. Synchronizer Assembly
32. Gear, 3rd Speed Input
33. Gear, Input Cluster
34. Bearing Assembly, Input
35. Screw
36. Shim, Input Gear Bearing Adjustment
37. Seal Assembly, Input Gear
38. Retainer, Input Gear
39. Retainer Assembly, Input Gear Bearing
40. Seal, Input Gear Bearing Retainer
41. Bearing Assembly, Clutch Release
42. Screw & Washer, Reverse Idler
43. Shaft, Reverse Idler
44. Gear Assembly, Reverse Idler
45. Spacer, Reverse Idler Shaft
46. Housing Assembly, Clutch & Differential
47. Screw
48. Retainer, Speedo Gear Fitting
49. Sleeve, Speedo Driven Gear
50. Seal, Speedo Gear Sleeve
51. Gear, Speedo Driven
52. Seat, Reverse Inhibitor Spring
53. Spring, Reverse Inhibitor
54. Pin
55. Lever, Reverse Shift
56. Stud, Reverse Lever Locating
57. Lever Assembly, Detent
58. Washer, Lock Detent Lever
59. Spring, Detent
60. Bolt
61. Shaft, Shift
62. Seal Assembly, Shift Shaft
63. Bolt
64. Nut
65. Interlock, Shift
66. Shim, Shift Shaft
67. Washer, Reverse Inhibitor Spring

68. Fork, 3rd and 4th Shift
69. Shaft, Shift Fork
70. Screw
71. Guide, Oil
72. Fork, 1st and 2nd Shift
73. Seal Assembly, Clutch Fork Shaft
74. Bearing, Clutch Fork Shaft
75. Shaft Assembly, Clutch Fork
76. Differential Assembly
77. Bearing Assembly, Differential
78. Case, Differential
79. Shaft, Differential Pinion
80. Gear, Speedo Drive
81. Shim, Differential Bearing Adjustment
82. Washer, Pinion Thrust
83. Gear, Differential Pinion
84. Washer, Side Gear Thrust
85. Gear, Differential Side
86. Lockwasher
87. Screw, Pinion Shaft
88. Gear, Differential Ring
89. Bolt

Figure 57-7. Parts of a transaxle assembly. PONTIAC MOTOR DIVISION—GMC

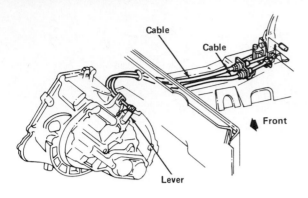

Figure 57-8. Cable gearshift linkage.
PONTIAC MOTOR DIVISION—GMC

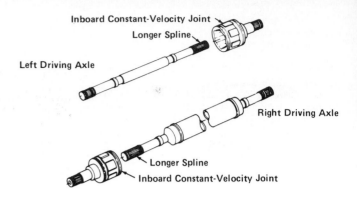

Figure 57-10. Solid and hollow driving axle assemblies.
FORD MOTOR COMPANY

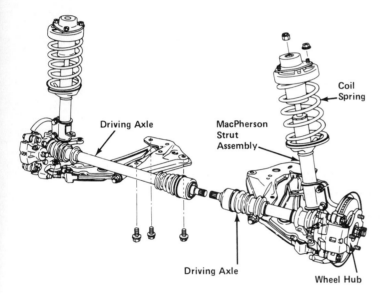

Figure 57-9. Typical driving axle system.
NISSAN MOTOR CORPORATION

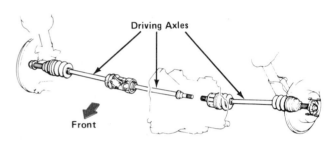

Figure 57-11. Driving axles with three shafts.
MAZDA MOTOR CORPORATION

longer driving axle. This is known as *torque steer*. Figure 57-9 shows a typical driving axle system.

Different methods can be used to help correct torque steer. The longer axle may be made thicker, but hollow inside (see Figure 57-10). Another solution is to use different types of steel, so that the longer axle is stiffer. A more complicated way to reduce torque steer is to make both drive axles the same length. A third, or connecting, shaft is used to make up for the length of the longer axle (see Figure 57-11).

Constant-velocity joints. Driving axles used with front-drive automobiles must steer from side to side as well as move up and down. Universal joints are *not* flexible enough to do the job. Power must be transmitted smoothly through the sharp angles necessary when steering the front wheels. To do this, a *constant-velocity joint* is used.

The most common constant-velocity (CV) joint is the *Rzeppa joint*. A Rzeppa joint has large-diameter

ball bearings that run in grooves in the inner and outer parts of the joint. See Figure 57-12. This type of joint can be used at the inner and outer ends of the drive axles.

Another type of joint may be used on the inner, or transaxle, ends of the axles. This is called a *tripot*, or *tripod, joint*. A tripod joint has a triangular-shaped center spider and needle bearings. It also has circular races that run in grooves machined into the outer portion of the joint (see Figure 57-13).

57.3 OTHER TRANSAXLE DIFFERENCES

To achieve lighter weight and greater fuel economy, modern transaxle cases usually are made of aluminum. Older transaxle cases were made of cast iron.

In addition, modern manual transaxles are designed to use lower viscosity, or thinner, lubricants. Lubricants such as automatic transmission fluid, multi-viscosity engine oils, or light mineral oils often are recommended. Thinner lubricant allows the gears to spin more easily, resulting in increased fuel economy and making the transaxle easier to shift.

Modern transaxles also use caged needle, roller, or ball bearings to support the transaxle shafts, instead of separate needle bearings. This makes disassembly and reassembly easier.

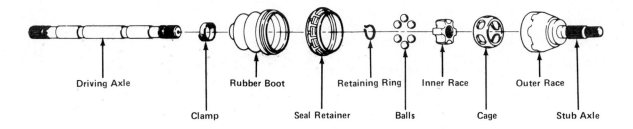

Figure 57-12. Rzeppa joint. PONTIAC MOTOR DIVISION—GMC

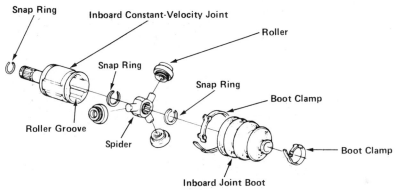

Figure 57-13. Tripod joint. HONDA MOTOR COMPANY

U N I T   H I G H L I G H T S

- A manual transaxle combines a transmission and a differential in one unit.
- Most front-drive power trains are mounted transversely.
- A manual transaxle drivetrain consists of a clutch, transaxle, and driving axles.
- Torquing-over is engine movement that is in a direction opposite to crankshaft rotation.
- Shift and clutch linkages usually are cable-operated in transverse-mounted power trains.
- Driving axles in transaxle power trains usually are of different lengths.
- A constant-velocity joint transmits power smoothly through sharp angles.
- Manual transaxles use lower viscosity, or thinner, lubricants than rear-drive transmissions and differentials.

T E R M S

torquing-over
torque steer
constant-velocity joint

Rzeppa joint
tripod joint
tripot joint

R E V I E W   Q U E S T I O N S

DIRECTIONS: The following questions are similar to those used on mechanic certification tests. On a separate sheet of paper, write the letter of the correct choice.

1. All of the following statements are true EXCEPT
A. A manual transaxle combines a transmission and a differential.
B. In an FWD automobile, the engine and drivetrain are combined at the front to drive the front wheels.
C. A transverse-mounted power train is mounted in a front-to-back direction.
D. Front-wheel-drive automobiles have humps and tunnels in the floorpan.

2. The parts of a manual transaxle include all of the following EXCEPT
A. a clutch.
B. a valve body housing.
C. driving axles.
D. constant-velocity joints.

3. Which of the following statements is correct?
   I. Torquing-over is a twisting action of the engine that helps to keep linkage in alignment.
   II. Torque steer is a method by which driving axles are controlled.
A. I only   B. II only   C. Both I and II   D. Neither I nor II

4. Mechanic A says that linkages used in transverse-mounted power trains usually are controlled by a cable.
   Mechanic B says that driving axles are always the same length.
   Who is correct?
A. A only   B. B only   C. Both A and B   D. Neither A nor B

5. All of the following statements about constant-velocity joints are true EXCEPT
A. Power must be transmitted at different speeds to eliminate torque steer.
B. A Rzeppa joint is the most common CV joint in use.
C. A tripot joint uses a triangular spider.
D. A tripod joint is used on the inner ends of driving axles.

S U P P L E M E N T A L   A C T I V I T I E S

1. Identify the locations where transaxles and engines can be found in modern automobiles.
2. Describe how the differential is driven off the transmission.
3. Explain the extra parts that are used to eliminate torque-over.
4. Explain how indirect gearing operates.
5. Describe the transaxle linkage system on a vehicle your instructor selects.
6. Explain what is meant by torque steer.
7. Identify and explain the operation of a constant-velocity joint.
8. Describe the flow of power from the engine crankshaft to the tires on a transaxle-equipped automobile.

Service procedures on a manual transaxle can be demanding because of its design and location on the vehicle. Several parts of the suspension, brake system, and steering must be removed to service a transaxle. Service procedures for the transmission portion are similar to those for manual transmissions. The proper service manual always must be consulted for transaxle and driving axle service because procedures vary widely.

LEARNING OBJECTIVES

When you have completed your assignments and exercises in this unit, you should be able to:

☐ Remove an indentation in a CV-joint boot.
☐ Remove a driving axle from a wheel assembly.
☐ Remove a driving axle from a transaxle.
☐ Disassemble an outer CV joint.
☐ Remove a transaxle.

SAFETY PRECAUTIONS

Several parts of an automobile must be supported independently when a transaxle is removed. Special supporting fixtures and special jacks are required when servicing a transaxle. When using a hoist to raise an automobile with a transaxle, always check the proper service manual for procedures. Use jackstands and safety glasses whenever working under an automobile.

Before servicing a transaxle, disconnect the battery. Many electrical connections are on or near parts that are to be serviced. Electrical connections can be activated by touch when the ignition switch is "on" or when the battery is connected. An electric cooling fan in the engine compartment may be controlled by a thermostat. This fan could start running, even with the ignition switch "off," and cause serious injury.

Hot transaxle lubricant, transaxles, exhaust systems, engines, and brakes can cause severe burns. When possible, allow the automobile to cool before working.

Be very careful when working around the clutch and brakes. Both assemblies contain asbestos.

Asbestos is easily inhaled and is dangerous to your health. Always wear a breathing mask. Always use a special vacuum cleaner to remove asbestos before continuing any service work.

58.1 PREVENTIVE MAINTENANCE

Manual transaxle preventive maintenance includes checking the oil and lubricating the gearshift linkage. A visual inspection should be made during any maintenance procedure.

Checking and Adding Lubricant

Lubricant is checked at a filler tube (see Figure 58-1) or filler plug at the end of the transaxle (see Figure 58-2). Unlike a separate transmission and differential, a transaxle has only one plug for these combined systems. Transaxle lubricant should always be at the "full" mark on the dipstick or just below the filler plug hole.

CAUTION: Always check the proper service manual before adding transaxle lubricant. Transaxles may require conventional 90W lubricant, automatic transmission fluid, engine oil, or light mineral oil. The wrong lubricant can cause serious damage to the transaxle.

Replacing Transaxle Oil

Manual transaxle oil is changed periodically, according to the manufacturer's recommendations. Some

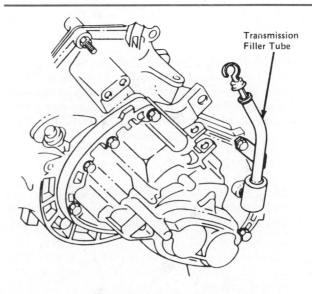

Figure 58-1. Filler tube location. BUICK MOTOR DIVISION—GMC

607

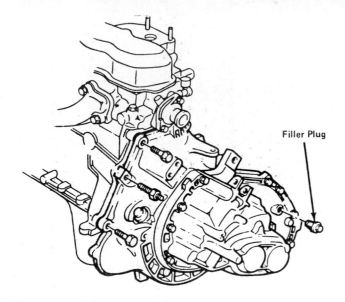

Figure 58-2. Filler plug location. BUICK MOTOR DIVISION—GMC

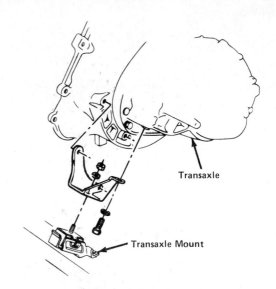

Figure 58-3. Transaxle mounting. PONTIAC MOTOR DIVISION—GMC

manufacturers do not recommend changing transaxle oil as a scheduled maintenance procedure.

A drain plug usually is located at the base of the transaxle. New oil is added through the filler tube or filler plug.

Checking and Adjusting Shift and Clutch Linkage

Transaxle and clutch linkages should be lubricated at the pivot points whenever a chassis lubrication is performed.

Visual Inspection

A visual inspection of a transaxle drivetrain is confined to the front of the automobile. That does not mean a visual inspection of a transaxle is easier. Many transaxle systems are squeezed into a small space, which may make it more difficult to see the areas clearly.

SAFETY CAUTION: Be sure that the vehicle being inspected has cooled sufficiently. You will be using your bare hands. Touching hot exhaust systems or other parts of the transaxle and engine can cause serious burns. Many transaxle-drive parts may have sharp edges that will cut. Move your hand slowly over these parts, and you will be able to feel danger in time to avoid injury.

Inspecting transaxle case and mounts. Check all parts for looseness and leaks. Also check the transaxle case for any casting porosity that shows up as leaks.

Push up and pull down on the transaxle case. Watch the mount to see if the rubber separates from the metal plate (see Figure 58-3). Also watch to see if the transaxle case moves up but not down. If the housing does not move down, the mount must be replaced.

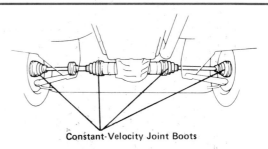

Figure 58-4. Constant-velocity joint boot locations. TOYOTA MOTOR SALES, U.S.A.

Inspecting the linkages. Move the clutch and transmission shift linkages around to check for looseness. Look for excessive or jerky movement. Look for damaged or missing parts. Cable linkage should have no kinks. Check the fluid level if a hydraulic clutch system is used.

Inspecting driving axles and CV joints. Driving axles should be checked for cracks, deformation, or damage.

The constant-velocity (CV) joints are covered with rubber boots to help prevent damage (see Figure 58-4). Inspect the boots for cracks, tears, or splits. Look for indentations in the boots. Check for leakage between the CV joints. Some CV joints can be repacked with grease, while others require replacement if they are leaking.

To check a CV joint, grasp the axle and try to move it up and down. If it moves, the CV joint should be serviced.

Bad CV joint boots must be replaced. Otherwise, dirt, salt, or other grit will enter the CV joint and cause it to fail. In most cases, the drive axle must be removed to replace a bad boot. An indentation in a

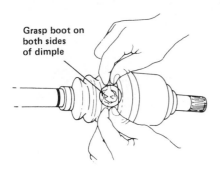

Figure 58-5. Removing boot indentations.
FORD MOTOR COMPANY

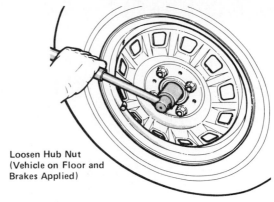

Figure 58-6. Loosening hub nuts. CHRYSLER CORPORATION

boot, however, usually can be removed. Remove the indentation by grasping the dimpled portion on both sides, as shown in Figure 58-5. Pull on the boot in opposite directions until the indentation pops out.

58.2 TRANSAXLE PROBLEM DIAGNOSIS

Diagnosing transaxle problems can be difficult, because the drivetrain parts are close together. Before servicing the transaxle, linkage, or clutch, the problem should be diagnosed thoroughly.

Most transaxle and clutch problems can be identified by shifting difficulties. Manual transmission and clutch diagnostic procedures are discussed in Units 50 and 52, respectively.

Diagnosing transaxle drivetrain noises can be confusing. As with manual transmissions, many noises are carried by the drivetrain. What is thought to be transaxle noise may actually be caused by tires, wheel bearings, the engine, or the exhaust system.

A thorough and careful check of all systems is essential in diagnosing transaxle problems. Always refer to the proper service manual and troubleshooting chart whenever making a diagnosis.

58.3 TRANSAXLE SERVICE

Removing and replacing a transaxle and drivetrain is complicated and requires considerable time. Service procedures vary considerably, so always consult the proper service manual.

Removing Driving Axles

Driving axle removal is necessary when servicing axle parts and removing a transaxle. Procedures vary so much that the following outline is only a brief description.

Place the transaxle shift lever in first or reverse. Set the emergency brake. Loosen the *hub nut,* as shown in Figure 58-6. Raise the vehicle on a hoist.

Remove the wheel and hub nut. Remove the brakes, steering, and suspension as the service manual indicates. Do *not* pull on the driving axle as this may cause the outer CV joint to separate and become damaged.

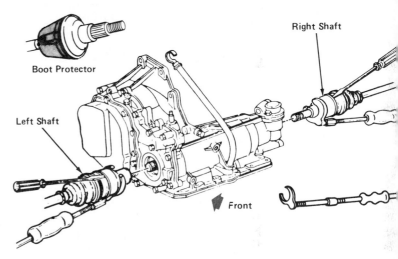

Figure 58-7. Removing driving axle shafts.
CHEVROLET MOTOR DIVISION—GMC

Use a special tool to remove the driving axle from the transaxle (see Figure 58-7). Do *not* allow the outer end of the driving axle to hang free and become damaged.

Servicing Driving Axles

Repairing or replacing constant-velocity joints and boots are the most common services performed on driving axles. Always inspect the shafts and splines for damage and wear when the driving axles have been removed. Figure 58-8 shows a driving axle assembly.

Outer constant-velocity joint service is shown in Figures 58-9 and 58-10. Inner constant-velocity joint service is shown in Figures 58-11 and 58-12.

Removing Transaxles

Transaxle removal requires removing braces, supporting the engine, and removing different parts of an automobile. The following procedure is a brief description of transaxle removal. Be sure to follow service manual procedures in completing this job.

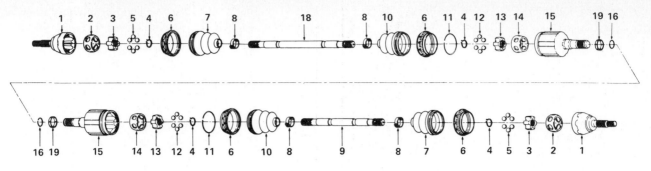

Automatic Transaxle
(LH Side Only)

1. Race, CV Joint Outer
2. Cage, CV Joint
3. Race, CV Joint Inner
4. Ring, Race Retaining
5. Ball (6)

6. Retainer, Seal
7. Seal, CV Joint
8. Clamp, Seal Retaining
9. Shaft, Axle (LH)
10. Seal, D/O Joint

11. Ring, Ball Retaining
12. Ball (6)
13. Race, D/O Joint Inner
14. Cage, D/O Joint
15. Race, D/O Joint Outer

16. Ring, Joint Retaining
17. Race, D/O Joint Outer
18. Shaft, Axle (RH)
19. Slinger

Figure 58-8. Driving axle assembly. CHEVROLET MOTOR DIVISION—GMC

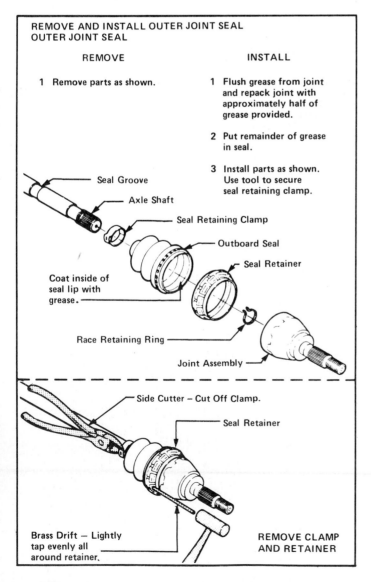

REMOVE AND INSTALL OUTER JOINT SEAL
OUTER JOINT SEAL

REMOVE

1 Remove parts as shown.

INSTALL

1 Flush grease from joint and repack joint with approximately half of grease provided.

2 Put remainder of grease in seal.

3 Install parts as shown. Use tool to secure seal retaining clamp.

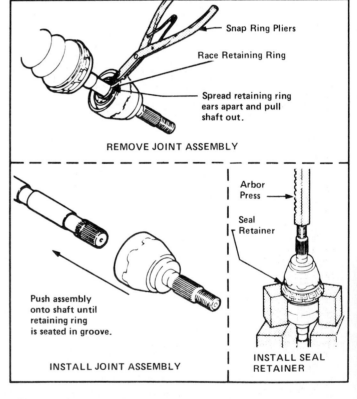

Figure 58-9. Removing and installing outer joints.
CHEVROLET MOTOR DIVISION—GMC

610

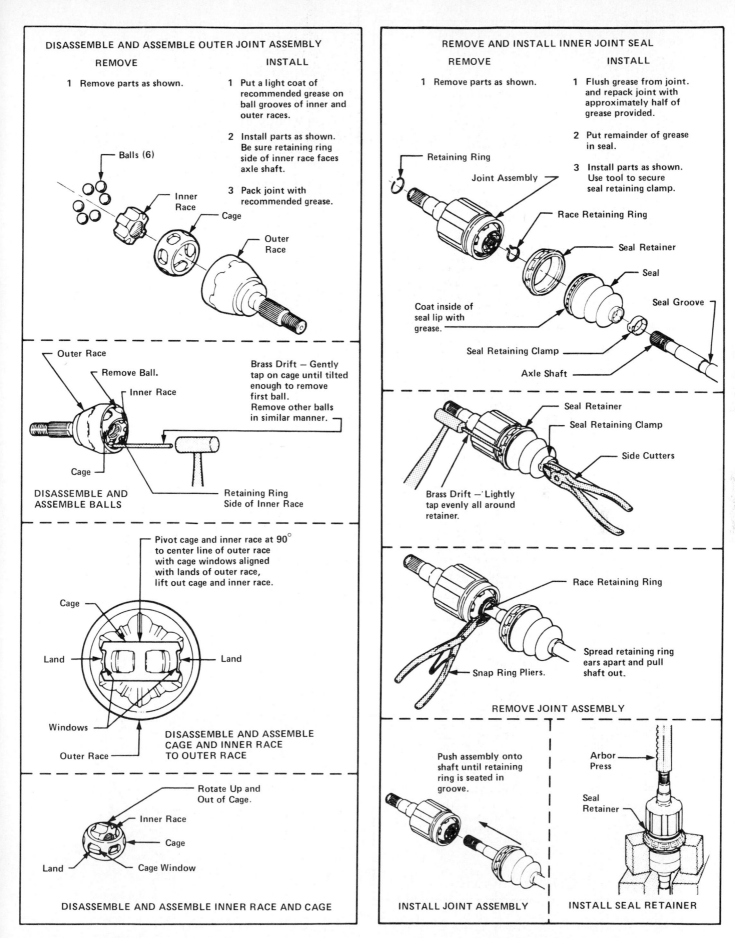

DISASSEMBLE AND ASSEMBLE OUTER JOINT ASSEMBLY

REMOVE	INSTALL
1 Remove parts as shown.	1 Put a light coat of recommended grease on ball grooves of inner and outer races.
	2 Install parts as shown. Be sure retaining ring side of inner race faces axle shaft.
	3 Pack joint with recommended grease.

Balls (6)

Inner Race

Cage

Outer Race

Outer Race

Remove Ball.

Inner Race

Cage

Brass Drift — Gently tap on cage until tilted enough to remove first ball. Remove other balls in similar manner.

Retaining Ring Side of Inner Race

DISASSEMBLE AND ASSEMBLE BALLS

Pivot cage and inner race at 90° to center line of outer race with cage windows aligned with lands of outer race, lift out cage and inner race.

Cage

Land

Land

Windows

Outer Race

DISASSEMBLE AND ASSEMBLE CAGE AND INNER RACE TO OUTER RACE

Rotate Up and Out of Cage.

Inner Race

Cage

Land

Cage Window

DISASSEMBLE AND ASSEMBLE INNER RACE AND CAGE

Figure 58-10. Disassembling and assembling outer joints.
CHEVROLET MOTOR DIVISION—GMC

REMOVE AND INSTALL INNER JOINT SEAL

REMOVE	INSTALL
1 Remove parts as shown.	1 Flush grease from joint. and repack joint with approximately half of grease provided.
	2 Put remainder of grease in seal.
	3 Install parts as shown. Use tool to secure seal retaining clamp.

Retaining Ring

Joint Assembly

Race Retaining Ring

Seal Retainer

Seal

Seal Groove

Coat inside of seal lip with grease.

Seal Retaining Clamp

Axle Shaft

Seal Retainer

Seal Retaining Clamp

Side Cutters

Brass Drift — Lightly tap evenly all around retainer.

Race Retaining Ring

Spread retaining ring ears apart and pull shaft out.

Snap Ring Pliers.

REMOVE JOINT ASSEMBLY

Push assembly onto shaft until retaining ring is seated in groove.

Arbor Press

Seal Retainer

INSTALL JOINT ASSEMBLY   **INSTALL SEAL RETAINER**

Figure 58-11. Removing and installing inner joints.
CHEVROLET MOTOR DIVISION—GMC

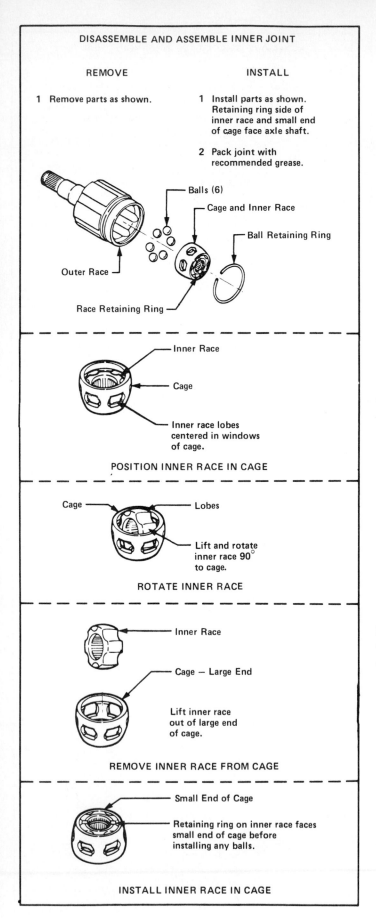

REMOVE   INSTALL

1 Remove parts as shown.

1 Install parts as shown. Retaining ring side of inner race and small end of cage face axle shaft.

2 Pack joint with recommended grease.

Balls (6)

Cage and Inner Race

Ball Retaining Ring

Outer Race

Race Retaining Ring

Inner Race

Cage

Inner race lobes centered in windows of cage.

POSITION INNER RACE IN CAGE

Cage

Lobes

Lift and rotate inner race 90° to cage.

ROTATE INNER RACE

Inner Race

Cage – Large End

Lift inner race out of large end of cage.

REMOVE INNER RACE FROM CAGE

Small End of Cage

Retaining ring on inner race faces small end of cage before installing any balls.

INSTALL INNER RACE IN CAGE

Figure 58-12. Disassembling and assembling inner joints.
CHEVROLET MOTOR DIVISION—GMC

Drain the transaxle. Disconnect the electrical system.

Install the proper *engine support fixture,* as shown in Figure 58-13. Engine support fixtures usually are not designed to support the entire weight of the engine and transaxle. Improper use of the support fixture can result in serious injury.

Remove the transaxle mount bolts and linkage systems. Remove the upper transaxle-to-engine bolts (see Figure 58-14). Raise the vehicle on a hoist and support all assemblies according to manufacturer's recommendations.

Remove the left front wheel and any body parts that are recommended in service manual procedures. Remove the necessary brake, suspension, and steering parts. Remove the driving axles.

Place a transaxle jack under the transaxle case. Remove the lower transaxle-to-engine bolts.

Remove the transaxle by sliding it away from the engine. Lower the jack carefully and guide the right

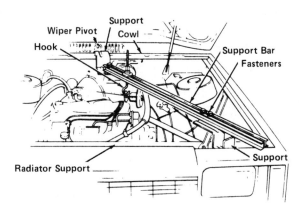

Wiper Pivot

Support

Cowl

Hook

Support Bar

Fasteners

Radiator Support

Support

Figure 58-13. Engine support fixture.
CHEVROLET MOTOR DIVISION—GMC

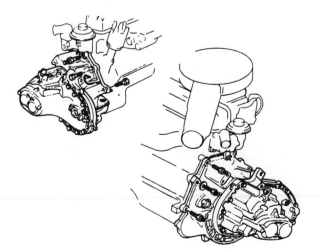

Figure 58-14. Transaxle bolt locations.
CHEVROLET MOTOR DIVISION—GMC

shaft out of the transaxle. Place the transaxle in a stand on a workbench (see Figure 58-15).

Servicing Transaxles

A manual transaxle is serviced in a manner similar to a manual transmission (see Topic 50.3) and a differential (see Topic 56.3). Figure 58-16 shows the parts of a manual transaxle. Always follow closely the service manual procedures.

Replacing Transaxles and Driving Axles

The procedure for installing a manual transaxle and driving axles is almost exactly the reverse of the procedure for removal. Follow carefully the manufacturer's recommendations in the service manual.

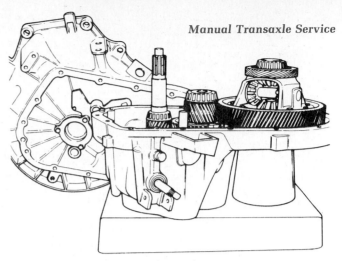

Figure 58-15. Transaxle with clutch cover removed.
CHEVROLET MOTOR DIVISION—GMC

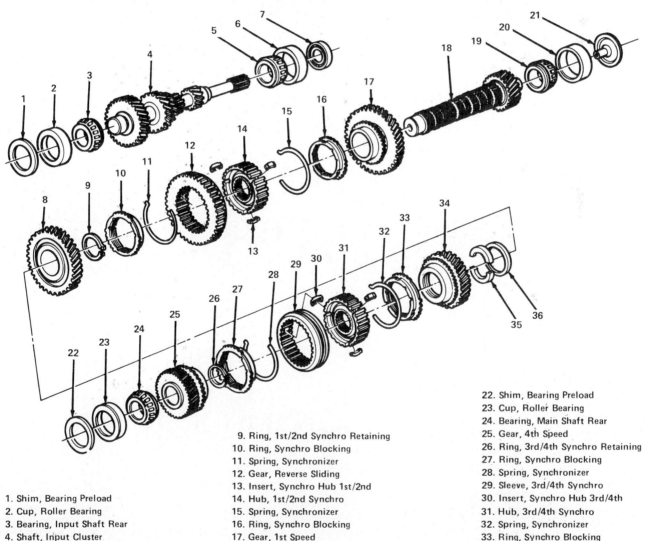

1. Shim, Bearing Preload
2. Cup, Roller Bearing
3. Bearing, Input Shaft Rear
4. Shaft, Input Cluster
5. Bearing, Input Shaft Front
6. Cup, Roller Bearing
7. Seal Assembly, Input Shaft
8. Gear, 2nd Speed

9. Ring, 1st/2nd Synchro Retaining
10. Ring, Synchro Blocking
11. Spring, Synchronizer
12. Gear, Reverse Sliding
13. Insert, Synchro Hub 1st/2nd
14. Hub, 1st/2nd Synchro
15. Spring, Synchronizer
16. Ring, Synchro Blocking
17. Gear, 1st Speed
18. Shaft, Main
19. Bearing, Main Shaft Front
20. Cup, Roller Bearing
21. Funnel, Mainshaft

22. Shim, Bearing Preload
23. Cup, Roller Bearing
24. Bearing, Main Shaft Rear
25. Gear, 4th Speed
26. Ring, 3rd/4th Synchro Retaining
27. Ring, Synchro Blocking
28. Spring, Synchronizer
29. Sleeve, 3rd/4th Synchro
30. Insert, Synchro Hub 3rd/4th
31. Hub, 3rd/4th Synchro
32. Spring, Synchronizer
33. Ring, Synchro Blocking
34. Gear, 3rd Speed
35. Washer, 2nd/3rd Gear Thrust
36. Ring, 2nd/3rd Thrust Washer Retaining

Figure 58-16. Parts of a transaxle assembly. FORD MOTOR COMPANY (Continued on next page.)

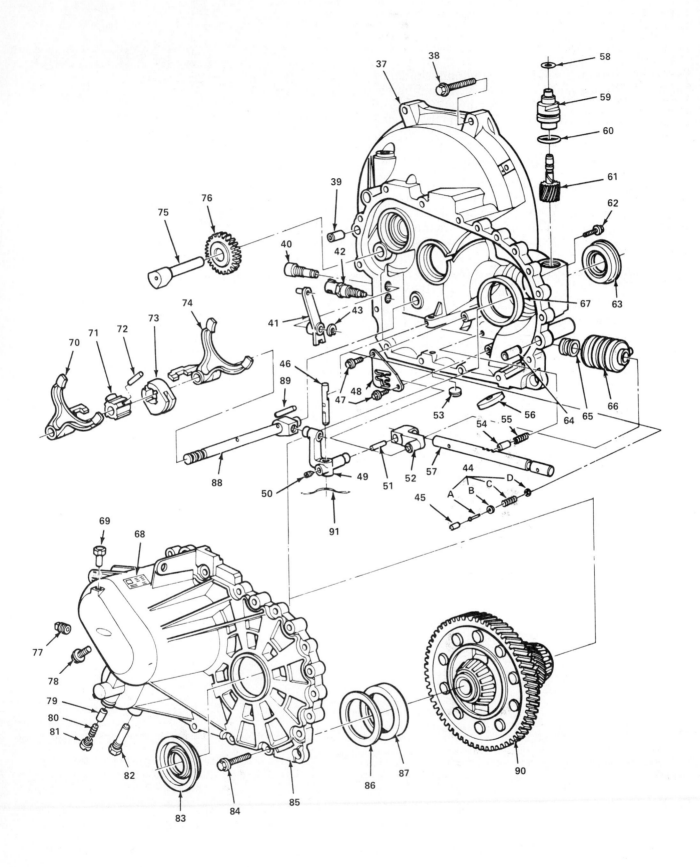

Figure 58-16. Continued.

37. Case, Clutch Housing
38. Bolt, Transaxle to Engine Attaching
39. Dowel, Trans Case to Clutch Housing
40. Pin, Reverse Relay Lever Pivot
41. Lever, Reverse Relay
42. Switch Assembly, Back Up Lamps
43. Ring, Retaining External
44. Spring and Retaining Assembly, Reverse Inhibitor
    A. Pin
    B. Washer
    C. Spring
    D. Ring
45. Plunger, Reverse Inhibitor
46. Shaft, Shift Lever
47. Bolt, Selector Plate Attaching
48. Plate, Selector
49. Lever, Shift
50. Screw, Shift Lever Shaft Set
51. Pin, Spring
52. Arm, Input Shift Shaft Selector Plate

53. Plug, Expansion
54. Plunger, Input Shift Shaft Detent
55. Spring, Input Shift Shaft Detent
56. Magnet, Case Ceramic
57. Shaft, Input Shift
58. Seal, 5.16mm x 1.6 O-Ring
59. Retainer, Speedo Driven Gear
60. Seal, Speedo Retainer to Case
61. Gear, Speedo Driven
62. Screw, Speedo Retaining
63. Seal Assembly (RH), Differential
64. Dowel, Trans Case to Clutch Housing
65. Seal Assembly, Shift Shaft Oil
66. Boot, Input Shift Shaft
67. Cup, Differential Bearing
68. Tag, Transaxle Identification
69. Vent, Case
70. Fork, 3rd/4th
71. Arm, Fork Selector
72. Pin, Spring
73. Sleeve, Fork Interlock
74. Fork, 1st/2nd

75. Shaft, Reverse Idler
76. Gear, Reverse Idler
77. Plug, Fill
78. Bolt, Reverse Shaft Retaining
79. Plunger, Main Shift Shaft Detent
80. Spring, Main Shift Shaft Detent
81. Screw, Detent Plunger Retaining
82. Pin, Fork Interlock Sleeve Retaining
83. Seal Assembly (LH), Differential
84. Bolt, Trans Case
85. Case, Trans
86. Shim, Differential Bearing Preload
87. Cup, Differential Bearing
88. Shaft, Main Shift
89. Pin, Reverse Relay Actuating Lever
90. Differential and Final Drive Ring Gear
91. Shift Bias Spring, 3rd/4th

Figure 58-16. Concluded.

U N I T   H I G H L I G H T S

- Special supporting fixtures and special jacks are required when servicing transaxles.
- A manual transaxle may require different lubricant than a manual transmission.
- Most transaxle and clutch problems can be identified by shifting difficulties.
- Driving axles are removed whenever the axles and transaxle are serviced.
- To remove a transaxle, parts of the suspension, brakes, and bracing members must be removed.

T E R M S

hub nut

engine support fixture

R E V I E W   Q U E S T I O N S

DIRECTIONS: The following questions are similar to those used on mechanic certification tests. On a separate sheet of paper, write the letter of the correct choice.

1. Which of the following statements is correct?

   I. A manual transaxle can use engine oil.

   II. A transaxle case mount can be checked only when the transaxle is removed.

   A. I only   B. II only   C. Both I and II   D. Neither I nor II

2. All of the following statements are correct EXCEPT

   A. Most transaxle and clutch problems can be identified by shifting difficulties.

   B. Driving axle removal is necessary when removing a transaxle.

   C. A special tool is used to remove a CV joint from a transaxle.

   D. The outer CV joint must be removed before loosening the hub nut.

3. Mechanic A says that the front wheels are removed when servicing a transaxle.

   Mechanic B says that an engine support fixture is used to raise the engine and transaxle out of the automobile.

   Who is correct?

   A. A only   B. B only   C. Both A and B   D. Neither A nor B

4. All of the following parts must be removed before the transaxle can be removed EXCEPT

   A. brakes.

   B. shift linkage.

   C. the driveline.

   D. clutch linkage.

5. Mechanic A says that a transaxle jack is used to remove a transaxle.

   Mechanic B says that a transaxle jack only supports a transaxle.

   Who is correct?

   A. A only   B. B only   C. Both A and B   D. Neither A nor B

S U P P L E M E N T A L   A C T I V I T I E S

1. Check the transaxle fluid level on a vehicle selected by your instructor.
2. Identify the type of transaxle fluid that is to be used in the vehicle selected.
3. Inspect the transaxle mounts on a vehicle selected by your instructor.
4. Inspect the boots on CV joints selected by your instructor.
5. Identify the parts that must be removed before the driving axles can be removed.
6. Disassemble an outer CV joint.
7. Study a service manual selected by your instructor and describe how to remove and replace a transaxle.

59 AUTOMATIC TRANSAXLES

UNIT PREVIEW

Automatic transaxles have many similarities to manual transaxles and automatic transmissions. This unit discusses the major differences in design and operation.

LEARNING OBJECTIVES

When you have completed your assignments and exercises in this unit, you should be able to:

☐ Describe the difference between an automatic transaxle and a manual transaxle.

☐ Describe how a torque converter is connected to a transaxle.

59.1 AUTOMATIC TRANSAXLE DESIGN

An automatic transaxle and manual transaxle are very similar. Both combine a transmission and differential in one housing. The main differences are that an automatic transaxle shifts gears automatically and has a torque converter instead of a manual clutch. Both are mounted to the engine and chassis in the same way. Both use the same type of driving axles.

59.2 AUTOMATIC TRANSAXLE OPERATION

The transmission portion of an automatic transaxle operates in the same way as an automatic transmission. See Figure 59-1. Automatic transmission operation is discussed in Unit 53. The differential of an automatic transaxle operates in the same manner as its manual transaxle counterpart, as discussed in Unit 57.

A torque converter is mounted inside the transaxle housing and behind the engine flywheel. Transaxle gear assemblies are mounted inside the same transaxle body, but either behind or to one side of the torque converter. Figure 59-2 shows a transaxle gear assembly mounted to one side of the torque converter. In a rear-drive automatic transmission, the transmission is mounted directly behind a torque converter.

Once the gearshift lever is set in the Drive position, automatic shifting is controlled by engine speed and throttle position. When the torque converter is operating, the oil pump creates hydraulic pressure. The valve body and other valve systems control hydraulic pressure and regulate shifting.

Engine torque is routed through two 90-degree turns in a transaxle. Power is transferred from the output end of the turbine shaft to the differential input shaft through a chain, shaft, or gears. When a chain is used, it is connected to sprockets at each shaft (see Figure 59-3). The valve body is connected over the sprockets.

Fluid in some automatic transaxles is stored in more than one oil pan, or reservoir. In some cases, an oil pan is mounted on the side of the transaxle. A thermostatic valve is used to regulate fluid flow between the two reservoirs, depending on transaxle temperature.

Some automatic transaxles have different kinds of parts. Examples of these differences include:

- Aluminum transaxle housings.
- Shifting linkages that operate off the engine electronically, mechanically, or by vacuum.
- Some converter lockup clutches may use silicone instead of mechanical parts to create lockup.
- Valve body locations may be on the top, side, or bottom of a transaxle.
- A valve body may be integral with the transaxle housing.
- A drive pinion gear may be integral with the transfer shaft.

Numerous minor differences also are found from one transaxle to the next.

59.3 DIFFERENT FRONT-DRIVE SYSTEMS

All front-drive automobiles do not use transaxles. Some front-drive systems use automatic transmissions and separate differentials. Oldsmobile Toronado, Buick Riviera, and Cadillac Eldorado use front-drive automatic transmissions. A front-drive transmission system is shown in Figure 59-4.

The engine in a front-drive transmission system usually is mounted longitudinally. The front-drive automatic transmission changes power flow from a rearward to a forward direction. The torque converter is connected to the engine with a flexplate. The remainder of the transmission system is located below the torque converter. The torque converter turbine shaft and transmission input shaft are connected with a chain, or *drive link assembly*. The drive link assembly is connected to sprockets on the ends of the turbine shaft and input shaft. As the turbine shaft rotates, the turbine sprocket rotates the drive link

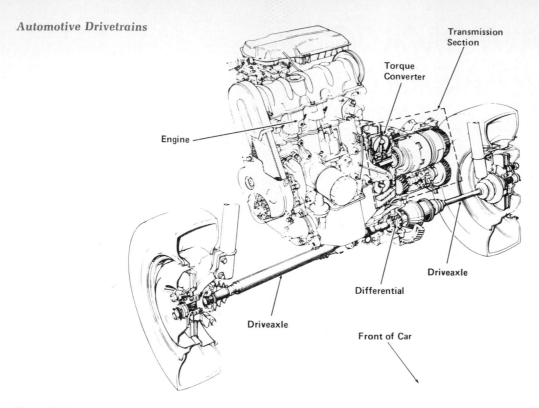

Transmission Section

Torque Converter

Engine

Driveaxle

Differential

Driveaxle

Front of Car

Figure 59-1. Automatic transaxle assembly. CHRYSLER CORPORATION

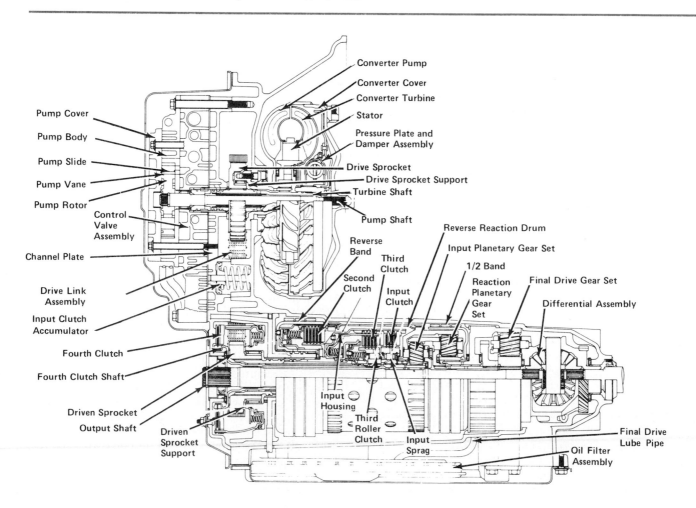

Converter Pump

Converter Cover

Converter Turbine

Stator

Pressure Plate and Damper Assembly

Drive Sprocket

Drive Sprocket Support

Turbine Shaft

Pump Shaft

Pump Cover

Pump Body

Pump Slide

Pump Vane

Pump Rotor

Control Valve Assembly

Channel Plate

Drive Link Assembly

Input Clutch Accumulator

Fourth Clutch

Fourth Clutch Shaft

Driven Sprocket

Output Shaft

Driven Sprocket Support

Reverse Band

Second Clutch

Third Clutch

Input Clutch

Reverse Reaction Drum

Input Planetary Gear Set

1/2 Band

Reaction Planetary Gear Set

Final Drive Gear Set

Differential Assembly

Input Housing

Third Roller Clutch

Input Sprag

Final Drive Lube Pipe

Oil Filter Assembly

Figure 59-2. Parts of an automatic transaxle assembly. CADILLAC MOTOR CAR DIVISION—GMC

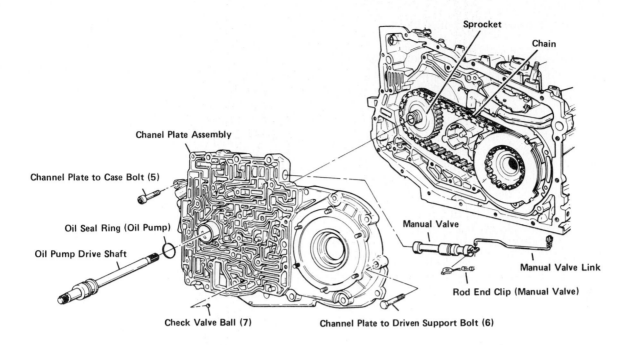

Sprocket

Chain

Chanel Plate Assembly

Channel Plate to Case Bolt (5)

Oil Seal Ring (Oil Pump)

Oil Pump Drive Shaft

Manual Valve

Manual Valve Link

Rod End Clip (Manual Valve)

Check Valve Ball (7)

Channel Plate to Driven Support Bolt (6)

Figure 59-3. Sprocket and chain drive assembly. CADILLAC MOTOR CAR DIVISION—GMC

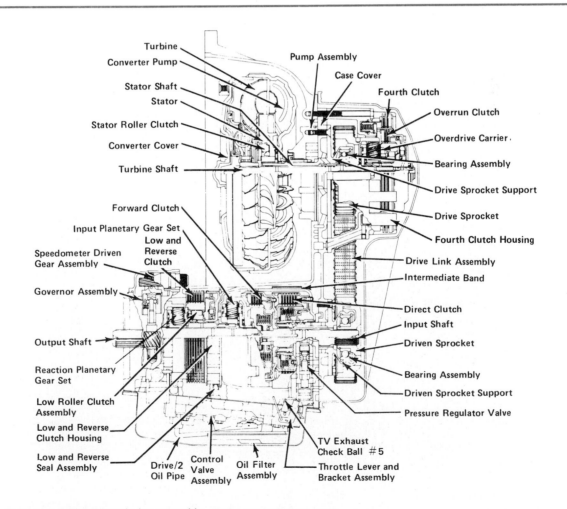

Turbine

Converter Pump

Stator Shaft

Stator

Stator Roller Clutch

Converter Cover

Turbine Shaft

Pump Assembly

Case Cover

Fourth Clutch

Overrun Clutch

Overdrive Carrier

Bearing Assembly

Drive Sprocket Support

Drive Sprocket

Fourth Clutch Housing

Forward Clutch

Input Planetary Gear Set

Low and Reverse Clutch

Speedometer Driven Gear Assembly

Governor Assembly

Output Shaft

Reaction Planetary Gear Set

Low Roller Clutch Assembly

Low and Reverse Clutch Housing

Low and Reverse Seal Assembly

Drive/2 Oil Pipe

Control Valve Assembly

Oil Filter Assembly

Throttle Lever and Bracket Assembly

TV Exhaust Check Ball #5

Pressure Regulator Valve

Driven Sprocket Support

Bearing Assembly

Driven Sprocket

Input Shaft

Direct Clutch

Intermediate Band

Drive Link Assembly

Figure 59-4. Front-wheel-drive transmission assembly. BUICK MOTOR DIVISION—GMC

assembly. As the drive link assembly rotates, it rotates the input shaft.

A separate differential assembly is bolted to the front of the transmission. No driveline is used. The pinion gear receives power directly from the transmission output shaft.

Power is delivered from the differential to the driving axles by *output shafts*. An output shaft has splines on one end that connect with the differential side gears. A flange on the outer end of an output shaft is bolted to a driving axle. Figure 59-5 shows a differential and driving axle assembly.

Constant-velocity joints are used at both ends of each driving axle. Constant-velocity joints and driving axles are discussed in Unit 57.

UNIT HIGHLIGHTS

- Automatic and manual transaxles are almost exactly the same.
- The transmission part of an automatic transaxle operates in much the same way as an automatic transmission.
- A torque converter is mounted to the side of the transmission assembly in an automatic transaxle.

TERMS

drive link assembly   **output shaft**

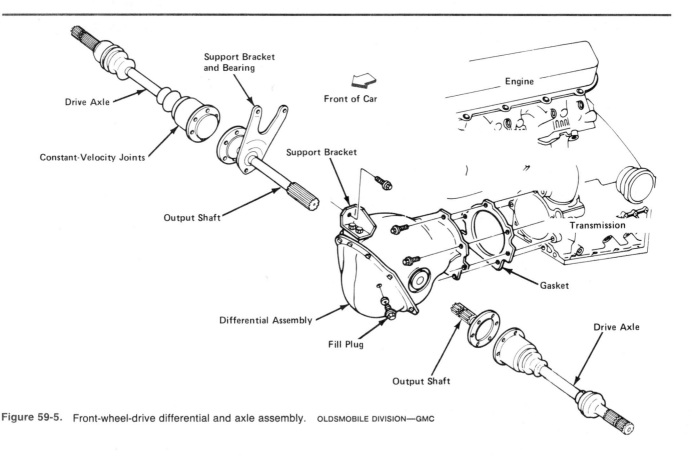

Figure 59-5. Front-wheel-drive differential and axle assembly. OLDSMOBILE DIVISION—GMC

R E V I E W   Q U E S T I O N S

DIRECTIONS: The following questions are similar to those used on mechanic certification tests. On a separate sheet of paper, write the letter of the correct choice.

1. Mechanic A says that automatic transaxles and manual transaxles are not mounted to the engine in the same way.
   Mechanic B says that automatic transaxles and manual transaxles are mounted to the engine in the same way.
   Who is correct?
   A. A only   B. B only   C. Both A and B   D. Neither A nor B

2. All of the following parts are used in or with an automatic transaxle EXCEPT
   A. a torque converter.
   B. two driving axles.
   C. an automatic transmission and a differential.
   D. a driveline.

3. Which of the following statements is correct?
   I. A torque converter is mounted outside of a transaxle housing.
   II. A torque converter is mounted between the automatic transmission and the engine.
   A. I only   B. II only   C. Both I and II   D. Neither I nor II

4. All of the following statements are true EXCEPT
   A. The oil pump increases hydraulic pressure when the torque converter is operating.
   B. The valve body helps to regulate hydraulic pressure.
   C. Automatic gearshifting is controlled by throttle speed.
   D. Automatic gearshifting is controlled by throttle pressure.

5. Mechanic A says that engine torque is routed through two 90-degree turns in the transaxle.
   Mechanic B says that oil pump pressure determines how many fluid reservoirs a transaxle contains.
   Who is correct?
   A. A only   B. B only   C. Both A and B   D. Neither A nor B

S U P P L E M E N T A L   A C T I V I T I E S

1. Describe the differences between an automatic transaxle and an automatic transmission.
2. Describe the operation of a torque converter with a chain and sprockets.

60 AUTOMATIC TRANSAXLE SERVICE

UNIT PREVIEW

Automatic transaxles use many of the same parts that are found in automatic transmissions and in manual transaxles. It is vital that you know these parts thoroughly before servicing an automatic transaxle. Different types of automatic transaxles may have considerably different service procedures. Always study the proper service manual before beginning service.

LEARNING OBJECTIVES

When you have completed your assignments and exercises in this unit, you should be able to:

☐ Change transaxle fluid and oil filter.

☐ Describe the procedures used to diagnose automatic transaxle problems.

☐ Identify which drivetrain assemblies have servicing procedures similar to those for an automatic transaxle.

SAFETY PRECAUTIONS

Many parts of an automobile must be supported when a transaxle is removed. Special supporting fixtures and jacks are required when servicing a transaxle. When using a hoist to raise an automobile with a transaxle, always check the proper service manual for procedures. Always use jackstands and safety glasses whenever you are working under an automobile.

A road test usually is necessary when checking out an automatic transaxle. Before starting, buckle up the seat belt and check the brakes. Drive in a safe manner. Jackrabbit starts, hard cornering, or sudden braking should be avoided. Driving techniques other than normal can worsen a problem or create a new one. Carelessness during the test drive can result in an accident. Drive only in a manner that is required to check or diagnose proper transaxle operation.

Whenever a transaxle is to be serviced, disconnect the battery. Many electrical connections are on or near parts that are to be serviced. Electrical connections can be activated by touch when the ignition switch is "on" or when the battery is connected. An electric cooling fan in the engine compartment may be controlled by a thermostat. This fan could start running, even with the ignition switch "off," and cause serious injury.

Many diagnostic tests on an automatic transaxle require that the engine be running. Be sure that proper ventilation removes dangerous exhaust fumes from an enclosed shop area. Do *not* allow anyone to stand in front of or behind the automobile during these tests. Block the wheels. Set the emergency brake and apply the service brakes, if possible. Carelessness or defective parts can make an automobile move and cause serious injury.

Some torque converters can be inspected by removing an inspection cover. This exposes part of the torque converter. Do *not* put your fingers near the moving torque converter while the engine is running.

Do *not* wipe transaxle parts with a cloth. Lint can remain inside the transaxle and cause problems. Lint can be blown out with dry compressed air. Do *not* use compressed air to spin-dry bearings. Compressed air can spin and damage bearings. Always wear safety glasses when using compressed air. Do *not* point a compressed air tool at another person.

Hot transaxle lubricant, transaxles, exhaust systems, engines, and brakes can cause severe burns. When possible, allow the automobile to cool before working on it.

Be very careful when working around the brakes. Brake systems contain asbestos. Asbestos is easily inhaled and is dangerous to your health. Always wear a breathing mask and use a special vacuum cleaner to remove asbestos before continuing any service work.

60.1 PREVENTIVE MAINTENANCE

Automatic transaxle preventive maintenance includes lubricating gearshift linkage, checking and diagnosing transmission fluid, and replacing filter and screen. Refer to Topic 54.1 for discussions of automatic transmission linkage lubrication and transmission fluid checks. Some manufacturers do not recommend changing fluid or filter unless a problem is evident. Make a visual inspection of the transaxle parts (see Topic 58.1).

Changing Transmission Fluid

Raise the automobile on a hoist and support it properly. Place a drain pan under the transaxle oil pan. Some transaxles have a drain plug that can be removed. On other transaxles, the oil pan bolts should be loosened or removed, depending on manufacturer's directions, to drain the fluid.

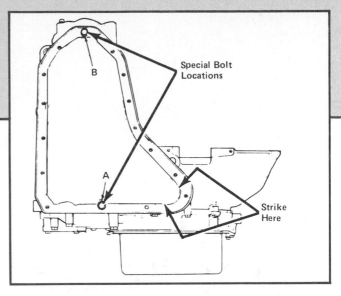

Figure 60-1. Special bolts are removed to permit removal of transaxle oil pan. BUICK MOTOR DIVISION—GMC

Figure 60-1 shows special procedures for draining and removing one type of transaxle that was assembled with a special sealant. Special bolts are placed in the locations shown in Figure 60-1. Remove all oil pan bolts, except the two special bolts. Loosen bolt B. If the oil pan will not separate from the housing, do not try to pry the oil pan loose. Damage can result. Instead, use a rubber mallet to strike the oil pan corner as indicated in Figure 60-1. Drain the transaxle. Remove the special bolts to remove the oil pan.

CAUTION: Some oil pans may have to be pried loose with a screwdriver. Be careful not to damage mating surfaces on the oil pan and case. Such damage can cause leaks.

Some transaxles use two different lubricants. One lubricant is used in the transmission, another in the differential. A special partition inside the transaxle separates the two fluids. Be sure to check the proper service manual and use the proper lubricant or lubricants. Incorrect lubricant can damage the transaxle.

Before replacing and refilling the transaxle with fluid, inspect and clean the pan. Look for metal, rubber, or organic particles. Clean the gasket mating surfaces and add a new gasket or silicone sealant.

Replacing the Filter or Screen

The filter or screen usually is located below the valve body (see Figure 60-2). Remove the filter or screen with a screwdriver, or special tool. See Figure 60-3. Replace the filter or screen with a new unit.

60.2 AUTOMATIC TRANSAXLE DIAGNOSIS

There are many different models of automatic transaxles. Use the proper service manual to identify the transaxle. Transaxle identification numbers usually are stamped into the transaxle case. Figure 60-4 shows the location of a transaxle identification number. It is important to identify the transaxle properly. Different automatic transaxles are diagnosed in different ways.

Always use the proper service manual. Troubleshooting charts are important when diagnosing an automatic transaxle problem. Refer to Topics 54.2 and 58.2 as a further guide for automatic transaxle diagnosis. Diagnostic test procedures are similar to those discussed in Topic 54.3.

60.3 AUTOMATIC TRANSAXLE SERVICE

Shift linkage and band adjustments are on-car service procedures. These procedures are similar to those

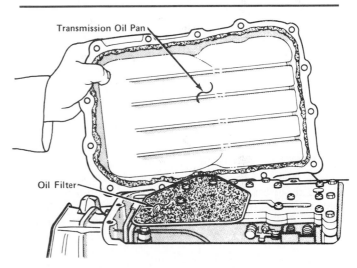

Figure 60-2. Typical transaxle filter location.
CHRYSLER CORPORATION

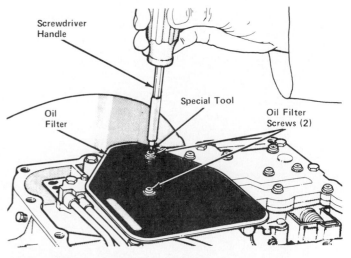

Figure 60-3. Removing a transaxle filter with a special tool.
CHRYSLER CORPORATION

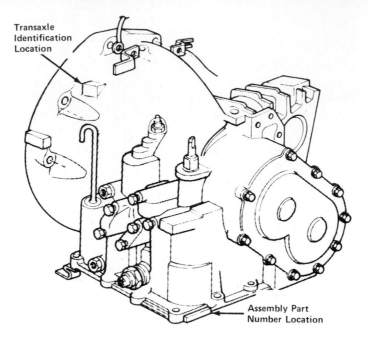

Transaxle
Identification
Location

Assembly Part
Number Location

Figure 60-4. Transaxle identification number location. CHRYSLER CORPORATION

discussed in Topic 54.4. Off-car service procedures include removing, inspecting, and reassembling an automatic transaxle.

Removing Transaxles

Transaxle and driving axle removal are identical to those discussed in Topic 58.3. On automatic transaxles, different control cables and electrical connections must be removed. Refer to the proper service manual for the exact procedures.

Servicing Automatic Transaxles

Servicing an automatic transaxle is similar to servicing an automatic transmission. Refer to Topic 54.4. Several differences in transaxles require the use of the proper service manual. Figure 60-5 shows the parts of an automatic transaxle.

Replacing Transaxles

Installing an automatic transaxle and driving axles is almost exactly the reverse of removing them. Refer to the proper service manual. Follow manufacturer's recommendations carefully.

U N I T   H I G H L I G H T S

- Some automatic transaxles may use two different types of fluids.
- Automatic transaxle diagnosis requires a road test and use of the proper service manual.
- Automatic transaxle removal is almost identical to manual transaxle removal.
- Automatic transaxle tests and disassembly are similar to those used for automatic transmissions.

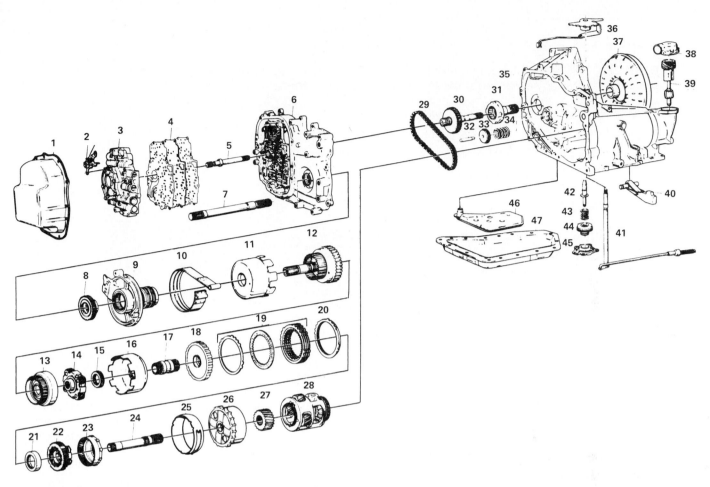

1.	Valve Body Cover	17.	Reaction Sun Gear	33.	1-2 Accumulator Piston	
2.	Throttle Lever Bracket & Link	18.	Low/Reverse Housing	34.	1-2 Accumulator Spring	
3.	Control Valve & Oil Gasket	19.	Low/Reverse Clutch Plates	35.	Case	
4.	Spacer Plate & Gaskets	20.	Low/Reverse Clutch Backing Plate	36.	Manual Detent Lever & Rod	
5.	Oil Pump Shaft	21.	Low Overrunning Clutch Race	37.	Converter	
6.	Case Cover	22.	Reaction Carrier	38.	Governor Cover	
7.	Output Shaft	23.	Reaction Internal Gear	39.	Governor	
8.	Driven Sprocket	24.	Final Drive Sun-Gear Shaft	40.	Parking Pawl	
9.	Driven Sprocket Support	25.	Final Drive Internal-Gear Spacer	41.	Actuator Rod & Manual Shaft	
10.	Intermediate Band	26.	Final Drive Internal Gear	42.	Intermediate Band Apply Pin	
11.	Direct Clutch Housing	27.	Final Drive Sun Gear	43.	Intermediate Servo Cushion Spring	
12.	Forward Clutch Housing	28.	Differential Carrier	44.	Intermediate Servo Piston	
13.	Input Internal Gear	29.	Drive Link	45.	Intermediate Servo Cover	
14.	Input Carrier	30.	Drive Sprocket & Turbine Shaft	46.	Oil Filter	
15.	Input Sun Gear	31.	Drive Sprocket Support	47.	Oil Pan	
16.	Input Drum	32.	1-2 Accumulator Pin			

Figure 60-5. Cutaway view of an automatic transaxle. CHEVROLET MOTOR DIVISION—GMC

R E V I E W   Q U E S T I O N S

DIRECTIONS: The following questions are similar to those used on mechanic certification tests. On a separate sheet of paper, write the letter of the correct choice.

1. All of the following statements are true EXCEPT

A. Special supporting fixtures are used when servicing an automatic transaxle.

B. Disconnect the battery whenever servicing an automatic transaxle.

C. Do not wipe parts with a cloth.

D. Wear a breathing mask and use a special vacuum cleaner to remove asbestos from an automatic transaxle clutch assembly.

2. Changing automatic transaxle fluid does *not* require

A. loosening bolts in the transaxle oil pan.

B. inspecting particles in the oil pan before cleaning.

C. checking the service manual to determine if different lubricants are needed for the transmission and differential sections of the transaxle.

D. valve body adjustment.

3. Which of the following statements is correct?

   I. The oil filter or screen is located above the valve body.

   II. A special tool may be required to remove the oil filter or screen.

A. I only   B. II only   C. Both I and II   D. Neither I nor II

4. Mechanic A says that all transaxles are serviced in the same way.

   Mechanic B says that transaxle identification numbers are stamped into the transaxle housing. Who is correct?

A. A only   B. B only   C. Both A and B   D. Neither A nor B

5. Which of the following statements is correct?

   I. Automatic transaxle parts can be serviced in a manner similar to automatic transmission parts.

   II. Each type of automatic transaxle is serviced differently.

A. I only   B. II only   C. Both I and II   D. Neither I nor II

S U P P L E M E N T A L   A C T I V I T I E S

1. Check the fluid level of an automatic transaxle.

2. Identify the type of fluid, or fluids, that must be used in an automatic transaxle chosen by your instructor.

3. Change a transaxle oil filter.

4. Describe diagnostic procedures for an automatic transaxle chosen by your instructor.

5. Remove and install an automatic transaxle chosen by your instructor.

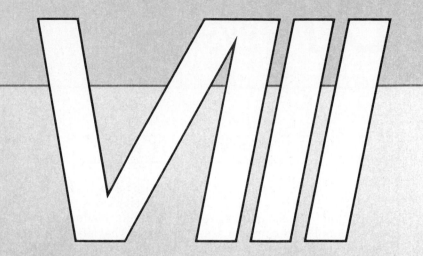

VIII

THE
AUTOMOTIVE
CHASSIS

61 THE SUSPENSION SYSTEM

UNIT PREVIEW

A suspension system supports an automobile and keeps its wheels in contact with uneven road surfaces. Modern suspensions provide a smooth ride for an automobile, its occupants, and its cargo. They also provide control for the driver. Automobile suspensions come in many different forms and are designed to meet a variety of motoring requirements. A suspension system can determine how an automobile turns a corner and how much weight can be carried safely. There are many aspects to suspension design. This unit discusses the important parts of the automobile's suspension system.

LEARNING OBJECTIVES

When you have completed your assignments and exercises in this unit, you should be able to:

☐ Describe the different types of springs used in suspensions.

☐ Explain the functions of a shock absorber.

☐ Describe the operation of an independent suspension system.

☐ Describe the operation of a MacPherson strut suspension system.

☐ Describe a trailing arm suspension.

61.1 SPRINGS

The main parts of a suspension system are the *springs*. Springs are used to support the automobile's frame, body, engine, and drivetrain above and between the wheels. Springs also permit the wheels to move upward and downward. As the wheels go over bumps and uneven road surfaces, the springs absorb much of the shock. The basic types of springs used on modern automobiles are:

- Coil springs
- Leaf springs
- Torsion bars
- Air springs.

All four corners of an automobile are supported by spring assemblies. However, many automobiles have different spring assembly designs at the front and rear. Most of the weight of an automobile is supported by the springs. *Sprung weight* refers to parts of the automobile suspended by the springs, such as the body, engine, and transmission. *Unsprung weight* identifies those parts that are *not* suspended by the springs, such as wheels, brakes, and axles.

Spring Function

Springs are designed to compress a certain amount when they support the sprung weight of an automobile. Enough additional movement is built into the springs to absorb road bumps when the automobile is driven. When traveling over uneven surfaces, wheels and other unsprung parts act to compress and expand springs, and cushion the ride.

Coil Springs

A *coil spring* is a steel wire that has been coiled. A coil spring is compressed under pressure and is expanded when the pressure is released. Coil springs can be used in both front and rear suspension assemblies. *Control arms* are connected from the frame to the bottom of a coil spring and to the wheel. Control arms allow a coil spring to expand and compress as road conditions affect the wheels. When wheel action stops, the coil spring returns to its original position. Figure 61-1 shows a coil spring suspension.

Leaf Springs

A *leaf spring* is made of one or more long, thin strips of metal. The metal strips, called *leaves,* are laid one atop another to form a curved assembly. Leaves bend and slip over one another when the spring is compressed or expanded.

Leaf springs can be mounted longitudinally or transversely at the front or rear of an automobile. Leaf springs usually are held in place at the center and at the eyes, or loops, at each end. Shackles attach the spring loops to the frame (see Figure 61-2).

Torsion Bars

A *torsion bar* is a steel bar that is capable of twisting to provide spring action. A torsion bar is attached to a control arm and to a frame crossmember (see Figure 61-3). Torsion bars are used as front suspension systems on many modern automobiles. As wheel movement causes the control arm to move up and down, the torsion bar is twisted. The rear of the torsion bar is held firmly in the crossmember and cannot be twisted. The torsion bar resists the twisting force, eventually untwisting to return the control arm to its original position. Torsion bars can be mounted longitudinally or transversely in an automobile.

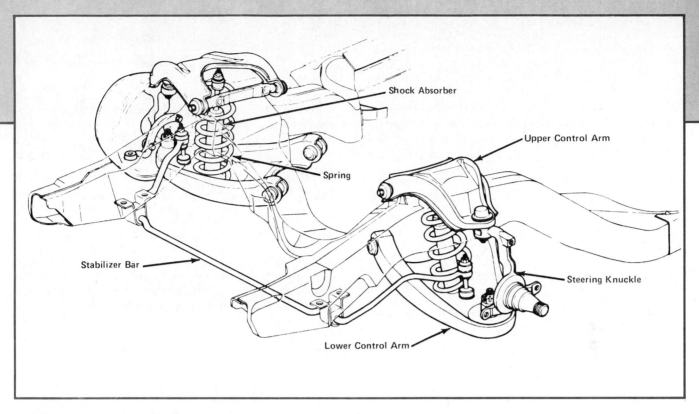

Figure 61-1. Coil spring suspension system. CHEVROLET MOTOR DIVISION—GMC

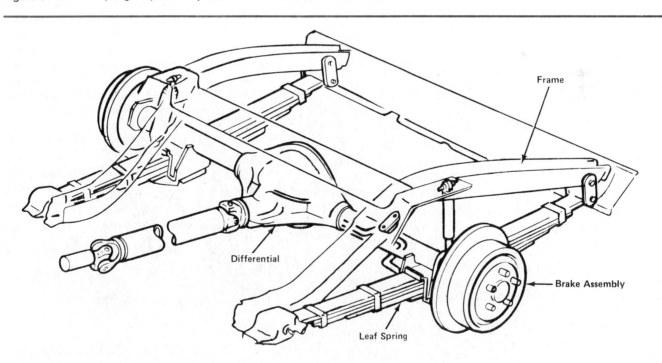

Figure 61-2. Leaf spring suspension system. CHEVROLET MOTOR DIVISION

Air Suspensions

An *air suspension* system consists of air bags, or air spring assemblies, which can replace or supplement conventional springs. See Figure 61-4. An air spring is a piston made of flexible rubber that operates on compressed air. An air suspension system may be controlled by a microprocessor that automatically levels all springs as needed.

61.2 SHOCK ABSORBERS

A *shock absorber* is a device that works with the springs to control movements of the body, wheel, and axle. A spring that is not controlled by a shock absorber will continue to expand and compress, or oscillate, several times. A shock absorber dampens, or limits, the number and extent of spring oscillations.

Four shock absorbers usually are used on an automobile, one at each wheel. Shock absorbers are said to be *double-acting.* Double-acting means that the shock absorber controls both upward and downward movements of a suspension.

When a wheel travels over a bump, the spring is compressed, or shortened, and the wheel moves upward. This *compression,* or *jounce,* builds up energy in the spring. As the energy is released, the spring expands beyond its normal length. This expansion is called *rebound.* A spring also expands when a wheel travels over a low spot in a road surface or falls into a hole. This expansion is followed by compression and rebound.

The tubular shock absorber lengthens and shortens, like a telescope, as it operates. A piston inside the shock absorber moves up and down in a fluid-filled chamber (see Figure 61-5). The piston forces fluid through small orifices, or holes, which slow the flow of the fluid. This slows the movement of the piston and the telescoping action of the shock absorber. This action also slows spring movement.

Shock absorbers may be controlled by a gas instead of hydraulic fluid. Some front suspensions also may have automatic shock absorbers that adjust to driving conditions. An automatic shock absorber is controlled by an electronic control module. The control module sends signals to an actuator that controls shock absorber action. The actuator is located on the shock absorber.

Automatic Level Control

Some automobiles use an *automatic level control,* or a *load leveling,* system. An automatic level control keeps the rear of the automobile at a normal level when a heavy load is added. An automatic level control is activated by a *height sensor* at the rear of the automobile. The height sensor signals an electronic control module when the rear suspension is compressed by a heavy load. Normal up-and-down movement from driving does not affect an automatic level control. A delay switch in the electronic control module prevents premature activation of the system. The signal must be on for several seconds before the load leveling system kicks in.

In operation, the electronic control module activates an electrically operated compressor under the hood. The compressor pumps air into lines that lead

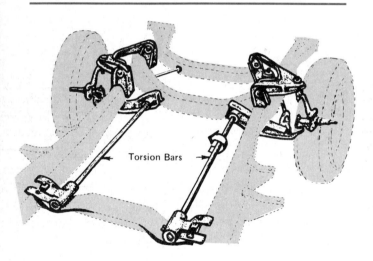

Figure 61-3. Torsion bar suspension system.
CHRYSLER CORPORATION

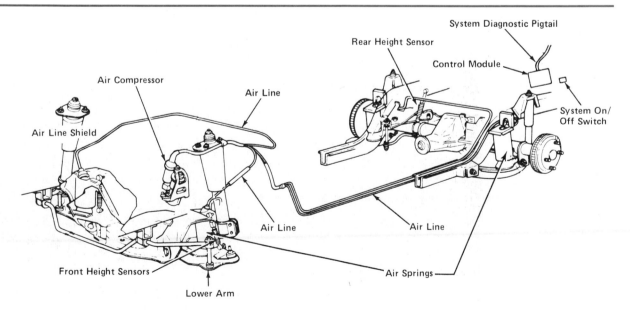

Figure 61-4. Air suspension system. FORD MOTOR COMPANY

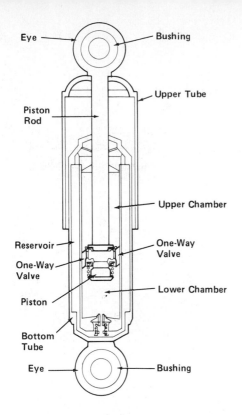

Figure 61-5. Parts of a shock absorber.

to special air chambers in the rear hydraulic shock absorbers. The air chambers are filled with compressed air, raising the rear of the automobile to a predetermined height. Figure 61-6 shows an automatic load leveling system.

61.3 FRONT SUSPENSION

Modern automobiles have *independent suspension* systems at the front wheels. An independent suspension system is designed to allow each wheel to move up and down separately, or independently. Each wheel assembly has its own suspension system. This type of suspension, illustrated in Figure 61-7, usually has coil springs or torsion bars. Other parts of an independent front suspension include:

- Control arms
- Wheel spindle assembly
- Ball joint
- Stabilizer bar.

Control Arms

Two control arms at each wheel direct the actions of the suspension system. One end of a control arm is

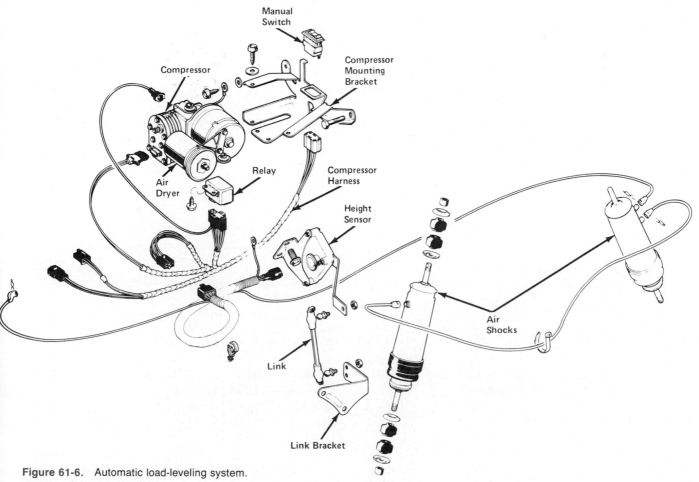

Figure 61-6. Automatic load-leveling system.

AMERICAN MOTORS CORPORATION

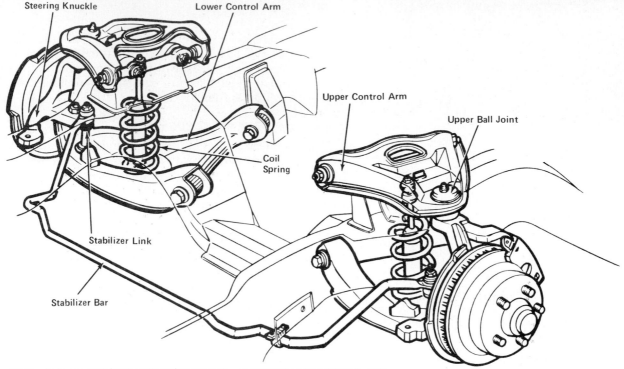

Figure 61-7. Independent front suspension system. CHEVROLET MOTOR DIVISION—GMC

connected to a frame member. The other end is connected to a wheel spindle assembly (see Figure 61-8). As the wheel moves up and down, it moves the control arms and the spring.

A control arm often is shaped like the letter "A." Because of this, a control arm may be called an A-arm or A-frame.

Upper and lower front control arms are made in different lengths. Short and long control arms, called SLA type, are used at each wheel. The upper control arm is shorter. As the wheels move up and down, this arrangement allows stable tire contact with the ground.

Figure 61-8 shows a suspension system with a spring located between the frame and lower control arm. It also shows how control arms operate when the wheel moves.

Wheel Spindle Assembly

A *wheel spindle assembly* consists of a *wheel spindle* and a *steering knuckle*. See Figure 61-9. A wheel spindle is connected to a wheel through wheel bearings. The wheel spindle is the point at which the wheel hub and wheel bearings are connected. See Figure 61-9. A steering knuckle is connected to control arms. In most cases, a steering knuckle and wheel spindle are forged to form a single piece.

Ball Joint

The steering knuckle and control arms are connected by a *ball joint*. See Figure 61-10. A ball joint has a ball stud that is positioned in a seal retainer, as shown in Figure 61-11. The ball stud pivots in a socket as the

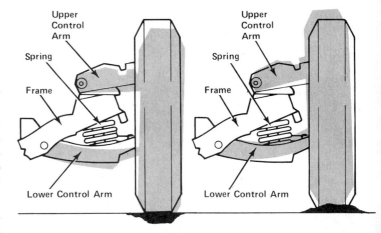

Figure 61-8. Front suspension movement.

control arms are moved up and down. Ball joints may be riveted or bolted in place.

Ball joints help to support the weight of an automobile. Ball joints also allow rotary (steering) movement and vertical (bumps and holes) movement.

Stabilizer Bar

A *stabilizer bar*, or sway bar, is a long steel rod. The ends of the rod are connected to the lower control arms. The center section of the rod is connected to the frame or subframe.

A stabilizer bar controls *body roll*. Body roll occurs when the automobile is turning and the body leans, or sways, toward the outer suspension. Body

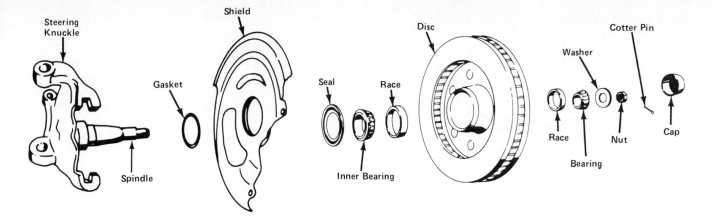

Figure 61-9. Steering spindle assembly.
CHEVROLET MOTOR DIVISION—GMC

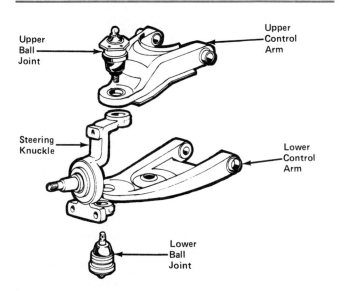

Figure 61-10. Ball joint locations. MOOG AUTOMOTIVE

roll shifts weight to the outside and moves the lower control arm upward to compress the spring. When the outer lower control arm moves upward, it twists the stabilizer bar. See Figure 61-12. The stabilizer bar resists the twisting and limits movement of the control arm. This action reduces body roll and improves driver control.

Types of Independent Front Suspensions

Although there are many variations of independent front suspensions, most share the same parts. The most common independent front suspension systems are:

- Double A-arm
- Straight control arm and strut rod
- Spring above upper control arm
- MacPherson strut
- Modified strut
- Longitudinal torsion bar
- Transverse torsion bar.

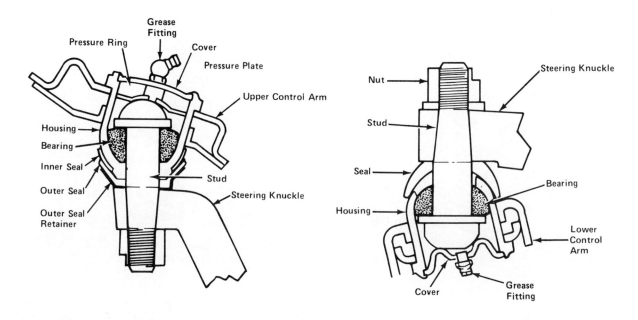

Figure 61-11. Ball joint assemblies.

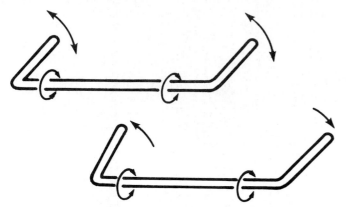

Figure 61-12. Sway bar operation. Sway bar does not offer torsional resistance when both parts of the frame move simultaneously (top). When frame is tipped on one side (bottom), it is pressed down on one end and is lifted up on the other end. This creates torsional resistance.

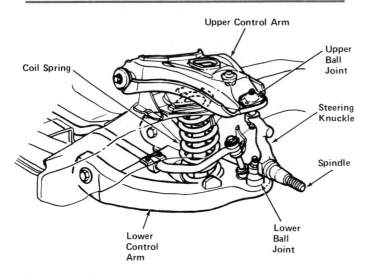

Figure 61-13. Double A-arm suspension.
CHEVROLET MOTOR DIVISION—GMC

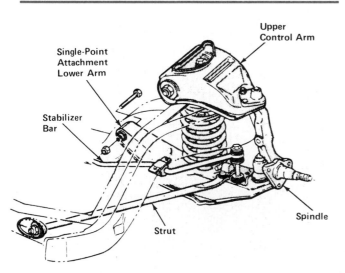

Figure 61-14. Straight control arm and strut-rod suspension.
FORD MOTOR COMPANY

Double A-arm. The *double A-arm* suspension is one of the oldest designs still in use (see Figure 61-13). It is used mostly on larger automobiles. Parts of this design were highlighted earlier in this section.

Straight control arm and strut rod. The *straight control arm and strut rod* design is a variation of the double A-arm system (see Figure 61-14). The upper control arm has an A-frame. The lower control arm is straight. The lower control arm is attached to the frame at a single point. It is stabilized by a strut rod. The strut rod is connected to the outer end of the control arm and to a front frame member.

Spring above upper control arm. A design similar to the straight control arm and strut rod system is the *spring above upper control arm*. In this type of suspension, the spring is mounted between the body spring tower and the upper control arm (refer to Figure 61-15). This suspension system is used in many smaller automobiles.

MacPherson strut. The *MacPherson strut* suspension is a single-arm system (see Figure 61-16). It has only a lower control arm. The remainder of the suspension parts act as an upper control arm and a shock absorber.

A strut assembly includes a large shock absorber and a coil spring. The bottom of the strut is connected to the steering knuckle/wheel spindle assembly. At the top, a coil spring is connected to a tower in the body sheet metal. The tower is part of a reinforced inner

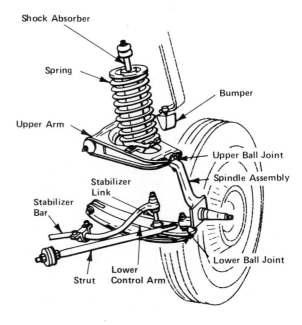

Figure 61-15. Spring above upper control arm suspension.
FORD MOTOR COMPANY

fender. The top of the strut assembly rotates in the tower when the steering system is activated.

The strut operates on hydraulic action from the shock absorber and on spring action. When the wheel causes suspension movement, the strut is telescoped to compress or rebound the spring and the shock absorber.

Modified strut. The *modified strut* is another type of strut suspension, actually a modified MacPherson strut system (see Figure 61-17). In this type of suspension, only the shock absorber is combined with a strut. The coil spring is mounted separately between the control arm and the frame.

Longitudinal torsion bar. A *longitudinal torsion bar* suspension system is similar to the straight control arm and strut system. However, the coil spring is replaced by a torsion bar (see Figure 61-18). The torsion bar is connected to the lower control arm at its pivot point on the frame.

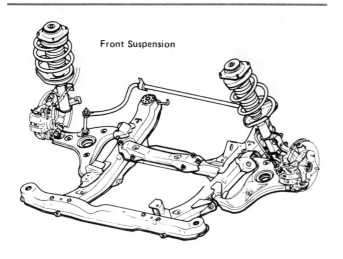

Figure 61-16. MacPherson strut suspension assembly.
MAZDA MOTOR CORPORATION

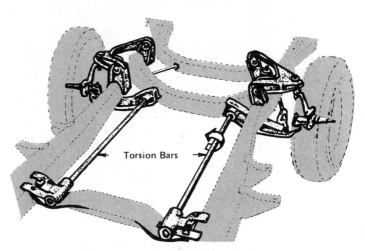

Figure 61-18. Longitudinal torsion bar system.
CHRYSLER CORPORATION

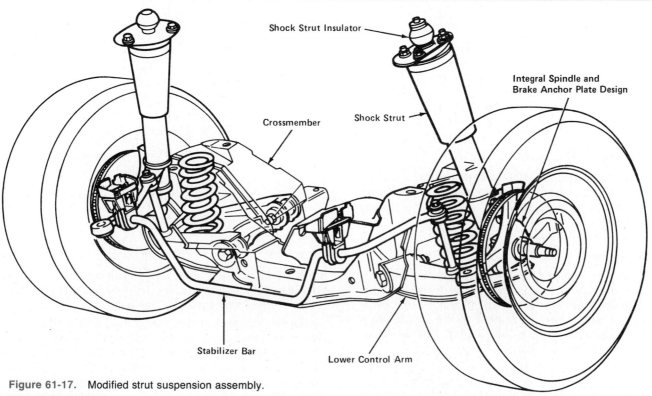

Figure 61-17. Modified strut suspension assembly.
FORD MOTOR COMPANY

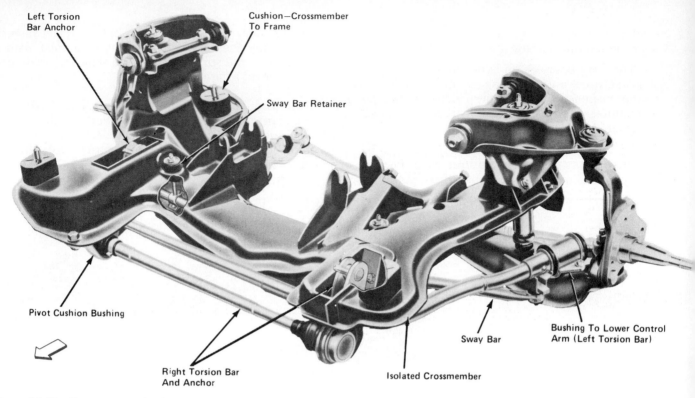

Figure 61-19. Transverse torsion bar system. CHRYSLER CORPORATION

Transverse torsion bars. *Transverse torsion bars* operate on the same principle as longitudinal torsion bars. However, the torsion bars are positioned across the front of the automobile (see Figure 61-19).

Fiberglass Springs

Chevrolet uses a fiberglass leaf spring design on the independent front suspension of the newest Corvette model, introduced in 1984. The ends of the leaf spring are connected to each lower control arm (see Figure 61-20). This type of front suspension shares many of the same parts used with coil springs.

61.4 REAR SUSPENSION

Designs similar to front suspension systems are used at the rear suspension. Since the rear wheels are not steered, a rear suspension system has fewer requirements.

Coil Springs

Coil springs are located between brackets on the rear-axle housing and *spring seats* in the frame or unit body. Spring seats are saucer-like brackets that position the springs. Springs are held in the spring seats by the weight of the automobile and by the shock absorbers (see Figure 61-21).

Coil springs can be flexed or moved in all directions. Control arms are used to control this random movement. Rear suspension control arms usually are

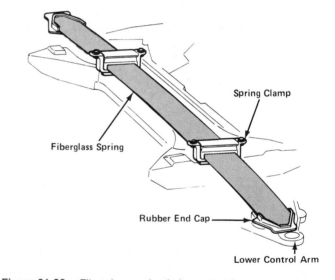

Figure 61-20. Fiberglass spring independent front suspension. CHEVROLET MOTOR DIVISION—GMC

made of channeled steel and mounted with rubber bushings to prevent damage from shock. Upper and lower control arms usually are used.

Upper control arms control *rear-end torque* and sideways movement of the axle housing assembly. Rear-end torque occurs when the driveshaft causes the differential and driving axles to twist. Upper control arms are connected to the frame or unit body and to the differential housing.

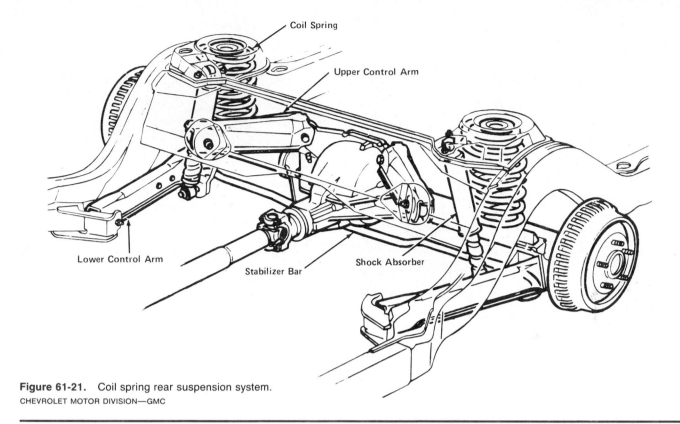

Figure 61-21. Coil spring rear suspension system.
CHEVROLET MOTOR DIVISION—GMC

Lower control arms are mounted between the axle assembly and the frame. Lower control arms maintain the fore-and-aft relationship of the axle housing to the chassis. The rigid axle, or axle housing, holds the rear wheels in proper alignment.

The Volvo coil-spring rear suspension uses only lower control arms. Upper control arms are replaced with a wishbone-shaped subframe. Rear-end torque is transferred to the subframe by two torque arms (see Figure 61-22).

A single, long *torque arm* also is used on some General Motors automobiles (see Figure 61-23). The front of the torque arm is connected to the transmission. The rear of the torque arm is connected to the differential housing.

Many Japanese automobiles have open axle shafts at the rear. The coil spring suspension used on these automobiles has only lower control arms. A suspension assembly crossmember supports the control arms (see Figure 61-24). The tops of the shock absorbers are mounted to the unit body. The springs are positioned on seats at the top and bottom.

MacPherson Strut

Many automobiles use MacPherson strut assemblies at the rear (see Figure 61-25). Rear suspension MacPherson strut assemblies operate in the same way as front suspension strut assemblies. A radius rod may be connected to the unit body and to the wheel spindle assembly. The radius rod keeps the lower control arm properly aligned.

Figure 61-22. Rear suspension with wishbone subframe and lower control arms. VOLVO CAR CORPORATION

MacPherson struts also are used at the rear in some mid-engined and rear-engined automobiles. Figure 61-26 shows the rear suspension of a Pontiac Fiero.

Another type of strut assembly also is used. On this type of suspension, shown in Figure 61-27, only the shock absorber is part of the strut assembly. The coil spring is located elsewhere on the lower control arm. A stabilizer bar also is used with this suspension.

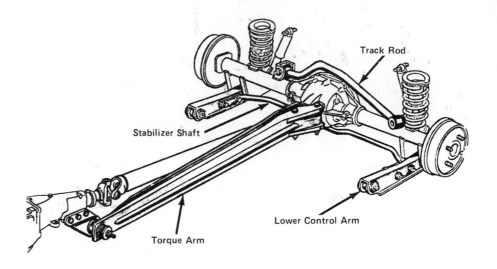

Figure 61-23. Rear suspension torque arm assembly. OLDSMOBILE DIVISION—GMC

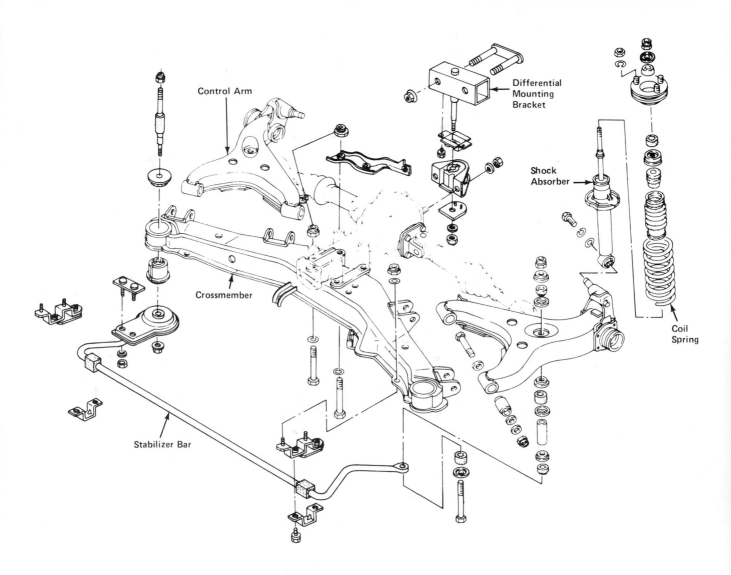

Figure 61-24. Rear suspension with lower control arms and open driving axles. NISSAN MOTOR CORPORATION

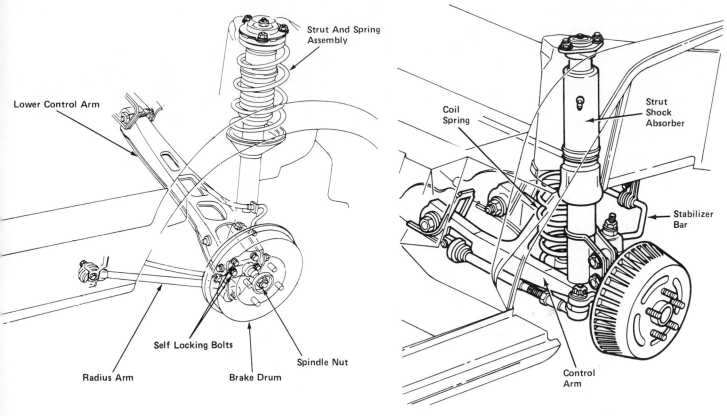

Figure 61-25. Rear suspension with MacPherson struts.
HONDA MOTOR COMPANY

Figure 61-27. Non-MacPherson strut assembly.
CADILLAC MOTOR CAR DIVISION—GMC

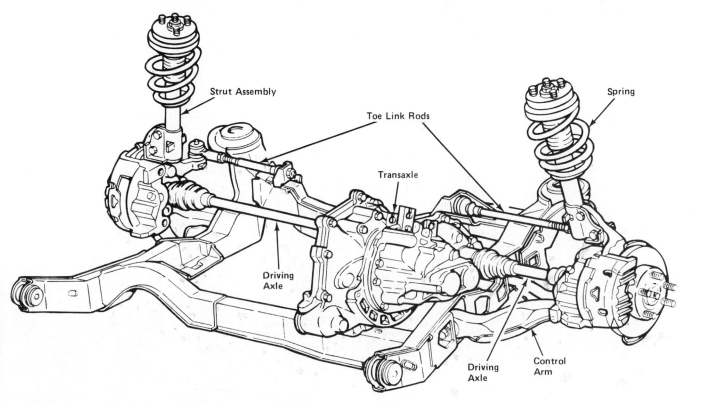

Figure 61-26. Pontiac Fiero rear MacPherson strut system.
PONTIAC MOTOR DIVISION—GMC

Semi-Independent Rear Suspension

Many automobiles with front transaxles have a *semi-independent suspension* system at the rear. A semi-independent system is one in which the two rear wheels are connected by a crossmember. In addition, each rear wheel is independently suspended by a spring.

One semi-independent rear suspension system uses a *trailing arm* design. A trailing arm extends rearward from the actual suspension mounting points on the body. This allows more interior room for occupants. A wheel spindle is attached to the trailing arm. The crossmember between the trailing arms may twist and act as a stabilizer bar. Figures 61-28 and 61-29 show trailing arm suspension systems.

A torsion bar also is used on some trailing arm suspensions. For example, Renault has utilized a transverse torsion bar built into the crossmember.

When a torsion bar is used, only a shock absorber and wheel spindle are connected to the trailing arm.

Leaf Springs

Leaf spring rear suspensions are used on many automobiles with conventional rear drive. This type of rear suspension usually has longitudinally mounted springs. Springs and shock absorbers are positioned below the rear-axle housing and are connected to the frame or unit body. See Figure 61-30.

The front eye of a leaf spring is attached to the frame. The rear eye is attached to a *spring shackle* (see Figure 61-31). A spring shackle allows the leaf spring to change length as the leaves bend. The center of each leaf spring is connected to the rear-axle housing with U-bolts. Rubber bumpers are located between the rear-axle housing and frame or unit body to dampen severe shocks.

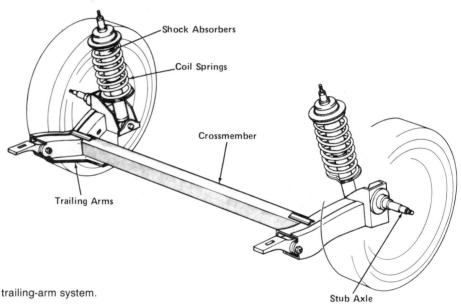

Figure 61-28. Integrated shock and spring trailing-arm system.
CHRYSLER CORPORATION

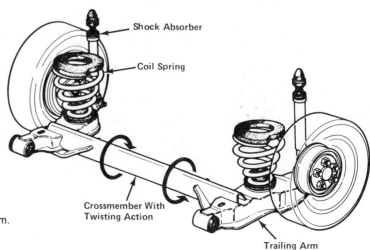

Figure 61-29. Separate shock and spring trailing-arm system.
PONTIAC MOTOR DIVISION—GMC

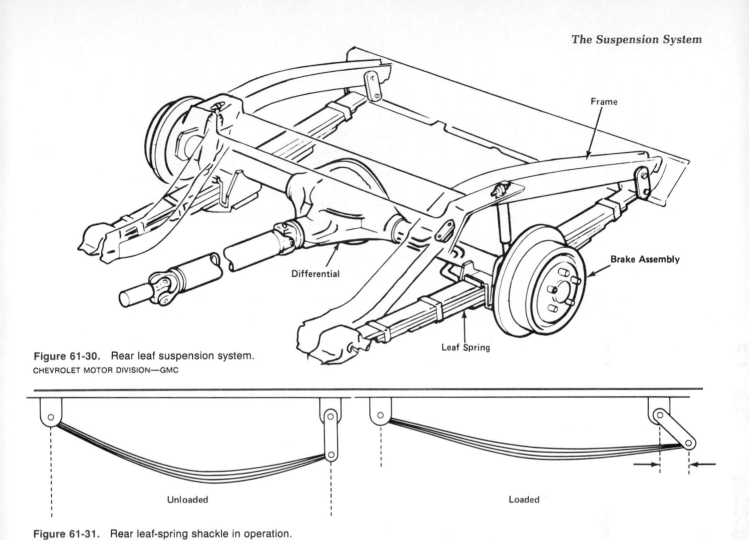

Figure 61-30. Rear leaf suspension system.
CHEVROLET MOTOR DIVISION—GMC

Figure 61-31. Rear leaf-spring shackle in operation.

Unloaded

Loaded

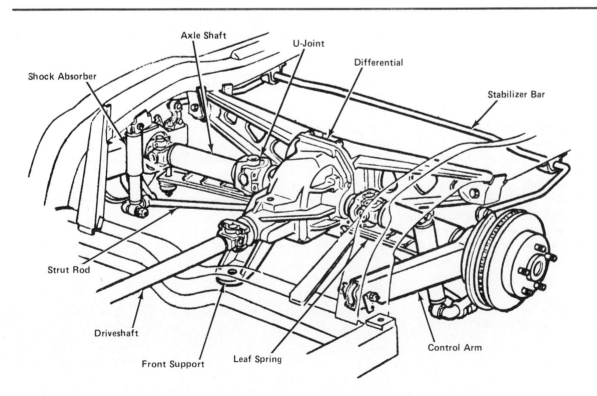

Figure 61-32. Transversely mounted multi-leaf rear springs. CHEVROLET MOTOR DIVISION—GMC

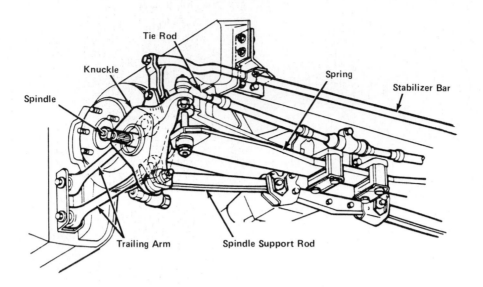

Figure 61-33. Transversely mounted single-leaf rear spring. CHEVROLET MOTOR DIVISION—GMC

Transverse-mounted leaf springs sometimes are designed to act as independent suspensions. A multileaf (see Figure 61-32) or single-leaf (see Figure 61-33) spring system may be used. The transverse leaf spring is mounted to the differential housing. The spring eyes are connected to wheel spindle assemblies.

On rear-drive automobiles, extra bracing is required for the suspension because of rear-end torque (see Figure 61-34). For leaf spring suspensions, the common methods of bracing are Hotchkiss drive and control rods.

Hotchkiss drive.   Automobiles with leaf spring rear suspensions have *Hotchkiss drive*. Hotchkiss drive is a design that allows spring action to control rear-end torque. When rear-end torque begins, the axle housing twists upward at the front. This action lifts the front of the leaf springs and lowers the rear of the leaf springs. Hotchkiss drive limits this movement to control rear-end torque.

Control rods.   .*Control rods* are used to brace a torque tube driveline. Control rods are solid steel rods that help strengthen the torque tube assembly. Two control rods are used (see Figure 61-35). The control rods are connected from the rear-axle housing to the frame.

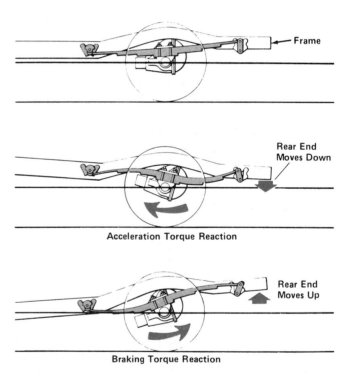

Figure 61-34. Rear-end torque reaction. FORD MOTOR COMPANY

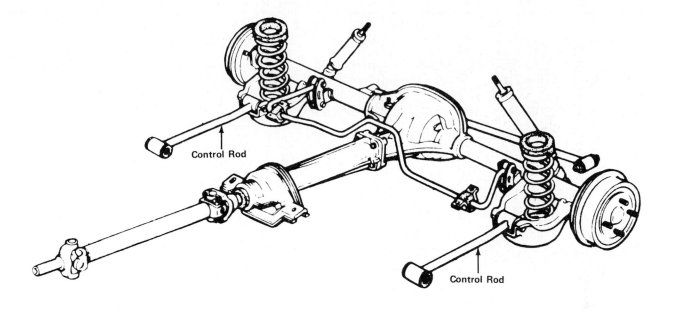

Figure 61-35. Control rods for torque-tube drive. CHEVROLET MOTOR DIVISION—GMC

U N I T H I G H L I G H T S	**T E R M S**	

- Different types of springs are used in different suspensions.
- Coil springs are coiled steel wire that expands and contracts.
- Leaf springs are metal strips in a semi-elliptical shape that are laid one on top of another.
- Torsion bars are solid steel bars that are twisted to provide spring action.
- Air suspension uses air bags instead of springs.
- A shock absorber dampens and controls spring action.
- An automatic level control raises and lowers the rear suspension automatically.
- An independent suspension is designed to allow each wheel to move independently.
- Control arms move with the wheel and expand or compress a coil spring.
- A wheel spindle assembly connects the wheel to the suspension.
- Ball joints provide pivot points at the steering knuckle.
- A MacPherson strut combines a spring and a shock absorber into one assembly.
- A stabilizer bar controls body roll.
- Rear suspension systems must control rear-end torque.
- Trailing arm suspensions extend rearward from their mounting points.

springs	ball joint
sprung weight	stabilizer bar
unsprung weight	body roll
coil spring	double A-arm
control arms	suspension
leaf spring	straight control arm
leaves	and strut suspension
torsion bar	spring above upper
air suspension	control arm
shock absorber	suspension
double-acting shock	MacPherson strut
absorber	modified strut
compression	longitudinal torsion bar
jounce	transverse torsion bar
rebound	spring seat
automatic level control	rear-end torque
load leveling system	torque arm
height sensor	trailing arm
independent	spring shackle
suspension	Hotchkiss drive
wheel spindle assembly	control rods
wheel spindle	semi-independent
steering knuckle	suspension

R E V I E W   Q U E S T I O N S

DIRECTIONS: The following questions are similar to those used on mechanic certification tests. On a separate sheet of paper, write the letter of the correct choice.

1. Which of the following is *not* used as a spring in a suspension?
A. Control arm
B. Leaf
C. Torsion bar
D. Air bag

2. Which of the following statements is true?
   I. A shock absorber dampens spring action.
   II. A shock absorber absorbs shock.
A. I only   B. II only   C. Both I and II   D. Neither I nor II

3. All of the following statements are true EXCEPT
A. A non-independent suspension uses a rigid axle.
B. An independent suspension allows each wheel to move independently.
C. Upper control arms are shorter than lower control arms.
D. Ball joints allow vertical and rotary motion.

4. Mechanic A says that a MacPherson strut assembly can be used as a front or rear suspension assembly.
   Mechanic B says that a MacPherson strut assembly uses only an upper control arm.
   Who is correct?
A. A only   B. B only   C. Both A and B   D. Neither A nor B

5. Which of the following is *not* an element of a rear suspension?
A. Hotchkiss drive
B. Spring seats
C. Trailing arm
D. U-joint

S U P P L E M E N T A L   A C T I V I T I E S

1. Explain how leaf springs, coil springs, and torsion bars differ.
2. Use a shock absorber selected by the instructor to explain how a shock absorber works.
3. Identify the parts of an automatic level control system selected by your instructor.
4. Describe how an independent suspension with coil springs operates under different road conditions.
5. Describe how MacPherson strut front and rear suspensions operate.
6. Explain the parts of a leaf spring rear suspension your instructor has selected.
7. Describe the operation of a coil spring rear suspension selected by your instructor.

62 SUSPENSION SYSTEM SERVICE

UNIT PREVIEW

Suspension system maintenance usually is performed as part of a routine "lube and oil change." Some manufacturers make little provision for maintenance, while others provide numerous grease fittings that must be serviced regularly.

During this service, or during an oil change, an inspection of suspension components should be performed.

Many different suspension systems are used in modern automobiles. However, service procedures are quite similar. This unit discusses how to identify and correct common suspension problems.

LEARNING OBJECTIVES

When you have completed your assignments and exercises in this unit, you should be able to:

☐ Repack wheel bearings.
☐ Inspect the parts of a suspension system for wear and damage.
☐ Replace a shock absorber.
☐ Replace a ball joint.
☐ Replace bushings.
☐ Replace a MacPherson strut assembly.

SAFETY PRECAUTIONS

Suspension systems are important to driver control and highway safety. An improperly repaired suspension system can lead to an accident and even serious injury. Always follow servicing instructions carefully. Suspension parts must be assembled in a specific order. Always use the proper service manual.

Use extreme caution when making road tests with an automobile that may have suspension problems. Before starting, buckle up the seat belt and check the brakes. Drive carefully and only enough to determine the problem.

When raising an automobile for suspension service, special precautions must be followed. Hoists, floor jacks, and safety stands must be used. Each automobile may require that the lifting devices or stands be placed only in specific places. Follow the instructions carefully. Jack and safety stand positions often control the action of a spring.

Springs are under extreme pressures when they are compressed on an automobile. Always follow the manufacturers' precautions. Learn the safety rules thoroughly before servicing. Disregard of precautions can lead to damage or serious injury.

Always use the proper tools. Many special tools are needed to service a suspension system. Learn how to use these special tools properly to avoid damage and injury.

Be careful with your hands. Suspension parts can move while being serviced. Keep your fingers and hands clear of parts that may move. A finger or hand can become wedged between suspension parts, causing serious injury.

A fastener must be replaced with one of the same part number or with an equivalent. Do *not* use a replacement part of lesser quality or substitute design. Fasteners are important attaching parts in the suspension. They can affect the performance of vital parts and systems. They also can result in major repair expense.

Always torque fasteners to the proper specifications. Improperly torqued fasteners can fail.

Never heat, quench, or straighten any suspension part. Always replace worn or damaged parts with new parts.

62.1 PREVENTIVE MAINTENANCE

The only preventive maintenance procedure recommended by manufacturers is periodic lubrication of the ball joints and wheel bearings. Recommended lubrication intervals may be as short as 10,000 miles or as long as 50,000 miles. Always check the proper service manual for preventive maintenance schedules. These recommendations may change as new systems are developed.

Ball Joint Lubrication

Ball joints are semipermanently lubricated at the factory. Lubrication may be recommended only every three years, but ball joints should be inspected every six months.

Before inspecting a ball joint, clean the dirt and grease from the outside surface. Seals can be damaged, causing lubricant to leak or to become contaminated, which can quickly damage the ball joint. Replace damaged seals and ball joints immediately. Lubricate undamaged ball joints, if necessary.

Ball joints usually have a lubrication plug or grease fitting at the top or bottom of the ball joint housing. See Figure 62-1. Clean the plugs and fittings to remove dirt from the grease inlet, thus avoiding grease contamination during lubrication. Install the proper lubrication fittings on the grease gun. Remove the lubrication plugs, if necessary, and install grease fittings. Use a low-pressure lubrication gun and the proper lubricant. Too much lubricant will damage the seals. Stop filling when either of the following occurs:

- Grease begins to flow freely from the bleed areas at the base of the seal
- The seal begins to balloon.

Always check the proper service manual before attempting lubrication procedures. When finished, remove the lubrication fittings if the customer does not wish to keep them. If fittings are removed, replace any plugs that were removed to permit lubrication.

Tie rod ends and other steering joints are lubricated in the same manner. These and other chassis lubrication tasks are discussed in Units 58 and 64.

Repacking Wheel Bearings

Wheel bearings normally are inspected and relubricated, or repacked, every 30,000 miles, or whenever the brake system is removed. *Never* add lubricant. Always repack wheel bearings.

Wheel bearing removal. Raise the automobile and safely support it so that the wheels to be packed are off the floor. Remove the wheel cover and wheel. If the wheel has a disc brake assembly, remove the brake caliper. Hang the caliper out of the way with wire, being sure that the brake hose is not stretched (see Unit 68). Remove the bearing dust cover and the cotter pin. Remove the locking device and the adjusting nut and washer (see Figures 62-2, 62-3, and 62-4).

Remove the thrust washer and outer bearing cone. Pull the drum or disc assembly off the spindle. Remove the inner grease seal and inner bearing according to the proper service manual. Discard the old grease seal. A new seal must be used when installing the wheel bearing assembly. A wheel bearing assembly for a disc brake assembly is shown in Figure 62-5.

Cleaning and inspection. Clean the hub and drum assembly. Use kerosene, mineral spirits, or a similar cleaning fluid.

CAUTION: Do not spin the wheel bearings dry with compressed air. This will damage the bearings.

Examine the bearing cups for pitting, scoring, or other damage. If the cups are damaged, remove them from the hub with a soft steel drift. The bearing cup areas in the hub should be smooth, with no scored or

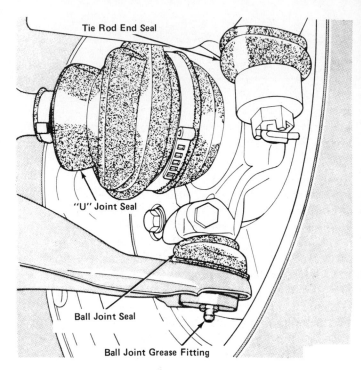

Figure 62-1. Ball joint grease fittings. CHRYSLER CORPORATION

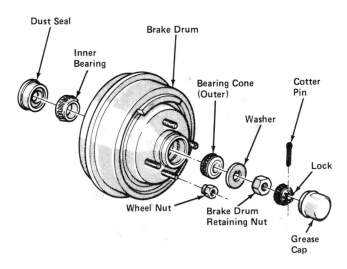

Figure 62-2. Parts of a drum brake wheel bearing assembly. CHRYSLER CORPORATION

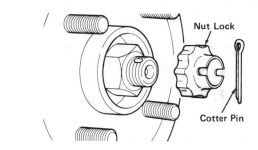

Figure 62-3. Removing cotter pin and nut lock. CHRYSLER CORPORATION

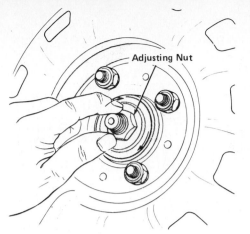

Figure 62-4.
Removing adjusting nut and washer.
CHRYSLER CORPORATION

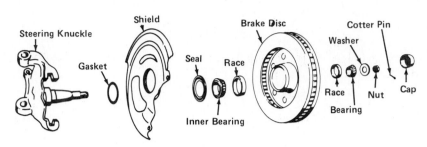

Figure 62-5. Parts of a disc brake wheel bearing assembly.
BUICK MOTOR DIVISION—GMC

raised metal. Bearing cones and rollers should be smooth and free of pits, chipping, or other damage.

Replace any damaged parts. Clean the spindle and apply a light coating of lubricant.

Wheel bearing installation. Force the recommended lubricant between the bearing cone rollers by hand, or repack using a suitable bearing packer.

Press in a new bearing cup, if it is being replaced. Coat the inside hub cavity with a small amount of grease. Install the inner cone. Place a new seal flush with the end of the hub.

Install the wheel hub and drum, or disc, onto the wheel spindle. Install the outer bearing cone, thrust washer, and adjusting nut. An assembled wheel bearing is shown in Figure 62-6. Do *not* tighten the adjusting nut at this point.

Wheel bearing adjustment. Use a lb.-in. torque wrench to tighten the adjusting nut to specifications (see Figure 62-7). Back off on the adjusting nut with a wrench to release bearing preload. Finger-tighten the adjusting nut. Install the lock nut and cotter pin (see Figure 62-8).

Clean and install the grease cap. On disc brake systems, install the caliper. Install the tire and wheel assembly.

62.2 DIAGNOSING SUSPENSION SYSTEM PROBLEMS

Suspension problems can show up in many forms. Noises, bouncing, erratic movements while driving, and improper tire wear are indications that a suspension problem may exist. Suspension, steering, wheel, and tire problems all can have similar effects on the operation of an automobile. For this reason, always refer to diagnostic charts in the proper service manual.

Mechanical Checks

A suspension inspection should be made during any routine maintenance and when a suspension problem is suspected. A visual inspection is made to locate

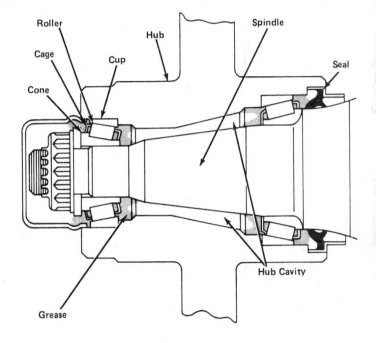

Figure 62-6. Assembled wheel bearing. CHRYSLER CORPORATION

Figure 62-7. Torque wrench adjustment.
CHRYSLER CORPORATION

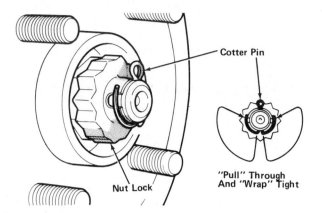

Figure 62-8. Nut lock and cotter pin installation.
CHRYSLER CORPORATION

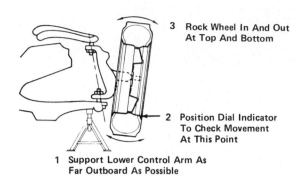

3 Rock Wheel In And Out At Top And Bottom

2 Position Dial Indicator To Check Movement At This Point

1 Support Lower Control Arm As Far Outboard As Possible

Figure 62-9. Checking upper ball joint.
BUICK MOTOR DIVISION—GMC

broken, bent, or worn suspension parts. The following procedures require that the automobile be raised on a hoist. Be sure all safety supports are in place before going under the automobile.

A check of tire wear patterns is usually the first visual inspection made. Always check tire inflation as part of an inspection. Tire and wheel inspection procedures are discussed in Unit 66.

Wheel bearings. Grasp each wheel at the top and bottom. Shake it to check for looseness. Looseness may indicate a bad bearing, improper bearing adjustment, or worn ball joints.

Rotate each tire by hand. The wheel should rotate quietly. If not, the wheel bearing should be checked for adjustment or removed and inspected for damage.

Ball joints. Before inspecting ball joints, the wheel bearings must be in proper adjustment.

To check upper ball joints, raise the automobile on a jack. Place safety stands under the lower control arms or the frame. Where the jack and safety stands can be placed will vary considerably from one automobile to another. Always check the proper service manual before proceeding with this inspection.

SAFETY CAUTION: Be sure the automobile is stable and does not rock on the safety stands. An improperly secured automobile could fall and cause serious injury.

Dial indicators are used to measure ball joint movement. Dial indicators usually are placed on the wheel rim. Always check the proper service manual for procedures. Figure 62-9 shows procedures for checking ball joint movement.

Grasp the wheel. Push in on the bottom of the tire and pull out on the top. Read the dial indicator. Reverse the push-pull procedure and read the dial indicator again. The dial indicator should not exceed the manufacturer's specifications.

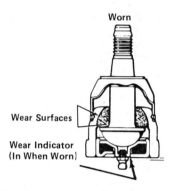

Worn

Wear Surfaces

Wear Indicator (In When Worn)

Figure 62-10. Ball joint wear indicator.
BUICK MOTOR DIVISION—GMC

If the dial indicator reading exceeds specifications, replace the ball joint. Also check the ball stud. If it has become disconnected from the steering knuckle, or if any looseness is detected, replace the ball joint.

The lower ball joint may have a *wear indicator.* Wear is indicated visually by a round nipple that projects beyond the surface of the ball joint cover.

To check the wear indicator, lower the automobile so that it rests on its wheels. The sprung weight of the automobile should be resting normally on the suspension, loading the ball joints. Always check the proper service manual for procedures.

To inspect the ball joint for wear, wipe the grease fitting and nipple free of dirt and grease. The nipple should extend outward from the cover surface (see Figure 62-10). If the nipple is flush or inside the cover surface, replace the ball joint.

Shock absorbers. Check each shock absorber for loose or broken mounts or mounting brackets. Look for leaks. Fluid on the outside of a shock absorber usually indicates a broken or worn seal or rod. Always double-check the source of the fluid leak because it could come from another part of the automobile.

If a defect is suspected, lower the hoist. At each corner of the automobile, push down firmly by hand to bounce the suspension. The suspension should stop bouncing after about two up-and-down motions. If not, the shock absorber may be bad. Disconnect or remove the shock absorber to make a further check (see Topic 62.3).

Some shock absorbers can be disconnected at the lower end to check damping action. Whether disconnected or removed, fully extend and push in on the shock absorber several times. If no resistance is felt, a worn shock absorber is indicated. If only light resistance is felt, compare it with the action of a new shock absorber.

Control arms and strut rods. Lower control arms and bushings can be inspected with the automobile on a hoist. Figure 62-11 shows a lower control arm and its bushings. Upper control arms and bushings usually are inspected off the hoist, with the wheel removed. Check the control arms for damage or wear. Check the bushings to make sure they are centered in the control arm. If the control arm moves excessively within the bushing or is noisy, replace the bushings.

If a strut rod is part of the suspension, it can be checked while the automobile is on a hoist. The strut rod, mounting bracket, and bushing should be replaced when any damage or wear is evident.

Stabilizer bar. Inspect the stabilizer bar for damage. Check the rubber bushings for wear. Replace them, if necessary.

Springs. Sagging and suspension-bottoming springs are the most obvious signs that new springs are needed. However, weak springs can be detected in other ways. Rapid tire wear, early failure of other suspension parts, and poor driver control are reasons to suspect weak springs.

Sagging springs are not always obvious. In this case, the *trim height* should be measured and all suspension parts inspected for damage. Trim height is a manufacturer's recommended height at different

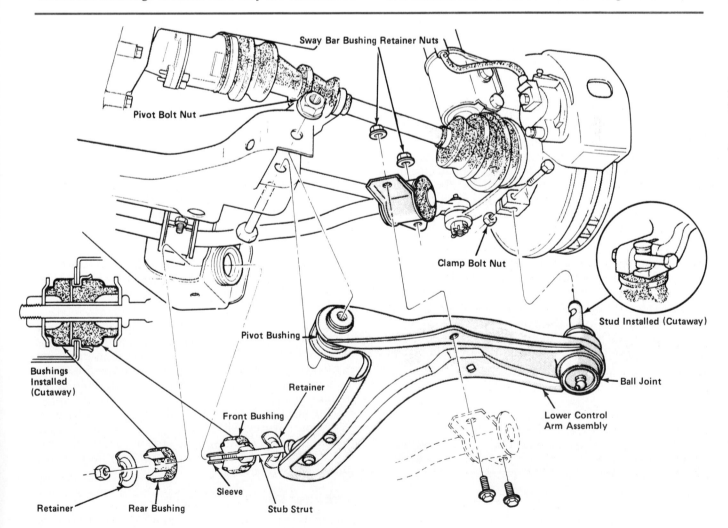

Figure 62-11. Lower control arm and bushings. CHRYSLER CORPORATION

parts of the chassis. Place the automobile on a level surface. Make sure the fuel tank is full, the trunk is empty, and the tires are properly inflated.

Figure 62-12 shows typical trim height measurement locations. The numbers in the following list correspond to the numbers in Figure 62-12. Types of information that can be obtained from trim height measurements include:

- The distance (1) between the lower control arm and the frame. One control arm measurement should be no more than ¼ inch [6.35 mm] different from the opposite control arm measurement.
- The distances (2, 3) between the pivot points on the lower control arm and the ground. The difference between both sides should not exceed ¾ inch [19.05 mm].
- The distance (4) between the bottom of the bumper and the ground. Before this measurement is made, be sure the bumper is straight. The difference between the measurements should not exceed ⅜ inch [9.525 mm].

There also are measurements taken from the road surface to various body points, front and rear. However, manufacturers' procedures may vary considerably. Always follow the proper recommendations when measuring trim height.

Inspect the leaf and coil spring assemblies for any problems. Check leaf spring systems for wear or damage around the hangers, shackles, bolts, and bushings. Also check for broken leaves. A pry bar usually is used between the spring eye and shackle. Pull down on the pry bar. If movement occurs between the spring eye and hanger bolts, replace the bushing. Little or no movement means the bushing is satisfactory.

Check coil spring assemblies for wear, damage, or missing parts. Generally, if the vehicle does not have proper trim height, and other parts are not defective, the springs must be replaced.

MacPherson struts. Diagnosing MacPherson strut suspensions is done in the same manner as for other coil spring suspensions. MacPherson strut assemblies may have to be replaced as complete units rather than

replacing only a worn part. Always refer to the proper service manual.

62.3 SUSPENSION SYSTEM SERVICE

Coil spring and MacPherson strut suspensions are both found on modern automobiles. This section discusses common service procedures for these two types of suspension systems.

Coil Spring Suspension

Figure 62-13 shows a typical General Motors front coil spring suspension. Service procedures for this suspension system include replacing:

- Shock absorbers
- Springs
- Stabilizer bars
- Control arms.
- Ball joints

Shock Absorber Replacement

Worn or damaged shock absorbers are a common suspension problem. Servicing this part requires removing and replacing it. Always follow the instructions enclosed with each replacement shock absorber because procedures can vary.

Locate the upper control arm. Place a wrench on the upper stem of the shock absorber to keep it from turning (see Figure 62-14). Use an open-end wrench and remove the upper retaining nut, retainer, and shock grommet. Parts of the shock absorber assembly are shown in Figure 62-15. If a nut is rusted, apply penetrating oil to the threads. When removing the nut, be careful not to damage mounting pins or studs that are to be reused.

Raise the automobile on a hoist. Remove the two bolts holding the bottom of the shock absorber to the lower control arm. Pull out the shock absorber assembly from the bottom.

Before installing the new shock absorber, carefully read all information on the instruction sheet. Be sure all parts needed for mounting are available. Hold the shock absorber upright and stroke through the full stroke several times to bleed out the air.

To install, place the retainer and grommet over the upper stem of the new shock absorber. Install the shock absorber, fully extended, up through the lower control arm and spring. Continue to insert the upper stem until it passes through the mounting hole in the upper control arm frame bracket. Install the upper rubber grommet, retainer, and nut. Hold the upper stem from turning with an open-end wrench. Tighten the nut to specifications. Install the bolts attaching the shock absorber to the lower control arm. Torque the nuts to specifications.

Stabilizer Bar Replacement

Stabilizer bar service usually requires the replacement of the bushings. Use Figure 62-16 as a guide during this replacement.

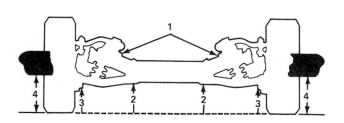

Figure 62-12. Measuring trim height.

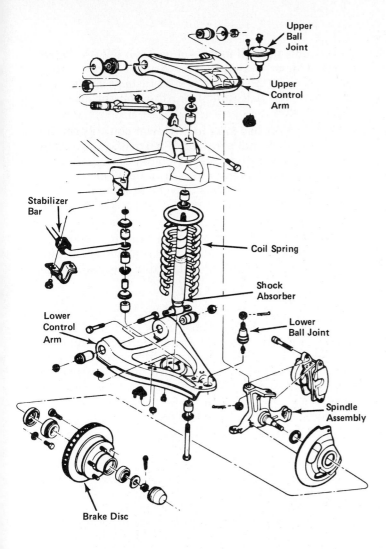

Figure 62-13. Front coil spring suspension.
OLDSMOBILE DIVISION—GMC

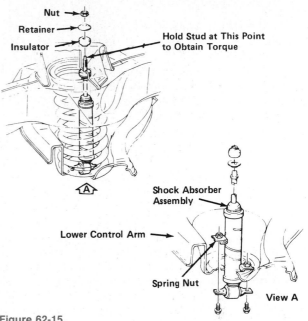

Figure 62-15.
Shock absorber attachments.
OLDSMOBILE DIVISION—GMC

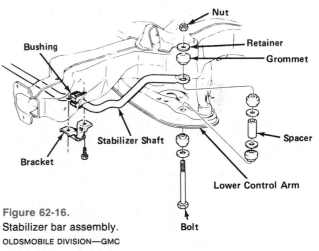

Figure 62-16.
Stabilizer bar assembly.
OLDSMOBILE DIVISION—GMC

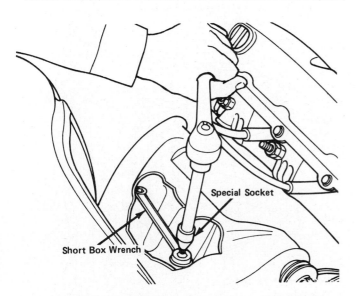

Figure 62-14. Removing nut at the top of the shock absorber.
CADILLAC MOTOR CAR DIVISION—GMC

Raise the automobile. If using a jack, position safety stands in the proper spots under the automobile before disassembly.

Disconnect the stabilizer linkage at each end of the bar. Remove the nuts, retainers, and grommets. Pull out the bolts and remove additional retainers, grommets, and spacers.

Remove the bolts that hold the mounting brackets to the frame. Remove the brackets and bushings. Remove the stabilizer bar.

To replace the stabilizer bar, position the bar under the front frame. Slide the rubber bushings into position on the stabilizer bar with the slits facing forward.

Install the mounting brackets over the bushings and tighten the bolts to specifications.

Install the grommets, retainers, spacers, and bolts on the ends of the stabilizer bar. Be sure all parts are arranged according to the manufacturer's recommendations. Install the upper grommets, retainers, and nuts. Tighten the nuts to specifications.

Ball Joint Replacement

It is not necessary to replace both lower and upper ball joints at the same time. Replace only a ball joint that is damaged or worn. The following procedures are for lower and upper ball joint replacement. These procedures differ, so be sure to follow the proper one.

SAFETY CAUTION: **A floor jack must remain under the lower control arm spring seat during removal and installation. The jack holds the spring and control arm. The spring is under great tension between the two control arms. Sometimes a special spring compressor tool is used to hold the spring. If the spring should come loose, it can cause serious injury.**

Lower ball joint.   Raise the automobile and support it with safety stands under the frame. Remove the tire and wheel assembly. Place a jack under the lower control arm spring seat. Take extreme care to be sure that the jack will not roll. Position the jack so that the wheels are parallel with the vehicle.

Remove the cotter pin from the ball joint stud. Loosen the stud nut two or three turns. Disconnect the lower control arm ball joint from the steering knuckle. A special tool, shown in Figure 62-17, is used to break the ball joint loose from the knuckle. Without this special tool, it is almost impossible to remove the ball joint.

After the ball joint breaks loose, remove the stud nut. Guide the lower control arm out of the splash shield with a putty knife or similar tool (refer to Figure 62-18).

Block the knuckle assembly out of the way by using a wooden block. Place the block between the frame and the upper control arm (see Figure 62-19).

Remove the ball joint seal by prying it off the retainer with a screwdriver or driving it off with a chisel. Remove the grease fittings. Install a special tool to remove the ball joint from the control arm (see Figure 62-20).

Position the ball joint in the lower control arm. Install the special tool shown in Figure 62-21. Position the bleed vent in the rubber boot so that it faces inward. Press the ball joint into the control arm until it bottoms. Remove the block of wood holding the upper control arm and align the steering knuckle hole with the ball joint stud.

Install the ball stud in the steering knuckle. Tighten the nut to specifications. Install the cotter pin. Lubricate the ball joint. Install the tire and wheel assembly.

Upper ball joint.   In the suspension being discussed, the lower ball joint is the load-carrying joint and always is under tension. The upper ball joint is a follower joint, a non-load-carrying joint. For this reason, safety stands must be positioned between the spring seats and the lower control arm ball joints. Always check the proper service manual for procedures. Remove the tire and wheel assembly.

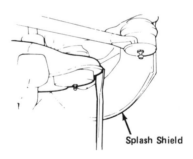

Figure 62-18. Guiding lower control arm past splash shield. OLDSMOBILE DIVISION—GMC

Splash Shield

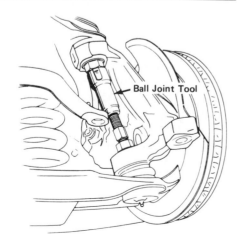

Figure 62-17. Breaking the ball joint loose. OLDSMOBILE DIVISION—GMC

Ball Joint Tool

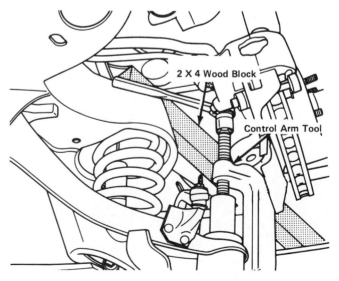

Figure 62-19. Blocking the steering knuckle assembly. OLDSMOBILE DIVISION—GMC

2 X 4 Wood Block

Control Arm Tool

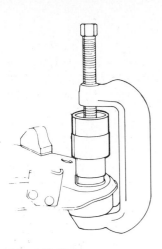

Figure 62-20.
Removing the lower ball joint.
OLDSMOBILE DIVISION—GMC

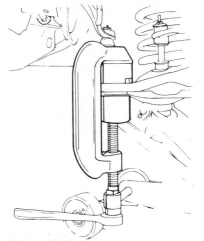

Figure 62-21.
Installing the lower ball joint.
OLDSMOBILE DIVISION—GMC

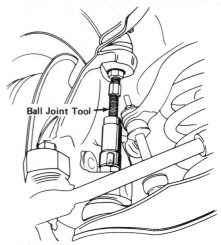

Figure 62-22.
Disconnecting the upper ball joint.
OLDSMOBILE DIVISION—GMC

On some automobiles, the brake caliper must be removed after the tire and wheel assembly have been removed.

Remove the upper ball joint cotter pin. Loosen, but do not remove, the nut three full turns. Install the special tool shown in Figure 62-22. Expand the tool until the stud is free of the steering knuckle. Remove the nut and raise the upper control arm. Support the knuckle assembly on the frame to prevent damage to the brake hose. Place a block of wood between the frame and the upper control arm.

Drill out the rivet heads (see Figures 62-23 and 62-24). Punch out the rivets using a small punch (see Figure 62-25). Remove the ball joint.

Position the new ball joint in the upper control arm. Replacement ball joints use bolts instead of rivets. Install and tighten the four bolts to specifications. Remove the block of wood. Install the ball joint onto the steering knuckle. Tighten the nut to specifications and install the cotter pin. Install and lubricate the ball joint fitting. Install the tire and wheel assembly.

Coil Spring Replacement

It is recommended that, when a coil spring is replaced, the opposite spring also be replaced. This ensures that both springs will operate identically, thus avoiding additional problems.

Spring removal. Place the transmission in neutral and unlock the steering wheel. Raise the automobile on a hoist and support it with safety stands. Remove the shock absorber.

Install a spring compressor tool (see Figure 62-26). Spring compressor tools vary in operation. Always follow instructions carefully when using this special tool. Compress the spring enough so that it is free in the spring seat.

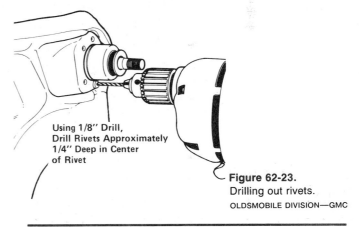

Using 1/8″ Drill, Drill Rivets Approximately 1/4″ Deep in Center of Rivet

Figure 62-23.
Drilling out rivets.
OLDSMOBILE DIVISION—GMC

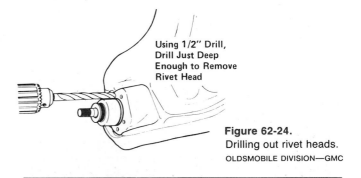

Using 1/2″ Drill, Drill Just Deep Enough to Remove Rivet Head

Figure 62-24.
Drilling out rivet heads.
OLDSMOBILE DIVISION—GMC

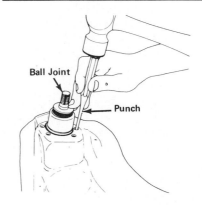

Ball Joint

Punch

Figure 62-25.
Punching out rivets.
OLDSMOBILE DIVISION—GMC

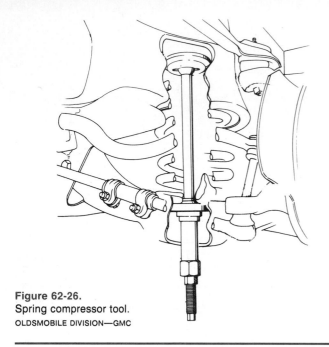

Figure 62-26.
Spring compressor tool.
OLDSMOBILE DIVISION—GMC

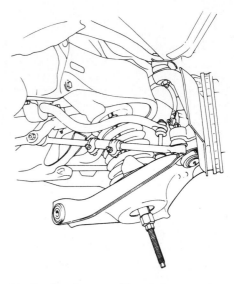

Figure 62-27. Rotate arm, with spring rearward, and remove spring from arm. OLDSMOBILE DIVISION—GMC

SAFETY CAUTION: A spring exerts great pressure. Learn thoroughly how to use a spring compressor tool. Improperly used, a spring compressor tool can cause serious injury.

Remove the two lower control arm pivot bolts. Disengage the lower control arm from the frame. Rotate the lower control arm rearward, with the spring (refer to Figure 62-27). Remove the spring from the arm.

On a workbench, remove the spring compressor tool according to the manufacturer's recommendations. Use extreme care, because a spring under pressure is very dangerous.

Spring installation. To install a new spring, assemble the spring compressor and install it in the new spring according to instructions. Compress the spring to the proper dimensions and curvature.

Position the top of the spring in the seat. Then, position the spring in the lower control arm. Install the lower control arm, using Figure 62-28 as a guide when positioning the spring. Remove the spring compressor. Install the shock absorber. Install the tire and wheel assembly. Be sure all nuts and bolts are tightened to the manufacturer's specifications.

Control Arm Replacement

Bushing replacement is the most common service procedure performed on a control arm. A control arm should be replaced if damaged or worn. A thorough inspection of control arms and bushings always should be made when ball joints are replaced. Service procedures for upper and lower control arms are discussed below.

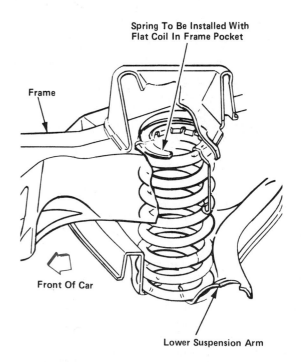

Figure 62-28. Spring installation guidelines.
CADILLAC MOTOR CAR DIVISION—GMC

Upper control arm. The automobile should be supported in the same manner as for upper ball joint removal. Remove the tire and wheel assembly. Loosen the upper ball joint. Loosen the nuts on the upper control arm pivot shaft where it is connected to the frame. Remove the alignment shims (see Figure 62-29). Alignment shims must be installed in the same position from which they were removed. Remove the upper control arm attaching bolts and the upper ball joint. Remove the control arm. Parts of an upper control arm are shown in Figure 62-30.

To replace bushings, press out the old ones and press in the new ones.

To reinstall, position the upper control arm bolts loosely in the frame. Install the pivot shaft and alignment shims. Tighten the nuts to specifications. Connect the ball joint to the steering knuckle. Install the tire and wheel assembly.

Lower control arm. Remove the coil spring. Break the lower ball joint loose from the knuckle. Remove the lower control arm.

Lower control arm bushings are pressed out. Replacement bushings are pressed in.

To reassemble the lower control arm, install the lower ball stud into the knuckle. Tighten to specifications. Install the spring, shock absorber, and lower control arm. Install the tire and wheel assembly.

MacPherson Strut Replacement

Servicing MacPherson strut suspensions usually requires replacing the shock absorber assembly only. Always use the proper service manual when servicing any MacPherson strut assembly. The following procedure is for front-wheel-drive Chrysler suspensions (see Figure 62-31).

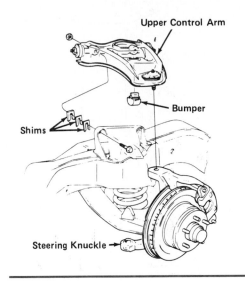

Figure 62-29. Upper control arm assembly. OLDSMOBILE DIVISION—GMC

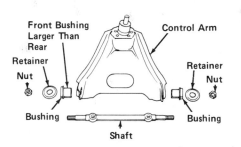

Figure 62-30. Parts of the upper control arm. OLDSMOBILE DIVISION—GMC

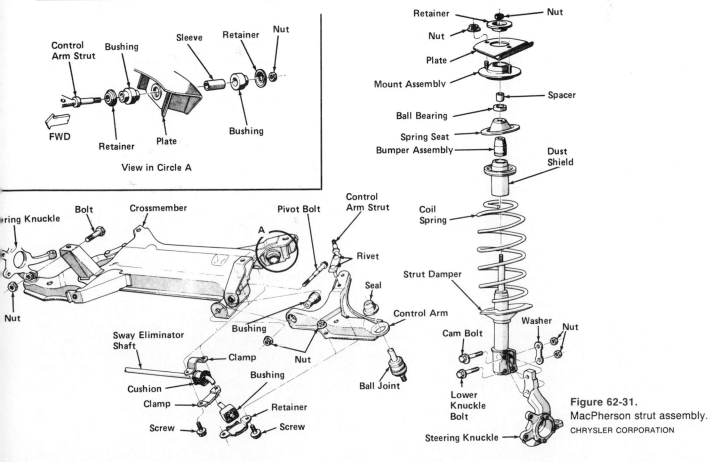

Figure 62-31. MacPherson strut assembly. CHRYSLER CORPORATION

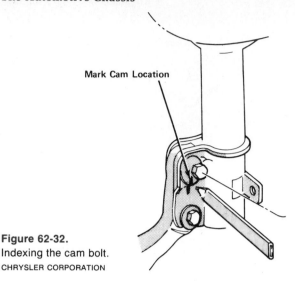

Figure 62-32.
Indexing the cam bolt.
CHRYSLER CORPORATION

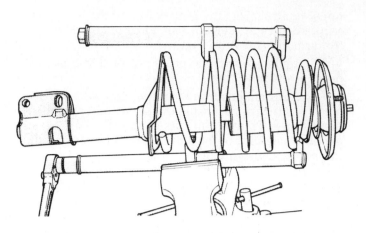

Figure 62-33. Spring compressor tool. CHRYSLER CORPORATION

Remove strut assembly. Raise the front of the automobile. Place safety stands under the frame *jack pads.* Jack pads are reinforced parts of an automobile where jacks can be positioned to raise the automobile safely.

Remove the tire and wheel assembly. Index (see Figure 62-32) and remove the two bolts that attach the strut to the steering knuckle. Remove the brake line from the strut.

At the top of the strut, and under the hood, remove the nuts holding the mounting assembly. Remove the strut/spring assembly.

Disassemble strut assembly. Strut disassembly is completed on the bench. Place the strut in a vise and compress the spring with a spring compressor tool (see Figure 62-33). Always follow instructions carefully when using a spring compressor. Mark the coil spring for reassembly on the same side of the vehicle.

SAFETY CAUTION: Use extreme caution when using a spring compressor. The spring is under great pressure and can cause serious injury if the spring compressor is not operated properly.

Remove the strut rod nut while holding the strut rod (see Figure 62-34).

Remove the strut assembly. Read the instructions carefully before removing the spring from the spring compressor tool. Remove the spring compressor tool.

Inspect the mount assembly (see Figure 62-35). Check for cracks, distortion, and other wear or damage. Replace any defective parts of the strut and mounting assemblies.

Reassemble strut assembly. Carefully follow the proper instructions and compress the spring with the proper tool. Place the compressed spring over the new strut and onto the lower spring seat.

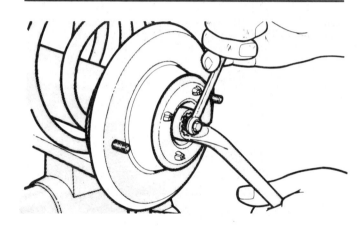

Figure 62-34. Removing strut-rod nut. CHRYSLER CORPORATION

Assemble the bumper, dust shield, upper spring retainer, bearing, and spacer on the strut rod. Mount the assembly over the strut, along with the rebound bumper, retainer, and rod nut. Align the spring, as shown in Figure 62-36. Use a special tool (see Figure 62-37) to tighten the rod nut to specifications. Release the spring compressor tool.

Install strut assembly. Place the top of the strut assembly into the fender reinforcement. Install and tighten the mounting nuts to specifications.

Place the lower end of the strut into the steering knuckle. Install the lower bolt that holds the parts together, but do not tighten. Attach the brake hose retainer to the strut and tighten to specifications.

At the steering knuckle, place the top bolt, or cam bolt, at its original index mark. Place a C-clamp on the strut and knuckle (see Figure 62-38). Tighten the clamp just enough to eliminate any looseness between the knuckle and the strut. Check alignment of the index marks. Tighten the bolts to specifications. Remove the C-clamp. Install the tire and wheel assembly. Wheel alignment always should be checked following strut replacement.

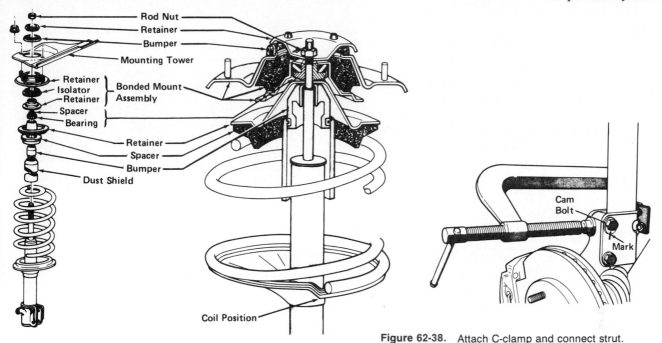

Figure 62-35. Strut damper assembly. CHRYSLER CORPORATION

Figure 62-38. Attach C-clamp and connect strut.
CHRYSLER CORPORATION

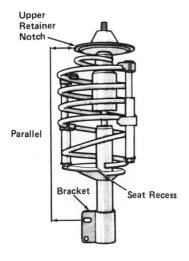

Figure 62-36. Align the spring. CHRYSLER CORPORATION

Figure 62-37. Tightening strut-rod nut. CHRYSLER CORPORATION

U N I T   H I G H L I G H T S

- Lubricate a ball joint about once a year and check it thoroughly.
- A wheel bearing should not have lubricant added to it, but should be repacked at periodic intervals.
- Check wheel bearings by shaking a wheel for looseness.
- A dial indicator is used to measure ball joint movement.
- Some ball joints have a wear indicator.
- Broken mounts and leaks are common shock absorber problems.
- Weak springs can be checked by measuring trim height.
- Carefully read all installation instructions that come with new shock absorbers.
- Ball joints must be broken free from the steering knuckle and control arm before they can be removed.
- When a coil spring is replaced, the opposite spring also must be replaced.
- Old control arm bushings are pressed out and new bushings are pressed in.
- MacPherson strut service usually involves replacing the shock absorber strut assembly.

T E R M S

wear indicator   jack pads
trim height

R E V I E W   Q U E S T I O N S

DIRECTIONS: The following questions are similar to those used on mechanic certification tests. On a separate sheet of paper, write the letter of the correct choice.

1. Which of the following statements is correct?

   I. Never add lubricant to the wheel bearings.

   II. Force grease between the wheel bearing cone rollers with an air gun.

   A. I only   B. II only   C. Both I and II   D. Neither I nor II

2. Which of the following statements is true?

   A. Wheel bearing inspection is made by shaking each wheel.

   B. Ball joint inspection is made by measuring the steering knuckle.

   C. A dial indicator also is called a wear indicator.

   D. A bad shock absorber can develop leaks.

3. Mechanic A says that, when replacing shock absorbers, don't worry about breaking an old mounting pin or stud.

   Mechanic B says that shock absorber bolts should be torqued to specifications.

   Who is correct?

   A. A only   B. B only   C. Both A and B   D. Neither A nor B

4. Which of the following procedures should *not* be done when replacing a ball joint?

   A. Support the vehicle with safety stands.

   B. Disconnect the ball joint from the steering knuckle.

   C. Break off the ball stud when replacing it.

   D. Tighten the bolts on a replacement upper ball joint.

5. Which of the following statements is true?

   I. A spring compressor tool is used when removing a coil spring.

   II. Coil springs should be replaced in pairs.

   A. I only   B. II only   C. Both I and II   D. Neither I nor II

S U P P L E M E N T A L   A C T I V I T I E S

1. Inspect and lubricate ball joints.
2. Repack a set of wheel bearings chosen by your instructor.
3. Make a visual inspection of the suspension system and record any problems that were found.
4. Make a trim height inspection on a vehicle chosen by your instructor.
5. Replace a shock absorber on a vehicle selected by your instructor.
6. Replace the bushings on a stabilizer bar or control arm chosen by your instructor.
7. Remove and replace a ball joint on a vehicle selected by your instructor.
8. Describe the proper use of a spring compressor tool.
9. Replace a MacPherson strut assembly on a vehicle selected by your instructor.

63 STEERING AND WHEEL ALIGNMENT

UNIT PREVIEW

A steering system gives a driver directional control of an automobile. Gears and a linkage system are used to transfer steering wheel rotation into a side-to-side motion at the turning wheels. Most steering systems can be either manually operated or power assisted. Proper wheel alignment is necessary for proper operation of a steering system. It also is important for safe handling characteristics and long tire life.

LEARNING OBJECTIVES

When you have completed your assignments and exercises in this unit, you should be able to:

□ Describe how the parts of a steering linkage are connected.

□ Describe the operation of a recirculating ball gearbox.

□ Describe how a rack and pinion gearbox operates.

□ Describe how an integral power steering works.

□ Explain the reasons for different column designs.

□ Describe the angles used in wheel alignment.

63.1 STEERING SYSTEM OPERATION

A steering wheel is the driver's direct contact with the steering system. A steering wheel is connected to a *steering shaft*. The steering shaft is rotated whenever the steering wheel is moved. A *steering column* is a tube, or housing, for a steering shaft. A steering column does not rotate.

The steering shaft extends from the steering wheel through the firewall and is connected to steering gears. Steering gears usually are housed in a *steering gearbox*. Steering gears change rotating motion from the steering wheel into side-to-side motion at the *steering linkage*. Steering linkage is a system of rods through which steering motion is transferred to the front wheels.

Steering Linkage

The rods that make up the steering linkage are mounted across the front portion of an automobile. The rods connect the front wheels to the steering gearbox. When the steering wheel is rotated, the steering gears drive the linkage assembly, turning both

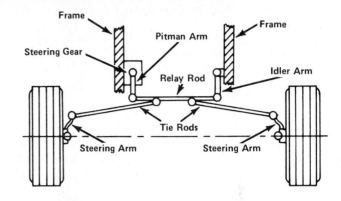

Figure 63-1. Parallelogram steering linkage.
AMERICAN MOTORS CORPORATION

front wheels simultaneously. The major parts of a steering linkage system are:

- Pitman arm
- Relay rod
- Idler arm
- Tie rod
- Steering arm.

Figure 63-1 shows a *parallelogram steering linkage*. A parallelogram is a four-sided figure in which the opposing sides are parallel to one another. Another type of steering linkage, shown in Figure 63-2, is used with rack and pinion steering. Refer to these illustrations as you read the following descriptions of steering linkage system parts.

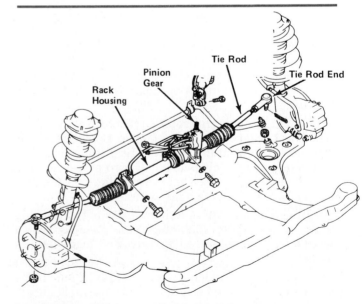

Figure 63-2. Rack and pinion steering assembly.
MAZDA MOTOR CORPORATION

Pitman arm.   A *Pitman arm* extends from the steering gearbox. This arm transmits gear movement to the relay rod.

Relay rod.   A *relay rod* transmits, or relays, steering movement toward both front wheels. A relay rod also is called a *center link* or *drag link*.

Idler arm.   An *idler arm* is connected to the relay rod and to the frame of the automobile. An idler arm supports the end of the relay rod that is opposite the Pitman arm.

Tie rod.   A *tie rod* is connected between the relay rod and the steering arm. There are two tie rods in a steering linkage system, one on each side. Tie rods usually are connected with *adjusting sleeves*. These sleeves are used when adjusting the steering system (see Topic 64.3).

Steering arm.   A *steering arm* is the last connection the steering linkage system makes. A steering arm is a separate rod or an extension of the steering knuckle (see Topic 61.3). A steering arm transmits movement to a turning wheel.

Notice that, in a parallelogram steering linkage system, the Pitman and idler arms are always parallel. These two arms also keep the relay rod in a position parallel to another part of the front suspension or frame. Thus, these parts make up three sides of a parallelogram.

Tie rods and steering arms usually are the only steering linkage parts used in a rack and pinion system.

Steering Ratio

Move a steering wheel to the left until it stops. Now, move the steering wheel to the right until it stops. That movement, from extreme left to extreme right, is called *stop-to-stop*, or *lock-to-lock*. During this steering wheel movement, the front wheels may have turned, from left to right, about 60 degrees. A circle is 360 degrees.

What is a 60-degree rotation? Picture the steering wheel as the face of a clock. Locate 12 o'clock at the top and 6 o'clock at the bottom. The distance between 12 o'clock and 6 o'clock is a half turn of the steering wheel, or 180 degrees. That is three times 60 degrees. On a clock face, 60 degrees is 10 minutes.

Imagine that the automobile has a 1:1 steering ratio. A 60-degree rotation of the steering wheel would then be required to turn the front wheels lock-to-lock.

Think of 12 o'clock as the position in which the automobile's front wheels are pointing straight ahead. Now, move the steering wheel from 12 o'clock to 11 o'clock (30 degrees left) or to 1 o'clock (30 degrees

right). If the steering ratio were 1:1, this slight movement would steer the automobile to extreme turns in both directions.

Obviously, a 1:1 ratio is too fast for normal driver reactions. The slightest movement of the steering wheel would cause the automobile to swerve. To control steering, a slower gear ratio is needed.

A gear ratio, or *steering ratio,* of 15:1 would be acceptable. This means the driver must turn the steering wheel 15 times more than the front wheels are turned. That translates to 900 degrees of steering wheel movement to 60 degrees of turning wheel movement, or 15:1. The steering wheel would go around 2½ times lock-to-lock at that ratio. A movement of 2½ to 3½ turns is considered normal. Fewer steering wheel rotations mean a faster steering ratio. More rotations mean a slower steering ratio.

63.2 MANUAL STEERING

An automobile may have either a manual or a power steering system. A *manual steering* system requires the driver to provide the steering effort. A *power steering* system uses hydraulic pressure developed by engine power to assist the driver when turning.

Manual steering systems are named for the types of steering gears that are used. Most manual steering gears have recirculating ball or rack and pinion systems.

Recirculating Ball

A *recirculating ball* gearbox has two gears: a driving gear and a driven gear (see Figure 63-3). The driving gear, called a *worm gear,* is connected to the steering shaft. A worm gear has spiral threads. The driven gear is a *sector gear* that is connected to the Pitman arm. A sector gear has teeth in a semi-circle, or on a section of a circle. The name "recirculating ball" is derived from what happens between the two gears.

The gearbox is attached to the frame and is filled with lubricant. In the gearbox, the worm gear is threaded into a *ball nut*. A ball nut is a nut with gear teeth on one side. Ball bearings fit into the internal thread, or groove, between the worm gear and the ball nut. Ball bearings roll through tubes, or *ball return guides,* that are connected to each end of the groove. These tubes provide a continuous loop that collects and recycles the ball bearings.

When the steering wheel is turned, the steering shaft will rotate the worm gear. Ball bearings will transmit turning force from the worm gear to the ball nut. Ball bearings help to reduce friction between the worm gear and ball nut. The ball nut will move up or down, depending upon which way the ball bearings are moving. The flow of ball bearings is determined by the rotation of the worm gear. Teeth on the edge of the ball nut move the sector gear and shaft which, in turn, swivel the Pitman arm. Parallelogram linkage is used with recirculating ball steering gears.

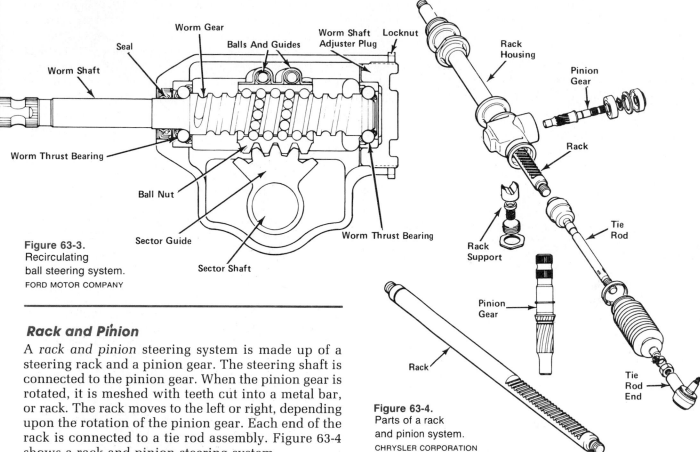

Figure 63-3.
Recirculating
ball steering system.
FORD MOTOR COMPANY

Figure 63-4.
Parts of a rack
and pinion system.
CHRYSLER CORPORATION

Rack and Pinion

A *rack and pinion* steering system is made up of a steering rack and a pinion gear. The steering shaft is connected to the pinion gear. When the pinion gear is rotated, it is meshed with teeth cut into a metal bar, or rack. The rack moves to the left or right, depending upon the rotation of the pinion gear. Each end of the rack is connected to a tie rod assembly. Figure 63-4 shows a rack and pinion steering system.

63.3 POWER STEERING

Hydraulic pressure is used to operate a power steering system, shown in Figure 63-5. Hydraulic principles are discussed in Topic 53.6. Many manual steering parts, such as steering linkage, are used with power steering systems. Parts added for power steering include:

- Pump
- Reservoir
- Hydraulic lines
- A special gearbox or assist assembly on the linkage.

Two types of power steering systems are used: *integral power steering* and *linkage power steering*. Integral power steering is the more popular of the two systems. An integral power steering system applies hydraulic pressure to the inside of a gearbox. The following discussions apply to parts of an integral power steering system. The differences in linkage power steering are discussed at the end of this topic.

Power Steering Pump

Hydraulic pressure for power steering is provided by a *power steering pump*. A pump usually is mounted near the front of the engine (see Figure 63-6). The

pump is driven off the crankshaft pulley by a belt. Hydraulic fluid for the power steering pump is stored in a reservoir. Fluid is routed to and from the pump by hoses and lines. Excessive pressure is controlled by a relief valve.

All power steering pumps operate in a similar manner. A typical pump is illustrated in Figure 63-7. The biggest difference in pumps is the manner in which the rotor seals in the elliptical pump ring. Spaces in the rotor hold inserts, which may be vanes, slippers, or rollers (see Figure 63-8). The inserts are forced outward by centrifugal force to seal the ring during pumping.

Power Steering Gears

A power steering gearbox is basically the same as a manual recirculating ball gearbox with the addition of a hydraulic assist. A power steering gearbox is filled with hydraulic fluid and uses a control valve. A power steering gearbox is illustrated in Figure 63-9.

The ball nut acts as a piston and separates the gearbox into two chambers. One chamber receives fluid for left turns. The other chamber receives fluid for right turns. When the ball nut is a piston, it is pushed by the hydraulic actions of the control valve one way or the other.

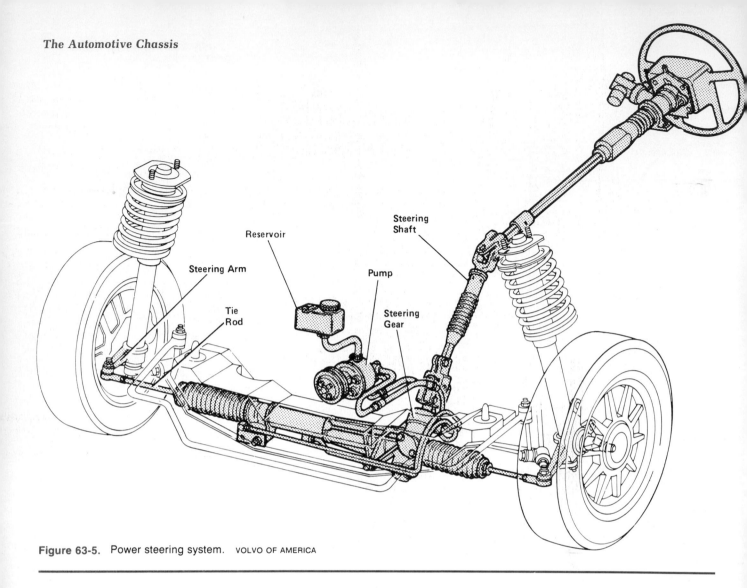

Figure 63-5. Power steering system. VOLVO OF AMERICA

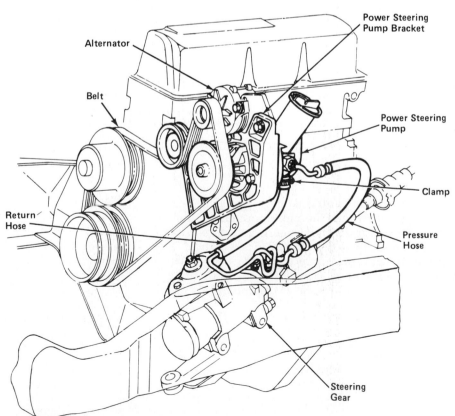

Figure 63-6.
Power steering pump location.
FORD MOTOR COMPANY

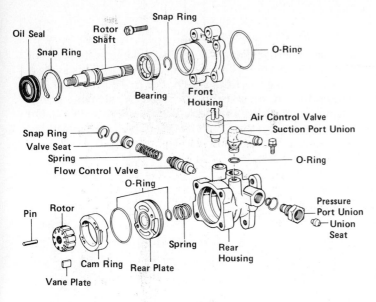

Figure 63-7. Parts of a vane-type pump.
TOYOTA MOTOR SALES, U.S.A.

The control valve is activated when the steering shaft is turned. The valve opens and closes passages to direct fluid into the proper chamber. The valve also directs return fluid back to the reservoir. Control valves are made in different configurations.

Variable ratio steering. A *variable ratio steering* system allows the steering ratio to be changed as steering wheel rotation is increased. The steering ratio may change from 15:1 to 10:1 to allow faster steering and less driver effort. Many power and some manual steering systems are designed with variable ratio steering.

Variable ratio steering is accomplished by redesigning the sector gear in a recirculating ball gearbox. A sector gear with a long middle tooth and two shorter teeth on each side is a variable ratio gear. See Figure 63-10. This feature provides for slower steering over the center and quicker steering at the ends.

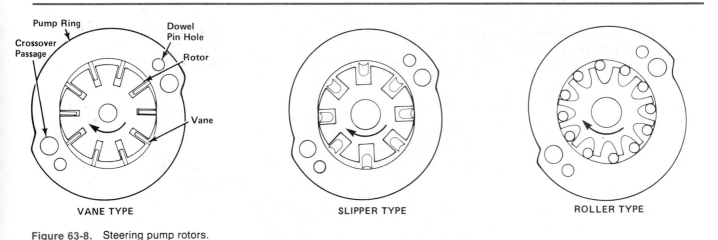

Figure 63-8. Steering pump rotors.

VANE TYPE   SLIPPER TYPE   ROLLER TYPE

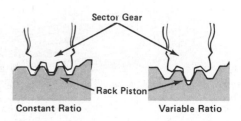

Figure 63-9. Power steering gearbox assembly. FORD MOTOR COMPANY

Figure 63-10. Variable-ratio steering.

Rack and Pinion Power Steering

A typical rack and pinion power steering assembly is shown in Figure 63-11. This is an integral power steering unit. The rack housing becomes the power cylinder where hydraulic fluid is moved under pressure (see Figure 63-12). Seals at each end eliminate leaks. A flange is mounted on the rack. The flange functions as a piston, which is activated by hydraulic pressure. Lines connect the cylinder with a rotating control valve. The control valve is located on the end of the steering shaft.

Linkage Power Steering

Power steering that operates the linkage system rather than the gearbox is arranged differently. This system uses a power cylinder and control valve that are mounted on the steering linkage. The steering pump is operated off an engine pulley (see Figure 63-13). On this type of system, the control valve is mounted between the Pitman arm and the relay rod.

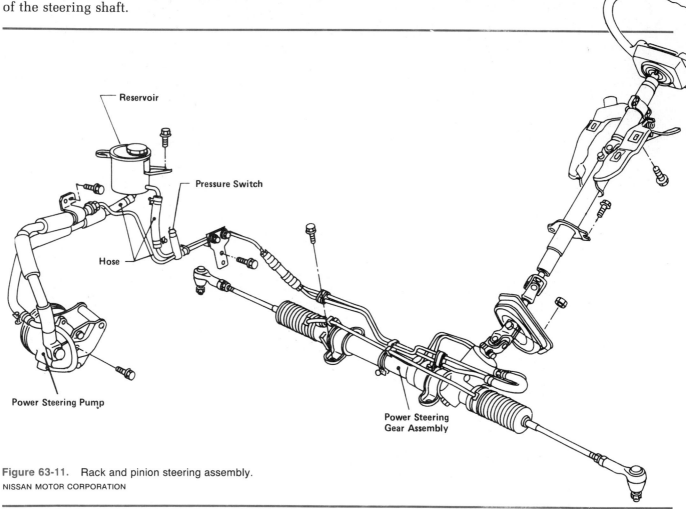

Figure 63-11. Rack and pinion steering assembly.

NISSAN MOTOR CORPORATION

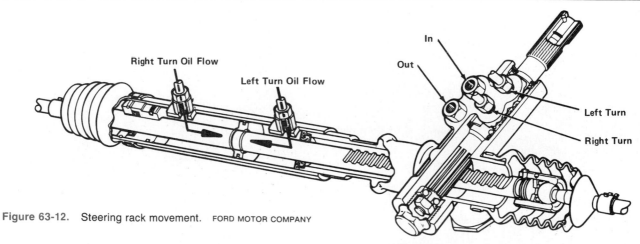

Figure 63-12. Steering rack movement. FORD MOTOR COMPANY

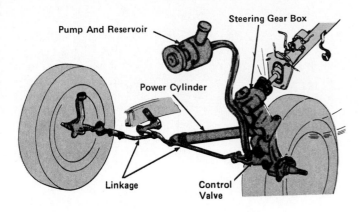

Figure 63-13. Linkage power steering system.
FORD MOTOR COMPANY

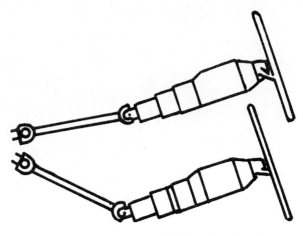

U-Joints Pivot To Absorb Crash Impact

When the Pitman arm is moved by turning linkage, the control valve is activated. The control valve moves in the direction of the turning wheel, routing power steering fluid to the cylinder for power assistance.

63.4 STEERING COLUMN

A steering column can hold several driver-operated controls, such as a shift lever, turn signal indicator, and hazard warning switch. Additional features may be built into the steering columns of many modern cars. These features include windshield wiper/washer, high beam, and horn switches.

Collapsible Steering Column

A *collapsible steering column* is a safety feature. A collapsible steering column is designed to absorb energy from an impact by bending or collapsing. Figure 63-14 shows how steering columns are designed to collapse.

Tilt Steering Wheels and Adjustable Columns

A *tilt steering wheel* allows the driver to adjust the angle of the wheel to a more comfortable driving position. To allow tilting of the steering wheel, a release mechanism is located on the steering column. A tilt wheel is illustrated in Figure 63-15. A release mechanism for a tilt steering column usually is mounted on a lever below (behind) the turn signal lever.

Some automobiles have steering columns that can be adjusted vertically. Vertically adjusting columns are offered in some small imported cars. Such adjustments usually permit only slight upward or downward adjustment of the entire column. The effect is different from that of a tilt wheel.

A steering column that telescopes is illustrated in Figure 63-16. A release mechanism usually is mounted on the steering wheel or below the turn signal lever.

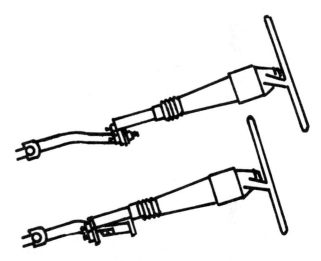

Plate Separates

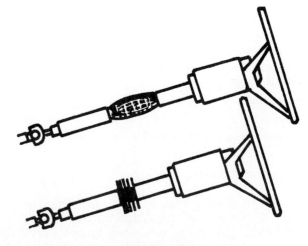

Mesh Compresses

Figure 63-14. Collapsible steering columns.

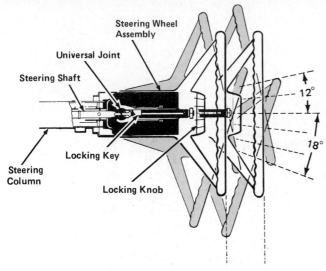

Figure 63-15. Tilt steering operation. CHRYSLER CORPORATION

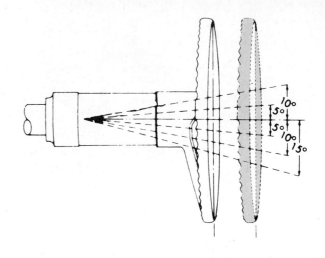

Figure 63-16. Telescoping steering operation.
CADILLAC MOTOR CAR DIVISION—GMC

Locking Steering Column

A *locking steering column* is part of an anti-theft device. The locking mechanism is activated by the ignition switch. When the ignition switch is turned off, the steering wheel and shift lever are locked and cannot be moved.

63.5 WHEEL ALIGNMENT

Wheel alignment refers to the positioning of certain front-end parts. The steering, front suspension, wheels, and frame must be aligned to the manufacturer's specifications. Proper wheel alignment gives the driver good control under many different circumstances. Improper wheel alignment causes steering problems, rapid tire wear, and damage to suspension and steering components.

Front-End Geometry

Steering geometry, or *front-end geometry,* is a term used to describe angles in the front suspension and steering of an automobile. The five angles of front-end geometry are:

- Camber
- Caster
- Steering axis inclination
- Toe
- Toe-out on turns.

Camber. A *camber* angle refers to the inward or outward tilt of a wheel, viewed from the front of an automobile. This tilt is measured in degrees as the angle between the tire centerline and vertical (see Figure 63-17). If the wheel tilts outward, the camber is positive. If the wheel tilts inward, the camber is negative. Incorrect camber will cause uneven tire wear. Camber angle is adjustable except on some MacPherson strut suspensions.

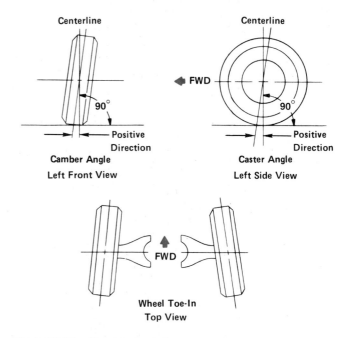

Figure 63-17. Steering geometry.
CHEVROLET MOTOR DIVISION—GMC

Caster. A *caster* angle is a forward or rearward tilt of the steering knuckle when viewed from the side (see Figure 63-17). If the steering knuckle is tilted forward at the top, the caster is negative. If the steering knuckle is tilted rearward at the top, the caster is positive. Caster does not have a great effect on tire wear but does affect handling characteristics. The caster angle is measured in degrees and is adjustable.

Steering axis inclination. *Steering axis inclination* refers to the angle at which the top of the steering knuckle slants inwardly from vertical (see Figure 63-18). This is a designed angle and cannot be changed or adjusted. It is measured in degrees.

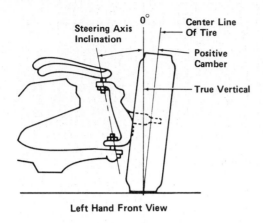

Figure 63-18. Steering axis inclination.
CHEVROLET MOTOR DIVISION—GMC

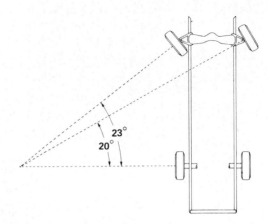

Figure 63-19. Toe-out on turns. CHEVROLET MOTOR DIVISION—GMC

Toe. If the wheels point inward at the front, this angle, viewed from above or below the wheel, is called *toe-in*. See Figure 63-17. Some toe-in is designed into rear-drive automobiles to assist in handling and to promote long tire life. Incorrect toe settings will cause rapid tire wear. The *toe* measurement can be made in either inches [cm] or degrees and is adjustable.

Toe-out on turns. On turns, *toe-out* is necessary for all cars. Toe-out on turns helps to keep the inner wheel turning at a sharper angle. *Toe-out on turns* refers to the difference in angles between the front wheels during turns (see Figure 63-19). Toe-out on turns is a design angle and cannot be adjusted. It is measured in degrees and will wear tires if not correct.

UNIT   HIGHLIGHTS

- A steering wheel is connected to a steering shaft, then to the steering gearbox.
- The steering linkage takes gearbox motion and directs it to the turning wheels.
- A steering ratio determines how many turns a steering wheel makes from lock to lock.
- A recirculating gearbox contains two gears, a ball nut rack, and ball bearings.
- Rack and pinion steering consists of a pinion gear and a metal bar with gear teeth cut into it.
- A power steering system relies on hydraulic pressure for power.
- A power steering gearbox is similar to a recirculating ball gearbox used in manual steering systems.
- A variable ratio steering system has steering ratios changed by a specially designed sector gear.
- Steering columns have features for safety, driver comfort, and theft prevention.
- Front-end geometry is a term that describes angles in the steering, suspension, wheels, and frame.

TERMS

steering shaft	rack and pinion
steering column	integral power steering
steering gearbox	linkage power steering
steering linkage	power steering pump
parallelogram steering	variable ratio steering
linkage	tilt steering wheel
Pitman arm	collapsible steering
relay rod	column
center link	adjustable steering
drag link	column
idler arm	locking steering
tie rod	column
adjusting sleeve	wheel alignment
steering arm	steering geometry
stop-to-stop	front-end geometry
lock-to-lock	camber
steering ratio	caster
manual steering	steering axis
power steering	inclination
recirculating ball	toe-in
worm gear	toe
sector gear	toe-out
ball nut	toe-out on turns
ball return guide	

REVIEW QUESTIONS

DIRECTIONS: The following questions are similar to those used on mechanic certification tests. On a separate sheet of paper, write the letter of the correct choice.

1. The relay rod is connected to the
A. drag link.
B. steering arm.
C. adjusting sleeve.
D. tie rod.

2. Which of the following statements is correct?
   I. Lock-to-lock steering is one complete turn of the steering wheel.
   II. A 15:1 steering ratio produces 2½ rotations of the steering wheel.
A. I only   B. II only   C. Both I and II   D. Neither I nor II

3. All of the following statements are true EXCEPT
A. A worm gear has spiral threads.
B. A ball nut has gear teeth on the inside.
C. Ball bearings roll through ball return guides.
D. The flow of ball bearings is determined by the rotation of the worm gear.

4. Mechanic A says that rotor inserts in a pump are of the spline type.
   Mechanic B says that a ball nut in a power steering gearbox is a piston.
   Who is correct?
A. A only   B. B only   C. Both A and B   D. Neither A nor B

5. Which of the following angles does not involve the position of the front wheels?
A. Camber
B. Steering axis inclination
C. Toe-in
D. Toe-out

SUPPLEMENTAL ACTIVITIES

1. Show how turning force is transferred from the steering wheel to the steering arm.
2. Determine how many turns it requires a steering wheel to go from lock to lock.
3. Identify the parts of a recirculating ball steering gearbox.
4. Explain how a rack and pinion steering system works.
5. On an automobile selected by your instructor, determine whether it has an integral or linkage power steering system.
6. Describe how hydraulic pressure enters and operates a power steering gearbox.
7. Explain how a steering column selected by your instructor collapses in a front-end accident.
8. Illustrate how front-end geometry is determined.

UNIT PREVIEW

Steering systems and wheel alignment require constant inspection and periodic adjustments. Steering and wheel alignment problems create excessive tire wear and reduce fuel economy. Whenever parts of a steering or suspension system are replaced, a wheel alignment is necessary. This unit discusses the maintenance and service of a steering system and how to make adjustments during a wheel alignment.

LEARNING OBJECTIVES

When you have completed your assignments and exercises in this unit, you should be able to:
- [ ] Check steering lubricant level.
- [ ] Diagnose steering problems.
- [ ] Adjust a steering gearbox.
- [ ] Replace a power steering pump.
- [ ] Make a wheel alignment.

SAFETY PRECAUTIONS

An automobile is raised on a hoist or placed on safety stands for many steering and wheel alignment service procedures. Be sure the hoist and safety stands are positioned at the proper locations on an automobile.

Be aware that ball joints which are worn excessively can break when the wheel assembly is moved. When a ball joint breaks, the vehicle will collapse from its own weight.

Be careful when working around an automobile that has just been driven. Hot parts and fluid around steering system parts can cause burns.

Do not use heat to straighten or correct a steering linkage problem. Replace any part that is damaged or worn excessively.

A power steering pump usually is located near the engine fan. Disconnect the battery before working around the engine fan assembly. A spinning fan can cause serious injury.

Use caution during road tests. A faulty steering system can be dangerous to you and other drivers. The automobile could swerve or make unusual movements. Buckle the safety belt before starting the road test. Do not speed or make extraordinary turning movements. Conduct the road test according to manufacturer's recommendations.

When using wheel alignment equipment, set the parking brake, place the gearshift lever in gear, and block the wheels. Follow all directions outlined by the equipment manufacturer.

Performing a wheel alignment requires the mechanic to work in tight areas around the wheel. Be alert at all times. A hand can become caught in parts, such as a coil spring. You could bump your head or get poked in the eye if you are careless.

All wheel alignment fasteners are important attaching parts. Improper fasteners can affect the performance of vital parts in the steering system. Do not use a replacement part of improper size or strength. Always tighten fasteners to the manufacturer's torque specifications.

64.1 PREVENTIVE MAINTENANCE

Periodic maintenance varies according to the vehicle. Always refer to the proper service manual for recommendations. Preventive maintenance for steering systems usually involves fluid level checks, lubrication, and visual inspection. Many parts of a steering system are permanently lubricated and seldom require maintenance.

Steering Gearbox Lubrication

Only manual steering gearboxes are checked for lubricant level. Power steering levels are checked at the hydraulic fluid reservoir. Some gearboxes are permanently sealed, and adding lubricant to them is not recommended.

A manual steering gearbox can be inspected for lubricant by removing a cover bolt (see Figure 64-1). First, wipe off the housing so that dirt will not enter the gearbox. Lubricant should be to the level of the

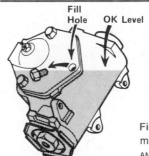

Figure 64-1. Checking manual gearbox lubricant.
AMERICAN MOTORS CORPORATION

bolt hole. Add the proper lubricant, if necessary. Replace the bolt and tighten to specifications.

Rack and pinion gears usually are permanently sealed. However, check to see if a universal joint is connected from the steering shaft to the pinion gear. Some universal joints require lubrication.

Power Steering Pump Lubrication

On some automobiles, the power steering lubricant level can be checked when the steering system is hot or cold. On others, the lubricant must be checked at driving temperature. To warm up power steering fluid, start the engine. Turn the steering wheel from lock to lock several times. This expels air from the system and warms the fluid.

Remove the cap on the power steering reservoir (see Figure 64-2). A dipstick is attached to the cap. Check the dipstick. Some dipsticks will have a reading for hot and cold fluid level. Add the proper lubricant, if necessary. Replace the cap.

Steering Linkage Lubrication

Parts of the steering linkage system that require periodic lubrication are shown in Figure 64-3. Clean the linkage parts to be lubricated, and remove the lube plug. Use a lubrication fitting to add the proper lubricant. Remove the fitting and install the lube plug.

Visual Inspection

During lubrication, check steering linkage for damage, excessive wear, and looseness. Areas around mountings, bushings, ball joints, and at gearboxes are especially critical. Look for leaks around gearboxes, power steering connections, and driving axle boots. Check the power steering belt for cracks, fraying, wear, and belt tension. Replace any parts that are worn or damaged.

64.2 DIAGNOSING STEERING PROBLEMS

Tire wear is a good indication of problems in the steering system and/or with wheel alignment (see

Topic 64.4). Always check tire wear patterns first. Refer to Topic 66.2 for tire tread wear patterns.

Steering problems may involve the suspension, wheels, and/or tires. All must be considered when diagnosing a steering condition. To avoid acting on the wrong symptom, always road test the automobile.

Before making a road test, make the following preliminary checks:

1. Check for proper tire inflation.
2. Check couplings and universal joints from the steering shaft to the gearbox for loose connections or wear. Check universal joints from the steering shaft to the rack and pinion.
3. Raise the automobile on a hoist. Check the front and rear suspensions and steering linkage for loose or damaged parts.
4. Spin the front and rear wheels. Check for out-of-round tires, out-of-balance wheel assemblies, bent rims, and loose and/or rough wheel bearings.
5. Check for leaks on the power steering system. Check power steering fluid level. Check tension on the drive belt.

If any defects are found, correct them. Then, road test the automobile to determine if the problem has been corrected. Vibration, steering response, and noise are indications of a possible steering problem. A troubleshooting chart from the proper service manual will provide extensive information on diagnostic procedures. The following symptoms and their probable causes will explain steering problems only. Other parts of an automobile may cause similar reactions.

Shimmy, shake, or vibration. These can be caused by worn steering linkage pivots, improper wheel balance, and/or bad tires.

Hard steering (manual). This can be caused by insufficient lubrication, bind in steering linkage, front

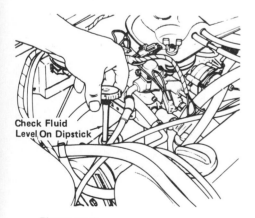

Figure 64-2.
Checking power steering lubricant.
CHRYSLER CORPORATION

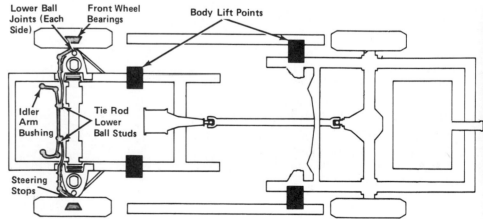

Figure 64-3. Steering linkage lubrication points. AMERICAN MOTORS CORPORATION

wheel misalignment, improper rack and pinion adjustment, or soft tires.

Hard steering (power). This can be caused by the hydraulic system, improper gearbox or rack and pinion adjustment, a loose belt, or low power steering fluid level. It also can be caused by binding in the steering linkage or in the rack and pinion assembly.

Excessive play. Play is the free movement of the steering wheel before the front wheels begin to turn. All steering systems have some play. Excessive play is caused by a loose or out-of-adjustment steering gearbox or rack and pinion. Also check the steering shaft coupling, universal joints, relay rod, tie-rod ends (for looseness or wear), and the idler arm.

Poor returnability (manual). *Returnability* is the tendency of the steering wheel to return to a straight-ahead position at the end of a turning maneuver. Poor returnability is caused by lack of lubrication at the steering linkage and at the rack and pinion. Other causes may be a bind in the steering column, front wheel alignment, or rack and pinion adjustment.

Poor returnability (power). This can be caused by lack of steering linkage lubrication, improper front end alignment, or a sticking hydraulic valve. Binds can occur in the steering shaft, lower coupling flange, or anywhere in the steering linkage. Adjustments may be required in the steering gearbox or the rack and pinion.

Wander. *Wander* shows up as poor steering stability, where the driver cannot keep the automobile moving straight ahead. Wander can be caused by a lack of lubrication at the steering linkage or an improper gearbox or rack and pinion adjustment. It also can indicate front or rear wheel alignment problems or loose parts almost anywhere in the steering system.

Pull during braking. This is caused by incorrect or uneven caster, soft tires, or loose and/or worn parts.

Kickback. *Steering wheel kickback* is a sharp, rapid movement of the steering wheel when the automobile strikes a bump or other obstruction. Kickback can be caused by lack of steering linkage lubrication, loose tie rod ends, or air in a power steering system. It also can be caused by loose gearbox or rack and pinion attachments or adjustments. A worn or loose steering shaft coupling or universal joint also could be the problem.

Steering wheel surge. *Steering wheel surge* describes the condition in which the steering wheel jerks in the driver's hands. Surge is caused by a steering hydraulic problem, sluggish control valve, or loose belt.

Abnormal power steering pump noise. A groan or whine is caused by low fluid level, air in the fluid, a loose pump mounting, or mechanical pump problems.

A rattle is caused by a pump rotor vane. A rattle or chuckle may indicate a loose gear, loose steering linkage, or a gearbox or rack and pinion adjustment. A rattle or chuckle in a rack and pinion system may be caused by improper lubrication or loose attachments. A pressure hose that is touching another part also may be the cause.

A squeal or chirp usually indicates a loose belt.

Abnormal front-end noise. Possible causes include lack of lubrication at the steering linkage. Also, check for worn linkage pivots or tie-rod ends, or rack and pinion adjustment.

64.3 STEERING SYSTEM SERVICE

Steering system service involves a steering gear adjustment and replacing parts. Procedures vary considerably among automobiles. Always consult the proper service manual.

Steering Gear Adjustment

Two adjustments can be made in a manual steering gearbox. The adjustments are for worm bearing preload and lash, or gear mesh, between the ball nut and sector gear. Preload adjustment is checked first. Always check the proper service manual for steering gear adjustment, because the adjustment sequence is critical. Improper adjustment procedures can result in a damaged gear or poor steering response. Adjustments are made by turning adjusters on the gearbox (see Figure 64-4).

Most adjustments require that the steering linkage be disconnected. Many power steering gearboxes must be removed from the automobile before adjustments can be made.

Rack and pinion adjustments require that pinion bearing preload be checked.

Steering Linkage Replacement

The automobile must be raised on a hoist to replace steering linkage. Figure 64-5 shows parts of the steering linkage system that can be removed. If the linkage

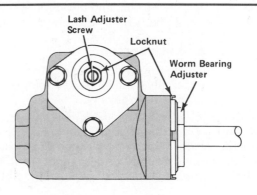

Figure 64-4. Steering gearbox adjustment points.
CHEVROLET MOTOR DIVISION—GMC

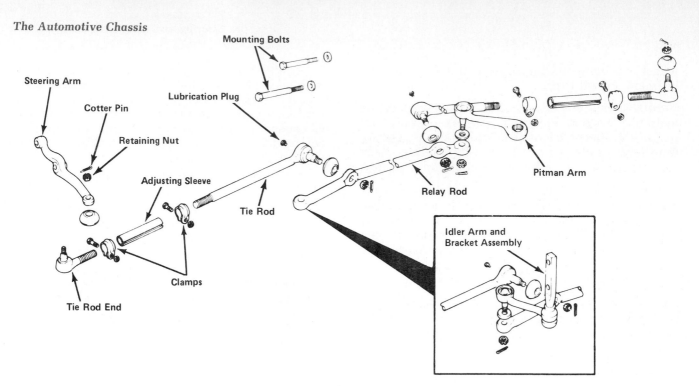

Figure 64-5. Parts of a steering linkage system. AMERICAN MOTORS CORPORATION

being disconnected will be reused, be sure to use a removing tool that will not damage the seal.

CAUTION: **Do not turn the steering wheel hard against the stop when the linkage is disconnected. This could damage the ball return guide in the gearbox.**

Whenever linkage parts are replaced, a wheel alignment must be made. See Topic 64.4.

Power Steering Pump Replacement

A typical power steering pump assembly is shown in Figure 64-6. Always disconnect the negative cable on the battery first. Parts of the engine fan assembly and air conditioning system may have to be removed. Remove the pump pulley, bracket, hoses, and pump.

When the pump is installed, be sure all fasteners are torqued properly, including the hose fittings. Fill the reservoir, tighten the belt, and bleed the system according to the manufacturer's recommendations.

Steering Gear Replacement

Procedures for removing and replacing steering gearboxes vary considerably. One type of steering gearbox attachment is shown in Figure 64-7.

Set the front wheels in a straight-ahead position. Remove any power steering attachments. Mark the relationship of the Pitman arm to the Pitman shaft. Remove the Pitman arm with a special puller. Remove the bolts holding the gearbox in position. Refer to Figure 64-8.

When replacing the gearbox, bolt it in place and install the Pitman arm according to the marks made

during removal. Attach any parts that were disconnected during assembly. Torque all fasteners to specifications.

Rack and Pinion Replacement

Before removing a rack and pinion assembly, raise the automobile on a hoist and remove the front wheels. Rack and pinion attachment points are shown in Figure 64-9. Remove the tie rods with a special puller and disconnect the steering shaft. Support the crossmember with a hydraulic jack. Remove all attachments, including power steering parts, according to the proper service manual. Remove the bolts holding the steering assembly, and then remove the assembly.

A rack and pinion assembly is installed in the reverse order of removal. Wheel alignment should be adjusted whenever a rack and pinion is removed.

64.4 WHEEL ALIGNMENT

Wheel alignment is not a periodic service. Alignment problems show up most often in the form of vibration, difficult steering, or abnormal tire wear. Wheel alignment should be made following suspension repair. As a preventive measure, wheel alignment frequently is checked and adjusted when new tires are installed on the front wheels. Always refer to the proper service manual when making a wheel alignment. Some suspensions can be adjusted only for certain geometric angles.

Prealignment Checks

Before any checks are made, the automobile must be on a level surface. The fuel tank must be full. All doors

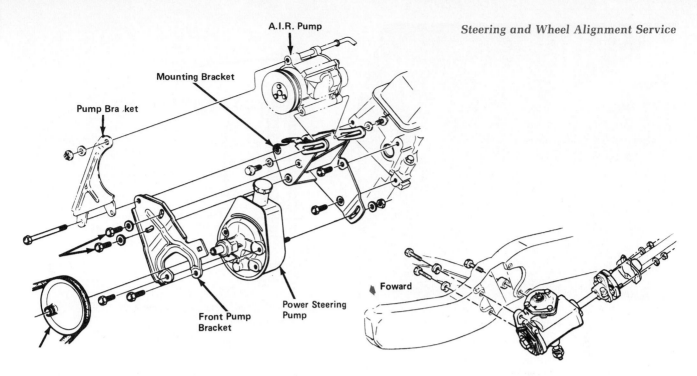

Figure 64-6. Power-steering pump assembly.
BUICK MOTOR DIVISION—GMC

Figure 64-7. Steering gearbox attachment.
CHEVROLET MOTOR DIVISION—GMC

must be closed, with no occupants or excess weight inside the automobile.

The following inspections should be made, and any faults should be corrected. Check:

1. All tires for proper inflation and approximately equal tread wear
2. Front wheel bearings for proper adjustment
3. For loose ball joints
4. Tie-rod ends and relay rod for looseness
5. For runout of wheels and tires
6. Vehicle height
7. For steering gear looseness at the frame
8. Shock absorbers for improper operation
9. For loose control arms
10. For loose or missing stabilizer bar attachments.

Wheel Alignment Measurement

Many different types of wheel alignment equipment are used. The equipment can be portable or permanently mounted. Figure 64-10 shows an example of wheel alignment equipment.

The method of checking alignment will vary depending on the type of equipment used. Instructions furnished by the equipment manufacturer always should be followed. Alignment checks are made for camber, caster, and toe.

Front-End Alignment

Three adjustments usually are made when correcting wheel alignment on coil spring front suspensions. These adjustments are for camber, caster, and toe-in.

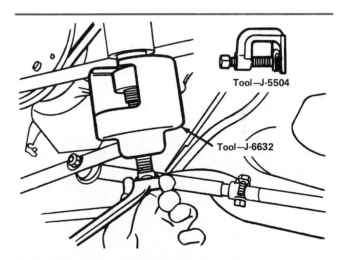

Figure 64-8. Removing bolts that hold gearbox.
CHEVROLET MOTOR DIVISION—GMC

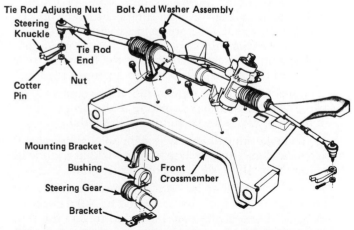

Figure 64-9. Rack and pinion assembly. CHRYSLER CORPORATION

Figure 64-10. Wheel alignment equipment.

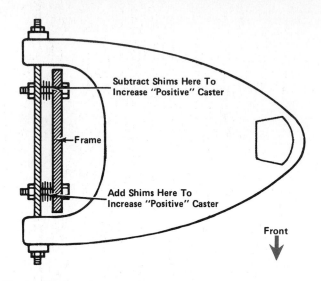

Figure 64-11. Shim caster adjustment.
CHEVROLET MOTOR DIVISION—GMC

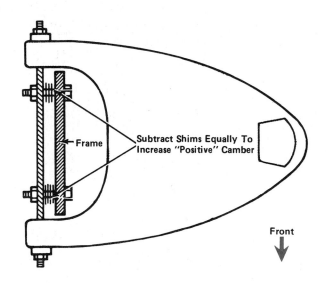

Figure 64-12. Camber adjustment with shims.
CHEVROLET MOTOR DIVISION—GMC

Alignment adjustments can vary considerably among automobiles. Always refer to the proper service manual. If both camber and caster must be adjusted, and they will be adjusted separately, always do caster first, then camber. If camber is done first, it may have to be redone after caster has been adjusted.

Caster. When making a shim adjustment for caster, a different number of shims is needed at the front and rear bolts. To correct caster, the shims are transferred from front to rear or from rear to front (refer to Figure 64-11).

Before adjusting caster and camber, bounce the car several times using the front bumper. This allows the automobile to settle to its normal height.

A caster change is made by turning each cam bolt to obtain one-half of the needed correction. Cam bolts are loosened, adjusted, and tightened in the same manner as for camber adjustment. Check the caster setting to make sure it is correct. If necessary, repeat the adjustments.

Camber. Two common camber adjustments are made with either shims or cam bolts. To adjust camber on a suspension with shims, the shims may be added or subtracted to correct the angle. Figure 64-12 shows where the shims are located. The same number of shims must be changed at both the front and rear of the control arm shaft to obtain a proper reading.

Loosen the frame nuts at the upper control arm. Add or subtract shims according to the proper alignment correction charts. Retorque the nuts.

To make adjustments with cam bolts, the cam bolt is loosened and turned. Use Figure 64-13 as a guide in making the following cam bolt adjustments.

Say that camber is –0.6 degrees. To obtain 0.0 degrees, camber must be corrected by +0.6 degrees. First, hold one of the cam bolts and loosen the nut. Turn the cam bolt to obtain a change that is equal to

half of the needed correction, or +0.3 degrees. Hold the cam bolt in this position to maintain the setting, and tighten the nut to specifications. Repeat the same procedure for the other cam bolt to get another correction of +0.3 degrees. The two corrections will total a change of +0.6 degrees.

Toe-in. The last wheel alignment adjustment should be toe-in. Caster and camber angle corrections may affect the toe-in setting. Toe-in usually can be increased or decreased by changing the length of the tie-rod ends. Toe-in adjustments vary among manufacturers. Therefore, always check the proper service manual for toe-in adjustments and specifications.

CAUTION: Never bend a tie rod as a method of adjusting toe-in. Bent tie rods must be replaced.

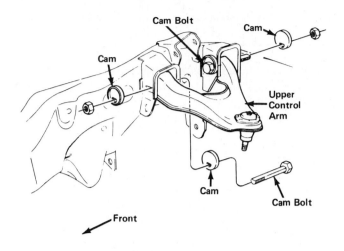

Figure 64-13. Cam bolt adjustments.
CHEVROLET MOTOR DIVISION—GMC

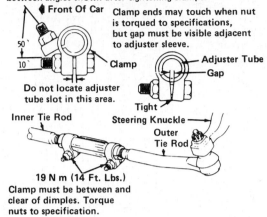

Bolts must be installed in direction shown, rotate both inner and outer tie rod housings rearward to the limit of ball joint travel before tightening clamps. With this same rearward rotation all bolt centerlines must be between angles shown after tightening clamps.

Figure 64-14. Tie rod adjustment. BUICK MOTOR DIVISION—GMC

If a tie-rod adjuster is heavily rusted, discard the nuts and bolts. Apply penetrating oil between the clamp and the tube. Rotate the clamps until they move freely. Install new nuts and bolts of the proper size and strength. Torque the nuts to specifications.

NOTE: Some tie rods are mounted ahead of the steering knuckle. These tie rods must be decreased in length to increase toe-in.

Use Figure 64-14 as a guide to adjusting toe-in. Loosen the clamp bolts at each end of the adjusting sleeves. With the steering wheel set in a straight-ahead position, turn the adjusting sleeves to obtain the proper toe-in adjustment.

When adjustment is completed, check that the tie-rod end housings are at proper angles to the steering arms. Place tie-rod clamps and sleeves in their proper positions.

Before locking the clamp bolts, be sure that the tie-rod ends are in alignment with their ball studs. To check alignment, rotate both tie-rod ends in the same direction as far as they will go. Tighten the clamps to specifications. Make sure the adjuster tubes and clamps are positioned properly. Torque the nuts to specifications.

MacPherson Strut Front-End Alignment

On many MacPherson strut front suspensions, only camber and toe-in adjustments are made. Caster adjustments usually cannot be made.

Camber. Use Figure 64-15 as a guide for camber adjustment. Loosen the bolts that connect the strut to the steering knuckle. The bolts should be just loose enough to allow movement between the strut and the knuckle.

Grasp the top of the tire firmly. Move the tire inward or outward until the correct camber adjustment

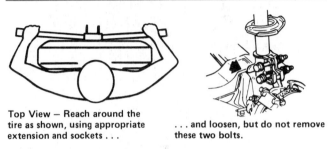

Top View — Reach around the tire as shown, using appropriate extension and sockets . . .

. . . and loosen, but do not remove these two bolts.

Then grasp the top of the tire firmly and move inboard or outboard until the correct reading is obtained.

If accessability is limited, it may be necessary now to remove the wheel and tire to apply final torque to bolts/nuts to retain the correct camber setting.

Figure 64-15. MacPherson strut camber adjustment.
BUICK MOTOR DIVISION—GMC

is obtained. At this point, it may be necessary to tighten one or both bolts. The torque will allow slight movement between the strut and the knuckle. The torque also will be sufficient to hold the correct camber reading while the tire-and-wheel assembly is removed. If bolts cannot be torqued completely because of accessibility, a *partial torque* is required. A partial torque means tightening the nuts just enough to hold the correct camber position. Remove the tire-and-wheel assembly and apply final torque. Install the tire-and-wheel assembly.

Toe-in. When adjusting toe-in on a front-drive automobile with MacPherson strut suspension, the tie-rod boots will be moved. Be careful that the boots are not damaged or twisted. Replace any boots that are worn or damaged.

Use Figures 64-16 and 64-17 as guides when adjusting toe-in. Loosen the jam nuts or clamp bolts on the tie rod. Rotate the tie rods to adjust the toe to specifications. Tighten the jam nuts or clamp bolts to specifications. Adjust the boot.

Rear-Wheel Alignment

Some manufacturers recommend rear-wheel alignment. Rear-wheel alignment procedures for coil spring suspensions are similar to those described above in Front-End Alignment. Always refer to the proper service manual when a rear-wheel alignment is necessary.

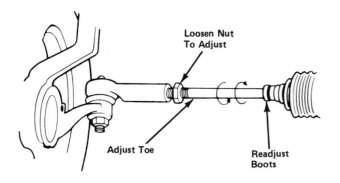

Figure 64-16. MacPherson strut toe adjustment.
BUICK MOTOR DIVISION—GMC

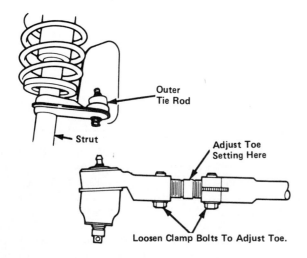

Figure 64-17. MacPherson strut toe adjustment.
BUICK MOTOR DIVISION—GMC

U N I T   H I G H L I G H T S

- Steering gearboxes are lubricated either at the gearbox housing or at the power steering reservoir.
- Steering linkage systems are lubricated with a lube gun.
- A visual inspection is made whenever the steering system is lubricated.
- Several preliminary checks must be made before an automobile is taken for a road test.
- A road test involves diagnosing vibration, steering response, and noise.
- Steering gearbox adjustment involves checking preload and backlash.
- A wheel alignment is necessary whenever a steering linkage part is serviced.
- To replace a steering gearbox, the steering shaft and Pitman arm must be disconnected.
- Servicing a rack and pinion system requires steering linkage and wheel removal.
- Prealignment checks are made to give an accurate reading during wheel alignment.
- Camber and caster alignments are made at the control arms.
- Toe-in adjustments are made on the adjusting sleeve.
- MacPherson strut suspensions usually cannot be adjusted for caster.

T E R M S

returnability
wander
steering wheel kickback

steering wheel surge
partial torque

REVIEW QUESTIONS

DIRECTIONS: The following questions are similar to those used on mechanic certification tests. On a separate sheet of paper, write the letter of the correct choice.

1. Which of the following statements is correct?

   I. All steering gearboxes are checked for lubricant level.

   II. Power steering lubricant level is checked at the reservoir.

   A. I only   B. II only   C. Both I and II   D. Neither I nor II

2. All of the following statements are true EXCEPT

   A. Play is free movement in a steering wheel.

   B. Returnability is the ability of a steering wheel to return to a straight-ahead position after it is turned.

   C. Kickback is the bending of a steering shaft during impact.

   D. Steering wheel surge causes a jerk.

3. Mechanic A says that a Pitman arm is removed with a puller.

   Mechanic B says that a Pitman arm on rack and pinion steering cannot be removed.

   Who is correct?

   A. A only   B. B only   C. Both A and B   D. Neither A nor B

4. Camber can be adjusted by

   A. subtracting shims.

   B. torquing cam bolts.

   C. replacing steering linkage.

   D. tightening cam nuts on the frame.

5. Which of the following statements is correct?

   I. Toe-in is adjusted by turning an adjusting sleeve.

   II. Toe-in on a MacPherson strut is adjusted by removing a front wheel.

   A. I only   B. II only   C. Both I and II   D. Neither I nor II

SUPPLEMENTAL ACTIVITIES

1. Check the lubricant level of a steering system selected by your instructor.
2. Lubricate a steering system.
3. Diagnose a steering problem presented by your instructor.
4. Make a steering gearbox or rack and pinion adjustment.
5. Replace a power steering pump.
6. Make wheel alignment measurements.
7. Adjust camber, caster, and toe-in on an automobile selected by your instructor.

65 TIRES AND WHEELS

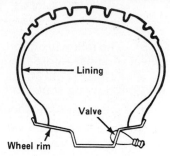

UNIT PREVIEW

Tires and wheels are responsible for the final actions of the power train, suspension, steering, and brakes. Tires provide traction when power and chassis performances are transferred to the road. Automobiles are designed to use only certain tires and wheels. Thus, it is important for the mechanic to understand how tires and wheels control automotive actions.

LEARNING OBJECTIVES

When you have completed your assignments and exercises in this unit, you should be able to:
- ☐ Identify the parts of a tire.
- ☐ Explain the different types of tires.
- ☐ Describe how to determine tire size.
- ☐ Describe the function of a safety wheel.
- ☐ Describe how a wheel is attached to an automobile.

65.1 THE PURPOSE OF A TIRE

A tire is the only part of an automobile that is in constant contact with the ground. The tire is a rubber ring that encircles the wheel. A tire is pneumatic, meaning it is filled with air. The air, and soft tire construction, help the tire flex and cushion an automobile when it rides over rough pavement. The tire also provides *traction* during turning, braking, and accelerating. Traction is the ability of a tire to grip the surface on which it is riding.

65.2 TIRE CONSTRUCTION

To hold air, a tire either has an *inner tube* or is *tubeless*. An inner tube is a separate rubber doughnut, or tube, that fits inside a tire and holds air. A tubeless tire has no tube. Instead, a tubeless tire is designed to fit tightly against the wheel to keep air from escaping.

A tire is designed to hold a specific amount of air pressure. The air in a tire is measured in pounds per square inch (psi) or in kilopascals (kPa). A typical car tire may have a maximum capacity of 35 psi [241.3 kPa]. Heavy-duty tires, such as those used on trucks, may hold 60–100 psi [413.7–689.5 kPa].

Air is forced into a tire through a *tire valve* (see Figure 65-1). A small spring and air pressure inside

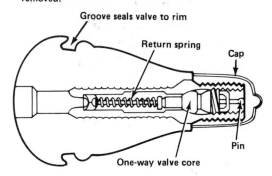

TUBELESS TIRE has a soft inner lining to keep air from leaking between the tire and rim. This inner lining often forms a seal around a nail or other object that punctures the tread. A self-sealing tire holds in air after a nail is removed.

TIRE VALVE has a central core that is spring-loaded to allow air to pass only inward, unless the pin is depressed. If the core becomes defective, it can be unscrewed and replaced. The airtight cap on the end of the valve provides extra precaution against valve leakage.

Figure 65-1.   Tire valves.

the tire keep the tire valve closed. When compressed air is used to inflate a tire, it acts against tire pressure and the spring to open the valve. A tire valve can be part of an inner tube or it can be mounted separately in the wheel. A tire valve usually has a cap over it to protect the valve from dirt and damage.

Parts of a Tire

Tires are constructed to combine the properties of ride, safety, and durability. There are a number of elements in tire construction (refer to Figure 65-2), including:

- Tread
- Sidewalls
- Carcass
- Plies
- Belts
- Beads
- Inner liner.

Tread.   *Tread* is the part of the tire that touches the ground. Tread provides traction and protects the tire from most road damage. Tread comes in a variety of patterns. Some patterns work better on dry pavement; other patterns work better on wet pavement. Most

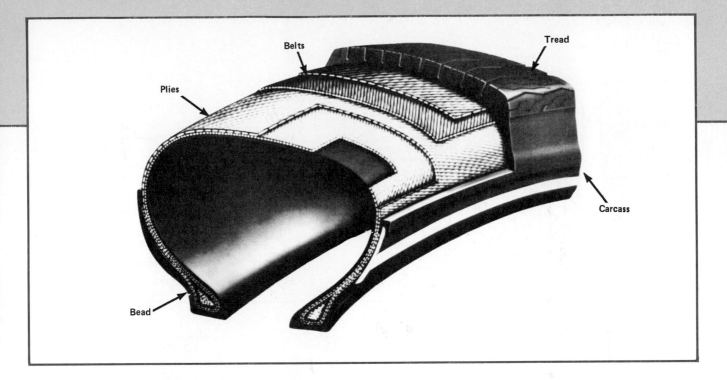

Figure 65-2. Parts of a tire.

patterns, however, are a compromise for both dry and wet road surfaces.

Sidewalls. *Sidewalls* are the sides of the tire. Sidewalls allow the tire to flex and absorb road shocks and loads. Sidewalls usually have the capability of being lettered or striped for added attractiveness.

Carcass. The *carcass* is the strong, inner part of the tire that holds in the air. The carcass is made up of layers, or plies, of fabric that are laid in different directions along the inside of a tire. A carcass gives the tire its strength.

Plies. The *plies* are layers of fabric that are impregnated with rubber to give a carcass great strength. Automobile tires may have 2, 4, or 6 plies. Extra-heavy-duty truck or heavy equipment tires may have 20 or more plies.

Belts. *Belts* are layers of material placed between the carcass and the tread. Belts reinforce the tread to keep it flat on the ground, reducing wear and improving traction.

Beads. *Beads* are the thick edges of the tire that are fitted onto a wheel rim and form a tight seal. A bead is formed at the edge of a sidewall. Metal wires are run through the beads to increase strength.

Inner liner. The inside of the tire has a soft rubber *inner liner* to ensure against air leaks. Some tires have an additional soft, sticky material to self-seal tread punctures.

Tire Materials

A tire has many layers of threads, or *cords,* that run through the plies and belts. These cords can be made of rayon, polyester, nylon, steel, fiberglass, or synthetic fibers.

Rayon and polyester are the least expensive and help to provide a soft ride. Both also are affected by heat. Nylon is more heat-resistant and has greater impact resistance, but it gives a somewhat harsher ride than rayon or polyester. Steel has the best impact and puncture resistance of any cord. Fiberglass is the most expensive. It provides great strength and a soft ride.

New synthetic fibers are being developed that combine the strength of steel and the light weight of fiberglass. Aramid ® is one of the best known of these new synthetics.

Types of Tires

Tires are classified by the ways in which the cords are arranged (see Figure 65-3). Types of tires in common use are:

- Bias ply
- Bias belted
- Radial ply.

Bias ply. *Bias ply tire* materials crisscross at angles, or are at a bias to one another, from bead to bead. This design allows the carcass to flex very little but does provide a soft ride. A disadvantage is that the tread is not always held firmly to the pavement. Also, the *rolling resistance* of these tires is relatively high. Rolling

679

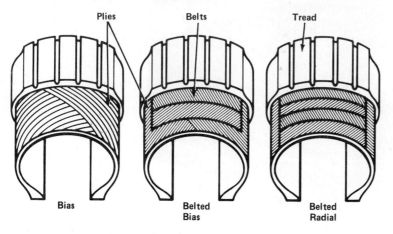

Figure 65-3. Types of tires.

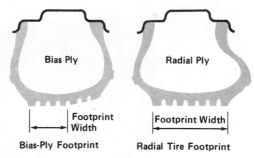

Figure 65-4. Tire footprints.

resistance is the amount of friction, or resistance, between the tread and the pavement when the automobile is moving. Bias ply tires should not be used with radial tires on the same vehicle.

Bias belted. A *bias belted tire* is a compromise between bias ply and radial construction. This tire basically is a bias ply tire with belts under the tread. The belts help stabilize the tread, resulting in longer tread/tire life and greater traction. The rolling resistance of this tire is somewhat less than that of a nonbelted bias ply tire.

Radial ply. Plies in a *radial ply tire* run straight across from bead to bead. In addition, belts, or extra plies, encircle the entire tire under the tread. This design allows radial tire sidewalls to flex more than the sidewalls of bias ply tires (see Figure 65-4). The sidewall flexing allows the belts to hold more of the tread on the pavement during cornering. A radial tire has a slightly firmer ride, but greater traction. Radial tires also improve fuel economy and give longer tread/tire life due to decreased rolling resistance.

Tread Design

Many different tread designs are made for tires. Some treads are better on dry pavement; others work better in rain or snow conditions. Figure 65-5 shows different types of tread designs.

Tire Information

Information about a tire is molded into the sidewall (see Figure 65-6). Included are tire size, construction, and quality ratings.

A tire size may appear in one of three ways on the sidewall. Examples are: P205/75R15 (P-metric), 175R13 (metric), and G78-14 (alphanumeric). These letters and numbers indicate the type of tire, section width, aspect ratio, construction type, and rim diameter. See Figure 65-7 for P-metric information.

Conventional Radial   All-Season Radial   Traditional Snow Tire

Figure 65-5. Tread designs.

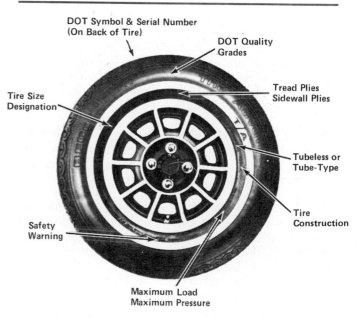

Figure 65-6. Sidewall markings.

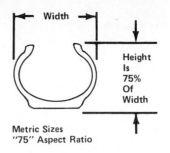

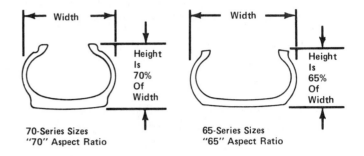

Metric Tire Sizes

P 205 / 75 R 15

Tire Type
P - Passenger
T - Temporary
C - Commercial

Section Width
185 mm
195 mm
205 mm
Etc.

Aspect Ratio   70
(Section Height)   75
(Section Width)   80

Construction Type
R - Radial
B - Bias-Belted
D - Diagonal (Bias)

Rim Diameter
(Inches)   13
           14
           15

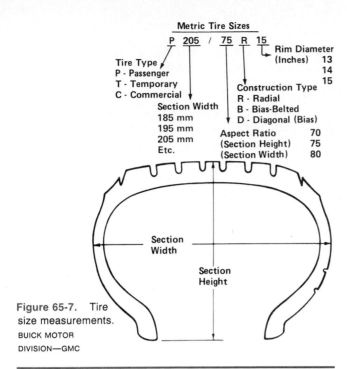

Figure 65-7. Tire size measurements. BUICK MOTOR DIVISION—GMC

Metric Sizes "75" Aspect Ratio

Height Is 75% Of Width

70-Series Sizes "70" Aspect Ratio

Height Is 70% Of Width

65-Series Sizes "65" Aspect Ratio

Height Is 65% Of Width

Figure 65-8. Tire size and aspect ratio. AMERICAN MOTORS CORPORATION

The "P" in P-metric stands for "passenger car." P-metric tires are manufactured in the United States. Tires with similar designations, but without a P, are made in foreign countries.

Section width is the distance from sidewall to sidewall. *Aspect ratio* indicates the height of a tire from bead to tread, expressed as a percentage of its section width. See Figure 65-8. *Rim diameter* is the size of the hole in the tire that fits over the wheel.

Another metric size—often referred to simply as "metric"—may be indicated as 175R13. This means the tire is 175 mm wide, is of radial construction (R), and fits a 13-inch wheel. Most P-metric and metric sizes have rim measurements in inches. Some metric sizes, however, indicate rim width in millimeters.

Alphanumeric sizes once were used for domestic automobile tires but now are used mostly for specialty tires. On a G78-14 tire, the G indicates tire width and the load-carrying capacity of the tire. The higher the alphabet letter, the wider the tire and the greater its load-carrying capacity. For example, an H tire can carry a greater load than an E tire. The number 78 is the aspect ratio, and the number 14 is the wheel diameter in inches.

Passenger car tires also must conform to federal safety requirements. Tires are graded by the Department of Transportation (DOT) for traction and for temperature qualities. These ratings are called the *Uniform Tire Quality Grading* system. They are based on tests conducted by DOT at a Texas test track. The grades are indicated on a tire by encircled letters or numbers.

Traction grades are A, B, and C, from highest to lowest. A traction grade represents a tire's ability to stop on wet pavement.

Figure 65-9. Compact spare tire.

Temperature grades also are A, B, and C, from highest to lowest. These gradings represent a tire's resistance to, and ability to dissipate, heat. Excessive heat can cause tire damage and rapid wear. All passenger car tires must meet the minimum standards necessary for a C rating.

Additional tire information markings are shown in Figure 65-6.

65.3 TEMPORARY USE TIRES

A compact spare tire and wheel assembly is used on many automobiles. This tire is smaller and narrower than the automobile's normal driving tires (see Figure 65-9). It is to be used only for emergency situations.

Another type of temporary tire is the collapsible spare. This tire is deflated, or collapsed, to save space. It is inflated from a supplied canister of compressed air before use.

65.4 RETREADED TIRES

Retreaded tires are used tire carcasses on which a new tread has been installed. Also called a *recap tire*, a retreaded tire is less expensive than a new tire. Retreaded tires are used by many large fleets.

65.5 WHEELS

A wheel performs a variety of functions on an automobile. The wheel must be strong enough to carry the weight of the car. It must be able to withstand extra forces caused by hard driving, braking, and engine torque.

Most passenger car wheels are made of steel. Steel wheels usually consist of a stamped center section welded to an outer section, called the rim. See Figure 65-10. Some wheels are made of aluminum alloy. Aluminum alloy wheels usually are made by casting.

To fit properly and safely with a tire, the inside of a wheel rim has a *drop center* and a *safety rim*. A drop center is a well inside the wheel rim. A safety rim has raised sections on both sides of the drop center (see Figure 65-11). When the tire is inflated, the bead is

forced over the raised sections of the safety rim. The raised sections help to hold the tire on the wheel if a failure occurs.

The wheel fits over studs, or *wheel lugs*, that are pressed into the *wheel hub*. *Lug nuts* fit over the studs, or lugs, to hold the wheel to the wheel hub. The wheel hub is mounted to the wheel spindle assembly.

Some automobiles have custom wheels. Custom wheels usually are aluminum alloy wheels that have been added to improve the appearance of an automobile. Stud holes in aluminum wheels are damaged easily, so special nuts, and often washers, are used to mount these wheels. In many cases, spacers are used to provide a precise fit or proper positioning of the wheel.

Figure 65-10. Parts of a wheel.

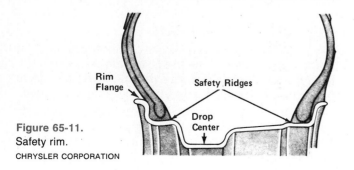

Figure 65-11. Safety rim.
CHRYSLER CORPORATION

U N I T   H I G H L I G H T S

* A tire cushions the ride of an automobile and provides traction.
* A tire may be tubeless or use an inner tube to hold air.
* A tire is inflated and deflated through the tire valve.
* Different parts are used to build a tire.
* Tires have cords that are made with different kinds of threads.
* Three basic types of tires are used on automobiles.
* Information about tire size, relative quality, and load-carrying capacity is imprinted on the sidewall.
* Smaller tires are used for spares on most modern cars.
* A safety rim helps hold a tire on the wheel rim.
* A wheel is mounted to a wheel hub.

T E R M S

traction	radial ply tire
inner tube	section width
tubeless tire	aspect ratio
tire valve	rim diameter
tread	Uniform Tire Quality
sidewall	Grading
carcass	traction grade
ply	temperature grade
belt	retreaded tire
bead	recap tire
inner liner	drop center
cord	safety rim
bias ply tire	wheel lugs
rolling resistance	wheel hub
bias belted tire	lug nuts

REVIEW QUESTIONS

DIRECTIONS: The following questions are similar to those used on mechanic certification tests. On a separate sheet of paper, write the letter of the correct choice.

1. Mechanic A says that a tire valve forces compressed air into a wheel well.
   Mechanic B says that a tire valve is held closed by air pressure.
   Who is correct?
   A. A only   B. B only   C. Both A and B   D. Neither A nor B

2. All of the following statements are true EXCEPT
   A. Tread provides traction.
   B. A carcass has plies.
   C. Beads are located at the edges of sidewalls.
   D. Belts are used to drive the wheels.

3. Which of the following statements is correct?
   I. A bias tire has plies that crisscross.
   II. A belted radial tire has belts under the tread.
   A. I only   B. II only   C. Both I and II   D. Neither I nor II

4. Which of the following statements about tire size is correct?
   A. Alphanumeric-sized tires are made in Japan.
   B. Section width is the distance between the edges of the tread.
   C. Aspect ratio is the roundness of a tire.
   D. P-metric tires are used on American cars.

5. Mechanic A says that a drop center and a safety rim are different styles of wheels.
   Mechanic B says that a drop center is a well in a wheel rim.
   Who is correct?
   A. A only   B. B only   C. Both A and B   D. Neither A nor B

SUPPLEMENTAL ACTIVITIES

1. Describe the operation of a tire valve.
2. Show where the parts of a tire are located.
3. Describe the different types of cords used in a tire.
4. Show how the plies and belts are positioned on the three types of tires.
5. Explain the sidewall information on a tire selected by your instructor.
6. Describe the parts of a wheel.
7. Show how a wheel is connected to an automobile selected by your instructor.

66 TIRE AND WHEEL SERVICE

UNIT PREVIEW

The tires and wheels of an automobile are a driver's direct contact with the highway. Many problems show up in the driver's hands through the steering wheel. A shimmy, thump, or vibration can indicate one or more possible areas for a mechanic to investigate. Through experience, a mechanic learns to identify many of these service problems simply by observing how tires are wearing. This unit discusses the use of tires for instant diagnosis. Tires also can reveal whether a driver is a drag racer or a normal highway driver.

LEARNING OBJECTIVES

When you have completed your assignments and exercises in this unit, you should be able to:

☐ Explain how inflation pressures affect tires.

☐ Describe how tire rotation is performed.

☐ Describe the differences between static and dynamic balance.

☐ Describe how tire and wheel runout is checked.

☐ Explain the differences between plug repair and patch repair.

SAFETY PRECAUTIONS

Tire pressure is controlled by compressed air. You will be working with compressed air frequently during tire and wheel service. Playing with compressed air can lead to damage and serious injury. Use proper judgment.

Much of the time, the automobile will be raised with a floor jack. Always be sure that the car is properly supported by safety stands.

Tire rotation should be performed in a specific order, according to the manufacturer's recommendations. Be sure to properly identify each tire and wheel assembly. Do not assume anything! Always mark the tire according to where it is to be located. An improperly positioned tire and wheel assembly could result in failure and serious injury for the driver and passengers.

High-speed balancing machines are used with wheel assemblies. Be sure all balancing attachments are securely tightened and all safety guards are in place. Improper use of balancing machines can result in serious injury.

When performing a road test to identify a problem, use proper safety equipment and drive within legal limits.

Air pressure builds up quickly in tires. Always watch the tire pressure gauge carefully. Never sit on, stand on, or straddle a tire that is being inflated. Serious injuries can result if a tire is overinflated and explodes.

Always be careful if a hot patch is being used to repair a tire. A hot patch usually requires an open flame to ignite it. Never use an open flame near an automobile's fuel system.

66.1 PREVENTIVE MAINTENANCE

Only a few periodic maintenance procedures are required to keep tires and wheels in good operating condition. These steps are:

- Checking tire inflation
- Visual inspection
- Tire rotation
- Wheel balancing.

Proper Inflation

Maintaining proper tire pressures is the most important procedure for ensuring long tire life. Tires that have wrong, or uneven, tire pressures will wear out quickly. Proper inflation also is important for proper handling and optimum fuel economy.

Before checking the tires, look at the sidewalls for the recommended inflation pressure. The tire pressure noted on the sidewalls is usually the maximum pressure. Actual tire pressure can be slightly lower than the maximum pressure to help improve ride. A more complete range of recommended tire inflations can be found in most automobile owners' manuals. Improper pressures can damage tires (refer to Figure 66-1).

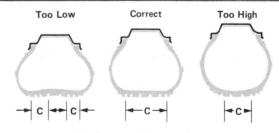

C = Contact of tire to surface.

Figure 66-1. Inflation and footprint patterns.

Figure 66-2. Checking tire pressure.

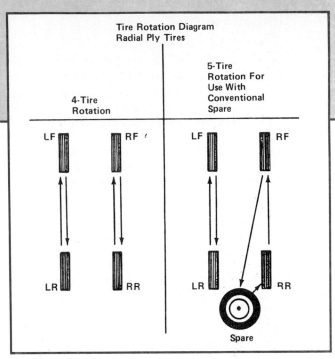

Figure 66-3. Tire rotation sequences. FORD MOTOR COMPANY

Too little tire pressure, or *underinflation,* will cause the outer edges of the tread to wear quickly. Low tires can cause hard steering, pulling to one side, tire squeal, front-end *shimmy,* and side-to-side wheel vibration. Underinflation also can damage sidewalls, plies, and, in extreme cases, wheel rims that come in contact with the road surface.

Excessive tire pressure, or *overinflation* of tires, will cause the center of the tread to wear quickly. Excessive pressure causes a harsh ride and loss of traction and makes tires susceptible to cuts and puncture. Overinflation also can damage the tire's cords.

Uneven pressures among the tires on an automobile can cause the vehicle to wander while driven or to pull when the brakes are applied.

Improper tire inflation reduces a tire's *footprint,* the amount of tire tread that makes contact with the road. This condition reduces traction.

To check tire pressure, remove the cap from the tire valve. Use a tire gauge, shown in Figure 66-2, to check the pressure. Be sure the tire gauge is accurate. All tire pressures should be equal, or within specifications. Front and rear tire pressures may not be the same due to automotive design or load requirements. Be sure to check the spare tire.

CAUTION: Always check inflation pressures when the tires are cold or after only a mile or two of driving. Tire pressures can increase considerably as heat builds up during driving. Never lower the pressure of a hot tire, because pressure will drop when it cools. If the automobile has been driven a long distance, wait about three hours before checking inflation.

If air is needed, use a compressed-air hose with the proper adapter. If air is to be removed, press in on the valve stem until the desired pressure is reached. Replace the valve cap.

Visual Inspection

Tires require constant inspection and inflation checks to eliminate improper wear. Once a tire begins to wear abnormally, its condition cannot be corrected. Make sure all tires are wearing the same. Different types of tires wear and react in different ways. On some automobiles, different types of tires can be added only in pairs either at both front wheels or at both rear wheels.

Look for abnormal tire wear, discussed in Topic 66.2. A badly worn tire should be replaced because it can affect driving qualities. Look for cuts and bruises. Check the tire valve for cracks or damage.

Inspect wheels for damage and cracks. Make sure the lug nuts are tight and that none are missing.

Tire Rotation

Tires usually are rotated every 5,000 miles [8,046 km] or when uneven tire wear begins to show. Greater tire wear often occurs at the *traction wheels,* or driving wheels.

Tire rotation involves switching tire-and-wheel assemblies to different locations on an automobile to increase tire life. Tire rotation usually is recommended in a specific order. Figure 66-3 shows typical tire rotation sequences. This rotation sequence allows the tires to turn in the same direction at all times. Some manufacturers may recommend an additional tire rotation sequence. Only normal sized spare tires can be used in rotation. Compact and collapsible spare tires cannot be used for tire rotation.

Refer to Topic 66.3 for removing and replacing tire-and-wheel assemblies. Always correct wheel balance and check air pressures after rotation.

CAUTION: **Wheel lug nuts always should be tightened in the proper order and to specifications. Check the proper service manual. Lug nuts that have been tightened improperly can damage brakes or result in a loose wheel.**

Wheel Balancing

Tire and wheel assemblies that are out of balance vibrate as they rotate. This can cause abnormal tire wear and noise. To rotate smoothly, a tire and wheel assembly must be balanced. Balancing involves locating a heavy spot on the assembly and counter-balancing it with an equal weight.

There are two types of tire and wheel balance: static and dynamic.

Static balance is the equal distribution of weight around a wheel (see Figure 66-4). A statically unbalanced wheel will hop, or *tramp,* as it rotates.

Dynamic balance is the equal distribution of weight on each side of the centerline of a vertical wheel (see Figure 66-5). A dynamically unbalanced wheel will shimmy at medium and high driving speeds.

Wheel balance usually is performed on an electronic balancer, shown in Figure 66-6. The tire and wheel assembly is removed from the automobile and placed on the electronic balancer. The balancer spins the assembly and identifies the heavy spots. The technician clips a lead weight to the rim at a location opposite that of the heavy spot. The lead weight should have the same weight as the heavy spot. However, there are many different methods of wheel balancing. Follow wheel balancer manufacturers' instructions for best results.

66.2 DIAGNOSING TIRE PROBLEMS

Many problems show up on tire treads, including bad road conditions, wheel misalignment, and suspension and steering wear. Tires, in fact, are a good diagnostic source for many chassis problems. Poor tire life often is caused by problems elsewhere. Nevertheless, tire problems must be separated from other automotive problems in order to make a proper diagnosis. The most common diagnostic procedures are a test drive and a tread wear inspection.

Driving Problems

It may not be necessary to test drive an automobile to diagnose a tire problem. Get the driver's description of any noise or unusual movement. If a tire or wheel problem is suspected, look for signs of overloading.

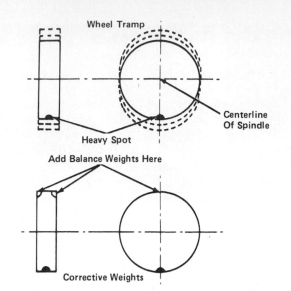

Figure 66-4. Static balance. FORD MOTOR COMPANY

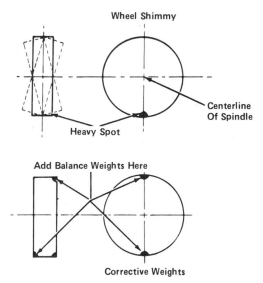

Figure 66-5. Dynamic balance. FORD MOTOR COMPANY

Figure 66-6. Adding lead weights for balance.

Check tire pressures and inspect the tread for abnormal wear. Tread wear patterns are discussed in the following section. If these procedures do not pinpoint a problem, make a test drive.

Most vibrations at highway speeds are caused by tires and wheels. A vibration results from rapid back-and-forth motion of an object. An unbalanced wheel assembly, or improper tire or wheel runout, will cause vibration. Also, radial tires are highly susceptible to vibration when mounted improperly.

A tire can make a thumping sound when running over a bump or if the tire has a defect. Check the tires for bulges.

Some noises result from tire design. Tires with heavy treads, such as all-weather tires or snow tires, can be noisy. Underinflated tires also can make noise.

Unusual movements while driving, such as sway and pull, can be caused by improper inflation or by a chassis problem.

Tread Wear

Automobile problems, road conditions, and poor driving habits can show up on tire treads. Tread wear can serve as a diagnostic "chart" for a mechanic (see Figure 66-7).

New tires have a built-in warning system called a *tread wear indicator*. A tread wear indicator, shown in Figure 66-8, alerts the owner that only $\frac{1}{16}$ inch of tread remains. In most cases, this is the legal limit of tread wear. The tire should be replaced when the indicator bands become visible.

Tire and Wheel Runout

Excessive radial and lateral runout of a tire or wheel can cause excessive noise, vibration, and wear. *Radial runout* is a measurement that determines how much the wheel assembly is out of round. *Lateral runout* is a measurement of the in-and-out movement, or wobble, of the assembly.

All runout measurements should be made with a dial indicator while the wheel assembly is on the automobile. Inflate the tires properly and adjust the wheel bearings.

The automobile must be driven at least seven miles [11.3 km]. This will eliminate false readings caused by temporary flat spots in the tires.

Tire runout is measured at the points indicated in Figure 66-9. Use chalk to mark the runout high points on the tire. Tire runout readings should not exceed manufacturer's specifications. If runout exceeds specifications, check wheel runout to determine whether the tire or the wheel is the problem.

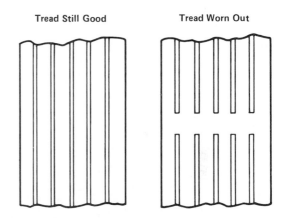

Tread Still Good   **Tread Worn Out**

Figure 66-8. Tread wear indicator.
AMERICAN MOTORS CORPORATION

Condition	Rapid Wear At Shoulders	Rapid Wear At Center	Cracked Treads	Wear On One Side	Feathered Edge	Bald Spots	Scalloped Wear
Effect							
Cause	Under-Inflation Or Lack Of Rotation	Over-Inflation Or Lack Of Rotation	Under-Inflation Or Excessive Speed*	Excessive Camber	Incorrect Toe	Unbalanced Wheel Or Tire Defect*	Lack Of Rotation Of Tires Or Worn Or Out-Of-Alignment Suspension
Correction	Adjust tire pressure to specifications when tires are cool. Rotate tires.			Adjust camber to specifications.	Adjust toe-in to specifications.	Dynamic or static balance wheels.	Rotate tires and inspect suspension.

*Have tire inspected for further use

Figure 66-7. Tire tread wear chart. CHRYSLER CORPORATION

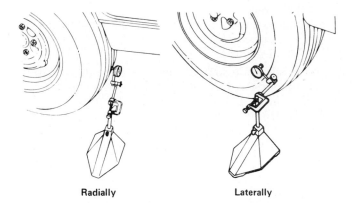
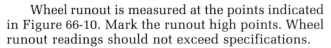

Figure 66-9. Tire runout measurement locations.
AMERICAN MOTORS CORPORATION

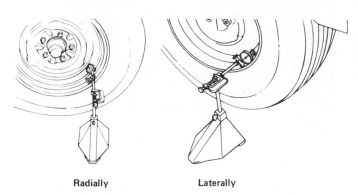

Figure 66-10. Wheel runout measurement locations.
AMERICAN MOTORS CORPORATION

Wheel runout is measured at the points indicated in Figure 66-10. Mark the runout high points. Wheel runout readings should not exceed specifications.

If tire runout exceeds specifications and wheel runout is satisfactory, relocate the tire. Deflate the tire and turn it on the wheel. Position the high-point marks 180 degrees from their original locations.

If tire runout cannot be brought to specifications, replace the tire. If wheel runout is not within specifications, replace the wheel.

66.3 TIRE AND WHEEL SERVICE

Servicing tires and wheels usually means replacing one or more tires. When the tire and wheel are removed and disassembled, all parts should be inspected thoroughly before any are reused.

Removing Wheels

Wheel covers and hubcaps usually are removed before the automobile is lifted on a hoist or jack. Be sure the automobile is supported properly. Place a wheel cover or hubcap near each wheel.

Loosen the lug nuts with a lug wrench or an impact wrench. Lug nuts can be loosened slightly before the automobile is raised. On some automobiles, the wheels on the left side of the automobile will have left-hand threads. The right side of the automobile will have right-hand threads. If this is the case, the ends of the studs will be marked "L" and "R."

Remove the lug nuts and place them inside the wheel cover or hubcap near each wheel to prevent loss. Remove the wheels.

Demounting Tires

If the tire is to be remounted after it is serviced, make a chalk mark across the sidewall and the rim. The tire should be replaced as close as possible to its original position. This could make wheel balancing easier. However, always rebalance a tire and wheel assembly after service. Tire repairs can change wheel balance.

Release air through the tire valve. Do *not* try to remove the beads from the wheel rim unless the tire is deflated completely. Always inspect the tire valve for cracks or damage. Replace the tire valve, if necessary.

Using a Tire Machine

Most tires are changed on a tire machine operated with compressed air. See Figure 66-11.

A special tool that is free of sharp edges is used to loosen, or break, the bead from the wheel rim. Use the proper lubricating solution to coat the wheel rim and tire beads. Follow the manufacturer's directions when using the tire machine. Procedures will vary among machines. Remove the tire from the wheel. Repair or replace the tire.

Before installing the tire, remove all rust scale from the wheel rim. Repaint the wheel, if necessary. Coat the wheel rim and tire beads with the proper lubricant. If necessary, align the tire and wheel chalk marks that were made during demounting. Install the tire, using the proper remounting tool. If the valve core was removed, install it now. Inflate the tire to the proper pressure.

CAUTION: Do not stand on or over a tire during inflation. Excessive pressure can cause a tire to explode and cause serious injury.

Balance the tire and wheel assembly. Place the wheel on the hub, and tighten the lug nuts to specifications. Replace the wheel cover or hubcap.

Repairing Punctures

Most punctured tires should be removed from the wheel. It is usually recommended that repairs be made from the inside of a tire, using a combination repair plug and patch.

Only punctures in the tread area are repairable. Never try to repair punctures in the shoulders or

Figure 66-11. Tire-changing machine.

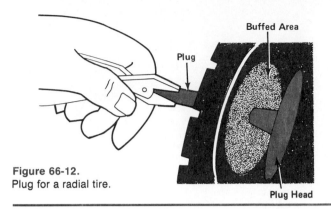

Figure 66-12.
Plug for a radial tire.

sidewalls. Never try to repair a tire with the following types of damage:

- Bulges or blisters
- Ply separation
- Broken or cracked beads
- Fabric cracks or cuts
- Tires worn to the fabric
- Visible wear indicators
- Punctures larger than ¼ inch [6.35 mm].

Many manufacturers do not recommend using externally applied repair plugs, blowout patches, and aerosol sealants except for emergency repair.

CAUTION: If a tire is to be replaced, manufacturers usually recommend replacement with the same type of tire. The replacement tire should be of the same size, load range, and type of construction as the original tire. *Never mix radial and bias-ply tires on the same axle.* Different types or sizes of tires on opposing wheels can result in damage to the power train, suspension, and body.

Plug repair. A permanent *tire plug* has a flat plug head at one end (see Figure 66-12). The narrow end of

the plug is inserted into the puncture. The head adheres to the inside of the tire. Other types of plugs are recommended only for emergency use.

To install a tire plug, remove the object that caused the puncture. Clean the puncture. A buffing tool usually is included with the tire kit. A buffing tool roughens up the tire's inner surface where the plug head will make contact. The roughened surface gives the adhesive a better gripping surface. The proper cement is applied to the plug and to the plug head. Follow the instructions given by the tire plug manufacturer for exact installation procedures.

Cold patch repair. A tire repair patch is placed over a puncture on the inside of a tire. The area around the puncture should be cleaned and buffed. The proper adhesive should be spread around the puncture, and the patch should be placed over the puncture. A stitching tool is run over the patch to help bind, or stitch, the patch to the tire.

Only special patches that are approved for radial tires should be used with radials. When using these patches, be sure that the arrow on the patch is parallel to the radial plies.

Hot patch repair. A tire hot patch is applied much as a cold patch. After cleaning and buffing, the hot patch is clamped over the puncture. Heat is applied to the patch to make it adhere.

Tube repair. Patches usually are used to repair punctures in tubes. Since the tube holds the air, it is not necessary to seal a small puncture in the tire.

Puncture-sealing tires. Some tires are made with a sealing substance on the inside of the tread area. If a nail punctures the tread, the nail can be removed without loss of air. The sealing compound will plug the puncture from the inside (see Figure 66-13).

Checking Wheels

Inspect the wheels for bending, dents, elongated bolt holes, and heavy rusting. Check for excessive runout and for air leaking through the welds. If any of these conditions are present, replace the wheel. Manufacturers do not recommend repairing wheels.

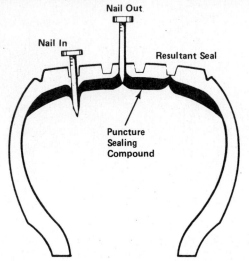

Figure 66-13. Puncture-sealing tire. BUICK MOTOR DIVISION—GMC

Replacement wheels should be equivalent to the original wheels. Check wheel load capacity, diameter, rim width, offset, and lug pattern. *Offset* is the measurement between the mounting point of the center section and the center of the rim. Front-wheel offset is especially critical on front-drive cars. *Lug pattern,* or *bolt pattern,* is the mounting configuration of the lug studs.

The use of improper wheels can affect wheel and wheel bearing life, brake cooling, and speedometer calibrations. Improper wheels also can affect ground clearance and the clearance between the tire and chassis or body.

Servicing Compact Spare Tires

A compact spare tire can be mounted and demounted from its wheel with normal tire-changing equipment and procedures. Though compact spare tires hold about 60 psi [413.7 kPa], the beads will seat at 40 psi [275.8 kPa]. This seating pressure is comparable to regular-size tires. Compact spare tires can be serviced with patches.

UNIT HIGHLIGHTS

- Inflation affects tire wear and traction qualities.
- Visual inspection involves knowing and checking for tire wear characteristics.
- Tire rotation is a procedure that increases tire life.
- Wheel balancing is performed by counterbalancing a known heavy spot in a tire and wheel assembly.
- Tire problems often show up as vibrations, thumps, and unusual movements while driving.
- A tread wear indicator is an indication of how much tire life is left.
- Tire and wheel runout are determined by radial and lateral motion.
- Lug nuts on wheels may rotate in different directions, depending on where they are located.
- Tires are demounted on a tire machine.
- Repairable punctures are small damaged areas on the tread of the tire.
- Tire repairs are made with plugs and patches.
- Defective wheels must be replaced, never repaired.

TERMS

underinflation	dynamic balance
shimmy	tread wear indicator
overinflation	radial runout
footprint	lateral runout
traction wheels	tire plug
tire rotation	offset
static balance	lug pattern
tramp	bolt pattern

R E V I E W   Q U E S T I O N S

DIRECTIONS: The following questions are similar to those used on mechanic certification tests. On a separate sheet of paper, write the letter of the correct choice.

1. All of the following statements are true EXCEPT
A. Tire pressure can be lower than the maximum pressure.
B. Underinflation means there is too little pressure in the tire.
C. Overinflation means the tire is heavier than it should be.
D. Footprint is the amount of tread that makes contact with the ground.

2. Mechanic A says that tire wear often is greater on the traction wheels.
Mechanic B says that tire rotation is switching the tires from one wheel to another.
Who is correct?
A. A only   B. B only   C. Both A and B   D. Neither A nor B

3. Which of the following statements about tires is correct?
A. Poor tire life can be caused by a bad suspension.
B. Driving problems can be caused by forethought.
C. A thumping indicates even tread wear.
D. Sway or pull can be caused when the P-metric measurement is wrong.

4. Which of the following statements is correct?
I. A tire has lateral runout when it wobbles.
II. A tire has radial runout when the cord is showing.
A. I only   B. II only   C. Both I and II   D. Neither I nor II

5. All of the following statements are true EXCEPT
A. Hubcaps must be removed after the tire bead has been broken.
B. You should not try to remove the beads until the tire is deflated completely.
C. Puncture repairs usually are made from inside the tire.
D. A cold patch should have stitches.

S U P P L E M E N T A L   A C T I V I T I E S

1. Check and record the tire pressures on an automobile selected by your instructor.
2. Perform a tire rotation.
3. Balance a wheel.
4. Explain how a tread wear indicator works.
5. Make runout readings on a tire and wheel assembly furnished by your instructor.
6. Remove a wheel from an automobile selected by your instructor.
7. Remove a tire from a wheel.
8. Repair a tire.
9. Install a tire and wheel assembly.

67 THE BRAKE SYSTEM

UNIT PREVIEW

A brake system is used to slow and stop an automobile. The operation of a brake system, obviously, is of utmost importance to every driver. Brakes are operated by hydraulic pressure and act at each wheel. Two basic brake systems are used in automobiles: disc brakes and drum brakes. Many cars combine these two types of brake systems. Disc or drum brakes may be operated directly or through a power assist. This unit discusses brake design and the various parts of brake systems.

LEARNING OBJECTIVES

When you have completed your assignments and exercises in this unit, you should be able to:

☐ Explain how friction is used to stop an automobile.

☐ Identify the parts of a basic brake system.

☐ Describe the differences between disc and drum brakes.

☐ Identify the valves in a disc and drum brake combination.

☐ Describe the operations of a power brake system.

67.1 BRAKE SYSTEM DESIGN

A brake is a device that uses *friction* to slow or stop a mechanism. Friction is an action that is caused when two parts rub against one another and resist motion. An automotive brake system uses stationary devices at all four wheels to act on rotating devices and produce friction.

Friction

Three factors that produce friction in automotive brakes are: pressure, friction material, and surface area. To illustrate, think of your hand as a brake. Grasp a fairly heavy object, such as a large wrench. Held too loosely, the wrench will begin to slip from your grasp. If you increase the pressure of your grip, your hand will stop the slipping motion of the wrench.

Friction material determines how much friction will be created between two parts. If you have oil or grease on your hand, the wrench will slip from your grip. If you wipe your hand clean, you can grip the wrench more effectively. The clean hand, then, has more friction material (skin) that is making contact with the wrench.

Surface area is the amount of surface that makes contact between two parts. If you use two hands on a wrench, it is easier to grip and hold the wrench. With two hands, you contact more surface area on the wrench than with one hand.

Friction also causes heat. Heat causes wear. An automobile's braking system must be able to withstand extremely high temperatures and still wear well.

Automotive Braking Friction

The braking friction of an automobile is created when pressure from the brake pedal is transmitted to the wheels. At the wheels, the braking system is mounted so that it remains stationary to the wheel rotation. Pressure moves a stationary part of the brake assembly to contact a rotating portion connected to the wheel. When these two surfaces make contact, friction is created. This friction slows—and, if continued, will stop—the rotation of the wheel.

Hydraulic Principles

Pressure is applied hydraulically in a braking system. Hydraulic principles are discussed in Topic 53.6.

A hydraulic system is activated when a driver steps on the brake pedal. Force from the brake pedal operates on a hydraulic piston mounted under a fluid reservoir. This unit is called a *master cylinder* (see Figure 67-1). Brake pedal action on the master cylinder piston forces fluid out of the cylinder, developing hydraulic pressure in the system. This hydraulic pressure is routed through hoses and tubing, called *brake lines*. The brake lines transfer that pressure to a *wheel cylinder* at each wheel. A wheel cylinder has pistons that move outward under direct hydraulic pressure. The outward movement of these pistons mechanically moves and applies the brakes.

67.2 BRAKE SYSTEM CONSTRUCTION

Parts within an automotive brake system may vary, but the basic system components are much the same (see Figure 67-2). These parts are:

- Brake fluid
- Master cylinder
- Brake lines
- Wheel cylinders
- Friction materials
- Stop light switch.

Brake Fluid

Temperatures in braking systems vary considerably. The fluid used in a brake hydraulic system must be

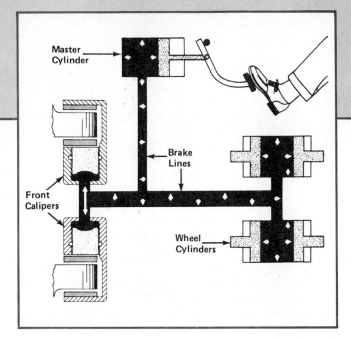

Figure 67-1. Automotive hydraulic system.
CHEVROLET MOTOR DIVISION—GMC

able to withstand these temperature changes and not corrode the parts. Brake fluid is a nonpetroleum liquid. Petroleum oils should not be used in brake systems. Petroleum oil will cause the rubberized cups and seals in the hydraulic system to swell, causing brake failure. Use only DOT 3 or higher brake fluids.

Master Cylinder

The automotive master cylinder has two main functions. The master cylinder is the source of hydraulic braking pressure through its cylinder bore and pistons. The master cylinder also serves as a reservoir for brake fluid used by the brake system (see Figure 67-3).

The force applied by the driver to the brake pedal is multiplied approximately six times by the pedal linkage. This force is multiplied even more by a power assist unit, if the automobile is so equipped. The pedal force is applied through a pushrod to the rearmost, or primary, piston. The primary piston has two rubber-type seals. The back seal is the secondary cup, which prevents fluid from leaking from the back of the master cylinder. The front seal, or primary cup, seals the hydraulic pressure chamber (see Figure 67-3).

As the primary piston is pushed forward under pedal pressure, the primary cup covers the primary compensating port. This traps fluid between the primary cup and the rear of the secondary piston. The trapped fluid acts on the secondary piston, moving it forward. As the secondary piston primary cup covers the secondary compensating port, fluid also is trapped in front of the secondary piston. Further pedal movement builds pressure in both primary and secondary pressure chambers, causing fluid to flow out into the system. This flow results in brake application.

When the brake pedal is released, the piston springs cause the pistons to return to a relaxed, or "home," position. During this time, additional fluid is drawn into the pumping chambers through holes in the pistons. This supplements the fluid already there, should the pedal be applied again immediately. This action is called pumping up the pedal.

During brake application, the heat generated is partially absorbed by the brake fluid, causing the fluid to expand. When the pedal is released and the pistons move back, the primary cups uncover the compensating ports. This allows the expanded volume of fluid

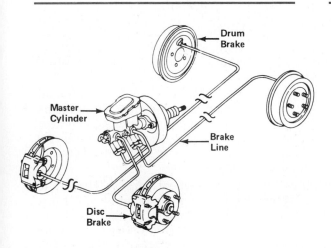

Figure 67-2. Brake system.
DELCO MORAINE DIVISION—GMC

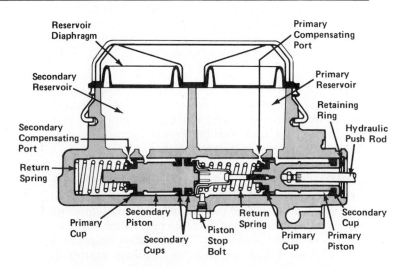

Figure 67-3. Parts of a master cylinder. BENDIX CORPORATION

693

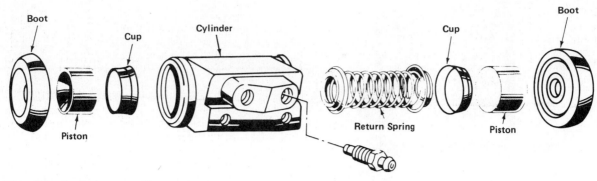

Figure 67-4. Wheel cylinder assembly. FORD MOTOR COMPANY

to be vented to the reservoirs through the compensating ports.

The master cylinder on a modern automobile has a *split reservoir,* or two chambers. One chamber feeds hydraulic fluid to the front brakes. The other chamber feeds hydraulic fluid to the rear brakes. This is a safety feature. If one chamber fails, or the brake lines or cylinders from one chamber fail, the automobile still can be stopped.

Brake Lines

The brake lines consist of steel tubes and hoses that carry hydraulic fluid from the master cylinder to the wheel cylinders. Steel tubes make up most of the brake lines. At the wheels, flexible brake hoses move with the wheels and suspension.

Wheel Cylinder

The wheel cylinders receive fluid and pressure from the master cylinder, causing them to activate the brake assemblies. As the brake assemblies are activated, friction slows or stops the automobile. A wheel cylinder is located at each brake assembly (see Figure 67-4).

When hydraulic pressure increases from brake pedal movement, pistons in the wheel cylinders are forced outward against the brake assembly. This makes frictional contact with the wheel.

Friction Materials

The friction materials used in automotive brakes usually are referred to as *brake linings*. Brake linings must have high heat resistance and durability. The most common material used is asbestos.

SAFETY CAUTION: Asbestos is associated with diseases such as cancer. When asbestos wears, it creates a fine dust that can be inhaled and can settle in the lungs. Always use extreme care when working around asbestos materials. Do *not* use compressed air to clean brake assemblies. Follow manufacturers' directions.

Asbestos has very good friction and heat-resistance characteristics. Most brake systems use asbestos. Sometimes the asbestos is impregnated with metal or a resinous compound. On some braking systems, a fiberglass compound is used instead of asbestos.

Stop Light Switch

A stop light switch is connected between the brake pedal and master cylinder. When the brake pedal is depressed, the switch is activated to illuminate the stop lights. Stop light switches are discussed under Topic 36.6.

67.3 DISC BRAKES

Brake assemblies are described according to the design of their braking, or friction-producing, parts. On an automobile, brake systems usually are referred to as *disc brakes* or *drum brakes*. A disc brake stops an automobile through action on a disc. A drum brake stops an automobile through action on a drum. Drum brakes are discussed in Topic 67.4.

A disc brake system has a metal disc, called a *rotor,* that is mounted on the axle. The rotor rotates with the wheel. A U-shaped gripping mechanism, or *caliper,* is mounted over the disc. The caliper is connected to an adapter that connects with the steering knuckle. *Brake pads,* or *shoes*, are mounted inside a caliper to grip the rotor. A disc brake assembly is shown in Figure 67-5.

A rotor may be ventilated or solid. A ventilated rotor has holes, or vents, in the center between the frictional surfaces. The vents help to dissipate heat more quickly. In some cases, these vents are unidirectional; in other words, they are either right side or left side. A solid disc has no vents.

A caliper operates as a wheel cylinder. Hydraulic pressure forces pistons out of a caliper. The pistons act on the pads, or shoes to push, or squeeze, them against the rotor to create friction. Disc brakes do not use return springs on the brake pads. During brake application, the square-cut caliper piston seal is stretched and distorted. When the brakes are released,

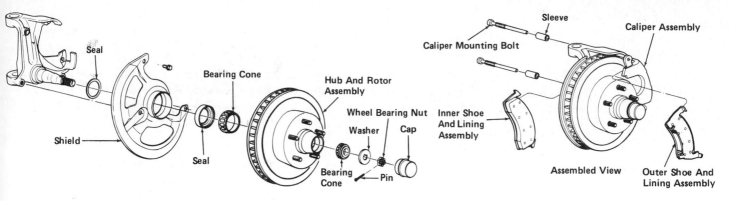

Figure 67-5. Disc brake assembly. CHEVROLET MOTOR DIVISION—GMC

the seal returns to its original position, retracting (releasing) the brake pads, or shoes.

Three common designs of disc brake systems are used:

- Fixed caliper
- Floating caliper
- Sliding caliper.

Fixed caliper is a brake design in which the caliper is bolted directly to the steering knuckle. Two or four pistons—one or two on each side of the caliper—operate against the pads or shoes (see Figure 67-6).

In the other two designs, the assemblies have one piston that holds a pad against one side of the disc. The non-piston side of the caliper holds the other shoe. A *floating caliper* assembly slides on bushings and caliper pins as it moves toward or away from the rotor (see Figure 67-7). The housing of a *sliding caliper*

assembly also slides in and out against the rotor when it is activated (see Figure 67-8).

67.4 DRUM BRAKES

A drum is mounted on an axle between the end of the axle and the wheel. Two curved pieces of metal lined with friction material push against the drum during braking. These curved metal pieces are called *brake shoes*. The brake shoes are pressed against the inside of the drum by a wheel cylinder. A drum brake assembly is shown in Figure 67-9.

The brake shoes are mounted on a *backing plate*. A backing plate is mounted to the steering knuckle or axle housing and holds the brake shoes from rotating with the drum during braking. Two brake shoes are used: a *primary brake shoe* and a *secondary brake shoe*. The primary shoe is positioned toward the front of an automobile. The secondary shoe is positioned toward the rear.

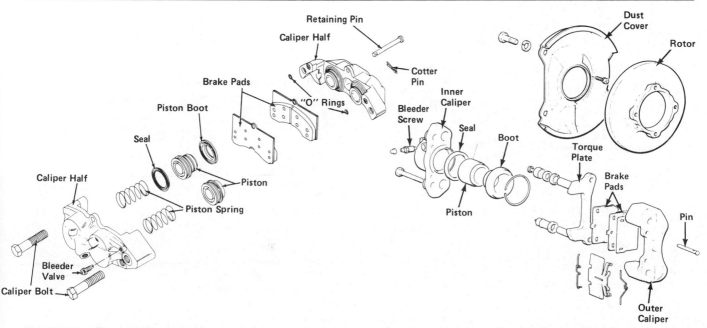

Figure 67-6. Fixed caliper disc brake assembly.
CHEVROLET MOTOR DIVISION—GMC

Figure 67-7. Floating caliper disc brake assembly.
CHRYSLER CORPORATION

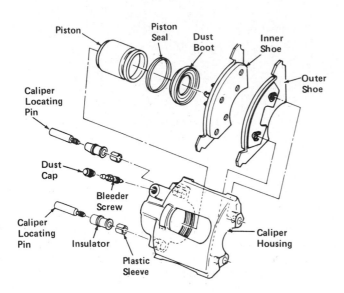

Figure 67-8. Sliding caliper disc brake assembly.
FORD MOTOR COMPANY

Brake shoes have linings that contact the drum. The *brake linings* are riveted or bonded (glued) to the brake shoes. Linings usually are made of asbestos. The linings provide the frictional surface needed for braking, in much the same way as disc brakes.

A wheel cylinder is mounted at the top of the backing plate, between the two brake shoes. Pistons in the wheel cylinder force the shoes to move outward and against the drum. The shoes are held in place by an *anchor pin,* which prevents them from rotating with the drum. A heavy spring holds the shoes together at the bottom. When the brake pedal is released, the brake shoe return springs return the shoes to their relaxed, nonbraking, position.

Self-Energizing

When brake shoes begin to rotate as they contact the drum, a *self-energizing* reaction takes place. Self-energizing means that a drum brake assembly increases braking performance by its own actions. This also means that less effort is required by the driver

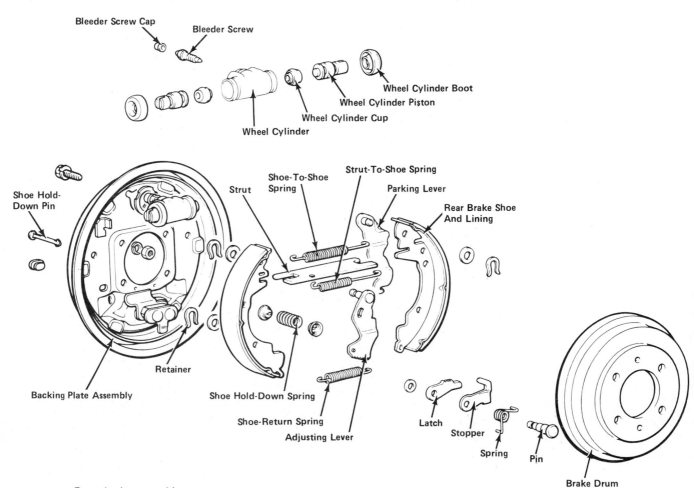

Figure 67-9. Drum brake assembly. TOYOTA MOTOR SALES, U.S.A.

when pushing down on the brake pedal. Most automobiles have self-energizing drum brakes.

As the primary shoe moves away from the anchor pin and downward, it exerts rearward force on the adjusting screw. At the same time, the secondary shoe is rotating upward until it contacts the anchor pin. Thus, forces of the primary shoe and the wheel cylinder, and the force from drum rotation, are transferred to the secondary shoe. This gives the secondary shoe additional braking force. A secondary shoe usually is larger than a primary shoe because of the additional force applied to it.

Self-Adjusting

Most drum brake systems on modern cars are self-adjusting. Adjustment maintains a proper clearance between the lining and the drum.

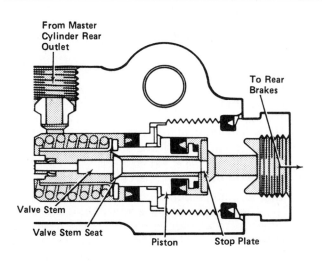

Figure 67-10. Proportioning valve.
CHEVROLET MOTOR DIVISION—GMC

A *self-adjuster* consists of a lever that is attached to the secondary shoe. The lever pivots and rotates an adjusting screw, or *star wheel,* during braking action when the automobile is moving in reverse. A star wheel has teeth, or gears, around its circumference.

67.5 DISC AND DRUM BRAKE COMBINATIONS

Many automobiles use a combination of brake systems. Disc brakes usually are located at the front wheels and drum brakes at the rear wheels. Since the two brake systems operate differently, control valves are used for proper braking action.

Proportioning Valve

Disc and drum brakes require different operating pressures. Disc brakes are operated at higher pressures. To furnish proper hydraulic pressures to each system, a *proportioning valve* is used. A proportioning valve is placed between the master cylinder and rear brakes (see Figure 67-10). The proportioning valve limits maximum pressure to the rear drum brakes during hard braking, effectively preventing rear-wheel lockup.

Metering Valve

A *metering valve* delays hydraulic pressure to the disc brakes. Disc brakes react quicker to braking action. The delay allows both disc and drum systems to operate simultaneously. A metering valve is shown in Figure 67-11.

Combination Valve

A *combination valve* combines a proportioning valve, metering valve, and *failure warning switch* into one system. A failure warning switch activates a warning light on the dashboard when a front or rear brake failure occurs. A combination valve is shown in Figure 67-12.

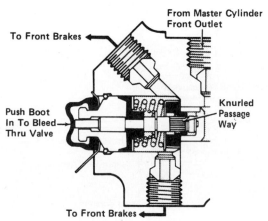

Figure 67-11. Metering valve.
CHEVROLET MOTOR DIVISION—GMC

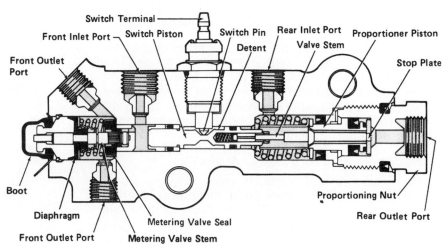

Figure 67-12. Combination valve. CHEVROLET MOTOR DIVISION—GMC

697

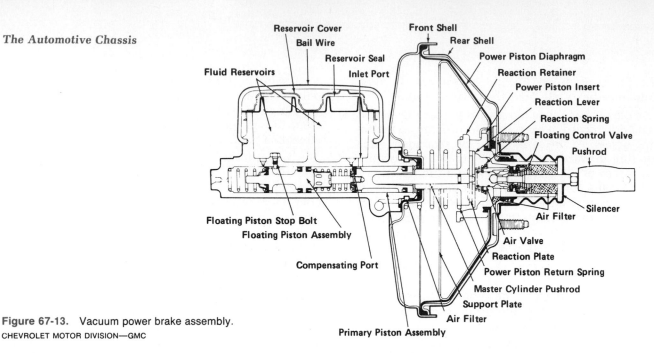

Figure 67-13. Vacuum power brake assembly.
CHEVROLET MOTOR DIVISION—GMC

Residual Check Valve

Drum brakes require some residual pressure to minimize leaking at the wheel cylinders. This is accomplished through a *residual check valve*. A residual check valve usually is located in the master cylinder.

67.6 POWER BRAKES

Power brakes are provided by adding a *power brake booster unit* between the firewall and master cylinder. The unit boosts pedal pressure, reducing the amount of effort required by the driver during braking. A power brake system is operated by either vacuum or hydraulic pressure.

Vacuum Power Brakes

Most power brakes are operated by vacuum and atmospheric pressure. A power unit between the brake pedal and master cylinder, on the firewall, holds a large diaphragm (see Figure 67-13). The diaphragm separates the power unit into two chambers. One chamber is·operated by engine vacuum. The other chamber is operated by atmospheric pressure.

When the brake pedal is depressed, air is removed from the power unit through a vacuum line. The vacuum line is connected to the intake manifold. As vacuum increases, atmospheric pressure pushes against the diaphragm. The diaphragm moves toward the master cylinder and assists the pushrod as it enters the master cylinder.

Hydraulic Pressure Power Brakes

Power steering fluid is used to assist braking on some automobiles. Fluid flows from the power steering pump to a brake booster. The booster is mounted between the brake pedal and master cylinder, on the firewall (see Figure 67-14). Fluid enters the booster and is controlled by a spool valve. The spool valve directs fluid to help drive the pushrod.

67.7 ANTI-SKID BRAKING SYSTEM

An *anti-skid braking system* keeps wheels from locking up during hard braking. A sensing device is mounted to each wheel. Some anti-skid systems control only the rear wheels. When a wheel begins to lock up or skid, the sensor transmits this information to a control unit. The control unit reduces pressure at that wheel until lockup or skidding stops.

67.8 PARKING BRAKE OPERATION

A *parking brake* is connected to the rear brake assembly. The parking brake is a mechanical braking system that operates independently of the hydraulic service brakes. A lever or pedal near the driver is set to lock the rear brakes. A cable or linkage is run from the parking brake lever or pedal to the rear of the automobile (see Figure 67-15). When the lever or pedal is activated, cables to the rear brakes are stretched to tighten the brake shoes against the drums.

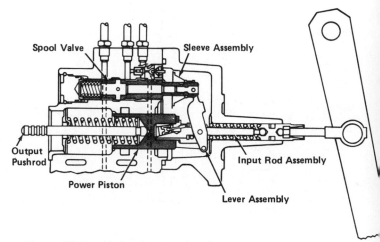

Figure 67-14. Hydraulic power booster.
GENERAL MOTORS CORPORATION

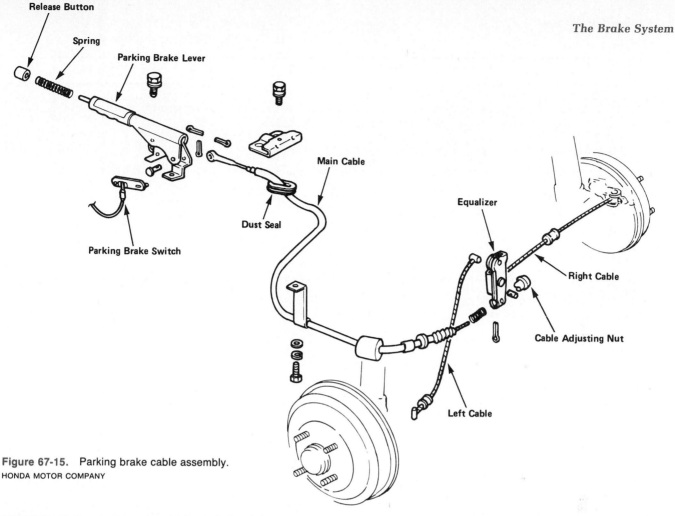

Figure 67-15. Parking brake cable assembly.
HONDA MOTOR COMPANY

U N I T   H I G H L I G H T S

- A brake uses friction to slow and stop an automobile.

- Hydraulic pressure transfers brake pedal action to the wheel cylinders.

- A master cylinder has two main functions. It is the source of hydraulic braking pressure and also serves as a reservoir for brake fluid.

- Wheel cylinders move the brake shoes to create friction.

- Brake lines carry hydraulic pressure from the master cylinder to the wheel cylinders.

- A disc brake assembly uses a rotor, caliper, and pads, or shoes, to stop an automobile.

- A drum brake assembly uses a drum, brake shoes, and brake linings to stop an automobile.

- Self-energizing increases the performance of drum brake systems.

- Various valves are used to control the actions of disc and drum brakes when they are used on the same automobile.

- Power brakes can be operated by vacuum and atmospheric pressure or by power steering fluid.

- A parking brake is used to lock the rear brakes.

T E R M S

friction
master cylinder
brake lines
wheel cylinder
split reservoir
brake linings
disc brakes
drum brakes
rotor
caliper
brake pads
fixed caliper
floating caliper
sliding caliper
brake shoes
backing plate

primary brake shoe
secondary brake shoe
anchor pin
self-energizing
self-adjuster
star wheel
proportioning valve
metering valve
combination valve
failure warning switch
residual check valve
power brake booster
  unit
anti-skid braking
  system
parking brake

R E V I E W   Q U E S T I O N S

DIRECTIONS: The following questions are similar to those used on mechanic certification tests. On a separate sheet of paper, write the letter of the correct choice.

1. All of the following statements are true EXCEPT
A. An automotive brake system uses stationary devices to act on rotating wheels and create friction.
B. Braking friction is created between the brake pedal and the master cylinder.
C. A hydraulic system is activated when a driver steps on the brake pedal.
D. The brake lines transfer pressure to a wheel cylinder.

2. Which of the following statements is correct?
I. A master cylinder transmits hydraulic pressure.
II. A wheel cylinder absorbs hydraulic pressure.
A. I only   B. II only   C. Both I and II   D. Neither I nor II

3. Which of the following statements is correct?
A. A disc brake uses a distributor rotor and caliper.
B. A caliper applies hydraulic pressure to a wheel cylinder.
C. A fixed caliper is a rebuilt caliper.
D. A floating caliper slides.

4. Mechanic A says that disc and drum brakes operate identically.
Mechanic B says that disc brake and drum brake systems often are combined on the same automobile.
Who is correct?
A. A only   B. B only   C. Both A and B   D. Neither A nor B

5. All of the following statements are true EXCEPT
A. A power brake system boosts brake pedal pressure.
B. A vacuum line in a power brake system runs to the intake manifold.
C. A diaphragm in a power brake booster is moved by hydraulic pressure.
D. A hydraulic pressure power brake system is operated by power steering fluid.

S U P P L E M E N T A L   A C T I V I T I E S

1. Describe the operation of a master cylinder.
2. Demonstrate the differences between good and bad friction materials.
3. Describe the operation of a disc brake system.
4. Identify the type of caliper selected by your instructor.
5. Describe the operation of a drum brake system.
6. Explain the term self-energizing.
7. Locate and identify the valves in a disc and drum brake combination system.
8. Explain what occurs in a power brake system when the brakes are applied.
9. Locate the parts of a parking brake system on an automobile selected by your instructor.

68 BRAKE SYSTEM SERVICE

UNIT PREVIEW

Brake service is relatively uncomplicated. However, it is a vital part of automobile service. Brake service must be performed carefully and precisely. The health, safety, and well-being of both the mechanic and the customer are at stake. The mechanic must guard against asbestos inhalation. The customer must have good, reliable brakes for safe driving.

This unit discusses the preventive maintenance and service procedures that are used for disc and drum brake systems.

LEARNING OBJECTIVES

When you have completed your assignments and exercises in this unit, you should be able to:
☐ Inspect a brake system for obvious problems.
☐ Check shoe and lining wear.
☐ Describe the procedures for conducting a safe and proper road test.
☐ Bleed a brake system.
☐ Service disc and drum brake systems.

SAFETY PRECAUTIONS

Inspection and servicing of brake systems require that the automobile be raised on a hoist or jack. Check the proper service manual to locate the proper jacking points on the vehicle that is being serviced. Always use the proper safety stands.

Brake shoes and linings usually are made of asbestos. Breathing asbestos dust is a health hazard. Always use a special, approved vacuum cleaner to remove asbestos dust from a brake assembly before working on the system. Never use compressed air or a brush to remove asbestos dust. Dispose of asbestos dust and dirt from the vacuum cleaner in a sealed bag.

Grinding or sanding on linings, rotors, or drums should be done while using the proper exhaust-ventilation equipment. Special equipment is designed for use with asbestos.

Never use gasoline, kerosene, motor oil, transmission fluid, or any mineral oil in the brake system.

Never clean a brake part with mineral oil. Mineral oils will damage rubber parts in the brake system and contaminate brake fluid.

Grease and other foreign material must be kept off the caliper, rotor, linings, drum, and hub during service.

Handle all brake parts with extreme care. Scratches, nicks, and any deformation can cause brake failure.

Always wear safety glasses or goggles when using compressed air.

68.1 PREVENTIVE MAINTENANCE

A thorough inspection of brake systems is required on a periodic basis. Preventive maintenance requires a careful visual inspection as well as the removal of wheel assemblies and brake parts.

Brake Fluid Inspection

A master cylinder usually is located under the hood and near the firewall on the driver's side. A master cylinder cover may be screwed on or held on by a bail-type retainer (see Figure 68-1). Remove the cover and check the gasket, or diaphragm. Inspect the cover for damage or plugged vent holes. Clean the vent holes, if necessary.

Check the brake fluid level in the master cylinder. A cast iron reservoir usually is filled to within ¼ in. [6.35 mm] of the top. A plastic reservoir may have fluid level marks. Do not overfill a reservoir. If fluid must be added, a leak probably has developed. Check the system carefully to locate the leak.

To check for contaminated fluid, place a small amount of brake fluid in a clear glass jar. If the fluid is dirty or separates into layers, it is contaminated. Contaminated fluid must be replaced.

CAUTION: Contaminated brake fluid can damage rubber parts and cause leaks. When replacing contaminated brake fluid, it is necessary to flush and refill the brake system with new fluid. Always use fluid with a DOT rating of 3 or higher, following manufacturer's recommendations.

Check the master cylinder for dampness and leaks around the body and fittings, especially at the rear. A leak where it is mounted to the firewall or power brake unit indicates a defective rear piston seal. The master cylinder must be rebuilt or replaced.

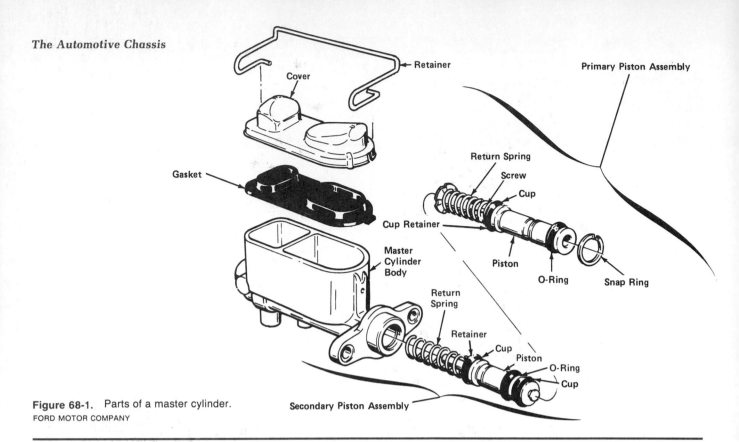

Figure 68-1. Parts of a master cylinder.
FORD MOTOR COMPANY

Brake Line Inspection

Check all tubing, hoses, and connections from under the hood to the wheels for leaks and damage. Wheels and tires also should be inspected for signs of brake fluid leaks. Check all hoses for flexibility, bulges, and cracks. Check parking brake linkage, cable, and connections for damage and wear. Replace parts where necessary.

Brake Pedal Inspection

Depress and release the brake pedal several times (engine running for power brakes). Check for friction and noise. Pedal movement should be smooth, with no squeaks from the pedal or brakes. The pedal should return quickly when it is released.

SAFETY CAUTION: When operating the engine, be sure the transmission lever is in neutral or park. Be sure the area is properly ventilated for the exhaust to escape.

Apply heavy foot pressure to the brake pedal (engine running for power brakes). Check for a *spongy pedal* and *pedal reserve*. Spongy pedal action is springy. Pedal action should feel firm. Pedal reserve is the distance between the brake pedal and the floor after the pedal has been depressed fully. The pedal should not go lower than 1 or 2 in. [25.4 or 50.8 mm] above the floor.

With the engine off, hold a light foot pressure on the pedal for about 15 seconds. There should be no pedal movement during this time. Pedal movement indicates a leak. Repeat the procedure using heavy pedal pressure (engine running for power brakes).

If there is pedal movement, but the fluid level is not low, the master cylinder has internal leakage. It must be rebuilt or replaced. If the fluid level is low, there is an external leak somewhere in the brake system. The leak must be repaired.

Depress the pedal and check for proper stoplight operation.

To check power brake operation, depress and release the pedal several times while the engine is stopped. This eliminates vacuum from the system. Hold the brake down with moderate foot pressure and start the engine. If the power unit is operating properly, the brake pedal will move downward when the engine is started.

Disc Brake Inspection

Raise the automobile on a hoist or support it with safety stands. Remove at least one front and one rear wheel. (If drum brakes are used at the rear wheels, refer to the discussion of Drum Brake Inspection below.) Whenever wear symptoms appear, or at recommended intervals, inspect the brake linings for wear.

SAFETY CAUTION: Use extreme care when working around the brake linings. Brake linings usually contain asbestos. Asbestos is a health hazard when inhaled. Use a special, approved vacuum cleaner to remove asbestos dust from the brakes before disassembly. Never use compressed air to blow off brake dust.

Lining wear. Lining should be thicker than the thickness of the shoe to which it is attached. It usually is not necessary to remove the caliper to check lining thickness. First, check both ends of the outer linings from the ends of the caliper. The inner linings often are checked through an inspection hole at the top of the caliper. If the lining is the approximate thickness of the pad, or less, remove the lining and replace it.

Shoe removal. The caliper must be removed to replace a brake shoe. Calipers can be removed in several different ways. One method of caliper removal is shown in Figure 68-2. Pins are removed to free the caliper housing. Remove the caliper housing from the rotor by sliding the caliper slowly out and away from the rotor. The inboard brake shoe may remain with the caliper housing.

NOTE: Support the caliper assembly on an upper control arm with a wire hanger. Do not kink or stretch the brake lines.

Remove the outer brake shoe by sliding it out from the rotor (see Figure 68-3). Remove the inner brake pad from the caliper housing (see Figure 68-4).

If linings are oil-soaked, imbedded with foreign material, too thin, or have loose rivets, replace them.

Lining thickness measurement. Check the brake shoes and linings for uneven or excessive wear. Measure the lining thickness. Lining thickness should be more than about ⅛ in. [3.18 mm] above a rivet or the shoe at any point.

Rotor measurement. A disc, or rotor, should be checked for wear, runout, parallelism, and flatness.

Visually check for scoring, rust, imbedded lining material, and worn ridges in the rotor. Rust causes noise and chatter. Wear and scoring can create an improper contact area with the lining. Some discoloration and wear is normal.

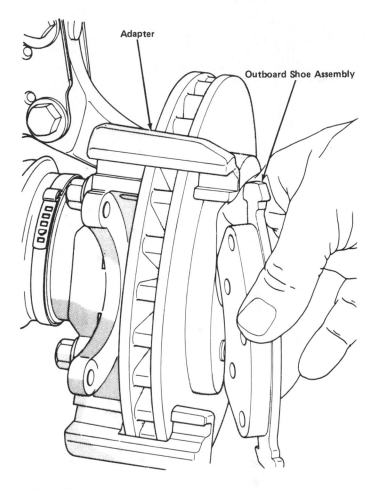

Figure 68-3. Outboard brake pad removal.
CHRYSLER CORPORATION

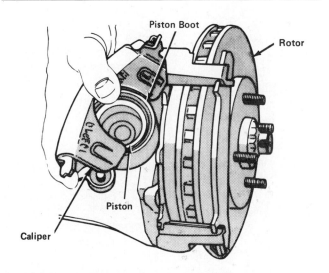

Figure 68-2. Caliper removal. CHRYSLER CORPORATION

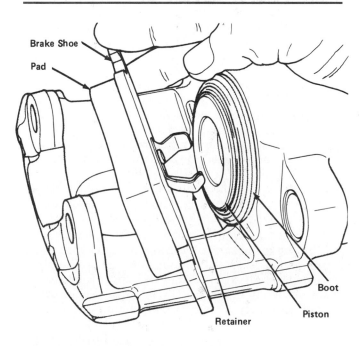

Figure 68-4. Inboard brake pad removal.
CHRYSLER CORPORATION

Excessive runout, or wobble, can increase pedal travel or cause pedal pulsation, and damage a caliper. Check runout with a dial indicator (see Figure 68-5). Slowly rotate the rotor while watching the dial indicator. A runout of 0.002 to 0.004 in. [0.05 to 0.10 mm] is cause for repair. Check the service manual for exact specifications.

Parallelism is the degree to which both surfaces of a disc, or rotor, are parallel to each other. Parallelism can cause brake pedal pulsation, or vibration. To check rotor parallelism, use a micrometer at equally spaced points around the rotor disc. (See Figure 68-6). Generally, any variation over 0.005 in. [0.13 mm] is reason for concern and repair.

Dishing and distortion are problems that affect the flatness of a rotor. A straightedge can be used to check flatness.

Reassembly inspection. Before reassembling a disc brake assembly, inspect all parts.

Check the linings for looseness, cracks, unusual wear, or imbedded foreign material. Check the shoes for cracks or distortion.

Check the caliper and hydraulic hose for leaks or damage. Check the mounting bolts and other attachment parts for corrosion and damage.

Correct any faults. Reassemble the disc brake and install the wheel assembly. Disc brakes do not need an adjustment.

Drum Brake Inspection

Raise the automobile on a hoist or support it with safety stands. Remove at least one front and one rear wheel. (If disc brakes are used at the front wheels, refer to the discussion of Disc Brake Inspection above.) Whenever wear symptoms appear, or at recommended intervals, inspect brake linings for wear.

SAFETY CAUTION: **Use extreme care when working around drum brakes. Brake linings usually contain asbestos. Asbestos is a health hazard when inhaled. Use a special vacuum cleaner to remove asbestos dust from the brakes before disassembly. Never use compressed air to blow off brake dust.**

Drum removal. Different procedures may be required when removing rear drum and front drum assemblies. Always check the proper service manual.

Remove the wheel assembly. The brake adjuster may have to be backed off through the adjusting hole. Remove the grease cap and wheel bearing assembly, as discussed in Topic 62.1. Carefully remove the drum, shown in Figure 68-7. Vacuum away the brake dust immediately with a special vacuum cleaner.

Brake inspection. Check the linings for looseness, cracks, unusual wear, and imbedded foreign material. No oil, grease, or brake fluid should be on the linings.

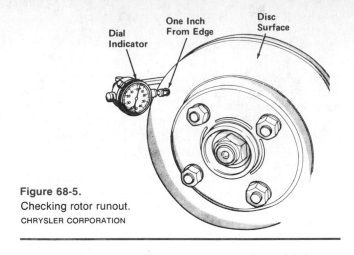

Figure 68-5.
Checking rotor runout.
CHRYSLER CORPORATION

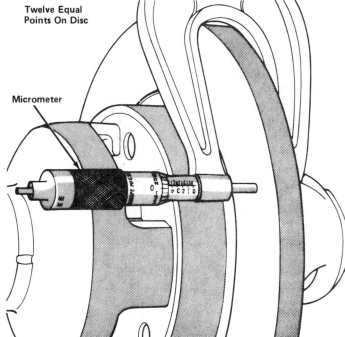

Figure 68-6.   Checking rotor parallelism.   CHRYSLER CORPORATION

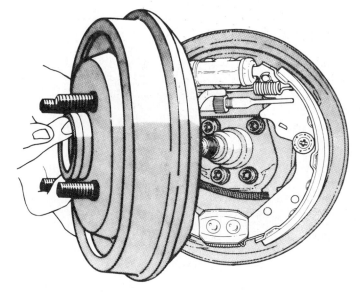

Figure 68-7.   Removing the brake drum.   CHRYSLER CORPORATION

Check the shoes for cracks, distortion, or broken parts. Check the springs, fasteners, and backing plate for damage or excessive wear.

Check for foreign objects or accumulations of dirt in the brake assembly. Brake parts must be reasonably clean to operate properly.

Lining thickness measurement. Check the linings for uneven or excessive wear. Measure the lining thickness. Lining thickness should be more than about ⅛ inch [3.18 mm] above a rivet or the shoe at any point.

Drum inspection. The drum surface should be clean, smooth, and free of damage. Check for hard spots, scoring, and imbedded foreign material.

Use a *clearance gauge,* shown in Figure 68-8, to measure drum and brake shoe clearances. Check drum runout.

Before reassembling brake and wheel bearing assemblies, check the flexible brake hoses for damage and wear. Check the backing plate, especially the brake shoe linings, for grooves. If they are deeply grooved, replace them. If they are still serviceable, lubricate the linings with special high-temperature lubricant. Replace the drum, repack the wheel bearings, and install the wheel assembly.

Most drum brake systems are self-adjusting. Manual adjustments seldom are required. If a manual adjustment is required, check the proper service manual for procedures.

68.2 BRAKE SYSTEM PROBLEM DIAGNOSIS

If no problems are found during a visual inspection of the automobile, prepare to make a road test. First, check that the stoplights and warning lights are operating properly. Be sure the brake fluid is at the proper level. Check tire pressures and wheel bearing adjustments. A road test should be made only when the operator is sure that the brakes will stop the automobile.

SAFETY CAUTION: Before driving, depress the brake pedal to make sure it will not bottom. Make a few slow-speed stops to determine if the brakes are safe for driving. Do not apply the brakes continually, because they might overheat and *fade,* or lose their holding power.

A road test is necessary to check brakes for safe, quiet operation. Road tests should be conducted on a level road that is dry, clean, and smooth. Use the proper service manual to identify problems and causes during the road test. The following tests will help to evaluate brake performance.

Pulls, Noises, and Braking Effectiveness

Make light and moderate stops from about 15 mph [24 km/h]. Stop the automobile completely each time.

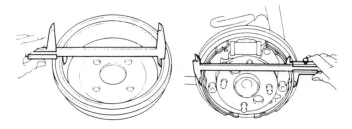

Figure 68-8. Checking brake drum clearances.
BUICK MOTOR DIVISION—GMC

Notice whether pedal effort is too light or too hard during each stop. Check for pulls. Front brakes pull in the direction of the brake doing most of the work. Rear brakes that pull may not be noticeable during low-speed stops. Check for noise. Open the windows and turn off all accessories. Listen to determine the type of noise and the wheel from which it is coming.

Make hard stops from 55 mph [88 km/h] and check in the same manner as for the low-speed test. A hard stop is one in which the automobile is stopped quickly, just short of skidding. Do not repeat a hard stop until the automobile has traveled about 2 miles [3.2 km].

SAFETY CAUTION: Use extreme caution when making high-speed tests. There should be no traffic where these tests are conducted. The area around the road test area should be clear of obstructions. Stay away from residential areas. If a brake pulls or locks up, or the automobile skids, release the brake pedal immediately.

Roughness or Pulsation

Make light stops from 55 mph [88 km/h]. Notice how the brake pedal feels when it is depressed. Check for a vibration that is rough or pulsating.

Brake Fade

A *fade* is a temporary loss, or reduction, of brake effectiveness. Fade is caused by heat. To test, make three hard stops from 55 mph [88 km/h] at ½-mile [0.8km] intervals. Check for pulling. Notice how much pedal effort is required. Check the pedal reserve after each stop.

Delayed Brake Fade

After performing the brake fade test, allow the automobile to stand for about 10 minutes. To test for delayed brake fade, accelerate to 55 mph [88 km/h] and make one hard stop. Check for pulling, pedal effort, and pedal reserve.

The results of brake tests, along with a service/diagnosis manual, will assist in pinpointing any problems.

68.3 BLEEDING BRAKES

The hydraulic system must be free of air for proper operation. Air in the system will affect the operation of the brakes to the point where they may not stop the vehicle. To eliminate air, it is necessary to *bleed* the brake system. Bleeding is a process of forcing fluid through the brake lines and out through a *bleeder valve* or *bleeder screw*. The fluid eliminates any air that may be in the system. Bleeder screws and valves are fastened to the wheel cylinders or calipers. The bleeder must be cleaned. A drain hose then is connected from the bleeder to a glass jar (see Figure 68-9).

Two types of brake bleeding procedures are used: manual bleeding and pressure bleeding. Always follow the manufacturer's recommendations when bleeding brakes. The sequence in which bleeding is performed can be critical. When bleeding a power brake system, remove the vacuum line from the power unit and plug the unit. To remove vacuum, the engine must be off. Pump the brake pedal several times.

CAUTION: **Always use fresh brake fluid when bleeding the system. Do not use fluid that has been drained. Drained fluid may be contaminated and can damage the system.**

Manual Bleeding

A *manual bleeding* procedure requires two people. One person operates the bleeder; the other, the brake pedal. Bleed only one wheel at a time.

CAUTION: **Be sure the bleeder hose is below the surface of the liquid at all times. Do not allow the master cylinder to run out of fluid at any time. If these precautions are not followed, air can enter the system, and it must be bled again. The master cylinder cover must be kept in place.**

Place the bleeder hose and jar in position. Have a helper pump the brake pedal several times and then hold it down with moderate pressure. Slowly open the bleeder valve. After fluid/air has stopped flowing, close the bleeder valve. Have the helper slowly release the pedal. Repeat this procedure until fluid that flows from the bleeder is clear and free of bubbles.

Discard all used brake fluid. Fill the master cylinder reservoirs. Check the brakes for proper operation.

CAUTION: **Clean the master cylinder and cover before adding fluid. This is important for preventing dirt from entering the reservoir.**

Pressure Bleeding

A *pressure bleeding* procedure can be done by one person. Pressure bleeding equipment uses pressurized fluid that flows through a special adapter fitted into the master cylinder (see Figure 68-10).

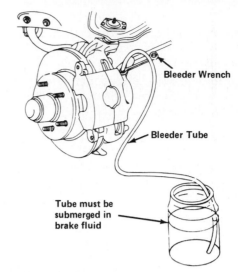

Figure 68-9. Brake bleeding attachments.
BUICK MOTOR DIVISION—GMC

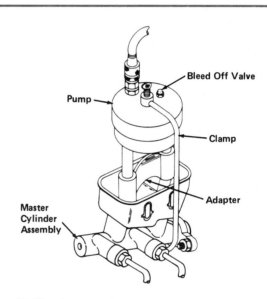

Figure 68-10. Pressure bleeder adapter.
BUICK MOTOR DIVISION—GMC

The use of pressure bleeding equipment varies with different automobiles and different equipment makers. Always follow the automobile manufacturer's recommendations when using pressure bleeding equipment.

On automobiles with metering valves, the valve must be held open during pressure bleeding. Figure 68-11 shows a special tool used to hold open the metering section of a combination valve.

Open the bleeder valves one at a time until clear, air-free fluid is flowing. Progress from the wheel cylinder farthest from the master cylinder to the cylinder closest.

Do not exceed recommended pressure while bleeding the brakes. Always release air pressure after bleeding. Clean and fill the master cylinder after pressure bleeding. Check the brakes for proper operation. Be sure to remove the special tool used to hold the metering valve.

68.4 MASTER CYLINDER REBUILDING

A master cylinder is rebuilt to replace leaking seals or gaskets. If a more serious problem exists, the master cylinder should be replaced.

To remove a master cylinder, disconnect the brake lines at the master cylinder. Install plugs in the brake lines and master cylinder to prevent dirt from entering. Remove the nuts that attach the master cylinder to the firewall or power brake unit, and remove the cylinder.

Remove the cover and seal. Drain the master cylinder and carefully mount it in a vise. Remove the piston assembly and seals according to the manufacturer's instructions. Figure 68-12 shows a master

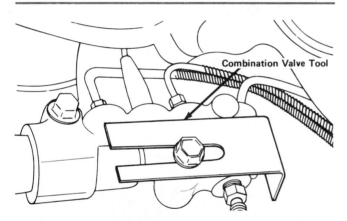

Figure 68-11. Metering valve tool. BUICK MOTOR DIVISION—GMC

cylinder assembly. New pistons, pushrods, and seals usually are included in rebuilding kits.

CAUTION: **Clean master cylinder parts only with brake fluid, brake cleaning solvent, or alcohol. Do not use a solvent containing mineral oil, such as gasoline. Mineral oil is very harmful to rubber seals.**

Inspect the master cylinder. Damage, cracks, porous leaks, and worn piston bores mean the master cylinder must be replaced. Check very carefully for pitting or roughness in the bore. If any is present, the cylinder must be replaced.

Reassemble, install, and bleed the master cylinder according to the manufacturer's directions.

68.5 DISC BRAKE SERVICE

Although disc brake operation is similar, some disc brake service procedures can vary considerably. Always check the proper service manual.

Disassembly

Raise the automobile on a hoist or safety stands at the proper locations. Remove the wheel assembly. Remove the caliper assembly as discussed in Topic 68.1. Disassemble the caliper according to the manufacturer's recommendations. A disc brake assembly is shown in Figure 68-13.

Cleaning and Inspection

All asbestos dust should have been removed from the disc brake assembly before further cleaning and inspection. Wipe off the remainder of the brake parts with a clean, dry shop towel.

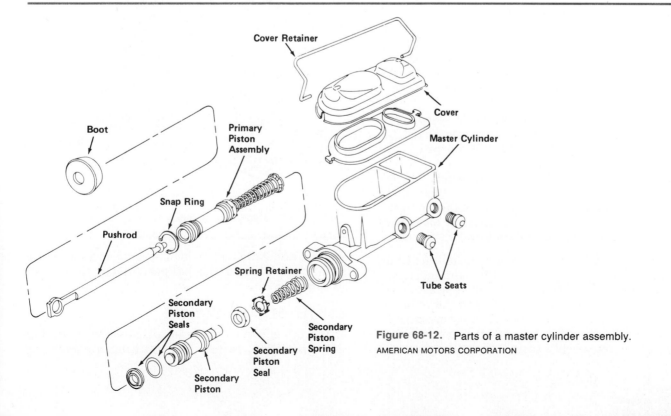

Figure 68-12. Parts of a master cylinder assembly.
AMERICAN MOTORS CORPORATION

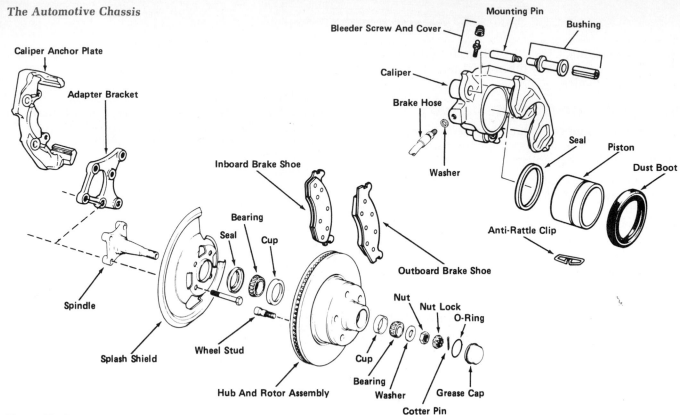

Figure 68-13. Parts of a disc brake assembly.
AMERICAN MOTORS CORPORATION

Check the linings and rotor for damage and wear. Check for leaks around the piston seal, boot area, and linings. Check the piston boot. Install a new seal, boot, and piston if they are leaking, damaged, or corroded. Rebuild the calipers, if necessary. Check the rotor for runout, parallelism, and flatness, as discussed in Topic 68.1.

Rotor Removal and Replacement

Once the caliper assembly has been removed, the rotor can be pulled off the hub or spindle (see Figure 68-14). On some automobiles, the rotor and hub are removed as a unit, then disassembled on a workbench.

A rotor can be resurfaced or refaced. Refacing requires a special rotor-turning tool. A rotor is refaced when the surface is deeply scored or warped.

SAFETY CAUTION: Always wear safety glasses when resurfacing or refacing a rotor. When using rotor-turning equipment, read the manufacturer's instructions carefully. The rotor must be cleaned of chips or other contamination before it is turned.

To replace the rotor, pack and install the inner wheel bearings. On some front-drive automobiles, a hub and sealed wheel bearings may be one assembly. Install the hub, if it was removed, and the rotor. Be sure that the rotor is installed on the correct side. Some rotors are made for right or left side installation. Install the outer wheel bearing, thrust washer, and

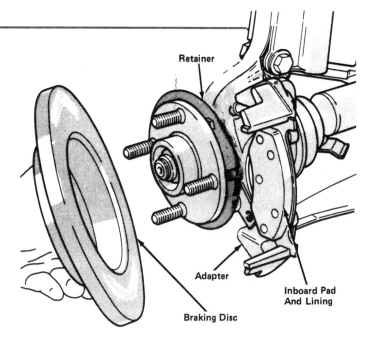

Figure 68-14. Removing the rotor. CHRYSLER CORPORATION

spindle nut. Adjust the wheel bearing and install the grease cap. Install the caliper. Install the wheel assembly.

68.6 DRUM BRAKE SERVICE

Drum brake service includes disassembly, cleaning and inspection, resurfacing the drums, rebuilding wheel cylinders, and replacing linings. Refer to Topic 68.1 for procedures to remove the drum and to inspect the drum brake parts. Service procedures can vary considerably. Always refer to the proper service manual.

Disassembly

Parts of a rear brake system are shown in Figure 68-15. For disassembly, place brake cylinder clamps over the wheel cylinders to hold them in place. Disconnect the parking brake on rear brake systems. Remove the springs with brake spring pliers. Remove the self-adjuster parts and the brake shoes.

SAFETY CAUTION: **Use extreme care when disassembling drum brakes. Brake linings usually contain asbestos, which is a health hazard when inhaled. Use a special, approved vacuum cleaner to remove asbestos-containing brake dust from the brakes before disassembly. Never use compressed air to blow off brake dust.**

Cleaning and Inspection

Clean all parts, except lining and drums, with brake cleaning solvent. Do not attempt to clean linings contaminated with brake fluid or axle lubricant. Contaminated linings must be replaced. Remove brake fluid contamination, except on linings, with denatured alcohol. Clean the brake drums only with a soap and water solution.

Pull back the wheel cylinder boots and check for leakage. If leakage is found, the wheel cylinders must be rebuilt, if possible. Some aluminum wheel cylinders cannot be rebuilt. Clean the metal portion of the brake shoes with fine emery cloth and inspect them for damage and excessive wear. Inspect for lining wear. If wear is uneven, the drums and shoes must be checked for distortion and damage. Inspect all parts for unusual wear and damage. Replace all defective parts.

Refacing Drums

The drums should be inspected for damage and excessive wear. Measure drum runout and diameter. If damage, excessive wear, or improper measurements are found, the drum must be refaced on a brake drum lathe.

A brake drum cannot be refaced if the drum diameter exceeds the maximum allowable diameter. The maximum allowable diameter usually is marked on the outside of the drum. Always follow the manufacturer's tolerances for refacing.

Rebuilding Wheel Cylinders

If the boot on a wheel cylinder has cuts, tears, or heat cracks, or the cylinder is leaking, the wheel cylinder should be removed. Wheel cylinders should be cleaned, inspected, and have new parts installed.

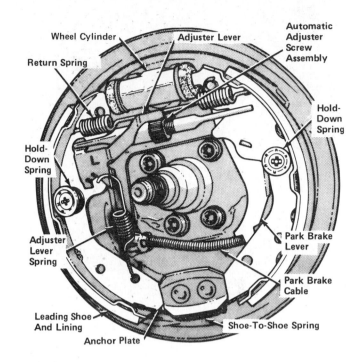

Figure 68-15. Parts of a drum brake assembly.
CHRYSLER CORPORATION

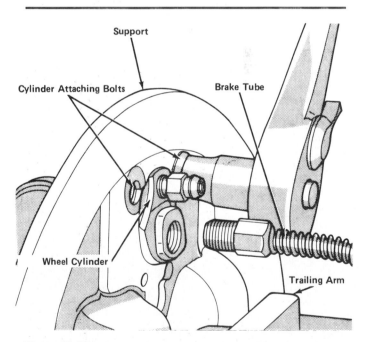

Figure 68-16. Removing brake lines. CHRYSLER CORPORATION

To remove a wheel cylinder, first disconnect the brake tube from the rear of the wheel cylinder (see Figure 68-16). Remove the bolts that hold the wheel cylinder in place. Remove the wheel cylinder (see Figure 68-17). Check the diameter of the wheel cylinder because automobiles of the same make may use different sizes.

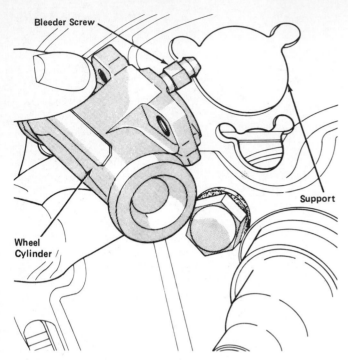

Figure 68-17. Removing a wheel cylinder.
CHRYSLER CORPORATION

First, carefully attempt to loosen the bleeder valve, using penetrating oil if necessary. After soaking, try to open the valve. It should open. If the valve twists off, a new cylinder is needed.

Disassemble the wheel cylinder by prying off the boots. Then slide out the piston assembly by pushing in on one end. Remove all wheel cylinder parts (refer to Figure 68-18).

Clean the metal parts thoroughly in brake fluid or alcohol. Do not use a rag when cleaning the bore surfaces. Lint will adhere to the surfaces and contaminate the brake fluid.

Check the cylinder bore and piston for damage or excessive wear. Light scratches can be cleaned with crocus cloth, using a circular motion. Black stains on the cylinder walls are caused by piston cups and will not affect cylinder operation. Pitting or roughness, however, would be reason to reject the cylinder and install a new one.

A wheel cylinder kit contains all the replacement parts necessary for reassembly. Dip the pistons and new cups in clean brake fluid. Coat the cylinder bore with clean brake fluid. Assemble all the parts according to the manufacturer's recommendations.

Install and tighten the cylinder assembly and brake tubing. Torque the fasteners to specifications.

Brake Springs

Check all brake springs for distortion and overheating. The spring coils should be tight against one another and should be painted. An absence of paint may indicate overheating. Replace any springs that are questionable.

Backing Plate

Inspect the backing plate for any looseness or wear. Pay special attention to the pads or bosses. They sometimes have deep grooves worn in them by the

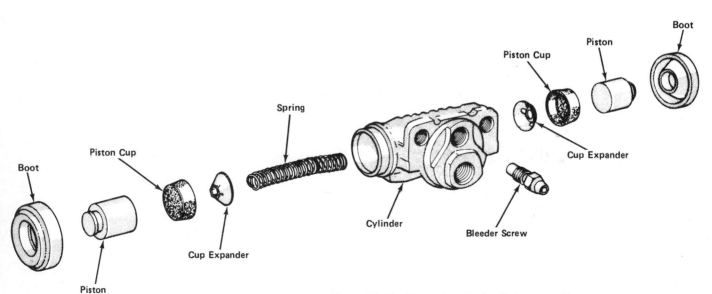

Figure 68-18. Parts of a wheel cylinder assembly. CHRYSLER CORPORATION

brake shoes. Lubricate the pads with a thin coat of special high-temperature brake lubricant.

Reassembly

Replace all damaged and excessively worn drums with new ones. Reassemble the brake assembly according to the manufacturer's recommendations. Install the drum and wheel assembly as discussed in Topic 68.1.

68.7 POWER BRAKE SERVICE

If diagnosis indicates an internal problem with the power brake unit, replace the entire power unit. Most manufacturers do not recommend disassembly, repair, or adjustment of power brake units.

To remove the power brake unit, first disconnect the vacuum hose. Remove the nuts and lockwashers that hold the power unit to the master cylinder and to the firewall. Remove the power unit. It usually is not necessary to disconnect the brake lines. A typical power unit installation is shown in Figure 68-19.

Install a new power unit in the reverse order of disassembly. A lubricant usually is used at the pushrod. Check the proper service manual for any special requirements.

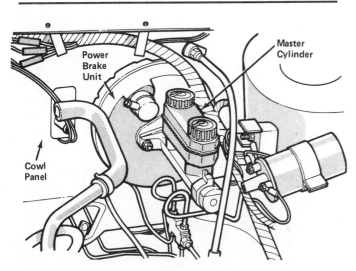

Figure 68-19. Power brake mounting. CHRYSLER CORPORATION

- Brake fluid is contaminated if it separates into layers in a glass jar.
- Brake lines that are swollen and deteriorated may be filled with contaminated fluid.
- The way a brake pedal feels when it is being depressed can be an indication that a brake problem exists.
- Brake pad wear can be checked by looking through the caliper.
- Shoe removal requires at least a partial disassembling of a caliper.
- A rotor is measured to determine runout, flatness, and parallelism.
- The drum must be removed to inspect drum brake linings.
- Drum and lining measurements are made with a clearance gauge.
- The brakes should be checked thoroughly before conducting a road test.
- Air is removed from a hydraulic system by a procedure called bleeding.
- A master cylinder can be rebuilt to correct a leakage problem.
- A rotor can be refaced when it is deeply scored or warped.
- A brake drum should not be turned if the inside diameter exceeds the maximum allowed diameter.
- Wheel cylinders can be rebuilt if the cylinder bore is not scored or pitted.
- Power brake units must be replaced when they fail to operate properly.

T E R M S

spongy pedal	bleed
pedal reserve	bleeder valve
parallelism	bleeder screw
clearance gauge	manual bleeding
fade	pressure bleeding

DIRECTIONS: The following questions are similar to those used on mechanic certification tests. On a separate sheet of paper, write the letter of the correct choice.

1. Mechanic A says that, to check brake lining wear, the caliper does not have to be removed. Mechanic B says that, to check drum brake lining wear, the backing plate must be disassembled. Who is correct?

A. A only   B. B only   C. Both A and B   D. Neither A nor B

2. All of the following statements are true EXCEPT
A. When removing a front brake drum, the brake adjuster should be disconnected.
B. Asbestos must be vacuumed away.
C. Brake parts are designed to operate properly even if damaged.
D. Drum and brake shoe clearances are measured with a clearance gauge.

3. Which of the following statements is correct?
I. Wheel bearing adjustment must be correct before conducting a road test.
II. Brake fade is a temporary loss of pedal pressure.

A. I only   B. II only   C. Both I and II   D. Neither I nor II

4. When bleeding a brake system, a mechanic should
A. remove a brake line.
B. have a helper push down on the metering valve.
C. not reuse the brake fluid.
D. bleed the master cylinder.

5. Mechanic A says that a rotor can be resurfaced. Mechanic B says that a drum should be turned when it is over the maximum allowed diameter. Who is correct?

A. A only   B. B only   C. Both A and B   D. Neither A nor B

S U P P L E M E N T A L A C T I V I T I E S

1. Check the level and condition of brake fluid in an automobile selected by your instructor.
2. Inspect the brake lining on an automobile selected by your instructor.
3. Show the proper use of a special vacuum cleaner used to remove asbestos dust from a brake system.
4. Remove a wheel assembly and inspect the condition of the brakes on an automobile selected by your instructor.
5. Replace the brake shoes on an automobile.
6. Measure lining thickness on a brake system selected by your instructor.
7. Explain the procedures that are used to perform a road test to check the braking system.
8. Bleed a brake system.
9. Rebuild a master cylinder.
10. Disassemble, inspect, and reassemble a brake assembly on an automobile selected by your instructor.
11. Rebuild wheel cylinders.
12. Remove and install a power brake unit.

IX

AUXILIARY SYSTEMS

69 HEATING AND AIR CONDITIONING SYSTEMS

UNIT PREVIEW

Occupant comfort is an important safety factor during driving. If a driver becomes too warm or too cold, driving judgment can be affected. To keep the driver and passengers comfortable and alert, hot or cold air can be introduced into the passenger compartment. Heating and air conditioning systems are added to most automobiles for this purpose. These systems should be understood by mechanics, because they are among the first to be noticed when they fail.

LEARNING OBJECTIVES

When you have completed your assignments and exercises in this unit, you should be able to:

☐ Describe the operation of a heating system.

☐ Explain how a refrigerant cools an air conditioning system.

☐ Identify the parts of an air conditioner.

☐ Explain how an evaporator uses refrigerant for cooling.

☐ Describe the airflow through doors and distribution plenums.

69.1 HEATING SYSTEM

An automotive heating system uses engine heat to provide occupant comfort. A heating system operates much as an engine cooling system. Heated coolant is mixed with cooler outside air in a heater assembly. The air mixture then is routed to the passenger compartment through a series of passages. The basic assemblies in a heating system, as shown in Figure 69-1, are:

- Air inlet
- Heater
- Heater controls.

Air Inlet Assembly

An *air inlet assembly* draws in outside air and forces it into the passenger compartment. Outside air usually is drawn into a heating system through a grille assembly in an opening below the windshield. A duct directs the incoming air to a *blower*. A blower is a fan that pushes, or blows, the incoming air through, or out of, a heater assembly. The blower is operated by an electric motor.

Heater Assembly

A *heater assembly* is a housing that usually is mounted to a firewall. A heater assembly contains a radiator, or *heater core*, and doors that direct heated air to the passenger compartment. A heater core, receiving hot coolant from the engine through hoses, operates in the same manner as an engine radiator. It draws heat from engine coolant. Doors in the heater assembly housing are opened and closed to direct heated air to the *distribution plenums*. A plenum is a chamber that accepts circulating air and distributes it.

Returning engine coolant flows through a *heater hose* between the engine block and heater core. Two heater hoses are used (see Figure 69-2). The outlet hose is connected to the suction port on the water pump. The suction port helps circulate engine coolant through the system.

Hot coolant warms the air around the core. The heated air is mixed with cooler outside air and pushed by the blower. The flow of air is controlled by heater controls that determine how the doors operate. Depending on which doors are opened, heated air can be directed to the floor, to the ceiling, and to the windows. Plenum chambers that direct airflow to the windshield usually are called *defrosters*.

Many heating systems also are used as *ventilation systems*. A ventilation system may draw in outside air, pass it through the heating system, then into the passenger compartment. A bypass plenum sometimes is used to direct airflow around the heater core. Coolant may not flow through a heating system unless the heater switch is in the proper position, depending upon heater design.

Airflow through a heater assembly is shown in Figure 69-3.

Heater Controls Assembly

A *heater controls assembly* regulates a heating system with manual, vacuum, and electric switches and levers. Coolant flow to the heater assembly is operated by a *heater control valve* in the inlet heater hose. Doors in the heater assembly are opened and closed by cables or vacuum motors. A blower is operated electrically. Parts of a heater control panel are shown in Figure 69-4.

69.2 AIR CONDITIONING SYSTEM

An air conditioning system, like a heating system, is designed for occupant comfort. It absorbs heat from the warm air inside the passenger compartment. This

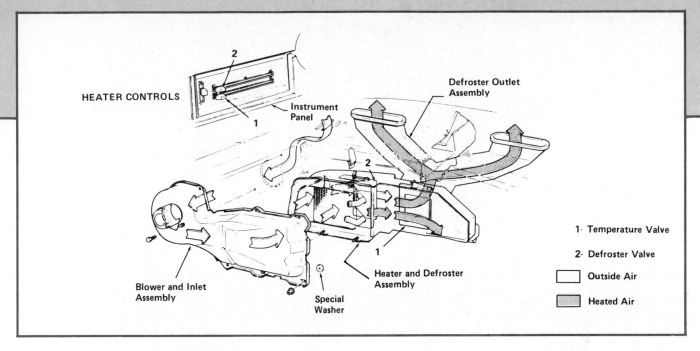

HEATER CONTROLS

1 - Temperature Valve

2 - Defroster Valve

□ Outside Air

▨ Heated Air

Instrument Panel

Defroster Outlet Assembly

Heater and Defroster Assembly

Blower and Inlet Assembly

Special Washer

Figure 69-1. Heating system assembly. CHEVROLET MOTOR DIVISION—GMC

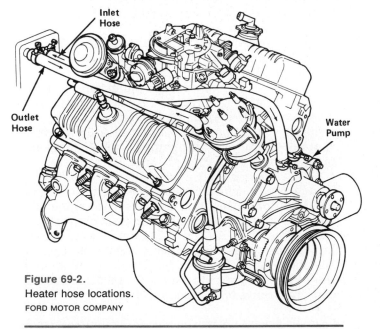

Inlet Hose

Outlet Hose

Water Pump

Figure 69-2. Heater hose locations. FORD MOTOR COMPANY

warm air is cooled, dehumidified, cleaned, and recirculated.

The principle behind air conditioning is an old one. When a liquid is converted to a gas, it absorbs heat. When the gas is liquified, it releases heat. You can feel this process by applying alcohol to the back of your hand. The cooling sensation you feel is caused by the alcohol absorbing heat from your skin as it evaporates. Evaporation is discussed below.

Evaporation

Refrigeration is a process that cools, or maintains cold. Most refrigeration systems operate on the principle of *evaporation*. Evaporation is the process in

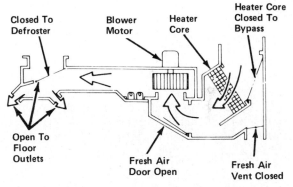

Closed To Defroster

Blower Motor

Heater Core

Heater Core Closed To Bypass

Open To Floor Outlets

Fresh Air Door Open

Fresh Air Vent Closed

View A — Max. Heat Airflow

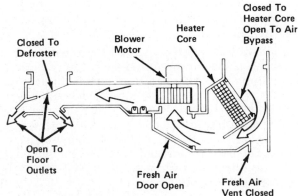

Closed To Defroster

Blower Motor

Heater Core

Closed To Heater Core Open To Air Bypass

Open To Floor Outlets

Fresh Air Door Open

Fresh Air Vent Closed

View B—Fresh (Unheated) Airflow

Figure 69-3. Airflow through a heater assembly.
AMERICAN MOTORS CORPORATION

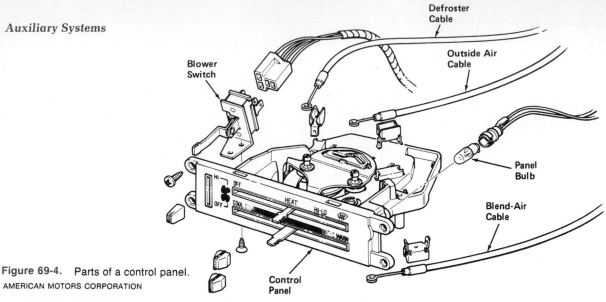

Figure 69-4. Parts of a control panel.
AMERICAN MOTORS CORPORATION

which a liquid turns into a gas, or vapor. As a liquid evaporates, it absorbs heat and cools.

In an air conditioning (refrigeration) system, this evaporation is completed inside a closed system. In this way, the refrigerant liquid can be used over and over again.

Refrigerants

A liquid that is used to cool by way of evaporation is called a *refrigerant*. A refrigerant usually is a liquid that will begin to boil and evaporate at a very low temperature. These temperatures are well below the freezing point of water, 32 degrees F [0 degrees C]. A good refrigerant also is nonpoisonous, nonexplosive, noncorrosive, and can be mixed with oil. Automotive air conditioning systems use a refrigerant that is identified as R-12.

Humidity Control

Humidity is the amount of water vapor that air can hold. A humidity of 100 percent means the air is saturated with water vapor. It can hold no more. A humidity rating of 50 percent means that the air is holding only half the amount of water vapor it is capable of holding.

Cold air holds less moisture than warm air. Consequently, as the warm, humid air is cooled by an air conditioning system, it becomes super-saturated with water vapor. This means that the air has more water vapor than it can hold. The excess moisture begins to separate from the air and collect on the cooler air conditioning surfaces. This process is called *dehumidification*. Dryer air is more comfortable than humid air. An air conditioning system not only cools the air but also dehumidifies it.

Air Conditioner Operation

Automotive air conditioning systems, called *air conditioners*, use the principle discussed earlier to cool the passenger compartment. For the refrigerant to vaporize and condense properly, it is routed through

many parts in the air conditioner. Refrigerant flow is shown in Figure 69-5. Parts of an air conditioner include:

- Compressor
- Condenser
- Receiver/dryer
- Refrigerant control
- Evaporator
- Controls.

Approximate locations of air conditioner parts are shown in Figure 69-6.

Compressor. A *compressor* is a pump that circulates refrigerant vapor through the system. A compressor takes heated refrigerant vapor, compresses it, and pushes it to the condenser under pressure. From a compressor, the vapor is pumped through hoses and into the condenser.

Condenser. A *condenser* changes the vapor into a liquid, or condenses it. A condenser is similar to a radiator. It usually is located just in front of the engine cooling radiator. As hot refrigerant vapor passes through the condenser, cooler air flows through the condenser core. The refrigerant cools and is condensed from a vapor to a liquid. This liquid refrigerant then flows to the receiver/dryer.

Receiver/dryer. A *receiver/dryer*, sometimes called a receiver/dehydrator, is a storage tank located near the condenser. A receiver/dryer stores liquid refrigerant and removes moisture from the refrigerant through the use of a *desiccant*. A desiccant is a special substance that absorbs moisture. Moisture in the refrigerant will cause an air conditioner to clog. A receiver/dryer is used only in systems that use expansion valves.

Refrigerant control. All systems have some sort of *refrigerant control*. The control device separates the high-pressure side of the air conditioning system from the low-pressure side. The sizing and operation of this control is very important. Too little or too much refrigerant will cause cooling problems.

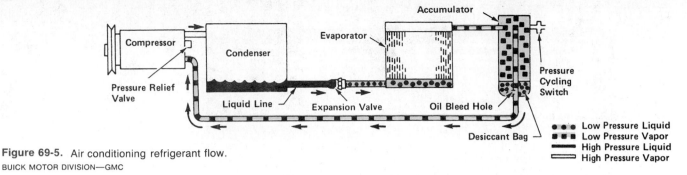

Figure 69-5. Air conditioning refrigerant flow.
BUICK MOTOR DIVISION—GMC

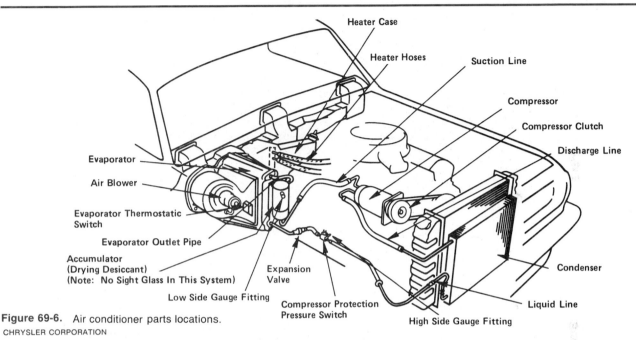

Figure 69-6. Air conditioner parts locations.
CHRYSLER CORPORATION

In older systems, some compressors ran continuously whenever the engine was operating. Cooling was controlled with expansion valves and with evaporator pressure regulators.

In more modern systems, the compressor cycles off and on during engine operation to maintain proper cooling. In this case, the refrigerant control is no more than a metered hole or face. The refrigerant control always is located on the high-pressure side of the evaporator.

Evaporator. Outside air, or recirculated air from the passenger compartment, passes over the *evaporator*. An evaporator is like a heater core. Heated air passes over the evaporator. As the refrigerant control releases liquid refrigerant, the refrigerant begins to boil inside the evaporator tubes. The heat is absorbed by coils in the evaporator. Cooled and dehumidified air from the evaporator is pushed by a blower and directed into the passenger compartment through plenum chambers.

As heat is absorbed by the evaporator, the refrigerant begins to evaporate. The evaporating gas passes into an *accumulator*, or holding tank. Any liquid refrigerant is held in the accumulator where it vaporizes before returning to the compressor. A desiccant in the accumulator helps remove moisture

from the refrigerant. The refrigerant continues on to the compressor, where the refrigeration process begins again.

Air Conditioner Controls

Control systems for air conditioners usually are connected with heater controls. Most heater and air conditioner systems use the same plenum chamber for air distribution. Two types of air conditioner controls are used: manual and automatic.

Manual controls. Air conditioner manual controls operate in a manner similar to heater controls. Depending on the control setting, doors are opened and closed to direct airflow (see Figure 69-7). The amount of cooling is controlled manually through the use of control settings and blower speed.

Automatic temperature control. An *automatic temperature control system* maintains a specific temperature automatically inside the passenger compartment. To maintain temperature, a microprocessor is used to sense temperature changes, and to control airflow and door operation. Warm and cool air usually are mixed to maintain the proper temperature. Airflow in an automatic temperature control system is shown in Figure 69-8.

717

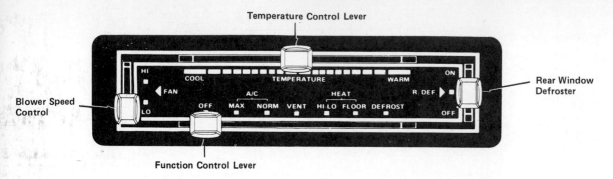

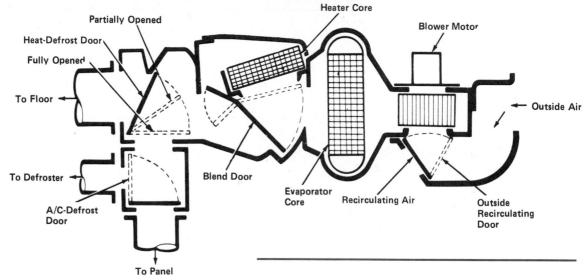

Figure 69-7. Manual control airflow. FORD MOTOR COMPANY

U N I T   H I G H L I G H T S

- Heating and air conditioning systems are designed for passenger comfort.
- A heater air inlet assembly draws air from the outside and forces it through the heating system.
- A heater assembly takes engine heat and directs it to the passenger compartment through distribution plenums.
- Many heating systems include a ventilation system.
- A heater control assembly controls the heating system by means of manual, vacuum, or electric switches and levers in the passenger compartment.
- An air conditioning system absorbs heat from the passenger compartment.
- Air conditioning systems cool air by evaporation.
- A refrigerant evaporates well below the freezing point of water.
- Humidity is the amount of water in the air.
- Ventilation, heating, and air conditioning systems are often combined into one unit.
- An automatic temperature control can be used with an air conditioner to maintain a desired passenger compartment temperature at all times.

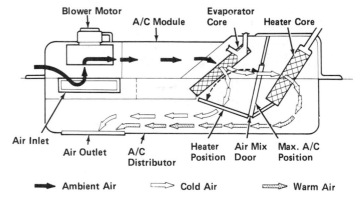

Figure 69-8. Automatic temperature airflow.
CADILLAC MOTOR CAR DIVISION—GMC

T E R M S

air inlet assembly	refrigerant
blower	humidity
heater assembly	dehumidified
heater core	air conditioner
distribution plenum	compressor
heater hose	condenser
defroster	receiver/dryer
ventilation system	desiccant
heater controls	refrigerant control
assembly	evaporator
heater control valve	accumulator
refrigeration	automatic temperature
evaporation	control system

DIRECTIONS: The following questions are similar to those used on mechanic certification tests. On a separate sheet of paper, write the letter of the correct choice.

1. A heating system includes all of the following parts EXCEPT
A. a grille opening below the windshield.
B. a distributor plexus.
C. a door.
D. a ventilation system.

2. Mechanic A says that a refrigerant is a liquid that boils at temperatures lower than the freezing temperature of water.
   Mechanic B says that cold refrigerant humidifies the air.
   Who is correct?
A. A only   B. B only   C. Both A and B   D. Neither A nor B

3. Which of the following is conditioned by refrigerant?
A. Compressor
B. Receiver/dryer
C. Passenger compartment air
D. Accumulator

4. Which of the following statements is correct?
   I. An evaporator is like a radiator.
   II. A blower pushes warm air over the evaporator.
A. I only   B. II only   C. Both I and II   D. Neither I nor II

5. All of the following statements are true EXCEPT
A. Air conditioner controls can be manual or power-assisted.
B. Heaters and air conditioners use the same plenum chambers.
C. A vacuum switch shuts off air conditioner power during peak engine loads.
D. A microprocessor control can keep the temperature level the same, regardless of weather.

SUPPLEMENTAL ACTIVITIES

1. Explain how a blower moves air through a heater assembly and into the distribution plenums.
2. Locate heater hoses and explain their function.
3. Locate a heater control valve.
4. Describe how doors to plenum chambers distribute heat and air conditioning to different parts of an automobile.
5. Explain evaporation and its role in cooling.
6. Explain the meaning of humidity.
7. Locate and identify the parts of an air conditioning system on an automobile selected by your instructor.
8. Explain how an air conditioner operates, beginning with the compressor.
9. Describe the process that takes place as each air conditioning control is moved.

70 HEATING AND AIR CONDITIONING SERVICE

UNIT PREVIEW

Heaters and air conditioners share some common systems, such as plenum chambers, doors, and controls. For the most part, however, service procedures for both vary considerably. Heating system service involves working with the engine coolant system. Air conditioning system service requires knowledge and safety awareness of the refrigerant used for cooling. This unit discusses how heating and air conditioning systems are maintained, diagnosed, and serviced.

LEARNING OBJECTIVES

When you have completed your assignments and exercises in this unit, you should be able to:
☐ Diagnose a heating system problem.
☐ Remove a heater assembly.
☐ Diagnose an air conditioning system problem.
☐ Check refrigerant level.
☐ Check for leaks with a leak detector.
☐ Recharge a system with refrigerant.

SAFETY PRECAUTIONS

A hoist or jack may have to be used to raise the automobile. If a jack is used, support the automobile properly with safety stands.

You will be working with hot coolant and around hot parts of the automobile. Use extreme care to avoid serious burns.

The engine will be running during some tests. Be aware of moving parts, such as the cooling fan, pulleys, and belts. Make sure your hands and loose clothing will not become caught.

Electrical parts, such as a blower, can begin operating without warning. When servicing electrical parts, always disconnect the battery.

The refrigerant used in air conditioning systems is called R-12. It is transparent and colorless in both liquid and vapor states. It will evaporate at normal temperatures and pressures, causing very low temperatures, in the vicinity of -21 degrees F [-29.5 C].

Any skin contact will cause instant frostbite. The R-12 vapor is heavier than air, nonflammable, and nonexplosive. It is nonpoisonous, except when it is in direct contact with an open flame. It is noncorrosive, except when combined with water.

Though R-12 is not poisonous, contact with an open flame can cause the vapor to become very poisonous. Do not discharge large quantities of refrigerant in an area that has an open flame or that is not well ventilated. Poisonous gas is produced when using a flame-type leak detector, so avoid inhaling fumes from a leak detector.

Always wear safety glasses when servicing a refrigeration system. Keep sterile mineral oil and a weak boric acid solution handy when working with refrigerant. Should any liquid refrigerant get into the eyes, use a few drops of mineral oil to wash them out. Then, wash the eyes with the boric acid solution. Call a doctor immediately, even though irritation may have ceased after the first-aid treatment.

Refrigerant evaporates so quickly that it will freeze anything it contacts. Extreme care must be taken to prevent liquid refrigerant from contacting skin and eyes. Special safety gloves are recommended when working on parts that may have come in contact with refrigerant.

Good ventilation is vital. Always discharge refrigerant into a service bay exhaust system or outside the building. Large quantities of refrigerant vapor can displace air and cause suffocation.

Do not heat a refrigerant container or store it in a hot portion of the building. Temperatures above a recommended safety level can increase refrigerant pressure and cause containers to explode. Do not weld or steam clean on or near system parts or refrigerant lines.

70.1 PREVENTIVE MAINTENANCE

Heating and air conditioning systems usually do not require periodic maintenance. A visual inspection, however, should be made whenever other parts of an automobile are being checked. Leaks or damage are the most frequent problems located during a visual inspection.

Check the heater and air conditioner hoses. There should be no leaks, frayed ends, cracks, or hardness when a hose is squeezed. Hose clamps should be tight and in good condition. If any of these problems are found, replace the hose or clamp. Further hose maintenance procedures are discussed in Unit 18.

Check the air inlet and heater assemblies for damage. Repair or replace any damaged parts. A hole in any duct can allow road debris to enter the heating system and cause further damage.

Control cables are routed to control valves through the firewall. Check these cables for wear, damage, or missing parts. Replace if necessary.

70.2 DIAGNOSING HEATER PROBLEMS

Heater operation often can be checked with a thermometer. Place a thermometer at an outlet duct in the automobile and set the heater controls according to the manufacturer's recommendations. The proper service manual will list minimum temperature requirements for a heater that is operating properly (see Figure 70-1). If heating problems exist, first check the heating system for leaks and damage.

Insufficient Heat

Any number of conditions can cause insufficient heating. First, check the heater controls to make sure they are at the proper setting. If heater controls are operated electrically, check the proper fuse. Check blower operation. Check control cables and vacuum hoses for wear, damage, and proper connections.

Blockage is a common cause of insufficient heat. Check heater outlets for obstructions and check doors for binding. A heater hose may be kinked or clogged. Check the heater core for obstructions, damage, or leakage.

Ducting problems may exist. Check fresh air ducting and all heater assembly ducts and doors for damage and adjustment. If one duct operates and another does not, a door or control cable problem may be indicated.

Engine cooling problems also can cause insufficient heat. Check for low engine coolant and for a stuck or missing thermostat.

A bad electrical connection at the control switch is a common problem. A defective temperature sensor on thermostatically controlled heaters will cause insufficient heat.

Cold spots can be caused by missing or damaged insulation, seals, or other material. Check around the firewall and floor areas.

Too Much Heat

When the heater puts out too much heat, the problem usually involves a control cable, a door, or a thermostatic switch.

Temperature Reference Chart			
Ambient Temperature		Minimum Heater Outlet Duct Temperature	
Celsius	Fahrenheit	Celsius	Fahrenheit
15.5°	60°	62.2°	144°
21.1°	70°	63.8°	147°
26.6°	80°	65.5°	150°
32.2°	90°	67.2°	153°

Figure 70-1. Temperature reference chart.
CHRYSLER CORPORATION

Blower Problems

If a blower is not operating properly, check the fuse circuit and other electrical connections. Check the relay switches and all thermostatically controlled switches. Check for electrical current at the blower motor when the switch is on. If current is present and the blower does not operate, replace the motor. If no current is present, check the switch, wiring, or heat resistors. Follow the procedures in the proper service manual.

70.3 HEATER SERVICE

Heater service may only require replacing a hose, or it could involve removing a heater assembly and dashboard. In many cases, cable and vacuum hose replacement can be completed without removing the heater assembly. Heater core leaks usually show up as a wet carpet on the passenger side. Should the heater core be leaking and need replacement, the heater assembly and, perhaps, the dashboard will have to be removed. Examples of heater assembly and dashboard removal are shown in Figures 70-2 and 70-3. Procedures can vary considerably between manufacturers. Always check the proper service manual. Heater hose, heater valve, and cooling system service is discussed in Unit 18.

Heater core and blower removal usually requires the removal and disassembly of the heater assembly. Engine coolant must be drained, and heater hoses and control cables must be disconnected from the heater assembly housing. Follow the manufacturer's disassembly and assembly procedures. After the heater assembly is removed and disassembled, inspect all parts for wear and damage.

A heater control assembly usually is removed from the dashboard to check connections and operation. See Figure 70-4. Doors, mechanical cables, and

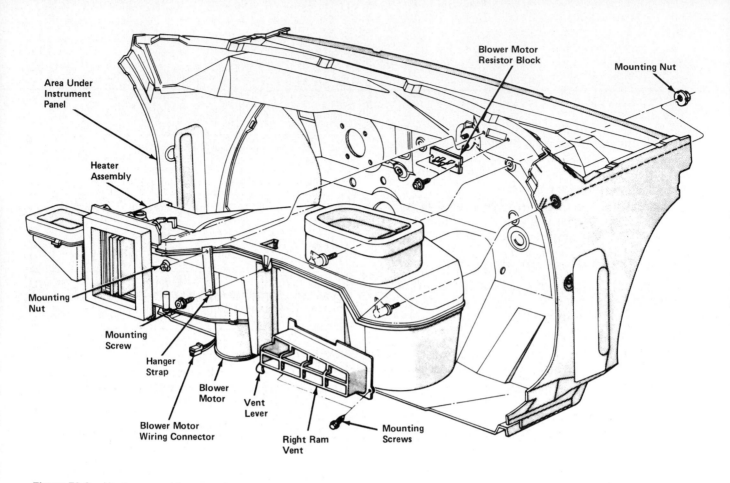

Figure 70-2. Heater assembly removal. CHRYSLER CORPORATION

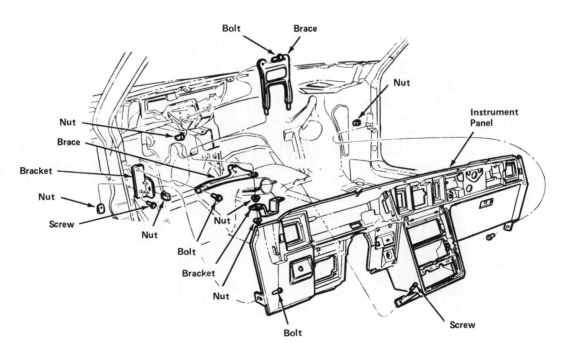

Figure 70-3. Dashboard removal. FORD MOTOR COMPANY

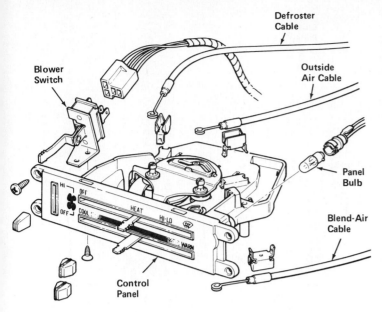

Figure 70-4. Parts of the control panel.
AMERICAN MOTORS CORPORATION

electrical switches can be checked at the heater housing or under the dashboard.

70.4 DIAGNOSING AIR CONDITIONER PROBLEMS

Air conditioner problems usually are noticed as lack of cooling, noises, and odors. When working around air conditioning systems, always wear safety glasses. Do not disconnect air conditioning lines without proper instruction or without instructor permission.

Insufficient Cooling

Insufficient cooling often is caused by low refrigerant level. Restricted evaporator and condenser cores can also be at fault. Check the receiver/dryer for proper operation. Hoses or tubes may be kinked or blocked.

No Cooling

An air conditioner that does not cool often has an electrical problem. Check the fuses, switches, and wiring systems. Other causes may be a bad clutch on the compressor or leaking vacuum lines that lead to the plenum doors. Check the outside of the condenser for blockage from debris. If the refrigerant system is empty, check for leaks.

If you notice oily spots around the compressor pulley, by connections, or by the condenser, a refrigerant leak is indicated. Repair the leak as outlined in the service manual.

No Air

If cold air is felt at the air conditioner outlets, but no air is blowing, check the fuses. Check the on/off switch and wires leading to the blower. No airflow also can mean that there are leaking vacuum lines to the plenum doors.

Noises

Most air conditioner noises come from a drive belt or the compressor. A squealing sound usually indicates a loose or badly worn drive belt. A rumbling sound indicates a compressor problem. Grinding or clashing noises indicate that compressor shaft or pulley bearings may be defective.

Odors

A musty smell occurs when material collects in the bottom of the evaporator housing. An evaporator drain plug also may be clogged.

70.5 AIR CONDITIONER MAINTENANCE

Periodic maintenance usually is not required for air conditioning systems. However, parts of an air conditioner should be inspected at least once a year to check for proper operation.

Condenser Cleaning

Check the outside of the radiator and condenser cores for blockage caused by dirt, leaves, insects, or other foreign material. To clean out debris, use a hose and water pressure, directing the water from the inside to the outside. Be sure the core is cleaned thoroughly. Use a brush, if necessary, but be careful not to damage the delicate tubes and fins on the condenser and radiator.

Drive Belt Inspection

The drive belt operates the compressor. It should be checked whenever you are working under the hood of an automobile. Check the belt for tension, cracks, or glazing.

Tubing and Hose Inspection

Check all hose connections and tubing for kinks, cracks, frayed ends, and loose or damaged connectors. Oil deposits on the hoses or tubing indicate a refrigerant leak.

SAFETY CAUTION: **Never disconnect an air conditioning hose or tube. If pressure is released, it will evaporate instantly and produce tremendously low temperatures. This can freeze your skin severely.**

Magnetic Clutch Inspection

A *magnetic clutch* connects and disconnects a compressor. A magnetic clutch is connected to the drive pulley and to the compressor. One part of the clutch rotates with the drive pulley whenever the engine is running. The clutch does not turn the compressor until the air conditioner control switch is turned on. When the switch is on, the clutch is connected magnetically to the compressor. The pulley, clutch, and compressor then rotate together. The magnetic connection is disengaged when the switch is off. A compressor and clutch assembly is shown in Figure 70-5.

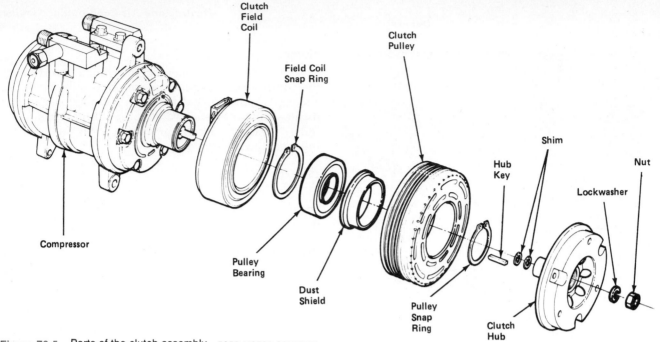

Figure 70-5. Parts of the clutch assembly. FORD MOTOR COMPANY

To check the operation of a magnetic clutch, raise the hood and have a helper start the engine and turn on the air conditioner. Watch the front of the clutch for operation. Listen for noises.

Refrigerant Level Inspection

Manufacturers often provide a *sight glass* to check refrigerant level. A sight glass is a glass-covered hole. It may be located either on the receiver/dryer or between the receiver/dryer and the expansion valve. A sight glass is shown in Figure 70-6.

To check refrigerant, the engine must be running and the air conditioning turned on. Be sure the automobile is in a well-ventilated area, or connect an exhaust gas ventilation system. Check the sight glass. If you see oil-streaking, bubbles, or foam, the refrigerant is low. A clear sight glass indicates that the system is either completely full or empty.

SAFETY CAUTION: You will be working near the engine fan and rotating belts. Keep hands, clothing, and tools away from those moving parts or serious injury can result. Be careful when touching any parts, because the engine will be hot and can cause serious burns.

If an air conditioning system has no sight glass, the system can be checked with gauges. To connect the gauges, follow the manufacturer's directions carefully. A gauge assembly that is connected to check operating pressures is shown in Figure 70-7. Gauge assemblies are discussed in Topic 70.6.

70.6 AIR CONDITIONER SERVICE

Servicing an air conditioner involves working with refrigerant under pressure. Refrigerant can be dangerous when not handled properly. Follow all safety

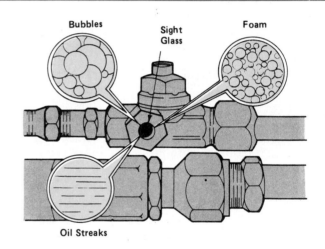

Figure 70-6. Sight glass diagnosis. FORD MOTOR COMPANY

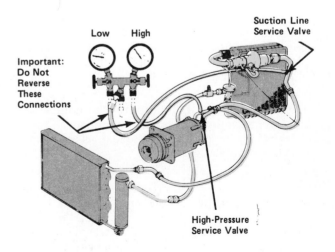

Figure 70-7. Checking refrigerant level. FORD MOTOR COMPANY

precautions carefully. Always heed the manufacturer's service recommendations.

Checking for Leaks

A system that is low on refrigerant usually has a leak. Most leaks can be located where two parts are connected. Possible leak locations are shown in Figure 70-8. The most common source of leakage is the compressor shaft seal.

Air conditioner leaks are checked with a *leak detector tool,* shown in Figure 70-9. A leak detector tool is a butane gas-burning torch used to locate a leak in the refrigeration system. Refrigerant is drawn into a hose, called a *sniffer,* that is connected to the tool. The sniffer is held near an air conditioner connection. A flame inside the tool will change color when a leak is detected.

SAFETY CAUTION: Do not use the lighted detector in any place where explosive gases, dust, or vapors may be present. Do not breathe the fumes that are produced by the burning refrigerant. Large concentrations of refrigerant that may enter the live flame can be toxic. Always use the detector in a well-ventilated area.

Pressure Testing

A pressure test is conducted with a *manifold gauge assembly.* A manifold gauge assembly determines high and low pressures and correct refrigerant charge. It also helps in the diagnosis of system problems. High and low pressures are compared to determine proper system operation. A manifold gauge assembly is shown in Figure 70-10.

When connecting a manifold gauge assembly, always follow the manufacturer's recommendations. Pressure readings on the gauge assembly should be compared with specifications in the proper service manual.

Refrigerant Recharging

To replace parts or clean an air conditioning system, the system must be discharged, evacuated, and charged. The refrigerant is under pressure, so it must be handled carefully. Always follow the manufacturer's recommendations.

SAFETY CAUTION: Always wear safety glasses. Never open the high-pressure valve on the gauge set when the engine is running. It could explode the refrigerant container.

Discharging

Refrigerant is discharged to eliminate pressure in an air conditioning system. Discharging must be done in a well ventilated area.

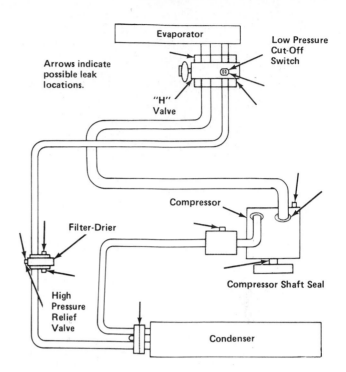

Figure 70-8. Possible refrigerant leak locations.
CHRYSLER CORPORATION

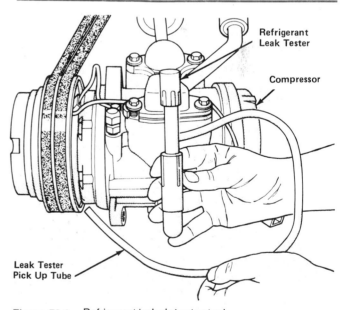

Figure 70-9. Refrigerant leak detector tool.
CHRYSLER CORPORATION

A gauge set is hooked up (see Figure 70-11). Be sure that the gauge set valves are closed before attaching hoses to the refrigerant system. Place the discharge hose in a collector can. Open the discharge and suction valves to release the refrigerant into the oil collector can. The refrigerant must be discharged slowly. If the refrigerant vapor is discharged too rapidly, it will carry refrigerant oil out with it. The oil

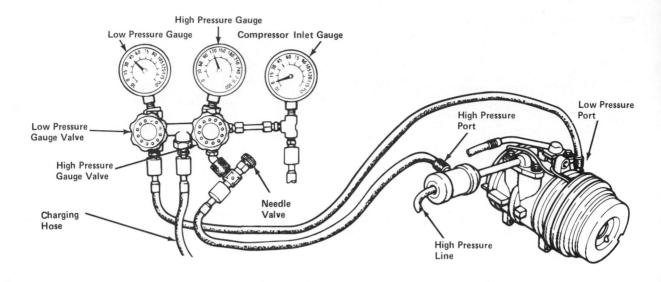

Figure 70-10. Manifold gauge assembly. CHRYSLER CORPORATION

must stay in the system. If some oil does come out, measure it and replace with new oil.

NOTE: When the system has been completely discharged, measure the amount of oil collected in the can. The same amount of oil should be added to the refrigerant system before it is recharged. Add new oil. Discard the used oil. It is important to have the correct amount of oil in the refrigerant system. Too little oil can cause a compressor failure. Too much oil can increase discharged-air temperature.

If any air conditioner parts are removed, immediately cap or plug any openings to keep out moisture and dirt. Replace or repair any parts as needed. Before the system is *evacuated,* or purged of air and moisture, add the proper amount of refrigerant lubricant.

Evacuating

Whenever an air conditioning system has been opened, it must be evacuated. A vacuum pump is used to evacuate, or remove air and moisture, from an air conditioner.

To evacuate a system, install a gauge set according to the manufacturer's directions (see Figure 70-12). Be sure the gauge set valves are closed before attaching hoses to the refrigerant system. If the gauge set indicates pressure, discharge the system.

Open the gauge set valves and operate the vacuum pump until the suction gauge registers the recommended reading. Continue to operate the vacuum pump for at least 15 minutes, or for as long the manufacturer recommends. Then, close the manifold valves. Turn off the vacuum pump. Watch the evaporator

suction gauge for several minutes. The vacuum level should remain constant. If it does not, the system has a leak. Locate and repair all leaks.

Charging

The system must be evacuated before charging. Use only the recommended refrigerant, which usually is R-12. This refrigerant is available in small cans or in bulk tanks. Before handling R-12, review the safety precautions discussed at the beginning of this unit.

Keep refrigerant tank or cans upright. If a refrigerant container is on its side or upside down, liquid refrigerant will enter the system and damage the compressor.

To charge a system with small cans, a special dispensing manifold is used. Figure 70-13 shows how a gauge set and refrigerant cans are connected for charging.

SAFETY CAUTION: Carefully follow the manufacturer's recommendations on the refrigerant can. Never use cans to charge into the high-pressure side of a system or into a system that is at high temperature. High pressures can cause the cans to explode.

Refrigerant manifold valves should be kept capped when not in use.

Once the gauge set and refrigerant cans are connected properly, turn the manifold valves to puncture the cans. Close the manifold valves. Purge air from the charging line by loosening the charging hose. Release refrigerant into the system, according to the manufacturer's instructions.

When refrigerant no longer flows into the system, start the engine. Turn on the air conditioner

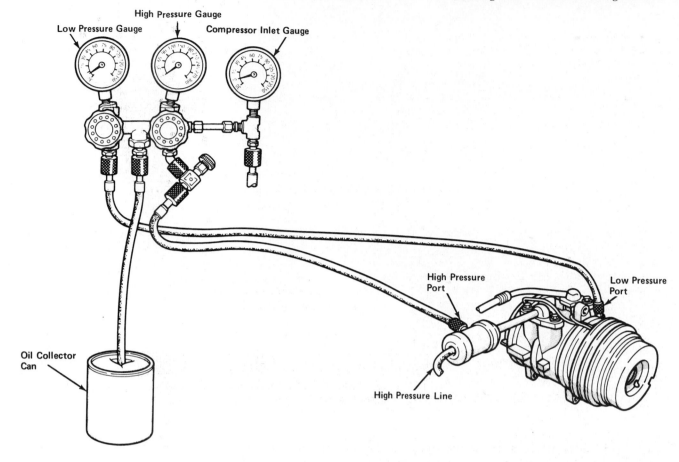

Figure 70-11. Manifold gauge set for discharging refrigerant. CHRYSLER CORPORATION

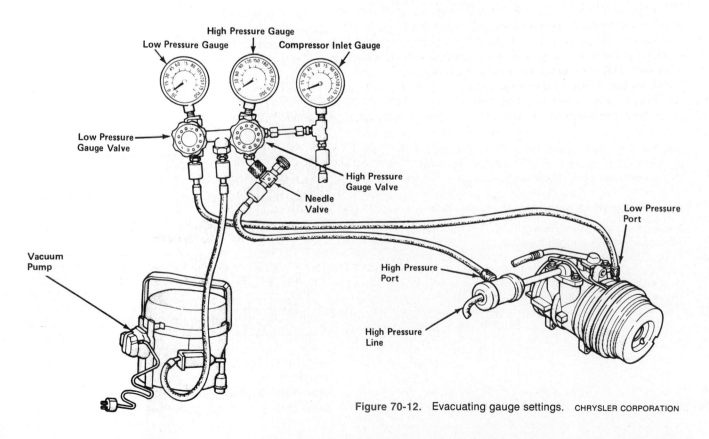

Figure 70-12. Evacuating gauge settings. CHRYSLER CORPORATION

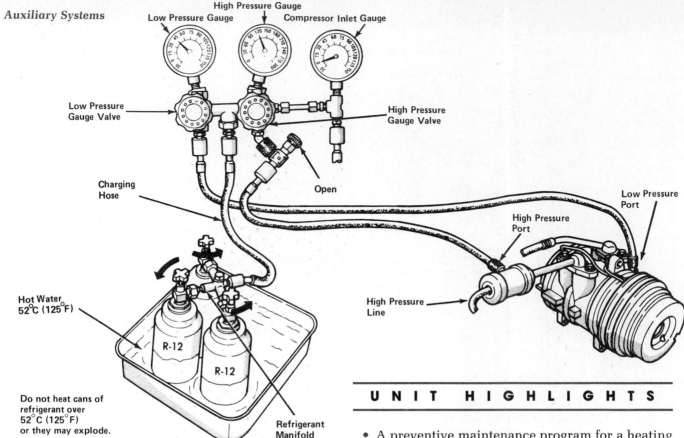

Figure 70-13. Charging hookup for manifold gauge set.
CHRYSLER CORPORATION

and set the blower. Continue charging according to instructions.

Use care when removing the charging assembly from the air conditioner. Any refrigerant on the fittings can freeze your hands. Place a shop towel on fittings when removing them, to protect your hands.

To add refrigerant, a system does not have to be discharged and evacuated. Manufacturers furnish directions on correcting low refrigerant level. Consult the proper service manual.

Replacing Air Conditioner Parts

Replace all worn or damaged parts according to the manufacturer's recommendations. Parts such as the cores, compressor, clutch, and blower usually are replaced with new or rebuilt ones. Parts replacement should be done only after a system has been discharged.

UNIT HIGHLIGHTS

- A preventive maintenance program for a heating system involves making a visual inspection.
- Heater diagnosis is based on the amount of heat generated by the system.
- Engine coolant often must be drained when servicing a heating system.
- The dashboard and heater assembly often must be removed when servicing a heater core and blower.
- Periodic maintenance of an air conditioning system requires an inspection and cleaning of parts.
- Refrigerant level sometimes can be checked through a sight glass.
- Checking the air conditioner for leaks is done with a leak detector.
- Pressure testing determines air conditioner pressures and the level of charge.
- Discharging a system means removing refrigerant and pressure from the air conditioner.
- Evacuating removes air and moisture from a system.
- Adding refrigerant to an air conditioner is called charging the system.

TERMS

magnetic clutch	manifold gauge
sight glass	assembly
leak detector tool	evacuate
sniffer	

R E V I E W   Q U E S T I O N S

DIRECTIONS: The following questions are similar to those used on mechanic certification tests. On a separate sheet of paper, write the letter of the correct choice.

1. Which of the following statements is correct?
   I. Heater operation can be checked with a thermometer.
   II. Too much heat can be caused by a blocked heater hose.
   A. I only   B. II only   C. Both I and II   D. Neither I nor II

2. All of the following statements are true EXCEPT
   A. A dashboard may be removed when servicing a heater assembly.
   B. The battery should be disconnected before a blower is serviced.
   C. Engine coolant should be drained before a heater assembly is disconnected.
   D. Electrical switches are disconnected at each vacuum hose.

3. Mechanic A says that a magnetic clutch is operated by a drive pulley.
   Mechanic B says that a magnetic clutch is operated by the on/off switch.
   Who is correct?
   A. A only   B. B only   C. Both A and B   D. Neither A nor B

4. A sight glass can indicate that
   A. the system is colder than normal.
   B. refrigerant is low.
   C. a leak is occurring in the condenser.
   D. the control lever is on.

5. Which of the following statements is correct?
   I. Discharging a system means evacuating air and moisture.
   II. Charging is done by connecting a refrigerant tank or can to a manifold gauge assembly.
   A. I only   B. II only   C. Both I and II   D. Neither I nor II

S U P P L E M E N T A L   A C T I V I T I E S

1. Explain how to use refrigerant safely.
2. Make a visual inspection of a heating system.
3. Diagnose a heater problem presented by your instructor.
4. Disassemble a heater assembly.
5. Diagnose an air conditioner problem presented by your instructor.
6. Clean a condenser.
7. Check refrigerant level.
8. Check for leaks in the air conditioning system.
9. Pressure test an air conditioning system.
10. Discharge a refrigeration system.
11. Evacuate a refrigeration system.
12. Recharge a refrigeration system.

71 SAFETY SYSTEMS

UNIT PREVIEW

Many parts of an automobile have safety systems built in. This means safety for the automobile and its parts in addition to safety for its occupants. Safety systems often affect the operation of an automobile. The major safety systems, and their operations, are discussed in this unit.

LEARNING OBJECTIVES

When you have completed your assignments and exercises in this unit, you should be able to:

☐ Explain the purpose of a safety device.

☐ Identify the safety devices in a brake system.

☐ Explain how lights and indicators act as safety devices.

☐ Describe how an active restraint is connected.

☐ Describe how an air bag is activated.

☐ Explain how an automobile body acts as a safety system.

71.1 SAFETY DEVICES

Certain safety devices have been part of the automobile since the first car was sold almost 100 years ago. Brakes, lights, and switches were among the first safety devices used. In the past two decades, however, government regulations and public demand have increased the number of safety devices now in use.

A safety device is a part or system that helps to avoid and prevent accidents, damage, or injury. For example, the brakes help a driver control an automobile. Indicators, such as dashboard gauges and warning lights, alert a driver that something is wrong and must be serviced or repaired. See Figure 71-1. Turn signals are warning devices that alert other drivers. Seat belts help prevent injury during an accident. A rollover switch prevents greater damage and injury after an accident.

As you can see, the safety functions of individual devices can vary. The following discussions describe safety devices built into modern automobiles.

Brakes

The brake system is, perhaps, the most important system for the safe operation of an automobile. Without it, an automobile would not be able to slow

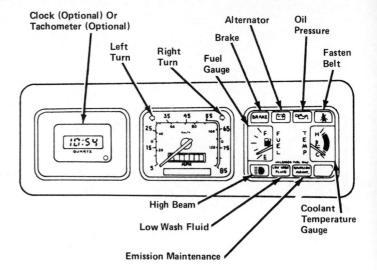

Figure 71-1. Safety indicators and gauges on dashboard. AMERICAN MOTORS CORPORATION

or stop. Brakes are so important, in fact, that a number of additional safety and warning devices are used in the system.

A dual braking system ensures continued operation of the brakes, even if one system fails. Two reservoirs in the master cylinder direct brake fluid to two separate brake line systems. If one system should fail, the automobile still can be stopped. Brake systems are discussed in detail in Unit 67.

A warning light on the dashboard alerts the driver if a brake hydraulic failure occurs. The switch for this light is located in the hydraulic pressure system. If pressure in the two systems is considerably different, the warning light will go on. The light will remain on until the problem has been corrected and, in many cases, until the switch has been released by a mechanic.

Numerous valves in the braking system control brake fluid flow. Some automobiles even use an anti-skid device to prevent wheel lockup and stop the automobile quicker and straighter.

Electrical Protection

Electricity is distributed throughout an automobile to provide power for many parts and accessories. Electricity, however, can present a fire hazard if a failure occurs. Safety devices—in the form of fuses, fusible links, and circuit breakers—are placed in all electrical

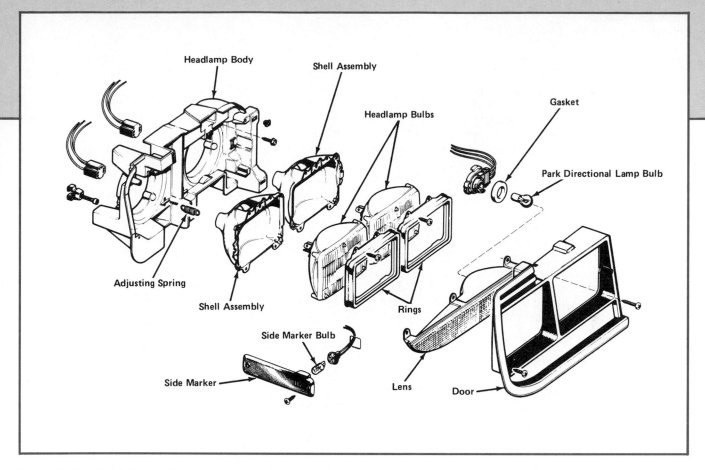

Figure 71-2. Headlight assembly. AMERICAN MOTORS CORPORATION

circuits. Without an electrical safety device, excess current would cause a wiring system to overload and catch fire. To prevent an overload, these safety devices are designed to stop current flow. Fuses, fusible links, and circuit breakers are discussed in Units 27 and 36.

Lights and Indicators

Lights originally were used only as a method for seeing the road after dark. Today, lights still have the same purpose, but a number of safety improvements and lighting systems have been added. For example, lights are used to signal a driver's intentions to turn or stop. Lights also are used as indicators to pinpoint numerous safety, mechanical, and electrical conditions. Lights and indicators are discussed in Unit 36.

Headlights, stop lights, turn signals. Headlights allow a driver to see the road ahead. A dimmer switch allows a driver to adjust the beams according to traffic conditions. Headlights also are angled away from oncoming traffic to help prevent temporary blindness. Some automobiles even have delay switches that turn off the headlights automatically when the engine is not running. This prevents accidental battery drain. A headlight assembly is shown in Figure 71-2.

A headlight switch also turns on taillights and marker lights so that the automobile can be seen more clearly at night. Indicator lights inside the automobile may be used to indicate light operation and condition.

Stop lights are connected so that movement of the brake pedal illuminates a bright bulb in the taillights or rear window. Turn signals are another warning device to alert other drivers. Turn signals are mounted so that they can be seen from the front, rear, or side of an automobile.

Emergency flashers. An emergency flasher flashes parking lights and taillights to warn others that the automobile is stopped and not moving. A flasher turns lights on and off much as a turn signal does.

Indicators. Indicators include dashboard lights that go on to catch a driver's attention. An indicator may signal that fuel is low or that a door is ajar. An indicator also may warn of a brake failure or a dead engine. Indicators even can relate a diagnostic problem to a mechanic. Indicators are important safety devices because they can warn of problems before damage occurs.

Not all indicators are operated electrically. Many parts have wear indicators that indicate the part should be replaced. These wear indicators are early warning signs that a damaging failure may result. They may be visual indicators (ball joints) or audio indicators (disc brake shoes).

Switches

Several safety, anti-theft, and convenience switches can be located close to a driver. A neutral-start switch, for example, prevents an automobile from being started in gear. A locking steering wheel switch is an anti-theft device. It prevents the steering wheel from being turned when the ignition key is removed. A seat-adjustment switch can affect safety as well as driver convenience. The adjustment allows a driver to be positioned for a better view of surroundings.

Some switches operate automatically, such as a rollover switch. If an automobile rolls over or is involved in another type of accident, fuel to the engine is shut off. This helps to prevent the possibility of fire. A safety switch also may shut off the engine when oil pressure becomes too low. It is important to be aware of how switches work and where they are located. Low oil pressure, of course, can cause engine damage.

Buzzers

To get a driver's attention immediately, annoying-sounding buzzers are used as safety warnings. If a key is left in the ignition switch and the driver's door is opened, a buzzer will sound. Unbuckled seat belts and headlights that are left on can activate buzzers. Some manufacturers use chimes or voices (either recorded or simulated) to make the warning less abrupt.

Windshield Wipers

Rain, snow, ice, and mist on the windows obstruct a driver's vision. A number of devices are used to clear a windshield, or other windows, when vision becomes obscured.

A windshield wiper is used to remove outside moisture and dirt from a windshield (see Figure 71-3). A windshield washer sprays a cleaning solvent on the windshield, or rear window, to help a wiper remove dirt. Rear-window wipers and washers are used on some automobiles.

A fogged or steamed window on the inside of an automobile can be cleared with a defroster. A defroster is part of a heating system. Defroster ducts are directed toward a windshield, and sometimes toward rear and side windows. Some automobiles use an electric defogger at the rear window. An electric defogger heats wires that are imbedded in, or attached to, the glass to melt snow or ice as well as to defog the window.

Collapsible Steering Column

A steering column and steering shaft can be pushed into the passenger compartment during a collision. To prevent this, steering columns are made to collapse, or bend, during impact. Special connections and joints are used to keep the steering wheel from striking and seriously injuring the driver. Collapsible steering columns are discussed in Topic 63.4.

Tires and Wheels

A tire can be made to be puncture-resistant or self-sealing. If a tire loses air and becomes flat suddenly, an automobile can become difficult to control, and an accident may result. Steel belts and a special sealant can be built into tires to help prevent flats. Some tires also are designed with strong sidewalls to reduce tire collapse and give the driver more control should the tire lose its air pressure.

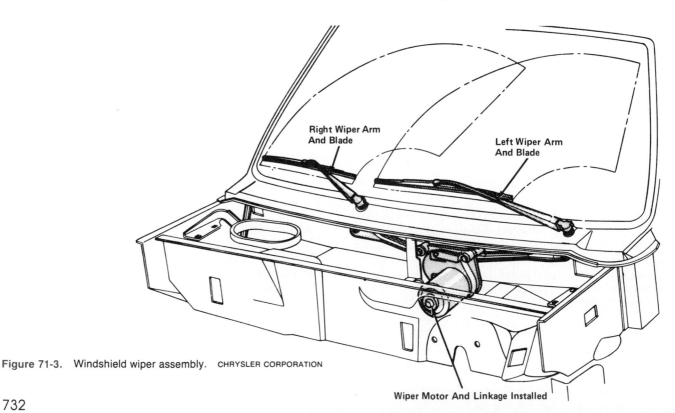

Right Wiper Arm And Blade

Left Wiper Arm And Blade

Wiper Motor And Linkage Installed

Figure 71-3. Windshield wiper assembly. CHRYSLER CORPORATION

A collapsed tire also can separate from a wheel. To prevent this, wheels are built with a safety rim. Wheels and tires are discussed in Unit 65.

Emissions Controls

An automobile emits gases and particles that can pollute the air. As a health precaution, a number of emission controls are used. Emissions controls are discussed in Unit 41.

The burning of fuel, as well as the control of exhaust, is affected by engine design and exhaust system parts. Some parts even reduce the amount of evaporation from fuel. Emissions control devices are integral parts of an automobile and will affect operation if they are faulty or removed.

71.2 OCCUPANT PROTECTION

Protection of driver and passengers is an important part of automobile construction. Many protection systems must be designed into an automobile before it is built. Special restraint systems must have sturdy anchors. Even the car body itself is designed to collapse in a certain way during a bad collision, thus absorbing the shock. These are all important considerations for occupant protection.

Active Restraints

An *active restraint* is one that must be activated by an occupant. A manual seat and shoulder belt is an active restraint. The occupant must activate it, or buckle it up, before it will restrain bodily movements in an emergency.

Seat and shoulder belts are required for front and rear seat occupants. The *restraint anchor,* or attachment point, is connected securely to a strong, unyielding part of the body or frame. A belt must be anchored properly so it will not break loose in an accident. A seat belt assembly is shown in Figure 71-4.

A restraint system belt is made from webbed, synthetic material. On modern cars, a one-piece belt serves as both lap and shoulder restraint. A sliding tongue fixture is connected to a stationary buckle to fasten the harness. The buckle may be attached to the end of a short length of webbed material or may be part of a swiveling anchor assembly. Most buckles have an easy-operating button release to enable quick occupant exit following an accident.

The restraint belt usually is passed through a *retractor.* A retractor is a reel that rotates and locks in place when a belt is tightened (see Figure 71-5). A retractor will allow the belt to move out slowly, permitting normal upper body movement by occupants. However, when a sudden movement occurs, the retractor locks up, preventing belt movement.

A wire is attached to the buckle end of a belt assembly. The wire operates a warning light and a buzzer. These devices operate for several seconds after the ignition is turned on, or until the belt is buckled up.

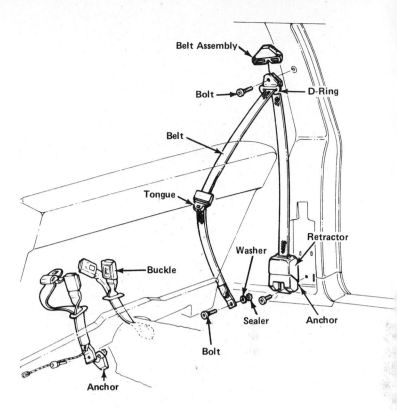

Figure 71-4. Safety belt assembly. FORD MOTOR COMPANY

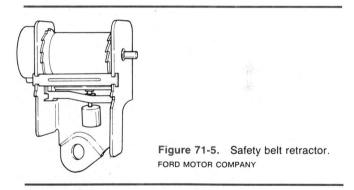

Figure 71-5. Safety belt retractor. FORD MOTOR COMPANY

Passive Restraints

A *passive restraint* is one that operates automatically. No action is required of the occupant to make it functional. Two types of passive restraints are automatic belts and air bags.

Automatic belts. An automatic seat and shoulder belt system usually is connected to an automatic retractor and to a door (see Figure 71-6). When a door is opened, the belt stretches out with the door. An occupant enters and sits in the seat. When the door is closed, the belt wraps around the occupant.

Air bags. An air bag system usually is used to protect only the driver, or the driver and front seat passengers. A driver's side air bag system is mounted in the steering wheel. When an air bag device is included for the front passenger side, it is mounted in the dashboard.

An air bag is called an *air cushion restraint system.* In a collision, a sensor activates a gas cartridge that

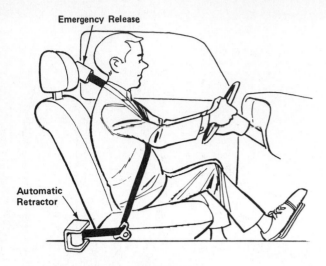

Figure 71-6. Passive restraint system.

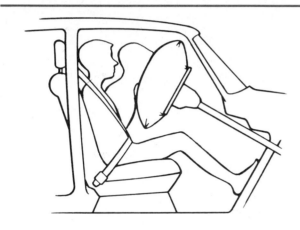

Figure 71-7. Air bag system.

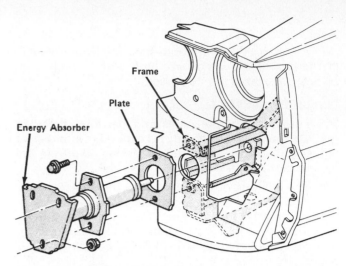

Figure 71-8. Energy-absorbing bumper. CHRYSLER CORPORATION

fills an air bag. The inflating air bag pushes out from the steering hub and provides a cushion for the occupant (see Figure 71-7).

Interior Design

An automobile interior has built-in protection. A dashboard is designed to "give" and is sometimes padded to cushion an occupant who might strike it. Safety knobs and latches on the doors are made to avoid accidental opening. Strong anchors hold the seats firmly in place during an impact. *Safety glass* is used in all windows. Safety glass crumbles into small pieces when broken. No sharp, jagged pieces of glass protrude to seriously cut an occupant.

Exterior Design

The outside of an automobile, too, is designed to protect occupants during an accident. Strong metal beams are built into doors and side panels to protect occupants in side collisions. Bumpers on modern cars have energy absorbers, which are much like shock absorbers. Energy absorbers allow bumper movement upon impact, with little damage up to a certain speed (see Figure 71-8).

Body panels are designed to collapse at specific rates in a collision. As it collapses, the automobile body absorbs much of the shock before it reaches the occupants.

UNIT HIGHLIGHTS

- A safety device helps to prevent accidents and to avoid or minimize damage and injury.
- A brake system is a safety device that has several other safety systems built into it.
- Lights enable an automobile to be seen in the dark, and they also indicate a driver's intentions.
- Indicators give signals that indicate a condition or problem with an automobile.
- Safety switches can be manual or automatic.
- An active restraint requires that it be connected by an occupant.
- A passive restraint is one that operates automatically.
- An air bag is activated by a sensor that acts on a gas cartridge.
- Automobile safety glass is designed to crumble into small pieces in a collision, avoiding injury to occupants.
- A bumper is made energy-absorbing by using a device similar to a shock absorber to cushion impact.

TERMS

active restraint
restraint anchor
retractor
passive restraint

air cushion restraint
system
safety glass

R E V I E W   Q U E S T I O N S

DIRECTIONS: The following questions are similar to those used on mechanic certification tests. On a separate sheet of paper, write the letter of the correct choice.

1. All of the following statements are true EXCEPT
A. A safety device helps to avoid or prevent an accident.
B. If one system fails, brakes still can stop an automobile.
C. Overloading the vehicle is prevented by an overloading switch.
D. An indicator light is designed to catch a driver's eye.

2. Which of the following statements is correct?
   I. A rollover switch operates only when an automobile is upside-down.
   II. A rollover switch turns off fuel flow.
A. I only   B. II only   C. Both I and II   D. Neither I nor II

3. A passenger restraint system
A. is passive if it does nothing.
B. is passive if it operates automatically.
C. uses a retractor to measure belt tension.
D. has a warning-light wire connected to the D-ring.

4. Mechanic A says that an air bag is an active restraint.
   Mechanic B says that an air bag comes out of the steering wheel.
   Who is correct?
A. A only   B. B only   C. Both A and B   D. Neither A nor B

5. All of the following are safety features designed into an automobile EXCEPT
A. stop lights.
B. breakaway anchors.
C. safety glass.
D. energy absorbers.

S U P P L E M E N T A L   A C T I V I T I E S

1. Locate the safety devices in a brake system.
2. Locate fuses, fusible links, and circuit breakers in an automobile selected by your instructor.
3. Locate and identify the safety indicators on an automobile selected by your instructor.
4. Describe and locate a rollover switch.
5. Locate the collapsible portion of a steering column on an automobile selected by your instructor.
6. Locate and identify all the parts of a seat and shoulder belt assembly on an automobile selected by your instructor.
7. Describe how passive restraint systems operate.
8. Name interior assemblies that are designed for safety.
9. Describe how an energy-absorbing bumper operates.

Allsystems in an automobile have safety devices that require service. Service procedures for many of these parts are discussed in earlier units. Occupant restraint systems also require service if they are to operate properly when they are needed. This unit discusses servicing of occupant restraints and energy-absorbing bumper cartridges.

LEARNING OBJECTIVES

When you have completed your assignments and exercises in this unit, you should be able to:
☐ Make a visual safety inspection.
☐ Inspect safety belt mounting areas for damage and distortion.
☐ Inspect an air bag assembly.
☐ Replace a safety belt assembly.
☐ Replace an energy-absorbing bumper cartridge.

SAFETY PRECAUTIONS

Working on occupant restraints requires working inside the automobile. Be careful not to cut or tear upholstery with tools. Always use the proper covers on seats to avoid soiling the cushions.

Air bags are inflated by gas cartridges. Use care when working around pressure-filled cartridges. Some manufacturers may recommend that the electrical system be disconnected or short-circuited while working on air bag systems. Follow air bag servicing procedures carefully. An air bag can be inflated accidentally and cause damage or injury.

Cartridges for energy-absorbing bumpers operate under extreme pressures. Do not drill or strike a cartridge. Serious injury can result.

72.1 PREVENTIVE MAINTENANCE

A visual inspection of all safety systems should be made routinely whenever an automobile is being serviced. Check tires, wheels, windshield wipers, and lights. Look for fluid leaks and damaged or worn parts. All safety systems should be in good condition so they will operate properly if needed.

72.2 DIAGNOSING OCCUPANT PROTECTION SYSTEM PROBLEMS

Seat and shoulder belt assemblies should be checked occasionally for wear and damage. Many belts have labels with the date of manufacture printed on them. This date is important, because belt material can lose its strength over a period of time. Check the proper service manual for the recommended life of a belt.

Check the belt for fraying and wear. A belt that has been bleached or dyed should be replaced. Bleaching and dying weakens the *webbing* of a belt. Webbing is the woven material in a belt.

Air bag systems should be checked according to the manufacturer's recommendations. Parts of an air bag system that should be inspected are shown in Figure 72-1.

Make sure that all warning indicators are operative. Check all anchors, retractors, and connections. Replace all parts that are damaged or that fail to function.

72.3 OCCUPANT PROTECTION SERVICE

Restraint systems should be replaced after they have been subjected to loading by occupants in a collision.

Belt Assembly Replacement

Before installing a new belt assembly, the attaching areas should be inspected for damage and distortion.

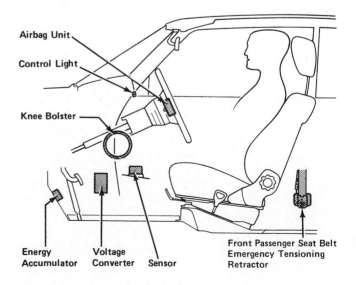

Figure 72-1. Parts of an air bag system.
MERCEDES-BENZ OF NORTH AMERICA

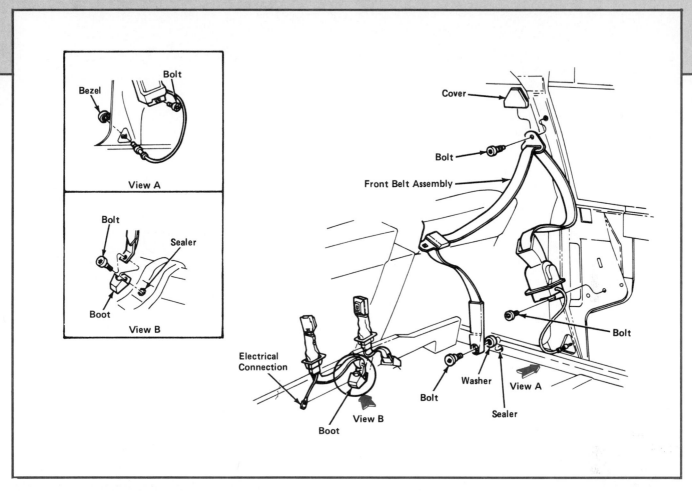

Figure 72-2. Front safety belt assembly. FORD MOTOR COMPANY

Sheet metal around the attaching points may have to be reworked back to its original shape.

To remove belt assemblies, refer to Figures 72-2 and 72-3. Disconnect the anchor assembly near the floor and the D-ring that is attached near the ceiling. At the rear seat, remove the seat cushion, then disconnect all assemblies. Replace all worn or damaged parts. Install the assemblies in the reverse order of removal. In doing this, be sure to torque all fasteners to specifications.

NOTE: Sometimes a new retractor will not operate properly after it has been bolted into a damaged or distorted mounting area. The new retractor could be warped and fail to function. Reshape the sheet metal at the mounting area and install another complete new belt assembly.

Air Bag Replacement

Air bags are replaced following a collision. However, some parts of an air bag system also can be replaced if a problem occurs. Methods for testing and replacing air bag parts vary considerably among manufacturers. Follow the proper procedures carefully.

SAFETY CAUTION: Air bag systems are operated by cartridges that are under pressure. Be sure that an air bag system is short-circuited properly so that it won't activate accidentally.

Energy-Absorbing Bumper Cartridge Replacement

A bumper usually is removed to replace a cartridge. On some automobiles, front bodywork also must be removed. Always refer to the proper service manual before replacing an energy-absorbing cartridge.

SAFETY CAUTION: Never drill into a cartridge to remove pressure. Cartridge pressures can be 10,000 psi [68,950 kPa]. A sudden release of pressure can cause serious injury.

To replace a cartridge, remove the push-on fasteners that hold a boot over the cartridge (see Figure 72-4). Support the bumper properly. Remove the nuts that hold the bumper to the energy absorber. Figure 72-5 shows parts of the bumper assembly. Lower the bumper to the floor. Replace the cartridge. Cartridge assembly parts are shown in Figure 72-6.

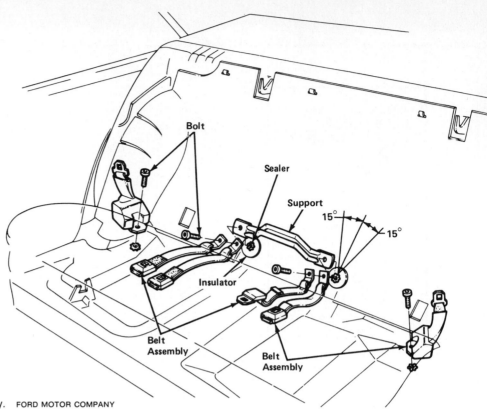

Figure 72-3. Rear safety belt assembly. FORD MOTOR COMPANY

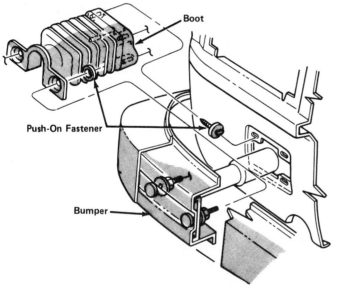

Figure 72-4. Bumper boot removal. CHRYSLER CORPORATION

U N I T   H I G H L I G H T S

- Labels on the webbing of a safety belt tell the date of manufacture.
- Belts should be replaced periodically.
- A safety belt assembly is replaced after a collision.
- Attaching points may have to be straightened when installing a safety belt assembly.
- Some parts of an air bag can be replaced without inflating the bag.
- Bodywork and bumpers may have to be removed to replace an energy-absorbing cartridge.

T E R M S

webbing

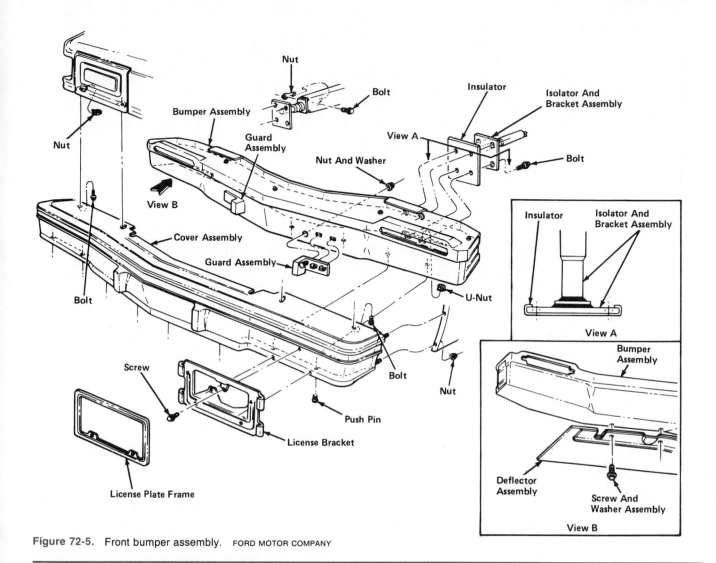

Figure 72-5. Front bumper assembly. FORD MOTOR COMPANY

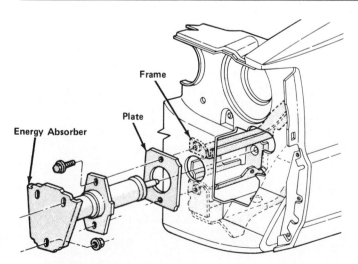

Figure 72-6. Bumper cartridge assembly.
CHRYSLER CORPORATION

R E V I E W   Q U E S T I O N S

DIRECTIONS: The following questions are similar to those used on mechanic certification tests. On a separate sheet of paper, write the letter of the correct choice.

1. Mechanic A says that labels on a belt assembly indicate when the belt was manufactured.
   Mechanic B says that belts will last the life of the automobile.
   Who is correct?
   A. A only   B. B only   C. Both A and B   D. Neither A nor B

2. All of the following statements are true EXCEPT
   A. A belt assembly that was used in a collision should be replaced.
   B. Sheet metal often must be reshaped when a new belt assembly is mounted.
   C. A new retractor that does not operate properly should be replaced.
   D. Anchor fasteners do not have to be torqued.

3. Which of the following statements is correct?
   I. An air bag assembly cannot be serviced.
   II. An air bag assembly uses high-pressure gas.
   A. I only   B. II only   C. Both I and II   D. Neither I nor II

4. To remove an energy-absorbing bumper cartridge, you must
   A. remove the bodywork.
   B. support the bumper.
   C. remove pressure from inside the cartridge.
   D. remove the wheel.

5. Mechanic A says that an energy-absorbing bumper must be supported before removal.
   Mechanic B says that the cartridge is bonded to the bumper.
   Who is correct?
   A. A only   B. B only   C. Both A and B   D. Neither A nor B

S U P P L E M E N T A L   A C T I V I T I E S

1. Inspect belt webbing for damage and wear.
2. Inspect an air bag assembly according to the manufacturer's recommendations.
3. Remove a safety belt assembly.
4. Check the warning light and buzzer system in a safety belt assembly.
5. Describe the procedure for replacing an energy-absorbing bumper cartridge on a vehicle selected by your instructor.

GLOSSARY

A

accelerator pump A small pump in the carburetor that supplies extra fuel when the throttle is depressed quickly for acceleration. It prevents a hesitation or flat spot when the fuel discharge changes from the idle circuit to the main metering circuit.

accumulator A shock absorber for apply devices in an automatic transmission; also, in an air conditioning system, a tank that holds and prevents liquid refrigerant from returning to the compressor. In some cases, the accumulator contains a desiccant, which removes moisture from the refrigerant.

acid fog Fog containing sulfuric, nitric, and other acids that are harmful to living things.

acid rain Rain containing sulfuric, nitric, and other acids that are harmful to living things.

activated charcoal A highly porous substance that can store large amounts of vapors.

active restraint A manual seat and shoulder belt assembly that must be activated by an occupant.

actuator A device that responds to a signal by producing an action, such as moving a mechanical device.

adhesive A glue to hold together two objects.

adjustable open-end wrench An open-end wrench with jaws that can be loosened or tightened to fit different sizes.

adjustable steering column Steering column that contains a mechanism to allow the steering wheel to be tilted or telescoped.

adjusting sleeve Part of a tie rod that is used during wheel alignment for an adjustment of tie rod length (toe).

advance To make ignition spark occur sooner.

advance timing light A timing light that allows a mechanic to determine ignition advance by reading a number scale.

aeration The presence or addition of air bubbles to a liquid.

after TDC (ATDC) A piston position after top dead center, specified in degrees of crankshaft rotation.

air bleed An orifice that controls the flow of air mixing with fuel.

air-bleed jet A jet through which air can be added progressively to a fuel flow to prevent overenrichment.

air chisel Air-powered hammering tool for removing bodywork and exhaust system parts.

air conditioner An automotive air conditioning system.

air cooled An engine cooling system that operates with air.

air cushion restraint system An air bag.

air drill A spark-resistant drill that operates on compressed air.

air filter A device to trap and hold airborne contaminants in an intake air charge.

air-hold adapter A hollow metal fitting of the same size as a spark plug; used to introduce compressed air into a cylinder.

air horn The top section (of three main sections) of the carburetor, through which air enters the barrel(s). Provides a base for the air cleaner housing.

air impact wrench A socket wrench powered by compressed air.

air injection The introduction of fresh air into an exhaust manifold for additional burning or to provide oxygen to a catalytic converter.

air inlet assembly The portion of a heating system that draws in outside air and forces it through the heating system with a blower.

air nozzle A device that controls and directs compressed air coming out of a line.

air pressure test Applying air pressure to an automatic transmission case to check operation of parts.

air ratchet An air-powered wrench similar to an air impact wrench but used for lighter parts.

air resistance Resistance to the motion of a body through the air.

air suspension A suspension that uses four air bags instead of conventional springs.

align boring The process of boring crankshaft bearing housings in a straight line.

Allen head screw A special screw head design on machine screws.

alloy A mixture of metallic elements with other metallic or nonmetallic elements. Usually produced by melting the elements and allowing them to fuse together.

alternator An electrical generator that produces alternating electrical current (AC) when turned by engine power. The AC is *rectified*, or changed, to direct current (DC) for vehicle systems and the battery.

ammeter An electrical measuring device used to measure current flow.

ampere A measurement of electrical current, equivalent to a given number of electrons (6,280,000,000,000,000,000,000) passing a point in one second.

analog Information in a form similar, or analogous, to the condition being measured. A typical dashboard gauge with a moving needle is an analog instrument.

anchor pin A pin that prevents brake shoe rotation during braking.

aneroid bellows A device that responds to atmospheric pressure and can be used to move a metering needle within a jet to automatically compensate for altitude changes.

anti-friction bearing A ball or roller bearing.

anti-seize compound A greasy type compound that prevents fasteners from seizing on one another.

anti-skid braking system A series of sensing devices at each wheel that control braking action to prevent wheel lockup.

anti-wear additive An oil additive that coats bearings and other moving parts to help prevent wear.

anvil The stationary measuring surface of a micrometer.

apply device A part that holds or drives the planetary gear system in an automatic transmission.

arbor A shaft to which other parts may be attached.

arbor press A device that applies strong force to objects through a rack and pinion gear arrangement.

arc-joint pliers Slip-joint adjustable pliers that can be adjusted to many different positions.

armature The inner, rotating part of an electrical motor or generator. *Also see* reluctor.

aspect ratio The height of a tire, from bead to tread, expressed as a percentage of the tire's section width.

atom The smallest portion of a type of matter that retains its unique characteristics.

atomization The process of reducing fuel to tiny droplets during carburetion.

automatic level control An electronically controlled system that keeps the rear suspension at a proper level when a heavy load is added.

automatic temperature control A ventilation, heating, and air conditioning control system that uses a microprocessor to maintain temperature automatically.

automatic transaxle A transaxle that shifts automatically once placed in the proper drive range.

automatic transmission A transmission that shifts automatically.

automatic transmission fluid An oil used in automatic transmissions.

automotive machinist A machinist who specializes in precision machining of automotive parts.

automotive specialty mechanic A mechanic who specializes in servicing one part of an automobile.

axle bearing A roller bearing, or ball bearing, that supports the weight of the vehicle through the axle housing and axle shafts.

B

backfire An explosion of air-fuel mixture in the intake manifold.

backing plate A stationary mount that holds brake shoes from turning when they contact the drum.

backlash The amount of free play between the ring gear teeth and the drive pinion gear teeth.

backpressure Pressure created by restriction in an exhaust system.

backpressure transducer A device that senses exhaust gas pressure and regulates a vacuum control valve.

balance To adjust the weight of a rotating part so that it rotates without vibration or whip.

balance pad A thick portion of a piston or connecting rod that can be ground down to lighten and balance the part.

balancing coil gauge A gauge that uses two coils of wire to create magnetic fields to move an indicating needle.

ballast resistor A primary ignition circuit electrical resistor that changes resistance in response to dwell angle and engine rpm.

ball joint A connection formed by a rounded, ball-shaped part that fits into a matching hollow socket; connects the control arms to the steering knuckle.

ball nut A nut with gear teeth on one side that fits over a worm gear and is rotated by ball bearings.

ball return guide Part of a recirculating ball gearbox that provides a continuous loop that collects and recycles ball bearings.

bank An area of a V-type or flat engine cylinder block that contains cylinders. This term applies to engines with more than one bank.

bar A unit of pressure measurement. One bar is equal to 14.5 psi [99.98 kPa].

barrel *See* throttle bore.

battery A chemical device that produces electrical energy to start an engine.

battery cell A group of battery elements connected in series, positive to positive and negative to negative. A single automotive battery cell produces approximately 2.1 volts.

battery charger A machine that changes line current (110V AC) to low-voltage DC current to charge vehicle batteries.

battery element Two battery plates (one positive and one negative) immersed in electrolyte and kept apart by a separator strip.

battery hydrometer A measuring tool used to check the density of electrolyte.

battery load tester An instrument used to measure a battery's electrical capacity.

battery post A round projection to which all negative or positive battery plates are connected.

battery starter tester An electrical testing device that includes a voltmeter, an ammeter, and a variable electrical resistance load.

battery voltage tester A voltmeter.

bead The edge of a tire's sidewall that helps hold the tire to the wheel.

bead blasting A process that uses compressed air to blow small glass beads and chips at metal parts. The glass beads gently abrade, or wear off, deposits.

bearing A component used to hold a rotating part and allow it to turn smoothly.

bearing cap A heavy, machined metal clamp used to attach a connecting rod bearing or main bearing to the crankshaft. Also, the sheet metal protective cap on a wheel bearing assembly, sometimes called a dust cover.

bearing crush The process of compressing a bearing into place as the bearing cap is tightened.

bearing spread The distance a larger bearing insert must be compressed to fit into its smaller machined opening.

before TDC (BTDC) A piston position before top dead center, specified in degrees of crankshaft rotation.

bellhousing A protective bell-shaped, metal case, that houses the clutch.

belt A layer of material placed between the carcass and tread of a tire.

bench adjustment An adjustment performed while a part or assembly is removed from the vehicle.

beveled The tapered end of a part or tool.

bezel A retainer around a light or instrument.

bias belted tire A tire with bias plies and belts.

bias current A small amount of current applied to the emitter-base junction of a transistor to enable it to conduct.

bias ply tire A tire with plies that crisscross diagonally.

big end The end of the connecting rod that bolts around the crankpin.

billing The cost of servicing.

binding force The force that attracts electrons and holds together atoms of matter.

black box A device that produces a certain output from a given input.

bleeder screw A variation of a bleeder valve.

bleeder valve A valve on a brake assembly that is opened when the brakes are bled.

bleeding A procedure that eliminates air from a hydraulic system.

blind rivet A small metal rivet inserted and fastened by expansion with a special tool.

blowby gases Vapors that leak past piston rings into the crankcase during combustion.

blower A fan that pushes, or blows, air through a ventilation, heater, and/or air conditioning system.

blowgun A tool that controls and directs compressed air.

blown Ruptured through pressure.

blue To soften and turn blue, as steel, from excessive heat.

body The part of the automobile that holds and protects the occupants and cargo.

bolt A fastener with external threads, used with a nut.

bolt pattern The mounting configuration of the lug studs on a wheel hub.

bonded Held in place with adhesive.

boost Manifold pressure created by a turbocharger.

booster valve A valve that boosts the mainline hydraulic pressure to clutches and bands in an automatic transmission.

bore The diameter of a machined hole.

boss A reinforced, protruding area around a hole.

bottom dead center (BDC) The position of the piston at the bottom of either the intake or power stroke.

bottom-feed injector An EFI injector in which fuel is fed in from the bottom.

Bourdon tube A springy, flexible metal tube that uncoils as pressure is applied; used in gauges and instruments.

box-end wrench A wrench with a closed head that encircles a fastener.

brake drum The part of a drum brake assembly that is slowed or stopped during braking.

brake dynamometer A dynamometer that applies a braking force to an engine to test its torque output.

brake horsepower (bhp) Output horsepower, as measured on a brake dynamometer.

brake lines Hoses and steel tubing that route hydraulic fluid from the master cylinder to the wheel cylinders.

brake lining Friction material riveted or bonded to a brake shoe.

brake pad *See* brake shoe.

brake shoe The part of a drum brake assembly that exerts pressure on the brake drum.

breakaway torque The point at which a driving wheel begins to rotate during a limited-slip clutch check.

breaker bar A long, hinged handle for a socket wrench.

breaker points A set of electrical contacts with a movable and a stationary contact. Used to interrupt the flow of current to the ignition primary coil.

brakes Assemblies at each wheel that slow or stop an automobile.

break-in The initial wear period when an engine or other assembly's moving parts begin to conform to each other.

bridge rectifier circuit An assembly of diodes used to transform AC current into DC current.

British thermal unit (BTU) A customary unit of heat energy. The heat required to raise the temperature of 1 pound of water 1 degree F.

brush A carbon or copper graphite conductor that rides against a commutator to transfer electricity.

bucket lifter A hollow lifter that fits over the valve stem, spring, and retainer; used in overhead camshaft engines.

bushing A removable, hollow bearing surface for a hole to limit the size of the opening, resist abrasion, and/or serve as a guide.

bypass valve A valve used to redirect unfiltered oil through a clogged full-flow oil filter.

bypass wiring New wiring used to bypass inaccessible, defective wires.

C

cable linkage Clutch linkage operated by a cable.

caliper A U-shaped hydraulic gripping device that forces brake pads against a rotor to provide braking action on a rotor.

cam A projection on a rotating part that is used to cause another part to move.

cam grinder A machine that grinds a round piston into an oval cam shape.

cam grinding A machining process that produces an oval-shaped piston to counteract the effects of expansion.

camber The tilting of a wheel inward or outward from true vertical.

camshaft A metal shaft onto which cams have been cast or machined.

camshaft bearing A bearing used to support a camshaft. May be a fully cylindrical bushing, or a split, insert-type bearing.

capacitor An electronic device that can hold an electrical charge.

capscrew A screw with a six-sided head, which screws directly into a part.

carbon monoxide An odorless, colorless, toxic gas produced by incomplete burning of hydrocarbon fuel.

carbon tracking Formation of a line of carbonized dust within a distributor cap or on a rotor.

carburetion The enrichment of a gas (usually air) by combining it with a hydrocarbon fuel such as gasoline.

carburetor A vacuum-operated device that atomizes gasoline into a stream of air passing through the device.

carcass The inner part or body of a tire that holds air.

carriage bolt A bolt with a raised, square shoulder on the underside of the head.

castellated nut A nut held in position by slots and a cotter pin to prevent loosening.

caster The tilting of a steering knuckle forward or rearward from true vertical.

casting A process of molding parts by liquifying material and pouring it into a shaped mold to solidify.

casting porosity A hole in a housing caused by a casting imperfection during manufacture.

catalyst A chemical that promotes a chemical reaction between other substances, without being consumed itself.

center link *See* relay rod.

centrifugal advance mechanism A device, operated by centrifugal force, that advances ignition timing according to rpm.

centrifugal force An outward pull from the center of a rotating axis.

ceramic Material made of clay hardened by baking in a high-temperature oven, like traditional household dishware.

cetane rating A rating that measures the ease with which diesel fuel will ignite under the heat and pressure of compression. Also, the fuel's anti-knock quality.

chafing Damage caused by friction and rubbing.

chain hoist A chain and pulley assembly attached to the ceiling or to a special structure. Used for lifting heavy parts, such as engines.

chamfer To produce an angled or beveled edge in a hole or around the end of a shaft.

charcoal canister A container that stores fuel vapors from the fuel tank and carburetor until they can be drawn into the engine by intake manifold vacuum and burned.

charge Electrical positivity or negativity.

charging Reversing the discharging process by connecting a source of DC current to a battery.

chassis The frame, unit body reinforcement, suspension, braking, and steering systems.

chassis dynamometer A dynamometer that tests the horsepower output of vehicles at the driving wheels.

check valve A valve that opens in the direction of flow and closes to prevent flow in the opposite direction.

chemical energy Energy produced or stored by chemical means.

chisel A wide, heavy tool used to separate or align parts.

choke plate A metal plate at the top of the carburetor air horn that can be closed to reduce airflow and provide a rich mixture for starting and warm-up.

chuck The part of a drill that holds a drill bit.

circuit A completed pathway through which electricity can travel from a source to a load, and return. Also, a carburetor system that provides air-fuel mixture for a given running condition.

circuit breaker A resettable device that interrupts a circuit to prevent excessive current flow.

clearance The distance between adjacent parts.

clearance gauge A tool used to measure brake drum and brake shoe clearances.

C-lock axle assembly A driving axle held in place by a C-lock in the differential.

closed loop A feedback control system that uses output information to modify its own input information.

clouding The formation of tiny wax particles in diesel fuel, giving the fuel a cloudy or milky appearance.

clutch An assembly that engages and disengages an engine from a manual transmission.

clutch chatter A shaking and shuddering from the clutch, felt everywhere in the automobile during clutch engagement.

clutch disc The part of the clutch that takes power from the flywheel and transfers it to the transmission.

clutch drag A condition in which the clutch disc and transmission input shaft do not come to a complete stop when the clutch is disengaged.

clutch fork A lever that pivots in the bellhousing and acts on the throwout bearing.

clutch-head screwdriver A screwdriver used to loosen or tighten clutch-head screws.

clutch linkage A series of parts that connect the clutch pedal and clutch fork.

clutch pedal pulsation A rapid up-and-down movement of the clutch pedal.

clutch plate *See* clutch disc.

clutch plate limited-slip A limited-slip differential system in which clutch discs lock up the driving axles.

clutch slippage A condition that causes the engine to run faster than the transmission.

clutch vibration A condition similar to clutch pedal pulsation but louder and not as rapid.

coefficient of drag (C$_d$) A factor that expresses the relative ease with which a shape passes through the air. The lower the coefficient of drag, the less air resistance.

coil spring A thick steel wire that is coiled to expand and compress under force.

coil wire An insulated cable that conducts secondary current from the coil to the central connection of a distributor cap.

coking Damage to lubricating oil consisting of gum, varnish, and carbon formation from excessive heat.

cold cranking amperes Current flow that can be maintained from a battery during a cold cranking test before voltage drops below 7.2. The test is performed at 0 degrees F [-18 degrees C].

cold tank A cleaning tank for aluminum and brass.

collapse To move downward or reduce a given distance.

collapsible steering column A steering column that collapses or bends upon impact.

collector A portion of a transistor to which electrons flow.

combination valve A valve in a disc/drum brake system that acts as a proportioning valve, metering valve, and failure warning switch.

combination wrench A wrench with one open end and one box end.

combustion chamber A space between the top of a piston at top dead center and the cylinder head, where combustion takes place.

combustion control computer (CCC) *See* electronic control unit.

combustion leak detector A diagnostic device used to detect the presence of combustion gases in the radiator.

commutator Part of an electrical motor or generator through which electricity flows to armature windings.

compound Combinations of molecules that form a distinct type of matter.

compressed air Air under pressure.

compression Upward suspension movement.

compression ignition A way of igniting an air-fuel mixture through the heat of compression.

compression ratio A ratio comparing the volume above the piston at BDC and the volume above the piston at TDC.

compression ring One of the upper rings on a piston that prevents combustion gases from escaping past the piston.

compression test A diagnostic test to determine cylinder pressure and sealing.

compression tester A tool for measuring compression in an engine cylinder.

compressor A pump that circulates refrigerant through an air conditioning system.

computer An electronic device that processes data into useful information.

computerized diagnostic tester A machine that sends electrical inputs to a computer, which compares engine performance against established criteria.

concave An inward-curved surface.

condenser Part of an air conditioning system that changes refrigerant from a gas to a liquid. *See also* capacitor.

conduction Heat transfer from a hotter object to a colder object upon contact.

conductor A material that allows the passage of electricity.

cone limited-slip A limited-slip differential system that uses friction-faced cones to lock up the driving axles.

configuration The shape, or layout, of an engine.

connecting rod A rod connected to the piston and to the crankshaft.

constant-mesh gears Multiple transmission gearsets on the transmission mainshaft and countershaft that are meshed at the same time.

constant-velocity joint Universal-like joints used on front-wheel-drive axles which transmit power flow smoothly through sharp angles.

contact disk A heavy copper washer, part of a relay or solenoid, that forms a connection between terminals.

continuous fuel injection Fuel injection that continues, in small amounts, without pause.

control arms Suspension parts that control coil spring action as a wheel is affected by road conditions.

control rods Solid steel rods that brace a torque-tube drive and control rear-end torque.

convection Upward heat transfer in a fluid-filled system.

conventional electrical theory The theory which states that electrical current flows from positive to negative.

coolant A mixture of antifreeze and water that passes through the engine to help maintain proper temperatures.

coolant bypass A passage or hose that allows coolant to flow from the cylinder head to the water pump inlet when the thermostat is closed.

coolant hydrometer A testing device used to measure the freezing point of a coolant mixture.

cooling fins Thin metal projections cast or machined into parts to increase their surface area heat dissipation.

cooling system pressure tester A diagnostic device used to check whether cooling system components will hold pressure.

cord One of several layers of threads that run through the plies and belts of a tire.

core A solid plug used to form hollow areas in a casting mold.

cornering light A light that burns steadily, when turn signals operate, to light up the area in the direction of a turn.

corona effect A "glow" around faulty spark plug wires that can be seen in the dark. It is not necessarily harmful.

corrected horsepower Horsepower ratings that have been corrected for atmospheric conditions present during a dynamometer test.

corrosion inhibitor An oil additive that helps to prevent the formation of acids.

cotter pin A steel wire that is bent at the end to hold a part in place.

countergear The gear on the countershaft driven by the main drive gear.

countershaft The shaft, turned by engine power, that drives the gears on the mainshaft.

counterweight A weight formed on a crankshaft to balance the weight of the offset crankpins.

crane A portable lifting device used to lift engines or other heavy assemblies from an automobile.

crankcase The lower inside part of the cylinder block to which the crankshaft is bolted.

crankpin The machined, offset area of a crankshaft where the connecting rod journals are machined.

crankshaft A shaft with offset journals to which the connecting rods are attached at the bottom of the engine. It rotates, converting reciprocating motion to rotary motion, when the piston is pushed downward by combustion.

crankshaft end play The movement of the crankshaft forward or rearward in the block.

crimp The use of pressure to force a thin holding part to clamp to, or conform to the shape of, a held part.

crimp-type clamp A small, metal hose clamp band that is crimped to form a seal.

crossover pipe A metal pipe that connects two exhaust pipes on a V-type engine.

cubic centimeter (cc) The volume contained in a cube one centimeter, or 10 millimeters, on each side. (1,000 cc = 1 liter.)

cup plug A type of soft plug, shaped like a cup, having flanges that face outward.

curb idle speed The normal idling speed of an engine.

cushioning springs Clutch disc springs between the facings that absorb shock when the clutch is engaged.

customary unit A unit of measurement in feet, inches, ounces, or other English-based measurement unit.

cutting out A condition in which an engine dies momentarily at irregular intervals.

cylinder A round passageway inside the cylinder block, in which a piston travels.

cylinder block The largest part of an automotive engine, which houses, or holds, the major mechanical parts of the engine.

cylinder head The upper part of an engine that closes off the tops of the cylinders. Located within the head are ports, valves, and threaded openings for spark plugs.

cylinder liner A cylindrical sleeve used to form the actual cylinder wall within a block. Associated mainly with aluminum engine blocks, but also may be used in cast iron blocks with badly damaged cylinders.

cylinder ridge An unworn section at the top of a cylinder formed by the friction of piston rings acting on the rest of the cylinder.

cylinder ridge remover A tool used to machine the cylinder ridge from a cylinder so that the piston and connecting rod assembly can be removed.

cylinder taper The difference between a cylinder's diameter at the top and bottom.

damper pulley A pulley that usually is bolted to the torsional vibration damper. Used to help damp, or reduce, irregular rotation.

dashpot A partially sealed, flexible diaphragm attached to a pushrod, which slows the closing action of the throttle when the accelerator is released.

data Uninterpreted raw facts and figures. (Singular form is *datum*.)

dead timing The process of correctly repositioning a distributor for engine starting purposes.

dealer An agent who sells new automobiles for an automobile manufacturer.

deceleration valve A valve that operates during deceleration to allow fresh air to bypass the carburetor to the intake manifold.

De Dion axle An independent-suspension driving axle system with open axles and U-joints.

defroster A distribution plenum system that directs heated air to the inside of the windshield.

dehumidified A condition in which moisture, or humidity, has been removed from air.

de-icer A chemical added to gasoline to prevent ice particles from forming and adhering to cold metal surfaces.

desiccant A special substance that absorbs moisture.

detergent-dispersant A chemical additive that keeps particles of carbon and other contaminants suspended in lubricating oil.

detonation Uncontrolled explosion of remaining air-fuel mixture from heat and pressure after spark ignition has occurred.

detonation sensor A device that senses sound waves produced by detonation and converts them into electrical signals.

diagnosis Investigation and analysis of an automotive service problem.

diagnostics Overall analysis of an automobile's operation.

diagonal cutting pliers Pliers with sharp-edged jaws, used to cut electrical and wire connections.

dial indicator An instrument used to measure runout and play.

diaphragm spring A single, thin sheet of convex-shaped metal in a pressure plate assembly, which "gives" when pressure is applied.

die A cutting tool used to form, or repair damaged, external threads.

dielectric compound An insulating material, often used to seal electrical connections against moisture and dirt.

diesel A hydrocarbon motor fuel, less refined and containing more heat energy than gasoline. Also, a condition in which a spark-ignition engine continues running after spark ignition ceases; may be called "run-on."

diesel engine A compression-ignition engine that operates on diesel fuel.

diesel injection pump A fuel injection pump, on a diesel engine, which creates high fuel pressures to force open a mechanical injection nozzle.

diesel knocking A condition similar to detonation in a gasoline engine. Fuel of too low a cetane rating ignites in an uncontrolled manner after an ignition lag.

differential An assembly of gears that drives the driving axles. The differential allows a difference in speed between the driving axles during turns.

differential bearing preload The load or pressure on bearings upon installation.

differential case A case that houses differential parts and is bolted to the ring gear. Sometimes called a *carrier*.

differential gearset A name given to the ring gear and drive pinion gear.

differential pinion gears Gears that help to direct more power to the outside wheel when the automobile is turning. They mesh with the side gears.

digital Information presented in the form of digits, or numbers.

dimple A tapered depression in sheet metal caused by an overtightened attachment device.

diode An electronic device that, in general, acts as a one-way valve and allows current to flow in only one direction.

diode trio Three diodes connected in parallel. Used in some alternators to supply rectified DC to the rotor coil and to apply bias current to regulator transistors.

direct current (DC) Electricity, such as that produced by a battery, that flows in only one direction, from one terminal of an electrical source to the other.

direct injection A diesel fuel injection system in which fuel is injected directly onto the top of the piston.

disc brake A brake assembly in which a caliper with shoes exerts pinching pressure on a disc to slow or stop the vehicle.

discharge nozzle A shaped opening for a main-metering or accelerator pump fuel discharge.

dispatch sheet A form to keep track of time schedules and appointments in a service area.

displacement The volume of a cylinder through which a piston moves from BDC to TDC.

display An oscilloscope pattern that shows cylinder firings one after another, in firing order.

display device An instrument or warning light that alerts the driver to the condition of a vehicle system.

distribution plenum A chamber that accepts circulating air and distributes it.

distributor A component of the ignition system that determines the firing order of the cylinders. It also directs electrical current to the correct spark plug at precisely the right time.

distributor cam A multi-lobed cam against which a rubbing block rides to open and close breaker points. It is driven by the distributor shaft.

D-Jetronic The first electronic fuel injection system, developed by Robert Bosch Corporation, applied to production passenger vehicles. Airflow is measured by means of a manifold absolute pressure (MAP) sensor.

doping The process of adding trace amounts of chemicals to semiconductors to produce positive (P) or negative (N) characteristics.

double-acting shock absorber A shock absorber that controls both the upward and downward movements of a suspension.

double Cardan U-joint A constant-velocity joint consisting of two closely connected conventional universal joints.

dowel A cylindrical part that fits through other parts to attach or position them.

dowel pin A cylindrically shaped fastener that aligns two parts.

downdraft carburetor A carburetor in which air flows through the barrel in a downward, vertical direction.

drag link *See* relay rod.

drain plug A pipe plug fitting used to drain lubricant.

drill bit A steel shaft that has a sharp, spiral groove and cuts into metal when turned.

driveability The degree to which a vehicle operates properly. Includes starting, running smoothly, accelerating, and delivering reasonable fuel mileage.

drive belt A belt, driven by the engine, which operates equipment in the engine compartment.

drive belt tension guide A tool to measure tightness of a drive belt.

drive link assembly A chain, or link, assembly that connects the turbine shaft to the input shaft in a front-drive automatic transmission.

drive member A gear that drives, or provides power for, other gears in a planetary gearset.

drive pinion gear A pinion gear that takes power from the driveline and transfers it to the differential through the ring gear. It is part of the ring and pinion gearset.

drive size The diameter of the drive in a socket wrench handle, or the socket drive end.

driveline The driveshaft and flexible joint assembly that transfers torque from the transmission to the differential in a rear-wheel-drive automobile.

driven member The output gear during planetary gearset operation.

driveshaft A solid or hollow metal shaft forming part of the driveline.

drivetrain A series of components that transmit power from the engine to the driving wheels.

driving axle A shaft that accepts power from the differential and turns the driving wheel.

drop center The well in a wheel rim.

drum brake A brake that exerts pressure inside a drum to slow or stop the vehicle.

dry friction Friction that occurs when unlubricated objects come in direct contact, such as metal rubbing against metal.

dry liner A cylinder liner whose outer surface does not contact the coolant in a liquid-cooled engine.

dual bed A catalytic converter with two areas where catalytic reactions occur.

dual bed converter A catalytic converter that promotes the oxidation of HC and CO to CO_2 and H_2O. It also promotes the reduction of NO_x to N_2 and O_2.

dual overhead camshaft (DOHC) An engine design with two camshafts—one for intake valves, the other for exhaust valves—mounted above the cylinder head.

duty cycle The amount of time that a mixture-control solenoid is activated so that fuel cannot flow.

dwell The length of time that contact points remain closed during operation.

dwell angle The amount of rotation through which breaker points remain closed to energize the ignition primary coil.

dwell-tachometer An instrument used for measuring dwell and the speed of the engine.

dynamic balance The equal distribution of weight on each side of the centerline of a wheel.

dynamometer A device for measuring horsepower.

E

early fuel evaporation (EFE) A system on General Motors vehicles that increases intake charge vaporization. Uses a heat riser valve to heat the intake manifold with heat from the exhaust manifold.

eccentric An off-center circular lobe that rotates to move a part, similar to a cam.

EGR valve A vacuum-operated valve that can open a passage between exhaust and intake manifold areas for exhaust gas recirculation purposes.

electric impact wrench An electrically powered socket wrench.

electrical capacity The ability of a battery to produce current.

electrical connector plug A plastic, two-part, male-female plug with metal electrical terminals in each half. When the halves are pushed together, an electrical connection is made.

electrical schematic A "map" of electrical components that uses symbols and lines to indicate electrical circuits.

electrical solenoid A device that uses electricity to create a magnetic force to push, pull, or hold a mechanical linkage.

electrical system Provides electrical current to start and operate all the electrical components of the automobile.

electricity A form of energy that can be used to create light, heat, or force to cause motion.

electrochemical action A chemical reaction that produces the potential for electrical flow, as in a battery.

electrolysis A chemical and electrical decomposition process that can damage metals such as brass, copper, and aluminum in the cooling system.

electrolyte A material whose atoms become ionized, or electrically charged, in solution. Automobile battery electrolyte is a mixture of sulfuric acid and water.

electromagnet A magnet formed by electrical flow through a conductor.

electron An extremely small particle that orbits the nucleus of an atom.

electron electrical theory A theory that states that electrical current flows from negative to positive.

electronic control module (ECM) *See* electronic control unit.

electronic control unit (ECU) A small computer mounted on board the vehicle to control engine operation, including air-fuel ratio and spark timing, and other vehicle functions.

electronic fuel injection (EFI) A gasoline fuel injection system in which a microprocessor is used to energize solenoid-controlled injection nozzles. The nozzles spray finely atomized gasoline into the incoming air.

electronic ignition control unit A transistorized device used to switch current on and off to the ignition primary coil.

electronic mixture control Air-fuel mixture control that operates by moving a tapered or stepped needle within a carburetor jet. Movement is based on signals from an electronic control unit.

electronics A branch of physics that deals with the behavior and effects of small amounts of electrons in semiconductor circuits.

element A specific, unique type of matter that cannot be reduced to a simpler form.

emission control Techniques and equipment that reduce the level of harmful gases in engine exhaust.

emitter A portion of a transistor from which electrons are emitted, or forced out.

emulsion tube A perforated tube immersed in a fuel. Air is passed through the tube to make a frothy air-fuel mixture.

end play The distance a shaft moves forward or rearward in a direction parallel to its length.

energy The capacity to do work. *See also* work, force.

engine A machine that converts energy produced by combustion into mechanical force.

engine calibration unit A separate computer module that contains the programs for a specific car model.

engine lift A crane used to remove or install an automobile engine.

engine support fixture A special support used to hold an engine in place while a transaxle is being removed.

English/metric conversion Tables or charts used to convert measurements from English to metric and from metric to English.

English system A system of measurement based on inches and pounds.

enrichment circuit A carburetor circuit that provides a richer air-fuel mixture during full-power operation.

epoxy cement An extremely strong plastic adhesive that is formed by mixing a base substance and an epoxy resin.

epoxy resin A thermosetting plastic material that hardens to form a strong adhesive bond when exposed to oxygen; the hardening agent in epoxy cement.

ethanol A form of alcohol used as a motor fuel and in spirits. Also known as *grain alcohol.*

evacuate The process of applying a vacuum to a closed refrigeration system to remove air and moisture.

evaporation A procedure by which a liquid is turned into vapor.

evaporative emission controls Parts and systems designed to prevent fuel vapors from escaping directly into the atmosphere.

evaporator A radiator-like part of an air conditioner that absorbs heat as air passes over it.

exhaust gas analyzer An electronic diagnostic instrument used to determine the amounts of harmful gases in engine exhaust fumes.

exhaust gas recirculation (EGR) Reusing exhaust gases in the intake charge to reduce NO_x.

exhaust manifold The hollow part connected to the cylinder head at the exhaust port that directs burned gases into the exhaust system.

exhaust pipe The metal pipe that connects the exhaust manifold to the rest of the exhaust system.

exhaust system A series of parts that direct heat and exhaust gases from the engine into the atmosphere.

exhaust valve A valve fitted into the exhaust port of a cylinder head.

expansion dome A raised portion of the upper fuel tank wall.

expansion plug A form of soft plug that expands to form a better seal as pressure is exerted against it.

extension A steel rod that adds distance between the drive and the socket on a socket wrench.

external combustion Term applied to an engine whose heat source is outside the area where force is applied to cause motion.

external threads Threads that are on the outside of a part.

external transmission cooler An automatic transmission cooler system that has a separate, external radiator.

face shield A clear, shatterproof bubble that protects a person's face while working.

failure warning switch A switch that activates a dashboard warning light when the front or rear brake system fails.

fast-idle cam A stepped or tapered part connected between the choke plate and the throttle plate; used to help the engine run faster during warm-up.

fatigue Cracking or breaking damage that results from repeated flexing and bending of a part.

feedback carburetor A carburetor with a mixture control solenoid activated by a control unit based on information fed back from sensing units.

feedback control A method of combining the functions of using sensors, a computer, and servomechanisms. Data about the effects of the computer's output commands are fed back into the computer. The computer constantly compares the input data to a set goal, and adjusts its output accordingly.

feeler gauge A tool containing a number of small, flat strips of metal or plastic used to measure the space between two surfaces.

ferrous Containing iron.

field coil A coil of wire on an alternator rotor or starter motor frame that produces a magnetic field when energized.

filament A metal element within a glass bulb that is heated to produce light.

file A steel tool with rows of teeth to remove, smooth, or polish metal.

fill plug A plug that is removed to check the oil level of, or add oil to, a manual transmission.

fillet A rounded area machined at the intersection of two flat sections that are at an angle to one another.

firing order A sequence in which ignition occurs in the numbered cylinders of an engine.

firing position The crankshaft, piston, and valve position at which the spark occurs to ignite the air-fuel mixture in a cylinder.

fixed caliper A disc brake design that uses four pistons to force pads against a rotor.

flame front The edge of the burning air-fuel mixture during combustion.

flange A projecting lip, rim, or edge.

flare An expanded, shaped end on a metal tube or pipe.

flare-nut wrench A special wrench meant for use on a tubular metal line fitting to prevent damage to the fitting.

flat rate An established length of time in which a repair should be completed.

flat rate manual A book that lists flat rates for different automotive jobs.

flat spot *See* hesitation.

flat washer A wide washer used to prevent damage to a part surface.

fleet A group of vehicles operated by an organization.

fleet garage A shop that services fleet vehicles for an organization.

flexplate A smaller version of a flywheel, used with an automatic transmission.

float A lightweight part that rests, or floats, on the surface of a liquid.

float bowl A hollow fuel reservoir area within a carburetor from which fuel is drawn during carburetion.

floating caliper A disc brake design in which the caliper slides in and out against a rotor.

flooding A condition in which excess unvaporized fuel in the intake manifold prevents the engine from starting.

floor jack A portable tool used to raise and lower an automobile.

fluid coupling A method of driving an automatic transmission by using a fluid to transfer rotation.

flushing gun A device that uses compressed air to force clean water and air through a cooling system for flushing purposes.

flywheel A heavy, circular wheel attached to a rotating part to increase its momentum when spinning.

foam inhibitor An additive that reduces the formation of foam in oil.

foot-pound (ft.-lb.) A customary unit of work, equivalent to the force necessary to move one pound through a distance of one foot.

footprint The portion of the tire tread that makes contact with the road surface.

force The cause of motion. *See also* energy, work.

forge A process of hammering or pounding a heated metal piece into a desired shape. Forging produces structurally stronger assemblies than casting.

forward-biased A transistor to which a small current is applied to the emitter-base connection, turning on the transistor. A large current can thus flow through the emitter-collector path.

four-stroke cycle Refers to the four up-and-down movements, or strokes, of the piston within the cylinder. The four strokes—intake, compression, power, and exhaust—complete one firing cycle.

frame The section of the automobile that supports the body, engine, and drivetrain.

free-floating piston pin A piston pin that is free to turn in the piston and connecting rod small end.

free travel The distance a clutch pedal moves before it begins to take up slack in the clutch linkage.

friction The resistance between two rubbing or sliding materials.

friction bearing A bushing, sleeve, or insert bearing.

friction pads The gripping surface of a brake caliper that slows the rotor.

frictional horsepower (fhp) The horsepower necessary to overcome internal friction within an engine.

frontal area The area against which air resistance is present as a vehicle travels forward.

front-end geometry A term used to describe the angles between front suspension parts on an automobile.

fuel bars Hollow tubes above the throttle body assembly used to spray fuel.

fuel filter A device to trap and hold sediment, rust particles, and other contaminants in fuel.

fuel injection A fuel system that sprays a measured amount of fuel into the incoming airflow or into the combustion chamber.

fuel rail A line that supplies fuel to multi-point fuel injectors.

fuel-vapor separator A device that uses gravity to separate liquid fuel from vaporized fuel.

fuel wetting The accumulation of excess fuel on the walls and floor of the intake manifold and on the port.

full field To bypass the regulator and apply full battery current to the alternator field windings to produce maximum output.

full-flow oil filtering system A filtering system in which all of the oil normally passes through the filter before it can flow through the galleries and to the moving parts of the engine.

fuse A safety device that conducts a given current of electricity, then melts to open a circuit and prevent excessive current flow.

fuse block A plastic block with connectors for wires, fuses, circuit breakers, turn signal flashers, and relays.

fusible link A wire, smaller in diameter than the circuit it is to protect, that can burn out like a fuse.

G

garter spring A small, narrow coil spring, connected to itself, that helps to apply pressure behind the lip of a seal against a rotating shaft.

gasket A soft material used to seal areas between non-moving parts.

gasohol A mixture of alcohol (up to 10%) and gasoline.

gasoline The most common hydrocarbon motor fuel.

gassing A discharge of large amounts of hydrogen gas and loss of water during charging.

gear A toothed wheel that meshes with, or fits into, another toothed wheel.

gear clash A noise made when a manual transmission is shifted improperly from one gear to another.

gear drive A method of using gears of varying sizes to coordinate and turn shafts.

gear ratio A number indicating the relative number of turns and rotating speeds of a driving and a driven gear.

gear tooth contact pattern test A diagnostic procedure in which the differential ring gear and drive pinion gear are marked with a compound. The gears then are rotated to determine how they mesh.

general automobile mechanic A mechanic who is certified in all areas of automobile servicing.

general repair manual A service manual in condensed form, covering several models and years of automobiles.

generator *See* alternator.

glass bead blaster A cleaning machine that shoots glass beads at parts to clean them off.

glazed Polished by heat and friction to a slick, poorly gripping surface.

glow plug An electrical heating element used in a diesel engine to preheat the air and surrounding metal to a temperature sufficient to ignite the fuel.

governor pressure A pressure lower than mainline pressure in an automatic transmission that assists in upshifting.

grade markings Marks on fasteners that indicate strength.

graphic displays Drawings or pictures of a vehicle that can be illuminated to indicate problem areas.

graphited oil A thin lubricant containing graphite particles.

grease points Areas where grease or oil is added when lubricating.

greasy friction Friction that occurs when a thin film of grease or oil is present between touching surfaces.

grinder A tool that uses an electric motor to drive a grinder on one side and, usually, a wire wheel on the other.

gross horsepower A rating of an engine's horsepower without any driven accessories.

ground A common connection through which electricity can flow to complete a circuit.

group number A number code that indicates the physical dimensions and terminal types of a battery.

growler An electrical test device that produces a strong magnetic field; used to test armatures.

H

hairspring A fine wire spring.

halogen light A small glass bulb containing a filament surrounded by halogen gas. The small bulb fits within a larger reflector and lens element.

hammer A striking tool with a metal, wooden, plastic, leather, or rubber head attached to a handle.

hand tool A tool that is operated by hand, without power.

hand vacuum pump A hand-operated device that produces and measures vacuum.

harmonic balancer A torsional vibration damper that has a central hub, an elastic intermediate sleeve, and an outer rim.

harness A bundled group of wires.

head The part of a wrench that grips a fastener.

head gasket The gasket between the cylinder block and the cylinder head.

header An aftermarket, high-performance combination of an exhaust manifold and a headpipe, custom-formed from steel tubing.

heat dam A small groove cut into the piston above the top ring groove or below the oil ring groove. This prevents excess combustion heat from being transferred.

heat energy Energy produced by burning.

heat exchanger A device that transfers heat from one fluid to another.

heat range The heat-transferring ability of a spark plug, indicated by a code on the side of the plug.

heat riser valve A flap or valve in an exhaust manifold that causes exhaust gases to flow out more slowly than in an unrestricted opening.

heat shield A device, usually made of pressed or perforated sheet metal, used to protect parts and people from excessive heat.

heat sink A device used to dissipate heat and protect parts.

heat stove A sheet metal enclosure around the exhaust manifold, through which air can flow and be heated by the manifold.

heater assembly A housing that holds the heater core and control doors for the distribution plenum chambers.

heater control system Switches and levers that are operated manually, by vacuum, and/or electrically to control heating system flow.

heater control valve A valve that controls coolant flow to the heater core inlet hose.

heater core A small radiator, or heat exchanger, used to heat air for the comfort of passengers.

heater hose A hose that connects the heater core to the engine cooling system.

heavy-duty cooling system cleaner Powdered phosphoric acid, usually packaged in a two-part container with a chemical neutralizer (baking soda).

height sensor An electronic sensing device that signals a control module when the suspension is compressed by a heavy load.

hesitation A momentary lack of response as the accelerator is pressed down, such as when moving away from a stop.

hoist A lift that is stored in the floor of a work area and that is used to raise or lower an entire automobile.

hollow-head screw *See* Allen head screw.

horsepower A unit of power based on the ability of a horse to pull a load. One horsepower is equivalent to 550 foot-pounds of work per second, or 746 watts. In an engine, horsepower is the rate at which an engine produces torque.

hot-idle compensator A device that opens an air passage to lean the mixture slightly when the engine is hot.

hot tank A tank filled with corrosive solvent; used to remove rust, corrosion, and deposits from large ferrous metal parts.

Hotchkiss drive A suspension design that uses leaf springs and the frame to control rear-end torque.

hub nut A fastener that holds a transaxle driving-axle assembly to the driving wheel.

humidity The water vapor content in air.

hunting gearset A differential gearset in which one drive pinion gear tooth contacts every ring gear tooth after several rotations.

hydraulic lash adjuster A device similar to a hydraulic lifter; used in overhead-camshaft valve trains.

hydraulic lifter A lifter mechanism that uses oil pressure to transfer force to the valve train.

hydraulic linkage Clutch linkage that is operated by hydraulic fluid.

hydraulic press An assembly that uses the pressure of a hydraulic jacking unit or hydraulic cylinder to produce pushing force.

hydraulic tools Tools that operate on oil pressure.

hydrocarbon A chemical substance made up primarily of hydrogen and carbon atoms. Petroleum products are hydrocarbon compounds.

hypoid gears A type of spiral, beveled ring and pinion gearset in a differential. Hypoid gears mesh below the ring gear centerline.

I

idle discharge port A fuel discharge port positioned just below the edge of the throttle plate when it is closed for idling.

idler arm A steering rod connected to the frame; helps to support the relay rod end opposite the Pitman arm.

idler gear A gear meshed between a driving gear and a driven gear.

idle-speed solenoid An electrical solenoid used to position the throttle plate for proper idle speed.

idling Normal slow-speed engine operation without the accelerator pedal depressed.

ignition interlock A theft prevention device that locks the steering wheel if the key is not inserted and turned. Also used to prevent vehicles with automatic transmissions from starting in gear.

ignition timing The point at which spark occurs, as referenced by piston position and crankshaft rotation.

ignition timing marks Marks on external engine and pulley or flywheel surfaces used to determine piston position in No. 1 cylinder.

impeller A fan-like propeller that forces a fluid to flow.

impeller pump A pump with radiating blades that operates by drawing fuel in at its center and forcing it outward through centrifugal action.

inches of vacuum A measurement of engine vacuum represented by the height of a column of mercury, sometimes written as "inches of Hg."

inclinometer An instrument used to measure driveshaft inclination, or angle.

independent garage An automotive service and repair shop that deals with all parts of an automobile.

independent suspension A system that allows wheels to move independently.

indicated horsepower (ihp) Theoretical horsepower calculated through pressure measurements within a cylinder.

indirect injection A diesel fuel injection system in which fuel is injected into a precombustion chamber for ignition.

induce To create another magnetic field and/or an electric current through the use of a magnetic field.

induction hardening A heat-treating process that hardens metals.

inductive ammeter An ammeter that reads current flowing through a wire by magnetic induction.

inductive pickup A device that can induce a signal current by being clamped around a conductor.

inductive timing light A timing light with an inductive pickup to trigger a flash.

information disclosure Protection for consumers against servicing frauds.

inline diesel injection pump A diesel injection pump using a camshaft similar to an engine camshaft to move plungers that pump diesel fuel.

inner tube A rubber tube that fits inside a tire and holds air.

input Data furnished for the use of a computer. Also, to supply data to a computer.

inside mircrometer A tool used to measure hole diameters, or distances between parallel surfaces.

instrument voltage regulator A voltage regulator used to stabilize and limit voltage for accurate instrument operation.

insulator A material that does not conduct electricity.

intake charge The air-fuel mixture drawn from the carburetor through the intake manifold and into the cylinder on its intake stroke.

intake manifold A hollow part that directs air-fuel mixture from the carburetor into the intake port of a cylinder head.

intake port The port on a cylinder head connected to the intake manifold.

integral-carrier differential A design in which the differential carrier bearings are mounted directly in the rear axle housing.

integral power steering A power steering system that applies hydraulic pressure to a piston in the steering gearbox.

integral valve guide A hole machined in the metal of the cylinder head to align and support the valve stem.

integral valve seat A valve seat machined into the cylinder head.

integrated circuit A miniaturized series of electronic components connected together to perform specific functions. Also known as a "chip."

integrated control system An electronic control system that combines many functions into a single control unit.

intercooler A type of radiator heat exchanger mounted in the airstream to cool the intake air charge after compression in a turbocharger.

interference angle The difference in angle between two mating parts.

internal combustion Term applied to an engine whose heat source is enclosed within the area where force is applied to cause motion.

internal short A short circuit between the positive and negative battery plates.

internal transmission cooler An automatic transmission cooler system that uses the engine radiator for cooling.

International System of Units (SI) Standard international units of measurement based on the metric system. *See also* metric system.

ion An element that has more or less electrons than the number needed to balance the number of protons in the nucleus of its atom.

iso-octane A hydrocarbon fuel assigned an octane rating of 100, to which other motor fuels are compared.

J

jack A portable tool that is used to raise an automobile off the floor.

jack pads Reinforced parts of a chassis where jacks can be placed to raise an automobile.

jackstand A support device to hold the automobile off the floor after it has been raised by a jack.

jet A precisely sized, calibrated hole in a hollow passage, through which fuel or air can pass.

jet spray booth A closed container in which large engine parts are cleaned with multiple high-pressure spray jets.

joule (J) A SI unit of energy or work, equivalent to one Newton-meter of force per second.

jounce Upward suspension movement.

journal The area of a rotating shaft that is in contact with a bearing.

jump starting Starting a vehicle with a weak battery by connecting its electrical system to a good battery.

jumper cables Heavy cables with color-coded clamps at each end, used for jump starting.

jumper wire Wires used to make connections for test or replacement wiring purposes.

junction block A plastic base with metal terminals and connectors for common wiring connections.

K

key A small, narrow piece of metal used to fasten two rotating parts.

keyway A slot that holds a key fastener.

kickdown linkage An automatic transmission linkage system that allows downshifting by depressing the throttle pedal to the floor.

kilowatt (kw) An electrical measurement equal to 1,000 watts.

K-Jetronic A form of EFI developed by Robert Bosch Corporation in which fuel is sprayed constantly from all injectors. Air-fuel ratio is adjusted by varying fuel pressure.

knurl A raised ridge on a cylindrical part, produced by a machining operation. Also, to produce a knurl.

L

land The areas on a piston between the grooves.

lateral runout A measurement of the in-and-out movement of a tire and wheel.

lead peroxide (PbO$_2$) A porous, chocolate-brown, crystalline substance that forms the positive plate of a battery element.

lead sulfate (PbSO$_4$) A combination of lead, sulfur, and oxygen that forms on the plates of a battery. Sulfate prevents electrolyte from penetrating the plate and impairs electrochemical action.

leaded gasoline Gasoline containing tetraethyl lead.

leaf spring A semi-elliptic suspension assembly that is made up of one or more long, thin strips of metal.

leak detector tool A butane-gas-burning tool used to locate refrigerant leaks in an air conditioning system.

leak-down tester A tester used to measure leakage from the combustion chamber through piston rings, intake and exhaust valves, and head gaskets.

lean mixture An air-fuel mixture containing more than 14.7 parts of air to one part of gasoline, by weight.

lever and shaft assembly Part of a rod and lever clutch linkage that connects two levers with one shaft.

LH-Jetronic A variation of L-Jetronic that uses microprocessors to control the injector timing and duration.

lifter A part that changes the rotating motion of the cam lobe into a reciprocating motion.

limited-slip differential A design that reduces individual wheelspin through a series of clutches in the differential that lock the two driving axles together.

line mechanic—heavy work A mechanic whose work involves complicated service on an automobile.

line mechanic—light work A mechanic who performs minor service on an automobile.

linkage power steering A power steering system that applies hydraulic pressure to the steering linkage system.

lip-type seal An assembly consisting of a metal or plastic casing, a sealing element made of rubber, and a garter spring to help hold the seal against a turning shaft.

liquid cooling A method of cooling heated parts by circulating a liquid through hollow areas of the parts.

liquid cooling system cleaners A mild solution of phosphoric acid dissolved in water and mixed with detergent.

L-Jetronic A form of EFI developed by Robert Bosch Corporation in which airflow is measured by a pivoting flap in the airstream. Fuel is injected twice each crankshaft revolution.

LN-Jetronic A variation of L-Jetronic EFI that uses low-pressure bottom-feed fuel injectors and a hot-wire mass air-flow sensor.

load A device or resistance that can cause work to be done by electrical energy.

load leveling system *See* automatic level control.

lobe An individual cam shape on a camshaft.

locking pliers Pliers with jaws that can be locked in position.

locking steering column A locking mechanism in the ignition switch. It keeps the steering wheel and shift lever from moving when the ignition switch is in the "lock" position.

locknut A nut used to keep a screw or bolt from loosening.

lock-to-lock The rotating distance of a steering wheel from extreme left to extreme right.

lockup system A friction assembly that locks the turbine and torque converter housing together in an automatic transmission.

lockwasher A washer with sharp edges that grip parts and keep them from moving.

longitudinal A mounting that is parallel to, or in line with, a front-to-back centerline.

longnose pliers Pliers with long, narrow jaws.

lubricant Slippery materials, such as oil and grease, that reduce friction.

lubrication The action of providing lubricant, usually oil or grease, to reduce friction between parts, thus reducing heat and wear.

lubrication system A number of parts, components, and passages, which function to keep engine parts lubricated.

lug nuts Nuts that hold a wheel on the wheel lugs.

lug pattern *See* bolt pattern.

machining A process of producing a desired size, shape, or finish on a part by using power machinery.

MacPherson strut A single-arm suspension system that combines a coil spring and shock absorber to act as an upper control arm.

magnetic clutch A clutch that rotates with a drive pulley and turns an air conditioning compressor on or off with a magnetic connection.

main body The central section of a carburetor which contains the float bowl and most passages, jets, and discharge ports.

main drive gear The gear, turned by the transmission input shaft, that drives the countergear.

main journal The central area of a crankshaft, where the main bearings support the shaft in the block.

main metering circuit A vacuum-operated fuel discharge system that draws fuel from a tube inserted into the float bowl. It discharges the fuel in the venturi area.

mainline pressure Pressure that is regulated in an automatic transmission hydraulic system.

mainshaft The shaft in the transmission that transfers torque to the driveline.

maintenance The care and upkeep of mechanical and other parts of an automobile.

maintenance-free battery A battery that, in normal service, does not require the periodic addition of water to maintain an electrolyte level.

major thrust face The side of the piston to which most force is applied by side thrust.

malleable Able to be shaped.

mallet A small hammer.

manifold absolute pressure (MAP) A measure of the degree of vacuum or pressure within an intake manifold; used to measure air volume flow.

manifold gauge assembly A set of gauges and hoses, used on air conditioning systems, which determines high and low pressures and correct refrigerant charge, and helps to diagnose air conditioner problems.

manifold vacuum Vacuum present at the intake manifold.

manual bleeding A method of bleeding the brakes by operating the brake pedal.

manual control valve Directs fluid to switching and pressure-regulating valves in an automatic transmission.

manual steering A system in which the driver provides the steering effort.

manual transaxle A transaxle that is shifted by the driver.

manual transmission A transmission that is shifted by the driver.

manufacturer's service bulletin A one- or two-page bulletin describing a service change instituted by the manufacturer.

manufacturer's service manual A service manual, published by the manufacturer, covering one or more models for one year of an automobile.

map A three-dimensional graph.

mass air-flow sensor An EFI air intake sensor that measures the mass, not the volume, of the air flowing into the intake manifold.

master cylinder A hydraulic fluid reservoir for the brake system that also develops hydraulic pressure.

mate To fit together, as parts.

matter The material of which all things are made.

measurement inspection The use of measurement tools and specific measurement procedures to locate problem areas.

mechanical efficiency A comparison of how much horsepower an engine produces at the flywheel, compared to the theoretical horsepower the engine could produce from the pressures generated within the combustion chamber.

mechanical energy Energy stored or produced by mechanical means.

mechanical fuel injector A fuel injection nozzle assembly held closed by strong spring pressure and open by fuel pressure.

mechanical fuel pump A pump driven by engine power, usually from the camshaft, through either an eccentric lobe or a lobe, a pushrod, and a rocker arm arrangement.

mechanical measuring tool A tool that is operated and adjusted by hand to obtain a measurement.

mechanic's stethoscope A device similar to a doctor's stethoscope for listening to mechanical noises.

memory A computer feature that stores, or saves, information.

mercury switch A switch that completes a circuit by allowing liquid mercury metal to flow and conduct across two contacts.

753

mesh To fit together, as gear teeth.

meshing spring A spring on a starter motor driveshaft used to prevent excessive damage to gear teeth during engagement.

metal spray To deposit molten metal on a surface by spraying.

metering In carburetion, the addition of a measured amount of fuel into the airstream passing through a carburetor.

metering rod A small, tapered or stepped rod within a jet. The rod's up or down movement controls the effective cross-sectional area of the jet and the amount of fuel flowing.

metering valve A valve that delays hydraulic pressure to a front disc brake assembly when drum brakes are used at the rear.

methanol A poisonous form of alcohol used as a motor fuel, a carburetor cleaner solvent, and, formerly, as an anti-freeze additive for liquid cooling systems. Also known as "wood alcohol."

metric system A system of measurement based on meters and kilograms. *See also* International System of Units.

micron A very small metric dimensional measurement, equal to 39 millionths of an inch.

microprocessor A computer chip used to process raw data into usable information.

minor thrust face The side of a piston to which least force is applied by side thrust.

misfueling Adding leaded gasoline to vehicles with catalytic converters.

missing A lack of power in one or more cylinders.

modulate To control by degrees.

module A replaceable unit, such as a computer processing unit.

molecule A combination of atoms that form a given type of matter.

motion transfer Hydraulic pressure being transferred from one part to another.

Motronic A Robert Bosch electronic control system that combines ignition timing control with fuel injection control.

muffler A formed metal container with holes, baffles, and chambers that muffle, or soften, exhaust noise.

multiple-disc clutch A series of friction and steel discs that operate as an apply device in an automatic transmission.

multi-point fuel injection Fuel injection at each individual intake manifold runner.

multi-viscosity oil A chemically modified oil that has been tested for viscosity at cold and hot temperatures.

N

national coarse thread A bolt, screw, or stud with relatively wide spaces between threads.

national fine thread A bolt, screw, or stud with relatively narrow spaces between threads.

needle valve A variable restriction consisting of a tapered (convex) part that can move in or out of a matching (concave) opening. Also, a blunt, pointed valve that fits into a seat to modulate or stop fluid flow.

negative ground A way of connecting a single-wire vehicle system so that the negative battery terminal is connected to the metal of the vehicle to form a ground.

net horsepower A rating of an engine's horsepower with all normal drive accessories connected.

neutral position The position of a synchronizer between two gears when neither is being engaged to the mainshaft.

neutral safety switch An electrical series switch in the starting control circuit that will not close unless the transmission is in park or neutral.

neutron Part of the nucleus of an atom that is without charge.

nodular iron A metal, used in pressure plates, that contains graphite, which acts as a lubricating agent.

no-load rpm test A test made to check the free rotational speed of a starter motor.

nonhunting gearset A differential gearset in which one drive pinion gear tooth contacts only three ring gear teeth after several rotations.

non-sequential fuel injection Fuel injection that occurs without regard for the opening of individual intake valves.

nonthreaded fasteners Fasteners without threads.

normally aspirated A fuel system that draws air due to atmospheric pressure.

nose The high spot of a cam.

nucleus The center portion of an atom, consisting of parts called protons and neutrons.

nut A fastener with internal threads, used to tighten bolts.

observed horsepower Horsepower readings from a dynamometer test that have not been corrected to standardized units.

octane rating A measure of a motor fuel's ability to resist ignition from heat and pressure. Also, the anti-knock rating.

odometer A digital instrument that records how far a vehicle has traveled.

off-idle port A fuel-discharge port located just above the idle discharge port. It serves as an air bleed during idle and a discharge port at off-idle speeds.

offset Placed off center. Also, the measurement between the center of the rim and the point where a wheel's center is mounted.

oil control ring The lower grooved or perforated ring on a piston that scrapes excess oil from the cylinder walls.

oil filter A filtering element enclosed in a metal container, used to remove foreign particles from engine oil before it flows to moving engine parts.

oil galleries Small passageways that carry oil within the engine.

oil pan A storage area for oil, that is bolted to the bottom of the engine block.

oil pump A part of the lubrication system that moves oil, under pressure, to keep engine parts lubricated. Also, a pump that pressurizes the hydraulic system in an automatic transmission.

oil pumping A condition in a worn engine in which oil is drawn past the piston rings by intake vacuum.

oil spurt hole   A small hole drilled in a connecting rod big end or bearing cap for external lubrication purposes.

open   A break in electrical flow at some point in a circuit.

open-end wrench   A wrench with two open ends.

open-loop   A feedback control system operating in such a way that output information does not affect input.

operating mode   A specific way in which a vehicle might operate.

organic compound   A material that contains carbon compounds.

orifice   A precisely sized hole that controls fluid flow. Also, an opening.

oscilloscope   A sophisticated electronic testing instrument that displays on a screen changing levels of voltage in an electrical system.

output   The results of processing data in a computer.

output device   A mechanism or indicating device that is controlled by computer output.

output shaft   A driveshaft that is connected to a differential and to a driving axle on a front-drive automatic transmission.

outside micrometer   An accurate measuring tool placed on the outside of a part to measure outside diameter.

overbore   The dimension by which a machined hole is larger than the standard size.

overdrive   The condition when a smaller driven gear turns faster than a larger driving gear.

overhead camshaft   A camshaft mounted in a cylinder head, above the combustion chambers.

overinflation   Excessive tire pressure that causes the center of a tire to wear quickly.

overrunning clutch   A mechanism used to disengage a driven part from its driving member when another, connected part turns faster.

oversize   Larger than the standard size.

oxidation   The chemical combination of a substance with oxygen to produce an oxygen-containing compound. Also, the chemical breakdown of a substance or compound caused by its combination with oxygen.

oxidation inhibitor   An oil additive that helps to prevent oil oxidation

oxygen sensor   A sensor that detects the amount of oxygen present in exhaust gases.

palladium   A rare metal, used with platinum as an oxidizing catalyst.

parallel   Lines that are the same distance apart no matter how far extended. Also, to have a close similarity in development or procedure.

parallelogram steering linkage   A linkage system in which the Pitman arm, idler arm, and relay rod form three sides of a parallelogram.

parking brake   A cable or linkage assembly that is operated by the driver to activate the rear brakes.

partial nonhunting gearset   A differential gearset in which one drive pinion gear tooth contacts six differential ring gears after several rotations.

partial torque   Tightening a fastener just enough to hold adjustment until final torque can be applied.

parts requisition   A place on a repair order to log in parts and parts prices.

passive restraint   A safety belt or air bag that operates automatically.

pedal reserve   The distance between a brake pedal and the floor of an automobile when the brake pedal is depressed fully.

penetrating solvent   A thin, oily solvent that flows between threads and helps to lubricate parts for removal.

pentroof   A combustion chamber shaped like the roof of a house.

percolation   Boiling of fuel within the carburetor.

phase   A portion of a cyclical event, such as a given section of an AC sine wave.

Phillips screwdriver   A screwdriver used to loosen or tighten Phillips head screws.

pickup coil assembly   A small, permanent magnet and coil assembly that, in combination with a reluctor, forms an electronic position sensor.

pinion depth setting   The in-and-out adjustment of the drive pinion gear.

pinion shaft   A differential part that is mounted in the carrier and that holds the differential pinion gears.

piston   A can-shaped part that moves inside a cylinder during combustion.

piston clearance   The distance between the piston and the cylinder wall.

piston pin   A tubular steel pin that attaches the piston to the connecting rod.

piston ring compressor   A tool used to compress piston rings around a piston so that it may be inserted into a cylinder bore.

piston ring expander   A tool to remove cast piston rings from a piston without breaking them.

piston side thrust   Force developed against the cylinder wall by the tilting of the piston at the top or bottom of its strokes.

piston slap   The noise made by the tilting of a piston against the cylinder wall on the power stroke. Caused by excessive piston clearance.

Pitman arm   A steering rod that connects the steering gearbox to the relay rod.

pivot stud   A stud that serves as a pivot point for a mechanism.

planetary gearset   A set of gears in an automatic transmission that are in constant mesh and that can be shifted while they are spinning.

Plastigage   Perfect Circle Plastigage, a thin thread of waxlike material that flattens when compressed between two parts. The amount of flattening indicates the clearance between the parts.

platinum   A rare metal, used as an oxidizing catalyst in catalytic converters.

play   Looseness in the connection of two parts.

plunger   Part of a dial indicator that transfers play or contour to the indicator.

ply   One of several layers of material that make up a tire carcass.

pneumatic tool   A tool powered by compressed air.

pole piece An iron core that increases magnetic reluctance; used within field coils.

pole shoe *See* pole piece.

polisher A tool that shines and polishes an automobile's finish.

poppet valve A valve that moves up and down to open and close a port.

porosity Tiny holes in a casting caused by air bubbles.

port A hole or passage.

portable electric drill An electric-powered drill that can be carried.

ported vacuum A vacuum source on the carburetor, slightly above the throttle plate, which provides vacuum only after the throttle plate has opened slightly.

port-type injection Fuel injection within an intake port.

positive crankcase ventilation system (PCV) An emission control system that routes blowby gases and unburned oil and fuel vapors to the intake manifold.

positive ground A way of connecting a single-wire vehicle system so that the positive battery terminal is connected to the metal of the vehicle to form a ground.

pour point depressant A chemical additive that helps cold oil to remain thin enough to flow to engine parts during starting.

power brake booster unit An assist device that reduces driver effort on the brake pedal.

power steering A system that uses hydraulic power to assist the driver when turning.

power steering pump A part that creates hydraulic fluid flow to operate a power steering system.

power tools Tools that are operated by electricity, compressed air, or hydraulic pressure.

power train Engine and drivetrain.

prechamber A small opening within a cylinder head where fuel is ignited prior to ignition in the main combustion chamber.

precision insert bearings Friction bearings made in two halves and precisely formed and machined to proper shape and size.

preignition Ignition caused by a glowing deposit or metal part heated enough to begin ignition before a spark occurs at the spark plug.

press *See* stamp.

pressure The amount of force pushing on a surface.

pressure bleeding A method of bleeding a brake system by using air pressure at the master cylinder.

pressure plate A heavy, flat ring that presses against the clutch disc.

pressure plate assembly Parts of the clutch that hold the clutch disc tightly against the flywheel.

pressure regulator valve A valve in an automatic transmission that controls hydraulic pressure from the oil pump.

pressure relief valve A valve that opens under pressure to allow excessive pressure to escape.

pressure test A check of hydraulic pressures in an automatic transmission.

pressure transfer The ability of pressure to be equal in all areas of a hydraulic system.

primary brake shoe The smaller of two brake shoes, positioned toward the front of an automobile.

primary throttle plate The first, or main, throttle plate in a multiple-barrel carburetor.

printed circuit A thin sheet of nonconductive plastic material on which strips of conductive metal have been deposited.

process To change data into meaningful information by following program instructions.

program A set of instructions for a computer.

programmable read-only memory (PROM) A computer module containing information and programs for a specific car model. The information and programs may be used as source information but may not be changed.

programmed Provided with instructions, as a computer.

propeller shaft *See* driveshaft.

proportioning valve A valve in a brake system that limits maximum pressures to rear drum brakes, preventing wheel lockup on hard braking.

proton Part of the nucleus of an atom that has a positive charge.

protractor An angle gauge.

prove-out sequence A display sequence that checks, or proves, that an indicating device's basic operation is correct.

pry bar A long, steel rod used to position or break free heavy parts.

pulse air valve A container with reed valves, used to provide small amounts of air for air injection.

pulse transformer A transformer that produces periodic surges of high voltage, such as an ignition coil.

pulse width The length of time in which energy is applied to open an EFI injector to spray fuel.

punch A thin, tapered metal tool used to remove rivets and pins.

quench area The narrow, confined area farthest from the center of the combustion chamber where the flame front is extinguished.

rack and pinion A steering system that operates with a steering rack and a pinion gear.

radial ply tire A tire with plies that run straight across the width of the tire. Radial tires also have belts between the carcass and the tread.

radial runout A measurement that determines how much a tire and wheel are out of round.

radiation Heat transfer from one location to another through empty space.

radiator A heat exchanger that transfers heat from liquid coolant to air passing through a finned core.

raster An oscilloscope pattern that displays all firing order traces separately, in a stack.

reach The length of the threaded part of a spark plug.

reaction member A gear that is held from moving during planetary gearset operation.

reamer A tool that machines holes to exact sizes.

rear-end torque   A reaction caused by torque transmitted to the differential that causes the differential and rear axle housings to rotate.

rebound   Downward suspension movement.

recap tire   *See* retreaded tire.

receiver/dryer   A liquid refrigerant storage tank that removes moisture from refrigerant.

recess   A shaped hollow space on a part.

reciprocating piston engine   An engine in which pistons are driven back and forth in the cylinders.

recirculating ball   A steering gearbox design that includes a worm gear, sector gear, ball nut rack, and ball bearings.

reduction   The chemical removal of oxygen from a compound containing oxygen.

reed valve   A valve device with a flexible diaphragm to open or block an opening, similar in operation to a check valve.

refrigerant   A liquid with a very low boiling point that is used to absorb heat in an air conditioning system.

refrigerant control   A control that regulates the amount of refrigerant passing from the high-pressure side to the evaporator, or low-pressure side, of an air conditioning system.

refrigeration   A process that maintains cold, or that cools.

regrind   To machine to a smaller size with a grinding device.

relay   An electromagnetically operated device that uses small amounts of electricity to operate a heavy-duty switch.

relay rod   A steering rod that transfers steering movement from the Pitman arm toward both front wheels.

release levers   Parts of a clutch pressure plate assembly that release the holding power of clutch springs when depressed by the throwout bearing.

reluctor   A device that conducts lines of magnetic force easily; part of a switching device for electronic ignition.

remote starter   A simple electrical switch with leads that can be connected to crank the engine with the starter motor.

remote starter switch   A spring-operated electrical momentary-contact switch and leads. Such a switch is used to activate the starter motor from a location away from the key switch.

removable-carrier differential   A design in which the differential carrier bearings are mounted in a removable casting, separate from the rear-axle housing.

repair   The replacement or fixing of automobile parts that wear out, break, or malfunction.

repair order   A form that shows information about a customer, a car (service description, parts used), and billing.

replaceable valve guide   A bushing pressed into a cylinder head to form a valve guide.

residual check valve   A brake valve that applies residual pressure to a drum brake assembly to prevent leakage at wheel cylinders.

resistance   The quality of a substance that opposes electrical flow, measured in ohms.

resistor   An electrical component that lowers the amount of voltage and current passing through an electrical circuit.

resonator   A small, muffler-like device added to an exhaust system to absorb additional sound frequencies.

restraint anchor   An attachment point where a seat and shoulder belt assembly is attached to the automobile.

retainer   A holding device.

retainer-plate axle assembly   A driving axle that is bolted to a retaining plate and to a wheel backing plate.

retaining ring   A ring with spring action that snaps into grooves and holds gears onto shafts.

retard   To make ignition spark occur later.

retractor   A reel that rotates and locks a seat belt in position.

retreaded tire   A used tire carcass with a new tread added.

returnability   The ability of a steering wheel to return to a straight-ahead position after it has been turned.

reverse biased   A transistor whose emitter-base junction receives a small current flow in a reverse direction. No current flow can flow through the emitter-collector path.

reverse flushing   A procedure of forcing clean liquid backwards through the cooling system to loosen and carry away rust, scale, corrosion, and other contaminants.

reversed polarity   A condition that occurs when the connections to a DC source are switched from one pole to another.

rhodium   A rare metal used with platinum as a reducing catalyst.

rich mixture   An air-gasoline mixture containing less than 14.7 parts of air to one part of gasoline, by weight.

rim diameter   The size of the hole in a tire that fits over the wheel rim.

ring gap   The space between the ends of a cylinder ring.

ring gear   A large gear that redirects torque rotation in the differential; part of the ring and pinion gearset.

ring seal   A ring-shaped seal made of rubber or hollow metal tubing; used to form a stationary or dynamic seal.

rivet   A soft metal pin used to fasten materials together permanently.

rocker arm ratio   The ratio between the distances moved by the pushrod end and the valve tip end of a rocker arm.

rocker follower   A pivoting rocker arm used in an overhead-camshaft engine.

rocker shaft   A shaft on which a rocker arm or rocker follower is mounted.

rod and lever linkage   Clutch linkage that is operated by a series of rods and levers.

rod bearing knock   A sharp knocking sound caused by excess connecting rod bearing clearance.

rod cap   A heavy metal clamp, used to attach the connecting rod to the crankpin.

rod journal   The offset crankpin area where a connecting rod is attached.

rolling resistance   Friction between the tires and the road.

rollover valve   A safety valve that automatically closes a fuel-vapor line to the front of the vehicle if the vehicle tilts excessively.

rope-type seal   A seal made up of fibers braided like a rope.

rotor   The shaft, rotating coil, and field pole assembly of an alternator that produces a magnetic field. Also, a metal disc that is part of a disc brake system and that rotates with the axle.

rotary distributor-type pump   A diesel injection pump in which a rotating device is used to pump and distribute the diesel fuel.

rotary engine   An engine whose internal movement is rotary rather than reciprocal.

rotary roller pump An EFI pump that uses rollers on a centrally mounted eccentric to pump fuel.

rubbing block A plastic or resin-impregnated fiber block attached to a movable breaker point contact. It rests against the distributor cam.

runner A hollow, tubular area of a manifold.

runout The distance the surface or edge of a rotating part moves, in or out, during rotation.

RTV A room-temperature vulcanizing, or hardening, synthetic rubber sealant.

Rzeppa joint A constant-velocity joint with large-diameter ball bearings that run in the inner and outer parts of the joint.

S

SAE Society of Automotive Engineers.

SAE (Society of Automotive Engineers) horsepower A customary, corrected horsepower rating.

safety glass Automobile glass that crumbles into small pieces to help prevent injuries from cuts.

safety glasses Goggles to protect eyes while working.

safety guards Shields over moving parts to protect the worker from flying debris.

safety rim A wheel rim with raised sections that hold a tire on a wheel.

sampling probe A device, inserted in a tail pipe, that allows small amounts of exhaust gas to enter an exhaust gas analyzer.

sand cast Referring to materials cast in a mold made of sand; rough-surfaced.

sander A tool that smooths and removes metal.

saturate To fully develop the primary coil's magnetic lines of force.

scoring Parallel grooves worn by friction around the inside or outside circumference of a part.

screwdriver A tool that consists of a shaft of metal with a handle and a blade to loosen or tighten screws.

screw extractor A steel tool that removes broken bolts or studs.

scuff Momentary welding of two rubbing surfaces because of excessive heat. When the weld is broken, a scuffed surface remains.

scuffing Damage caused by greasy friction between parts.

seal A part or assembly used to form a leak-proof seal around a rotating part.

sealed-beam A large, sealed, evacuated glass bulb reflector and lens housing that contains a filament.

seam A line of contact where two parts join.

seat To rub by friction until rubbing edges match each other almost perfectly.

secondary brake shoe The larger of two brake shoes, positioned toward the rear of an automobile.

secondary circuit The high voltage side of an ignition system. Includes the ignition secondary coil, coil cable, rotor, distributor cap, spark plug cables, and spark plugs.

secondary progression system A system to open a secondary throttle plate in relation to the amount of opening of the primary throttle plate.

section width The distance between sidewalls on a tire.

sector gear A gear that has teeth in a semi-circle, or on a section of a circle.

segment A lighted area of a gauge or other display device with a meaningful shape.

segments Copper sections of a commutator that are connected to each end of an armature coil on a motor or generator.

seize To melt and stick, such as when an aluminum piston melts and sticks to the cylinder wall.

self-adjuster Part of a drum brake system that adjusts drum brake clearances automatically.

self-diagnostics The capability of a computer system to diagnose its own problems.

self-energizing A reaction that creates additional braking performance in drum brake systems.

self-locking nut A hump-shaped nut that locks to the bolt when tightened.

self-tapping screw A screw that cuts its own threads into metal.

semi-centrifugal clutch A clutch with weighted release levers, or fingers, that ease clutch pedal operation.

semiconductors Materials that partially conduct electricity.

semi-floating axle A driving axle that helps to support the weight of the automobile.

semi-floating piston pin A piston pin that is fixed to either the piston or the connecting rod.

sending unit A device with variable resistance that operates a dashboard gauge.

sensor A device that senses a condition and modifies an electrical signal in response to changes in the condition.

separator strip A porous plastic or paper insulator between battery plates.

sequential fuel injection (SFI) Fuel injection that occurs at an individual multi-point injector just before the opening of its intake valve.

series A number of things that follow one another in order.

series circuit A circuit in which each electrical load, in order, forms part of a circuit.

series-parallel A combination of series and parallel flow patterns. *See also* series and parallel.

service bay A working area, especially in a garage, where automobiles are serviced.

service manager Head of a service department.

service manual A book that explains how to service and repair an automobile.

service station A gas station with one or more service bays.

service writer A person who greets customers in a service department, makes a preliminary diagnosis of service requirements, and prepares a cost estimate.

servicing Maintenance and repair of automobiles.

servo A hydraulically operated part that controls a transmission band in an automatic transmission.

servomechanism A force amplifier used for positioning control.

SFI (Sequential Fuel Injection) A system of electronic fuel injection in which fuel is sprayed just before the opening of each individual intake valve.

shell A spherical shape formed by spinning electrons that orbit the nucleus of an atom.

shifting arms Short levers attached to the shifting shafts on the side of a manual transmission.

shifting forks Semi-circular yokes that push or pull the synchronizers toward, or away from, a gear to be engaged to, or disengaged from, the mainshaft.

shifting shafts Metal shafts inside a manual transmission case that move the shifting forks.

shift lever A lever that transfers motion from one part to another.

shift quadrant The letters that designate gear positions on an automatic transmission gearshift indicator.

shift valve A switching valve that selects the correct gear in an automatic transmission.

shimmy Side-to-side wheel vibration.

shock absorber A hydraulic suspension part that dampens spring action and works with the springs to control movements of the body, wheel, and axle.

shop foreman A person in charge of several mechanics, who also provides quality control on repair and service operations.

shop layout The location of work areas and equipment in a shop.

short circuit A condition created when electricity accidentally flows incompletely through a circuit, bypassing a part of the intended circuit.

short finder An electrical testing device used to find the location of a shorted or broken wire.

shroud A hollow duct that helps to direct air toward the cooling system fan for better engine cooling.

shunt An electrical bypass.

SI *See* International System of Units.

siamese To form two adjacent intake or exhaust ports into a common port, perhaps separated by a thin center separation.

sidedraft carburetor A carburetor in which air flows through the barrel in a horizontal direction.

side gears Differential gears that are connected to the driving axles and mesh with the differential pinion gears.

side marker light A light visible from the side of a vehicle that increases vehicle visibility in poor lighting conditions.

side terminals An internally threaded connector to which all negative or positive battery plates are connected.

sidewall The side of a tire.

sight glass A glass-covered hole in an air conditioning system through which refrigerant level is checked.

sine wave A pictorial representation of an alternating current (AC) voltage.

single overhead camshaft (SOHC) An engine design with a single camshaft mounted in the cylinder head.

single-point fuel injection Fuel injection at a single point, rather than at each individual intake manifold runner.

single-viscosity oil An engine oil tested for viscosity at 212 degrees F [100 degrees C] or at 0 degrees F [−18 degrees C], but not both.

single-wire circuit A method of wiring a vehicle so that the metal of the vehicle forms a ground connection.

skirt The lower part of a piston, below the ring grooves.

slant Term describing an angle that is not perpendicular to the horizontal.

sleeve A thin cylinder that is inserted or pressed into the block as a replacement for a damaged or worn cylinder bore. Also, the part of a micrometer between the spindle and the thimble, with a scale that gives a measurement reading.

slide valve A device that slides back and forth to open or close an opening.

sliding caliper *See* floating caliper.

slip A condition caused when a driving part rotates faster than a driven part.

slip joint A tubular splined assembly that allows two rotating parts to remain connected as one or both move along a common horizontal axis.

slip-joint adjustable pliers Pliers whose jaws adjust to two different sizes; sometimes called *combination pliers*.

slip ring A circular, smooth ring on an alternator rotor through which electrical connections are made by brushes. It passes current between a rotating and a stationary surface.

slip yoke A yoke attached to a slip joint.

slotted screwdriver A screwdriver with a flat blade.

slow charging Slow battery charging done at rates less than 3 amperes, sometimes called "trickle charging."

sludge A thick, soft, tarry substance formed in oil by water vapor and contaminant particles.

sluggishness A condition in which the engine will not deliver sufficient power under load or at high speed.

small hole gauge A tool for measuring holes too small for an inside micrometer.

snap ring *See* retaining ring.

sniffer A hose on a leak detector tool through which refrigerant can flow.

socket wrench A wrench with a handle and a drive that turns a socket.

soft plug A plug made of stamped sheet metal; used to seal holes, especially in cast metal parts.

solder An alloy, or mixture, of lead and tin that when heated can be used to join metals such as brass, copper, and iron. Also, to join by using solder.

solderless connector Metal devices used for joining or terminating wires. Stripped wires are placed in a tubular metal device which is crimped to hold wires securely.

solenoid A device that uses electromagnetism to exert a pulling or holding force.

solid lifter A lifter made from a single piece of solid metal.

solvent A chemical used to clean automotive parts.

solvent cleaner A tank used for cleaning small parts with cleaning solvent.

space frame A unitized body with additional body parts and braces built into it.

spaghetti tubing A hollow, straw-shaped flexible insulating material that can be slipped over wires.

spark ignition A way of igniting an air-fuel mixture by using a high-voltage electrical arc.

spark plug A removable part that screws into the cylinder head, extending into the combustion chamber, and ignites the air-fuel mixture. A spark plug consists of an outer metal shell with one electrode and a center ceramic insulator with another electrode. The electrodes are separated by a small air gap, across which a high-voltage current can arc.

specialty repair manual A manual published by someone other than the manufacturer. It covers in great depth a particular component or system of an automobile.

specialty shop A shop that specializes in one type of automotive service, such as transmissions, mufflers, or tune-ups.

specifications Measurements for tightening, fitting, and testing parts of an automobile.

specific gravity The relative density of a material when compared to the density of pure water.

speed handle A long cranking handle for a socket wrench.

speed nut A flat nut that is pressed onto a bolt or stud.

speedometer cable A cable that connects to the transmission and operates the speedometer.

spindle The movable measuring surface on a micrometer.

spindown time The time required for the clutch disc, input shaft, and transmission gears to come to a complete stop.

splash lubrication A method of distributing oil in which moving parts splash and throw oil to adjacent parts.

splay To spread or move outward from a central point.

splice To join. Electrical wires can be joined by soldering or by using crimped connectors.

spline A machined ridge on the inner or outer circumference of a round part, used to connect and drive another part.

split driveshaft A driveshaft consisting of multiple sections connected by universal joints.

split reservoir A master cylinder design that has two chambers to direct brake fluid to the front and rear brakes.

sponge lead (Pb) Porous lead that forms the negative plate of a battery element.

sponginess A condition in which the engine does not speed up as much as expected when the accelerator is depressed, especially during cruising.

spongy pedal A brake pedal action that feels springy.

spray painting A process that uses compressed air to spray paint on an automobile.

spring The part of the suspension that absorbs road shock and supports the frame, body, engine, and drivetrain above the wheels.

spring seat A saucer-like bracket that holds coil springs in position.

spring shackle A part that allows a leaf spring to change length as its leaves bend.

sprocket Any of the teeth on a cogwheel used to drive a chain. Also refers to the wheel itself.

sprung weight The weight of all parts suspended by the springs.

stabilizer bar A long steel rod mounted longitudinally to the lower control arms and to the body to control body roll.

stagger To arrange parts in an alternating or zigzag pattern.

stalk A lever, usually attached to the steering column that contains switches for electrical devices.

stalling A condition in which the engine dies after starting.

stall speed The maximum engine rpm achieved by pressing the accelerator with the automatic transmission in gear and the brakes applied.

stamp To form parts from sheet metal by pressing in metal forms.

starter drive The unit mounted on the armature shaft; it combines the overrunning clutch and the drive pinion gear into a single unit.

star wheel An adjusting screw that is used to adjust drum brake clearances.

static balance The equal distribution of weight around a wheel.

stator A part between the impeller and the turbine in a torque converter that redirects and accelerates fluid flow. Also, a stationary coil within an alternator, in which current is induced.

steam cleaner A machine that produces steam and mixes it with a soap solution to clean parts of an automobile.

steering A turning system that moves the front wheels.

steering arm Linkage that connects a steering knuckle to a tie rod.

steering axis inclination An angle created when the steering knuckle slants inward.

steering column A housing that encloses the steering shaft and holds control devices, such as shift and turn signal levers.

steering gearbox A set of gears in a housing. These gears change rotating motion from the steering shaft to side-to-side motion at the steering linkage. Often referred to as a *steering gear*.

steering kickback A sharp, rapid movement of a steering wheel when an automobile strikes a bump or other obstruction.

steering knuckle A part of the wheel spindle assembly that connects to the ball joints. In many cases, a part that is forged into a unit with the wheel spindle.

steering linkage A system of rods that transfers steering motion from the steering gearbox to the front wheels.

steering ratio A gear ratio in the steering gearbox that determines the steering wheel rotations required to turn the wheels from lock to lock.

steering shaft A shaft that connects the steering wheel to the steering gearbox.

steering wheel surge A sudden jerk of the steering wheel.

stellite An extremely hard alloy of cobalt, chromium, and tungsten.

step-down transformer A transformer in which the voltage produced in the secondary coil is less than that in the primary coil.

stepping motor An electrical motor that can move a plunger in or out a precise distance in response to electrical signals. Also called a *stepper motor*.

step-up transformer A transformer in which the voltage created in a secondary coil is greater than that in the primary, or first, coil.

stoichiometric A chemical term that indicates the proper or ideal mixture of chemicals for a particular reaction.

straightedge A tool shaped like a ruler; has straight edges to measure for warpage.

stratified charge An intake charge that is layered, with a richer mixture on top and a leaner mixture beneath it.

streamlining The practice of reducing the coefficient of drag of a vehicle's body.

stress Applied force that may cause a part to crack or break.

strip To remove insulation from a wire.

stroke The distance a piston moves in a cylinder, up or down.

struts A flat structural piece that controls expansion.

stub frame A short frame used to help support the weight of the engine and the transmission at the front of some automobiles.

stud A fastener with external threads at each end.

substrate A ceramic honeycomb grid structure coated with catalyst materials.

sulfation The formation of lead sulfate on battery plates.

sulfuric acid A powerfully corrosive substance formed from water and sulfur.

supercharger A compressor driven by mechanical engine power to force air into an intake manifold under pressure.

superimposed Placed one on top of the other, as oscilloscope patterns for comparison of all cylinder firings.

surface plate A steel plate, accurately machined until it is almost perfectly flat; used to check the flatness of other parts.

surging A condition in which the engine speeds up and/or slows down with the throttle held steady.

suspension Springs and shock absorbers connected to the frame or underbody to provide a smooth ride over uneven surfaces.

swing axle A driving axle that pivots from the differential and moves, or "swings," the axle in an up-and-down motion.

swirl A circular or whirlpool-shaped flow of the intake charge.

switch A device that can complete (close) or interrupt (open) an electrical circuit.

synchronizer An assembly that can engage a gear to turn the mainshaft.

T

tampering Intentionally removing, modifying, disconnecting, or disabling emission control devices or other parts.

tang A projecting piece that fits into a matching opening.

tap A cutting tool used to form, or repair damaged, internal threads.

taper A difference in measurement (i.e., width or diameter) between two ends of a component.

telescoping gauge A spring-loaded tool for measuring the inside size of a hole.

temperature grade A grading system that indicates how well a tire resists and dissipates heat.

terminal A location at which an electrical connection is made.

test drive A form of troubleshooting that requires specific driving procedures by a mechanic.

testing by substitution Substituting a known good part for a suspected defective part.

tetraethyl lead An extremely toxic chemical lead compound added to gasoline to increase its octane rating.

T-handle A socket wrench handle used in tight working areas and for greater working force.

thermal efficiency A comparison between the energy present in fuel and the energy output of an engine.

thermal gauge A gauge in which a heating coil and a bimetallic spring move an indicating needle.

thermodynamics The scientific study of the mechanical action or relations of heat.

thermostat A temperature regulating mechanism.

thermostatic coil A bimetallic coil, or spring, that responds to heat by curling or uncurling.

thermostatically controlled air cleaner An air cleaner assembly that can provide relatively hot, warm, or cool air to a fuel atomization system.

thermostatically operated air cleaner A device that mixes hot and cool air to promote fuel vaporization in the intake charge.

thimble The adjusting portion of a micrometer that moves the spindle and has a bevel scale to give a reading.

thread gauge A tool for measuring the number of threads per inch.

thread pitch The distance between each thread of a fastener.

thread sealant A sealing gel used over fasteners before installation.

threaded fasteners Fasteners that connect parts with grooves, or threads.

three-phase AC current Alternating current induced in three coils at slightly staggered times.

three-way catalyst A catalytic converter that changes HC, CO, and NO_x into H_2O, CO_2, N, and O_2. Also called a three-way catalytic converter.

throttle body The lower section of a carburetor, which contains the throttle plates, idle mixture passages, and adjusting screws.

throttle body injection (TBI) Fuel injection with one or two injectors located in a throttle body.

throttle bore The opening in a carburetor through which air passes.

throttle plate A movable plate, or flap, in an opening at the bottom of a carburetor barrel.

throttle position sensor An electrical sending unit that relays information to a control system about how far the throttle plate of the carburetor is open.

throttle positioner An electrical device that mechanically holds a throttle plate open.

throttle pressure An increase in automatic transmission mainline pressure to help control shifting.

throttle valve A balancing valve that controls throttle pressure in an automatic transmission.

throttle valve cable See kickdown linkage.

throw An offset area on a crankshaft.

throw-off lubrication A system of lubrication in which oil is thrown from crankshaft main bearings onto cylinder walls.

throwout bearing A prelubricated ball bearing that is moved against the pressure plate release levers when the clutch is operated.

tie rod A steering rod connected between the relay rod and steering arm.

timing gear A gear that drives or is driven in a synchronized gear assembly.

timing light An instrument that produces a brief (0.0010 second), repeated flash of light that appears to "freeze" a moving pulley or flywheel.

tire pressure gauge A tool for checking air pressure in a tire.

tire plug A tire repair kit that contains a plug to fill the puncture and a head to seal the puncture.

tire rotation The switching of tire-and-wheel assemblies to different locations on an automobile to increase tire life.

tire valve A valve through which a tire is inflated or deflated.

toe-in A condition in which the front edges of the tires on the same axle are closer than the rear edges.

toe-out A condition in which the front edges of the tires on the same axle are farther apart than the rear edges of the tires.

toe-out on turns The difference in angles between the front wheels during turns.

top dead center (TDC) The position of the piston at the top of either the compression or exhaust stroke.

top-feed injector An EFI injector in which fuel is fed in from the top.

torque A turning or twisting force, such as that used to turn a shaft, measured in pounds-feet (lb.-ft.). *See also* work.

torque arm A long steel rod that is connected between the rear axle and the transmission to control rear-end torque.

torque converter An assembly that produces a fluid coupling between the engine and automatic transmission.

torque converter housing A case that encloses the parts of a torque converter.

torque specifications Required amount of tightening for fasteners.

torque steer A twisting axle movement in front-wheel-drive automobiles that causes a pulling action under acceleration toward the side with the longer driving axle.

torque-tube drive A method of controlling rear-end torque by connecting a rigid tube between the differential and transmission or vehicle frame.

torque wrench A tool that measures the torque, or turning force, applied to a fastener.

torquing-over Engine twisting motion in a direction opposite to crankshaft rotation.

torsion bar A steel bar that is twisted to provide spring action in a suspension.

torsional coil springs Clutch disc springs in the hub that help smooth out rotation by absorbing torsional vibration.

Torx screwdriver A screwdriver used to loosen or tighten Torx head screws.

trace A characteristic oscilloscope pattern. Also, a very small amount.

tracer A contrasting colored stripe on plastic insulation, used to help trace a particular wire.

traction The ability of a tire to grip the surface on which it is riding.

traction grade A grading system that indicates a tire's ability to stop on wet pavement.

traction wheels Driving wheels.

trailing arm An arm on the rear suspension that extends rearward from the actual suspension mounting point.

tramp Wheel hop caused by static balance.

transaxle A driving system in which the transmission and differential are combined in one unit.

transfer port *See* off-idle port.

transformer A device with coils in which electricity can be produced through induction.

transitional port *See* off-idle port.

transistor A semiconductor device used to control or amplify current flow.

transmission A series of gears that take power from the engine and transfer it to more usable speeds while driving.

transmission band A friction-lined, steel strip that wraps around a clutch drum in an automatic transmission.

transmission input shaft The shaft through which engine power enters the transmission.

transverse Perpendicular, or at right angles, to a front-to-back centerline.

tread The part of a tire that touches the road surface.

tread wear indicator A series of bands, or bald spots, that appear on a tire when only 1/16 in. remains.

trim height A manufacturer's recommended height, from ground level, of certain suspension and body parts.

tripod joint A constant-velocity joint with a triangle-shaped center spider, needle bearings, and circular races in the outer part of the joint.

tripot joint *See* tripod joint.

trouble code Information in the form of numbers stored by an on-board computer to indicate specific problems.

trouble light A caged, insulated light bulb that is used during work on automobiles.

troubleshooting A step-by-step procedure for diagnosing an automotive problem.

troubleshooting chart A listing of problem conditions, possible sources of problems, and actions to be applied to resolve the problems.

trunnion One of the arms of the cross-shaped central part of a universal joint.

tubeless tire A tire that fits tightly against the wheel to keep air from escaping.

turbine A wheel with curved blades that can be used to turn a shaft or to pump fluids under pressure. Also, a fan-like part connected to the transmission input shaft and driven by a fluid coupling.

turbine-type pump A centrifugal EFI pump similar to a water pump or turbocharger compressor wheel.

turbo lag The time necessary for a turbocharger to begin compressing the intake air charge.

turbocharger A method of supercharging that uses the power of exhaust gases to turn a compressor. The compressor forces air, or an air-fuel mixture, into the intake manifold under pressure.

turbulence An irregular pattern of flow of an intake charge.

two-stroke cycle An engine operating cycle that combines the functions of intake and exhaust, and compression and ignition. This causes a power stroke to occur once each revolution of the crankshaft.

two-way catalyst A catalyst that promotes the oxidation of HC and CO exhaust emissions.

U

U-joint *See* universal joint.

underinflation Low tire pressure; causes the outside of a tire to wear quickly.

uneven firing Term used to characterize an engine whose crankshaft receives power pulses at uneven intervals.

Uniform Tire Quality Grading A federal government testing program that grades tires for traction wear and temperature resistance qualities.

unitized body A reinforced body structure that eliminates the need for a frame.

universal joint A joint that allows the driveshaft to transmit torque at different angles as the suspension moves up and down.

universal-joint adaptor A socket-wrench adapter that allows the socket to be turned from an angle.

unpowered test light An electrical testing device that can be used to check for power and/or ground connections.

unsprung weight The weight of parts that are not suspended by the springs.

updraft carburetor A carburetor in which air flows through the barrel in an upward, vertical direction.

V

vacuum advance mechanism A mechanism that can advance ignition timing in response to engine load.

vacuum and pressure gauge A tool for measuring engine vacuum and fuel system pressure.

vacuum diaphragm tester A tool used to check for proper operation and for leaks in vacuum systems.

vacuum modulator A diaphragm-operated part that controls throttle valve action in some automatic transmissions.

vacuum motor A vacuum diaphragm attached to a pull rod that can provide a mechanical pulling or pushing action.

vacuum relief valve A valve that opens to allow outside air into a sealed container to prevent the formation of a vacuum.

vacuum retard A mechanism that can retard ignition timing to decrease combustion pressures and lengthen combustion time.

valve A part that moves to open or close a port.

valve adjusting screw A threaded shaft located in a rocker arm or rocker follower; used to adjust valve clearance.

valve adjustment The process of adjusting valve clearance.

valve adjustment shim A thin, replaceable, precisely sized metal insert used to adjust valve clearance. Generally used with bucket lifters.

valve body A housing in an automatic transmission that contains a maze of passages and valves to direct hydraulic pressure to the proper locations.

valve clearance Distance between the tip of the valve stem and the rocker arm when the camshaft is positioned on its base circle. Also, distance between a bucket lifter and the tip of valve stem when camshaft is positioned on its base circle.

valve float A condition in which the valves fail to follow the actions of the valve train, remaining open.

valve guide The area within the head that guides and supports the valve stem. May be integral or replaceable.

valve lash *See* valve clearance.

valve overlap A situation in which both the intake and exhaust valves are open at the same time.

valve rotator A mechanism that rotates a poppet valve while it is being opened and closed.

valve seat insert A circular, hardened metal ring pressed into a cylinder head to form a valve seat.

valve spring surge A valve spring vibration that causes erratic valve action.

valve train The parts that operate the valves, driven by the camshaft. May include lifters, pushrods, rocker arms, cam followers, bucket tappets, and adjusting shims.

vane-type pump A pump with flat vanes, or blades, that move within an enclosure to trap and compress fluids.

vapor canister *See* charcoal canister.

vapor/fuel separator A unit that separates fuel vapor from liquid fuel.

vapor lock A collection of vapor in an area of a liquid fuel system, which prevents an engine from receiving fuel.

vapor recovery canister A container that stores fuel vapors for a vapor recovery system.

vapor recovery system A system that traps and holds fuel vapors until they can be drawn into an engine with an intake charge.

variable ratio steering A steering system within the steering gearbox that changes steering ratios as the steering wheel is turned.

varnish A dark, partially transparent hard coating caused by lubricant oxidation that can increase friction and reduce the size of oil passages.

ventilation system A passenger comfort system that circulates outside air through the passenger compartment.

venturi A narrow restriction in a carburetor bore that increases the velocity of air passing through the barrel.

vernier calipers A tool for measuring inside and outside diameters.

viscosity The thickness or thinness of a fluid and its ability to resist flowing.

viscosity index improver A chemical additive that helps oil to maintain an adequately thick lubricating film as the oil is heated.

viscous drive fan clutch A mechanism that uses fluid between an impeller and a stator to drive a fan.

viscous friction Friction between layers of liquid, such as oil.

voice simulator A device that produces sounds like human speech.

voice warning device A device that plays a recorded message or produces speech sounds to warn the driver of problems or conditions.

volatile Able to vaporize.

voltage drop Voltage lost by the passage of electrical current through resistance.

voltage drop test A test to measure the amount of voltage drop, or loss, across a conductor while electrical current is flowing. Excessive voltage indicates high resistance.

voltage regulator A device to control alternator current and voltage charging output to the battery.

voltage spike A pulse, or surge, of electricity that creates momentary high voltage. Usually caused by connecting or disconnecting a heavy electrical load in an electrical system.

voltmeter A measuring instrument used to check battery voltage level.

volumetric efficiency A comparison between how much fuel and air are actually drawn into an engine and how much could be drawn in.

vortex flow A swirling, twisting motion of fluid.

W

warpage Bending.

washer A thin spacer used between a screw or nut and the automotive part being tightened.

wastegate A pressure relief valve for a turbocharger.

water cooled An engine cooling system that operates with liquid.

water jacket Hollow spaces filled with coolant surrounding, the cylinders in the block and combustion chamber areas in the cylinder head.

water pump A belt-operated pump that forces liquid coolant through an engine cooling system.

water sludge A soft, light-colored foamy substance formed from water whipped into engine oil by the action of the crankshaft.

watt A unit of power equivalent to an electrical current of one ampere at one volt. Also, the work done at the rate of one joule per second. Equals 1/746 horsepower.

wear indicator A round nipple mounting surface whose position on a ball joint surface indicates wear.

webbing Woven material, such as that in a seat or shoulder belt.

weep hole A ventilation hole located at the bottom of a water pump shaft housing.

wet compression test A compression test conducted after a small amount of engine oil has been added through the spark plug hole. Used to determine if piston rings are sealing properly.

wet liner A cylinder liner whose outer surface is in contact with the coolant in a liquid-cooled engine.

wheel alignment The positioning of steering and front suspension components, and wheels.

wheelbase The distance between the center of a front wheel and the center of a rear wheel.

wheel cylinder A cylinder in the brake assembly that transfers hydraulic pressure to the brake shoes.

wheel lugs Studs in a wheel hub on which a wheel is mounted.

wheel spindle assembly A suspension part that consists of a wheel spindle and a steering knuckle.

whip Flexing of a shaft that occurs during rotation.

wide-open throttle (WOT) An operating mode in which the accelerator pedal is held to the floor for maximum engine power production.

winding The loops of wire that form a coil, as in an electric motor or generator.

wire gauge A feeler gauge that contains round, not flat, measuring strips.

wiring diagram A diagram that, like a road map, shows how wires are connected in circuits.

work The result of applying force to an object and causing it to move. *See also* energy, force.

work order Instructions to a mechanic on a repair order.

worm-drive clamp A metal clamping band with a screw that engages slots on the band.

worm gear A gear with spiral threads.

wrench A tool used to loosen or tighten a fastener.

wrist pin *See* piston pin.

Y

yoke A U-shaped part used to connect two other parts.

Z

zener diode A special form of diode that conducts in the opposite direction when sufficient voltage is applied.

INDEX

A